W9-CCN-858

43rd Edition

Warman's®

Antiques&
Collectibles

2010 Price Guide

Mark F. Moran

©2009 Krause Publications

Published by

kp **krause publications**

A subsidiary of F+W Media, Inc.

700 East State Street • Iola, WI 54990-0001
715-445-2214 • 888-457-2873
www.krausebooks.com

Our toll-free number to place an order or obtain
a free catalog is (800) 258-0929.

ISSN 1076-1985
ISBN-13: 978-0-89689-807-3
ISBN-10: 0-89689-807-5

Designed by Wendy Wendt and Kay Sanders
Edited by Mark F. Moran

Printed in China

ON THE COVER:

Jacket, Donald Brooks, black silk paisley, 1960s, in black, cream and yellow, with a standup collar, flared fit, hidden pockets, fully lined. Labeled: Donald Brooks, **$360**

Overbeck vase incised with stylized figures of children amidst red hollyhock blossoms, on a matte mustard ground. Restoration to rim chip. Incised OBK F with paper label possibly covering E, 10 1/2" x 7". **$72,000**

Maurice Logan, (American, 1886-1977), oil on canvas of the San Francisco ferry dock and skyline, **$80,500**

Contents

WARMAN'S® IDENTIFICATION AND PRICE GUIDES

American & European Art Pottery Guide
Carnival Glass
Children's Books
Civil War Collectibles
Civil War Weapons
Coca-Cola® Collectibles
Coins and Paper Money
Cookie Jars
Costume Jewelry Figurals
Depression Glass
Dolls: Antique to Modern
Duck Decoys
English & Continental Pottery & Porcelain
Fenton Glass
Fiesta
Flea Market Price Guide
Gas Station Collectibles
Hull Pottery

Jewelry
John Deere Collectibles
Little Golden Books®
Majolica
McCoy Pottery
Modernism Furniture and Accessories
North American Indian Artifacts
Political Collectibles
Red Wing Pottery
Rookwood Pottery
Roseville Pottery
Sporting Collectibles
Sterling Silver Flatware
Vietnam War Collectibles
Vintage Jewelry
Vintage Quilts
Weller Pottery
World War II Collectibles

WARMAN'S® COMPANIONS

Carnival Glass
Collectible Dolls
Collectible Fishing Lures
Depression Glass
Fenton Glass
Fiesta
Hallmark Keepsake Ornaments

Hot Wheels
McCoy Pottery
PEZ®
Roseville Pottery
U.S. Coins & Currency
Watches
World Coins & Currency

WARMAN'S® FIELD GUIDES

Action Figures
Antique Jewelry
Barbie Doll
Bean Plush
Bottles
Buttons
Coca-Cola®
Depression Glass
Disney Collectibles
Dolls
Farm Toys
Precious Moments®
Fishing Lures
G.I. Joe

Hot Wheels
Kitschy Kitchen Collectibles
Lionel Train 1945-1969
Lunch Boxes
Matchbox
Pepsi
Star Wars
Tools
Transformers
U.S. Coins & Currency
U.S. Stamps
Vintage Guitars
Watches
Zippo Lighters

Introduction

WELCOME TO THE NEW WARMAN'S GUIDE FOR 2010

The 43rd edition of *Warman's Antiques & Collectibles Price Guide* is bigger and better than ever, and brings a fresh, 21st-century perspective to the collecting world.

Our list of auction houses has been dramatically expanded to more than 70 businesses from coast to coast, covering hundreds of collecting categories. The number of consulting experts in various fields has also grown, and we have included new sections on both established and emerging collecting areas.

An important new feature is a focus on the "Future of the Markets," advising collectors on the best places to invest in five key areas:

For the first time, *Warman's* features a comprehensive view of the art markets, featuring hundreds of listed artists. This section is highlighted by the contributions of Mary P. Manion, acting director of Landmarks Gallery and Restoration Studio in Milwaukee. Manion also appears along with Senior Editor Mark F. Moran in an informative DVD included with this edition, discussing fakes and reproductions.

On the subject of folk art, we welcome dealer Tim Chambers of Sikeston, Mo. Tim and his wife, Charline, are active dealers in folk art and Americana, doing business at shows across the country as Missouri Plain Folk. In 2001, Tim authored the book, *The Art of the Game,* showcasing the game-board collection of Selby Shaver. As a result, Chambers works extensively with collectors in this field. Besides game boards, Missouri Plain Folk is known for vintage Americana with an emphasis on surface, form, color and graphic impact. An ever-changing selection of game boards and Americana may be found on their Web site: *www.missouriplainfolk.com.*

Our section of vintage clothing and couture features prices realized and images from Leslie Hindman Auctioneers of Chicago, plus an overview of the market by Caroline Ashleigh, owner of Birmingham, Mich.-based Caroline Ashleigh Associates LLC. She is a graduate of New York University in Appraisal Studies in Fine and Decorative Arts and is a board-certified senior member of the Appraisers Association of America. Ashleigh is an internationally known appraiser and regularly appears on the PBS program *Antiques Roadshow.* Caroline Ashleigh Associates conducts fully catalogued online auctions. Visit *www.appraiseyourart.com* or *www.auctionyourart.com.*

Another new category is our Modernism section, with an introduction by Noah Fleisher, former editor of *Antique Trader* magazine. Fleisher has also written extensively for *New England Antiques Journal, Northeast Journal of Antiques and Art* and all their online components in the recent years. He has also written for *www.wondertime.com*, a division of the Disney publication of the same name, as well as for *Goldmine* magazine, and a Massachusetts style magazine called *Living Spaces*, where he wrote about a Modern-design pool house in the Amherst, Mass., area.

Finally, we are honored to include an overview of all things Tiffany written by Reyne Haines, a specialist in 20th-century decorative arts. Haines, owner of Reyne Gallery in Cincinnati, is a regular appraiser on PBS' *Antiques Roadshow*. She is the author of *The Art of Glass: The Collection from the Dayton Art Institute* and has contributed to numerous books and articles on collecting. Haines is also the co-owner and founder of *www.JustGlass.com*.

You will find hundreds of new, detailed color photos in the 43rd edition of Warman's, and expanded information with each image, as well. Every new photo caption will include not only the name of the contributing auction house, but also its location and its Web address.

The Warman's Advantage

The Warman's Advantage manifests itself in several new ways in the 2010 edition. As we reviewed past volumes, we wanted to make this book as easy to use as possible. To that end, we've consolidated and reorganized how we present several key categories. Our new mantra is, "What is it first?"

For instance, an antique clock may also have an advertising component, an ethnic element (like black memorabilia), reflect a specific design theme (like Art Deco) and be made of cast iron. But first and foremost, it's a clock, and that's where you'll find it listed, even though there are other collecting areas involved.

Of course, there are always going to be certain antiques and collectibles that cross lines of interest, but we hope that our newly reconfigured index will help collectors locate that special treasure quickly.

There are a few categories that remain iconic in the collecting world. Coca-Cola collectibles cross many interests, as do folk art, Oriental antiques and Tiffany designs, to name just a few. These still have their own broad sections.

In addition to art and Modernism, newly expanded sections include autographs, vintage doorstops, fishing and hunting items, lighting, sports memorabilia and western/cowboy collectibles. We are also highlighting new sections on paperback books, salt- and peppershakers, and objects associated with the Vietnam War.

Prices

The prices in this book have been established using the results of auction sales all across the country, and by tapping the resources of knowledgeable dealers and collectors. These values reflect not only current collector trends, but also the wider economy. The adage that "an antique (or collectible) is worth what someone will pay for it" still holds. A price guide measures value, but it also captures a moment in time, and sometimes that moment can pass very quickly.

Beginners should follow the same advice that all seasoned collectors have learned: Make mistakes and learn from them; talk with other collectors and dealers; find reputable resources (including books and Web sites), and learn to invest wisely, buying the best examples you can afford.

Words of Thanks

This 43rd edition of the Warman's guide is the best we've ever published. Dozens of auction houses have generously shared their resources, but a few folks deserve special recognition: Susan "BFF" Pinnell and Jeff Evans, Green Valley Auctions, Mt. Crawford, Va.; Andrew Truman, assisted by Lisa Oakes, at James D. Julia Auctioneers, Fairfield, Maine; Anthony Barnes at Rago Arts and Auction Center, Lambertville, N.J.; Anne Trodella at Skinner Inc., Boston; Greg Martin Auctions, San Francisco; Jeff Belhorn at Belhorn Auction Services LLC, Columbus, Ohio; Lang's Sporting Collectibles, Waterville, N.Y.; Treadway Toomey Galleries, Cincinnati and Oak Park, Ill.; Waasdorp Inc., Clarence, N.Y.; Slotin Auction, Buford, Ga.; Heritage Auction Galleries, Dallas; Morphy Auctions, Denver, Pa.; Swann Auction Galleries, New York; Bertoia Auctions, Vineland, N.J.; Abigail Rutherford at Leslie Hindman Auctioneers, Chicago; and Guyette & Schmidt Inc., St. Michaels, Md.

Special thanks also go to Noah Fleisher, who contributed to a dozen sections, and editor Sharon Thatcher, who helped to edit miles of text.

Read All About It

There are many fine publications that collectors and dealers may consult about antiques and collectibles in general. Space does not permit listing all of the national and regional publications in the antiques and collectibles field; this is a sampling:

- **Antique Trader Weekly**, published by Krause Publications, 700 E. State St., Iola, WI, 54990 – *www.antiquetrader.com*
- **Antique & The Arts Weekly**, 5 Church Hill Road, Newton, CT 06470 – *www.antiquesandthearts.com*
- **AntiqueWeek**, P.O. Box 90, Knightstown, IN 46148 – *www.antiqueweek.com*
- **Maine Antique Digest**, P.O. Box 358, Waldoboro, ME 04572 – *www.maineantiquedigest.com*
- **New England Antiques Journal**, 24 Water St., Palmer, MA 01069 – *www.antiquesjournal.com*
- **The Journal of Antiques and Collectibles**, P.O. Box 950, Sturbridge, MA 01566 – *www.journalofantiques.com*
- **Southeastern Antiquing & Collecting** magazine, P.O. Box 510, Acworth, GA 30101 – *www.go-star.com/antiquing*

Reproductions

Reproductions are a major concern to all collectors and dealers. Throughout this edition, boxes will alert you to known reproductions and keys to recognizing them (this is in addition to the DVD mentioned earlier). Most reproductions are unmarked; the newness of their appearance is often the best clue to uncovering them. We recommend a visit to *www.repronews.com*, an online database that reports on past and current reproductions, copycats, fantasies and fakes.

Let us know what you think

We're always eager to hear what you think about this book and how we can improve it. Contact:

Mark F. Moran
Senior Editor,
Antiques & Collectibles Books
Krause Publications
700 E. State St.
Iola, WI 54990-0001
mark.moran@fwmedia.com

Visit an antique show

One of the best ways to really enjoy the world of antiques and collectibles is to take the time to really explore an antiques show. Some areas, like Manchester, N.H., turn into antique meccas for a few days each summer when dealers and collectors come for both specialized and general antiques shows, plus auctions.

Here are a few of our favorites:

Atlantique City, Atlantic City, N.J., Convention Center; *www.atlantiquecity.com*

Brimfield, Mass., shows, held three times a year in May, July and September, *www.brimfield.com.*

Round Top, Texas, antique shows, held spring and fall, *www.roundtop.com/antique1.htm*

Antiques Week in and around Manchester, N.H., held every August.

Palmer/Wirfs Antique & Collectible Shows, including the Portland, Ore., Expos, *www.palmer-wirfs.com*

The Original Miami Beach Antique Show, *www.dmgantiqueshows.com*

Merchandise Mart International Antiques Fair, Chicago, *www.merchandisemart.com/chicagoantiques*

High Noon Western Americana Show & Auction, Phoenix, *www.highnoon.com*

Ask an expert

Many contributors have proved invaluable in sharing their expertise during the compilation of the 43rd edition of the Warman's guide. For more information on their specialties, call or visit their Web sites.

Caroline Ashleigh
Caroline Ashleigh Associates LLC
1000 S. Old Woodward, Suite 105
Birmingham, MI 48009-6734
248-792-2929
www.auctionyourart.com
Vintage Clothing, Couture and Accessories, Textiles, Western Wear

Al Bagdade
The Country Peasants
1325 N. State Parkway, Apt 15A
Chicago, IL 60610
312-397-1321
Quimper

Dudley Browne
James D. Julia, Inc.
P.O. Box 830
Fairfield, ME 04937
207-453-7125
www.juliaauctions.net
E-mail: dbrowne@jamesdjulia.com
Glass & Lamps

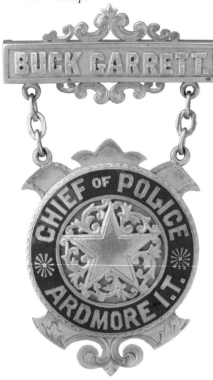

Photo courtesy Greg Martin Auctions, San Francisco;
www.GregMartinAuctions.com

*Badge (suspension), multicolor gold and blue enamel,
for Buck Garrett (1871-1929), Chief of Police, Ardmore,
Indian Territory.* **$36,800**

Tim Chambers
Missouri Plain Folk
501 Hunter Ave
Sikeston, MO 63801-2115
573-471-6949
E-mail: plainfolk@charter.net
Folk Art

Wes Dillon and Bill Taylor
James D. Julia, Inc.
P.O. Box 830
Fairfield, ME 049370
207-453-7125
www.juliaauctions.net

E-mail: wdillon@jamesdjulia.com
btaylor@jamesdjulia.com
Firearms

Joel Edler
Iola, Wis.
715-445-4080
Postcards

Noah Fleisher
E-mail: noah.fleisher@yahoo.com
Modernism

Bill Gage
James D. Julia, Inc.
P.O. Box 830
Fairfield, ME 04937
207-453-7125
www.juliaauctions.net
E-mail: antiques@jamesdjulia.com
Antiques & Fine Art

Reyne Haines
Reyne Gallery
17 E. 8th St.
Cincinnati OH 45202
513-504-8159
www.reyne.com
E-mail: reyne@reyne.com
Tiffany, 20th Century Decorative Arts

Ted Hake
Hake's Americana & Collectibles Auctions
P.O. Box 1444
York, PA 17405
717-848-1333
www.hakes.com
E-mail: auction@hakes.com
Disneyana, Political

Mark B. Ledenbach
P.O. Box 2421
Orangevale, CA 95662
www.HalloweenCollector.com
Halloween Items

Mary P. Manion
Landmarks Gallery & Restoration Studio
231 N. 76th St.
Milwaukee, WI 53213
800-352-8892
www.landmarksgallery.com
Fine Art & Restoration

Mark F. Moran
Senior Editor, Antiques & Collectibles Books
Krause Publications
700 E. State St.
Iola, WI 54990-0001
800-726-9966, Ext. 13461
Mark.Moran@fwmedia.com

Suzanne Perrault
Perrault Rago Gallery
333 N. Main St.
Lambertville, NJ 08530
609-397-1802
www.ragoarts.com
E-mail: suzanne@ragoarts.com
Ceramics

David Rago
Rago Arts and Auction Center
333 N. Main St.
Lambertville, NJ 08530
609-397-9374
www.ragoarts.com
Art Pottery, Arts & Crafts

Dennis Raleigh Antiques & Folk Art
P.O. Box 745
Wiscasset, ME 04578
207-882-7821
3327 Cones Court
Midland, MI 48640
989-631-2603
www.dennisraleighantiques.com
E-mail: dgraleigh@verizon.net
Decoys, Silhouettes, Portrait Miniatures

Henry A. Taron
Tradewinds Antiques
P.O. Box 249
Manchester-By-The-Sea, MA 01944-0249
(978) 526-4085
www.tradewindsantiques.com
Canes

Andrew Truman
James D. Julia, Inc.
P.O. Box 830
Fairfield, ME 04937
207-453-7125
www.juliaauctions.net
E-mail: atruman@jamesdjulia.com
Toys, Dolls & Advertising

Auction Houses

A&S Antique Auction Co.
900 East Loop 340
Waco, TX 76716
254-799-6044
www.asauctions.com
Full service, western memorabilia, firearms

Photo courtesy Sanford Alderfer Auction & Appraisal, Hatfield, Pa.; www.AlderferAuction.com

Walter Emerson Baum, (American, 1884-1956), winter scene of village with snow falling, oil on canvas, signed lower right, 25" x 30". **$31,625**

Sanford Alderfer Auction & Appraisal
501 Fairgrounds Road
Hatfield, PA 19440
215-393-3000
www.alderferauction.com
Full service

All Out Auctions & Delivery Inc.
5015 Babcock St.
Palm Bay, Fl 32905.
321-984-8484
www.alloutauctions.com
Full service

American Bottle Auctions
2523 J St. Suite 203
Sacramento, CA 95816
800-806-7722
www.americanbottle.com
Antique bottles, jars

American Pottery Auction
Waasdorp Inc.
P. O. Box 434
Clarence, NY 14031
716-759-2361
www.antiques-stoneware.com
Stoneware, redware

Photo courtesy Belhorn Auction Services LLC, Columbus, Ohio; www.Belhorn.com

Rose Cabat "Feelie" with rare performance trial glaze. Marked 84T Cabat 28N. Mint. 2 1/2" h x 2 1/4" w. **$700** *(Rose Cabat, born 1914, New York, is a Tucson, Ariz.-based potter known for her "feelies" — small, narrow-necked porcelain pots with soft glazes that feel feathery to the touch.)*

Photo courtesy Cowan's, Cincinnati; www.CowanAuctions.com

O.S. Goff, albumen photograph of a Crow soldier and his wife, mounted on cream card stock; titled on mount in script, "Indian soldier and wife;" portrait shows a Crow man dressed as a sergeant of the 1st U.S. Calvary; his wife, wearing a gingham dress and beaded hide moccasins, stands besides him. Lacks Goff's imprint, but taken at Fort Custer, Mont., post 1885, 9" x 7 1/4". **$1,265**

Americana Auctions

Glen Rairigh
P.O. Box 337
Sunfield, MI 48890
800-919-1950
www.americanaauctions.com
Full service

Auctions Neapolitan

1100 First Ave. S.
Naples, FL 34102
239-262-7333
www.auctionsneapolitan.com
Full service

Belhorn Auction Services LLC

P.O. Box 20211
Columbus, Ohio 43220
614-921-9441
www.belhorn.com
Full service, American art pottery

Bertoia Auctions

2141 DeMarco Drive
Vineland, NJ 08360
856-692-1881
www.bertoiaauctions.com
Toys, banks, holiday, doorstops

Brunk Auctions

P.O. Box 2135
Asheville, NC 28802
828-254-6846
www.brunkauctions.com
Full service

Burley Auction Group

134 Deborah Drive
New Braunfels, TX 78130
830-237-3440
www.burleyauction.com
Full service, western memorabilia, firearms

Caroline Ashleigh Associates LLC

1000 S. Old Woodward, Suite 105
Birmingham, MI 48009-6734
248-792-2929
www.auctionyourart.com
Full service, vintage clothing, couture and
    accessories, textiles, western wear

Clars Auction Gallery

5644 Telegraph Ave.
Oakland, CA 94609
888-339-7600
www.clars.com
Full service

Cowan's
6270 Este Ave.
Cincinnati, OH 45232
513-871-1670
www.cowanauctions.com
Full service, historic Americana, Native American

Craftsman Auctions
109 Main St.
Putnam, CT 06260
800-448-7828
www.craftsman-auctions.com
Arts & Crafts furniture and accessories

Cyr Auction Co.
P.O. Box 1238
Gray, ME 04039
207-657-5253
www.cyrauction.com
Full service

Eagles Basket Auction
110 S. Main St.
Travelers Rest, SC 29690
864-506-4649
864-483-8785
www.eaglesbasket.com
Full service

Early Auction Co. LLC.
123 Main St.
Milford, OH 45150
513-831-4833
www.earlyauctionco.com
Art glass

Elder's Antiques
901 Tamiami Trail (US 41) S.
Nokomis, FL 34275
941-488-1005
www.eldersantiques.com
Full service

Greg Martin Auctions
660 Third St., Suite 100
San Francisco, CA 94107
800-509-1988
www.gregmartinauctions.com
Firearms, edged weapons, armor, Native
    American objects

Green Valley Auctions Inc.
2259 Green Valley Lane
Mt. Crawford, VA 22841
540-434-4260
www.greenvalleyauctions.com
Full service, glass

Grey Flannel
8 Moniebogue Lane
Westhampton Beach, NY 11978
631-288-7800
www.greyflannel.com
Sports jerseys, memorabilia

Guyette & Schmidt Inc.
P.O. Box 1170
24718 Beverly Road
St. Michaels, MD 21663
410-745-0485
www.guyetteandschmidt.com
Antique decoys

Photo courtesy Guyette & Schmidt Inc., St. Michaels, Md.; www.GuyetteandSchmidt.com

Hooded merganser by Lloyd Tyler. **$170,000**

Photo courtesy Joel Edler, Iola, Wis.

Halloween, John Winsch, girl in red devil costume, 1912 copyright. **$75+**

Hake's Americana & Collectibles Auctions
P.O. Box 1444
York, PA 17405
717-848-1333
www.hakes.com
Character collectibles, pop culture

Heritage Auctions Inc.
3500 Maple Ave., 17th Floor
Dallas, TX 75219-3941
800-872-6467
www.ha.com
Full service, coins, pop culture

iGavel Inc.
229 E. 120th St.
New York, NY 10035
866-iGavel6 or 212-289-5588
auction.igavel.com
Online auction, arts, antiques and collectibles

Ivey-Selkirk
7447 Forsyth Blvd.
Saint Louis, MO 63105
314-726-5515
www.iveyselkirk.com
Full service

Photo courtesy Leslie Hindman Auctioneers, Chicago; www.LeslieHindman.com

Dress, Christian Francis Roth, Crayon motif, late 1980s, in yellow and blue wool knit, swing fit, one sleeve in form of sky-blue Crayon, patch pocket at front with scribbling throughout. Labeled: Christian Francis Roth/New York City. Small moth holes. **$840**

Jackson's International Auctioneers and Appraisers
2229 Lincoln St.
Cedar Falls, Iowa 50613
319-277-2256
www.jacksonsauction.com
Full service, religious and Russian objects, postcards

James D. Julia Inc.
P.O. Box 830
Fairfield, ME 04937
207-453-7125
www.juliaauctions.net
Full service, toys, glass, lighting, firearms

John Moran Auctioneers Inc.
735 W. Woodbury Road
Altadena, CA 91001
626-793-1833
www.johnmoran.com
Full service, California art

Kaminski Auctions
564 Cabot St.
Beverly, MA 01915
978-927-2223 or
5171 Santa Fe St., Suite B
San Diego, CA 92119
508-328-5967
www.kaminskiauctions.com
Full service

Lang's Sporting Collectibles
663 Pleasant Valley Road
Waterville, NY 13480
315-841-4623
www.langsauction.com
Antique fishing tackle and memorabilia

Leslie Hindman Auctioneers
1338 W. Lake St.
Chicago, Il 60607
312-280-1212
www.lesliehindman.com
Full service

McMasters Harris Auction Co.
5855 John Glenn Hwy
P.O. Box 1755
Cambridge, OH 43725
740-432-7400
www.mcmastersharris.com
Dolls and accessories

Michael Ivankovich Auction Co.
P.O. Box 1536
Doylestown, PA 18901
215-345-6094
www.wnutting.com
Wallace Nutting objects

Leland Little Auctions & Estate Sales Ltd.
246 S. Nash St.
Hillsborough, NC 27278
919-644-1243
www.llauctions.com
Full Service

Litchfield County Auctions Inc.
425 Bantam Road (Route 202)
Litchfield, CT 06759
860-567-4661
212-724-0156
www.litchfieldcountyauctions.com
Full service

Mark Mattox Auctioneer & Real Estate Broker Inc.
3740 Maysville Road
Carlisle, KY 40311
859-289-5720
www.mattoxrealestate.com
Full service

Morphy Auctions
2000 N. Reading Road
Denver, PA 17517
717-335-3435
www.morphyauctions.com
Toys, banks, advertising, pop culture

New Orleans Auction Galleries Inc.
801 Magazine St.
New Orleans, LA 70130
800-501-0277
www.neworleansauction.com
Full service, Victorian

Noel Barrett Vintage Toys @ Auction
P.O. Box 300
Carversville, PA 18913
215-297 5109
www.noelbarrett.com
Toys, banks, holiday, advertising

Photo courtesy Old Town Auctions LLC, Boonsboro, Md.; www.OldTownAuctions.com

A&A American Metal Toy Co., Desi Arnaz, conga drum, retains original tag copyrighted 1952 by Lucille Ball – Desi Arnaz; bottom metal band has dent; small dent to body at top band; drum head intact with some wrinkling; rare original box: complete, split on one seam. **$6,600**

Old Town Auctions
P.O. Box 91
Boonsboro, MD 21713
240-291-0114
781-771-3998
www.oldtownauctions.com
Toys, Advertising, Americana; no Internet sales

Old World Auctions
2155 W. Hwy 89A, Suite 206
Sedona, AZ 86336
800-664-7757
www.oldworldauctions.com
Maps, documents

Past Tyme Pleasures
39 California Ave., Suite 105
Pleasanton, CA 94566
925-484-6442
www.pasttyme1.com
Internet catalog auctions

Philip Weiss Auctions
1 Neil Court
Oceanside, NY 11572
516-594-0731
www.prwauctions.com
Full service, comic art

Pook & Pook Inc.
463 East Lancaster Ave.
Downingtown, PA 19335
610-629-0695
www.pookandpook.com
Full service, Americana

Professional Appraisers & Liquidators LLC
16 Lemington Court
Homosassa, FL 34446
800-542-3877
www.charliefudge.com
Full Service

**Quinn's Auction Galleries &
    Waverly Rare Books**
431 N. Maple Ave.
Falls Church, VA 22046
703-532-5632
www.quinnsauction.com
www.waverlyauctions.com
Full service, rare books and prints

Photo courtesy Rago Arts and Auction Center, Lambertville, N.J.;
www.RagoArts.com

Lamp, table, Dirk Van Erp, hammered copper and mica, its four-panel conical shade atop a two-socket trumpet-shaped base. Original patina and mica. Open box windmill mark, 18" x 17". **$14,400**

Rago Arts and Auction Center
333 N. Main St.
Lambertville, NJ 08530
609-397-9374
www.ragoarts.com
Arts & Crafts, modernism, fine art

Red Baron's Antiques Inc.
6450 Roswell Road
Atlanta, GA 30328
404-252-3770
www.redbaronsantiques.com
Full service, Victorian, architectural objects

Rich Penn Auctions
P.O. Box 1355
Waterloo, IA 50704
319-291-6688
www.richpennauctions.com
Advertising and country-store objects

Richard D. Hatch & Associates
913 Upward Road
Flat Rock, NC 28731
828-696-3440
www.richardhatchauctions.com
Full service

Photo courtesy Robert Edward Auctions, Watchung, N.J.;
www.RobertEdwardAuctions.com

Babe Ruth, 1914 Baltimore News rookie card. Ruth just happened to be with the Baltimore Orioles in 1914, as a complete unknown, when the Baltimore News issued the card set that included him. **$517,250**

Photo courtesy Slotin Auction, Buford, Ga.; www.SlotinFolkArt.com

Finster, Howard. Cutout Coke Sign. **$1,500**

Robert Edward Auctions LLC
P.O. Box 7256
Watchung, NJ 07069
908-226-9900
www.robertedwardauctions.com
Baseball, sports memorabilia

Rock Island Auction Co.
4507 49th Ave.
Moline, IL 61265-7578
800-238-8022
www.rockislandauction.com
Firearms, edged weapons and accessories

St. Charles Gallery Inc.
1330 St. Charles Ave.
New Orleans, LA 70130
504-586-8733
www.stcharlesgallery.com
Full service, Victorian

Samuel T. Freeman & Co.
1808 Chestnut St.
Philadelphia, PA 19103
215-563-9275
www.freemansauction.com
Full service, Americana

Seeck Auctions
P.O. Box 377
Mason City, IA 50402
641-424-1116
www.seeckauction.com
Full service, carnival glass

Showtime Auction Services
22619 Monterey Drive
Woodhaven, MI 48183
734-676-9703 Michigan Office
909-392-4707 California Office
316-721-5236 Kansas Office
www.ShowtimeAuctions.com
Coin-ops, advertising

Skinner Inc.
357 Main St.
Bolton, MA 01740
978-779-6241
www.skinnerinc.com
Full service, Americana

Sloans and Kenyon
7034 Wisconsin Ave.
Chevy Chase, MD 20815
301-634-2344
www.sloansandkenyon.com
Full service

Slotin Folk Art
Folk Fest Inc.
5619 Ridgetop Drive
Gainesville, GA 30504
770-532-1115
www.slotinfolkart.com
Naïve and outsider art

Stover's Auctions
302 S. Dickerson St.
Burgaw, NC 28425
910-259-0570
www.stoversauctions.com
Full service

Strawser Auctions
P.O. Box 332, 200 N. Main
Wolcottville, IN 46795
260-854-2859
www.strawserauctions.com
Full service, majolica, Fiesta ware

Swann Galleries Inc.
104 E. 25th St.
New York, NY 10010
212-254-4710
www.swanngalleries.com
Rare books, prints, photographs, posters

Theriault's
P.O. Box 151
Annapolis, MD 21404
800-638-0422
www.theriaults.com
Dolls and accessories

Tom Harris Auction Center
203 S. 18th Ave.
Marshalltown, IA 50158
641-754-4890
www.tomharrisauctions.com
Full service, clocks, watches

Tradewinds Antiques
P.O. Box 249
Manchester-By-The-Sea, MA 01944-0249
978-526-4085
www.tradewindsantiques.com
Canes

Treadway Gallery
2029 Madison Road
Cincinnati, OH 45208
513-321-6742

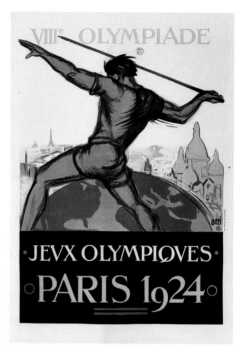

Photo courtesy Swann Auction Galleries, New York; www.SwannGalleries.com

Jeux Olympiques / Paris, 1924, by Orsi, Phogor 92, Paris, vertical and horizontal folds; minor creases and abrasions in image; repaired tears and restoration in image. A taut, poised and powerful image set against the Parisian skyline. One of two posters chosen by the French Olympic Committee to advertise the 8th Olympiad. French version, 46 7/8" x 31 1/4". **$4,400**

John Toomey Gallery
818 North Blvd.
Oak Park, IL 60301
708-383-5234
www.treadwaygallery.com
Arts & Crafts, modernism, fine art

Victorian Casino Antiques
5585 S. Valley View Blvd., Suite 1
Las Vegas, NV 89118
702-382-2466
www.vcaauction.com
Coin-ops, gambling

Wiederseim Associates Inc.
P.O. Box 470
Chester Springs, PA 19425
610-827-1910
www.wiederseim.com
Full service

Advertising

ADVERTISING

Commercial messages and displays have been found in the ruins of ancient Arabia. Egyptians used papyrus to create sales messages and wall posters, while lost-and-found advertising was common in ancient Greece and Rome. As printing developed in the 15th and 16th centuries, advertising expanded to include handbills. In the 17th century, advertisements started to appear in weekly newspapers in England.

Also see Coca-Cola, Posters, Toys.

Ashtray, plates, Moxie, lot of six items, sandwich plates feature Moxie girl logo and ashtray features pointing Frank Archer. Plates, 8 1/4" d. Ashtray, 5 1/2" d. Plates: three good to very good while other three have some spider cracks. Ashtray has some cigarette staining. .... **$201 all**

Calendar, Firestone Tires, 1935, deco image on textured paper from the Rome, N.Y., Tire and Battery Service, 20 3/4" w x 42" h; original metal hanging strip and full date pad. Two small punctures to field but otherwise very good condition with strong bright colors. **$288**

Calendar, Hercules Powder Co., 1916, four-page calendar with cover illustration of ring-neck pheasant. Other images include farm scene, black-breasted plovers and a gold miner; 11 1/2" w x 27 1/2" h; retains original metal hanging strip, subtle edge tears... **$1,725**

Calendar, Lykens Brewing Co., 1912, springtime illustration by Arthur J. Elsley of mother and daughter with their faithful St. Bernard companion; 17" w x 23 1/4" h in frame. **$172**

Calendar, S.S. Patterson, 1904, stone lithographed image of reclining damsel with her beer from this Dillon, Mont., distributor of Val Blatz Brewing Co.'s Milwaukee Beer; 16" w x 24" h in frame; small circular surface cut at bottom margin, possibly a minor repair. One or two tiny edge tears... **$632**

Calendar, Peters Cartridge Co., 1909, hunting dog illustration by A. Muss-Arnolt titled, The First Lesson-Steady; 13 3/4" w x 27 1/4" h; soft roll creases; retains top and bottom metal bands; December date sheet only. **$2,415**

Containers, Planter's Peanuts, lot of six includes five glass peanut jars and one 10-pound peanut tin for Pennant-brand salted peanuts. Two "octagon jars" with lids; two "fishbowl" jars with lids, one with most of its original label; one square jar with lid. Good to very good condition, a few lids and necks of jars show light chips and nibbles. **$201**

Calendar, Dubuque Malting Co., 1902, scarce, colorful calendar from this Iowa brewer promoting their line of Banquet Beer, 17" w x 22 3/4" h in frame; top and bottom margins have been replaced; professional restoration to bottom right corner; repaired horizontal tear through entire image just above trademark logo; two pages of calendar date sheets in-painted. **$1,035**

Calendar, Bowler Bros. Ltd. Brewing Co., 1900, scarce stone lithograph depicting a bathing-suit-attired young beauty at the shore, Image 13 3/4" w x 22 3/4" h in frame; areas of professional restoration and in-painting, particularly along several horizontal creases and to the blue water background. **$1,020**

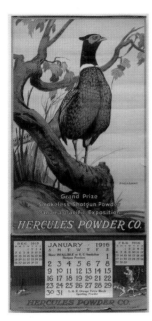

Calendar, Hercules Powder Co., 1916, four-page calendar with cover illustration of ring-neck pheasant. Other images include farm scene, black-breasted plovers and a gold miner; 11 1/2" w x 27 1/2" h; retains original metal hanging strip, subtle edge tears. **$1,725**

Calendar, Prospect Brewing Co., 1893, a seldom-seen advertisement from this Philadelphia brewer. Small colorful vignettes flank the calendar dates and commemorate a variety of national holidays, 18 1/2" w x 28" h in frame; horizontal fold crease four inches from the top; vertical scuff at top center. **$4,370**

Calendar, Peters Cartridge Co., 1908, one of the rarest of the Peters calendars, showing duck hunters in a marsh by the Strowbridge Litho. Co., Cincinnati; 13 3/4" w x 27 1/4" h; some edge wear and fingernail-sized hole at bottom left corner. Retains both metal bands and what appears to be the balance of a June date pad. **$7,762**

Calendar, Weisbrod & Hess Brewing Co., 1906, elusive calendar from this Philadelphia brewer, with a variety of vignettes showing outdoor activities in the surrounding Pennsylvania countryside. Lower portion of calendar has illustrations of their Rheingold and Shakespeare brews, 19" w x 28" h in frame; some flattened paper creases across top; small area of paper loss to the "S" in Shakespeare; minor in-painting at bottom. **$1,380**

Calendar, Firestone Tires, 1935, deco image on textured paper from the Rome, N.Y., Tire and Battery Service, 20 3/4" w x 42" h; original metal hanging strip and full date pad. Two small punctures to field but otherwise very good condition with strong bright colors. **$288**

Calendar, Peters Cartridge Co., 1909, hunting dog illustration by A. Muss-Arnolt titled, The First Lesson-Steady; 13 3/4" w x 27 1/4" h; soft roll creases; retains top and bottom metal bands; December date sheet only. **$2,415**

Opening page:

Calendar, Peters Cartridge Co., 1906, illustration of moose hunters captioned "Coming Out a Head," Strobridge Litho. Co., Cincinnati; 13 3/4" w x 27 1/4" h; slight paper loss where date pad used to be, horizontal roll creases; retains both metal bands. **$3,737**

*Calendar, Lykens Brewing Co., 1912,
springtime illustration by Arthur J.
Elsley of mother and daughter with their
faithful St. Bernard companion; 17" w x
23 1/4" h in frame.* **$172**

*Calendar, S.S. Patterson, 1904, stone lithographed
image of reclining damsel with her beer from this
Dillon, Mont., distributor of Val Blatz Brewing
Co.'s Milwaukee Beer; 16" w x 24" h in frame;
small circular surface cut at bottom margin,
possibly a minor repair. One or two tiny edge tears.*
$632

Dispenser, Hires, ceramic, classic hourglass-shaped soda fountain dispenser, complete with pump and Hires ceramic insert, 14" h. Light discoloration to bottom of dispenser, small stress crack to exterior. **$420**

Dispenser, Kola Mint keg/syrup dispenser with original crate, thick wooden barrel keg with copper rings, painted with red and white lettering stating "Demonstrating Dept., Williamsport Penna." Lid with porcelain knob. Barrel has plaque that reads "U.C. Water Cooler, Union Cooperage Co., St. Louis". Rests on separate round wooden base on four bent steel legs. Original wooden crate with similar lettering style "K-M-Co., Williamsport PA 2" with hinged side handles. Interior has partial paper label on inner lid showing contents. Barrel only, 19" h. Crate with various chips and scratches. **$920**

Dispenser, Liberty Root Beer, ceramic, lettering to two sides with the logo "Try a Stein-It's Fine". Includes correct style pump with "Root Beer" ceramic insert, 13 3/4" h. **$3,450**

Display, Baker Chocolate, thick cardboard die-cut window advertisement featuring the Baker Chocolate girl with tray of goodies approaching a group of Revolutionary War-era nobles enjoying Baker's hot chocolate. Large banner at top reads, "The Mills of Walter Baker & Co. Ltd. 52 Highest awards." Shown with vignettes around perimeter of various Baker products. Center section is open suggesting that this was a window display to have presentation behind; 38 1/4" w x 28" h. Some restoration to top section and showing some edge wear and crease at top corner, overall very good. **$345**

Photo courtesy Hake's Americana & Collectibles, York, Pa; www.Hakes.com

Display, Baranger Honeymoon Rocket, motion display, with original shipping crate, working, minor age wear, minor paint wear to base, 19" h, 20" w, 14" deep. **$12,100**

Photo courtesy Green Valley Auctions, Mt. Crawford, Va., www.GreenValleyAuctions.com

Display, American carved and painted wood and painted wrought iron figure of a hackney, viceroy and driver, the horse features a braided mane and is fitted with harness, the driver is outfitted in a suit and top hat with a red lap robe covering his legs, the cart features an iron chassis and shafts, a "W" is carved on each side. A note indicates that this was part of a St. Louis tack shop window display. Second quarter 20th century; 22 1/2" h, 47" l, excellent condition, minor repairs to driver, reins detached. **$12,100**

Photo courtesy Hake's Americana & Collectibles, York, Pa; www.Hakes.com

Display dolls (theatrical size), Mickey Mouse and Minnie Mouse, giant display-model dolls, made by Charlotte Clark, early 1930s, 44" h Mickey and 48" h Minnie (smaller dolls shown for comparison). **$151,534 pair**

Photo courtesy James D. Julia Auctioneers, Fairfield, Maine; www.JuliaAuctions.com

Display, Lone Star Beer, chalkware, reclining armadillo wrapped around a bottle of Lone Star Beer; 12" w x 11 1/2" h x 6" deep. Good to very good condition with a few tiny chips to base. **$402**

Photo courtesy Old Town Auctions LLC, Boonsboro, Md.; www.OldTownAuctions.com

Display, Gem Damaskeene Razor, clockwork mechanical, depicting a man shaving as he rocks his baby, in original shipping crate, light edge wear to top of man's head, scattered light spotting to paper, sign at bottom as minor paper damage on right side, clockwork housing retains paper labels, has original key, works fine, 29 1/4" h, 20 3/4" w, wood crate still retains original shipping labels, lid has cracked board. **$3,850**

Photo courtesy James D. Julia Auctioneers, Fairfield, Maine; www.JuliaAuctions.com

Display, Nut House, uncommon mahogany figural countertop display complete with two embossed glass jars and scoop. The roof and sides of the house retain their original gilt lettering; 18" w, 16" h x 8" deep. Very good to excellent condition, backside of the house reveals two wood chips, one at the roof and one at the lower edge of one side. **$480**

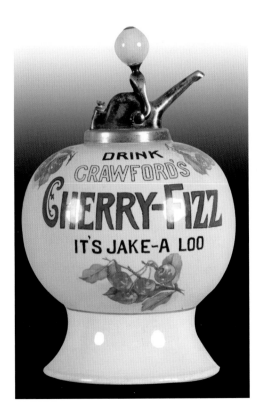

Photo courtesy Morphy Auctions, Denver, Pa.; www.MorphyAuctions.com

Dispenser, Crawford's Cherry-Fizz, circa 1920s, ceramic with original ball pump. Light soiling and minor wear. No chips or cracks. **$10,350**

Photo courtesy James D. Julia Auctioneers, Fairfield, Maine; www.JuliaAuctions.com

Figure, Red Goose Shoes, plaster, figure on a green base was a counter decoration. Has raised lettering on the chest reading "Red Goose Shoes." Approximately 11 1/4" h. Generally, very good condition. A few scattered paint chips over the surface; retains almost all of its paint. **$115**

Fan pull or hanging sign, Hires Root Beer, circa 1900, cardboard lithograph, two-sided, depicts an early version of the Ugly Kid holding a mug feeding a living planet Earth. Minor bend, minor edge wear, and a few mildew spots on back. One small closed crack, 11" x 10". **$52,000**

Display, Bear Brand Hosiery, papier-mâché, countertop store advertisement featuring Papa Bear, Momma Bear and Baby Bear; 18 1/2" h. Spots of wear to base but otherwise very good condition. **$1,035**

Display, Buster Brown Shoes, chalkware, uncommon countertop display featuring Buster Brown and his dog, Tighe, for the "Tread Straight" line of shoes; 16 1/2" h. Generally good condition; several chips to base and Buster's hat; paint loss to base, shoe sign and Buster's leg. **$460**

Display, Crawford Cigars, wood, countertop display is hand lettered on all four sides "Smoke the Crawford 5 cent Cigar." It appears this display originally had smoke pumped through a tube located in the back to a pipe that extends up from the top, possibly having held at one time a cigar or figural smoking head; 20 1/2" w, 28" h x 12" deep. Appears to be all original surfaces; a few chips to wooden base. **$805**

Display, Crystal Rock Beer, chalkware, from the Cleveland and Sandusky Brewing Co. of a bartender wearing a Crystal Rock apron pouring a mug of brew; 10" w x 13 1/2" h x 7" deep. A few surface nicks and a few fine age lines, but otherwise very good condition. **$575**

Display, Edison Mazda Lamps light bulbs, with the colorful "Get Together" front panel illustration by Maxfield Parrish. Features twelve porcelain sockets radiating around a figural light-bulb shaped counter top display. Each socket has an individual on/off switch, which collectively held a variety of Edison Mazda-GE light bulbs; 15 3/4" w x 23 1/2" h. Good to very good condition; front panel shows areas of discoloration but the Parrish graphics remain unaffected with the exception of a few fine scratches. Back base panel has some loss of color; one porcelain socket and switch have old break, original cord is frayed and has not been tested. **$2,300**

Display, Indian brave seated cross-legged, holding pennant – Quoddy Moccasins – on pole, painted wood, red painted 20" square base, 30" h overall, minor paint loss, crazing to surface on back and chest; braided hair possibly repaired. **$977**

Displays, "Amos" and "Andy" Pepsodent Toothpaste, sardboard, die cut featuring the popular radio personalities of Amos and Andy promoting Pepsodent Toothpaste. Copyright 1930. Andy 22" w x 61" h, Amos 21" w x 54" h. Fair to good condition; some cardboard and paper loss, staining, creases and edge tears. .... **$460 pair**

Displays, Ritz Ice Cream Cone, composition, pair, feature bathing boy and girl clutching colossal ice cream cones standing atop stylized Art Deco bases, which read "Ice Cream with a Facchino Cone;" 22" h. Bathing girl figure shows some cracking to the base, which doesn't effect its stability, otherwise both figures in good to very good condition. **$1,035**

Fan, Lucky Strike, Frank Sinatra appears on this tobacco leaf fan given to audience members during the 1950-1959 telecast of "Your Hit Parade" show, sponsored by Lucky Strike. Lot includes two glossy photos; 7 1/2" w x 13" h in frame. Good condition; repair to paper tear at top; cellophane tape left side; slight paper loss right side. **$690**

Lithograph, Frank Abbott, colorful image of buckskin-clad Indian maiden for this Chicago retailer of lumber, bank and office fittings. Paul B. King illustration printed on textured paper. Image size, 16 1/4" w x 20 1/4" h. Near excellent with bright strong colors. **$604**

Photo courtesy James D. Julia Auctioneers, Fairfield, Maine; www.JuliaAuctions.com

Display, Whitman's Chocolate, scarce Lego-style messenger boy with original Whitman's Sampler candy box under arm. These were distributed in limited numbers during the 1920s to the sales force for selected accounts where Whitman's was sold. Base bears an aluminum tag which reads, "Designed and produced by W.L. Stensgaard & Associates, Inc., Chicago, Illinois;" 18 3/4" h. Some wear to corners of cardboard box but the balance of the display in very good to excellent condition. **$2,645**

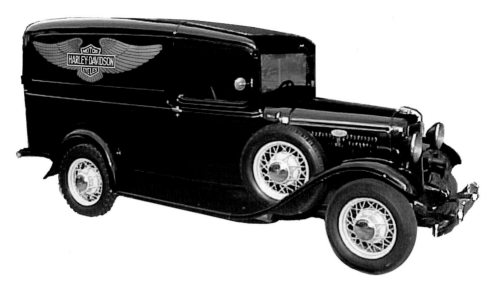

Photo courtesy Old Town Auctions LLC, Boonsboro, Md.; www.OldTownAuctions.com

Panel truck, Harley-Davidson 1934 Ford panel truck with old "wings" logo on both sides, purportedly used by a Harley dealer in the early 1950s as a delivery vehicle, running, flathead V-8, one of about 800 built. **$15,950**

Photo courtesy James D. Julia Auctioneers, Fairfield, Maine; www.JuliaAuctions.com

Sign, Campbell's Soups, tin, the Holy Grail of all advertising signs, rarely seen and seldom ever appearing on the auction block. When Campbell's introduced this sign to their selected retail accounts, it created such a public controversy by using an image of the American Flag for commercial self-promotion that most of the signs were quickly withdrawn and destroyed. Lithographed by the Standard Adv. Co., Coshocton, Ohio; 39 1/4" l x 27 1/4" h. Overall fair to good condition. Perimeter edges exhibit bending, nail holes, scuffs and scratches. Field of sign shows multiple nail holes and two 1/2" diameter holes, cause unknown. Bottom left corner of the "flag" and the word "Just" show some corrosion with a build up of some tar-like substance. **$18,400**

Lithograph, Bunker Hill Breweries, 1896 illustration by Leon Moran and lithographed by Louis Prang for A. G. Van Nostrand, Bunker Hill Breweries of Charlestown, Mass. Complete with original mat. Matted image measures 17 1/2" w x 23 1/2 " h in frame. Some moisture stains around perimeter of mat board, and to the far right margin of the lithographed image, otherwise in good condition. **$240**

Lithograph, Phoenix Brewing Co., springtime farmyard illustration from this Rice Lake, Wis., brewer. Image 14 1/4" w x 18 3/4" h in frame. Good to very good condition with some light surface scuffs. Staple marks would indicate this was probably used as a calendar................................ **$862**

Lithograph, Sweet Home Soap, little girl with roses, copyright 1895. Lithograph appears to be in original ornate frame. Image size, 13 1/2" w x 27 1/2" h. Water stain along bottom edge; a few areas of discoloration from original wood backing boards; light soiling overall to white background............................ **$345**

Lithograph, Yardley's Old English Lavender, on textured paper laid down on cardboard of colorful English street peddlers with their baskets of lavender. The textured surface and lithographic quality of this advertisement lend it the look of an oil painting. Image size, 27 1/2" w x 21 1/2" h. Very good condition with some light surface scuffs........ **$805**

Plaque, Goodyear Tires Zeppelin, brass, manufactured by the Medallic-Art Co., N.Y., and given to tire dealers of distinction to commemorate ten years of working relationships; 12" w x 17" h. Very good condition.........**$345**

Pocket mirror, Garrett's Rye, celluloid, mirror featuring a semi-nude Diana the Huntress standing in a landscape with her bow. The caption, "Garrett's XXXX Baker Rye, Oldest Rye in Baltimore." Approximately 2 3/4" l. A small blister spot on celluloid surface by Diana's wrist; otherwise, very good condition. Retains original mirror. **$345**

Pocket mirror, Pepsi-Cola, celluloid, features a Lillian Russell-type figure holding a glass of Pepsi-Cola at a soda fountain. Above, "The Pepsi-Cola Girl 5¢;" 2 3/4" l. Celluloid generally in good condition. The mirror on the reverse side broken...**$575**

Sign, Albis Barber Shop, painted wood, American, late 19th/early 20th century, (weathered surface), old gilt surface shows through top and bottom bulbed areas, 35 1/2" h, 9 1/2" w. **$296**

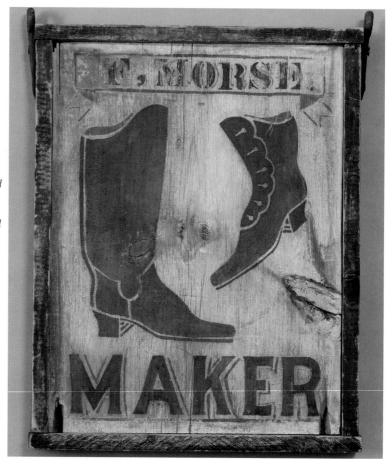

Photo courtesy Skinner Inc., Boston,
www.SkinnerInc.com

Sign, boot maker, painted wood and iron, American, late 19th century, double-sided rectangular painted panel with applied molding, painted with a man's and woman's boot and lettering "F. MORSE MAKER," iron hardware, (weathered surface), about 2" x 1 1/2" loss to lower right corner of panel reverse side, 24" x 17 3/4". **$2,014**

Photo courtesy Morphy Auctions, Denver, Pa.;
www.MorphyAuctions.com

Sign, Alaska Fur Co., double sided with detailed carving, original finish, circa 1890. Manufactured by the City Sign Co. Comes with mounting bracket, 55" l x 53" h. **$79,000**

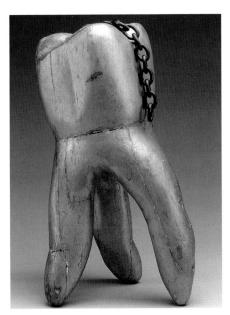

Photo courtesy James D. Julia Auctioneers, Fairfield, Maine; www.JuliaAuctions.com

Sign, dentist tooth, carved wood with chain, which likely was displayed outside the dentist's office; 9" w x 15 1/2" h. Good to very good condition, appears to have multiple layers of gilt paint. **$2,243**

Photo courtesy Skinner Inc., Boston, www.SkinnerInc.com

Sign, Father Time, painted cast iron and tin, American, late 19th century, double sided sign, (dial repainted), 29" h, 25" w. **$829**

Sign, The Berengaria Steamship, tin, illustration of this triple-stack passenger steamer entering New York City harbor with the Statue of Liberty in the background. Original illustration by A.F. Bishop, 1924; 39 1/2" w x 29 1/2" h. Sign nailed to wood stretchers at perimeter edge and in center; light scattered scuffs, stains, scratches. **$480**

Sign, Brown's Shoes, tin, early embossed advertisement with graphic pointing finger from the company that introduced the Buster Brown brand in 1904. Image 19 1/2" w x 11 1/2" h, in wood frame. Fair condition, several nail holes, creasing, margin tear and surface discoloration. **$57**

Sign, Canada Dry Spur, cardboard, aviatrix leaning against her airplane taking time out for a refreshing Spur; 27" w x 44" h. Fair to good condition; horizontal crease with some cellophane tape; multiple staple holes across top and bottom. **$115**

Sign, Carter's Ink Bottle/Mucilage, tin, rare embossed sign, circa 1870s with stereotyped black youth attempting to extricate a fashionably attired gent stuck to a crate of Carter's Mucilage, captioned "The Great Stickist." Image size 13 1/4" w 9 1/4" h. Strong graphic appeal and rarity offsets some of its condition drawbacks, which include nail holes at corners, light surface pitting and loss of pigment bottom right corner. **$3,738**

Sign, Chicago, Rock Island & Pacific reverse-on-glass, train panorama of engine tender and five cars, painted and highlighted with slices of mother-of-pearl. This 1902 version showing the Rocky Mountain Limited train with the Colorado Rockies in the background; 89" l x 14" h. Overall very good to excellent condition. Some spots of discoloration to background of cars and tender. **$9,775**

Sign, Chiclets Gum, tin, die cut, fox character, one of a set of six animals produced by Chiclets Gum circa 1916. Includes tin easel back for counter display; 7" w x 10" h. Good to very good condition. Matte surface with some soiling and wear. **$402**

Sign, Clark's Mile-End Spool Cotton, cardboard with profile view of portly man in red striped pants and blue coat carrying a sample of Clark's thread, all on black background. Bottom reads, "Thos. Russell & Co., Sole Agents." In old, possibly original, frame; 28 1/2" h x 22" w. Some in-painting, predominantly to oval logo in top left corner, but also various spots to the background. Some light warping, overall good. **$230**

Sign, Cleveland and Sandusky Brewing Co., tin, oval advertisement featuring a raised simulated wood-grain frame, depicting a satisfied consumer. Lithographed by the H.D. Beach Co., Coshocton, Ohio, circa 1902; 22 1/4" w x 28 1/2" h. Generally good condition with some light wear; nail hole at top; and some spotting and yellowing to original surface finish. **$258**

Sign, Clossman Hardware Company, tin, circa late 1920s to early 1930s, embossed with open touring car and bi-plane graphics from this Zanesville, Ohio, company. Lithographed V. Crystal Adv. Co., Zanesville; 27 3/4" w x 19 3/4" h. Has a vertical crease with some paint loss just to the back of the touring car; a few other light soft creases with paint chips; otherwise in good to very good condition. **$403**

Sign, Cooks Beer, tin on cardboard, southern plantation scene with black waiter and maid promoting Cooks Goldblume beer for this Evansville, Ind., brewer; 21" w x 13" h. Good to very good condition; some light surface pitting, a few soft perimeter bends and a vertical scratch to waiter's leg. Retains original brass chain hanger. **$287**

Photo courtesy Skinner Inc., Boston, www.SkinnerInc.com

Sign, figural, painted molded tin, American, late 19th/early 20th century, depicting a figure of a black man holding a sign inscribed, "A Word to the Wise/See Miller," scattered small paint losses, possible line of retouch on lower portion of shirt, 33 3/4", 27" w. **$2,251**

Photo courtesy James D. Julia Auctioneers, Fairfield, Maine; www.JuliaAuctions.com

Sign, Hire's Root Beer, celluloid over cardboard, with original manufacturer's label on reverse. Features an illustration of the Hires Root Beer boy and mug. Lithographed by Bastian Bros. Co., Rochester, N.Y.; 6" w x 8" h. Edge wear concentrated at corners with a few chips along edges, otherwise very good condition. **$3,162**

Photo courtesy James D. Julia Auctioneers, Fairfield, Maine; www.JuliaAuctions.com

Sign, Job Cigarette papers, cardboard, Art Nouveau illustration of red-headed damsel by the artist Edgard Maxence, 1900; 14 3/4" w x 20" h. Good to very good condition; has some light surface foxing, a few paper ripples along top margin; and two small vertical punctures to lower right corner, which may have held a sample packet of rolling papers. **$345**

Photo courtesy James D. Julia Auctioneers, Fairfield, Maine; www.JuliaAuctions.com

Sign, Home Run Cigarettes, cardboard, stone-lithographed advertisement with baseball illustration. Copyright 1909 by the American Tobacco Co. Image 11 1/2" w x 17 1/2" h. Very good condition; outer white border has a couple chips, but only one at the bottom actually extends slightly into the printed image. **$5,750**

Photo courtesy James D. Julia Auctioneers, Fairfield, Maine; www.JuliaAuctions.com

Sign, I.W. Harper Whiskey, vitrolite, hunting lodge illustration on milk glass, captioned "Here's Happy Days." Image 17 1/2" w x 23 1/2" h in frame. Very good condition. **$805**

Photo courtesy Skinner Inc., Boston, www.SkinnerInc.com

Sign, L. Coe's House of Entertainment, tavern, painted wood, American, early 19th century, oval sign with brass hanging ring, with black lettering on a gray-blue ground over previous white-painted ground, (loss, lacks frame), 33 3/4" h, 20 1/4" w. **$2,014**

Photo courtesy James D. Julia Auctioneers, Fairfield, Maine; www.JuliaAuctions.com

Sign, Mentor Comfort Underwear, die-cut countertop advertisement with metal easel features an illustration of mom with young daughter, both comfortably clad in their Mentor long johns; 19 1/2" w x 27 1/4" h. Generally good to very good condition with a few soft creases and light surface scuffs. **$3,335**

Sign, Dutch Baby, porcelain, convex advertisement for Dutch Baby Condensed Milk with tin can illustration of Holland countryside with windmill; 35 1/2 w x 24" h. Good to very good condition with some perimeter edge chips and two areas of fine surface stress cracks. **$1,093**

Sign, Ericsson Steamship, tin, self-framed illustration of the steamship Lord Baltimore leaving the dock with a full accompaniment of passengers, which emphasizes their speedy "20 Knot Day Boat" service between Philadelphia and Baltimore. Lithographed by Meek Co., Coshocton, Ohio, after the painting by H.C. Greaves; 33" w x 23" h. Sign has had professional paint restoration. Displays good to very good with some light surface discoloration, paint chips and light spotting. **$2,875**

Sign, Fleet Bros. Department Store, tin, flat die-cut tin advertisement for a Florida department store depicting a portly gent in red, white, and black encouraging the viewer to "Visit the Big Store First." Mounted to newer wooden backing with similar cut for support; 48" h x 18" w. Overall weather-related chipping and wear. **$210**

Sign, Fry's Chocolate, porcelain, English candy manufacturer with humorous images of a young boy in various stages of anticipation of a Fry's chocolate treat, circa 1910; 30" w x 22" h. Large chip to top middle mounting hole, otherwise only minor chips to perimeter edge. Some very light spotting to white background, otherwise very good condition. **$1,680**

Sign, H.P. Hood & Sons Ice Cream, porcelain, colorful version of this truck sign, with illustration of dairy cow in a summer pasture. Manufactured by the Ingram-Rich Co., Beaver Falls, Pa., circa 1934; 30" d. Good condition; chips to mounting holes and several in field; some light iron stains to the blue sky; some scattered light surface scuffs; some waviness to perimeter edge. **$3,738**

Photo courtesy Old Town Auctions LLC, Boonsboro, Md.; www.OldTownAuctions.com

Sign, Moxie, self-framed tin, featuring the company's mascot horse in a convertible, scarce size and design, some light edge wear and marks to mounting holes, 36 3/8" x 12 3/8". **$4,675**

Photo courtesy James D. Julia Auctioneers, Fairfield, Maine; www.JuliaAuctions.com

Sign, R.G. Sullivan's cigars, porcelain, four-color advertisement for this Manchester, N.H., company's 7-20-4 cigar products; 23" l x 10 1/2" h. Near excellent condition, missing several grommets. **$201**

Sign, Hire's Root Beer, cardboard, embossed with image of bottle on one side and root-beer syrup box on the other; 11" w x 7" h. A few spots of light soiling, otherwise very good condition..**$2,875**

Sign, Hood's Ice Cream, tin, two embossed advertisements back-to-back in their original steel sidewalk sign holder. Overall 20 1/2" w x 33 1/2" h. Sign is good to very good condition; holder good with weathered surface. **$660**

Sign, Iver Johnson Revolver, tin, Double-sided, die cut captioned, "Hammer the Hammer" with graphics to match; 15 3/4" w x 11 3/4" h. Two minor soft bends to bottom, otherwise near excellent condition with original surface gloss....................**$5,750**

Sign, J.B. Lewis Shoemaker, tin, illustration of shoemaker at work in his shop to promote this Boston shoe manufacturer. Image size 13 1/4" w x 19 1/4" h. Generally good condition; a few filled nail holes, in-painted "S" to work apron dent, overall soiling and wear, and what appears to be a clear coat that has left some spotting..**$477**

Sign, J.G. Goodwin Slippers, wood, curved, hand-carved sign with original sand paint and gilt highlights, circa late 1800s; 17 1/4" w x 30" h. Very good to excellent condition with nice surface patina.......................................**$230**

Sign, Kool Cigarettes, NRA, illustration of penguin smoking a cigarette for this circa-WWII advertisement from the Brown & Williamson Co.; 17 1/2" w x 11 3/4" h. Good to very good condition. **$201**

Sign, Lakeside Club Bouquet Whiskey, vitrolite, lithograph on milk glass of a Victorian couple sampling a round or two from the Wm. Drueke Co., Grand Rapids, Mich.; 20" w x 17" h. Loss of coloring to portions of litho; chip bottom left corner. **$460**

Photo courtesy James D. Julia Auctioneers, Fairfield, Maine; www.JuliaAuctions.com

Sign, Old Diamond Wedding Rye, reverse on glass, gilt lettering against a blue background. Advertisement from Aug. Baetzhold distributor Buffalo, N.Y. Image 25 1/2" w x 15 1/2" h in period frame. Some lifting to blue background, otherwise good condition. **$258**

Sign, Maumee Brewing Co., cardboard, illustration of Colonialists enjoying the ale, porter and brown stout from this Toledo, Ohio, brewery. Image 13 3/4" w x 17 1/4" h in vintage frame. Repaired break bottom right with in-painting; repair to top right corner; some chips to image at top margin.........**$517**

Sign, Pepsi-Cola, tin, die-cut bottle form, circa 1941, embossed; 12" w x 44 1/2" h. Very good condition with some scattered light black paint overspray....................**$360**

Sign, pointing finger, tin, with contemporary plywood reinforcement. Age uncertain; 46" w x 19" h. Fair to good condition..**$230**

Sign, Procter & Gamble's Soaps reverse-on-glass, elaborate lettering highlighted with foil and mother-of-pearl flank this Cincinnati company's trademark logo of the Man in the Moon. Manufactured by the Meuttmann Co., Cincinnati. Image size: 29 1/2" l x 21 1/2" h. Good to very good condition with several areas of paint lifting and loss, notably to the black background surrounding the stars and some of the letters where what appears to be ground mother-of-pearl has been lost. **$1,668**

Sign, Schlitz Brewing Co., tin, fanciful characterization of a gent with the embodiment of the Schlitz trademark logo. Background is realistically lithographed to imitate quarter-sawn oak. Chas. W. Shonk Litho., Chicago. Image 13" w x 19" h in vintage frame. Very good condition with a few soft bends to top and bottom edges...................................**$1,495**

Photo courtesy Skinner Inc., Boston, www.SkinnerInc.com

Sign, T. Doty Tavern, painted wood, Canton, Mass., 18th century, double-sided sign flanked by baluster-turned posts, one side painted with the figure of a shackled rampant lion, over the inscription "T. Doty," the other side is painted with a faint standing horse figure over an earlier bust of Washington, but shows weathering, on original iron hardware, (surface imperfections), retouch to lion figure on body, legs, tail, areas surrounding lettering, 71 1/2" h overall, 44" w. **$28,440** (The Marquis de Lafayette, on his first visit to America, rested at Doty's while journeying from Taunton, Mass., to Boston. The tavern was also a refuge during the siege of Boston. It burned down on Dec. 20, 1888.)

Sign, Sen-Sen Mints, cardboard, illustration of fashionably attired lady singing on stage with background of chrysanthemums to promote this maker's line of throat and breath lozenges; 12" w x 48" h. Generally good condition; water stain to lady's dress; in-painting at top left margin; surface scuffs and a few small punctures. **$518**

Sign, Sherwin Williams Paints, porcelain, larger version of the die-cut "Cover the Earth" trademark logo; 35 1/2" w x 63" h. Good condition, with some fading and oxidation in places. **$210**

Sign, Sun Oil Co. "two-fisted," tin, die cut, unusual embossed sign to promote their gasoline's performance. Copyright 1932; 39" w x 16" h. Fair condition; several rust spots, pitting, and color loss. Sign reverse features contemporary wood support bracket. **$920**

Sign, Sweet-Orr Overalls, curved corner advertisement created using both printed lithography and traditional ground-glass firings. Illustration of men engaged in a tug-of-war with a pair of this maker's overalls as testimony to their durability; 18" w x 14" h. Very good condition with only a few small edge chips and nibbles. Retains original corner mounting bracket. **$1,610**

Sign, Thixton, Millett & Co. Distillers, tin, Louisville, Ky., featuring a rustic log cabin whiskey distillery with a buckskin clad "Daniel Boone" character guarding the door. Copyrighted 1904 by Thixton, Millett & Co. Lithographed by Hafusermann Co., N.Y.; 22 1/4" l x 14" h. Very good condition with scattered spots of surface pitting, some of which are difficult to see except upon close inspection. **$1,265**

Photo courtesy Old Town Auctions LLC, Boonsboro, Md.; www.OldTownAuctions.com

Sign, Standard Oil, 1940, painted tin, with Mickey Mouse, some discoloration to finish, minor bends, 24" d. **$2,090**

Sign and tray, Carnation Gum advertisements, includes square tin sign with raised simulated wood grain frame with an illustration of the Carnation Girl. Also includes tip tray with gum package and carnation graphics. Lower left is marked, "Copyright 1906 by the American Art Works, Coshocton, Ohio;" sign measures 13 3/4" square; tip tray 4 1/4" d. Frame of sign appears professionally restored while the field appears to have one small spot of in-painting; tip tray generally good. ....**$805 pair**

String holder, Moxie Soda, traditional bent-wire bottom attached to upper milk-glass panel that advertises "Drink Moxie-Clean-Safe" on one side; 8" w x 26" h. Good to very good condition...**$360**

Thermometer, Moxie, tin, version with Frank Archer image at the bottom and a Moxie bottle at the top. Complete with working thermometer tube and wood holder; 9 3/4" w x 25 1/2" h. Very good condition with scattered scuffs and some minor dents to bottom edge...**$1,020**

Tray, City Brewing Co., pre-Prohibition tray from this Toledo, Ohio, brewer for their Preferred Stock beer featuring the Carnation Girl illustration; 13" d. Very good to excellent condition with a dry, very finely crazed surface finish. .. **$316**

Tray, Eagle Brewing Co., circa 1908, captioned "Good Morning" lithographed by The Meek Co. for this Waterbury, Conn., brewer. 13 1/4" square. Good to very good condition with some professional in-painting concentrated around raised perimeter rim....................**$345**

Tray, Evans & Giehl Brewing Co., illustration of thoroughbred filly and her colt used to promote this Rome, N.Y., brewer's line of pure ales; 13 1/4" square. Some professional restoration and in-painting especially to the sky. **$840**

Tray, Finlay Brewing Co., pre-Prohibition tray with young woman holding aloft a bottle of this Toledo, Ohio, brewer's Salvator beer; 12" d. Good, overall matte surface with some crazing to the paint. **$316**

Tray, Moerlein Brewing Co., pre-Prohibition tray from this Cincinnati brewer lithographed by the Chas. W. Shonk Co., Litho, Chicago; 12" d. A few spots of light flaking, otherwise good condition. **$270**

ARCHITECTURAL ELEMENTS

Architectural elements, many of which are handcrafted, are those items that have been removed or salvaged from buildings, ships or gardens.

Beginning about 1840, decorative building styles began to feature carved wood and stone, stained glass, and ornate ironwork. At the same time, builders and manufacturers also began to use fancy doorknobs, doorplates, hinges, bells, window locks, shutter pulls and other decorative hardware as finishing touches on new homes and commercial buildings.

Hardware was primarily produced from bronze, brass and iron, and doorknobs also were made from clear, colored and cut glass. Highly ornate hardware began appearing in the late 1860s and remained popular through the early 1900s. Figural pieces that featured animals, birds and heroic or mythological images were popular, as were ornate and graphic designs that complimented the many architectural styles that emerged in the late 19th century.

Photo courtesy Skinner Inc., Boston, www.SkinnerInc.com

Finials (pair), white-and black-painted sheet iron spires, American, 19th century, paint wear, minor dents, 43 1/2" h. **$355 pair**

Cupola, circa 1860s, from the Universalist Unitarian Church of Waterville, Maine. Eight-sided with cathedral window openings, topped by two areas of wide molding and having a shingled rooftop. Weight approximately 8,000 pounds. Approximately 24' h x 13' d. Interior open section is 8 feet tall. **$1,150**

Fragments (pair), Chinese, gilt and red lacquer, the first of an audience scene between an official and warrior, the floral patterned floor and wall with mother-of-pearl inlay; the second of an official watching women on a garden terrace, overall: 16" h x 17" w. .... **$140 pair**

Window, Arts & Crafts style, leaded-glass with a balustrade, column and flower vase. Frame size, 70 3/4" h x 29" w... **$1,920**

Window, Frank Lloyd Wright design, vertical leaded-glass, after ones in the Coonley Playhouse, Riverside, Ill.; unmarked. Frame: 54 3/4" h x 20 1/4" w. **$1,200**

Window, leaded glass with seashells, unusual window motif with a border incorporating real scallop shells alternating with what appears to be stylized glass seaweed designs. Glass panel measures 23" w x 16 1/2" h, in original wood window frame. **$2,990**

Photo courtesy Skinner Inc., Boston, www.SkinnerInc.com

Finial, tin, pigeon form, American, late 19th century, 11 1/4" h, several cracks and small losses on wings and sides. **$829**

Photo courtesy Skinner Inc., Boston, www.SkinnerInc.com

Finial, tin, with star and flag, American, late 19th century, including stand, 21" h, some rusty surface, dents on lower cone. **$2,607**

Photo courtesy Skinner Inc., Boston, www.SkinnerInc.com

Finials (two), metal, American, 19th century, including a sheet copper obelisk with verdigris surface and a sheet iron spire with weathered black paint, (minor dents), 33" and 37" h. **$385 pair**

Art

FUTURE OF THE MARKET: ART

Everything is a niche nowadays

By Mary P. Manion

Acting Director, Landmarks Gallery and Restoration Studio, Milwaukee

The cable television cliché about 500 channels with nothing on is almost – but not entirely – true. Most of us have discovered a handful of channels that reflect our tastes and echo our interests. It's a long way from a nation of three networks where virtually everyone was exposed to the same programming.

Enter the world of niche audiences, where the masses count for little if a small, devoted coterie can be secured. The phenomenon has always been with us, especially for high-end products, but has been democratized with the spread of cable, satellite dishes and the Internet.

Likewise, the art market has never been without niche collectors, whether of Southwestern art, wildlife prints or Byzantine icons. But in recent years, niche collecting has been accentuated by the trend in art toward no real trend at all. There are no longer any over-arching movements, no Abstract Expressionism or Pop Art, to capture the public's imagination. The "shock of the new," as critic Robert Hughes memorably described Modern Art, is no longer especially shocking or even relevant to many art buyers. The last new artist everyone was talking about, Andy Warhol, made his mark more than 40 years ago and has been dead for two decades.

Everything in art is a niche nowadays, but some niches will have greater staying power than others. Many contemporary artists from the 1990s and later have fulfilled Warhol's prophesy about the diminishing shelf life of celebrity. After enjoying their 15 minutes of fame in the galleries of Manhattan and the pages of Art Forum, they have often been supplanted by new faces. In this environment, the most obvious future indicator for market prices points to the work of stellar artists that has only increased in value over time, whether an El Greco, a Van Gogh or a Hopper. But despite the proliferation of wealth and prestige collecting in rising societies such as China, Russia, India and the Persian Gulf states, this is a game relatively few can play.

In any event, collectors of Hudson River School, folk art and 20th-century Modernism are themselves niches in a world where no one group of taste makers can legislate for everyone else. In these well-explored peaks of the art market, prices will continue to climb into the stratosphere. In recent years auction results for naturalist and Hudson River School painter Martin Johnson Heade (1819-1904) have reached new levels. Unless the global economy sinks into depression, there is every likelihood that artworks by renowned figures in these areas will gain in value.

Below these peaks stretch vast continents of collectible

Andy Warhol (American, 1928-1987), Mobil, limited-edition screen print, image of the Mobilegas sign with Pegasus. Signed lower left and numbered "20/190". The right corner having two embossed stamps. Housed in a modern metal frame with linen backing, 38" x 38". **$31,200**

artwork; some well explored, others less so. Some are still on the frontier of the art market, where unknown artists await discovery and bargains can be found. Many of these genres are islands unto themselves. Fanciers of John James Audubon avian prints have little to say to aficionados of Montague Dawson nautical paintings. Devotees of the Harlem Renaissance seldom cross paths with collectors of black-and-white fashion photography. It makes little difference. There is value to be found and investments to be made in most of these areas.

One of the most familiar niche markets involves art produced during the Great Depression by the Works Progress Administration (WPA). The federal program launched by the Roosevelt Administration provided employment for artists by commissioning them to paint murals and produce other artworks for schools, courthouses and other public buildings. Many of the paintings were idealized depictions of America at a time when American values were being tested. Many of the artists who worked for the WPA were involved with various forms of social realism. and including the Midwest Regionalism of Grant Wood (1891-1942) and Thomas Hart Benton (1889-1975). As with other genres, Midwest Regionalism nurtured many obscure but talented artists along with a handful of familiar figures. The work of the lesser-knowns can still sometimes be found in local antique or resale stores; the value of even the unknowns has seen modest growth.

Like the Midwest Regionalists, the California Plein Air Impressionist and scene painters of the 1930s-1950s continue to captivate collectors with their representations of the beauty of a particular landscape during a time when the countryside was abundant and relatively untouched by development and environmental pollution. Big names in the genre – such as Edgar Payne (1882-1947) and Alson Skinner Clark (1876-1949) – command big prices. Many galleries in the Southwest feature fine art from this era and have Web sites providing histories of the artists, as well as online purchasing of inventory.

The Harlem Renaissance refers to an African-American cultural movement that flourished in 1920s New York. It is historically important as an early turning point where black Americans began to represent themselves and their lives, endowing their experience with dignity. Painters such as Aaron Douglas (1898-1979) and Jacob Lawrence (1917-2000) command interest beyond collectors of black heritage on the strength of their artistry and have gradually produced gains at the auction block. Imitators of the genre can be found at estate sales and antique shops throughout the country. If a painting from the 1920s through mid-century bears the signature of a black artist, chances are the style was influenced by the Harlem Renaissance.

The advent of photography in the 19th century resulted in a new mode of expression. Of course, many photographs were intended as documents, not artworks, freezing families and public events in time; others were composed and rendered with the intention of being taken seriously as art. The line between art and commerce in photography was often blurry, especially in the areas of portraiture and fashion photography. From Margaret Bourke White (1904-1971) to Henri Cartier Bresson (1908-2004), the market for fine-art photography continues to grow among collectors. Ansel Adams (1902-1984), environmentalist and photographer, was instrumental in calling attention to the natural beauty of the landscape and the preservation of nature. His black-and-white photos are often highly detailed studies of trees, mountain peaks and desert ground, executed with a contrasting palette in which every nuance of black and gray is exquisitely composed against the stark, white sky. His influence can be seen in many works of many contemporary photographers who believe in the conservation of nature. As the world recognizes the importance of "going green," this niche market has a growing interest for many environmentalists.

The first edition of Audubon's portfolio, Birds of America, has enjoyed a niche in fine art collecting since the day they were produced. When the print production began in 1827, the enormous project yielded 456 hand-colored prints of different species in editions of 100 prints each,

Photo courtesy James D. Julia Auctioneers, Fairfield, Maine; www.JuliaAuctions.com

Edward S. Curtis (American, 1868-1952), "The Vanishing Race," sepia-toned photograph showing a line of Native Americans on horseback below a mesa. The image has a blurred hue and is stamped, "Copyright 1904 by ES Curtis." Photograph is mounted on gray cut paper on top of a brown frayed-edge paper on gray backing paper in what appears to be its original frame. Photograph is 6" x 7 7/8". **$1,495**

published on a subscription basis. Reproductions of the series have been printed since his death in 1851, making the original series all the more attractive to the collector.

Audubon wasn't the only visual exponent of Americana. The frontier legend of the American West was indelibly stamped by painters of the 19th and early 20th centuries, who captured the folklore, history and culture of this vast expanse of territory. Frederic Remington (1861-1909) was an American sculptor and painter who rendered cowboys and Indians in bronze. Edward Curtis (1868-1952) turned the new medium of photography on the Western landscape, artfully rendering the vanishing culture of the Plains Indians. Examples of his work perform well at auction, although his photos can still be found in antique shops and estate sales by the astute collector.

Some niche venues have broader range. Works on paper, such as etchings and mezzotints, can be collected not only for individual artists, but according to subject, aesthetic appeal or historical significance. Many collectors of works on paper have a keen interest in history and collect antique pictures that record a period of historical interest. They can be a window onto the past, preserving a simple moment from a different era.

In many respects, the future of collecting will focus on genres or artists that have attracted devoted followings under the radar of the media and in more modest price ranges. Often, scarcity will drive the market upward, as well as speculation by investors who are looking to turn over artwork for profit the way they might sell real estate. Everyone knows that the market price of a Rothko or a Rembrandt can only continue to climb because so few are available for sale. Likewise, if on a smaller scale, the same will hold true for Meiji Era Japanese woodblock prints, 18th-century Persian miniatures and other pieces of fine art that may never reach the heights of the market, but will continue to gain value as demand rises and supply in private hands diminishes.

Also see Folk Art, Oriental Objects, Photographs, Tiffany.

Photo courtesy James D. Julia Auctioneers, Fairfield, Maine; www.JuliaAuctions.com

Thomas Hart Benton (American, 1889-1975), The Corral, pencil signed lithograph, shows horses being rounded up and placed in a corral with barn and windmill. Housed in a modern gilt wood frame with white matte, 10 1/4" x 14 1/4" (sight). **$4,680**

Anonymous or undocumented artists

Erotic painted miniature on copper, circular, partially disrobed woman with man on recamier, ebonized frame, 3" d, two chips at left edge. **$115**

Erotic painted miniature on copper, circular, partially disrobed woman on couch as two figures approach her from behind drapery, 3" d, worn frame. **$57**

The Pink Pillow, (American, 19th century), unframed oil on thick paper interior scene shows a small infant dressed in white nightgown and seated on a pink pillow. The right hand holds up a small whip against a green wall background. Attached to a wood stretcher, 11 1/4" x 8 1/4", very good condition. **$6,600**

Carved and painted picture of ducks in marshland, painting on board of water and marsh grasses with a hillside background under blue and white skies. Five ducks are seen in full relief carving and painted. Signed lower left "Bowman". Housed in a pine frame, 17 1/2" x 23" (sight). **$230**

Portrait miniature on ivory, bust-length of lady with flowers in hair and at breast, signed "S.C. 1853" at right edge, oval ebonized frame with gilt metal tied bow cresting, 2 1/2" x 2" (sight); inscribed on reverse and identified as "Madame De Chivoigne"; ebonized oval frame with scraps of green and red seals on reverse. **$345**

Profile of woman with red cape, oval, waist length, right profile; framed, inscribed on back "At the back of the /picture is written/Mm. Grauheion/ Miss Sarah Tully/Born Jan1769/ Drawn by J. Moseley." **$431**

Alphabetical Listings

Charles Partridge Adams, (American, 1858-1942), San Juan Mountains, large oil on canvas, scene shows partially snow covered peaks reflecting a pink sunset, a crescent moon is seen under a blue sky and shadows are cast on the mountains backside. Signed on reverse of canvas and titled on the stretcher. Housed in a gesso decorated period fame, which is "as is", 36" x 29", craquelure with surface dirt. **$10,925**

Milton Clark Avery, attributed (American, 1885-1965), The Purple Sofa, oil on canvas, scene shows two women seated facing each other on a purple sofa. One wears blue, the other brown. Signed bottom right, "Milton Avery 1951". Housed in what appears to be its original gilt wood frame, 18" x 25 3/4". **$6,000**

Reynolds Beal, (American, 1867-1951), The Circus is in Town, pastel on paper, summer scene shows a multi-tent circus with wagon set up for business. Several figures are seen around tents and flags fly off the big top. Pencil signed lower right. Housed in a modern carved and gilt double frame with glass, 8 1/2" x 11 1/2" (sight). **$2,990**

Reynolds Beal, (American, 1867-1951), Sparks Circus, mixed media, scene shows a number of circus workers and participants outside a big top flying two American flags. A large crowd is seen along with an elephant and figure on horseback. Signed lower right, dated "1931" and titled. Housed in a gesso decorated modern frame with double matte, 14 1/2" x 16 1/4" (sight). **$4,312**

Photo courtesy James D. Julia Auctioneers, Fairfield, Maine; www.JuliaAuctions.com

Robert Bateman (Canadian, 1930-), Bull Moose Studies, mixed media, study of two bull moose heads. Watercolor and black chalk work. Pencil signed, dated "1992" and titled. Housed in a gilt molded wood frame with multiple mattes, 9 1/2" x 7" (sight). **$2,185**

Johann Berthelsen, (American, 1883-1972), Times Square, New York City, oil on board, winter street scene shows the intersection at Times Square. Several pedestrians cross in front of stopped cars. Signed lower right. Housed in a partial gilt French-style frame, 20" x 14". **$18,400**

Carrie Horton Blackman, (American, 1856-1935), Nasturtiums Still Life, oil on canvas glued to cardboard, scene shows colorful flowers in a rose-colored pitcher. Two flowers are seen on tabletop. Signed lower right. Housed in a period carved wood gold frame, 17 3/4" x 13 3/4". Inconsistent varnish. **$900**

Rosalie (Rosa) Bonheur, (American, 1822-1899), Comanche Red River, water-colored pencil sketch of an Indian brave standing, holding a shield, bow and arrows in one hand and a spear in the other. Pencil titled above figure. Signed lower right "Rosa B-" and dated lower left "1876". Housed in a gilt frame with watercolor highlighted matte, 9" x 5 1/2" (sight). Some wrinkling to paper. **$5,750**

Albert Thompson Bricher, (American, 1837-1908), Rocks and Seaweed, watercolor, coastline scene of a beach at low tide with seaweed-covered rocks and pine-covered bluff. Signed lower left with conjoined first initials "A. T. Bricher". Housed in a dark-stained molded wood period frame, 10" x 20", top edge with some loss, generally good. Some toning. **$4,600**

Alfred Thompson Bricher, (American, 1837-1908), Rock-Strewn Beach, watercolor on paper, shows a beach with large and small rocks, small waves with sailboat nearby and one in distance. A grass-covered sand dune is seen at the end of a beach. Signed lower right with conjoined "AT Bricher 35". Housed in a gilt reeded-edge frame with white matte. Deeley Gallery, Manchester Village, Vt., label affixed to reverse, 10 1/4" x 26 1/2". **$6,325**

John Bunyan Bristol, (American, 1826-1909), Ausable Lake, New York, oil on canvas, scene shows a small sailboat on calm water with mountain background and green tree shoreline in foreground. Lifting clouds and mist blanket some of the mountain view. Signed lower right "J B Bristol". Housed in a modern gilt molded wood frame, 18" x 30"; five small patches to reverse with corresponding in-painting, visible stretcher lines. **$6,900**

Harrison Bird Brown, (American, 1831-1915), Coastal Landscape, oil on canvas, scene shows waves crashing upon steep cliffs having grass-covered tops. Signed bottom right "H.B 1874". Housed in a gesso decorated gilt frame, 9" x 15". **$2,530**

Photo courtesy James D. Julia Auctioneers, Fairfield, Maine; www.JuliaAuctions.com

Walter Emerson Baum, (American, 1884-1956), Edge of the Old Dam at Sellersville, oil on board, scene shows flowing water over rocks with a tree-lined bank. Signed lower right "WE Baum". Titled and signed on back of board. Also several taped titles, "River Valley No 10", housed in a carved wood frame. 8" x 10". **$3,450**

Photo courtesy Sanford Alderfer Auction & Appraisal, Hatfield, Pa.; www.AlderferAuction.com

Walter Emerson Baum, (American, 1884-1956), winter scene of village with snow falling, oil on canvas, signed lower right, 25" x 30". **$31,625**

Photo courtesy James D. Julia Auctioneers, Fairfield, Maine; www.JuliaAuctions.com

Reynolds Beal, (American, 1867-1951), Downey Bros. Circus, Elephants and Appaloosa, mixed media, scene shows a wide view of a circus with three large tents flying American flags, two large elephants with riders, a man on horse and other performers. Signed lower left, dated "1934" and inscribed "Downey Bros. Circus". Housed in a carved and gilt double frame with white matte, 14 1/4" x 17 3/4" (sight). **$2,640**

Photo courtesy James D. Julia Auctioneers, Fairfield, Maine; www.JuliaAuctions.com

Albert Bierstadt, (American, 1830-1902), Mediterranean Coast with Railway, oil on wood panel, shows a railway line with tunnel having a stone castle front with locomotive coming through it next to water with boat. The railway hugs the steep coastline. Signed lower right "A.B." Set in a gilt carved wood frame with linen lining, 4 1/2" x 6 1/2". Fine craquelure. **$4,600**

Photo courtesy James D. Julia Auctioneers, Fairfield, Maine; www.JuliaAuctions.com

Mary Cable Butler, (American, 1865-1946), Low Tide, oil on board, coastal scene shows red and yellow skiffs on dry land. Rocky shoreline with grass-topped bluff. Signed lower left. Housed in a modern carved gilt and wood frame having name plaque, 10" x 12". **$2,587**

Photo courtesy James D. Julia Auctioneers, Fairfield, Maine; www.JuliaAuctions.com

Augusto Chartrand (Dubois), (Cuban, 1828-1899), Sunset Matteanzas Harbour, 1875, small scene shows a panoramic view of a river harbor with two-mast schooner off a cliff-side house. In the distance is a city under large mountains, all under a sky filled with soft colors, with the foreground having detailed vegetation and rock outcroppings. Signed, titled and dated on the reverse. Housed in a modern gilt molded wood frame. This work is sited in the Smithsonian American Art Museum's Inventory of American Painting and Sculpture database, 8" x 12". **$9,775**

Aleksandr Aleksandrovich Deineka, (Russian, 1899-1969), High Jump, pastel/gouache on heavy paper, scene shows a red and blue track and field high bar being successfully jumped by a woman in black and red track attire. She is seen against a blue-sky background over a green field stadium setting. Signed in Cyrillic bottom right and dated "62", 14 1/4" x 19 3/4". **$6,900**

Raoul Dufy, (French, 1877-1953), Inner City Harbor, oil on masonite, scene shows several sailboats with tall buildings as background. Signed center bottom. Housed in a modern gesso decorated gilt frame. Back of masonite with black stamp "Heller Collection" also "Raoul Dufy 34" and an attached French postcard, 12 3/4" x 16 1/4". Some minor scratches. **$29,900**

Photo courtesy James D. Julia Auctioneers,
Fairfield, Maine; www.JuliaAuctions.com

*Colin Campbell Cooper,
(American 1856-1937),
California Mission, unsigned
oil on wood panel, scene
shows a red-roofed white
stucco building with arched
openings, colorful flower-
lined lawn and large tree.
Housed in a period gesso
decorated frame and having
written on the back panel
the artist's name, 12" x 16".*
$1,320

Emile Bulcke, (Belgian, 1875-1963), The Flute Player, large oil on canvas, woodland pond scene shows a child playing a flute only draped in a blue cloth sitting on a grassy bank next to a pond filled with lilies. Housed in its original decorated wood frame having an artist name plaque and dated "1926". Painting is unsigned, 34" x 44". Some in-painting. **$2,400**

Sir David Young Cameron, (United Kingdom 1865-1945), Luxor, Egypt, watercolor and graphite, scene shows the ruins with large pillars and grand entrance. Watercolor highlights to background, buildings and sky. Pencil signed bottom right. Housed in modern gilt frame with a double matte with lined highlights and artist name. Original label from Jas. McClure & Son, Glasgow, with artist name and title, dated "16/10/28". 16 1/2" x 9" (sight). **$632**

Mary Helen Carlisle, (American, 1869-1925), Water Garden at Newton, Tipperary, oil on canvas mounted on wood panel, scene shows a colorful garden landscape with water, trees, flowers and Greek-style building with columns. Initialed bottom right. Also having partial labels and a full title label. Housed in wide gilt frame with inner liner. This artist is best known for her pastel and oil paintings of famous gardens in the United States and Great Britain, 32" x 24". **$2,300**

Mauritz Frederik De Haas, (American, 1832-1895), Hudson Under the Moonlight, large oil on canvas, scene shows a large paddle-wheel steamer plying a waterway while a small boat with three men net fish. A ferry landing with several sailboats is seen on right side with buildings and dock. Mountains are seen on right side. Signed lower left "MFH de Haas N.A." Housed in a wide gilt frame, 27 1/2" x 41". **$34,500**

Photo courtesy Skinner Inc., Boston, www.SkinnerInc.com

*A.E. Crowell, (American, 1862-1951), carved and
painted miniature Baltimore Oriole, East Harwich,
Mass., mid-20th century, the figure with wire legs
mounted on a wooden mound, signed "A.E. Crowell
Cape Cod" and with impressed rectangular mark on
base, 4" h.* **$2,666**

Cornelia DeHaaf, (American, 20th century), The Flower Seller, oil on canvas board, scene shows an outdoor market with flower seller setup with colorful flowers all in front of a large arch entrance and city backdrop. Signed lower left "C. DeHaaf". Housed in a modern gilt carved wood frame, 16" x 12". **$575**

Thomas Colman Dibdin, (British, 1810-1893), Abbeville, watercolor street scene shows a large cathedral in background with busy street in foreground. Storefronts line both sides. People ride in carriages on a dirt street. Titled and signed lower left with date "1877". Housed in a modern burl-type frame with white matte, 21 1/4" x 14 1/2" (sight). **$575**

Walt Disney Studios, limited-edition framed animation art, Villainous Portraits, COA affixed verso, 16" h x 30" w. **$100**

Mstislav Valerianovich Dobujinsky, (Russian, 1875-1957), Monument to Peter the Great in St. Petersburg, Russia, lithograph, heightened by china white, blue green and pale red applied by the artist. The scene shows E.M. Falconet sculpture of man on rearing horse on rock plinth. Pencil signed bottom right and dated "22" in the print. Note: Accompanying lot is a copy of the artist obituary and small memorial exhibition pamphlet. Housed in a modern silver frame with white matte, 9 1/2" x 14 1/4" (sight). **$1,380**

David Y. Ellinger, (American, 1913-2003), framed theorem, basket of fruit with bird perched on grape cluster to right, signed "D.V.E." lower right below basket, oil on velvet, 10 3/4" x 13 3/4" (sight); red and black painted frame. **$3,450**

Nicolai Fechin, (Russian-American, 1881-1955), The Wood Engraver, this image won the 1924 Thomas R. Proctor Award for Portraiture at the National Academy of Design; **$1,092,500**

Photo courtesy James D. Julia Auctioneers, Fairfield, Maine; www.JuliaAuctions.com

Abbott Fuller Graves, (American, 1859-1936), Nature's Color Pallet, oil on canvas still life shows a variety of colorful flowers in a tiered arrangement against a mottled background. Flowers include red, pink and white zinnias, blue lupines, yellow and white wildflowers. All with different shades of green leaves. Signed lower right "Abbott Graves". Housed in its original gilt frame liner, 30" x 15", professionally cleaned, some light craquelure. **$31,625**

Philip Howard Evergood, (American, 1901-1973), Flowers by the Lake, oil on canvas scene shows a young blonde girl in yellow bikini at the top of a stairway holding an earthenware bulbous vase full of red poppies. The red poppies with green stems fill half of the painting and partly obscure the scene behind her, which includes several large boats on water, one of which is going through a railroad bridge, which has rotated to allow it through. A lighthouse is seen next to multi-storied house and the open ocean is beyond. Signed lower left "Philip Evergood" and dated "55". Housed in a period partial gilt molded wood frame with linen liner. There are three labels, one from the Wadsworth Atheneum, Hartford Conn., with artist, title and owner as Whitney Museum of American Art. The other label of Terry Dintenfass, Inc., New York; and a third label which is only a fragment, 48 1/2" x 30", very good condition, some craquelure. There are several small white-painted sections that fluoresce under UV light, which appear to be the same white in other areas. **$201,250**

Washington F. Friend, (Canadian, 1820-1886) A View of Cheltenham, Pennsylvania, historical watercolor panoramic view on bluff above a large river. The oval watercolor shows the river full of large three-mast sailing vessels along busy wharfs dotted with large buildings. A man and woman sit on the river's edge in the foreground looking out over this view. The city with large buildings, one having a dome, others with spires and on the left hand hill there appears to be a large fort with flag. Mountains are seen in the background. Along the wharf are two white river side-wheel boats. Signed lower left "W F Friend". Housed in what appears to be its original gilt frame with oval cutout gilt matte. Old label attached to back with location, 13" x 21 3/4" sight. Some toning, generally in good condition. **$3,450**

Gertrude Gazelle Gardner, (American, 1878-1975), New England Harbor Scene, oil on canvas scene shows a schooner moored in a calm harbor with building on tall posts and grass-lined shore. Beyond is a hillside with many buildings. Possibly a Maine setting. Signed lower left. Housed in a carved and gesso decorated gilt frame, 16" x 20", very good condition. **$960**

Charles C. Gruppe, (American, 1928-), Winter Solitude, large oil on canvas, scene shows snow-covered water surrounded by low hills and trees. A fence-lined road leads to the frozen water. Signed lower right "C Gruppe". Housed in a modern aluminum frame, 48" x 32". **$1,150**

Charles P. Gruppe, (American, 1860-1940), Fishing Boat, oil on canvas, seascape shows two fishing boats passing each other under gray skies. Signed lower right "C.P. Gruppe". Elliot Galleries label affixed to reverse. Housed in its original gesso decorated gilt frame, 8" x 10". Frame with losses. **$1,840**

Margo Hoff, (American, mid-20th Century), Balcony View New York City, oil on canvas, view of city looking across a wide street with cars and tree-lined water. A white pigeon in foreground is seen on a fancy wrought-iron railing. Signed lower left "M. Hoff". Housed in a partially painted blue molded wood frame, 30" x 15". **$1,150**

Josef Israels, (Dutch, 1824-1911), Preparing the Meal, oil on canvas interior scene shows a young mother with infant seated at a table with a man and woman peeling vegetables. Another woman pours coffee while a cat watches the infant. A window is on left side, cascading light on the scene. Signed lower left. Housed in a modern gesso decorated frame, 22 1/4" x 26 1/4". Several old patches to reverse, in-painting, stretcher lines. **$13,200**

Eduard Kasparides, (Austrian, 1858-1926), The Courtship, large unframed oil on canvas scene shows a young maiden being wooed by a young man wearing a green hat with feather. They sit together in a tavern interior. Signed lower left "E. Kasparides", 33 1/4" x 26 1/4", craquelure, two old patches to reverse, some in-painting. **$1,955**

Walt Francis Kuhn, (American, 1877-1949), Parade, watercolor, scene shows a parading horse with man dressed in fancy uniform. Signed lower right and dated "41". Titled bottom left of a hand-line highlighted matte, which is housed in a modern frame with wide white matte, 7" x 8" (sight). **$1,955**

Ernest Lawson, (American, 1873-1939), Autumn Landscape, pastel with fall colors shows a line of trees in front of a body of water with rolling hills. Signed lower right "E. Lawson." Housed in a gilt replacement frame, 14 3/4" x 20 3/4". One corner chipped. Mounted on light cardboard. **$9,200**

John Frederick Kensett, (American, 1818-1872), Portrait of a Young Woman, oil on canvas, portrait shows a young woman with dark hair and dark dress wearing a printed scarf. Signed in period writing on back of canvas "J. K. 237". Housed in a partial gilt wood frame with linen and gold liner, 24" x 20". Masking varnish, some in-painting, small chip at center. **$1,725**

James Lapham, Dennisport, Mass., mid-20th century, carved and painted Kingfisher with fish, signed by the maker on the base, mounted on a piece of driftwood, 6 1/2" h. **$1,896**

Photo courtesy James D. Julia Auctioneers, Fairfield, Maine; www.JuliaAuctions.com

Emile Albert Gruppe, (American, 1896-1978), Motif #1, oil on canvas, Rockport Harbor scene shows two men on floating dock with another man in lobster boat beside. A green fishing boat is moored next to a red connected building on stone wharf. Another is beyond to the right. Signed lower right "Emile A. Gruppe." Housed in a modern carved wood gilt frame with gilt name plaque; 30" x 25", very good condition. **$18,400**

Photo courtesy James D. Julia Auctioneers, Fairfield, Maine; www.JuliaAuctions.com

George Inness Jr., (American, 1854-1926), After the Storm, oil on canvas, panoramic scene shows a valley landscape with cultivated fields and a village nestled on the valley floor. Hills are seen in the background, partially obscured by dark rain clouds, and a rainbow is present. Two travelers follow a hay wagon in the foreground. Signed "G Inness 18_8". Housed in an antique gilt frame, 14" x 20". Relined, restored with in-painting. **$2,990**

Photo courtesy James D. Julia Auctioneers, Fairfield, Maine; www.JuliaAuctions.com

Edwin Henry Landseer, (British 1802-1873), Study of a Deer, graphite, drawing of a bleating stag standing in shallow water. Title and signed lower left. Housed in an antique painted frame with white matte, 10 1/2" x 14 3/4". **$1,840**

Photo courtesy Sanford Alderfer Auction & Appraisal, Hatfield, Pa.; www.AlderferAuction.com

Harry Leith-Ross, (American, 1886-1973), Gray Day in the Harbor, oil on canvas, signed lower left, titled verso, 18" x 24", **$14,950**

Photo courtesy John Moran Auctioneers Inc., Altadena, Calif.; www.JohnMoran.com

Maurice Logan, (American, 1886-1977), oil on canvas of the San Francisco ferry dock and skyline, **$80,500**

Reginald Marsh, (American, 1898-1954), Train Yard with Locomotives, watercolor on paper, scene shows several black locomotives with tenders passing each other in a multi-track yard. Signed lower right "Reginald Marsh". Housed in a gilt wood frame with beige matte. Label on reverse from DeMatteteis Gallery, Annapolis, Md., 13 1/2" x 19" (sight). **$8,050**

Charles E. Prendergast, (American, 1863-1948), Day at the Beach, mixed-media crayon and watercolor beach scene shows people on a sandy beach and in the water. A long black pier is on left side under a sun and blue sky. Signed lower left "Prendergast". Housed in a modern gilt wood frame with silk matte and gold inner liner, 7 1/4" x 10 3/4" (sight), very good condition. **$4,025**

Photo courtesy John Moran Auctioneers Inc., Altadena, Calif.; www.JohnMoran.com

William Joseph McCloskey, (American, 1859-1941), Florida Oranges, signed and dated oil on canvas of his best-known subject of oranges with paper wrappers, **$546,250**

Sadie H. Lowes, (American, 1870-?), Winter in Chicago, oil on panel, shows heavy snow that has fallen on a residential area with tall building in background. Signed lower right "Lowes". Housed in a stepped gilt wood carved frame, 24" x 18 1/4". Minor in-painting.
.... **$920**

George Benjamin Luks, (American, 1867-1933), Memorial Library, watercolor, scene shows a column-front library with figures on stairs. The library sits on a small grassy knoll surrounded by trees. Signed lower left. Housed in a modern gilt wood frame with white matte, 15 1/2" x 19 1/4" (sight). **$9,200**

Photo courtesy John Moran Auctioneers Inc., Altadena, Calif.; www.JohnMoran.com

Anton Robert Leinweber, (Czech Republic, 1845-1921), Arab Bazaar, signed, inscribed and dated lower left: Robert Leinweber Munich 1889, 72" x 53". **$195,500**

Rene Magritte, (Belgian, 1898-1967), Vignette Sketches, pencil and watercolor, small sketches on a folded hotel card bearing an engraving of the hotel on one quarter of it with the other three quarters having a variety of sketches, some of which are in black watercolor. Most have a title and most are of single objects. Signed lower left "Magritte". Housed in a modern frame with black and gold matte which has the backside matted also with viewing glass, 3 1/2" x 8 1/4" (sight). **$6,325**

John Marin, (American, 1870-1953), Lobsterman's Pier, Port Clyde, Maine, watercolor scene shows harbor with buildings, docks and boats. A green forested shoreline. Signed bottom right "Marin '23". A typed piece of paper on the back indicates, "This watercolor scene painted by John Marin at Port Clyde, Maine, in June of 1923 and given to Dock Attendant Avery Bullock in appreciation, for his Yeoman's work." Housed in what appears to be its original oak frame, 11 1/4" x 15 1/2" (sight), all over even toning, scratch to upper left, otherwise very good condition. **$2,300**

Harry McChesney, hand-carved and painted Canada goose, black and white neck and head, glass eyes, brown feathers with white tips. Original business card taped to bottom with artist name, 13 1/2" h x 27" l. **$201**

Willard Leroy Metcalf, (American, 1858-1925), Pastel Impressions, oil on canvas, scene shows a stream curving through flat grassy area towards woods that have a lavender hue. Artist monogrammed with a capital "M" in circle bottom right. Housed in a modern gilt molded wood frame, 14 3/4" x 19 1/2". **$14,375**

Lucille (Mrs. H.M. Dingley Jr.) Mudgett, (American, 1911-), Still Life with Flowers in Blue Vase, oil on canvas board, shows a blue glass pedestal vase having colorful wildflower arrangement. Next to the vase is a brass figural lighter. Signed lower right. Housed in a wide gilt molded wood frame, 30" x 20". Discolored varnish, in need of cleaning. **$345**

H. Murray, (British, 19th/20th century), Stuck in the Snow, watercolor shows a stagecoach laden with passengers and luggage, stuck in a snowdrift. A man from a nearby house walks with shovel to help. The sign indicates they are between London and Brighton. Signed lower left, "H. Murray". In a decorative gilt frame with a watercolor highlighted matte, 11 1/4" x 17". **$480**

Anthony Oberman, (Dutch, 1781-1845), Still Life with Flowers, Bird and Butterfly, unframed oil on canvas, flowers including roses and chrysanthemums, and blue, white and purple wild flowers. Lion-decorated pedestal urn rests upon a tabletop, which has one flower and a finch-type bird which looks up at a butterfly. At the right edge of table is signature of the artist "A. Oberman," 32 1/2" x 22 1/4", relined with several layers of restoration and masking varnish. ... **$14,950**

Fried Pal, (American/Hungarian 1893-1976), Nude with Red Shawl, pastel on paper, three-quarter portrait of a nude woman with a red drape over lower part of body. Arm rests on a linen-covered table and her eyes are closed. Signed lower left. Housed in a white-highlighted carved wood frame with white matte and anti-glare glass, 22" x 18". **$1,080**

Petro Pavesi (Italian, early 20th century), Cardinals Visit with the Pope, interior watercolor shows two cardinals having tea with the pope. Library setting has a fancy interior with bookshelves and hung tapestry. Chairs and table rest on a Caucasian Oriental rug. Signed lower left

Photo courtesy James D. Julia Auctioneers, Fairfield, Maine; www.JuliaAuctions.com

Norman Rockwell, (American, 1894-1978), Catching His Eye, watercolor and light oil illustration on paper laid on board, scene shows a woman in Spanish-type dress with shawl, fan, black and gold dress and shoes and silk stockings. She looks over her shoulder with a smile at a man dressed in brown Army outfit with hat and coat. His hand is at his chin pondering what the evening might bring. Between them are lush, tropical plants. Signed bottom right "Normal Rockwell," unframed, 23 1/2" x 16 3/4"; 1 1/2" split in the top center margin, appears to have some paint loss at edges and on woman's arm. **$18,400**

"P. Pavesi 1901". Housed in a gesso decorated period frame with gold liner, 17 1/4" x 12 3/4" (sight). **$460**

Elizabeth Vaughan Okie Paxton, (American, 1877-1971), Copper jug with Apples, oil on canvas scene of a table top still life shows a large copper-handled jug on a white tablecloth with green cup and saucer and three apples. Signed upper right. Housed in its original period carved and gilt Arts & Crafts frame. Title in pencil on back of stretcher, 20" square, very good condition. **$4,600**

William McGregor Paxton, (American, 1869-1941), Portrait of a Woman, oil on canvas, half portrait of a woman in a red dress. She looks off to the right against a green and black background. Signed lower right "Paxton". Housed in a gilt wood frame, 20" x 16". **$920**

Margaretta Angelica Peale, attributed (American, 1795-1882), Fruit on a Plate, oil on canvas, still life shows a pear, apple, banana and grapes on a gold-trimmed white plate. Unsigned. Housed in a period gesso decorated gilt frame, 7" x 9". Some in-painting. **$2,880**

George W. Sotter, (American, 1879-1953), The Valley of the Delaware, hillside view of the Delaware River, oil on canvas, 22" x 26", signed lower left, Sotter; complemented by a signed gilt floral-carved Ben Badura frame, minor loss to frame, sight: 21 1/2" x 25 1/2", width: 2 1/2", painting titled verso. **$97,750**

Charles Rollo Peters, (American, 1862-1928), Yerba Buena, a nocturne scene depicting San Francisco Bay, with an original note from the artist,.............................. **$40,250**

Jane Peterson, (American, 1876-1965), Gloucester Harbor, oil on board harbor scene shows a green schooner tied up to dock with other rowboats beside. Hillside beyond with many houses under a white and blue sky. Signed lower right "Jane Peterson". Housed in a period molded wood frame with a Marshall Field & Co. label, 20" x 23". Surface dirt, very good condition. **$8,625**

Lucien Pissaro, (French, 1863-1944), Summer Fields, watercolor, landscape shows tall grassy field with trees and walkway. Monogrammed "LP" in a circle and dated "1930" in lower right. Housed in a modern wood frame with linen and wood matte, 4 1/2" x 6 1/2" (sight). **$1,495**

Diego Rivera, (Mexican, 1886-1957), Femme Nue, pen and ink drawing, of a nude female with hand held up and finger pointing. Signed lower right. Housed in a modern gilt frame with blue matte and inner gold liner. Accompanying the drawing is a catalog entry from the sale at auction of the Hemingway Collection by Kruse Auctioneers, Oct. 29, 1978. This study was probably done in Italy, 1920-1921, 7 1/2" x 5" (sight). **$3,738**

Guy Rose, (American, 1867-1925), California Coastline, oil on board, scene shows an ocean bay surrounded by mountains under colorful sky. Signed lower right. Housed in a deep walnut Victorian frame with gilt liner, 4 1/2" x 6 1/2" (sight). **$3,105**

Tadeusz Rybkowski, (Polish, 1848-1926), Crimean Scene of Two Soldiers with Troika, oil on panel, depicting a wounded Crimean soldier in a straw-lined litter drawn by a horse with Troika, another soldier tends to him in the snow. Signed lower left, "TAD. RYBKOWSKI, 1877," In original Eastlake-style frame with gilt gesso design and black and gilt decorated liner. Retains old paper label on reverse, 6 1/2" x 4 1/2". **$3,450**

James Seymour, (in the manner of, British, 1702-1752), The Prince of Wales at Newmarket, 1797, large 19th-century oil on canvas panoramic scene shows the Prince of Wales in an elegant carriage pulled by six white horses in the center of a large field and slight hill. There are many horses and riders galloping and being led. Other spectators are seen in a carriage and on foot, with the English hillside in the background under a blue and cloudy sky. Unsigned and by an accomplished hand. Housed in a modern gilt molded wood frame with title plaque, 23 1/2" x 49 1/2", some in-painting, relined. **$5,400**

Ben Shahn, (American, 1898-1969), City Tenements, oil on masonite, scene shows inner-city buildings with narrow alley. Signed lower right, also signed on reverse. Housed in a carved molded wood frame, 22 1/4" x 15 1/4". Some old chipping and loss. **$2,875**

Dorothea Sharp, (British, 1874-1955), Study for 'Vivi at Play', 1926, oil on canvas interior scene shows a young blonde-haired girl in green dress holding doll in one arm and walking stick in other. A ball sits on rag runner, doorway in background. Titled at bottom center "Vivi," bottom right dated with artist cipher and signed "Dorothea Sharp". Back of canvas has title, date and artist name. Housed in a gilt oak frame, 22" x 18 1/2". **$15,525**

William Matthew Prior, (American, (1806-1873), portrait of a young boy, circa 1852, oil on canvas, the child seated wearing a red dress bordered in white, holding a white rose with a whip laid across his legs. Signed and inscribed on reverse, "Wm. M. Prior East Boston Trenton Street./Kingly Express," 26" x 20", unframed. Good condition, minor retouch. **$112,575**

Paul Signac, (French, 1863-1935), Barfleur, ink and watercolor scene shows several boats at low tide in a harbor with large buildings. Lower left is titled and dated "32," signed bottom right. Housed in a gesso decorated gilt frame with linen matte and gold liner, 8 1/4" x 11" (sight). **$18,400**

Raphael Soyer, (American, 1899-1987), Out of Work and Keeping Warm, watercolor, outdoor scene shows five black men seated and standing around a trashcan fire. Several bottles of wine are seen at their feet and there is a building with trees in the background. Signed upper left, "R. Soyer," 7 3/4" x 8 1/4". **$632**

Marion Williams Steele, (American, 1912-2001), Sunset-Gloucester Harbor, oil on canvas scene shows a colorful sky reflecting in harbor water. Two figures work on a two-mast schooner next to dock with building. Other boats dot the docksides surrounding the harbor. Housed in a period carved gold frame; 25" x 30", very good condition. .. **$3,680**

Seth W. Steward, (American, 1844-1927), Squaw Mtn from East of Greenville, Moosehead Lake, Maine, 1897, oil on board landscape shows early fall scene, cows, pasture and house in foreground with lake and mountains under a colorful sky. Signed lower left "S. W. Steward 97," housed in a gesso decorated gilt frame. Titled and initialed on reverse, 11 1/2" x 17 1/2", very good condition. **$2,875**

Harry P. Sutton Jr., (American 1897-1984), By the Light of the Window, oil on canvas, interior scene shows a woman sitting on a windowsill, which is bathed with outside light, a chair stands beside her. Window shade is partially down. Signed lower right "Sutton". Housed in a modern gilt molded wood frame with Guido Frame Studio label, 20" x 16". **$11,500**

Anthony Thieme, (American, 1888-1954), Back Beach, Rockport, Ma., large oil on canvas scene shows a dirt road winding along the northern section of Rockport Harbor alongside Back Beach with two figures under a tree, rocky shoreline with the town on a peninsula beyond. A sailboat exits the harbor area on a blue ocean. Along the dirt road are houses with a solitary figure in red. Scene is framed with large trees and light blue sky. Housed in a fine carved gilt custom frame with a Guido Frame Studio label. Several labels are attached to reverse including an exhibit label from the Lynn (Mass.) Museum & Historical Society. The back has title and artist number "1508," 30" x 36", very good condition. **$54,625**

Martha C. Walter, (American, 1875-1976), Ellis Island, oil on masonite, Scene shows immigrants crowded in a interior of a building. Signed lower left. Housed in an antique gold frame, 10 1/2" x 14". **$6,727**

Mary E. Loring Warner, (American, 1860-?), Woodland Pool, oil on canvas laid on board, scene shows a stream with small waterfall cascading into a pool. Sunlight shines in the background, trees reflect on water. Signed lower right "M E Loring" (her maiden name). Housed in an Art Nouveau-style wide period frame, 12 1/2" x 18 1/4". Spot in-painting, generally very good. **$1,265**

Mary L. Weiss, (American, early 20th Century), Hollyhocks, large oil on canvas, floral scene shows a large group of colorful white, red and pink hollyhocks. Signed lower right "Mary L. Weiss". Housed in its original gilt and gesso decorated frame, 30" x 28". **$4,140**

Daniel F. Wentworth, (American, 1850-1934), Spring Time, large oil on canvas landscape shows five cows under a blossoming apple tree. Farmhouse is seen in distance and three of the cows look toward viewer. Signed lower left "DF Wentworth". Housed in an antique gesso decorated frame. Title on back of canvas, 24" x 36", good condition, some surface dirt with in-painting. **$5,175**

Constantin Aleksandrovich Westchiloff, (Russian, 1877-1945), The Street Merchant, oil on board, scene shows a merchant next to a small tent of wares with nearby white stucco buildings. A small burro carrying produce is tied to a tree all under a blue sky. Signed "C. Westchiloff" on bottom right. Unframed, 10 1/2" x 8 1/2". Some roughness at very edge of corners. **$1,150**

Photo courtesy John Moran Auctioneers Inc., Altadena, Calif.; www.JohnMoran.com

Nell Walker Warner, (American, 1891-1970), signed oil on canvas, depicting cherry blossoms in a still-life setting against an unusual gauze-effect background created by cross-hatching into the wet paint. **$12,650**

Photo courtesy James D. Julia Auctioneers, Fairfield, Maine; www.JuliaAuctions.com

Arthur Fitzwilliam Tait, (American, 1819-1905), After a Hard Chase, Raquette Lake, Adirondacks, oil on canvas scene shows a deer struggling through a pond-lily-filled water scaring up three mallard ducks with tall marsh grass beyond. Signed lower right, "AF Tait N. Y. 1873." Housed in a period gesso decorated gilt frame. Red Fox Fine Art label on reverse, 19" x 28", very good condition. Wax relining, minor in-painting. **$22,425**

Guy Carleton Wiggins, (American, 1883-1962), The Public Library, oil on canvas, active scene of Manhattan in the snow, with the focal point being the New York Public Library, with its well-known lion statues. Depiction includes seven American Flags, pedestrians with umbrellas, a bus and taxicabs. Snow is blowing at an angle, and awnings are visibly out. Signed lower right. Guy Carleton Wiggins was born in Lyme, Conn., and was educated there at his father's (Carleton Wiggins, seldom used his given name, John) art school. Before he settled on a career as a painter, the younger Wiggins worked with the Foreign Service. He would paint local scenes wherever he was posted. After taking an early retirement from the job, Wiggins entered the Art Students League in New York, followed by a course of study in the artists colony of Old Lyme. Wiggins is best known for his Impressionistic paintings of New York in the snow, as well as for his renderings of Connecticut landscapes, 29 1/2" x 23 1/4" (framed). **$17,250**

Guy Carleton Wiggins, (American, 1883-1962), 5th Avenue and 2nd Street, oil on canvas, signed Guy Wiggins. N.A. Manhattan snow scene features pedestrians walking with umbrellas, city traffic, a row of apartment buildings and two American Flags, 15 1/2" x 11 1/2" (framed). **$23,000**

Photo courtesy Clars Auction Gallery, Oakland, Calif.; www.Clars.com

Yellow Submarine (1968), framed animation celluloid depicting the four Beatles following two Apple Bonkers, 10" h x 12" w sight. **$1,600**

Gustave Adolph Wiegand, (American, 1870-1957), Tending the Sheep, large oil on canvas summer scene shows a shepherd resting under birch trees with small flock of sheep. A dirt road leads to water with trees and hills beyond. Light blue sky with puffy white clouds. Signed lower left. Housed in a gesso decorated gilt frame that may be original, 28" x 36", Very good condition. **$4,887**

(John) Carleton Wiggins, (American, 1848-1932), A Holstein Cow, oil on canvas, cow is prominent in a grassy field leading to a wood's edge. Seen under a gray and white cloudy sky. Signed lower left. Also signed and titled on reverse of canvas. Housed in a gilt molded wood antique frame, 25" x 30". One old patch to reverse with corresponding in-painting. **$2,012**

Yellow Submarine (1968), framed animation celluloid depicting John Lennon and three of the Blue Meanies, 11" h by 15" w sight. **$900**

Photo courtesy James D. Julia Auctioneers, Fairfield, Maine; www.JuliaAuctions.com

Andrew Nathaniel Wyeth, (American, 1948-), New England Cemetery, watercolor, scene shows a cemetery with 18th/19th-century gravestones on a colorful grass and leaf ground with trees in autumn colors under a gray/white cloudy and blue sky. Initialed lower left. Housed in a molded wood frame with white matte, 12 3/4" x 15 3/4" (sight). **$3,220**

Photo courtesy James D. Julia Auctioneers, Fairfield, Maine; www.JuliaAuctions.com

Stanford White frame, in an Arts & Crafts Taos style by LeBrocq. Top and bottom frame pieces have been rabbitted an extra 1/2" to accommodate oil on canvas portrait of a socialite by Florence Thaw, student of Abbott Thayer. Frame has a ripple outside border, inner molding border with turret type corners with an inner border design having gesso decorated liner. (A rare form with the inner design.) Overall 54" x 44 3/4"; opening 40 3/4" x 30 1/2". Some gesso loss, generally good condition. **$14,950**

Photo courtesy James D. Julia Auctioneers, Fairfield, Maine; www.JuliaAuctions.com

Aesthetic-influence frame, top crest having a bird perched on a fruit-laden branch, decorative square block corners with flowers. Flowers and corn stalks decorate the sides with small flower panels below. An interior red velvet liner and pebble-finish liner complete the frame. Back retains a partial label from Newark, N.J., with the name "Devausney Mossop". Overall 37 1/2" x 32"; opening 26 1/4" x 22 1/4". One small loss to bottom flower panel. **$402**

Photo courtesy James D. Julia Auctioneers, Fairfield, Maine; www.JuliaAuctions.com

Gesso decorated frame, 19th century, set with two inner liners. Overall 36 1/2" x 53"; opening 23" x 40". **$747**

Picture Frames

Arts & Crafts carved gilt frame, (period), corners with carved leaf rows. Overall 47 1/4" x 57 1/4"; opening 40 1/4" x 50 1/4". **$575**

Art Nouveau frame, (period), bronze-colored gilt frame having double scroll design with large bead interior. Liner has dash-and dot-motif. Overall 31" x 47"; opening 20 1/4" x 36 1/4". **$345**

Shadowbox frame, 19th/20th Century, inner gold frame with gesso decorated leaves and petals have interior gilt liner. A large box frame surrounds. Overall 55 3/4" x 46 1/4"; opening 30 1/4" x 40 1/4". One 3" x 1" section of gesso missing, otherwise very good. **$805**

Gilt gesso decorated frame, with bead and leaf design with an inner liner having dash-and-dot decoration. Overall 59" x 48 1/2"; opening 40 1/4" x 50 1/4". Some minor losses and gold rub. **$862**

Gilt frame, gesso decorated frame with gold liner. Decoration of scrolled flower and leaf design against a textured background. Overall 41" x 49"; opening 29" x 36 1/4". Some minor gesso loss to outside edge, generally very good. .. **$575**

Ornate frame, 20th century, with gilt surface and decorative corner and central elements. Overall 47 3/4" x 61"; opening 41" x 54". Minor losses. **$172**

Prints

Nathaniel Currier

American Field Sports-Retrieving, by N. Currier, in large color folio showing hunter with two retrievers. Print after a painting by A.F. Tait and lithographed by N. Currier, N.Y., 1857. Image, 18" x 26". Print exhibits toning/foxing with some reverse burning with show-through and glue residue near matt opening. Puncture at left side. **$70**

The Pursuit by N. Currier, in large color folio showing man on horseback chasing an Indian with spear on horseback. Print after a painting by A.F. Tait and lithographed by N. Currier, N.Y., 1856. Image, 24" x 31". Print exhibits toning/foxing with some reverse burning with show-through. **$750**

Currier & Ives

American Farmyard – Evening, colored large folio lithograph shows a farmyard filled with livestock with the farmhouse beyond a white picket fence, dated 1857. Housed in a Victorian deep walnut frame with gold liner. Image, 19" x 25 1/2". Very good condition. Not examined out of frame. **$1,150**

Photo courtesy Skinner Inc., Boston, www.SkinnerInc.com

The Whale Fishery "Laying On" 1852, by N. Currier, small folio lithograph with hand coloring on paper, sheet size 13 3/8" x 17 1/2", in a contemporary molded gilt-wood frame. Margins of 2 1/4" or more, repaired tear into image center right, light toning, creases, foxing, light moisture stains in margins, hinged at the top with archival tape. **$1,125**

Photo courtesy Skinner Inc., Boston, www.SkinnerInc.com

Bass Fishing, undated, small folio lithograph with hand-coloring on paper, sheet size 9 7/8" x 13 7/8", unframed. Margins of 5/8" or more, light toning. **$711**

Photo courtesy Skinner Inc., Boston, www.SkinnerInc.com

Central Park in Winter, undated, small folio lithograph with hand coloring on paper, sheet size 9 7/8" x 13 7/8", in a contemporary bird's-eye maple veneer frame. Margins of 5/8" or more, 1/2" old repaired tear left center through the letter "N" in title, minor toning, hinged at the top with old tape. **$2,725**

Photo courtesy Skinner Inc., Boston, www.SkinnerInc.com

The Express Train, 1870, small folio lithograph with hand coloring on paper, sheet size 9 7/8" x 13 1/2", in a contemporary bird's-eye maple veneer frame. Margins of 5/8" or more, repaired tears, several into image, light toning, strong color. **$1,303**

Photo courtesy Skinner Inc., Boston, www.SkinnerInc.com

The Great East River Bridge. To Connect the Cities of New York & Brooklyn, 1872, small folio lithograph with hand coloring on paper, sheet size 11 3/8" x 14 7/8", unframed. Margins of 1 1/4" or more, two repaired tears, creases, minor toning. **$592**

Photo courtesy James D. Julia Auctioneers, Fairfield, Maine; www.JuliaAuctions.com

The Great Fire at Chicago Octr 8th, 1871, fine colored lithograph showing the city of Chicago ablaze with many ships and people in and at edge of water. Bottom legend complete, and dated 1871. Back having pencil inscription, "Purchased from Walter M. Hill Oct, 1914." Housed in a gilt and black old frame. Image, 17" x 25". Examined out of frame. Colors are bright and vibrant. There are small water stains to bottom margin and the right quarter showing a water stain in the margins. **$18,400**

Photo courtesy Skinner Inc., Boston, www.SkinnerInc.com

New York Bay. From Bay Ridge L.I., 1860, medium folio lithograph with hand coloring on paper, sheet size 18" x 23 7/8", in a molded mahogany frame. Margins of 1 3/8" or more, toning, some light vertical acid stains from previous wood backing. **$474**

Photo courtesy Skinner Inc., Boston, www.SkinnerInc.com

Wild Turkey Shooting, 1871, small folio lithograph with hand coloring on paper, sheet size 10 3/4" x 14 3/4", in a molded wooden frame. Margins of 7/8" or more, minor toning, small loss upper left corner. **$592**

Gold Mining in California, 1871, small folio lithograph with hand coloring on paper, sheet size 10 3/4" x 13 1/2", unframed. Margins of 1/2" or more, light toning and mat stains. **$3,199**

Kiss Me Quick, undated, small folio lithograph with hand coloring on paper, sheet size 13 3/4" x 10 1/2", unframed. Margins of 1" or more, toning and light stains prevalent in margins, two tape hinges at the top, angled corner crease in margin upper left. **$829**

James Abbott McNeill Whistler, (American, 1834-1903), The Rag Gatherers, etching, signed and dated in the plate, fifth state. Housed in a gilt wood frame with wide white double matte, 6 1/2" x 4" (sight). **$1,495**

John Steuart Curry (American 1897-1946), John Brown, pencil-signed lithograph, shows John Brown in a wild demeanor with a tornado behind him and a sword on his side. Pencil signed bottom right and having an Associated American Artist label affixed to the reverse. Housed in simple ivory frame with white matte, 15 1/2" x 11 1/2" (sight). Some toning at edges. **$4,600**

Rockwell Kent, (American, 1882-1971), Sacco & Vanzetti, pencil-signed engraving shows two heads on a pole with crosses in the background. Housed in silver gilt molded wood frame and double matte, 5" x 3" (sight). Light signature and minor foxing. **$300**

Four Civil War Brown Water Navy lithographs, C&I, titles include; Bombardment and Capture of Fort Henry, Tenn.; Admiral Porter's Fleet Running the Rebel Blockade of the Mississippi at Vicksburg, April 16th 1863; Brilliant Naval Victory on the Mississippi River, Near Fort Wright, May 10th 1862; Bombardment of "Island Number Ten" in the Mississippi River. .... **$920 set**

Four Civil War medium-folio lithographs, C&I, titles include: The Battle of Antietam, MD. Sept. 17th 1862; The Night After The Battle; Capture of Roanoke Island, Feby. 8th 1862; Surrender of Fort Hudson, LA. July 8th 1863. All 16" x 12" (unframed) 12 1/2" x 7 3/4" (sight). .... **$1,380 set**

Four Civil War medium-folio lithographs, C&I, titles include: General Stoneman's Great Cavalry Raid, may, 1863; Battle of Chancellorsville, Va. May, 3rd 1863; The Storming of Fort Donelson, Tenn. Feby. 15th 1862; The Battle of Pittsburg, Tenn. April 7th 1862. All 16" x 12" (unframed) 12 1/2" x 7 3/4" (sight). .... **$805 set**

Four Civil War medium-folio lithographs, C&I, titles include: Battle of Fredericksburg, VA. Dec. 13th 1862; Battle of Williamsburg VA. May 5th 1862; The Battle of Fair Oaks, Va. May 31st 1862; Genl. Shields at the Battle of Winchester, Va. 1862. All 16" x 12" (unframed) 12 1/2" x 7 3/4" (sight). .... **$805 set**

Prints, Alphabetical by Artist

Karel Appel, (Dutch, 1921-2006), Cat Suite, color serigraph shows a colorful cat against a black background. Pencil signed and numbered "55/125" lower right. A certificate of authenticity from Genesis Galleries affixed to reverse. Housed in a metal frame with double matte (frame with tape marks), 23 1/2" x 30 1/2" (sight). **$300**

Frank Weston Benson, (American, 1862-1951), In Dropping Flight, drypoint on paper, scene shows four ducks landing in clear water. Pencil signed lower left, 1926 edition of 134, housed in a hinged matte, 10 3/4" x 13 3/4" (plate). **$1,725**

Thomas Hart Benton, (American, 1889-1975), Island Hay, limited-edition signed original lithograph, showing several men with scythes haying a field with barn in background. Pencil signed bottom right "Benton". Housed in a modern molded wood frame with beige matte, 10 1/2" x 13" (sight). Light toning to edges, very good condition. **$3,680**

Paul Cadmus, (American, 1904-1999), Waiting for Rehearsal, limited-edition etching, shows three dancers outside a doorway rehearsing for the New York City Ballet. Signed lower right. Titled and numbered "53/175". Housed in a modern silver black-edged frame with wide white matte, 11 3/4" x 8 1/2" (sight). **$1,560**

Roland H. Clark, (American, 1874-1957), A Memory, drypoint on paper, scene shows a flock of ducks coming into a marshy area. Signed in pencil lower right and titled in the print, 1928 from an edition of 75. Housed in a hinged matte. Along with a book, To Keep a Tryst with the Dawn: An Appreciation of Roland Clark by John T. Ordman, limited edition numbered 1006 and signed, 16" x 12 3/4" (plate). Slight overall toning. **$977**

Photo courtesy Rago Arts and Auction Center, Lambertville, N.J.; www.RagoArts.com

Gustave Baumann, (American, 1881-1971), color woodblock print, Fox River Farmyard, 1908. Soiled paper, dime-sized stain to lower margin. Matted. Pencil-signed and dated, 6 3/4" x 8 3/4" image. **$1,320**

Salvador Dali, (Spanish, 1904-1989) Untitled, signed limited-edition color lithograph, depicts a man's head and torso against green tree background. Protruding from the man's mouth are human legs and an object protrudes from his head. Numbered "128/150". Signed bottom right. Housed in a gilt frame with wide matte and inner gold liner. Also pen signed on back with cutout for viewing, 11 3/4" x 8 1/4" (sight). **$540**

Herbert Thomas Dicksee, (British, 1862-1942), Leopard Cubs at Play and Danger, pair of large etchings, both pencil signed "Herbert Dicksee". 1) Scene shows two leopards on a fallen tree trunk with two butterflies in grasses. Below image "Copyright 1907 by Frost & Reed, Bristol, England in the United States of America." Above is "Published at 8 Clare Street, Bristol by Frost & Reed Printsellers of Bristol, Clifton & London May 1st 1907 Berlin Stiefbold & Co., No. 25, Markgrafemstrasse, Copyright Registered." Housed in its period oak frame with thick white matte. 2) Scene shows a lion and lioness with her cubs in amongst a cleared area with grass. Above image "Copyright 1905 by Mess'rs Arthur Tooth & Sons 586 Hay Market, London 14 Boulevard Des

Capucineo Paris 299 Fifth Avenue, New York & Mess'rs Stiefbold & Co., Berlin." Housed in a flat oak frame with thick matte. 1) Image, 19 1/2" x 26 1/2". 2) Image, 16" x 27 1/2". 1) Image is very good; the border has foxing, matte with stains. 2) Image is very good with foxing to borders. ..... **$1,035 pair**

Arthur Wesley Dow, (American, 1857-1922), color woodblock print of illustrated poem by Everett S. Hubbard, Rain in May. Matted and framed, 7 1/2" x 6" sight. .. **$1,200**

Arthur Wesley Dow, (American, 1857-1922), four woodblock prints, Little Venice, 5 1/2" x 3"; Seashore Landscape, sheet, 6 1/2" x 9"; Lily, colored drawing from Ipswich prints series F, 5 1/2" x 4"; and Emerson House Greeting Cards, 3 3/4" x 3". All matted and framed, last two marked. .... **$3,600 set**

Arthur Wesley Dow, (American, 1857-1922), color woodblock print, The Lost Boat. Matted and framed, unsigned, 5 3/4" x 4" image. **$4,200**

Erte, (Romain de Tirtoff, Russian, 1892-1990), The Zodiac Suite, 1982, 12 serigraphs in original portfolio. Each signed, titled and numbered 341/350, 25 1/2" x 20" (sheet) each. Tristar Publishing Ltd., New York. **$2,040**

Photo courtesy Rago Arts and Auction Center, Lambertville, N.J.; www.RagoArts.com

Margaret Patterson, (American, 1867-1950), color woodblock print, Pink Dogwood. Matted and framed. Pencil-titled and signed, 7" x 10 1/4" image. **$5,700**

Photo courtesy Rago Arts and Auction Center, Lambertville, N.J.; www.RagoArts.com

Arthur Wesley Dow, (American, 1857-1922), color woodblock print, Gables by the Bridge, circa 1893. Matted and framed, unsigned, 2 1/4" x 4" image. **$1,020**

Our Heroes and Our Flags, copyright 1896 by Southern Lithograph Co. Print features central vignette of full standing portraits of Generals Lee, Jackson and Beauregard, surrounded by 17 small vignettes of other generals and Confederate flags. Print measures 24" x 18" and is framed. **$115**

Aiden Lassell Ripley, (American, 1896-1969), Ruffled Grouse in Winter, unframed etching shows two grouse in a sunlit snow-covered scene. Pencil titled and signed. Accompanying the lot is the book Sporting Etchings by A. Lassell Ripley. This etching is illustrated on page 90. Image 11" x 9 1/4". Very good condition. **$1,380**

Rufino Tamayo, (Mexican 1899-1991), Watermelon Man, silkscreen (?), scene shows a man seated at a table eating a section of watermelon with pieces on the table and a piece

Photo courtesy James D. Julia Auctioneers, Fairfield, Maine; www.JuliaAuctions.com

Roger Tory Peterson, (American, 1908-1996), Snow Owl, limited-edition lithograph, pencil signed and marked "Publisher's Proof." Published by Mill Pond Press Inc., Venice, Fla. Scene shows two snowy owls perched on a rock with lichen in an arctic setting. Housed in a modern gilt-wood frame. Image 30 1/4" x 22". Very good condition. **$230**

resting on a stand behind him, watermelon seeds scattered around. Bright colors on masonite. Housed in a painted molded wood frame. Signed lower left "Tamayo 40", 28" x 22". One small scrape below watermelon. **$920**

Rembrandt Harmenszoon Van Rijn, (Dutch, 1606-1669), Joseph's Coat Brought to Jacob, 1633, 18th-century impression), etching (framed), signed in the plate, 4 3/8" x 3 3/8" (sheet). **$2,280**

Stow Wengenroth, (American, 1906-1978), The Church, lithograph on paper, scene shows the side view of the front of a Wiscasset Maine church in October, 1947. Pencil signed and numbered "Ed/60". Housed in a silver gilt frame with white matte, 15 1/2" x 11 1/4" (image). **$780**

James Abbott McNeill Whistler, (American, 1834-1903), Billingsgate, 1859, etching on tan woven paper (framed). Signed, 5 5/8" x 8 7/8" (sheet). **$480**

The Worship of Bacchus, large framed colored engraving, after a painting housed in the National Gallery; printed by R. Holdgate and published June 20, 1864, by Wilhelm Tweedie, London. Figures outlined on the steel plate by George Cruikshank, and the engraving finished by Charles Mottram. Scene showing a monument surrounded by hundreds of people in a chaotic scene with vignettes. Housed in an antique molded wood frame with gold liner and glass; 28 1/2" x 44 1/2". Toned with slight fading, otherwise good condition. **$300**

Statuary

Also see Oriental Objects.

Eugene Bormel, (19th century), bronze sculpture of winged goddess with flowers and a basket, on a marble socle, 1897. Cast in two separate pieces and joined at the hip. Signed "Bormel 1897", 16 5/8" h. **$480**

Continental bronzes, Ovide Yencesse (French, 1869-1947) bronze plaque of a mother and child reading, framed, signed upper right O. Yencesse; and Ernest Sanglan (French, 19th-20th century) two-handled vase with sleeping satyr, signed on side E. Sanglan with foundry seal and #7537 on base. Vase: 7 1/4". .... **$900 pair**

Edmond Drappier, (French, 19th-20th century), bronze statue of a bull, on wooden base. Signed E. Drappier, 10" x 16" x 9". **$2,040**

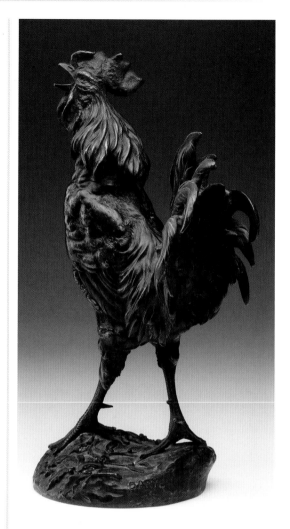

Photo courtesy Rago Arts and Auction Center, Lambertville, N.J.; www.RagoArts.com

Alfred Barye (French 1839-1882), bronze animalier statue of a rooster on round base. Signed Barye, 13" h. **$1,920**

Photo courtesy Rago Arts and Auction Center, Lambertville, N.J.; www.RagoArts.com

Austrian bronze, horse-drawn coach on green marble base, 20th century, stamped "Made in Austria," circled AT monogram. 9 1/2" x 28 3/4" x 7 1/2". Reportedly one of only two made, commissioned by the Winmill family of Warrenton, Va. A copy of the book, "Gone Away with the Winmills" (1877) by Virginia Winmill Livingstone Armstrong, accompanies bronze. **$4,800**

Photo courtesy Rago Arts and Auction Center, Lambertville, N.J.; www.RagoArts.com

Henry Étienne Dumaige, (French, 1830-1888), untitled (Young Couple), gilt bronze statue on rotating gilt bronze base. Provenance: Signed "Henr. Dumaige" and with foundry mark "E. Colin", 22" h, 25" w (with base). **$4,200**

Photo courtesy Rago Arts and Auction Center, Lambertville, N.J.; www.RagoArts.com

Hyppolyte Francois Moreau, (French, 1832-1927), "La Vigne," gilt bronze sculpture on base, signed "HMOREAU", 22 3/4" h, 24" w (with base). **$2,400**

Emmanuel Fremiet, (French, 1824-1910), bronze figurine of a dog, signed E. Fremiet; together with a bronze horse on a rectangular base, by unknown maker, broken tail, slightly rubbed patina and one ear bent forward, 19th center, taller: 9 1/4". .... **$840 pair**

Adrien Étienne Gaudez, (French, 1845-1902), "Etoile du Matin," bronze statue with base. Signed "A. GAUDEZ H.C" and titled "ETOILE/DU MATIN", 21 3/4" h, 22 3/4" w (with base). **$1,800**

P.J. Mene, (French, 1810-1877), bronze sculpture of a horse standing by a makeshift fence, freestanding on black marble base. Signed on base P.J. Mene, Susse Freres & Co. foundry mark. With base: 14" x 19" x 8 1/2". **$4,800**

P.J. Mene, (French, 1810-1877), bronze quail hunting group. Signed PJ Mene on the bronze, 8" x 16" x 8". **$1,680**

Jules Moigniez, Patinated bronze sculpture of an owl preparing to land, signed (after), 33" h x 24" w.

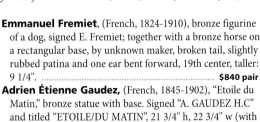

.... **$325**

Louis-Auguste Moreau, (French, 1855-1919), "David," bronze sculpture, signed "L. Moreau," 29" h. **$3,240**

Mathurin Moreau, (French, 1822-1912), "Echo," bronze sculpture, signed "Math Moreau / Hors. Concours" and stamped "MEDAILLE HONNEUR", 26 3/4" h. **$3,000**

Jean Jules Salmson, (French, 1823-1902), bronze sculpture of a woman in the Oriental style, a jar in her hand. Drilled for lamp, with small repair on back of neck. Marked Salmson, 21" h. **$2,640**

Vaclaw Bernard (Victor) Szczeblewski, (Polish, 19th century), bronze sculpture, "Boy Whisting," on marble base, 1889. Signed and dated. With base: 9" h. **$780**

Charles Valton, (French 1851-1918), bronze statue of a mastiff with sign 'Passez au Large.' Signed C.H. Valton, 18 1/4" h. **$2,640**

Vienna bronzes, cold painted: two bird figurines, late 19th/ early 20th century, both marked on underside of tail, one with Geschutzt 1801, the other initialed FB with illegible writing, taller: 3 1/2". .... **$900 pair**

Photo courtesy Rago Arts and Auction Center, Lambertville, N.J.; www.RagoArts.com

Dog group, bronze, two hunting dogs (dachshunds) on a red marble plinth, 19th century, each stamped with numbers and Geschutzt, 2 1/2" x 4 1/2". **$480**

Photo courtesy Rago Arts and Auction Center, Lambertville, N.J.; www.RagoArts.com

R. Clark, cowboy bronze, figure on horseback leading two horses and covered wagon, the packhorses with a deer, antlers and supplies, 20th century, signed R. Clark. 32" x 13". **$1,440**

Russian bronze, horse-drawn buggy and rider, 20th century, marked on base "Fabr. by C.F. WOERFELL", signed in Cyrillic, 4" x 9 1/2". **$3,000**

Henry Schonbauer (American, b. 1895), bronze sculpture, "The Stone Roller," 1936. Signed and dated, with accompanying paperwork, 18 1/4" x 30" x 10 1/2". **$11,400**

Mathurin Moreau, (French, 1822-1912), "La Muse des Bois," bronze sculpture on rotating bronze base, signed "Math. Moreau", 27 1/2" h, 28 1/2" w (with base). **$4,500**

GETTING INSIDE OUTSIDER ART

By Mary P. Manion

Acting Director, Landmarks Gallery & Restoration Studio, Milwaukee

Reprinted from *Antique Trader* magazine

Eugene von Bruenchenhein (1910-1983), a self-taught artist living in obscurity in Milwaukee, handcrafted a plaque that hung in his kitchen and identified his metier: "Freelance artist, Poet and sculptor, inovater (sic) Arrow maker and Plant man, Bone artifacts constructor, Photographer and Architect, Philosopher." Shortly after his death, when his enormous lifetime collection of works was discovered in his tiny home (which was more of a working studio than a comfortable living space) the art world proclaimed him as an Outsider Artist. He never realized the reputation he gained.

Unknown, his insular life was of his own creation, devoted to his skill at handcrafting found objects into sculpture, photographing his wife and projecting his apocalyptic vision of mankind's future threatened by nuclear destruction through paintings on cardboard, and by writing poetry and prose on scraps of old paper. Most of his creations were crafted from scraps others would discard as junk. His fantastic vision filled every inch of the humble living space he shared with his wife, Marie. Stacked floor to ceiling were paintings on cardboard, masonite and pages of discarded wallpaper sample books depicting atomic mushroom clouds and fantastic sea-monsters, ceramics constructed from dug-up dirt with ruddy, ghoulish features, sculptures of chairs and towers constructed from chicken bones, and hundreds of photos of Marie, playfully posing in costumes of his making, some fashioned from drapery and other handy materials.

Ernest Rancoulet, (French, 1870-1915), untitled (Woman Carrying Wheat), bronze figure, signed "Rancoulet", 21 1/2" h. **$1,440**

Eugene Von Bruenchenhein. Photo of Marie with Snake (artist's wife). Original silver gelatin print, 8" x 10". Archival frame. **$1,955**

Photo courtesy Slotin Auction, Buford, Ga.; www.SlotinFolkArt.com

Eugene Von Bruenchenhein. Abstract Dragon. Oil on board, framed, 26" w x 26" h. **$8,050**

His life was his art, his home was his studio and his wife was his model. Her photographs, often semi-nude and very beguiling, were pin-ups for their use only, adorning the walls along with self-made masks of gothic expression and chicken-bone regal crowns for Marie to wear.

Von Bruenchenhein, also referred to as an "obsessive visionary," fits the profile of an Outsider Artist, a term he likely never heard. Strictly defined, Outsider Art refers to work produced by artists usually living in self-imposed isolation with no ties to the art world or any other community, little social contact and often sporadic employment. Characteristics of the category include the artist rendering a unique and nontraditional vision of the world. Expressing the view repeatedly, the outsider often produces extensive quantities of work and seldom veers from the obsessive vision. The outsider artist is self-taught and seeks no influence from the mainstream art world.

Although the term was coined in 1972, Outsider Art grew from the label "Art Brut," a term defined by the French artist Jean DuBuffet in the late 1940s. Translated as raw or rough art, DuBuffet's focus was on mentally ill and often disturbed patients he observed in psychiatric clinics. Recognizing creative impulses in them, he believed that art could be created from a genuine expression from within, with no outside influence dictating, distracting or intimidating the creator of the art. As Dubuffet stated: " works created from solitude and from pure and authentic creative impulses – where the worries of competition, acclaim and social promotion do not interfere." He began obtaining works by these artists, both institutionalized and others bearing a non-conventional approach to art. In 1971 he donated his collection to the city of Lausanne, Switzerland, where it remains today as one of the most important compilations of the genre.

The definition of Outsider Art has prompted widespread debate in recent years, with many artists eagerly adopt-

ing the label as a marketing tool. The "Outsider Art movement" is a contradiction in terms. True outsiders know of no movements and belong to no clubs.

Another classic Outsider Artist was the subject of a 2004 documentary, *In the Realms of the Unreal: The Mystery of Henry Darger.* Filmed by Oscar-winning director Jessica Yu, the film reconstructs the life a Chicago recluse who spent his childhood in an asylum and his adulthood working as a janitor. Until after his death, few knew that Darger spent his life writing and illustrating a 15,000–page fantasy called *In the Realms of the Unreal,* as well as executing hundreds of paintings to accompany his narrative.

Early on in life, Darger (1892-1973) determined existence was too difficult and painful for him to bear. Rather than give in to the depths of his misery and despair, he invented a fantastic new world for himself, through writing and painting. His singular epic of biblical proportions centered on seven heroines he called the Vivian Girls and, for 60 years, they filled his life with their struggles and triumphs. Culling from his own life experience, the girls faced good and evil as they fought hard battles, at times featuring profane and disturbing imagery.

As with von Bruenchenhein, his alternative world was shared with few and it was not for show or sale. After his death, his works were discovered in the apartment he occupied most of his life. The cramped rooms were filled with the materials from which he shaped his vision. Art supplies, stacks of old newspapers and periodicals, religious items and pictures of children were among his belongings.

The lives of von Bruenchenhein and Darger illustrate the importance of the power of art. They found purpose through their vision, which became their raison d'etre. Both worked within the classic Outsider Art dictum, creating not to earn a living or gain recognition but simply to stay alive amidst a kind of madness that lurked within.

The John Michael Kohler Arts Center in Sheboygan, Wis., has showcased a permanent collection of more than 600 examples of von Bruenchenhein's work, which includes bone chairs and towers, ceramic crowns, sculpture and vessels, concrete masks, miscellaneous artifacts, paintings and photographs.

Authentic Outsider Art has been a pursuit of collectors

Photo courtesy Slotin Auction, Buford, Ga.; www.SlotinFolkArt.com

Adkins, Minnie and Garland. Black and White Hog. Carved and painted wood. 35" x 12" x 6 1/2". **$1,495**

Photo courtesy Slotin Auction, Buford, Ga.; www.SlotinFolkArt.com

Darger, Henry. Untitled. Watercolor on paper, double-sided, 47" w x 19" h, framed to see both sides. **$25,000**

for several decades, with auction prices remaining substantial. In 2003, Christies (New York) auctioned several of Darger's sizable works with prices ranging from $35,850 (including buyer's premium) for an 18 3/4" x 92" watercolor/graphite/collage on paper titled *Violet Goes on Dangerous Mission/Surprised Again,* to $89,625 (including buyer's premium) for a larger watercolor/graphite/collage on paper (24" x 107 1/8") *While inside they await developments they are cleverly Outwitted*

Von Bruenchenhein auction prices are lower but respectable. A 2004 sale also at Christies (New York), brought $5,975. (including buyer's premium) for an untitled oil on masonite, 24" square. Gallery prices for his works can be found in the same range.

While much of the commercially inspired "Outsider Art" of recent years will probably prove to have ephemeral value, at best, the work of prominent, genuine outsiders is likely to retain value and interest based on their compelling life stories.

Almon, Leroy. Untitled. Latex paint on bas-relief carved wood, signed and dated 1991 on reverse, 24" w x 23" h. **$4,025**

Archuleta, Felipe. Donkey, 1984. Carved and painted wood, 50" h x 69" l by 12" w. **$12,650**

Arning, Eddie. Three Men at the Beach. Crayon on paper, 1968, 22" w x 16" h. **$5,750**

Ashby, Steve. Large Woman, 1974. Natural and cut wood, acorns, paint, metal, cloth and a pair of old sunglasses, 48" h x 11" w x 8" deep. **$5,865**

Barker, Linville. Buffalo, 1994. Carved wood. 16 1/2" w x 11 1/2" h. **$5,462**

Birnbaum, Aaron. Early Settlers. Acrylic on masonite with a coat of varnish, 39 1/2" w x 25 1/2" h. **$6,900**

Burnside, Richard. Two-Headed Dog. Paint on masonite, signed and dated, 2002, 30" w x 20" h. **$805**

Cartledge, Ned. Our Kind of Devil, 1981. Carved and painted bas-relief, 17 1/2" h x 19" w x 1 1/2" deep. .. **$5,750**

Castle, James (1900-1977). Double-Sided Drawing, circa 1940-1950, 9" w x 6" h, framed 17 1/2" w x 15". **$10,025**

Clark, Henry Ray. I Will Eventually Kill You All if You Mess with Me. Ink on paper, 30" w x 18" h. **$3,335**

Coins, Raymond. Dream. Carved stone, 16" w x 23" h.
.... **$5,290**

Photo courtesy Slotin Auction, Buford, Ga.; www.SlotinFolkArt.com

Black, Calvin and Ruby. Miss Sherion (or Sharion) Rose Possum Trot doll. Carved and painted wood with silk fabric clothing, crochet knit hat, wig hair, wearing a necklace with a stone pendant. Mounted on stand with a homemade tag, 34" h, extremely rare. **$92,000**

Photo courtesy Slotin Auction, Buford, Ga.; www.SlotinFolkArt.com

Dey, Uncle Jack. Acupuncture Moose Style. Oil-based enamel on board with wood frame, 29 1/2" w x 18" h. **$12,650**

Craig, Burlon (B.B.). Five-Gallon Face Jug. Ash glaze, gas-burn kiln, some glass drips. In script: B.B. Craig on bottom, 18" h. **$3,737**

Cunningham, Earl. Night Harbor. Thick oil on board, heavy brush strokes, signed, 21 1/2" w x 21" h. **$9,775**

Davis, Ulysses. Fantasy Creature. Carved and painted wood, 9" w x 20" h x 18" diameter. **$10,350**

Dawson, William. Carved Couple, circa 1980s. Carved and painted wood with feathers and a tassel, 16 1/2" h each. Articulated arms, unsigned. **$4,255**

Dieter, Charlie. Lyria Band, Palmerton. Graphite and crayon on paper, 21" w x 17" h. **$1035**

Doyle, Sam. Penn State Football Player. Paint on tin, environmental piece, 27" w x 43" h. **$36,800**

Drgac, Peter Paul (Uncle Pete). Horses and Animals. Paint on paper. **$2,750**

Edmondson, William. Squirrel Holding a Nut, circa 1937. Carved limestone, 5" w x 13" h x 8 1/4" deep. **$48,300**

Esteves, Antonio. Reclining Nude, 1973. Paint on board, 30" w x 24" h. **$3,450**

Evans, Minnie. Flowers. Mixed media on paper floral collage, signed, 9" w x 12" h. **$3,910**

Farmer, Josephus. King Cotton, 1987. Painted wood-relief carving, 36" w x 29 1/2" h. **$7,475**

Fasanella, Ralph. Marc Antonio for Mayor. Oil on canvas, 71 1/2" w x 51 1/2" h. **$69,000**

Finster, Howard. Deluxe Glass Panel Box. Enamel on cut wood, glass and mirror in wood box, 24 1/2" w x 31" h x 2 1/2" deep. **$11,500**

Photo courtesy Slotin Auction, Buford, Ga.; www.SlotinFolkArt.com

Dial, Thornton. Lady with Tigers. Mix media and paint, backed on a wooden sign, 49" x 49". **$8,625**

Photo courtesy Slotin Auction, Buford, Ga.; www.SlotinFolkArt.com

Finster, Howard. Daniel Boone and Wolf Dogs. Paint on wooden panel with artist-decorated wood-burned frame, 48" w x 48" h. **$20,700**

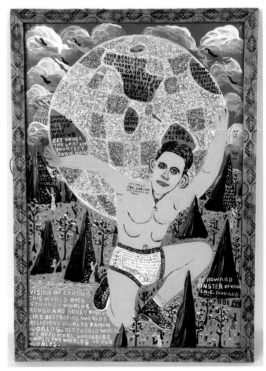

Photo courtesy Slotin Auction, Buford, Ga.; www.SlotinFolkArt.com

Finster, Howard. Visions of Carrying this World, circa 1981. Paint and glitter on metal. Signed on front and back, 13 1/2" w x 19 1/2" h. **$9,200**

Photo courtesy Slotin Auction, Buford, Ga.; www.SlotinFolkArt.com

Golding, William. Rosa Lee, circa 1932. Colored pencil on paper. 12" w x 9" h. Framed: 17" w x 14" h. Signed, "W.O.G. 5/20/32 Savannah, GA." (American shanghaied From Savannah as an 8-year-old boy. In 1932, while in poor health, he returned to Savannah for a hospital stay. There he documented his travels from memory in approximately 70 maritime drawings. **$4,600**

Finster, Howard. Cutout Red Angel. **$1,600**

Finster, Howard. Cutout Coke Sign. **$1,500**

Garrett, Carlton. The Café. Carved and painted wood, 10" h x 9 1/2" w. **$2,070**

Gatto, Victor Joseph. Soldiers In Training. Oil on canvas, 30" w x 24" h. **$10,925**

Gibbs, Ezekial. Texas Baptism. Crayon on paper, 23" w x 17" h. **$2,415**

Gibson, Sybil. Pink Floral Blooms. Tempera on newsprint, signed, 38 1/4" w x 33" h. **$1,035**

Godie, Lee. Self Portrait. Watercolor on paper, 19 1/2" w x 29 1/2" h. **$1,495**

Gordon, Ted. Lodge Official, circa 1994. Ink on paper, 9 1/2" w x 11 3/4" h. **$431**

Hall, Dilmus. Early environmental piece with hands in relief and date cut into cement, circa 1962. 14 x 14 x 14. Blue Hands refers to an African American charm called a mojo. **$6,900**

Harvey, Bessie. Days of the Week Working Girls. Fabric on painted wood. Tallest is 16" h. **$2,415**

Hawkins, William. Three Kids and a Dog. House paint on wood, 35" x 35". **$23,000**

Hayes, Rev. Herman. Ten Carved Wooden Totems, circa 1990-1993, 7" h x 17" h. .... **$690 all**

Holley, Lonnie. Crown of Thorns. Wire, organic material, fabric, wheel bolts, lamp parts, 89" w x 32" h. **$1,437**

Howard, Jesse. Sorehead Dalton. Enamel paint on metal with wood backing, 60 1/2" w x 11" h. **$3,162**

Hunter, Clementine. Bucket Lilies, self-portrait of the artist at work, circa 1960. Paint on board, 23 1/2" w x 14" h. ... **$21,850**

Hunter, Clementine. Pickin' Haulin' and Weighin' Cotton, circa 1960. Paint on board, 23 1/2" w x 18" h. **$20,700**

Hussey, Billy Ray. Large Lion, 20" h x 18" w. **$5,750**

Jones, S.L. Woman Wearing Scarf Bust, 9" w x 13" h. **$10,925**

Kinney, Charlie. Hoot Owl. Paint on poster board, 22" w x 28" h. **$2,415**

Klumpp, Gustav. Nude in the Woods, 22" w x 18" h. . **$33,350**

Lebduska, Lawrence. Pintos. Oil on board, 20" x 24" h. **$5,750**

Lieberman, Harry. Children's Children are the Crown, circa 1977. Oil on canvas paper, 14" w x 18" h. **$5,462**

Long, Woodie. Man on Bicycle, tempera on paper, 24" w x 12" h, frame, 32" w x 20" h. **$805**

Lucas, Charlie. Horse Sculpture. Metal assemblage, life size, ... **$3,500**

Lucas, Charlie. Theatre Masks. Metal assemblage, 23 1/2" w x 18" h x 5" deep. **$718**

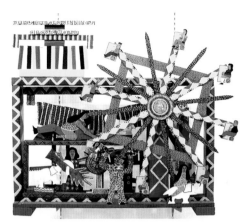

Jennings, James Harold. Circus World. Acrylic on wood assemblage. Multiple layer kinetic piece, as the star wheel turns the figures move, 40" w x 33" h x 11" deep. **$6,210**

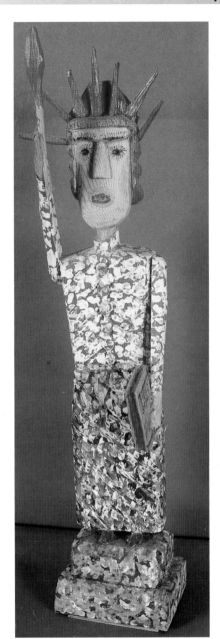

Massey, Willie. Cat with Birds in Tree, circa 1980. Oil on board, 16" x 24". **$1,150**

McKenzie, Carl. Statue of Liberty, circa 1988. Carved and painted wood, 22" h x 11" x 5". Articulated arms. **$575**

McCarthy, Justin. Jesus Carrying the Cross. Paint on board, 32" w x 32" h. **$8,050**

McCord, Jake. Cats and Birds, enamel on wooden board, 32" w x 48" h. **$4,312**

Meaders, Arie. Owl, Bristol glaze with cobalt decoration. Signed, 7" h. **$9,200**

Meaders, Edwin. Voodoo Jug #6. Signed and dated 1994. Blue with runny green eye glaze, 10" h. **$3,565**

Meaders, Lanier. Devil Face Jug. No signature, rare. Ash glaze, 7" h. **$16,100**

Miller, R.A. Pair of Blow Oskars. Painted tin cutouts, approximately 36" h. .... **$100.**

Monza, Louis. Old Man Vesuvius, circa 1944. Oil on canvas, 17" w x 22" h. **$7,130**

Morgan, Sister Gertrude. Jesus is My Airplane. Ink and paint on cardboard, 11 1/2" w x 10" h. **$20,700**

Morgan, Sister Gertrude. The Shepherds Voice, acrylic on paper. Signed, with a long poem incorporated into the work on the front, 19" w x 21 1/2" h. **$28,750**

Photo courtesy Slotin Auction, Buford, Ga.; www.SlotinFolkArt.com

Rowe, Nellie Mae. Emerald Rabbit, circa 1981. On paper, 19 3/4" h x 15" w. **$6,727**

Photo courtesy Slotin Auction, Buford, Ga.; www.SlotinFolkArt.com

Serl, Jon. Us Kids Were Punished. Oil on board. Full description on back says, "Us kids were punished by being locked in a dark room," 30" w x 24" h. **$2,000**

Photo courtesy Slotin Auction, Buford, Ga.; www.SlotinFolkArt.com

O'Kelley, Mattie Lou. Untitled, circa January 1983. Signed and dated. Oil on canvas. **$27,600**

Photo courtesy Slotin Auction, Buford, Ga.; www.SlotinFolkArt.com

Tolliver, Mose. "Mose, Willie Mae, Moose Lady," 1990. House paint on plywood, 8' w x 4' h. **$6,095**

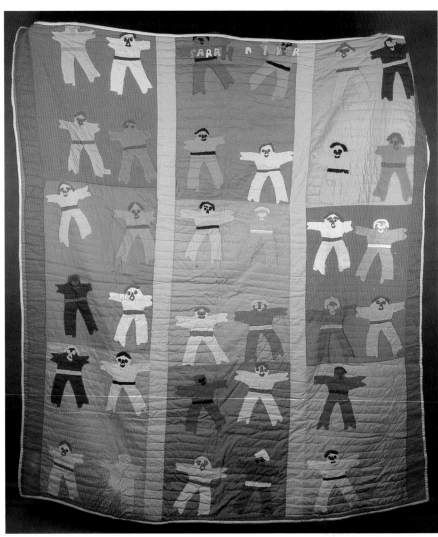

Taylor, Sarah Mary. Figure Quilt - African American. Hand-stitched, 72" x 82". **$1,265**

Mumma, Mr. Eddy. Goat. Paint on artist board, 17 1/2" w x 13 1/2" h. **$1,265**

Murry, J.B. Birth of the Blue Spirits. Watercolor and marker on poster board, 37" w x 31" h. **$4,887**

Perkins, B.F. Alabama Map. Acrylic on canvas, 40" w x 50" h. **$2,012**

Pierce, Elijah. Tiger, circa 1979. Signed, dated and priced on bottom. Carved wood in a three-dimensional style. Latex paint with jeweled eyes, 19 1/2" l x 12" h x 3 1/2" w. **$18,400**

Pressley, Daniel. Moses and the Promised Land. Bas-relief wood carving, signed on back, name carved on front, 16 1/2" h x 28" w. **$11,500**

Pry, Old Ironsides. Fishing, paint on canvas. **$4,000**

Ramirez, Martin. Caballero, circa 1953. Graphite on paper, 24" w x 34" h. **$48,300**

Reed, Ernest "Popeye." Indian Chief Seated With Arms Folded, carved sandstone. Signed, "E. Reed", 11" x 29" h. **$3,450**

Robertson, Royal. Mrs. Mekia, enamel paint and glitter on wood, 14" w x 62 1/2" h. **$2,875**

Rogers, Sultan. Boxing Match. Three carved and painted wooden figures. The tallest in the red trunks is just over 10" h. Mint condition. **$920**

Ruley, Ellis. Stag. Oil on poster board. Featured in book, "Discovering Ellis Ruley," page 73, 22" h x 28" w. Framed: 25 1/2" x 32". **$18,400**

Savitsky, Jack. A Day In the Mines, circa 1974. Oil on canvas board, 20" w x 18" h. **$4,887**

Scott, J.P. Shrimp Boat, circa 1987. Carved and painted wood with found objects, 36" h x 58" w. **$8,050**

Scott, Lorenzo. Harmony in Heaven. Paint on canvas, 54" x 54" including hand-carved bondo frame (his signature style frame designed to replicate the fancy gold frames he once saw at a museum). **$4,600**

Sims, Bernice. My Neighborhood, acrylic on canvas, 26" x 24" including frame. **$1,265**

Photo courtesy Slotin Auction, Buford, Ga.; www.SlotinFolkArt.com

Sudduth, Jimmy Lee. Wild Hog. Heavy mud and paint on wooden panel, 48" w x 24" h. **$7,187**

Photo courtesy Slotin Auction, Buford, Ga.; www.SlotinFolkArt.com

Traylor, Bill. Blue Cat, circa 1939-1942. Not signed. Show-card color on cardboard, 7" x 11". **$42,550**

Photo courtesy Slotin Auction, Buford, Ga.; www.SlotinFolkArt.com

Woolsey, Clarence. Blue Face Bunny. Bottle-cap construction on wood. Excellent condition. 39" h x 19" w. **$9,775**

Singleton, Herbert. Am I My Brother's Keeper? Paint on bas-relief wood carving, 19 1/2" w x 60" h. **$3,220**

Smith, Mary T. Mr. and Mrs. Bull. Paint and marker on roofing tin, 96" w x 48" h. **$1,840**

Speller, Henry. Woman with House, circa 1980. Crayon and pencil on paper, 24" w x 18" h. **$1,150**

Swearingen, Johnnie, Adam and Eve in the Garden. Oil on canvas panel. Signed upper left, 33 1/2" w x 27" h, including wooden frame. **$8,050**

Thomas, James Son. Black and White Skulls. Gumbo clay, tin foil, dentures. The taller is 8" h. .... **$900 both**

Tolson, Edgar. Sodom and Gomorrah, circa 1980. Model airplane paint and radiator paint on wood with small stones. Signed on the bottom, 16" x 11 1/2" x 14". . **$15,000**

Traylor, Bill. Black Horse. Paint and graphite on paper, 13 1/2" h x 11" w. **$35,650**

Traylor, Bill. Woman in a Polka Dot Skirt. Pencil and poster paint on shirt cardboard, circa 1939-42, 7 1/2" w x 13 1/2" h. **$33,350**

Walker, Inez Walker. Bad Girls with Cigarettes. Graphite and crayon on paper, 23" w x 17 1/2" h. **$2,702**

Willings, George. Statue of Liberty, circa 1990. Carved and painted wood. Signed, 24" x 9" x 5". **$1,610**

Wireman, Philadelphia. Wire Sculpture, circa 1970s-1980s. Wound wire around various found objects, 8" h with display stand. **$3,450**

Wolfli, Adolf. Masked Man. Central figure surrounded by abstract shapes and figures, colored pencil and crayon on paper. Excellent condition. Image: 10" w x 13" h. Framed: 22" w x 25". **$29,900**

Yoakum, Joseph. Ester's Bay in Pacific Ocean, Watercolor and ink on paper. Titled, signed and dated in upper left corner. 19" w x 12" h. **$11,500**

Young, Purvis. Inferno. Oil on board. Very early piece. circa 1975. 18" w x 24" h. Frame is 21" w x 27" h. **$9,775**

Zeldis, Malcah. New York Street Scene, circa 1979. Oil on board, 20" w x 15 1/2" h...**$2,185**

AUTOGRAPHS

Autographs appear on an amazing array of objects: letters, photographs, books, cards, clothing, etc. Most collectors focus on a particular person, country or category, like movie stars, musicians or athletes.
Also see Sports Memorabilia.

Photo courtesy Heritage Auction Galleries, Dallas; www.HA.com

Hank Aaron, single-signed baseball. **$95**

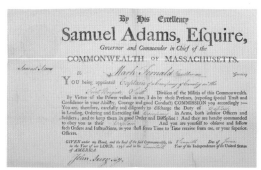

Photo courtesy Swann Auction Galleries, New York; www.SwannGalleries.com

Samuel Adams, 1796, partly printed document signed as Governor of Massachusetts, appointing Mark Fernald "captain of a Company of Cavalry in the First Brigade, Sixth." Countersigned by Secretary John Avery. Approximately 9" x 14 1/2"; diagonal tear lower right (not affecting text), docketed on verso, paper seal intact. **$2,280**

Woody Allen, 5" x 6" headshot postcard, signed in black ink. $59
"All in the Family", signatures from co-stars Sally Struthers, Rob Reiner, Carroll O'Connor and Jean Stapleton, matted with a 5" x 6" color photo of the cast. $215
Louis Armstrong, white silk handkerchief signed in black ink, matted and framed along with a color 12" x 12" photo of Armstrong to an overall size of 17" x 21". $717
Fred Astaire and Ginger Rogers, vintage promotional photo. $298
Pearl Bailey, 1990, pictorial greeting card: "You stand so majestic – you invite the world to look up past you to the heavens. '100 years old –' amazing – your youth overpowers your age, I love you." (Marking the 100th anniversary of the Eiffel Tower.) $360

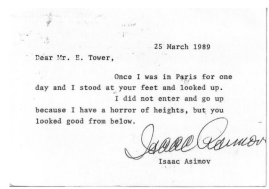

Photo courtesy Swann Auction Galleries, New York; www.SwannGalleries.com

Isaac Asimov, 1989, typed note on a card: "Dear Mr. E. Tower, Once I was in Paris for one day and I stood at your feet and looked up. I did not enter and go up because I have a horror of heights, but you looked good from below." (Marking the 100th anniversary of the Eiffel Tower.) **$660**

Photo courtesy Heritage Auction Galleries, Dallas; www.HA.com

Chuck Berry, white Signature Series electric guitar with Chuck Berry logo and image on the body, signed on the pick guard. **$478**

Photo courtesy Heritage Auction Galleries, Dallas; www.HA.com

Ray Bolger, vintage promotional photo from "The Wizard of Oz." **$298**

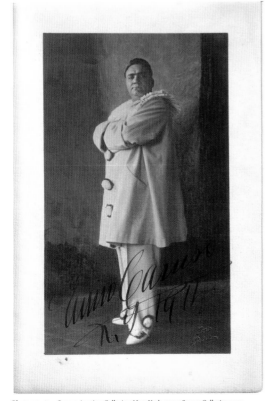

Photo courtesy Swann Auction Galleries, New York; www.SwannGalleries.com

Enrico Caruso, 1911, photograph, showing him standing, arms crossed, in costume as Pagliacci. Signed in the image. Approximately 9" x 5" (image). **$1,800**

Photo courtesy Swann Auction Galleries, New York; www.SwannGalleries.com

George Armstrong Custer, 1868, letter to Captain W.J. Lough, concerning the alleged poor treatment of Custer's horses, Phil and Mack, under Lough's care. Custer writes in part: "I do not want him kept from his regular full account of work merely because he shys . . . I certainly do not intend to pay for any time not even a day that my horse does not receive the work and care on the track which I intended he should . . . I distinctly told you that I did not want my horses taken outside the track enclosure and I still desire that except for shoeing." Four pages, written on a single folded sheet; soiling on terminal page, vertical fold through signature, small stain through text on terminal page. With Captain Lough's letter in response to Custer, defending his work. **$7,200**

Leonard Bernstein (1918-1990), photograph showing him sitting behind a music stand at the New York Philharmonic Young People's Concert in 1964. Signed in the image. Approximately 9" x 7"; some dings, staining at right edge. **$330**

Napoleon Bonaparte, 1814, letter, written as the Continental powers march toward Paris, to the Duke of Feltre, in French, ordering the deployment of two troop divisions and requesting to be informed about their prompt arrival, as "[t]he fate of the capital may depend on it." One page, folds, tiny holes in lower left (not affecting signature). **$6,000**

James Brown, B&W 8" x 10" photo, circa 1992, in blue ballpoint. **$149**

James Cagney, photo from the 1931 movie, "The Public Enemy." **$107**

Johnny Cash and June Carter Cash, 22-page tour book from the mid-'70s, full of color photos, signed on the inside front cover in black ballpoint. Some mild wear and moderate spine stress. **$179**

James Fenimore Cooper, 1841, letter to the Boston publisher George Roberts, rejecting the idea of writing a novel because, "It would not tally with my notions to publish a novel in the way you mention," and offering other projects. One full page, small tear in left margin, closed tear in right margin repaired, folds. **$2,040**

Dwight D. Eisenhower and Douglas MacArthur, photograph signed by both, silver print image by Thomas Shafer showing the two generals side by side in a car during Eisenhower's visit to Tokyo in May 1946. Approximately 8" x 10"; minor creases and dings, marginal chips, photographer's stamp on verso. **$36,000** *(Eisenhower and MacArthur's enmity toward each other is well documented, making this image an exceptional association piece. Shafer was a combat photographer during World War II and spent most of the war in the Pacific Theater. He made some 18 troop landings with the 1st Cavalry division, and took many of the widely distributed photos of MacArthur wading ashore on his "I have returned" landing in the Philippines. After the Japanese surrender, Shafer spent time in Japan and took the first close-up photos of Emperor Hirohito and became essentially MacArthur's personal photographer. In May 1946, Eisenhower was Army Chief of Staff and MacArthur the head of the U.S. occupation of Japan. Ike was in Tokyo on an inspection trip visiting U.S. troops stationed in the Far East. In the photograph, the two generals are seated in MacArthur's official Cadillac limousine. It appeared in newspapers on June 2, 1946, but Shafer personally had the two generals sign the photograph in his presence while Ike was still in Tokyo.)*

Dallas Cowboys, 1992 Super Bowl Champions helmet, including Troy Aikman, Emmitt Smith, Michael Irvin, Jerry Jones, Dave Wannstedt, Daryl Johnston, Bill Bates, Jay Novacek and many more. **$1,075**

Bobby Darin, signed contract, 1967. Initialed and signed in blue ink with his real name, Bob Cassotto. Overall age toning and smudging of the ink in a couple spots, while the signature reads clearly. **$155**

James Dean (1931-1955), photograph, bust portrait in jacket and t-shirt, signed in the image. Approximately 10" x 8"; minor handling, circa 1955. ....**$6,240**

Cecil B. DeMille, signed contract, dated Nov. 22, 1950, negotiating the use of cinematographer and visual effects designer Gordon Jennings for the 1952 drama, "The Greatest Show on Earth," signed by in blue ink. Minimal edge wear and mild discoloration. **$239**

Frederick Douglass, 1891, letter written as Minister and American Consul in Haiti, to a Mr. Halford, asking for a bigger portrait of President Harrison. In full: "I have a very excellent picture of President Harrison, but it is too small for the size of the U.S. Legation at this place. I want our American sea captains to see a good picture of our President. Could you cause one to be sent to me? I would be much obliged to you. My fervent best wishes of the season;" 1 1/2 pages, written on the first and third pages of a single folded sheet.............**$4,320**

Clint Eastwood, poster for "Unforgiven" (1992) in gold ink. The poster has an overall size of 28" x 40". **$567**

Edward, Duke of Windsor, 1922, letter signed, "Edward P.," as Prince of Wales, to Lord Richard: "Thank you very much for your kind present; it was very nice of you to think of me on my birthday. I hope you are keeping well." One page, St. James' Palace stationery; horizontal fold, minor soiling. **$210**

Albert Einstein, 1934, typed letter to Charles D. Hart, in German, thanking him for an invitation to a Stokowski concert and declining due to his obligations. One-half page, usual folds; notes in pencil in another hand in lower left on recto, two holes punched in left margin. **$2,280**

"Messieurs Tichnor & Fields": "Please send to the 'Union Club' a copy of 'Emerson's Works' entirely bound in calf, with my compliments, & charge them to the account of your obed't serv't." One page, small numerals written in ink in top left on recto, horizontal folds...**$1,200**

Gerald Ford, 1976, his signature as President, and date, added to a typed letter signed by Susan Ford, which offers thanks for a letter and responds to a photograph request. One page, White House stationery; horizontal fold thorough GRF signature; matted and framed. Not examined out of frame. **$120**

Aretha Franklin, signed contract for "Shindig" television appearances, 1965. A 15" x 9" matted display, accompanied by an image of Franklin. Minor age-toning to contract. **$107**

Robert Fulton, 1813, affidavit excusing himself from appearing at the arbitration of a patent dispute with John Sullivan, and appointing John Devereux Delacy to act on his behalf. Additionally Signed by DeWitt Clinton as Mayor of New York, affirming Delacy's power of attorney. Two pages, with integral blank; damp stained, separations at folds repaired, docketed on terminal page. **$2,880**

(The dispute concerned Fulton's request for a patent for towing boats by steam and warping them over rapids. Despite the competency of Delacy, Fulton's personal secretary, and the legal assistance of Elihu Whitney, arbitration at Hartford found in favor of Sullivan and denied the patent.)

Photo courtesy Swann Auction Galleries, New York; www.SwannGalleries.com

Theodore Geisel (Dr. Seuss) (1904-1991), book, If I Ran the Zoo (1950), inscribed with a small original drawing, on the verso of the front free endpaper, "For Susan West! With best wishes – Dr. Seuss." Publisher's pictorial boards, covers worn, back strip replaced by tape; lacking rear free endpaper. **$900**

George and Ira Gershwin, framed, ex-Kaye Ballard collection. **$657**

Ulysses S. Grant, 1867, partly printed letter signed as Secretary of War ad interim, to Miles W. Keogh, informing him of the president's appointing him Lieutenant Colonel by brevet for his service at the Battle of Dallas, Ga. One page, with integral blank; horizontal folds. **$2,040**

Horace Greeley, 1862, letter to Thomas A. Hillbanse (?), opining that Thomas I. Sawyer, whose two sons were "enlisted as privates at the first tidings of the attack on Sumter," should have been appointed Lieutenant, and requesting that he contact Mr. Sawyer about whether there had been a mistake. One full page, Daily Tribune stationery; small closed tear at right edge repaired, minor soiling, vertical fold. **$270**

Hank Greenberg, 8" x10" black and white photo. **$537**

John Hancock, 1783, letter with initials, a retained draft of a letter to George Washington, praising him for his virtues and past service on the occasion of his retiring to his Mount Vernon plantation: "May you long live, my dear General, and long have the joy to see the increasing splendor and prosperity of a rising nation aided by your councils and defended by your sword." Two pages, with integral blank; folds, minor foxing, minor soiling on terminal page, docketed on the terminal page. **$78,000**

Ernest Hemingway (1899-1961), book, The Sun Also Rises (1927), inscribed on the front blank, to Donald R. Williams. Publisher's cloth, some chipping at spine ends, spine label chipped at edges and darkened; front blank (signature page) nearly completely separated at gutter. Later printing. **$2,880**

Patrick Henry, 1777, letter signed as Governor of Virginia, to Colonel Evan Shelby, requesting him to "order Capt. Joseph Martin, agent in the Cherokee Nation, to be supply'd with provisions for himself & his servants among that people." With a two-line autograph postscript signed with initials. One page, folds, minor soiling, docketed on verso. **$5,760**

Photo courtesy Swann Auction Galleries, New York; www.SwannGalleries.com

Thomas Jefferson, 1824, signed letter written in the hand of his granddaughter, Virginia, to the poet Lydia H. Sigourney, thanking her for her letter and for her notice of the part he played in the Revolution, agreeing with her views regarding the advocacy of "Indian rights," and expressing the wish that these wrongs were "the only blot in our moral history, and that no other race had higher charges to bring against us." One and 1/2 pages, with integral address leaf, detached; addressed in his hand and with franking signature. Small hole at fold of address leaf with loss to "J" of signature, seal tear, and minor soiling; docketed. **$48,000**

Sir Edmund Hillary (1919-2008), drawing in ink on a card, image of a man atop a mountain, followed by a Sherpa. ...**$850**

Buddy Holly and the Crickets, twice-autographed British Tour souvenir program, also been signed by Holly on the interior pages along with Des O'Connor (supporting act). With mild overall wear and bent lower left rear corner. **$5,078**

Langston Hughes, 1944, book, Shakespeare in Harlem (1942), inscribed, and dated on the front free endpaper, to "Libby Holman with happy good wishes from Langston Hughes." Publisher's cloth, chipping at spine ends; pages evenly toned; dust jacket, front inside panel separated at fold, chipped at all edges. First edition. **$425**

Washington Irving, 1857, letter to later critic, William Alfred Jones, thanking him for sending a copy of a book which is "in a department of literature very much to my taste, and in which you have proved yourself a master," and saying of him that "your worthy father was one of the first to applaud and encourage my early attempts at authorship ..." Two and 1/2 pages, written on a single folded sheet; minor soiling. **$1,020**

Reggie Jackson, "563 HR" single-signed baseball. **$89**

Lyndon B. Johnson (1908-1973), photograph inscribed, "[t]o George Ball with high regard," image of LBJ, Ball and another man seated beside someone speaking at the presidential podium. Approximately 11" x 14"; minor fading to signature, mounted; matted and framed. **$390**

Kaleleonalani, Queen Consort of the Hawaiian Islands, signature, 1862. One page, approximately 5 1/2" x 3 1/2", personal stationery, bold signature. **$720**
(Kaleleonalani [1836-1885] was Queen to King Kamehameha IV of Hawaii between 1856 and 1863. For a short period after the death of her son, she went by the name "Kaleleokalani," a name that is reflected in the signature.)

Robert Kennedy, 1960, book, inscribed first-edition copy of The Enemy Within, "For Deda with love, Bobby, XX OO XX," on the front free endpaper. Publisher's cloth, back strip faded, lacks the dust jacket. **$720**

Rudyard Kipling (1865-1936), letter to Gabriel Hanotaux, apologizing for being unable to meet the day before, arranging a meeting for the next day, and thanking Hanotaux "for all your kindness in suggesting to us so charming a retreat as we have found here." One and 1/2 pages, written on recto and verso of a single sheet; horizontal fold. Circa 1926. .... **$390**

Marquis de Lafayette, Gilbert Du Motier, 1823, letter to an unnamed recipient ("mon cher ami"), in French, following up on a mission and delivery of paperwork by Mechin, and writing "I was forced to leave for Lagrange immediately after the funeral of M. Savoie-Rollin, who is so justly missed; I will return to Paris Saturday morning for four or five hours and will use this chance to see my two colleagues." One page, remnants of prior mounting in left margin recto. **$900**

John Lennon, twice-inscribed photo, color 8" x 10", signed "John Lennon to Bill" on the front in blue ball point, and features the following inscription on the reverse in black ink: "Dear Bill, A lot of water under the bridge, and over the wall! A sad story, love, John." Slight wear. **$3,585**

Charles Lindbergh, 1930, First Flight airmail cover, mounted in front of a Lindbergh print titled "The Lone Eagle". The cover postmarked from Grand Central Station, New York, April 25, 1930, a green 20-cent airmail stamp with a First Flight stamp commemorating the first direct Caribbean flight and the seven-day flight from New York to Buenos Aires. The cover is signed upper left "CA Lindbergh, Dec. 1934". Housed in a modern gilt molded wood frame with double matte, 14 3/4" x 19" (sight). Print shows some folds but generally very good, the cover has a dog-ear fold through first part of signature, otherwise good. **$360**

Photo courtesy Swann Auction Galleries, New York; www.SwannGalleries.com

Rev. Martin Luther King Jr. (1929-1968), photograph inscribed, "[t]o Mrs. Libby Shanker with great respect & admiration, Martin Luther King Jr.," image by Faingold of MLK standing behind a chair. Signed in the image, approximately 7 1/2" x 9 1/2"; signature in blue ink against a dark background, some dings; matted and in a silver frame engraved with the words, "Libby with my love, Clifton [Webb]." **$3,120**

Photo courtesy Heritage Auction Galleries, Dallas; www.HA.com

B.B. King, black six-string Epiphone Junior electric guitar signed on the body, with wall-mountable metal carrying case with a Plexiglas viewing window on one side. **$597**

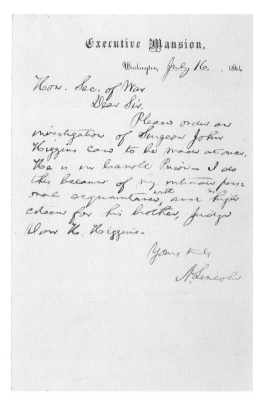

Abraham Lincoln, 1864, letter to Secretary of War Edwin M. Stanton, requesting that an investigation be made into the case of a friend's brother in Carroll Prison. One page, Executive Mansion stationery; vertical fold through "A" of signature, mounted along top edge verso to a larger sheet, recent owner's gift inscription in ink on verso, minor soiling. **$22,800**
("Please order an investigation of Surgeon John Higgins case to be made at once. He is in Carroll Prison – I do this because of my intimate personal acquaintance with and high esteem for his brother, Judge Van H. Higgins.")

Charles Lindbergh (1902-1974), photo by Underwood & Underwood, shows a young Lindbergh with flight cap and goggles. Signed on side "CA Lindbergh", 6 1/4" x 4 1/2". Margin shows frame toning, otherwise very good.
....**$862**
Henry Wadsworth Longfellow, 1855, quotation, five lines from his poem, Excelsior: "The shades of night were falling fast / As through an Alpine village passed / A youth, who bore, 'mid snow and ice, / A banner with the strange device / Excelsior!" Approximately 4 1/2" x 6 3/4" 1; stained at edges on verso from prior mounting, mounted to bottom is a strip of paper on which is written in HL's hand, "With W. Longfellow's compliments." **$570**
Douglas MacArthur (1880-1964), book, Reminiscences, McGraw-Hill, photographic illustrations, with publisher's slipcase. First limited edition, number 204 of 1750 copies signed by MacArthur. **$600**

Pete Maravich photo features an action shot of Maravich and he keeps the ball away from fellow Hall of Famer John Havlicek. Photo was clipped from a periodical and measures about 4" x 5". **$310**

Roger Maris, 1976 diamond jubilee card. **$358**

Groucho Marx, childhood photograph, signed "This is the way I looked as a kid." **$956**

James A. Michener, 1990, typed note on a card [in all capitals]: "I have said many times that a nation or a city is fortunate if it has some architectural feature which represents it to the world. No symbol is more universally known and loved that [sic] the Eiffel tower. It sets the standard that others strive to equal. My salute!!!!" (Marking the 100th anniversary of the Eiffel Tower.) **$240**

James Monroe, 1821, letter signed as President, to an unnamed recipient ("Dear Sir"), sending $350 "with great pleasure." One-half page, folds. .... **$2,280** ("I send you with great pleasure a check for $350 to which I will add more if at all material to you. The payment of this sum is extended with no inconvenience to me. Very sensible of your kindness be assured of my constant & sincere friendship.")

Franklin D. Roosevelt (1882-1945), signature as President, on a White House card. Approximately 2 3/4" x 4 1/4"; partially mounted; framed, circa 1933-45. .... **$960**

Theodore Roosevelt, 1893, book, Wilderness Hunter, publisher's cloth; covers stained, spine soiled and darkened; front blanks nearly loose. One of 200 numbered copies, signed by Roosevelt. **$2,160**

Jonas Salk (1914-1995), inscribed copy of The Survival of the Wisest (1973). Signed on the front free endpaper. Publisher's cloth; dust jacket. **$270**

William H. Seward, 1839, letter, as Governor of New York, to Peter B. Porter, responding to a letter recommending that Mr. Bird be considered for the office of Canal Commissioner and remarking that he "shall have great pleasure in making known your wishes on the subject to our common friends in the legislature ..." One page, with integral address leaf; folds, docket and postal stamp on terminal page. **$270**

Philip H. Sheridan, 1866, letter to J.G. Foster, Commanding General, Department of Florida, informing him that "I was obliged under orders from Genl Grant to order the muster out of one thousand more of your colored troops," and of the "fuss and feathers over on the Rio Grande," because "[t]he black troops over there have become much incensed at the Franco Mexicans in

Eleanor Roosevelt (1884-1962), photograph inscribed, to "Roberta dear, with my love, Eleanor Roosevelt," an image by Harris & Ewing showing her seated in a gown, signed in the image. Approximately 9 1/2" x 6 1/2"; minor soiling; matted, circa 1930s. **$780**

Frank Sinatra, 2 1/2" x 2" autograph, cut, framed along with a color 8" x 10" photo. **$143**

Alex Rodriguez, 8" x10" photo depicts the day he signed with the Yankees. **$179**

Leon Trotsky (1879-1940), typed document, signed in blue pencil in Russian, ordering authorities to drive away animals upon the approach of Mamontov gangs and to search anyone suspicious, especially plant managers. One page, two small holes punched in left margin, docketed at top in pencil in Russian, bottom margin trimmed (not affecting signature). **$2,280**

Kurt Vonnegut (1922-2007), ink drawing, signed twice, self-portrait on a card with a note: "Why should it make me so happy every time I see it? That's crazy." **$480**

Tiger Woods, Masters flag, 2002. Framed against green velvet background to final measurement of 20" x 25". **$844**

consequence of the abuse of them in a paper published in Matamoras so that we have to watch them closely." Two pages, with integral blank leaf, written on recto and verso of first leaf, Headquarters stationery; docketed on terminal page, minor soiling... **$1,560**

James Stewart, 2" x 2" photo, inscribed, "To Michael, Jimmy Stewart." Two small sets of staple holes and a bit of tape on the top left corner. **$143**

Leo Tolstoy, 1903, letter in Russian, to Pyotr Petrovich Nikolaev, in which the master advises a fellow writer on his manuscript. Three pages, written on the first and third page of a folded sheet and the first page of another folded sheet, Japan paper; folds. **$14,400**

John Travolta, "Saturday Night Fever" soundtrack LP (1977). **$155**

Harry S. Truman, 1943, letter, signed as senator, to William B. Welling, responding to a note involving the proposal of a Committee on the Progress of the War: "... I don't think tactics and strategy has any place in the United States Senate." One page, U.S. Senate stationery; horizontal folds. **$960**

Artemas Ward, July 9, 1776, letter to Ebenezer Hancock, Deputy Paymaster General of the Army of the United States, requesting him to "Pay to Col John Glover eight hundred & eighty pounds three shillings, equal to two thousand nine hundred & thirty three dollars . . . it being for one month's pay of the Regiment of Foot in the service of the United Colonies ..." Countersigned by Glover, acknowledging receipt of the money. Written on verso is Colonel Glover's itemized list of his regiment and their monthly wages, which is additionally signed and dated by Glover: "Camp in Beverly, July 7, 1776." One page, folds, minor bleed-through. **$2,880**

(Ward [1727-1800] was commissioned as general and commander-in-chief of the Massachusetts troops in 1775 and resigned in 1776 when his rank was reduced to major-general upon Washington's being given supreme command.)

George Washington (1732-1799), undated letter signed with initials, to Mr. [James?] Madison, in full: "At as early an hour this evening as you can make it convenient I should be glad to see you. Y's Sincerely & affect'y." One-half page, with integral address leaf; minor soiling, small edge tears, remnants of prior soiling along left edge of terminal page, staining and offsetting from seal in corners of each page. **$7,200**

Daniel Webster (1752-1852), undated letter, to Dr. Parsons, thanking him for his "kind advice & attendance, which I feel to have been highly instrumental in relieving me from an indisposition which threatened to be serious." One page, with integral address leaf; closed separation at fold just below signature repaired, toned, damp staining and repairs on terminal page. **$300**

Chuck Yeager (1923-), letter with a drawing..............**$330**

("Dear Miss Tower, Happy birthday! The first time I saw you, you were 55 years old and I was 21. You looked like this [the drawing] because I was in the cockpit of a P-51 Mustang at 3000 meters above you. The date was Feb 13, 1944, my 21st birthday! Things were very hostile in the sky above you that day. Later I learned to like you very much. I hope that we have many more birthdays.")

BADGES AND MEDALS

Badges and medals have been used for centuries to designate rank or official duties, and to commemorate events and public observances.

42nd Pa. Buck Tails, Co. A "ladder" badge, German silver, four-part with braided brass tassel, each bar stamped with recessed area painted black, top bar/pin-back reads "Co. A., 42, Penn. Buck Tails," 2" x 5". **$862**
(The Buck Tails got their name by wearing the tail of a deer on their headgear.)

Army of the Potomac, 5th Corps badge, German silver, border engraved around the outline of a Maltese cross with sunburst in the center. **$632**

Photo courtesy Greg Martin Auctions, San Francisco; www.GregMartinAuctions.com

Badge (presentation), 19th century, engraved gold, made for Benjamin Franklin Rogers, Chief of Police, Stockton, Calif. **$36,800**

Photo courtesy Greg Martin Auctions, San Francisco; www.GregMartinAuctions.com

Badge (presentation), eagle and shield, gold, enamel and diamonds, for Bodie A. Wallman, Chief of Police, Oakland, Calif., by B.J. Co. **$19,550**

Black Hawk War, pin-back bronze and silk badge, undated, alternating red and black silk stripes with gold lettering, mint condition with the original storage envelope and backing with St. Louis Button Co. logo; 5" l. **$2,415**
(The short-lived Black Hawk War fought during the spring and summer of 1832 forcibly ejected the last native tribes, the Sauk and Fox, from the old Northwest Territory. It ushered in an era of active Indian removal. Roughly 4,000 Illinois militia and regulars commanded by Winfield Scott were marshaled to defeat Black Hawk and all were later accorded the status of "veterans.")

Photo courtesy Greg Martin Auctions, San Francisco; www.GregMartinAuctions.com

Badge (suspension), multicolor gold and blue enamel, for Buck Garrett (1871-1929), Chief of Police, Ardmore, Indian Territory. **$36,800**

Photo courtesy Greg Martin Auctions, San Francisco; www.GregMartinAuctions.com

Badge, U.S. Marshal, five-pointed star, cloisonné and 14K gold. **$23,000**

Brotherhood of Locomotive Engineers medals (six), including 1st, 2nd, 3rd, chief engineer and chaplain, housed in case with gilt title "Easton (Pa.), Div. No 259". Medals made by the Webb C. Ball Watch Co. of Cleveland, feature a locomotive motif, each 3" x 2". .... **$228 all**

Eagle Scout medal, cased, 3" x 1 1/2"; reverse of bar marked "Sterling." Interior of case marked "Eagle Scout Badge Awarded by the Boy Scouts of America." Housed in Art Deco-style case measuring 4" x 2", early 20th century. **$69**

GAR badge and medal from 15th Iowa, in German silver, two-part with arrow-form pin-back with "War 1861-5" with shield-shaped hanger reading "Wm. Makinster./Co. A/15 Iowa/Vol. Inf.," 2" x 2", plus a typical cast-bronze and silk three-part GAR medal, 1 1/2" x 4 3/4", and enameled brass shoulder bar with black enameled ground and applied sterling silver Bird Colonel spread-winged eagle, 1 1/2" l. .... **$690 both**

GAR presentation past officer's badge, fancy jeweler-made enameled and gold-plated pattern, 1887 five-pointed GAR star with T-bar clasp suspended from a silver eagle rank strap, engraved on reverse, "Presented to/ J.F. Crichton/Julius White Post/740/1900" with flag ribbon edged in faded light blue indicating past post commander. With original folding leatherette case gold stenciled, "Chas. H. Pfeil/182 State Street/Chicago, Ill" with push-button closure. **$373**

Grant's Tomb dedication badge, New York, April 27, 1897, for Pennsylvania Legislature member, in red, white and blue silk, with attached U.S. flag and aluminum alloy medal, made by the Shaw Co. of Philadelphia. **$144**

Police badge, presentation, solid gold jeweler-made, six-pointed star pin-back, with enamel decoration and gemstone center, Chicago Police Post No. 207 American Legion, reverse marked "Solid Gold" and engraved "Presented to National Commander American Legion Raymond J. Kelly by Chicago Police Post No. 207 Feb. 11, 1940," with original black leather case, tested 10K. **$300**

Prussian Order of the Black Eagle, including breast star, medal and sash. Enameled silver gilt breast star measuring 80mm. Wide pin on reverse exhibits hallmark "900" and "835" struck over other mark. Orange watered sash presenting enameled silver gilt medal measuring 75mm. Blue enameling on medal exhibits some light abrasions and sash exhibits some light soiling. **$3,450**

Sheriff's badge, gold, engraved and inscribed: "To/Pat Garrett/with the Best/Regards of/A.J. Fountain/1881." **$115,000**
(Patrick Floyd Garrett [1850–1908] was a lawman, bartender and customs agent who was best known for killing the outlaw Henry McCarty, a.k.a. Billy the Kid. He was also the sheriff of Lincoln County, N.M.)

Harvard University Hasty Pudding Club silver medallion, circa 1860, octagonal medallion, one side with the symbol of hands holding a bowl and spoon dipping into the pudding pot over a banner with inscribed motto "Seges Votis Respondet," the reverse with "Concordia Discores" over a sphinx, a wreath of flowers inscribed with the name "J.T. Morse," and the year "1795" (date of club's founding), 1 1/2" d. **$385**

Quaker's pin-back badge, coin silver, shield-shaped with engraved heart and S/F and motto at top, "One Heart One Way," 0.8" x 1". **$180**

Washington Monument dedication badge, Philadelphia, May 15, 1897, for Pennsylvania Legislature member, in red, white and blue silk with bronze medal, made by the Shaw Co. of Philadelphia. **$60**

Twelve law enforcement badges, including a Sheriff Oakland County, Mich.; Dearborn County; Deputy Sheriff Wayne County; 1981 Official Inauguration badge for D.C. Police; Captain's Police; Official CTS; Deputy Sheriff Wayne County; Department of Police Edgewater PK; Special Detective Atlantic City, N.J.; Conservation Officer State of Michigan; Serg't Of Police M.C. RR; and Sheriffs Assn. badge. ......**$460 all**

Four 18th and 19th century European silver badges, all have inscriptions in German. Oldest is oval-shaped 4" x 3" inscribed "Der Schutzen Campagne Zu Osterberg zu Ehren," dated 1752. Second-oldest is star-shaped 4 1/2" x 3" with inscription "W. Stengel" and dated 1839. Third-oldest is star shaped 3 1/2" with 13 points (14th is missing) and dated 1871. Fourth-oldest is octagonal 1 1/2" and inscribed "Leht Konig," 1875. ....**$431 all**

Grouping of Civil War veterans/reunion ribbons (23), includes nine reunion ribbons for the 3rd Pennsylvania Heavy Artillery, seven ribbons from the Juniata County Veteran's Association, with the balance being military related; with two Civil War belt plates. ....**$575 all**

Photo courtesy Cowan's, Cincinnati; www.CowanAuctions.com

Texas Rangers three-part bronze medal with pin-back bar, embossed "Veteran," black and red silk with gilt lettering "Texas Rangers" and Maltese cross hanger with mounted plains warrior stamped on reverse; St. Louis Button Co. 2 1/5" x 5". **$1,150**

Photo courtesy Cowan's, Cincinnati; www.CowanAuctions.com

United Confederate Veterans ribbon and cello badge; a white silk ribbon with metal braids and tassels with gold printed text "United/Confederate/Veterans/Reunion/July 18 19 1898/Atlanta/Ga.," 3 1/2" x 7 3/4"; and a chromolithographed shield-shaped cello badge with uniformed shoulder-length portrait of Gen. Lee with CSA canteen and stars-and-bars shield with palm leaf surround, text above "Reunion U.C.V." and below "Louisville./May, 1900," marked The Whitehead & Hoag Co., Newark, N.J. with red silk ribbon hanger, 2 1/2" x 3". **$287 pair**

Photo courtesy Cowan's, Cincinnati; www.CowanAuctions.com

U.S. Navy badge, 1841, C.P.O., with fouled anchor and eagle. **$920**

BANKS, MECHANICAL

Banks displaying some form of action while accepting a coin are considered mechanical. Most collectors are interested in those made over a period of about 60 years, from the late 1860s to the late 1920s.

More than 80 percent of all cast-iron mechanical banks produced between 1869 and 1928 were made by J. & E. Stevens Co., Cromwell, Conn.

While rarity is a factor in value, appeal of design, action, quality of manufacture, country of origin and provenance also are important.

Reproduction Alert. Reproductions, fakes and forgeries exist for many banks. Forgeries of some mechanical banks were made as early as 1937, so age alone is not a guarantee of authenticity.

Photo courtesy Morphy Auctions, Denver, Pa.; www.MorphyAuctions.com

Charles A. Bailey, Cobalt, Conn., Darky Fisherman, 1880s, when a coin is placed in the slot at the front of the bank and the lever is pressed, the boy raises his pole to discover he has caught a fish. His cap flips up and the fish nudges coin into bank slot, ex-Stephen and Marilyn Steckbeck collection. **$287,500**

Photo courtesy Morphy Auctions, Denver, Pa.; www.MorphyAuctions.com

Kyser & Rex, Mikado, circa 1886, the cast-iron bank's complex interior mechanism enables the character to perform a "shell game" illusion, ex-Stephen and Marilyn Steckbeck collection. **$287,500**

Photo courtesy Morphy Auctions, Denver, Pa.; www.MorphyAuctions.com

Kyser & Rex, Merry-Go-Round, late 1880s, when the handle is turned, bells chime, the figures revolve, and the attendant raises the stick and gathers in any coins deposited on the stand, ex-Stephen and Marilyn Steckbeck collection. **$172,500**

Photo courtesy James D. Julia Auctioneers, Fairfield, Maine; www.JuliaAuctions.com

Kyser & Rex, Boy Stealing Watermelon Bank, when lever is pressed, dog appears from the doghouse. Boy is slinking through the garden in an attempt to steal the watermelon and raises his right hand. While along the fence, a boy runs off with another watermelon in hand. Probably in the 1880s, it was considered a very comical bank, 5" h x 6 1/2" l. Bank is missing spring and trap. Needs cleaning. **$6,325**

Photo courtesy James D. Julia Auctioneers, Fairfield, Maine; www.JuliaAuctions.com

Shepherd Hardware, Mason Bank with original box; the mason, constructing a wall of brick, is being assisted by the hod carrier, who has the coin contained within the hod. Upon depressing the lever, the hod tips forward depositing the coin into the wall as the mason raises his trowel to even out the cement on the bricks. (Typical of most mechanical and steel banks, they depicted various nationalities of their time. This bank features two Irishmen.); 7 1/2" h x 7 1/4" l. Near excellent condition and would be greatly enhanced by a cleaning. Original box is lacking slide lid. **$13,225**

Kyser & Rex, Zoo Bank, push gorilla's face and shutters open to reveal a bear and a lion. Coin is deposited into bank, 4 1/2" h x 4" w. Trap is missing but bank is in near-excellent condition. **$1,840**

Mechanical Novelty Works, Initiating Bank 2nd Degree, press lever and man riding goat springs forward and deposits coin in frog's mouth. This is a fairly rare bank, 7" h x 7 1/2" l. The bank was over-painted gold at some point. **$2,300**

Shepard Hardware, Stump Speaker and Uncle Sam banks, Uncle Sam throws coin in satchel and Stump Speaker drops coin in carpetbag, 11 1/2" h x 4 7/8" w x 10" h x 5" w. Stump Speaker has a replaced coin trap; otherwise both banks are in good to very good condition.............................**$2,300 pair**

Photo courtesy Morphy Auctions, Denver, Pa.; www.MorphyAuctions.com

Kyser & Rex, Roller Skating, 1880s, bank is comprised of a rink and skaters that glide around the perimeter when a coin is deposited, man turns as if to present a wreath to the little girl, ex-Stephen and Marilyn Steckbeck collection. **$195,500**

Photo courtesy Morphy Auctions, Denver, Pa.; www.MorphyAuctions.com

Stevens, Germania Exchange, 1880s, when a coin is placed on the goat's tail and the faucet on the beer keg is turned, the goat deposits the money and presents a glass of beer to the depositor, ex-Stephen and Marilyn Steckbeck collection. **$149,500**

Stevens, Chief Big Moon Bank with red base; Chief sits by tepee holding a fish in hand. When lever is pressed, frog springs from under pond and the chief pulls back the fish and coin is deposited in bank. This also is the rare version of the bank with a red and yellow base; 6" h x 10" l. Colors are bright and bank is in excellent condition with some minor scratches and chipping. **$3,910**

Photo courtesy James D. Julia Auctioneers, Fairfield, Maine; www.JuliaAuctions.com

Stevens, Girl Skipping Rope Bank, when the clockwork mechanism is wound, the girl gracefully skips rope while at the same time her head sways from left to right and her feet swing back and forth in a very realistic manner. Some of the collectors of these banks take pride in how many revolutions of swinging their bank can accomplish, 8 1/4" h x 8" l. Appears all original with even wear throughout bank. Overall very good condition. **$13,225**

Photo courtesy James D. Julia Auctioneers, Fairfield, Maine; www.JuliaAuctions.com

Stevens Boy Scout Camp Bank, boy looks out from tepee while another boy cooks over a cauldron. When lever is pressed, a third boy raises flag announcing "Boy Scout Camp," 6" h x 9 3/4" l. Bank appears all original and is in very good to excellent condition. **$6,900**

Photo courtesy James D. Julia Auctioneers, Fairfield, Maine; www.JuliaAuctions.com

Stevens, Columbus World's Fair Bank, painted gold and silver with green vines and copper-colored log. This is the slightly more rare painted version, with the embossed lettering. Flip lever and Indian rises from under log. Columbus raises his hand greeting the Indian; 6 3/4" h x 8 1/2" l. Near excellent condition. **$4,600**

Photo courtesy Morphy Auctions, Denver, Pa.; www.MorphyAuctions.com

Stevens, Jonah and the Whale/Jonah Emerges, late 1880s, pull back the knob located behind the whale's tail to lock it into position. Place a coin in the small slot shaped like a boat next to the whale's tail and press the lever. The coin falls into the bank as the whale opens his mouth and Jonah emerges. The whale's tail flips up during the action, all original and one of the finest known examples of its type, ex-Stephen and Marilyn Steckbeck collection. **$414,000**

Photo courtesy Morphy Auctions, Denver, Pa.; www.MorphyAuctions.com

Stevens, Darky and Watermelon, circa 1888, features a gentleman in top hat who kicks a football over the watermelon as a coin is deposited. Early repair to one leg. Touch-up to jacket and arms. One of only four examples known, ex-Stephen and Marilyn Steckbeck collection. **$195,500**

Stevens, Eagle & Eaglets Bank, glass-eyed eagle on rocky outcropping feeds eaglets and deposits coin in bank, 6" h x 7" w. Uniform wear throughout, overall good to very good. **$720**

Stevens, I Always Did 'Spise a Mule Bank, place coin in the black jockey's mouth and when lever is pressed, mule bucks jockey over, hitting his head on log and depositing coin, 8" h x 10" l. Very good overall condition. Replaced trap. **$517**

Stevens, Magic Bank, painted red, white and blue. When door is opened, cashier appears with tray in hand. Place coin on tray, press lever. Door closes and the coin is deposited in bank; 5 1/2" h x 4 1/2" l. Bank has very strong paint, needs a good cleaning but otherwise is in near-excellent condition. **$4,370**

Photo courtesy Morphy Auctions, Denver, Pa.; www.MorphyAuctions.com

Stevens, North Pole, circa 1910, when a coin is placed in the slot and pressed forward, it causes an American Flag to pop up at the top, ex-Stephen and Marilyn Steckbeck collection. **$149,500**

Brass, beehive, well detailed, base marked "A.B. Dalames Bank," 4" h, 4 1/2" d..**$385**

Cast iron

Bungalow, Grey Iron Ceiling Co., porch, painted, 3 3/4" h.
....**$470**

Cab, Arcade, Yellow Cab, painted orange and black, stenciling on doors, seated driver, rubber tires, painted metal wheels, coin slot in roof, 7 3/4" l.....................**$935**

Cat With Ball, A.C. Williams, painted gray, gold ball, 2 1/2" x 5 11/16"...**$190**

Circus Elephant, Hubley, colorfully painted, seated position, 3 7/8" h. **$180**

Coronation, Syndeham & McOustra, England, ornately detailed, embossed busts in center, England, circa 1911, 6 5/8" h. **$200**

Duck, Hubley, colorfully painted, outstretched wings, slot on back, 4 3/4" h. **$165**

Dutch Boy and Girl, Hubley, colorfully painted, boy on barrel, girl holding flowers, circa 1930, 5 1/4" and 5 1/8" h. ....**$260 pair**

Egyptian Tomb, green finish, pharaoh's tomb entrance, hieroglyphics on front panel, 6 1/4" x 5 1/4".................**$275**

Elk, painted gold, full antlers, 9 1/2" h. **$155**

Hall Clock, swinging pendulum visible through panel, 5 3/4" h..**$110**

Horseshoe, Arcade, Buster Brown and Tiger with horse, painted black and gold, 4 1/4" x 4 3/4".......................**$125**

BANKS, STILL

Banks with no mechanical action are known as still banks. The first still banks were made of wood or pottery. Redware and stoneware banks, made by America's early potters, are prized possessions of today's collectors.

Still banks reached a golden age with the arrival of the cast-iron bank. Leading makers include Arcade Mfg. Co., J. Chein & Co., Hubley, J. & E. Stevens, and A.C. Williams. The banks often were ornately painted to enhance their appeal. Still bank were often used as a form of advertising.

The tin lithograph bank reached its zenith from 1930 to 1955. The tin bank was an important premium, whether a Pabst Blue Ribbon beer can bank or a Gerber's Orange Juice bank. Most tin advertising banks resembled the packaging of the product.

Many of the early glass candy containers also converted to a bank after the candy was eaten. Thousands of varieties of still banks were made, and hundreds of new varieties appear on the market each year.

Photo courtesy Morphy Auctions, Denver, Pa.; www.MorphyAuctions.com

Barrel-shaped man with outstretched arms. **$1,100**

*Kenton State
Bank, near mint,
6" h.* **$400**

*Lindberg with
Goggles, 6" h.* **$75**

Husky, Grey Iron Casting Co., painted brown, black eyes, yellow box, repaired, 5" h. **$365**

Jewel Chest, ornate casting, footed bank, brass combination lock on front, top lifts for coin retrieval, crack at corner, 6 1/8" x 4 5/8". **$90**

Kodak, J. & E. Stevens, nickeled, highly detailed casting, intricate pattern, embossed "Kodak Bank" on front opening panel, circa 1905, 4 1/4" x 5" w. **$225**

North Pole, nickeled, Grey Iron Casting Co., depicts wooden pole w/handle, embossed lettering, 4 1/4" h. **$415**

Mailbox, Hubley, painted green, embossed "Air Mail," with eagle, standing type, 5 1/2" h. **$220**

Maine, Grey Iron Casting Co., japanned, gold highlights, circa 1900, 4 5/8" l. **$660**

Mammy, Hubley, hands on hips, colorfully painted, 5 1/4" h. **$300**

Pagoda, England, gold trim, circa 1889, 5" x 3" x 3". ...**$240**

Pershing, General, Grey Iron Casting Co., full bust, detailed casting, 7 3/4" h. **$65**

Professor Pug Frog, A.C. Williams, painted gold, blue jacket, new twist pin, 3 1/4" h. **$195**

Radio, Kenton, metal sides and back, painted green, nickeled front panel in Art Deco style, 4 1/2" h. **$445**

Reindeer, A. C. Williams, painted gold, full rack of antlers, replaced screw, 9 1/2" h, 5 1/4" l. **$55**

Rumplestiltskin, painted gold, long red hat, base and feet, marked "Do You Know Me," circa 1910, 6" h............**$210**

Safe, Kyser & Rex, Young America, japanned, intricate casting, embossed at top, circa 1882, 4 3/8" h. **$275**

Sharecropper, A. C. Williams, painted black, gold, and red, toes visible on one foot, 5 1/2" h. **$240**

Spitz, Grey Iron Casting Co., painted gold, repaired, 4 1/4" x 4 1/2" h. **$165**

Stove, Gem, Abendroth Bros., traces of bronzing, back marked "Gem Heaters Save Money," 4 3/4" h. **$275**

U.S. Mail, Kenton, painted silver, gold painted emb eagle, red lettering large trap on back panel, 5 1/8" h. **$180**

World Time, Arcade, paper timetables of various cities around the world, 4 1/8" x 2 5/8". **$315**

Chalk

Cat, seated, stripes, red bow, 11" h. **$200**

Winston Churchill, bust, painted green, back etched "Save for Victory," wood base, 5 1/4" h. **$55**

Glass

Charles Chaplin, Geo Borgfeldt & Co., painted figure standing next to barrel slotted on lid, name embossed on base, 3 3/4" h. **$220**

Lead

Boxer, Germany, head, painted brown, black facial details, lock on collar, bent in back, 2 5/8" h. **$130**

Burro, Japan, lock on saddle marked "Plymouth, VT," 3 1/2" x 3 1/2". **$125**

Ocean liner, bronze electroplated, three smoking stacks, hinged trap on deck, small hole, 2 3/4" x 7 5/8" l. ...**$180**

Pug, Germany, painted, stenciled "Hershey Park" on side, lock on collar, 2 3/4" h. **$300**

Pottery

Dresser, redware, Empire chest of drawers shape, Philadelphia, loss to feet, roughness on edges, 6 1/2" w, 4" deep, 4 1/2" h..**$220**

Jug, redware, bulbous, bird atop mouth, green and yellow graffito dev, Jim Seagreaves, signed "JCS," 7 1/2" h...**$515**

Steel

Lifeboat, pressed, painted yellow and blue, boat length decal marked "Contributions for Royal National Life Boat Institution," deck lifts for coin removal, over painted, 14" l...**$360**

Postal Savings, copper finish, glass-view front panel, paper registering strips, embossed "U.S.Mail" on sides, top lifts to reveal four coin slots, patented 1902, 4 5/8" h, 5 3/8" w. ...**$95**

Stoneware

Dog's Head, white clay, yellow glaze, two-tone brown sponging, shallow flakes, 4" h. **$175**

Ovoid, brushed cobalt blue flowers, leaves, and finial, minor flakes at coin slot, 6" h. **$6,875**

Pig, sitting, signed in dark green "Delight M. Caskey Merry Christmas," 6 1/4" l. **$3,000**

Tin litho

Keene Savings, Kingsbury, bank building shape, non-working tally wheels, 6 1/2" x 6" x 3". **$70**

White metal

Amish Boy, seated on bale of straw, U.S., painted in bright colors, key lock trap on bottom, 4 3/4" x 3 3/8"..........**$55**

Gorilla, colorfully painted in brown hues, seated position, trap on bottom. **$165**

Pig, painted white, decal marked "West Point, N.Y." on belly, 4 3/8" h. **$30**

Rabbit, seated, painted brown, painted eyes, trap on bottom, crack in ear, 4 1/2" h..**$30**

Spaniel, seated, painted white, black highlights, 4 1/2" h. **$470**

Uncle Sam Hat, painted red, white, and blue, stars on brim, slot on top, trap on bottom, 3 1/2" h. **$135**

Wood

Burlwood inlaid with exotic woods, top decorated with geometric banding, front with sailing vessels, end panels with flags, Prisoner of War, late 19th century, imperfections, 5" x 8" x 5 1/4".......................................**$1,150**

BASKETS

Today's collectors often focus on baskets made of splint, rye straw or willow. Emphasis is placed on handmade examples. Nails or staples, wide splints that are thin and evenly cut, or a wire bail handle may denote factory construction, which can date back to the mid-19th century.

Baskets are collected by (a) type—berry, egg or field; (b) region—Nantucket or Shaker; and (c) composition—splint, rye or willow.

Also see Native American.

Nantucket basket, woven cane, early 20th century, cane losses, 5 5/8" h, 7 1/4" d. **$1,292**

Shaker pine and ash picnic basket, red-stained, New Lebanon, N.Y., mid- to late 19th century, pine sides and bottom on rectangular form with two hinged lids, upright ash handle, imperfections, 13" h, 10 3/4" w, 18 1/4" l. ..**$440**

Shaker woven splint basket, found in Shirley, Mass., 19th century, round basket over square base with four runners, carved handles and double-wrapped rim, 15 3/4" h, 21" d. **$763**

Shaker woven splint hamper basket, possibly Canterbury, N.H., second half 19th century, deep oblong form with carved upright handle, two lids hinged at the center with copper wires, few minor breaks and losses, 16 1/2" h, 9 3/4" w, 15 5/8" l. **$293**

Woven splint basket, with carved wooden handles, large. **$235**

Woven splint basket, with handholds, deep rectangular..**$88**

Woven splint basket, American, 19th century, oval rim on rectangular base with carved wooden handles, base corner breaks, 13 3/4" h, 23" w, 25" l. **$176**

Woven splint feather basket, American, late 19th century, painted green with conforming cover, (loss to lashing on basket rim), 13 1/2" h. **$940**

Woven splint ribbed basket, American, 19th century, with entwined bentwood handle, 14 1/2" h, 15" w, 25" l. **$176**

Photo courtesy Sanford Alderfer Auction & Appraisal, Hatfield, Pa.; www.AlderferAuction.com

Buttocks basket with fixed handle, fine-weave splint oak, 11" h, 14 1/2" w. **$2,300**

Photo courtesy Skinner Inc., Boston; www.SkinnerInc.com

Woven splint basket, American, 19th century, round with square bottom with carved wooden swing handle, painted sea-foam green, 5 3/8" h to rim, 8 3/4" d. **$558**

Photo courtesy Skinner Inc., Boston; www.SkinnerInc.com

Nantucket basket, woven rattan, American, circa 1950, wooden bottom with pyrographic inscriptions, "Frances B. Smith/F.H. Dewey III" and "Nantucket Lightship P.B. + B.S. Heywood 1-28-50.", 13 1/2" to top of handle, 11 1/8" d. **$881**

Photo courtesy Skinner Inc., Boston; www.SkinnerInc.com

Nantucket basket, John Kittla Jr., 1961, cylindrical form, cover centered with a carved ivory floral medallion, the base inscribed "Nantucket Light Ship Basket 1961 by John Kittla Jr.," (break on latch), 7 3/4" h. **$503**

CHILDREN'S BOOKS

In the 19th century, books were popular gifts for children, with many of the children's classics written and published during this time. Developments in printing made it possible to include more attractive black and white illustrations and color plates.

A Child's Garden of Verses, illus by Myrtle Sheldon, Donahue Pub, 1st ed, 1916. .... **$25**

A Christmas Carol, Charles Dickens, Garden City Pub, color and black and white illus by Everett Shinn, red cover, fancy gold trim, ©1938. .... **$28**

Adventures of Tom Sawyer, Mark Twain, American Pub. Co., Hartford, Connecticut, blue and gold cover, 1899. ...... **$45**

Alice's Adventures in Wonderland in Words of One Syllable, Saalfield, illus by John Tenniel, dj, ©1908. ...... **$18**

American Girl Beauty Book, Bobbs-Merrill, New York, illus, 1945. .... **$9**

And To Think That I Saw It On Mulberry Street, Dr. Seuss, Vanguard Pub., 3rd printing, ©1937. .... **$15**

An Old Fashioned Girl, Louisa M. Alcott, Robert Bros. Pub, 1870, 1st ed. **$35**

Bobbsey Twins At The County Fair, The, Grossett & Dunlap, 1st ed., dj, 1922. .... **$28**

Book of the Camp Fire Girls, Rev. Ed., paperback, 1954. **$6**

Boys Story of Lindbergh, The Lone Eagle, Richard Beamish, John C. Winston Co., dj, 1928. .... **$20**

Bunny Rabbit Concert, Lawrence Welk, illus Carol Bryan, Youth Pub. Sat Evening Post, 2nd printing, 1978. .... **$8**

By the Shores of Silver Lake, Laura Ingalls Wilder, illus Garth Williams, Harper Collins, dj, 1953. .... **$10**

Christmas Eve on Lonesome and Other Stories, John Fox, Jr., Grossett & Dunlap, 1904. .... **$15**

Erick & Sally and Other Stories, Johanna Spyri, Grossett & Dunlap, 342 pgs, 1932. .... **$7**

Freckles, Grossett & Dunlap, illus by E. Stetson Crawford, 1904. .... **$8**

Girl Scout Handbook, Rev. Ed., 1930. .... **$7**

Hardy Boys, Missing Chums, Franklin Dixon, illus by Walter Rogers, Grossett & Dunlap, 1st ed, 1928. .... **$25**

Helen's Babies, John Habberton, J. H. Sears & Co., colorful illus by Christopher Rule. **$10**

How the Grinch Stole Christmas, Dr. Seuss, Random House, Grinch on red and green cover, ©1957. .... **$25**

Little Britches, Father and I Were Ranchers, Ralph Moody, illus Edward Shenton, Peoples Book Club, Chicago, 1950. .... **$8**

Lullaby Land, Eugene Field, Scribner, 1st ed, 1897. .... **$35**

Marcella Stories, Johnny Gruelle, M. A. Donahue Co., color and black and white illus, dj, 1930s. **$95**

Metropolitan Mother Goose, Elizabeth Watson, Metropolitan Insurance Co. promo, 1930s, 20 pgs. **$18**

Mickey Mouse Book, second to fourth printing, Wynn Smith daily strips on page 8 and back cover, "Printed in USA" on front, complete copy, Bibo and Lang ©, light age, VG/Fine, 9" x 12". **$925**

Mother Goose and Nursery Rhymes, Anthemum Pub., colored wood engravings by Philip Reed, 1st ed, Mother Goose and gander on orange cover, 1963. .... **$35**

Mother Goose or The Old Nursery Rhymes, Warne, Kate Greenaway illus, pictures on both front and back cov, c1900, 44 rhymes. **$45**

Moving Picture Boys and the Flood, Victor Appleton, Grossett & Dunlap, pictorial cover, 1914. .... **$15**

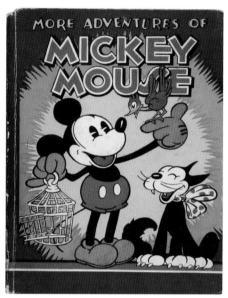

Photo courtesy Hake's Auctions, www.hakes.com.

More Adventures Of Mickey Mouse, English version, Dean & Son Ltd. ©1932, scattered aging, cover with spine/edge wear, 32 pgs, 5 1/2" x 7 1/2", **$380.**

Mr. Winkle Goes to War, Theodore Pratt, Duell, Sloan & Pearce, 1st ed, dj, 1943. .... **$8**

Mrs. Appleyard's Year, Louise Andrews Kent, Hough. Mifflin, 195 pgs, rooster on cover, 1941. .... **$9.50**

Mrs. Wiggs of the Cabbage Patch, Alice Hegan Rice, Appleton-Century Co., hardbound, lady in red dress on cover, 1941. .... **$10**

My Very Own Fairy Stories, Johnny Grulle, P. F. Volland Co., 30th ed, color illus, 1917. .... **$65**

Nancy Drew, The Password to Larkspur Lane, illus by Russell Tandy, Grossett & Dunlap, some fading to blue cover, 1933. .... **$65**

Nelly's Silver Mine, Helen Hunt Jackson, Little Brown & Co., illus by Harriet Richards and Henry Pitz, dj, 1924. .... **$20**

Peter Rabbit and the Little Boy, Linda Almond, Platt & Munk, 1935. .... **$15**

Raggedy Ann's Wishing Pebble, Johnny Gruelle, M. A. Donohue Co., color and black and white illus, dj, 1930s. **$85**

Riley's Songs O'Cheer, James Whitcomb, Bobbs Merrill Pub, six color illus, black and white illus by Will Vawter, 1905. .... **$35**

Six White Horses, Candy Geer, illus Leslie Bennet, M & W Quill Pub, 2nd printing, 1964. .... **$6**

Smoky The Cow Horse, Will James, Aladdin Books. **$8**

Swiss Family Robinson, The, Johann Wyss, illus by Lynd Ward, Grosset & Dunlap, Junior Library edition, 1949. .... **$8**

Tarzan and City of the Gold, Edgar Rice Burroughs, Whitman, dj, 1952. .... **$15**

The Cat In The Hat Comes Back, Dr. Seuss, Random House, dj, 1958. ....$185

The New Our Friends, Dick and Jane, Scott Foresman, 1951. ....$38

The Night Before Christmas, A Little Golden Book, Simon Schuster, illus Cornelius DeWitt, 1946. ....$45

Tom Sawyer Detective, Mark Twain, Grossett & Dunlap, 1924. ....$15

Uncle Remus His Songs and Sayings, Joel Chandler Harris, 112 illus by A. B. Frost, D. Appleton & Co., 1916......$75

Uncle Wiggily and the Runaway Cheese, Howard R. Garis, color illus by A. Watson, Platt & Munk, oversize, 1977. ....$13

When We Were Very Young, A. A. Milne, Dutton, 3rd printing, 1924. ....$18

COMIC BOOKS

Shortly after comics first appeared in newspapers of the 1890s, they were reprinted in book format and often used as promotional giveaways by manufacturers, movie theaters and candy and stationery stores. The first modern-format comic was issued in 1933.

The magic date in comic collecting is June 1938, when DC issued Action Comics No. 1, marking the first appearance of Superman. Thus began the Golden Age of comics, which lasted until the mid-1950s and witnessed the birth of the major comic-book publishers, titles and characters.

In 1954, Fredric Wertham authored *Seduction of the Innocent*, a book that pointed a guilt-laden finger at the comics industry for corrupting youth, causing juvenile delinquency and undermining American values. Many publishers were forced out of business, while others established a "comics code" to assure parents that their comics were in compliance with morality and decency standards established by the code authority.

The Silver Age of comics, mid-1950s through the end of the 1960s, saw the revival of many of the characters from the Golden Age in new comic formats. The era began with Showcase No. 4 in October 1956, which marked the origin and first appearance of the Silver-Age Flash.

While comics survived into the 1970s, it was a low point for the genre. But in the early 1980s, a revival occurred. In 1983, comic-book publishers, other than Marvel and DC, issued more titles than had existed in total during the previous 40 years. The mid- and late 1980s were a boom time, a trend that has continued with mammoth movie projects and product licensing.

Reproduction Alert. Publishers frequently reprint popular stories, even complete books, so the buyer must pay strict attention to the title, not just the portion printed in oversized letters on the front cover. If there is any doubt, look inside at the fine print on the bottom of the inside cover or first page. The correct title will be printed there in capital letters. Also pay attention to the dimensions of the comic book. Reprints often differ in size from the original.

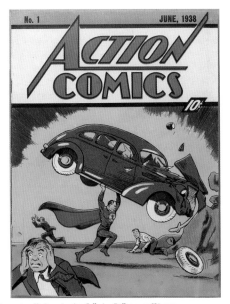

Photo courtesy Heritage Auction Galleries, Dallas; www.HA.com

Action Comics #1 (DC, 1938) The first appearance of Superman. Restoration includes: color touch, pieces added, tear seals, cleaned, reinforced. **$116,512**

Photo courtesy Heritage Auction Galleries, Dallas; www.HA.com

The Amazing Spider-Man #1 (Marvel, 1963) The issue that had the first Fantastic Four crossover and the first appearances of John Jameson, J. Jonah Jameson and the Chameleon. Autographed by Stan Lee. **$5,078**

Photo courtesy Heritage Auction Galleries, Dallas; www.HA.com

Aquaman #1 (DC, 1962) Glossy copy of first issue. It features the first appearance of Quisp the Water Sprite. Howard Purcell drew the cover, Nick Cardy handled the interior art. **$2,151**

Photo courtesy Heritage Auction Galleries, Dallas; www.HA.com

Captain America Comics #1 (Timely, 1941) The origin and first appearance of the title character. Joe Simon and Jack Kirby drew the origin story, while the cover is a solo effort by Kirby. Restoration includes: color touch, pieces added, tear seals, cleaned, reinforced. **$15,535**

Photo courtesy Heritage Auction Galleries, Dallas; www.HA.com

Batman #1 (DC, 1940) The first appearances of the Joker and Catwoman. Classic (and much-imitated) cover by Bob Kane and Jerry Robinson. **$51,750**

The Amazing Spider-Man, #129 (Marvel, 1974) The first appearance of the Punisher and a striking Gil Kane/John Romita Sr. cover. **$717**

The Amazing Spider-Man, #194 (Marvel, 1979) The first appearance of the Black Cat. Al Milgrom cover. Keith Pollard art. **$657**

The Avengers, #1 (Marvel, 1963) Origin and first appearance of the Avengers (Thor, Iron Man, Hulk, Ant-Man and Wasp), with appearances by Loki, the Teen Brigade and the Fantastic Four. Jack Kirby provided cover and interior art. Slight, professional color touch. **$717**

The Avengers, #57 (Marvel, 1968) The first appearance of the Silver Age Vision and the death of Ultron-5. John Buscema provides the cover and interior art. **$3,346**

Batman Annual, #2 (DC, 1961) Includes a 1962 pin-up calendar. Batman Family pin-up on back cover. Curt Swan cover art. Dick Sprang, Sheldon Moldoff and Lew Schwartz art. **$286**

Captain America Comics, #45 (Timely, 1945) Human Torch story. Alex Schomburg cover. **$1,260**

Captain America, #100 (Marvel, 1968) Captain America's origin is retold. Black Panther appearance. First issue of the title, with numbering continued from Tales of Suspense. Jack Kirby cover. Kirby and Syd Shores art. **$77**

Fantastic Four, #53 (Marvel, 1966) Origin and second appearance of the Black Panther. First appearance of Klaw. Jack Kirby cover. Kirby and Joe Sinnott art. **$131**

Photo courtesy Heritage Auction Galleries, Dallas; www.HA.com

Captain Marvel Adventures (#1) (Fawcett, 1941) High-grade, un-restored. This is the only issue of the title to have Jack Kirby art, and it was drawn on the "night shift" at the time Kirby was working on Captain America by day. This first issue's cover art is by C. C. Beck. **$10, 755**

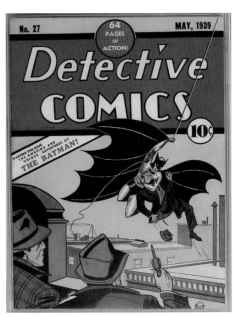

Photo courtesy Heritage Auction Galleries, Dallas; www.HA.com

Detective Comics #27 (DC, 1939) Batman's first appearance, with a backing board autographed by Bob Kane with the inscription, "For Duncan -- 'Bats' wishes" inside a sketched Batman silhouette. Restoration includes: color touch, pieces added, tear seals, cover cleaned, reinforced. **$65,725**

Photo courtesy Heritage Auction Galleries, Dallas; www.HA.com

Daredevil #1 (Marvel, 1964) The origin and first appearance of Daredevil (Matt Murdock) and the first appearances of Karen Page and Foggy Nelson. Jack Kirby and Bill Everett provide the cover. Everett adds interior art. **$2,629**

Photo courtesy Heritage Auction Galleries, Dallas; www.HA.com

Fantastic Four #1 (Marvel, 1961) The comic that started Marvel's Silver Age. Stan Lee wrote the story, Jack Kirby penciled the issue. In addition to having the origin and first appearance of the Fantastic Four, the issue also has the debut of the Mole Man. **$1,314**

Photo courtesy Heritage Auction Galleries, Dallas; www.HA.com

The Flash #139 (DC, 1963) Featured this issue is the origin and first appearance of Professor Zoom (aka Reverse-Flash). **$3,882**

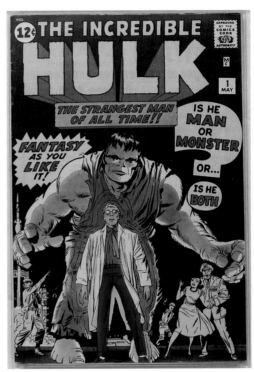

Photo courtesy Heritage Auction Galleries, Dallas; www.HA.com

The Incredible Hulk #1 (Marvel, 1962) This is the origin and first appearance of the Hulk. Stan Lee and Jack Kirby signed first page in pen and marker. **$12,082**

Photo courtesy Heritage Auction Galleries, Dallas; www.HA.com

Green Lantern #1 (DC, 1941) Howard Purcell is the cover artist. **$7,468**

The Flash, #137 (DC, 1963) Here the Golden Age Flash makes an appearance (his third), Vandal Savage makes his first Silver Age appearance, and the Justice Society of America makes its second Silver Age appearance. Carmine Infantino and Murphy Anderson team up for the cover, with Infantino also providing the interior art. **$1,075**

The Flash, #145 (DC, 1964) Weather Wizard appearance. Carmine Infantino and Murphy Anderson cover. Infantino and Joe Giella art. **$119**

The Incredible Hulk, #3 (Marvel, 1962) The Hulk's third appearance, and his origin is retold. First appearance of the Ringmaster. Jack Kirby cover, interior art by Kirby and Dick Ayers. **$107**

The Incredible Hulk, #103 (Marvel, 1968) Second issue of the title. Marie Severin cover and art. Frank Giacoia art. **$155**

Justice League of America, #12 (DC, 1962) The origin and first appearance of Dr. Light. Murphy Anderson is the cover artist. **$2,868**

Justice League of America, #29 (DC, 1964) First Silver Age appearance of Starman. Justice Society of America crossover. "Crisis on Earth-Three" story. Mike Sekowsky cover and art. **$454**

Marvel Team-Up, #133 Spider-Man and the Fantastic Four (Marvel, 1983) Al Milgrom and John Byrne cover. **$48**

Superman, #18 (DC, 1942) Lex Luthor appearance. Contains a half-page ad for Wonder Woman #1. Fred Ray cover. John Sikela and Ed Dobrotka art. **$334**

Photo courtesy Heritage Auction Galleries, Dallas; www.HA.com

Iron Man #1 (Marvel, 1968) One of the key issues in Marvel's late-1960s offerings, and one of Gene Colan's most memorable and dynamic covers. Colan and Johnny Craig art. **$2,868**

Photo courtesy Heritage Auction Galleries, Dallas; www.HA.com

The Silver Surfer #1 (Marvel, 1968) Origin of the Silver Surfer. **$264**

Photo courtesy Heritage Auction Galleries, Dallas; www.HA.com

Justice League of America #1 (DC, 1960) JLA #1 has been a tough book to find in high grade. **$35,850**

Photo courtesy Heritage Auction Galleries, Dallas; www.HA.com

Superman #1 (DC, 1939) Restoration includes: color touch, pieces added, tear seals, reinforced. **$28,680**

Photo courtesy Heritage Auction Galleries, Dallas; www.HA.com

Wonder Woman #1 (DC, 1942) This first issue of Wonder Woman's own title came out just half a year or so after her debut in All Star Comics #8 (she had appeared in Sensation Comics in the meantime). H. G. Peter is the cover artist. **$10,157**

Giant-Size X-Men, #1 (Marvel, 1975) First appearance of the new X-Men (Nightcrawler, Storm, Colossus and Thunderbird). Second full appearance of Wolverine. Gil Kane cover. Dave Cockrum art. **$388**

Photo courtesy Heritage Auction Galleries, Dallas; www.HA.com

X-Men #1 (Marvel, 1963) Origin and first appearance of the X-Men (the Angel, the Beast, Cyclops, Iceman and Marvel Girl). First appearances of Professor X and Magneto. Jack Kirby cover and art. **$2,151**

X-Men, #125 (Marvel, 1979) Chris Claremont story. John Byrne and Terry Austin art. Dave Cockrum and Terry Austin cover. **$310**

PAPERBACK BOOKS

The first mass-market, pocket-sized, paperback book printed in the U.S. was an edition of Pearl Buck's *The Good Earth*, produced by Pocket Books in late 1938, sold in New York City.

At first, paperbacks consisted entirely of reprints, but publishers soon began publishing original works. Genre categories began to emerge, and mass-market book covers reflected those categories. Mass-market paperbacks had an impact on slick magazines (slicks) and pulp magazines. The market for cheap magazines diminished when buyers went to cheap books instead. Authors also turned from magazines and began writing for the paperback market. Many pulp magazine cover artists were hired by paperback publishers to entice readers with their alluring artwork. Several well-known authors were published in paperback, including Arthur Miller and John Steinbeck, and some, like Dashiell Hammett, were published as paperback originals.

For more information and details on condition grades, consult *Antique Trader Collectible Paperbacks Price Guide* by Gary Lovisi, or visit www.gryphonbooks.com. (Camera icons in this section indicate that the book's cover is pictured.)

	G	VG	F		G	VG	F

Adams, John Paul, *Picture Quiz Book*, Popular Library #223, 1950, paperback original, cover by Alex Schomburg.
$35 $75 $165

--- *Puzzles For Everybody,* Avon Book #295, 1951, paperback original, the scarce second Avon puzzle book, girly photos inside. 📷 $90 $175 $450

Addams, Charles, *Addams and Evil*, Pocket Book #50063, 1965, first paperback printing, cover by Charles Addams, cartoons. 📷 $4 $20 $65

--- *Black Maria*, Pocket Book #50059, 1964, first paperback printing, cover by Charles Addams, cartoons.
$5 $20 $50

--- *Drawn and Quartered*, Bantam Book #37, 1946, the first of his cartoon books, predates "The Addams Family" TV series. $4 $30 $90

--- *Drawn and Quartered*, Pocket Book #50058, 1964, reprints Bantam #37, cover by Charles Addams, cartoons.
$4 $15 $40

--- *Homebodies*, Pocket Book #50062, 1965, first paperback printing, cover by Charles Addams, cartoons.
$4 $20 $45

--- *Monster Rally*, Pocket Book #50061, 1965, first paperback printing, cover by Charles Addams, cartoons.
$4 $20 $45

--- *Nightcrawlers*, Pocket Book #50060, 1964, first paperback printing, cover by Charles Addams, cartoons.
$5 $25 $50

Alverson, Chuck, *Wonder Wart-Hog*, Captain Crud & Other Super Stuff, Gold Medal Book #d1781, 1967, first book edition, reprints counter-culture comics that lampoon super heroes, predates *Zap*, Harvey Kurtzman introduction, art by Gilbert Shelton, Vaughan Bode. 📷 $1 $60 $165

Anderson, Poul, *Golden Slave, The*, Avon Book #T-388, 1960, paperback original, scarce historical novel by famed SF author. 📷 $4 $20 $75

Anonymous, *1000 Facts Worth Knowing*, LA Bantam #10, 1940, text cover, the most common LA Bantam but still rare. $35 $100 $155

--- *Avon Book of Modern Short Stories, The,* Avon, no number (#15) 1942, anthology, with Globe endpapers.
$20 $50 $125

--- *Best Cartoons From Argosy*, Zenith Book #ZB-5, 1958, first book edition. 📷 $3 $16 $40

--- *Best From True, The,* Gold Medal Book, no number (#99), 1949, first book edition, photo cover, first Gold Medal Book and only Gold Medal in short format. 📷 $12 $40 $120

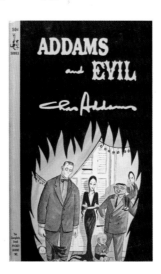

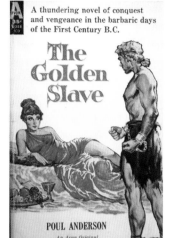

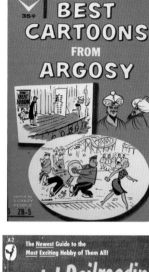

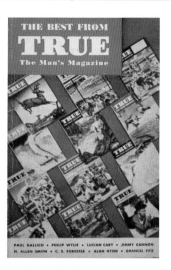

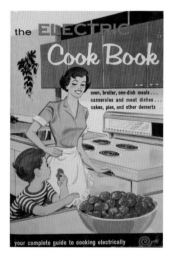

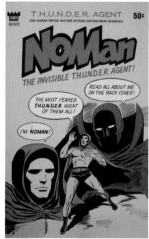

	G	VG	F

--- *Challenger Crossword Puzzles*, Readers Choice #34, 1952, paperback original, digest-size.
| | $60 | $225 | $550 |

--- *Crossword Puzzles*, Popular Library #107, 1946, paperback original.
| | $45 | $155 | $250 |

--- *Electric Cook Book, The,* Philadelphia Electric Co., 1959, paperback original, 1950s kitchen cover art makes this book collectible, recipes for "cooking electrically."
| | $4 | $15 | $40 |

--- *Everybody's Dream Book*, LA Bantam #4, 1940, text cover, rare.
| | $55 | $150 | $220 |

--- *I Was a Nazi Flyer*, Dell Book #21, Map Back, cover by Gerald Gregg, World War II aviation novel.
| | $10 | $45 | $140 |

--- *Man Story*, Gold Medal Book #102, 1950, first book edition, reprints adventure stories from *True* magazine.
| | $10 | $30 | $90 |

	G	VG	F

--- *Model Railroading*, Bantam Book #A-2, 1950, paperback original, cover by Walter Popp, written by Lionel editors, many photos and drawings of layouts.
| | $4 | $20 | $50 |

--- *Noman*, Tower Book #42-672, 1966, paperback original, comic book in paperback format, T.H.U.N.D.E.R. agents.
| | $10 | $40 | $120 |

--- *Pony Book of Puzzles*, Pony Book #65, 1946.
| | $50 | $125 | $225 |

--- *Proceed at Your Own Risk*, Quick Reader #146, 1946, jokes, stories and gags, rare.
| | $35 | $100 | $300 |

--- *Smile, Brother, Smile!,* Trophy Book #401, 1946, humor anthology, one of two books in the Trophy series.
| | $20 | $75 | $225 |

--- *Superman*, Signet Book #D-2966, 1966, first book edition, comic book in paperback format, Superman comics, includes origin, scarce in condition.
| | $10 | $30 | $100 |

	G	VG	F

--- *Terrific Trio, The,* Tower Book #42-687, 1966, paperback original, comic book in paperback format, includes Noman, Dynamo, and Menthor.

| | $10 | $30 | $100 |

Archer, Jules and Sawyer, Maxine, *Sex Life and You,* Red Circle Book #1, 1949, paperback original, text cover, first pre-Lion, scarce.

| . | $10 | $60 | $150 |

Arenson, D. J., *Zorro and the Pirate Raiders,* Bantam Book #24670, 1986, paperback original, continues Johnston McCulley's hero, Zorro, recalled for copyright purposes, scarce.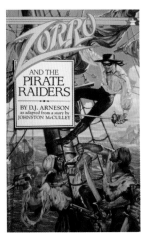

| | $4 | $20 | $50 |

--- *Zorro Rides Again,* Bantam Book #24671, 1986, paperback original, Zorro novel, recalled for copyright purposes, scarce.

| | $5 | $20 | $55 |

Balchin, Nigel, *Small Back Room, The,* Lion Book #31, 1950, cover by Wesley Snyder.

| | $5 | $18 | $60 |

Baldwin, Faith, *Bride From Broadway,* Dell Ten-Cent Book #5, 1950, first book edition, cover by Wesley Snyder, sexy siren cover art captures the feel of the 1930s era in New York City.

| | $5 | $25 | $65 |

Barnett, Lincoln, *Universe and Dr. Einstein, The,* Mentor Book #M71, second printing 1952, cover by Robert Jonas shows Albert Einstein.

| | $3 | $12 | $35 |

Beach, Edward L., *Run Silent, Run Deep,* Perma Book #4061, cover by Clark Hulings, submarine warfare.

| | $2 | $14 | $30 |

--- *Submarine!,* Signet Book #S1043, 1953, submarines in World War II.

| | $2 | $14 | $35 |

Benefield, Harry, *Valiant is the Word For Carrie,* Bantam Book #24, 1946, in dust jacket.

| | $20 | $45 | $100 |

Bengtsson, Fran G., *Long Ships, The,* Signet Book #D1391, 1957, historical novel.

| | $3 | $20 | $60 |

Beveridge, Elizabeth, *Pocket Book of Home Canning, The,* Pocket Book #217, 1943, rare text dust jacketed edition.

| | $35 | $100 | $175 |

Bradley, David, *No Place to Hide,* Bantam Book #421, 1949, in dust jacket.

| | $20 | $70 | $140 |

Brande, Dorothea, *Wake Up and Live,* Pocket Book #2, 1939, only 10,000 copies sold in New York City area.

| | $55 | $150 | $350 |

Brandon, Michael, *Nonce,* Avon Book #506, 1953, voodoo magic and sex.

| | $4 | $20 | $45 |

Brennan, Dan, *Naked Night, The,* Lion Book #197, 1954, paperback original, war novel.

| | $5 | $20 | $65 |

Brewer, Gil, *Appointment in Hell,* Monarch Book #187, 1961, paperback original, cover by Robert Stanley, survivors of a plane crash.

| | $10 | $65 | $125 |

Brock, Rose, *Longleaf,* Avon Book #10482, 1974, paperback original, gothic romance; pseudonym of Joseph Hansen.

| | $10 | $45 | $100 |

--- *Tarn House,* Avon Book #5450, 1971, paperback original, gothic romance.

| | $15 | $50 | $135 |

Brockman, Susan, *Ladies Man,* Bantam Loveswept Book #0648, 1997, paperback original, scarce romance.

| | $70 | $200 | $300 |

Bromfield, Louis, *What Became of Anna Bolton?,* Bantam Book #462, 1948, in dust jacket.

| | $35 | $90 | $175 |

Brontë, Emily, *Wuthering Heights,* Pocket Book #7, 1939, only 10,000 copies sold in New York City area.

| | $40 | $150 | $290 |

Brown, Douglas, *Anne Bonny Pirate Queen,* Monarch Book #MA320, 1962, cover by Robert Stanley, historical novel about female pirate; pseudonym of Walter B. Gibson.

| | $10 | $55 | $125 |

Brown, Harry, *Walk in the Sun, A,* Lion Book #76, 1952 war novel.

| | $5 | $15 | $55 |

Brown, Harry C., *Favorite Poems,* LA Bantam Book #8, 1940, paperback original, text cover, rare.

| | $40 | $100 | $200 |

Buchanan, Jack, *Saigon Slaughter,* Jove Book #09107, 1987, paperback original, #7 in the M.I.A. Hunter men's action series, written by Joe Lansdale.

| | $5 | $25 | $80 |

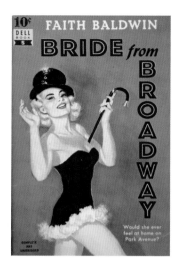

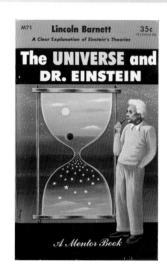

	G	VG	F			G	VG	F

Buck, Pearl, *Good Earth, The,* no number, 1938, the first mass-market paperback, only 2,000 copies distributed in the New York City area on a trial basis, less than a dozen copies known, later reprinted with similar cover art and a number as #11 in the regular Pocket Book series, rare.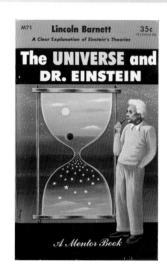

	$1,500	$6,000	$15,000

--- *Good Earth, The,* Pocket Book #11, 1939, first printing this number, reprints Pocket no number with new number.

	$20	$50	$150

Butler, Samuel, *Way of All Flesh, The,* Pocket Book #8, 1939, only 10,000 copies sold in New York City area.

	$45	$150	$275

Capote, Truman, *Other Voices Other Rooms,* Signet Book #700, 1949, cover by Robert Jonas, another version of the "keyhole" cover, novel, gay interest.

	$3	$25	$75

Capp, Al, *World of Li'l Abner, The,* Ballantine Book #8, 1953, paperback original, cover by Al Capp, cartoons.

	$10	$30	$100

Carnegie, Dale, *How to Win Friends and Influence People,* Pocket Book #68, 1940, photo cover, for some reason yet determined the first printing of this book was only distributed in Texas, scarce.

	$25	$50	$100

--- *Little Known Facts About Well Known People,* LA Bantam Book #2, 1940, text cover, rare.

	$50	$160	$300

Castle, Jayne, *Queen of Hearts,* MacFadden Book #132, circa 1975, paperback original, romance novel; pseudonym of Jayne Bentley.

	$10	$40	$100

--- *Vintage of Surrender,* MacFadden Book #157, 1975, paperback original, romance novel.

	$10	$40	$100

Cavannah and Weir, *Dell Book of Jokes, The,* Dell Book #89, 1945, paperback original, cover by Gerald Gregg, anthology.

	$20	$75	$175

Chambliss, William C., *Boomerang!,* Bantam Book #156, 1948, war novel, Infantry Journal edition in Bantam dust jacket.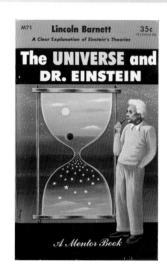

	$22	$75	$135

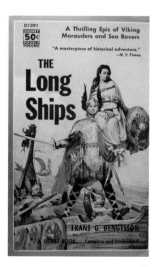

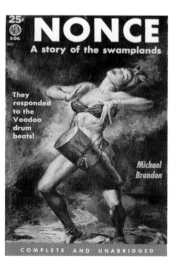

	G	VG	F

Clagett, John, *Cradle of the Sun,* Popular Library #566, 1954, historical novel.  $2 $12 $30

Clark, Comer, *England Under Hitler,* Ballantine Book #512K, 1961, paperback original, true story of Nazi plans for conquered England in World War II. $4 $20 $60

Collins, Norman, *Black Ivory,* Pocket Book #632, 1949, cover by Barye Phillips, historical novel about African slave trade. $6 $25 $80

Corbett, Jim, *Man-Eaters of Kumaon,* Pennant Book #P23, 1953, true adventure, big-game hunter tracks man-eating tigers in India. $3 $15 $38

Cotlow, Lewis, *Amazon Head-Hunters,* Signet Book #S1094, 1954, first paperback printing, cover by James Meese, true adventures among tribes in Amazon, photos. $4 $20 $45

Crane, Aimee, *G.I. Sketch Book, The,* Infantry Journal #S225, 1944, for soldiers overseas, oblong book, soldier art includes future paperback artists John J. Floherty and John McDermott. $10 $30 $100

Cuppy, Will, *How to Tell Your Friends From the Apes,* Quick Reader #118, 1944, cover by Axelrod shows caricature of Tarzan author Edgar Rice Burroughs, humor and satire, Tarzan-related. $8 $30 $75

Currie, S. M. A., *How to Make Friends Easily,* LA Bantam #5, 1940, paperback original, text cover, rare. $55 $125 $175

Cushman, Dan, *Tongking!,* Ace Book #D-49, 1954, paperback original, cover by Rafael DeSoto, pirate novel, Ace Double backed with *Golden Temptress* by Charles Grayson, historical novel. $12 $50 $125

David, Eddie, *Campus Joke Book,* Ace Book #S-171, 1956, paperback original, cover by Pierce. $5 $20 $60

Davies, Valentine, *Miracle on 34th Street,* Pocket Book #903, 1952. $4 $15 $55

--- *Miracle on 34th Street,* Pocket Book #903, second printing 1959, cover by Frederick Banbery. $2 $10 $30

Davis, Franklin M., *Bamboo Camp #10,* Monarch Book #236, 1962, paperback original, cover by Robert Stanley, American soldiers brutalized in Japanese POW camp in World War II. $10 $40 $100

--- *Naked and the Lost, The,* Lion Book #221, 1954, paperback original, military prisoners. $5 $25 $75

Dean, Robert George, *On Ice,* Bantam Book #148, 1948, Superior reprint in dust jacket. $25 $60 $145

De Camp, L. Sprague, *Bronze God of Rhodes, The,* Bantam Book #2589, 1963, first paperback printing, scarce historical novel. $5 $35 $70

--- *Elephant For Aristotle, An,* Curtis Book #09059, no date, circa 1970, first paperback printing, scarce historical novel by SF/F author. $10 $40 $100

--- *Golden Wind, The,* Curtis Book #07091, no date, circa 1970, first paperback printing, scarce historical novel. $5 $20 $50

Dodd, Christina, *Castles in the Air,* Harper Book #08034, 1993, paperback original, cover by Robert Maguire, historical romance, error cover art shows "3-armed lady," the book was recalled and copies destroyed, later reprinted with a new cover by another artist. $5 $25 $75

Erskine, John, *Private Life of Helen of Troy, The,* Popular Library #147, 1948, cover by Rudolph Belarski, historical novel with famous "nipple" cover art. $10 $50 $120

Ewing, Frederick R., *I, Libertine,* Ballantine Book #165, 1956, paperback original, cover by Kelly Freas, satire of historical novels; pseudonym of Theodore Sturgeon. $12 $40 $100

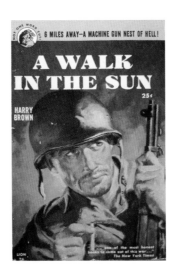

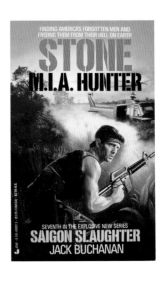

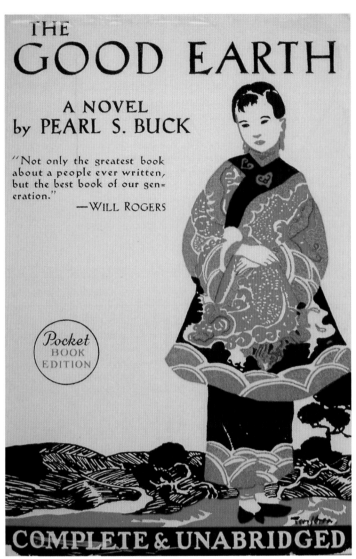

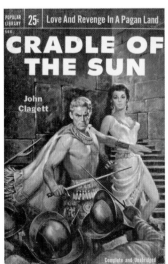

	G	VG	F

Farr, John, *She Shark,* Ace Book #S-159, 1956, paperback original, modern pirate novel; pseudonym of William Ard. 📷

| | $5 | $25 | $65 |

Faulkner, William, *Intruder in the Dust,* Signet Book #S1253, 1956, murder and racial violence in a Southern town.

| | $10 | $30 | $100 |

--- *Mosquitoes,* Avon Book, no number (#12), 1941, with Globe endpapers.

| | $45 | $175 | $425 |

--- *Rose For Emily, A,* Armed Service Edition #825, no date, circa 1945, paperback original, the hardcover on the cover was made up and does not exist.

| | $75 | $250 | $750 |

Fishbein, M. D., Morris, *Your Questions on Health,* LA Bantam Book #3, 1940 paperback original, text cover, rare.

| | $55 | $150 | $250 |

Fitzgerald, F. Scott, *Diamond As Big As the Ritz and Other Stories, The,* Armed Service Edition #1043, no date, circa 1947, first book edition.

| | $75 | $250 | $700 |

--- *Great Gatsby, The,* Armed Service Edition #862, no date, circa 1946.

| | $45 | $160 | $325 |

--- *Great Gatsby, The,* Bantam Book #8, 1945, in dust jacket. 📷

| | $55 | $175 | $400 |

--- *Tender Is the Night,* Bantam Book #A867, 1950.

| | $10 | $40 | $90 |

Flaubert, Gustave, *Salambo,* Berkley Book #G-5, 1955, cover by Rudy Nappi, historical novel with sexy cover art.

| | $10 | $35 | $120 |

Forester, C. S., *Beat to Quarters,* Armed Service Edition #Q-18, no date, circa 1944, historical novel.

| | $10 | $35 | $100 |

--- *Commodore Hornblower,* Armed Service Edition #804, 1945, historical novel.

| | $10 | $35 | $100 |

--- *Flying Colours,* Armed Service Edition #F-157, no date, circa 1944, historical novel.

| | $10 | $35 | $100 |

--- *Lord Hornblower,* Armed Service Edition #1187, 1946, vertical format, historical novel. 📷

| | $12 | $45 | $100 |

--- *Ship of the Line,* Armed Service Edition #E-133, no date, circa 1944, historical novel.

| | $10 | $40 | $100 |

Fox, William Price, *Southern Fried,* Gold Medal Book #k1232, 1962, paperback original, satire with cover art and inside drawings by Jack Davis. 📷

| | $8 | $35 | $100 |

Frey, Richard L., *How to Play Canasta,* Novel Library #43, 1950, card game rules.

| | $3 | $12 | $25 |

Friedman, Stuart, *Rasputin: The Mad Monk,* Monarch Book #241, 1962, paperback original, cover by Robert Maguire, historical novel. 📷

| | $8 | $35 | $90 |

Gibbons, Floyd, *Red Knight of Germany, The,* Bantam Book #A1919, 1959, abridged, true story of World War I ace Baron Von Ricthofen. 📷

| | $5 | $15 | $40 |

Gibson, Walter B., *Magic Explained,* Perma Book #P-54, 1949, first book edition, simultaneous with Perma hardcover with same number, the paperback is scarce.

| | $15 | $40 | $100 |

Glay, George Albert, *Oath of Seven,* Ace Book #S-102, 1955, paperback original, historical novel about Mau Mau terror in Kenya. 📷

| | $5 | $22 | $75 |

Goulart, Ron, *An Informal History of the Pulp Magazine,* Ace Book #37070, 1973, cover shows pulp magazine covers, original title *Cheap Thrills,* collectible reference.

| | $10 | $25 | $50 |

Gregory, Jerome, *Everybody's Book of Jokes and Wisecracks,* LA Bantam #6, 1940, paperback original, anthology of jokes, text cover, rare.

| | $55 | $155 | $225 |

Gruenberg, Sidonie, *Your Child and You,* Gold Medal Book #112, 1950, first book edition, photo cover. 📷

| | $3 | $20 | $65 |

Hatch, Richard Warren, *Go Down to Glory,* Dell Book #D-114, 1952 in dust jacket.

| | $100 | $300 | $650 |

Heard, Gerald, *Is Another World Watching?,* Bantam Book #1079, 1953, early UFO book.

| | $3 | $20 | $60 |

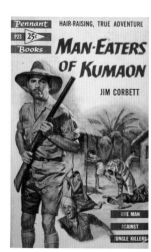

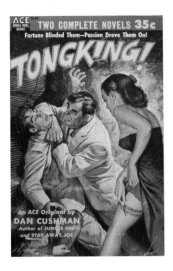

	G	VG	F
Hecht, Ben, *Count Bruga,* Avon Book, no number (#11), 1941, with Globe endpapers.	$25	$75	$155
Hemingway, Ernest, *Farewell to Arms, A,* Bantam Book #467, 1949.	$10	$25	$65
--- *Selected Short Stories of Ernest Hemingway,* Armed Service Edition #K-9, no date, circa 1944, first book edition.	$75	$180	$450
--- *Sun Also Rises, The,* Bantam Book #717, 1949, cover by Ken Riley.	$5	$15	$65
--- *To Have and Have Not,* Armed Service Edition #667, no date, circa 1946.	$15	$75	$180
Henry, O., *Selected Stories of O. Henry,* Armed Service Edition #K-16, no date, circa 1946.	$10	$40	$100
Hibbs, Ben, *Great Stories From the Saturday Evening Post,* Bantam Book #116, 1947, first book edition, cover by Steven Dohamos.	$3	$25	$65

	G	VG	F
Higgins, Marguerite, *War in Korea,* Lion Book #82, 1952, cover by Floherty.	$5	$20	$50
Hilton, James, *Ill Wind,* Avon Book, no number (#4), 1941, in Globe endpapers.	$35	$75	$150
Hinds, Arthur, *Complete Sayings of Jesus, The,* Pocket Book #291, 1945, arranged by Hinds, very scarce.	$15	$50	$100
House, Brant, *Cartoon Annual #2,* Ace Book #S-132, 1955 paperback original.	$5	$20	$50
--- *Little Monsters,* Ace Book #S-145, 1956, paperback original.	$5	$20	$55
Hull, E. M., *Sheik, The,* Dell Book #174, 1947, Map Back, early Dell romance novel.	$2	$18	$45
--- *Sons of the Sheik,* Dell Book #279, 1949, Map Back, cover by F. Kenwood Giles, Dell Romance with heart in keyhole logo.	$2	$20	$50

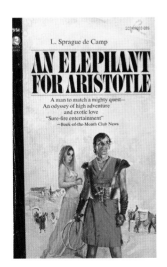

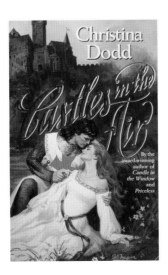

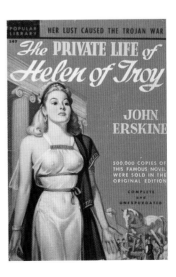

	G	VG	F

Hunt, George P., *Coral Comes High,* Signet Book #1440, 1957, cover by Paul Lehr, with the Marines in the Pacific in World War II. $4 $16 $40

Ibanez, V. Blasco, *Blood and Sand,* Dell Book #500, 1951, Map Back, cover by Robert Stanley.
   $3 $15 $60

Ilton, Paul, *Last Days of Sodom and Gomorrah, The,* Signet Book #1399, 1957, cover by Robert Maguire, biblical historical novel. $10 $30 $100

Infantino, Carmine, *Green Lantern and Green Arrow #1,* Paperback Library #64-729, 1972, first book edition, cover by Neal Adams, comic book reprints, contains art by Adams, Gil Kane. $10 $45 $100

--- *Green Lantern and Green Arrow #2,* Paperback Library #64-755, 1972, first book edition, cover and interiors by Neal Adams, comic book reprints.
   $12 $50 $120

Jacobs, Bruce, *Korea's Heroes,* Lion Book #172, 1953, paperback original, the story of the Medal of Honor winners in Korean War. $6 $20 $75

Kamal, Ahmad, *High Pressure,* Bantam Book #716, 1949, in dust jacket. $55 $150 $225

Kane, Bob, *Batman,* Signet Book #D-2939, 1966, first book edition, comic reprints.
   $10 $20 $50

--- *Batman vs the Joker,* Signet Book #D-2969, 1966, first book edition, comic reprints, book #3 in series.
   $10 $20 $60

--- *Batman vs the Penguin,* Signet Book #D-2970, 1966, first book edition, contains the Penguin and Catwoman comic reprints, book #4 in series. $12 $35 $90

Keel, John A., *Fickle Finger of Fate, The,* Gold Medal Book #d1719, 1966, paperback original, satire, scarce.
   $10 $40 $100

Kells, Susannah, *Aristocrats, The,* St. Martins Press #91009, 1988, first paperback printing, romance; pseudonym of Bernard Cornwell, uncommon.
   $4 $20 $45

--- *Crowning Mercy, A,* Penguin Book #10148, 1987, first paperback printing, cover by Michael Tedesco, historical romance, uncommon.
   $4 $20 $50

Kelly, F., and Ryan, C., *MacArthur Man of Action,* Lion Book #67, 1951, his story "from Bataan to Truman."
   $5 $18 $55

Kendricks, James, *She Wouldn't Surrender,* Monarch Book #MA301, 1960, paperback original, historical novel about Confederate spy Belle Boyd; pseudonym of Gardner F. Fox.
   $5 $20 $60

--- *Sword of Casanova,* Monarch Book #111, 1959, paperback original, historical novel.
   $6 $20 $65

Ketchem, Jack, *Cover,* Warner Book #30245, 1987, paperback original, Vietnam novel; pseudonym of Dallas Mayr. $10 $25 $75

Key, Alexander, *Wrath and the Wind, The,* Popular Library #608, 1954, historical novel, cover shows slave girl whipping male slave trader.
   $3 $15 $40

Keyhoe, Donald, *Flying Saucers Are Real, The,* Gold Medal Book #107, 1950, paperback original, cover by Frank Tinsley, early UFO book.
   $6 $30 $90

Khayyam, Omar, *Rubaiyat of Omar Khayyam,* Avon Book, no number (#2), 1941, with Globe endpapers.
   $20 $100 $200

Kinnaird, Clark, *Avon Complete Crosswords and Cryptograms, The,* Avon Book #162, 1948, the second Avon crossword book.
   $125 $350 $750

Krentz, Jayne Ann, *Maiden of the Morning,* MacFadden Book #249, 1979, paperback original, scarce romance novel; pseudonym of Jayne Bentley.
   $20 $75 $200

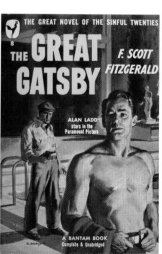

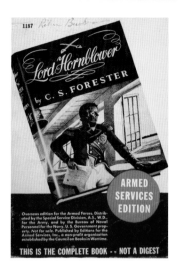

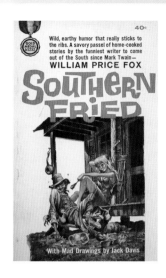

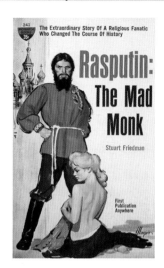

	G	VG	F

--- *Moment Past Midnight, A*, MacFadden Book #224, 1979, paperback original, scarce romance novel.

	$20	**$60**	**$175**

--- *Turning Toward Home*, MacFadden Book #192, 1979, paperback original, scarce romance novel.

	$25	**$75**	**$200**

Kurtzman, Harvey, *Executive's Comic Book,* MacFadden Book #50-159, 1962, first book edition, reprints Goodman Beaver superhero parody and other strips, Will Elder art.

	$10	**$40**	**$125**

--- *Help!*, Gold Medal Book #s1163, 1961, first book edition, photo cover, satire.

	$5	**$30**	**$90**

--- *Jungle Book*, Ballantine Book #338K, 1959, paperback original, cover by Jack Davis.

	$6	**$30**	**$90**

--- *Mad Reader, The*, Ballantine Book #93, 1954, cartoons from *Mad* magazine.

	$8	**$40**	**$100**

--- *Second Helping!*, Gold Medal Book #s1225, 1962, first book edition, humor.

	$5	**$15**	**$60**

Lamott, Kenneth, *Stockade, The,* Dell Book #703, 1953, cover by Griffith Foxley, prisoners on Pacific island during World War II. 📷

	$3	**$14**	**$35**

Lardner, Ring, *Love Nest and Other Stories, The,* Bantam Book #145, 1948, Superior reprint in dust jacket.

	$35	**$70**	**$145**

Lawrence, D. H., *Love Among the Haystacks,* Avon Book #248, 1950, collection.

	$5	**$20**	**$55**

--- *Virgin and the Gypsy, The*, Avon Book #98, 1946, cover by Paul Stahr. 📷

	$8	**$25**	**$60**

Lawson, Ted W., *Thirty Seconds Over Tokyo,* Bantam Book #S221, sixth printing 1945, text cover, rare.

	$20	**$50**	**$125**

Lay, Margaret Rebecca, *Ceylun,* Lion Book #32, 1950, cover by Julian Paul, "She was his untouched wife."

	$5	**$18**	**$70**

Lee, Stan, *Amazing Spider-Man, The,* Lancer Book #72-112, 1966, first book edition, cover by Steve Ditko, comic book reprints in the Lancer "Mighty Marvel Collector's Album" series of six books.

	$10	**$30**	**$90**

--- *Fantastic Four, The*, Lancer Book #72-111, 1966, first book edition, cover and interior art by Jack Kirby, comic book reprints. 📷

	$10	**$30**	**$90**

--- *Fantastic Four Return, The*, Lancer Book #72-169, 1967, first book edition, cover and interior art by Jack Kirby, comic book reprints.

	$10	**$35**	**$100**

--- *Here Comes…Daredevil*, Lancer Book #72-170, 1967, first book edition, comic book reprints, art by Bill Everett, Johnny Romita, and Gene Colon.

	$10	**$30**	**$90**

--- *Incredible Hulk, The*, Lancer Book #72-124, 1966, first book edition, cover and interior art by Steve Ditko and Jack Kirby, comic book reprints.

	$10	**$35**	**$100**

--- *Mighty Thor, The*, Lancer Book #72-125, 1966, first book edition, cover and interior art by Jack Kirby, comic book reprints.

	$10	**$30**	**$90**

Lewis, Ellen, *Children's Favorite Stories,* LA Bantam Book #12, 1940, paperback original, edited anthology, rare.

	$60	**$120**	**$200**

Lewis, Sinclair, *Babbitt,* Bantam Book #22, 1948, in dust jacket.

	$25	**$60**	**$125**

--- *Elmer Gantry*, Avon Book, no number (#1), 1941, the first Avon paperback, with Globe endpapers only. 📷

	$30	**$125**	**$245**

--- *Ghost Patrol, The*, Avon Book #74, 1946, first book edition, collection. 📷

	$5	**$35**	**$100**

--- *Kingsblood Royal*, Bantam Book #705, 1949, cover by James Avati, early racial novel, a white man learns he has black blood in his veins and is proud of it. 📷

	$4	**$20**	**$75**

Libby, Martin, *How to Win and Hold a Husband,* LA Bantam Book #11, 1940, text cover, rare.

	$55	**$125**	**$220**

	G	VG	F

Lindsey, Johanna, *Love Only Once,* Avon Book #89953, 1985, paperback original, cover by Robert McGinnis is a twist on traditional romance art. 📷

| | $3 | $14 | $40 |

Locke, Charles O., *Last Princess, The,* Popular Library #622, 1954, historical novel of the Aztecs. 📷

| | $3 | $14 | $30 |

London, Jack, *Call of the Wind,* Armed Service Edition #K-3, no date, circa 1945.

| | $6 | $40 | $100 |

--- *Curse of the Snark, The,* Armed Service Edition #H-221, no date, circa 1945.

| | $10 | $50 | $120 |

--- *Sea Wolf, The,* Armed Service Edition #F-180, no date, circa 1945.

| | $8 | $45 | $120 |

--- *South Sea Tales,* Lion Book #92, 1952. 📷

| | $6 | $35 | $100 |

--- *White Fang,* Armed Service Edition #G-182, no date, circa 1945.

| | $5 | $30 | $75 |

	G	VG	F

Lupoff, Dick and Thompson, Don, *All in Color For a Dime,* Ace Book #01625, no date, circa 1972, first paperback printing, comic book history, photos.

| | $5 | $20 | $55 |

MacDonald, John D., *House Guests, The,* Gold Medal Book #m2894, 1973, first and only paperback, mystery writer tells story about family pets.

| | $10 | $25 | $90 |

MacIsacc, Fred, *Love On the Run,* LA Bantam Book #18, 1940, text cover, rare.

| | $50 | $150 | $225 |

Mailer, Norman, *Barbary Shore,* Signet Book #1019, 1953, cover by Stanley Zuckerberg, postwar stories of people in a seedy Brooklyn, New York boarding house. 📷

| | $3 | $20 | $75 |

Mannix, Daniel P., *Those About to Die,* Ballantine Book #275K, 1958, paperback original, Roman gladiators.

| | $5 | $25 | $50 |

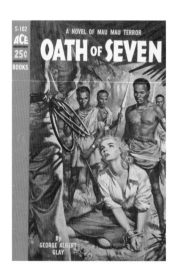

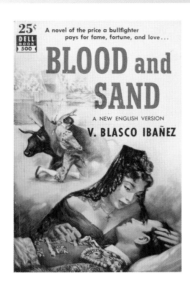

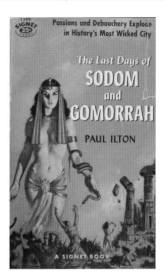

	G	VG	F

Marais, Claude, *Saskia,* Lion Book #116, 1952, cover by Geygan, the story of Rembrandt.

	$5	$18	$60

March, William, *Company K,* Lion Book #111, 1952, cover by Rafael DeSoto, World War II novel.

	$5	$25	$70

Marshall, Edison, *Caravan to Xanadu,* Dell Book #D157, 1955, cover by George Gross, historical novel.

	$2	$12	$35

--- *Great Smith,* Dell Book #D102, 1952, cover by Robert Stanley, historical adventure.

	$3	$12	$40

--- *Love Stories of India,* Dell Book #530 1951, Map Back, romance and adventure.

	$3	$14	$50

--- *Yankee Pasha,* Dell Book #353 1949, Map Back, cover by Robert Stanley.

	$3	$12	$50

	G	VG	F

Mason, Ernst, *Tiberius,* Ballantine Book #361K, 1960, paperback original, biography of debauched Roman emperor; pseudonym of Frederick Pohl.

	$6	$30	$75

Matheson, Richard, *Beardless Warriors, The,* Bantam Book #F2281, 1961, first paperback printing, World War II novel by horror master.

	$9	$45	$120

Maugham, W. Somerset, *Rain,* Dell Ten-Cent Book #2, 1950, first book edition, cover by Victor Kalin.

	$8	$20	$75

McClintock, Marshall, *How to Build and Operate a Model Railroad,* Dell First Edition #D72, 1955, paperback original, photo cover with inside photos of train layouts for hobbyists.

	$6	$30	$75

Millard, Joseph, *Mansion of Evil,* Gold Medal Book #129, 1950, paperback original, done in color comic book format, scarce.

	$40	$100	$250

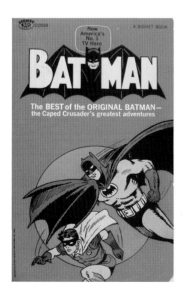

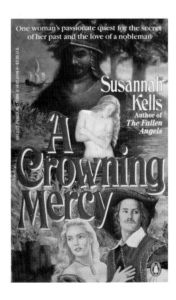

	G	VG	F

Miller, Arthur, *Focus,* Popular Library #230, 1950, cover by Rudolph Belarski, sexy cover art belies the seriousness of this brutal but important novel on anti-Semitism. 📷

| | $3 | $30 | $85 |

Moore, Robin, *Tales of the Green Berets,* Signet Book #D3001, 1966, first book edition, cover by Joe Kubert, in comic book format, Green Berets in Vietnam War.

| | $5 | $25 | $75 |

Moravia, Alberto, *Woman of Rome, The,* Signet Book #S844, 1951, cover by James Avati, Italy in postwar era. 📷

| | $4 | $16 | $55 |

Murray, Ken, *Giant Joke Book,* Ace Book #D-62, 1954, paperback original. $5 $20 $70

Nathan, Robert, *One More Spring,* Bantam Book #19, 1945, with dust jacket, romance novel.

| | $15 | $45 | $100 |

O'Hara, John, *Butterfield 8,* Avon Book #94, 1944.

| | $6 | $30 | $75 |

Olson, Lloyd E., *Skip Bomber,* Ace Book #D-441, 1960, paperback original, B-29 bomber cover art. 📷

| | $4 | $15 | $40 |

Palmer, Diana, *Now and Forever,* MacFadden Book #127, 1979, paperback original, scarce romance novel, her first novel. $30 $90 $250

--- *Sweet Enemy,* MacFadden Book #179, 1979, paperback original, scarce romance novel.

| | $25 | $60 | $135 |

Parker, Dorothy, *Enough Rope,* Pocket Book #6, 1939, only 10,000 copies sold in New York City area. 📷

| | $40 | $125 | $250 |

Parker, Eleanor, *Humorous Anecdotes and Funny Stories,* LA Bantam Book #24, 1940, paperback original, anthology, text cover, rare. $75 $150 $225

--- *Humorous Anecdotes and Funny Stories,* LA Bantam Book #24, 1940, paperback original, anthology, illustrated cover edition, rare. 📷 $90 $300 $525

--- *World's Great Love Affairs, The,* LA Bantam Book #12, 1940, paperback original, text cover, rare.

| | $65 | $200 | $350 |

Patherbridge, Margaret, *Pocket Book of Crossword Puzzles, The,* Pocket Book #210, 1943, paperback original.

| | $20 | $50 | $125 |

Payne, Robert, *Blue Negro, The,* Avon Book #373, 1951, first book edition, adventure stories.

| | $8 | $30 | $90 |

Pei, Mario, *Swords For Charlemagne,* Graphic Book #G-208, 1955, cover by Robert Maguire, historical novel. 📷

| | $4 | $20 | $50 |

Pernikoff, Alexander, *Bushido,* Quick Reader #109, 1943, cover by Axelrod shows World War II terror. 📷

| | $7 | $35 | $85 |

Petersen, Clarence, *Bantam Story, The,* Bantam Book, no number, 1970, paperback original, no price, giveaway, photo cover, publisher history from 1945 to 1970.

| | $4 | $20 | $45 |

--- *Bantam Story, The,* Bantam Book, no number, second printing 1975, no price, giveaway, updates and expands 1970 edition to 35 years of Bantam paperback publishing.

| | $4 | $20 | $45 |

Prouty, Olive Higgins, *Now, Voyager,* Dell Book #99, no date 1946, Map Back, classic romance novel with Dell heart in keyhole romance logo. 📷

| | $5 | $20 | $50 |

Rafferty and O'Neill, *Dell Crossword Puzzles,* Dell First Edition #60, 1955, paperback original.

| | $40 | $110 | $250 |

--- *Second Dell Book of Crossword Puzzles,* Dell Book #278, 1949, paperback original. $130 $300 $625

Remarque, Erich Maria, *All Quiet on the Western Front,* Lion Book #49, 1950, novel of trench warfare in World War I. 📷

| | $4 | $14 | $55 |

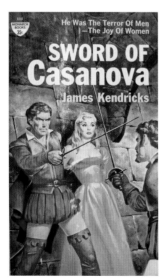

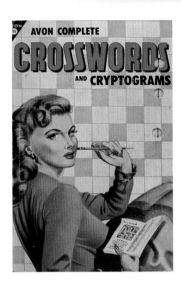

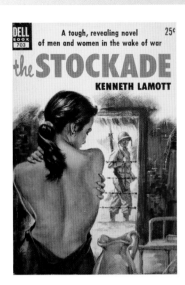

	G	VG	F

Roberts, Nora, *Irish Thoroughbred,* Silhouette Romance #57081, 1981, paperback original, #81 in Silhouette series, her first novel. **$20 $90 $200**

--- *Promise Me Tomorrow,* Pocket Book #47019, 1984, paperback original, scarce romance novel. **$15 $50 $150**

Runyon, Charles W., *Bloody Jungle, The,* Ace Book #G-594, 1966, paperback original, cover by G. McConnell, Vietnam novel about the Green Berets. **$5 $25 $65**

Sabatini, Rafael, *Captain Blood,* Pocket Book #82, 1940, classic pirate adventure novel **$5 $25 $100**

--- *Mistress Wilding,* Avon Book #84, 1946, historical novel. **$5 $25 $85**

--- *Scaramouche,* Bantam Book #5, 1945, cover by Calin. **$4 $18 $55**

Sandburg, Carl, *Selected Poems of Carl Sandburg,* Armed Service Edition #N-6, no date, circa 1946, first edition thus. **$10 $40 $100**

Seagrave, Gordon S., *Burma Surgeon,* Infantry Journal, no number, 1944, Penguin Books imprint published for soldiers in World War II. **$3 $15 $40**

Siegel, Jerry, *High Camp Super-Heroes,* Belmont Book #B50-695, 1966, paperback original, comic book stories scripted by Siegel, creator of Superman, contains costume heroes Steel Sterling, Fly Man, the Shield, and Web. **$10 $35 $125**

Shakespeare, William, *Five Great Tragedies,* Pocket Book #3, 1939, only 10,000 copies sold in New York City area. **$55 $175 $350**

--- *Jokes, Gags and Wisecracks,* Dell Book #152, 1947, anthology of jokes, gags. **$25 $90 $165**

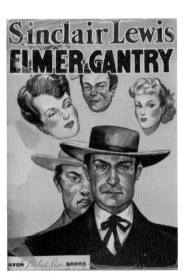

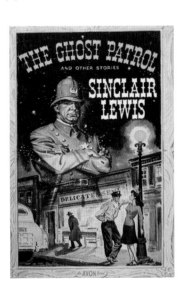

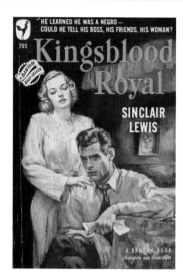

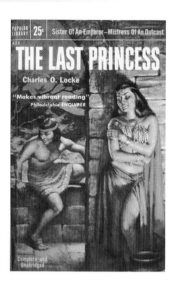

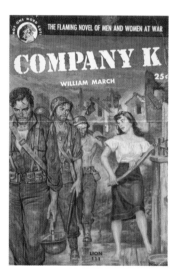

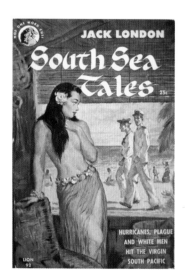

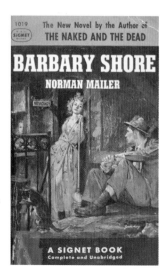

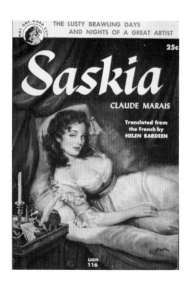

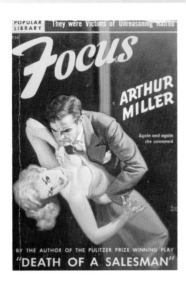

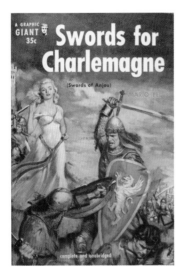

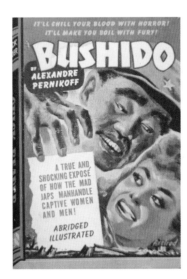

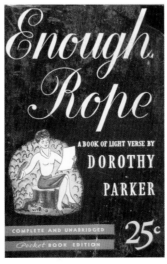

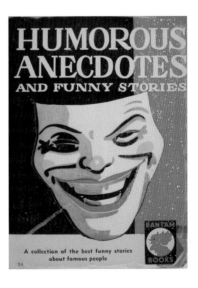

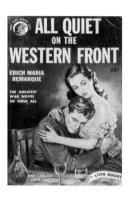

	G	VG	F		G	VG	F

Shaplen, Robert, *Love-Making of Max-Robert, The,* Signet Book #789, 1950, cover by James Avati, postwar angst in the Orient.  $3 $20 $55

Shay, Frank, *Pirate Wench,* Pyramid Book #G-75, 1953, historical novel about female pirate Mary Reed. $3 $20 $55

Shea, Vernon, *Strange Desires,* Lion Book #191, 1954, anthology with William Faulkner. $5 $30 $75

Silver, Stuart, *Faster Than a Speeding Bullet,* Playboy Press #16760, 1980, paperback original, golden age of radio history and quiz, with Isidore Haiblum. $5 $15 $45

Silverstein, Shel, *Grab Your Socks,* Ballantine Book #163, 1956, paperback original, cover by Shel Silverstein, joke book. $10 $60 $160

Slaughter, Frank G., *Fort Everglades,* Perma Book #P155, 1952, historical novel, bondage cover. $2 $15 $40

Smith, H. Allen, *Rude Jokes,* Gold Medal Book # t2347, 1970, paperback original, very scarce. $10 $25 $65

Southern, Terry, *Magic Christian, The,* Berkley Book #BG500, 1961, cover by Richard Powers, predates the film, wild satire. $5 $35 $90

Stagg, Delano, *Bloody Beaches,* Monarch Book #210, 1961, paperback original, cover by Robert Stanley, World War II novel, "Marines die hard!"; unknown pseudonym. $4 $15 $50

Steinbeck, John, *Cannery Row,* Armed Service Edition #T-5, no date, circa 1944. $15 $55 $120

--- *Cannery Row,* Bantam Book #75, 1947, in dust jacket. $35 $100 $275

--- *Cup of Gold,* Armed Service Edition #750, no date, circa 1945, pirate novel. $15 $55 $120

--- *Cup of Gold,* Popular Library #216, 1950, cover by Rudolph Belarski, pirate novel. $6 $35 $90

--- *Cup of Gold,* Bantam Book #1184, 1953, cover by Earl Mayan, pirate novel. $3 $20 $50

--- *Grapes of Wrath, The,* Armed Service Edition #C-90, no date, circa 1945. $20 $55 $150

--- *Grapes of Wrath, The,* Armed Service Edition #690, no date, circa 1945, reprints ASE #C-90. $15 $35 $85

--- *Grapes of Wrath, The,* Bantam Book #7, 1945, cover by Bratz. $5 $20 $75

--- *Long Valley, The,* Armed Service Edition #794, no date, circa 1945. $32 $75 $155

--- *Pastures of Heaven, The,* Penguin Book #509, 1942. $30 $75 $150

--- *Pastures of Heaven, The,* Armed Service Edition #703, no date, circa 1945. $20 $55 $120

--- *Pastures of Heaven, The,* Bantam Book #899, 1951. $3 $18 $55

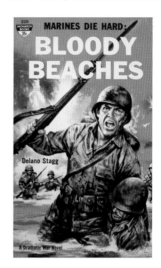

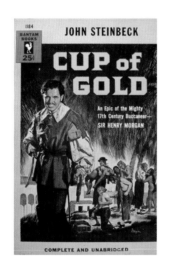

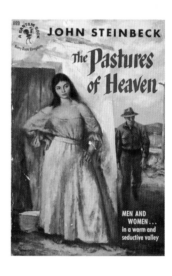

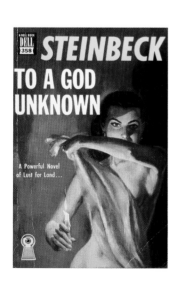

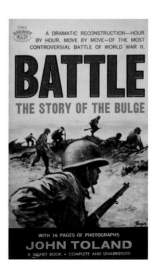

	G	VG	F
--- *Steinbeck Pocket Book, The*, Pocket Book #243, 1943, first book edition, cover by Leo Manso, collection.	$10	$30	$75
--- *To a God Unknown*, Dell Book #358, 1949, Map Back.	$6	$30	$75
--- *Wayward Bus, The*, Armed Service Edition #1232, no date, circa 1947.	$35	$100	$200
Stevenson, Robert Louis, *Treasure Island*, Quick Reader #130, 1945, cover by Cirkel, abridged, pirate classic, very scarce.	$25	$85	$150
Stolberg, Charles, *Avon Book of Puzzles, The*, Avon Book #27, 1943, first Avon puzzle book.	$60	$150	$400
Stuart, Anne, *Barrett's Hill*, Beagle Book #26585, 1974, paperback original, gothic romance, her first book.	$20	$50	$100
Talbot, Daniel, *Damned The*, Lion Library #LL6, 1954, first book edition, anthology with stories by Jim Thompson, Ernest Hemingway, James Joyce.	$8	$35	$80
Tebbel, John, *Paperback Books, A Pocket History*, Pocket Book, no number, 1964, paperback original, silver text cover, giveaway, publisher history from 1939 to 1964, scarce.	$15	$50	$120
Terrill, Rogers, *Argosy Book of Adventure Stories, The*, Bantam Book #A1158, 1953, first book edition, anthology, contains Robert A. Heinlein.	$3	$20	$50
Toland, John, *Battle: The Story of the Bulge*, Signet Book #T-1862, 1960, cover by Barye Phillips, the World War II battle by a famed historian.	$2	$16	$45
Tracy, Don, *Carolina Corsair*, Cardinal Book #C-228, 1957, cover by James Meese, historical novel about Blackbeard the pirate. $2	$14	$35
Van Loon, Hendrik Willem, *Story of Rabelais and Voltaire, The*, LA Bantam Book #20, 1940, text cover, rare.	$65	$150	$275
Vidal, Gore, *Dangerous Voyage*, Signet Book #1003, 1953, first paperback printing, original title *Williwaw*.	$4	$30	$75
Voltaire, *Candide*, Lion Book #107, 1952, a classic gets the sexy cover treatment.	$5	$20	$75
Webster, Miriam, *Avon Webster English Dictionary*, Avon Book #G-1007, 1951, very scarce.	$25	$100	$200
--- *Self-Pronouncing New Webster's Pocket Size Dictionary and Spelling Helper*, Quick Reader #108, 1942.	$10	$35	$75
--- *Self-Pronouncing New Webster's Pocket Size Dictionary and Spelling Helper*, Quick Reader, no number, 1943, same as #108 but says "special edition for service men" on cover, scarce.	$20	$70	$155
Weegee, *Naked Hollywood*, Berkley Book #G-9, 1955, first book edition, photo cover, written with Mel Harris, 150+ photos by ace crime photographer.	$10	$35	$100
Wilcox, Ella Wheeler, *Poems of Passion*, LA Bantam Book #15, 1940, first book edition, text cover, rare.	$60	$120	$200
Wilder, Thornton, *Bridge at San Luis Rey, The*, Pocket Book #9, 1939, only 10,000 copies sold in New York City area.	$50	$150	$250
--- *Heaven is My Destination*, Avon Book #59, 1945.	$8	$20	$90
Wilson, Gahan, *Gahan Wilson's Graveside Manner*, Ace Book #F-331, 1965, first book edition, satire, macabre cartoons.	$6	$30	$75
Wodehouse, P. G., *Quick Service and Code of the Woosters, The*, Ace Book #D-25, 1953, cover by Norman Saunders.	$5	$20	$65
Wolfe, Thomas, *Web and the Rock, The*, Dell Book #LY-103, 1961, Bill Lyles told me only 640 copies of this edition were ever sold, scarce.	$15	$30	$75
Young, Chic, *Blondie & Dagwood in Footlight Folly*, Dell Books, no number (#1), 1947, paperback original.	$25	$75	$175

CANES AND WALKING STICKS

Canes and walking sticks have existed through the ages, first as staffs or symbols of authority. They evolved into a fashion accessory that might incorporate carved ivory, precious metals, jewels, porcelain and enamel.

Canes have also been a favorite form of expression for folk artists, with intricate pictorial carving on shafts and handles. Another category of interest to collectors features gadget canes or "system sticks" that contain hidden objects, from weapons to drinking flasks, telescopes, compasses and even musical instruments.

Agate and tortoiseshell with jewels, brown agate handle is 3 1/4" high and 1" at its widest. It is encased in four long gilded silver strands with dozens of turquoise and garnet stones set in raised bezels. There is a fancy 1" gilded silver collar on a slender tortoiseshell-veneer shaft that ends with a 1 1/4" brass and iron ferrule. It comes in original leather-covered case with brass fittings and gold velvet lining. The overall length is 37 1/4" and there is a small gap of normal age shrinkage just above the ferrule. Possibly French, circa 1880.. **$2,300**

Art glass with garnets, one-piece blown glass handle is 2 1/4" high with a gold-decorated flat knob top that is 1 1/8" in diameter. A 1/8" rose-cut garnet is at its center and there are several other tiny garnets in various locations. The handle has a central core of deep cobalt blue. The stem is octagonal-shaped and highlighted with bright gold areas that have tiny raised decoration. There is a 2/3" decorated gilded collar on a stepped partridgewood shaft with a 7/8" brass ferrule. The overall length is 34 1/3". A few of the tiny are garnets missing. Possibly continental, circa 1895..................... **$1,955**

Ball and hand, elephant ivory handle is 2 1/3" high and 1 1/2" at its widest. It is carved in the form of a hand clutching a ball. There are four ring separators, two of ebony. With 3/4" ivory ferrule. The overall length is 34 3/4". Possibly Anglo-Indian, circa 1890. .... **$431**

Battle of Gettysburg Memorial, made from a single piece of hickory, it has an "L" handle that is 4 3/4" to the side and 1 1/2" thick. The butt end of the handle is inscribed in ink: "Round Top" (probably where the wood was cut), "Gettysburg July 63", and "made Aug. 94". The entire cane is highlighted with poker-burned dots and lines under the finish. Extending down the shaft are inked images and identification of most of the Union units that fought at the Battle. There is a house marked "Mead's Headq'ters" above another marked "Lee's Headquarters". Created in fine detail, are monuments to, and identification of, 27 units that participated in the Battle, with where they fought identified on some of the images. A sampling of them includes the "8th Penn. Cavalry", "93rd. N.Y., Wolf Hill", "10th N.Y. Battery, Peach Orchard", "73rd Penn., Cemetery Hill", etc. It is signed at the base: "C.N. Sneads, Artist, Gettysburg". The piece ends with a 7/8" white metal ferrule. The overall length is 34 3/4". (The cane belonged to Rufus K. Hamlin, who fought with the Maine 12th Infantry and was the cousin of Hannibal Hamlin, prominent Maine politician and vice president under Lincoln.) **$2,990**

Bears motif, elephant ivory handle is 11 3/4" long and 1" at its widest. It depicts a chain of seven full-bodied bears standing on each other's backs. Signed in red characters by the maker. There is a 1/3" silver collar on a black enameled hardwood shaft and a 3/4" burnished brass ferrule. The overall length is 37". Possibly English with an imported handle, circa 1895... **$632**

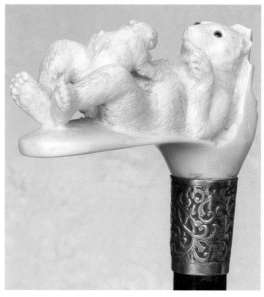

Photo courtesy Tradewinds Antiques & Auctions, Manchester-by-the-Sea, Mass.; www.TradewindsAntiques.com

Bears motif, elephant ivory "L" handle is 2 1/4" high and 4" to the side. It depicts a mother bear on her back, feeding her two cubs. Each bear has brown glass eyes. There is a 1 1/3" decorated silver collar on an ebony shaft with a 1" replaced brass ferrule. The overall length is 36 1/4". Possibly continental, circa 1890. **$460**

Beer or wine measure, elephant ivory handle is 2" high and 1 1/3" in diameter. The top is inlaid with a 1" gilt disc with an image of a stag with an arrow through its neck, presumably the logo of the maker. The cap unscrews and reveals the underside of the gilt disc that is marked "Enfield-Birmingham", probably the locations of the purveyor. A 36" long, round wooden measure can be withdrawn from the shaft. It is calibrated in inches as well as in markings to gauge the amount of the beer or wine that might remain in a cask. There is a 1/4" brass collar on a malacca shaft that ends with a 3 3/4" burnished brass and iron ferrule. The overall length is 37 1/4". It is English, circa 1850. .... **$1,380**

Bird motif, elephant ivory handle is 5 3/4" high and 1 3/4" at its widest. It depicts a stylized tropical bird with a long curved beak and 1/3" round abalone discs at the shoulders of its wings. Two carved feet are at the base. The shaft is dark-stained tropical wood with a crisscross pattern of incised carving that extends for 13". The cane ends with a 1" brass ferrule. The overall length is 35 1/2". Possibly South Pacific in origin and was made in about the mid-20th century. **$115**

Cat with animated mouth, painted wood and burl handle is 5" high and 2" at its widest. It depicts a white, brown and black domestic cat with yellow glass eyes. When a lever at its throat is engaged, the cat's mouth opens to reveal a pink interior. Upon release, it snaps shut on a strong spring. There is a 3/4" silver collar on a malacca shaft with a 1" horn ferrule. The overall length is 33 1/2". Possibly Black Forest, circa 1900. **$1,150**

Black man, mahogany handle is 3 1/4" high and 2 3/4" at its widest. It depicts the head of a black man with amber glass eyes and detailed features. There is a 1/3" lined brass collar on a dark palmwood shaft with round ivory eyelets and a 7/8" brass ferrule. The overall length is 35 3/4". Possibly Continental, circa 1880. .... **$316**

Boar's tusk, handle measures about 6 1/2" along the arc and is 1" at its widest point. It has mottled brown staining and is carved with decorative grooves. There is a 1 1/2" silver collar rimmed with two hammered rings and marked "Sterling". The shaft may be cherry with a 1 1/2" horn ferrule. The overall length is 36 1/4". American, circa 1895. .... **$230**

Cigar cutter and match safe, "L" silver handle is 2 1/8" high and 3 3/4" to the side. At the end, there is a cap that covers a spring-loaded device with a thin rod at its center. When a cigar was pushed downward on it, a hole was created that made a channel for smoking. At the shoulder of the handle, a lid provided access to a chamber for holding matches and the underside of the lid was scored as a striker. The stem of the handle is inscribed: "Willie Lewellen Palmer, 20th Hussars" and there is a registration number, the name and address of the Regent Street purveyor, as well as London hallmarks for 1902. The shaft is stepped partridgewood with a 3/4" worn brass ferrule. The overall length is 36". **$805**

Dagger cane, hardwood shaft is carved to simulate bamboo and it has a short knob top that is 7/8" high and 7/8" in diameter. Five and one quarter inches down the shaft there is a 2/3" silver collar London hallmarked

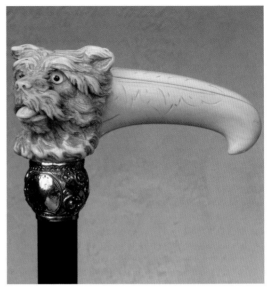

Dog motif, substantial elephant ivory "L" handle is 2 1/8" high and 5" to the side. It is incised with two long leaves and is carved at the shaft end with the shaggy head of a terrier with yellow glass eyes and tongue protruding. There is a 1 1/8" blown-out gold-filled collar that is decorated and initialed "C.G.H." The shaft is ebony with a 1" replaced brass ferrule. The overall length is 35 3/4". Possibly American, circa 1880. **$3,450**

for 1910. At that point the dagger can be withdrawn. It is 14" long, ends in a sharp point, and has a squared configuration. The cane ends with a 1 1/2" worn brass and iron ferrule. The overall length is 34 1/4", with some cosmetic repair to an age crack in the shaft. **$345**

Dog motif, elephant ivory "L" handle is 1 1/2" high and 4 1/4" long. It depicts a detailed greyhound with amber glass eyes. There is a 1/2" silver collar fashioned as a belt and buckle. The shaft is rosewood with a 7/8" replaced brass ferrule. The overall length is 33", with minor roughness on the ear tips. Probably English, circa 1880. .... **$805**

Dog motif, ivory and silver, walrus ivory "L" handle is 2 1/2" high and 3 3/4" to the side. It is overlaid with reticulated silver so the ivory shows through, and there are owner's initials on the end-cap. The silver is elaborately engraved with scrolls and the underside is scored for secure gripping. On the stem portion, a 3/4" silver face of a terrier is fashioned in high relief. The shaft is tan bamboo with a 3/4" worn brass ferrule. The overall length is 34 1/4" and the condition is very good. By style and appearance, the piece is undoubtedly American, circa 1870. .... **$1,150**

Eagle motif, elephant ivory "L" handle is 1 3/4" high and 4" to the side. It depicts a fierce looking eagle head with brown glass eyes. There is a 1/2" coin silver collar on a full-bark malacca shaft with a 7/8" burnished brass and iron ferrule. The overall length is 35". Probably American, circa 1870. .... **$4,830**

Eagle motif, German Art Deco, silver "L" handle is 2 3/4" high and 5" long. It is fashioned with lines and acute edges to give it a classic Art Deco flavor. It depicts an eagle with yellow glass eyes. It is marked "800" and "Geschutz" the mark meaning "registered" in Germany and Austria. The shaft is stepped partridgewood with a 1" worn brass and iron ferrule. The overall length is 34 1/2", with light denting of the bird's beak. It is circa 1920.. **$2,645**

Eating tools, silver collar, initialed "F.S.", is 1" high and 1 3/4" in diameter. It can be removed to reveal two compartments, one holding two ivory and pewter serving spoons, and the other two silver open salts. The compartments are designed to accept their contents in a tight fit. The shaft is thick hardwood with lacquered ring of whipping for decoration. About 11" down the shaft the cane opens again at a silver fitting to reveal eating implements placed in their own compartments. At the center is an ebony-handled carving knife, ringed by two sets of ivory and silver chopsticks, a pair of tools with twin tines, a metal knife sharpener, and a long pointed ivory device of unknown purpose. The cane ends with a 3 3/4" long metal ferrule. The overall length is 37". Possibly Chinese, circa 1900, exported to England. **$3,737**

English piqué and enamel, mid-17th century, elephant ivory cylindrical handle is 3 3/4" high and 1" in diameter. It is decorated in silver hollow dots, string inlay, and red and green enamel highlights. The top is decorated with a 3/4" circle rimmed with piqué. Around a solid smaller circle at the center is silver string inlay that identifies the maker, John Pointer. The sides are decorated with rings of piqué as well as lines of tiny spherules of green and red enamel that frame eight panels. The panels have birds, animals and flowers done in string inlay with enamel highlights. There is a 1/3" silver collar that is scalloped and punch-decorated in the style of the handle. The shaft is Malacca and terminates with a 4 1/2" brass ferrule with a rusty iron tip. The overall length is 37 7/8" and the general condition is very good with most of the piqué and string inlay still intact.. **$29,900**

English ivory piqué pomander, elephant ivory handle is 3 1/2" high and 1 1/3" in diameter. It has a lid that is decorated with a small central circle of piqué and eight star-shaped holes, as well as "R.C." for the owner and "92", (1692), in a frame of pique. The lid unscrews to reveal a shallow receptacle that was designed to hold a bit of wool or cloth that was soaked with healing herbs and potions that the user could sniff through the holes to ward off illness. The handle is pierced with eyelets for a cord, and it has a raised central ring. It is elaborately decorated with piqué in flowers and scrolls. There is a 1" silver collar with line decoration on a shaft of malacca with a 1 3/4" brass and iron ferrule. The overall length is 36 1/3". **$6,325**

Elephant on a horn ball, elephant ivory handle is 3 1/8" high and 2 1/8" at its widest. It depicts a baby elephant with pale yellow glass eyes, struggling to hold its footing on a large horn ball that is resting on an ivory pedestal. There is a 2/3" smooth silver collar on an exotic snakewood shaft with a 1 1/2" white metal and iron ferrule. The overall length is 38 1/2". Possibly American, circa 1900, an unusual interpretation of the circus theme. **$3,450**

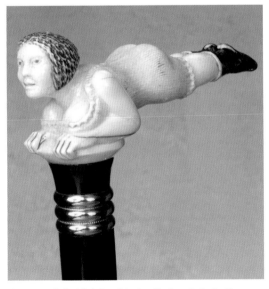

Female acrobat, walrus ivory "L" handle is 1 3/4" high and 4 3/4" to the side. It depicts a detailed performing acrobat. She is fully stretched out and is holding onto the edge of a stand. She has short brown hair, black boots and is wearing a short, form fitting costume with a revealing décolletage. There is a 2/3" ringed silver collar on a black hardwood shaft with a 1" horn ferrule. The overall length is 36". Possibly French, circa 1880. **$1,150**

Fire screen/sunshade, plain silver handle is 1 3/4" high and 1 1/4" in diameter. There are worn hallmarks, perhaps French. The handle unscrews at its mid-point to reveal a 3/4" upright ivory knob in an acorn shape. By gently lifting the knob, a 6 3/4" pleated, round, stiff-linen screen emerges from a cardboard storage tube to which it is attached. It is painted with purple flowers and green leaves with brown stems. The screen is in good condition. The shaft is dark bamboo with a 1" white metal and iron ferrule. The overall length is 36" and the condition is very good with some wear to the silver at the lower half of the handle. It is circa 1870. Fire screen/sunshades were used by women to protect their complexions from the heat of open fireplaces, and also from the sun. **$2,300**

Folk art, polychrome, made from a single piece of hardwood, it has a thin 1" tin disc affixed with a nail as a protector at the top. It has a crazed, painted finish. There is a brown and red eagle, a long brown snake, a bathing beauty in a modest red suit, a black sailboat with three masts, a red cricket, a red, green and brown bulls-eye, another bather in green and red, a brown and red rooster, a brown and red airplane with open cockpit and pilot, a brown and green star, a boat with red keel, a dirigible, and a brown fox. The piece ends with a 2/3" brass homemade pipe ferrule. The overall length is 34". American, circa 1915, found in the Midwest. **$575**

Frog motif, stained elephant ivory handle is 3 1/4" high and 2" at its widest. It depicts a greenish frog with brown glass eyes sitting on the 1/2" silver collar at the top of the cane. The shaft is tan bamboo with a 7/8" replaced brass ferrule. The overall length is 36 1/3". Probably English, circa 1890. .... **$2,415**

GAR veteran's cane, by Edwin H. Smith. Fashioned from a single piece of basswood, it has a burnished bronze octagonal handle that is 1" high and 1 1/8" in diameter. It is carved for its entire length in raised relief. Below the handle is an American flag around which is inscribed: "In God We Trust" and "We Will Stand By The Flag". There are numerous GAR corps badges around a long encircling ribbon that says: "To William J. Copeland from Edwin H. Smith, National Soldiers Home, Va.". A 1 1/2" white metal and iron ferrule completes the piece. The overall length is 34 3/4". It is circa 1885. (The carver, Edwin H. Smith, was a disabled veteran who served as a private in the N.Y. 72nd Infantry. He was wounded and discharged for disability in 1863. William J. Copeland was a private in the N.Y. 123rd Infantry and was discharged in 1865. Smith carved canes for comrades at several of the Soldiers Homes.) **$1,725**

Gargoyle, Art Nouveau, silver "L" handle is 3" high and 4 1/2" to the side. It depicts a gargoyle with the head of a wild cat, long wings, a scaly snake's body, and claws of a raptor. There are French hallmarks as well as those of a maker. The shaft is ebony with a 1" worn brass and iron ferrule. The overall length is 37 1/4", with some wear to the shaft's finish. It is circa 1900. .... **$1,150**

Gun cane, 19th century, smoothbore, .36 caliber, 28 3/4" steel barrel, threaded at breech. Brass mount to horn handle. **$1,092**

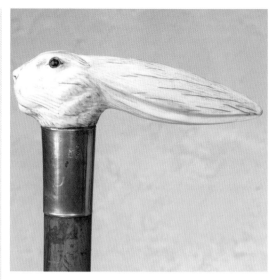

Photo courtesy Tradewinds Antiques & Auctions, Manchester-by-the-Sea, Mass.; www.TradewindsAntiques.com

Hare motif, elephant ivory "L" handle is 4 1/2" to the side and 1 1/4" at its widest. It depicts a detailed long-eared hare with brown glass eyes. There is a 1 1/2" smooth sterling collar Chester hallmarked for 1862. The shaft is malacca with a 1 1/2" burnished brass and iron ferrule. The overall length is 34". **$690**

Gun cane, Remington dog head, "L" handle is 2 1/3" high and 3 1/4" long. It depicts the Remington gutta-percha large hound head. It has the model number "539" near the base of the handle. There is a 1/3" lined nickel collar and the gun unscrews 7" down the shaft so that a .32 caliber rim-fire cartridge could be inserted. It is cocked with a straight pull that allows a notched gun sight to pop up. A round trigger under the handle fires the piece and all mechanics are in working order. The shaft is covered in gutta-percha that is all intact except for a small semi-circular chip near the opening. Some of the Remington marks on the surface of the gutta-percha above the opening are faint and barely visible using a strong glass. However, the patent date "Feb. 9, 1858" is visible as is "N.Y." from the Remington address in Ilion. The piece ends with a 1 3/4" hollow nickel ferrule. The overall length is 35 1/4". Circa 1860s. **$9,200**

Gun cane, Remington percussion, semi-crook gutta-percha handle is about 4" long and 1" thick. Below it is a 1/3" lined nickel collar. The remainder of the shaft is gutta-percha veneer. The piece unscrews 4 1/4" down the shaft so it could be loaded. It cocks with a pull that allows a notched sight to pop up, and so that a percussion cap could be placed on the hollow nib. After closing it was fired by a round trigger below the handle that caused a hammer to strike the percussion cap. All mechanics are working. There is a 2" hollow steel ferrule that is marked: "T.E.. Thomas, patent Feb. 9, 1858, Remington & Sons, Ilion, N.Y." and the registration number "12" which means it was the 12th number of this model made. Since the percussion type was the first gun cane made by Remington, this piece would be one of the earliest examples. The overall length is 34 1/2". **$5,462**

Hunting motif, made of a single piece of elephant ivory, the pistol-grip handle is 8" high and 2 1/2" to the side. It is carved on the stem portion in high relief. Depicted is a hound with a calling horn on a cord around its neck. There is also a flintlock rifle and powder horn, a dagger in a sheath, and a game bag hung on a tree branch. Finally, there is the head of a majestic elk sporting a large antler rack. At the base of the handle there is an etched and inked ducal crown along with owner's initials above a carved ivory belt and buckle. The overall length is 34 3/4" with an almost imperceptible tiny chip on the side of the hound's nose. It is continental, circa 1850. .... **$4,312**

Andrew Jackson, presentation cane, gold and hickory, solid gold knob, tested to be at least 18k, is 1 1/3" high and 1" in diameter. Inscribed on top is "Andrew Jackson to Silas E. Burrows, June 12th, 1832". The sides of the handle have two decorated raised rings. The shaft is crooked, natural hickory with fancy gold eyelets and a 5 1/4" burnished brass and rusted iron ferrule. The overall length is 38 1/4" and the condition is very good with some minor loss of bark above the ferrule. (Jackson and Burrows are linked in U.S. history to the creation of a monument for Mary Ball Washington, George Washington's mother. When her grave was in jeopardy of being moved, Burrows wrote the mayor of Fredericksburg, Va., protesting the removal and offered to pay for a monument to be erected at her chosen site. In 1833, Jackson laid the cornerstone for the Burrows Monument. Because the date on the cane is 1832, the year before the dedication ceremony, it is believed that it was a gift from Jackson to thank Burrows. Burrows, the stonemason and the contractor all died before the monument could be completed, leaving the project in disarray. It was not completed until Grover Cleveland's administration in 1894.) **$9,200**

Jade ball, handle is 1 1/2" diameter and it rests on a silver "crown" mount. The mount has eight points that cradle the stone that is moss green with mottled white shading. The silver is engraved with a cloverleaf maker's mark. The heavy shaft is exotic snakewood. It terminates with a 7/8" replaced brass ferrule. The overall length is 36 1/4" and the condition is very good with a small area of surface roughness near the top of the jade ball. Possibly continental, circa 1900. .... **$1,150**

Jolly monk, handle is 3" high and 2" at its widest. It depicts a smiling monk with his face carved in elephant ivory and wearing a carved wood cloak. There is a 1 1/4" decorated silver collar on a full-bark malacca shaft with a 1" replaced brass ferrule. The overall length is 37 1/2". Possibly English, circa 1880. .... **$1,955**

Monkeys clinging to a tree, handle made of elephant ivory over snakewood is 2 1/2" high and 2" at its widest. It depicts a pair of long-tailed monkeys with arms, legs and tails intertwined on the side of a tree, with an ivory umbrella of palm fronds at the top. The monkeys have dark-brown glass eyes. There is a 1 1/3" gilt silver collar decorated with "C" scrolls and a shield cartouche. The shaft is dark exotic wood with a 1" white metal and iron ferrule. The overall length is 37". Probably English, circa 1905. .... **$1,495**

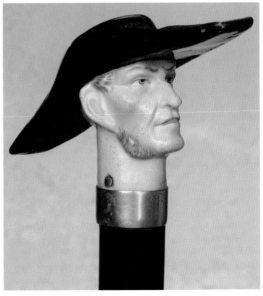

Photo courtesy Tradewinds Antiques & Auctions, Manchester-by-the-Sea, Mass.; www.TradewindsAntiques.com

Lady's leg, walrus ivory "L" handle is 1 1/4" high and 4 1/4" to the side. It depicts a young lady's leg in a pointed-toes pose. There is a 1 1/2" scroll-decorated silver collar on a rosewood shaft with a 7/8" black horn ferrule. The overall length is 34 1/4". Possibly English, circa 1910. **$690**

Photo courtesy Tradewinds Antiques & Auctions, Manchester-by-the-Sea, Mass.; www.TradewindsAntiques.com

Man with a long hat, porcelain handle is 2 1/4" high, 4 1/2" long and 1 3/4" at its widest. It depicts a fashionable man with a very long black hat. There are blue maker's marks in the porcelain on the back of his neck. There is a 1/2" silver collar on a black hardwood shaft with a 1" replaced brass ferrule. The overall length is 34 3/4". Possibly Italian, circa 1880. **$2,300**

Franklin Murphy, Governor of New Jersey, elephant ivory handle is 1 1/2" high and 4 2/3" long. It is relief-carved with classical scrolls and is accented with 15 small, beaded silver bars. It has a fancy end cap that is initialed "F.M." for Franklin Murphy. There is 7/8" silver collar that matches the end cap. It is inscribed with Murphy's Newark, N.J., address and is also marked: "Gorham Mfg. Co., Sterling". The shaft is exotic coromandel that ends with a 1 1/2" white metal and iron ferrule. The overall length is 36 3/4". It is circa 1890. (Franklin Murphy [1846-1920] served in the Union Army during the Civil War, fighting at Antietam, Chancellorsville, Gettysburg and the Atlanta Campaign. He then was active in commerce and New Jersey politics and eventually became governor.) **$1,840**

Nautical cane with fist, whale ivory handle is 2 1/2" high and 1 1/2" wide. It depicts a detailed clenched fist with a hole for a carrying cord. The lower portion of the handle is octagonal-carved and blends into the thick palm wood shaft, also octagonal-carved for 11 1/2", and then a smooth taper. (Such configuration was in vogue in cane construction from about 1840 to about 1860.) A 1/3" old hand-made brass ferrule completes the piece. The overall length is 33 3/4". Probably American, circa 1850. ...... **$3,680**

Nude maiden, German Art Nouveau, silver crook handle measures about 7 1/2" long and is 1 1/3" at its widest. It depicts a nude maiden astride a fish among other swimming fish, cattails and reeds. It is inscribed on a ring at the base: "Geschuz" (registered) and "900", for the silver purity, and there are maker's marks. It is mounted on a shaft of macassar ebony with a 1 1/3" black horn ferrule. The overall length is 36 1/4". Circa 1900. .... **$1,380**

Odd Fellows, made of a single piece of elephant ivory, the knob handle is 3 7/8" high and 1 2/3" in diameter. The top is inlaid with a 3/4" silver disc that is engraved with Odd Fellows symbols including the three-link chain and the heart in hand. There is a 3/4" coin silver collar that is inscribed: "John Morrill, Nashua N.H." and "Feb. 5, 1844". The shaft is rosewood with round silver eyelets and a 3 1/3" brass and iron ferrule. The overall length is 34 2/3", with age lines at the top of the ivory knob. (John Merrill was a blacksmith and a founding member of the Grand Lodge of Odd Fellows established in Nashua on Sept. 11, 1843.) **$431**

Pike with a trout, elephant ivory "L" handle is 1 1/2" high and 4" to the side. It depicts a full-bodied pike grasping its prey, a small trout, in its jaws. Each fish has yellow glass eyes. There is a 1 1/2" gold-filled collar fashioned as a buckle on a honey-toned malacca shaft with a 1" burnished brass and iron ferrule. The overall length is 36". Probably American, circa 1890. .... **$805**

Pistol grip, damascene handle is 3" high and 1 1/2" at its widest. It is decorated in two colors of gold with several differently styled panels that feature the distinctive flying dragon seen on pieces made in Toledo, Spain. The shaft is snakewood. It terminates with a 1" brass and iron ferrule. The overall length is 35 3/4". It is circa 1900. .... **$3,220**

Pitch pipe, ivory and silver handle is 2 1/2" long and 3/4" thick. It is made with eight blowing holes that are marked with various major and minor keys, (A, D, G, F, etc.) There are vent holes on the underside to expel the air, and it is in working order. There is a 1 2/3" silver collar on a fine snakewood shaft with a 1" brass ferrule. The overall length

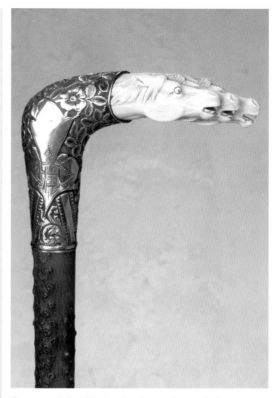

Photo courtesy Tradewinds Antiques & Auctions, Manchester-by-the-Sea, Mass.; www.TradewindsAntiques.com

Racing horses, ivory and silver, elephant ivory and silver "L" handle is 3 1/3" high and 4 1/4" to the side. Three racing horses are carved nose to nose in a racing motif and are rendered in fine detail. The silver portion of the handle is chased in flowers and leaves and there is an unusually fashioned cartouche with owner's initials, "A.H." It is also marked "Sterling." The shaft is scarred medlar with a 1 1/2" white metal and iron ferrule. (Medlar is a flowering shrub whose branches were scarred with a special tool while still growing. When harvested, it has an unusual texture.) The overall length is 34 1/4" and the condition is very good. It is American, circa 1895. **$1,495**

is 34" and the condition is very good. Possibly English, circa 1900. .... **$1,725**

Pool cue, textured silver knob handle is 1 1/2" high and 1 1/4" in diameter. It unscrews from a rosewood shaft in order to withdraw the long maple end of a cue stick. After removing the 7/8" brass ferrule, the maple end can be screwed into the shaft to form a real working cue. The ferrule can be screwed into the silver handle for safe-keeping, and when the handle is re-attached to the rosewood shaft, the 58" cue is ready to have a fresh cue tip affixed to the ivory top for use. The overall length when a cane is 34", with minor dents in the silver handle and some surface cracks in the rosewood. Possibly English, circa 1900. .... **$977**

a total of 5 1/4". Within each separate chamber is a freely moving whalebone ball that rolls up and down as the cane is tilted. (This type of whimsy is often seen in wood "ball and chamber" canes.) The carving continues down the shaft with an area of tiny diamond configuration, then fluting with lines, and finally, rope-twist above a short tapered base. It never had a ferrule. The overall length is 33 1/4" and the condition is very good. It is quite straight indicating that it came from the center of the panbone. Possibly American, circa 1850............ **$21,850**

Shakespeare motif, elephant ivory handle is 3 1/4" high and 1 1/4" at its widest. It depicts a detailed bust of William Shakespeare on a fancy base. There is a 1" textured silver collar on a Macassar ebony shaft with a 1 2/3" white metal and iron ferrule. The overall length is 37 1/2" and the condition is very good. It is English, circa 1880. .... **$690**

Shibayama, Japanese ivory, one-piece elephant ivory handle is 8" long and 7/8" in diameter. It is inlaid in the Shibayama manner with various colored hard stones and mother-of-pearl, as well as having inked etching. It depicts a multicolored bird perched in a trailing floral vine. All of the inlay is intact. It is signed in an oval cartouche by the Japanese artist. There is a 3/4" sterling collar inscribed, "Nina," and there are London hallmarks for 1913. The shaft is figured snakewood with a 7/8" burnished brass and iron ferrule. The overall length is 37 1/4" and the condition is excellent.. **$1,150**

Shibayama insects, elephant ivory "L" handle is 1 1/4" high and 3 3/4" long. It is scored on the underside for a better grip and there are eight different insects randomly inlaid in the Japanese Shibayama manner. They are fashioned with various polished hardstones, mother-of-pearl and abalone, with each insect having etched legs and antennae. It is signed by the maker. There is a 1" silver collar with a presentation done in initials. The shaft is malacca with a 3/4" ivory ferrule. The overall length is 33". Probably fashioned in England with an imported handle, circa 1890. .... **$3,220**

Silver and turquoise enamel, cylindrical silver handle is 3" high and 7/8" in diameter. Inlaid on top is a 3/4" turquoise colored guilloche-worked enamel disc rimmed with a thin vermeil ring, and another of white enamel. Below the top is a ring of silver acanthus leaves, a white enamel ring, and then the long turquoise enamel body, also worked in guilloche. Another white enamel ring as well as one of silver acanthus leaves completes the decoration on the handle. The base is marked "925" and there are hallmarks, perhaps Irish. The shaft is dark brown hardwood with a 1" horn ferrule. The overall length is 36". First half of the 20th century...................................... **$1,725**

Snake and frog, folk art made from a single piece of wood, perhaps red oak, it has a black-painted round knob handle that is 1" high and 1 1/3" in diameter. The top is inlaid with a round disc and six teardrops of mother of pearl. There are pale blue beads inlaid around the sides. Below the handle, a green and black frog is wrapped around the shaft, above a thick black ring. Below the ring is a long, menacing snake painted black and green. The snake has a forked tongue of copper protruding out of its red mouth as well as mother-of-pearl eyes. Its long body encircles the shaft all the way down. A 2" gilded metal homemade ferrule completes the piece. The overall length is 36". Possibly American, circa 1900. .... **$488**

Photo courtesy Tradewinds Antiques & Auctions, Manchester-by-the-Sea, Mass.; www.TradewindsAntiques.com

Rose quartz and crystal, rose quartz handle is 2" high and 1 1/4" in diameter. One large and two smaller rock-crystal rings span the handle. The quartz is pale pink with the internal crystalline fissures for which this stone is noted. The shaft is ebony and it never had a ferrule. The overall length is 37 ". Probably American, circa 1890. **$1,725**

Rock crystal, enamel and silver with an amethyst stone, cylindrical handle is 3 1/2" high and 3/4" in diameter. The top is fully inlaid with a faceted amethyst set into a guilloche-turned silver mount with blue enamel rings as highlights. The long tapered rock crystal stem is surmounted with a double festoon of silver laurel roping. A 1/2" silver mount at the base has matching blue enamel showing through the reticulated silver, and there are continental hallmarks. The shaft is natural applewood with a 1 2/3" white metal and iron ferrule. The overall length is 36". It is circa 1900. .... **$1,495**

Roman Empress, large elephant ivory handle is 4 3/4" high and 2 1/4" at its widest. It depicts the bust of a Roman lady, perhaps Pompeia, the wife of Julius Caesar, upon a plinth, adorned in regal finery. The shaft is honey-toned malacca with a 1 1/4" horn ferrule. It is staff length at 41 1/4", with a fine creamy patina. Possibly Continental, circa 1860. .... **$7,475**

Sailor's whimsy nautical cane, whale ivory handle is 1 3/4" high and 1 1/3" in diameter. The round top is done in melon configuration with concentric grooves meeting at the center. There is another 2 1/2" of octagonal-carved whale ivory that joins the whalebone shaft that is carved as follows: There are two chambers with concave posts that measure

Stallion motif, elephant ivory handle is 1 1/2" high and 3 3/4" long. It depicts a detailed stallion with brown glass eyes, mouth agape, veins protruding and a flowing mane. There is a decorated sterling collar initialed "F.H.B." in script with Birmingham hallmark for 1913. The shaft is honey-toned malacca with a 1" replaced brass ferrule. The overall length is 35 3/4"... **$862**

"Sunday Stick" golf driver, elephant ivory handle measures about 3" long and is 1 1/2" at its widest point. It is fashioned as a golf driver complete with a simulated foot and a simulated weight on the side opposite the club-face, much like the construction of an early club. It is inscribed with "special". There is a 2/3" brass collar on a dark bamboo shaft with a 7/8" replaced brass ferrule. The overall length is 35". It is English, circa 1900. (Canes fashioned as golf clubs were sometimes called "Sunday Sticks" because some avid golfers liked to stroll on the golf course sporting their club canes on Sundays when playing was not allowed.).. **$517**

Sword cane, ivory and malacca, elephant ivory knob handle is 2" high and 1 1/3" in diameter. There is a 1/3" silver collar on a malacca shaft with silver oval eyelets followed by a 2/3" silver band. At that point a 15 1/2" triangular short sword can be withdrawn from a tight and well-hidden juncture. A 5 1/4" burnished brass and iron ferrule completes the piece. It has numerous dings and a slight bend from two centuries of age and use. The overall length is 36". American, circa 1790. .... **$1,150**

Sword cane, 1826, stag horn and gold, straight stag-horn handle is 3 1/2" high and 1 1/2" at its widest. There is a square solid gold cartouche on top that is engraved with a Masonic square and compass. There is a 7/8" solid gold collar inscribed: "Presented to Br. Edw'd Arents by Morton Lodge No. 108 as a testimony of esteem, N.Y. Aug. 17th, AL5826 (Masonic method of dating for 1826)". The shaft is dark bamboo with gold oval eyelets ending with a 2 2/3" brass ferrule. At the second step of the bamboo, the sword withdraws from a well-hidden juncture. It is 27 1/2" long, in early concave "small sword" configuration, with 12" of engraving. The overall length is 36"............................ **$1,150**

Sword cane, with quillons, silver knob handle is 1 1/8" high and 1 1/4" in diameter. It has a round cartouche on top that contains an applied silver ducal crown. The body of the handle is also engraved in a floral pattern. Six inches down the malacca shaft there is a 1/3" silver band at which point the blade can be withdrawn with a straight pull from a tight fitting. As it is withdrawn, two brass spring-driven quillons (hand guards) snap into place. The 23 1/3" steel blade is diamond-shaped and comes to a sharp point. The cane ends with a 1 1/4" worn metal ferrule. The overall length is 36". Possibly continental, circa 1885. .... **$1,610**

Thousand Faces motif, sterling knob handle is 2" high and 1" in diameter. It is London hallmarked for 1895 and "J.H." for the English maker. It is fashioned "a la japonais" with 14 round smiling faces in raised repousse. The shaft is malacca with a 1 1/8" burnished brass and iron ferrule. The overall length is 36"..................................... **$1,035**

Webb cameo glass, ball handle is 1 1/2" in diameter. It is fashioned with off-white clematis leaves, vines and flowers on a deep blue background that has a lightly glossed finish. It is beautifully crafted resembling a cameo, hence the name. (English cameo glass was produced primarily by Thomas Webb, the inventor of this glassmaking technique in which a design was etched onto the surface of blown glass with white acid.) There is a 1/3" gold collar on a malacca shaft with a 1 1/2" old brass and iron ferrule. The overall length is 35 1/2". English, circa 1895............. **$2,185**

Whale ivory and whalebone, with mother of pearl, single whale tooth handle is 3 1/2" high and 1 1/3" in diameter at the flat knob top. It is line decorated and inlaid with a large 1" MOP disc on top. There is a 1/4" baleen separator on a whalebone shaft that is octagonal-carved for 13" followed by 1" of angled lines, then twist-carved for the remaining 16 3/4". It never had a ferrule. The overall length is 34 1/2". It is American and undoubtedly sailor-made, circa 1860. .... **$3,737**

Whale ivory and whalebone, with elaborate inlay, constructed of two pieces, the whale ivory handle measures about 5" along the arc and is 2" wide at the foot end. There is a 2/3" oval inlay of exotic wood set into the foot and two ring spacers set off the parts of the handle. Going down the shaft there is 6 1/2" of elaborate inlay done in whale ivory and exotic wood. The decoration includes rings, squares, spherules and triangles. The remainder of the shaft is a smooth taper ending in a 2/3" brass ferrule. The overall length is 34". Possibly English, circa 1860.................. **$8,625**

Ceramics

CERAMICS, AMERICAN

Also see Tiffany, Redware, Stoneware.

Arequipa

Arequipa Sanatorium operated in Marin County north of San Francisco, treating tuberculosis patients from 1911-1918. The facility's art directors included Frederick Rhead, Albert Solon and Fred Wilde.

Batchelder and Brown

Ernest Allan Batchelder founded the Batchelder Tile Co. in Pasadena, Calif., in 1909. He took on Frederick L. Brown as his partner, renaming the pottery Batchelder and Brown in 1912. The firm closed in 1932.

Batchelder, triptych of an ox cart caravan with blue engobe. A few small chips to edges, some grout on back. No visible mark. 8" x 18" each....................................**$5,100**

Burley, and Burley Winter

Several generations of the Burley and Winter families operated potteries in and around the Ohio communities of Crooksville, Zanesville and Mt. Sterling from the early 19th to the early 20th centuries.

Photo courtesy Belhorn Auction Services LLC, Columbus, Ohio; www.Belhorn.com

Burley Winter, floor vase with Grecian women and green over brick red glazes. Marked 'Burley Winter, Crooksville, O.' Mint. 17" h x 10 1/2" w. **$575**

Photo courtesy Rago Arts and Auction Center, Lambertville, N.J.; www.RagoArts.com

Arequipa flaring bowl by Frederick Rhead, its interior decorated in squeezebag with clusters of stylized trees in front of dark mountains and white clouds. (One of only a few Arequipa landscapes known). Ink mark with Arequipa California 269. 2 1/4" x 6 1/4" d. **$20,400**

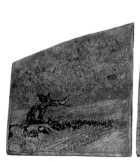

Photo courtesy Rago Arts and Auction Center, Lambertville, N.J.; www.RagoArts.com

Batchelder and Brown early and large triptych of pumpkin field. (Featured in the exposition, "California Tile: The Golden Era 1910-1940," The California Heritage Museum, Santa Monica, 2001.) A few small edge chips. Stamped BATCHELDER PASADENA. 19 1/2" x 63". **$10,800**

Rose Cabat

Rose Cabat, born 1914, New York, is a Tucson, Ariz.-based potter known for her "feelies" — small, narrow-necked porcelain pots with soft glazes that feel feathery to the touch.

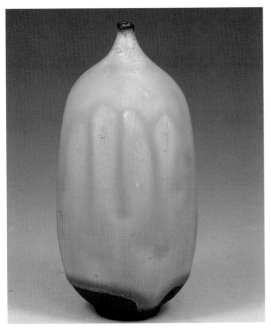

Photo courtesy Belhorn Auction Services LLC, Columbus, Ohio; www.Belhorn.com

Rose Cabat "Feelie" in turquoise with color streaking down the sides. Marked 841 Cabat 48. Mint. 3 3/4" h x 1 5/8" w. **$500**

Photo courtesy Belhorn Auction Services LLC, Columbus, Ohio; www.Belhorn.com

Rose Cabat fig "Feelie" with shades of lime green and tan. Marked Cabat 12 43. Mint. 3 1/8" h x 2" w. **$575**

Photo courtesy Belhorn Auction Services LLC, Columbus, Ohio; www.Belhorn.com

Rose Cabat "Feelie" with rare performance trial glaze. Marked 84T Cabat 28N. Mint. 2 1/2" h x 2 1/4" w. **$700**

Opening page:

Photo courtesy Belhorn Auction Services LLC, Columbus, Ohio; www.Belhorn.com

Rose Cabat minaret "Feelie" with subtle glaze treatment. Marked Cabat 841 38P. Mint. 3 5/8" h x 1 3/4" w. **$800**

Camark

Camark Art Tile and Pottery Co. operated in Camden, Ark., from 1926 until the mid-1970s. Art director John Lessell created many of the firm's distinctive glazes.

Camark, Blue Crackle Bright folded-rim vase in deep cobalt blue with gold crackle effect. Marked with die impressed Arkansas stamp. 7 1/8" h x 7 3/8" w. **$700**

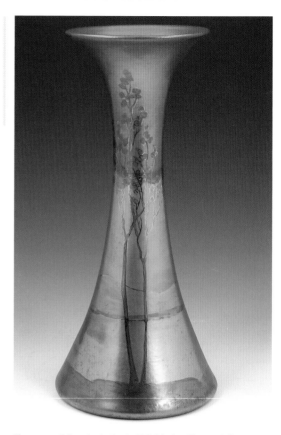

Photo courtesy Belhorn Auction Services LLC, Columbus, Ohio; www.Belhorn.com

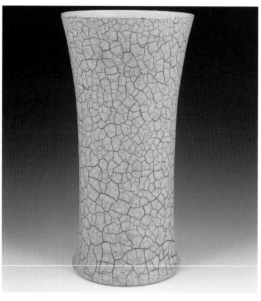

Photo courtesy Belhorn Auction Services LLC, Columbus, Ohio; www.Belhorn.com

Camark, Ivory Crackle Matte vase. Marked with a gold Arkansas ink stamp over an impressed mark. Mint. 10 3/8" h x 5 1/4" w. **$525**

Camark Lessell, tapered trumpet vase with scene of trees on a lake with deep red upper sky and golden iridescent tones. Marked Lessell. 10" h. **$1,100**

Photo courtesy Belhorn Auction Services LLC, Columbus, Ohio; www.Belhorn.com

Photo courtesy Belhorn Auction Services LLC, Columbus, Ohio; www.Belhorn.com

Camark, Jeanne vase with a plethora of iridescent flowers on a black background with gold trim. 9 3/8" h x 4 3/4" w. **$800**

Camark Lessell (LeCamark), vase with scene of trees on a lake with deep red upper sky and golden iridescent tones. Marked Le-Camark. 6" h. **$675**

Camark Lessell (LeCamark), vase with scene of palm trees on a shore, mountains in the far background and the sun behind a cloud. Decorated in iridescent gold and bronze tones. Marked Le-Camark. 9 7/8" h x 5" w. **$925**

Clewell Pottery Co., (Canton, Ohio, 1902-1940, 1951-1965) copper-clad vase with a good verdigris patina. Incised Clewell 351-2-9. 7" x 3 3/4". **$1,320**

Clifton Art Pottery

The Clifton Art Pottery, Newark, N.J., was established by William A. Long, once associated with Lonhuda Pottery, and Fred Tschirner, a chemist.

Production consisted of two major lines: Crystal Patina, which resembled true porcelain with a subdued crystal-like glaze, and Indian Ware or Western Influence, an adaptation of the American Indians' unglazed and decorated pottery with a high-glazed black interior. Other lines included Robin's-Egg Blue and Tirrube. Robin's-Egg Blue is a variation of the Crystal Patina line, but in blue-green instead of straw-colored hues and with a less-prominent crushed-crystal effect in the glaze. Tirrube, which is often artist signed, features brightly colored, slip-decorated flowers on a terra-cotta ground.

Marks are incised or impressed. Early pieces may be dated and impressed with a shape number. Indian wares are identified by tribes.

Clewell Pottery Co. (Canton, Ohio, 1902-1940, 1951-1965) tall copper-clad vase, modeled around a stylized Arts & Crafts landscape, rare. Fine original patina. A few splits to copper. Pottery body stamped X2. 13 1/2" x 4". **$3,900**

Clifton, vases (two) in matte green glaze, one embossed with poppies. Both marked, poppy vase hand-incised Clifton First Fire October 1905. 5 1/2" and 6 1/2". **$1,200 pair**

J.B. Cole, Seagrove, N.C., vase with ring handles attributed to Waymon Cole with chrome red treatment. Unmarked. Excellent condition. 16 1/2" h x 16" w. **$675**

Common Ground, (Madison, Wis.), tile, contemporary, calla lily design, held in an Arts & Crafts-style frame, marked, signed by Eric Olson, #262, 8" sq. $75

Cowan Pottery

R. Guy Cowan was born in 1884 in East Liverpool, Ohio, and educated at the New York State School of Ceramics at Alfred. He founded the Cowan Pottery Studio in Lakewood, Ohio (a suburb of Cleveland) in 1912. The firm closed in 1931.

Cowan, Art Deco figurine titled, "Introspection." Finish in black semi-matte glaze. Designed by A. Drexler Jacobson, the piece is marked with die-impressed circular Cowan mark and the artist's monogram on the plinth. Mint and uncrazed. 8 3/8" h. **$1,600**

Cowan, Elephant bookends in Oriental Red by Margaret Postgate. Marked with die-impressed circular Cowan mark and COWAN in die-impressed letters. Mint and uncrazed. 7 3/8" h. **$1,000 pair**

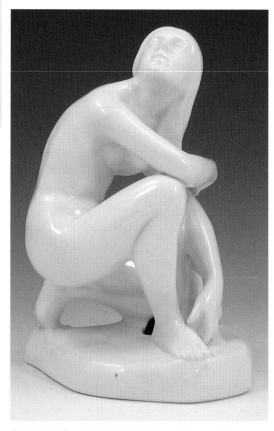

Cowan, Kneeling Nude flower figure in Original Ivory attributed to Walter Sinz. Unmarked. Mint and uncrazed. 6" h. **$800**

*Cowan, Lorelei
lamp base in April
Green by Wayland
Gregory. Marked
COWAN in die-
impressed letters.
There is a tight 1"
stress line to the
base. 16 3/4" h.*
$875

*Cowan, F-9 Pan flower figure in Special Ivory. Marked with
die-impressed circular Cowan mark and COWAN in die-
impressed letters and F9 in crayon. Mint. 9 3/8" h.* **$325**

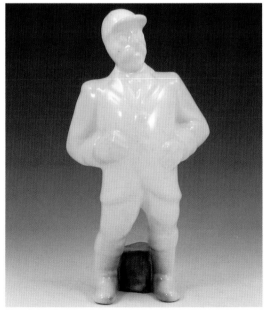

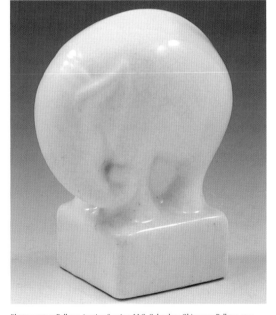

*Cowan, Hunting Set, Standing Gentleman in Shadow
White. Marked COWAN in die-impressed letters. Mint.
7 3/4" h.* **$350**

*Cowan, D-3 elephant paperweight designed by Margaret
Postgate (circa 1930) in ivory semi-gloss glaze. Marked
with die-impressed circular Cowan mark and COWAN in
die-impressed letters. Mint. 4 3/8" h x 3 1/2" w.* **$300**

Photo courtesy Belhorn Auction Services LLC, Columbus, Ohio; www.Belhorn.com

Cowan, V-99 handled vase in Lemon yellow designed by Viktor Schreckengost. Marked twice with die-impressed circular Cowan mark and V99 in black crayon. 6" h. **$375**

Photo courtesy Belhorn Auction Services LLC, Columbus, Ohio; www.Belhorn.com

Cowan, V-99 vase by Viktor Schreckengost in Egyptian Blue. Marked with die-impressed circular Cowan mark and V99 in black crayon. Mint. 5" h x 7" w. **$300**

Photo courtesy Belhorn Auction Services LLC, Columbus, Ohio; www.Belhorn.com

Cowan, #552 vase with Mulberry over Copper flambe. Marked Cowan Pottery 552 in block letters. 7 1/2" h. **$240**

Photo courtesy Belhorn Auction Services LLC, Columbus, Ohio; www.Belhorn.com

Cowan, V-853-A Modernist or Stepped Parfait vase in April Green. Marked with die-impressed circular Cowan mark. Mint. 5 7/8" h x 4 5/8" w. **$450**

Photo courtesy Belhorn Auction Services LLC, Columbus, Ohio; www.Belhorn.com

Cowan, V-932 vase in uncommon Feu Rouge glaze. Marked with die-impressed circular Cowan mark and COWAN in die-impressed letters. Mint and uncrazed. 8" h. **$290**

Photo courtesy Belhorn Auction Services LLC, Columbus, Ohio; www.Belhorn.com

Cowan, #933 vase in Feu Rouge. Marked with die-impressed circular Cowan mark and 933 in black crayon. Mint. 5 1/2" h. **$230**

Photo courtesy Belhorn Auction Services LLC, Columbus, Ohio; www.Belhorn.com

R. Guy Cowan, mustard pot, rare and early, with sterling silver lid by Horace E. Potter and an ivory finial. The spoon is also ivory and marked "FRANCE." Incised with RGC monogram and signed R.G. Cowan. Mint. 4 1/4" h x 2 7/8" w. **$3,000**

Photo courtesy Belhorn Auction Services LLC, Columbus, Ohio; www.Belhorn.com

Cowan, vase with unusual matrix glaze of purple and yellow. Marked with die-impressed circular Cowan mark. Also marked with illegible shape notation and 881X/Purple. Mint and uncrazed. 6 1/2" h x 4 3/4" w. **$525**

Photo courtesy Rago Arts and Auction Center, Lambertville, N.J.; www.RagoArts.com

Albert Cusick exceptional and tall vase, probably done at the Craven Art Pottery, East Liverpool, Ohio, completely decorated in squeeze bag with a large scenic band flanked by curvilinear flowers and tulips in polychrome. Cusick's work of this caliber is extremely rare. Incised Cusick on side. 14 1/2" x 5". **$9,000**

Dedham Pottery

Alexander W. Robertson established a pottery in Chelsea, Mass., in about 1866. After his brother, Hugh Cornwall Robertson, joined him in 1868, the firm was called A. W. & H. C. Robertson. Their father, James Robertson, joined his sons in 1872, and the name Chelsea Keramic Art Works Robertson and Sons was used.

The pottery's initial products were simple flower and bean pots, but the firm quickly expanded its output to include a wide variety of artistic pottery. It produced a fine redware body used in classical forms, some with black backgrounds imitating ancient Greek and Apulian (an Iron and Bronze Age Greek colony) works. It experimented with under-glaze slip decoration on vases. The Chelsea Keramic Art Works also produced high-glazed vases, pitchers and plaques with a buff clay body, with either sculpted or molded applied decoration.

James Robertson died in 1880 and Alexander moved to California in 1884, leaving Hugh alone in Chelsea, where his experiments eventually yielded an imitation of the Chinese Ming-era blood-red glaze. Hugh's vases with that glaze were marked with an impressed "CKAW." Creating these red-glazed vases was expensive, and even though they received critical acclaim, the company declared bankruptcy in 1889.

Recapitalized by a circle of Boston art patrons in 1891, Hugh started the Chelsea Pottery U.S., which produced gray crackle-glazed dinnerware with cobalt-blue decorations, the rabbit pattern being the most popular.

The business moved to new facilities in Dedham, Mass., and began production in 1896 under the name Dedham Pottery. Hugh's son and grandson operated the business until it closed in 1943, by which time between 50 and 80 patterns had been produced.

The following marks help determine the approximate age of items:

• "Chelsea Keramic Art Works Robertson and Sons," impressed, 1874-1880.

• "CKAW," impressed, 1875-1889.

• "CPUS," impressed in a cloverleaf, 1891-1895.

• Foreshortened rabbit only, impressed, 1894-1896.

• Conventional rabbit with "Dedham Pottery" in square blue-stamped mark along with one impressed foreshortened rabbit, 1896-1928.

• Blue rabbit stamped mark, "reg. stamp" beneath, along with two impressed foreshortened rabbit marks, 1929-1943

Photo courtesy Rago Arts and Auction Center, Lambertville, N.J.; www.RagoArts.com

Breakfast plate, no. 2, Mushroom design, pale pink overglaze, indigo stamp and impressed stamp, 8 1/2" d. **$960**

Photo courtesy Jim Kaufman

Teapot, Rabbit pattern, six cup size, blue stamp, 8 1/8" h. **$875**

Photo courtesy Rago Arts and Auction Center, Lambertville, N.J.; www.RagoArts.com

Vase, bulbous, experimental, by Hugh Robertson, fine, frothy, dripping green, brown, and amber glazes, incised "Dedham Pottery/HCR/tr/B.W.," ink mark "DP7/A#53," 8" x 6 3/4". **$1,000**

Lonhuda

Lonhuda Pottery Co. of Steubenville, Ohio, was organized in 1892 by William Long, with investors W.H. Hunter and Alfred Day. "Lonhuda" combines the first two letters of the partners' last names.

Denver Denaura/Lonhuda, baluster vase modeled and incised with daffodils, covered in vellum matte green glaze, rare form. 1 1/2" tight hairline from rim. Stamped indigo arrow mark, Denaura 85 18?, incised Lonhuda. 8 1/2" x 5". **$3,000**

Photo courtesy Belhorn Auction Services LLC, Columbus, Ohio; www.Belhorn.com

Ephraim Faience Pottery, (Deerfield, Wis.), #817 Dragonfly vase in matte green. Retired 12/31/02 with an edition of 301 pieces. Marked with circular 2000 Ephraim mark and Kevin Hicks' impressed name. Mint. 12" h. **$625**

Photo courtesy Belhorn Auction Services LLC, Columbus, Ohio; www.Belhorn.com

Ephraim Faience Pottery, (Deerfield, Wis.), #318 Underwater Crab vase in dark green matte and tan. One of 61 made. 9 1/2" w x 4 1/2" h. **$450**

Fiesta

The Homer Laughlin China Co. introduced Fiesta dinnerware in January 1936 at the Pottery and Glass Show in Pittsburgh. Frederick Rhead designed the pattern; Arthur Kraft and Bill Bensford molded it. Dr. A.V. Bleininger and H.W. Thiemecke developed the glazes.

The original five colors were red, dark blue, light green (with a trace of blue), brilliant yellow and ivory. A vigorous marketing campaign took place between 1939 and 1943. In mid-1937, turquoise was added. Red was removed in 1943 because some of the chemicals used to produce it were essential to the war effort; it did not reappear until 1959. In 1951, light green, dark blue and ivory were retired and forest green, rose, chartreuse and gray were added to the line. Other color changes took place in the late 1950s, including the addition of "medium green."

Fiesta was redesigned in 1969 and discontinued about 1972. In 1986, Homer Laughlin reintroduced Fiesta. The new china body shrinks more than the old semi-vitreous and ironstone pieces, thus making the new pieces slightly smaller than the earlier pieces. The modern colors are also different in tone or hue, e.g., the cobalt blue is darker than the old blue.

Homer Laughlin has continued to introduce new colors in the popular Fiesta pattern. It's important for collectors to understand when different colors were made.

Fiesta Ware, carafe, cobalt blue. **$320**

Color Guide

Color Name	Color palette	Years of Production
Red	Reddish-orange	1936-43, 1959-72
Blue	Cobalt blue	1936-51
Ivory	Creamy yellow-white	1936-51
Yellow	Golden yellow	1936-69
Green	Light green	1936-51
Turquoise	Sky blue	1937-69
Rose	Dark dusky rose	1951-59
Chartreuse	Yellow-green	1951-59
Forest green	Dark hunter green	1951-59
Gray	Light gray	1951-59
Medium green	Deep bright green	1959-69
Antique gold	Dark butterscotch	1969-72
Turf green	Olive green	1969-72
Cobalt blue	Very dark blue, almost black	1986-
Rose	Bubblegum pink	1986-
White	Pearly white	1986-
Black	High gloss black	1986-
Apricot	Peach-beige	1986-98
Turquoise	Greenish-blue	1988-
Yellow	Pale yellow	1987-2002
Periwinkle blue	Pastel gray-blue	1989-
Sea mist green	Pastel light green	1991-
Lilac	Pastel violet	1993-95
Persimmon	Coral	1995-
Sapphire (Bloomingdale's exclusive)	Blue	1996-97
Chartreuse	More yellow than green	1997-99
Pearl gray	Similar to vintage gray, more transparent	1999-2001
Juniper green	Dark blue-green	1999-2001
Cinnabar	Brown-maroon	2000-
Sunflower	Bright yellow	2001-
Plum	Rich purple	2002-
Shamrock	Grassy green	2002-
Tangerine	Bright orange	2003-

Fiesta Ware, coffeepot, turquoise, 10 3/8" x 8". **$170**

Fiesta Ware, salt and pepper shakers, cobalt blue, 2 3/8" x 2 3/4". **$35**

Fiesta Ware, individual salad bowl in medium green. **$115**

Fiesta Ware, ashtray, cobalt blue, 6 1/4" x 1 1/4". **$55**

Fiesta Ware, Tom & Jerry mug, medium green, 3 1/8" x 4 3/8". **$120**

Fiesta Ware, covered onion soup bowl, ivory. **$700**

Fiesta Ware, sugar bowl, covered, turquoise. **$50**

Fiesta Ware, teapot, rose, 8 1/2" x 5 5/8" with lid. **$275**

Ashtray
Ivory $55
Red...$60
Turquoise...$50
Yellow $48
Bowl, green, 5 1/2" d.......................................$60
Cake plate, green..................................$1,950
Candlesticks, pr, bulb
Cobalt blue...$125
Ivory $125
Red...$120
Turquoise...$110
Candlesticks, pr, tripod, yellow $550
Carafe
Cobalt blue...$495
Ivory $385
Casserole, covered, two handles, 10" d
Ivory $195
Yellow $160
Chop plate, gray, 13" d..............................$95
Coffeepot
Cobalt blue...$235
Ivory $390
Red...$250
Turquoise...$250
Yellow $185
Compote, low, ftd, 12" d
Cobalt blue...$175
Ivory $165
Red...$185
Yellow $165
Creamer
Cobalt blue...$35
Ivory $30
Red...$65
Yellow $30
Creamer and sugar, figure-eight server, yellow creamer
and sugar, cobalt blue gray $315
Cream soup bowl
Cobalt blue...$60
Ivory $55
Red...$65
Turquoise...$48
Yellow $45

Fiesta Ware, dessert bowl, medium green, 6 1/4" x 1 1/4". **$750**

Cup, ring handle
Cobalt blue...$35
Ivory...$30
Red..$30
Turquoise..$25
Yellow..$25
Demitasse cup, stick handle
Cobalt blue..$75
Ivory...$80
Red..$85
Turquoise...$75
Yellow..$65
Demitasse pot, covered, stick handle
Cobalt blue..$650
Ivory...$535
Red..$575
Turquoise...$650
Yellow...$465
Dessert bowl, 6" d
Cobalt blue..$50
Ivory...$45
Turquoise...$40
Yellow..$40
Egg cup
Cobalt blue..$75
Ivory...$72
Red..$80
Turquoise...$55
Yellow..$70
Fruit bowl, 5 1/2" d
Ivory...$33
Turquoise...$25
Yellow..$25
Fruit bowl, 11 3/4" d, cobalt blue.............................$485
Gravy boat
Cobalt blue..$75
Ivory...$65
Red..$85
Turquoise...$45
Yellow..$50
Juice tumbler
Cobalt blue..$40
Rose..$65
Yellow..$40

Fiesta Ware, fruit bowl, chartreuse, 5 1/2". **$35**

Fiesta Ware, oval platter, yellow. **$55**

Fiesta Ware, plate, medium green, 9" d. **$75**

Fiesta Ware, cream soup bowl, turquoise, 6 5/8" x 5 1/16" x 2 1/4". **$48**

Fiesta Ware, mixing bowl #6, red, 6 1/4" x 9 3/4". **$340**

Fiesta Ware, footed salad bowl, red, 11 3/8" x 5 1/2". **$585**

Marmalade jar, covered

Cobalt blue $335
Red $345
Turquoise $325
Yellow $250

Mixing bowl

#1, red, 5" d $375
#2, cobalt blue $195
#2, yellow $140
#4, green $195
#5, ivory $275
#7, ivory $580

Mixing bowl lid, #1, red $1,100

Mug

Dark green $90
Ivory, marked $125
Rose $95

Mustard, covered

Cobalt blue $325
Turquoise $275

Nappy, 8 1/2" d

Cobalt blue $55
Red $55
Turquoise $42
Yellow $45

Nappy, 9 1/2" d

Cobalt blue $65
Ivory $65
Red $70
Turquoise $55
Yellow $60

Onion soup, covered, turquoise $8,000

Pitcher, disk

Chartreuse $275
Turquoise $110

Pitcher, ice lip

Green $135
Turquoise $195

Plate, deep

Gray $42
Rose $42

Plate, 6" d

Dark green $15
Ivory $7
Light green $9
Yellow $5

Plate, 7" d

Chartreuse $12
Light green $9
Medium green $30
Rose $14

Turquoise $9

Plate, 9" d

Cobalt blue $15
Ivory $14
Red $15
Yellow $13

Plate, dinner, 10" d

Gray $42
Light green $28
Medium green $125
Red $35
Turquoise $30

Platter, oval

Gray $35
Ivory $25
Red $45

Relish

Ivory base and center, turquoise inserts $285
Red, base and inserts $425

Salad bowl, large, ftd

Cobalt blue $375
Red $585
Turquoise $335
Yellow $400

Salt and pepper shakers, pr

Red $24
Turquoise $135

Saucer

Light green $5
Turquoise $5

Soup plate

Ivory $36
Turquoise $29

Sugar bowl, covered

Chartreuse $65
Gray $75
Rose $75

Syrup

Green $450
Ivory $600
Red $695

Sweetmeat compote, high standard

Cobalt blue $95
Red $100
Turquoise $125
Yellow $400

Teacup, flat bottom, cobalt blue $100

Teapot, covered

Cobalt blue, large $335
Rose, medium $275
Tumbler, cobalt blue $75

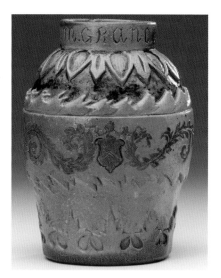

Photo courtesy Rago Arts and Auction Center, Lambertville, N.J.; www.RagoArts.com

Susan Frackelton, (1848-1932), rare stoneware vase carved in a foliate and heraldic pattern and covered in green and indigo matte glazes, 1879. Dedicated to her husband and incised around the rim CUM. GRANO. SALIS. AD1879 (Translation: "With a grain of salt," which, according to family history, is a play on words, remarking both on the use of salt in the glaze, as well as a gentle dig at her husband, Richard Goodrich Frackelton, who apparently disapproved of her profession, and to whom this was a gift.) Incised on bottom SF No 2 6/3/79 For RGF. 7" x 5 1/4". **$18,000**

Photo courtesy Belhorn Auction Services LLC, Columbus, Ohio; www.Belhorn.com

Fraunfelter, vase with hand decorated flowers on a shimmering silver-gray background by John Lessell. Signed Lessell at the base and marked Fraunfelter USA 93. Mint. 6 1/4" h. **$500**
(Fraunfelter China Co., Indiana and Ohio, 1923-1939.)

Fulper Pottery Co.

The firm that became Fulper Pottery Co. of Flemington, N.J., originally made stoneware pottery and utilitarian wares beginning in the early 1800s. Fulper made art pottery from about 1909 to 1935.

The company's earliest artware was called the Vase-Kraft line (1910-1915). Its middle period (1915-1925) included some of the earlier shapes, but they also incorporated Oriental forms. Their glazing at this time was less consistent but more diverse. The last period (1925-1935) was characterized by Art Deco forms.

FULPER in a rectangle is known as the "ink mark" and dates from 1910-1915. The second mark, as shown, dates from 1915-1925; it was incised or in black ink. The final mark, FULPER, die-stamped, dates from about 1925 to 1935.

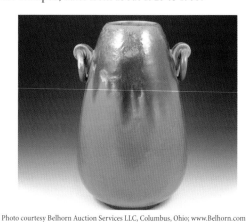

Photo courtesy Belhorn Auction Services LLC, Columbus, Ohio; www.Belhorn.com

Fulper, vase, in green over rose flambe glaze with ring handles. Marked with vertical oval Fulper ink stamp. Mint. 12 3/4" h. **$450**

Photo courtesy Rago Arts and Auction Center, Lambertville, N.J.; www.RagoArts.com

Galloway, (Philadelphia, early 20th century), pair of large oil jars covered in a fine mottled blue-purple and amber. Some glaze chips. Unmarked. 23 1/2" x 16". **$1,440 pair**

Grueby Faience Co.

William Grueby was active in the ceramic industry for several years before he developed his own method of producing matte-glazed pottery and founded the Grueby Faience Co. of Boston in 1897.

The art pottery was hand thrown in natural shapes, hand molded and hand tooled. A variety of colored glazes, singly or in combinations, was produced, but green was the most popular. In 1908, the firm was divided into the Grueby Pottery Co. and the Grueby Faience and Tile Co. The Grueby Faience and Tile Co. made art tile until 1917, although its pottery production was phased out about 1910.

Photo courtesy Rago Arts and Auction Center, Lambertville, N.J.; www.RagoArts.com

Grueby tile incised and modeled with polar bear on iceberg, rare. Small chip to one corner and flake to back. Stamped GRUEBY BOSTON. 5 1/2" x 7". **$11,400**

Photo courtesy of Treadway Toomey Galleries, Cincinnati and Oak Park, Ill.; www.treadwaygallery.com

Grueby tile, carved and painted landscape, signed PS, held in a contemporary Arts & Crafts oak frame; tile 6" sq; overall 11 3/4" sq. **$3,500**

Photo courtesy Rago Arts and Auction Center, Lambertville, N.J.; www.RagoArts.com

Grueby gourd-shaped vase with tooled and applied full-height ribbed leaves, covered in a superior feathered matte green glaze. (Extremely rare, one of Grueby's most important forms.) Professional restoration to small chip at rim and to a couple of leaf tips, several minor glaze nicks to leaf edges. Stamped GRUEBY. 9 1/4" h. **$84,000**

Photo courtesy Rago Arts and Auction Center, Lambertville, N.J.; www.RagoArts.com

Grueby seven-tile frieze of "The Pines," decorated in Cuenca style, with stylized trees in a hilly landscape, along with surrounding matte green tiles, thirty-five 2" x 6" (chips to edges), and twenty-four 2" x 3" (cut-down, as-is). Small chip to one edge of pine, unmarked, rectangular marked. 6" sq. each. **$18,000** *(This Spanish style of pottery is named for Cuenca, Ecuador.)*

Photo courtesy Rago Arts and Auction Center, Lambertville, N.J.; www.RagoArts.com

Grueby squat vessel with tooled and applied leaves, covered in a superior leathery matte glaze. Restoration to small chip at rim. Circular Pottery stamp AAP166. 6" x 6 1/2". **$2,280**

Grueby, two-color vase-form lamp base, matte green glaze, yellow buds on a corseted neck, above tooled full-height leaves, impressed "GRUEBY POTTERY / BOSTON, USA" circular mark, retains partial circular label. Early 20th century. 11 1/2" h, 5 1/2" d rim, 5 3/8" d base. Minute nicks/spots of wear to leaf edges. **$5,500**

Grueby, Cuenca-style tile depicting St. George Slaying the Dragon in rich matte colors, extremely rare. Artist signed. 8" sq. **$10,800**
(This Spanish style of pottery is named for Cuenca, Ecuador.)

Grueby, tile with stylized tree on blue ground, rare. Small chip to corner, light abrasion to surface. Stamped GRUEBY BOSTON M.B. 6" sq.....................................**$5,400**

Grueby, two-tile frieze decorated in Cuenca style, with a procession of horses. Restoration to corners. Mounted in new Arts & Crafts frame. Each tile 6" sq. **$7,200**
(This Spanish style of pottery is named for Cuenca, Ecuador.)

Grueby, frieze of three red clay tiles decorated in Cuenca style, with ivory water lilies and light green lily pads on dark green water. A few flakes to edges. Stamped GRUEBY BOSTON. 6" sq. ea...**$2,400**

Grueby, unusual and large squat bulbous vase by Wilhelmina Post, completely cut back with stylized alternating razor clam leaves, under an exceptional matte green glaze. Impressed pottery mark/WP. 7 1/2" x 8". **$8,400**

Grueby, vase by Wilhelmina Post with three full-height leaves alternating with yellow buds. Restoration to a couple of rim chips. Circular stamp WP. 8 1/2" x 5".
....**$6,600**

Grueby, vase with full-height tooled and applied leaves covered in a frothy matte green glaze. Touch-ups to tips of three leaves. Circular stamp. 8" x 4 1/2". **$2,280**

Grueby, large melon-shaped vase by Ruth Erickson with full-height leaves alternating with yellow buds, covered in fine leathery matte green glaze. Circular pottery stamp RE 36. 11" x 7 3/4"..**$22,800**

Hall China Co.

Robert Hall founded the Hall China Co. in 1903 in East Liverpool, Ohio. He died in 1904 and was succeeded by his son, Robert Taggart Hall. After years of experimentation, Robert T. Hall developed a leadless glaze in 1911, opening the way for production of glazed household products.

The Hall China Co. made many types of kitchenware, refrigerator sets, and dinnerware in a wide variety of patterns. Some patterns were made exclusively for a particular retailer, such as Heather Rose for Sears.

One of the most popular patterns was Autumn Leaf, a premium designed by Arden Richards in 1933 for the exclusive use by the Jewel Tea Co. Still a Jewel Tea property, Autumn Leaf has not been listed in catalogs since 1978, but has been produced on a replacement basis with the date stamped on the back.

Cookie jar, covered

Autumn Leaf, Tootsie...$265
Blue Blossom, Five-Band shape................................$275
Chinese Red, Five-Band shape..................................$150
Gold Dot, Zeisel...$95
Meadow Flower, Five-Band shape............................$230
Owl, brown glaze...$90
Red Poppy...$50

Kitchen ware and advertising

Bean pot, New England, #1, Orange Poppy..................$80
Casserole, covered, Chinese Red, Sundial, #4, 8" w......$65
Coffeepot, percolator, ducks and partridge dec...........$100
Cuspidor, green and white, 7 1/4" d, 4 1/4" h...............$90
Drip jar, Little Red Riding Hood, 4 1/2" h, 5" w........$3,300
Jug, Primrose, rayed...$20
Mixing bowl, nested set of three, pink, basketweave and floral dec, gold trim, 6" d, 7 1/2" d, 8 1/2" d..................$85
Mug, Braniff International Airlines, 4" h, 2" d..............$18

Hall Dripolator, light blue base and lid with gold leaf decoration, marked. **$75**

Hall front: batter pitcher, "ear handle," $90; rear: ball-shaped pitcher, both Autumn Leaf pattern, gold trim. **$75**

Refrigerator bowl, Addison Gray and Daffodil, ink stamped "GE Refrigerators, Hall Ovenware China, Made for General Electric," circa 1938 ....**$12**

Sauceboat, Quartermaster logo emblem near handle on both sides, circa 1940, 10" l **$25**

Patterns

Autumn Leaf
Bowl, 5 1/2" d	$8
Coffeepot, electric	$300
Cup and saucer	$18
Juice reamer	$250
Pepper shaker, gold trim, 4 1/4" h	$20
Pie bird, 5" h	$40
Plate, 8" d	$15
Tidbit tray, three tiers	$125
Utensil holder, marked "Utensils," 7 1/4" h	$275

Blue Bouquet
Bowl, 7" d, 3" h	$30
Creamer, Boston	$25
Cup and saucer	$28
Soup, flat	$30
Spoon	$100
Teapot, Aladdin infuser	$165

Cameo Rose
Bowl, 5 1/4" d	$3
Butter dish, 3/4 lb.	$30
Casserole	$25
Creamer and sugar	$10
Plate, 8" d	$2.50
Teapot, covered, six-cup	$35
Tidbit, three-tier	$40

Gamebirds
Percolator, electric	$140
Teapot, covered, two-cup size, ducks and pheasant	$200

Mount Vernon
Coffeepot	$125
Creamer	$12
Cup	$10
Fruit bowl	$8
Gravy boat	$20
Saucer	$4
Soup bowl, flat, 8" d	$17

Red Poppy
Bowl, 5 1/2" d	$5
Cake plate	$18
Casserole, covered	$25
Coffeepot, covered	$12
Creamer and sugar	$15
Cup and saucer	$8
French baker, fluted	$15
Jug, Daniel, Radiance	$28
Plate, 9" d	$7
Salad bowl, 9" d	$14
Teapot, New York	$90

Silhouette
Bean pot	$50
Bowl, 7 7/8" d	$50
Coffeepot, covered	$30
Mug	$35
Pretzel jar	$75
Trivet	$125

Tulip
Bowl, oval, 10 1/4" l	$36
Condiment jar	$165
Mixing bowl, 6" d	$27
Plate, luncheon, 9" d	$16
Platter, oval, 13 1/4" l	$42
Shakers, bulge-type, price for pair	$110
Sugar, covered	$25

Teapots

Camellia, gold roses, windshield, gold trim on handle, spout, rim, and finial, mkd "Hall 0698 6 cup made in USA" **$100**

Chinese Red, donut, 9 1/2" w, 7 1/2" h **$500**

Cleveland, turquoise and gold **$165**

Lipton Tea, off white stoneware, aluminum cozy, 9 1/2" l, 7 1/2" h **$30**

Hampshire Pottery Co.

In 1871, James S. Taft founded the Hampshire Pottery Co. in Keene, N.H. Production began with redware and stoneware, followed by majolica in 1879.

Until World War I, the factory made an extensive line of utilitarian and artware, including souvenir items. After the war, the firm resumed operations, but made only hotel dinnerware and tiles. The company was dissolved in 1923.

Photo courtesy Rago Arts and Auction Center, Lambertville, N.J.; www.RagoArts.com

Hampshire, vases (two) in fine blue and green frothy glazes. Both marked, 5 1/2" and 8 1/2". **$1,140 pair**

Hull Pottery Co.

In 1905, Addis E. Hull purchased the Acme Pottery Co. of Crooksville, Ohio. In 1917, the A.E. Hull Pottery Co. began making art pottery, novelties, stoneware and kitchenware, later including the famous Little Red Riding Hood line. Most items had a matte finish, with shades of pink and blue or brown predominating.

After a flood and fire in 1950, the factory reopened in 1952 as the Hull Pottery Co. New pieces, mostly with a glossy finish, were produced. The firm closed in 1985.

Pre-1950 vases are marked "Hull USA" or "Hull Art USA" on the bottom. Many also retain their paper labels. Post-1950 pieces are marked "Hull" in large script or "HULL" in block letters.

Each pattern has a distinctive letter or number, e.g., Wildflower has a "W" and a number; Water Lily, "L" and number; Poppy, numbers in the 600s; Orchid, in the 300s. Early stoneware pieces are marked with an "H."

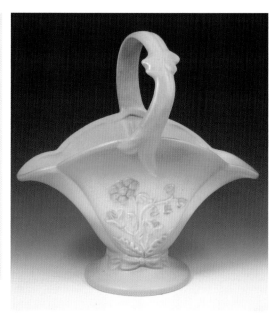

Photo courtesy Belhorn Auction Services LLC, Columbus, Ohio; www.Belhorn.com

Hull, Bow Knot basket in pink and blue. Marked Hull Art USA B-12-10 1/2. 11 1/4" h. **$350**

Photo courtesy Belhorn Auction Services LLC, Columbus, Ohio; www.Belhorn.com

Hull, experimental Blossom Flite T3 pitcher in green with yellow and pink flower and gold swirl. Unmarked. Mint. 8 3/4" h. **$500**

Photo courtesy Belhorn Auction Services LLC, Columbus, Ohio; www.Belhorn.com

Hull, Bow Knot basket in pink and blue. Marked USA Hull Art B-29-12". Mint. 11 3/4" h x 11" w. **$950**

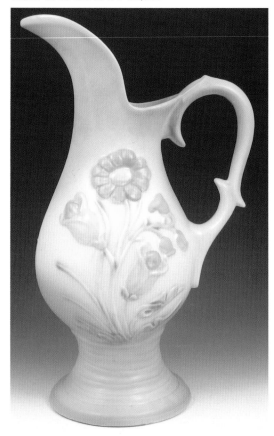

Photo courtesy Belhorn Auction Services LLC, Columbus, Ohio; www.Belhorn.com

Hull, Bow Knot pitcher in blue and turquoise. Marked Hull Art USA B-15-13 1/2". 14" h. **$375**

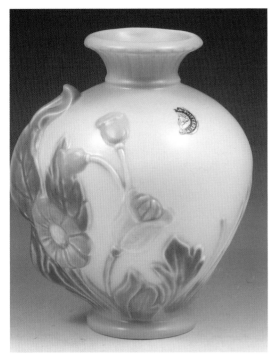

Hull, Bow Knot vase in blue and turquoise with partial original label. Marked Hull Art USA B-4-6 1/2". Mint. 6 5/8" h. **$130**

Hull, Corky Pig bank in blue and pink with gold trim. Marked Pat Pend Corky Pig Copyright USA 1957 HPCo. 7 1/2" long x 5" h. **$230**

Hull, Corky Pig bank in gray. Marked Pat. Pend. Corky Pig HPCo Copyright 1957 USA. 6 3/4" long x 5" h. **$650**

Hull, Continental #55 Basket in Mountain Blue. Marked Hull USA 55. Mint. 12 3/8" h. **$325**

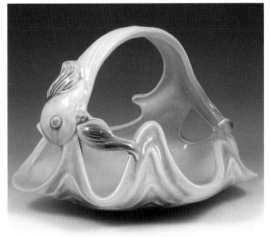

Hull, Ebb Tide E-5 fish basket in pink and turquoise. Unmarked. Mint. 6 5/8" h x 9 1/8" w. **$550**

Hull, Gingerbread Man cookie jar in sand. Marked Hull Copyright Crooksville, Ohio Oven Proof USA. 11 3/4" h. **$500**

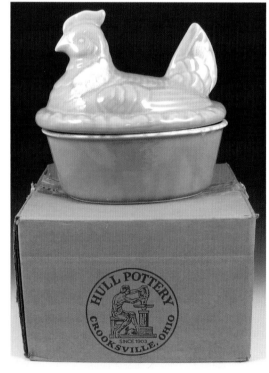

Hull, House & Garden chicken covered casserole in gray in the original box. Marked Hull Oven Proof USA. Mint. 10" long x 9 3/4" h. **$400**

Hull, Hull Pottery Association commemorative piece from 1996, a small Corky Pig bank. Marked Copyright USA HP 58 on the base and H.P.C. 96 on the "rear." Mint. 3 1/4" h x 4 1/2" l. **$300**

Hull. Hull Pottery Association Commemorative Gingerbread Man bank from 1999 in gray. Marked Hull Pottery Association Commemorative 1999. Mint and uncrazed. 9 3/8" h x 7 1/2" w. **$200**

Hull, Little Red Riding Hood Baby Feeding Dish, exceptionally rare. Unmarked. 8" w x 4 3/4" h. **$1,400**

Hull, Magnolia Matte tea set in pink and blue with original label on the teapot's lid. All marked. All mint. 3 1/8" to 5 3/4" h. **$250 set**

Hull, early novelty donkey planter. Marked with original Hull Sample 1 1/2" label with Style No. 953 Donkey, yellow, Large. 7 1/8" h. **$375**

Hull, unusually colored llama planter in white and green high gloss. Unmarked. Mint. 11 3/4" long x 10 3/4" h. **$210**

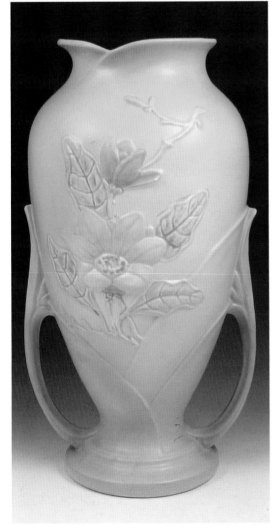

Hull, Magnolia Matte 16-15" floor vase in pink and blue. Marked Hull Art USA 16-15". Mint. 15 1/4" h. **$240**

Hull, early novelty #936 monkey scratching his head. Unmarked. Mint with the exception of some loss to the cold-painted decoration. 5 3/4" h. **$275**

Hull, Orchid bookends in pink and blue. One is faintly marked Hull USA 316-7. 5 1/4" h x 7 1/8" w. **$550 pair**

Hull, early stoneware flared bowl in shades of blue and rose high glaze. Marked with a circle H and the number 8. Mint. 8" w x 4" h. **$220**

Hull, early stoneware small pitcher. Marked with a circled H, 27, 36. Mint. 5 1/8" h x 7" w. **$550**

Hull, Supreme basket in brown. Considered experimental, the line was never entered into full production. Unmarked. Mint. 8 3/4" h. **$200**

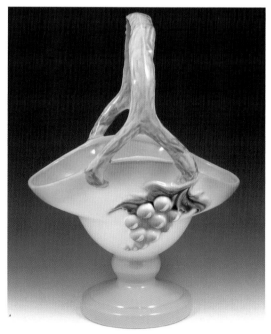

Hull, Tokay basket in multicolored finish. Marked 15 Tokay USA. Mint. 12" h. **$210**

Hull, Tokay basket with unusual test or experimental glaze with white highlights on deep olive green. Marked Tokay #6 with an original Hull label. Mint. 7 3/4" h x 7 1/4" w. **$210**

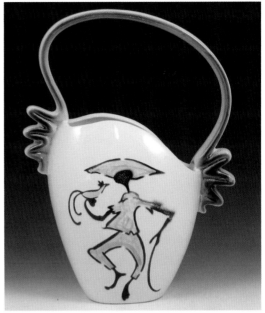

Hull, Tropicana basket with Caribbean man and bird. Marked Hull USA 55. Mint and uncrazed. 12 3/8" h x 9 1/4" w. **$750**

Hull, Tokay three-piece tea set in multicolored finish. All marked. All mint. 3 1/2" to 7 1/2" h. **$210 set**

Hull, Tropicana ashtray with Caribbean swimmer and fish. Marked Hull USA 51. 15 1/2" l. **$425**

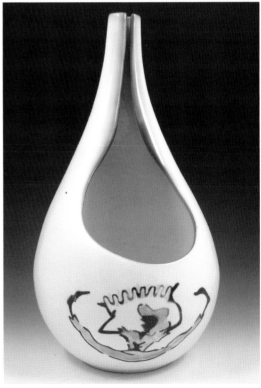

Hull, Tropicana hanging planter vase with Caribbean musician. Marked Hull USA 57. Mint and uncrazed. 14 3/8" h x 7 3/4" w. **$750**

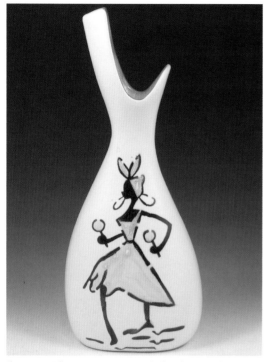

Photo courtesy Belhorn Auction Services LLC, Columbus, Ohio; www.Belhorn.com

Hull, Tropicana vase with female Caribbean musician. Marked Hull USA 54. Mint and uncrazed. 12 1/4" h. **$700**

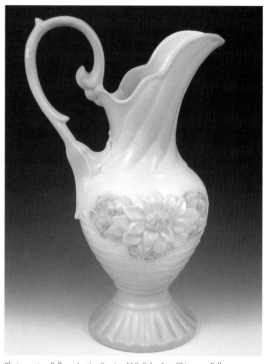

Photo courtesy Belhorn Auction Services LLC, Columbus, Ohio; www.Belhorn.com

Hull, Water Lily ewer in pink and turquoise. Marked Hull Art USA L-17-13 1/2. Mint with a factory kiln flaw to the handle. 14 1/8" h. **$250**

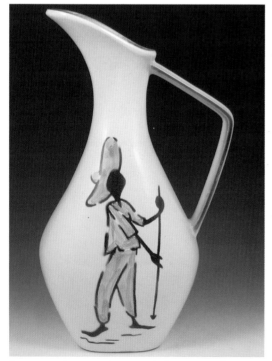

Photo courtesy Belhorn Auction Services LLC, Columbus, Ohio; www.Belhorn.com

Hull, Tropicana vase with Caribbean man holding a spear for fishing. Marked Hull USA 56. Mint and uncrazed. 12 5/8" h. **$700**

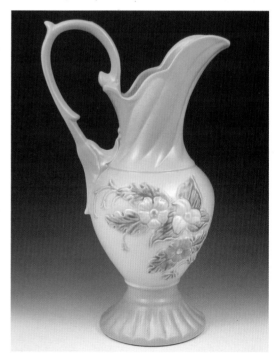

Photo courtesy Belhorn Auction Services LLC, Columbus, Ohio; www.Belhorn.com

Hull, Wildflower pitcher in pink and blue. Marked Hull Art USA W-19-13 1/2". Mint. 13 5/8" h. **$275**

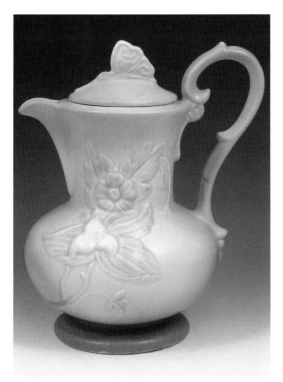

Photo courtesy Belhorn Auction Services LLC, Columbus, Ohio; www.Belhorn.com

Hull, Wildflower No. Series 72-8" teapot in pink and beige. Marked Hull Art USA 72-8". Some repairs. 8 1/8" h. **$325**

Photo courtesy Belhorn Auction Services LLC, Columbus, Ohio; www.Belhorn.com

Hull, Woodland Gloss W24 pitcher lamp (factory original). 20 3/4" h. **$300**

Photo courtesy Belhorn Auction Services LLC, Columbus, Ohio; www.Belhorn.com

Hull, Woodland Gloss jardiniere in white with gold trim. Marked Hull USA W21-9 1/2". 10 1/2" w x 7 1/4" h. **$375**

Photo courtesy Belhorn Auction Services LLC, Columbus, Ohio; www.Belhorn.com

Hull, Woodland Gloss tea set in chartreuse and pink. Each marked Hull USA with the respective shape number W26, W27 or W28. Mint. 3 3/8" to 6 1/2" h. **$200 set**

Photo courtesy Belhorn Auction Services LLC, Columbus, Ohio; www.Belhorn.com

Hull. Woodland Gloss vase in white with gold trim. Marked Hull USA W25-12 1/2". Mint. 12 5/8" h. **$210**

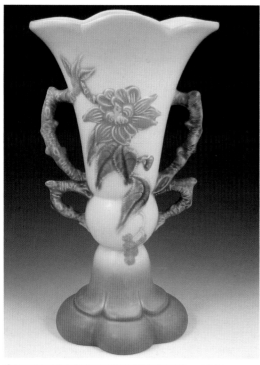

Photo courtesy Belhorn Auction Services LLC, Columbus, Ohio; www.Belhorn.com

Hull, Woodland Pre-50 Matte vase in Dawn Rose. Marked Hull W25-12 1/2" USA. Mint. 13 1/8" h x 7 3/8" w. **$280**

Lenox Inc.

In 1889, Jonathan Cox and Walter Scott Lenox established The Ceramic Art Co. at Trenton, N.J. By 1906, Lenox formed his own company, Lenox Inc. Using potters lured from Belleek, Lenox began making an American version of the famous Irish ware. The firm is still in business.

Older Lenox china has one of two marks: a green wreath or a palette. The palette mark appears on blanks supplied to amateurs who hand painted china as a hobby. The Lenox company currently uses a gold stamped mark.

Lenox, plates (six), porcelain hand painted with nymphs in landscapes. Five signed Wirkner, one signed Pohl, all with green Lenox mark and markings in gold, 10 1/4" d. . **$2,160 set**

Lenox, plates (six), hand painted by William and George Morley with floral decoration. Five signed W.H. Morley, one G. Morley, all marked with various green and gold marks, 10 1/2" d...**$900 set**

Lenox, plates (eight), three painted with portraits by H. Nosek; four painted with birds by William Morley; and one hand-painted with a wood nymph with fishing pole and fish. All but last artist-signed, most have Lenox stamp. Largest: 10 3/8" d...................................**$1,320 all**

J. & J.G. Low, large format Plastic Sketch by Arthur Osborne, "Tuning Up," covered in amber glaze. A few small chips to edges. Incised AO, and stamped J & JG LOW ART TILE WORKS CHELSEA, MASS., U.S.A. COPYRIGHT 1882 BY J & JG LOW. 16 1/2" x 10 1/2".................................**$1,920**

Photo courtesy Rago Arts and Auction Center, Lambertville, N.J.; www.RagoArts.com

Jugtown ridged urn with two small handles covered in rare mirror black glaze. Some bursts to body. Circular Jugtown Ware stamp. 9 1/2" x 7". **$600**

Photo courtesy Rago Arts and Auction Center, Lambertville, N.J.; www.RagoArts.com

J. & J.G. Low, plastic sketch by Arthur Osborne, "Spring Time," covered in amber glaze and mounted in new frame. Incised AO, back covered. Sight: 10" x 5". **$1,080**

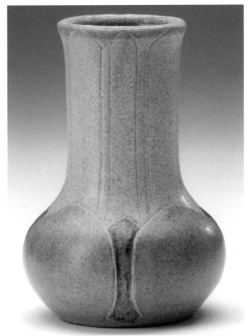

Photo courtesy Rago Arts and Auction Center, Lambertville, N.J.; www.RagoArts.com

Marblehead early bulbous vase by Arthur Baggs incised with a stylized design in blue-grays and pale yellow. Small glaze flake to rim. Incised M with seagull, AB. 4 3/4" x 3 1/4". **$45,000**

Marblehead

This hand-thrown pottery was first made in 1905 as part of a therapeutic program introduced by Dr. J. Hall for the patients confined to a sanitarium located in Marblehead, Mass. In 1916, production was removed from the hospital to another site. The factory continued under the directorship of Arthur E. Baggs until it closed in 1936.

Most pieces found today are glazed with a smooth, porous, even finish in a single color. The most desirable pieces have a conventional design with one or more subordinate colors.

Marblehead, ovoid vase by Hannah Tutt incised with brown oak leaves and acorns on a mustard ground. Stamped ship mark, HT. 7" x 4". **$3,900**

Marblehead, tapered vase incised and painted with stylized green leaves on a speckled rich brown ground. Stamped ship mark. 6" x 4 1/4". **$3,900**

Marblehead, vase carved by Hannah Tutt with crouching panthers and stylized trees on matte olive green ground. (Strong color and modeling.) Very short, very tight line to rim, almost impossible to see. Stamped ship mark/HT. 6 3/4" x 5". **$15,600**

Photo courtesy Rago Arts and Auction Center, Lambertville, N.J.; www.RagoArts.com

Marblehead tall and unusual vase designed by Arthur Baggs with incised and surface-painted blue flower stalks on a pebble gray ground. Impressed ship mark, incised AEB cipher. 8 1/2" x 4". **$6,000**

Marblehead, squat bulbous vase with a repeating design of yellow and blue flowers on green and brown foliage against a gray ground. Impressed ship mark. 3 1/2" x 5"........**$3,240**

Marblehead, cabinet vase incised with yellow blossoms and brown leaves. Stamped ship mark. 3 1/2" x 3".....**$1,440**

Marblehead, early and exceptional geometric-decorated vase with deep brown incised decoration repeating against a rich pea green ground. (Probably done within the first several years of Marblehead's production, the quality typical of this period). Pinhead-sized fleck inside rim. Impressed ship mark, incised N T. 5" x 4 3/4". **$13,200**

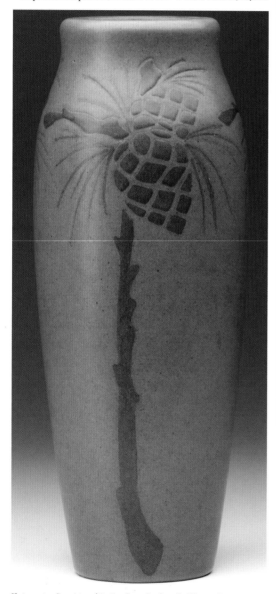

Photo courtesy Rago Arts and Auction Center, Lambertville, N.J.; www.RagoArts.com

Marblehead tall vase by Arthur Baggs, tooled and surface painted with brown pine boughs on green speckled ground. (Perhaps the only surviving example of this form without post-manufacturing flaws). Restoration to two kiln kisses. Ship mark AB. 12" x 4 1/2". **$8,400**

MCCOY POTTERY

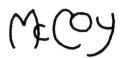

The J. W. McCoy Pottery Co. was established in Roseville, Ohio, in September 1899. The early McCoy company produced both stoneware and some art pottery lines, including Rosewood. In October 1911, three potteries merged, creating the Brush-McCoy Pottery Co. This firm continued to produce the original McCoy lines and added several new art lines. Much of the early pottery is not marked.

In 1910, Nelson McCoy and his father, J. W. McCoy, founded the Nelson McCoy Sanitary Stoneware Co. In 1925, the McCoy family sold their interest in the Brush-McCoy Pottery Co. and started to expand and improve the Nelson McCoy Co. The new company produced stoneware, earthenware specialties, and artware.

Marks: The Nelson McCoy Co. made most of the pottery marked "McCoy."

Reproduction Alert. Unfortunately, Nelson McCoy never registered his McCoy trademark, a fact discovered by Roger Jensen of Tennessee. As a result, Jensen began using the McCoy mark on a series of ceramic reproductions made in the early 1990s. While the marks on these recently made pieces copy the original, Jensen made objects that were never produced by the Nelson McCoy Co. The best-known example is the Red Riding Hood cookie jar, originally designed by Hull, and also made by Regal China.

The Jensen McCoy are an example of how a mark on a piece can be deceptive. A mark alone is not proof that a piece is period or old. Knowing the proper marks and what was made in respect to forms, shapes and decorative motifs is critical in authenticating a pattern.

Bean pot, cov, Suburbia Ware, brown, blue lid **$48**
Cookie jar, cov
    Aunt Jemima..**$275**
    Barn, cow in door, McCoy USA mark, lid, 1960s **$375**
    Bobby Baker...**$95**

McCoy strawberry jar, McCoy USA mark, 1950s. **$125**

Bugs Bunny, cylinder, 1971-72 .... **$185**
Chef, "Cookies" on hat band **$85**
Clown, bust, circa 1943 .... **$95**
Clown in Barrel, marked "McCoy USA," overall crazing, circa 1953-56 .... **$145**
Davy Crocket, circa 1956, 10" h **$325**
Engine, black **$175**
Kangaroo with Joey, 12" h **$525**
Little Red Riding Hood, 10 1/2" h **$650**
Panda, upside down, Avon label in heart logo on paw **$150**
Rooster, shades of brown, light tan head, green highlights **$225**
Strawberry **$125**
Touring Car, marked "McCoy USA," circa 1962-64, 6 1/2" h **$155**

Creamer and sugar, Sunburst **$120**
Decanter, Pierce Arrow **$90**
Decanter set, Jupiter 60 Train, Central Pacific locomotive, circa 1969 .... **$350**
Dresser caddy, buffalo, ... **$55**
Frog, naturalistic coloring, 8" l **$165**
Flower pot, saucer, hobnail and leaf **$40**
Hanging basket, Pine Cone Rustic **$45**
Jardinière, green, brown and gold, emb lion's heads and columns, 5 3/4" d, 5 1/4" d **$45**
Jardinière pedestal, Onyx glaze, signed "Cusick," circa 1909, 16 1/4" h **$400**
Lamp base, cowboy boots, circa 1956, 14" h **$150**
Low bowl, turtle flower frog, polychrome squeezebag dec, swastikas on bowl, 9" d, 2 3/4" h **$500**
Mug, green **$24**
Pitcher, Ring Ware, glossy green, unmarked, 1920s, 9" h ... **$90**
Planter
    Brown, white drip dec, 7 1/2" l, 4 1/2" w, 3" h **$20**
    Hunting Dog, No Fishing on sign, 12" l **$275**
    Three large pink chrysanthemums, marked "McCoy," 8" h **$155**
Spoon rest, yellow, foliage, overall crazing, 1940s, 8" l ... **$145**
Strawberry jar, stoneware, 12" h **$150**
Tankard pitcher, Buccaneer, green, 8 1/2" h **$135**
Tassel, glossy raspberry, stoneware, unmarked, 1930s, 8" h ... **$80**
Tea set, cov teapot, open creamer and sugar, Pinecone, circa 1946 .... **$350**
Umbrella stand, maroon, rose and yellow glaze, circa 1915, 11" d, 22" h **$795**
Valet
    Eagle **$75**
    Smiling horse, tail brush missing **$70**
Vase
    Bulbous, flaring rim, jeweled, pastel Squeezebag dec, green base, mkd "042," 8 3/4" h **$575**
    Cornucopia, green, 7 1/4" h **$125**
    Hyacinth, McCoy mark, early 1950s, 8" h **$175**
    Swan, white, gold trim, 9 1/2" h **$250**
Wall pocket
    Basketweave horn of plenty McCoy USA mark, 1950s, 8" **$110**
    Bellows **$60**
    Cuckoo Clock, brown, green, white, yellow bird ... **$225**
    Fan, blue **$65**
    Post Box, green **$70**
    Sunflower, blue **$80**
Window box, Pine Cone Rustic **$40**

McCoy, strap pitcher in glossy burgundy, McCoy mark, late 1940s. **$80**

McCoy urn wall pocket in speckled pink glaze with gold trim, McCoy USA mark, 4 1/2" l. **$80**

Photo courtesy of David Rago Auctions, Inc

McCoy jardinière and pedestal, decorated with trees and birds, sheer green glaze, signed "A. Cusick" in mold, abrasions and several small nicks, 27" h. **$325**

McCoy ivy jardinière in brown and green, unmarked, early 1950s, 8" h. **$100**

McCoy, large fan vase, also called "Blades of Grass," glossy black, McCoy USA mark, late 1950s, 10" h. **$200**

McCoy decanter, 1932 Pierce Arrow made for Jim Beam, 1960s, McCoy mark, 11" l. **$80**

McCoy, two strap-handleberry pitchers in glossy brown and green, unmarked, 1930s, each. **$95**

McCoy, two fish pitchers, McCoy mark, late 1940s, each. **$950**

Photo courtesy Rago Arts and Auction Center, Lambertville, N.J.; www.RagoArts.com

Merrimac (Newburyport, Mass., 1902-1908) cabinet vase with applied rows of leaves under a fine feathered semi-matte green glaze, 1903. A couple of small glaze flakes. Incised E.Q. 1903. 2 3/4" x 4". **$1,920**

Merrimac, (Newburyport, Mass., 1902-1908) jardinière carved and embossed with lotus leaves under a feathered microcrystalline matte green glaze. Abrasion to high points, some glaze flakes. Incised EB. 5 1/4" x 8 1/2"................ **$3,000**

Newcomb College

The Sophie Newcomb Memorial College, an adjunct of Tulane University in New Orleans, was originated as a school to train local women in the decorative arts. While metalworking, painting and embroidery were among the classes taught, the production of handcrafted art pottery remains its most popular and collectible pursuit.

Pottery was made by the Newcomb women for nearly 50 years, with earlier work being the rarest and most valuable. This is characterized by glossy finishes and broad, flat-painted and modeled designs. More common, though still quite valuable, are the matte-glaze pieces, often depicting bayou scenes and native flora. All bear the impressed NC mark.

Newcomb College, bowl, decorated with an incised band of animal figures, dark blue at rim and foot, cream interior, base with stamped "N within C" cipher, incised "MWS" for Mary Williamson Summey, decorator; impressed "JM" cipher for Joseph Fortune Meyer, potter; painted "DQ-44" for 1910, and impressed "B" for clay body. First quarter 20th century. 2" h, 5 1/2" d. **$8,250**

Newcomb College, tall vase carved by A.F. Simpson with a moonlit landscape of Spanish moss and live oak trees, 1927. Marked NC/AFS/JM/150QC32. 10 1/2" x 4 1/2". **$10,800**

Photo courtesy Rago Arts and Auction Center, Lambertville, N.J.; www.RagoArts.com

Newcomb College, transitional chocolate set by Ora Reams, complete with six cups and saucers, carved with yellow daisies. Small chip to edge of two saucers, tight opposing lines to one cup. Chocolate pot marked NC/JM/B/ORA REAMS 1913/FH2. Pot: 10 1/2" x 6". **$15,600**

Photo courtesy Belhorn Auction Services LLC, Columbus, Ohio; www.Belhorn.com

Newcomb College, moss and moon vase, large, by Sadie Irvine from 1931. Marked TB66 with the artist's mark. 9 3/4" h x 6 1/2" w. **$3,700**

Newcomb College, tall and early vase carved by Marie Ross with light blue blossoms and rich blue-green leaves, 1903. Very short, very tight line to rim. Stamped NC/S11/JM/Ross. 9 1/4" x 6"..**$7,200**

Newcomb College, transitional vase carved by Cynthia Littlejohn with stylized trees, 1913. Marked NC/JM/B/231/CL13/FX16. 7" x 5 1/2"..**$6,000**

Newcomb College, early and exceptional high-glaze vase by S. Massegale, brightly decorated as a stylized sunflower blossom in yellow, blue, and green on a cream ground, circa 1900. Marked NC/Massegale/P. 4 1/2" x 5". **$5,100**

Newcomb College, vase crisply carved in the Espanol pattern by A.F. Simpson, 1929. Marked NC/RM77/77/JH/AFS. 7" x 3 1/2"...**$6,600**

Newcomb College, exceptional, early bulbous vase by Marie De Hoa LeBlanc with deeply incised jonquil blossoms in cream, yellow, and green on an alternating dark, medium, and light blue ground, 1909. Invisible repair to very small rim chip. Marked NC/JM/Q/DD52/MHLB. 6 1/2" x 7 1/2"..........**$13,200**

Photo courtesy Rago Arts and Auction Center, Lambertville, N.J.; www.RagoArts.com

Newcomb College bulbous vase by Corinna Luria with ring handles in a stylized geometric design. (Rare form). Bruise to rim, firing line to shoulder. Marked NC/C.L./KD18/192. 6" x 5". **$3,240**

Photo courtesy Belhorn Auction Services LLC, Columbus, Ohio; www.Belhorn.com

Nicodemus, matching pair of handled vases in mottled green and brown semi-gloss glaze. Both marked Nicodemus. Mint. 7 1/2" h x 6" w. **$350 pair**
(Chester Nicodemus, 1901-1990, Ohio teacher and potter.)

NILOAK POTTERY

Niloak Pottery was made near Benton, Arkansas. Charles Dean Hyten experimented with native clay, trying to preserve its natural colors. By 1911, he perfected Mission Ware, a marbleized pottery in which the cream and brown colors predominate. The company name is the word "kaolin" spelled backward.

After a devastating fire, the pottery was rebuilt and named Eagle Pottery. This factory included enough space to add a novelty pottery line in 1929. Hyten left the pottery in 1941, and in 1946 operations ceased.

Marks: The early pieces were marked "Niloak." Eagle Pottery products usually were marked "Hywood-Niloak" until 1934, when the "Hywood" was dropped from the mark.

Note: Prices listed here are for Mission Ware pieces.

Ashtray, Mission Ware, 3 1/2" w..$80
Bowl, marbleized swirls, blue, tan, and brown, 4 1/2" d ..$65
Box, covered, Mission Ware, lid chip, 5" d.................$190
Bud vase, Mission Ware, imp mk, 6" h $180
Candlesticks, pr, marbleized swirls, blue, cream, terra cotta, and brown, 8" h $250
Chamber pot, infant's, Mission Ware, 5 1/2" w $550
Flower pot, ruffled rim, green matte glaze, circa 1930.
....$155
Jug, Mission Ware, 6" h..$325
Rose Jar, Mission Ware, 8" h.....................................$850
Shot glass, Mission Ware, set of six, one chip, 2 1/2"h .$425
Tobacco jar, Mission Ware, 5 1/2" w, 5 1/2" h $700
Toothpick holder, marbleized swirls, tan and blue......$100
Urn, marbleized swirls, brown and blue, 4 1/2" h.............$45
Vase
    Applied twisted handles, Ozark Dawn glaze, circa 1930, 6" h.
....$120
    Early foil label, circa 1920-30, 3 1/4" h...................$95
    Ozark Dawn glaze, circa 1930, 8 3/4" h, ...$140
    Second art mark, circa 1925, 4 1/2" h....................$75
    Starved rock mark, circa 1925, 4 1/2" h..................$95

Photo courtesy of David Rago Auctions, Inc.

Niloak Mission Ware vase, ovoid, marbleized clays, stamped "Niloak," spider line to base, 4" d, 8" h. **$115**

Niloak Mission Ware cordial set, four matching tumblers, all marbleized clay, paper labels and stamps, 12" h stoppered bottle. **$900**

North Dakota School of Mines, fine bulbous vase by Margaret Cable with cutback daffodils in light brown on a deep brown ground. Circular ink mark/M. Cable/273. 8" x 5 1/2". **$3,120**

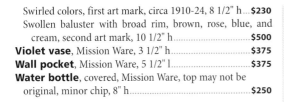

Swirled colors, first art mark, circa 1910-24, 8 1/2" h ...**$230**
Swollen baluster with broad rim, brown, rose, blue, and cream, second art mark, 10 1/2" h **$500**
Violet vase, Mission Ware, 3 1/2" h **$375**
Wall pocket, Mission Ware, 5 1/2" l **$375**
Water bottle, covered, Mission Ware, top may not be original, minor chip, 8" h **$250**

North Dakota School of Mines

The North Dakota School of Mines was established in 1890. Earle J. Babcock, a chemistry instructor, was impressed with the high purity level of North Dakota potter's clay. He tried to interest commercial potteries in the North Dakota clay, but had limited success.

In 1910, Babcock persuaded the school to establish a ceramics department. Margaret Cable, who studied under Charles Binns and Frederick H. Rhead, was appointed head. She remained until her retirement in 1949.

Decorative emphasis was placed on native themes, including flowers and animals. Art Nouveau, Art Deco and fairly plain pieces were made.

The pottery is often marked with a cobalt blue under-glaze circle of the words "University of North Dakota/Grand Forks, N.D./Made at School of Mines/N.D. Clay." Some early pieces are marked only "U.N.D." or "U.N.D./Grand Forks, N.D." Most pieces are numbered (they can be dated from University records) and signed by both the instructor and student. Cable-signed pieces are the most desirable.

North Dakota School of Mines, bulbous vase carved by Haesle with Viking ships in brown on a matte green ground, 1944. Indigo stamp, signed Haesle, 4-4-'44. 7 1/2" x 5". **$2,040**

North Dakota School of Mines, vase carved by H. Leigh with an Art Deco floral design under matte green and brown glaze, 1935. Circular indigo stamp, carved HLeigh Nov. 35. 8" x 6"..**$4,200**

North Dakota School of Mines, unusual, tall vase incised and enamel-decorated with white blossoms on matte green ground, 1927. Indigo stamp, DK1927. 9 1/2" x 5"......**$14,400**

North Dakota School of Mines, bulbous vase incised with fish under green and gunmetal glaze. Indigo stamp and incised Marie. 8 1/2" x 7"....................................**$6,600**

North Dakota School of Mines, squat vessel by Margaret Ruder incised with large brown leaves on a green ground, 1950. Indigo stamp. Incised MARgARET RudER Nov8 1950. 5 1/4" x 6 3/4"..**$570**

North Dakota School of Mines, high-walled vessel excised with an abstract pattern in black and ivory. 1/4" flake to base. Indigo stamp, carved cipher. 5" x 5 1/4". **$1,320**

Photo courtesy Rago Arts and Auction Center, Lambertville, N.J.; www.RagoArts.com

North Dakota School of Mines, bulbous vase painted in the Persian style in rich jewel tones. Indigo stamp, artist's cipher. 5" x 5 1/2". **$600**

Photo courtesy Belhorn Auction Services LLC, Columbus, Ohio; www.Belhorn.com

North Dakota School of Mines, vase by Ruth Schnell from 1944, matte-brown glaze and decoration consisting of stylized flowers. Marked with circular UND stamp and the artist's name and date 4/4/44 incised into the bottom. Mint and uncrazed. 5" h x 6" w. **$825**

George E. Ohr

Ohr pottery was produced by George E. Ohr in Biloxi, Miss. There is a discrepancy as to when he actually established his pottery; some say 1878, but Ohr's autobiography indicates 1883. In 1884, Ohr exhibited 600 pieces of his work, suggesting that he had been a potter for some time.

Ohr's techniques included twisting, crushing, folding, denting and crinkling thin-walled clay into odd, grotesque and sometimes graceful forms. His later pieces were often left unglazed.

In 1906, Ohr closed the pottery and stored more than 6,000 pieces as a legacy to his family. The entire collection remained in storage until it was rediscovered in 1972.

Today, Ohr is recognized as one of the leaders in the American art-pottery movement.

Much of Ohr's early work was signed with an impressed stamp including his name and location in block letters. His later work was often marked with the flowing script designation "G. E. Ohr."

G.E. OHR,
BILOXI.

George Ohr, teapot covered in cobalt blue glaze. Restoration to 4" chip and touch-up to finial. Script signature. 5" x 9"..**$4,800**

Photo courtesy Rago Arts and Auction Center, Lambertville, N.J.; www.RagoArts.com

George Ohr oversized teapot with an ear-shaped handle and serpentine spout on a dimpled body, covered in green and brown flambe glaze with gunmetal sponging. Small flat chip at rim, lid is original but not a match, as customary. (When Ohr's pottery was stored in 1907, the lids were packed separately from the teapots. As a result, perhaps a third were mismatched. This piece descended directly through Ohr family.) Stamped G. E. OHR Biloxi, Miss, twice. 7 1/4" x 8". **$10,800**

George Ohr, sculptural vessel of marbleized clay. Script signature. 4" x 6"............................$12,000

George Ohr, flaring vase covered in a fine raspberry, green, and gunmetal mottled glaze. Minute fleck to rim. Script signature. 3 1/2" x 5 1/2".............................$3,480

George Ohr, goblet covered in a fine purple, green, and brown mottled glaze. Tiny glazed hole to side. Script signature. 3 3/4" x 3 1/2".............................$3,900

George Ohr, squat vessel with deep in-body twist, covered in indigo and plum speckled glaze. G.E.OHR Biloxi, Miss. 4" x 4 1/2".............................$5,700

George Ohr, bulbous vase with deep in-body twist covered in brown speckled glaze, with black sponged-on pattern. G. E. OHR, Biloxi, Miss. 5 1/4" x 3 1/2".............................$4,500

George Ohr, tapering vessel with deep in-body twist at rim, covered in emerald green and black gunmetal glaze. GEO. E. OHR, BILOXI MISS. 3 1/2" x 4".............................$3,900

George Ohr, vessel with ribbed body and pinched floriform rim, covered in dark brown mottled glaze. G.E.OHR, Biloxi, Miss. 3 1/2" x 4".............................$3,120

Photo courtesy Rago Arts and Auction Center, Lambertville, N.J.; www.RagoArts.com

George Ohr Joe Jefferson mug, its incised motto entirely covered with raspberry, green, white, and indigo sponged-on glaze, 1896. Stamped G.E.OHR Biloxi, Miss. Incised 3-18-96. 4 1/2" x 4 1/2". **$5,700**

Photo courtesy Rago Arts and Auction Center, Lambertville, N.J.; www.RagoArts.com

George Ohr vase with pinched top, covered in green speckled mustard glaze. Stamped GO. E. OHR BILOXI, MISS. 4" x 4 1/2". **$6,600**

Overbeck Pottery

Four Overbeck sisters – Margaret, Hannah, Elizabeth and Mary Frances – established the Overbeck Pottery in their Cambridge City, Ind., home in 1911. Production ended with the death of Mary Frances in 1955.

Overbeck, large barrel-shaped vase excised with stylized birds and blossoms in matte mustard glaze on a rich chocolate brown ground. Incised OBK E F. 9 1/4" x 6".............$15,600

Overbeck, squat vessel excised with elephants and birds in russet against a pale orange ground. Incised OBK, E F. 3 1/2" x 5 1/2".............................$10,200

Photo courtesy Rago Arts and Auction Center, Lambertville, N.J.; www.RagoArts.com

Overbeck, bulbous vase excised with panels of stylized birds in green and brown. Incised OBK E F. 4 3/4" x 5 1/4". **$5,700**

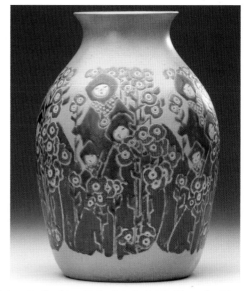

Photo courtesy Rago Arts and Auction Center, Lambertville, N.J.; www.RagoArts.com

Overbeck vase incised with stylized figures of children amidst red hollyhock blossoms, on a matte mustard ground. (An important piece, pictured in The Chronicle of Overbeck Pottery by Kathleen Postle, 1978, plate XXVIII.) Restoration to rim chip. Incised OBK F with paper label possibly covering E. 10 1/2" x 7". **$72,000**

Owens Pottery

J.B. Owens began making pottery in 1885 near Roseville, Ohio. In 1891, he built a plant in Zanesville and in 1897, began producing art pottery. After 1907, most of the firm's production centered on tiles.

Owens Pottery, employing many of the same artists and designs as its two cross-town rivals, Roseville and Weller, can appear similar to that of its competitors, e.g., Utopian (brown glaze), Lotus (light glaze) and Aqua Verde (green glaze).

There were a few techniques used exclusively at Owens. These included Red Flame ware (slip decoration under a high red glaze) and Mission (over-glaze, slip decorations in mineral colors) depicting Spanish Missions. Other specialties included Opalesce (semi-gloss designs in luster gold and orange) and Coralene (small beads affixed to the surface of the decorated vases).

Photo courtesy Belhorn Auction Services LLC, Columbus, Ohio; www.Belhorn.com

Owens, Utopian portrait vase by Mary F. Stevens. Well-executed portrait of Native American Indian Jack Red Cloud of the Ogallala Sioux (titled and signed on back of vase). Marked J.B. Owens Utopian 1010 8. Mint. 10 3/8" h x 5" w. **$4,500**

Photo courtesy Rago Arts and Auction Center, Lambertville, N.J.; www.RagoArts.com

Owens, large tile decorated in Cuenca style, with a cottage in a bucolic landscape. Framed. Unmarked. 11 1/2" x 17 1/2". **$4,200**
(This Spanish style of pottery is named for Cuenca, Ecuador.)

Photo courtesy Belhorn Auction Services LLC, Columbus, Ohio; www.Belhorn.com

Owens, Utopian standard-glaze handled vase with clover decoration signed MS by the artist. Marked J.B. Owens Utopian 953. Excellent condition. 4 7/8" h. **$160**

Photo courtesy Belhorn Auction Services LLC, Columbus, Ohio; www.Belhorn.com

Owens, matte blue Utopian jardiniere with slip-decorated tulips in white, unmarked. Mint. 7 5/8" h x 9 3/4" w. **$300**

Photo courtesy Belhorn Auction Services LLC, Columbus, Ohio; www.Belhorn.com

Pennsbury, Bluebird. Marked #103 Blue Bird Pennsbury Pottery K. Mint and uncrazed. 3 1/2" h. **$190**
(Pennsbury Pottery, Morrisville, Pa., 1950-1971.)

Peters & Reed, Landsun vase finely decorated with a farm scene and cottage. Short underglaze line to rim. Unmarked. 7 1/2" x 4". **$600**

Peters & Reed

J.D. Peters and Adam Reed founded their pottery in South Zanesville, Ohio, in 1900. Common flowerpots, jardiniéres and cooking wares comprised the majority of their early output. Occasionally, art pottery was attempted, but it was not until 1912 that their Moss Aztec line was introduced and widely accepted. Other art wares include Chromal, Landsun, Montene, Pereco and Persian.

Peters retired in 1921 and Reed changed the name of the firm to Zane Pottery Co.

Marked pieces of Peters & Reed Pottery are not known.

Peters & Reed, Landsun vase decorated with tree-lined hills. Minor grinding around base. Unmarked. 9 1/2" x 3 3/4". **$480**

Peters & Reed, Moss Aztec jardinière and pedestal set decorated with bands of poppies. A few minor nicks and abrasions to edges. Unmarked. 30" x 15" overall. **$960**

Providential Tile Works, Trenton, N.J., tiles, pair, with pendant portraits, head of bearded man, head of classical woman, teal glaze, both Design C, 6" x 6"; framed; 1896 wedding gift. .... **$360 pair**

Providential Tile Works, Trenton, N.J., tiles, two pair, with pendant portraits, head of lady wearing net cap and head of lady wearing plain cap, mottled brown and green glaze, 6" x 6"; framed. Lady and gentleman, greenish brown glaze, 6" x 6"; framed. .... **$373 all**

Pigeon Forge, Kingfisher by Douglas Ferguson. Signed by the artist. Mint. 9 3/4" h. **$350**

RED WING POTTERY

The Red Wing pottery category includes several potteries from Red Wing, Minn. In 1868, David Hallem started Red Wing Stoneware Co., the first pottery with stoneware as its primary product. The Minnesota Stoneware Co. started in 1883. The North Star Stoneware Co. was in business from 1892 to 1896.

The Red Wing Stoneware Co. and the Minnesota Stoneware Co. merged in 1892. The new company, the Red Wing Union Stoneware Co., made stoneware until 1920 when it introduced a pottery line that it continued until the 1940s. In 1936, the name was changed to Red Wing Potteries, Inc. During the 1930s, this firm introduced several popular patterns of hand-painted dinnerware, which were distributed through department stores, mail-order catalogs, and gift-stamp centers. Dinnerware production declined in the 1950s and was replaced with hotel and restaurant china in the early 1960s. The plant closed in 1967.

Marks: Red Wing Stoneware Co. was the first firm to mark pieces with a red wing stamped under the glaze. The North Star Stoneware Co. used a raised star and the words "Red Wing" as its mark.

Ashtray No. 54, Nokomis glaze, 4" w **$600**

Bean pot, covered, "It Pays to Trade with Shors & Alexander Pocahontas, IA" **$85**

Red Wing, "Woman with Two Tubes," double bud vase No. 1175, designed by Charles Murphy, 1942, 10 1/2" h. **$1,300**

Red Wing, teapot, No. 260, early 1940s, 7 3/4" h. **$150**

Red Wing two-gallon white stoneware churn with birch leaves, and cover, 12 1/2" h without cover. **$500-$700**

Bookends, pr, polar bears, jet black glaze, Rumrill........**$525**
Bowl
    Brown shoulder, bottom mkd, 7" d.......................**$45**
    Greek Key, 6" d......................................**$115**
    Shoulder, mkd, 13" d.................................**$175**
    Sponge dec, cap shape, 7" d.........................**$95**
    Spongeband, 4" d....................................**$275**
    Spongeband, 9" d....................................**$145**
    Spongeband, "Merry Christmas from Weigolb & Nordby Stores, Mix With Us," 8" d.........................**$125**
Butter churn, two gallons, 2" wing and oval mark........**$250**
Butter crock
    One gallon, "Polly Ann Boston Baked Beans".............**$175**
    Three lb, "Fresh Butter Model Dairy Inc.".............**$75**

Three lb, "North American Creameries, Inc., Meadowbrook Butter"......................................**$125**
Three lb, "White & Mathers" adv......................**$200**
Five lb, "Goodhue County Co-operative Co.," minor nick on top edge...**$95**
Casserole, spongeband, large............................**$125**
Casserole, covered, "Merry Christmas Hokah Co-Op Creamery," 8" d.......................................**$195**
Chicken water, half gallon, "Oak Leaf Simmon's Hardware Co."...**$250**
Churn, four gallons
    Oval mark and 4" wing................................**$175**
    Oval over birch leaf, hairline in bottom...............**$145**
    Salt glaze, lazy 8 and target dec....................**$375**
Churn, six gallon, white stoneware churn with birch leaves called "elephant ears," 17 1/2" h...............**$950**
Churn lid, 5/6 gallon.................................**$120**
Crock
    One gallon, 2" wing..................................**$350**
    Two gallon, 4" wing mark..............................**$90**
    Two gallon, tilted birch leaves and oval stamp with "Minnesota Stoneware Company" (spelled out, commonly found as "Co."), 12" h with lid, otherwise unmarked.........**$1,500**
    Three gallon, circle oval mark and 2" wing..............**$90**
    Three gallon, "Potteries" oval, 2" wing................**$65**
    Eight gallons, chip on base, oval mark and 6" wing.......**$75**
    Ten gallon, oval mark and 6" wing, "10" and oval in black-ink...**$125**
    Ten-gallon, Washington advertising that includes crockery...**$1,500**
    Twenty gallon, oval mark and 6" wing..................**$125**
Crock, salt glaze
    Two gallon, target, bottom mkd.......................**$100**
    Two gallon, salt-glaze crock with strong cobalt decoration of "target with tail," marked on bottom, "Minnesota Stoneware Co. Red Wing, Minn.," circa 1890...............**$475**
    Three gallon, tornado, front stamped "Red Wing Stoneware Company," large chip at bottom...................**$250**
    Five gallons, birch leaf, Union label, chip on handle.......**$55**
    Six gallons, leaf dec................................**$175**
    Ten gallons, leaf, front stamped "Minnesota Stoneware," hairline...**$250**
    Twenty lbs, butterfly, back stamped, hairlines.............**$175**
Crock lid
    One-gallon size......................................**$90**
    Fifteen gallons, nick where wire handle enters lid.........**$65**
    Two gallon...**$225**
Custard, spongeband
    Large, tight hairline.................................**$65**
    Small..**$85**
Funeral vase, Brushware................................**$65**
Fruit jar, "Union Stoneware Co., Red Wing Minn".......**$300**
Hotplate, Minnesota Centennial, 1958..................**$45**
Jug
    One-eighth pint, Michigan advertising.................**$225**
    One gallon, ball top shoulders, bottom mkd.............**$95**
    One gallon, brown top shoulders, "The Banner Liquor Store, Winona, Minn".......................................**$175**
    One gallon, brown top shoulders, wing mark.............**$195**
    One gallon, "Fargo Creamery Supply House St. Paul, Minn" in oval, bottom marked...............................**$150**

Red Wing four-gallon white stoneware water cooler without gallon mark, lid impressed "3W"; 12 3/4" h without lid; lid, 9 1/2" d. **$800-$1,000**

Red Wing four-gallon salt-glaze water cooler, cobalt lazy 8 decoration, original cover, unmarked, circa 1890, 11" h without lid. **$3,000**

Red Wing white stoneware "Koverwates," two sizes, which were placed inside crocks to keep foods submerged in preserving liquid, sizes shown are for three and four gallons, found up to 20-gallon size; three-gallon, 8" d; four-gallon, 9" d, depending on size. **$250-$500**

One gallon, tomato, brown top, wing mark $395
Three gallon, shoulder, no oval mark, 2" wing $35
Five gallons, Imperial, shoulder, 4" wing and oval mark
....$125
Five gallon, shoulders, "Union" oval and 4" wing............$80
Five gallon, shoulder, "The Mason House & Mineral Springs, Colfax Iowa," shield and Union label..........................$775
Five gallon, white stoneware, "beehive" two-handles, advertising, 17" h...$4,000
Dome top, "bird jug," about 1 1/2 gallons, in Albany slip glaze, circa 1895, 9 1/4" h.....................................$150
Salt-glaze "beehive" jug with cobalt "tornado" decoration, with glaze drippings called "turkey droppings," unmarked, circa 1890, 17" h..$2,900

Koverwate
Three gallon, "3" on side with instructions $450
Fifteen gallon, mkd "15," small nick..............................$125

Mason jar, stoneware screw top, metal lid, mkd "Stone Mason Fruit Jar," Union Stoneware Co., Red Wing, Minn
....$310

Mug
Blue bands, "Certainly"...$150
Blue bands, "Good Luck Malt Syrup," hairline..............$135
Blue bands, "I Came From Atlas Malt Products Co., Janesville, WI," hairline $115
Blue bands, "Souvenir West End Commercial Club, St. Paul June 21-26, 1909"..$185
Spongeband...$575

Nappy
Blue and white..$120
Saffronware, "Compliments of C. A. Habergarten & Co., Waconia, Minn"...$195

Pitcher
Blue mottled, large, minor bottom edge chips..............$200
Cherry band, large..$175
Cherry band, large, with Marble Rock, Iowa, advertising, 9 1/2"...$1,000
Cherry band, small..$195
Spongeband, large..$195
Sponge, mottled..$165
Spongeband, small..$335

Planter, Belle Kogan called "The Nymphs," No. B2500, part of the "Deluxe Line," 16 1/2" w, 6 3/4" h..............................$180

Plaque, Minnesota Centennial, maroon, 1958................$60

Refrigerator jar, small size, hairline $65

Salt shaker, Spongeband, white glaze $120

Sewer tile $70

Snuff jar, covered, North Star, Albany slip, minor chip under lid..$125

Souvenir jug, 1992 Red Wing Collctors Society $55

Spittoon, German-style, bottom edge chip $375

Thrashing jug, five gallons, beehive, six-sided spigot hole, oval mark and 4" wing..$1,650

Urn, No. 252, pale yellow glaze, blue circle stamp mark, 11" h..$290

Vase, Brushed Ware, No. 133, ink-stamped in a circle, "Red Wing Union Stoneware Co.—Red Wing, Minn," 8 1/4" h
....$175

Water cooler
Two gallon white stoneware water cooler, small wing and bail handles, 11" h without lid; lid, 9" d $2,200
Five gallon, 4" wing mark $350

Rhead/Santa Barbara, footed bottle-shaped vase, hand modeled by Frederick Rhead with an applied lizard, glazed green against a pale yellow body. Potter at the wheel stamp. 7 1/2" x 3 3/4". **$22,800**

Adelaide Alsop Robineau, (1865-1929) porcelain kylyx bowl-form with a cafe-au-lait exterior with full-blown blue crystals, black handles, and a rose-to-brown interior. Very short and tight line to rim, restoration to small chip at rim. Unmarked. 3 1/2" x 8". **$1,680**

Rockingham, glazed pottery cat figure, American, late 19th century, unobtrusive repaired cracks on base, 13 3/4" h. ...**$474**

Rookwood

Maria Longworth Nichols Storer of Cincinnati founded Rookwood Pottery in 1880. The name of the pottery came from her family estate, Rookwood, named for the crows that inhabited the grounds.

Though the Rookwood pottery filed for bankruptcy in 1941, it was soon reorganized under new management. Efforts at maintaining the pottery proved futile, and it was sold in 1956 and again in 1959. The pottery was moved to Starkville, Miss., in conjunction with the Herschede Clock Co. It finally ceased operating in 1967.

There are five elements to the Rookwood marking system: the clay or body mark, the size mark, the decorator mark, the date mark and the factory mark. The best way to date Rookwood art pottery is from factory marks.

From 1880 to 1882, the factory mark was the name "Rookwood" incised or painted on the base. Between 1881 and 1886, the firm name, address and year appeared in an oval. Beginning in 1886, the impressed "RP" monogram appeared and a flame mark was added for each year until 1900. After 1900, Roman numerals, indicating the last two digits of the year of production, were added at the bottom of the "RP" flame mark.

Rookwood, vase from 1922 decorated by Louise Abel. Double Vellum example with mottling to the glaze and color. Marked with Rookwood logo, XXII, the shape number 2308 and the artist's incised mark. Mint. 7" h. **$675**

Photo courtesy Belhorn Auction Services LLC, Columbus, Ohio; www.Belhorn.com

Rookwood, 1923 matte glaze vase by Katherine Jones. Decorated with red berries and green leaves on a red and pink mottled background. Marked with Rookwood logo, XXIII, 919E and the artist's mark. Mint and uncrazed. 4 1/8" h. **$750**

Photo courtesy Belhorn Auction Services LLC, Columbus, Ohio; www.Belhorn.com

Rookwood, vase from 1939 with Art Deco motif and blue-green matte crystalline glaze. Marked with Rookwood logo, XXXIX and the shape number 6462. Mint. 5 1/8" h. **$300**

Photo courtesy of Treadway Toomey Galleries, Cincinnati and Oak Park, Ill.; www.treadwaygallery.com

Rookwood, plaque, covered in a Vellum glaze with painted landscape, executed by Fred Rothenbusch in 1904, held in an Arts and Crafts oak frame; plaque 14 1/2" w x 9 1/2" h; overall 20" w x 15" h. **$10,000**

Rookwood, experimental Iris Glaze crescent-shaped vase by Ed Diers with a purple iris, covered in a silvered modeled iris, 1900. Tight 2" hairline from rim. Flame mark/T1236/ED/W. 4 1/2" x 4"..................**$7,200**

Rookwood, Jewel Porcelain faceted vase painted by Elizabeth Barrett with large clematis blossoms, 1944. Two small burst bubbles to rim. Flame mark/XLIV/6864/artist's cipher. 7 1/2" x 5 1/2"..................**$1,200**

Rookwood, Jewel Porcelain vase finely painted by Arthur Conant with large chrysanthemums on a deep blue ground, 1918. Flame mark/XVIII/999C/P/artist's cipher. 8 3/4" x 6 3/4"..........................**$10,800**

Rookwood, Jewel Porcelain barrel-shaped vase painted by Lorinda Epply with amber fish on a butter-yellow ground, 1930. Uncrazed. Flame mark/XXX/6203C/LE. 8" x 6 1/4"....................................**$4,500**

Rookwood, Jewel Porcelain vase by Kataro Shirayamadani with an all-over, chintz-like pattern of cherry blossoms on a raspberry pink ground, 1922. Uncrazed, superficial glaze fleck to rim. Flame mark/XXII/589F/artist's Japanese cipher. 7 1/2" x 3"..................**$4,200**

Rookwood, Jewel Porcelain vase by Kataro Shirayamadani with white and orange blossoms and green leaves against a shaded peach to gray ground, 1919. Uncrazed. Flame mark/XIX/1929/Japanese cipher. 5" x 7"....................**$1,920**

Rookwood, large Jewel Porcelain bulbous vase painted by Sara Sax with birds and magnolias on a rich blue and black ground, 1917. Uncrazed. Flame mark/XVII/2272/P/artist's cipher. 12 1/4" x 7 1/2"................................**$4,500**

Rookwood, Later Mat/Mat Moderne squat vessel by William Hentschel with sprigs in brown and indigo on ivory ground, 1931. Flame mark/XXXI/6199F/WEH. 4" x 4 1/2"..**$840**

Rookwood, Later Mat/Mat Moderne squat vessel William Hentschel with beige leaves on a yellow ground, 1931. Flame mark/XXXI/1110F/WEH. 3 3/4" x 5 1/4"........**$1,320**

Rookwood, Scenic Vellum vase by Sallie Coyne with lake landscape, 1921. Flame mark/XXI/2067/V/artist's cipher. 7 3/4" x 3 1/2"................................**$1,920**

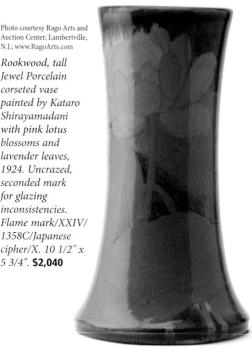

Rookwood, tall Jewel Porcelain corseted vase painted by Kataro Shirayamadani with pink lotus blossoms and lavender leaves, 1924. Uncrazed, seconded mark for glazing inconsistencies. Flame mark/XXIV/ 1358C/Japanese cipher/X. 10 1/2" x 5 3/4". **$2,040**

Rookwood, tall Painted Mat vase executed by A.R. Valentien with purple orchids on green ground, 1901. Flame mark/I/188VZ/ A.R. VALENTIEN. 12 1/4" x 4 1/2". **$7,800**

Rookwood, vase with hand-painted image of Sioux chief Black Bird, 13" h. **$15,500**

Rookwood, Scenic Vellum vase by Sallie Coyne with a full moon over a lake landscape, 1913. Overall crazing. Flame mark/XIII/2064/V/artist's cipher. 7 1/2" x 3 1/2". **$1,320**

Rookwood, Scenic Vellum vase by Sallie Coyne with lake landscape, 1920. Minimal crazing. Flame mark/XX/808/V/ artist's cipher. 8" x 3 1/2". **$2,040**

Rookwood, Scenic Vellum by Sallie Coyne with a banded moonlit lake landscape, 1908. Flame mark/VIII/1657/SEC/ V/C. 8" x 4 1/4". **$2,400**

Rookwood, Scenic Vellum vase by Ed Diers with a misty landscape, 1909. Some peppering to upper half. Flame mark/IX/1658D/V/ED. 9 3/4" x 4 3/4". **$1,440**

Rookwood, Scenic Vellum vase by Ed Diers with a lake landscape, 1919. Flame mark/XIX/1369D/V/ED. 9 1/4" x 5 1/4". **$2,040**

Rookwood, Scenic Vellum plaque by Fred Rothenbusch with a snow-covered alpine landscape, 1913. In original frame. 1/3" glaze flake to edge. Flame mark/XIII/V/FR. Plaque: 8 1/2" x 10 3/4". **$5,400**

Rookwood, Scenic Vellum vase by Fred Rothenbusch with lake landscape, 1921. Flame mark/XXI/614E/V/FR. 8 3/4" x 4". **$2,520**

Rookwood, large terra cotta garden urn and stand decorated in the Italian Renaissance style with blue engobe. A few small chips commensurate with age, largest 2". Stamped 3041Y RP. Overall: 43" x 26". **$3,900**

Rookwood, Vellum vase painted by Carl Schmidt with two large dragonflies, 1904. Seconded mark for peppering. Flame mark/IV/915D/artist's cipher/X. 7" x 5 1/2". **$9,000**

Rookwood, Later Mat/Mat Moderne squat vessel by William Hentschel with beige leaves on a caramel ground, 1931. (Seconded mark for no apparent reason.) Flame mark/XXXI/6199F/WEH/X. 4" x 4 3/4". **$1,440**

Rookwood tall Scenic Vellum vase by Lorinda Epply with a lake landscape in deep and vivid colors, 1916. Light peppering. Flame mark/XVI/977/V/LE. 11" x 5 1/2". **$2,520**

Rookwood, Vellum vase with a banded scene of bamboo by Lorinda Epply from 1908. Marked with Rookwood logo, VIII, the shape number 1124E, V (twice) and the artist's incised initials. Mint. 7" h x 3 1/8" w. **$1,200**

Rookwood, Sung Plum vase by Sara Sax with fleshy poppies on raspberry ground, 1927. (The crispness of the piece suggests some hand tooling by Sax). Flame mark/ XXVII/6006/artist's cipher. 12" x 7". **$20,400**

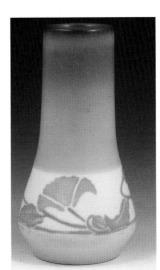

Rookwood, vase with Vellum Glaze and stylized floral decoration by Elizabeth Lincoln from 1908. Marked with Rookwood logo, VIII, the shape number 1278E, V for Vellum Glaze (twice) and the artist's mark. Mint. 7 3/8" h x 3 5/8" w. **$600**

Roseville

In the late 1880s, a group of investors purchased the J.B. Owens Pottery in Roseville, Ohio, and made utilitarian stoneware items. In 1892, the firm was incorporated and joined by George F. Young, who became general manager. Four generations of the Young family controlled Roseville until the early 1950s.

A series of acquisitions began: Midland Pottery of Roseville in 1898, Clark Stoneware Plant in Zanesville (formerly used by Peters and Reed), and Muskingum Stoneware (Mosaic Tile Co.) in Zanesville. In 1898, the offices also moved from Roseville to Zanesville.

In 1900, Roseville introduced Rozane, an art pottery. Rozane became a trade name to cover a large series of lines. The art lines were made in limited amounts after 1919.

The success of Roseville depended on its commercial lines, first developed by John J. Herald and Frederick Rhead in the first decades of the 1900s. In 1918, Frank Ferrell became art director and developed more than 80 lines of pottery.

In the 1940s, a series of high-gloss glazes were tried in an attempt to revive certain lines. In 1952, Raymor dinnerware was produced. None of these changes brought economic success and in November 1954, Roseville was bought by the Mosaic Tile Co.

Photo courtesy Belhorn Auction Services LLC, Columbus, Ohio; www.Belhorn.com

Roseville, Blackberry 569-5" volcano vase. Marked 596 in red grease pencil and with partial foil label. Mint. 5 1/4" h x 4 1/4" w. **$250**

Photo courtesy Belhorn Auction Services LLC, Columbus, Ohio; www.Belhorn.com

Roseville, Blue Falline candleholders 1092-3 1/2". Both marked 1092 in red grease pencil and with original foil label. Mint. 4 1/4" h. **$575 Pair**

Photo courtesy Rago Arts and Auction Center, Lambertville, N.J.; www.RagoArts.com

Roseville, bulbous Baneda-style (introduced 1932) factory lamp base decorated with band of yellow flowers and leaves on a green to blue ground. Unmarked. 10". **$960**

Photo courtesy Rago Arts and Auction Center, Lambertville, N.J.; www.RagoArts.com

Roseville, Blue Falline two-handled vase with stepped neck. Foil label. 7 1/4" x 6 1/2". **$1,320**

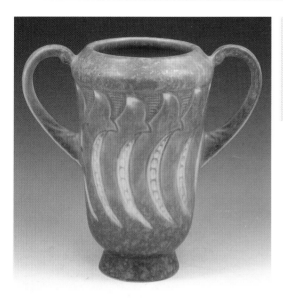

Roseville, Blue Falline 642-6″ vase with large, looping handles in blue. Unmarked. Mint. 6 1/8″ h x 6 3/8″ w. **$725**

Roseville, Columbine basket in blue. Marked Roseville USA 366-8″. Mint. 8″ h x 8 1/4″ w. **$200**

Roseville, Aztec vase decorated in squeeze bag with swags and blossoms on blue-gray ground. A few minor flecks to decoration. Unmarked. 11 1/4″ x 4 3/4″. **$390**

Roseville, Blackberry jardinière and pedestal set. Unmarked. 28 1/2″ x 13 1/2″. **$2,760**

Roseville, Crystalis massive vase covered in frothy matte mustard glaze. Post-factory drill hole to bottom. Unmarked. 29″ x 12″. **$2,400**

Roseville, Crystalis massive vase with tall neck over squat base, covered in a fine golden crystalline glaze. Post-factory drill hole to bottom. Unmarked. 25″ x 13 1/2″. **$4,200**

Roseville, Dahlrose 1069-3″ candleholders (pair). Unmarked. Mint. 3 1/2″ h x 5 1/2″ w. **$200 pair**

Photo courtesy Rago Arts and Auction Center, Lambertville, N.J.; www.RagoArts.com

Roseville, bulbous lamp base decorated with white and yellow flowers on a green ground. Unmarked. 9" x 6 1/2". **$960**

Photo courtesy Belhorn Auction Services LLC, Columbus, Ohio; www.Belhorn.com

Roseville, Windsor 545-5" handled vase in rust with green motif. Nice mold and glaze. Unmarked. Mint. 5 1/8" h x 5" w.
$425

Photo courtesy Belhorn Auction Services LLC, Columbus, Ohio; www.Belhorn.com

Roseville, Decorated Matte 468-7" jardiniere, signed in slip by the artist near the base. Marked only with an impressed 8. 8 3/4" w x 6 1/8" h. **$725**

Roseville, Della Robbia (Rozane) early and rare vase carved with concentric rings of incised daisies on a blue ground. Two chips to rim, some glaze nicks. Rozane Ware medallion, marked MF. 8 1/2" x 6 1/2". **$11,400**

Roseville, Della Robbia bottle-shaped vase carved with peach-colored gardenias on a blue-gray ground, with reticulated rim. Rozane Ware medallion and marked W.M. (to both side and bottom). 10" x 6 3/4". **$6,000**

Roseville, Della Robbia exceptional vase excised with lavender tulips and blue and green leaves on celadon ground. Light peppering on blossoms, missing lid. Marked G. 7 3/4" x 7". **$6,600**

Roseville, Della Robbia exceptional and tall vase with blossoms in apricot, yellow, and blue on a celadon ground. Restoration to base and rim. 15 3/4" x 4 1/2". **$21,600**

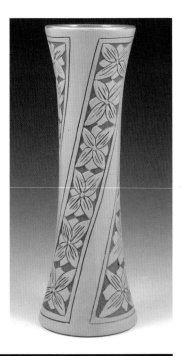

Photo courtesy Belhorn Auction Services LLC, Columbus, Ohio; www.Belhorn.com

Roseville, Della Robbia 9-10 1/4" vase in two colors with hand carved flowers. 10" h x 3 3/8" w. **$1,400**

Photo courtesy Rago Arts and Auction Center, Lambertville, N.J.; www.RagoArts.com

Roseville, Della Robbia gourd-shaped vase with penguins and trees in celadon on blue-gray. Restoration to chips on rim and base. Rozane medallion and marked EL. 8 1/4" x 4 1/2". **$2,760**

Photo courtesy Belhorn Auction Services LLC, Columbus, Ohio; www.Belhorn.com

Roseville, Early Velmoss matte green Arts & Crafts jardiniere. Very fine glaze and form. Unmarked. Mint. 15" w x 10" h. **$1,650**

Roseville, Egypto rare four-sided vase embossed with medallions, covered in frothy matte green glaze. Professional restoration to a few small chips at base. Rozane Ware Egypto medallion. 12 1/2" x 3 1/2". **$1,080**

Roseville, Early Lily planter with insert, decorated in squeeze bag with yellow and black water lilies on a green ground. A few flecks overall, 1/4" bruise to rim of liner, dark crazing to rim of planter (lines do not go through). Unmarked. 8 3/4" x 11"...**$300**

Roseville, Early Velmoss 130-8" vase in matte green and mustard yellow with strong Arts & Crafts motif. Unmarked. Mint. 7 7/8" h. **$525**

Roseville, Freesia basket in green. Marked Roseville USA 391-8". Mint. 8 1/4" h x 8 5/8" w. **$275**

Roseville, Ferella handled 510-9" vase, red. Unmarked. Mint. 9 1/4" h. **$1,150**

Roseville, Fuchsia jardinière and pedestal set, green. 3" bruise and faint spider lines to base of jard. Faint impressed mark to jard. 32" x 16". **$960**

Roseville, Fuchsia vase, brown, 904-15". Restoration to 3" area at rim. Impressed mark. **$360**

Roseville, Fudjiyama twisted, four-sided vase finely decorated with deep blue poppies, and designs in tan, blue and green around rim and body. A few extremely minor areas of wear on body, excellent condition overall. Rozane Ware seal. 9 1/2" x 3 1/2". **$2,280**

Roseville, Futura four-footed, four-sided vase with floral pattern on burgundy ground. Small glazed-over chip to inner foot. Unmarked. 9" x 5". **$1,140**

Roseville, Imperial II ovoid vase covered in a rich, mottled blue and yellow glaze over a ribbed body. Restoration to two drill holes, one on side and one on bottom. Foil label. 11 1/4" x 6 1/2"..**$840**

Roseville, Mostique jardinière and pedestal set. A few small nicks overall. Unmarked. 28 1/4" x 14"........................**$1,320**

Roseville, Pauleo vase covered in a dark black and green mottled glaze. Post-factory drill hole to bottom. Unmarked. 2 1" x 1 1". **$2,040**

Roseville, Pine Cone massive urn, brown, 912-15". Impressed mark. 15 1/4" x 1 1". **$1,440**

Roseville, Pink Foxglove jardinière and pedestal set, 659-10". Tight line to rim of jard. Raised marks..................**$570**

Roseville, Russco-type (introduced 1934) factory lamp base covered in a mottled orange to green glaze. Unmarked. 10 1/2". **$480**

Roseville, Russco-type (introduced 1934) factory lamp base covered in a mottled orange to yellow glaze. Unmarked. 10 1/2" x 4". **$480**

Photo courtesy Belhorn Auction Services LLC, Columbus, Ohio; www.Belhorn.com

Roseville, Futura 435-10" Elephant Leg vase. Unmarked. Mint. 10" h x 7 1/2" w. **$1,450**

Photo courtesy Rago Arts and Auction Center, Lambertville, N.J.; www.RagoArts.com

Roseville, Imperial II triple wall pocket covered in a frothy orange and green glaze. Unmarked. 6 1/2" x 8 1/4". **$600**

Photo courtesy Belhorn Auction Services LLC, Columbus, Ohio; www.Belhorn.com

Roseville, Pauleo floor vase with hand-decorated band of strawberries, leaves, blossom and branches on a golden-orange luster background. Marked 312 in slip. Mint. 16 7/8" h. **$875**

Photo courtesy Belhorn Auction Services LLC, Columbus, Ohio; www.Belhorn.com

Roseville, Luffa 687-8" vase in brown and green. Unmarked. Mint. 8 1/4" h x 5 7/8" w. **$250**

Photo courtesy Belhorn Auction Services LLC, Columbus, Ohio; www.Belhorn.com

Roseville, Pine Cone vase, brown. Marked Roseville 838-6". Mint. 6 1/4" h x 5" w. **$140**

Photo courtesy Belhorn Auction Services LLC, Columbus, Ohio; www.Belhorn.com

Roseville, Pauleo vase with metallic luster glaze tones of red, copper and gold, unmarked. 18 7/8" h. **$1,050**

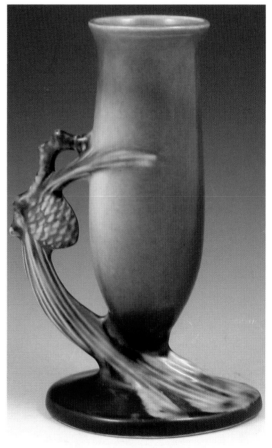

Photo courtesy Belhorn Auction Services LLC, Columbus, Ohio; www.Belhorn.com

Roseville, Pine Cone bud vase in blue. Marked Roseville 112-7. Mint. 7 5/8" h. **$120**

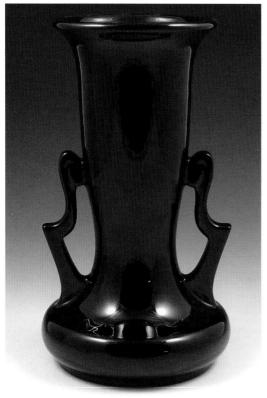

Roseville, Rosecraft Black 316-10" vase with handles. Unmarked. Mint and uncrazed. 10 3/8" h x 5 3/4" w. **$230**

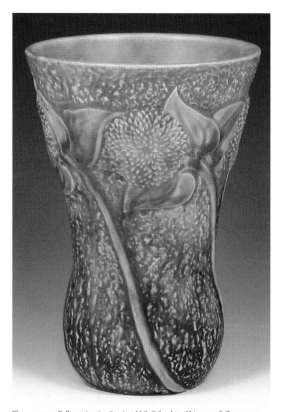

Roseville, Sunflower 487-7" flaring vase. Marked 487 in red grease pen. Mint. 7 1/4" h x 5" w. **$525**

Roseville, Savona vase in light blue high glaze. Partially marked 372 in red crayon. Mint. 6" h x 5" w. **$275**

Roseville, Sunflower 485-6" vase. Marked with original black paper label. Mint. 6 1/8" h x 5" w. **$450**

Roseville, spherical factory lamp base decorated with yellow, purple, and blue flowers with green leaves, on a mottled orange ground. Unmarked. 8 1/2" x 7 1/2". **$960**

Roseville, Windsor large squat vessel, brown. Good color. Professional restoration to small chip under each handle. Remnant of foil label. 7" x 9 1/2"..................................**$780**

Roseville, Wisteria bulbous vase, blue. Foil label. 7" x 8 1/2". **$840**

Roseville, Topeo 245-6" rose bowl in matte blue, green and pink pastel tones. Marked with original foil label, 7 1/2" w x 6" h. **$300**

Roseville, Thornapple rose bowl in blue. Marked Roseville 305-8". Mint. 10 1/2" w x 6 1/4" h. **$100**

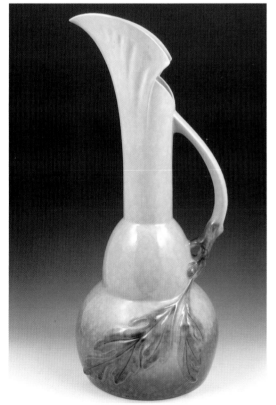

Roseville, Wincraft oak and acorn ewer in blue, uncommon. Marked Roseville USA 218-18". Mint. 18 3/4" h. **$525**

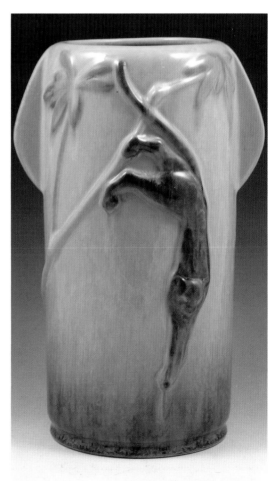

Roseville, Wincraft panther vase in blue. Marked Roseville USA 290-11". Mint. 10 1/2" h x 6 3/4" w. **$500**

Saturday Evening Girls, Paul Revere Pottery

Paul Revere Pottery, Boston, was an outgrowth of a club known as the Saturday Evening Girls. The S.E.G. was composed of young female immigrants who met on Saturday nights to read and participate in craft projects, such as ceramics.

Regular pottery production began in 1908, and the name "Paul Revere" was adopted because the pottery was located near the Old North Church. In 1915, the firm moved to Brighton, Mass. Known as the "Bowl Shop," the pottery grew steadily. In spite of popular acceptance and technical advancements, the pottery required continual subsidies. It finally closed in 1942.

Items produced range from plain and decorated vases to tableware to illustrated tiles. Many decorated wares were incised and glazed either in an Art Nouveau matte finish or an occasional high glaze.

In addition to an impressed mark, paper "Bowl Shop" labels were used prior to 1915. Pieces also may be found with a date and "P.R.P." or "S.E.G." painted on the base.

Saturday Evening Girls, low bowl decorated in "Cuerda Seca" technique with a band of pine boughs on matte green, 1917. 2 1/2" Y-shaped line from rim. Signed A M 1-17 SEG. 2 1/2" x 8 1/2"...**$1,320**
(Cuerda Seca literally means "dry string." A wax outline is drawn on the pottery and glaze is applied with a syringe. During the firing process, the glaze beads up against the wax barrier creating subtle flooded areas. Sometimes the outline is done with black wax and serves as a black outline in the design.)

Shawsheen, vase incised with stylized flowers in matte pastel colors. Signed SAP. 4" x 5"................................**$1,680**
(Several potteries were called Shawsheen, and were found in Iowa, Kansas and Massachusetts.)

Photo courtesy Rago Arts and Auction Center, Lambertville, N.J.; www.RagoArts.com

Saturday Evening Girls, cylindrical vase decorated in "Cuerda Seca" technique with a village seen through tall trees. Professional restoration to rim chip. Signed 2?8.11.11.SEG IG, 6 3/4" x 3". **$57,000**

Photo courtesy Rago Arts and Auction Center, Lambertville, N.J.; www.RagoArts.com

Saturday Evening Girls, cereal bowl decorated in "Cuerda Seca" technique with a band of hens and chicks around "ELIZA" in yellow and white, 1909. Light wear around rim. Signed F.L. 241-4-09. SEG in vessel. 1 3/4" x 6". **$1,140** *(Cuerda Seca literally means "dry string." A wax outline is drawn on the pottery and glaze is applied with a syringe. During the firing process, the glaze beads up against the wax barrier creating subtle flooded areas. Sometimes the outline is done with black wax and serves as a black outline in the design.)*

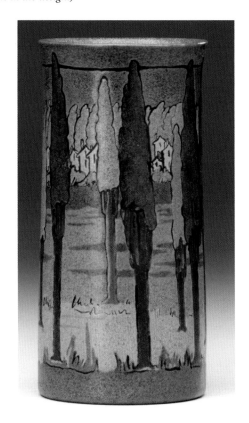

Photo courtesy Rago Arts and Auction Center, Lambertville, N.J.; www.RagoArts.com

Shawsheen covered box, its four panels incised with a castle landscape in matte glazes. Signed SAP. 5 1/2" x 3 1/2" sq. **$3,900**
(Several potteries were called Shawsheen, and were found in Iowa, Kansas and Massachusetts.)

Photo courtesy Belhorn Auction Services LLC, Columbus, Ohio; www.Belhorn.com

Shearwater, (founded 1928, Ocean Springs, Miss.), vase with swirl decoration in deep cobalt blue and finished in high glaze. Marked with impressed, semi-circular 'SHEARWATER' mark. Mint. 5 7/8" h. **$975**

Stangl

Stangl ceramic birds and animals were made from 1940 until the Stangl factory closed in 1978. They were produced at Stangl's Trenton, N.J., plant and either decorated there or shipped to its Flemington, N.J., outlet.

During World War II, the demand for the birds, and other types of Stangl pottery, as well, was so great that scores of decorators could not keep up with the demand. Orders were contracted out, to be decorated by individuals in their own homes. These orders then were returned for firing and finishing. Colors used to decorate these birds varied according to the artist.

As many as 10 different trademarks were used. Almost every bird is numbered; many are artist signed.

Note: Several birds were reissued between 1972 and 1977. These reissues are dated on the bottom.

Stangl, Magpie Jay and Spotted Owl. Impressed marks on owl, "Stangl USA," oval Stangl pottery birds mark and V.3758 under glaze. Taller, 10 1/2" h.......................... **$840 pair**

Photo courtesy Belhorn Auction Services LLC, Columbus, Ohio; www.Belhorn.com

Stangl, Della Ware Pheasant in natural colors. Marked 3586 with blue ink Della Ware stamp and WK by the decorator. Mint and uncrazed. 15 1/4" long x 8 1/4" h. **$675**

Photo courtesy Belhorn Auction Services LLC, Columbus, Ohio; www.Belhorn.com

Stangl, #3285 Rooster and #3286 Hen figures with open bases. Marked only with BB by Betty Bittner. Mint. 4" and 3" h. **$130 pair**

Photo courtesy Belhorn Auction Services LLC, Columbus, Ohio; www.Belhorn.com

Stangl, Double Red Headed Woodpeckers with matte red over-glaze color. Marked with brown STANGL POTTERY BIRDS oval, 3752D and MW for Margaret Walsh and BM. Mint and uncrazed. 7 3/4" h x 7" w. **$325**

Photo courtesy Belhorn Auction Services LLC, Columbus, Ohio; www.Belhorn.com

Stangl, #3244 Draft Horse with blue and black dappled colors and original label. Mint and uncrazed. 2 7/8" h. **$120**

Photo courtesy Rago Arts and Auction Center, Lambertville, N.J.; www.RagoArts.com

Taylor Tilery, six-tile panel, "San Juan Capistrano Mission". Previously mounted as a table top, still grouted. No visible mark. Panel, with grout: 16 1/2" x 24 3/4". **$1,920**
(The California company was called Santa Monica Brick until 1930. After one partner vanished, it was renamed for the remaining partner.)

Photo courtesy Rago Arts and Auction Center, Lambertville, N.J.; www.RagoArts.com

Teco, large double-gourd factory lamp base with buttressed handles covered in leathery matte green glaze. Restoration to several hairlines and small chips. Stamped Teco 287A. 13 1/4" x 10 1/2". **$4,200**

Photo courtesy Rago Arts and Auction Center, Lambertville, N.J.; www.RagoArts.com

University City, squat bowl attributed to Frederick Rhead, incised with stylized squirrels in dead matte glaze. Hairlines and restoration around rim. Incised UC mark/5148. 2" x 4 3/4". **$4,500**
(Between 1909 and 1914, University City, Mo., was the site of an art academy and porcelain works, divisions of a correspondence school called the Peoples University.)

Teco, vase surrounded with reticulated handles of narrow leaves against a ribbed, flaring neck, covered in matte green glaze. Touch-up to rim tip, stamped Teco. 11 1/2" x 4 1/4". **$12,000**
(American Terra Cotta Tile and Ceramic Co. was founded in 1881 in Terra Cotta, Ill.)

Union Porcelain Works, (Brooklyn, N.Y., established 1848) three shell-shaped oyster plates, each with five wells and raised, colored and gilded decoration of sea life, 19th C. Minor wear. All stamped UNION PORCELAIN WORKS and PAT.JAN.4.1881. 8 1/2" x 6 1/2". ....**$1,200 all**

University City, bud vase covered in matte mustard glaze with fully-formed celadon crystals. Two circular stamps. 8" x 2 1/4". **$3,120**
(Between 1909 and 1914, University City, Mo., was the site of an art academy and porcelain works, divisions of a correspondence school called the Peoples University.)

Van Briggle

Artus Van Briggle, born in 1869, was a talented Ohio artist. He joined Rookwood in 1887 and studied in Paris under Rookwood's sponsorship from 1893 until 1896. In 1899, he moved to Colorado for his health and established his own pottery in Colorado Springs in 1901.

The Art Nouveau designs he had seen in France heavily influenced Van Briggle's work. He produced a wide variety of matte-glazed wares in this style. Colors varied. Artus died in 1904, but his wife, Anne, continued the pottery until 1912.

The "AA" mark, a date, and "Van Briggle" were incised on all pieces prior to 1907 and on some pieces into the 1920s. After 1920, "Colorado Springs, Colorado" or an abbreviation was added. Dated pieces are the most desirable.

Van Briggle, large vase embossed with daisies under a superior frothy matte green glaze, 1908-11. 2 1/2" chip to base, from manufacturing. Incised AA VAN BRIGGLE COLO SPGS 767. 10 1/4" x 12". **$8,400**

Van Briggle, early vase embossed with poppy pods and covered in robin's-egg-blue glaze, the dark brown clay showing through, 1905. Incised AA 173 VAN BRIGGLE VX 1905. 9 1/2" x 4 3/4". **$4,200**

Photo courtesy Rago Arts and Auction Center, Lambertville, N.J.; www.RagoArts.com

Van Briggle early bud vase embossed with trillium and covered in a frothy lime green glaze, the pale clay showing through, 1903. Incised AA VAN BRIGGLE 121 1903. 6 1/2" x 3". **$1,920**

Photo courtesy Rago Arts and Auction Center, Lambertville, N.J.; www.RagoArts.com

Van Briggle, unusual flaring vase embossed with blossoms under a fine yellow and pearl gray frothy glaze, 1906. AA VAN BRIGGLE COLO. SPRINGS 1906 495. 9 1/2" x 4 1/2". **$1,320**

Photo courtesy Belhorn Auction Services LLC, Columbus, Ohio; www.Belhorn.com

Van Briggle, Arts & Crafts vase, early, with hand-tooled leaves and matte-green glaze (circa 1907-1912). Marked Van Briggle with logo, Colo. Spgs., 840 and 18. Mint with a 1/4" factory-grinding flake to the glaze at the base. 4 1/2" h x 3 1/2" w. **$675**

Photo courtesy Rago Arts and Auction Center, Lambertville, N.J.; www.RagoArts.com

Vance/Avon, (Tiltonville, Ohio, early 20th century) large jardinière and pedestal designed by Frederick Rhead, incised and painted in squeeze bag with stylized lotus blossoms and heart-shaped leaves, rare. A few flakes and 1 1/2" chip to pedestal, Y-line to jardinière. 33" x 16". **$9,600**

Van Briggle, early bulbous vase embossed with tobacco leaves under a frothy green and brown matte glaze, 1906. AA VAN BRIGGLE 389 1906. 4 1/2" x 4 3/4". **$1,680**

Van Briggle, flaring vase embossed with morning glories under a fine frothy green glaze, 1908-11. Grinding chips to base, the largest 3/4". AA Van Briggle, Colo Spgs 591. 8" x 6". **$1,440**

Van Briggle, horned toad figural paperweight in amber and green. No visible mark. 1 1/4" x 4 1/2". **$1,140**

Volkmar, tiles (set of three) matte-painted in the Impressionist style with a landscape in tones of green, framed together. (Descended through the Volkmar family). Each signed B. Each tile: 8" sq. .... **$6,600 set**

(Volkmar pottery was made by Charles Volkmar of New York from 1882 to 1911. His designs resemble oil paintings.)

Walrath, vase matte-painted with stylized water lilies. Stilt-pull chip. Incised Walrath Pottery. 7" x 4 1/2". **$6,000**
(Walrath Pottery was operated by Frederick E. Walrath from 1903 to 1918 in Rochester, N.Y.)

Walrath, vase matte-painted with a landscape, 1" hairline from rim. Signed Walrath Pottery. 6 1/4" x 4 1/2". **$3,000**
(Walrath Pottery was operated by Frederick E. Walrath from 1903 to 1918 in Rochester, N.Y.)

Photo courtesy Rago Arts and Auction Center, Lambertville, N.J.; www.RagoArts.com

W.J. Walley, (1852-1917) tall vase covered in curdled semi-matte and lustrous green glaze. Impressed WJW. 16 1/2" x 8". **$5,100**
(Walley was an English immigrant who bought a small pottery in West Sterling, Mass., in about 1890 and operated it until his death.)

Photo courtesy Rago Arts and Auction Center, Lambertville, N.J.; www.RagoArts.com

Walrath, unusual vase with wooded landscape and cabin, 1915. Incised Walrath Pottery. 7 1/4" x 4 1/4". **$14,400**
(Walrath Pottery was operated by Frederick E. Walrath from 1903 to 1918 in Rochester, N.Y.)

Weller

In 1872, Samuel A. Weller opened a small factory in Fultonham, near Zanesville, Ohio. There he produced utilitarian stoneware, such as milk pans and sewer tile. In 1882, he moved his facilities to Zanesville. In 1890, Weller built a new plant in the Putnam section of Zanesville along the tracks of the Cincinnati and Muskingum Railway. Additions followed in 1892 and 1894.

Weller entered into an agreement with William A. Long in 1894 to purchase the Lonhuda Faience Co., which had developed an art pottery line under the guidance of Laura A. Fry, formerly of Rookwood. Long left in 1895, but Weller continued to produce Lonhuda under the new name "Louwelsa." Replacing Long as art director was Charles Babcock Upjohn. He, along with Jacques Sicard, Frederick H. Rhead and Gazo Fudji, developed Weller's art pottery lines.

At the end of World War I, many prestige lines were discontinued and Weller concentrated on commercial wares. Rudolph Lorber joined the staff and designed lines such as Roma, Forest and Knifewood. In 1920, Weller purchased the plant of the Zanesville Art Pottery and claimed to produce more pottery than anyone else in the country.

Art pottery enjoyed a revival when the Hudson Line was introduced in the early 1920s. The 1930s saw Coppertone, and Graystone Garden ware was added. However, the Depression forced the closing of the Putnam plant and one on Marietta Street in Zanesville. After World War II, inexpensive Japanese imports took over Weller's market. In 1947, Essex Wire Co. of Detroit bought the controlling stock, but early in 1948, operations ceased.

Photo courtesy Rago Arts and Auction Center, Lambertville, N.J.; www.RagoArts.com

Weller, Baldin jardinière and pedestal set. Y-line to top of pedestal. Both with kiln stamp. 31 1/2" x 13". **$1,680**

Photo courtesy Belhorn Auction Services LLC, Columbus, Ohio; www.Belhorn.com

Weller, Barcelona vase with three vertical handles. Marked Weller with blue ink stamp. Mint. 13 7/8" h x 7 1/2" w. **$525**

Photo courtesy Belhorn Auction Services LLC, Columbus, Ohio; www.Belhorn.com

Weller, Coppertone lily bowl with frog. Marked with Weller Pottery ink stamp and the numbers 12 and 29. Mint. 11" long x 3 3/4" h. **$300**

Photo courtesy Rago Arts and Auction Center, Lambertville, N.J.; www.RagoArts.com

Weller, Coppertone rare pitcher with fish handle. Unmarked. 7 3/4" x 7 1/2". **$2,520**

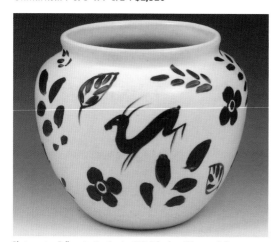

Photo courtesy Belhorn Auction Services LLC, Columbus, Ohio; www.Belhorn.com

Weller, Cretone vase with deer, flowers and leaves, decorated in black slip on white x hand. Marked Weller Pottery by hand with incised initials TM. Mint. 6 1/4" w x 5 1/2" h. **$475**

Weller, Burntwood vase with battle scene. Very crisp decoration. Two small nicks to body. Unmarked. 7" x 4 3/4". **$300**

Weller, Clinton Ivory jardinière and pedestal set with panels of vines and roses. Unmarked. 25 1/2" x 11"................. **$420**

Weller, Coppertone jardinière with a fish and frog. Crisply detailed. Kiln stamp. 7 1/2" x 7 1/2"............................. **$1,800**

Weller, Coppertone double bud vase in the form of two jumping fish, rare. Kiln stamp. 8" x 7"......................... **$3,900**

Weller, Coppertone large frog sprinkler. Includes fittings. Short line, possibly in the firing, to bottom at opening. Unmarked. 10 1/4" x 10 1/4". **$2,760**

Weller, Coppertone jardinière with frog. Kiln stamp. 7 1/2" x 7 1/2". **$1,920**

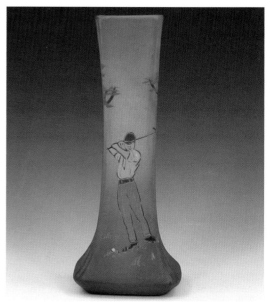

Photo courtesy Belhorn Auction Services LLC, Columbus, Ohio; www.Belhorn.com

Weller, Dickensware II (circa 1900-1905) tapered vase with male golfer in period attire. Golfer is in mid-swing with ball at foot and trees to either side. Marked with Weller Dickensware stamp. Mint and uncrazed. 8 1/2" h x 3 3/8" w. **$1,250**

Photo courtesy Rago Arts and Auction Center, Lambertville, N.J.; www.RagoArts.com

Weller, Dickensware ewer decorated with an American Indian, "Wolf Robe". Dickensware stamp, artist signed ELK or ELH, stamped 176. 11" x 5 1/2". **$840**

Weller, Dresden tall cylindrical vase painted by Levi J. Burgess with Dutch scene. 5" line, small glaze miss at rim. Etched Weller Matt L. J. B. 16" x 4 1/2". **$510**

Weller, Coppertone vase with two frogs at the rim, rare. Kiln stamp. 8" x 8 1/2"...**$2,400**

Weller, Coppertone flaring vase with two frogs. Restoration to chip on foot. Script mark. 8" x 9 1/2". **$840**

Weller, Etched Matt jardinière incised by Frank Ferrell with pink tulips. 1/4" flake to decoration. Incised Ferrell mark, hand-incised Weller mark on bottom. 8" x 10 1/2". **$1,080**

Weller, Eocean large vase (1898-1918) painted with purple, yellow, and white irises around the body. Firing flaw to 1/8" area around base (without glaze). Impressed Weller. 17 1/2" x 7 1/4". **$1,920**

Weller, Etched Matt ovoid vase decorated with daisies. Overfiring around rim. Impressed mark. 10 1/4" x 3". **$420**

Weller, Hudson vase painted by McLaughlin with irises. Circular ink stamp, Weller, and artist's mark. 9 1/4" x 4"....**$900**

Weller, Hudson vase painted by Mae Timberlake with nasturtium blossoms. Stamped kiln mark and signed Timberlake. 12 3/4" x 4 3/4".......................................**$1,080**

Photo courtesy Rago Arts and Auction Center, Lambertville, N.J.; www.RagoArts.com

Weller, large and rare Gardenware swan figure. 1/2" chip to bottom tip of tail. Marked in script. 18 1/2" x 21". **$10,800**

Photo courtesy Belhorn Auction Services LLC, Columbus, Ohio; www.Belhorn.com

Weller, Hudson vase, brown, in a broad, hand-thrown form with handles. Finely decorated on both the front and back by Hester Pillsbury (signed HP). Marked with original Weller Ware label. Mint and uncrazed. 12" w x 9 3/4" h. **$2,200**

Photo courtesy Rago Arts and Auction Center, Lambertville, N.J.; www.RagoArts.com

Weller, Jewell, vase with ribbed, buttressed handles, decorated with fruit and leaves. Stamped Weller. 11 1/2" x 6 1/2". **$4,500**

Photo courtesy Rago Arts and Auction Center, Lambertville, N.J.; www.RagoArts.com

Weller, Knifewood jardinière with daisies and butterflies. Unmarked. 7 3/4" x 8 1/2". **$600**

Photo courtesy Belhorn Auction Services LLC, Columbus, Ohio; www.Belhorn.com

Weller, Late Line Eocean flower holder, uncommon. Unmarked. 8 3/4" w x 3 1/4" h. **$900**

Weller, Sicard cabinet vase painted with stars. Stamped 6. 4" x 3". **$540**

Weller, Jewell, rare and tall vase incised with fiddlehead ferns, and embossed with a band of birds against a purple ground. Clean post-factory drill hole through bottom. Impressed Weller. 13" x 7". **$3,600**

Weller, Kenova vase with lizard. Some staining around rim. Impressed Weller. 6 1/4" x 5 1/2". **$480**

Weller, Knifewood ovoid vase with squirrels and oak branches. A few flecks to high points. Impressed mark. 11" x 5 1/4". **$2,280**

Weller, Knifewood corseted vase with colorful peacocks and roses. Impressed mark. 11" x 4 3/4"....................**$1,200**

Weller, Knifewood vase with owls, squirrels, and birds on oak branches. Stamped Weller. 7"..................................**$720**

Weller, Knifewood ovoid vase with owls in trees under crescent moons. 1/2" glaze miss at base. Impressed mark. 8" x 4 1/4"..**$900**

Weller, blue Louwelsa tear-shaped vase painted with clusters of pansies. Very tight opposing lines to rim, one goes through. Impressed Louwelsa mark. 8 1/2" x 3 1/2"........ **$600**

Weller, Sicard floor vase with grapevine design. Spider line to base. Marked #6 210 Sicard Weller. 25 1/4" x 9"....**$5,100**

Weller, Sicard vase with daisies. Nicely fired. Flat glaze chip to bottom, possibly from grinding. Script mark. 5 1/2" x 3"...**$720**

Weller, vase decorated by Rudolph Lorber with swimming fish. Tight firing lines and restoration around rim. Impressed mark/artist's initials. 13 1/4" x 4 3/4". **$960**

Weller, Woodcraft tall tree-shaped vase with climbing squirrel and owl. Short, tight line to rim, restoration to another line. Unmarked. 18" x 7 1/2". **$1,080**

Weller, Sicard cabinet vase with uncommon wheat or barley decoration in green, purple, gold and blue luster finish. Unmarked. Mint. 3 3/8" h x 2 1/4" w. **$700**

Weller, Woodcraft large and rare vase with owl perched on an apple tree branch. Restoration to small area in hole, hairline (possibly from firing) to interior (does not go through). Impressed mark. 15 3/4" x 6 1/2". **$2,040**

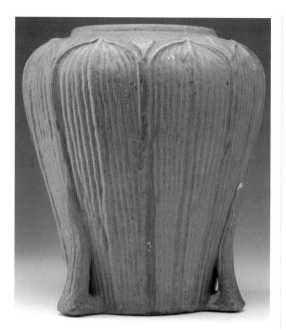

Wheatley, lamp base in the Kendrick style with three buttressed feet, full-height leaves, and buds, covered in matte brown glaze. Enlarged factory hole to base, abrasion around rim, some chips to feet. WP 6. 12 1/2" x 10". **$1,560**
(George Prentiss Kendrick was a designer for Grueby Faience Co., Boston.)

Weller, Woodcraft planters (two), one with mushroom (firing separation), the other partitioned with foxes in their den (nick to edge of branch). Both impressed Weller. 5 1/4" each.. **$660 pair**

Zark, vase with four buttressed handles, carved with dragonflies in two-tone matte blue. Incised ZARK C.C.B. 4 3/4" x 7 1/4". **$3,900**
(Zark Pottery was produced by the Ozark Pottery Co. of St. Louis from about 1907 to 1910.)

Wheatley, lamp base with buttressed feet and leaf and bud decoration under matte green glaze. Incised WP 609. 10" x 8 1/2". **$1,680**

Rick Wisecarver, pillow vase with buffalo. Mint. 7 1/4" w x 7" h. **$190**

REDWARE, STONEWARE

Also see Red Wing Pottery.

Redware

The availability of clay, the same used to make bricks and roof tiles, accounted for the great production of red earthenware pottery in the American colonies. Redware pieces are mainly utilitarian: bowls, crocks, jugs, etc.

Lead-glazed redware retained its reddish color, but a variety of colored glazes were obtained by the addition of metals to the basic glaze. Streaks and mottled splotches in redware items resulted from impurities in the clay and/or uneven firing temperatures.

Slipware is the term used to describe redware decorated by the application of slip, a semi-liquid paste made of clay. Slipwares were made in England, Germany and elsewhere in Europe for decades before becoming popular in the Pennsylvania German region and other areas in colonial America.

Pitcher, small dark-glazed redware, band of flower heads in relief, flower and paired leaves applied beneath spout, 4" h, slight damage to applied flower...................................... **$46**

Pitcher, Stahl green-glazed redware, inscribed on bottom, "Made/In/Stahl's Pottery/By/Thomas Stahl/April 25/1938"; 6 3/4" h. **$156**
(Three generations of the Stahl family operated a small pottery in Powder Valley, Pa., intermittently from about 1850 to 1956.)

Plate, shallow slipware, three wavy lines, mottled outer border, redware ground, coggled rim, 8 1/2" d. **$517**

Plate, "William & Mary" slip-decorated redware, attributed to the Smith Pottery, Norwalk, Conn., 1825-1850, round with coggled rim, yellow slip-trailed inscription, 11 1/8" d, slip is in very good condition, 1/2" d. shallow surface chip, few small rim chips. **$15,405**

Pot, covered, Stahl redware, brownish-green glazed; cover with knop, twin twist handles, two incised green bands, inscribed on bottom, "Made By I.S. Stahl/12-12/1938/S.P."; 6" h, repaired rim. **$57**
(Three generations of the Stahl family operated a small pottery in Powder Valley, Pa., intermittently from about 1850 to 1956.)

Stoneware

Made from dense kaolin and commonly salt-glazed, stoneware was hand thrown and high fired to produce a simple, bold vitreous pottery. Stoneware crocks, jugs and jars were made to store food products and fill other utilitarian needs. These intended purposes dictated shape and design: solid, thick-walled forms with heavy rims, necks and handles and with little or no embellishment. Any decorations were usually simple: brushed cobalt oxide, incised, slip trailed, stamped or tooled.

Stoneware has been made for centuries. Early American settlers imported stoneware items at first. As English and European potters refined their earthenware, colonists began to produce their own wares.

By the late 18th century, stoneware was manufactured in all regions of the country. This industry flourished during the 19th century until glass fruit jars appeared and the use of refrigeration became widespread. By 1910, commercial production of salt-glazed stoneware was phased out.

Batter jug with handle, cobalt blue leaves, wire and wood handle, impressed, "Cowden & Wilcox/ Harrisburg PA"; 7 5/8" h. **$4,887**

Photo courtesy Waasdorp Inc., Clarence, N.Y.; www.antiques-stoneware.com

Cream pot, 3 gallon, ovoid, T. Harrington, Lyons, N.Y., circa 1850, slip blue 3s on either side of a Thomas Harrington folk-art "Star Face" design, some interior Albany glaze loss in the bottom from use, tight hairline at the rim on the left, just touching the "3", 12 1/2" h. **$15,400**

Photo courtesy Waasdorp Inc., Clarence, N.Y.; www.antiques-stoneware.com

Cream pot, 2 gallon, ovoid, Cowden & Wilcox, Harrisburg, Pa., circa 1870, with bird in a bush design, additional blue at the maker's mark and handles, minor lime staining and a worn chip at the base on the front. Also, a tight hairline up from the bottom on the front just touching the design, 10" h. **$3,190**

Photo courtesy Waasdorp Inc., Clarence, N.Y.; www.antiques-stoneware.com

Crock, approximately 1/2 gallon, cylinder shape, circa 1800, S. Amboy, N. Jersey, deep blue incised swag design below the maker's mark. Further enhanced with reeded shoulder design. There is an old, tight hairline to the left of the name. Stone "ping" at the base on the front, 7 1/2" h. **$3,190**

Ceramics

Photo courtesy Waasdorp Inc., Clarence, N.Y.; www.antiques-stoneware.com

Crock, approximately 1 gallon, unsigned, circa 1850, with original lid, blue vine and leaf decoration all around with matching blue on the lid. Stone ping at the rim of the crock occurred in firing. Chip in the knob handle of the lid, 9" h. **$1,815**

Photo courtesy Waasdorp Inc., Clarence, N.Y.; www.antiques-stoneware.com

Crock, 2 gallon, circa 1880, Fulper Bros., Flemington, N.J., rare with dinosaur design, blue at the maker's mark. There is some minor lime staining, 9" h. **$14,300**

Photo courtesy Waasdorp Inc., Clarence, N.Y.; www.antiques-stoneware.com

Crock, approximate 1 1/2 gallon, ovoid, stamped "LIBERTY FOREV WARNE & LETTS 1807 S. AMBOY N. JERSEY," incised and blue-filled scallop designs above the name, blue accents under the ears. Additionally accented with impressed dental molding around the rim. There is a large "blow out" stack mark just below the name with an additional stack mark on the side. Minor surface wear and staining from use, 10" h. **$26,400** *(Cup not included.)*

Photo courtesy Waasdorp Inc., Clarence, N.Y.; www.antiques-stoneware.com

Crock, 2 gallon, P.H. Webster, North Bay, circa 1870, rare design of standing cat amid groundcover, 9 1/2" h. **$13,750**

Churn, 5 gallon, brushed cobalt and manganese tree-like decoration, additional manganese includes signature – "G N Fulton" (Alleghany County, Va.,) – across base, "5" and feathered wings under handles and across reverse, squared rim with five incised rings below, two double-rib handles; 1867-1885, 18" h, 9" d. Professional restoration to body cracks and losses. **$9,900**

Crock, with Fulper bird, cobalt blue decoration, twin molded handles, 12 3/4" h, cover with chipped edge. **$230**

Photo courtesy Waasdorp Inc., Clarence, N.Y.; www.antiques-stoneware.com

Crock, 2 gallon, A.O. Whittemore, Havana, N.Y., circa 1870, with house design, minor surface chip at front rim, 8 1/2" h. **$4,620**

Photo courtesy Waasdorp Inc., Clarence, N.Y.; www.antiques-stoneware.com

Crock, 3 gallon, W.A. MacQuoid Pottery Works, Little 12th St., N.Y., circa 1870, two hearts with "First Love" in blue script, beside cupid holding bow and arrow, minor interior rim chip, 10" h. **$41,800**

Photo courtesy Waasdorp Inc., Clarence, N.Y.; www.antiques-stoneware.com

Crock, 4 gallon, unsigned, circa 1870, rare decoration of a flower-decorated crock, probably New York State origin, minor glaze spider on back, 11 1/2" h. **$1,485**

Photo courtesy Waasdorp Inc., Clarence, N.Y.; www.antiques-stoneware.com

Crock, 4 gallon, J. & E. Norton, Bennington, Vt., circa 1855, rare double-deer decoration, only a few known examples of this design exist, some old glaze spidering throughout, 11 1/2" h. **$45,100**

Crock, 5 gallon, John Burger, Rochester, N.Y., circa 1865, detailed pine tree, standing buck and palm tree, minor staining and there are a few minor flake spots on the right front, tight line and some old glaze flake spots on the back, 12 1/2" h. **$42,900**

Crock, 5 gallon, N. Clark & Co., Lyons, N.Y., circa 1880, spread-eagle motif, minor old horizontal age line at the base under the right ear, minor surface chip in the left ear, 10" h. **$26,400**

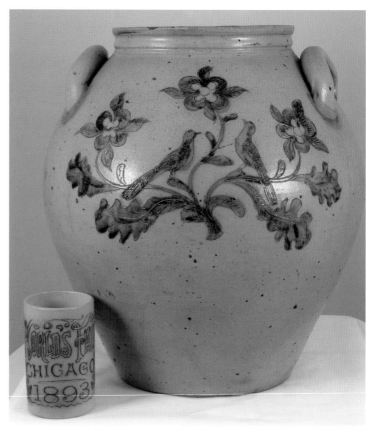

Crock, 5 gallon, ovoid, circa 1840, sharply incised design depicts birds in a flower tree, on the back is an equally well-executed design of Germanic-style tulips. The characteristics seen in this decoration are similar to a signed William Farrar (Geddes, N.Y.) jug in the Onondaga County, N.Y., Historical Society collection. There is some old age spidering below the flower design; clay separation that occurred in the making on the bottom, 16" h; cup not included. **$42,900**

Crock, 5 gallon, Hubbell & Chesebro, Geddes, N.Y., circa 1870, decorated with a fanciful, folky standing lion, long mane and dot-filled body; professional restoration to glaze loss at and under the rim. Both handles have been replaced, few minor flake spots in the blue have been restored, 12 1/2" h. **$17,050**

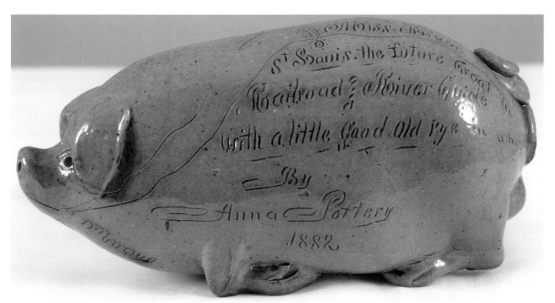

Photo courtesy Waasdorp Inc., Clarence, N.Y.; www.antiques-stoneware.com

Flask, salt-glaze stoneware "railroad pig," left side is scribed, "Ohio River/St. Louis the future Great/Railroad and River Guide/With a little Good Old Rye in a Hogs/By/Anna Pottery/1882." Right side has a railroad map which includes the

towns of Bloomington, Springfield, Alton/Chester, Grandtourgi, Jonesboro, Cairo, Anna, Gordondale, Duquoin, Tamaroa, Odin. The bottom is scribed "Mounds, Vinggus, Cincinnati the Pork City, Chicago the Corn City," 7" l, 3 1/2" h. **$12,650**

Photo courtesy Waasdorp Inc., Clarence, N.Y.; www.antiques-stoneware.com

Flask, barrel shape, circa 1830, rare, C. Crolius Manufacturer New York, brushed blue accents at the top and bottom. A form not generally found with a maker's mark. Excellent condition, 6 1/4" h. **$7,700**

Photo courtesy Waasdorp Inc., Clarence, N.Y.; www.antiques-stoneware.com

Crock, 5 gallon, Hubbell & Chesebro, Geddes, N.Y., circa 1870, with prancing deer (gazelle?) and palm tree, minor lime staining on back and interior, 12 1/2" h. **$12,650**

Photo courtesy Waasdorp Inc., Clarence, N.Y.; www.antiques-stoneware.com

Crock, 10 gallon, Midwest origin, rare design of double partridge, one holding a cherry in its beak. The birds are perched on a branch. There is a rabbit scampering across the bottom. The gallon designation is framed with a double "fishing lure" design, a few minor glaze spiders, 16" h. **$14,850**

Photo courtesy Waasdorp Inc., Clarence, N.Y.; www.antiques-stoneware.com

Jar, approximately 1/2 gallon, ovoid, marked, "C. Crolius Manufactured Manhattan-Wells – New York Pickles New York," circa 1800, six-line impressed maker's mark is accented in a squiggled blue frame. Blue squiggled drapes accent the back, old hairline down from the rim on the right, old surface chipping at the rim and base with some staining from use, 8" h. **$4,290**

Crock, 2 gallon with eagle decoration, impress marked "2" with a 6" x 5" spread-winged eagle holding arrows and olive branch. Eagle in deep blue with dot and dash decoration presenting a shield on breast, 9 1/4" h x 10" d without handles. Blue decoration is very good, small chips to base and one to inside of upper rim. **$660**

Jug, 3 gallon salt glazed with blue decoration, Ballard & Brothers, Burlington, Vt., mid-19th century, with applied handle and incised with the "3" above a large stylized blue floral spray, 16" h. Base rim chips, one repaired, an in-painted chip within flower head. **$460**

Jug, 6 gallon salt glazed with blue decoration, mid-19th century, with applied handle incised with the mark, "Satterlee & Mory, Fort Edward, N.Y.," above a large stylized blue-decorated floral spray, 19" h x 11 3/4" d. Very good overall with good color, 1/2" d. small shallow chip on surface, left shoulder. **$115**

Pitcher, advertising, impressed, "Made for/Wright Smith & Pearsall No. 5. North 5 St./Philadelphia"; cobalt blue leaves, 8 3/4" h. **$3,737**

Pitcher, 1 gallon, brushed cobalt double-tulip decoration, high-shoulder form, single incised ring below rim and on neck, three incised upper shoulder rings, handle with medial channel and squared lower terminal, additional petal decoration above and below neck ring. Attributed to the Zigler Pottery, Timberville, Rockingham County, Va., probably from Andrew Coffman's first period, 1830-1850, 10" h, 5" d. Shallow chip to top of spout and minor flakes to base. **$9,350**

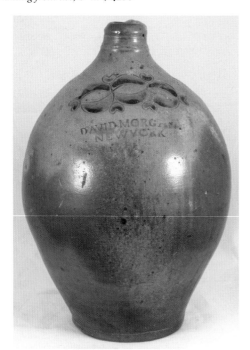

Photo courtesy Waasdorp Inc., Clarence, N.Y.; www.antiques-stoneware.com

Jug, approximately 2 gallons, David Morgan, New York, circa 1790, with three blue-accented scallop designs at the shoulder, additional blue accents at the handle. Mottled clay color in the making and there is a tight, old hairline up from the bottom on the front. 14 1/2" h. **$17,050**

Photo courtesy Waasdorp Inc., Clarence, N.Y.; www.antiques-stoneware.com

Pitcher, miniature, with Albany slip interior, incised and blue-accented "Clayton/1871," more accents on handle, New York State origin, 3 1/4" h. **$7,150**

Preserve jar, approximately 1/2 gallon, unsigned, attributed to M. Woodruff, Cortland, N.Y., rare design of a church and trees filling the front of this small piece, with original lid, 7 1/4" tall. **$7,700**

Preserve jar, 2 gallon, Fenton & Hancock, St. Johnsbury, Vt., circa 1852, with design of a lion and trainer, blue at the maker's mark, tight line on bottom that comes up 3" on back, long chip mark on bottom that may have occurred in making, 11" h. **$3,630**

Preserve jar, approximately 1 gallon, Cowden & Wilcox, Harrisburg, Pa., circa 1870, with stoneware lid, decorated with variation on "man in the moon" design, additional blue at the maker's mark and under the ears. There is an old surface chip at the rim in front of the left ear, 9 1/2" h. **$8,250**

Preserve jar, 2 gallon, L. Marsilliot (one of Ohio's first potters), date "1836" in blue below the deeply impressed and blued pottery mark. Mottled clay color occurred in the making, 12" h. **$6,875**

Photo courtesy Waasdorp Inc., Clarence, N.Y.; www.antiques-stoneware.com

Preserve jar, 3 gallon, Taft & Company, Keene, N.H., circa 1870, decorated with a large Fort Edward-style bird on a stump design. There are a few minor flake spots on the front, possibly occurring when the piece was made, 12 1/2" h. **$2,310**

Photo courtesy Waasdorp Inc., Clarence, N.Y.; www.antiques-stoneware.com

Umbrella stand, Whites, Utica, N.Y., circa 1850, salt glazed, with alligator design in relief, plus dragonflies and cattails, 20 1/2" h. **$2,750**

Photo courtesy Waasdorp Inc., Clarence, N.Y.; www.antiques-stoneware.com

Preserve jar, 4 gallon, J. Norton & Co., Bennington, Vt., circa 1861, bright blue pheasant on stump design, blue at the maker's mark, minor clay separation at the base that occurred in the making. Professional restoration to chips in the right ear, 14" h. **$3,410**

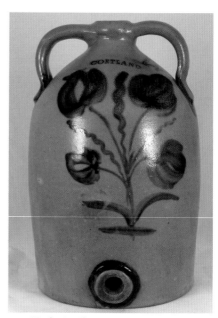

Photo courtesy Waasdorp Inc., Clarence, N.Y.; www.antiques-stoneware.com

Water cooler, 4 gallon, Cortland, circa 1870, double handles, with four large flowers, 17 1/2" h. **$3,300**

Pitcher, 1 gallon, exuberant brushed cobalt floral, double chain and feather decorations, incised ring below rim, at neck and on shoulder, grooved handle, pronounced foot, greenish brown interior glaze. Attributed to Philadelphia, 1860-1880, 9 1/2" h, 4 1/2" d. Minor chip to rim and foot, glazed-over chip on outer rim. **$6,600**

Pitcher, miniature, brushed cobalt floral decoration, pronounced foot, additional cobalt surrounds handle terminals. Baltimore origin, 1860-1880, 3 5/8" h, 2" d. Small chip to foot. **$4,125**

Preserve jar, stenciled in cobalt "Plumbs" above a brushed cobalt sprig, straight-sided form with rounded rim. Attributed to the Bustleburg-Firebaugh Pottery, Rockbridge County, Va., 1830-1867, 9" h, 4" d, narrow angled chip to base. **$12,100**

Correction

In the 2009 edition of the Warman's guide, this item was misidentified:

Photo courtesy Green Valley Auctions, Mt. Crawford, Va., www.GreenValleyAuctions.com

Pitcher, decorated salt-glazed stoneware, pint, impressed "JT", mid-Atlantic, 6 1/4" tall. **$1,650**

CERAMICS, EUROPEAN

Selected English and European Makers

The **Amphora Porcelain Works** was one of several pottery companies located in the Teplitz-Turn region of Bohemia in the late 19th and early 20th centuries. It is best known for art pottery, especially Art Nouveau and Art Deco pieces. Several markings were used, including the name and location of the pottery and the Imperial mark, which  included a crown. Prior to World War I, Bohemia was part of the Austro-Hungarian Empire, so the word "Austria" may appear as part of the mark. After World War I, the word "Czechoslovakia" may be part of the mark.

Belleek is thin-bodied, ivory-colored, almost-iridescent porcelain, first made in 1857 in County Fermanagh, Ireland. Production continued until World War I, was discontinued for a period of time, and then resumed. The Shamrock pattern is most familiar, but many patterns were made, including Limpet, Tridacna and Grasses.

Several American firms made a Belleek-type porcelain. The first was Ott and Brewer Co. of Trenton, N.J., in 1884. Other firms producing this ware included The Ceramic Art Co. (1889), American Art China Works (1892), Columbian Art Co. (1893) and Lenox Inc. (1904). Irish Belleek bore specific marks during given time periods, which makes it relatively easy to date. Variations in mark color are important, as well as the symbols and words.

Capo-di-Monte: In 1743, King Charles of Naples established a soft-paste porcelain factory. The firm made figurines and dinnerware. In 1760, many of the workmen and most of the molds were moved to Buen Retiro, near Madrid, Spain. A new factory, which also made hard-paste porcelains, opened in Naples in 1771. In 1834, the Doccia factory in Florence purchased the molds and continued production in Italy.

Capo-di-Monte was copied well into the 20th century by makers in Hungary, Germany, France and Italy.

In 1749, **Josiah Spode** was apprenticed to Thomas Whieldon and in 1754 worked for William Banks in Stoke-on-Trent, Staffordshire, England. In the early 1760s, Spode started his own pottery, making cream-colored earthenware and blueprinted whiteware. In 1770, he returned to Banks' factory as master, purchasing it in 1776.

Spode pioneered the use of steam-powered, pottery-making machinery and mastered the art of transfer printing from copper plates. Spode opened a London shop in 1778 and sent William Copeland there in about 1784. A number of larger London locations followed. At the turn of the 18th century, Spode introduced bone china. In 1805, Josiah Spode II and William Copeland entered into a partnership for the London business. A series of partnerships between Josiah Spode II, Josiah Spode III and William Taylor Copeland resulted.

In 1833, Copeland acquired Spode's London operations and seven years later, the Stoke plants. William Taylor Copeland managed the business until his death in 1868. The firm remained in the hands of Copeland heirs. In 1923, the plant was electrified; other modernization followed.

In 1976, Spode merged with Worcester Royal Porcelain to become Royal Worcester Spode, Ltd.

Delftware is pottery with a soft, red-clay body and tin-enamel glaze. The white, dense, opaque color came from adding tin ash to lead glaze. The first examples had blue designs on a white ground. Polychrome examples followed.

The name originally applied to pottery made in the region around Delft, Holland, beginning in the 16th century and ending in the late 18th century. The tin used came from the Cornish mines in England. By the 17th and 18th centuries, English potters in London, Bristol and Liverpool were copying the glaze and designs. Some designs unique to English potters also developed.

Augustus II, Elector of Saxony and King of Poland, founded the Royal Saxon Porcelain Manufactory in the Albrechtsburg, **Meissen**, in 1710. Johann Frederick Boettger, an alchemist, and Tschirnhaus, a nobleman, experimented with kaolin from the Dresden area to produce porcelain. By 1720, the factory produced a whiter, hard-paste porcelain than that from the Far East. The factory experienced its golden age from the 1730s to the 1750s under the leadership of Samuel Stolzel, kiln master, and Johann Gregor Herold, enameler.

The Meissen factory was destroyed and looted by forces of Frederick the Great during the Seven Years' War (1756-1763). It was reopened, but never achieved its former greatness.

In the 19th century, the factory reissued some of its earlier forms. These later wares are called **"Dresden"** to differentiate them from the earlier examples. There were several other porcelain factories in the Dresden region and their products also are grouped under the "Dresden" designation.

Many marks were used by the Meissen factory. The first was a pseudo-Oriental mark in a square. The famous crossed swords mark was adopted in 1724. A small dot between the hilts was used from 1763 to 1774, and a star between the hilts from 1774 to 1814. Two modern marks are swords with a hammer and sickle, and swords with a crown.

Gouda and the surrounding areas of Holland have been principal Dutch pottery centers for centuries. Originally, the potteries produced a simple utilitarian, tin-glazed Delft-type earthenware and the famous clay smoker's pipes.

When pipe making declined in the early 1900s, Gouda turned to art pottery. Influenced by the Art Nouveau and Art Deco movements, artists expressed themselves with freeform and stylized designs in bold colors.

In 1842, American china importer **David Haviland** moved to **Limoges**, France, where he began manufacturing and decorating china specifically for the U.S. market. Haviland is synonymous with fine, white, translucent porcelain, although early hand-painted patterns were generally larger and darker colored on heavier whiteware blanks than were later ones.

Haviland revolutionized French china factories by both manufacturing the whiteware blank and decorating it at the same site. In addition, Haviland and Co. pioneered the use of decals in decorating china.

Haviland's sons, Charles Edward and Theodore, split the company in 1892. In 1936, Theodore opened an American division. In 1941, Theodore bought out Charles Edward's heirs and recombined both companies under the original name of H. and Co. The Haviland family sold the firm in 1981.

Charles Field Haviland, cousin of Charles Edward and Theodore, worked for and then, after his marriage in 1857, ran the Casseaux Works until 1882. Items continued to carry his name as decorator until 1941.

Thousands of Haviland patterns were made, but not consistently named until after 1926. The similarities in many of the patterns make identification difficult. Numbers assigned by Arlene Schleiger and illustrated in her books have become the identification standard.

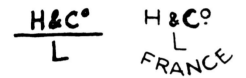

The **"KPM"** mark has been used separately and in conjunction with other symbols by many German porcelain manufacturers, among which are the Königliche Porzellan Manufactur in Meissen, 1720s; Königliche Porzellan Manufactur in Berlin, 1832-1847; and Krister Porzellan Manufactur in Waldenburg, mid-19th century.

Collectors now use the term KPM to refer to the high-quality porcelain produced in the Berlin area in the 18th and 19th centuries.

Creamware is a cream-colored earthenware created about 1750 by the potters of Staffordshire, England, which proved ideal for domestic ware. It was also known as "tortoiseshellware" or "Prattware" depending on the color of glaze used.

The most notable producer of creamware was Josiah Wedgwood. Around 1779, he was able to lighten the cream color to a bluish white and sold this product under the name "pearl ware." Wedgwood supplied his creamware to England's Queen Charlotte (1744-1818) and Russian Empress Catherine the Great (1729-1796), and used the trade name "Queen's ware."

The **Leeds Pottery** in Yorkshire, England, began production about 1758. Among its products was creamware that was competitive with that of Wedgwood. The original factory closed in 1820, but various subsequent owners continued until 1880. They made exceptional cream-colored ware, either plain, salt glazed or painted with colored enamels, and glazed and unglazed redware.

Early wares are unmarked. Later pieces are marked "Leeds Pottery," sometimes followed by "Hartley-Green and Co." or the letters "LP."

Liverpool is the name given to products made at several potteries in Liverpool, England, between 1750 and 1840. Seth and James Pennington and Richard Chaffers were among the early potters who made tin-enameled earthenware.

By the 1780s, tin-glazed earthenware gave way to cream-colored wares decorated with cobalt blue, enameled colors and blue or black transfers.

Bubbles and frequent clouding under the foot rims characterize the Liverpool glaze. By 1800, about 80 potteries were working in the town producing not only creamware, but soft paste, soapstone and bone porcelain.

The reproduction pieces have a crackled glaze and often age cracks have been artificially produced. When compared to genuine pieces, reproductions are thicker and heavier and have weaker transfers, grayish color (not as crisp and black), ecru or gray body color instead of cream, and crazing that does not spiral upward.

In 1793, **Thomas Minton** joined other entrepreneurs formed a partnership to build a small pottery at Stoke-on-Trent, Staffordshire, England. Production began in 1798 with blueprinted earthenware, mostly in the Willow pattern. In 1798, cream-colored earthenware and bone china were introduced.

A wide range of styles and wares was produced. Minton introduced porcelain figures in 1826, Parian wares in 1846, encaustic tiles in the late 1840s, and majolica wares in 1850. In 1883, the modern company was formed and called Mintons Limited. The "s" was dropped in 1968.

Many early pieces are unmarked or have a Sevres-type marking. The "ermine" mark was used in the early 19th century. Date codes can be found on tableware and majolica. The mark used between 1873 and 1911 was a small globe with a crown on top and the word "Minton."

Mocha decoration usually is found on utilitarian cream-ware and stoneware pieces and was produced through a simple chemical action. A color pigment of brown, blue, green or black was made acidic by an infusion of tobacco or hops. When the acidic colorant was applied in blobs to an alkaline ground, it reacted by spreading in feathery designs resembling sea plants. This type of decoration usually was supplemented with bands of light-colored slip.

Types of decoration vary greatly, from those done in a combination of motifs, such as Cat's Eye and Earthworm, to a plain pink mug decorated with green ribbed bands. Most forms of mocha are hollow, e.g., mugs, jugs, bowls and shakers.

English potters made the vast majority of the pieces. Collectors group the wares into three chronological periods: 1780-1820, 1820-1840 and 1840-1880.

William Moorcroft was first employed as a potter by James Macintyre & Co. Ltd. of Burslem, Staffordshire, England, in 1897. He established the Moorcroft pottery in 1913.

The majority of the art pottery wares were hand thrown, resulting in a great variation among similarly styled pieces. Colors and marks are keys to determining age.

Walter Moorcroft, William's son, continued the business upon his father's death and made wares in the same style.

The company initially used an impressed mark, "Moorcroft, Burslem;" a signature mark, "W. Moorcroft" followed. Modern pieces are marked simply "Moorcroft," with export pieces also marked "Made in England."

In 1794, the **Royal Bayreuth** factory was founded in Tettau, Bavaria. Royal Bayreuth introduced its figural patterns in 1885. Designs of animals, people, fruits and vegetables decorated a wide array of tableware and inexpensive souvenir items.

Tapestry wares, in rose and other patterns, were made in the late 19th century. The surface of the pieces feel and look like woven cloth.

The Royal Bayreuth crest used to mark the wares varied in design and color.

Derby Crown Porcelain Co., established in 1875 in Derby, England, had no connection with earlier Derby factories that operated in the late 18th and early 19th centuries. In 1890, the company was appointed "Manufacturers of Porcelain to Her Majesty" (Queen Victoria) and since that date has been known as "Royal Crown Derby."

Most of these porcelains, both tableware and figural, were hand decorated. A variety of printing processes were used for additional adornment.

Derby porcelains from 1878 to 1890 carry only the standard crown printed mark. After 1891, the mark includes the "Royal Crown Derby" wording. In the 20th century, "Made in England" and "English Bone China" were added to the mark.

Doulton pottery began in 1815 under the direction of John Doulton at the Doulton & Watts pottery in Lambeth, England. Early output was limited to salt-glazed industrial stoneware. After John Watts retired in 1854, the firm became Doulton and Co., and production was expanded to include hand-decorated stoneware such as figurines, vases, dinnerware and flasks.

In 1878, Doulton's son, Sir Henry Doulton, purchased Pinder Bourne & Co. in Burslem, Staffordshire. The companies became Doulton & Co., Ltd. in 1882. Decorated porcelain was added to Doulton's earthenware production in 1884.

Most Doulton figurines were produced at the Burslem plants, where they were made continuously from 1890 until 1978. After a short interruption, a new line of Doulton figurines was introduced in 1979.

Dickensware, in earthenware and porcelain, was introduced in 1908. The pieces were decorated with characters from Dickens' novels. Most of the line was withdrawn in the 1940s, except for plates, which continued to be made until 1974.

Character jugs, a 20th-century revival of early Toby models, were designed by Charles J. Noke for Doulton in the 1930s. Character jugs are limited to bust portraits, while Royal Doulton Toby jugs are full figured. The character jugs come in four sizes and feature fictional characters from Dickens, Shakespeare and other English and American novelists, as well as historical heroes. Marks on both character and Toby jugs must be carefully identified to determine dates and values.

Doulton's Rouge Flambé (Veined Sung) is a high-glazed, strong-colored ware.

Production of stoneware at Lambeth ceased in 1956.

Beginning in 1872, the "Royal Doulton" mark was used on all types of wares produced by the company.

Beginning in 1913, an "HN" number was assigned to each new Doulton figurine design. The "HN" numbers, which referred originally to Harry Nixon, a Doulton artist, were chronological until 1940, after which blocks of numbers were assigned to each modeler. From 1928 until 1954, a small number was placed to the right of the crown mark; this number, when added to 1927, gives the year of manufacture.

ROYAL DOULTON FLAMBE

In 1751, the **Worcester Porcelain Co.,** led by Dr. John Wall and William Davis, acquired the Bristol pottery of Benjamin Lund and moved it to Worcester. The first wares were painted blue under the glaze; soon thereafter decorating was accomplished by painting on the glaze in enamel colors. Among the most-famous 18th-century decorators were James Giles and Jeffery Hamet O'Neal. Transfer-print decoration was developed by the 1760s.

A series of partnerships took place after Davis' death in 1783: Flight (1783-1793); Flight & Barr (1793-1807); Barr, Flight & Barr (1807-1813); and Flight, Barr & Barr (1813-1840). In 1840, the factory was moved to Chamberlain & Co. in Diglis, Worcester. Decorative wares were discontinued. In 1852, W.H. Kerr and R.W. Binns formed a new company and revived the production of ornamental wares.

In 1862, the firm became the Royal Worcester Porcelain Co. Among the key modelers of the late 19th century were James Hadley, his three sons, and George Owen, an expert with pierced clay pieces. Royal Worcester absorbed the Grainger factory in 1889 and the James Hadley factory in 1905. Modern designers include Dorothy Doughty and Doris Lindner.

The principal patron of the French porcelain industry in early 18th-century France was Jeanne Antoinette Poisson, Marquise de Pompadour. She supported the Vincennes factory of Gilles and Robert Dubois and their successors in their attempt to make soft-paste porcelain in the 1740s. In 1753, she moved the porcelain operations to **Sevres,** near her home, Chateau de Bellevue.

The Sevres soft-paste formula used sand from Fontainebleau, salt, saltpeter, soda of Alicante, powdered alabaster, clay and soap.

In 1769, kaolin was discovered in France, and a hardpaste formula was developed. The baroque designs gave way to rococo, a style favored by Jeanne du Barry, Louis XV's next mistress. Louis XVI took little interest in Sevres, and many factories began to turn out counterfeits. In 1876, the factory was moved to St. Cloud and was eventually nationalized.

Louis XV allowed the firm to use the "double L" in its marks.

Spatterware generally was made of common earthenware, although occasionally creamware was used. The earliest English examples were made about 1780. The peak period of production was from 1810 to 1840. Firms known to have made spatterware are Adams, Barlow, and Harvey and Cotton.

The amount of spatter decoration varies from piece to piece. Some objects simply have decorated borders. These often were decorated with a brush, requiring several hundred touches per square inch to achieve the spatter effect. Other pieces have the entire surface covered with spatter. Marked pieces are rare.

Notes: Collectors today focus on the patterns—Cannon, Castle, Fort, Peafowl, Rainbow, Rose, Thistle, Schoolhouse, etc. The decoration on flatware is in the center of the piece; on hollow ware, it occurs on both sides.

Aesthetics and the colors of spatter are key to determining value. Blue and red are the most common colors; green, purple, and brown are in a middle group; black and yellow are scarce.

In 1754, **Josiah Wedgwood** and Thomas Whieldon of Fenton Vivian, Staffordshire, England, became partners in a pottery enterprise. Their products included marbled, agate, tortoiseshell, green glaze and Egyptian black wares. In 1759, Wedgwood opened his own pottery at the Ivy House works, Burslem, Staffordshire. In 1764, he moved to the Brick House (Bell Works) at Burslem. The pottery concentrated on utilitarian pieces.

Between 1766 and 1769, Wedgwood built the famous works at Etruria. Among the most-renowned products of this plant were the Empress Catherine of Russia dinner service (1774) and the Portland Vase (1790s). The firm also made caneware, unglazed earthenwares (drabwares), piecrust wares, variegated and marbled wares, black basalt (developed in 1768), Queen's or creamware, and Jasperware (perfected in 1774).

Bone china was produced under the direction of Josiah Wedgwood II between 1812 and 1822 and revived in 1878. Moonlight Luster was made from 1805 to 1815. Fairyland Luster began in 1920. All luster production ended in 1932.

A museum was established at the Etruria pottery in 1906. When Wedgwood moved to its modern plant at Barlaston, North Staffordshire, the museum was expanded.

Vilmos Zsolnay (1828-1900) assumed control of his brother's factory in Pécs, Hungary, in the mid-19th century. In 1899, Miklos, Vilmos' son, became manager. The firm still produces ceramic ware.

The early wares are highly ornamental, glazed and have a cream-colored ground. Eosin glaze, a deep, rich play of colors reminiscent of Tiffany's iridescent wares, received a gold medal at the 1900 Paris exhibition.

Originally, no trademark was used, but in 1878 the company began to use a blue mark depicting the five towers of the cathedral at Pécs. The initials "TJM" represent the names of Miklos' three children.

Ceramics Listed by Form or Type

Ceramic styles produced by many makers—including Flow Blue, Majolica and Quimper—are found at the end of this section. *Also see Oriental Objects.*

Bottles (pair), Italian, Cantagalli, of flattened shape, hand-painted with mythological scenes of Hermes and Venus, 20th century, Bottles topped with differing stoppers, marked with Cantagalli rooster symbol. 13 7/8". **$25,200**

Bowl, British pearlware, mochaware, circa 1830. Footed bowl having a wide grayish band with undulating earthworm design. Top rim having a blue border and below decoration, four black lines, 4" h x 7 1/2" d. Discolored with old discolored hairline in base. No chips. **$180**

Bowl and dish, Moorcroft, bowl with fish, and a "Pomegranate" small dish with pewter foot. Dish marked TUDRIC MOORCROFT/H/MADE IN ENGLAND/01339. Dish: 2 3/4" x 4 1/4"..**$1,320 pair**

Box, china, covered, brown-haired child wearing pink garment cuddles with rabbits; carrots, foliage and two more rabbits below, 4 3/4" h, 5 7/8" w, 3/4" hairline inside at back, not visible from outside. **$402**

Box, coach form, porcelain, young girl in coach shows doll to baby; "11.86" inscribed in black on side of coach and also on bottom of cover, 5 3/4" h, 6" l. **$258**

Box, figural, porcelain, covered, lady holds picture frame around upper body of young girl who sits in a chair, "LL.1" inscribed on each piece, 6 1/4" h, 6 3/4" w. **$480**

Box, French, circular, lidded, china, putti in landscape decoration in bas relief, ormolu mounts, marked "France" on bottom, cobalt blue crowned "N" mark, 5 1/8" h, 4 3/4" d. Hairline to base...**$92**

Box, French, oblong, lidded, china, three putti in landscape, iron red swag border, marked "Made in France" on bottom, cobalt blue crowned "N" mark, 5" w, 3 1/4" d. Separation of metal mount below hinge.......................................**$92**

Box (vanity), Sevres, pink ground, 18th century, reserves with grisaille scenes, interior with painted floral sprays, 3" h, 5 1/2" w. **$1,200**

Butter pat, creamware, marked "And three weeks after the wedding day"; "Happy" and when inverted "Sad", pair of heads, floral border, 3 1/8" d, chips to rim.......................**$57**

Charger, Delftware, England, mid-18th century, blue and white decorated with central floral landscape, 2 1/2" h, 12 1/4" d; 1" repaired chip, several glaze losses around rim and a few shallow rim chips. **$355**

Barber's bowl, English Delft, painted floral sprays, 13" w, 9 1/2" (inner width). Repaired crack across bowl. **$75**

Bowl, Moorcroft, china with fruit motif, grapevine and leaves in blue, purple and yellow on green ground, 8 3/4" d, 2 3/4" h. **$184**

Charger, Italian, ceramic, painted with a rampant lion against a floral ground. Marked on back C. Novelli Roma 1896, 18 1/2" d. **$1,140**

Charger, Italian, Melandri & Foccaccia, faience painted with a portrait in profile, the wide border with a repeating decorative motif, 20th century, Marked Faenza with an MF monogram and company logo, also large oval spur mark, 16" d..**$480**

Charger, Meissen, porcelain painted with chrysanthemums on a blue ground, 20th century, under-glaze blue mark, impressed numerals, 18" d. **$10,200**

Photo courtesy Skinner Inc., Boston, www.SkinnerInc.com

Coffeepot and cover, creamware, England, circa 1780, attributed to Liverpool, pear shape with black transfer "tea party" and "shepherd" prints, strap handle and ball knop, (spout restored, slight rim lines), 10" h. **$355**

Photo courtesy Skinner Inc., Boston, www.SkinnerInc.com

Coffeepot and cover, Staffordshire, creamware, early 19th century, pear shape with black transfer "tea party" prints to either side, strap handle, (pot with spout and foot rim chips, rim line, cover damaged), 9" h. **$266**

Dinnerware service, (partial), Doulton "Madras" blue and white, circa 1891-1902; consisting of eleven 7 1/2" plates, eight saucers, five demi-saucers, two demi-cups, eighteen 5 3/8" fruit bowls, fifteen 6 1/2" plates, eleven 7 1/2" bowls (one chip), one 9 3/4" oblong vegetable bowl, two 10 1/2" oblong vegetable bowls, eleven 10 1/2" plates, six 9 3/4" plates (one cracked), one 7 3/4" oblong gravy boat liner, two 4 3/4" finger bowls, (one chipped), one 5 1/2" pitcher, one 15 1/2" platter and one covered soup tureen. .... **$1,150 all**

Dinnerware service, (partial), "Iris" pattern, Royal Staffordshire, Burslem; consisting of one 13" platter, one 14 1/2" platter, one 10 1/2" platter, one covered sugar, one gravy boat, ten 8" bowls, eight cups (one chipped), eleven saucers, twelve 8" plates, thirteen 7" plates (3 chipped), eleven 9" plates, one 13 1/2" oval covered vegetable bowl, one 11 1/4" round covered vegetable bowl, one creamer, one 9 1/4" open vegetable bowl, one 10 1/4" open vegetable bowl, one 5" pitcher, one covered butter with liner, six butter pats, two 6" bowls and five 5 3/8" bowls. .... **$862 all**

Dinner service, (partial), Spode "New Stone" china, Stoke, Staffordshire, England, circa 1825, the floral design in underglaze blue highlighted in gilt, each with impressed maker's mark "Spode New Stone," most with painted iron-red pattern number "3702," comprising two square cut-corner bowls, seven dinner plates, two round serving trays, two covered oval tureens with undertrays, two small oval covered sauce dishes, three oblong platters and a small square covered serving dish, nineteen pieces total, (minor gilt wear). .... **$1,125 set**

Dish, Clews, historical blue china, "Winter View of Pittsfield, Mass.", and spread-wing American Eagle; also an impressed Clews mark with crown, 10 1/2" d. Repair to slight chip on rim. **$218**

Dish (figural), Dresden blue and white, young girl holding nosegay seated on handled baskets; bottom with blue crossed swords mark, impressed "132" or "182"; incised "3024"; 4 3/4" h, 5 1/2" w. **$138**

Envelope, KPM porcelain, crying putto climbs out of envelope, with applied flowers, tasseled blue pillow beneath; marked "1099"; 6 1/8" h. **$195**

Figural groups (pair), Napoleonic, porcelain, possibly Vienna, depicting the defeat of Napoleon by the Russians in 1812, 19th century, one titled, "Bautzen 21 Mai 1813," the other, "La Retraite de Russie 1812." Unmarked, 9" x 10 1/2" x 6 1/2". .... **$840 pair**

Figural stand, European, Chinoiserie porcelain, with a seated Asian elder flanked by stepped cups, possibly for condiments or eggs, late 19th century, iron-red markings on side of cup, likely the maker. 6" x 8 3/4" x 4 1/2"..... **$480**

Figure, Italian, ceramic, life-sized, poodle, well modeled and finely rendered detail, 20th century, marked on the base Made in Italy. 30" x 20" x 14". **$960**

Figure, Meissen porcelain, Diana retrieving an arrow from a quiver, holding a bow in her left hand, 19th century, under-glaze mark and incised numerals on base. Repair to bow. 11". **$1,800**

Figures (pair), French, Chinoiserie porcelain, two gentleman and lady on cushions, painted in Kakiemon style enamels, 18th-19th century, impressed marks D.V., possibly Mennecey. Height: 5". .... **$1,440 pair**

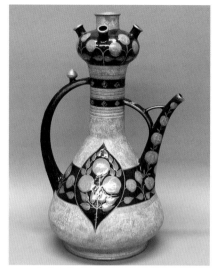

Photo courtesy Sanford Alderfer Auction & Appraisal, Hatfield, Pa.;
www.AlderferAuction.com

Ewer, Austrian pottery, Teplitz, flask form with five spouts at top, stylized yellow flowers on dark blue bands and medallions, cream ground, gilt trim, circa 1910, impressed "1169/7" and red Teplitz mark on bottom, 16 7/8" h. **$460**

Photo courtesy Sanford Alderfer Auction & Appraisal, Hatfield, Pa.;
www.AlderferAuction.com

Figures (pair), Capo-di-Monte, classical females, one at desk with compass and scroll, other sculpting helmeted bust on stand, oval base, porcelain, Capo-di-Monte, 19th century, 6 1/2" h. **$510 pair**

Photo courtesy Sanford Alderfer Auction & Appraisal, Hatfield, Pa.;
www.AlderferAuction.com

Figures (pair), Staffordshire, lady and gentleman in Scottish attire, each standing next to sheep, approximately 7 3/4" h, figure of lady with 5/8" hairline running horizontally just above base. **$345 pair**

Figures (pair), French porcelain, parrot and ceramic basket, with birds and flowers in high relief, 20th century, losses to both. Parrot marked France. Taller: 17 1/4". .... **$480 pair**

Figures (pair), Venus and Cupid on round bases, KPM porcelain, both with under-glaze and incised marks, 15 1/2". .... **$2,160 pair**

Figures (three), porcelain putti with instruments, each seated on leaf-molded urn, one playing panpipes, second playing two horns, third playing cymbals, approximately 6" h, crowned G mark, Italian, 20th century. .... **$184 set**

Figures (23), Meissen porcelain, monkey band, including the music stand, 20th century, all bear Meissen marks and incised numbers. Conductor: 7"........... **$22,800 set**

Game service, Limoges, Rococo, hand-painted bird and flower decoration on molded ground, gilt trim; consisting of 18 1/4" oval platter, ten 9 1/4" plates and two 5 3/4" shallow bowls... **$431 set**

Ice cream set, tray and six plates, English majolica, with fan design, maker unknown, 19th century, tray stamped with maker's mark and registration numbers, all illegible. Tray: 1 1/2" x 14 3/4" x 9". .... **$390 set**

Jar (figural), Martin Brothers, stoneware, grotesque bird, a couple of minor flecks. Base inscribed RW Martin & Brothers London + Southall 1893, head inscribed Martin Brothers London + Southall 12-93, 15" x 9"............. **$54,000**

Jardinière, Fives-Lille (France), organic motif with curled leaf-like handles under a dynamic and flowing white, blue, gold, and pink crystalline glaze. Restoration to small chip on edge of leaf. Die-stamp mark L'ISLE – ADAM, 9" x 12". **$2,040**

Jardinières and pedestals (pair), Doulton Lambeth, stoneware, by Frank A. Butler, the jardinières with a row of carved angels over lotus leaves, the pedestals with complementary leaf designs, 1876. Some losses to angels on jardinières, bottom of one has crude restoration to breaks, which cannot be seen from interior, probably done in factory. Each piece stamped DOULTON LAMBETH 1876, one jardinière inscribed FAB. Jardinières: 14" x 19", pedestals: 38" x 18 1/2" and 37" x 17 3/4". .... **$7,800 pair**

Photo courtesy Sanford Alderfer Auction & Appraisal, Hatfield, Pa.;
www.AlderferAuction.com

Figures (pair), Staffordshire, whippets with catch, each with rabbit in mouth, rocky plinth, 11" h. **$330 pair**

Jug, Liverpool creamware, England, early 19th century, transfer designs of Masonic symbols, signed by the engraver "Kennedy" (probably J. Kennedy of Burslem), under the spout with various Masonic elements with a ribbon inscribed "Mason Form'd out of the Meteirals [sic] of His Lodge," one side with Masonic symbols woven into a wreath surrounding a motto, (imperfections), 11 1/2" h. Old repairs-spout repaired, three repaired cracks on side, handle repaired, brownish discoloration. **$651**

Lamp base, Clement Massier, gourd-shaped with four scalloped buttressed handles, painted with mistletoe in luster glaze. One re-glued handle, a few small glaze chips. Incised MCM 1900 R, 6" x 10 1/2". **$1,020**

Mugs, (three), British creamware, mochaware, two similar with blue background and seaweed stalks. One having wide green band with seaweed stalks and upper blue band. Some discoloring, generally very good. .... **$360 all**

Pitcher, Masonic, commemorative, for the Ancient Landmark Lodge, Portland, Maine. Flow blue pitcher by Royal Doulton, Burslem, to commemorate the Ancient Landmark Lodge No. 17, Portland, Maine Centennial Celebration, 1806-1906, marked in a cartouche and presented at the Centennial celebration June 10th, 1906. Sides with Masonic emblems and writing, "Instituted 5806 A.L.M. Lodge Portland". Decorated overall with foliate sprays and Masonic symbols. Marked on base Royal Doulton England, 8 1/2" h. Small fleck to gold gilding on lip of pitcher. **$172**

Pitcher, Royal Worcester, porcelain, bold lavender flowers on yellow ground, stag horn-form handle side, gilt trim, Reg. No. 37112. .... **$92**

Pitcher, Royal Worcester, porcelain, gilt bas relief flowers below rim, handle side, gilt trim, Registry No. 117049, 8 3/4" h. .**$103**

Plaque, Zsolnay, Art Nouveau, painted with a maiden by a pond with swans, and "framed" with three-dimensional gargoyles, entirely covered in blue and gold luster glaze. A few professional touch-ups to edges. Five churches stamp with ZSOLNAY PECS, 19" x 18". **$31,200**

Plate (cabinet), George Jones & Sons Crescent China, hand-painted with the Three Graces in landscape, and raised gilt decoration. Partially erased puce mark stamped Made In England, signed H. Nosek, 19th century, 10" d. **$5,700**

Plate, (cabinet), porcelain, hand-painted, "Lady Harrington and her two sons," 19th century, signed Wagner, Dec. 314, Depose, spurious over-glaze blue crest mark, Clairon Germany with green star mark, 9 3/4". **$1,920**

Plate, (cabinet), Royal Vienna, hand-painted with a classical scene, 19th century, signed Fiala, under-glaze blue crest mark, 9 1/4" d. **$660**

Plate, (cabinet), Royal Vienna, hand-painted with classical scene, 19th century, marked Grazien, signed Knoeller, under-glaze blue crest mark, 9 5/8" d. **$960**

Plates, (pair, cabinet), Royal Vienna, hand-painted, one titled "Die Musik," the other "Sehnsucht," 19th century, both signed Riemer, with under-glaze blue crest marks, 9 1/2" d. **$660 pair**

Plates, (pair), historical blue, J. & W. Ridgway, "Beauties of America" and "City Hall/New York"; floral border, 9 3/4" d. .... **$258 pair**

Plates, (two), Delftware, England, 18th century, polychrome-decorated with bird and floral landscape, (larger plate with repaired crack, crazing, rim chips), 13 1/4" and 8 7/8" d. .... **$533 both**

Photo courtesy Skinner Inc., Boston, www.SkinnerInc.com

Mug, mochaware, quart, England, early 19th century with thin brown and reeded green bands flanking a wide pumpkin band with brown dendritic decoration, 5 1/2" h. Some segments of brown glaze are missing on the thin bands on rim and base, done in the making, scattered light brownish discoloration. **$1,066**

Photo courtesy Skinner Inc., Boston, www.SkinnerInc.com

Plate, Delftware, England, 18th century, with polychrome decorated floral and bird designs, (rim chips), 11 3/4" d. **$444**

Plates, (four) with scenes, Sarreguemines, French faience, interior scenes with Dr. Herr Maire and figures; three signed "Frederic Regainey" and one signed "M. Loux"; 8 5/8" d..**$138 set**

Plates, (eight), Royal Copenhagen, Flora Danica, porcelain painted with various fruit, openwork border with gilding; all marked 'Royal Copenhagen, Denmark', and under-glaze blue stamp; together with two larger plates, one with a moose, the other with a wolf, all 20th century, Flora Danica: 9" d, animal plates: 10" d...........................**$9,000 all**

Plates, (eight), Sevres porcelain, with portraits of famous women on green enameled ground and stylized gilt decoration, 19th century, some signed Georget, some titled, all stamped M. Imple de Sevres [Manifacture Imperiale de Sevres], 9 1/2" d...**$3,480 set**

Plates, (10), Meissen porcelain, with four fan-shaped vignettes of alternating flowers and amorous couples, 19th century, 8 3/4" d...**$1,020 set**

Plates (11), creamware, reticulated, Leeds Pottery, England, late 18th century, a luncheon plate with raised bowknot and swag rim border, two plates with entwined strap handles and openwork center and rims, and eight dessert plates, with bowknot and pendant leaf border, each impressed, "Leeds Pottery," (minor discoloration), 10 1/4" and 9 1/2" d. The luncheon plate pattern has a slightly different border than the rest of the plates, it has swag and bowknots, the others have pendant leaf and swag borders. The luncheon plate has a small 1/3" hairline at the top of one scallop on rim edge, some small areas of glaze wear on the rim edge also; one dessert plate with 1 1/2" area rim repair, three with faint light brownish discoloration. ....**$1,540 set**

Plates, (11), Royal Doulton, "Famous English Inns," painted by C. Hart with gilt rims, 19th century, each titled and signed. 10 1/2" d...**$720 set**

Plates, (12), Derby, porcelain, with under-glaze blue Imari pattern and over-glaze red and gilt decoration, 18/19th century, 10 1/4" d...**$660 set**

Plates (12), Royal Doulton, with hand-painted botanicals and gilt fish roe border, signed D. Dewsberry, 19th/20th century, 10 5/8" d..**$6,600 set**

Plates, (12), Spode Copeland's china, with hand-painted botanicals and Renaissance-style gilt decoration. Marked Spode Copeland's China England Made for Davis Collamore & Co. Ltd. New York, 10 1/2" d. **$3,900**

Plates, (15), Meissen, porcelain with molded design on cavetto, hand-painted floral decoration, basket weave on border and gilt rims. Together with a hand-painted teapot with floral decoration, rose finial and gilt decoration, all 19th century, with Meissen crossed sword mark on bottom. Plates: 9 3/4" d. ....**$2,880 all**

Platter, Staffordshire, England, early 19th century, scallop rim oblong platter decorated with flowering tree branches and flower blossoms in under-glaze blue and polychrome enamel highlighted with gilt, (scattered surface scratches), 14 7/8" x 19 1/4". **$503**

Sugar bowl, Spatterware, floral decorated, yellow, bulbous form with five-petal red flower and green leaves, unmarked. English, mid-19th century. 5" h overall, 4 3/4" d overall. Undamaged with interior discoloration.........**$3,850**

Photo courtesy Skinner Inc., Boston, www.SkinnerInc.com

Platter, ironstone, "Boston Mails," England, circa 1841, blue transfer-decorated chamfered rectangular platter depicting the "Ladies' Cabin" motif, with the border showing four steamships with "Acadia," or "Columbia," printed below, representing the historic mail ship service between England and North America, blue back stamp mark with "Boston Mails" over a vessel, 12 x 15 3/8". **$474**

Photo courtesy Skinner Inc., Boston, www.SkinnerInc.com

Platter, Staffordshire, "Landing of La Fayette," James and Ralph Clews, Cobridge, 1819-36, blue and white transfer-decorated oblong platter with title below "Landing of Gen. La Fayette at Castle Garden in New York, 16 August, 1824," impressed maker's mark, (repaired crack across platter, surface scratches), 12 1/2" x 9". **$503**

Photo courtesy Skinner Inc., Boston, www.SkinnerInc.com

Punchbowl, Delftware, England, late 18th century, blue and white with large interior flower design, the exterior with floral panels, 6" h, 12" d; 3" hairline from rim, several rim chips and glaze losses around rim, glaze losses around table rim. **$2,014**

Tile, glazed ceramic, with frog in relief, 9 7/8" square, framed. **$216**

Tiles, (pair), English, glazed, floral, "Oranges on Bough"; green fruit and pink and blue flowers, brown ground, attributed to Maw and Benthald, 12" h, 6" w., framed. .... **$287 pair**

Tiles, (12, panel), Rozenburg, painted after Johannes Christiaan Karel Klinkenberg (Dutch, 19th century), depicting a Dutch cityscape with canal. Small chip to one tile, 3" corner line to other. Framed. Signed N. Klinkenberg. B. Rozenburg. Panel: 18" x 24". **$2,760**

Tureen and an under tray, Staffordshire, England, circa 1830, the tureen blue transfer-decorated with a scene titled "ESKE ESTAMBOUL", together with an under tray decorated with a scene titled "MOSQUE IN LATACHIA", (cover repaired), 11 1/2" h, 14 1/2" and 14 1/4" d. .... **$325 pair**

Vase, (cabinet), Royal Vienna, with hand-painted young woman and roses, gilt-work in relief on a green ground, 19th century, signed Wagner, lower left, titled 'Les Lebens Moi', under glaze blue crest mark. Restoration to 1" chip at rim, 12 1/4" d. **$2,520**

Photo courtesy Skinner Inc., Boston, www.SkinnerInc.com

Tureen with under tray (covered, sauce), Staffordshire, historic blue, Clews, second quarter, 19th century, depicting the "Landing of Gen. La Fayette at New York 1824", impressed maker's marks on base, 4 1/2" h. Very small spots of glaze loss to edges of cover, a few small chips to interior fitter rim of cover, one handle shows a darker glazed area, done in the making, not a repair. **$1,422**

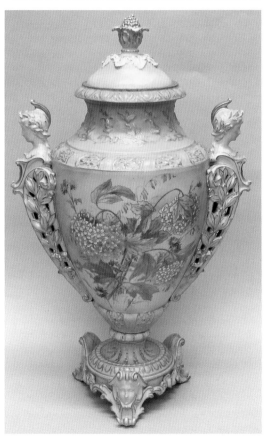

Photo courtesy Sanford Alderfer Auction & Appraisal, Hatfield, Pa.; www.AlderferAuction.com

Urn, Royal Rudolstadt, porcelain, twin reticulated handles with classical busts, berry and leaf finial, circular base with three scroll feet and classical head, hand-painted floral decoration on shaded pink and off-white ground, gilt trim, 19 1/4" h. **$345**

Photo courtesy Sanford Alderfer Auction & Appraisal, Hatfield, Pa.; www.AlderferAuction.com

Urn, Sevres, 18th century, polychrome, twin-handled ormolu mount with mask heads, domical cover with gilt pineapple finial, mid-band painted with musicians in garden signed, "A. Harel" lower left, opposite scene with chateau in landscape, gold enriched cartouches above with couple in landscape and another chateau scene, bleu du roi ground, square ormolu base with ovolo cut-outs, 25" h. **$3,162**

Photo courtesy Sanford Alderfer Auction & Appraisal, Hatfield, Pa.; www.AlderferAuction.com

Urns (pair), Sevres, with putti reserves, twin-handled covered oval urn form with Egyptian heads, oval medallions with painted putti and garden scenes, blue ground, gold trim, signed, 16 1/2" h (with cover), 14 1/2" w. (across handles). Lacks one cover, other repaired. **$805 pair**

Vase, Dresden porcelain, baluster form with maidens and baskets of flowers, 19th century, the front is painted with classical figures, the obverse with bouquet of flowers and the lid surmounted by two cherubs with a crown and armorial crest, marked, 23 1/2" h. **$2,160**

Vase, KPM porcelain, baluster with female busts on shoulders and applied metal ribbons, the tall neck with raised tassels, 19th century, restoration to lid, Under-glaze blue mark. 20"...**$1,320**

Vase, Martin Brothers, stoneware, embossed and incised with fish and sea life, 1891. Signed 10-11-91, Martin Bros. London + Southall. 8 1/2" x 5 1/2".............................**$7,200**

Vase, Martin Brothers, four-sided stoneware, incised with grotesque fish and sea life, 1913. Restoration to short line at rim. Incised 9-1913 Martin Bros. London + Southall, 6" x 3"
....**$4,500**

Vase, Martin Brothers, four-sided stoneware, incised with crabs and anemones, 1903. (Unusual subject matter). Incised 10-1903 Martin Bros. London + Southall. 8 3/4" x 4"...........**$6,000**

Vase, Moorcroft, Florian pattern, with all-over decoration of black-eyed Susans, circa 1902, 1" area of glaze scaling at base, restoration to one handle. Stamped registration mark, W Moorcroft Des in green, 10" x 7 1/4". **$4,500**

Vase, Moorcroft, Hazledene pattern, bulbous, in blue and green. Green script W. Moorcroft Des, stamped RDNO397964 MADE FOR LIBERTY & CO., P., 5" x 3 3/4". **$4,800**

Vase, Moorcroft, in "Leaves and Fruit" design. Short under-glaze line at bottom. Signed in green, stamped signature, POTTER TO THE QUEEN, MADE IN ENGLAND, 13" x 8 1/4". **$3,600**

Vase, Moorcroft, in the "Pomegranate" pattern, bulbous two-handled, green signature, MOORCROFT MADE IN ENGLAND, 8" x 7 1/2"..**$1,200**

Vase, painted china, baluster form, earth tones on pale mint green ground with blossoming trees, butterfly and insect, 13 3/8" h; impressed on bottom "ES" and "999." **$230**

Vase, Rorstrand porcelain, modeled with blue and taupe tulips on tall swerving stems. Chip to petal, rim, and base. Green ink stamp Rorstrand, crown, AE, 40443, EG, 50, 16 1/2" x 8".
....**$2,160**

Vase, Royal Vienna porcelain, tall narrow baluster form with scroll handles and entwined snakes painted with putti and goddess, 19th century, the obverse with a wood nymph sitting on a rock. Marked on base with under-glaze crest mark. 20 1/2"..**$4,200**

Vase, Royal Worcester, porcelain, twin-handled bulbous form, Rd. No. 124679/1142, angular feet, 13 1/4" h. **$230**

Vase, Sevres-style porcelain, conical with gilt metal mounts painted with Cupid and Venus in woodland landscape, obverse with classical ruins, 19th century, lid restored, 29 1/2" h. **$2,640**

Vase, Sevres-style porcelain, painted with a cherub assisting Arachne carding wool, the obverse with gilt floral ribbons, turquoise ground and gilt metal mounts, 19th century, 18 1/2" h. **$1,440**

Vase, (tapestry), Doulton and Slater's, flattened gourd shape hand-painted in the Aesthetic Movement style with geese and flowers, 1880s. Impressed Doulton & Slater's patent mark, 15"..**$480**

Vase, Wedgwood Jasperware, black basalt, Portland, Wedgwood mark and dots, England, 9 3/4" h. **$720**

Vase, Zsolnay, embossed with a classical scene of goddess and putti sheltered by deep purple trees. Some over-firing, restoration around base, V-shaped bruise to rim, scratches. Five churches medallion, 3119, 12" x 6".....................**$1,200**

Vases, (pair), continental porcelain, baluster form with bisque winged cherubs sitting atop scroll handles, painted with cupids and violets on obverse, 19th century, rose ground neck and bases. Marked HA & Co. 435, 17" h.
....**$2,640 pair**

Vases, (pair), Sevres, covered, ormolu-mounted blue celeste with twin mask heads and loop handles, molded ormolu base; painted scenes with cavaliers and ladies (one signed "Leber"); floral reserves opposite, 11 5/8" h................**$1,725**

Wall bracket, Wedgwood, majolica with a putto holding up a curtain, 19th century, stamped Wedgwood YZW, 9" x 6" x 7 1/2". **$540**

Wall brackets, (pair), Dresden, with putti, each of reticulated half-cone shape with putto and painted applied flowers, signed, 6 1/2" h, 9 3/4" w. Restored. ....**$345 pair**

FLOW BLUE

Flow Blue is the name applied to china of cobalt blue and white, whose color, when fired in a kiln, produced a flowing or blurred effect. The color varies from dark royal cobalt blue to navy or steel blue. The flow may be very slight to a heavy blur, where the pattern cannot be easily recognized. The blue color does not permeate through the body of the china. The amount of flow on the back of a piece is determined by the position of the item in the "sagger" (a case of fire clay) during firing.

Known patterns of flow blue were first produced around 1830 in the Staffordshire area of England. Credit is generally given to Josiah Wedgwood, who worked in that area. Many other potters followed, including Alcock, Davenport, Grindley, Johnson Brothers, Meakin, Meigh and New Wharf. They were attempting to imitate the blue and white wares brought back by the ship captains of the tea trade. Early flow blue, 1830s to 1870s, was usually of the pearlware or ironstone variety. The later patterns, 1880s to 1900s, and the modern patterns after 1910, were of the more delicate semi-porcelains. Most flow blue was made in England but it was made in many other countries as well. Germany, Holland, France, Spain, Wales and Scotland are also known locations. Many patterns were made in the United States by several companies: Mercer, Warwick, Sterling and the Wheeling Pottery to name a few.

Addison, Upper Hanley, 1900
Small punchbowl...$185
Alaska, Grindley, 1891
Bone dish...$85
Plate, 10"...$110
Tea cup and saucer...$95
Amoy, Davenport, 1844
Butter dish insert, restored chip on edge $150
Child's teapot with lid...$575
Child's cup and saucer..$275
Child's creamer...$400
Child's sugar bowl with lid...$450
Creamer..$325
Cup plate..$55
Gravy boat...$225
Ramekin, 3 1/2" x 2"...$200
Soup tureen undertray..$195
Tea cup and saucer...$150
Waste bowl..$145
Arabesque, Mayer, 1845
Platter, 15 1/2"..$265
Arcadia, Wilkinsen, 1900
Platter, 18"...$175
Platter, 20"...$200
Rimmed soup bowl, 10 1/2"..$100
Argyle, Grindley, 1890
Butter pat..$55
Butter dish with lid...$195

Collector's Note: The Flow Blue International Collectors' Club Inc. has studied new vs. reproduction flow blue. There are still areas of personal judgment as yet undetermined. The general rule has been "new" indicates recent or contemporary manufacture and "reproduction" is a copy of an older pattern. Problems arise when either are sold at "old" flow blue prices.

The club continues to inform members through its conventions, newsletters and the Web site: www.flowblue.com.

The following is a listing of "new" flow blue, produced since the 1960s.

Blossom: Ashworth Bros., Hanley, 1962. Washbowl and pitcher made for many years now.

Iris: By Dunn, Bennett, Burslem, has been reproduced in a full chamber set.

Romantic Flow Blue: Blakeney Pottery, 1970s. Resembles Watteau. The old patterns never had the words "flow blue" written on them.

Touraine: By Stanley, by far the most prolific reproduction made recently, in 2002. Again, the "England" is missing from the mark, and it is made in China. Nearly the entire dinnerware set has been made and is being sold.

Victoria Ware: Mark is of lion and uniform, but has paper label "Made in China," 1990s. Made in various patterns and designs, but the giveaway is the rough-

ness on the bottoms, and much of it has a pea-green background.

Vinranka: Upsala-Ekeby, Sweden, 1967-1968. Now discontinued and highly collectible, a full dinnerware set.

Waldorf: By New Wharf, cups and saucers are found, but missing "England" from their mark and are made in China.

Floral pitchers (jugs) and teapots bearing a copied "T. Rathbone England" swan mark.

Williams-Sonoma and Cracker Barrel have released a vivid blue-and-white line. Both are made in China. One line is a simplified dahlia flower on white; the other has summer bouquets. Both are well made and readily available, just not old. The reproductions are more of a threat to collectors.

In all cases, regarding new pieces and reproductions, be aware of unglazed areas on the bottoms. The foot rings are rough and too white. The reproductions, particularly the Touraine, are heavier in weight, having a distinctive thick feel. The embossing isn't as crisp and the pieces are frequently slightly smaller in overall size than the originals.

Check the Flow Blue International Collectors' Club, Inc. Web site and also www.repronews.com. Join the club, study the books available, and always work with a trusted dealer. Good dealers guarantee their merchandise and protect their customers.

Flow Blue, Syria, slop jar with lid, Grindley, 1892. **$550**

Flow Blue, pitcher, Stag and Hound, unknown maker, 1850, 8". **$425**

Flow Blue, Touraine, hot water pitcher, Stanley, 1898. **$375**

Creamer and sugar with lid **$550**
Milk pitcher, 7" **$250**
Platter, 18" **$395**
Platter, 19" **$475**
Sauce tureen with lid **$295**
Soup ladle **$225**
Vegetable tureen with lid **$350**

Ashburton, Grindley, 1891
Gravy boat with tray **$110**
Plate, 10" **$60**

Aster and Grape, unknown maker, 1855
Teapot with lid **$425**

Babes In Woods, Doulton, 1890
Ewer, 10" **$375**
Mug **$150**
Two handled vase **$375**

Bamboo, Alcock, 1843
Teapot with lid **$375**

Basket, unknown maker, 1860
Child's cup and saucer **$85**
Creamer, 4" **$175**
Sugar with lid **$250**
Toast rack **$750**

Beaufort, Grindley, 1902
Oyster bowl **$90**

Belmont, Grindley, 1891
Dessert dish, 4 1/4" **$38**
Plate, 6 1/2" **$48**
Plate, 8" **$60**

Bleeding Heart, unknown maker, 1835
Sugar with lid, finial restored **$175**
Teapot with lid **$295**

Blossom, unknown maker, 1914
Cheese dish with lid **$295**
Platter, 12" **$155**
Vegetable tureen with lid **$225**

Bluebell, Ridgway, 1840
Pitcher, 8 1/2" **$425**
Sauceboat **$195**
Sauce tureen with lid and undertray **$550**

Blue Diamond, Wheeling, 1890
Orange bowl **$975**
Brair, Burleigh Ware, unknown date
Teapot with lid **$350**

Brushstroke, Ridgeway, 1845
Footed cake plate **$255**

Brushstroke, unknown maker, 1830-1840
Chocolate pot with lid **$350**
Creamer, 3 1/2" **$140**
Pitcher, relief, copper lustre, 8" **$265**

Cabul, Challinor, 1847
Toothbrush box with lid **$285**

Calico, Warwick, 1900
Pinched spout pitcher, 7 1/2", has 1" hairline **$255**
Tea tile **$175**
Tray, 5" x 7" **$135**

Cashmere, Ridgway, Morley, 1845
Handless cup and saucer **$175**
Honey dish **$225**
Sauce tureen base **$325**
Sugar with lid **$550**
Soup tureen undertray **$975**

Chain of States, unknown maker, 1891
Tea cup and saucer **$85**
Chapoo, Wedgwood, 1850
Honey dish **$150**
Pitcher, 7 1/2" **$355**
Plate, 8 1/2" **$115**
Sauce tureen, 4 pieces. **$500**
Teapot with lid, finial restored **$550**
Vegetable tureen with lid **$400**
Chatsworth, Keeling, 1886
Plate, 10 1/2" **$95**
Chusan, Clementson, 1830
Chestnut bowl with base **$500**
Child's sugar with lid **$250**
Creamer, 5" **$175**
Grandfather cup and saucer **$150**
Mug, 3 1/2" **$125**
Sugar bowl with lid **$195**
Claremont Group, Hancock, 1850
Cheese dish with lid **$450**
Clayton, Johnson Bros., 1890
Platter, 18" **$265**
Conway, New Wharf, 1891
Gravy boat with tray **$235**
Platter, 18 1/2" **$275**
Waste bowl **$150**
Cracked Ice, Warwick, 1898
Cake plate, pierced handles, 10 1/2" **$225**
Charger, round, 10 1/2" **$175**
Jardinière, pedestal, 3 pieces. **$550**
Croydon, Keeling, 1891
Bucket with wicker handle **$325**
Crumlin, Myott, 1900
Demitasse cup and saucer **$80**
Plate, 7" **$45**
Dahlia, Challinor, 1850
Child's cup and saucer **$65**
Creamer **$155**
Vegetable bowl, open, 9 1/4" **$185**
Daisy Chain, Doulton, 1891
Pitcher, 8" **$385**
Delph, Warwick, 1900
Jardinière **$250**
Vegetable bowl, round, 10" **$100**
Doreen, Grindley, 1897
Wash basin **$150**
Dover, Royal Doulton, 1900
Chamber pot with lid **$165**
Pitcher, 7 1/2" **$130**
Dresden Sprigs, Cochrane, 1855
Pitcher, 10" **$375**
Dudley, Ford & Sons, 1900
Plate, 9 1/2" **$40**
Plate, 10 1/2" **$60**
Fairy Villas, Adams, 1891
Butter dish with lid **$245**
Platter, 15 1/2" **$260**
Soup tureen with lid and undertray **$450**
Vegetable tureen with lid. **$275**
Fasan, Villeroy & Boch, 1860
Fish platter **$800**
Soup bowl, 9" **$65**

Flow Blue, Polychrome, plate, unknown maker, 1855, 9". **$110**

Flow Blue teapot with lid, Abbey, Jones, 1900. **$295**

Flow Blue bowl, La Belle, Wheeling, orange, 1890. **$2,550**

Ceramics

Floral, unknown maker, 1900
Clock, 15 1/2" x 12 1/2"..................................... **$375**
Fleur de Lis, Meakin, 1891
Platter, 16".. **$225**
Soup bowl, 9"... **$45**
Waste bowl.. **$150**
Florida, Grindley, 1895
Pitcher, 7 1/2"... **$400**
Platter, 14"... **$285**
Under tray for soup tureen............................. **$150**
Vegetable tureen with lid................................ **$350**
Gainesborough, Ridgway, 1900
Bacon platter, well and tree............................ **$375**
Cereal bowl, 7 1/2".. **$45**
Platter, 16"... **$325**
Gaudy Strawberry, unknown maker, 1865
Teapot with lid.. **$1000**
Gironde, Grindley, 1890
Creamer... **$110**
Cream soup... **$45**
Platter, 17 1/2".. **$275**
Soup tureen with lid...................................... **$395**
Glenwood, Bursley Crown Pottery, 1890
Pitcher and wash basin................................... **$675**
Georgia, Johnson Bros., 1900
Vegetable tureen with lid................................ **$295**
Grace, Grindley, 1891
Butter pat.. **$65**
Pitcher, 7 1/2"... **$300**
Hawthorne, Mercer, 1890
Ice-cream set, 9 pieces................................... **$600**
Hindustan, Wood & Baggaley, 1884
Water pitcher.. **$200**
Holland, Johnson Bros., 1891
Butter dish with lid....................................... **$250**
Tea cup and saucer.. **$95**
Vegetable tureen with lid................................ **$225**
Hong Kong, Meigh, 1850
Pitcher, inverted loop shape, 9"........................ **$400**
Platter, 14"... **$275**
Sauce tureen, lid, base, undertray..................... **$195**
Sugar with lid.. **$225**
Vegetable tureen with lid................................ **$250**
Water pitcher.. **$500**
Hong Kong, Ridgways, 1845
Pickle dish, polychromed................................ **$185**
Humphreys Clock, Unknown, 1898
Chamber pot... **$150**
Hyson, Alcock, 1843
Dessert set, blue ground, 15 pieces.................... **$3,000**
Vase, red ground, 9 1/4"................................. **$1,100**
Indian, Phillips, 1850
Sugar with lid.. **$155**
Teapot with lid.. **$350**
Indian Jar, Furnival, 1843
Paneled pitcher.. **$375**
Vegetable tureen with lid................................ **$255**
Indian Stone, Walley, 1850
Creamer... **$150**
Iris, Doulton, 1850
Creamer... **$155**
Stag pitcher.. **$175**

Flow Blue bowl, Brushstroke, unknown maker, Scotland, 1860s, 8" d. **$150**

Flow Blue, unknown pattern, unknown maker, polychromed tea caddy with lid, 1875. **$450**

Flow Blue tea cup and saucer, unknown pattern, K & G, France, 1880. **$110**

Flow Blue round vegetable bowl, Astoria, Upper Hanley, 10". **$225**

Ivy, unknown maker, 1890
Pitcher, 8"..**$225**
Soap dish with insert and lid.....................**$250**
Japonica, B & L, 1890
Tea tile, polychromed................................**$195**
Janette, Grindley, 1890
Plate, 10"...**$90**
Teapot with lid...**$365**
Jenny Lind, Royal Staff. Pott., 1900
Charger, 13 1/2".......................................**$155**
Jewel, Johnson Bros., 1900
Bone dish, large.......................................**$85**
Platter, 14"...**$225**
Kew, Bourne & Leigh, 1912
Plate, 10 1/2"..**$50**
Kinshaw, Challinor, 1855
Shaving mug...**$250**
Kremlin, Alcock, 1843
Creamer, polychromed...............................**$325**
Pitcher, 9" polychromed.............................**$1,600**
La Belle, Wheeling, 1890
Biscuit jar with lid....................................**$355**
Butter dish with lid...................................**$245**
Charger, 10"..**$275**
Chocolate pot with lid...............................**$685**
Clock...**$1,600**
Creamer, 5"...**$225**
Hot water pot with lid...............................**$1,000**
Ice pitcher..**$2,400**
Jardinière...**$1,200**
Nut dish, 4"..**$425**
Pitcher, 7"...**$325**
Plate, 10"..**$150**
Ribbon handled bowl.................................**$250**
Teapot with lid...**$850**
Ladas, Ridgway, 1895
Plate, 9"..**$65**
Rimmed soup bowl, 10".............................**$55**

Lancaster, New Wharf; 1890
Oval bowl, 12"...**$250**
Vegetable tureen with lid...........................**$275**
Linda, Maddock, 1898
Creamer..**$125**
Sauce tureen with lid................................**$260**
Soup ladle..**$275**
Tea cup and saucer...................................**$95**
Lahore, Phillips, 1840
Mitten relish...**$150**
La Pavot, Grindley, 1896
Butter dish with lid, insert.........................**$275**
Linton, Godwin, 1840
Pancake dish with lid.................................**$250**
Lonsdale, Ford, 1898
Plate, 10"..**$80**
Platter, 18"..**$290**
Luzern, Mercer, 1890
Soup tureen with lid and undertray..............**$375**
Madras, Doulton, 1902
Creamer, 5"...**$135**
Vegetable tureen with lid...........................**$275**
Manhatten, Alcock, 1890
Teapot with lid...**$450**
Manilla, Podmore Walker, 1850
Pitcher, 5 1/2"...**$250**
Pitcher, 7 1/2"...**$525**
Sauce tureen undertray..............................**$100**
Marie, Grindley, 1895
Oyster bowl..**$135**
Marguerite, Grindley, 1890
Creamer..**$225**
Sugar bowl with lid....................................**$225**
Well and tree platter..................................**$650**
Melbourne, Grindley, 1890
Bone dish..**$50**
Creamer, 4"...**$120**
Gravy boat with undertray..........................**$225**
Platter, 16 1/2"...**$295**
Mongolia, unknown maker, 1850
Posset cup..**$110**
Nankin, Edwards, 1850
Plate, 9 1/4"...**$85**
Tea cup and saucer...................................**$100**
Waste bowl...**$125**
Normandy, Johnson Bros., 1890
Child's plate..**$125**
Chocolate pot with lid...............................**$750**
Non-Pariel, Burgess & Leigh, 1896
Fish sauceboat..**$150**
Platter, 13"...**$225**
Sauce ladle...**$250**
Sugar with lid..**$250**
Oriental, Alcock, 1840
Gravy boat with red ground........................**$500**
Plate, 10 1/2"...**$125**
Platter, 12"...**$175**
Vegetable bowl, oval, 10"...........................**$150**
Oriental, Dimmock, 1850
Meat drainer...**$375**

Flow Blue pitcher, John Westwood, Low Toryburn, 1866. **$575**

Oregon, Mayer, 1845
Creamer **$300**
Gravy boat **$200**
Mug **$275**
Relish **$150**
Sugar with lid **$260**
Tazza, stemmed **$295**

Pansy, Warwick, 1896
Cheese dish with lid **$275**
Chocolate pot with lid **$250**
Syrup with lid, underplate **$250**
Tea tile **$195**

Pekin, Royal Staff, 1891
Tea cup and saucer **$110**

Persian Spray, Pinder Bourne, 1855
Gravy boat with lid, footed **$425**
Platter, 18 1/2" **$250**
Vegetable tureen with lid, footed **$350**

Polychrome, unknown maker, 1855
Footed tazza with green ground **$145**

Scinde, Alcock, 1840
Creamer, 5 1/2" **$275**
Gravy boat **$250**
Sauce tureen with lid and undertray **$425**
Sauce ladle **$600**
Soup bowl, 10 1/2" **$225**
Teapot with lid, gothic **$525**
Tea cup (handled) and saucer **$165**
Vegetable bowl, open **$250**

Shapoo, Boote, 1842
Sugar with lid **$250**
Teapot with lid **$325**

Shell, Challinor, 1860
Bowl, 10" **$275**
Creamer, gothic **$200**
Platter, 12" **$385**
Tea cup (handless) and saucer **$110**

Shell, Dimmock, 1844
Sugar bowl with lid **$225**

Stanley, Johnson Bros., 1900
Bone dish **$45**

St. Louis, Johnson Bros., 1890
Charger, 12" **$300**
Chowder tureen with lid **$325**
Soup bowl, 9" **$55**

The Hofburg, Grindley, 1891
Pitcher, 8 1/2" **$125**

The Temple, Podmore Walker, 1845
Plate, 9" **$145**

Tonquin, Heath, 1845
Handless cup and saucer **$175**

Touraine, Alcock, 1898
Creamer **$150**
Pitcher, 7 3/4" **$300**
Plate, 6 1/2" **$45**
Vegetable bowl, individual, oval **$95**

Touraine, Stanley, 1898
Bone dish **$75**
Creamer, 5" **$185**
Plate, 8 1/2" **$100**

Tulip, Copeland Spode, 1850
Pitcher, 7 1/2" **$275**

Victoria, Grindley, 1900
Soup tureen with lid **$250**

Water Nymph, Wedgwood, 1872
Low tazza **$200**

Watteau, Doulton, 1915
Demitasse cup and saucer **$85**
Plate, 9" **$75**

Waverly, Grindley, 1890
Bone dish **$70**

Willow, Keeling, 1886
Watercress drainer, 2 piece. **$325**

MAJOLICA

Majolica, an opaque, tin-glazed pottery, has been produced in many countries for centuries. It was named after the Spanish Island of Majorca. Today, however, the term "majolica" denotes a type of pottery made during the last half of the 19th century in Europe and America.

Majolica frequently depicts elements of nature: leaves, flowers, birds and fish. Designs were painted on the soft-clay body using vitreous colors and fired under a clear lead glaze to impart the rich color and brilliant characteristic of majolica.

Victorian decorative art philosophy dictated that the primary function of design was to attract the eye; usefulness was secondary. Majolica was a welcome and colorful change from the familiar blue and white wares, creamwares and white ironstone of the day.

Wedgwood, George Jones, Holdcroft and Minton were a few of the English majolica manufacturers who marked their wares. Most of their pieces can be identified through the English Registry mark and/or the potter-designer's mark. Sarreguemines in France and Villeroy and Boch in Baden, Germany, produced majolica that compared favorably with the finer English majolica. Most Continental pieces have an incised number on the base.

Although 600-plus American potteries produced majolica between 1850 and 1900, only a handful chose to identify their wares. Among these manufacturers were George Morely, Edwin Bennett, the Chesapeake Pottery Co., the New Milford-Wannoppee Pottery Co. and the firm of Griffen, Smith and Hill. The others hoped their unmarked pieces would be taken for English examples.

Notes: Prices listed here are for pieces with good color and in mint condition. For less-than-perfect pieces, decrease value proportionately according to the degree of damage or restoration.

Reproduction Alert. Majolica-style pieces are a favorite of today's interior decorators. Many exact copies of period pieces are being manufactured. In addition, fantasy pieces incorporating late Victorian-era design motifs have entered the market and confused many novice collectors.

Modern majolica reproductions differ from period pieces in these ways: (1) modern reproductions tend to be lighter in weight than their Victorian ancestors; (2) the glaze on newer pieces may not be as rich or deeply colored as on period pieces; (3) new pieces usually have a plain white bottom; period pieces almost always have colored or mottled bases; (4) a bisque finish either inside or on the bottom generally means the piece is new; and (5) if the design prevents the piece from being functional—e.g., a lip of a pitcher that does not allow proper pouring—it is a new piece made primarily for decorative purposes.

Some reproductions bear old marks. Period marks found on modern pieces include "Etruscan Majolica" (the mark of Griffen, Smith and Hill) and a British registry mark.

Basket
Bird on branch, pink ribbon on handle, 10" x 6 1/2" **$250**
Floral and basketweave with bird perched on twig handle, bird missing beak, 8" h **$300**
Yellow, angel faces on each side, 8" **$200**
Yellow basketweave, flowers, attributed to Holdcroft, 10" l **$300**
Bread tray
Floral, butterflies, pastel colors, "Waste Not Want Not".. **$250**
Geranium and basketweave, "Eat thy bread with thankfulness," 12 3/4" **$300**
Strawberry blossom dec, George Jones, impressed registry mark, date code for 1873, 10 1/2" l, 2 3/4" h **$700**
Bud vase, Minton, yellow, green ribbon, triple holes, 6" . **$450**
Butter pat
Cobalt blue, sunflower **$140**
Copeland pansy, good color **$150**
Holdcroft, fan shape, bird in flight **$175**
Wedgwood, chrysanthemum **$150**
Cachepot, Rorstrand, hairline, rim and base chip, 8" h, 8 3/4" d **$25**
Cake stand
Etruscan, morning glory, 8 1/4" **$175**
George Jones, leaf on napkin, white ground, 9" w, 6" h **$450**
Low, bird on branch, 8 3/4" d **$60**
Wedgwood, green leaf, green ground, 8" d, 2 1/2" h **$125**
Candlestick, figural
Dolphin, Minton, professional repair to top, 8 1/4" h ... **$450**
Palmer Cox Brownie, 8 1/2" h **$250**
Wardle, water lily form, all green **$125**
Cheese keeper, covered
Bird on branch, yellow ground, ribbon and bow accents ... **$375**
George Jones, apple blossom and basketweave, 10" d .. **$1,900**
Mottled brown and green, wedge shape, florals, 12" l .. **$250**
Turquoise, blackberry and cow, 11 1/2" h **$700**

Photo courtesy of Strawser Auction Group by Michael G. Strawser.

Majolica, Continental jardinière, two Blackamoor hunters hunting lion, one figure holds cubs, other aims at lion, gun and leaf repair, 17" h. **$5,000**

Majolica, George Jones, Picket Fence and Daisy full-size cheesekeeper, cobalt, outstanding color, minor professional rim repair to underplate, 12" h, 12" d. **$10,000**

Majolica, Holdcraft, oyster plate, pink wells, blue spaces, seaweed and shells, 11" w. **$1,700**

Majolica, George Jones, comport, fox looking into rabbit hole at rabbit under tree, 8" h. **$8,000**

Majolica, Minton vase with basket-weave and applied floral motif, hairline, shape no. 1287, good color, date code for 1870, 6 3/4" h. **$700**

Majolica match striker, "B Block" figural Blackamoor with baskets, minor repair to rim of basket, head reattached, 10 1/2" h. **$350**

Photo courtesy of Strawser Auction Group by Michael G. Strawser.

Majolica, two-handled jardinière, cobalt blue, acorns, holly, oak leaves, mythological figures, hounds, panthers, Minton, No. 1992, professional repairs, **$3,500.**

Photo courtesy of Strawser Auction Group by Michael G. Strawser.

Majolica, two putti harvestors, barrel flower holder, professional barrel rim repair, 9 1/2" h, **$1,200.**

Photo courtesy of Strawser Auction Group by Michael G. Strawser.

Majolica, George Jones, game tureen, cover depicts boar's head with oak leaves and acorns, boar's head handles, sides depict boar and hunting dogs, cover rim repair, 12 1/2", **$6,000.**

Centerpiece
Double dolphin supports, nautilus, Wedgwood, also marked with impressed "GA," circa 1880, 16 3/8" h **$1,800**

Putto riding dolphin atop shell and coral base while holding shell, George Jones, rim chip to one shell and hairline to another, outstanding color and detail, 15" h, 13 1/2" w **$3,500**

Compote
Shallow, Etruscan maple leaf, with early mark for Griffen, Smith and Hill, 9" d, 5 1/2" h **$250**

Wedgwood, double dolphin, nautilus shell top, 16" **$800**

Cup and saucer
Banks and Thorley, Basketweave and Bamboo, butterfly handle **$275**

Etruscan, bamboo **$125**

Lovebirds on branch, green and tan **$75**

Shell shape, pink, yellow and brown **$175**

Humidor, covered, figural
Clown head, yellow hat and collar, 6" h **$75**

Man, night cape and pipe, 4 1/2" h **$75**

Oriental lady, hat, 5" h **$75**

Policeman, pot bellied, 10 1/2" h **$150**

Sailor, hat and beard, 5" **$50**

Jardinière
Bamboo and Fern, Wardle, 8" **$550**

Large, French, birds on branch, blackberry, floral and leaves oval, good detail, 8" h, 15" w **$500**

Jardinière on stand, large Austrian Rococo Revival ovoid,
scroll handles and feet, shaped rocaille rim with diaper cartouches, yellow and light blue ground, enamel dec with scattered bees, foliates and dragonflies, conforming waisted stand, late 19th C, 33" h **$1,057**

Jug, Palissy Ware with oak leaves, acorns and snake wrapped
around jug with frog on spout, professional rim, handle and spout repair, 10" h **$1,100**

Match striker, Continental
Happy Hooligan, hat **$100**

Lady with tambourine, 10 1/2" **$100**

Man with violin, 12" **$125**

Monk, stein and brick barrels, 8" **$100**

Monkey, cobalt blue cape, 5 1/2" **$125**

Mug
Etruscan, Water Lily **$250**

Samuel Lear, classical urn **$100**

Wedgwood, grape and vine **$150**

Mustache cup and saucer, Wild Rose and Rope **$250**

Oyster plate
French Orchies, blue and beige, 10" d **$150**

Minton, pink wells, 9" d **$450**

Russian, Imperial eagle, 9 1/2" d **$500**

Seaweed and Shell, cobalt blue center, 10" d **$375**

Pedestal, Argenta ware "Corinthian," Wedgwood, England,
fluted column, relief neoclassical oval portrait pendants, fruiting grapevine garland, leopard masks, trophy drops, impressed mark, foot rim restoration, rim hairline, chip, circa 1878, 33 1/2" **$1,410**

Pitcher
Bird and bird nest, 9" h **$225**

Gnarled tree trunk and florals, 8" h **$150**

Robin, mottled, 9 1/4" h **$100**

Stork in marsh, 11" h **$225**

Photo courtesy of Strawser Auction Group by Michael G. Strawser.

Majolica, George Jones, leaf and ferns plate with turquoise ground, surface wear, 8 1/2" d. **$200**

Photo courtesy of Wiederseim Associates, Inc.

Majolica jardinière, two parts, English, late 19th century, 44" h, bowl 17" h x 17 1/2" d. **$600**

Photo courtesy of Strawser Auction Group by Michael G. Strawser.

Majolica, George Jones, covered butter dish, cobalt blue, butterfly handle, yellow flowers, green foliate. **$1,350**

Water lily, green and yellow, 8" h **$175**
Water lily and iris, George Jones, turquoise, outstanding
    color and detail, Bacall Collection, 8 1/4" h **$2,500**
Placement tray, yellow rope trim and red tassels,
    French, 12 1/2" w **$60**
Plate
    Bellflowers, cobalt blue, 8 3/4" d **$225**
    Bird and Fan, pebbles, cobalt blue, 9" d **$150**
    Bird in flight, fern and cattail, white ground, 8 1/2" d .. **$125**
    Blackberry and basketweave, brown, 9" d **$125**
Platter
    Dragonfly and leaf, pink border, 11 1/2" l **$200**
    Eureka, bird and fan, diamond shaped, 15 1/2" l **$250**
    Leaves and ferns, oval, greens and brown, 12" **$250**
Sardine box, covered
    English, green and brown mottled **$250**
    Fielding, Fan and Scroll, attached underplate, blue and
        yellow **$500**
    Wedgwood, boat shaped anchor finial **$550**
Server, Holdcroft, double leaf, squirrel handle, 13" **$675**
Spittoon, Etruscan, Pineapple, yellow and green **$500**
Syrup, pewter top
    Holdcroft, Pond Lily, turquoise, 3 3/4" **$300**
    Wedgwood, Caterer jug, turquoise and brown, 7 1/2" .. **$250**
    Wedgwood, Doric, mottled cobalt blue and brown, 7 1/2" h
    .... **$125**

Teapot, covered
    Basketweave and floral, pink and turquoise, pewter lid,
        6 3/4" h **$275**
    Bird and Bird's Nest, figural, brown and green, 9" **$225**
    Dragon-handled, birds, flowers and vine in relief, Royal
        Worcester, strong color and detail, minor professional
        spout repair, rare, 7 1/2" h **$3,000**
    Fielding, Fan and Scroll, insect, pebble ground, cream and
        purple, 7" **$275**
    Pyramid shape, brown, yellow and green, 8 1/2" **$250**
    Wild Rose, yellow pebble ground, white flowers, 5 1/2" .. **$225**
Tray
    Etruscan oak leaf, 12" w **$175**
    Minton, bird, oak leaf shape, 8" **$500**
Tureen, George Jones, mackerel on bed of ferns, 19" .. **$4,250**
Vase, lily, Minton cobalt and turquoise shape No. 293, great
    detail, professional rim repair and base repair, 6 1/2" h .. **$20**

Quimper

Quimper faience, dating back to the 17th century, is named for Quimper, a French town where numerous potteries were located. Several mergers resulted in the evolution of two major houses—the Jules Henriot and Hubaudière-Bousquet factories.

The peasant design first appeared in the 1860s, and many variations exist. Florals and geometrics, equally popular, also were produced in large quantities. During the 1920s, the Hubaudière-Bousquet factory introduced the Odetta line, which used a stone body and Art Deco decorations.

The two major houses merged in 1968, the products retaining the individual characteristics and marks of the originals. The concern suffered from labor problems in the 1980s and was purchased by an American group.

The "HR" and "HR Quimper" marks are found on Henriot pieces prior to 1922. The "Henriot Quimper" mark was used after 1922. The "HB" mark covers a long time span. Numbers or dots and dashes were added for inventory purposes and are found on later pieces. Most marks are in blue or black. Pieces ordered by department stores, such as Macy's and Carson Pirie Scott, carry the store mark along with the factory mark, making them less desirable to collectors.

Adviser: Al Bagdade.

Additional Terms:

A la touche border decor—single brush stroke to create floral

Breton Broderie decor—stylized blue and gold pattern inspired by a popular embroidery design often used on Breton costumes, dates from the 1920s.

Croisille—criss-cross pattern

Decor Riche border—acanthus leaves in two colors

Fleur-de-lys—the symbol of France.

Bell, 4" h, bagpipe shape, male peasant on front, female on reverse, scattered typical florals, green grass base, molded black pipe handle, molded blue ribbon top, "HR Quimper" mark. **$100**

Biberon, 7" h, bold coloring, male peasant on side holding long pipe, flanked by usual red, green, blue and yellow verticals, band of similar florals on reverse, blue and yellow striped base, blue dash side handle and overhead handle, blue knob and spout, "HR Quimper" mark.................. **$295**

Bowl, covered, 6 1/2" h, female peasant on cover with scattered red, green, and blue foliage, band of red, green, and blue florals on base, yellow and blue striped rims, blue dash curled handles, blue pointed knob, glaze chip, "HenRiot Quimper France" mark. **$100**

Box, covered, 7" w, octagonal, two male peasants playing horn or bagpipe, on cover, dark blue acanthus borders, orange line rims, four small feet, "HenRiot Quimper" mark. **$300**

Bud vase, 4 3/4" h, ball shape, flared brown-lined rim, cream ground, bust of male peasant in large hat, brown shades on front, female bust on reverse, brown shades with orange and white accents, white coif, "HB Quimper" mark. **$125**

Cake stand, 9 1/2" d x 2" h, circa 1880s, frontal views of female peasant holding apron hem and basket, male with nets on shoulder and at side, border of alternating bunches of red, blue, and green florals or blue-dot designs, shaped rim, circular base, "HB Quimper" mark...................**$1,100**

Chamberstick, 2 1/4" h x 6" l, ivoire corbelle designs, bagpipe shape, molded brown pipes and blue ribbon on margins, red dashes, chains of red centered blue circles on base, hex nozzle with similar designs, blue and gold outlined rim, blue handle, "HenRiot Quimper" mark...**$265**

Charger, 12" d, Breton Broderie design, center scene of fisherman with net on shoulder, boy at side watching sailboats, cobalt border ground with enameled gold and white dot floral inner border, gold band of arrowheads between gold wave drapes, brown rim, "HB Quimper" mark. **$1850**

Creamer, 5 1/2" h, figural bust of female peasant, blue-dot shawl, green dress, lighting pipe, white coif forms spout, "HenRiot Quimper" mark................**$175**

Cruet set, 8" h, two bottles, yellow ground, male or female peasant on front of bottles, cobalt, green and red single stroke flowers, cobalt lined rims, blue striped circular center handle, blue sponged knobs, "HB Quimper" mark. **$125**

Cup and saucer, heart shape with three feet, male peasant on front of cup and center of saucer, laurel band of red, green, yellow, and yellow-centered blue dot flower heads, blue rims, blue dash handle, "HR Quimper" marks......**$125**

Cup and saucer, pink ground, female peasant on side with light-blue clouds and band of blue centered dark-red dot florals, light-blue and green foliage, green handle, saucer with band of blue centered dark-red dot florals, green foliage, sprig in center, light-blue rim, "HenRiot Quimper France" mark. **$65**

Egg cup, 3" h, kneeling peasant woman, blue dress, black jacket with orange stripes, white coif, red-brown shawl, holding brown-accented conch shell egg holder, "HenRiot Quimper, C. Maillard" marks. **$95**

Figure, 5 1/2" h, "St. Anne," light-blue head shawl, medium-blue robe, yellow gown with black ermine tail designs, red accents, baby Jesus at side in white gown with blue vertical stripes containing red dots, octagonal base with green grass, "St. Anne" on front, corners with blue X's and red dots, "HenRiot Quimper France 109" mark.................**$225**

Figure, 8 1/2" h, standing young male peasant, green sponged shirt, yellow-lined cobalt jacket, yellow trousers, square base with cut corners and "PERRIK" on front, rock on back, "HenRiot Quimper France" mark. **$195**

Inkwell, 6 1/4" l x 5 1/8" w, hat shape with rolled rim, cover with seated male peasant, blue-dot flowers, brown acorn knob, yellow band on side with green herringbone overlay repeated as blue-dash-outlined ribbons on base and band of red, green and yellow centered blue dot flowers, blue sponged rim, "HenRiot Quimper France" mark...........**$225**

Jardiniere, 6" h x 7 1/2" l, figural swan, double gold outlined cartouche of seated female peasant with egg basket and bouquet on swans breast, gold and blue sponged circular feathers on base, blue circlets above, blue dash borders, gold feet, green crown, orange bill resting on neck, "HenRiot Quimper France" mark. **$750**

Jug, 9" h, bulbous, female peasant under spout, flanked by vertical red, green, blue, and yellow foliage, horizontal florals on reverse with four blue-dot designs, yellow and

Plaque, 15" w x 18" h, relief molded, black Porquier Beau mark. **$1,850**

blue banded borders, fleur-de-lis spout, blue-dash handle, "HR Quimper" mark under handle. **$195**

Lamp base, 12" h, Modern Movement, circa 1930, figural standing female peasant with mustard-yellow jar on shoulder, white coif, orange-striped cobalt dress, pink apron, brown and orange wooden shoes, molded blue-striped white circular base with green leaves, "C. Maillard," "HenRiot Quimper" marks. **$575**

Oyster plate, 8 3/4" d, six wells around center lemon well, ivoire corbeille designs, center well with bust of male peasant in yellow border, three wells with red, blue, and yellow slashes, dots, and circles, three wells with red dashes and red centered blue circles, blue sponged rim, red dashes between wells, "HenRiot Quimper" mark. **$300**

Pie plate, 7 1/2" d, female peasant holding folded umbrella in center, flanked by red, yellow, blue and green florals, four bunches of similar florals on border with scattered four-blue-dot designs, orange edge and blue sponged rim with eight pinches, "HR Quimper" mark on front. **$195**

Plate, 8 1/2" d, multicolored exotic bird in center with blue basket, light-blue and yellow or red and yellow florals, border of red, yellow and green single-stroke flowers and foliage between blue lines, "HB Quimper France" mark. **$125**

Plate, 9" d, kneeling old man, peasant woman, two children before wayside cross, green acanthus border between orange lines, crest of Brittany at top of border, Porquier Beau mark. **$950**

Plate, 9 1/4" d, female peasant holding bale of hay on head flanked by green trees, border of scattered sprigs separated by four-blue-dot designs, shaped rim, "HB Quimper" mark on front. **$350**

Plate, 9 5/8" d, circa 1920s, standing female with basket on arm, umbrella under other arm, border of meandering orange and green florals alternating with orange crisscross designs, blue outlined scalloped rim, "HB Quimper" mark. **$250**

Platter, 16 1/2" l x 11 1/4" w, female seated on rock holding bouquet, bunches of red, yellow, blue, and green flowers on each side, band of single-stroke red, green, yellow and blue sprays on border, blue indented rims, unmarked. **$300**

Porringer, 5 3/4" h, blue florals in bowl with scattered four-blue-dot designs and crisscross patches, inner border of blue hanging lambrequins and swags, blue-outlined fan handles, "HenRiot Quimper France" mark. **$90**

Relish tray, 9 1/2" w, oval, center scene of peasant sitting on rock in meadow blowing horn, blue swag inner border, two border panels of blue crisscross and red-dot designs, blue and gold outlined end panels of single-stroke flowers and red and yellow flower blossom, paneled rim, blue-and-gold dash open handles, "HenRiot Quimper" mark. **$195**

Salt, 7" l x 5 1/2" w, double, two oval dishes joined by blue-and-gold dash heart-shaped handle, female or male peasant in bowl, flanked by typical florals, gold and blue striped shaped rims, "HB Quimper France" mark. **$120**

Shaving bowl, 10 1/2" l x 8 1/2" w, oval, standing male peasant with cane and pipe in meadow in center, border of scattered multicolored florals and four-blue-dot designs, blue outlined rim, "Quimper" mark. **$225**

Snuff bottle, 3 1/4" h, oblong, multicolored coq on front, male peasant on reverse, orange-yellow molded border with teardrops, cobalt spout and sides. **$175**

Soup tureen, 15 1/2" H-H, melon-lobed shape, base with seated female in meadow on side, scattered ajonc florals on sides and reverse, scattered ajonc on cover, blue sponged open handles and arched knob, yellow border bands with blue scalloping, "Henriot Quimper" mark. **$450**

Teapot, 6 1/2" h, bulbous, "Petit Breton" pattern, male peasant on side, band of red, green and yellow flowers on reverse and blue dots, yellow- and blue-striped borders, rim and cover, blue sponged handle, knob and spout tip, "Henriot Quimper France 754" mark. **$295**

Tea set, pot 8" h, creamer 5" h, covered sugar bowl, 6 3/4" h, salt glaze, chips, "HR Quimper" marks. **$900**

Tulipiere (flower holder), 5 1/2" h, fan shape with three gold-outlined nozzles, front with female and bale of flax and male peasant watching in meadow, crest of Brittany below, green- and gold-sponged handles, gold-outlined semi-circular base, white back, "HB" mark. **$575**

Tray, 11" H-H, reclining male peasant blowing horn in meadow, scattered floral border, blue-lined shaped and waisted rim, two blue-sponged handles, "HB Quimper" on front. **$225**

Vase, 5 1/4" h, bulbous, flared rim, male peasant in blue coat, yellow pantaloons, flanked by vertical blue, red, and yellow foliage, band of blue arches and dots on shoulder, red and green stripes, "HenRiot Quimper France" mark. **$95**

Vase, 10" h, circa 1935, narrow base, swollen bulbous shoulder, flared neck and rim, alternating green or red vertical stripes with black accents, brown interior, "Quimper Kenilworth Studios France" mark. **$375**

Wall pocket, 7 1/2" h, double-cone shape, male or female peasant on cones, blue-dash bases, scattered flowers on sides, three blue-outlined, red-dash back plates, blue-dash center hanging loop, "HB Quimper" mark. **$125**

Wall pocket, 7 5/8" h, pouch-shaped bowl with molded blue drawstrings and hanging molded tassels, large blue-shaded fleur-de-lis on front, molded hanging tassel from base, scattered black ermine tails on pouch and back plate, center hanging hole, "HR Quimper" mark. **$175**

COLLECTIBLE CERAMICS, FIGURINES

HOLT-HOWARD

Three young entrepreneurs, Grant Holt and brothers John and Robert Howard, started Holt-Howard from their apartment in Manhattan in 1949. All three of the partners were great salesmen, but Robert handled product development, while John managed sales; Holt was in charge of financial affairs and office management. By 1955, operations were large enough to move the company to Connecticut, but it still maintained its New York showroom and later added its final showroom in Los Angeles.

The company's first successful imported product was the Angel-Abra, followed closely by its Christmas line. This early success spurred the partners to expand their wares. Their line of Christmas and kitchen-related giftware was popular with 1950s consumers. Probably the most famous line was Pixieware, which began production in 1958. Production of these whimsical pieces continued until 1962. Other lines, such as Cozy Kittens and Merry Mouse, followed.

The founders of this company sold their interests to General Housewares Corp. in 1968, where it became part of the giftware group. By 1974, the three original partners had left the firm. By 1990, what remained of Holt-Howard was sold to Kay Dee Designs of Rhode Island.

Holt-Howard pieces were marked with an ink-stamp. Many were also copyright dated. Some pieces were marked only with a foil sticker, especially the small pieces, where a stamp mark was too difficult. Four types of foil stickers have been identified.

Christmas

Air freshener, Girl Christmas Tree $65
Ashtray, Snow Baby $35
Ashtray/cigarette holder, Starry-eyed Santa $45
Bells, Elf Girls, pair $55
Bottle opener, wooden
   Santa $28
   Snowman $28
Candle climbers, Ole Snowy, snowman, set $48
Candleholders
   Camels $38
   Carolers trio $30
   Elf Girls, NOEL, set of four $38
   Ermine Angels with snowflake rings, set $48
   Green Holly Elf, pair $35
   Madonna and Child $25
   Naughty Choir Boy, set of two $30
   Reindeer, pair $38
   Santa driving car candleholders, traffic light candle rings,
     pair $55
   Santa riding stagecoach, pair $38
   Santas, NOEL, set of four $90
   Snow Babies, igloo, set of two $55
   Three Choir Boy $60
   Three Snowmen $50
   Totem Pole, Santa $25
   Wee Three Kings, set of three $60
   Cigarette holder with ashtrays, Santa King, stackable $70
   Coffee mug, Green Holly Elf $23
Cookie jar, pop-up, Santa $150
Cookie jar/candy jar combination, Santa $155
Creamer and sugar
   Reindeer $48
   Winking Santas $55
   Decanter and glasses, Santa King $100
   Dish, divided, Green Holly Elf $50
   Floral ring, Green Holly Elf $48
Head vase, My Fair Lady $75
Letter and pen holder, Santa $55
Napkin holder, Santa, 4" $25
Nutmeg shaker, Winking Santa $55
Pitcher and mug set, Winking Santa $75
Place card holders, Green Holly Elf, set of four $40

Dworkin collection, photo by Van Blerck Photography.

Holt-Howard, Pixieware, Cocktail Olives, **$130;** *Plain Olives.* **$100**

Holt-Howard, Pixieware, Sam n' Sally salad cruet set, one for oil, other for vinegar, copyrighted 1958, 9″ h, each. **$185**

Planter
Camel	$40
Elf Girl in Sleigh	$58
Ermine Angel	$38
Green Holly Elf, pair	$75

Punch bowl set, punch bowl and eight mugs, Santa ...$145

Salt and pepper shakers, pair
Cloud Santa	$38
Holly Girls, pair	$23
Rock 'N' Roll Santas, on springs	$75
Santa and Rudolph sleeping in bed	$105
Santa and snowman in NOEL candleholder	$95
Snow Babies	$35

Server, divided tray, Santa King ...$60

Wall pocket
Green Holly Elf	$65
Santa on ornament	$58

Cozy Kittens
Ashtray, with match holder	$60
Bud vase, pair	$95
Butter dish, covered	$105
Condiment jar, Cat	
Instant Coffee	$190
Jam 'N' Jelly	$180
Ketchup	$180
Mustard	$180
Cookie jar, pop-up	$260
Cottage cheese crock	$55
Creamer and sugar	$295
Kitty catch clip	$50
Letter holder/caddy	$58
Match dandy	$80
Memo minder	$78
Meow milk pitcher	$130
Meow mug	$38
Meow oil and vinegar	$195
Salt and pepper shakers, pair	$20
Sewing kit, Merry Measure	$80
Spice set of four, with rack	$120
String holder	$60
Sugar pour	$85
Totem pole stacking seasons	$70

Cows
Creamer and sugar	$75
Milk glass, moo cow	$32
Salt and pepper shakers, pair	
Cow's heads	$38
Cow's heads with moveable tongues	$38

Easter
Candelabra, three rabbits	$65
Candle climbers, four-piece set	
Feathered Chicks, cracked egg floral frog bases	$78
Honey Bunnies, floral frog bases	$78
Candleholder	
Totem pole, chicks	$70
Totem pole, rabbits	$50

Collection of, and photo by, Jane Tischler.

Holt-Howard, Cozy Kittens sugar and creamer, set. **$300**

Dworkin collection, photo by Brenner Lennon Photo Productions.

Holt-Howard, Pixieware, Onion Annie. **$688**

Dworkin collection, photo by Van Blerck Photography.

Holt-Howard, Pixieware, Berries. **$750**

Egg cups, Slick Chick, pair of egg cups with Chick salt and
    pepper shaker, four-piece set $50
Salt and pepper shakers with napkin holder, Winking
    Wabbits $60
Salt and pepper shakers, pair
    Bunnies in baskets $35
    Rabbits, pink and yellow $25

Jeeves, butler
Ashtray $65
Chip dish $80
Liquor decanter $165
Martini shaker set $185
Olives, condiment jar $135

Merry Mouse
Cocktail kibitzers, mice, set of six $120
Coaster, ashtray, corner $55
Crock, "Stinky Cheese" $55
Desk pen pal $90
Match mouse $80
Salt and pepper shakers, pair $45

Minnie & Moby Mermaids
Ashtray, Moby $60
Cotton ball dispenser, Minnie $85
Matchbox holder, Moby $70
Pill box, Moby $60
Planter, seahorse, Minnie & Moby, pair .... $100 each
Powder box, Minnie $60

Miscellaneous
Ashtray
    Golfer Image $110
    Li'l Old Lace $50
Bank, bobbing, Dandy Lion $135
Bud vase, Daisy Dorable $70
Candelabra, Li'l Old Lace, spiral $50
Candleholder, Market Piggy $28
Candle rings, Ballerina, with bases, set $58
Cookie jar, pop-up, Clown $225
Desk organizer, Market Piggy $78

Letter holder, Pheasant $60
Memo holder, Pheasant $60
Napkin doll, Sunbonnet Miss $75
Pencil holder and sharpener, two-piece set
    Chickadee $80
    Cock-A-Doodle $85
    Professor Perch $65
Planter, Doe & Fawn $35
Salt and pepper shakers, pair
    Bell Bottom Gobs (sailors) $55
    Chattercoons, Peppy and Salty $38
    Daisy Dorables, ponytail girls $40
    Goose 'N' Golden Egg $35
    Pink cat, white poodle $65
    Rock 'N' Roll Kids, on springs $85
Tape dispenser
    Chickadee $50
    Pelican Pete $68
Tea maker, Tea Time Tillie $55

Peepin' Tom & Tweetie Birds
Butter dish, covered $65
Candleholder/floral holder $40
Creamer, sugar and saccharin holder, 4 1/2" $85
Egg cups, thermal salt and pepper tops, 4" h $60
Salt and pepper shakers, set $30
Stackable condiment bowls, set of three $45

Pixiewares, 1958
Bottle bracelets
    Bourbon $105
    Gin $105
    Scotch $105
    Whiskey $105
Child's Pixie spoon
    Carrot nose, flesh-colored Pixie $145
    Green head Pixie $145
    Orange head Pixie $145
    Yellow chicken beak Pixie $145
Condiment jar
    Cherries $120
    Cocktail Cherries $140

Cocktail Olives	$130
Cocktail Onions	$155
Instant Coffee	$255
Jam 'N' Jelly	$75
Ketchup	$75
Mustard	$75
Olives	$100
Onions	$145

L'il sugar and cream crock ... $155

Liquor decanter

"Devil Brew"	$590
"300 Proof"	$590
"Whisky"	$590

Oil cruet, Sally ... $185
Oil cruet, Sam ... $185
Stacking seasons, shakers, set of four ... $180

Pixiewares, 1959

Ashtray Pixie

Blue stripe	$160
Green stripe	$160
Pink stripe	$160
Red stripe	$160

Condiment jar

Chili Sauce	$365
Honey	$725
Mayonnaise	$190
Relish	$225

Hanging planter, rare ... $450

Party Pixies hors d'oeuvre dish

Green stripe boy pixie	$200
Orange stripe girl pixie, Australian	$475
Pink stripe girl pixie	$200

Salad dressing jar

Flat head, French Pixie	$140
Flat head, Italian Pixie	$140
Flat head, Russian Pixie	$140
Round head, French Pixie	$125
Round head, Italian Pixie	$125
Round head, Russian Pixie	$125

Salty & Peppy shakers ... $350

Snack Pixie bowl

Berries	$750
Goo	$1,100
Ketchup Katie	$675

Mustard Max	$675
Nuts	$600
Onion Annie	$685
Oscar Olives	$575
Peanut Butter Pat	$675
Pickle Pete	$675
Tartar Tom	$850

Teapot candleholder hurricane vase, complete with glass globe

Blue stripe boy	$285
Pink stripe girl	$285

Towel hook

Brother	$150
Dad	$150
Mom	$150
Sister	$150

Red Rooster, "Coq Rouge"

Butter dish, covered	$65
Candleholders, pair	$30
Coffee mug	$14
Coffee server, 36 oz	$65
Cookie jar	$100
Creamer and sugar	$55
Dinner plate	$18
Electric coffee pot, six cups	$70
Mustard condiment jar	$60

Pitcher

12 oz	$45
32 oz	$60
48 oz	$75

Salt and pepper shakers, pair, 4 1/2"	$25
Snack tray	$18
Spoon rest	$25

Wooden

Canister set, four pieces	$145
Cigarette carton holder	$45
Recipe box	$70
Salt & pepper shakers, pair	$25

Tigers

Child's cup	$20
Cookie jar	$45
Napkin holder	$20
Salt and pepper shakers, pair	$23

Dworkin collection, photo by Brenner Lennon Photo Productions.

Holt-Howard, Daisy 'Dorables, salt and pepper set.
$40

HUMMEL ITEMS

Hummel items are the original creations of Berta Hummel, who was born in 1909 in Massing, Bavaria, Germany. At age 18, she was enrolled in the Academy of Fine Arts in Munich to further her mastery of drawing and the palette. Berta entered the Convent of Siessen and became Sister Maria Innocentia in 1934. In this Franciscan cloister, she continued drawing and painting images of her childhood friends.

In 1935, W. Goebel Co. in Rodental, Germany, began producing Sister Maria's sketches as three-dimensional bisque figurines. The Schmid Brothers of Randolph, Mass., introduced the figurines to America and became Goebel's U.S. distributor.

In 1967, Goebel began distributing Hummel items in the U.S. Controversy developed between the two companies, the Hummel family, and the convent. Lawsuits and countersuits ensued. The German courts finally effected a compromise: the convent held legal rights to all works produced by Sister Maria from 1934 until her death in 1946 and licensed Goebel to reproduce these works; Schmid was to deal directly with the Hummel family for permission to reproduce any pre-convent art.

All authentic Hummel pieces bear both the signature "M. I. Hummel" and a Goebel trademark. Various trademarks were used to identify the year of production. For purposes of simplification the various trademarks have been abbreviated in the following list.

In August 2008, Goebel announced that it would discontinue production of Hummel figurines on Oct. 31, 2008.

Trademark	Abbreviations	Dates
Crown	TMK-1	1934-1950
Full Bee	TMK-2	1940-1959
Stylized Bee	TMK-3	1958-1972
Three Line Mark	TMK-4	1964-1972
Last Bee	TMK-5	1972-1979
Missing Bee	TMK-6	1979-1991
Hummel Mark	TMK-7	1991-1999
Millennium Bee (Current)	TMK-8	2000-present

Note: The first seventeen Hummels made are highly prized by collectors. We have included the eleven to thirteen in this book with listings for all of the known marks. For additional information see *Luckey's Hummel® Figurines & Plates Identification and Price Guide*.

All photos appear courtesy of Goebel of North America unless otherwise indicated.

Hum No. 11 Merry Wanderer. **$165-$750**

Hum No. 12 Chimney Sweep. **$145-$850**

Hum No. 13 Meditation. **$160-$5,000**

The First Seventeen, Numbers Eleven to Thirteen

Hum 11: Merry Wanderer

This is the same design as the Hum 7, *Merry Wanderer*, and it, too, was first modeled by sculptor Arthur Moeller in 1935.

Although most of these figures have five buttons on their vest, there are six- and seven-button versions of the 11/2/0 size. These bring a bit more than the five-button version, but it is not significant (about 10%).

The Hum 11 model of the *Merry Wanderer* has been found with a faience finish.

In 1993, as part of a special Disneyland and Disney World promotion, an unknown number of the small *Merry Wanderers* were given a special decal transfer mark beneath the base to commemorate the occasion. The piece was supposed to be sold along with a similar-sized limited-edition Mickey Mouse. Mickey has an incised mold number of 17322, a limited-edition indicator, and TMK-7. The *Merry Wanderer* is a regular production 11/2/0.

The problem was that the *Merry Wanderers* did not make it to the theme parks in time for the promotion. The edition for the pair on a wooden base was 1,500. The first sales of them on the secondary market apparently took place at the site of the M.I. Hummel Club Member Convention in Milwaukee in May 1993. Some private individuals were selling the figures out of their hotel room for $650 per set. They have been advertised for as high as $1,000 since then.

11, 4 3/4"

TMK-1	$600-$750

11/2/0, 4 1/4"

TMK-1	$450-$550
TMK-2	$250-$325
TMK-3	$225-$250
TMK-4	$190-$225
TMK-5	$175-$190
TMK-6	$170-$175
TMK-7	$165-$170
TMK-8	$170

11/0, 4 3/4"

TMK-1	$550-$700
TMK-2	$400-$500
TMK-3	$325-$375
TMK-4	$300-$325
TMK-5	$275-$300
TMK-6	$250-$275
TMK-7	$225-$230

Hum 12: Chimney Sweep

When first introduced in 1935 as part of the original group displayed at the Leipzig Fair, this figure was called "*Smoky.*" It was first designed by sculptor Arthur Moeller in 1935 with several restylings through the years.

The small 4" size was not added to the line until well into the 1950s, and consequently, no Crown Mark (TMK-1) pieces are found in that size. There are many variations in size, but none are significant. Examples found in sales lists are 4", 5 1/2", 6 1/4", and 6 3/8".

There was a surprise in store for those who bought the 1992 Sampler (a Hummel introductory kit). In it was the usual club membership discount and that year's figurine, *Chimney Sweep*. Along with the figure came a special display base of a rooftop and chimney.

In 1995, Goebel produced a special edition of the *Chimney Sweep* for German retail promotion with a gilded base. The edition was limited to 500 pieces.

12/2/0, 4"

TMK-2	$250-$325
TMK-3	$175-$200
TMK-4	$160-$175
TMK-5	$150-$160
TMK-6	$145-$150

12, 5 1/2"

TMK-1	$700-$850
TMK-2	$425-$500

12/I, 5 1/2"

TMK-1	$700-$850
TMK-2	$425-$500
TMK-3	$350-$410
TMK-4	$325-$350
TMK-5	$270-$300
TMK-6	$260-$270
TMK-7	$255-$260
TMK-8	$260

Hum 13: Meditation

The Hum 13/0 and the Hum 13/II sizes were the first to be released in 1935 and were first modeled by Reinhold Unger.

The most significant variations involve flowers and baskets. When first released, the 13/II had flowers in the basket, but sometime in the Last Bee (TMK-5) era, the piece was restyled by sculptor Gerhard Skrobek without flowers in the basket, and the style remains so today.

Other variations in the Hum 13/0 include the pigtails. The first models of the figure in the Crown Mark (TMK-1) era sported short pigtails with a painted red ribbon. By the time the Full Bee (TMK-2) was being used, the ribbon had disappeared and the pigtails had grown longer.

The larger Hum 13/V was copyrighted in 1957 and has a basket filled with flowers. It is scarce in the older trademarks and hardly ever found for sale. It was temporarily withdrawn from production on Dec. 31, 1989. Also temporarily withdrawn were 13/2/0 and 13/0 pieces in January 1999.

There is an unusual and probably unique Meditation that has a bowl attached to its side. There have been three different figurines found with bowls attached. The other two are Goose Girl and Congratulations.

13/2/0, 4 1/4"

TMK-2	$250-$350
TMK-3	$225-$250
TMK-4	$190-$225
TMK-5	$175-$190
TMK-6	$160-$170

13/0, 5"

TMK-4	$325-$350
TMK-5	$270-$300
TMK-6	$260-$270
TMK-7	$245-$260

13/0, 5 1/4"

TMK-1	$700-$850
TMK-3	$350-$400

13/0, 6"

TMK-2	$425-$500

13/II (13/2), 7"

TMK-1	$4,000-$5,000 with flowers
TMK-2	$3,500-$4,000 with flowers
TMK-3	$3,000-$3,500 with flowers

13/II, 7"

TMK-5	$410-$455
TMK-6	$350-$410

13/V, 13 3/4"

TMK-1	$4,000-$5,000
TMK-2	$3,000-$3,500
TMK-3	$1,700-$2,200
TMK-4	$1,350-$1,500
TMK-5	$1,300-$1,350
TMK-6	$1,200-$1,300

Hum No. 264 Heavenly Angel. **$500-$750**

Bell, Annual

Anniversary Bell, Hum 730, 1985	$1,500-$2,000
Busy Student, Hum 710, 1988	$58
Farewell, Hum 701, 1979	$25
Favorite Pet, Hum 713, 1991	$58
Festival Harmony With Flute, Hum 781, 1995	$35
In Tune, Hum 703, 1981	$38
Knit One, Hum 705, 1983	$35
Latest News, Hum 711, 1989	$58
Let's Sing, Hum 700, 1978	$38
Mountaineer, Hum 706, 1984	$35
She Loves Me, Hum 704, 1982	$35
Sing Along, Hum 708, 1986	$58
Sweet Song, Hum 707, 1985	$35
Thoughtful, Hum 702, 1980	$25
What's New?, Hum 712, 1990	$58
Whistler's Duet, Hum 714, 1992	$58
With Loving Greetings, Hum 709, 1987	$58

Bell, Christmas

Angel With Flute, 1972	$45
Angelic Gifts, 1987	$48
Angelic Messenger, 1983	$58
Angelic Procession, 1982	$45
Cheerful Cherubs, 1988	$53
Echoes Of Joy, Hum 784, 1998	$28
Gift From Heaven, 1984	$45
Herald Angel, 1977	$45
Nativity, 1973	$45
Parade Into Toyland, 1980	$45
Sacred Journey, 1976	$45
Starlight Angel, 1979	$47

Cottages, Bavarian Village

Angel's Duet, 1996	$50
Bench & Pine Tree, The/Set, 1996	$25
Christmas Mail, 1996	$50
Company's Coming, 1996	$50

Hum No. 257/0 For Mother. **$255**

Hum No. 47/0 Goose Girl. **$290-$900**

Sled & Pine Tree, The/Set, 1996	$25
Village Bridge, The, 1996	$25
Winter's Comfort, 1996	$50
Wishing Well, The, 1996	$25

Dolls and Plush

Anderl 1718	$150
Birthday Serenade/Boy, 1984	$275
Birthday Serenade/Girl, 1984	$275
Brieftrager 1720	$175
Carnival, 1985	$275
Christl 1715	$150
Easter Greetings, 1985	$275
Felix 1608	$175
Felix 1708	$175
Gretel 1501	$200
Gretel 1901, 1964	$160
Hansel 1504	$200
Hansel 1604	$175
Konditor 1723	$175
Lost Stocking 1926, 1964	$125
Mariandl 1713	$150
Max 1506	$200
Merry Wanderer 1906, 1964	$125
On Secret Path 1928, 1964	$85
Peterle 1710	$150
School Boy 1910, 1964	$130
School Girl 1909, 1964	$130
Skihaserl 1722	$175
Valentine Gift Doll, Hum 524	$200-$250
Visiting An Invalid 1927, 1964	$130
Wanderbub 1507	$200

Figurine, M.I. Hummel

Due to space constraints, a range of pricing has been provided. Please consult the 12th edition of *Luckey's Hummel® Figurines & Plates Identification and Price Guide* for individual pricing based upon trademark variations.

Accompanist, The, Hum 453, 1988	$140
Accordion Boy, Hum 185, 1947	$200-$750
Adoration With Bird, Hum 105, 1938	$7,000-$8,000
Angel Duet, Hum 261, 1968	$270-$850
Angel Lights, Candleholder, Hum 241	$300-$500
Angel With Accordion, Hum 238 B, 1967	$73-$125
Angel With Lute, Hum 238 A, 1967	$73-$125
Angel With Trumpet, Hum 238 C, 1967	$73-$125
Angel/Accordion, Candleholder, Hum 1/39/0	$80-$200
Angel/Accordion, Candleholder, Hum 111/39/0	$60-$200
Angel/Accordion, Candleholder, Hum 111/39/1	$200-$350
Angel/Lute, Candleholder, Hum 111/38/1	$200-$350
Angel/Trumpet, Candleholder, Hum 1/40/0	$73-$200
Angel/Trumpet, Candleholder, Hum 111/40/0	$60-$200
Angel/Trumpet, Candleholder, Hum 111/40/1	$200-$350
Angelic Conductor, Hum 2096/A, 2002	$135
Apple Tree Boy, Hum 142	$650-$950
Apple Tree Boy, Hum 142/3/0	$180-$550
Apple Tree Boy, Hum 142/I	$350-$800
Apple Tree Boy, Candleholder, Hum 677	$200-$250
Apple Tree Boy/Girl-Bookends, Hum 252 A&B	$300-$425
Apple Tree Girl, Hum 141	$650-$950
Apple Tree Girl, Hum 141/3/0	$180-$550
Apple Tree Girl, Candleholder, Hum 676	$200-$250
Ba-Bee-Ring, Hum 30/0 A&B	$245-$700
Band Leader, Hum 129/4/0	$125-$140

Hum No. 50/0 Volunteers. **$375-$1,100**

Hum No. 88/I Heavenly Protection. **$540-$750**

Barnyard Hero, Hum 195/2/0 .... $205-$450
Barnyard Hero, Hum 195/I .... $350-$700
Chimney Sweep, Hum 12 .... $425-$800
Chimney Sweep, Hum 12/2/0 .... $145-$325
Christ Child, Hum 18 .... $165-$550
Christmas Gift, 1999 .... $95
Christmas Song, Hum 343/4/0, 1996 .... $135
Come Back Soon, Hum 545, 1995 .... $180-$500
Congratulations, Hum 17/0 .... $230-$750
Coquettes, Hum 179, 1948 .... $325-$1,100
Culprits, Hum 56 .... $900-$1,100
Culprits, Hum 56 A .... $365-$650
Dearly Beloved, Hum 2003, 1999 .... $200-$520
Delicious, Hum 435/3/0 .... $170-$175
Doll Mother, Hum 67 .... $257-$900
Duet, Hum 130 .... $300-$1,000
Evening Prayer, Hum 495, 1991 .... $135
Eventide (Rare), Hum 99 .... $3,000-$3,500
Eventide, Hum 99 .... $360-$1,250
Farewell, Hum 65 .... $275-$1,000
Farewell, Hum 65/I .... $325-$1,000
Farewell, Hum 65/0 .... $5,000-$8,000
Farm Boy, Hum 66 .... $270-$900
Farm Boy/Goose Girl Bookends, Hum 60 A&B
.... $400-$1,250
Favorite Pet, Hum 361 .... $335-$5,000
Feeding Time, Hum 199 .... $525-$1,000
Feeding Time, Hum 199/I .... $315-$575
Feeding Time, Hum 199/0 .... $250-$500
Festival Harmony (Flute), Hum 173/0 .... $350-$650
Festival Harmony (Mandolin), Hum 172 .. $1,000-$3,500
Festival Harmony (Mandolin), Hum 172/4/0 .... $135
Festival Harmony (Mandolin), Hum 172/II .... $450-$800

Festival Harmony (Mandolin), Hum 172/0 ..... $350-$650
Flying Angel, Hum 366 .... $150-$275
Flying High, Hum 452, 1984 .... $175-$300
Follow The Leader, Hum 369 .... $1,390-$5,000
For Father, Hum 87 .... $270-$800
Forest Shrine, Hum 183 .... $595-$1,900
Free Flight, Hum 569, 1993 .... $215
Friend Or Foe, Hum 434, 1991 .... $275
Girl With Doll, Hum 239B .... $73-$200
Girl With Nosegay, Hum 239A .... $73-$200
Girl With Sheet Of Music, Hum 389 .... $110-$275
Girl With Trumpet, Hum 391 .... $110-$275
Globe Trotter, Hum 79 .... $200-$750
Going To Grandma's, Hum 52 .... $850-$1,600
Good Friends, Hum 182 .... $250-$750
Good Hunting, Hum 307 .... $300-$5,000
Goose Girl, Hum 47 .... $800-$900
Grandma's Girl, Hum 561, 1990 .... $185
Grandpa's Boy, Hum 562, 1990 .... $185
Guardian, The, Hum 455, 1991 .... $205
Guiding Angel, Hum 357 .... $110-$150
Happiness, Hum 86 .... $170-$500
Happy Days, Hum 150 .... $900-$1,600
Happy Days, Hum 150/2/0 .... $210-$400
Happy Pastime, Hum 69 .... $190-$650
Happy Traveller, Hum 109/II .... $375-$900
Happy Traveller, Hum 109/0 .... $185-$350
Hear Ye, Hear Ye, Hum 15/2/0 .... $185-$190
Hear Ye, Hear Ye, Hum 15/I .... $280-$900
Hear Ye, Hear Ye, Hum 15/II .... $450-$1,500
Hear Ye, Hear Ye, Hum 15/0 .... $230-$750
Heavenly Angel, Hum 21/0 1/2 .... $270-$850
Heavenly Lullaby, Hum 262 .... $270-$850

Hum No. 94/3/0 Surprise. **$190-$550**

Hum No. 3 Book Worm. **$365-$4,000**

Holy Water Font, Angel Cloud, Hum 206 .... **$60-$500**
Holy Water Font, Angel Duet, Hum 146 .... **$60-$225**
Holy Water Font, Angel Joyous News, Hum 241, 1955
.... **$1,500-$2,000**
Holy Water Font, Angel Joyous News, Hum 242, 1955
.... **$1,500-$2,000**
Holy Water Font, Angel Shrine, Hum 147 .... **$68-$275**
Horse Trainer, Hum 423, 1990 .... **$268-$280**
Hosanna, Hum 480, 1989 .... **$140**
I'll Protect Him, Hum 483, 1989 .... **$115**
I'm Here, Hum 478, 1989 .... **$145**
In D Major, Hum 430, 1989 .... **$255**
In The Meadow, Hum 459, 1987 .... **$255**
Joyful, Hum 53 .... **$140-$450**
Joyous News, Hum 27/3 .... **$280-$2,000**
Joyous News, Hum 27/I .... **$250-$500**
Joyous News, Hum 27/III **$253**
Jubilee, Hum 416, 1985 .... **$500-$600**
Just Dozing, Hum 451, 1984 .... **$265**
Just Resting, Hum 112 .... **$700-$850**
Just Resting, Hum 112/I .... **$320-$800**
Kindergartner, Hum 467, 1987 .... **$255**
Knit One Purl One, Hum 432, 1983 .... **$160**
Latest News, Hum 184 .... **$360-$1,100**
Let's Play, Hum 2051/B, 1999 .... **$95**
Let's Sing, Hum 110 .... **$325-$600**
Let's Sing, Hum 110/0 .... **$160-$500**
Letter To Santa Claus Prototype, Hum 340, 1956
.... **$15,000-$20,000**
Letter To Santa, Hum 340 .... **$400-$1,000**
Little Architect, The, Hum 410, 1978 .... **$3,000-$4,000**
Little Band (On Base), Hum 392 .... **$275-$450**
Little Bookkeeper, Hum 306 .... **$335-$1,500**

Little Cellist, Hum 89 .... **$1,250-$1,600**
Little Cellist, Hum 89/I .... **$270-$850**
Little Cellist, Hum 89/II .... **$450-$1,500**
Little Fiddler, Hum 2/4/0 .... **$130-$140**
Little Fiddler, Hum 2/I .... **$415-$1,500**
Little Fiddler, Hum 2/II .... **$1,110-$3,500**
Little Fiddler, Hum 2/III .... **$1,205-$4,000**
Little Fiddler, Hum 2/0 .... **$325-$850**
Little Gabriel, Hum 32, 1935 .... **$2,000-$2,500**
Little Goat Herder, Hum 200 .... **$500-$850**
Little Goat Herder, Hum 200/I .... **$270-$550**
Little Hiker, Hum 16 .... **$450-$750**
Little Hiker, Hum 16/I .... **$245-$700**
Little Sweeper, Hum 171/4/0 .... **$130**
Little Sweeper, Hum 171/0 .... **$185**
Little Tailor, Hum 308 .... **$305-$350**
Little Thrifty, Bank, Hum 118 .... **$185-$650**
Lost Sheep, Hum 68 .... **$350-$750**
Lost Sheep, Hum 68/2/0 .... **$160-$350**
Lost Sheep, Hum 68/0 .... **$200-$450**
Lost Stocking, Hum 374 .... **$185-$1,500**
March Winds, Hum 43 .... **$180-$600**
Message Of Love, Hum 2050/A, 1999 .... **$95**
Mountaineer, Hum 315 .... **$250-$1,000**
Old Man Reading Newspaper, Hum 181, 1948
.... **$15,000-$20,000**
Old Woman Walking To Market, Hum 190, 1948
.... **$15,000-$20,000**
Ooh, My Tooth, Hum 533, 1995 .... **$145**
Out Of Danger, Hum 56 B .... **$345-$650**
Out Of Danger, Table Lamp, Hum 44 B .... **$325-$650**
Photographer, Hum 178 .... **$335-$1,100**
Pixie, Hum 768, 1995 .... **$145**

Hum No. 1 Puppy Love. **$305-$1,000**

Hum No. 2 Little Fiddler. **$130-$4,000**

Playmates, Hum 58 .... $500-$1,050
Playmates, Hum 58/2/0 .... $185-$200
Postman, Hum 119/2/0 .... $185
Postman, Hum 119/0 .... $250
Puppy Love, Hum 1 .... $305-$1,000
Ring Around The Rosie, Hum 348, 1957
.... $3,200-$5,000
Run-A-Way, Hum 327 .... $310-$325
Saint George, Hum 55 .... $350-$3,000
School Boy, Hum 82 .... $625-$775
School Boy, Hum 82/2/0 .... $170-$600
School Boy, Hum 82/II .... $500-$1,600
School Boy, Hum 82/0 .... $235-$775
School Girl, Hum 81 .... $350-$750
School Girl, Hum 81/0 .... $225-$700
Seraphim Soprano, Hum 2096/R, 2002 .... $135
Serenade, Hum 85 .... $775-$1,550
Serenade, Hum 85/4/0 .... $130
Serenade, Hum 85/II .... $500-$1,500
Serenade, Hum 85/0 .... $160-$500
Shepherd Boy, Hum 395, 1996 .... $280-$315

Shepherd's Boy, Hum 64 .... $330-$900
Sing Along, Hum 433, 1987 .... $330
Sister, Hum 98 .... $325-$700
Sister, Hum 98/2/0 .... $180-$250
Sister, Hum 98/0 .... $230-$325
Soloist, Hum 135/4/0 .... $135
Soloist, Hum 135/0 .... $175
Spring Cheer, Hum 72 .... $200-$650
Standing Boy, Plaque, Hum 168 .... $200-$1,100
Standing Madonna With Child, Hum 247, 1955
.... $10,000-$15,000
Star Gazer, Hum 132 .... $258-$800
Stitch In Time, Hum 255 .... $325-$800
Stitch In Time, Hum 255/4/0 .... $115-$140
Teacher's Pet, Hum 2125, 2002 .... $175
Trumpet Boy, Hum 97 .... $150-$525
Village Boy, Hum 51 .... $900-$1,150
Wash Day, Hum 321 .... $275-$1,000
Wash Day, Hum 321/I .... $355-$365
Wonder Of Christmas, Hum 2015 With Steiff Bear, 1999
.... $575

LLADRÓ PORCELAINS

Brothers Vicente, Jose and Juan Lladró formally incorporated themselves as a company in 1953 and, by 1955, were selling their porcelain creations in their own retail shop in Valencia, Spain. By 1958, they had acquired the land to build a small factory, probably not operational until the early 1960s. Production started in 1969, also the year of first export to the United States. Today, Lladró exports all over the globe. Management of the company has passed to the second generation of the Lladró family.

Lladró is entirely handmade of fine porcelain, with many molds and artisans involved in the production of each item, using traditional porcelain-making techniques that have changed little in the centuries since the Meissen manufactory of Germany first developed them. Lladró is famous for its floral work, in which each stamen, petal and leaf is separately applied. Items with floral work in mint condition command premium prices on the secondary market.

Oldest Lladró items found on today's secondary market would have been fired as early as the mid-1960s, and some of these made their way to the United States in tourist suitcases prior to 1969. Marks of these oldest items are impressed or etched into the porcelain base and include the word "Lladró" as well as the words "Made in Spain" and sometimes "España". The Lladró cobalt-blue backstamp was first used in the late 1960s to early 1970s, with the accent missing. The mark went through several minor changes throughout the 80s and 90s.

"Seconds" are sold at the factory in Spain and in the company's outlet stores in the U.S. Seconds are indicated by the scraping off of the logo flower in the backstamp. Serious collectors avoid these, as they are worth only a fraction of the value of a first-quality piece.

As Lladró has grown in popularity and value, the backstamp has also been counterfeited. Counterfeit marks have disproportionately large accent marks over the "o" and are a pale grayish purple in color rather than the deep cobalt blue of the genuine mark.

Other genuine Lladró and Lladró-affiliated brands have included NAO (still in production), Zaphir and Golden Memories. Production of the latter two brands ceased more than a decade ago, but they are still seen on the secondary market. Each can be readily identified by its own unique backstamp.

Lladró has many Valencian competitors who are working "in the Lladró style," but such products have little or no following among serious collectors.

All photos appear courtesy of Lladró, USA, Inc.

"A" IS FOR AMY, L5145G/M, 1982 .... **$1,500**
"E" IS FOR ELLEN, L5146G, 1982 .... **$1,200**
"I" IS FOR IVY, L5147G, 1982 .... **$600**
"O" IS FOR OLIVIA, L5148G, 1982 .... **$450**
"U" IS FOR URSULA, L5149G, 1982 .... **$450**
ABRAHAM, L5169G, 1982 .... **$725**
ADMIRATION, L4907G/M, 1974 .... **$650**
AEROBICS FLOOR EXERCISE, L5335G, 1985 .... **$300**
AEROBICS PULL-UPS, L5334G, 1985 .... **$300**
AEROBICS SCISSOR FIGURE, L5336G, 1985 .... **$300**
AFGHAN, L1069G/M, 1969 .... **$625**
AFTER THE DANCE, L5092G, 1980 .... **$350**
AFTERNOON JAUNT, L5855G, 1992 .... **$550**
AFTERNOON PROMENADE, S7636G, 1995 .... **$350**
AFTERNOON TEA, L1428G/M, 1982 .... **$320**
AGGRESSIVE DUCK, L1288G/M, 1974 .... **$525**
ANDALUSIANS GROUP, L4647G, 1969 .... **$1,100**
ANGEL DREAMING, L4961M, 1977 .... **$185**
ANGEL PRAYING, N0010G, 1969 .... **$75**
ANGEL RECLINING, N0012G, 1969 .... **$75**
ANGEL WITH BABY, L4635G, 1969 .... **$165**
ANGEL WITH BABY, L4635M, 1969 .... **$250**
ANGEL WITH CLARINET, L1232G/M, 1972 .... **$450**
ANGEL WITH FLUTE, L1233G/M, 1972 .... **$450**
ANGEL WITH FLUTE, N0015G, 1969 .... **$80**
ANGEL WITH LUTE, L1231G/M, 1972 .... **$450**
ANGEL WITH LYRE, N0013G, 1969 .... **$80**
ANGEL WITH MANDOLIN, N0016G, 1969 .... **$80**
ANGEL WITH TAMBOURINE, N0011G, 1969 .... **$75**
ANGEL WONDERING, L4962M, 1977 .... **$275**
ANGORA CAT, N0113M, 1970 .... **$90**
ANTELOPE DRINKING, L5302G, 1985 .... **$640**
ARACELY WITH HER PET DUCK, L5202G, 1984 .... **$350**
AVOIDING THE GOOSE, L5033G, 1979 .... **$400**
AZTEC DANCER (GRES), L2143M, 1984 .... **$600**
AZTEC INDIAN (GRES), L2139M, 1984 .... **$1,100**
BABY DOLL, L5608G, 1989 .... **$220**

Lladró, "Santa Claus with Toys," L4905G, 1974. **$1,200**

BABY JESUS, L4670G, 1969 .... $65
BABY JESUS, L4670M, 1969 .... $95
BABY ON FLOOR/LEARNING TO CRAWL, L5101G, 1982 .... $275
BABY WITH PACIFIER (TEETHING), L5102G, 1982 .... $275
BABY'S OUTING, L4938G, 1976 .... $850
BALLERINA/WAITING BACKSTAGE, L4559G/M, 1969 $500
BALLET FIRST STEP, L5094G, 1980 .... $425
BALLET TRIO, THE, L5235G, 1984 .... $1,775
BARRISTER, THE, L4908G, 1974 .... $450
BASKET OF ROSES, L1073M, 1969 .... $400
BASKET OF ROSES, L1544M, 1988 .... $700
BEAGLE PUPPY (LYING), L1072G/M, 1969 .... $300
BEAGLE PUPPY (POUNCING), L1070G/M, 1969 .... $350
BEAGLE PUPPY (SITTING), L1071G/M, 1969 .... $300
BEARLY LOVE, L1443G, 1983 .... $175
BETH, L1358G, 1978 .... $225
BIG PARTRIDGE (GRES), L2087, 1978 .... $375
BIRD, L1053G, 1969 .... $250
BIRD, L1054G, 1969 .... $250
BIRD ON CACTUS, L1303G, 1974 .... $850
BLUE CREEPER, L1302G, 1974 .... $675
BOLIVIAN MOTHER, L4658, 1969 .... $450
BONGO BEAT, L5157G, 1982 .... $250
BOY & HIS BUNNY, L1507G/M, 1986 .... $275
BOY BLOWING/KISSING, L4869G, 1974 .... $175
BOY BLOWING/KISSING, L4869M, 1974 .... $200
BOY FROM MADRID, L4898G/M, 1974 .... $175
BOY MEETS GIRL, L1188G, 1972 .... $425
BOY POTTERY SELLER, L5080G, 1980 .... $600
BOY WITH CORNET (BUST), L1105G, 1971 .... $400
BOY WITH CYMBALS, L4613G/M, 1969 .... $350
BOY WITH DOG, L4522G/M, 1970 .... $225
BOY WITH DOUBLE BASS, L4615G/M, 1969 .... $400
BOY WITH DRUM, L4616G/M, 1969 .... $350
BOY WITH GOAT (BUST), L2009, 1970 .... $900
BOY WITH GOAT (WHITE), L2009.3, 1970 .... $800

Lladró, "Cathy and her Doll," L1380G. **$700**

BOY WITH GOAT/BOY WITH KID, L4506G/M, 1969 ... $375
BOY WITH GUITAR, L4614G/M, 1969 .... $400
BOY WITH LAMBS, L4509G, 1969 .... $375
BOY WITH YACHT/YOUNG SAILOR, L4810G, 1972 ... $215
BOY (BIG HAT), N0182G, 1975 .... $150
BOY (BIG HAT), N0182M, 1975 .... $200
BOYS PLAYING WITH GOAT, L1129G, 1971 .... $2,500
BUDDHA, L1235G, 1972 .... $700
CALF, L4680G, 1969 .... $110
CALF, L4680M, 1969 .... $175
CAMEL (GRES), L2027, 1971 .... $2,000
CAREFREE ANGEL WITH FLUTE, L1463G, 1985 .... $650
CARESS AND REST, L1246G/M, 1972 .... $325
CARMENCITA, L5373G, 1986 .... $250
CAT GIRL/KITTY, L5164G, 1982 .... $475
CAT, HEAD DOWN (EARLY, RARE) L0008G/M, 1965 .... $150
CAT, HEAD UP (EARLY, RARE) L0010G/M, 1965 ... $150
CENTAUR BOY, L1013G/M, 1969 .... $450
CENTAUR GIRL, L1012G/M, 1969 .... $450
CHICK ON THE WATCH, L4630G, 1969 .... $400
CHILDREN AT PLAY, L5304, 1985 .... $500
CHILDREN IN NIGHTSHIRTS, L4874G, 1974 .... $250
CHILDREN IN NIGHTSHIRTS, L4874M, 1974 .... $350
CHILDREN'S GAMES, L5379G, 1986 .... $675
CHINESE BOY (GRES), L2153M, 1982 .... $300
CHINESE FARMER (GRES), L2068, 1977 .... $1,000
CHINESE GIRL (GRES), L2152M, 1982 .... $300
CHINESE NOBLEMAN, L4921G, 1974 .... $2,000
CHINESE NOBLEWOMAN, L4916G, 1974 .... $2,000
CHRISTMAS CAROLS, L1239G, 1973 .... $750
CHRYSANTHEMUM, L4990G, 1978 .... $350
CHRYSANTHEMUM W/BASE, L5189M, 1984 .... $225
CINDERELLA, L4828G, 1972 .... $275
CLEAN UP TIME, L4838G/M, 1973 .... $300
CLOSING SCENE, L4935G, 1974 .... $550
CLOSING SCENE, WHITE, L4935.30M, 1983 .... $400
CLOWN, L4618M, 1971 .... $450
CLOWN WITH CLOCK, L5056G, 1980 .... $800
CLOWN WITH CONCERTINA, L1027G/M, 1969 .... $800
CLOWN WITH VIOLIN, L1126G, 1971 .... $2,000
CLOWN'S HEAD (BUST), L5129G, 1982 .... $500
COMFORTING BABY/MOTHER KISSING CHILD (BUST), L1329M, 1976 .... $1,200
CONCERT VIOLINIST, L5330G, 1985 .... $475
CONSIDERATION (BUST), L5355M, 1986 .... $250
COUNTRY GIRL N0522G/M, 1978 .... $100
COUNTRY LADY, L1330, 1976 .... $1,600
COW WITH PIG, L4640G/M, 1969 .... $750
CUPID (BLINDFOLDED), L4607G/M, 1969 .... $400
DALMATIAN (BEGGING), L1262G, 1974 .... $400
DALMATIAN (SITTING), L1260G, 1974 .... $400
DALMATIAN (TAIL IN AIR), L1261G, 1974 .... $400
DANCERS RESTING, L4992G, 1978 .... $750
DANCING PARTNER, A, L5093G, 1980 .... $380
DANCING THE POLKA, L5252G, 1984 .... $525
DANTE, L5177G, 1982 .... $700
DAUGHTERS/SISTERS, L5013G/M, 1978 .... $850
DEATH OF THE SWAN, L4855G/M, 1973 .... $350
DEATH OF THE SWAN (WHITE), L4855.30M, 1983 ..... $250
DEBUTANTE, L1431G/M, 1982 .... $320

C

Ceramics

DEEP IN THOUGHT, L5389G, 1986 .... **$350**
DEER, L1064G/M, 1969 .... **$395**
DEMURE CENTAUR GIRL, L5320G/M, 1985 .... **$400**
DENTIST, L4762G, 1971 .... **$550**
DERBY, L1344G, 1977 .... **$2,500**
DEVOTION, L1278G, 1974 .... **$450**
DIVERS WITH CHICKEN (GRES), L2116, 1980 .... **$1,400**
DOCTOR, L4602G, 1969 .... **$400**
DOG (COLLIE), L1316G, 1974 .... **$500**
DOG (LLASA APSO), L4642G/M, 1969 .... **$500**
DOG AND CAT IN HARMONY, N1048G, 1987 .... **$125**
DOG AND CAT/LITTLE FRISKIES, L5032G, 1979 ...... **$285**
DOG IN THE BASKET, L1128G, 1971 .... **$450**
DOG PLAYING BASS FIDDLE, L1154G, 1971 .... **$500**
DOG PLAYING BONGOS, L1156G, 1971 .... **$550**
DOG PLAYING GUITAR, L1152G, 1971 .... **$550**
DOG SINGER, L1155G, 1971 .... **$450**
DOGS BUST (GRES), L2067, 1977 .... **$875**
DON JUAN, L4609G, 1969 .... **$715**
DON QUIXOTE & SANCHO PANZA, L4998G, 1978 . **$2,800**
DON QUIXOTE DREAMING (GRES), L2084, 1978 .. **$1,900**
DON QUIXOTE, L1030M, 1969 .... **$1,550**
DONKEY IN LOVE/DONKEY W/DAISY, L4524G/M, 1969 .... **$400**
DONKEY, L4678M, 1969 .... **$175**
DONKEY, L4679G, 1969 .... **$125**
DORMOUSE, L4774G, 1971 .... **$450**
DOVE GROUP, L1335G, 1977 .... **$1,500**
DOVE, L1015G/M, 1969 .... **$150**
DOVE, L1016G/M, 1969 .... **$225**
DOVE N0060G, 1970 .... **$50**
DOVE N0062G, 1970 .... **$50**
DOVE N0063G, 1970 .... **$50**
DRESS REHEARSAL, L5497G, 1988 .... **$450**
DRESSMAKER, L4700G/M, 1970 .... **$450**
DUCK JUMPING, L1265G, 1974 .... **$110**
DUCK, L1056G, 1969 .... **$275**
DUCK RUNNING, L1263G, 1974 .... **$110**
DUCKLINGS, L1307M, 1974 .... **$175**
DUCKS GROUP, N0006M, 1969 .... **$75**
DUTCH GIRL, L4860G/M, 1974 .... **$335**
EGYPTIAN CAT (GRES), L2130, 1983 .... **$650**
EGYPTIAN CAT (WHITE), L5154G/M, 1982 .... **$650**
ELEPHANT FAMILY, L4764G, 1971 .... **$1,000**
EMBROIDERER, L4865G, 1974 .... **$725**
ESKIMO BOY (GRES), L2007, 1970 .... **$300**
ESKIMO BOY (WHITE PARKA GRES), L2007.3, 1970 **$300**
ESKIMO BOY AND GIRL (GRES), L2138, 1971 .... **$650**
ESKIMO GIRL (GRES), L2008, 1970 .... **$300**
EXQUISITE SCENT/SCHOOLGIRL, L1313G, 1974 ...... **$650**
FAIRY, L4595G/M, 1969 .... **$200**
FAWN HEAD (GRES), L2040, 1971 .... **$575**
FEEDING THE DUCKS, L4849G/M, 1973 .... **$325**
FEEDING TIME, L1277G/M, 1974 .... **$400**
FEMALE EQUESTRIAN, L4516M, 1969 .... **$800**
FEMALE TENNIS PLAYER, L1427M, 1982 .... **$350**
FISH A'PLENTY, L5172G, 1982 .... **$435**
FISH VENDOR, L2162, 1985 .... **$275**
FISHER BOY/GOING FISHING, L4809G/M, 1972 ...... **$175**
FISHERMAN (BUST), L2108, 1978 .... **$1,150**
FLOWER HARMONY, L1418G, 1982 .... **$335**

FLOWER HARVEST, L1286G, 1974 .... **$535**
FLOWER PEDDLER, L5029G, 1979 .... **$1,550**
FLYING DUCK, L1264G, 1974 .... **$110**
FOX AND CUB, L1065G/M, 1969 .... **$425**
FRIAR JUNIPER (GRES), L2138, 1984 .... **$350**
FRIDAY'S CHILD (BOY), L6019G, 1993 .... **$285**
FRIENDSHIP, L1230G/M, 1972 .... **$450**
FULL OF MISCHIEF, L1395G, 1982 .... **$1,000**
GATHERING BUTTERFLIES, N0181G, 1975 .... **$175**
GATHERING BUTTERFLIES, N0181M, 1975 .... **$200**
GAZELLE, L5271G, 1985 .... **$525**
GAZELLE RESTING (GRES), L2048, 1971 .... **$600**
GEESE GROUP, L4549G/M, 1969 .... **$250**
GEISHA, L4807G/M, 1972 .... **$550**
GELSIE/LITTLE BALLET GIRL, L5108G, 1982 .... **$350**
GENTLEMAN EQUESTRIAN, L5329G, 1985 .... **$500**
GERMAN SHEPHERD W/PUP, L4731G, 1970 .... **$950**
GIRL AT THE FOUNTAIN, N0136G, 1971 .... **$175**
GIRL AT THE FOUNTAIN, N0136M, 1971 .... **$200**
GIRL CLOWN WITH TRUMPET, L5060G, 1980 ...... **$550**
GIRL FROM THE FOUNTAIN, N0115G, 1970 .... **$265**
GIRL FROM THE FOUNTAIN, N0115M, 1970 .... **$300**
GIRL GATHERING FLOWERS, L1172G/M, 1971 ...... **$365**
GIRL MANICURING, L1082G/M, 1969 .... **$300**
GIRL POTTERY SELLER, L5081G, 1980 .... **$600**
GIRL SHAMPOOING, L1148G/M, 1971 .... **$300**
GIRL WATERING/GROWING ROSES, L1354G, 1978 .. **$625**
GIRL WITH BASKET/SHEPHERDESS WITH DOG, L1034G/M, 1969 .... **$235**
GIRL WITH BONNET, L1147G/M, 1971 .... **$300**
GIRL WITH BRUSH, L1081G/M, 1969 .... **$300**
GIRL WITH CALF, 4513G/M, 1978 .... **$550**
GIRL WITH CALLA LILIES, L4650G, 1969 .... **$170**
GIRL WITH CATS, L1309M, 1974 .... **$375**
GIRL WITH COCKEREL/SHEPHERDESS W/BASKET, L4591G/M, 1969 .... **$300**
GIRL WITH DOLL, L1083G/M, 1969 .... **$300**

Lladró, "The Gossips", L4984G. **$950**

Lladró, "Ballerina" L4559G/M. **$500-$700**

Lladró, "A Lady of Taste" L1495G. **$1,100**

GIRL WITH DOLL, L1211G/M, 1972 .... $450
GIRL WITH DUCK, L1052G/M, 1969 .... $235
GIRL WITH DUCKS, N0026G/M, 1969 .... $150
GIRL WITH FLAX, N0089G, 1970 .... $175
GIRL WITH FLOWERS IN TOW, L5031G, 1979 .... $1,500
GIRL WITH FLOWERS, L1088G/M, 1969 .... $725
GIRL WITH GEESE, L1035G/M, 1969 .... $235
GIRL WITH GOOSE AND DOG, L4866G/M, 1974 .... $325
GIRL WITH GOOSE, L4815G/M, 1972 .... $335
GIRL WITH GOOSE, N0025G/M, 1969 .... $90
GIRL WITH LAMB, L1010G/M, 1969 .... $250
GIRL WITH LAMB, L4505G, 1969 .... $145
GIRL WITH LAMB, L4505M, 1969 .... $165
GIRL WITH LAMB, L4584G/M, 1969 .... $250
GIRL WITH LAMB/SHEPHERDESS, L4835G/M, 1972

.... $295
GIRL WITH LILIES SITTING, L4972G, 1977 .... $180
GIRL WITH MANDOLIN, L1026G, 1969 .... $625
GIRL WITH MILK PAIL, L4682G/M, 1970 .... $325
GIRL WITH MOTHER'S SHOE, L1084G/M, 1969 .... $300
GIRL WITH PIG, L1011G, 1969 .... $125
GIRL WITH PIG, L1011M, 1969 .... $175
GIRL WITH PIGEONS, L4915G, 1974 .... $400
GIRL WITH PUPPIES, L1311G, 1974 .... $375
GIRL WITH RABBIT, N0003G/M, 1969 .... $75
GIRL WITH SLATE, N0117G, 1970 .... $110
GIRL WITH SLATE, N0117M, 1970 .... $135
GIRL WITH UMBRELLA AND GEESE, L4510G/M, 1969

.... $300

GIRL WITH WATER CARRIER (BUST), L2014, 1970

.... $1,000

GIRL WITH WATERING CAN/BLOOMING ROSES,
  L1339G, 1977 .... $500
GIRLS IN THE SWING/SWINGING, L1366G, 1978 ... $1,850
GOOSE (13"), N0052G, 1969 .... $100
GOOSE (13"), N0052M, 1969 .... $150
GOOSE (9"), N0053G, 1969 .... $100
GOOSE (9"), N0053M, 1969 .... $125
GOOSE-REDUCED (11-3/4"), N0054/2G, 1969 .... $75
GOOSE-REDUCED (8"), N0055/3G, 1969 .... $75
GOYA LADY/AMPARO, L5125G, 1982 .... $350
GRACEFUL DUO, L2073, 1977 .... $1,700
GREAT BUTTERFLY NO. 13 (CAPRICHO), L1685M,
  1989 .... $235
GREAT DANE, L1068G, 1969 .... $575
GREAT GRAY OWL, L5419G, 1987 .... $225
GRETEL/DUTCH GIRL HANDS AKIMBO, L5064G,
  1980 .... $400
GROUP OF MUSICIANS, L4617G/M, 1969 .... $550
GUARDIAN CHICK, L4629G, 1969 .... $400
GYPSY WOMAN, L4919G, 1974 .... $1,300
HAMLET AND YORICK, L1254G, 1974 .... $1,300
HAPPY HARLEQUIN, L1247G/M, 1974 .... $1,000
HARLEQUIN "A", L5075G, 1980 .... $475
HARVESTER, WOMAN, L4582G, 1969 .... $650
HATS OFF TO FUN, L5765G, 1991 .... $600
HEATHER, L1359G, 1978 .... $225
HEN, L1041G/M, 1969 .... $300
HINDU GODDESS, L1215G, 1972 .... $900
HORNED OWL, L5420G, 1987 .... $225
HORSE GROUP (2), L4655G/M, 1969 .... $785
HORSE HEADS (GRES), L3511, 1978 .... $650

Lladró, "Preparing for the Sabbath," L6183G. **$435**

HUNTERS, L1048G/M, 1969 .... **$1,500**
HUNTING DOG (EARLY/RARE), L308.13G, 1963 ..... **$2,000**
I HOPE SHE DOES, L5450G, 1987 .... **$375**
IDYLL, L1017G/M, 1969 .... **$700**
IN THE FOREST, N0092G, 1970 .... **$200**
INFANTILE CANDOR, L4963G, 1977 .... **$1,200**
JOCKEY AND LADY, L5036G, 1979 .... **$2,615**
JOCKEY, L1341G, 1977 .... **$500**
JULIA, L1361G, 1978 .... **$225**
KING BALTHASAR, L4675G, 1969 .... **$125**
KING BALTHASAR, L4675M, 1969 .... **$175**
KING GASPAR, L4674G, 1969 .... **$125**
KING GASPAR, L4674M, 1969 .... **$195**
KING MELCHIOR, L4673G, 1969 .... **$125**
KING MELCHIOR, L4673M, 1969 .... **$175**
KISSING DOVES, L1169M, 1971 .... **$250**
KISSING DOVES W/PLAQUE, L1170G, 1971 .... **$300**
LADY AT DRESSING TABLE, L1242G, 1973 .... **$3,200**
LADY WITH SHAWL, L4914G, 1974 .... **$800**
LADY WITH YOUNG HARLEQUIN, L4883G, 1974 ... **$2,000**
LAMB IN ARMS, N0120M, 1970 .... **$200**
LANDAU CARRIAGE, THE, L1521G, 1987 .... **$4,000**
LANGUID CLOWN, L4924G, 1976 .... **$1,200**
LATEST ADDITION (GRES VERSION), L2262, 1989 ..... **$600**
LAURA, L1360G, 1978 .... **$225**
LAWYER, L1089G, 1971 .... **$900**
LAWYER, L1090G, 1971 .... **$900**
LETTERS TO DULCINEA (NUMBERED SERIES, GRES),
L3509, 1978 .... **$2,200**
LITTER OF KITTENS, N0104G/M, 1970 .... **$150**
LITTLE BIRD, L1301, 1974 .... **$650**

LITTLE BOY BLUE, N0521G/M, 1978 .... **$150**
LITTLE DUCK, 4551G, 1969 .... **$55**
LITTLE DUCK, 4551M, 1969 .... **$75**
LITTLE DUCK, 4552G, 1969 .... **$55**
LITTLE DUCK, 4552M, 1969 .... **$200**
LITTLE DUCK, 4553G, 1969 .... **$55**
LITTLE DUCK, 4553M, 1969 .... **$150**
LITTLE DUCK, N0242M, 1979 .... **$50**
LITTLE DUCK, N0243M, 1979 .... **$50**
LITTLE DUCK, N0244M, 1979 .... **$50**
LITTLE DUCK, N0245M, 1979 .... **$50**
LITTLE EAGLE OWL (GRES), L2020, 1971 .... **$400**
LITTLE FLOWER JUG, L1222G, 1972 .... **$475**
LITTLE GIRL W/GOAT/GETTING HER GOAT, L4812G,
1972 .... **$450**
LITTLE JUG ROSE WITH FLOWERS, L1220G, 1972 .. **$475**
LITTLE RED RIDING HOOD, L4965G, 1977 .... **$550**
LITTLE SHEPHERD WITH GOAT, L4817G/M, 1972 ..... **$475**
LONG RABBIT (EARLY/RARE), 352.13G, 1965 .... **$800**
LOVERS FROM VERONA, L1250G, 1974 .... **$1,200**
LOVERS IN THE PARK, L1274G/M, 1974 .... **$1,400**
MADAME BUTTERFLY, L4991G, 1978 .... **$350**
MAN'S BEST FRIEND N0032G, 1969 .... **$175**
MARY, L4671G, 1969 .... **$85**
MARY, L4671M, 1969 .... **$125**
MATERNAL ELEPHANT, L4765G, 1971 .... **$800**
MAYOR, L1728, 1981 .... **$1,200**
MAYORESS (BUST), L1729, 1989 .... **$750**
MEDIEVAL LADY, L4928G, 1974 .... **$1,150**
MIME ANGEL, L4959M, 1977 .... **$185**
MINIATURE FLOWER VASE, L1219G, 1972 .... **$475**

MONKEYS (GRES), L2000, 1970 .... $650
MOTHER AND CHILD, L4575G, 1969 .... $300
MOTHER AND CHILD, L4701G, 1970 .... $325
MOTHER WITH PUPS, L1257G, 1974 .... $700
MY GOODNESS, L1285G, 1974 .... $450
NAUGHTY DOG, L4982G, 1978 .... $325
NIGHTINGALE PAIR, L1228G, 1972 .... $650
NUDE (FULL FIGURE), L4511M, 1969 .... $650
NUDE (TORSO), L4512M, 1969 .... $500
NUDE IN WHITE, L4511.3M, 1969 .... $700
NURSE, L4603G, 1971 .... $400
OBSTETRICIAN, L4763G/M, 1971 .... $450
OLD DOG, L1067G, 1969 .... $625
OLD FOLKS, L1033G/M, 1969 .... $1,400
OLYMPIC PUPPET, L4968G, 1977 .... $900
ON THE FARM, L1306G, 1974 .... $335
ORCHESTRA CONDUCTOR, L4653G, 1969 .... $875
ORIENTAL GIRL/ORIENTAL FLOWER ARRANGER, L4840G/M, 1973 .... $550
ORIENTAL WOMAN (GRES), L2026, 1971 .... $450
OSTRICHES (EARLY/RARE), L297.13G, 1963 .... $2,000
OTHELLO, L3510 (GRES), 1978 .... $1,050
OWL (GRES), L2019, 1971 .... $400
PAINFUL ELEPHANT, L5020G, 1978 .... $850
PAINFUL GIRAFFE, L5019G, 1978 .... $850
PAINFUL KANGAROO, L5023G, 1978 .... $900
PAINFUL LION, L5022G, 1978 .... $850
PAINFUL MONKEY, L5018G, 1978 .... $850
PAINTER, L4663G, 1969 .... $900
PAN WITH CYMBALS, L1006G, 1969 .... $550
PAN WITH PIPES, L1007G, 1969 .... $550
PEKINESE SITTING, L4641G/M, 1969 .... $450
PELUSA CLOWN, L1125G, 1971 .... $1,500
PERUVIAN GROUP, L4610G, 1969 .... $1,700
PHARMACIST, L4844G/M, 1973 .... $1,500
PHYLLIS, L1356G, 1978 .... $225
PICKING FLOWERS, L1287G, 1974 .... $475
PLATERO AND MARCELINO, L1181G, 1971 .... $400
PLAYFUL DOGS, L1367G, 1978 .... $725
POLAR BEAR OBSERVING (EARLY/RARE), L075G, 1966 .... $300
POODLE, L1259G/M, 1974 .... $475
PROFESSOR, L5208G, 1984 .... $600
PUPPY LOVE, L1127G, 1971 .... $365
QUIXOTE ON GUARD/BRAVE KNIGHT, L1385G, 1978 .... $800
RABBIT EATING (BROWN & WHITE), L4772G/M, 1971 .... $165
RABBIT EATING (GRAY & WHITE), L4773G/M, 1971 $165
RABBIT SCRATCHING (EARLY/RARE), 278.12G $700
RABBIT'S FOOD, L4826G/M, 1972 .... $300
RACE, THE, L1249G, 1974 .... $2,200
RAIN IN SPAIN, THE/UNDER THE RAIN, L2077, 1978 .... $525
RAM, L1046G, 1969 .... $600
READING, L5000G/M, 1978 .... $325
REMINISCING, L1270G, 1974 .... $1,400
ROMANCE, L4831G/M, 1972 .... $1,500
ROMEO AND JULIET, L4750M, 1971 .... $1,450
SAD HARLEQUIN, L4558G/M, 1969 .... $625
SANCHO PANZA, L1031G/M, 1969 .... $600

SANTA CLAUS, L4904G, 1974 .... $1,000
SATYR GROUP, L1008G, 1969 .... $975
SATYR WITH FROG (VERY RARE), L1093G, 1971 .... $750
SATYR WITH SNAIL (VERY RARE), L1092G, 1971 .... $750
SCOTTISH LASS, L1315G, 1974 .... $2,800
SEA BREEZE/WINDBLOWN GIRL, L4922G, 1974 .... $400
SEA CAPTAIN, L4621G/M, 1969 .... $325
SEAMAN/HELMSMAN, THE, L1325M, 1976 .... $1,250
SEATED BALLERINA, L4504G/M, 1969 .... $350
SEATED HARLEQUIN, L4503G/M, 1969 .... $400
SEESAW, L1255G/M, 1974 .... $625
SEESAW, L4867G, 1974 .... $425
SETTER'S HEAD (GRES), L2045, 1971 .... $650
SHELLEY, L1357G, 1978 .... $225
SHEPHERD, L4659G, 1969 .... $325
SHEPHERD RESTING, L4571G/M, 1969 .... $450
SHEPHERD SLEEPING, L1104G, 1971 .... $2,000
SHEPHERD WITH LAMB, L4676G, 1969 .... $135
SHEPHERD WITH LAMB, L4676M, 1969 .... $225
SHEPHERDESS SLEEPING/SHEPHERDESS W/LAMB (BUST, GRES) L 2005M, 1970 .... $700
SHEPHERDESS W/DUCKS/GIRL W/GEESE, L4568G/M, 1969 .... $300
SHEPHERDESS WITH BASKET, L4678G, 1969 .... $135
SHEPHERDESS WITH BASKET, L4678M, 1969 .... $225
SHEPHERDESS WITH DOVE, L4660G/M, 1969 .... $300
SHEPHERDESS WITH GOATS, L1001G/M, 1969 .... $750
SHEPHERDESS WITH ROOSTER, L4677G, 1969 .... $125
SHEPHERDESS WITH ROOSTER, L4677M, 1969 .... $250
SHEPHERD'S REST, L1252G, 1974 .... $675
SHERIFF PUPPET, L4969G, 1977 .... $650
SINGING LESSON/CHOIR LESSON, L4973G, 1977 .... $1,350
SKIER PUPPET, L4970G, 1977 .... $625
SLEEPY CHICK, L4632G, 1969 .... $400
SMALL DOG (PAPILLON), L4749G, 1971 .... $250
SPRING BIRDS, L1368G, 1978 .... $2,700
ST. JOSEPH, L4672G, 1969 .... $100
ST. JOSEPH, L4672M, 1969 .... $135
SWAN, L4829G/M, 1972 .... $350
SWEET HARVEST, L5380G, 1986 .... $900
SWEETY/HONEY LICKERS, L1248G, 1974 .... $550
SWINGING/VICTORIAN GIRL ON SWING, L1297G, 1974 .... $1,850
TEACHER, THE (MALE), L4801G, 1972 .... $500
TENNIS PLAYER PUPPET, L4966G, 1977 .... $550
THOUGHTS, L1272G, 1974 .... $3,600
TORSO IN WHITE, L4512.3, 1969 .... $600
TROUBADUOR, L4548G/M, 1969 .... $800
TWO ELEPHANTS, L1151G, 1971 .... $475
TWO HORSES, L4597M, 1969 .... $1,400
TWO WOMEN CARRYING WATER JUGS, L1014G/M, 1969 .... $850
UNDER THE WILLOW, L1346G, 1978 .... $2,200
VALENCIANS GRP/VALENCIAN COUPLE-HORSEBACK, L4648G/M, 1969 .... $1,200
VIOLINIST AND GIRL, L1039G/M, 1969 .... $1,000
WATCHING THE PIGS, L4892G, 1974 .... $1,200
WOMAN GOLFER/LADY GOLFER, L4851M, 1973 .... $400
WOMAN/LADY WITH DOG, L4761G, 1971 .... $365
WOODCUTTER, L4656G, 1969 .... $650

PRECIOUS MOMENTS

Artist Sam Butcher's artwork was spotted by Enesco Corp. CEO Eugene Freedman at a booksellers' covention in 1975. At that time, Butcher and his business partner, Bill Biel, had a greeting-card company. The characters depicted in Butcher's designs were wide-eyed children with inspiring messages. Freedman arranged to have a figurine created from one of Butcher's drawings by sculptor Yasuhei Fujioka.

Butcher liked the figurine and agreed to Enesco's creation of 20 others based on his artwork. The public embraced the original 21 figurines, which were released in 1978 and a collectible legacy was born.

Marks:

1981	Triangle	1993	Butterfly
1982	Hourglass	1994	Trumpet
1983	Fish	1995	Ship
1984	Cross	1996	Heart
1985	Dove	1997	Sword
1986	Olive Branch	1998	Glasses
1987	Cedar Tree	1999	Star
1988	Flower	2000	Cracked Egg
1989	Bow & Arrow	2001	Sandal
1990	Flame	2002	Cross in Heart
1991	Vessel	2003	Crown
1992	Clef		

Images appear courtesy of Enesco Group Inc.

Additional Listings: See *Price Guide To Contempory Collectibles and Limited Editions*, 9th edition by Mary L. Sieber, Krause Publications.

Advisor: Mary L. Sieber

Bell, Annual
God Sent His Love, 15873, 1985 .... $38
I'll Play My Drum For Him, E2358, 1982 .... $50
Let The Heavens Rejoice, E5622, 1980 .... $148
Love Is The Best Gift Of All, 109835, 1987 .... $33
Surrounded With Joy, E-0522, 1983 .... $57
Time To Wish/Merry Christmas, 115304, 1988 .... $38
Wishing You A Cozy Christmas, 102318, 1985 .... $38
Wishing You A Merry Christmas, E5393, 1984 .... $44

Figurine, Precious Moments
3 Mini Nativity Houses/Palm Tree, E2387, 1982 .... $54
Animal Collection, Bunny, E9267c, 1982 .... $26
Animal Collection, Dog, E9267b, 1982 .... $26
Animal Collection, Kitty w/Bow, E9267d, 1982 .... $26
Animal Collection, Lamb w/Bird E9267e, 1982 .... $26
Animal Collection, Pig w/Patches
  E9267f, 1982 .... $26
Animal Collection, Teddy Bear E9267a, 1982 .... $26
Baby Figurines Six Piece. Set, E2852, 1983 .... $165
Baby's First Trip, 16012, 1985 .... $258
Be Not Weary In Well Doing, E3111, 1979 .... $127
Bear Ye One Another's Burdens, E5200, 1980 .... $90

Bless This House, E7164, 1981 .... $204
Bless You Two, E9255, 1982 .... $47
Blessed Are The Peacemakers, E3107, 1979 .... $87
Blessed Are The Pure In Heart, E3104, 1980 .... $46
Blessings From My House To Yours, E0503, 1983 ... $76
Bringing God's Blessing To You, E0509, 1983 .... $79
Bundles Of Joy, E2374, 1982 .... $89
But Love Goes On Forever, E3115, 1979 .... $68
But Love Goes On Forever, E6118, 1981 .... $95
But Love Goes On Forever Plaque, E-0102, 1982 .... $88
Camel, E2363, 1982 .... $43
Christmas Is A Time To Share, E2802, 1979 .... $80
Christmas Joy From Head To Toe, E2361, 1982 .... $72
Christmastime Is For Sharing,
  E-0504, 1983 .... $81
Cow With Bell Figurine, E5638, 1980 .... $43
Crown Him Lord Of All, E2803, 1979 .... $82
Donkey Figurine, E5621, 1980 .... $23
Dropping In For Christmas, E2350, 1982 .... $76
Dropping Over For Christmas, E2375, 1982 .... $88
End Is In Sight, **The**, E9253, 1982 .... $98
Especially For Ewe, E9282c, 1982 .... $42
First Noel, **The**, E2365, 1982 .... $70
First Noel, **The**, E2366, 1982 .... $70
Forgiving Is Forgetting, E9252, 1981 .... $73
God Has Sent His Son, E-0507, 1983 .... $79
God Is Love, E5213, 1980 .... $83
God Is Love, Dear Valentine, E7153, 1981 .... $43
God Is Love, Dear Valentine, E7154, 1981 .... $43
God Is Watching Over You, E7163, 1981 .... $89
God Loveth A Cheerful Giver, E1378, 1979 .... $850
God Understands, E1379b, 1979 .... $104
Hand That Rocks The Future, **The**, E3108, 1979 .... $79

Precious Moments, You Suit Me To a Tee, 526193. **$38**

He Leadeth Me, E1377a, 1979.................................$105
He Watches Over Us All, E3105, 1979..............$74
Heavenly Light, The, E5637, 1980.....................$53
His Burden Is Light, E1380g, 1979,.................$108
His Sheep Am I, E7161, 1981.............................$80
I Believe In Miracles, E7156, 1981..................$83
If God Be For Us...Against Us, E9285, 1982....$82
I'll Play My Drum For Him, E2356, 1982.........$86
I'll Play My Drum For Him, E2360, 1982.........$40
Isn't He Wonderful, E5639, 1980......................$67
Isn't He Wonderful, E5640, 1980......................$68
It's What's Inside That Counts, E3119, 1979....$106
Jesus Is Born, E2012, 1979...............................$118
Jesus Is Born, E2801, 1979...............................$306
Jesus Is The Answer, E1381, 1979...................$143
Jesus Is The Light, E1373g, 1979.....................$79
Jesus Loves Me, E1372b, 1979..........................$72
Jesus Loves Me, E1372g, 1979..........................$72
Jesus Loves Me, E9278, 1982.............................$30
Jesus Loves Me, E9279, 1982.............................$31
Joy To The World, E2344, 1982.........................$95
Let Heaven And Nature Sing, E2347, 1982.....$43
Let Not The Sun Go Down...Wrath, E5203, 1980....$149
Let The Whole World Know, E7165, 1981.......$107
Lord Bless You And Keep You, The, E3114, 1979....$68
Lord Bless You And Keep You, The, E4720, 1980....$43
Lord Bless You And Keep You, The, E4721, 1980....$54
Lord Give Me Patience, E7159, 1981................$56
Love Beareth All Things, E7158, 1981.............$55
Love Cannot Break/True Friendship, E4722, 1980..$113
Love Is Kind, E1379a, 1979..............................$103
Love Is Kind, E2847, 1983.................................$43
Love Is Patient, E9251, 1982.............................$79
Love Is Sharing, E7162, 1981..........................$149
Love Lifted Me, E1375a, 1979.........................$106
Love Lifted Me, E5201, 1980.............................$92
Love One Another, E1376, 1979.......................$79
Loving Is Sharing, E3110b, 1979.....................$94
Loving Is Sharing, E3110g, 1979.....................$68
Make A Joyful Noise, E1374g, 1979.................$75
May Your Christmas Be Cozy, E2345, 1982.....$77
May Your Christmas Be Warm, E2348, 1982....$109
Mother Sew Dear, E3106, 1979.........................$57
My Guardian Angel, E5207, 1980....................$187
Nativity Buildings & Tree, E2387, 1982.........$102
Nativity Set Of 9 Pcs., E2800, 1979................$158
Nativity Wall, E5644 (Set Of 2), 1980............$122
Nobody's Perfect, E9268, 1982.........................$262
O Come All Ye Faithful, E2353, 1982..............$79
Oh, Taste & See That The Lord Is Good, E9274,
   1982..$69
Our First Christmas Together, E2377, 1982.....$80
Peace Amid The Storm, E4723, 1980................$83
Peace On Earth, E2804, 1979...........................$125
Peace On Earth, E4725, 1981.............................$80
Perfect Grandpa, The, E7160, 1981..................$67
Praise The Lord Anyhow, E1374b, 1979..........$79
Prayer Changes Things, E1375b, 1979............$165
Prayer Changes Things, E5214, 1980..............$121
Precious Memories, E2828, 1983.......................$88
Purr-Fect Grandma, The, E3109, 1979.............$54

Purr-Fect Grandma, The, E7242, 1982..............$83
Rejoice O Earth, E5636, 1980.............................$53
Rejoicing With You, E4724, 1980......................$74
Sharing Our Joy Together, E2834, 1982..........$55
Silent Knight, E5642, 1980...............................$360
Smile, God Loves You, E1373b, 1979................$76
Tell Me The Story Of Jesus, E2349, 1982.........$98
Thank You For Coming To My Aide, E5202, 1980..$122
Thanking Him For You, E7155, 1981................$51
Thee I Love, E3116, 1979...................................$99
There Is Joy In Serving Jesus, E7157, 1981.....$57
They Followed The Star, E5624, 1980.............$245
They Followed The Star, E5641, 1980.............$196
Thou Art Mine, E3113, 1979.............................$58
To A Special Dad, E5212, 1980.........................$50
To Some Bunny Special, E9282a, 1982............$47
To Thee W/Love, E3120, 1979...........................$74
Trust In The Lord, E9289, 1982........................$69
Unto Us A Child Is Born, E2013, 1979...........$102
Walking By Faith, E3117, 1979.........................$93
We Are God's Workmanship, E9258, 1982.......$44
We Have Seen His Star, E2010, 1979................$90
Wee Three Kings, E5635, 1980..........................$99
We're In It Together, E9259, 1982....................$73
You Have Touched So Many Hearts, 527661, 1982..$41
You're Worth Your Weight In Gold, E9282b, 1982...$38

Figurine, Nativity
Come Let Us Adore Him, E2011, 1979............$312
Come Let Us Adore Him, E2395 (Set Of 11), 1982.....$135
Come Let Us Adore Him, E2800 (Set Of 9), 1980......$255
Come Let Us Adore Him, E5619, 1980..............$42

Plate, Christmas Collection
Come Let Us Adore Him, E5646, 1981..............$50
Let Heaven And Nature Sing, E2347, 1982......$43

Plate, Joy Of Christmas
Christmastime Is For Sharing, E-0505, 1983..........$70
I'll Play My Drum For Him, E2357, 1982.........$58
Tell Me The Story Of Jesus, 15237, 1984..........$70

*Precious Moments, Mother's Day, Thinking Of You Is
What I Really Like To Do, 1993.* **$50**

COOKIE JARS

Cookie jars, colorful and often whimsical, are popular with collectors. They were made by almost every manufacturer in all types of materials. Figural character cookie jars are the most popular with collectors.

Cookie jars often were redesigned to reflect newer tastes. Hence, the same jar may be found in several different variations and these variations can affect the price.

Many cookie-jar shapes were manufactured by more than one company and, as a result, can be found with different marks. This often happened because of mergers. Molds also were traded and sold among companies.

Abingdon Pottery
Bo Peep, No. 694D, 12" h **$425**
Choo Choo, No. 561D, 7 1/2" h **$120**
Daisy, No. 677, 8" h **$50**
Pumpkin, No. 674D, 8" h **$550**
Three Bears, No. 696D, 8 3/4" h **$245**
Windmill, No. 678, 10 1/2" h **$500**

Brayton Laguna Pottery
Partridges, Model No. V-12, 7 1/4" h **$200**
Provincial Lady, high-gloss white apron and scarf, red, green and yellow flowers and hearts, marked "Brayton Laguna Calif. K-27," 13" h **$455**
Swedish Maid, incised mark, 1941, 11" h **$600**

Hull Pottery
Barefoot Boy **$320**
Duck **$60**
Gingerbread Boy, blue and white trim **$400**
Gingerbread Man, 12" h **$550**
Little Red Riding Hood, open basket, gold stars on apron
.... **$375**

Metlox Pottery
Bear, blue sweater **$100**
Chef Pierre **$100**
Pine Cone, gray squirrel finial, Model No. 509, 11" h ... **$115**
Rex Dinosaur, white **$120**
Tulip, yellow and green **$425**

Red Wing Pottery
French Chef, blue glaze **$250**
Grapes, yellow, marked "Red Wing USA," 10" h **$125**
Rooster, green glaze **$165**

Shawnee Pottery
Cinderella, unmarked **$125**
Dutch Boy, striped pants, marked "USA," 11" h **$190**
Dutch Girl, marked "USA," 11 1/2" h **$175**
Great Northern Boy, marked "Great Northern USA 1025," 9 3/4" h **$425**
Jo-Jo the Clown, marked "Shawnee USA, 12," 9" h **$300**
Little Chef **$95**
Muggsy Dog, blue bow, gold trim and decals, marked "Patented Muggsy U.S.A.," 11 3/4" h **$850**
Smiley Pig, clover blossom decoration, marked "Patented Smiley USA," 11 1/2" h **$550**

Granny, Brayton Laguna, with decoration in cold paint and under glaze, impressed mark on bottom, "Brayton Laguna California 40-85," various applied decorations, 11 1/2" h, late 1940s. **$900**

Leprechaun, McCoy, red, unmarked, never put into wide production, but no one is certain just how many were made, widely reproduced slightly smaller, 1950s, 12" h. **$3,000**

Winnie Pig, clover blossom decoration, marked "Patented Winnie USA," 12" h...**$575**

Stoneware, cobalt blue decoration, unknown maker
Basketweave and Morning Glory, marked "Put Your Fist In," 7 1/2" h...**$625**
Flying Bird, 9" h...**$1,250**

Watt Pottery
Apple, No. 21, 7 1/2" h...**$400**
Cookie Barrel, wood grain, 10 1/2" h...**$50**
Goodies, No. 76, 6 1/2" h...**$150**
Happy/Sad Face, No. 34, wooden lid...**$165**
Starflower, No. 503, 8" h...**$350**

Pumpkin, Metlox, ink-stamped on bottom, "Original California Pottery Metlox," 1960s, 9 1/4" h. **$450**

Big Orange, McCoy USA mark, cold-painted stem and leaves, early 1970s. **$90-$110**

Hamm's Bear, McCoy, USA mark, also found with white tie, early 1970s. **$225-$250**

Mickey Mouse on Birthday Cake, Japanese, impressed mark of conjoined letters (MR?), ink-stamped, "Copyright (symbol) Walt Disney Productions," 11" h. **$500**

Pretty Ann, Metlox, marked on bottom, "Made in Poppytrail California" over an outline of the state, not to be confused with the Raggedy Ann jar by Metlox, which has glazes matching the doll created by illustrator Johnny Gruelle in 1908 and is valued at about **$300**; 1960s, 11" h. **$500**

Woodsy Owl jar and bank, USA mark on jar, cold-painted details, 1970s. **$275**

Photo courtesy of David Rago Auctions, Inc.

Art Pottery, raspberry-colored ground, white painted clematis and green leaves, signed M.R. Avon/65, 7" x 6 1/2". **$960**

Herringbone Black Butler, rattan handle, ink-stamped, "Japan," Japanese, early 1950s, 8 3/4" h with handle down. **$2,500**

CLOCKS

The clock is one of the oldest human inventions. The word clock (from the Latin word clocca, "bell"), suggests that it was the sound of bells that also characterized early timepieces.

The first mechanical clocks to be driven by weights and gears were invented by medieval Muslim engineers. The first geared mechanical clock was invented by an 11th century Arab engineer in Islamic Spain. The knowledge of weight-driven mechanical clocks produced by Muslim engineers was transmitted to other parts of Europe through Latin translations of Arabic and Spanish texts.

In the early 14th century, existing clock mechanisms that used water power were being adapted to take their driving power from falling weights. This power was controlled by some form of oscillating mechanism. This controlled release of power—the escapement—marks the beginning of the true mechanical clock.

Also see Tiffany.

American brass Chelsea ship's clock, retailed by George B. Carpenter & Co., Chicago, circa first half 20th century. The brass case with brushed steel dial attached to it's original mahogany bracket both with the serial number 76554 and additionally numbered "6008". This model patented December 30, 1901, 7" d. Overall height including bracket 10" x 10 1/4" x 5 1/4". **$862**

Ansonia crystal regulator, Excelsior eight-day clock with overall gilding and elaborate decoration, 19th century. Complete with original pendulum. 20 1/2" x 11". **$1,680**

Ansonia gilt metal clock, with Rococo-style case surmounted by a cherub playing a flute, circa 1900. 19 1/2" x 9" x 8". **$960**

Ansonia Rococo-design mantel clock, cast metal with seated figure (possibly Mercury) to left, case with C-scrolls, S-scrolls and shell work, circular porcelain dial with exposed escapement, gilt egg-and-dart molded bezel, Ansonia Clock Co., New York; 15" h, 16" w. **$517**

Ansonia Royal Bonn mantel clock, Rococo cresting, porcelain dial with exposed escapement, floral painted, brass works marked on back: "Ansonia Clock Co., patented June 14, 81, New York, U.S.A."; pink shaded case, leaf-decorated scroll feet, 13 7/8" h, 10 1/4" w. **$840**

Banjo clock, with reverse painting, white-painted dial, circular glazed brass door, twin pierced brass brackets, reverse-painted throat panel with leaf-scroll, American eagle and shield, reverse-painted pendulum door with ship battle between Americans and British, 32 1/2" h, 10" w.
.... **$1,610**

Banjo clock, Simon Willard, circa 1810, eight-day, weight-driven works, inlaid mahogany case, gilt metal American eagle finial, circular glazed dial door with brass mount, glazed throat panel with reverse-painted gold on white lattice motif and gilt bead border flanked by twin curved brass brackets. Reverse-painted glazed pendulum door with lattice work reserve marker, "S. Willard's/ PATENT", 35" h (including finial), 9 5/8" w, 3 1/2" deep, some reverse paint damage to gilt bead border on pendulum door.
....**$13,800**

Brass two-day marine chronometer, by Chadwick, Liverpool, late 19th or 20th century. The silver dial with subsidiary seconds dial within a brass gimbal, the dial

Ansonia porcelain mantel clock with Royal Bonn "La Vendee" case and open escapement, 14 3/4" h. **$793**

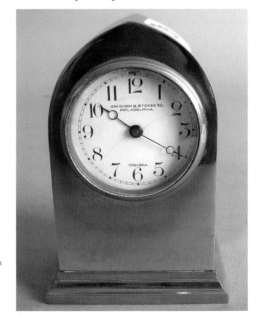

Chelsea "Gothic" silver over brass time only desk clock retailed by Van Dusen & Stokes Co., Philadelphia, 5 1/4" h. **$263**

*French black marble mantel
clock by Henri Jullien with open
escapement, 13" h. (broken glass).*
$293

marked "Chadwick, 69 Lord Street, Liverpool. No. 386".
Fitted in a brass-bound mahogany case. Retains original
key. Dimensions of box 7 1/2" x 7 1/2" x 7 1/2". The case
and exterior of chronometer in very good condition overall.
The back plate, once removed, reveals a bent spring. The
dial was not removed to inspect interior. **$1,438**

Ephraim Downes, pillar-and-scroll mantel clock, Bristol,
Conn., three brass urn and steeple finials, scrolled
pediment, white-painted dial with cornucopia spandrels,
twin colonnettes, reverse-painting on door with sailboat
and house, bracket feet, 27 7/8" to top of central plinth,
16 1/2" w, pediment damaged with some pieces retained.
.... **$575**

Ever-Ready Safety Razor clock, wood face features
graphic of lathered gent shaving. Includes original
pendulum, 18" w x 28" h. Generally good condition; Roman
numerals and dial graphics have had older paint touch-up
that extends into black outlines. Original pendulum.
.... **$1,725**

Four-hundred-day clock, exceptionally large, German or
French, its porcelain dial painted with musical instruments
and champlevé decoration on columns, dome and base,
disc pendulum, circa 1900. With wooden base and glass
dome, 26". **$8,400**

French bracket clock of baluster form, with a
porcelain dial above an elaborate brass coat of arms, circa
1870-1880, 36" x 21". **$1,800**

French bronze and champlevé clock, oval case flanked
by two columns with champlevé enamel, painted dial and
double vial mercury pendulum, movement marked L.
Marti & Co. 1889 Made in France. 14 1/2" x 9 1/2" x 5 1/2".
.... **$2,520**

French champlevé crystal regulator, with painted
champlevé panels, dial and pendulum surrounded by
rhinestones, circa 1890. 16 1/2". **$9,000**

French country cottage clock, painted metal dial has
raised cartouches with Roman numerals, inlaid mother-of-
pearl, brass and exotic woods, 19th century. 23" x 20".
.... **$570**

French Marti & Cie, eight-day time and strike crystal
regulator shelf clock, circa 1900, the dial inscribed "Bigelow
Kennard & Co., Boston", 10 1/2" h. **$305**

*French bronze and rouge marble shelf clock, late 19th
century, by Lemerle-Charpentier & Cie, the bronze figure
of a woman signed "Moreau Mathurin," 22 1/2" h.* **$3,042**

French wall clock, late 19th century, inscribed "Georges Chazottes Chateau-Gontier" on the mother of pearl inlaid dial, 24 1/2" h. **$234**

French painted mantel clock with ormolu mounts, 16" h. **$439**

French porcelain mantel clock, 19th century, ormolu-mounted, surmounted by basket of flowers on cobalt blue glazed vase, glazed dial door opening to circular porcelain dial inscribed "1/Hry Marc/A Paris"; festoons of ormolu flowers supported by pair of ram's heads at sides, base having seated child at each side with book, porcelain panel at center with two putto, molded base with leaf-scrolled supports, 25" h, 20" w. **$4,600**

French slate clock, beveled glass on front and back doors, marked H & F Paris 2877, 19th century. 18 1/2" x 12 1/2" x 8". **$840**

French spelter shelf clock, late 19th century, with figure of a knight, 15 1/2" h. **$410**

Gilt bronze mantel clock, blue porcelain urn flanked by cherubs holding a garland of flowers, on a breakfront base with enamel clock dial, 19th century. The top with a floral bouquet and two doves. Restoration to porcelain urn, 18 1/2" x 16" x 5 1/2". **$2,760**

Chauncey Ives pillar-and-scroll mantel clock, Bristol, Conn.; mahogany case, twin scroll pediment, three brass urn finials, white-painted dial, twin colonnettes; reverse-painted

Ithaca No. 3 calendar clock, circa 1875, 38 1/2" h. **$1,404**

Photo courtesy Pook & Pook Inc., Downingtown, Pa.; www.pookandpook.com

Marlow's Atlantic advertising clock by the Electric Neon Clock Co., Cleveland, 31" h, 36" w. **$549**

Photo courtesy Pook & Pook Inc., Downingtown, Pa.; www.pookandpook.com

Swiss enamel decorated sterling silver peacock desk clock, marked "Yocs Paris", 3 1/4" h. **$2,808**

glass panel with ship and water surrounded by flowers and leafage in earth tones, 28 3/4" h, 16 1/2" w, 4 1/2" deep, reverse-painted glass panel cracked. **$1,035**

Jaeger Le Coultre Atmos clock, square form with glass sides and top, revealing the movement and dial, 20th century. 9" x 8 1/2" x 5 1/2". **$1,200**

Japy Freres, marble and bronze three-piece clock garniture, 19th century, the porcelain dial inscribed "Boursier Jne Paris," the bronze figure of mother and child signed Faillot (Edme-Nicolas Faillot, 1810-1849). 16" h. overall. **$380**

Mantel clock, L. & J.G. Stickley, designed by Peter Hanson with an etched copper face, square wooden details, and a small glass window. Unmarked. 22" x 16" x 8". **$7,200**

McClintock Co. clock, with stained-glass door and face in the style of Purcell and Elmslie. Brass McClintock Co. tag, Minneapolis, 45 3/4" x 17" x 10 3/4". **$2,520**

Sessions clock, with cast iron frog surround, whimsical copper-flashed cast-iron group of frogs playing musical instruments, 9 1/2" w x 11 1/2" h. **$517**

Seth Thomas, faux marble shelf clock, 11 1/2" h. **$176**

Seth Thomas ship's clock, first half 20th century, brass, mounted on custom bracket, the clock now mounted with a brass ship's wheel, the dial marked "Seven jeweled eight day ships bell," 9" x 13" x 3". Appears to be in untouched original condition. Clock has not been disassembled for condition. **$288**

Swiss Omega square eight-day brass desk clock, #10600650, 5 1/2" h. **$1,404**

Waterbury Sage eight-day repeater carriage clock, 5 1/2" h. **$214**

Sevres shelf clock, decorated with ormolu and rhinestones with painted dial, late 18th century. Porcelain crack upper right of frame. Signed Duryea & Potter, Paris. 14 1/4". **$4,200**

Waterbury, mahogany eight-day mantel clock, patented 1914, with a four-train movement, 16 1/2" h. **$205**

Tall-Case Clocks

British tall-case clock, of traditional design in profusely inlaid walnut, early 19th century. Signed "Thomas Heywood, Bangor," probably signature of owner, 90" h. **$2,400**

Cherry tall-case clock, shaped, arched cresting with twin brass hexagonal urn finials, glazed arched door, white painted wood dial, yellow flowers at top, gold spandrels, second hand dial, calendar dial, molded door, molded base, bracket feet, 83" h, 17 1/4" w, 10" deep. **$632**

Dark-stained tall-case clock, quarter-spool-turned cornice, arched glazed door, twin fluted colonnettes flanking, brass dial, painted-moon dial, second hand dial, calendar dial, engraved fruit decoration; glazed beveled pendulum door flanked by fluted quarter-columns, molded base, ogee bracket feet, 92 3/4" h, 20 3/4" w, 12 1/8" deep, hands broken. ... **$1,092**

Henry Deyken, inlaid mahogany and oak tall-case clock, broken-scroll pediment with two roundels, glazed door, flanked by two reeded colonnettes, opening to brass dial inscribed "Henry Deyken Worcester No. 1172," gilt metal spandrels, second hand dial, molded base with inlaid bird, bracket feet, 82 3/4" h, 17 1/2" w, 9" deep, alteration to back probably to accommodate works. **$900**

Federal inlaid mahogany tall-case clock, probably New Jersey, circa 1815, the arch molded hood below conforming scrolled cresting with brass terminals centering three ball finials, the center with displayed eagle above an astragal glazed door flanked by fluted colonnettes and unusual brass stop fluting. Painted enameled moon-phase dial with pink rose spandrels centering an Arabic and Roman numeral chapter ring. Dial centered with a sweep second hand and calendar aperture. Eight-day brass works with iron plate stamped "Wilson", probably Thomas Wilson, London, 1790-1825. Waisted case fitted with rectangular door with molded edges and string inlay flanked by engaged fluted quarter columns with brass capitals and brass stop fluting above a molded box base raised on flared French feet with shaped apron. Clock with two door keys, winder, both weights and pendulum, 90" h x 13 1/2" throat w x 9" deep. Fine condition with original clean surfaces **$6,038**

French Morbier tall-case clock, with porcelain dial and articulating pendulum in pine case, 19th century. 90". **$1,920** (Morbier clocks were made in the Franche-Comté region of eastern France for more than 200 years, beginning in the late 17th century.)

French oak tall-case clock, arched molded cornice, cast-pewter spandrels and dial, arched glazed dial door, twin brackets carved with husk pendants, molded paneled door with carved emblem, bombe form base, 81 3/4" h, 21" w, 11" deep. **$4,600**

Jacob Gothart walnut tall-case clock, Lebanon, Pa., twin scroll pediment with pair of urn finials, white-painted dial, moon dial, gilt spandrels, trunk with American Eagle inlay, 99 3/8" h, 18 3/4" w. **$9,000**

Inlaid mahogany tall-case clock, twin scrolled pediment, centering brass ball and steeple finial (replaced), glazed arched door opening to white painted dial inscribed "E. Winftanles/Wigan"; second hand dial, calendar aperture, pointed arch pendulum door with thumb-molded border, two reeded flanking corners, conforming inlaid chamfered base, French bracket feet, 87 3/4" h. **$2,185**

Joseph Krout, (Bucks County, Pa.) cherry tall-case clock, broken-scroll pediment, pair of rosettes, three urn finials, arched glazed door, four slender colonnettes flanking, painted dial and moon dial, sweep second hand, brown painted monograms ("JK" and "BC"); American red, white and blue shield motif; eight-day brass works with strike by "Joseph Krout", 1815; pendulum door with brass plate inside detailing family history of clock; rounded front corners, trunk and base, French bracket feet, 97" h, 17 3/4" w, 10" deep, pendulum door replaced. **$6,600**

Mahogany tall-case clock, twin scrolled pediment with twin brass rosettes (one missing), three brass ball-and-steeple finials, twin colonnettes, arched glazed door opening to painted dial, brass 8-day works, oval gilt reserve with thistles and arch of flowers above, floral painted spandrels, arched pendulum door, twin quarter-columns flanking, serpentine apron, bracket feet, early 19th century, 87 1/4" h, 18 3/8" w, 9" deep. **$1,725**

Oak tall-case clock, pewter eagle on spire (replaced), shaped top, painted leaf scroll, bearing "1776"; square glazed door (flanked by twin columns) opening to steel dial marked "Dav'd Collier Gatley"; works with strike, moon dial, gilt metal mask head and scrollwork spandrels, pendulum door flanked by two rounded corners, molded chamfered base, bracket feet, 85 1/2" h, 19" w, 10" deep. **$2,300**

Secessionist grandfather clock, with brass face and base molding, beveled glass door with added glass shelves where pendulum originally swung, possibly imported by Gustav Stickley. Partial Eastwood label. 78" x 15 1/4" x 9 1/2". **$1,800**

Walnut tall-case clock, cove-molded cornice with large metal inlaid "1776"; steel dial, four gilt metal mask head spandrels; "Franz Iacob/ Braun Eber Bach/ A.M. Kecken"; glazed dial door, low bracket feet, 90 3/4" h, 16 1/4" w, 9" deep, replaced brass H-hinges on right side of dial door. **$1,725**

Walnut tall-case clock, inlaid, twin scroll pediment with twin roundels, inlaid scrolled plinth, brass ball and steeple finial, twin wooden urn finials, arched glazed door flanked by turned spindles, painted dial marked "Blomagerus"; second hand dial, calendar aperture, gilt floral spandrels, inlaid trunk with pendulum door (bird inlay), conforming inlaid base, bracket feet, 83 1/4" h (without finial), 18" w, 8 1/2" deep. **$1,840**

Photo courtesy of Pook & Pook Inc.
Tall case clock, mahogany, painted dial, 8-day works, inlaid case, New England, Federal, circa 1810. **$3,500**

Clothing

FUTURE OF THE MARKET: VINTAGE CLOTHING

Make your own fashion statement

By Caroline Ashleigh
Caroline Ashleigh Associates, Birmingham, Mich.

The definition of "vintage clothing" varies from expert to expert. Alison and Melissa Houtte, authors of *Alligators, Old Mink & New Money* (Avon Books, 2006), state that "in the industry, people say that 20 years or older is 'vintage.' However, television programs like Sex in the City have started a whole new trend of buying 'newer' vintage fashion to a generation of sophisticated women who want to stand out from the crowd, like Carrie Bradshaw, to make a true fashion statement."

Valuable vintage does not necessarily have to be expensive to be fresh, carefree and sleek. If you are in the market for tomorrow's vintage fashion today, look for design that breaks the rules, and has classic staying power with a distinctive, singular trademark style. Check out regional designers in your own locale, rather than the off-the-rack regulars.

Boutiques like Hooti Couture in Brooklyn, N.Y., and Resurrection in New York and California, rummage and estate sales, flea markets, and online auctions are all wonderful sources of vintage fashion if you want to stand out at any party. The "hip" gal of today is not afraid to mix new with vintage, bringing a little whimsy, fun and touch of glam to her wardrobe. She can create miles of look on a minimal budget by adding a vintage beaded or sequined jacket or top, over a smart skirt or slacks and jeans, with a great pair of Manolos, and voila!

A different fashion statement is being made by men across the country who turn out in their crease-free synthetics every year at the National Leisure Suit Convention. And then there are those with a personal affection for the custom-crafted detail and originality in vintage western wear. Authentic western wear embodies the antithesis of mass production in each shirt, chap and cowboy hat that carries with it the unique personality of the designer. Western clothing is the iconic American style, because deep in the soul of practically every American kid is just a little bit of cowboy or cowgirl achin' to get out.

There's value in vintage Western wear because it transcends the fickleness of fashion. These clothes are perennial. If we can no longer roam the range, at least we can dress the part! At the same time, we're seeing elements of Western style returning to fashion magazines and runways every year.

For decades, avid collectors have flocked to Goodwill and Salvation Army stores hoping to find a hidden Western wear diamond in the rough. Today, collectors scour the flea market fields of Brimfield in Massachusetts, the Rose Bowl in Pasadena, Calif., and the Pier Show in New York, among countless others, for indigenous Western textile art in the form of a rare Nathan Turk embroidered shirt or regular "store-stock" items with original tags.

Meanwhile, the Internet has ushered in mail order as the most popular method for purchasing Western wear, taking the genre from a regional audience to the national and international marketplaces.

My older brother had a penchant for anything Hopalong Cassidy. He especially treasured a Hopalong drinking mug. And he insisted on wearing only "Hoppy" underpants. Too bad he didn't keep them in their original packages. At one auction run by Ted Hake of Hake's Americana & Collectibles, a pair of vintage "Hoppy" boy's underpants sold for $173.

The modern-day master tailor who brought mass-media attention and razzle-dazzle to the Western-wear scene was a Russian immigrant by the name of Nuta Kotlyarenko, better known as Nudie Cohn (1902-1984), a.k.a. "King of the Cowboy Couturiers," "Dior of the Sagebrush," and "The Original Rhinestone Cowboy." Cohn influenced the Western-wear industry for nearly 40 years, whipping up costumes for Hank Williams, Hopalong Cassidy, Clayton Moore, Ronald Reagan, Liberace, Elton John, the Rolling Stones and Elvis Presley, among others.

Photo courtesy Leslie Hindman Auctioneers, Chicago; www.LeslieHindman.com

Dress, Christian Dior, black silk, cocktail, 1956, with three-quarter-length sleeves, a V-neckline, fitted waist with pleated gathering at waist for a full skirt. No label. **$192**

In 1957, he was commissioned to create the most expensive suit he had ever made: a 14k gold lame outfit bejeweled with 10,000 rhinestones. Over the years, Nudie is said to have sold Elvis $100,000 worth of clothes, today worth $400,000-$500,000.

Another immigrant who created a market niche was Nathan Turk from Minsk, Poland. Beginning in the 1930s, movie studios began commissioning Turk to design costumes for Westerns. By the 1940s, Western musicians began frequenting Turk's shop in Van Nuys, Calif. He created the blueprint for most of the successful country bands: a unique ensemble for group leaders to set them apart, with the advertising slogan, "With real western wear from the movie."

Caroline Ashleigh owns Birmingham, Mich.-based Caroline Ashleigh Associates LLC. She is a graduate of New York University in Appraisal Studies in Fine and Decorative Arts and is a board-certified senior member of the Appraisers Association of America. Ashleigh is an internationally known appraiser and regularly appears on the PBS program Antiques Roadshow. Caroline Ashleigh Associates conducts fully catalogued online auctions. Visit www.appraiseyourart.com or www.auctionyourart.com.

Helpful Hints for the Care and Storage of Clothing

Wash your hands thoroughly before handling fine vintage garments. Use white cotton gloves when handling vintage fabric; soiled gloves may transfer dirt.

Before handling textiles, remove any sharp jewelry that could snag or pull delicate threads.

Do not smoke, drink or eat near your garments. Accidents may result in stains on textiles, and food attracts insects.

Avoid prolonged exposure of textiles to direct sunlight as it can weaken fibers.

Roll fabrics—do not fold—as creases can weaken fibers and cause them to become brittle and crack.

Resist cleaning. It is best to clean fabric with a hand vacuum.

Check periodically for mildew and insect damage.

Whenever possible, do not wear makeup when putting on or trying on a valuable vintage garment.

Do not use mothballs or crystals to protect your garment from insects. They are extremely toxic and leave a permanent odor.

Storage

Use acid-free textile storage containers. Do not store textiles in brown cardboard boxes, as they release acids.

Acid-free buffered tissue can be used for cottons, linens, synthetics.

Use acid-free, un-buffered tissue for wool, silk, leather.

Use padded wood hangers to hang garments.

Do not store vintage garments in a damp basement or hot attic.

Do not store fabrics in plastic bags as they hold moisture and can release chemicals. Store in unbleached muslin.

Enjoy your vintage piece! With the proper care, you will have it to treasure for many years to come and perhaps pass in on to another family member.

Sources for Archival Materials for Clothing

Gaylord Bros., Syracuse, N.Y.: 800-962-9580; www.gaylordmart.com

Talas, New York, N.Y.: 212-219-0770; www.talas-nyc.com

Light Impressions, Santa Fe Springs, Calif.: 800-828-6216; www.lightimpressionsdirect.com

Textile Terms

Brocade: Rich silk fabric with raised patterns.

Cashmere: Soft twilled fabric made of goat's wool.

Chantilley (pronounced shan-tee-yee): Bobbin lace most commonly found in black.

Chenille: Velvety silk, wool or cotton fabric, with a protruding pile.

Chintz: Glazed printed cotton fabric.

Cutwork: Fabric made "lacy" by cutting away and binding edges with satin or buttonhole stitches. It is not needle lace, but rather cutwork embroidery. Also known as embroidered lace.

Damask: Fine lustrous fabric with flat patterns and a satin weave.

Denim: Firm and durable twilled cotton.

Dresden: Lace that combines a number of embroidery techniques including satin stitch, tambour (chain stitch) and pulled stitches to create a lace-like surface. Also known as white work.

Gabardine: Closely woven cotton or wool twill.

Georgette: Thin silk.

Gingham: Striped cotton cloth.

Grosgrain: Heavy close-woven corded silk.

Hairpin Lace: Lace that is formed over a U-shaped wire frame called a hairpin, with the help of a crochet hook. Also known as Portuguese lace.

Haute Couture: The term "haute couture" is French. *Haute* means "high" or "elegant." *Couture* literally means "sewing" or "tailoring," but has come to indicate the business of creating, designing and selling high-fashion women's clothes. Haute couture originated in the 19th century by Charles Frederick Worth. Made from scratch for each customer, it usually takes from 100 to 400 hours to make one dress.

Jacquard: Name of the mechanism invented by Joseph Marie Jacquard in 1801. A term used to describe coverlets with complex floral and pictorial designs; most typical period from 1830s-1860s.

Moire: Watered silk.

Nylon: First synthetic fiber, invented in 1935.

Organdie: Fine translucent cotton.

Organza: Transparent thin silk or nylon.

Pique: Stiff durable corded fabric or cotton, rayon or silk.

Satin: Closely woven silk with lustrous face.

Shantung: Plain rough silk or cotton.

Stevengraphs: Colorful silk pictures invented by Thomas Stevens, beginning in the 1860s, and also produced by other English makers. Collectors seek examples in original mats with all labels complete.

Taffeta: Thin glossy silk.

Tatting: Tatting is made with a shuttle and is distinguished by rings of knots.

Ticking: Strong cotton or linen fabric used for pillowcases and mattresses.

Tulle: Sheer and delicate silk.

Clothing and Accessories

Also see Native American, Textiles, Western/Cowboy.

Belt plate, Civil War Confederate, lead-filled brass featuring pelican and young (Louisiana). Plate measure approximately 2 1/8" by 3", with brass hooks on reverse, some bends to edges. **$3,000**

Blouse, Emilio Pucci, cotton, 1960s, in a blue, green and purple geometric print with matching covered buttons. Labeled: Emilio Pucci. Left shoulder needs to be re-stitched about 1". **$156**

Bustier with leggings ensemble, Emilio Pucci, 1970s, in a pink, brown and black geometric print, strapless bustier top. Together with two pairs of leggings. All labeled: Emilio Pucci. ....**$180 all**

Photo courtesy Leslie Hindman Auctioneers, Chicago; www.LeslieHindman.com

Blouse, Hermes, silk, 1980s, black knit sleeves, yellow and red key-and-tassel motif. Labeled: Hermes/Paris. **$180**

Photo courtesy Leslie Hindman
Auctioneers, Chicago;
www.LeslieHindman.com

*Coat, Balenciaga
Couture, hound's-
tooth wool, barrel,
1961, in grey and
cream, with cropped
sleeves, a shawl collar,
double breasted with
round grey buttons,
fully lined. Labeled:
Balenciaga/65333.
Pilling to the wool,
lining is coming apart
at neckline, there
are a couple small
rips in lining. Tag is
unattached at one side.*
$1,800

Coat, Balenciaga Couture, cream wool, 1955, with cropped
sleeves, small collar, cream buttons, fully lined. Labeled:
Balenciaga/69262, small tear in lining near the tag, small
stain on lining. **$1,020**

Coat, Eisa, cream faux fur, early 1960s, ready-to-wear from
the house of Balenciaga, with full length sleeves, straight fit
with cream buttons at front, pockets at side, fully lined in
silk faille. Labeled: Eisa. Some buttons are loose. **$360**

Coat, Geoffrey Beene, black silk, dress, 1960s, with cropped
sleeves, a wrap style, empire waist, full skirt with hidden
pockets, fully lined. Labeled: Geoffrey Beene. **$204**

Coat, Givenchy Couture, green, early 1960s, streamlined
silhouette, small collar, green round buttons with
additional snap closures, center and hem framed in
seam lines, two slits at side, fully lined in silk. Labeled:
Givenchy/46.178. ....**$420**

Photo courtesy Leslie Hindman Auctioneers, Chicago;
www.LeslieHindman.com

*Coat, Christian Dior Couture, red wool,
fall 1952, with a rounded collar, two red
buttons at front, swing fit, fully lined.
Labeled: Christian Dior/Paris 21981.
Total length 48".* **$1,440**

Costume, patriotic flag motif, 19th century, satin, machine-sewn, with blue top decorated with six silver painted stars, puckered waist, and red and white printed polished cotton skirt; dress lined with cotton, length 33" and chest 38". This was likely made for the American Centennial celebration. **$431**

Coat, Givenchy Couture, red wool, travel, early 1960s, in a mod fit, with double welt seams throughout, double-breasted with round black buttons. Labeled: Givenchy/98.484. Buttons show some wear, one of the interior seams needs to be re-stitched. **$300**

Coat, Hattie Carnegie, black silk, evening, 1950s, with two frog closures at front, fully lined. Labeled: Hattie Carnegie. Total length 48". **$240**

Coat, Holly Harp, brown silk chiffon, duster, 1970s, with all-over velvet leaves, three-quartered sleeves with beaded detail, closureless. Labeled: Holly's Harp. **$108**

Coat, dark-brown, three-quarter-length mink, Herbert's Furs, San Francisco label. **$150**

Coat, brown three-quarter-length mink, with shawl collar and floral embroidered lining, I. Magnin, size 10/12. ....**$250**

Coat, dark-brown, three-quarter-length mink, with notch lapel, I. Magnin, size 14/16. ....**$275**

Coat, Teal Traina, black velvet, 1950s, double-breasted, full skirt, fully lined. Labeled: Teal Traina. Total length 55". **$96**

Coat, winter fox, full-length, size 10/12. ....**$1,000**

Coat, early 1940s, wool, black and white herringbone with black wool trim, accentuated shoulders, swing fit, slit pockets, fully lined. Total length 41". **$90**

Coat, gray wool, cape, 1960s, with a notched collar, sleeveless with a cape extension at back covering arms, fitted waist, flared skirt, fully lined. **$216**

Cocktail ensemble, 1940s, navy, jacket with cropped sleeves, a sculptured sweetheart neckline, buttoned bodice. Dress with a floral lace bust, fitted bodice, flared skirt. **$120**

Cover up, Emilio Pucci, cotton, 1960s, blue and white floral print with a matching self belt. Labeled: Emilio Pucci/Florence-Italy. Two small stains at the front hem area. **$300**

Dress, Adele Simpson, floral silk, cocktail, 1950s, with a fitted bodice, two bows at waist. No label. **$72**

Dress, Ben Reig, taupe satin, cocktail, 1950s, with thick straps, a fitted bodice with a panel of brown satin and beading at bust, full skirt. Labeled: Ben Reig. **$132**

Photo courtesy Leslie Hindman Auctioneers, Chicago; www.LeslieHindman.com

Dress, Adele Simpson, 1960s, black and white with all-over ducks, slit neckline with hook-and-eye closure, right side slit, fully lined. Labeled: Adele Simpson. **$60**

Photo courtesy Leslie Hindman Auctioneers, Chicago; www.LeslieHindman.com

Dress, Christian Francis Roth, crayon motif, late 1980s, in yellow and blue wool knit, swing fit, one sleeve in form of sky-blue crayon, patch pocket at front with scribbling throughout. Labeled: Christian Francis Roth/New York City. Small moth holes. **$840**

Dress, Bob Meyer, green wool, 1960s, with cropped sleeves, mock collar, with a cream panel at front and a peach panel at back, fully lined. Labeled: Bob Meyer/Chicago. **$120**

Dress, Chloe, yellow, 1960s, with a round neckline with full length sleeves, rows of clear beading throughout, matching slip underneath. Labeled: Chloe. One area where the beads are loose. **$570**

Dress, Claire McCardell, black velvet, 1950s, with elastic band sleeves, "ruched" (a ruffle or pleat of lace, muslin or other fine fabric) front at closures, skirt in a sheer black silk with a cream underlay with glitter dots throughout.

Labeled: Claire McCardell Clothes/by Townley. There are missing glitter spots throughout the skirt, the velvet is slightly worn in spots. There is an area where the velvet in the armpit has ripped and been repaired. There is some wear around the closures at front. There is also some wear around the waist to the skirt. **$240**

Dress, Courreges, cream wool, day, 1969, in an A-line fit, with short sleeves, a V-neck and front and back, two patch pockets at front, fully lined. Labeled: Courreges Paris/38139. Slight surface stain at back and two single threads sticking out at the back. **$960**

Dress, Courreges, yellow wool, day, 1969, A-line fit, with short sleeves, a V-neck, two faux pockets, fully lined. Labeled: Courreges/Paris/Made in France. **$780**

Dress (flapper), 1920s, pink, beaded, matching slip, overall good condition, some missing beads and also surface stains at front. Total length 41". **$270**

Dress, Emilio Pucci, cotton, 1960s, strapless in a brown, pink and orange geometric print. Labeled: Emilio Pucci/Florence-Italy. **$540**

Dress, Emilio Pucci, velvet, 1960s, in a geometric print, full-length sleeves, V-neck, A-line skirt, fully lined. Labeled: Emilio Pucci. **$600**

Dress, Frederick Starke, pink floral, cocktail, 1950s, strapless with a fitted bodice, bow at front, full skirt. Labeled: Frederick Strake. **$450**

Dress, Galanos, floral print with matching shoes, 1958, with cap sleeves, a boat neckline, asymmetrical fitted bodice, decorative buttons at the left side, V back buttoning

at right, pleating at waist leading into a full skirt with crinoline underneath, fully lined. No label. Together with matching pumps. Labeled Saks Fifth Avenue/Fenton Last. (This dress was worn to Sammy Davis Jr.'s wedding to Loray White.) .... **$720 ensemble**

Dress, Galanos, black lace, cocktail, 1950s, with cape sleeves, round neckline, fitted throughout, fully lined. Labeled: Galanos. **$720**

Dress, Galanos, black silk chiffon, cocktail, 1950s, with flutter sleeves leading into a tier of pleated ruffles at back, banded waist, pleated skirt, fully lined. Labeled: Galanos.
.... **$450**

Photo courtesy Leslie Hindman Auctioneers, Chicago; www.LeslieHindman.com

Dress, Geoffrey Beene, pink linen, day, late 1960s, trimmed in cream, with short sleeves, two cream buttons at waist, hidden pockets at side. Labeled: Geoffrey Beene. Slight discoloration at hemline, lining needs to be restitched. **$240**

Photo courtesy Leslie Hindman Auctioneers, Chicago; www.LeslieHindman.com

Dress, Geoffrey Beene, mulit-color floral print, 1960s, with puff sleeves, mock neck, empire waist with sash belt, flared skirt, fully lined. Labeled: Geoffrey Beene. **$330**

Dress, Galanos, 1960s, short sleeves, A-line fit, front panel has cream silk pleating, fully lined. Labeled: Galanos. Minor imperfections in pleating. **$330**

Jacket, Geoffrey Beene, floral print, late 1960s, in a flared fit, with round clay buttons, large patch pockets, fully lined. Labeled: Geoffrey Beene. **$60**

Dress, Geoffrey Beene, navy, 1960s, with a button front, breast pocket, oversized belt, pleated skirt. Labeled: Geoffrey Beene. **$120**

Dress, Geoffrey Beene, plaid wool, 1967, with decorative gold-tone buttons at front, fitted waist, flared skirt, fully lined. Labeled: Geoffrey Beene. **$72**

Dress, Leslie Fay, black, 1950s, with a ruffled round-banded neck, with short ruffles in a crisscross pattern. Labeled: Leslie Fay Knits. Hem has been let out. **$120**

Dress, Lilly Pulitzer, tropical print, halter, 1960s, multicolored tropical pattern, inverted pleat at neckline, tie halter. Labeled: The Lilly/Lilly Pulitzer Inc. **$72**

Dress, Marimekko, prototype, pink cotton, 1963, swirl print with full-length sleeves, zipper front, A-line fit, side pockets. Labeled: Marimekko/Suomi-Finland. **$120**

Dress, Mollie Parnis, ivory satin, 1950s, with a scoop neck, empire waist with floral belt, full skirt with hidden pockets, fully lined. Labeled: Mollie Parnis/New York. Possible zipper replacement, slight overall discoloring at hem line. **$204**

Dress, Mollie Parnis, silk, cocktail, 1950s, one-shoulder taupe bodice gathering at side, fitted waist, full skirt with a cream, grey and orange print, orange taupe and grey panels at side. No label. The printed silk easily rips so there is a lot of ripping throughout. **$540**

Photo courtesy Leslie Hindman Auctioneers, Chicago; www.LeslieHindman.com

Dress, Moschino Couture!, 1988, strapless with men's ties sewn throughout, fully lined. Labeled: Moschino Couture! Some areas where the silks ties have been slightly snagged. **$510**

Dress, Pauline Trigere, silk chiffon, blue floral print, 1960s, two piece, over blouse with sheer sleeves, cream cuffs, cream collar tying at front, slip with matching floral top and a blue skirt. Labeled: Pauline Trigere. Some slight discoloration at the collar. **$180**

Dress, Suzy Perette, floral brocade, 1950s, with a fitted bodice, sashes at side waist tying at back, full skirt. Labeled: Suzy Perette/New York. Hanger strap on the interior is broken. **$192**

Dress, Tassel, orange, 1960s, with full-length sleeves, rolled collar tying at back, hidden pockets, fully lined. Labeled: Tassel. **$60**

Dress, Traina Norell, floral print, silk, 1950s, original model, with gold metallic yarn throughout, short sleeves, boat neckline, fitted waist, together with a matching fabric and gold leather belt, full skirt. Labeled: Traina Norell/New York/Joan 163. Shoulders are ripping and the cloth belt is in fair condition. **$360**

Photo courtesy Leslie Hindman Auctioneers, Chicago; www.LeslieHindman.com

Dress, Yoshiki Hishinuma, laminated, full length with cutout flaps of laminated urethane exposing sheer material. Labeled: Yoshiki Hishinuma. Stretch to exposed mesh parts. **$4,080**

Photo courtesy Leslie Hindman Auctioneers, Chicago; www.LeslieHindman.com

Hat, Christmas motif, label reads Adolfo II. **$120**

Ensemble, Christian Dior, pink moire silk, daywear, 1960s, sleeveless dress with a rolled collar, empire waist. Jacket with cropped sleeves, covered buttons. All fully lined. Labeled: Christian Dior New York. **$480**

Ensemble, Courreges, cream, 1965, sleeveless dress with a netted top, mod skirt with faux pockets, fully lined. Jacket in cropped sleeves, closureless ending at waist, fully lined. No label. Spots with slight fading throughout so the overall color is inconsistent. **$780**

Ensemble, Emilio Pucci, maroon silk and velvet, late 1960s, with a blue print throughout, silk blouse with an asymmetric collar. Skirt in velvet, high-waisted with adjustable buckles, flared, fully lined. All labeled: Emilio Pucci. **$120**

Hat, Hattie Carnegie, cream, straw, with patchwork throughout, blue ribbon at brim. Labeled: Miss Carnegie.
....**$36**

Hat, Yves Saint Laurent, blue, with a petal brim. Labeled: Yves Saint Laurent. **$108**

Photo courtesy Leslie Hindman Auctioneers, Chicago; www.LeslieHindman.com

Gown, Galanos, paisley silk and sequins, evening, 1970s, with all-over sequins following the pattern, sequined straps, a ruched bust, straight-fit skirt, fully lined. Labeled: Galanos. Couple areas of missing sequins. **$2,640**

Photo courtesy Leslie Hindman Auctioneers, Chicago; www.LeslieHindman.com

Jacket, Donald Brooks, black silk paisley, 1960s, in black, cream and yellow, with a standup collar, flared fit, hidden pockets, fully lined. Labeled: Donald Brooks. **$360**

Photo courtesy Leslie Hindman Auctioneers, Chicago; www.LeslieHindman.com

Ensemble, Bonnie Cashin, multicolor wool tweed, 1960s, coat with an attached capelet, trimmed in black leather, buckle closure. Labeled: Sills/A Bonnie Cashin Design. Together with a matching skirt. Some pilling to the wool that can simply be removed. Leather is worn. The button missing at waist of the skirt. **$180**

Photo courtesy Leslie Hindman Auctioneers, Chicago; www.LeslieHindman.com

Jacket, Courreges, orange vinyl, cropped, 1970s, with white snaps, cream Courreges logo at chest, orange jacquard lining with logo. Labeled: Courreges/Paris Made in France/C. Slight rippling in vinyl. **$720**

Gown, Valentino, red jersey, evening, 1980s, with full-length sleeves, gathered at shoulders leading into a V at back, with fabric draping into three rhinestone pods. Small snags at chest. **$600**

Jacket, Courreges, brown, bomber, 1960s, with brown wool collar sleeves and hem, leather at both front and back, zipper front. Together with matching brown wool pants. All labeled: Courreges/Paris Made in France. ....**$360 set**

Kepi (officer's), Civil War-period, chasseur-style, exhibits some light moth damage and soiling with detached bill and damage to liner. Bill features old attached numbers "18 2". No label. **$1,035**

Photo courtesy Leslie Hindman Auctioneers, Chicago; www.LeslieHindman.com

Pants, Emilio Pucci, silk, 1960s, palazzo style in a geometrical print. Labeled: Emilio Pucci. Small hole from wear at the front thigh, surface stain hemline. **$120**

Scarf, Hermes, silk, in blue, white and yellow, in a golden wheel motif. Labeled: Hermes at Bonwit Teller, 35" square. **$330**

Scarf, Emilio Pucci, in a pink and cream geometric print. Labeled: Emilio Pucci/Firenze. 22" square. **$36**

Scarf, Hermes, cashmere, in a jewel motif at center, signed J. Abadie. Labeled: Hermes, 56" square. **$510**

Scarf, Hermes, silk, white with a circus motif. Labeled: Hermes/Paris, 35" square. **$330**

Shawl, Hermes, black, cashmere, with fringe. Labeled: Hermes/Paris, 54" x 68". **$510**

Skirt, Emilio Pucci, silk, 1960s, in a peach and purple print, flared fit. Labeled: Emilio Pucci. **$60**

Skirt, Moschino, "Art Is Love," black leather, 1990, in a pencil fit, with green and gold leather trim at waist, with the words "Art is love" at the hemline, fully lined. Labeled: Cheap and Chic by Moschino. Slight wear to waistband. **$480**

Skirt, Pierre Cardin, orange wool, 1960s, in a flared fit, with a large patch pocket at hip, white leather lace up side from the hip to the waist, slit at side. Labeled: Pierre Cardin. Grommets are slightly tarnished, there is some fading to the leather belt, skirt has one small spot on it. **$300**

Skirt, "Wonder Woman" motif, 1970s, multicolored with a yellow starred waistline, fully lined. No label. Small stain on one of the stars. **$60**

Skirt suit, Balenciaga Couture, black and white wool, 1965, jacket with full-length sleeves, double-breasted, fully lined in silk crepe. Skirt in an A-line fit, fully lined in silk crepe. Labeled: Balenciaga/87786. Small rust stain at left hip lining from hanger. **$720**

Skirt suit, Balenciaga Couture, green wool, 1961, jacket with cropped sleeves, notched collar, three green plastic buttons, fitted, fully lined in silk taffeta. Skirt in a pencil fit, fully lined in silk taffeta. Labeled: Balenciaga/76452. Fading to jacket lining. **$720**

Skirt suit, Balenciaga Couture, green wool, 1960, jacket with a notched collar, full-length sleeves, double-breasted with black buttons, fully lined in silk taffeta. Skirt in an A-line fit, fully lined in silk taffeta. Labeled: Balenciaga/87414. Hem has been let out on skirt, fading to jacket lining, some areas of pilling to wool. **$480**

Skirt suit, Balenciaga Couture, tan wool herringbone, 1961, jacket with full-length sleeves, notched collar, fitted with tan plastic buttons, two flap pockets at waist, fully lined in silk taffeta. Skirt in an A-line fit, fully lined in silk taffeta. Labeled: Balenciaga/80925. Minor spots that appear to be on the surface stains on buttons. **$1,020**

Photo courtesy Leslie Hindman Auctioneers, Chicago; www.LeslieHindman.com

Photo courtesy Leslie Hindman Auctioneers, Chicago; www.LeslieHindman.com

Skirt suit, Chanel Couture, mauve and black tweed, 1960s, comprised of waist-length boxy jacket with stacked patch pockets, open notched lapels, buttons on jacket rimmed with jersey and centered with gilt-metal granulated domes, fully lined in mauve jersey and with chain at hem. Jersey blouse, sleeveless with a button front. Skirt in a straight fit. Labeled: Chanel/10026. Skirt may have been relined, underarms on blouse and jacket have slight discoloration. **$1,080**

Skirt suit, Mainbocher, 1950s, cropped fitted jacket with a shawl collar, double-breasted, fully lined. High waisted A-line skirt, fully lined. Labeled: Mainbocher. The lining in the skirt has been partially replaced and the waist area is shredded. **$600**

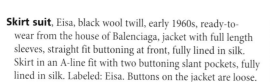

Skirt suit, Eisa, black wool twill, early 1960s, ready-to-wear from the house of Balenciaga, jacket with full length sleeves, straight fit buttoning at front, fully lined in silk. Skirt in an A-line fit with two buttoning slant pockets, fully lined in silk. Labeled: Eisa. Buttons on the jacket are loose. **$660**

Skirt suit, Eisa, cream wool, 1960s, ready-to-wear from the house of Balenciaga, jacket with a purple velvet collar, gold-tone buttons, fully lined. Skirt in an A-line fit, fully lined. Labeled: Eisa. Missing a button, wear to velvet collar. **$120**

Suit, Bonnie Cashin, yellow tweed, cape, 1960s, flared capelet sleeves, round collar, sides laced up with suede, suede-covered buttons, slant pockets, fully lined. Labeled: Sills/A Bonnie Cashin Design. Together with matching tweed A-line skirt. **$180**

Suit, Ceil Chapman, cream, dress, 1960s, jacket with all-over floral lace, straight fit with covered buttons at front, fully

lined. Labeled: Ceil Chapman for Miss Winston. Dress sleeveless with a silk top, ruched waist, lace skirt, fully lined. **$120**

Tunic, Emilio Pucci, brown silk, 1960s, in a brown and grey print, with long sleeves and silk-covered buttons. Labeled: Emilio Pucci. One armpit has slight discolorations and needs reinforcement stitches and the other has been repaired. The buttons were moved; small surface stain. **$144**

Tunic with pants, Geoffrey Beene, navy wool, 1960s, sleeveless with hook-and-eye closures on left shoulder, round neckline, matching belt at waist, hidden pockets, fully lined. Flared pants, fully lined. Labeled: Geoffrey Beene. **$570**

Vest, floral print, full length, 1960s, mandarin neckline, loop closure buttons at bust, ribbon hemline, fully lined. Labeled: Wilson Folmar. **$84**

Bags, Clutches, Purses and Totes

Though these terms are often used interchangeably, the listings here reflect actual auction house catalog entries, divided into subcategories.

Bag, Andrea Pfister, animal print, 1980s, quilted in a boxy shape, gold-tone chain handle, fully lined. Stamped: Andrea Pfister, 13 1/2" x 10". **$72**

Bag, Barry Kieselstein-Cord, evening, 1999, in a bronze satin with floral embroidery, gold-tone handle, gold dragon at front, lined in red satin. Stamped: Barry Kieselstein-Cord, 11" x 5". **$360**

Bag, beaded, early 20th century, in an Asian motif, with a drawstring handle, fringe at base, fully lined in silk, 7" x 8". Small stain to lining and one section of fringe is loose. **$84**

Bag, Christian Dior, leopard print, with tan leather trim, wide shoulder strap, detachable cell-phone compartment, gold-tone hardware, fully lined. Stamped: Christian Dior/Paris, 12" x 6". **$204**

"Birkin" Bag, Hermes Barenia Haut a Courroies, 2000, with palladium hardware, blind stamp D. Stamped: Hermes/Paris, 12 1/2" x 10" x 6 1/4". **$7,200**

"Birkin" Bag, Hermes, black Ardennes leather, 2002, with gold hardware, lock key and sheath, blind stamp D. Stamped: Hermes/Paris, 14" x 9 1/2" x 7". **$8,400**

Photo courtesy Leslie Hindman Auctioneers, Chicago; www.LeslieHindman.com

Bag, Swedish, beaded, peacock design, early 20th century, with a silver handle closure. **$180**

Photo courtesy Leslie Hindman Auctioneers, Chicago; www.LeslieHindman.com

Bag, Moschino, "Siamo alla Frutta," in black leather with two matching shoulder straps, multiple felt fruit appliques at front with the phrase " ... siamo alla frutta," zipper closure. Stamped: Moschino, 10" x 12". **$180**

Photo courtesy Leslie Hindman Auctioneers, Chicago; www.LeslieHindman.com

"Charm" Bag, Louis Vuitton, limited edition, trimmed in brown leather, with gold-tone hardware, chain and leather handles, canvas charm print laminated with plastic, lock at front, fully lined in leather. Stamped: Louis Vuitton/Paris, 12" x 9". **$900**

Photo courtesy Leslie Hindman Auctioneers, Chicago; www.LeslieHindman.com

"Kelly" bag, Hermes, sable Taurillon Clemence leather, 2002, with gold hardware, a matching shoulder strap, lock key and sheath, blind stamp F. Stamped: Hermes/Paris, 12 1/2" x 9 1/2" x 5". Hardware slightly worn. **$5,760**

Bags, beaded, one in a black floral motif, drawstring style with fringe at base. One in cream satin with all-over beads in a floral motif, gold-tone chain handle, with a faux pearl and gold-tone closure, fully lined in cream satin. Stamped: Made in France/Handmade. Black: 6 1/2" x 8 1/2". Cream: 7" x 5". .... **$48 pair**

Bags, beaded, early 20th century, one in a floral motif, a gold-tone frame with rhinestones throughout, fringe at base, fully lined in silk. One in navy silk, with crocheted floral beaded a top, fully lined. Cream: 6" x 6". Navy: 6" x 9". .... **$390 pair**

Belt purse, Hermes, red leather, 2000, with a thin tie belt strap, and small purse with snap closure, gold hardware. Stamped: Hermes/Paris, 4" x 5 1/2". **$168**

Clutch, burgundy alligator, in an envelope style, fully lined in red leather. Stamped: Saks Fifth Avenue/Made in France, 10" x 6". **$360**

Clutch, gray patent leather, envelope, alligator embossed, V-shaped flap at front. Stamped: Campanile Spatarella, 10" x 7". **$180**

Handbag, Hermes, tan canvas, 1960s, with caramel leather trim and handle, flap closure, multiple interior pockets, fully lined in leather. Stamped: Hermes-Paris/24 fg St Honore, 9 1/2" x 6". **$300**

Handbag, Roberta di Camerino, eagle design, 1960s, in a navy velvet with navy leather trim and handle, with a cream velvet flap with an eagle symbol at front, lifting into a hidden pocket, gold-tone hardware, fully lined in leather. Stamped: Made in Italy by Roberta di Camerino, 10" x 8" x 4". **$240**

Purse, black calfskin and lizard skin, with a chain handle, silver etched closure, fully lined in silk, 8" x 6". **$156**

Purse, black suede, with gold-tone hardware, flap closure, white leather crocodile embossed trim and braided strap, fully lined, 9" x 8". **$96**

Purse, brown crocodile, with a matching handle, gold-tone hardware, 20" x 5". **$132**

Purse, brown eel skin, in a round shape with a matching adjustable shoulder strap, zipper expander at base, zipper closure, fully lined, 16" x 12". Minor wear on bottom of bag. **$168**

Photo courtesy Leslie Hindman Auctioneers, Chicago; www.LeslieHindman.com

Purse, brown leather, with a Lucite flamingo-form handle, flap closure. Stamped: Saks Fifth Avenue, 11" x 10". **$300**

Purse, Gucci, nautical motif, 1980s, khaki canvas bag, a rope handle with a leather-wrapped top, white and blue striped lining with a matching nautical wallet. Labeled: Gucci, 9" x 8". **$60**

Purse, Gucci, tan leather, with a long shoulder strap, flap closure with gold-tone logo buckle at front, adjustable buckle at base, fully lined. Stamped: Gucci/Made in Italy, 14" x 11". Several minor scratches from use; four small stains on interior of bag. **$180**

Purse, Pierre Cardin, with blue leather trim and handles, canvas with navy logos at both front and back, fully lined in leather. Labeled: Pierre Cardin/Paris New York, 14 1/2" x 13". **$156**

Purse, Louis Vuitton, in monogram canvas, trimmed in tan leather, long shoulder straps, full zipper closure, fully lined in suede. Stamped: Louis Vuitton Paris, 16" x 12". **$600**

Purse, Louis Vuitton, in monogram canvas, with a long shoulder strap and a flap front opening. Stamped: Louis Vuitton Paris, 14" x 12". **$240**

Purse, Lucille de Paris, crocodile, with two long chain handles, fully lined in leather. Stamped: Lucille de Paris, 9" x 6". **$156**

Purse, Midas, poodle motif, wicker, 1950s, bucket shape with white-painted wicker, painted flowers and a beaded poodle detail, gold-tone hardware with white and gold woven leather handles. Labeled: Midas of Miami, 10" x 8". **$180**

Purse, Midas, roadrunner motif, wicker, 1950s, with gold painted wicker, green roadrunner at front, gold-tone hardware with gold woven leather handles. Labeled: Midas of Miami, 13" x 10". **$84**

Purse, Nancy Gonzalez, black crocodile, in a woven style with a cream canvas bag underneath, matching crocodile handles, toggle closure. Stamped: Nancy Gonzalez/Columbia New York, 8" x 7". **$420**

Purse, Nettie Rosenstein, cream, ostrich, 1970s, with gold-tone hardware, matching handle. Stamped: Nettie Rosenstein, 9 1/2" x 7". **$108**

Purse, Nettie Rosenstein, silver lamé, 1950s, with a silver-tone, metal-detailed handle and knob closure, together with matching compact mirror, fully lined. Labeled: Nettie Rosenstein, 6" x 7". Wear to the edges at back where the fabric and piping has separated slightly. **$120**

Purse, Rayne, gold silk, with a rhinestone detail at center, two matching straps, fully lined in brown satin. Stamped: Rayne, 9" x 6". **$96**

Purse, yellow Lucite, 1950s, plastic with octagonal shape, flower-top design with gold-tone hardware, 7" x 6". **$60**

Tote, Gucci, canvas shopper, with logo print throughout, red and green handles. Stamped at front: GG, 12" x 14". Slight wear to the corners and Gucci logo is slightly discolored. **$132**

Photo courtesy Leslie Hindman Auctioneers, Chicago; www.LeslieHindman.com

Purse, Judith Leiber, alligator, suitcase style, with gold-tone hardware, two long chain shoulder straps. Stamped: Judith Leiber, 6 1/2" x 4". With matching coin purse, mirror and care card, mirror needs to be cleaned, exterior hardware has minor scratches from use. **$540**

Photo courtesy Leslie Hindman Auctioneers, Chicago; www.LeslieHindman.com

Purse, Midas, elephant form, wicker, 1950s, with rhinestone and sequin detailing, white glitter tusks, red with gold tassel saddle, gold-tone hardware with a gold leather handle. Labeled: Midas of Miami, 13" x 13". Slight wear and fading. **$450**

Boots and Shoes

Boots, cowboy, in red leather and lizardskin. Stamped: Rios of Mercedes. **$120**

Shoe tights, silver lamé, 1960s, thigh high, with a round rhinestone decoration. Labeled: Design by Evins. **$180**

Geoffrey Beene, black satin shoes. **$50**
Joseph LaRose, orange rafia shoes. **$80**
Versace, red patent leather thigh-high boots. **$1,100**
Roger Vivier, black satin shoes. **$50**
Roger Vivier, multicolor pumps. **$150**
Vivienne Westwood, white patent leather shoes. **$1,300**

Other Accessories

Back Pack, Louis Vuitton, in monogram canvas, with tan leather straps, round football shape. Stamped: Louis Vuitton, 11" x 13". **$132**

Eyeglass case, Louis Vuitton, in monogram canvas, trimmed in suede. Stamped: Louis Vuitton/Paris, 3" x 6 1/2". **$96**

Umbrella, Courreges, red with clear vinyl heart-shaped windows throughout. Labeled: Courreges Paris. **$144**

Photo courtesy Leslie Hindman Auctioneers, Chicago; www.LeslieHindman.com

Roger Vivier, black satin shoes with a triangular rhinestone detail at toe. Labeled: Saks Fifth Avenue. **$96**

COCA-COLA

Originally intended as a patent medicine when it was invented in the late 19th century by John Pemberton of Columbus, Ga., Coca-Cola was bought out by businessman Asa Griggs Candler, whose marketing tactics led Coke to its dominance of the world soft drink market throughout the 20th century.

The famous Coca-Cola logo was created by Pemberton's bookkeeper, Frank Mason Robinson, in 1885. It was Robinson who came up with the name, and he also chose the logo's distinctive cursive script.

Coca-Cola's advertising has had a significant impact on American culture, and is frequently credited with the "invention" of the modern image of Santa Claus as an old man in red-and-white garments.

Bottles

Coca-Cola Bottling Works, Los Angeles, 8 1/2" tooled crown top, "CCBW" on base. Little wear. **$160**

Coca-Cola San Francisco, Cal., 8" tooled top with slight purplish tint. Some wear. **$240**

Photo courtesy American Bottle Auctions, Sacramento, Calif.; www.AmericanBottle.com

Coca-Cola Denver, 8 3/4" crown top, made between 1905-16, number "30" near the front base. Slight interior stain. **$200**

Photo courtesy American Bottle Auctions, Sacramento, Calif.; www.AmericanBottle.com

The Best By A Dam Site, Boulder Products, Las Vegas, Nev., 7 1/2", automatic bottling machine, wear around the base. **$190**

Photo courtesy American Bottle Auctions, Sacramento, Calif.; www.AmericanBottle.com

The Salt Lake Coca-Cola Bottling Co., Red Seal Brand, automatic bottlling machine, 7 1/2" crown top, 1/4" chip off the lip, a little wear and a few scratches. **$40**

Photo courtesy Old Town Auctions LLC, Boonsboro, Md.; www.OldTownAuctions.com

Brunhoff, illuminating countertop display, 1930s, all original except replaced electric cord, round lens has tiny spot of discoloration, minor wear to case finish, 14" h, 12 1/2" w. **$9,350**

Coca-Cola Bottling Co., Las Cruces-Deming New Mexico, 8", automatic bottling machine, slight wear near the base and a couple scratches, scarce. **$120**

Property Of Salt Lake Coca-Cola Bottling Co., Registered (in circle), some wear and a little stain with a tiny ding on the right base of the seam. **$160**

Salt Lake Coca-Cola Bottling Co., Salt Lake City, Utah, 10" with tooled top, brilliant bluish aqua, there is wear around the shoulders and some scratching along with a chip from the bottom front base. **$425**

Assorted Advertising

Photo courtesy Morphy Auctions, Denver, Pa.; www.MorphyAuctions.com

Calendar, 1898, embossed cardboard, with miniscule marks or edge wear. Two missing chips in lower left and right corners, 7 1/4" x 13". **$23,000**

Photo courtesy James D. Julia Auctioneers, Fairfield, Maine; www.JuliaAuctions.com

Calendar, 1920, illustration of a girl in yellow sundress at the golf links enjoying a glass of Coke, 12" w x 31 1/2" h. Good to very good condition with a few light roll creases; strong color; appears to retain original full date pad and top metal band. **$862**

Photo courtesy James D. Julia Auctioneers, Fairfield, Maine; www.JuliaAuctions.com

Display, 1937, scarce four-piece window display of a soda fountain complete with pedestrian die cuts. Remarkably realistic scene of a soda shop full of customers being waited on by two soda jerks. Unique perspective views the shop through a revolving glass door from the sidewalk outside with other customers about to enter. Marquee reads "The Pleasantest Place in Town." Lithograph by the Niagara Litho Co., Buffalo, N.Y. (This display was found in the log storage bin at the estate of a prominent Little Rock, Ark., family who owned the largest soda fountain in town. According to the family it was never put on display, but placed in the log bin as potential fuel.) Approximately 52" w x 46" h. Some edge chips and surface scuffs, but overall in very good condition. **$40,250**

Photo courtesy James D. Julia Auctioneers, Fairfield, Maine; www.JuliaAuctions.com

Display, cardboard, nine-piece variation of the Toonerville display typically found in the books, showing another large building in addition to the general store. Lithographed by Snyder & Black, New York, circa 1930. Illustrations on the individual pieces include comic-book character residents in the fictional town of Toonerville. Overall good condition, some pieces show folds, wear and breaks and a few could use some reinforcement. **$2,012**

Photo courtesy James D. Julia Auctioneers, Fairfield, Maine; www.JuliaAuctions.com

Glasses, eight, flared, red, of unknown age, purchased in 1960, etched with fill lines. Each 3 3/4" h. Very good to excellent condition. **$120 set**

Photo courtesy James D. Julia Auctioneers, Fairfield, Maine; www.JuliaAuctions.com

Globe, milk-glass, with original hardware, circa 1930s, lettered Coca-Cola on two sides in script, 11 1/2" d. Hardware has lost most of its gilt finish. **$360**

"Glo-Glass" easel-back sign, 1930s, retains original cardboard back and attached bent-metal easel and paper label on lower right corner of back, few minor rubs on reverse painted areas from raised bumps, normal for these signs. One tiny nick, quarter inch, in upper right glass edge corner area, nearly concealed by frame. Frame is probably not original, 12 1/2" x 13 3/4". **$15,000**

Sign, cardboard, produced in 1936 to commemorate Coca-Cola's 50th anniversary while also comparing the evolution of women's bathing fashions. Image 26" w x 46 1/2" h. Some prominent creasing, surface wear and multiple BB sized punctures at the top. **$575**

Sign, button, tin on cardboard, NOS, showing Coke bottle behind "Coca-Cola" in script with gold border. Back of sign has cardboard easel back for display (unopened), red string hanger, and decal reading "Philadelphia Badge Co., Agent J. Paul Cobb, Atlanta, GA". Complete with original unused mailer, 9" d. Like new with light dent to side border and small edge ding. **$287**

Sign, cardboard, "Hospitality," large advertisement with image of woman lighting a candle, 54" w x 25" h. Some mildew spots along far left edge. **$517**

Sign, cardboard, 1945, small version of this WWII-themed advertisement of army soldier and young woman, 15 3/4" w x 27" h. Some light soiling to border, and a few small spots of color touch-up to soldier's uniform and girl's dress. **$517**

Sign, "Umbrella Girl," cardboard, 1926, scarce early die cut with illustration of bathing beauty at the beach enjoying a Coca-Cola refreshment, boasting "7 Million drinks a day," 17 3/4" w x 31" h in frame. Hole at top; a few perimeter chips mostly just to top and bottom corners; three small nail holes approximately six inches up from center bottom. **$4,025**

Photo courtesy Old Town Auctions LLC,
Boonsboro, Md.; www.OldTownAuctions.com

*Vendo machine, on original
stand, unrestored, 57 1/2" h.*
$2,860

Signs, pair, includes large cardboard advertisement, circa 1940s, in its original gold frame. It pictures two women looking at a globe, pointing to Europe with one stating, "Here's to Our G.I. Joes" while enjoying a Coke. Also, 1930s Canadian paper poster picturing a 36-cent six-pack of Coke with snowy letters stating, "Add Zest to the Holiday." Matted and framed. Sign: 62" w x 34" h. Poster: 23 1/2" w x 9" h. Cardboard sign has scratch in lower left and some scattered touch-up. Poster shows light vertical creases. .... **$1,380 pair**

Photo courtesy Morphy Auctions, Denver, Pa.; www.MorphyAuctions.com

Sign, straight-sided with bottle, embossed tin, circa 1910. Few minor crimps and shallow dents. One small hole at top center border for mounting. Minor edge rust and light wear, 20" x 28". **$2,750**

Photo courtesy James D. Julia Auctioneers, Fairfield, Maine; www.JuliaAuctions.com

Sign, trolley, 1926, illustration of young couple toasting one another captioned, "It had to be good to get where it is," 20 3/4" w x 11" h. Some water stains to margins, a horizontal scuff mark through the middle, light scattered pigment loss to green background. **$2,012**

Photo courtesy James D. Julia Auctioneers, Fairfield, Maine; www.JuliaAuctions.com

Sign, trolley, 1905, early cardboard advertisement which reads, "Delicious and Refreshing – Drink Coca-Cola at Fountains in Bottles," 20 3/4" w x 11" h. Paper loss top right corner, nail holes at other corners, right margin tear, several small scattered scuffs. **$1,495**

Photo courtesy James D. Julia Auctioneers, Fairfield, Maine; www.JuliaAuctions.com

Women of the Military die cuts, set of five, WWII-era women from the various military branches have attached cardboard easels for countertop display. Lithographed by Snyder & Black, Inc., N.Y., 1943. Each 17 1/2" h. All appear in near excellent condition, with one or two having slight creases at the necks. **$5,175 set**

COINS

Collecting Modern U.S. Commemorative Coins

1982-S proof Washington silver half dollar. **$6.50**

For more information, see *The Instant Coin Collector* by Arlyn G. Sieber, 2009, Krause Publications.

Congress has authorized myriad commemorative coin series since 1982. Commemorative coins honor events, people, organizations or other things, and are authorized by law. They are official U.S. government issues and legal tender, but they are not intended to circulate. Instead, the U.S. Mint—at a premium above face value—sells them directly to collectors. Laws authorizing commemorative coins usually mandate that a certain amount of the purchase price benefit a group or event related to the coin's theme.

In terms of cost, collecting modern commemoratives is a step up from collecting coins from circulation at face value or buying them at shops

The story behind the coins

The first U.S. commemorative coin was an 1892 half dollar for the Columbian Exposition. The exposition was held May 1-Oct. 30, 1893, in Chicago to commemorate the 400th anniversary of Columbus' arrival in the New World. The U.S. Mint struck 950,000 Columbian half dollars dated 1892 and more than 1.5 million dated 1893.

The Columbian half dollar opened the door to many other commemorative coins from the 1910s and continuing into the 1950s. Most were silver half dollars, but there was also an 1893 quarter (also for the Columbian Exposition), a number of gold dollars, two gold $2.50 coins and two gold $50 coins.

The coins were sold by the Mint at a premium above face value. Some commemorated state anniversaries or national themes, such as the U.S. Sesquicentennial in 1926.

There were no less than 18 commemorative half dollars issued in 1936 alone. Among them was an issue commemorating the 75th anniversary of the Battle of Gettysburg. Others, however, were of little national importance, such as issues for the Cincinnati Music Center and the centennial of Elgin, Ill.

Congress grew weary of U.S. coinage being used as local fundraisers, and the flow of commemorative coins slowed in the 1940s and '50s. The last issue among what are commonly called "early" commemoratives was a 1954 half dollar honoring Booker T. Washington and George Washington Carver.

A 28-year hiatus on commemorative coinage ensued until Congress authorized a half dollar in the traditional 90-percent-silver composition to honor the 250th anniversary of George Washington's birth in 1982. Thus began the "modern" commemoratives.

The Washington coin was a winner in many respects: First, its theme was of truly national significance and worthy of commemoration. Second, its design by Mint engraver Elizabeth Jones featured a striking depiction of Washington on horseback, a departure from the staid busts used for portraiture on coins since the Lincoln cent of 1909. The reverse, also designed by Jones, features a view of Washington's Mount Vernon home.

These factors, combined with the long break in commemorative coinage, made the coin popular with collectors. The Mint sold more than 2.2 million uncirculated versions ("D" mintmark) and almost 4.9 million proof versions ("S" mintmark).

1997-W proof Franklin Delano Roosevelt five dollar gold. **$565**

The first U.S. commemorative coin: 1892 Columbian Exposition half dollar (AU-50). **$18.50**

The proliferation of commemorative coins in the 1930s included a half dollar for the Cincinnati Music Center (AU-50). **$315**

The last of the "early" commemoratives honored Booker T. Washington and George Washington Carver (AU-50). **$40**

Like the Columbian half dollar 90 years earlier, the George Washington half dollar opened the door to more commemorative coinage, and like the commemorative coinage of the 1930s, an undesirable proliferation resulted. The coins' themes in the 1990s weren't as localized as many of those in the 1930s, but commemorative coinage became an easy mark for senators and U.S. representatives looking to do a favor for a constituency, or for a fellow lawmaker by offering their vote for a commemorative coin program. Commemoratives could raise funds for a pet cause through surcharges on the Mint's sales of the coins, and a vote for a program went largely unnoticed by the general public.

The year 1994 alone brought five commemorative coin programs: World Cup soccer, National Prisoner of War Museum, U.S. Capitol Bicentennial, Vietnam Veterans Memorial and Women in Military Service Memorial. Although each theme had its virtues, the market for commemorative coins couldn't keep up with all the issues, and sales plummeted from the highs of the Washington half dollar and other early issues in the modern era.

In response, Congress passed the Commemorative Coin Reform Act of 1996. Among other provisions, it limits the number of commemorative themes to two per year. In addition, congressional proposals for commemorative coins must be reviewed by the Citizens Coinage Advisory Committee, which reports to the Treasury secretary. The 10-person committee consists of members from the general public and those with credentials in American history, sculpture and numismatics.

1994 commemoratives included issues for World Cup soccer, National Prisoner of War Memorial, Bicentennial of the United States Capitol, Vietnam Veterans Memorial and the Women in Military Service Memorial.

Where to get them

Current-year commemoratives can be purchased directly from the U.S. Mint (www.usmint.gov). Issues from previous years can be purchased at shows, shops or through advertisements in hobby publications, such as *Coins* magazine.

Collecting strategies

A complete collection of every commemorative half dollar, silver dollar and gold coin issued since 1982 is a commendable but daunting goal for many collectors, especially beginners. Following are suggestions for getting started in collecting modern commemoratives, which can lead to expanding the collection in the future:

Collect what you like

If you see a modern commemorative coin and you like it, buy it. The coin may appeal to you because of its theme or design. Whatever the reason, if you like the coin and are willing to pay the asking price, it will make a great addition to your collection.

By denomination

A new collector may want to focus on just the commemorative half dollars issued since 1982 or just the silver dollars. With a good value guide in hand and more money to spend, a new collector could also venture into gold coins and select one or more of the many commemorative gold $5 coins.

By theme

Collectors of modern commemoratives can also focus on a particular theme that appeals to them, such as presidents, the Olympics or other sports, women or military themes. Again, collect what you like.

1996-P proof Atlanta Olympics silver dollar, high-jumper design. **$60**

1988-W proof Olympiad gold five dollars. **$190**

1990-P proof Eisenhower Centennial silver dollar. **$17**

1986-S proof Statue of Liberty Centennial clad half dollar. **$5.50**

1993-S proof Thomas Jefferson silver dollar. **$28**

1986-S proof Statue of Liberty Centennial silver dollar. **$13.50**

As a complement to a circulating-coin collection

One or more commemorative coins can complement a collection of circulating coins with similar design themes. For example, a 1993 silver dollar commemorating the 250th anniversary of Thomas Jefferson's birth can complement a collection of Westward Journey nickels. A 1990 silver dollar commemorating the centennial of Dwight Eisenhower's birth can complement a collection of Eisenhower dollars.

By set

When selling a current-year commemorative series, the U.S. Mint often offers various sets containing individual coins in the series in uncirculated and proof versions. For example, the 1986 Statue of Liberty Centennial coin series consisted of a base-metal half dollar, silver dollar and gold $5. Various sets of the series offered by the Mint that year included a two-coin set consisting of an uncirculated silver dollar and clad half dollar; a three-coin set consisting of uncirculated versions of each coin; and a six-coin set consisting of proof and uncirculated versions of each coin.

These and sets of other series can be found in their original Mint packaging from online sellers, at shops and shows, and through advertisements in hobby publications such as *Coins* magazine.

How much?

Some of the least popular commemorative coins at the time of their issue are the most expensive on the secondary market today, and some of the most popular commemorative coins at the time of their issue are the most affordable today. Why? The least popular coins didn't sell as well, which resulted in lower mintages. Generally speaking, the scarcer coins are more valued by collectors, which increases demand and drives up their asking prices on the secondary market.

For example, the 1982 George Washington silver commemorative half dollar was popular and sold well at the time of issue. With millions of coins produced, either an uncirculated or proof example can be purchased for under $10.

1986-W proof Statue of Liberty Centennial gold five dollars. **$190**

1993-S proof James Madison clad half dollar. **$16.50**

1996-S proof Atlanta Olympics clad half dollar, swimmer design. **$36**

1991-S proof Mount Rushmore Golden Anniversary clad half dollar. **$20**

In contrast, less than 50,000 uncirculated versions of the 1996 Atlanta Olympics commemorative clad half dollar with the swimmer design were produced. Expect to pay more than $150 for one on the secondary market.

Coin Prices magazine, available on many newsstands, provides a complete list of modern U.S. commemorative coins and a guide to current retail values.

Mintmarks

Modern U.S. commemorative coins have either a "P" mintmark for Philadelphia, "D" for Denver, "S" for San Francisco, or a "W" for West Point, N.Y. Mintmark location varies by coin.

Condition

Commemorative coins are specially handled and packaged at the mints. Thus, grading is less of a factor in purchasing and collecting them.

Still, check each coin before you purchase it or after you receive it in the mail. Make sure its surfaces are clean and free of scratches or other significant blemishes.

The U.S. Mint has a 30-day return policy for coins purchased directly from it. Mail-order dealers, such as those who advertise in *Coins* magazine, also offer return policies. Check individual ads for specific terms.

1989-S proof Bicentennial of the Congress silver dollar. **$18.50**

1997-S proof Jackie Robinson silver dollar. **$85**

1992-P proof Columbus Quincentenary silver dollar. **$39**

2004-P proof 125th Anniversary of the Light Bulb silver dollar. **$41**

1995-S proof Civil War silver dollar. **$78**

How to store them

Keep commemorative coins in their original U.S. Mint packaging, whether purchased directly from the Mint or on the secondary market. The packaging is suitable for long-term storage and protects the coins from wear and blemishes that occur when handled directly.

Modern commemorative coin specs

Commemorative coins are struck in traditional specifications for the denomination and composition. Future issues may be subject to change from the specs listed.

Clad half dollars

Diameter: 30.6 millimeters.

Weight: 11.34 grams.

Composition: clad layers of 75-percent copper and 25-percent nickel bonded to a pure-copper core.

Silver half dollars

Diameter: 30.6 millimeters.

Weight: 12.5 grams.

Composition: 90-percent silver, 10-percent copper.

Actual silver weight: 0.3618 troy ounces.

Silver dollars

Diameter: 38.1 millimeters.

Weight: 26.73 grams.

Composition: 90-percent silver, 10-percent copper.

Actual silver weight: 0.76 troy ounces.

Gold $5

Diameter: 21.5 millimeters.

Weight: 8.359 grams.

Composition: 90-percent gold, 10-percent alloy.

Actual gold weight: 0.24 troy ounces.

Gold $10

Diameter: 27 millimeters.

Weight: 26.73 grams.

Composition: 90-percent gold, 10-percent alloy.

Actual gold weight: 0.484 troy ounces.

1999-W proof George Washington gold five dollars. **$475**

2006-P proof Benjamin Franklin Tercentenary silver dollar, Franklin portrait design. **$54**

1993-W James Madison gold five dollars. **$265**

2003-P proof First Flight Centennial gold 10 dollars. **$560**

COIN-OPERATED DEVICES

Coin-operated devices fall into three main categories: amusement or arcade games, trade stimulators and vending machines.

Also see Music Boxes.

"Advice for Single Men", electrified with one-cent mechanism, tells how to win love, fame and fortune. Wood cabinet with reverse-painted glass front, 11 1/2" w x 25" h x 10" deep. Appears to be working. Some bulbs may need replacement. **$287**

Atlas, baseball countertop penny flip, cast aluminum front on a wood cabinet. Player inserts a penny and bats it into play. Resulting score tracked on bottom abacus. Manufactured by Atlas Indicator Works, Chicago, circa 1931, 12" w x 13" h x 7 1/2" deep. Some staining to baseball lithograph, otherwise good condition, with key. **$2,070**

Arcade crane, tabletop model, manufactured by Buddy Sales of Brooklyn, N.Y., 1920s arcade game in all-original, untouched condition. It features a fanciful cast-aluminum front with a plethora of information and is adorned with two small children similar to those on the Jennings Dutch boy and girl machine. Surrounded by glass on three sides, the rear of the machine depicts an industrial location with a traveling crane. Machine is activated by depositing coin, wheel directs crane to haul up prize, 20" w x 18" deep x 41" h. Crack to glass on right door, lacking keys, machine has not been tested, needs new electrical cord. **$4,600**

Bluebird, gumball machine and trade stimulator, one cent, dispenser mounted atop a wood-cased penny drop that would give your penny back if you deflected it through the opening below, 9 1/4" w x 21 1/2" h x 8 1/4" deep. Lower wood cabinet refinished and metal parts repainted. **$805**

Condom vendor, mid-20th century, wall mount with 25-cent mechanism, in crackled black paint with illegible partial label. Includes key and is filled with more than 20 double packs, various chips and scratches, overall good. **$210**

Fortuneteller, tabletop machine issued by the National Institute for the Blind, featuring a blind man with a cane under a dome that sits atop the machine. Insert a coin and the man spins, pointing his cane to one of several fortunes. The front is emblazoned with directions suggesting to make "A good turn for the blind", 10" h x 10" w x 7" deep. Uniform wear to paint. **$3,105**

Gottlieb, strength tester, insert a penny and squeeze the handles to measure your grip strength. Machine has two side and front decals, 8 1/2" w x 15" h x 10 1/4" deep. Missing rear door and possibly some interior parts; not working. **$230**

International Mutoscope Co., Silver Gloves boxing-theme arcade game from 1962 Seattle World's Fair. **$9,755**

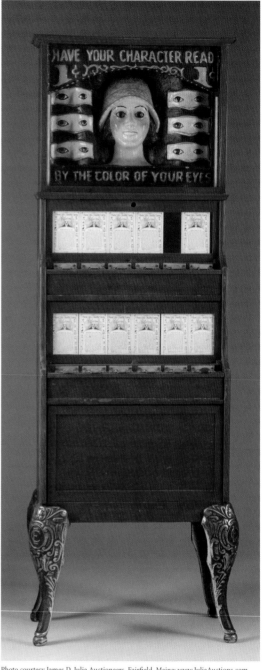

Fortuneteller, arcade machine, future predicted based on the color of one's eyes. Wood case rests on four elaborate cast-iron cabriole-type legs. Encased behind glass are a large papier-mâché woman's face and six masks that show different eye colors. Customer chooses their astrological sign, deposits a coin and receives their fortune in the form of a small card, 72" h x 23" w x 14" deep. Older restoration to wood case with some possible replacements to wooden parts. Mechanism appears to be professionally restored. **$4,600**

Digger machine, Esco (Exhibit Supply Co.), Art Deco style, restored, slight use wear, works but cable needs to be adjusted, 71" h. **$9,350**

*Little Dream, gum machine,
penny drop, trade stimulator
with walnut case with glass front,
behind which is a series of pins.
Drop a penny in and it would fall
to any one of several baseball-
related outcomes (runs, outs, etc.).
Retains original directions card,
14" w x 18 1/2" h x 9 1/2" deep.
Lacking key, front door is locked.
Lacking marquee. Overall good to
very good condition with some old
chips.* **$230**

*Match vendors (two) by Advance
Machine Co., Chicago, with
cast-iron bases with ornate feet.
Insert penny and pull lever.
Matches fall to tray below. One
with original dome (cracked),
one without. Stacks with what
appear to be original cardboard
marquees, other with painted
lettering (paint is redone), 14" h
each. Some wear and corrosion
to cast iron. Lacking keys to
padlocks.* **$1,437 pair**

Photo courtesy James D. Julia Auctioneers, Fairfield, Maine; www.JuliaAuctions.com

Peanut vendor, Freeport Dragons, in untouched, as-found, original condition. Made by Goo Goo Gum Co. of Chicago. Retaining its original glass (both front and side viewing windows) with paper on front window detailing how to operate the machine. Decals on the right and left side depict an American eagle clutching the U.S. flag with a banner encompassing the eagle. A small sliver of wood from the right side of the base is missing. The front iron casting is in fair original paint, 17" h. Mechanism not fully tested. Dispensing cup is "frozen" in place. Padlock heavily rusted. One foot on front casting is present but detached. **$10,350**

Photo courtesy of Skinner, Inc.

"Penny-Pack" bandit, 1 cent operation, three cigarette packet reels, gum dispenser lacking button, arched Art Deco metal case, period paintwork, 11" h, **$265.**

"Pull the Tiger's Tail and Make Him Roar!", made by Exhibit Supply Co., 1928, wood and painted cast-iron. With original 5-cent coin slide and rope release, the "roar" was originally via an ah-oo-ga horn that was activated as the rope was pulled; the horn sat in the bottom, mounted inside, and flush to the side in a brass screened speaker grille; a replacement electric device has been rebuilt a few times; 64" h x 31" w x 20" deep. **$42,550**

Regina, upright 26" disc, elaborate two-part music box with turned columns and large front glass to view disc, with later quarter coin-op mechanism. Rests on detailed, carved base with pull-out door with disc storage in which 10 are stored, 74" h x 36" w x 16 1/4" deep. Replaced back panel, lacking crown molding and small strip of side molding. Uniform wear. Mechanics are good and intact except for broken spring. **$6,900**

"Shake Hands with Uncle Sam", strength tester, circa 1940s-50s by Mechanical Antiques & Amusement Co., reproduction of 1908 original, features cast-iron Uncle Sam

Postcard dispenser, French, cast iron, circa 1900-1910. One of two known, it depicts a young woman adorned in a sweeping gown, giving a postal card to Cupid himself to mail to her lover. Seated in a garden setting with flowers and vines, a glass window shows a card that is available for purchase. Mechanism is activated by dropping a coin in the slot and pulling lever next to Cupid. Card is then dispensed to holder under machine, 28" h (including marquee) x 13" w x 12" deep. Mechanism and castings appear to be intact. Paint is old, but not original. **$12,650**

bust figure with arm extended. Quarter coin mechanism. Squeeze hand and electrified apparatus reveals strength of contestant's personality. Cast marquee mounted to shoulders, all mounted to wooden base, 76" h. Allover repaint of casting and modern electric wiring. Various small chips and usual wear to paint on Sam's hand. **$2,415**

Stella, upright disc music box, with ample record storage below, egg-and-dart molding in cornice, shelf and base. Two turned and fluted columns on upper doors with pierced panels on the bottom and tops of doors. Gracefully

Photo courtesy of David Rago Auctions, Inc.

Slot machine, "Little Duke" fortune teller, sideways mechanism, minor wear, O.D. Jennings & Co., 1932, 20 1/2" x 8 3/4" x 13", **$2,000.**

Photo courtesy Morphy Auctions, Denver, Pa.; www.MorphyAuctions.com

Unicum Chocolate, dispenser, circa 1900, German, made by Gischol & Spenler, Berlin, all original paint. When coin is deposited, black man dances and rolls eyes side to side. Original key and coins, one of few known, overall 68" h. **$43,700**

Slot machine, Mills, 1938, 25 cents, Jewel Hightop, **$1,800.**

arched glass in the center of the two top doors. Large raised panel on the bottom center of the door. Coin operated but can be played manually by inserting a key in the side. Mahogany case has original finish, includes thirty-three 26" discs; 78" h x 36" w x 20 1/2" deep. Carved top gallery is apparently missing, evidenced by three mounting holes in top. Has original keys and crank. Mechanism appears unrestored. **$8,625**

Wurlitzer, 1015 jukebox, "bubbler" of WWII era with walnut case and colored lights that fade through a rainbow of colors. Has 24-record changer and 12" speaker. Volume adjusted by key in back. Front opens for change of records and removable back panel for servicing, 60" h x 32" w x 25" deep. Unrestored, lower back corner of right side needs to have veneer re-glued, various dings and scratches, finish is slightly flaking. **$4,715**

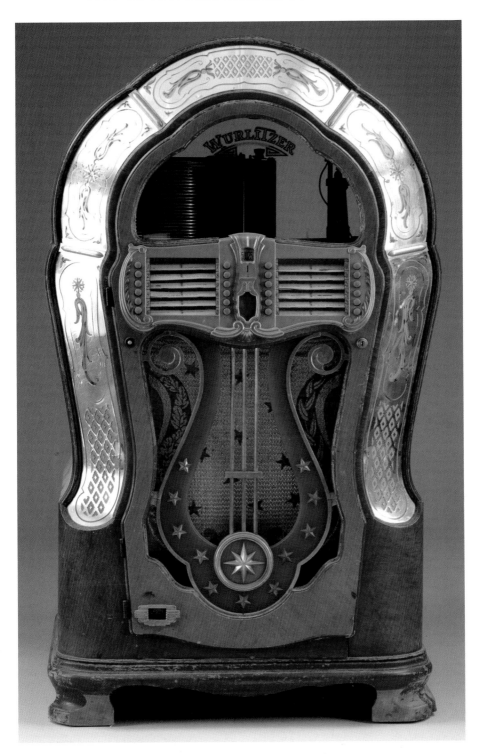

Photo courtesy James D. Julia Auctioneers, Fairfield, Maine; www.JuliaAuctions.com

Wurlitzer, Victory Model 1080 jukebox, walnut case with decorative mirrors on front and music lyre and stars on front, 24-selection changer, 58" h x 34" w x 25" deep. Appears complete except for back panel and one tube. Light corrosion, finish is generally good. Two small pieces and one large piece of molding missing from base. Accompanied by box of records. **$6,325**

COPPER

Copper objects, such as kettles, warming pans and measures, played an important part in the 19th-century household. Outdoors, the apple-butter kettle and still were the two principal copper items. Copper culinary objects were lined with a thin protective coating of tin to prevent poisoning. They were relined as needed.

Collectors place great emphasis on signed pieces, especially those by American craftsmen. Since copper objects were made abroad as well, it is hard to identify unsigned examples.

Many modern reproductions exist.

Bookends, hammered copper, possibly by Potters Studio, inset large Grueby scarab paperweights, matte brown glaze, original dark patina, scarabs marked, 5 1/2" x 6". .... **$2,500 pair**

Breadbox, chamfered oblong rectangular form, hinged cover, paneled domical form, brass finial rising from lozenge-shaped plaque over brass ring handles, brass bottom, Neoclassical, possibly Dutch, circa 1800, 12" l x 7 1/2" w x 11" h. **$165**

Carpenter's pot, globular, dovetailed body, raised on three plain strapwork iron legs, conforming handle, 11" l x 8" h. **$70**

Censer, lobed, carved and pierced lid set with white jade, China, 19th century, 13" d. **$1,300**

Charger, hand hammered, embossed high relief of owl on branch, naturally forming patina, Liberty paper label, 29 1/2" d. **$3,110**

Desk set, hammered blotter, letter holder, bookends, stamp box, each with bone-carved cabochon, branch-and-berry motif, Potter Studio, fine original patina, die-stamp mark. .... **$750 set**

Fish poacher, covered, oval, rolled rim, iron swing ball handle, 19th century, 20 1/2" l. **$350**

Inglenook hood, hammered, embossed Glasgow roses, English, small tear at bottom, 30" w, 8" d, 34 1/2" h. **$1,610**

Panel, repoussè of Bodhisattva seated on lotus seat, high relief figure, chased detail, traces of red pigment and gilding, Southeast Asia, slight bends, 18th century, 6 3/8" h x 2 7/8" w. **$500**

Pot, covered, twin handles, oval, raised on four strapwork legs, fitted with tubular end handles, shallow domed cover stamped with shield design, center stationary handle, English, 19th century, 19 1/2" l, 12" w, 16" h. **$215**

Screen, Arts & Crafts, ruffled edges, repoussè design of oak tree, acorns, sun behind it, iron supports with copper coils wrapped around on front, 24" w x 38 1/4" h. **$495**

Teakettle, gooseneck, dovetailed construction, swivel handle, brass finial, stamped "W. Wolfe," 12" h. **$3,520**

Tray, Stickley Brothers, hammered copper, lobed rim embossed with dots, stamped "36", no patina, 13 1/2" d. **$800**

Umbrella stand, hand hammered, flared rim, cylindrical body, two-strapwork loop handles, repoussè medallion, riveted flared foot, circa 1910, 25" h. **$650**

Vase

Hammered, ovoid, Dirk Van Erp, fine original mottled patina, D'Arcy Gaw box mark, small shallow dent on rim, 5 1/2" d x 7" h. **$8,100**

Roycroft, hammered, four-sided, two rows of pierced squares below rim, minor cleaning, orb and cross mark. **$7,200**

Vessel, hammered, ovoid, closed-in rim, original dark patina, Dirk Van Erp closed box mark, 4" d, 3 1/4" h. **$2,300**

Wall sconce, hammered, flame head, riveted Arts & Crafts details, attributed to Dirk Van Erp, cleaned patina, 4 1/2" w x 11" h **$425**

Water urn, copper body, interior with capped warming tube, applied brass ram's head handles, urn finial, brass spout, square base with four ball feet, unmarked, repairs to lid, 14" h. **$125**

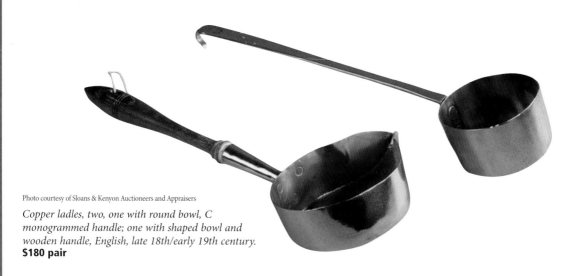

Photo courtesy of Sloans & Kenyon Auctioneers and Appraisers

Copper ladles, two, one with round bowl, C monogrammed handle; one with shaped bowl and wooden handle, English, late 18th/early 19th century.
$180 pair

Copper charger, hammered, Arts & Crafts, Onodaga Metal Shops, embossed with leaves and pods, stamped "OMS 100," cleaned patina, 20" d. **$1,400**

Copper candy kettle, iron handles, interior worn, 18 1/2" d. **$150**

Copper coal bucket, hammered, Arts & Crafts, Dirk Van Erp, riveted brass bands, flame-shaped brass finial, original dark patina, stamped open box mark, normal wear around rim, 10" d, 17" h. **$4,600.**

Copper kettle, gooseneck spout, signed "G. Tryon," Philadelphia, 19th century, 11 1/2". **$440**

Photo courtesy of Green Valley Auctions

Copper, coffeepot, conical form, hinged lid, applied handle, side spout, American, mid-19th century, 10″ h, 4 1/4″ d rim. **$88**

Copper vessel, hammered, Dirk Van Erp, flaring rim, original patina, open box mark with remnant of D'Arcy Gaw, 3″ x 6″. **$600**

Photo courtesy of David Rago Auctions, Inc.

Copper basket, hammered, Dirk Van Erp, pierced and riveted handle, some cleaning, open box mark, 7 1/2" x 11 1/2". **$660**

Photo courtesy of David Rago Auctions Inc.

Copper humidor, hammered, riveted base, cast leaf-shaped finial, cedar-lined, new patina, Gustav Stickley, stamped Als-ik-kan, 4 1/2" x 7" x 5". **$2,280**

DOORSTOPS

Decorative cast-iron doorstops date from around the turn of the 19th century, and have attracted collectors with their myriad depections of flowers, people and animals. Beware of modern reproductions that simulate aged and worn paint.

Accordion Player, cast iron, rare example of black gentleman musician wearing orange and red suit; stands on brown base, pristine, 6 3/4" h. **$977**

Ann Hathaway Cottage, Hubley, two-piece cast iron, cottage with a multitude of blooming flowers in foreground, near mint, 6 1/2" x 8 3/8". **$1,380**

Amish Woman, cast iron, full-figured Amish woman standing on base holding wicker basket, pristine, 8 1/4" x 4". $258

Bathing Beauties, Hubley, cast iron, signed "FISH," Art Deco design featuring two bathers sharing a parasol, excellent, 10 7/8" x 5". $345

Bellhop, H.L. Judd Co. Inc., cast iron, uniformed bellhop at attention on carpeted station, very good/excellent, 4 5/8" x 8 7/8". $373

Bloodhound, marked "SPENCER" on reverse, cast iron, wedge back, Art Deco style elongated figure of painted in green, excellent, 15" h. $287

Boston Terrier, cast iron, realistic depiction, facing left, hard to find, excellent, 7" x 6". $431

Bridesmaid Holding Flowers, cast iron, young girl in formal dress with bouquet in hand, excellent/pristine, 8 1/4" h. $373

Cairn Terrier, Bradley & Hubbard, cast iron, seated dog with open mouth in playful pose, pristine, 6" x 8 7/8".
.... $143

Cape Cod, Hubley, cast iron, ocean-side home with colorful climbing flowers, pristine, 5 1/2" x 7 3/4". $230

Castle on the Hill, cast iron, fairytale castle sits high atop a hill with painted foliage and winding pathway, pristine, 5 1/4" x 8". $546

Black Man on Cotton Bale, bale is cast iron, figure is pot metal, figure is preparing to strike a match, excellent, 6 7/8" x 6 7/8". **$1,380**

Cat Scratch Girl, H.L. Judd Co. Inc., highly detailed portrayal of little girl examining recent scratch from nearby pet, signed A. Diougy, excellent, 4" x 9". **$373**

Crossed Out, cast iron, depicts clown in turmoil, twisted whimsically amidst strewn books and pamphlets, "CROSSED OUT" embossed on base, originally meant to commemorate the N.Y. Times crossword puzzle phenomenon, near mint/pristine, 7 1/8" h. **$4,025**

Cat Licking Paw, Waverly Studios, 1926, cast iron, hard-to-find example of seated cat cleaning its paw, excellent, 4" x 7 5/8". **$460**

Colonial Man With Flowers, cast iron, portrays stumpy caricature of man with giant bouquets of flowers in each hand, pristine, 5" x 9". **$488**

Colonial Woman, Littco Products, cast iron, elegantly dressed lady in green dress with cream bustle and matching flowered bonnet; tip of shoe appears from beneath gown, very good, 10 1/4" x 5 3/4". **$258**

Cottage in the Woods, cast iron, with smoke billowing from chimney; surrounded by trees, flowers and a small path, excellent/pristine, 7 1/4" x 8 1/4". **$345**

Covered Bridge, cast iron, dark-red covered bridge with running water beneath, very good, 8 1/4" x 4 3/4". **$431**

Ducks, Hubley, cast iron, in nature setting, excellent, 8 1/2" h. **$316**

Elephant, Hubley, cast iron, full figure of gray elephant with raised trunk exposing white tusks, heavily cast, near mint, 8" x 11". **$345**

Fireside Cat, Hubley, cast iron, realistic appearing, full figured piece with embossed bell on pink painted collar, pristine, 5 5/8" x 10 3/4". **$172**

Floral Medallion, Bradley & Hubbard, cast iron, embossed floral decor inside "framed" medallion with embellished handle at top, excellent, 3 1/2" x 7 1/2". **$57**

Flapper Girl, cast iron, marked "8", fashionably attired flapper in layered dress, umbrella in hand, detailed casting, very good/excellent, 9 1/2" h. **$690**

Flower Basket, Hubley, cast iron, marked "471", tulips and starflowers in basket with pink base, near mint, 5 1/2" x 9 3/4". **$316**

Jungle Boy, cast iron, boy in leopard skin pelt, on one knee with arm out stretched, pristine, 12" h. **$1,092**

Flower Basket, Hubley, cast iron, arrangement of morning glories, zinnias and more in crosshatch wicker basket, embossed flower on base; fine casting and strong colors, pristine, 7" x 9 1/2". **$316**

Flower Basket, Hubley, cast iron, colorful, marked "182"; mixed bouquet of flowers rests in black & cream striped basket with black base, pristine, 8 1/4" h. **$230**

Flower Basket, Hubley, cast iron, marked "471", tulips & starflowers in basket with pink base, near mint, 5 1/2" x 9 3/4". **$316**

Flower Basket, cast iron, with thick base depicting wicker basket with woven handle and blue bow holding mixed bouquet, excellent/pristine, 6" x 8 1/2". **$230**

Flowerpot, Hubley, cast iron, marked "288", modern styling, heavy casting for size, excellent, 5 1/4" x 9". **$92**

Fruit Basket, Judd Co., cast iron, wicker basket with embossed pink bow and arrangement of fruit spilling over, heavy green painted base, near mint/pristine, 9 3/4" x 6 1/4". **$316**

Gamecock, Hubley, cast iron, rare full-figured example of strutting bird, painted in vibrant red with fanned out tail, excellent, 5 3/8" x 7". **$632**

German Shepherd Dog, cast iron, wedge style; lifelike casting, reverse marked with triangle logo, pristine, 14 3/8" x 12 3/8". **$402**

Grapes, Albany Foundry, cast iron, elaborate with fruit and foliage painted in vibrant colors, near mint, 6 1/2" x 7 7/8". **$460**

Heron, cast iron, detailed feathers, excellent, 7 1/2" x 5 1/8". **$345**

King Tut, cast iron, rare, elaborately cast and colorfully painted, pristine, 10 5/8" h. **$2,300**

Photo courtesy Bertoia Auctions, Vineland, N.J.; www.BertoiaAuctions.com

Little Red Riding Hood and the Wolf, cast iron, embossed "NUYDEA" and "LITTLE RED RIDING HOOD" on reverse, crisp overall casting details, pristine, 7 1/2" x 9 1/2". **$1,840**

Jonquils, Hubley, cast iron, colorfully painted depiction of jonquil blooms bending in the breeze, pristine, 7 1/2" x 8". **$230**

Lighthouse, cast iron, with keeper's house, depicted on landscaped yard with recessed shoreline, excellent, 6 1/4" x 8". **$287**

Little Red Riding Hood and the Wolf, Albany Foundry, cast iron, forward-facing example with ominous wolf peering from behind, near mint, 7 1/4" h. **$862**

Mad Hatter, cast iron, full-figured character stands with nose in air, sporting a top hat and red jacket, excellent/pristine, 2 7/8" x 6 5/8". **$172**

Mammy, Hubley, cast iron, with hands on hips; expressive facial features, wears blue dress and polka-dot head wrap. Minor touch-up, otherwise pristine, 8 3/4" h. **$345**

Nathanael Green House, cast iron, Colonial-era house embossed on back "NATHANAEL GREEN", old repaint, 4 3/4" x 7 7/8". **$460**
(His last name was actually spelled Greene (1742-1786). He was a major general of the Continental Army in the American Revolutionary War. When the war began, Greene was a militia private, the lowest rank possible. He emerged from the war with a reputation as George Washington's most gifted and dependable officer.)

Old Salt, cast iron, full-figure example depicting bearded fisherman, vibrant colors, pristine, 4 1/8" x 11". **$402**

Old Woman, Bradley & Hubbard, cast iron, woman walking in profile on Art Deco "carpeted" base; wearing a ruffled Victorian dress and shawl, she holds a basket of flowers and parasol, pristine, 11" x 7". **$1,380**

Oriental Boy, Hubley, "TOKO", cast iron, colorful, three-piece casting, boy seated on tufted pillow, near mint, 5 1/4" x 6". **$172**

Oriental Girl, cast iron, full-figured girl on base, hand painted in colorful attire, pristine, 7 3/4" h. **$316**

Parlor Maid, Hubley, cast iron, Art Deco design, features maid serving cocktails; signed "FISH" on base, very good/excellent, 3 1/2" x 9 1/2". **$258**

Penguin in Top Hat, Hubley, cast iron, Art Deco style depiction, dressed in tuxedo, standing in proud pose, excellent/pristine, 3 3/4" x 10". **$632**

Pheasant, Hubley, designed by Fred Everett, cast iron, finely detailed, hand-painted depiction in underbrush, near mint, 1 1/4" x 8 1/2". **$488**

Poppies, Hubley, cast iron, marked "440", vibrant colors, features red poppies in classic-style vase; black base, excellent/pristine, 10 5/8" x 7 1/8". **$172**

Quails, Hubley, cast iron, marked with copyright symbol and "Everett" fine painted details, near mint, 7 1/4" h. **$575**

Rabbit in Top Hat, Albany Foundry, cast iron, vivid overall coloring with blue top hat and coattails, excellent, 4 3/4" x 9 7/8". **$632**

Popeye, Hubley, cast iron, rare full-figured example of United Features Syndicate cartoon figure; vibrant colors overall, near mint, 9″ h. **$17,250**

Sitting Black Cat, marked, "Copyright 1927 A.M. Greenblatt Studios #20," wedge-back design, animated side-glancing expression on face, excellent, 9″ h. **$402**

Rose Vase, Hubley, cast iron, one-sided piece depicts pastel roses in pierced handle, urn-shaped vase, pristine, 6 1/8" x 10 3/8". **$402**

Senorita, Hubley, cast iron, young woman in dress and shawl with fan in hand, near mint, 9" x 5". **$1,495**

Sitting Cat, cast iron, unusual flat-back example, seated facing forward with mischievous painted eyes and finely detailed fur on chest, pristine, 6 3/8" h. **$316**

Terrier, Creations Co., cast iron, attentive pose, painted in white with tan markings and brown collar, excellent, 6 3/4" x 7". **$86**

Terrier, Hubley, cast iron, dog seated on green base, excellent/pristine, 6" x 7 1/8". **$287**

Twin Cats, Hubley, Drayton design, cast iron, marked "73" on reverse side; colorful depiction of two side-glancing, arm-in-arm felines, one in a dress and the other in a jumper, excellent, 5 1/4" x 7". **$546**

Wine Merchant, cast iron, full-figured merchant grasping multiple wine bottles in each hand; white wines in right hand, red wines in left, pristine, 9 3/4" x 7". **$1,265**

Zinnias, Hubley, cast iron, in various colors, hand-painted pot done in blue & cream color scheme with embossed design, pristine, 9 3/4" x 8 1/2". **$230**

Zinnias (Basket of), cast iron, depicting pastel-colored flowers overflowing from basket, crisp casting details, pristine, 10 1/2" x 8". **$287**

Rabbit, Bradley & Hubbard, cast iron; one of the largest animal doorstops, jackrabbit on hind legs, embossed base, excellent/pristine, 8″ x 15″. **$4,025**

FIREARMS

Laws regarding the sale of firearms, especially modern-era weapons, continue to evolve. Be sure to buy and sell firearms through auction houses and dealers properly licensed to transact business in this highly regulated area.

Photo courtesy Greg Martin Auctions, San Francisco; www.GregMartinAuctions.com

Gatling Gun, U.S. Model 1883, with U.S. inspector markings "D.F.C." for David F. Clark on field carriage, with accompanying limber marked "F. Bannerman, New York". **$172,500**

Machine gun, A.O.S.A American Historical Foundation, semiautomatic, "50th Anniversary of the Thompson Machine Gun," serial no. 26982, 19" barrel including the muzzle break, complete with 50-round drum magazine, checked walnut stocks. New and unfired. **$862**

Pistol, A.A. Arms Inc. Model AP9, 9mm, 5" barrel, military-type sights and black composition grip. **$172**

Pistol, Accu-Tek Model AT-380, semiautomatic, serial no. 014558, .380 caliber, 2 3/4" barrel, satin-gray finish with polished sides, black plastic grips. **$86**

Pistol, Advantage Arms Model 422, breech loading, serial no. 2107, .22 caliber, 2 3/8" four-barrel cluster. **$143**

Pistol, Advantage Arms Model 422 Pocket, serial no. 3024, .22 magnum caliber, 2 1/2" four-barrel tip-over breech **$230**

Pistol (air), Benjamin Franklin, no visible serial number, .22 caliber. 8 5/8" barrel. Primarily brass, silver-plated, with unfinished gray cast-metal frame. **$115**

Pistol, American Arms Co. P98, semiautomatic, serial no. 006246, .22 caliber, 5" barrel. Contained in factory box with literature. **$230**

Pistol, AMT "Back Up" Model, semiautomatic, serial no. A76153, 9mm, 2 3/4" barrel. Sold together with factory box, manual and extra magazine **$258.75**

Pistol, AMT "Lightning," semiautomatic, serial no. G12287, .22 caliber, 5" barrel with target sights. Contained in original factory box with magazine. **$201**

Pistol, AMT Automag II, semiautomatic, serial no. H41859, .22 rim-fire magnum, 4 3/4" barrel. **$431.25**

Pistol, Argentinian Bersa Model 83, semiautomatic, serial no. 262301, .380 caliber, 3 5/8" barrel. Contained in original factory box with factory literature. **$172**

Pistol, Auto Ordnance 1927 A-5 Thompson, semiautomatic, serial no. 392, .45 caliber, 13 1/2" ventilated barrel and top-bolt toggle. **$920**

Pistol, Beretta Model 92F, semiautomatic, serial no. BER045077Z, 9mm, 5.9" barrel. Black Bruniton finish. **$345**

Pistol (pocket), Beretta Model 950 "Minx," semiautomatic, with extra magazine, serial no. 71503CC, .22 caliber, 2 1/2" barrel. **$230**

Pistol, Bersa Model 23, semiautomatic, serial no. 183858, .22 long-rifle caliber, 3 1/2" barrel. Frost nickel-plated finish. Made in Argentina. **$201**

Pistol, Bersa Model 85, semiautomatic, serial no. 167673, .380 caliber, 3 1/2" barrel. Made in Argentina. **$230**

Pistol (derringer), American Derringer Corp. Model M-1, serial no. 120630, .45 caliber, 3 1/8" over-and-under barrels, stainless steel. **$143**

Pistol (derringer), BJT Model DA, serial no. 006617, .38 caliber, 3" barrels. **$287**

Pistol (pocket), Belgian Bayard, semiautomatic, serial no. 76244, .380 caliber, 3 1/2" barrel. **$201**

Pistol, "protector," semiautomatic, serial no. 31330, 6.35mm, 2" barrel. **$69**

Photo courtesy Greg Martin Auctions, San Francisco; www.GregMartinAuctions.com

Pistol (revolver), J.H. Dance & Brothers, Confederate Dragoon, with history of original ownership by Private Mile C. Bell, Co. F, 23rd Brigade of Texas Cavalry. **$57,500**

Pistol, Navy, Volcanic, lever action. **$31,625**

*Pistol
(revolver), Colt
Second Model
Dragoon with
accessories,
U.S. martially
marked, cased.*
$97,750

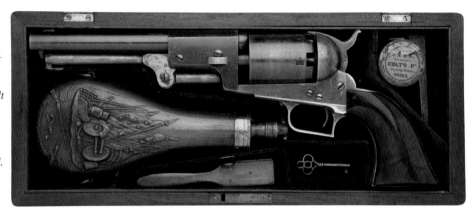

*Pistol (revolver), Colt Texas Paterson No. 5, holster model,
rare 9".* **$97,750**

*Pistol (revolver), Colt Texas Paterson, U.S. martially marked,
accompanied by leather-flap holster.* **$69,000**

Pistol (revolver), Beretta Model 950B "Minx" Long Barrel, serial no. H02129, .22 caliber, 3 1/2" barrel. **$287**

Pistol (revolver), Charter Arms "Off Duty" Double Action, serial no. 1018679, .38 special caliber, 1 7/8" barrel with florescent front sight. **$115**

Pistol (revolver), Dolne, Apache folding knife with steel knuckles, serial no. 1641, 6.35mm pin-fire caliber, six-shot blued fluted cylinder, case-hardened frame and steel knuckle, with double-action folding trigger and spurless hammer; engine-turned finish to dagger. Light patina on dagger blade. **$4,887**

Pistol (revolver), L. Dolne, Apache "knuckleduster" with dagger, serial no. 5770, 7mm, six-shot cylinder with long flutes, folding steel knuckleduster grips. Frame marked: L. Dolne Invor. Folding trigger and dagger blade. (Named for the infamous "Apache" Parisian gang known to use them.) Metal with gray age patina. **$2,875**

Pistol, (revolver, composite), Colt Bisley, single action, serial no. 292547, .45 caliber, 3 3/4" barrel, marked, "COLT'S PT F.A. CO. HARTFORD CT. U.S.A." **$488**

Pistol (revolver), Colt "Viper" Double Action, serial no. 61894R, .38 caliber, 4" barrel. Contained in original factory box with factory literature. **$431**

Pistol (revolver), Colt Detective Special Double Action, serial no. 540662, .38 caliber, 2" barrel. Contained in original brown factory box with cleaning rod and instruction sheet. **$862**

Pistol (revolver), Colt Diamondback 22 Magnum Double Action, serial no. D90630, .22 long-rifle caliber, 4" barrel with vented rib and target sights. **$1,725**

Pistol (revolver), Colt Lawman Mark V Trooper Double Action, serial no. 21521V, .357 magnum caliber, 2" barrel. Contained in original factory box with literature. **$632**

Pistol, Colt Mark IV/Series 70 Gold Cup National Match, semiautomatic, with special customizing, serial no. 19553N70, .45 caliber, 5" barrel with target sights. Contained with extra slide spring in original factory box. **$1,092**

Pistol, Colt Mark IV Series 80 "El Jefe," semiautomatic, serial no. EL JEFE 376, .38 Super caliber, 5" barrel. Nickel-plated finish. Pearl grips. **$920**

Pistol, Colt Mark IV/Series 70 Government Model 1911, semiautomatic, serial no. 70L01267, 9mm. Contained in original factory box. **$862**

Pistol (revolver), Colt Model Python Double Action, serial no. VO5958, .357 magnum caliber, 2 1/2" barrel with elevated rib and target sights. Contained in factory carton with factory literature. **$1,150**

Pistol, Colt M1911A1, "World War II American Legion" commemorative, semiautomatic, serial no. FR11615, .45 ACP caliber, 5" barrel, cased, left side of slide marked, "1941 THE AMERICAN LEGION WORLD WAR II VICTORY M1911A1 'FOR GOD AND COUNTRY' 1945." **$805**

Pistol, Colt Mark IV, Series 80, Gold Cup National Match commemorative, semiautomatic, serial no. FN06278E, .45 ACP caliber, 5" barrel, cased, slide marked, "GOLD CUP SERIES' 80 COLT MARK IV GOLD CUP NATIONAL MATCH LIMITED EDITION." **$747**

Pistols (revolvers, pair), Colt Baby Dragoon transition, book-cased with consecutive serial numbers and accessories. **$28,750 pair**

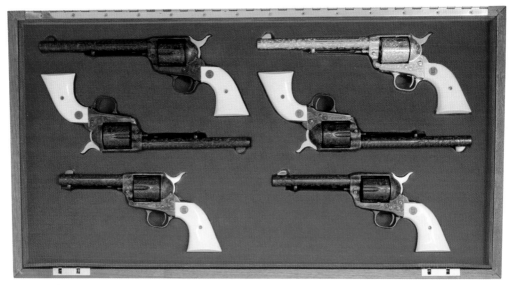

Photo courtesy Greg Martin Auctions, San Francisco; www.GregMartinAuctions.com

Pistol (revolver) ensemble, Colt Custom Shop, single-action, each is Type D, factory engraved, individually designed and sold as a factory-cased group, with Colt factory letters for the six revolvers. **$23,000 set**

Photo courtesy Greg Martin Auctions, San Francisco; www.GregMartinAuctions.com

Pistol (revolver), Smith & Wesson, hand ejector, engraved and inscribed to Sheriff Buck Garrett (1871-1929), with documentation, photographs and memorabilia. **$25,875**

Pistol, Hungarian Model 37M, semiautomatic, serial no. 155056, 9mm Kurz caliber, 4" barrel. **$230**

Pistol, Ruger, standard semiautomatic, with rare serial no. 444444, .22 long-rifle caliber, 6" barrel, blued, standard markings. **$690**

Pistol (revolver), Smith & Wesson Model 25-2 Double Action, serial no. N301067, .45 long Colt caliber, 6 1/2" barrel with target sights. Case-hardened hammer and trigger. Contained in original shipping carton. **$632**

Pistol (revolver), Smith & Wesson Model 10 (.38 military and police), serial no. C 60207 on butt, .38 S&W Special, 2"

barrel, customary trademark and maker/address markings on right side of frame, circa 1951. .... **$345**

Pistol (revolver), Smith & Wesson Model 640 Centennial, hammerless, double action, serial no. BFV8288, .38 Smith & Wesson caliber, 2" barrel, varnished Smith & Wesson medallion, boxed. **$345**

Pistol, Sturm-Ruger KP-85 Mark IIC, semiautomatic, serial no. 303-00001, 9mm x 19, 4 3/8" barrel, satin stainless steel finished slide. Round hammer spur. Case contained in original brown cardboard shipping box.

.... **$345**

Photo courtesy Greg Martin Auctions, San Francisco; www.GregMartinAuctions.com

Pistol, Walther MP hammerless model, semiautomatic in .45 ACP caliber, Pre-World War II Prototype, circa 1935-36. **$126,500**

Pistol, "Titan," semiautomatic, by F.I.E. Corp., serial no. 156904, .25 caliber, 2 3/8" barrel, chrome-finished barrel, slide, hammer and trigger, gray-alloy metal frame. **$86**

Pistol, Walther ac43 Code P-38, semiautomatic, serial no. 7749, 9mm, 5" barrel, Waffenamt markings. **$345**

Pistol, Carl Walther engraved P 38, semiautomatic, serial no. 351006. 9mm caliber, 5" barrel. Oak leaf and border engraved, with front of grip strap with crosshatched pattern. Silver-plated finish. Appears to be unfired. **$1,955**

Pistol, Carl Walther P 38/II, semiautomatic, with extra magazine, serial no. 322122, 9mm caliber, 5" barrel. Brown box with manual, extra magazine and cleaning rod. Made at Ulm factory for Interarms, Alexandria, Va. **$460**

Rifle, Adler-Jager Model AT74, with telescopic sight, serial no. 101029, .22 caliber, 21" barrel including flash hider, military-type sights. **$258**

Rifle, (air), .20 Caliber Beeman Model R1, with Leupold telescopic sight, serial no. 1517378, 20 1/2" barrel. **$517**

Rifle, (air), Beeman Model HW 50S, serial no. 715999, Marked "Kal. 4.5," 18 3/8" round barrel. Wear, patina (more pronounced at muzzle), storage marks. **$86**

Rifle, (air), .177 Daisy/Feinwerkbau 300, serial no. 189917, 19" barrel, side-lever cocking, hooded front sight, adjustable aperture sight. **$488**

Rifle, (air, target), BAIKAL (Russia) Model 1ZH-61, serial no. 9817677, 4.5mm caliber, 17 1/2" round barrel. **$57**

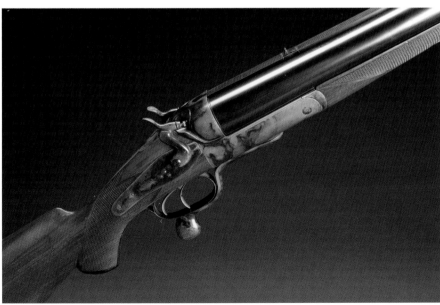

Photo courtesy Greg Martin Auctions, San Francisco; www.GregMartinAuctions.com

Rifle (double), massive four-bore, British, black powder. **$86,250**

Photo courtesy Greg Martin Auctions, San Francisco; www.GregMartinAuctions.com

Rifle, Henry, repeating, with walnut stock. **$28,750**

Photo courtesy Greg Martin Auctions, San Francisco; www.GregMartinAuctions.com

Rifle (cut down), Winchester Model 1873, belonging to Pat Garrett, "PAT" carved on right side of stock, with detailed provenance, game-skin repair to butt stock. **$34,500**

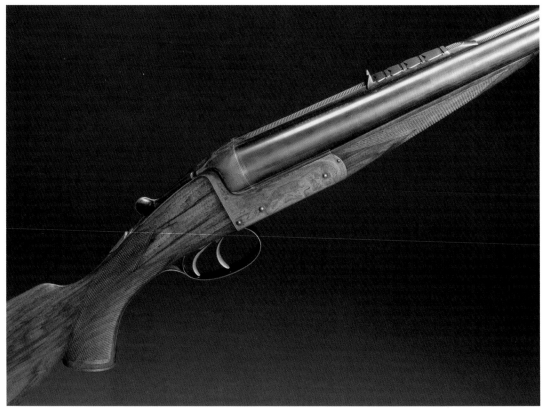

Photo courtesy Greg Martin Auctions, San Francisco; www.GregMartinAuctions.com

Rifle, W.J. Jeffery, double barrel, cased .475 Number 2 Nitro, box-lock ejector. **$25,875**

Photo courtesy Greg Martin Auctions, San Francisco; www.GregMartinAuctions.com

Rifle (sporting), Winchester Model 1873, lever action, deluxe gold and silver inlaid and engraved, with custom sights and relief-carved and checkered walnut stocks. **$54,625**

Rifle, Armalite AR-10T, semiautomatic, serial no. US50040, 308 caliber, 24" round barrel with fiberglass free-floating armguard tube, together with four 20-round and four 10-round magazines and canvas pouch. .... **$920 all**

Rifle, American Historical Foundation Commemorative, Winchester M-1 Garand, "1 of 100," serial no. 2355102, barrel date 5-44, this is the showcase edition, 30/06 caliber, 24" barrel, military front and rear sights. **$1,035**

Rifle, Armi Jaeger Model AP80, serial no. 019408, .22 long-rifle caliber, 17" barrel. **$230**

Rifle, Armscorp of America M14, semiautomatic, serial no. A004741, 7.62mm, 22" barrel, adjustable military sights. Frame marked Armscorp of America, Baltimore, MD. Rifle is unassembled. **$920**

Rifle, .303 British No. 3 (Pattern 1914), bolt action, .30 caliber, serial no. ERA7211, 26" barrel, standard markings, and British proof marks, War Department broad arrow, with olive-drab canvas sling. **$488**

Rifle, Birmingham Small Arms, Martini action, single shot, serial no.16577, 25" barrel, marked "Commonwealth of Australia." **$402**

Rifle, Camo U.S. Springfield Model M1-A, semiautomatic, with telescopic sight, serial no. 147618, .30-06 caliber, 24" barrel with recoil compensator. Box with scuffs and wear. **$1,265**

Rifle (carbine), A.O.S.A. American Historical Foundation U.S. Marine Corps Commemorative, serial no. 27515, 45ACP caliber, 19" barrel including muzzle brake, walnut stock complete with sling and sling swivels. **$805**

Rifle (carbine), Winchester Model 94, lever action, serial no. 1836624, .32 Winchester Special, 19 1/2" barrel. **$402**

Rifle, German, Mauser-action magazine, .30 caliber, unmarked, serial no. 3225, 24" replacement barrel, spear front sight on a matted ramped base, action with Redfield aperture sight, wood shows a few nicks and handling marks. **$575**

Rifle, Mossberg Targo 42TR, bolt action, serial no. M336, 20" barrel. **$230**

Rifle, percussion, with octagonal barrel, including ramrod, tiger maple stock, brass mounts, 51 3/4" l (overall); crazed surface on one side. **$632**

Rifle, Siamese Model 1903 Mauser, bolt action, military, produced in Japan, serial no. not visible. Appears to be 7.92 x 57mm caliber, 29" barrel, Thai Chakra stamped on top of breech. **$316**

Rifle, .22 Winchester Magazine RF 61, slide action, serial no. 326996, 24" barrel, standard iron sights. **$1,495**

Rifle, Winchester pre-64 Model 70 National Match, bolt action, serial no. 159460, .30/06, 24" standard-weight barrel, marked Winchester. **$1,725**

Rifle, (sporting), Barrett Model 99, bolt action, high power, single shot, serial no. 0262, .50 caliber, approximately 32" heavyweight barrel, with folding bipod; matte-blue finish, with olive-drab breech. Fitted with IOR 10 x 56 scope for extremely long distance shooting. **$3,162**

Rifle, (sporting), "1 of 1000" Winchester Model 70 Featherweight, gold inlaid and engraved, serial no. UG 485; .270 Winchester caliber, 22" barrel; Big Horn sheep head panel scene engraved on floor plate; two gold-inlaid barrel bands at muzzle; "1 of 1000" flush gold-inlaid on right side of barrel at breech. **$1,840**

Rife, unmarked .30 caliber custom Springfield 1903, bolt-action magazine, no visible serial number, possibly .30-06, 24" barrel. **$287**

Shotgun, .410 Browning Citori Lightning Grade 6, over and under, serial no. 240477PN983, 26" barrels with ventilated rib, marked Made in Japan, boxed. **$2,875**

Shotgun, Browning A-5, light semiautomatic, 12 gauge, serial no. 73G 32290, 27 1/2" barrel with ventilated rib. **$862**

Shotgun, .410 Iver Johnson Skeeter, double barrel, hammerless, serial no. 25148, 28" barrels, automatic safety. **$3,162**

Shotgun, Frank Malin .410 side lock, "The Royal Presentation," gold inlaid, engraved and cased, commemorating the wedding of Prince Charles and Lady Diana Spencer, serial no. 81003, .410 gauge, 27 3/4" side-by-side barrels, British scroll-engraved, solid rib gold inlaid: "F.E. Malin, London, Ont." **$6,900**

Shotgun, Remington Model 11-48, slide action, serial no. 4033682, 28 gauge, 25" ventilated-rib barrel. **$460**

Shotgun, Remington Model 1100 LW, slide action, serial no. L335956H, 24 1/2" barrel. **$402**

Shotgun, Ruger Red Label, 20 gauge, over and under, serial no. 400-12054, 26" barrels with ventilated rib. **$1,495**

Shotgun, L.C. Smith Grade 3, double barrel, hammerless, by Hunter Arms Co., serial no. 202801, 12 gauge, 30" blued barrels with textured rib. **$1,840**

Shotgun, Winchester, 12 gauge, slide action, serial no. 1918194, 28" barrel, wood shows marks and three 1" long scratches on right side. **$258**

Shotgun, Winchester Model 12, pump action, skeet, serial no. 1586740, 20 gauge, 24" ventilated-rib barrel with Cutts compensator. **$546**

Shotgun, Winchester Model 97, slide action, serial no. 380017, 12 gauge, 28" barrel. **$517**

FIREPLACE EQUIPMENT

In colder climates throughout the world, the fireplace or hearth has traditionally been a central feature of the house-hold. The sensation of direct heat, and the mesmerizing spectacle of a wood fire, make it a favored refuge at all times of the year. *Also see Modernism.*

Photo courtesy of Treadway Toomey Galleries, Cincinnati; www.treadwaygallery.com

Andirons, Arts & Crafts style, large hammered form with spherical top over a column base with applied details, original black finish, 13" w x 26" d x 24" h, very good condition. **$700**

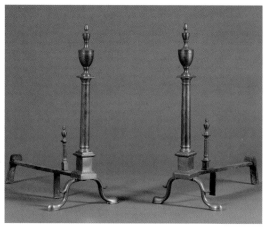

Photo courtesy Skinner Inc., Boston; www.SkinnerInc.com

Andirons, brass, urn-top, Philadelphia, last quarter 18th century, acorn finials on urn tops with punch-scallop borders, columnar shaft, on square plinths, cabriole legs and slipper feet, with conforming log stops, 23 5/8" h, 10 1/2" w, 20 1/2" deep. **$1,303**

Photo courtesy Skinner Inc., Boston; www.SkinnerInc.com

Andirons, cast iron, brownie figural, American, late 19th/early 20th century, male and female figures, each modeled standing with legs spread and hands on hips, log supports may not be original, 15 3/4" h, 8" w, 16 1/2" deep. **$355**

Photo courtesy Skinner Inc., Boston; www.SkinnerInc.com

Andirons, Chippendale brass and iron, New York, third quarter 18th century, with flame finials on faceted ball, (lacking swirled bulbous columns), over square plinths, cabriole legs and ball-and-claw feet, (losses, seam separations), 18" h, 15" w, 19 1/4" deep. **$355**

Andirons, beehive form, brass, turned finials above a baluster-turned standard, raised on arched legs, on ball feet, 18 1/2" h, 17" deep. Normal wear. **$150**

Andirons, duck form, bronze, unmarked, 20th century, shoulder bust ducks are made in two part separating above shoulders. This allows for a turning of the head, heavy iron dogs attached, 11 1/2" h x 20" l. **$978**

Andirons, Gustav Stickley, with swag chain, rings and ball tops. Circular Craftsman stamp, one firedog stamped Sweden. 20 1/2" h x 14" w x 24" d. **$9,600**

Andirons, Victorian, brass, with elaborate decoration, faceted ovoid tops and matching log stoppers, base with overlapping leaves and paw feet, 19th century, 24" h.
.... **$960**

Photo courtesy Skinner Inc., Boston; www.SkinnerInc.com

Andirons, polychrome painted cast iron, Indian figures, American, late 19th/ early 20th century, minor rust, 13" h, 7 1/4" w, 12 3/4" deep. **$2,607**

Andirons, wrought iron, knife-blade, brass urn-form finials, small in-curved feet, 15 3/4" h. **$143**

Screen, carved mahogany, needlepoint and petit point insert, two arched trestles with leaf carving, 37 1/2" h, 26 1/4" w.
.... **$143**

Screen, pole, George III, mahogany, fluted bun-form finial on round shaft (with fluted knops) supported by four cabriole legs with acanthus-carved knees, adjustable molded screen with ovolo corners, having beaded image of angel and child on light brown woven cloth background, 59" h overall, screen 19 1/2" h, 15" w. **$460**

Screens, pair, George III, mahogany; panel fitted with light brown pleated silk, two ring-turned horizontal stretchers, twin trestle base with four saber legs, bun feet, small folding shelf with two brass supports, circa 1820, 38" h, 17" w, 14 1/4" deep (at base). Repairs to bases of some stiles. .... **$977 pair**

Photo courtesy Skinner Inc., Boston;
www.SkinnerInc.com

Bellows, polychrome painted "North Wind" decorated, wood and leather, American, early 19th century, with indistinct impressed maker's mark, "WM DO-----MAKER," bellows torn but still works, 19" l. **$325**

Photo courtesy Old Town Auctions LLC, Boonsboro, Md.;
www.OldTownAuctions.com

Mantel, heavily carved, circa 1885, with heads of mythological beasts, flat top has some staining and scratches with an area of deep scratching, chip to nose of one creature and rear corner trim piece missing, some overall age wear, opening is 48" w, 39" h; overall 79 1/2" w, 16 5/8" deep, 48 1/2" h. **$4,400**

FISHING, HUNTING EQUIPMENT

Bird Decoys

Carved wooden decoys, used to lure waterfowl to the hunter, have become widely recognized as an indigenous American folk-art form. Many decoys are from 1880 to 1930, when commercial gunners commonly hunted and used rigs of several hundred decoys. Fine carvers also worked through the 1930s and 1940s. Individuals and commercial decoy makers also carved fish decoys.

The skill of the carver, rarity, type of bird, condition and age all affect the value.

Black-bellied plover by Obediah Verity. **$94,875**

Black duck by Jess Heisler. **$28,175**

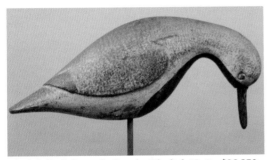

Black-bellied plover, feeding, by Obediah Verity. **$86,250**

Bluebill, "fat jaw," by Charles Perdew. **$15,525**

Black duck by John Blair Sr. **$97,750**

All photos courtesy Guyette & Schmidt Inc., St. Michaels, Md.; www.GuyetteandSchmidt.com

Bluebill hen by Wilfred Benham. **$1,610**

Brant duck by Joseph Lincoln. **$106,375**

Bufflehead drake by the Mason Decoy Factory. **$35,650**

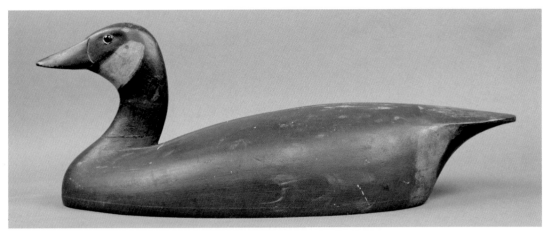

Canada goose by Tom Chambers. **$46,000**

Canvasback by the Ward Brothers. **$43,700**

Curlew by the Mason Decoy Factory. **$24,725**

Golden plover by William Bowman. **$46,000**

Green-wing teal by Charles Perdew. **$43,125**

Hooded merganser hen by Art Herron. **$1,725**

Hooded merganser from Ontario, Canada. **$86,250**

Mallard drake by Huck Caines. **$34,500**

Mallard drake by Elmer Crowell. **$61,525**

Mallards (pair) by Heck Winnington. **$8,913**

Merganser hen by Joseph Lincoln. **$83,375**

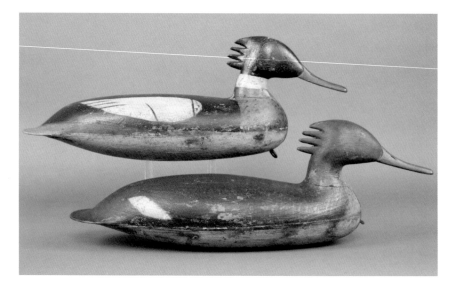

Mergansers (pair) by Harry V. Shourds. **$46,000**

Peep, running, by Obediah Verity.
$36,800

Pintail by Ivar Fernlund.
$126,000

Pintail hen by John English.
$225,000

*Redhead by
Harry V. Shourds.*
$28,175

*Redhead drake by
Mark Whipple.*
$11,500

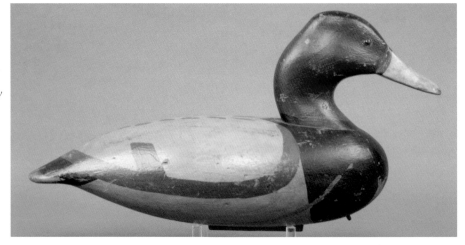

*Ruddy duck by
Ben Dye.* **$12,650**

Ruddy duck by Lee Dudley. **$269,000**

Sanderling by Daniel Lake Leeds. **$25,300**

Swan, 19th century, from Oregon. **$54,625**

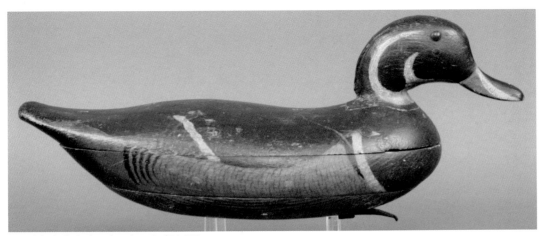

Wood duck drake by John Blair, Sr. **$54,625**

FISHING EQUIPMENT

Lures and Fish Decoys

Chapman # 3 minnow propeller. **$240**

Creek Chub gar minnow. **$354**

Carl Christiansen whitefish decoy. **$280**

DAM Ever Ready "Punkinseed" minnow. **$240**

Creek Chub baby jigger. **$398**

Dicken's Weedless Wonder in box. **$287**

Froglegs Mechanical Fishing Lure in box. **$230**

Creek Chub Deluxe wagtail. **$673**

All photos courtesy Lang's Sporting Collectibles,
Waterville, N.Y.; www.LangsAuction.com

Heddon Crackleback # 100 minnow. **$172**

Heddon near-surface wiggler. **$360**

Hosmer Mechanical Froggie in box. **$13,437**

Manhattan top-water casting bait in box. **$306**

Paw Paw pike caster minnow. **$245**

Immell Bait Co. Chippewa minnow. **$918**

Oscar Peterson trout fish decoy. **$6,944**

Pflueger Crackleback Surprise minnow. **$316**

Lovelace breathing minnow. **$168**

Frank Mizra 9" fish decoy. **$1,163**

Pflueger Ketch-Em wooden minnow. **$776**

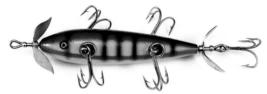

Pflueger Neverfail underwater minnow. **$316**

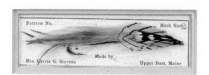

Carrie Stevens streamer fly. **$1,715**

Polly Rosborough flies (two). **$90 pair**

9" Bud Stewart sucker fish decoy. **$300**

Shakespeare Midget minnow. **$120**

Wilson fluted wobbler in box. **$252**

Helen Shaw Indian Bass Devil fly. **$300**

Winchester five-hook underwater minnow. **$460**

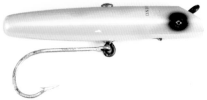

South Bend King-Oreno in box. **$460**

Lee Wulff dry fly. **$280**

Reels

Abel Super 11 fly reel. **$431**

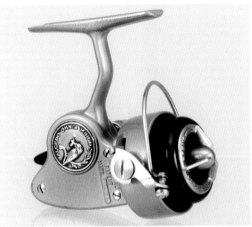

Alcedo Omnia Minor ultra-light reel. **$198**

Acme First Click trout reel. **$488**

Ambassadeur 2500C Deluxe reel. **$252**

Billinghurst birdcage fly reel in box (record price for an American reel at auction). **$40,320**

Cargem Mignon No. 33 ultra-light reel. **$510**

Dame, Stoddard & Kendall reel. **$280**

Charlton fly reel in box. **$862**

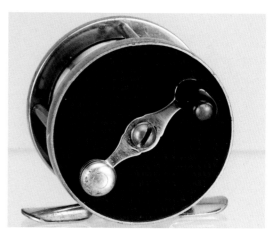

Four Brothers Delite trout reel. **$172**

Cozzone marbleized fly reel. **$2,070**

Hardy Elarex reel with box. **$150**

Hardy reel with case, ex-Zane Grey collection. **$11,480**

Horton # 3 Blue Grass reel. **$90**

Haywood brass-clamp fly reel. **$1,120**

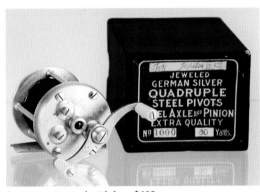

Jupiter casting reel with box. **$402**

Heddon 3-25 German-silver reel. **$300**

Hendryx aluminum trout reel. **$920**

Kopf raised-pillar casting reel. **$2,587**

Leonard-Mills grilse reel. **$896**

Kovalovsky 14/0 big-game reel. **$9,520**

Record Ambassadeur 5000 casting reel. **$258**

H.L. Leonard marbelized fly reel. **$29,120**

Redington large arbor fly reel. **$172**

Saracione Monarch fly reel. **$546**

Silas Terry fly reel. **$252**

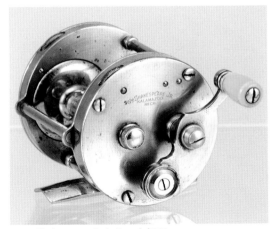

Seamaster Mark III fly reel with bag. **$1,150**

A.B. Shipley & Son ball-handle reel. **$501**

Wm. Shakespeare Style B reel. **$240**

Edward Vom Hofe Restigouche salmon reel. **$1,495**

Edward Vom Hofe tournament casting reel. **$3,307**

Yawman & Erbe Automatic reel. **$214**

Julius Vom Hofe perforated fly reel. **$14,375**

Zwarg 1/0 salmon fly reel. **$2,082**

*Arthur Walker Model
TR-2 fly reel.* **$2,180**

Rods

6' Airex-Uslan spinning rod. **$224**

8' L.L. Bean trout rod. **$367**

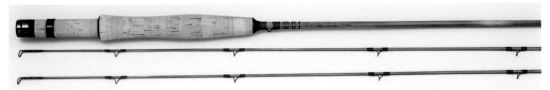

7 1/2' Sam Carlson "Four" trout rod. **$7,043**

8 1/2' Walt Carpenter fly rod. **$3,480**

11 1/2' Conroy Bissett salmon rod. **$1,200**

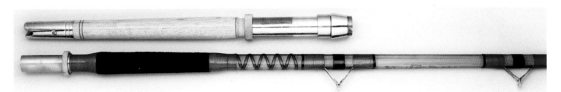

6' 10" Custom Tycoon rod. **$805**

9' Edwards Quadrate trout rod. **$857**

8' Gene Edwards DeLuxe fly rod. **$532**

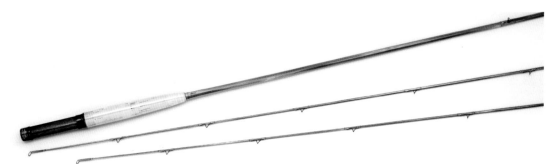

7 1/2' Leonard Ausable 39-5 fly rod. **$2,072**

7' Leonard Model # 38 fly rod. **$2,200**

9' Orvis antique fly rod. **$1,041**

8' Orvis Battenkill fly rod. **$420**

6' Orvis Superfine fly rod. **$918**

9 1/2' Payne salmon rod. **$517**

7' 9" Spring Creek Series fly rod. **$390**

8' Thomas & Thomas Hendrickson rod. **$977**

Other Objects

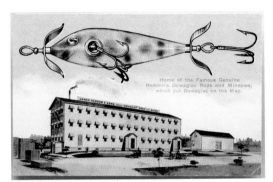

1912 Heddon postcard. **$560**

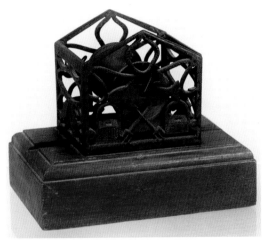

Davis ice fishing tip-up. **$448**

Antique slide-top wooden fly box. **$510**

Copper minnow bucket. **$390**

1880s Chubb Rod Co. catalog. **$402**

"The Fisherman" ship pennant, ex-Zane Grey collection. **$21,450**

Fighting chair, ex-Zane Grey collection. **$24,640**

George Lawrence creel. **$1,792**

Leather-covered tackle box. **$390**

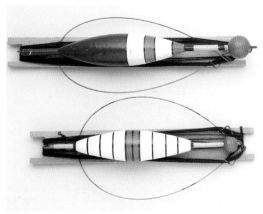

W.B. Griggs carved trout plaque. **$9,890**

Ideal bobbers (two). **$210 pair**

Leather-bound turtle creel. **$1,020**

Native American Salish creel. **$4,255**

Walnut and brass fly chest. **$3,024**

Tackle shop fish sign, metal. **$2,990**

Julius Vom Hofe 1912 catalog. **$690**

Zane Grey record broadbill photograph, 1926. **$4,287**

Folk Art

FUTURE OF THE MARKET: FOLK ART

Folk art captivates, but what is it?

By Tim Chambers

Missouri Plain Folk, Sikeston, Mo.

Folk art? What in the world is it? Where can I find it? How do I know what it is worth when I do find it? This is, in fact, what I deal with every day in my line of work. Work? Yes, Mother. After almost 20 years I still have close friends who can't figure out what it is I do when I get up in the morning! By accident or choice, I've become a dealer in early and vintage folk art, almost exclusively American.

This seemingly ambiguous material in the world of antiques captivated my wife and me early on in my dawning desire to become an antiques dealer in the late 1980s. My wife, Charline, is equally attracted to folk art. She shares many of the duties of the business with me, but she will also be the first to tell you it's "Tim's business," and a business it is. So, as in any other business, a working knowledge is needed to perform to the best of one's ability. Whether in the business of buying and selling folk art, which I am, or in the "business" of collecting folk art, the rules remain the same. We should gather as much information about our interests in order to be more educated. The more knowledge and understanding of the task at hand, the greater the confidence we have in our pursuits. The satisfaction we derive from a job well done only adds to our enjoyment in doing what we like!

Folk art as a classification of antiques very likely offers more opportunity to express our individuality based on the pieces we purchase. The almost endless variety of material that falls under the category of folk art makes this possible. Experts have a difficult time agreeing on a conclusive definition of what constitutes folk art, but can agree on the attraction to be found in its many forms. For example, two items commonly referred to as folk art today are early manufactured weathervanes, as well as handmade weathervanes, which were created in more humble circumstances. What is important to note are the similarities in such diverse objects and not their obvious differences. Consider a horse weathervane of finely molded copper by one of America's commercial makers around the turn of the 20th century. The other a simpler but well conceived silhouette of a horse made of sheet iron or wood by a capable farmer. In either case the objects were intended for a utilitarian purpose, but a sense of beauty is found in both. It is that beauty which they have in common. An awareness of this link between two such dissimilar objects is of utmost importance when it comes to an understanding of folk art. It is an appreciation of this innate beauty that must be achieved by collectors and dealers to develop the skills needed to recognize a great piece of folk art.

"Beauty is in the eye of the beholder." Regarding folk art, this old cliché is probably as accurate and to the point as anything I could write. Simply put, we are most inclined

to pursue an object we're drawn to. That beauty we're beholding in any piece of folk art must resonate on a personal level. This is one of the great attractions folk art offers for the dealer and the collector: the freedom to follow one's own interests. If we're going to acquire folk art that pleases us, this is perhaps one of the most important aspects to be understood. Even as a dealer, it is my experience that when it comes to folk art, my customers expect me to be passionate about the piece. If I'm not passionate, then the chances are my customer won't be either. At that point it becomes very difficult to make a sale! Likewise, if you're buying for your collection, isn't it logical to surround yourself with pieces for which you have great affection? Buy what you like!

Don't know what you like? Let's see if we can work on that! Due to the vast array of categories that fall under the heading of folk art, perhaps the most important first step is to simply look at some. This may sound incredibly naïve, but it really is the best way to begin forming your own opinions, likes, and dislikes. When you've looked at enough, trust me, you will know what I mean.

There are any number of ways this can be accomplished. Without a doubt the very best approach is to see and touch pieces firsthand. Go to an antiques show. These venues offer the chance to see a broad selection of pieces from a wide variety of dealers. My wife and I participate in about 15 antiques shows a year, from California to Connecticut. I can tell you plainly that nothing makes us happier than to have someone interested in learning about a piece we have in our display. The majority of dealers I know enjoy sharing information concerning the material they have for sale. It is this constant dialogue that provides the ongoing education in folk art for collectors and dealers alike. The point is, if you have real interest in something, engage the dealer in conversation regarding your interests. What you learn can become groundwork for the future. From a dealer's perspective I can tell you it is time well spent for both my customer and myself. Such conversations may not result in a sale at that time, but every effort is made to see that the customer leaves my space knowing more about the item of interest than when they entered. Even if it ultimately turns out to be something that would never interested them to the point of purchase, they leave with a greater insight and more information to add to a growing knowledge of folk art.

Single-owner shops also offer excellent opportunities. Besides the same hands on shopping that a show provides, a single-owner shop can be especially helpful from a regional stand point. Often the inventory found in a local shop is just that, local. The shop owner may be able to provide more details as to the maker and origin of a given piece. It is always a bonus to get the history along with the object. This may also increase the object's value.

Group shops and antiques centers are also helpful in terms of looking at and comparing different items. Although some are not equipped to field a lot of questions concerning the goods they have for sale, they do allow the methodical shopper ample time to peruse the aisles at their own speed. Undoubtedly, museums as well as reference books offer a wealth of information that can be turned to on a regular basis. Collectors themselves can be one of the best sources for information due to their experience over a period of time. Virtual shopping can also be helpful. With the information available on the Internet, anyone with access to a computer has a world of knowledge at their fingertips. Web sites specializing in antiques and folk art are increasing daily.

We are now to the point where I tell you what folk art is. I wish I could. Actually that's not entirely true. There are many accepted areas of collecting when it comes to folk art. Most of these categories by definition refer to goods made by hand. Countless objects were made down on the farm, up in the city, or somewhere in between. Whether driven by necessity or a desire to create, folks hooked rugs, sewed quilts, painted game boards or constructed a whirligig just to see which way the wind was blowing. Maybe a sign was needed to show the way

to the apple orchard. A means was needed to hold an ashtray, so a cutout painted butler extending his arm was created for the job. The list goes on. Children made things at church or school, soldiers made things while in training or on the frontlines. And who can forget the tramps? Look at all the tramp art that exists. (Actually there's no proof that tramps were that prolific when it came to chip carving.) Frankly, it is human nature to create and most of those objects created fall somewhere in the definition of folk art. What is considered the most desirable in this abundance of choices? That, of course, varies from person to person. However, it is safe to say the best example of anything in its field becomes the standard by which all other examples are judged.

The central questions remains: Why the attraction and what gives folk art value? As I've tried to point out, the attraction is and should be personal. It may simply come from an appreciation of the object and the maker's ability to create it. Folk art often represents a slower, less complicated time, which resonates with many of us. Then there's just plain old American ingenuity, which can be intriguing. Something was needed and something was made. Just because it was a necessity didn't mean it couldn't be artfully accomplished.

Value: If you think it's hard to completely understand what folk art is, let me tell you, value can be even harder to define. Consider the fact that, by definition, nearly all examples of folk art are essentially one of a kind. Value, on the other hand, is generally determined by comparing two similar objects. One is deemed better than the other and is thus given a higher value. That's tough to do when there's only one exactly like this one. That being said, comparison is still the closest means of assigning a value to a piece. This is another example of the importance of looking at as much material as you can to create your own database regarding prices. Like any other field of collecting, there are the basics of age, condition and desirability that come into play. As a dealer, I'm often asked why a piece is priced higher than another piece. I always try to give the simplest answer: "More people want this one. It was that way when I bought it and will be that way when I sell it."

Photo courtesy Skinner Inc., Boston, www.SkinnerInc.com

"Black Hawk," running horse, molded copper, "Harris & Co." Boston, late 19th century, flattened full-body figure with zinc ears, mounted on a copper rod over a small sphere, maker's mark impressed on side, no stand, dents, seam separations, 20 1/2" h, 26 1/2" l. **$3,081**

If you have read this far then you are well aware that you have learned everything there is to know about folk art. Just kidding! I do hope you have a better understanding of the subject. We have discussed what it is and places to look for it. Now let's get to the fun part and talk about buying some! Let's say we have $10,000 available to purchase folk art. Where should we spend it? Well, let's understand a basic principal first. Folk art, and antiques in general for that matter, are very much a "fashion" business. Things rise and fall in popularity/desirability. It's not quite Seventh Avenue, but there are trends. What's hot now? Most things of a visual, colorful nature seem to be right at the top of the list. I'm known for painted game boards, having written a book on the subject. I can tell you firsthand the more colorful a game board the more desirable, hence the more expensive, as I explained earlier. To put it another way, I would take some of that $10,000 and purchase one great colorful game board, not four mediocre brown ones (sorry, brown!). A great weathervane is always desirable. Again, the wise buy is the one in the budget in the best condition with wonderful form. Hand-painted trade signs remain at the top of the list. Here are a couple of pointers in making a choice: consider the subject matter and the graphics. A colorful sign advertising strawberries will generally be more desirable than a more colorful sign advertising funerals.

The truth of the matter is, with $10,000 you could absolutely fill a house and have money left over with some types of folk art. On the other hand, $10,000 would not even be a decent down payment on some single pieces. To me this is the beauty of this area of collecting. No matter how deep your pockets, I can promise you one thing. It's not what it costs you that will bring satisfaction in folk art. It's what living with it does for you. So far, no one has been able to put a price on that!

I would like to close with some encouraging words. First, for those of us attracted to folk art, it is an endless source of pleasure and we welcome those new to this area of collecting. It is truly an adventure. This material, in all its forms, has been produced all over the world since man's arrival. Even as this country was being formed some 400 years ago, folk artists were among the colonists. As the population spread west, so did they. Folk art in one form or another can be found almost anywhere we are. I haven't really talked about age, but folk art is generally accepted from its earliest origins up to the mid-20th century. That's a large body of work. Ultimately there is plenty to go around. Now, get out there and find it! And remember, buy what you like!

Tim Chambers and his wife, Charline, are active dealers in folk art and Americana, doing business at shows across the country as Missouri Plain Folk. In 2001, Tim authored the book, *The Art of the Game,* showcasing the game-board collection of Selby Shaver. As a result, Chambers works extensively with collectors in this field. Besides game boards, Missouri Plain Folk is known for vintage Americana with an emphasis on surface, form, color and graphic impact. An ever-changing selection of game boards and Americana may be found on their Web site: www.missouriplainfolk.com.

Photo courtesy Susan D. Jones, sdjones.net

The bottle whimsies created by itinerant Carl Worner have become highly prized by folk-art collectors. Many of his bottles feature taverns and tobacco shops. The best examples sell for thousands of dollars.

Cabinet, tramp art, possibly for sheet music, with one drawer over double doors, two interior shelves and mirrored back, circa 1930. Featured at the Clarion Exhibit of American Folk Art, New York, summer 1978, 41 1/4" x 19 1/2" x 13 1/2". **$9,000**

Also see Advertising, Art.

Carousel chariot boards, set of two, red-painted wood, possibly by Gustav Dentzel, circa 1900, 46" x 78". **$300 both**

Carousel horse, Karl Muller (attributed), prancer with original paint and detailed overall carvings, late 19th/early 20th century, 64" x 62". **$3,600**

Carousel horse, Parker, 19th-20th century, outside row "Flying Horse" is shown with all legs up, turned head and intricately carved mane, head and tail. The old park paint surface shows a light brown horse with white mane and tail, with a green, blue and orange blanket with brown and orange-trimmed saddle. There is a large grape cluster carving on hindquarters. Glass jewel decoration on bridle,

Figure of a rooster, carved and painted wood, attributed to S.F. Welsh, Grayson County, Va., in a standing position with boldly carved tail, inset metal eyes, one retaining a quartz-stone pupil, red-painted comb and wattles, applied legs mortised into original block-form stand, original dry crackled varnished surface; with a letter of provenance and a group of research material. Fourth quarter 19th century, 13 1/2" h, 11 3/4" l, old (possibly when produced) repair to lower tip of beak, minor loss/wear to top of comb, slight wear and flaking to surface. **$41,800**

blanket and front. Marked on bottom of all four hooves "Parker, Leavenworth, Kansas". With display stand, approx. 51" h x 60" l, minor defects. **$4,830**

Eagle, American, late 19th century, with yellow beak, carved with spread wings clutching three arrows and green-painted branch in talons, 17" l, repair to left wing and small losses to both wingtips, good patina. **$575**

Eagle, American, carved and paint-decorated wall plaque in the manner of John Haley Bellamy, late 19th century, depicted with shield, 47" w. Retains all original surfaces, with repairs to upper and lower beak and old repair to right upper wing facing. Head retains original dowel fastener. **$3,335**

Eagle, carved and gilded, depicted in full flight with good details to the wings. Carved from pine, 34" x 15",

Photo courtesy Skinner Inc., Boston; www.SkinnerInc.com

Figure, polychrome carved bird, American, 19th century, with applied carved agate eyes, copper feet, mounted on a wall bracket, repair to crack on beak, overall 26 1/4" h. **$1,896**

Photo courtesy Skinner Inc., Boston; www.SkinnerInc.com

Fire bucket, painted leather, American, early 19th century, with leather handle painted dark blue with polychrome scrolled foliage and lettering "No. 1, Semper Fidelis," and "Thomas Carter 1815," paint losses, 12 1/4" h to top of collar. **$1,185**

Photo courtesy Skinner Inc., Boston; www.SkinnerInc.com

Bust, carved marble, of "Jim," American, 19th century, (small loss), 6" h. **$237**

Photo courtesy Skinner Inc., Boston; www.SkinnerInc.com

Fencepost whimsy, green-painted, carved, wooden with birds, American, late 19th/early 20th century, including stand, minor wear, overall 15 1/4" h, 15 3/4" d. **$1,070**

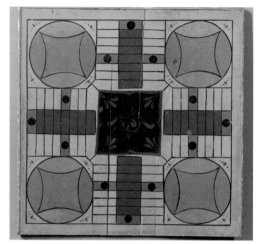

Photo courtesy Skinner Inc., Boston; www.SkinnerInc.com

Game board, Parcheesi, American, late 19th century, square wooden panel with polychrome-painted playing field, the "Home" area at center with black-painted scrolled foliage on a red ground, the board is composed of two thin wide square panels sandwiched together, surrounded by a thin applied molding, the boards are a little bowed causing three cracks on the playing surface, 20 1/4" square. **$3,081**

Photo courtesy Green Valley Auctions, Mt. Crawford, Va.; www.GreenValleyAuctions.com

Key basket, Virginia, leather, oblong form with subtle V-shaped rim, black exterior with stitched decoration featuring a shield on each end, red rim and interior, natural brown arched handle attached on exterior. Together with a group of three early iron keys on a forged iron ring and attached wooden fob carved "WBG". Mid-19th century, light wear to handle and rim, minor insect damage to interior and base, 6 1/2" x 5 1/4" x 8 1/2". **$13,200**

Photo courtesy Skinner Inc., Boston; www.SkinnerInc.com

Panel, painted, Masonic, walnut, American, early to mid-19th century, signed "J.R. Warren" lower right, appears to be original paint, panel slightly bowed, about 4" crack to panel at left center, 25 3/4" x 19 1/4". **$355**

Photo courtesy Green Valley Auctions, Mt. Crawford, Va.; www.GreenValleyAuctions.com

Picture frame, Shenandoah Valley, carved walnut, diminutive slightly arched top surmounted by boldly scrolled ears and a central crosshatched inverted heart, original yellow pine backboard, original dry surface. Contains a cutout and woven paper heart in hand mounted on lined paper. Second half 19th century, 6 1/4" h, 4 1/8" w. **$4,950**

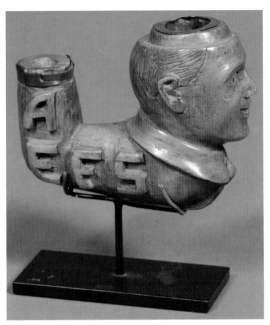

Pipe, figural, carved wood, American, early 20th century, the bowl carved with the head of a man, the shaft with the letters "AEFS," with stand, overall 5 3/4" h, 4 1/2" l. **$177**

Whirligig figure, carved and painted wood, "Dewey Boy" sailor, possibly Nantucket, Mass., late 19th/early 20th century, with tin hat brim, mounted on a wooden stand, lacking paddles, shrinkage crack on right-facing leg, overall 15 1/4" h. **$1,422**

Shooting gallery target, clown wearing mask, dated 1911, made by Dickman, cast iron, 20" x 16". **$16,000**

modern replaced gilding, chip to upper beak and seam repairs along the body extending into the right wing facing. **$345**

Paperweight, carved in form of an ear of corn, bone or horn, realistically depicting a partially husked ear of corn with graduated kernels and tipped with silk, 11 1/4" l, original patina, corn-silk tips showing dark patina, overall mellow ivory color. **$1,610**

Sculpture, carved wood and burl, three-dimensional scene showing building landscape and train with locomotive, tender and two cars. Carved wooden portrait surmounts frame, exhibits some minor wood loss and crazing to some varnish, 28" x 39". **$1,035**

Sign, carved and painted wood, "Post Office," American, 19th century, arched pine panel with applied molding, the lettering painted mustard yellow on a cream-colored ground, (minor molding losses), 16 1/2" h, 31 3/4" w. **$2,962**

Whimsy bottle, rack with birds, flower pots, etc., signed "Adam Selig" and dated "1891"; fan-like form below signature; painted blue, brick red on wood, large bottle, 11 1/8" h.
.... **$316**

Whimsy bottle with animals by Daniel Rose, two squirrels on pedestals and three stylized trees below, fan-form upper section, 7 3/4" h. **$1,380**
(Daniel Rose [1871-1926] was a master whittler and bottle-whimsy maker living in Johnstown, Pa. He created elaborate and delicate folk art despite suffering with debilitating rheumatism from an early age.)

Whimsy bottle, with Christ on cross, interior with meticulous wood construction, 10" h. **$316**

Whimsy bottle, red and white yarn, wood stopper, 6 3/4" h, inscribed on paper on bottom: "Made by/H. H. Hutchins Feb. 14, 1914". **$420**

SCRIMSHAW

Scrimshaw is the name given to handiwork created by whalers made from the byproducts of harvesting marine mammals. It is most commonly made out of the bones and teeth of sperm whales, the baleen of other whales, and the tusks of walruses. It takes the form of elaborate carvings of pictures and lettering on the surface of the bone or tooth, with the engravings highlighted using a pigment.

Warning: To avoid illegal ivory, contemporary collectors and dealers check provenance and deal only with other established and reputable sellers. Scrimshaw that is found to have an illegal source may be seized by customs officials worldwide.

Reproduction Alert: The biggest problem in the field is fakes, although there are some clues to spotting them. A hot needle will penetrate the plastics and resins used in reproductions, but not the authentic material. Ivory will not generate static electricity when rubbed, plastic will. Patina is not a good indicator; it has been faked by applying tea or tobacco juice.

Busk

Bone, scratch carved eagle, pinwheels, vining foliage, compass stars, and heart at top, black coloring with red in eagle's shield and one flower, small chip at top, 12 3/8" l. **$550**

Wood, decorated with eagle, shield, lovebirds, and ship under sail, heart and foliate devices, inscribed "GC & EW" and dated 1840, 13 7/8" l. **$345**

Cribbage board, carved walrus tusk

Carved in relief with Northwest fish and sea life, polychrome decoration, late 19th century, 11" l. **$360**

Carved on both sides, obverse, board in floral decorated panel flanked by scenes of Northwest animals and fish, reverse with scenes of life in Northwest region, minor age splits, late 19th century, 23" l. **$475**

Photo courtesy Sloans & Kenyon Auctioneers and Appraisers

Scrimshaw whale's tooth, one side incised with strolling couple, reverse with amorous couple, mounted on wood base, 19th century, 5 3/4" h. **$2,010**

Domino box, bone and wood, shoe form, pierced carved slide top with star and heart decoration, domino playing pieces, Prisoner of War, cracks, minor insect damage, 19th century, 6 7/8" l. **$520**

Game box, bone, pierced carved box with geometric decoration, three slide tops, compartmented interior, backgammon and other playing pieces, traces of paint decoration, Prisoner of War, repair, warping to tops, minor losses, 19th century, 5 3/4" x 6 1/2". **$690**

Obelisk, inlaid mahogany, with various exotic woods, abalone and ivory in geometric and star motifs, minor losses, minute cracks, 19th century, 13 3/8" h. **$815**

Plaque, sailing ship, pencil inscription "Whale bone found in England by Mrs. Fred Rich," circa 1800, 14 1/2" l.
.... **$13,000**

Salt horn, engraved "John Snow March…1780 by S. H.," crosshatched borders enclosing reserve of ship, geometric, and foliate devices, insect damage, 5 1/2" l. **$460**

Seam rubber, whalebone, geometric designs on handle, traces of orig paint, 19th century, 4" l. **$850**

Snuff box, horn, architectural and marine motifs, dated "AD 1853" and "William Sandilands Plumber," English, 5" l.
.... **$950**

Swift, all whale bone and ivory, copper pegs, yarn ties, pincushion socket on top, age cracks, minor edge damage, possible replaced section, 16" h. **$900**

Walrus tusk

Reserves of animals, courting couples, ships under sail, memorials, sailors and armaments, later engraved brass presentation caps, "Presented by George M. Chase to Ike B. Dunlap Jan. 25th 1908," cracks, one restored, pair, 17 3/4" h.. **$2,530 pair**

Walrus, decorated with two eagles, lady, Indian and vulture, age cracks, 19th century, 18 7/8" l. **$1,840**

Watch hutch, bone, pierce carved floral and figural decoration, brass backing, polychrome foliate highlights, Prisoner of War, custom-made case, minor cracks, losses, repairs, 19th century, 11 7/8" h. **$750**

Whale's tooth, 19th century

Decorated with ship, woman resting on anchor holding flag, two potted plants, chips, minor cracks, 4 3/8" l.
.... **$690**

Historic landmarks, decorated on both sides, minor cracks and chips, 6 5/8" h. **$865**

Various ships under sail and young lady, cracks, 6 7/8" h.
.... **$1,380**

Photo courtesy of Pook & Pook Inc.

Scrimshaw whale's tooth, romantic couple on one side, young girl on other, red-stained highlights, mid-19th century, American, 16 1/4" l. **$1,170**

Weathervanes

Photo courtesy James D. Julia Auctioneers, Fairfield, Maine; www.JuliaAuctions.com

Banner, from the Universalist Unitarian Church of Waterville, Maine, branded "S. H. & W. C. Hunneman". In the shape of an arrow having a cast zinc/lead front part, which includes an arrow flanked by two C-scrolls attached to a cast-zinc rectangular area set for rod insert. The back section has two open S-scrolls leading to an 11-rayed star with four round cutouts. Back section appears to be flat sheet metal. Central rod receiving area has a hand-forged top with open prongs. The maker's brand on the central pole receiving area, 61" l x 21 1/2" h (without wrought-iron rod). Bend in one cast scroll, a break 1" from the central vertical support, several bends and loss of green patina throughout. Remnants of the original gilt can be seen. The weathervane has a green over-paint. **$6,612**

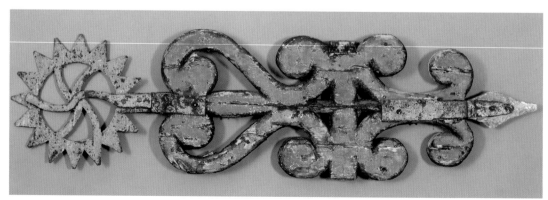

Photo courtesy Skinner Inc., Boston, www.SkinnerInc.com

Banner, wood, iron and zinc, American, late 19th century, zinc arrow tip joined to carved scrolled wooden banner with iron mounts ending with a "spur" tail, weathered surface with vestiges of paint and gilding, rusty surface on iron, joinery separations, 18" h, 68" l. **$3,851**

*Eagle, oversized, copper,
spread-wing on ball and
arrow, detailed feathers,
slightly turned head and
open mouth. Detail of
the feathers on top and
bottom having a verdigris
patina. Fully restored
by Valerie Hunt at the
Shelburne Museum in
1991, a videotape of the
restoration procedures
is included along with
color slides showing
some of the progress of
the restoration. Vane
comes with its original
directionals. Wingspan
56"; approximately 32"
from tail to beak. Arrow,
58" l.* **$23,575**

*Chicken, carved and painted wood, three-dimensional fully sculpted chicken stands on a wood ball resting on a long
wood and sheet-metal arrow. White and green body with red tail. Ball is painted green and the arrow a light blue.
Weathervane with ball is 16" h; chicken is 17 1/2" l; arrow is 60" l. Some wear to paint, some cracking at lamination,
cracks in ball.* **$2,588**

Eagle, gilt copper, American, early 20th century, full-body molded copper spread-wing figure, mounted on a large sphere, arrow and small sphere, including stand, 6" dent on wing, overall 27" h, 30" w, 31" l. **$1,066**

Fish, carved wood, Virginia, second quarter 19th century, flat body with V-shape open mouth, faint eyes, crescent-shape gills and simple tail, fins mortised into upper and lower edges of body and secured with wooden pins, top to bottom mounting hole located to the rear of the front fins, weathered natural surface 48" l, 11" h. Loss to upper rear fin, small hole below upper front fin, expected wear. **$17,600**

Biplane, with a heavily rusted body, rubber wheels and cracks on edges of wings, circa 1920, 44" x 20" x 53 3/4" wingspan. **$300**

Cow, molded copper, with verdigris patina, 19th-20th century, original copper globe directionals, iron rod and arms, four bullet holes, 17 3/4" x 27 1/2". **$900**

Fishing trawler, gilt copper, Massachusetts, early 20th century, molded sheet copper and wirework vessel, including stand, gilt wear, overall 32" h, 25" l. **$3,851**

Photo courtesy Skinner Inc., Boston, www.SkinnerInc.com

Gabriel, tin and iron, American, late 19th/early 20th century, cutout tin angel figure with iron wire reinforcement and vestiges of creamy white paint, mounted on an iron pipe, including stand, overall 14 3/4" h, 28 1/2" l. **$2,962**

Photo courtesy James D. Julia Auctioneers, Fairfield, Maine; www.JuliaAuctions.com

Running horse, full-body copper, attributed to Harris & Co., second half 19th century, with zinc head and molded copper body, with extended sheet mane and flowing tail. Vane comes with its original directionals and pole, 18" overall h x 27 1/2" l. horse. With old patina, brown tones to head. Multiple repaired bullet holes to body, with dents, crease in tail at hindquarters, base rod bent at front support. **$2,070**

Photo courtesy James D. Julia Auctioneers, Fairfield, Maine; www.JuliaAuctions.com

Schooner, carved wood and metal, made by Frank Adams, Martha's Vineyard, Mass., first quarter of the 20th century. Painted in brown and white, the hull black with dinghies, 20" h x 38 1/2" l. **$920**

Photo courtesy Skinner Inc., Boston, www.SkinnerInc.com

Leaping stag, gilt copper, attributed to the E.G. Washburne & Co., New York, and Danvers, Mass., late 19th century, flattened full-body molded copper figure, mounted on a copper rod and small copper sphere, including stand, minor dents, overall 24" h, 29" l, surface regilded some time ago with traces of verdigris, one hind quarter area dented inward, few small bullet dents on rod. **$7,702**

Photo courtesy Skinner Inc., Boston, www.SkinnerInc.com

Running horse, yellow-painted molded copper, American, late 19th/early 20th century, full-body figure mounted on a copper rod, no stand, dents, 16 1/4" h, 28 1/2" l. **$1,422**

Furniture

FURNITURE AND ACCESSORIES

Furniture styles

Furniture styles can be determined by careful study and remembering what design elements each one embraces. To help understand what defines each period, here are some of the major design elements for each period.

William and Mary, 1690-1730: The style is named for the English King William of Orange and his consort, Mary. New colonists in America brought their English furniture traditions with them and tried to translate these styles using native woods. Their furniture was practical and sturdy. Lines of this furniture style tend to be crisp, while facades might be decorated with bold grains of walnut or maple veneers, framed by inlaid bands. Moldings and turnings are exaggerated in size. Turnings are baluster-shaped and the use of C-scrolls was quite common. Feet found in this period generally are round or oval. One exception to this is known as the Spanish foot, which flares to a scroll. Woods tend to be maple, walnut, white pine or southern yellow pine. One type of decoration that begins in the William and Mary period and extends through to Queen Anne and Chippendale styles is known as "japanning," referring to a lacquering process that combines ashes and varnish.

Queen Anne, 1720-1760: Evolution of this design style is from Queen Anne's court, 1702 to 1714, and lasted until the Revolution. This style of furniture is much more delicate than its predecessor. It was one way for the young Colonists to show their own unique style, with each regional area initiating special design elements. Forms tend to be attenuated in New England. Chair rails were more often mortised through the back legs when made in Philadelphia. New England furniture makers preferred pad feet, while the makers in Philadelphia used triffid feet. Makers in Connecticut and New York often preferred slipper and claw and ball feet. The most popular woods were walnut, poplar, cherry, and maple. Japanned decoration tends to be in red, green and gilt, often on a blue-green field. A new furniture form of this period was the tilting tea table.

Chippendale, 1755-1790: This period is named for the famous English cabinetmaker, Thomas Chippendale, who wrote a book of furniture designs, *Gentlemen and Cabinet-Maker's Director*, published in 1754, 1755 and 1762. This book gave cabinetmakers real direction and they soon eagerly copied the styles presented. Chippendale was influenced by ancient cultures, such as the Romans, and Gothic influences. Look for Gothic arches, Chinese fretwork, columns, capitals, C-scrolls, S-scrolls, ribbons, flowers, leaves, scallop shells, gadrooning and acanthus leaves. The most popular wood used in this period was mahogany, with walnut, maple and cherry also present. Legs become straight and regional differences still existed in design elements, such as feet. Claw and ball feet become even larger and more decorative. Pennsylvania cabinetmakers used Marlborough feet, while other regions favored ogee bracket feet. One of the most popular forms of this period was a card table that sported five legs instead of the four of Queen Anne designs.

Federal (Hepplewhite), 1790-1815: This period reflects the growing patriotism felt in the young American states. Their desire to develop their own distinctive furniture style was apparent. Stylistically it also reflects the architectural style known as Federal, where balance and symmetry were extremely important. Woods used during this period were mahogany and mahogany veneer, but other native woods, such as maple, birch or satinwood, were used. Reflecting the architectural ornamentation of the period, inlays were popular, as was carving and even painted highlights. The motifs used for inlay included bellflowers, urns, festoons, acanthus leaves and pilasters, to name but a few. Inlaid bands and lines were also popular and often used in combination with other inlay. Legs of this period tend to be straight or tapered to the foot. The foot might be a simple extension of the leg, or bulbous or spade shaped. Two new furniture forms were created in this period. They are the sideboard and the worktable. Expect to find a little more comfort in chairs and sofas, but not very thick cushions or seats.

Photo courtesy Sanford Alderfer Auction & Appraisal, Hatfield, Pa.; www.AlderferAuction.com

Cabinet on stand, continental, walnut, top section with molded cornice with sides extended, panel below, carved cartouche and scrolling stems with flowers; intricately carved paneled door below flanked by two tapered round columns, door with border of bas relief leafage, twin vertical panels with conforming cartouche and leafage; lower section with molded midband, single drawer with conforming leaf scroll and flowers, two free-standing front columns with drapery swags, stretcher shelf; twin vertical panels with neo-classic portrait heads, leafage with rosettes; urns with birds below, bun feet, late 19th century; tin plate reinforces top of right front corner; left column with repaired split at top; damage to left top corner of cornice, 68 5/8" h, 31" w, 18" deep. **$1,035**

When a piece of furniture is made in England, or styled after an English example, it may be known as Hepplewhite. The time frame is the same. Robert Adam is credited with creating the style known as Hepplewhite during the 1760s and leading the form. Another English book heavily influenced the designers of the day. This one was by Alice Hepplewhite, and titled *The Cabinet Maker and Upholsterer's Guide,* published in 1788, 1789 and 1794.

Sheraton, 1790-1810: The style known as Sheraton closely resembles Federal. The lines are somewhat straighter and the designs plainer than Federal. Sheraton pieces are more closely associated with rural cabinetmakers. Woods would include mahogany, mahogany veneer, maple and pine, as well as other native woods. This period was heavily influenced by the work of Thomas Sheraton and his series of books, *The Cabinet Maker and Upholsterer's Drawing Book*, from 1791-1794, and his *The Cabinet Directory*, 1803, and *The Cabinet-Maker, Upholsterer, and General Artist's Encyclopedia* of 1804.

Empire (Classical), 1805-1830: By the beginning of the 19th century, a new design style was emerging. Known as Empire, it had an emphasis on the classical world of Greece, Egypt and other ancient European influences. The American craftsmen began to incorporate more flowing patriotic motifs, such as eagles with spread wings. The basic wood used in the Empire period was mahogany. However, during this period, dark woods were so favored that often mahogany was painted black. Inlays were popular when made of ebony or maple veneer. The dark woods offset gilt highlights, as were the brass ormolu mountings often found in this period. The legs of this period are substantial and more flowing than those found in the Federal or Sheraton periods. Feet can be highly ornamental, as when they are carved to look like lion's paws, or plain when they extend to the floor with a swept leg. Regional differences in this style are very apparent, with New York City being the center of the design style, as it was also the center of fashion at the time.

New furniture forms of this period include the sleigh bed, with the headboard and footboard forming a graceful arch. Several new forms of tables also came into being, especially the sofa table. Because the architectural style of the Empire period used big, open rooms, the sofa was now allowed to be in the center of the room, with a table behind it. Former architectural periods found most furniture placed against the outside perimeter of the walls and brought forward to be used.

Victorian, 1830-1890: The Victorian period as it relates to furniture styles can be divided into several distinct styles. However, not every piece of furniture can be dated or definitely identified, so the generic term "Victorian" will apply to those pieces. Queen Victoria's reign affected the design styles of furniture, clothing and all sorts of items used in daily living. Her love of ornate styles is well known. When thinking of the general term, think of a cluttered environment, full of heavy furniture, and surrounded by plants, heavy fabrics and lots of china and glassware.

French Restoration, 1830-1850: This is the first sub-category of the Victoria era. This style is best simplified as the plainest of the Victorian styles. Lines tend to be sweeping, undulating curves. It is named for the style that was popular in France as the Bourbons tried to restore their claim to the French throne, from 1814 to 1848. The Empire (Classical) period influence is felt, but French Restoration lacks some of the ornamentation and fussiness of that period. Design motifs continue to reflect an interest in the classics of Greece and Egypt. Chair backs are styled with curved and concave crest rails, making them a little more comfortable than earlier straight-back chairs. The use of bolster pillows and more upholstery is starting to emerge. The style was only popular in clusters, but did entice makers from larger metropolitan areas, such as Boston and New Orleans, to embrace the style.

The Gothic Revival period, 1840-1860: This is relatively easy to identify for collectors. It is one of the few styles that celebrates elements found in the corresponding architectural themes: turrets, pointed arches and quatrefoils—designs found in 12th through 16th centuries that were adapted to this mid-century furniture style. The furniture shelving form known as an étagère was born in this period, allowing Victorians to have more room to display their treasured collections. Furniture that had mechanical parts was also embraced by the Victorians of this era. The woods preferred by makers of this period were walnut and oak, with some use of mahogany and rosewood. The scale used ranged from large and grand to small and petite. Carved details gave dimension and interest.

Rococo Revival, 1845-1870: This design style features the use of scrolls, either in a "C" shape or the more fluid "S" shape. Carved decoration in the form of scallop shells, leaves and flowers, particularly roses, and acanthus further add to the ornamentation of this style of furniture. Legs and feet of this form are

Photo courtesy Rago Arts and Auction Center, Lambertville, N.J.; www.RagoArts.com

Chair, Egyptian Revival, with carved winged figure, pierced skirt and light rose upholstery, 19th/20th century, 39" x 24" x 21".
$1,680

Photo courtesy Sanford Alderfer Auction & Appraisal, Hatfield, Pa.; www.AlderferAuction.com

Highboy, William and Mary, maple and ebonized in two sections; upper section with two small drawers over three wide graduated drawers, brass drop handles; lower section with frieze drawer flanked by two deep drawers, trumpet-turned legs joined by flat shaped stretcher, short turned feet, 60" h, 37 3/4" w, 17 1/2" deep. **$3,450**

cabriole or scrolling. Other than what might be needed structurally, it is often difficult to find a straight element in Rococo Revival furniture. The use of marble for tabletops was quite popular, but expect to find the corners shaped to conform to the overall scrolling form. To accomplish all this carving, walnut, rosewood, and mahogany were common choices. When lesser woods were used, they were often painted to reflect these more expensive woods. Some cast-iron elements can be found on furniture from this period, especially if it was cast as scrolls. The style began in France and England, but eventually migrated to America where it evolved into two other furniture styles, Naturalistic and Renaissance Revival.

Elizabethan, 1850-1915: This sub-category of the Victorian era is probably the most feminine-influenced style. It also makes use of the new machine-turned spools and spiral profiles that were fast becoming popular with furniture makers. New technology advancements allowed more machined parts to be generated. By adding flowers, either carved or painted, the furniture pieces of this era had a softness to them. Chair backs tend to be high and narrow, having a slight back tilt. Legs vary from straight to baluster-turned forms to spindle turned. This period of furniture design saw more usage of needlework upholstery and decoratively painted surfaces.

Louis XVI, 1850-1914: One period of the Victorian era that flies away with straight lines is Louis XVI. However, this furniture style is not austere; it is adorned with ovals, arches, applied medallions, wreaths, garlands, urns and other Victorian flourishes. As the period aged, more ornamentation became present on the finished furniture styles. Furniture of this time was made from more expensive woods, such as ebony or rosewood. Walnut was popular around the 1890s. Other dark woods were featured, often to contrast the lighter ornaments. Expect to find straight legs or fluted and slightly tapered legs.

Naturalistic, 1850-1914: This furniture period takes the scrolling effects of the Rococo Revival designs and adds more flowers and fruits to the styles. More detail is spent on the leaves—so much that one can tell if they are to represent grape, rose or oak leaves. Technology advances enhanced this design style, as manufacturers developed a way of laminating woods together. This layered effect was achieved by gluing thin layers together, with the grains running at right angles on each new layer. The thick panels created were then steamed in molds to create the illusion of carving. The woods used as a basis for the heavy ornamentation were mahogany, walnut and some rosewood. Upholstery of this period is often tufted, eliminating any large flat surface. The name of John Henry Belter is often connected with this period, for it was when he did some of his best design work. John and Joseph W. Meeks also enjoyed success with laminated furniture. Original labels bearing these names are sometimes found on furniture pieces from this period, giving further provenance.

Renaissance Revival, 1850-1880: Furniture made in this style period reflects how cabinetmakers interpreted 16th- and 17th-century designs. Their motifs range from curvilinear and florid early in the period to angular and almost severe by the end of the period. Dark woods, such as mahogany and walnut, were primary with some use of rosewood and ebony. Walnut veneer panels were a real favorite in the 1870s designs. Upholstery, usually of a more generous nature, was also often incorporated into this design style. Ornamentation and high relief carving included flowers, fruits, game, classical busts, acanthus scrolls, strapwork, tassels and masks. Architectural motifs, such as pilasters, columns, pediments, balusters and brackets, are another prominent design feature. Legs are usually cabriole or have substantial turned profiles.

Néo-Greek, 1855-1885: This design style easily merges with both the Louis XVI and Renaissance Revival. It is characterized by elements reminiscent of Greek architecture, such as pilasters, flutes, column, acanthus, foliate scrolls, Greek key motifs and anthemion high-relief carving. This style originated with the French, but was embraced by American furniture manufacturers. Woods are dark and often ebonized. Ornamentation may be gilded or bronzed. Legs tend to be curved to scrolled or cloven hoof feet.

Eastlake, 1870-1890: This design style is named for Charles Locke Eastlake, who wrote a popular book in 1872 called *Hints on Household Taste*. It was originally published in London. One of his principles was the relationship between

Feet

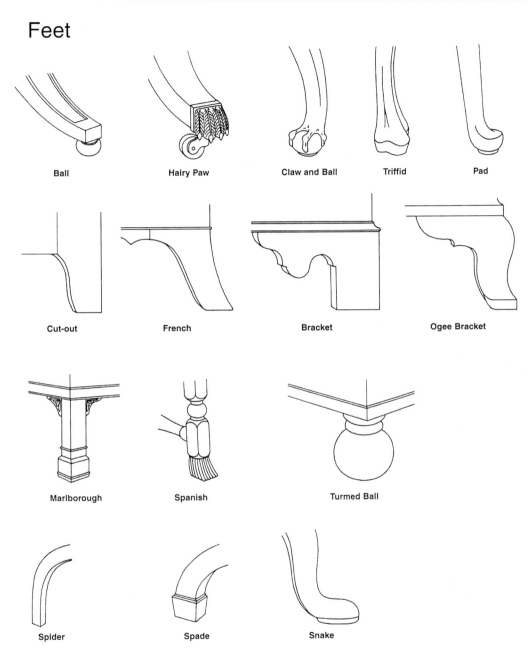

Ball

Hairy Paw

Claw and Ball

Triffid

Pad

Cut-out

French

Bracket

Ogee Bracket

Marlborough

Spanish

Turned Ball

Spider

Spade

Snake

function, form and craftsmanship. Shapes of furniture from this style tend to be more rectangular. Ornamentation was created through the use of brackets, grooves, chamfers and geometric designs. American furniture manufacturers were enthusiastic about this style, since it was so easy to adapt for mass production. Woods used were again dark, but more native woods, such as oak, maple and pine, were incorporated. Legs and chair backs are straighter, often with incised decoration.

Art Furniture, 1880-1914: This period represents furniture designs gone mad, almost an "anything goes" school of thought. The style embraces both straight and angular with some pieces that are much more fluid, reflecting several earlier design periods. This era saw the wide usage of turned moldings and dark woods, but this time stained to imitate ebony and lacquer. The growing Oriental influence is seen in furniture from this period, including the use of bamboo, which was imported and included in the designs. Legs tend to be straight; feet tend to be small.

Arts & Crafts, 1895-1915: The Arts & Crafts period of furniture represents one of the strongest trends for current collectors. Quality period Arts & Crafts furniture is available through most of the major auction

Legs

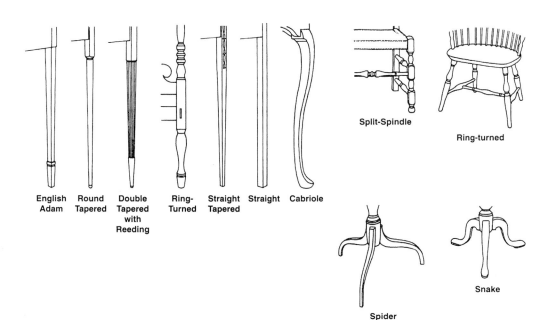

English Adam | Round Tapered | Double Tapered with Reeding | Ring-Turned | Straight Tapered | Straight | Cabriole

Split-Spindle

Ring-turned

Spider

Snake

Hardware

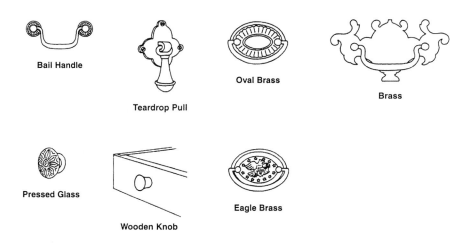

Bail Handle

Teardrop Pull

Oval Brass

Brass

Pressed Glass

Wooden Knob

Eagle Brass

houses. And, for those desiring the look, good quality modern furniture is also made in this style. The Arts & Crafts period furniture is generally rectilinear and a definite correlation is seen between form and function. The primary influences of this period were the Stickley brothers (especially Gustav, Leopold and John George), Elbert Hubbard, Frank Lloyd Wright and Harvey Ellis. Their furniture designs often overlapped into architectural and interior design, including rugs, textiles and other accessories. Wood used for Arts & Crafts fur-

niture is primarily oak. Finishes were natural, fumed or painted. Hardware was often made in copper. Legs are straight and feet are small, if present at all, as they were often a simple extension of the leg. Some inlay of natural materials was used, such as silver, copper and abalone shells.

Art Nouveau, 1896-1914: Just as the Art Nouveau period is known for women with long hair, flowers and curves, so is Art Nouveau furniture. The Paris Exposition of 1900 introduced furniture styles reflecting what

Construction Details

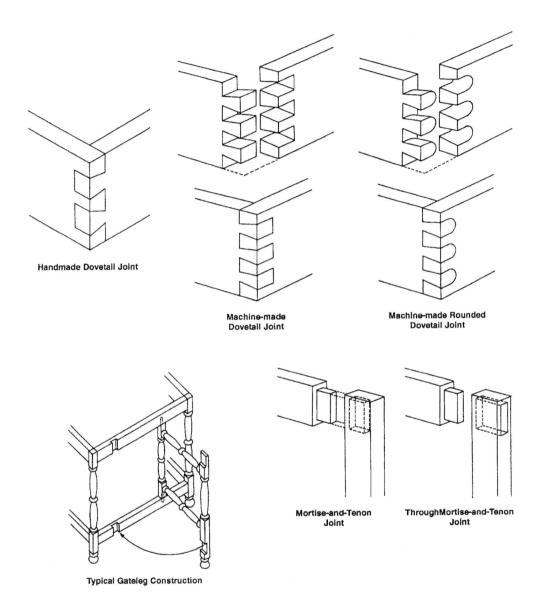

Handmade Dovetail Joint

Machine-made
Dovetail Joint

Machine-made Rounded
Dovetail Joint

Typical Gateleg Construction

Mortise-and-Tenon
Joint

ThroughMortise-and-Tenon
Joint

was happening in the rest of the design world, such as jewelry and silver. This style of furniture was not warmly embraced, as the sweeping lines were not very conducive to mass production. The few manufacturers that did interpret it for their factories found interest to be slight in America. The French held it in higher esteem. Legs tend to be sweeping or cabriole. Upholstery becomes slimmer.

Art Deco, 1920-1945: The Paris *"L'Exposition International des Arts Décorative et Industriels Modernes"* became the mantra for designs of everything in this period. Lines are crisp, with some use of controlled curves. The Chrysler Building in New York City remains among the finest example of Art Deco architecture and those same straight lines and gentle curves are found in furniture. Makers used expensive materials, such as veneers, lacquered woods, glass and steel. The cocktail table first enters the furniture scene during this period. Upholstery can be vinyl or smooth fabrics. Legs are straight or slightly tapered; chair backs tend to be either low or extremely high.

Modernism, 1940-present: Furniture designed and produced during this period is distinctive, as it represents the usage of some new materials, like plastic, aluminum and molded laminates. The Bauhaus and also the Museum of Modern Art heavily influenced some designers. In 1940, the museum organized competitions for domestic furnishings. Designers Eero Saarien and Charles Eames won first prize for their designs. A new chair design combined the back, seat and arms together as one unit. Tables were designed that incorporated the top, pedestal and base as one. Shelf units were also designed in this manner.

Also see Modernism, Nautical, Oriental Objects.

Beds

Bed, Art Deco, France, single curvilinear bed frame with hanging shelf compartments, price for pair, circa 1930, 82" l...**$1,410**

Bed, Limbert, #651, daybed, angled headrest with spade cut-out, original finish, recovered cushions, branded, numbered, 74" w, 25" d, 23" h **$650**

Bed, Stickley Bros, attributed to, headboard with narrow vertical slats and panels, tapered feet, original side rails, original finish, minor scratches, stenciled "9001-1/2," 80 1/2" l, 56 1/2" w, 30" h..**$1,355**

Bed, Biedermeier, figured mahogany veneer, octagonal posts, turned feet and finials, paneled head and footboards, original rails, veneer damage, 38" w, 72" l, 45" h, pair. **$750**

Bed, Chippendale, tall post, curly maple, turned posts, scrolled headboard with poplar panel, original side rails, old mellow refinishing, minor repairs to posts, 60" w, 72" l, 80" h **$3,000**

Bed, country, American, rope, high post, curly maple, areas of tight curl, evidence of old red wash, turned and tapered legs, boldly turned posts taper toward the top, paneled headboard with scrolled crest, turned top finial, pierced restorations, 53 1/2" w, 70" l rails with original bolts. **$1,890**

Bed, Renaissance Revival, walnut, double, high headboard topped by rounded pediment, pointed finial.............**$1,700**

Bed, Gustav Stickley, a custom order variation of No.924, Prairie School influence, well-proportioned low form with double horizontal rail above 12 vertical spindles, fine original finish, branded signature, 58" w x 79" l x 37" h, excellent condition...**$3,500**

Bed, Sheraton, tester, straight headboard, carved baluster-turned posts, turned legs and feet, 88 1/2" h, tester incomplete. **$373**

Daybed, No.292, L. & J.G. Stickley, flared legs with through tenon construction and four vertical slats at sides, original spring cushion recovered in leather, includes two back bolsters, original finish, signed with Handcraft decal, 80" w x 30" d x 28" h, excellent condition. **$3,500**

Bookcases

Bookcase, American Renaissance Revival, carved cherry, circa 1890. The center cabinet with acorn and oak-leaf carved frieze, the bowed cornice surmounted by brass gallery, fitted with a bowed glass door opening to an interior of four adjustable shelves, flanked by bookcase sections, the pilasters rope-twist and acanthus-carved, on a conforming base fitted with three aligned drawers on

a molded plinth, 78 1/2" overall h x 71" w x 20 1/2" deep. All original, including cast-brass hardware; various scuffs and mars overall. Bowed glass door with L-shaped crack in glass lower right facing. **$2,588**

Bookcase, American Victorian, carved walnut, circa 1875. In three parts; the arched molded cornice with incised scrolled crest fitted to the upper case having a step-molded cornice fitted with a pair of astragal-glazed doors opening to an interior of adjustable shelves, stepped back on the lower case fitted with two aligned short drawers on a molded plinth, 8' 6 1/2" h x 53" overall w x 17" overall deep. Professionally cleaned and repolished, otherwise original. **$1,898**

Photo courtesy Rago Arts and Auction Center, Lambertville, N.J.; www.RagoArts.com

Bookcase (no. 359), Limbert, triple door with nine adjustable shelves, branded mark, 58 3/4" x 66 1/2" x 14". **$5,400**

Photo courtesy Rago Arts and Auction Center, Lambertville, N.J.; www.RagoArts.com

Bookcase, Victorian, oak with carved vine detail, three leaded-glass doors over three drawers and turned columns, 19th century, 65 3/4" x 68 1/2" x 16 1/4". **$2,160**

Bookcase, (no. 357), Limbert, single door with three adjustable shelves, branded mark, 57" x 29 1/2" x 14". **$5,700**

Bookcase, (no. 358), Limbert, double door with six adjustable shelves, branded mark, 57" x 48" x 14". **$4,200**

Bookcase/secretary, Governor Winthrop, American carved mahogany, 20th century. In two parts; the upper bookcase section with molded swans' neck pediment and carved floral terminals centering a turned finial above a pair of astragal glazed doors fitted to the lower section with sloping writing surface opening to an interior of cubby holes, drawers and prospect door above four serpentine drawers on a molded base. Raised on short cabriole legs with scalloped returns terminating in ball and claw feet, 82" h x 36" case w x 20 1/2" deep. Original finish and hardware. There is some damage to the left and right lower moldings and one chip of veneer off the right side of case between the second and third drawer. **$288**

Boxes

Pipe box, cherry, American, early 19th century, two-section box with pierced backboard, lower drawer, shrinkage crack on right side, 20 1/4" h, 6" w, 4 3/4" deep. **$237**

Pipe box, red-painted pine, American, early 19th century, shaped box with pierced backboard, lower drawer, shrinkage cracks, loss of drawer back causing loose drawer joinery, probable later paint, 20 1/4" h, 6" w, 4 3/4" deep.
....**$829**

Photo courtesy Sanford Alderfer Auction & Appraisal, Hatfield, Pa.; www.AlderferAuction.com

Knife boxes (pair), Hepplewhite, inlaid mahogany with sloping lid having shell-inlaid patera, geometric inlaid edges, serpentine front with four "stop fluted" inlaid pilasters, small ring handle with back-plate, reverse of lid inlaid with compass star, sloping fitted interior with numerous slots framed by line inlay, circa 1790, 14 1/2" h, 8 1/2" w, 11" deep. **$8,050 pair**
(A patera is a circular ornament, resembling a dish, often worked in relief on friezes.)

Photo courtesy of Treadway Toomey Galleries, Cincinnati and Oak Park, Ill.; www.treadwaygallery.com

Cabinet, Arts & Crafts style, single door with strap hinges and original hardware, interior contains one shelf, refinished, 20" w x 20" d x 29" h, very good condition. **$450**

Cabinets

Vitrine, gilt "vernis Martin" design, raised molded top, shaped swell-front glazed door, molded glass side panels, mirror back, ormolu border and mounts; base of door with painted garden scene with musician and lady, signed "Ch Olivier" lower left; painted side panels, flaring cabriole legs, 65 1/4" h, 24 1/2" w, 14 5/8" overall depth. ....**$1,610** *(In interior design, "vernis Martin" is a type of lacquer named for the French brothers Guillaume and Etienne-Simon Martin. It is an imitation of Chinese lacquer and was applied to a wide variety of items, from furniture to coaches.)*

Photo courtesy of Treadway Toomey Galleries, Cincinnati and Oak Park, Ill.; www.treadwaygallery.com

Map cabinet, circa 1910, manufactured for Rand McNally and Co., tambour front with two adjustable shelves, original label, cleaned original finish, 21" w x 14 1/2" d x 28" h, very good condition. **$700**

Photo courtesy Sanford Alderfer Auction & Appraisal, Hatfield, Pa.;
www.AlderferAuction.com

Vitrine, Hepplewhite-style, mahogany, lift lid top, four glazed sides, all glass beveled, line-inlaid apron and tapered square legs, casters, 35 1/2" h, 22" w, 30" l.
$1,440

Chairs

Photo courtesy Sanford Alderfer Auction & Appraisal, Hatfield, Pa.;
www.AlderferAuction.com

Armchair, Battleship Maine, oak, back with battleship carved in relief, "Maine" below; cresting of crossed flags with "1898" between paired C-scrolls, saddle seat, cabriole legs, tapered feet, baluster-and-ball turned H-stretcher, 40" h, 26" across arms. (The sinking of the Maine on Feb. 15, 1898, precipitated the Spanish-American War.) **$720**

Photo courtesy of Treadway Toomey Galleries, Cincinnati and Oak Park, Ill.;
www.treadwaygallery.com

Armchair, No. 349A, Gustav Stickley, heavy ladder-back form with three horizontal slats to back, original hard leather seat, original finish, signed with red decal, 26" w x 22" d x 38" h, very good condition. **$950**

Photo courtesy
Skinner Inc., Boston;
www.SkinnerInc.com

Armchair, polychrome, Sweden, late 18th century, scrolled cresting with a beaded paneled back with shaped arms on block, vase, and ring-turned legs and square stretchers, old surface, worn paint, back is dated "1790," 40" h, seat height 16".
$1,540

Armchair, Chippendale style, mahogany, strapwork splat, flame needlework-covered slip seat, shell-carved serpentine apron and knees, cabriole legs, claw and ball feet, 40 3/4" h. **$258**

Armchair, Empire, mahogany, with inverted C-scroll armrests and later tufted brown leather upholstery, 19th century, 39 1/2" x 32" x 26 1/2". **$1,020**

Armchair, Gothic Revival, walnut, crest with center spire and twin acorn finials, crockets on pointed arch; earth-toned oriental design fabric on back, arm-pads and seat, tapered round legs, 71" h, 27 1/2" w, 25 1/2" deep......**$1,840** *(A crocket is an architectural ornament of curved foliage used at the edge of a spire or gable.)*

Armchair, griffon carved, Victorian, Gothic carved pediment, paneled back, scrolled arm, conforming carving on frieze. **$780**

Armchair, Shop of the Crafters, tall back, inlaid with tacked-on red leather seat. Unmarked. 47 3/4" x 27 1/2" x 23". **$1,800**

Armchair, Windsor, branded under saddle seat "J.B. Ackley" (John Brientnall Ackley, Philadelphia, working 1791-1802); old black surface, arched back, nine bamboo-turned spindles, down-scrolled arms, turned legs with stretchers, 38 3/4" h. Replaced arm support. **$1,380**

Armchairs (pair), No. 318, Gustav Stickley, five vertical slats to back over a recovered leather drop-in spring cushion, corbel supports to sides, original finish, branded signature, 27 1/2" w x 24 1/2" d x 37" h, excellent condition. .... **$1,500 pair**

Chairs, (six), painted balloon backs, shell and fruit cresting, floral splat, green-bordered plank seat, conforming splayed legs and stretchers, circa 1870. .... **$330 set**

Photo courtesy Rago Arts and Auction Center, Lambertville, N.J.; www.RagoArts.com

Armchair, Roycroft, rare, with tooled leather, carved Orb and Cross mark, 36 1/2" x 24" x 25". **$7,200**

Photo courtesy of Treadway Toomey Galleries, Cincinnati and Oak Park, Ill.; www.treadwaygallery.com

Arm rocker, No.715, Stickley Brothers, massive form with five vertical slats to back and three under each arm, through tenon construction, recovered leather cushion, back cushion included, refinished, unsigned, some chips to edges, 28 1/2" w x 39" d x 35" h, very good condition. **$950**

Photo courtesy Sanford Alderfer Auction & Appraisal, Hatfield, Pa.; www.AlderferAuction.com

Armchair, Windsor, continuous arm, eight spindles, saddle seat, baluster and tapered round legs, H-stretcher, 35" h, early 19th century, split from back left leg to front of seat. **$270**

Photo courtesy James D. Julia Auctioneers, Fairfield, Maine; www.JuliaAuctions.com

Chairs (six), Southern Chippendale, carved fruitwood, possibly Virginia, second half 18th century. Each with serpentine crest rail with flared backswept ears above the upswept pierced five-ribbed splat with urn-form base set in a cove-molded cleated shoe, joined to the trapezoidal molded rail fitted with slip seat raised on frontal square legs, with shaped returns, the rear legs backswept joined by a recessed box stretcher, 38 1/2" h. Chairs retain original cleaned finish and framing, no visible restoration or repairs, ears with old losses. **$7,475 set**

Photo courtesy of Treadway Toomey Galleries, Cincinnati and Oak Park, Ill.; www.TreadwayGallery.com

Chalet chair, No. 2578, Gustav Stickley, single broad slat at back over a recovered leather seat, original finish, signed with box mark, 16" w x 16" d x 29" h, very good condition. **$350**

Photo courtesy Sanford Alderfer Auction & Appraisal, Hatfield, Pa.; www.AlderferAuction.com

Corner chair, maple, three ring-turned tapered round supports, conforming turned legs with X-stretcher, needlework seat with musical trophies, early 19th century, 33 3/4" h, 27 3/8" w. **$230**

Dining chairs (eight), Chippendale-style, carved mahogany with shaped crest rail with centering shell, strapwork splat, upholstered slip seat, apron with shell, cabriole legs, claw and ball feet; including open armchair and seven side chairs, 42" h, 21 1/4" w. .... **$4,800 set**

Dining chairs, (12), upholstered, possibly by R.J. Horner; mahogany; consisting of two armchairs and 10 side chairs; armchairs with acanthus leafage near back, acanthus hand rests, tapered square legs headed by scrolled, under-cut carving above husk pendants; garden upholstery on backs, arm-pads and over-upholstered seats, 50 3/8" h.
.... **$3,105 set**

Dining chairs, (four), Gustav Stickley, early U-back style with rush seats, circa 1901, unmarked, 34 3/4" x 19" x 17".
.... **$6,600 set**

Dining chairs, (six), Gustav Stickley, V-Back, one armchair (no. 354) and five side chairs, circa 1905, small red decals. Armchair 36" x 26" x 22", side chairs 35 1/2" x 19" x 19".
.... **$7,200 set**

Dining chairs, (six), Victorian, walnut, carved with barley-twist columns, circa 1900, 39 1/2" x 16 1/2" x 19".
.... **$1,140 set**

Morris chair, No. 332, Gustav Stickley, classic flat-arm form with five vertical slats under each arm and original leatherette cushions, complete with original pegs and washers, branded signature, lightly re-coated original finish, 31" w x 38" d x 41" h, very good condition......**$6,000**

Photo courtesy Rago Arts and Auction Center, Lambertville, N.J.; www.RagoArts.com

Hall chairs (pair), Charles Rohlfs, with tall cutout backs and saddle seats, 1901, carved R 1901, 54 3/4" x 18" x 17". **$19,200 pair**

Photo courtesy of Treadway Toomey Galleries, Cincinnati and Oak Park, Ill.; www.treadwaygallery.com

Hall chair, Stickley Brothers, Prairie School influence, three vertical slats at back over a replaced leather drop-in seat, original finish, signed with Quaint tag, 17" w x 17" d x 42" h, very good condition. **$400**

Photo courtesy Rago Arts and Auction Center, Lambertville, N.J.; www.RagoArts.com

Rocker (no. 393), Gustav Stickley, rare, high back with inverted V arm supports, drop-in spring seat with new leather cover, red decal, 44" x 27 3/4" x 24". **$7,200**

Rocker, L. and J.G. Stickley, similar to No. 1321, large high-back form with 13 spindles at back over a replaced leather sling seat, original finish, 31" w x 32" d x 42" h, unsigned, very good condition. **$900**

Side chair, Windsor, fan-back, deeply bowed crest rail, seven spindles, saddle seat, splayed bamboo-turned legs with stretcher, circa 1790, 35" h. **$575**

Morris chair, (no. 410), L. and J.G. Stickley, drop-arm with slats to the floor and original drop-in spring seat, branded mark, 38" x 32 1/2" x 38". **$8,400**

Side chair, No. 354, Gustav Stickley, "V"-back form with five vertical slats over a replaced seat, refinished, unsigned, 19" w x 19" d x 36" h, very good condition. **$375**

Side chair, No. 394, Gustav Stickley, "H"-back form with recovered drop-in seat, original finish, unsigned, some looseness, 17" w x 16" d x 40" h, very good condition.
....**$225**

Side chair, banister-back, rush seat, bun-form finials, four flat spindles, turned round legs with stretchers, circa 1720, 45 3/8" h. **$92**

Side chair, William & Mary, circa 1730, shaped crest rail over vase splat, turned and blocked front legs with ball-turned front stretcher. **$240**

Side chairs, (eight), Chippendale style, carved crest rail over strapwork splat back, serpentine apron with carved shell, cabriole legs with acanthus knees, claw and ball feet; mahogany. **$1,150**

Side chairs, (four), Old Hickory, with woven seats. Old Hickory metal tag on one, 39" x 20" x 16 1/2". .... **$1,800 all**

Side chairs, (eight), upholstered, carved oak, possibly by R.J. Horner, crest rail with oval cartouche flanked by twin lion figures, fluted round stiles with banded ball finials; urn-turned round front legs with casters, twin leaf-scroll apron, upholstered back rest and over-upholstered seat, 44 1/8" h; missing some casters, loss to finial. ... **$1,265 set**

Wing chair, upholstered, carved walnut, carved leaf-scrolled crest rail; upholstered small wings, back support, arm-pads and seat, all in pastel-shaded flame stitch; scrolled acanthus hand-rests, ring-turned and blocked legs with carved stretchers, 53 3/4" h, 29 1/2" w, 27" deep. **$345**

Photo courtesy James D. Julia Auctioneers, Fairfield, Maine; www.JuliaAuctions.com

Blanket chest in old blue paint, American, pine, bootjack legs, circa 1820. Rectangular molded top hinged on the conforming case fitted with till, case ends arched, wear to painted surfaces, top with normal shrinkage split, 19 1/2" h x 42 1/2" l x 14" deep. **$1,035**

Chests

Blanket chest, English, Victorian, oak, with carved decoration of geometric shapes, 19th century, 29" x 50" x 20 3/4". **$780**

Chest, English, 17th century, walnut, three carved reserves with interlaced scroll forms, raised supports at ends, front hinged at bottom and drops down, 29 1/2" h, 43" w, 18 3/4" deep. **$575**

Chest, green painted pine, inscribed "Peter Michel Anno 1785"; two oblong reserves with brown sponge decoration; interior with till to left; wrought-iron strap hinges, two skid supports, 21 1/2", 48 7/8" l, 22 3/4" deep. **$1,495**

Photo courtesy James D. Julia Auctioneers, Fairfield, Maine; www.JuliaAuctions.com

Sea chest, New England, paint-decorated pine, circa 1850. The rectangular hinged lid with applied molding painted with a fully rigged ship above the conforming case, the interior fitted with till, the sides with beckets, the front decorated with opposing dolphins centering a ship's wheel. The whole painted on a blue-green ground on a plinth base, 16" h x 46" l x 17 1/2" deep. **$1,150** *(Beckets are short lines with an eye at one end and a knot at the other; used to secure loose items on a ship.)*

Photo courtesy of Treadway Toomey Galleries, Cincinnati and Oak Park, Ill.; www.treadwaygallery.com

Chest, Arts & Crafts style, paneled top and sides, original finish, 40" w x 21" d x 20" h, very good condition. **$800**

Chests of drawers

Chest of drawers, blonde mahogany, molded oblong top, four graduated cock-beaded drawers, oval brasses (replaced), straight bracket feet, split near right front top corner, 37 3/8" h, 37 3/8" w, 20 5/8" deep. **$805**
(A cock bead is a narrow half-round trim detail that surrounds a drawer front or door.)

Chest of drawers, Bucks County, Pa., walnut, cove-molded cornice above band of dentil molding, three small drawers over two small drawers over five graduated drawers, all thumb-molded and with oval sickle and sheaf brasses (replaced), twin fluted quarter-columns flanking, ogee bracket feet, 64" h, 43 5/8" w, 23" deep. **$2,875**

Chest of drawers, Chippendale, cherry, molded top, four graduated thumb-molded drawers, brass bail handles (replaced), fluted quarter-columns flanking, ogee bracket feet, Pennsylvania, circa 1780, 36 1/2" h, 37 3/8" w, 20 1/2" deep. **$3,450**

Chest of drawers, Chippendale, cherry, top section with three small over four wide graduated thumb-molded drawers, flanking fluted chamfered corners with lamb's tongues; lower section with four graduated wide drawers, flanking fluted chamfered corners with lamb's tongues, brass bail handles (replaced), bracket feet, 74 1/2" h, 43 1/2" w, 22" deep. **$4,025**

Chest of drawers, Chippendale, mahogany, molded top, four graduated cock-beaded drawers, brass bail handles, flanked by twin fluted quarter-columns, ogee bracket feet, circa 1780, 32 7/8" h, 37 1/2" w, 22 1/8" deep. **$2,070**
(A cock bead is a narrow half-round trim detail that surrounds a drawer front or door.)

Chest of drawers, Hepplewhite, mahogany, two small drawers over three wide graduated cock-beaded drawers, oval brasses (replaced), French bracket feet, 40 1/4" h, 37" w, 18 3/8" deep; interiors of two small drawers refinished. **$660**
(A cock bead is a narrow half-round trim detail that surrounds a drawer front or door.)

Chest of drawers, inlaid, cherry, four graduated thumb-molded drawers, brass bail handles and escutcheons, line-inlaid vertical bands, twin fluted quarter columns, ogee bracket feet, circa 1800, 41 5/8" h, 39 1/2" w, 20 1/2" deep. **$2,300**

Cupboards

Corner cupboard, cherry, two sections, glazed 12-light door, hinges on right, painted shelved interior, chamfered corners, 86" h, 42" w. **$2,990**

Cupboard, walnut, single door, top thumb-molded on three sides, door with two wrought-iron H-hinges, shelved interior, bracket feet, early 19th century, 43 1/4" h, 30 1/4" w, 16 1/2" deep. **$1,440**

Photo courtesy Sanford Alderfer Auction & Appraisal, Hatfield, Pa.; www.AlderferAuction.com

Chest of drawers, Chippendale, cherry, molded top, four graduated scratch-molded drawers, brass bail handles and escutcheons, ogee bracket feet, 37 5/8" h, 38 3/4" w, 18 1/4" deep, replaced glue blocks on feet. **$920**

Photo courtesy Sanford Alderfer Auction & Appraisal, Hatfield, Pa.; www.AlderferAuction.com

Corner cupboard, cherry, two section, cove-molded cornice, glazed 12-light door, hinges on right, off-white painted butterfly shelves, twin cabinet doors, chamfered corners, bracket feet, 87 1/2" h, 43" w. **$2,587**

Photo courtesy James D. Julia Auctioneers, Fairfield, Maine; www.JuliaAuctions.com

Corner cupboard, New England Sheraton, birch and maple, upper case with molded cornice and canted sides centering a pair of glass paneled doors opening to two fixed shelves, fitted to the lower case having a pair of cupboard doors opening to a shelf. Base with shaped and arched apron, 79" h, 46 1/2" w, 23 1/2" deep. Early refinished medium-brown surface. Retains original backboards with hand-cut nails, original feet. **$2,300**

Photo courtesy Sanford Alderfer Auction & Appraisal, Hatfield, Pa.; www.Alderfer-Auction.com

Hanging cupboard, Pennsylvania, walnut, cove-molded cornice, six-light glazed door with brass H-hinges, pale green painted interior, thumb-molded drawer below, oval molded brasses, flanking fluted quarter-columns, early 19th century, 38" h, 39 1/2" w (overall), 9 7/8" deep (overall). **$3,162**

Wall cupboard, Rococo Revival, oak, upper section with bowed cresting with fruit and scrollwork above, beveled mirror, oblong beveled mirrors at sides, twin mirror-back glazed cabinets at sides with two beveled mirrors flanking below and twin acanthus-carved supports; lower section with lower leaf-scroll-carved center frieze drawer flanked by two drawers with large carved mask-head pulls, opening below above conforming drawer; four fluted tapered round columns flanking twin leaf-carved cabinet doors, bun feet, circa 1880s; 82" h, 82" w, 25 1/2" deep. **$2,875**

Cupboard section, Chippendale, walnut, circa 1780, cove-molded cornice, twin doors, each with two raised panels, twin flanking quarter columns, front molding with conforming right molding. Shelved interior, 44 3/4" h, 39" w, 11 1/2" deep. Left side molding missing; repair at lower hinge on right door. **$1,150**

Desks

Desk, English, Victorian, oak, slant front with four graduated drawers, 19th century, 42" x 37" x 19 1/2" (when closed). **$480**

Desk, George III, mahogany, slant-front, fitted interior with five open pigeonholes, two banks of six small drawers to each side; case with four graduated cock-beaded drawers, brass bail handles and back plates, pair of lopers, bracket feet, 41" h, 42 5/8" w, 21" deep; writing board broken out; splits and damage to outer edge of writing board. **$575**
(A cock bead is a narrow half-round trim detail that surrounds a drawer front or door.)

Photo courtesy James D. Julia Auctioneers, Fairfield, Maine; www.JuliaAuctions.com

Desk, American Chippendale, maple and curly maple, slant lid, last half of the 18th century, rectangular dovetailed case fitted with a sloping lid opening to an interior of six valanced cubby holes over five aligned drawers above four long graduated and thumb molded drawers. Raised on a molded plinth with shaped bracket feet, 41 1/2" h x 32 1/2" h writing surface x 36" case w x 18 1/2" deep, fully restored and refinished with replaced hardware. **$4,485**

*Desk, Chippendale, inlaid mahogany, slant-front writing
board opening to prospect door with inlaid three-pointed
star, pair of document drawers, six small drawers, over eight
pigeonholes; pair of lopers, case with four graduated cock-
beaded drawers with oval brasses (replaced), fluted quarter-
columns flanking, ogee bracket feet, 43" h, 41 1/4" w, 20"
deep; backboards replaced; piece of outside sheathing of left
front foot is missing.* **$1,150**
*(A cock bead is a narrow half-round trim detail that
surrounds a drawer front or door.)*

Desk, inlaid, mahogany slant-front, English, early 19th
century, prospect door with satinwood border, twin half-
column document drawers, six arched pigeonholes over
six small drawers and two wide drawers, lightwood band
on slant lid, four graduated ebonized drawers, oval brasses
with thistles (replaced), bracket feet, 42 1/4" h, 39 1/4" w,
19 1/4" deep. **$517**

Desk, Lancaster County, Pa., inlaid cherry, slant front;
writing board opening to fitted interior with inlaid arched
prospect door with five small drawers behind, twin
flanking document drawers, four arched pigeonholes,
six small drawers; case with four cock-beaded graduated
drawers, oval brasses, two lopers, French bracket feet,
44 7/8" h, 38" w, 20 1/2" deep. **$5,462**
*(A cock bead is a narrow half-round trim detail that surrounds a
drawer front or door.)*

Drop-front desk, (no. 91), Roycroft, with gallery interior,
carved Orb and Cross mark, 44 1/4" x 38 1/2" x 19 1/2".
....**$6,600**

Drop-front desk and cabinet, Gustav Stickley, rare, with
strap hinges, chamfered back, interior gallery, early red
decal, 56" x 38" x 15". **$18,000**

Slant-front desk, carved oak, possibly by R.J. Horner,
circa 1880; oblong top, mask head and patera-carved
shallow map drawer, scroll-carved writing board; fitted
interior with three convex-front drawers and pigeonholes,
serpentine-front case with three conforming frieze drawers
and small drawers beneath, supported by carved griffons,

*Sea captain's travel desk, line-inlaid mahogany with
centering foil inlay marked "JH"; folding writing surface,
green felt lined, including wood inkwell and wood sand
shaker, three small interior drawers, twin brass handles,
turned feet, 8 1/2" h, 19 5/8" w, 12" deep (closed).* **$1,610**

*Slant-front desk, Chippendale, cherry, fitted interior with
prospect door, two document drawers, six small drawers
and six pigeonholes; case with four graduated cock-beaded
drawers, brass bail handles and escutcheons, bracket feet,
circa 1780, 44 1/4" h, 37 38" w, 21 1/8" deep.* **$2,280**
*(A cock bead is a narrow half-round trim detail that
surrounds a drawer front or door.)*

resting on stretcher shelf, molded set-back for feet,
conforming carved side paneling, low square molded feet,
45 1/2" h, 42 1/2" w, 22" deep. **$8,625**

Traveler's desk, Hepplewhite, inlaid, oblong lift lid with
centering blonde wood patera, four quarter-fans at corners,
dark figured exotic wood with blonde wood borders,
dovetailed drawer in base with brass bail handle, when
open, sloping surface revealed with dark blue felt, glass ink
bottle and pen tray, circa 1790, 6" h, 16 3/8" w, 10" deep.
.... **$747**
*(A patera is a circular ornament, resembling a dish, often worked
in relief on friezes.)*

Settees, Settles and Sofas

Photo courtesy Rago Arts and Auction Center, Lambertville, N.J.; www.RagoArts.com

Drop-arm settee (no. 219), Gustav Stickley, with slatted back and original drop-in spring seat recovered in black leather, unmarked, 37 1/2" x 71 1/2" x 26". **$2,160**

Photo courtesy Rago Arts and Auction Center, Lambertville, N.J.; www.RagoArts.com

Cube settle, Gustav Stickley, spindle sides with drop-in spring seat recovered in brown leather, red decal, 30 3/4" x 68 1/2" x 30". **$21,600**

Photo courtesy of Treadway Toomey Galleries, Cincinnati and Oak Park, Ill.; www.treadwaygallery.com

Settle, No. 775, L. and J.G. Stickley, even-arm paneled form with recovered cushion, original finish, signed with Handcraft decal, re-pegged, 84" w x 32" d x 40" h, very good condition. **$6,500**

Sofa, William & Mary style, oak, high-back, double-arched top, outward scrolled arms, center ball-turned support flanked by molded scrollwork, domical foot; two conforming supports at front corners, turned and blocked stretchers; covered in pink, red and ivory flame-stitch patterned upholstery; 56 1/2" h, 64" w, 37" deep. **$2,400**

Sideboard, Baroque Revival, mahogany, three "Atlas" figures providing support, three protruding mask head frieze drawers, two cabinet doors carved with women figural drawers, carved feet with mask heads, sides carved with shells, scrolls and flowers, 50" h, 73" w, 26 1/2" deep, top section missing. **$6,325**

Settle, No. 220, L. & J.G. Stickley, paneled Prairie School form with wide arms supported by corbels, nicely recovered leather cushions, branded signature, cleaned original finish, rarely comes to market, 84" w x 37" d x 29" h, very good condition. **$18,000**

Settle, Arts & Crafts style, even-arm form with an upholstered seat and back, refinished, reupholstered, 72" w x 27 1/2" d x 39 1/2" h, very good condition. **$800**

Sideboards

Sideboard, Jacobean style, oak, oblong molded top, three drawers, each with recessed molded X-forms, brass drop

Sideboard (no. 814), Gustav Stickley, with plate rack and strap hardware, branded mark, 48" x 66" x 24". **$8,400**

Sideboard, Sheraton, mahogany, two small cock-beaded drawers with brass ring handles, over arched opening, tapered round legs with vase-turned feet, 33 3/4" h, 37 1/8" w, 19 1/4" deep. **$2,587**
(A cock bead is a narrow half-round trim detail that surrounds a drawer front or door.)

handles, three vase-form and ring-turned front legs, bun feet, 35 1/4" h, 74 3/8" w, 20" deep. **$1,725**

(Jacobean style is the name given to the second phase of Renaissance design in England, following the Elizabethan style. It is associated with King James I, reign 1603–1625.)
Sideboards, (pair), marble tops, mahogany, beige marble tops, early 20th century, with dentil molding, canted corners, each with paw foot below and lion head above, 35" h, 72" w, 25 3/4" deep. .... **$920 pair**

Tables

Banquet table, Sheraton, mahogany, two sections, each with rounded corners, single leaf, five reeded tapered round legs (one support leg swings out), ball feet, circa 1820, 28 1/2" h, 48" w, 84 1/2" l, additional bracing underneath. **$920**

Boulle table, ormolu-mounted, shield-form top, center with chariot driver holding spear, conforming serpentine front drawer, mask heads at corners, cabriole legs, ormolu paw feet, 30 1/4" h, 35 1/4" l, 21" w, inlay damage at one rounded end. **$977**
(André-Charles Boulle [1642–1732], was a French cabinetmaker generally considered the preeminent artist in the field of marquetry.)

Center table, marquetry inlaid, center reserve with profusion of flowers, stems, leafage and birds, heavily leaf-scrolled border, single frieze drawer, marquetry drawer front, apron, tapering square legs and shaped stretcher, bun feet, 28" h, 42 3/4" w, 33" deep, refinished. **$1,955**

Center table, oval, late 19th century, mahogany, conforming inner top band of low relief scroll- and latticework; conforming acanthus leaf apron, four acanthus-carved vase and ball supports on oval platform base with narrow acanthus apron and four bold paw feet with casters, 29 1/2" h, 53 3/4" x 35 3/4" (top). **$2,300**

Dining table, massive mahogany, circular, possibly by R.J. Horner, late 19th century, molded extension top, paneled octagonal pedestal supported by carved S-scrolled braces, resting on shaped stretchers, square paneled legs headed by scrolled, undercut carving above husk pendants, molded square feet, casters, 29 1/2" h, 65 1/2" d. With additional leaves. **$5,750**

Dining table, mahogany, made by Baker, extension top with rounded ends and corners, cross-banded blonde

Card table, Hepplewhite, inlaid, mahogany; folding top, "ovolo" corners, oval blonde wood reserve, geometric border inlay, tapered square legs with line inlay; diamond-form inlay above legs, 30" h, 35 3/4" w, 16 7/8" deep (closed). **$1,380**
(Ovolo refers to a convex molding having a cross section in the form of a quarter of a circle or of an ellipse.)

mahogany, twin tapered round ringed pedestals, each on four splayed reeded saber legs with brass caps and casters, including three 18" leaves, 28 1/2" h, 72" l (no leaves in place), 46" w. **$6,000**

Dining table, mahogany, early 19th century, deep drop leaves, tapered square legs; two legs swing out for support, 29" h, 42" w, 58" l (leaves up). **$201**

Dining table and five side chairs, Shop of the Crafters, with one leaf. Unmarked. Table, 28" x 54", 11" leaf, chairs 43 1/2" x 19" x 18". .... **$9,600 set**

Dining table and eight chairs, Federal style, extension-top dining table with cross-banded border and rounded corners, twin pedestals, each with fluted urn, four down-swept reeded legs with acanthus decoration, brass paw feet with casters; 29 1/8" h, 42" w (leaves down), 60" l) including five 12" leaves in case and set of pads; together with eight mahogany square-back chairs (2 armchairs and 6 side chairs); strapwork urn splat with drapery swags; over-upholstered gold and pale green seat; molded tapered square legs with spade front feet, 36 5/8" h, 23" w. .... **$2,875 set**

Drop-leaf table, birch, deep overhang at ends, slender tapered square legs, 28 3/8" h, 31 1/2" w (leaves up).
.... **$126**

Drop-leaf table, Sheraton, mahogany, reeded round legs (two swing out to support leaves), circa 1820, 29 1/8" h, 68 3/8" l (leaves up). **$270**

Drop-leaf table, Victorian, mahogany, with D-end flaps and ball-and-claw feet, 19th century, 28" x 43" x 20".
.... **$480**

Gaming table, inlaid, exotic mixed-wood circular top with checkerboard, faceted apron, small drawer, three legs with carved zigzag motif. **$632**

Library table, Arts & Crafts style, rectangular top with four vertical slats to each side over a lower shelf, through tenon construction, original brass hardware, worn original finish, some damage to side, 36" w x 24" d x 30" h, good condition. **$275**

Library table, Arts & Crafts style, possibly Harden, rectangular top over two drawers with original hardware, slatted sides with through tenon construction, refinished, 49" w x 29" d x 30" h, good condition.............................**$450**

Dining table, oak, circa 1900, extension top, circular top with gadrooned border, four carved lion heads with acanthus, short curved legs, massive paw feet; including five 12" leaves in case and turned central support, 28 3/4" h, 59 1/4" d. **$5,750**

Dressing table, State of Maine, Sheraton faux-grained paint-decorated pine, circa 1825, shaped splash guard with paint-decorated cluster of fruit and ochre striping fitted to the rectangular top above the conforming frieze with long drawer raised on cylindrical swelled and ring-turned legs on ball feet, 31 1/2" h, 32 1/2" w, 17" deep. Retains good original surface and patina. Paint mostly intact showing nominal and normal wear. **$1,380**

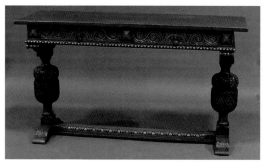

Library table, Elizabethan style, oak, molded apron with two drawers with brass drop handles, twin leaf-carved bulbous supports resting on trestles connected by carved stretcher, 34" h, 60" w, 22" deep. **$517**

Occasional table, Samuel Yellin, wrought iron, tripod with hammered copper tray, normal cleaning to tray, authenticated by Samuel Yellin Metalworkers, unmarked, 33" x 21". **$4,200**

Pembroke table, English, mahogany, molded drop-leaf top with rounded corners, cock-beaded end drawer with two brass pulls, conforming opposite mock drawer, tapered square legs, casters; circa 1840, 28" h, 36" w, 45 1/4" l. (leaves up). **$316**

(A cock bead is a narrow half-round trim detail that surrounds a drawer front or door. The characteristic that gives a table the name of Pembroke involves the drop leaves,

Luncheon table (no. 647), Gustav Stickley, with stretcher on edge, mortised with keyed-through tenons, unmarked, 29 1/2" x 40" x 28". **$2,160**

Pembroke table, mahogany, with reeded legs and shaped corner flaps, 19th century, 29" x 36" x 21 1/2". **$420**

Refectory table, English, oak, with single drawer on frieze, barley-twist legs and stretchers, 19th century, 32" x 45 1/2" x 22". **$780**

Photo courtesy James D. Julia Auctioneers, Fairfield, Maine; www.JuliaAuctions.com

Sewing table, Massachusetts, Sheraton, circa 1810, figured mahogany inlaid three-drawer, rectangular top with canted corners and figured birch cross banding above the conforming case, fitted with three long string-inlaid drawers, two with ivory escutcheons and the third fitted for a bag. Raised on cylindrical reeded and ring-turned slender legs with multiple ring cuffs. Old dry finish with minor losses to cross banding on top; top two drawers with original escutcheons and hardware. Bag slide has original front and slide but has been reconstructed into a drawer. Old repairs rejoining the four legs to the table top, professionally done. Other minor veneer chips, 30" h x 20 1/2" w x 14 3/4" deep. **$690**

Photo courtesy Rago Arts and Auction Center, Lambertville, N.J.; www.RagoArts.com

"Rocket" occasional table, Bradley & Hubbard / Longwy, embossed brass, top and shaft inlaid with Longwy tiles, circa 1880-1885, 33 1/4" x 14" sq. **$6,600**

which are held up, when the table is open, by brackets that turn under the top.)

Side table, Chippendale, walnut, top with invected front corners, thumb-molded frieze drawer, two brass bail handles, straight legs with molded outer corners, chamfered inner corners, 28 3/4" h, 35" w, 19 1/8" deep.
....$1,265
(Invected means having a border or outline composed of semicircles with the convexity outward; the opposite of engrailed.)

Side table, gilt wood, white alabaster top, apron with acorn and oak leaf decoration, conforming out-set fluted tapered round legs with ball feet, 19th century, 29 1/4" h, 28 1/4" w, 19 1/2" deep. **$480**

Side table, tiger maple, single drawer with pressed glass pull, tapered round legs with vase-form feet, 28 3/4" h, 25" w, 15" deep...$920

Side table, walnut, oblong top, single drawer with two brasses (replaced), ring-turned round legs, ball feet, 19th century. **$201**

Table, Bucks County, Pa., red painted, molded top, drawer with brass pull, splayed tapered square legs, 19th century, 29" h, 16 1/4" w, 17" deep. **$1,150**

Table with lift top, cherry, three small compartments to rear, single drawer with figured cherry facing and brass pull, twin half-spindle sides flanking, ring-turned tapered round legs, circa 1840, 28 3/4" h, 22" w, 21 7/8" deep.
....**$575**

Table, marble top, walnut, octagonal black marble top with white striations, walnut tripod base with three partially disrobed women at corners, low relief images of birds, musicians and other figures; bold paw feet, 30 1/4" h. (not including marble top), vertical shrinkage splits in base.
....**$3,900**

Table, attributed to Old Hickory, with quarter-sawn oak veneered oval top over five legs. Unmarked, 30" x 66" x 36". **$1,560**

Taboret (no. 46), Gustav Stickley, rare, with hexagonal top over six angled legs and corbels, circa 1901, unmarked, 21" x 19" sq. **$7,200**

Work table, pine, drawer with wood pull, tapered square legs with splay, 19th century, 29 1/2" h, top 19" x 18 7/8". **$184**

Other Forms

Bench, Arts & Crafts style, spindle form with 18 vertical spindles to back over a recovered leather seat, cleaned original finish, 44 1/2" w x 22" d x 39" h, very good condition. **$600**

Bench, circa 1910, rectangular top with pyrographic cattail design, original finish, 38 1/2" w x 15" d x 19" h, very good condition. **$550**

Bookstand, wrought iron, slanting scrolled rests for two books, "spear" point at center, pair of swiveling candleholders, twist standard with tripod scrolled base, 61 1/2" h. **$1,150**

Cradle, red finish, heart-form cutout in headboard and footboard, twin rocker base, 19th century, 22 1/2" h, 40" l. **$86**

Footstool, No. 300, Gustav Stickley, original leather and tacks over a base with original finish, signed with red decal and partial paper label, 20 1/2" w x 16 1/2" d x 16" h, excellent condition. **$1,800**

Butler's tray on stand, mahogany, 19th century, oblong with shaped gallery and pierced hand-holds, dovetailed corners, folding stand; tray, 27 1/2" x 17 1/4". **$570**

Footstool, Arts & Crafts style, contemporary, in mahogany, similar to Gustav Stickley No. 395, seven vertical spindles to each side, 20" w x 16" d x 16" h, very good condition. **$150**

Photo courtesy Sanford Alderfer Auction & Appraisal, Hatfield, Pa.; www.AlderferAuction.com

Footstool, Berks County, Pa., made by Marks DeTurk, Jan. 5, 1920; oblong with splayed tenoned legs, finely detailed bird and tree decoration, 6" h, 12" l, 5 5/8" w. **$1,560**

Photo courtesy Rago Arts and Auction Center, Lambertville, N.J.; www.RagoArts.com

Magazine stand (no. 80), Roycroft, tall trapezoidal, carved Orb and Cross mark, 64" x 17 3/4" sq. **$18,000**

Photo courtesy Rago Arts and Auction Center, Lambertville, N.J.; www.RagoArts.com

Hanging wall shelf, Charles Rohlfs, with scrolled sides, 1905, carved R 1905, 44" x 27" x 7 1/2". **$5,100**

Footstool, Victorian, American, carved mahogany with floral bouquets on the skirt, Spanish feet and needlepoint upholstery of a reclining dachshund, 17" x 23" x 16".
.... **$360**

Parlor suite, Victorian, mahogany, 19th century: armchair with carved rams heads and paw feet on metal casters; fire screen with needlework panel and applied glass beads; and Chippendale-style side table. Tallest: 43". .... **$1,800 set**

Screen, Arts & Crafts style, in mahogany, peaked top over leaded amber glass panels, original strap hardware, original finish, each panel: 24" w x 63" h, very good condition.
.... **$325**

Photo courtesy Rago
Arts and Auction Center,
Lambertville, N.J.
www.RagoArts.com

*Picnic set,
Old Hickory,
with table and
two benches.
Branded marks.
Table 30" x 60"
x 30", benches
18" x 48" x 14".*
$3,600 set

Photo courtesy James D. Julia Auctioneers, Fairfield, Maine; www.JuliaAuctions.com

*Shaving stand, Federal, mahogany and boxwood, inlaid,
circa 1810. Oval mirror suspended on cyma-curved arms
resting on a rectangular box with serpentine front fitted
with three aligned drawers each with a brass knob pull,
the whole raised on ogee bracket feet, minor staining on
surface of glove box probably due to perfume or cologne
bottles leaving ring outlines. Brackets for mirror appear
original as do the feet, 22 1/2" h x 17" w x 8" deep.* **$402**

Stand, Arts & Crafts style, rectangular top over a drop-front
cabinet door with original strap hinges, slatted sides with
through tenon construction, original finish, 25" w x 14" d x
30" h, very good condition...**$500**

Tabouret, circa 1915, Moorish influence, octagonal top with
deeply carved and inlaid designs in mother-of-pearl, some
wear and separation, 16 1/2" w x 16 1/2" d x 20" h, good
condition...**$250**

Photo courtesy James D. Julia Auctioneers, Fairfield, Maine; www.JuliaAuctions.com

*Umbrella stand, stick & ball design, oak with curled feet,
ball finials and central stylized hourglass and abacus
designs, 26 3/4" h. One central hourglass design has old
repair with one replaced dowel.* **$172**

Vanity and mirror (no. 110), Roycroft, with single drawer, carved Orb and Cross mark, 56" x 39" x 17 1/2". **$3,900**

Barometers

Mahogany-cased barometer, C-scroll cresting over mercury thermometer, barometer with steel dial marked "Royal Hotel," 47 3/8" h, 15" w. **$632**

Mahogany-cased barometer, unsigned, 19th century, having a single dial with thermometer and mirror. In an older refinish, 38" l. **$345**

Stick barometer, walnut, baluster form, with mercury tube covered with a turned half-column along most of its length, with a turned rosette at the base. Printed dial marked "S. Bennett" across the bottom, with different weather conditions along the sides. Mounted to the face and flanking the dial is a thermometer and indicator; retains old varnish, 42" l. **$287**

Stick barometer, telescope form, in walnut and ebonized walnut with tombstone top, silvered dial with barometer vertical through center and thermometer mounted along right margin, marked "The Standard" at top and "Storm King/Barometer/Warranted Correct/Manufactured/And Sold by/C. Spooner/Boston," with original cover glass, in original finish, 42" l. **$287**

Mirrors

Convex mirror, classical gilt gesso and wood, England or America, circa 1800, re-gilded, (imperfections), 43" d, may lack candle sconces; most of the frame is repainted; chips to gesso. **$2,370**

Dressing table mirror, Hepplewhite, mahogany veneer, early 19th century, shield-shaped mirror, bowed base with three drawers on ogee bracket feet, cross-banded borders, 23" h, 16 1/2" w, 8" deep, one drawer pull replaced, unobtrusive crack to top surface, missing one circular ivory disk decoration, crack across on side. **$207**

Washstand, mahogany, lift top revealing circular basin opening and openings for two glasses, cabinet door below flanked by twin spiral molded pilasters, spiral turned round legs, ball feet, circa 1840, 32 3/4" h, 18" w, 16 1/4" deep; split at right rear corner of lid. **$805**

Wardrobe, Gustave Serrurier-Bovy, with mirrored door next to five-drawer cabinet, wrought-iron hardware. Branded Serrurier Liege, 82 1/2" x 58 1/4" x 23 1/2". **$10,200**

(Gustave Serrurier-Bovy [1858-1910] was a Belgian architect and furniture designer.)

Chippendale-style mirror, with carved and gilded bird's eye maple frame, circa 1900, 47" x 25". **$900**

Classical gilt and black-painted mirror, split-baluster, Massachusetts, circa 1825, tablet with a fruit-filled cornucopia, (minor imperfections), 44" h, 20 3/4" w. **$2,962**

Federal parcel-gilt mirror, American, with reverse-painted panel, circa 1820, stepped cornice with 12 spherules above the rectangular painted panel depicting a basket of fruit within stylized green and red spandrels over the rectangular mirror plate. Flanked by engaged concave balusters, housing rope twist columns on a concave plinth, 33" h x 17" w, panel is original with some paint loss above the basket of fruit and at the foot rim of basket. Minor rubbing to gilding. **$1,265**

Federal gilt-wood mirror, circa 1840, oval mirror plate within opposing cornucopia surmounted by a displayed eagle perched on leafy boughs, 23" x 26". **$2,300**

Federal carved gilt wood over-mantel mirror, American, circa 1830, stepped cornice above the rectangular frame, frieze with carved draperies flanked by fluted columns with anthemion leaves and oval reeded patera centering three rectangular mirror plates. Surrounds with attached floral garlands. Lower molded apron with acorn leaf carvings, 27" h x 60" l, retains original glasses and backboards. Original surfaces are somewhat chipped with losses to gesso and some of the gilt work throughout the entire mirror frame, overall probably 3-4 percent. **$2,990**

Fret-scrolled mahogany mirror, gilt molded bezel, original beveled glass, 29 3/4" h. **$488**

Fret-scrolled mahogany frame mirror, molded bezel, circa 1800, 41 1/4" h, 22" w, replaced glass; shrinkage splits to cresting. **$690**

Hall mirror, No. 65, L. & J.G. Stickley, arched top over original glass and hammered iron hooks, signed with Handcraft decal, original finish, some restoration, 40" w x 26 1/2" h, very good condition. **$700**

Hall Mirror, L. & J.G. Stickley, long rectangular form with original dark finish, signed "The Work of ...," original glass, 56" w x 17" h, excellent condition. **$650**

Over-mantel mirror, classical gilt gesso and wood, probably New England, circa 1825, (minor imperfections), 25" h, 56" l, gesso loss and some gilding loss, minor clouding in mirrors. **$948**

Patriotic mirror frame, with eagle and shield motifs, carved walnut, American, late 19th century, the crest with carved spread-wing eagle flanked by foliage with acorns, and carved drapery and tassels and an American shield below the mirror, 28 3/4" h, 19 1/2" w. **$8,887**

Photo courtesy of Treadway Toomey Galleries, Cincinnati and Oak Park, Ill.; www.treadwaygallery.com

Dresser mirror, Gustav Stickley, original peaked mirror and glass supported by a tapered stand with through tenons on a shoe-foot base, fine original finish, branded signature, 24" w x 7" d x 21" h, excellent condition. **$1,200**

Glass

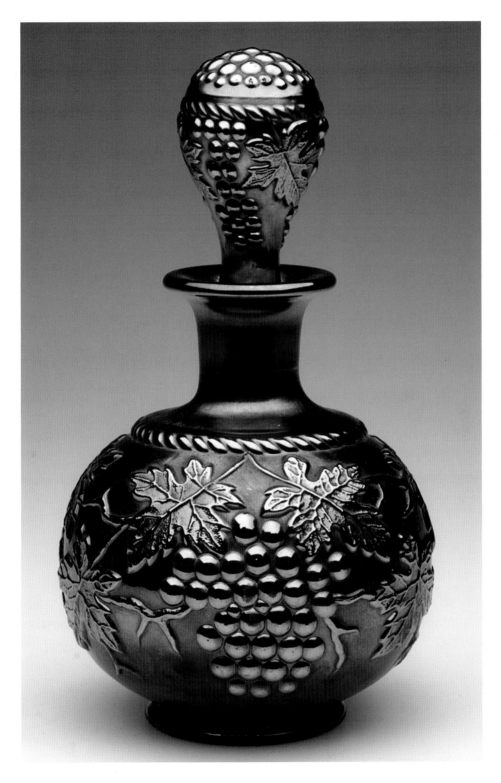

GLASS

Listed by Form, Style or Type

For glass grouped by specific makers, see end of this section. *Also see Perfume Containers, Tiffany.*

Art Glass

Art Deco, Decorated Rib Optic Cylindrical Vase, colorless with polychrome enameled flower decoration, pink enameled background signed "Leg." near base. Possibly Legras. First quarter 20th century. 4 3/4" h, 1 5/8" d. **$96**

Art Deco, Tinted Crystal Vase, colorless to green with spaced blue and green spirals, random embedded mica flakes to upper half, polished bottom with ground pontil mark. Possibly French. First half 20th century. 12" h, 5" d rim. Several bruises to edge of base. **$108**

Cluthra-Type Vase, mottled green, polished pontil mark. Possibly Steuben or Kimball. First half 20th century. 4 3/4" h, 3 5/8" d rim. **$172**

Daum Nancy, Art Deco Vase, smoky topaz with some amethyst, flattened hexagonal rim with cut and polished edges, polished base, signed "Daum (cross) Nancy, France" at the edge of base. Second quarter 20th century. 6 7/8" h, 10" d overall. Minute nick to the edge of rim. **$270**

Dorflinger Honesdale, Cameo Pinch Vase, green cut to clear Art Nouveau pattern with textured background, gilt decoration, polished pontil with gilt signature. Early 20th century. 7 1/4" h. Some wear to gilt and an open bubble to rim interior. **$460**

Etling, art glass figural vase with nude, opalescent glass, circa 1930. Marked Etling France, 7 7/8" h. **$1,800**

Durand, Lustre Ware Vase, gold iridescent, polished pontil mark signed "Durand / V / 1982-14". Vineland Flint Glass Works. First quarter 20th century. 14" h. **$920**

English Cameo Vase, white cut to yellow, intricate floral decoration on body and neck, leaf-like decoration at polished rim, slightly concave base. Fourth quarter 19th century. 6 5/8" h, 5 1/8" d overall. Two minute nicks to outer rim, a tiny open bubble on one leaf, small scuffs to reverse. **$2,070**

Gallé, Cameo Vase, brown cut to yellow green cut to peach, landscape decoration full round, signed, polished slightly concave base. First quarter 20th century. 6 1/2" h, 4" d overall. **$1,320**

Gallé, Enameled and Etched Vase, ice green with polychrome and gilt decoration, icicle-like decoration at rim and all-over roughed background, signed "GaLLé / Nancy, Paris / Depose / g.g" in gold under base. Emile Gallé. Late 19th/early 20th century. 8" h, 4 3/4" d overall. Flake to edge of foot, loss of majority of gilding. **$1,092**

Gilt-Decorated, Spangle and Crackle Basket, heavy olive green glass with red, white and blue mottling, embedded gold foil, crackled interior, and gilt floral decoration, polished table ring and slightly concave base. Late 19th/early 20th century. 9 3/4" h, 6 1/2" d overall. Wear to handle and rim gilding. **$360**

Gold Iridescent Vase, tooled rim, scratched "3689" under base, polished pontil mark. Shape number not identified although similar shapes were produced by Durand and Steuben, among others. First half 20th century. 8" h, 7 3/4" d overall. **$517**

English Cameo Footed Vase, white cut to yellow, intricate floral decoration on body, stylized scrollwork on neck, polished rim, slightly concave base. Probably Thomas Webb & Sons. Fourth quarter 19th century. 9" h, 3 1/4" d overall. **$3,737**

Photo courtesy Green Valley Auctions, Mt. Crawford, Va.;
www.GreenValleyAuctions.com

Loetz, Giant Clam-Like Fan Vase, red to yellow green swirling mottled iridescent, unmarked, partially polished pontil mark. Late 19th/early 20th century. 12" h, 5 1/2" x 12 1/4" rim, 6" d base. **$488**

Imperial, Lead Lustre Vase, swirling blue and opal mosaic exterior with blue luster interior, shape no. 623, decoration 11, polished pontil mark. Imperial Glass Co. Circa 1925. 9 3/4" h, 3 1/4" d rim...........**$517**

Kew-Blas, Water Pitcher, shaded gold iridescent, applied handle, polished pontil mark with engraved signature. Union Glass Co., Somerville, Mass. Late 19th/early 20th century. 7 1/2" h overall. **$373**

Libbey-Nash, Threaded Jug, colorless with blue decoration, shape K-540, colorless applied handle and foot, polished pontil mark signed with Libbey trademark. Libbey Glass Manufacturing Co. Second quarter 20th century. 9" h, 3 3/4" d foot. **$287**

Libbey-Nash-Type, Hat-Form Vase, colorless with green wavy thread decoration, not signed, polished pontil mark. Possibly Libbey Glass Manufacturing Co. Second quarter 20th century. 2" h, 5 1/8" d. **$57**

Locke Art-Style, Buster Brown and Tige Mug, colorless, the front featuring Buster Brown holding a jumping jack toy with his dog by his side, back with floral decoration. First quarter 20th century. 3 1/4" h..................**$805**

Loetz, Karneol Pair of Pinch Vases, marbled red with opal interior, gilt decoration on neck and shoulder with tiny white enamel dots. Fourth quarter 19th century. 11" h. Some wear to gilt.....................**$575 pair**

> **Collector's Note: Loetz is a type of iridescent art glass that was made in Austria by J. Loetz Witwe in the late 1890s. The Loetz factory at Klostermule produced items with fine cameos on cased glass, as well as the iridescent glassware commonly associated with the Loetz name.**

Loetz, Neptune Vase, green iridescent, three-point rim, polished pontil mark. Early 20th century. 6 5/8" h........**$517**

Loetz, Papillon Decorated Covered Jar, deep cobalt blue with mottled iridescent, hexagonal form with polished rim. First quarter 20th century. 5 1/4" h overall, 4 3/4" d overall. Minute flake to cover rim. **$460**

Loetz-Type, Diamond Quilted Bowl, opal cased beige iridescent, raised on three green scrolled feet, polished rim. First quarter 20th century. 4 1/8" h, 5 3/4" d rim, 8 1/4" d overall.....................**$126**

Loetz-Type, Marmorierte-Style Vase, cased red and deep green with tiny mica flecks, gilt decoration, square pinched-side form with four small applied handles on shoulder, polished rim. First quarter 20th century. 12 1/4" h, 5 3/4" sq base. Wear to gilt on handles and rim. **$480**

Loetz-Type, Phanomen-Style Decorated Vase, opaque black with purple iridescence, slightly swirled pinched-side form, polished rim, kick-up to base. First quarter 20th century. 12 1/4" h, 5 1/4" d overall.....................**$149**

Loetz-Type, Ribbed Waisted-Form Vase, amethyst iridescent, crimped rim and pinched base, rough pontil mark. First quarter 20th century. 12" h, 4 1/2" d rim. Small shear mark to one lower rib. **$144**

Loetz-Type, Thread-Decorated Vase, amethyst iridescent, applied random threading, polished rim. Late 19th/early 20th century. 6 1/4" h. Losses to threading, flake to base, possibly reduced in height. **$84**

Moser, Cameo-Frieze Decorated Vaseline Low Vase, Amazon warrior frieze above cut panels, polished base signed, "Made in Czechoslovakia, Moser, Karlsbad" in script. First quarter 20th century. 3 3/4" h, 3 3/8" d rim. Inner rim with two minute flakes and a small polished area. **$330**

> **Collector's Note: Ludwig Moser (1833-1916) founded his polishing and engraving workshop in 1857 in Karlsbad, Czechoslovakia. In 1900, Moser and his sons, Rudolf and Gustav, incorporated Ludwig Moser & Söhne. Moser art glass included clear pieces with inserted blobs of colored glass, cut colored glass with classical scenes, cameo glass and intaglio-cut items. Many inexpensive enameled pieces also were made.**

Moser-Style, Cobalt Blue to Colorless Nut Cup, gilt dogwood decoration, unusual cut and tooled "finger" rim and single applied hook-like handle, polished table ring. Fourth quarter 19th century. 3 1/4" h overall, 2 1/4" h rim, 3" d rim. **$69**

Moser-Style, Footed Mug, colorless, six panels each with finely detailed gilt filigree and amber-stained cabochon, two panels and reserve with applied handle, base with cut rays and polished pontil mark. First quarter 20th century. 5 3/4" h, 2 3/4" d rim, 3 3/4" d base. Minute nick to end of one ray, slight wear to gilt at rim. **$92**

Moser-Type, Persian-Style Urn, smoky amethyst with bright polychrome enamel decoration, two gold applied handles, polished table ring. Late 19th/early 20th century. 12" h. Some light residue in base. **$2,185**

*Cameo glass vase, mottled
amber bulbous cylindrical
form, crimson wheel carved
tobacco flowers, engraved
Daum Nancy, 8 1/2" h.*
$1,300

*Cameo glass vase,
stick form, citron glass,
decorated with ruby thistle
branches and leaves, signed
in cameo, D'Argental SL,
12" h.* **$700**

*Cameo glass miniature vase, broken-egg form, opalescent
crimson and yellow, green summer trees against red tree-
lined horizon, signed - Daum Nancy, 2" h.* **$1,200**

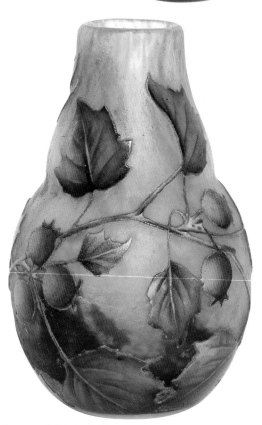

*Cameo glass vase, double gourd form, mottled yellow, red
and amethyst, vitrified red berries on green and amber
stems, signed Daum Nancy with cross of Lorraine,
4 1/2" h.* **$2,100**

Cameo glass vase, frosted yellow and amethyst tapered body, purple flowers and leaves decoration, signed in cameo Gallé with star, circa 1904, 8" h. **$1,100**

Cameo glass vase, tapered cylindrical form, frosted gray decoration with windblown trees, raised cameo raindrops, signed in enamel Daum Nancy, 3 1/2" h. **$3,100**

Cameo glass vase, cylindrical form, footed, frosted glass decoration with elongated stemmed flowers towering over pond scene, signed Gallé, 13" h. **$1,500**

Cameo glass cabinet vase, pink and gray body, cameo and enameled rain scene, signed in enamel Muller Fres Luneville, 3" h. **$450**

Photo courtesy Early Auction Co. LLC

Cameo glass vase, peach cylindrical shouldered body, cascading blue leafy branches, pastoral scene of shepherd, flock, and farmhouse with surrounding trees, slight rim grinding, signed in cameo, Devez, 12" h. **$1,650**

Photo courtesy David Rago Auctions Inc.

Cameo glass vase, blossoming carnations in deep red and yellow on polished and mottled red ground, engraved signature, Muller Freres, circa 1900, 17". **$3,120**

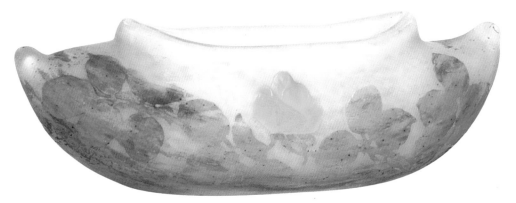

Photo courtesy Early Auction Co. LLC

Cameo glass vessel, boat form, mottled pink, yellow and blue ground, wheel carved rose on both sides, overall green and reed vitrified cameo leaves, engraved Daum Nancy signature, 6 1/2" l. **$5,250**

Photo courtesy Early Auction Co. LLC

Cameo glass vase, three color canoe shape, citron body, crimson and yellow pond scene of water lilies and foliage, signed in cameo Gallé, 16" l. **$2,600**

Photo courtesy Early Auction Co. LLC

Cameo glass bowl, footed, textured frosted glass, red flowers on green leafy stems dec, signed in cameo Daum Nancy, 6" w. **$2,100**

Photo courtesy Early Auction Co. LLC

Cameo glass tumbler, orange mottled glass cylindrical form, barren snow covered trees against gray forest, signed Daum Nancy, 5" h. **$2,100**

Photo courtesy Early Auction Co. LLC

Cameo glass vase, bulbous form, flaring rim, girl and geese in pink and gray enamel, signed Daum Nancy, 3 1/2" h. **$1,605**

Photo courtesy Early Auction Co. LLC

Cameo glass vase, frosted to yellow bulbous form, mountain lake with trees against blue mountain range decoration, signed in cameo Gallé, 6" h. **$1,400**

Cameo glass vase, bulbous stick form, blue to gray, summer scene of green pasture and trees with mountain range decoration, signed in enamel Daum Nancy, 3" h. **$1,100**

Cameo glass vase, footed cylindrical form, green and frosted mottled glass, variegated green and yellow leaves, blueberry stems decoration, signed in cameo Daum Nancy, 22" h. **$4,500**

Photo courtesy Green Valley Auctions, Mt. Crawford, Va.,
www.GreenValleyAuctions.com

Moser, Engraved Art Nouveau Vase, colorless to dark green, floral and gilt decoration, polished base engraved "D.357." and with another number. First quarter 20th century. 4 1/8" h, 2 1/4" d rim. Some wear to gilt. **$316**

Photo courtesy Green Valley Auctions, Mt. Crawford, Va.;
www.GreenValleyAuctions.com

Mt. Washington, Bowl, shaded blue to white with polychrome pansy decoration, satin finish, ground pontil mark. Mt. Washington Glass Co. Fourth quarter 19th century. 2 3/8" h, 3 3/8" d rim. **$115**

Collector's Note: The Mt. Washington Glass Works began operating in 1837 in the Mount Washington area of South Boston. The factory was relocated to New Bedford, Mass., in 1870. From 1880 until 1894, Mt. Washington supplied glass to the Pairpoint Manufacturing Corp. Pairpoint purchased Mt. Washington in 1894. Production of reverse-painted and "puffy" lampshades continued until about 1915.

Mt. Washington, Burmese No. 60 1/2 Toothpick Holder, satin or plush finish, bulbous base with square top, undecorated, polished pontil mark. Mt. Washington Glass Co. Fourth quarter 19th century. 2 3/4" h, 2" sq rim.....**$195**

Mt. Washington, Burmese No. 146 Gourd Vase, satin or plush finish, undecorated, partially ground pontil mark. Mt. Washington Glass Co. Fourth quarter 19th century. 7 3/4" h, 4 1/8" d overall. Minute burst surface bubble and a small scuffs to body. **$168**

Mt. Washington, Burmese No. 146 Gourd Vase, satin or plush finish, undecorated, ground pontil mark. Mt. Washington Glass Co. Fourth quarter 19th century. 7 7/8" h, 4 1/8" d overall.........**$345**

Mt. Washington, Burmese No. 151 Toothpick Holder / Whiskey Tumbler, satin or plush finish, cylindrical, undecorated, polished pontil mark. Mt. Washington Glass Co. Fourth quarter 19th century. 2 3/4" h, 2 1/4" d. **$115**

Mt. Washington, Burmese No. 181 Vase, satin or plush finish, undecorated, ground pontil mark. Mt. Washington Glass Co. Fourth quarter 19th century. 9 3/4" h, 5 1/2" d overall.....**$373**

Mt. Washington, Burmese Vase, satin or plush finish, applied low collared foot with rough pontil mark. Probably Mt. Washington Glass Co. Fourth quarter 19th century. 6 3/8" h, 2 1/8" d foot. With a 3/4" x 1/2" area and several nearby small spots of crizzling to body....**$115**

Mt. Washington, Colonial Ware Square Tray, free-hand polychrome floral decoration, turned-up sides, worn gold on rim, ground pontil mark inscribed "100". Mt. Washington Glass Co. Fourth quarter 19th century. 1 1/2" h, 5 1/2" x 5 3/4". **$80**

Mt. Washington, Creamer, shaded pink to white with polychrome violet decoration, applied reeded handle, satin finish, gilt rim, ground pontil mark inscribed 401. Mt. Washington Glass Co. Fourth quarter 19th century. 3 5/8" h, 3 1/4" d overall.........**$138**

Mt. Washington, Crown Milano Covered Jar, with two reeded curled handles and a steeple top, delicate polychrome floral decoration, polished pontil mark, unsigned. Mt. Washington Glass Co. Fourth quarter 19th century. 5 3/4" h overall, 4 1/4" d overall. One handle has a faint hairline and spot of professional restoration. **$316**

Mt. Washington, Crown Milano Cracker Jar, leaves, flowers and berries decoration, silver-plated repoussé decorated lid which fits over the decorated and gilded rim, base inscribed with "537". Mt. Washington Glass Co. Fourth quarter 19th century. 6 3/4" h overall. Several flakes and roughness to jar rim. **$240**

Mt. Washington, Crown Milano Cracker Jar, with two glossy reserves, the front depicting two colonial-dressed

Photo courtesy Green Valley Auctions, Mt. Crawford, Va.;
www.GreenValleyAuctions.com

Mt. Washington, Crown Milano Mushroom Sugar Sifter / Flower Holder, shape No. 535, polychrome daisy-like decoration on a shaded ground, "Albertine / Mt. W. G. Co." paper label under base of undetermined association. Mt. Washington Glass Co. Fourth quarter 19th century. 2 3/4" h, 5 1/4" d overall. **$862**

children, the boy blowing bubbles, the back with simple gilt floral decoration, original plated-silver rim, bail handle and lid marked "M W / 4419," jar inscribed "520." only under base. Mt. Washington Glass Co. Fourth quarter 19th century. 5" h rim, 7" d overall. **$460**

Mt. Washington, Crown Milano Diamond Quilted Spoon Holder, opal with heavy gilt and enamel floral decoration on a mottled ground, ten-petal rim, polished pontil mark. Mt. Washington Glass Co. Fourth quarter 19th century. 4 1/4" h, 3" d rim. Some high-spot wear to decoration, wear to rim gilt. **$240**

Mt. Washington, Crown Milano Large Rose Bowl, fired-on Burmese with polychrome floral decoration, satin finish, ground pontil mark. Mt. Washington Glass Co. Fourth quarter 19th century. 5" h, 6 1/4" d overall. Light wear and scuffs, worn rim gilt. **$168**

Mt. Washington, Crown Milano Pickle Jar, blue and white with polychrome floral decoration, unusual molded design at top and bottom, marked "M W" plated-silver lid with embossed flowers and twig finial. Mt. Washington Glass Co. Fourth quarter 19th century. 4 3/4" h overall, 4 1/2" d overall, 2 1/2" d base. Minor bruise and flake to inner rim, light wear to decoration, wear to edge of lid. **$316**

Mt. Washington, Decorated Peach Blow No. 145 Vase, rich decoration No. 30, "Lace Embroidery, Queen's patt.," original dark red painted top rim, ground pontil mark. Mt. Washington Glass Co. 1886-1890. 7 3/4" h, 4 1/2" d overall. **$6,325**

Collector's Note: Peach Blow derives its name from a fine Chinese glazed porcelain, resembling a peach or crushed strawberries in color. Three American glass manufacturers and two English firms produced Peach Blow glass in the late 1800s.

Photo courtesy Green Valley Auctions, Mt. Crawford, Va.;
www.GreenValleyAuctions.com

Mt. Washington, Lava/Sicilian Glass Vase, virtually opaque black amethyst with multi-color inclusions, square rim, polished pontil mark. Produced for a short period of time. Mt. Washington Glass Co. 1878-1880. 3 3/8" h, 3" sq. **$4,887**

Mt. Washington/Pairpoint, Burmese Vase, satin finish, eight-crimp rim, applied button stem and circular foot with polished pontil mark. Pairpoint Corp. at the Mt. Washington factory. Late 1920s/early 1930s. 10 1/2" h, 6 3/4" d, 4 1/2" d foot. **$207**

Nakara, Portrait Dresser Box, shaded pink ground, top featuring the bust of a lady with flowing hair, brass mounts, lid interior with original mirror, signed under base. C.F. Monroe Co. Late 19th/early 20th century. 2 1/2" h, 4 1/2" d overall. Loss of some white enamel dots on top and lacking rim clasp. **$230**

Nash, Chintz Footed Tumbler, colorless with blue and green vertical decoration, polished pontil mark engraved "Nash 178L". A. Douglas Nash Corp. 1928-1931. 4" h, 2 7/8" d rim.
.... **$156**

Nash-Attributed, Chintz Vase, colorless with vertical decoration, unsigned, polished pontil mark. Probably A. Douglas Nash Corp. 1928-1931. 5 5/8" h, 5 1/2" d overall.
.... **$192**

Nash-Attributed, Chintz Vase, shaded blue green with vertical decoration, unsigned, rough pontil mark. Probably A. Douglas Nash Corp. 1928-1931. 4 3/4" h, 3 5/8" d base.
.... **$84**

New England Glass Co., bride's bowl, pink overlay Mount Washington cameo on Pairpoint quadruple silver-plated stand, 19th century, marked on the base Pairpoint Mfg. Co. 10" h (with stand) x 7 5/8" d. **$1,320**

Pairpoint, Burmese Footed Cup, glossy finish, applied handle, rough pontil mark. Mid 20th century. 3 1/2" h overall, 3 1/4" h rim, 3 1/2" d rim. **$96**

Pairpoint, Burmese Goblet, satin finish, applied stem and slightly domed foot, rough pontil mark, paper label. Pairpoint Glass Co. Second half 20th century. 7" h. **$120**

Pairpoint, Melon Rib Presentation Cracker Jar, shaded green opal with gilt and green floral decoration, original plated-silver rim, bail handle and lid marked with P in Diamond and "3914", jar inscribed "3914/1112" under base, lid engraved "From Myrtle Chapter, No. 6, O.E.S. for Luella W. Stearns, G.M., June 18th, 1903" around edge. Pairpoint Mfg. Co. Late 19th/early 20th century. 4 3/4" h rim, 6 3/4" d overall. Normal wear to plating. **$316**

Schneider, "Le Verre Francais" Cameo-Etched Ewer, mottled mauve overlaid with plum, stylized floral design, boldly applied handle with the lower terminal trailing across the lower body, engraved signature, polished pontil mark. Retains a partial Maude B. Feld paper label. Second quarter 20th century. 12 1/2" h. Annealing crack to handle tail between lower terminal and first peak, open bubble near end of tail. **$1,150**

Steuben, Aurene Centerpiece Bowl, blue iridescent, shape #5061, polished base signed "Aurene / 5061". First quarter 20th century. 2 1/2" h, 10 3/8" d. Some wear to interior.
.... **$373**

> **Collector's Note: Frederick Carder, an Englishman, and Thomas G. Hawkes of Corning, N.Y., established the Steuben Glass Works in 1904. In 1918, the Corning Glass Co. purchased Steuben. Carder remained with the firm and designed many of the pieces bearing the Steuben mark. Probably the most widely recognized wares are Aurene, Verre De Soie and Rosaline.**

Steuben, Aurene Footed Bowl, gold iridescent, signed "Aurene" and "3067", rough pontil mark. First quarter 20th century. 3" h, 6" d. With a 3/8" embedded annealing crack in lower shoulder, does not break the surface. **$180**

Steuben, Aurene Low Bowl, gold iridescent, applied disk-like foot, signed "Aurene" and what appears to be "5061", rough pontil mark. First quarter 20th century. 2 1/4" h, 10" d. Part of signature obscured by scratches. **$230**

Steuben, Crystal Covered Dish, colorless, cover with applied bold ram's head finial, signed under base. Designed by Irene Butler. 20th century. 7 1/4" h overall, 5" d rim.
.... **$172**

Steuben, Footed Shallow Bowl, Sea Green and Amber, shape #3379, short swirled-rib stem, polished pontil mark. Second quarter 20th century. 5 1/2" h, 10" d overall. **$330**

Steuben, Ivrene Rib Optic Three-Piece Console Set, iridized, consisting of a shape #7563 footed center bowl with polished pontil mark and a pair of shape #7564 footed candleholders, both with a rough pontil mark and factory engraved signature. Second quarter 20th century. 7" h, 9 1/4" x 14 1/8", and 3 1/4" h. .... **$540 set**

Steuben, Ivrene Rib Optic Footed Vase, iridized, shape #7564, rough pontil mark and factory engraved signature. Second quarter 20th century. 9 1/2" h, 7 1/4" x 10".......**$420**

Steuben, Rib Optic Footed Vase, Pomona Green, probably shape #938 or #6629, polished pontil mark with block letter acid-stamped signature. Second quarter 20th century. 13" h, 9 3/8" d rim, 6 1/8" d foot. **$345**

Steuben-Type, Footed Bowl, gold calcite lead glass, small rough pontil mark. Possibly Steuben or Quezal. First quarter 20th century. 3 5/8" h, 4 7/8" d. **$149**

Steuben-Type, Low Bowl, Rosaline, rolled-over rim, polished pontil mark. First half 20th century. 1 1/2" h, 10 1/4" d overall. open bubble and light wear to interior.
.... **$144**

Photo courtesy Green Valley Auctions, Mt. Crawford, Va.;
www.GreenValleyAuctions.com

Smith Brothers, Decorated Ball Vase, delicate daisy decoration on soft beige ground, gilt and white enamel dot rim, marked with lion shield trademark under base. Fourth quarter 19th century. 4" h, 4 1/8" d overall. Undamaged except for the loss of one rim dot, no wear to decoration. **$103**

Photo courtesy Green Valley Auctions, Mt. Crawford, Va.;
www.GreenValleyAuctions.com

Steuben, Grotesque Vase, amethyst to crystal, shape #7091, polished base. First half 20th century. 6" h, 7 3/4" x 8 1/4". **$316**

*Igloo Inkwell, 2",
ground lip. With
vertical lines running
down the side, in
amethyst.* **$1,100**

*Keach Balt, torpedo-
type soda, 9 1/2" with
applied top. These
unusual soda bottles
came in various colors.
This example is an
apricot-puce. Medium
tone with significant
"whittle" (marks caused
by a reaction of the hot
glass hitting the surface
of a colder mold) and
overall crudity. Minor
scratches, possibly from
taking it in and out of
the holder. Comes with
holder.* **$16,000**

*H.P. Herb Wild Cherry Bitters, tooled top, 9". There are a
couple variants of the Herb Wild Cherry Bitters, including
this pure green example, also comes in amber. Minor
scratches and a tiny flake off the bottom.* **$4,600**

Loomis's Cream Liniment, 5". Early flared mouth, tooled lip, pontiled. Six-sided, corset waisted. Rare. **$3,400**

A Merry Christmas and Happy New Year, Label Under Glass with Santa, 6", with the ground lip and original screw cap. With crisscross design on reverse and label under glass is perfect. **$1,300**

Pacific Congress Water Springs, Saratoga California, with Running Deer. A pint olive-amber example. Often seen in lime green, overall crudity and bubbles. **$8,000**

Masonic Eagle, Pint, sheared lip. Pontil. Variation in color, going from deep olive amber to a light green, back to an almost black color in the base. There is some highpoint wear on both sides. Unusual crimped lip. **$9,000**

M. McCormack's Celebrated Ginger Ale, Nashville Tenn. Applied top, 8 1/4". Light to medium blue with embossing and the large blob top. There are a few minor imperfections including the tiniest of pings on the base and one letter disturbed. **$550**

McKeon & McGrann, Washington DC. These torpedoes come in two variants, both being equally rare. This example has the two names and is a light to medium sapphire blue. Significant whittle, minor wear and probably been cleaned at some point. **$4,000**

Molded Chestnut-Shaped Cologne, or Pocket Flask, 4". With tooled mouth and pontil. Possibly the beginning of the 1700s or older. Near mint. **$1,900**

National Bitters, Patent 1867 on base. Applied top. Yellow-olive variant. There is an open bubble on the left side. Significant whittle on the label area. **$3,000**

Mohawk Whiskey, Pure Rye Patented Feb. 11, 1868. With much of the original paint. It is a light amber and varies in hue throughout the arms and head area. The top has a chip, which was most likely done during the making. There is a tiny nick on the base. **$1,500**

Palmer's Perfumes, Tea Rose, 9" with stopper. The gold lettering is backed by a rose-colored background. In addition, this has a 2-cent revenue stamp on the base, featuring George Washington. **$3,200**

Poison, in Shape of Skull, 2 7/8". Small amount of crudity throughout the piece. A hard-to-find poison. **$5,000**

Teakettle Inkwell, with fancy design. Turquoise with the original brass lid and gold paint. Unusual to find the original paint and lid intact, especially in this color. It has little gold painted stars on the top and gold painting around the middle and stem of the ink. **$1,400**

Pacific Congress Springs, blob-style top. For many years, this variant of the Pacific Congress Springs bottle was largely unknown by Western collectors and virtually unheard of in the East. Light blue, made in the mid to late 1860s. **$2,200**

Pacific Congress Water Springs, Saratoga California/ Pacific Congress Springs. Pint with smooth base. These have variants and a number of different colors. The most prominent color is a bright green. Teal coloration with strong strike. **$3,400**

Poison, with Diamond Design, 8" tooled top. One of the larger, amber, diamond cornered poisons. Light to medium amber and pristine. **$350**

Poison, Triangular with original contents and label, 5". An example with the entire original label and contents. The label says it contains mercury bichloride. **$750**

Poison, Quilted with stopper, 11" without stopper. This is the second-largest of the 12 sizes known for the quilted, round poisons. This example has no embossing on the base. These are considered extremely rare. **$650**

Pold & Co., Barnums Building Balto. Applied top, smooth base. Sapphire-blue color, heavy whittle (marks caused by a reaction of the hot glass hitting the surface of a colder mold) and overall crudity, extremely rare. Some light wear. Comes with holder. **$4,000**

Race & Sheldon's, Magic Waterproof Boot Polish, 5 1/2", applied top with open pontil. The embossing is crude. Lockport green color with significant whittle. **$3,200**

Return to Joe Gribble, Old Crow Saloon Douglas, A.T., 6" screw cap with ground lip. Close to a half-pint. An Arizona Territory flask. In 1903, Joe Gribble opened a saloon called "The Whitehouse" and another called "The Old Crow". Rare. **$4,600**

Rowlers Rheumatism Medicine, Prepared by Dr. J.R. Boyce Sacramento, 7 1/2". Applied top and smooth base. These Western medicines come with and without a pontil mark. Probably made in the mid-1860s. This has an unusual and smaller than normal applied top and the overall odd shape. **$1,200**

Star Whiskey, W.B. Crowel Jr. New York, 8 1/4" with applied handle and mouth. Pontil. A yellowish amber with bubbles and overall crudity. **$1,200**

Thos. Taylor & Co., Sold, Agents P. Vollmer's Old Bourbon Louisville KY. Virginia, Nev. Tooled top, pint coffin flask.

*Umbrella Inkwell, Rolled lip, 2 1/2" h, in a brilliant blue.
The pontil is quite a bit off center, which gives the base an
unusual look.* **$1,300**

*W & Co. N.Y. Pineapple
Bitters, 8 1/2". Applied top,
graphite pontil. These usually
show up in amber. There are
a few variants, one reads J.C.
& Co. and another has no
embossing on the front panel.
Deep bluish green. Original
graphite intact. There is a little
interior stain.* **$9,000**

Mid-1880s. Thomas Taylor is a colorful and intriguing
name in the history of the Nevada wholesale liquor
business. **$1,800**

U.S.A. Hosp Dept., applied top and smooth base. Orange-
puce with some strawberry. Significant whittle (marks
caused by a reaction of the hot glass hitting the surface
of a colder mold) and overall crudity. Possibly an earlier
variant. Areas of dullness where the glass may have
touched the surface of another bottle during manufacture,
minor. **$1,400**

Victorian Inkwell, 2" h. Circa 1870s into the 1890s.
Embossed design. This was an inkwell used by a person
of substance. Its blue color is accented by ornate flower
design. **$1,000**

Warner's Safe Nervine, London. 9 1/2". Applied top.
This example does not have the slug plate, and has quotes
around the word "safe." A crude bottle, yellowish olive,
light scratches on the reverse. **$475**

The Wellington Saloon, the F.G. McCoy Co Inc. Prescott
Ariz. 6 1/2" half-pint. The Wellington Saloon was located
on Montezuma Street in 1902 and it is believed that it
closed in 1906. The bottom also reads, "Design Pat. Aug 9
1898." Considered a rare bottle. Some light stain. **$900**

WFJ, Socorro, N.M. Applied top. The embossing is quite
bold. **$600**

*W.B. Co. S.F. Trademark,
with sun design in center. It
is believed these odd-looking
bottles were made for beer,
but little is known about the
company. Significant whittle
(marks caused by a reaction of
the hot glass hitting the surface
of a colder mold) and bubbles.
Brilliant bluish-aqua.* **$2,200**

Wheeler's Berlin Bitters Baltimore, variant, also comes in aqua, amber and olive colorations. It is a little fatter and about a half an inch wider at the base. It has the graphite pontil and is yellowish amber with some green. It appears it may have been cleaned at some point and is crude. Minor scratches. **$7,000**

Bottles, Barber

In the 19th century, barbers filled their own bottles with hair tonic and oil, bay rum, shampoo and rosewater. The bottles came in distinctive colors/shapes so the barber could identify what was in each one of them. Barber bottles stopped being made after the 1906 Pure Food and Drug Act made it illegal to refill non-labeled bottles.

Hobbs, No, 323 Dew Drop / Hobnail Barber's Bottle, blue opalescent, ceramic pourer, polished pontil mark. Hobbs, Brockunier & Co. Fourth quarter 19th century. 6 3/4" h, 3 3/4" d overall. Loss of one hob and chip to two others, lowest row of hobs with multiple flakes. $120

Seaweed/Coral Barber's Bottle, cranberry opalescent, polished pontil mark. Late 19th/early 20th century. 7" h, 3 1/2" d overall. **$452**

Hobnail Barber's Bottle, cranberry opalescent, rough pontil mark. Late 19th/early 20th century. 8 1/4" h, 4 1/4" d overall. One flake to a hob and several with manufacturing roughness. $144

Inverted Thumbprint Barber's Bottle, amber, polished pontil mark. Fourth quarter 19th century. 7" h, 3 1/4" d overall. $34

L.G. Wright, Swirl Barber's Bottle, cranberry opalescent. L.G. Wright Glass Co. Second half 20th century. 7" h, 3 1/2" d overall. $120

L.G. Wright, Opal Rib Barber's Bottle, opalescent. L.G. Wright Glass Co. Second half 20th century. 7" h, 3 1/2" d overall. $115

Seaweed/Coral Barber's Bottle, blue opalescent, polished pontil mark. Late 19th/early 20th century. 7" h, 3 1/2" d overall. Pattern flake. $345

Stars and Stripes Barber's Bottle, opalescent, polished pontil mark. Late 19th/early 20th century. 6 7/8" h, 3 1/2" d overall. **$373**

Swirl Barber's Bottle, blue opalescent, polished pontil mark. Late 19th/early 20th century. 7" h, 3 1/2" d overall. **$195**

Swirl Barber's Bottle, cranberry opalescent. Late 19th/early 20th century. 7" h, 3 1/4" d overall. **$184**

Vesta/Hobnail in Square, Barber's Bottle and Tumbler, colorless opalescent, bottle slightly tinted. Aetna Glass & Mfg. Co. Fourth quarter 19th century. 6 3/4" and 4" h. Bottle with the partial loss of one hob and a flake to another, also some interior dirt/residue. .... **$92 both**

Victorian, Enamel Decorated Barber's Bottle, cobalt blue with white enamel stylized floral decoration, rough pontil mark. Late 19th/early 20th century. 7 1/2" h, 3 3/4" d overall. **$46**

Photo courtesy Green Valley Auctions, Mt. Crawford, Va.;
www.GreenValleyAuctions.com

Victorian, Enamel Decorated Rib Optic Barber's Bottle, green with polychrome floral decoration, rough pontil mark. Late 19th/early 20th century. 7 1/8" h, 3 1/2" d overall. **$56**

Carnival Glass

Carnival glass is colored, pressed glass with a fired-on iridescent finish. It was first manufactured about 1905 to imitate the more expensive art glass made by Tiffany and other firms. More than 1,000 different patterns have been identified. Production of old carnival glass ended in the 1920s. Most of the popular patterns of carnival glass were produced by five companies: Dugan, Fenton, Imperial, Millersburg and Northwood. The term "carnival glass" did not arise until the 1960s.

Acorn Bowl, red/Amberina, scalloped edge. Fenton Art Glass Co. First quarter 20th century. 2" h, 7 1/2" d. **$460**

> **Collector's Note: Joseph Locke developed Amberina glass in 1883 for the New England Glass Works. "Amberina," a trade name, describes a transparent glass that shades from deep ruby to amber. It was made by adding powdered gold to the ingredients for an amber-glass batch. A portion of the glass was reheated later to produce the shading effect. Usually it was the bottom that was reheated to form the deep red; however, reverse examples have been found.**

The New England Glass Co., Cambridge, Mass., first made plated Amberina in 1886; Edward Libbey patented the process for the company in 1889. Plated Amberina was made by taking a gather of chartreuse or cream opalescent glass, dipping it in Amberina, and combining the two, often using a mold. The finished product had a deep-amber to deep-ruby-red shading, a fiery opalescent lining and often vertical ribbing for enhancement.

Acorn Bowl, red, scalloped rim with points. Fenton Art Glass Co. First quarter 20th century. 2 3/8" h, 7 1/2" d. Minor nicks on two points. **$316**

Big Basket-weave Vase, amethyst. Dugan Glass Co. First quarter 20th century. 10" h, 3 1/4" d base. **$204**

Blackberry Spray Whimsical Hat, red, scalloped rim. Fenton Art Glass Co. First quarter 20th century. 3" h, 6 1/2" d. **$138**

Blackberry Spray Whimsical Hat, red/Amberina, scalloped rim. Fenton Art Glass Co. First quarter 20th century. 3" h, 6 1/2" d. Annealing fissure on side. **$184**

Bushel Basket Dish, amethyst, four-footed novelty basket with round rim, "N" in circle in base. Northwood Glass Co. First quarter 20th century. 4 5/8" h, 4 1/4" d. **$80**

Bushel Basket Dish, blue opalescent, four-footed novelty basket with round rim, "N" in circle in base. Northwood Glass Co. First quarter 20th century. 4 5/8" h, 4 1/4" d. **$120**

Bushel Basket Dish, aqua opalescent, four-footed novelty basket with round rim, "N" in circle in base. Northwood Glass Co. First quarter 20th century. 4 5/8" h, 4 1/4" d. Annealing fissure to rim. **$230**

Bushel Basket Dish, ice green, four-footed novelty basket with round rim, "N" in circle in base. Northwood Glass Co. First quarter 20th century. 4 5/8" h, 4 1/4" d. **$168**

Double-Stem Rose, Round Footed Bowl, cobalt blue, beaded rim. Dugan Glass Co. First quarter 20th century. 3 1/2" h, 8 3/8" d. Minor mold roughness on foot. **$101**

Bushel Basket Dish, white, four-footed novelty basket with eight sided rim, "N" in circle in base. Northwood Glass Co. First quarter 20th century. 4" h, 4 7/8" d. Tiny nick to rim. **$115**

Corn Vases, Pair, ice green, "N" in circle in base. Northwood Glass Co. First quarter 20th century. 6 1/2" h, 3 1/8" d base. One with significant crack at rim.
.... **$345 pair**

Grape and Cable, Cologne Bottle with Stopper, amethyst. Northwood Glass Co. First quarter 20th century. 8 3/4" h overall. Minor flake to stopper tip. **$192**

Drapery Rose Bowl, aqua opalescent, crimped top. Northwood Glass Co. First quarter 20th century. 3 7/8" h, 5 1/4" d. Several small manufacturing flaws. **$184**

Embroidered Mums Bowl, ice blue, scalloped rim with beaded edge. Northwood Glass Co. First quarter 20th century. 2 1/2" h, 8 3/4" d. **$575**

Fine Cut Roses Rose Bowl, green, crimped rim, plain interior. Northwood Glass Co. First quarter 20th century. 4" h. **$161**

Fine Rib Vase, red/Amberina, scalloped rim. Fenton Art Glass Co. First quarter 20th century. 10 1/2" h, 2 7/8" d base. **$230**

Fisherman Mug, amethyst. Dugan Glass Co. First quarter 20th century. 4" h. Annealing fissure on rim. **$72**

Fruits and Flowers Bon-Bon, aqua opalescent, footed bowl with two handles, beaded rim. Northwood Glass Co. First quarter 20th century. 3 3/4" h, 5" d. Minute flake to handle and minor interior scratches. **$431**

Good Luck Bowl, blue, crimped rim, ribbed exterior. Northwood Glass Co. First quarter 20th century. 2" h, 9" d.
.... **$517**

Grape and Cable Bowl, red, ruffled rim. Fenton Art Glass Co. First quarter 20th century. 2" h, 7 3/4" d. Minute pattern flake. **$240**

Grape and Cable, Hat Pin Holder, amethyst, on three feet. Northwood Glass Co. First quarter 20th century. 6 1/2" h. Minute mold flake on foot. **$207**

Grape and Cable, Sweetmeat Compote with Lid, amethyst. Northwood Glass Co. First quarter 20th century. 8 3/4" h overall. **$168**

Photo courtesy Green Valley Auctions, Mt. Crawford, Va.; www.GreenValleyAuctions.com

Kittens Child's Cup and Saucer, marigold, embossed with a series of three kittens. Fenton Art Glass Co. First quarter 20th century. Saucer 4 1/2" d, cup 2 1/8" h. **$207**

Hearts and Flowers Bowl, amethyst, scalloped rim with beaded edge. Northwood Glass Co. First quarter 20th century. 2 1/2" h, 9" d. **$258**

Hearts and Flowers Bowl, ice blue, scalloped rim with beaded edge. Northwood Glass Co. First quarter 20th century. 8 1/4" d. Expected wear to base. **$258**

Hearts and Flowers, Footed Compote, ice green. Northwood Glass Co. First quarter 20th century. 5 7/8" h, 6 3/4" d. **$690**

Heron Mug, amethyst. Dugan Glass Co. First quarter 20th century. 4" h. Annealing fissure to rim, does not sit level.... **$69**

Inverted Feather, Cracker Jar with Lid, green, Hobstar and Feather design. Cambridge Glass Co. First quarter 20th century. 6 1/2" h overall, 6 3/4" d. Lid rim with 1 1/4" x 3/16" filled-in chip.................................... **$72**

Lined Lattice Vase, amethyst. Dugan Glass Co. First quarter 20th century. 10" h, 3 1/4" d overall base. **$180**

Mikado Compote, blue, Cherry pattern on exterior, scalloped rim with beaded edge. Fenton Art Glass Co. First quarter 20th century. 7 7/8" h, 9 1/2" d. Wear to base..... **$575**

Nippon Bowl, ice blue, ruffled rim with beaded edge. Northwood Glass Co. First quarter 20th century. 8 7/8" d. **$228**

Open-Edge Basket-weave, Whimsy Hat with Jack-in-the-Pulpit Rim, red, reticulated rim. Fenton Art Glass Co. First quarter 20th century. 2 3/4" h, 5 3/4" x 4 1/4". Annealing lines to rim. **$184**

Orange Tree Mug, red/Amberina. Fenton Art Glass Co. First quarter 20th century. 3 1/2" h. Undamaged except for a minute flake on handle, expected wear to base. **$184**

Panther Small Footed Bowls, two, blue, Butterfly and Berry exterior, one example with scalloped rim, the other with plain rim. Fenton Art Glass Co. First quarter 20th century. 2 1/4" h, 5" to 5 1/4" d............................ **$144 pair**

Peacock and Urn, Large Ice Cream Bowl, amethyst, scalloped rim, "N" in circle in base. Northwood Glass Co. First quarter 20th century. 2 1/2" h, 9 7/8" d. **$460**

Photo courtesy Green Valley Auctions, Mt. Crawford, Va.; www.GreenValleyAuctions.com

Rose Show Bowl, amethyst, scalloped. Northwood Glass Co. First quarter 20th century. 2 3/4" h, 8 5/8" d. Minute pattern flake. **$734**

Peacock on the Fence Bowl, aqua opalescent, scalloped rim with beaded edge. Northwood Glass Co. First quarter 20th century. 2 3/8" h, 9" d. Minute interior nick. **$690**

Pony Bowl, amethyst, scalloped rim. Dugan Glass Co. First quarter 20th century. 2 3/4" h, 8 3/4" d. Minute wear to iridescence on pattern. **$287**

Poppy Pickle Dish, amethyst, scalloped, crimped rim. Northwood Glass Co. First quarter 20th century. 2" h, 5 1/4" x 8". **$172**

Poppy Show Plate, amethyst, scalloped rim. Northwood Glass Co. First quarter 20th century. 1 3/4" h, 9 3/8" d. **$1,035**

Photo courtesy Green Valley Auctions, Mt. Crawford, Va.;
www.GreenValleyAuctions.com

*Rose Show Bowl, aqua opalescent, scalloped rim.
Northwood Glass Co. First quarter 20th century. 3" h,
8 3/4" d.* **$678**

Rose Show Bowl, marigold, scalloped rim. Northwood
 Glass Co. First quarter 20th century. 3" h, 8 3/4" d. **$345**
Rustic Vase, amethyst. Fenton Art Glass Co. First quarter
 20th century. 10 1/2" h, 3 1/4" d base. **$48**
Rustic Vase, marigold. Fenton Art Glass Co. First quarter
 20th century. 16 1/2" h, 4 1/8" d base. **$126**
Singing Birds Mug, amethyst, plain background, "N"
 in circle in base. Northwood Glass Co. First quarter 20th
 century. 3 1/2" h. **$46**
Singing Birds Mug, marigold, stippled background, "N"
 in circle in base. Northwood Glass Co. First quarter 20th
 century. 3 1/2" h. Minute nick on handle. **$23**

Photo courtesy Green
Valley Auctions, Mt.
Crawford, Va.;
www.GreenValleyAuc-
tions.com

*Tornado Vase,
amethyst,
ribbed, "N" in
circle in base.
Northwood
Glass Co. First
quarter 20th
century.
6 1/4" h,
2 3/4" d base;
3/8" chip in spot
of exfoliation
on foot, flake to
rim.* **$300**

Thin Rib Vases, Pair, blue. Fenton Art Glass Co. First
 quarter 20th century. 14" h, 3 3/4" d base. Minute rim nick
 to one. .... **$69 pair**
Three Fruits Bowl, amethyst, stippled interior, ribbed
 exterior. Northwood Glass Co. First quarter 20th century.
 1 7/8" h, 8 3/4" d. Minute wear to iridescence on pattern.
 .... **$228**
Three Fruits Medallion, Spatula Footed Bowl, aqua
 opalescent, Meander pattern on exterior of bowl, scalloped
 rim with beaded edge, stippled background. Northwood
 Glass Co. First quarter 20th century. 3 1/4" h, 8 3/4" d. A
 few minute scuffs to interior of bowl. **$373**
Tree Trunk Vase, green. Northwood Glass Co. First quarter
 20th century. 10" h, 3 3/4" d base. **$57**
Trout and Fly Bowl, green, scalloped rim. Millersburg
 Glass Co. First quarter 20th century. 2 3/4" h, 8 3/4" d.
 Annealing line and some light interior scratches. **$360**
Victorian Bowl, amethyst, ruffled rim. Dugan Glass Co.
 First quarter 20th century. 3" h, 11 3/4" d. Pattern nick.
 .... **$161**
Wishbone and Spades Plate, amethyst. Northwood
 Glass Co. First quarter 20th century. 6 1/2" d. **$230**

Children's Glass, including Mugs

Castle, Boat and Church Medallion Mug, vaseline, stippled
 handle. Fourth quarter 19th century. 3 1/8" h, 2 3/4" d rim.
 Faint annealing line at top of handle. **$69**
Children's ABC Plates, two, amber, consisting of Clock
 with Scalloped Edge and an unidentified example with
 stippled background, beaded swag and fine-cut center,
 each with numbers as well as ABCs. Fourth quarter 19th
 century. 7" d. Unidentified example with minor mold
 roughness to interior rim and a flake to a heavy fin, clock
 undamaged. .... **$30 pair**
Children's ABC Plates, two, amber, consisting of Emma
 and Rover. New Martinsville Glass Co. Fourth quarter 19th
 century. 6 3/8" d. Each with normal mold roughness to
 interior rim. .... **$57 pair**
Child's Fish Platter, colorless with frosted center, polished
 table ring. Late 19th/early 20th century. 7/8" h, 3 1/8" x 5 1/4".
 .... **$180**
Garfield Memorial Toy Mug, colorless, bust on front and
 dates on reverse, 1880 to top of handle, beaded under base.
 Fourth quarter 19th century. 2 1/4" h, 1 7/8" d. Minute
 bruise under base. **$34**
Menagerie Fish, Child's Spooner, blue. Bryce, Higbee &
 Co. Fourth quarter 19th century. 3 1/2" h, 2 5/8" d base.
 .... **$126**
Mephistopheles Mug, opaque white/milk glass, plain
 handle. Fourth quarter 19th century. 3 1/8" h, 3 3/4" d rim.
 Small open bubble to base. **$60**
Ribbon Candy, Child's Cake Stand, green. Fourth quarter
 19th century. 3 1/2" h, 6" d. Minor mold roughness to foot.
 .... **$92**
Seesaw/Children at Play Plate, colorless with frosted
 center, detailed scene also features dogs and chickens, 24-
 scallop rim. Fourth quarter 19th century. 10 1/8" d. Light
 wear. **$144**

Depression Glass

Depression glass is clear or colored translucent glassware that was distributed free, or at low cost, around the time of the Great Depression. Some food manufacturers and distributors put a piece of glassware in boxes of food, as an incentive to purchase. Movie theaters and businesses would hand out a piece simply for coming in the door.

Dozens of manufacturers made scores of patterns. In addition to clear or crystal, common colors include pink, pale blue, green and amber. Depression glass has been highly collectible since the 1960s. Some manufacturers continued to make popular patterns after World War II, or introduced similar patterns, which are also collectible. Popular and expensive patterns and pieces have been reproduced, and reproductions are still being made.

For more information, see *Warman's Depression Glass Identification and Price Guide 4th Edition* by Ellen T. Schroy.

ADAM

Manufactured by Jeannette Glass Co., Jeannette, Pa., from 1932 to 1934.

Made in crystal, Delphite blue, green, pink, some topaz and yellow. Delphite 4" h candlesticks are valued at $250 a pair. A yellow cup and saucer are valued at $200, and a 7 3/4" d yellow plate is valued at $115. Production in topaz and yellow was very limited. Crystal prices are approximately 50 percent of the prices listed for green.

Reproductions: † Butter dish in pink and green.

Item	Green	Pink
Ashtray, 4 1/2" d	$28	$30
Berry bowl, small	22.50	18.50
Bowl, 9" d, cov	90	75
Bowl, 9" d, open	45	30
Bowl, 10" l, oval	40	40
Butter dish, cov †	395	135
Cake plate, 10" d, ftd	38	40
Candlesticks, pr, 4" h	125	100
Candy jar, cov, 2 1/2" h	120	135
Casserole, cov	95	80
Cereal bowl, 5 3/4" d	50	40
Coaster, 3 1/4" d	32	35
Creamer	30	35
Cup	30	28
Dessert bowl, 4 3/4" d	25	25

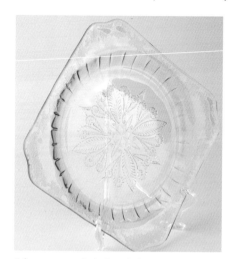

Adam, green salad plate. **$18.50**

Item	Green	Pink
Iced tea tumbler, 5 1/2" h	$72	$75
Lamp	500	500
Pitcher, 32 oz, round base	-	125
Pitcher, 32 oz, 8" h	48	45
Plate, 6" d, sherbet	15	18
Plate, 7 3/4" d, salad, sq	18.50	19.50
Plate, 9" d, dinner, sq	37.50	42
Plate, 9" d, grill	37.50	35
Platter, 11 3/4" l, rect	38	38
Relish dish, 8" l, divided	27	20
Salt and pepper shakers, pr, 4" h	130	95
Sherbet, 3"	40	38
Sugar, cov	48	65
Tumbler, 4 1/2" h	35	40
Vase, 7 1/2" h	60	550
Vegetable bowl, 7 3/4" d	30	40

Adam, green ashtray **$28**, *and pink pitcher.* **$45**

Adam, pink covered butter. **$135**

BOWKNOT

Unknown maker, late 1920s.

Made in green.

Item	Green
Berry bowl, 4 1/2" d	$25
Cereal bowl, 5 1/2" d	30
Cup	20
Plate, 7" d, salad	18
Sherbet, low, ftd	25
Tumbler, 10 oz, 5" h, flat	20
Tumbler, 10 oz, 5" h, ftd	25

Bowknot, green tumbler **$25**, *and footed berry bowl.* **$25**

COLONIAL BLOCK

Manufactured by Hazel Atlas Glass Co., Clarksburg, W.V., and Zanesville, Ohio, early 1930s.

Made in black, cobalt blue (rare), crystal, green, pink, and white (1950s).

Item	Black	Crystal	Green	Pink	White
Bowl, 4" d	$-	$6	$10	$10	$-
Bowl, 7" d	-	16	35	20	-
Butter dish, cov	-	35	50	45	-
Butter tub, cov	-	35	40	40	-
Candy jar, cov	-	30	45	40	-
Compote, 4" h, 4 3/4" w	-	12	-	-	-
Creamer	-	15	16	15	7.50
Goblet, 5 3/4" h	-	9	12	15	-
Pitcher, 20 oz, 5 3/4" h	-	40	50	50	-
Powder jar, cov	30	20	24	24	-
Sherbet	-	6	10	9.50	-
Sugar, cov	-	20	25	25	20
Sugar, open	-	10	8	8	10

Colonial Block, green covered butter dish. **$50**

DOGWOOD

Manufactured by Macbeth-Evans Co., Charleroi, Pa., from 1929 to 1932. Made in Cremax, crystal, green, Monax, pink and yellow. Yellow is rare; a cereal bowl is known and valued at $95. Crystal items are valued at 50 percent less than green.

Item	Cremax or Monax	Green	Pink
Berry bowl, 8 1/2" d	$40	$100	$65
Cake plate, 11" d, heavy solid foot	-	-	650
Cake plate, 13" d, heavy solid foot	185	135	165
Cereal bowl, 5 1/2" d	12	35	35
Coaster, 3 1/4" d	-	-	450
Creamer, 2 1/2" h, thin	-	48	35
Creamer, 3 1/4" h, thick	-	-	25
Cup, thin	-	32	20
Cup, thick	36	40	20
Fruit bowl, 10 1/4" d	100	250	550
Pitcher, 8" h, 80 oz (American Sweetheart style)	-	-	1,250
Pitcher, 8" h, 80 oz, decorated	-	550	295
Plate, 6" d, bread and butter	25	10	10
Plate, 8" d, luncheon	-	12	12
Plate, 9 1/4" d, dinner	-	-	45
Plates, 10 1/2" d, grill, AOP or border design only	-	24	35
Platter, 12" d, oval	-	-	725
Salver, 12" d	175	-	45
Saucer	20	10	8.50
Sherbet, low, ftd	-	95	42
Sugar, 2 1/2" h, thin	-	50	30
Sugar, 3 1/4" h, thick, ftd	-	-	20
Tidbit, 2 tier	-	-	90
Tumbler, 10 oz, 4" h, decorated	-	100	55
Tumbler, 11 oz, 4 3/4" h, decorated	-	95	125
Tumbler, 12 oz, 5" h, decorated	-	125	75
Tumbler, molded band	-	-	25

Dogwood, pink sugar **$20**, *creamer* **$25**, *and luncheon plate.* **$12**

FLORAGOLD

Manufactured by Jeannette Glass Co., Jeannette, Pa., 1950s.

Made in iridescent. Some large comports were later made in ice blue, crystal, red-yellow, and shell pink.

Item	Iridescent
Ashtray, 4" d	$7
Bowl, 4 1/2" sq	5
Bowl, 5 1/4" d, ruffled	15
Bowl, 8 1/2" d, sq	20
Bowl, 8 1/2" d, ruffled	10
Butter dish, cov, 1/4 pound, oblong	30
Butter dish, cov, round, 5 1/2" w sq base	800
Butter dish, cov, round, 6 1/4" w sq base	55
Candlesticks, pr, double branch	60
Candy dish, one handle	12.50

Floragold, 5 1/4" d iridescent dinner plate **$40** *and ruffled berry bowl.* **$15**

Item	Iridescent
Candy or cheese dish, cov, 6 3/4" d	**$130**
Candy, 5 3/4" l, four feet	12
Celery vase	420
Cereal bowl, 5 1/2" d, round	40
Coaster, 4" d	10
Comport, 5 1/4", plain top	750
Comport, 5 1/4", ruffled top	850
Creamer	15
Cup	8
Fruit bowl, 5 1/2" d, ruffled	8.50
Fruit bowl, 12" d, ruffled, large	12
Nappy, 5" d, one handle	12
Pitcher, 64 oz	55
Plate, 5 1/4" d, sherbet	12
Plate, 8 1/2" d, dinner	48
Platter, 11 1/4" d	28
Salad bowl, 9 1/2" d, deep	50
Salt and pepper shakers, pr, plastic tops	60
Saucer, 5 1/4" d	15
Sherbet, low, ftd	15
Sugar	15
Sugar lid	15
Tidbit, wooden post	35
Tray, 13 1/2" d	50
Tray, 13 1/2" d, with indent	65
Tumbler, 11 oz, ftd	20
Tumbler, 10 oz, ftd	20
Tumbler, 15 oz, ftd	110
Vase	420

HARP

Manufactured by Jeannette Glass Co., Jeannette, Pa., from 1954 to 1957.

Made in crystal and crystal with gold trim; limited pieces made in ice blue, pink, and shell pink.

Item	Crystal	Ice Blue	Shell Pink
Ashtray	$10	$-	$-
Cake stand, 9" d	35	45	50
Coaster	6	-	-
Cup	30	-	-
Parfait	20	-	-
Plate, 7" d	25	25	-
Saucer	14	-	-
Snack set, cup, saucer, 7" plate	48	-	-
Tray, two handles, rectangular	35	35	65
Vase, 7 1/2" h	30	-	-

Harp, crystal with gold trim, 7" plate **$25** *and cake stand.* **$35**

LACED EDGE

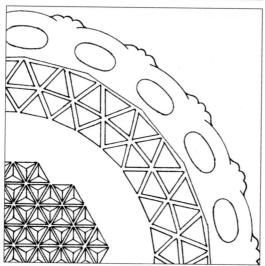

Manufactured by Imperial Glass Co., Bellaire, Ohio, early 1930s.

Made in blue and green with opalescent edges.

Item	Blue	Green
Basket, 9" d	$265	$
Bowl, 5" d	40	40
Bowl, 5 1/2" d	42	42
Bowl, 5 7/8" d	42	42
Bowl, 11" l, oval	295	285
Bowl, 11" l, oval, divided	165	165
Candlesticks, pr, double lite	175	180
Creamer	45	40
Cup	35	35
Fruit bowl, 4 1/2" d	32	30
Mayonnaise, three pieces	100	125
Plate, 6 1/2" d, bread and butter	24	24
Plate, 8" d, salad	35	35
Plate, 10" d, dinner	95	95
Plate, 12" d, luncheon	90	90
Platter, 13" l	185	165
Saucer	18	15
Soup bowl, 7" d	85	80
Sugar	45	40
Tidbit, two tiers, 8" and 10" plates	110	100
Tumbler, 9 oz	60	60
Vegetable bowl, 9" d	110	95

Laced Edge,
5 1/2" d blue bowl.
$42

MELBA

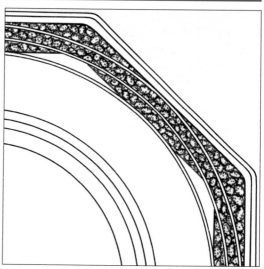

Manufactured by L.E. Smith Glass Co., Mount Pleasant, Pa., in the early 1930s.

Made in amethyst, black, green, and pink.

Item	Amethyst	Black	Green	Pink
Baker, oval	$20	$22	$18	$18
Bowl, 10 1/2" d, ruffled	18	20	15	15
Candleholder	15	17	12	12
Creamer	15	18	12	12
Cup	6.50	8.50	5	5
Dessert bowl	4.50	5	3.50	3.50
Plate, 6" d, bread and butter	5	7.50	4	4
Plate, 7" d, salad	7	9.50	6	6
Plate, 9" d, luncheon	9	12	8	8
Platter	15	18	12	12
Salad bowl	18	20	15	15
Saucer	3.50	4.50	3	3
Serving plate, 9" d, handles	15	18	12	12
Sugar	15	18	12	12
Vegetable bowl, 9 1/2" l	18	20	15	15

Melba,
amethyst
luncheon plate.
$9

NORMANDIE

*Normandie,
iridescent
dinner plate.*
$12

Manufactured by Federal Glass Co., Columbus, Ohio, from 1933 to 1940.

Made in amber, crystal, iridescent, and pink.

Item	Amber	Crystal	Iridescent	Pink
Berry bowl, 5" d	$9.50	$6	$7.50	$14
Berry bowl, 8 1/2" d	35	24	30	80
Cereal bowl, 6 1/2" d	30	20	12	35
Creamer, ftd	20	10	10	15
Cup	7.50	4	10	12.50
Iced tea tumbler, 12 oz, 5" h	45	-	-	-
Juice tumbler, 5 oz, 4" h	40	-	-	-
Pitcher, 80 oz, 8" h	115	-	-	245
Plate, 7 3/4" d, salad	13	5	55	14
Plate, 9 1/4" d, luncheon	25	6	16.50	100
Plate, 11" d, dinner	55	15	12	18
Plate, 11" d, grill	15	8	8	25
Platter, 11 3/4" l	24	10	12	80
Salt and pepper shakers, pr	50	20	-	4
Saucer	4	1.50	2.50	10
Sherbet	7.50	6	7.50	9.50
Sugar	10	6	9.50	12
Tumbler, 9 oz, 4 1/4" h	25	10	-	50
Vegetable bowl, 10" l, oval	27.50	12	25	45

PARROT

Manufactured by Federal Glass Co., Columbus, Ohio, from 1931 to 1932.

Made in amber and green, with limited production in blue and crystal.

Item	Amber	Green
Berry bowl, 8" d	$75	$80
Butter dish, cov	1,250	475
Creamer, ftd	65	55
Cup	35	40
Hot plate, 5" d, pointed	875	900
Hot plate, round	-	950
Pitcher, 80 oz, 8-1/2" h	-	2,500
Plate, 5-3/4" d, sherbet	45	35
Plate, 7-1/2" d, salad	-	60
Plate, 9" d, dinner	50	95
Plate, 10-1/2" d, grill, round	35	-
Plate, 10-1/2" d, grill, square	-	60
Platter, 11-1/4" l, oblong	65	70
Salt and pepper shakers, pr	-	270
Saucer	18	18

Item	Amber	Green
Sherbet, ftd, cone	$22.50	$27.50
Sugar, cov	450	320
Tumbler, 10 oz, 4 1/4" h	100	130
Tumbler, 10 oz, 5 1/2" h, footed, Madrid	145	-
Tumbler, 12 oz, 5 1/2" h	115	160
Tumbler, 5 3/4" h, footed, heavy	100	120
Vegetable bowl, 10" l, oval	75	65

Item	Black	Crystal	Green
Candy dish, cov	$45	$35	$45
Cereal bowl, 5" d	-	20	25
Creamer, ftd	-	10	18
Cup	-	4.50	6.50
Plate, 6 1/4" d, sherbet	-	3.50	4.50
Plate, 8" d, luncheon	15	7	10
Salt and pepper shakers, pr	45	36	32
Saucer	-	2	3.50
Sherbet	-	6	8
Sugar, ftd	-	12	18.50
Tumbler, 10 oz, 6" h	-	28	30

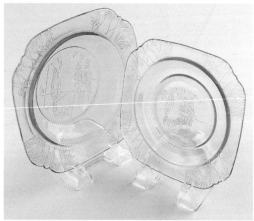

Parrot, amber jam dish **$75**, *and green sherbet plate.* **$35**

Ribbon, green cup **$6.50**, *and creamer* **$18**.

RIBBON

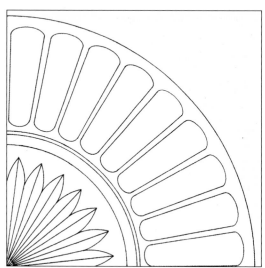

Manufactured by Hazel Atlas Glass Co., Clarksburg, W.V., and Zanesville, Ohio, early 1930s.

Made in black, crystal, green, and pink. Production in pink was limited to salt and pepper shakers, valued at $40.

Item	Black	Crystal	Green
Berry bowl, 4" d	$-	$20	$22
Berry bowl, 8" d	-	27.50	45
Bowl, 9" d, wide bands	-	-	35

SHARON

Manufactured by Federal Glass Co., Columbus, Ohio, from 1935 to 1939.

Made in amber, crystal, green, and pink.

Reproductions: † Reproductions include the butter dish, covered candy dish, creamer, covered sugar, and salt and pepper shakers. Reproduction colors include dark amber, blue, green, and pink.

Item	Amber	Crystal	Green	Pink
Berry bowl, 5" d	$8.50	$5	$18.50	$16.50
Berry bowl, 8 1/2" d	7.50	12	40	35
Butter dish, cov †	50	20	85	65
Cake plate, 11 1/2" d, ftd	30	10	65	45
Candy dish, cov †	45	15	100	65
Cereal, 6" d	24	12	32	30
Champagne, 5" d bowl	-	-	-	12
Cheese dish, cov †	225	1,500	-	950
Cream soup, 5" d	28	15	60	52.50
Creamer, ftd †	15	14	22	24
Cup	9	6	18	18
Fruit bowl, 10 1/2" d	24	18	40	50
Iced tea tumbler, ftd	85	15	-	65
Jam dish, 7 1/2" d	45	-	48	215
Pitcher, 80 oz, ice lip	165	-	150	165
Pitcher, 80 oz, without ice lip	140	-	150	150
Plate, 6" d, bread and butter	12	5	9	9.50
Plate, 7 1/2" d, salad	22.50	6.50	8	30
Plate, 9 1/2" d, dinner	17	9.50	27.50	26.50
Platter, 12 1/2" l, oval	24	-	35	35
Salt and pepper shakers, pr †	50	-	80	65
Saucer	6.50	4	36	12
Sherbet, ftd	12.50	8	35	20
Soup, flat, 7 3/4" d, 1 7/8" deep	55	-	-	60
Sugar, cov †	35	12	55	60
Tumbler, 9 oz, 4 1/8" h, thick	30	-	65	47.50
Tumbler, 9 oz, 4 1/8" h, thin	38	-	65	50
Tumbler, 12 oz, 5 1/4" h, thick	55	-	95	50
Tumbler, 12 oz, 5 1/4" h, thin	55	-	95	62
Tumbler, 15 oz, 6-1/2" h, thick	125	18	-	65
Vegetable bowl, 9-1/2" l, oval	22	-	45	36

*Sharon, (counterclockwise) pink sherbet **$20**, 5" d berry bowl **$16.50**, creamer **$24**, and 8 1/2" d berry bowl. **$35***

THISTLE

Manufactured by Macbeth-Evans, Charleroi, Pa., about 1929 to 1930.

Made in crystal, green, pink, and yellow. Production was limited in crystal and yellow.

Reproductions: † Recent reproductions have been found in pink, a darker emerald green, and wisteria. Several of the reproductions have a scalloped edge. Reproductions include the cake plate, fruit bowl, pitcher, salt and pepper shakers, and a small tumbler.

Item	Green	Pink
Cake plate, 13" d, heavy †	$195	$225
Cereal bowl, 5 1/2" d	50	50
Cup, thin	36.50	24
Fruit bowl, 10 1/4" d †	295	495
Plate, 8" d, luncheon	30	32
Plate, 10 1/4" d, grill	35	30
Saucer	12	12

*Thistle, green luncheon plate. **$30***

VERNON

Manufactured by Indiana Glass Co., Dunkirk, Ind., from 1930 to 1932.

Made in crystal, green, and yellow.

Item	Crystal	Green	Yellow
Creamer, ftd	$12	$25	$30
Cup	10	15	18
Plate, 8" d, luncheon	7	10	15
Sandwich plate, 11 1/2" d	14	25	30
Saucer	4	6	6
Sugar, ftd	18	25	30
Tumbler, 5" h, ftd	16	40	45

Vernon, yellow tumbler.
$45

YORKTOWN

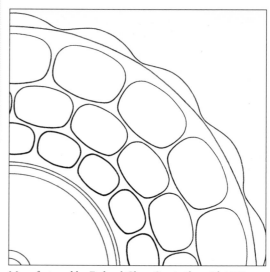

Manufactured by Federal Glass Co., in the mid-1950s.

Made in crystal, iridescent, smoke, white, and yellow. Values for all the colors are about the same.

Item	Crystal, etc.
Berry bowl, 5 1/2" d	$4.50
Berry bowl, 9 1/2" d	10
Celery tray, 10" l	10
Creamer	5
Cup	3.50
Fruit bowl, 10" d, ftd	18
Iced tea tumbler, 5 1/4" h, 13 oz	7.50
Juice tumbler, 3 7/8" h, 6 oz	4.50
Mug	15
Plate, 8 1/4" d	4.50
Plate, 11 1/2" d	8.50
Punch bowl set	40
Punch cup	2.50
Relish	5
Sandwich server	7.50
Saucer	1
Sherbet, 7 oz	3.50
Snack cup	2.50
Snack plate with indent	3.50
Sugar	5
Tumbler, 4 3/4" h, 10 oz	6
Vase, 8" h	15

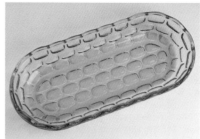

Yorktown, yellow relish.
$5

Early American Pattern Glass, Flint, Etc.

Early pattern glass (flint) was made with a lead formula, giving many items a ringing sound when tapped. Lead became too valuable to be used in glass manufacturing during the Civil War, and in 1864, Hobbs, Brockunier & Co., Wheeling, W.V., developed a soda lime (non-flint) formula. Pattern glass also was produced in transparent colors, milk glass, opalescent glass, slag glass and custard glass.

Collector's Note: Fostoria Glass Co. began operations at Fostoria, Ohio, in 1887, and moved to Moundsville, W.V., in 1891. By 1925, Fostoria had five furnaces and a variety of special shops. In 1924, a line of colored tableware was introduced. Fostoria was purchased by Lancaster Colony in 1983. See more Fostoria beginning on page 465.

Artichoke – Frosted, Finger Bowl with Under Plate, colorless, each with polished table ring. Fostoria Glass Co. Fourth quarter 19th century. 3" h overall, 6" d overall. Bowl with a flake to the table ring and light wear above pattern, plate with flake/roughness and manufacturing frosted-over chip to table ring. **$92**

Artichoke – Frosted, Open Compote, colorless, pillared stem and circular foot, wafer construction. Fostoria Glass Co. Fourth quarter 19th century. 8 3/4" h, 8" d. Molding flaw to stem. **$103**

Ashburton, Large Flip Glass, colorless flint, polished pontil mark. Third quarter 19th century. 6 7/8" h, 5 5/8" d rim. **$115**

Barred Ovals Water Pitcher, colorless and frosted, applied handle. George Duncan & Sons. Fourth quarter 19th century. 9 3/4" h overall, 5" d. Minor high point wear. **$80**

Collector's Note: George Duncan, his sons, Harry and James, and Augustus Heisey, his son-in-law, formed George Duncan & Sons in Pittsburgh in 1872. After a devastating fire in 1892, James Duncan relocated the firm to Washington, Pa. Designer John E. Miller was responsible for creating many fine patterns, the most famous being Three Face. Miller became a partner in 1900 and the firm used the name Duncan and Miller Glass Co. until the plant closed in 1955.

Bowtie Salt Shaker, colorless with a slight tint, period lid. Fourth quarter 19th century. 3" h overall. Lid with small spots of rust and light denting. **$57**

Brilliant – Amber Stained, Salt Shaker, colorless, period lid. Riverside Glass Works. Fourth quarter 19th century. 3" h overall. Minor pattern flakes/roughness, lid with denting and short splits. **$138**

California / Beaded Grape, Tankard Water Pitcher, green with gilt decoration. Fourth quarter 19th century. 10 1/8" h overall, 4 5/8" d. Wear to gilt decoration. **$80**

Photo courtesy Green Valley Auctions, Mt. Crawford, Va.; www.GreenValleyAuctions.com

Artichoke – Frosted, Bulbous Water Pitcher, colorless, applied handle with pressed fan design to upper terminal. Fostoria Glass Co. Fourth quarter 19th century. 8 1/2" h overall, 5 3/4" d overall. Two flat chips, area of roughness and manufacturing frosted-over chips to table ring. **$192**

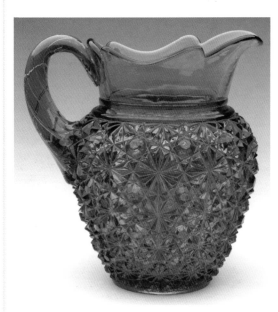

Photo courtesy Green Valley Auctions, Mt. Crawford, Va.; www.GreenValleyAuctions.com

Belmont, No. 100 / Daisy and Button – Scalloped Edge, Water Pitcher, amber, applied air-twist handle with pressed fan design to upper terminal. Belmont Glass Co. Fourth quarter 19th century. 8 3/4" h overall. Two pattern chips. **$192**

Photo courtesy Green Valley Auctions, Mt. Crawford, Va.; www.GreenValleyAuctions.com

Colorado, Four-Piece Table Set, green with very good gilt decoration, consisting of a butter dish, covered sugar bowl, creamer and spooner. U.S. Glass Co. Late 19th/early 20th century. 4 1/4" to 7" h overall, 4" to 6 7/8" d overall. **$218 set**

California / Beaded Grape, Nine-Piece Berry Set, green, consisting of a master berry bowl and eight berry dishes. Fourth quarter 19th century. 2 3/4" h, 8 1/4" sq and 1 1/4" h, 3 1/2" sq. Light interior wear to master berry bowl. .... **$46 set**

Cambridge Peacock, Seven-Piece Water Set, colorless, consisting of a tankard water pitcher and six tumblers. First quarter 20th century. Pitcher 11 1/2" h overall, 4 1/2" d base, tumblers 4 1/4" h, 3" d rim. One tumbler with small bruise to rim, one with a base flake and another with a 3/8" bruise under base, all tumblers with normal expected wear. .... **$360 set**

Central, No. 796 / Rope and Thumbprint Water Pitcher, vaseline, applied reeded handle. Central Glass Co. Fourth quarter 19th century. 8 1/2" h overall, 5 1/2" d overall. **$184**

Champion, Butter Dish, colorless with gilt decoration. McKee & Brothers. Late 19th/early 20th century. 5 1/4" h overall. Wear to gilding. **$36**

> **Collector's Note:** McKee & Brothers Glass Works was established in 1853 in Pittsburgh. In 1888, the factory was relocated to Jeannette, Pa., and began to produce many types of glass kitchenware. Production continued until 1951, when McKee-Jeannette Co. was sold to the Thatcher Manufacturing Co.

Chandelier, Salt Shaker, colorless, period lid. Fourth quarter 19th century. 3 1/2" h overall. Some flakes/roughness, lid with small spots of rust. **$34**

Classic Butter Dish, colorless and frosted, log feet. Gillinder & Sons. Fourth quarter 19th century. 6 3/4" h overall, 6 1/2" d overall. Single flake to interior rim of base, one foot with annealing crack, and another with a flake. **$192**

Coach Bowl, amber, three wheels with front tongue. Fourth quarter 19th century. 4 1/2" h, 5 1/4" x 9" overall. **$120**

Colorado, Five-Piece Beverage Set, green with good gilt decoration, consisting of footed pitcher with applied handle, and four tumblers with polished bases. U.S. Glass Co. Late 19th/early 20th century. 8" h overall, 5 1/2" d overall. Two tumblers with minute roughness to edge of base. **$230**

Photo courtesy Green Valley Auctions, Mt. Crawford, Va.; www.GreenValleyAuctions.com

Colorado, Celery Vase, green with gilt decoration, on three feet. U.S. Glass Co. Late 19th/early 20th century. 6" h, 4" d rim. Nick on one foot. **$270**

*Early Thumbprint, Salver/Cake Stand, colorless flint glass,
curved rim with 32 even scallops, double-step hollow
stem with 12 flutes, circular foot with 24 scallops, single
band of 24 thumbprints under foot, wafer construction.
Bakewell, Pears & Co. Third quarter 19th century.
6" h, 11 1/2" d rim, 5 3/8" d foot. Small area of pattern
roughness under the plate and a flake on one point of the
stem.* **$1,073**

*Daisy and Button with Ornament, Celery Vase, vaseline.
Fourth quarter 19th century. 6 3/4" h, 4 7/8" d overall.*
$108

Colorado, Pair of Footed Salt and Pepper Shakers, green
with gilt decoration, period lids. U.S. Glass Co. Late 19th/
early 20th century. 2 3/4" h. One with chip to exterior of
foot, both with minor flakes on rim. **$120**

Colorado-Maiden's Blush, Footed Toothpick Holder, gilt
decoration, beaded rim. U.S. Glass Co. Late 19th/early 20th
century. 2 1/2" h, 2 1/2" d rim. **$115**

Colorado Vase, colorless, on three feet. U.S. Glass Co. Late
19th/early 20th century. 14 3/4" h, 5 1/4" d rim. Minute
nick to one foot. **$120**

Columbian Coin, Pair of Salt and Pepper Shakers, colorless
with frosted coins, matching period lids. Central Glass
Co. Fourth quarter 19th century. 3" h overall. Both with
moderate to heavy wear, lids with minor imperfections.
.... **$115**

Daisy and Button, Inkwell, vaseline, original glass cover.
Fourth quarter 19th century. 2 1/4" h, 2" sq. Minor flake
and hint of mold roughness to cover rim. **$172**

Daisy in Oval Panels, Seven-Piece Beverage Set, green
with gilt decoration, consisting of a tankard pitcher and
six tumblers. Fourth quarter 19th century. 9 3/4" h overall,
4 3/4" d and 3 3/4" h, 2 7/8" d. Pitcher with one chip and
polished area to a lower rib. **$84**

Deer and Pine Tree, Bread Tray, vaseline. Fourth quarter
19th century. 1 1/4" h, 7 3/4" x 12 7/8". Minor mold
roughness to inner rim. **$80**

Dewdrop with Flowers, N.S. Starflower Water Pitcher,
colorless. Fourth quarter 19th century. 8 1/4" h overall,
5" d. Interior crizzeling/stretching, minor mold roughness.
.... **$48**

Diamond Quilted Tray, vaseline, leaf shape. Fourth
quarter 19th century. 1" h, 10" d overall. Some surface
wear. **$46**

Early Thumbprint, Open Compote, colorless flint glass,
rim with 32 even scallops, double step hollow stem with
12 flutes, circular foot with 24 scallops, single band of 24
thumbprints under foot, wafer construction. Bakewell, Pears
& Co. Third quarter 19th century. 10 3/4" h, 12 3/4" d,
6 7/8" d foot. Single chip under the rim and an open bubble
to one scallop. **$632**

Ellrose – Amber Stained, Goblet, colorless. George
Duncan & Sons. Fourth quarter 19th century. 6 3/8" h.
.... **$126**

Ellrose – Amber Stained, Butter Pats, Set of Four,
colorless. George Duncan & Sons. Fourth quarter 19th
century. 2 3/4" sq. Two with a single corner flake, two with
flake/roughness to two or more corners. .... **$132 all**

Eye-Winker Salt Shaker, colorless, period lid. Dalzell,
Gilmore & Leighton Co. Late 19th century. 3" h overall.
Normal manufacturing roughness under lid, lid with
scratches and light corrosion. **$57**

Feather, Pair of Salt and Pepper Shakers, colorless, period
lids. Late 19th century. 2 3/4" h overall. Several minor
flakes to shoulder rib and a small spot of roughness to one,
one lid with corrosion and minor denting. **$72**

Fine Cut and Block – Amber Stained, Sugar Bowl,
colorless, domed lid. Fourth quarter 19th century. 8 3/8" h
overall, 5 1/2" d. **$115**

Fine Cut and Block, Marmalade / Pickle Jar, amber.
Fourth quarter 19th century. 7" h overall, 3 3/4" d rim.
Minute mold roughness to interior of lid. **$36**

*Fine Cut and Block – Amber Stained, Goblet, colorless.
Fourth quarter 19th century. 6 1/4" h.* **$96**

Florida / Emerald Green, Herringbone Water Pitcher.
Fourth quarter 19th century. 9 3/4" h overall, 4 1/2" d.
Minute open bubble to one herringbone panel. **$34**

Fostoria, No. 183 / Victoria Boat-Shaped Relish, colorless.
Fostoria Glass Co. Fourth quarter 19th century. 3 1/2" h
overall, 2 3/4" x 8". **$48**

Frosted Dolphin, Creamer, colorless. Hobbs, Brockunier &
Co. Fourth quarter 19th century. 6 3/4" h overall, 3 1/2" d
rim. Lightly tinted. **$57**

Heart with Thumbprint, Ruby Stained Goblet, colorless.
Fourth quarter 19th century. 5 7/8" h. **$1,610**

Hexagon Block, Ruby Stained, Tumbler, colorless, with leaf
engraving. Fourth quarter 19th century. 3 7/8" h. Minute
wear to stain on rim. **$57**

Hobbs, No. 339 / Leaf and Flower – Amber Stained Four-
Piece Table Set, colorless, consisting of a butter dish,
covered sugar bowl, creamer with applied handle and
spooner, later three with polished pontil mark. Hobbs,
Brockunier & Co. Late 19th/early 20th century. 3 1/2" to
5" h overall, 3 1/2" to 8" d overall. Butter with chip to lid
rim and base flange, and other minor nicks and roughness,
sugar lid with flake to rim, each example with minor to
moderate roughness to scalloped line above pattern.
.... **$96 set**

*Flying Birds Goblet, colorless. Fourth quarter 19th
century. 5 5/8" h. Flake to line above pattern.* **$147**

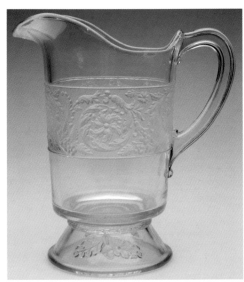

*Frosted Flower Band, Water Pitcher, colorless,
collared foot. Fourth quarter 19th century. 9 3/8" h
overall, 5" d.* **$96**

*Leaf Umbrella, Northwood No. 263 cracker jar, ruby/
cranberry, colorless applied finial, 8 3/4" h overall, 6"
greatest d. Small area of polishing and several interior
flakes to rim of cover, finial with roughness to tip; base
having minor flaking/roughness to exterior rim.* **$2,090**

*Jumbo – Ribbed, Covered Sugar, colorless with frosted
finial, lid and base with interior ribbing, additional
ribbing under the circular foot. Canton Glass Co. Fourth
quarter 19th century. 8 1/4" h overall, 3 1/8" x 4 3/4" rim.
Cover with a chip to two outer corners along with another
chip and several flakes under the rim, finial with a minute
flake to tip of tail and one to trunk.* **$1,080**

Hummingbird, Three-Piece Water Set, amber, consisting
of a water pitcher and two goblets. Fourth quarter 19th
century. Pitcher 9 1/4" h, goblets 6" h. .... **$184 set**

Hummingbird, Tumbler, colorless. Fourth quarter 19th
century. 3 3/4" h. Hint of mold roughness under base.
.... **$287**

Jeweled Moon and Star, Water Pitcher, colorless with
amber and blue staining, alternating frosted moons,
applied handle. Fourth quarter 19th century. 9 3/4" h
overall. Areas of light to moderate wear to interior and
exterior lower body. **$258**

Klondike – Curved, Amber Stained Salt Shaker, colorless
and frosted, period lid. Dalzell, Gilmore & Leighton Co.
Fourth quarter 19th century. 3 1/4" h overall. Minor
highpoint flakes/wear to corners, lid with normal wear.
.... **$103**

Klondike – Amber Stained, Tumbler, colorless and
frosted. Dalzell, Gilmore & Leighton Co. Late 19th/early
20th century. 3 7/8" h, 2 7/8" d. With two manufacturing
frosted-over nicks on base. **$126**

Klondike – Amber Stained, Square Bowl, colorless and
frosted, flared sides. Dalzell, Gilmore & Leighton Co. Late
19th/early 20th century. 3" h, 7 1/4" sq. Single flake and
minor roughness to rim. **$92**

Klondike – Amber Stained, Oval Bowl, colorless and
frosted. Dalzell, Gilmore & Leighton Co. Late 19th/early
20th century. 2 3/4" h, 5 3/4" x 9"............................ **$132**

Leaf Umbrella, Northwood No. 263 breakfast covered sugar
and creamer, ruby/cranberry, colorless applied handle and
finial. Sugar 5 3/8" h overall, 3 7/8" greatest d, creamer 4" h,
3 1/4" greatest d. Rim of sugar lid with several minor flakes
and a bruise, base rim with minute rim nicks, creamer with
several minute nicks and lightly polished spout edge.
.... **$935 pair**

Leaf Umbrella, Northwood No. 263 syrup, ruby/cranberry,
colorless applied handle with feather design at upper
terminal, period metal lid with patent date, 6 1/2" h overall,
4 1/4" greatest d. **$990**

Leaf Umbrella, Northwood No. 263 syrup, rose du Barry,
colorless applied handle, period metal lid with patent date,
6 1/2" h overall, 4 1/4" greatest d. **$1,210**

Leaf Umbrella, Northwood No. 263 four-piece table set,
ruby/cranberry, consisting of a butter dish, covered sugar

Loop and Crystal Tumbler, cobalt blue lead glass, faint pontil ring. Probably Pittsburgh. Mid 19th century. 3 1/2" h. **$138**

bowl, each with colorless applied finial, creamer with colorless applied handle, and spooner, 4" to 6 1/4" overall. Butter with bruise on the interior rim of the lid, creamer with a crack in the upper terminal of the handle, spooner having two minute rim flakes, the sugar is undamaged except for the base rim being polished. .... **$1,430 set**

Leaf Umbrella, Northwood No. 263 cruet, ruby/cranberry, colorless applied handle, original colorless facetted stopper, 6 3/4" h overall, 3 1/2" greatest d. **$935**

Lyon, Crystal/Madison Covered Sugar Bowl, colorless flint glass, hexagonal finial, and short hexagonal stem with circular foot. James B. Lyon & Co. Third quarter 19th

century. 7 1/2" h overall, 4 1/2" d. Lid with normal minor flaking/roughness to rim and finial, one small pattern flake and several minute nicks, base with a shallow pattern chip and several minute nicks. **$103**

Mid-Western, Free-Blown Pitcher, amber, tooled rim, high shoulder, applied hollow handle, rough pontil mark. Probably Pittsburgh or surrounding area. Second quarter 19th century. 7" h, 4 3/8" d rim. Handle with loss to lower terminal (lacking curl). **$862**

New Hampshire/Bent Buckle, Water Pitcher, maiden's blush stain with traces of gilt at rim. Fourth quarter 19th century. 8" h overall 4 1/2" d. **$108**

Oaken Bucket/Wooden Pail, Water Pitcher, amethyst. Fourth quarter 19th century. 8 1/8" h, 5 1/4" d rim. **$60**

Owl Water Pitcher, amber. Bryce, Higbee & Co. Fourth quarter 19th century. 9" h overall, 5" d. **$207**

Paneled Daisy, Four-Piece Table Set, opaque white/milk glass, consisting of a butter dish, covered sugar bowl, creamer and spooner. Late 19th/early 20th century. Sugar 7 1/2" h overall, 4 1/4" d. Creamer with annealing lines to rim, cover rims of butter and sugar with minor flaking/ roughness. .... **$108 set**

Portland – Banded, Sugar Shaker, colorless, period lid. Fourth quarter 19th century. 5" h overall, 3" d base. Minor high point wear to pattern and minor denting to lid. **$57**

Priscilla – Ruby Stained, Cruet, colorless, lacking stopper. Dalzell, Gilmore & Leighton Co. Late 19th/early 20th century. 5 3/4" h. **$632**

Priscilla Cake Stand, colorless. Dalzell, Gilmore & Leighton Co. Late 19th/early 20th century. 6 1/4" h, 10" d. One chip to scallop under plate and area of roughness to another. **$103**

Priscilla Variant, Footed Vase, colorless, lacking stars to vase. Late 19th/early 20th century. 14 3/4" h, 4 1/2" d rim, 5 1/2" d base. **$46**

Regent/Leaf Medallion, Master Berry Bowl, amethyst with gilt decoration. Northwood Glass Co. Fourth quarter 19th century. 4" h, 9" d. Less than normal wear to gilt decoration. **$115**

Riverside, No. 462 / X-Ray Four-Piece Table Set, green with worn gilt decoration, consisting of a butter, covered sugar,

Red Block – Ruby Stained, Wines, Set of Eight, colorless. Various makers. Fourth quarter 19th century. 4" h. One with pattern flake, one having rim nick. **$80 set**

Stippled Fleur-De-Lys, Seven-Piece Water Set, green with traces of gilt decoration, consisting of a water pitcher and six tumblers. Fourth quarter 19th century. Pitcher 8" h overall, 5" d, tumblers 3 3/4" h, 2 3/4" d. Pitcher with a single foot flake. **$72**

creamer and spooner. Riverside Glass Works. Late 19th/ early 20th century. 4 3/4" to 5 1/2" h overall. Creamer with crack to upper handle terminal. ....**$115 set**

Riverside, No. 484 / Croesus Breakfast Covered Sugar and Creamer, green with above-average gilt decoration. Riverside Glass Works. Late 19th/early 20th century. 4 1/8" and 5 3/4" h overall. Creamer with ghost-like crack to right side of upper terminal of handle, sugar with several minute nicks to edge of lid. ....**$84 both**

Riverside, No. 484 / Croesus Three-Piece Beverage Set, green with good gilt decoration, consisting of a water pitcher with an applied handle with impressed feather at upper terminal, and two tumblers with polished table rings. Riverside Glass Works. Fourth quarter 19th century. 11 1/4" h overall, 5 1/4" d overall, and 3 7/8" h, 2 3/4" d. ....**$132 set**

Rose in Snow, Water Pitcher, amber, applied amber handle. Bryce Bros. Fourth quarter 19th century. 8 1/2" h overall, 5" d overall. **$103**

Rose Sprig, Cake Stand, amber. Fourth quarter 19th century. 6 1/4" h, 9 1/8" sq. Mold roughness to interior of base. **$84**

Royal Oak, Three-Piece Table Set, colorless and frosted, consisting of a covered sugar bowl, creamer with applied handle and spooner. Northwood Glass Co. Late 19th/early 20th century. 3 3/4" to 6" h overall, 3 1/2" to 4" sq. Chip to rim of sugar base. ....**$108 set**

Shoshone/Victor, Cake Stand, green. U.S. Glass Co. Fourth quarter 19th century. 4 1/4" h, 9" d. **$57**

Snail, Covered Sugar Bowl, colorless, engraved foliate decoration. George Duncan & Sons. Fourth quarter 19th century. 7 1/4" h overall, 4 1/8" d. Minor high-point wear to base. **$57**

Sunken Primrose/Florida, Ruby and Amber Stained Tumbler, colorless, polished table ring. Greensburg Glass Co. Fourth quarter 19th century. 3 3/4" h. **$115**

Swan, Four-Piece Table Set, opaque white/milk glass, consisting of a butter base, covered sugar bowl, creamer and spooner. Fourth quarter 19th century. Sugar 7 1/8" h, 4 1/2" d rim. Creamer with rim roughness and annealing fissure to foot, butter base with annealing crack to rim, spooner with flaking/roughness and annealing fissure to rim, with graphite speckles. ....**$108 set**

Photo courtesy Green Valley Auctions, Mt. Crawford, Va.; www.GreenValleyAuctions.com

Riverside, No. 135 / Cabbage Leaf, Water Pitcher, amber, twisted-rib applied amber handle. Riverside Glass Works. Fourth quarter 19th century. 9 3/4" h overall, 6 3/4" d overall. Area of wear to un-patterned portion. **$1,685**

Photo courtesy Green Valley Auctions, Mt. Crawford, Va.; www.GreenValleyAuctions.com

Rose Sprig Milk Pitcher, vaseline, hexagonal foot. Fourth quarter 19th century. 7 3/4" h overall, 4 1/4" d. **$115**

Photo courtesy Green Valley Auctions, Mt. Crawford, Va.;
www.GreenValleyAuctions.com

Swirled Feather and Diamond Point, Covered Nappy / Butter, fiery opalescent flint, cover with acorn-like finial, base with alternating large and medium scallop rim, eight-petal rosette in base. Possibly Boston & Sandwich Glass Co. Mid 19th century. 6 1/8" d overall. Some light mold roughness. **$226**

Collector's Note: In 1818, Deming Jarves was listed in the Boston directory as a glassmaker. That same year, he was appointed general manager of the newly formed New England Glass Co. In 1824, Jarves toured the glassmaking factories in Pittsburgh, left New England Glass and founded a glass factory in Sandwich, Mass.

Originally called the Sandwich Manufacturing Co., it was incorporated in April 1826 as the Boston & Sandwich Glass Co. The firm closed on Jan. 1, 1888.

Texas – Maiden's Blush, Cruet, colorless, original colorless stopper. Late 19th/early 20th century. 6 1/2" h overall, 4" d base. Several spots of manufacturing roughness to shoulder ribs and light to moderate wear to lower ribs and stain. **$450**

Thousand Eye, Three-Piece Water Set, amber, consisting of a water pitcher, goblet and oval tray. Adams & Co. Fourth quarter 19th century. Pitcher 9 5/8" h overall, tray 12" x 13 7/8". Pitcher with chip to end of one support under bowl. **$57**

Tulip, Covered Sweetmeat, opaque white flint with fiery opalescence, on a simple six-panel standard, wafer construction. Third quarter 19th century. 7 1/4" h overall, 6" d rim. Minor chip under bowl rim. **$450**

Wildflower, Five-Piece Water Set, amber, consisting of a water pitcher, three tumblers and an oval tray. Adams & Co. Fourth quarter 19th century. Pitcher 8 1/2" h, tumblers 3 7/8" h, tray 11" x 13". Flake on the base of the water tray. .... **$72 set**

Willow Oak, Four-Piece Table Set, amber, consisting of a butter dish, creamer, sugar base and a spooner. Bryce Bros. Fourth quarter 19th century. 5" to 5 1/2" h overall. Minor mold roughness to rim of butter cover. .... **$149 set**

Photo courtesy Green Valley Auctions, Mt. Crawford, Va.;
www.GreenValleyAuctions.com

Wildflower, Water Pitcher, blue. Adams & Co. Fourth quarter 19th century. 8 3/4" h overall, 5 1/4" d rim. **$69**

Early Cut and Engraved Glass

Bowl, Free-Blown and Engraved, Footed, colorless, deep U-shape bowl with cross-hatched swag and tassel decoration below rim, small crude applied foot with rough pontil mark. Probably continental. 19th century. 4 3/4" h, 4" d rim, 2 3/8" d foot. **$67**

Celery Glass, Cut Laurel Wreath and Roundels, colorless, plain rim, cut lined panel base, applied button stem and plain circular foot with polished pontil mark. Probably Bakewell, Page & Bakewell. 1820-1830. 7 7/8" h, 5 1/4" d rim, 4 1/8" d foot. **$282**

Celery Glass, Cut Strawberry Diamonds and Rayed Roundels, colorless, cut laurel wreath below the delicately notched rim, panel cut base, applied knop stem and star-cut circular foot. Probably Bakewell, Page & Bakewell. 1820-1830. 8" h, 5 1/4" d rim, 4 1/8" d foot. Light 1/2" scratch below rim. **$270**

Compote, Cut Strawberry Diamonds and Fans, colorless, delicately notched rim, band of short panels cut below diamonds, applied knop stem and star-cut circular foot. Bowl is somewhat tilted. Probably Bakewell, Page & Bakewell. 1820-1830. 6 1/2" to 6 3/4" h, 9" d rim, 4 1/4" d foot. Several short scratches under bowl and some light wear to interior. **$282**

Chalice, Free-Blown, Cut and Engraved, colorless soda-lime glass, conical bowl elaborately engraved with birds, daisies, grapes and floral wreaths, along with cut punties, applied inverted baluster stem and wide sloping foot with light rough pontil mark. Probably continental. First half 19th century. 7 1/4" h, 4 3/4" d rim, 5" d foot. Light wear to interior base. **$450**

Celery Glass, Heavy Cut, colorless, bowl cut with 10 panels and pointed arches, raised on a panel-cut stem and star-cut foot. American or English. Mid-19th century. 7" h, 4 5/8" d rim, 3 5/8" d foot. Light interior wear. **$45**

*Flip Glasses (two), Free-Blown and Engraved, colorless,
each decorated with a similar bird within a circular
sunburst frame, additional simple flower on reverse, each
with a rough pontil mark. Probably continental. 19th
century. 3 3/4" h, 3" d rim, and 4 3/8" h, 3 5/8" d rim.
Smaller with unusually heavy wear under base and some
wear to interior.* **$390 both**

Decanter (pint) and Tumbler, Cut Strawberry Diamonds
and Fans, colorless, decanter with three applied neck rings
above shoulder flutes, applied circular foot with large cut
star, and hollow matching stopper, tumbler with basal
flutes and star-cut base. Probably Pittsburgh. 1820-1840.
Decanter 9 1/2" h overall, 7 1/4" h bottle, 3 1/8" d foot;
tumbler 3 1/2" h. Decanter with minute pattern nicks,
polishing to edge of foot, stopper is a different tint, tumbler
with minor base flakes. .... **$390 both**

Flip Glass, Free-Blown and Engraved, colorless, stylized
tulip decoration, rough pontil mark. Probably continental.
19th century. 5 3/4" h, 4 3/8" d rim. **$330**

Flip Glasses (two), Free-Blown and Engraved, colorless,
first with basket of flowers decoration, second with stylized
daisy and tulip decoration, ground and rough pontil marks.
Probably continental. 19th century. 3 1/8" h, 2 5/8" d rim,
and 5 3/8" h, 4" d rim. One with a ring of interior wear
above base. .... **$300 both**

Goblet, Free-Blown, Cut and Engraved, colorless soda-lime
glass, conical six-panel bowl, three panels elaborately
engraved with a different landscape reserve surrounded
by foliage, separated by single roughed panels each with
a cut daisy and quatrefoil, applied panel-cut stem and
wide sloping foot with light rough pontil mark. Probably
continental. 19th century. 6" h, 3" d rim, 3 5/8" d foot.
Minute flake to rim. **$192**

Jars (pair), sweetmeat, colorless cut glass, American, late
19th century, each with oval body with floral and flute
cuts, domed lid with oval faceted finial on a flute cut shaft
and stepped square base, 12" h, lids each with a couple of
minute nicks, some base corners and edges ground slightly,
one base edge has a small clamshell chip. .... **$770 pair**

Jug (panel), Cut Diamond, colorless, body features six
diamond panels with plain panels above and rays below,
step-cut neck and partially serrated rim, applied solid
handle with cut and polished lower terminal, wide polished
pontil mark. Probably Irish. 1815-1830. 6 1/8" h, 4 1/4" d
rim. Minute nicks to numerous points, light interior wear.
.... **$156**

*Celery Glass, Free-Blown, Pattern-Molded and Engraved,
colorless with a light gray tint, superimposed 20-rib
gadrooning around lower body, applied compressed knop
stem and slightly sloping foot with rough pontil mark.
Decoration consists of a flower basket and two floral
plumes within intricate floral swags with tassels. Probably
Pittsburgh region, possibly Bakewell, Page & Bakewell.
1815-1830. 8 1/2" h, 5 3/8" d rim, 4" d foot.* **$1,243**

Decanter (quart), Cut Strawberry Diamonds, Fans and
Rayed Roundels, colorless, three applied neck rings above
shoulder flutes, applied circular foot with large polished
pontil mark, hollow roundel and star-cut stopper. Probably
Pittsburgh, possibly Bakewell, Page & Bakewell. 1820-1830.
10 1/4" h overall, 8" h bottle, 3 3/4" d foot. Two minute
flakes to cuttings and a small chip to the lower ring of
stopper. **$214**

Decanter, colorless cut glass with white sulfide bust of
Washington, American, late 19th century, the decanter
throat and shoulder cut with concentric circles, the sides
with ribs, one section inset with a white sulfide bust of
George Washington, with an acorn-form cut-glass stopper,
(small chips), overall 12 1/4" h, roughness to two ribs
below right of bust about 1/2" and 1/4" long, several small
unobtrusive chips on the ribbed cuts, some cloudy, grimy
residue around lip and interior and some darkish residue
on the interior bottom, loss on bottom of stopper. ... **$5,925**

Jug (quart), Panel Cut and Engraved, colorless, eight neck flutes and 12 basal flutes, medial engraved Vintage decoration, applied handle, factory-polished sides of rim and handle terminal, polished pontil mark. Probably New England or New York. Third quarter 19th century. 8 3/4" h overall, 4 1/4" d rim, 4 1/4" d base. Two minute nicks to one base flute. **$113**

Mug, Free-Blown and Engraved, lead glass, short cylindrical form with thick base and applied solid handle, simple leaf and spray decoration, rough pontil mark. American or European. 19th century. 3" h, 2 1/2" d. **$158**

Mug, Free-Blown and Engraved Barrel-Form, colorless, stylized tulip decoration, applied strap handle, rough pontil mark. Probably continental. 19th century. 6 1/4" h, 3 7/8" d rim. **$254**

Wine Glasses, Cut Plumes and Roundels, Set of Six, colorless, each with an applied bladed-button stem and plain foot, one with rough pontil mark and others with polished pontil mark. Probably Pittsburgh. 1820-1840. 4" to 4 1/4" h. One with a foot flake and under-fill, one with a stem flake. **$228**

Early Pressed and Lacy Glass

Covered Sugar Bowl, California, canary, octagonal with circular foot, an unusually crude and thick example with a very slight cover seat causing a poor fit. New England Glass Co. or Curling, Robertson & Co. 1850-1870. 6" h overall, 5" d rim overall, 3" d foot. One large and two moderate chips to base rim, chip and two flakes to foot, several moderate chips to cover. **$84**

Creamer, Heart and Scale, colorless, molded handle and plain circular foot. Boston & Sandwich Glass Co. 1835-1850. 4 1/2" h overall, 3" d rim, 2 3/4" d foot. Shallow 3/4" spall to upper edge of spout, minor mold roughness. ... **$67**

Nappy on Foot, Heart and Sheaf of Wheat, colorless, double-scallop alternating with single-scallop rim, four overlapping hearts in center, attached by a sloping wafer to a medial-knop stem and sloping foot, rough pontil mark. New England. 1828-1835. 3 3/8" h, 4 7/8" d rim, 3 1/8" d foot. Three shallow chips to rim edge and two spalls (one 1" long) to upper rim. **$367**

Plate, Heart and Fleur-De-Lis central star and scrolls surrounded by a wide band of strawberry diamonds, broad scroll and scallop rim. Probably French. 1840-1860. 7 3/4" d. Some under-rim mold roughness. **$22**

Window Pane, Heavy Pressed Glass, Square, colorless, quatrefoil acanthus leaf and scroll design with a central bull's eye, lightly pebbled background, upper edge molded with a "J" initial and a bobbin and disk chain. While the design of this pane parallels those of the Lacy period, its soda-lime content indicates a later production date. Probably American. Fourth quarter 19th to first quarter 20th century. 1 1/4" thick, 8 1/4" sq. Large bruise and numerous chips to outer edge. **$30**

Covered Rectangular Dish, Extremely Rare, Midwestern, Lacy, colorless, dish with lancet and ellipse design on sides, bold scroll and fan rim, and 28 bull's-eye scallops around the base, stepped cover with Gothic arches and a bold fan-form finial. Probably Pittsburgh. 1830-1840. 5 5/8" h overall, 3 1/4" h rim, 4" x 6 1/4" overall. Dish rim with the partial loss of one corner scroll and a few small chips to fan tips, cover with light chip to one corner and minor flaking under the rim. This casket is one of only three or four recorded examples. **$11,300**

Window Pane, Marked "J.&.C. Ritchie," Lacy, colorless, central reserve depicting a side-wheel steamboat below the lettering and a draped tassel, surrounded by neo-classical style urns and flowers with a thistle centered below. A previously unrecorded example. Wheeling Flint Glass Works, Wheeling, W.V., John and Craig Ritchie, proprietors. 1833-1836. 7" x 5". Minute flake and hint of mold roughness to reverse edge. **$11,300**

Free-Blown Glass

Bowl (deep), Free-Blown, slightly cloudy aquamarine bottle glass, slightly tapered sides with folded rim, domed base with rough pontil mark. Probably Midwestern. First half 19th century. 7 1/4" h, 11" d. Minor wear, numerous light open bubbles. **$339**

Bowl (deep), Free-Blown, bottle green, slightly tapered sides with a boldly folded rim, domed base with rough pontil mark. Probably Midwestern. First half 19th century. 5 1/2" h, 8 1/2" d. Light wear, primarily on rim, small open bubble on outer edge of rim. **$367**

Bowl (deep), Free-Blown, swirling cobalt blue, somewhat crudely formed, slightly flaring rolled and folded rim, slightly domed base with rough pontil mark. First half 19th century. 4 1/8" h, 6 3/4" d rim. Areas of light wear. **$480**

Bowl (deep), Free-Blown, bottle green, nearly straight-sided with a narrow rolled rim, slightly domed base with rough pontil mark. Probably South Jersey. First half 19th century. 5 1/2" h, 7 1/8" d rim. Rim with a small open bubble and wear, interior with several open bubbles, scattered light wear. **$240**

Bowl (deep), Free-Blown, light bottle green, tapered sides with a boldly folded rim, domed base with rough pontil mark. Probably Midwestern. First half 19th century. 6 3/4" h, 9 1/4" d. Crack in side from below rim to near base. **$56**

Cracker Bowl, Free-Blown, colorless, applied lower knop stem and thick foot with partially polished pontil mark, original tin hinged cover with Britannia knob held in place by a tin band around rim. Probably Pittsburgh. Mid-19th century. 6" h rim, 7" d rim, 4 3/4" d foot. Light flake to inner rim, expected wear to cover. (The 1859 McKee & Brothers catalog illustrates this unusual form in a pressed-panel pattern, which they called a cracker bowl. The form continued to appear in their subsequent catalogs through 1871.) **$791**

Dome, Free-Blown, green bottle glass, elongated cylindrical form rough cut at one end. Probably 19th century. 20 3/4" h, 7" d. Several scratches and scuffs. **$56**

Egg Cup or Pedestal Salt, Free-Blown, deep cobalt blue with applied opal galleried rim, applied button stem and plain foot with rough pontil mark, high lead content. Probably English. Mid-19th century. 3 3/8" h, 2 1/4" d rim. **$101**

Ewer, Free-Blown, cobalt blue, pear-shape body with threaded neck, wide folded rim with long drawn spout, and applied hollow handle, kick-up base with rough pontil mark. 19th century. 7 1/2" h overall, 4 1/8" d overall. Loss to the lower end of threading, expected wear to rim and body, light interior residue. **$156**

Fish Globe on Foot, Free-Blown, colorless, tooled flattened rim and flared foot, rough pontil mark. American. 19th century. 14 1/2" h, 6 3/4" d rim, 8 1/4" d foot. Minor flake to rim. **$621**

Fish Globe on Foot, Free-Blown, colorless, tooled flattened rim and flared foot, rough pontil mark. American. 19th century. 11 1/4" h, 6 1/8" d rim, 7 1/8" d foot. Scratches and wear to bowl. **$423**

Inkwell, Free-Blown and Decorated, Teakettle-Form, strong aquamarine, bell-form body molded with faint

Photo courtesy Green Valley Auctions, Mt. Crawford, Va.; www.GreenValleyAuctions.com

Inkwell, Free-Blown Bird-Form, light green, globular body with applied head, wings and tail, raised on a short drawn stem and applied wide irregular sloping foot with light rough pontil mark. Possibly South Jersey. Probably 20th century. 4 3/4" h overall, 4 1/2" d foot. Chip and short crack to one tail feather, minor flake to beak. **$158**

ribs and fitted with two applied spouts, topped with a tooled triangular-shaped ornament mounted with a swan, additional applied prunts and threading on body, base with light four-point pontil mark. Possibly South Jersey. 19th or 20th century. 6 1/4" h, 3 1/4" d base. A 1" and 1/2" loss to threading at base and a light crack to another piece of threading. **$214**

Jar and Ball Cover, Free-Blown, pale aquamarine, crude jar with slight shoulder and faint rough pontil mark, well-formed ball with a 2 1/2" open rough pontil. Possibly Connecticut. 19th century. 5 1/4" h overall, jar 3" h x 2" d rim, ball 2 1/2" d overall. Two small pieces of rough extra glass near jar base. **$45**

Jug (cream), Free-Blown, medium violet, squat low-shoulder body with pulled spout, applied solid delicate handle, rough pontil mark. 19th century. 3" h, 2 1/8" d rim. **$791**

Jug (cream), Free-Blown, Footed, aquamarine, pear-shaped body with delicate applied three-rib handle, short drawn stem, applied oversized domed foot with boldly folded rim and rough pontil mark. Undetermined origin. 19th or 20th century. 5 5/8" h, 2 5/8" d rim, 4" d foot. Lacking handle curl and tip is polished, cloudy interior. **$734**

Jug (quart), Cains-Attributed, Double-Chain-Decorated, colorless with light gray tint, applied strap handle, kick-up base with rough pontil mark. Probably Thomas Cains, South Boston Flint Glass Works or Phoenix Glass Works. First quarter 19th century. 6 5/8" h overall, 4 3/4" d rim. **$2,147**

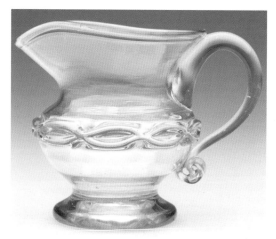

Photo courtesy Green Valley Auctions, Mt. Crawford, Va.; www.GreenValleyAuctions.com

Jug (cream), Free-Blown, Cains-Attributed, Chain-Decorated, colorless with light gray tint, tooled rim, applied handle, thick drawn foot with rough pontil mark. No other examples this size known. Probably Thomas Cains, South Boston Flint Glass Works or Phoenix Glass Works. First quarter 19th century. 3 7/8" h overall, 3 3/8" d rim, 2 3/8" d foot. **$4,237**

Jug (quart), Free-Blown, colorless, low shoulder, three tooled rings below rim, bold applied hollow handle, kick-up base with rough pontil mark. Probably Pittsburgh. First half 19th century. 7 3/4" h overall, 4 3/4" d rim, 3 3/4" d base...**$367**

Pan, Free-Blown, slightly cloudy medium amber, slightly flared boldly folded rim, slightly domed base with light rough pontil mark. Probably Midwestern. First half 19th century. 4 1/4" h, 10" d. Expected wear, heavier on rim, small spot of extra glass on exterior. **$1,469**

Pan, Free-Blown, colorless soda-lime, folded pale blue rim, slightly domed base with rough pontil mark having traces of olive green. Possibly Midwestern. Probably 19th century. 2" h, 6" d. Small rough area under the rim fold. **$124**

Ring Jar, Free-Blown, colorless, tall cylindrical form with two applied rings, domed cover with pinched flange and hollow button-top finial, domed base with rough pontil mark. American. Second half 19th century. 12 1/2" h overall, 5 7/8" d..**$144**

Salver, Free-Blown, colorless lead glass, plate with a slight upper and lower rim, raised on an applied multi-knop, tiered stem and domed foot with folded rim and rough pontil mark. English. 19th century. 4 1/2" h, 6 1/4" d rim, 3 3/4" d foot. Two short, light scratches under the plate. **$621**

Salver, Free-Blown, colorless soda-lime glass, plate with galleried rim, raised on a wafer-joined hollow Silesian stem with lower rings and a domed foot with tooled edge and rough pontil mark. 19th or 20th century. 6 1/4" h, 10 3/8" d rim, 6 1/2" d foot. Light usage wear to plate..................**$360**

Specie Jar, Free-Blown, colorless, tall cylindrical form with sharp shoulder and tin cover, domed base with rough pontil mark. American. Mid-19th century. 14 1/2" h

Photo courtesy Green Valley Auctions, Mt. Crawford, Va.; www.GreenValleyAuctions.com

Specie Jar, Free-Blown, light bottle green, tall cylindrical form with sharp shoulder and tin cover, domed base with rough pontil mark. American. First half 19th century. 10" h overall, 3 1/2" d rim, 4 3/4" d base. Scattered light scratches/wear, wear to cover. **$203**

overall, 4 1/2" d rim, 7" d base. Minor scattered wear, two light dents and wear to cover. **$146**

Specie Jar, Free-Blown, colorless, tall cylindrical form with domed cover featuring an applied hollow prunt-top finial, domed base with rough pontil mark. American. Mid-19th century. 13" h overall, 5" d...............................**$101**

Specie Jars, Free-Blown, Graduated Set of Four, colorless, one with a faint green tint, each of squat cylindrical form with sharp shoulder, tin cover, and domed base with rough pontil mark. American. Mid 19th century. 5 1/4" to 8" h overall, 3 1/2" to 6 1/8" d bases. Flake to rim of the largest and holes and corrosion to cover of the smallest, minor scattered wear to jars and expected wear to covers.
....**$339 set**

Storage Jar, Free-Blown, colorless, squat cylindrical form with wide folded rim and rough pontil mark, well-fitting stained composition cover of unknown association.

Sugar Bowl, Free-Blown, Footed, fiery opalescent, cup-shape bowl raised on an applied compressed baluster stem and circular folded foot with rough pontil mark. First half 19th century. 5" h, 4 1/2" d rim, 3 5/8" d foot. **$124**

Soda fountain straw holder, circa 1880, with applied glass "jewels," rare to find with original glass top, 14" h. **$6,900**

American. 19th century. 8" h, 9 1/2" d. Scattered light scratches and wear. **$180**

Storage Jar, Free-Blown, colorless, somewhat crude globular form with folded rim and kick-up base with thick rough pontil mark. Probably 19th century. 12" h, 7" d rim, 13" d overall. Scattered scratches and wear. **$79**

Sugar Bowl, Free-Blown Footed, medium yellowish-green bottle glass, somewhat crude deep U-shape bowl raised on a compressed-funnel foot with folded rim and faint rough pontil mark. Midwestern, probably Gallatin-Kramer or a nearby glasshouse. Late 18th or early 19th century. 4 1/4" h, 4 5/8" d rim, 3 3/8" d foot. Interior wear and scratching, some cloudiness, ring of wear under bowl. **$1,808**

Sugar Bowl With Cover, Free-Blown, Footed, cobalt blue, U-shape bowl with an applied sloping foot and polished pontil mark, cover with an applied solid spire finial, which is factory polished at the top, rough pontil mark under cover. American or English. Late 18th or early 19th century. 6 5/8" h overall, 4" d rim, 2 7/8" d foot. Some wear to lower exterior of bowl. **$423**

Sugar Bowl With Ball Cover, Free-Blown, aquamarine, bowl with galleried rim, pronounced shoulder, and a

Sugar Bowl With Cover, Heavy Free-Blown Footed, colorless, applied short solid stem and thick foot with rough pontil mark, flattened cover with applied button finial and interior rough pontil mark. Probably Pittsburgh. First half 19th century. 7 1/4" h overall, 5 1/4" h bowl, 4 3/4" d rim, 4 1/2" d foot. Moderate wear to interior and exterior of bowl. **$1,130**

Photo courtesy Green Valley Auctions, Mt. Crawford, Va.;
www.GreenValleyAuctions.com

*Vase or Chalice, Free-Blown Marbrie Decorated, colorless
flared bowl with opaque white loops, blown into a
pale yellow-green cup supported on a heavy solid stem
and circular foot with rough pontil mark. Probably
Midwestern or South Jersey. Mid-19th century. 8 1/2" h,
4 7/8" d rim, 4 3/4" d foot. Wear under foot.* **$1,073**

slightly domed base with rough pontil mark, ball is a
slightly bluer color and features an open 1" rough pontil.
Probably New York State. Mid-19th century. 8" h overall,
4 1/8" h bowl, 4 1/8" d rim, 5" d ball. Slight wear at
shoulder. **$734**

Twine Holder, Free-Blown, colorless with applied cobalt
top ring and lower rim, top of ring factory polished.
Probably Midwestern. Second half 19th century. 4 1/4" h,
4 3/4" d rim. Minute flake to ring hole. **$169**

Vase, Free-Blown, trumpet form, amethyst, plain rim,
applied inverted baluster solid stem and sloping foot with
polished pontil mark. Probably New England, possibly New
England Glass Co. Third quarter 19th century. 11 7/8" h,
4 1/2" d rim, 4" d foot...**$847**

Whimsy Powder Horn, Free-Blown, Marbrie Decorated,
deep amber with internal opaque white loops, tooled
mouth, applied bottle green ring, amber applied end cap
with rough pontil mark. Probably Pittsburgh or South
Jersey. Mid-19th century. 14" long. Small surface bruise,
which displays two 1/8" refractions under strong light, light
wear. **$101**

Whimsy Powder Horn, Free-Blown, opaque white,
applied mouth and neck ring, rough pontil mark. Second
half 19th century. 13" long. Several areas of light wear.
.... **$67**

Flint Glass, Colored

Bowl (footed low), O'Hara/Loop, deep fiery opalescent
teal blue, made from the large sugar bowl base which was
flattened and expanded outward and the rim turned up,
six large scallops, short hexagonal stem and circular single
step foot, one-piece construction. Probably Jas. B. Lyon &
Co., Pittsburgh (as identified in company catalogs). 1860-
1870. 3 1/4" h, 9" to 9 1/4" d rim, 3 7/8" d foot. Interior
with scattered small areas of wear, numerous impurities
and striations to glass. **$847**

Photo courtesy Green Valley Auctions, Mt. Crawford, Va.;
www.GreenValleyAuctions.com

*Bowl (footed low), O'Hara/Loop, deep fiery opalescent
teal blue, made from the large sugar bowl base which was
flattened and expanded outward and the rim turned up,
six large scallops, short hexagonal stem and circular single
step foot, one-piece construction. Probably Jas. B. Lyon &
Co., Pittsburgh (as identified in company catalogs). 1860-
1870. 2 3/8" to 2 5/8" h, 8 3/4" d rim, 3 7/8" d foot. Minute
flake to foot, interior with light to moderate wear.* **$452**

Photo courtesy Green Valley Auctions, Mt. Crawford, Va.;
ww.GreenValleyAuctions.com

*Covered Dish and Under Plate, melon form, translucent
starch blue, dish of oval form, the base with 11 ribs, the
cover with nine ribs, bent-stem finial, and rough pontil
mark to interior, both with factory polished rims, the plate
of leaf form with an oval seat to accept the melon, factory
rough ground under base. Boston & Sandwich Glass Co.
1850-1870. 5 3/4" h overall, 4" x 5 3/8" cover, 6 1/4" x
7 3/8" plate. Cover with a minor flake to finial, and a
shallow chip and two flakes to outer rim edge, plate with
two small potstones and associated light bruises, a chip
under one leaf point and a flake to several others.* **$3,672**

Photo courtesy Green Valley Auctions, Mt. Crawford, Va.; www.GreenValleyAuctions.com

Match Tray, Onion/Eaton, translucent soft blue with a slight lavender tint, rectangular form with a ribbed gallery, deep concave well, striker sides and a ribbed base. Boston & Sandwich Glass Co. 1860-1880. 1 1/2" h, 3 1/2" x 5" base. Two shallow chips and several flakes to rim scallops, base with flakes and roughness to a moderate fin at one end. **$1,073**

Photo courtesy Green Valley Auctions, Mt. Crawford, Va.; www.GreenValleyAuctions.com

Tumbler, Ringed Framed Ovals, bright yellow green, polished table ring. 1850-1870. 3 1/4" h, 2 3/4" d rim. **$270**

Goblet, Fedora Loop, unrecorded brilliant deep amethyst, deep polished pontil mark. Probably New England or Pittsburgh. 1840-1860. 5 7/8" h. Foot exhibits a uniform polished bevel to the top edge, which most likely was executed at the factory since it shows the expected wear. **$791**

Toothpick Holder, Pressed Covered Basket, alabaster/clam broth, base with decorative handles, cover with ribbed finial. Boston & Sandwich Glass Co. 1850-1870. 3 7/8" h overall, 2 1/4" d. Cover with shallow sliver chip to finial side and light inner-rim flaking. **$101**

Tumbler, Eight-Flute, brilliant fiery opalescent with strong pooling, faint pontil ring. Probably Midwestern. 1850-1870. 3 1/4" h, 3 1/4" d rim. Minute roughness to base points. **$254**

Tumbler, Loop and Arch, unusual slightly translucent soft blue, no resonance. Probably Pittsburgh. 1850-1870. 3 1/2" h, 3 1/8" d rim. Minor flake under base. **$180**

Tumbler, Loop and Arch, brilliant cobalt blue, faint pontil ring. Probably Pittsburgh. 1850-1870. 3 3/8" h, 3 3/8" d rim. Minute roughness to base points. **$79**

Tumbler, Six-Flute, medium golden amber, faint pontil ring, no resonance. Probably Pittsburgh. 1850-1870. 3 3/8" h, 3 1/4" d rim. Minute flake to one base point. **$192**

Tumbler (footed), Excelsior, brilliant fiery opalescent with strong pooling of color, short hexagonal stem, polished pontil mark. New England or Pittsburgh. Third quarter 19th century. 4 1/4" h, 3 5/8" d rim, 2 3/4" d foot..........**$960**

Tumbler (footed), Excelsior Variant, deep fiery opalescent, short hexagonal stem, rough pontil mark. Probably Pittsburgh. Third quarter 19th century. 4 1/2" h, 3 3/8" d rim, 2 7/8" d foot. Small shallow chip under foot, numerous flakes and roughness to pattern, small rim under-fill. **$84**

Vase, Blown-Molded, Five-Petal Rosette, translucent jade green, trumpet top, polished base. Boston & Sandwich Glass Co. 1850-1870. 6 1/4" h, 2 1/2" d rim. Minute rim flake. **$508**

Vase, Loop, canary, gauffered six-flute rim, single-piece construction, factory polished under base. New England. 1850-1870. 9 1/2" h, 3 7/8" d rim. Two base edges reduced by polishing, which may have been done at the factory. **$282**

Vase, Three-Printie Block, deep violet blue, gauffered six-flute rim, single-piece construction. New England. 1850-1870. 9 3/4" h, 4 1/4" d rim. Minute flakes/roughness to base mold lines, light residue to lower bowl. **$960**

Vase, Three-Printie Block, medium amethyst, gauffered six-flute rim, single-piece construction. New England. 1850-1870. 9 1/4" h, 4 1/8" d rim. Moderate chip to three base corners, manufacturing separation below stem knop. **$330**

Vases (pair), Circle and Ellipse, canary, each with gauffered six-petal rim, hexagonal base, one-piece construction, factory polished lower mold lines and under base. New England. 1850-1870. 7 1/2" h, 3 1/4" d rims, 3 3/4" d bases overall..**$536 pair**

Vases (pair), tulip form, brilliant medium amethyst, panels continue to peg extension, octagonal base, wafer construction. Boston & Sandwich Glass Co. 1845-1865. 10" h, 5 1/8" and 5 3/8" d rims, 4 3/4" d foot overall. One with a minor flake to one lower panel and two shallow chips and minor mold roughness to base. ...... **$6,780 pair**

FRUIT JARS

Fruit and canning jars used to preserve food. Thomas W. Dyott, one of Philadelphia's earliest and most innovative glassmakers, was promoting his glass canning jars in 1829. John Landis Mason patented his screw-type canning jar on Nov. 30, 1858. (This date refers to the granting of the patent, not the age of the jar.) There are thousands of different jars and a variety of colors, types of closures, sizes and embossings.

Collectors often refer to fruit jars by the numbering system "RB," which was established by Douglas M. Leybourne Jr. in *The Collector's Guide to Old Fruit Jars, Red Book No. 10.*

Photo courtesy American Bottle Auctions, Sacramento, Calif.; www.AmericanBottle.com

Airtight, barrel-shaped quart, solid wax sealer groove. Iron pontil instead of the sticky ball. All of its original graphite intact. Includes metal cap; may not be original. **$1,000**

All Right

Half gallon, aqua, reverse marked "Patd Jan. 28th 1868," base marked "Pat Nov 26 1867," ground lip, unmarked metal dome-shaped lid, wire clamp, two rim chips, 7 1/4" h, 4 1/2" d base, RB 61-3.............**$90**

Quart, aqua, reverse marked "Patd Jan 26th 1868," base marked "PAT Nov 26 1867" and "12" in center, ground lip, unmarked metal dome shaped lid, wire clamp, 7 3/4" h, 3 3/4" d base, RB 59. ....**$110**

Almy (arched), quart, aqua, base marked "Patented Dec 25, 1877 (star)" and "B," lid marked "C," ground lip, Mason shoulder seal, glass screw-on lid, chips on lid, 7 1/8" h, 3 7/8" d base, RB 63..........**$100**

Banner, encircled by, "Patd Feby 9th 1864 Reisd Jan 22D 1867," quart, aqua, ground lip, press-down glass lid, neck indentation in rear, several rim flakes, 7 1/2" h, 3 3/4" d base, RB 403.............**$135**

Beaver, facing right, chewing log, over word "Beaver," midget pint, Ball blue, base marked "3," unmarked glass insert and screw band, stippled tail, 5 5/8" h, 3 1/4" d base. **$385**

Bloeser Jar, quart, aqua, ground rim, glass lid marked "Pat Sept 27, 1887," original wire and metal clamp with necktie wire, rim chip, 8" h, 3 3/4" d, RB 468............**$90**

Cohansey Glass Mf'g Co., "Pat Mar 20. 77" (on base), half gallon, aqua, barrel shape, base also marked "3," glass lid marked "Cohansey Glass Mfg Co., Philada. PA," and "Y" in center, groove ring wax sealer, roughness, bruise on lid rim, 9 1/8" h, 4" d base, RB 633-1..............**$70**

Cunningham & Co., Pittsburgh (on base), half gallon, deep aqua, bottom push up, bare iron pontil mark, applied lip to receive cork stopper, 9 3/4" h, 4 5/8" d base, RB 721. ....**$310**

Eagle

Half gallon, aqua, unmarked glass lid, iron yoke clamp with six-pointed star-shape thumbscrew, applied lip, 10" h, 4 1/2" d base, RB 872. ....**$110**

Quart, aqua, applied smooth lip, fabricated closure, 7 5/8" h, 3 7/8" d base, RB 871. ....**$90**

Fahnestock Albree & Co., quart, dark aqua, pushed up bottom, pontil mark, Willoughby stopple marked "J. O. Willoughby Patented, January 4, 1859," replaced wing nut, surface wear, 8 1/2" h, 3 3/4" d base, RB 970. ....**$360**

Gem, three gallon, aqua, reverse marked "Manufactured by The Hero Glass Works, Philadelphia PA," ground lip, glass insert marked "Pat. Feb 12. 56. Dec 17.61. Nov 4.62. Dec 6.94, June 9.68. Sept 1.68. Sep 8.68. Dec.22.68. Jan 9 69," screw band, 17 5/8" h, 8 3/8" d base, RB 1058...........**$3,575**

Glass Pail, one-half pint, teal, base marked "Glass Pail Pat. Boston Mass June 24. 84," unmarked metal two-piece lid with bail handle, 4 1/2" h overall, 3" d base, RB 20. ......**$525**

Globe, quart, red amber, base marked "65," ground lip, red amber glass lid marked "Patented May 15 1886," iron clamp and metal band around neck, 8 1/8" h, 3 3/4" d base, RB 1123. .... **$135**

Griffen's, Patent Oct 7 1862 (on lid), quart, amber, ground lip, glass lid with cage-like clamp, rim chip and flake, 7" h, 3 3/4" d base, RB 1154. .... **$70**

Hansee's, (PH monogram) Palace Home Jar, quart, clear, base marked "Pat. Dec 19 1899," ground lip, monogrammed glass lid, wire clamp and neck tire wire, edge chips and flakes, 7 1/2" h, 3 3/4" d base, RB 1206. .. **$50**

Johnson & Johnson, New York (vertically), quart, cobalt blue, ground lip, cobalt lid, screw band, 7-1/8" h, 3 3/8" square base, RB 1344. .... **$360**

Joshua Wright Philada, half gallon, aqua, barrel shape, applied lip, 10 1/2" h, 3 3/4" d base, RB 3036 variant.....**$180**

Lafayette, (in script, underlined), quart, aqua, base marked "2," stopper neck finish three-piece glass and metal stopper, marked "Patented Sept 2 1884 Aug 4 1885," 8 1/2" h, 3 5/8" d, RB 1452....................................**$110**

Mansfield

Pint, clear, base marked "Mansfield Knowlton May '03 Pat. Glass W'K'S," and "2" in circle, glass lid, metal screw cap, light 1/4" crack, lid marked "Mansfield Glass W'ks Knowlton Pat. May .03," 5 1/8" h, 3 1/8" d base, RB 1619. .... **$15**

Quart, clear with light aqua tint, base marked "Mansfield Knowlton May '03 Pat. Glass W'K'S," glass lid, metal screw cap, lid marked "Mansfield Glass W'ks Knowlton Pat. May .03," rim flake, 7" h, 3 5/8" d base, RB 1619. .. **$80**

Mansfield Improved Mason, quart, lavender tint, glass insert, screw band, rim flake, 7" h, B 1621 variant......... **$60**

Mason's (cross), Patent Nov. 30th 1858, ("The Pearl" erased), gallon, dark aqua, ground lip, Mason shoulder seal, plain zinc lid, rim flakes, 12" h, 5 7/8" d base, RB 1943. .... **$1,100**

Mason's CFJCO Improved, half gallon, amber, base marked "H43," ground lip, amber insert marked "P," screw band illegibly marked, rim chip and flake, 9 1/8" h, 4 1/2" d base, RB 1711. .... **$190**

Mason's Patent, Nov. 30th, 1858, half gallon, green, amber swirls, smooth lip, metal "Ball" lid with milk glass insert marked "Boyd's Genuine Porcelain Lined Cap 18V," 8 3/4" h, 4 3/8" d base, RB 1787. .... **$360**

Mason's Patent, Nov. 30th, 1858, quart, Ball blue, reverse marked with Tudor rose emblem, base marked "A 83," ground lip, disk immerser lid, exterior marked "TradeMark The Mason Disk Protector Cap Patd. Nov 30 1880," and Tudor rose emblem in center, bottom of disk marked "Pat. Nov 23.75. Sept 12.76. Nov 30.80, July 20. 1886," 7 1/4" h, 3 3/4" d base, RB 1875. .... **$125**

Millville Atmospheric Fruit Jar, 56 ounce, aqua, reverse marked "Whitall's Patent June 18th 1861," glass lid, squared iron yoke clamp with thumbscrew, 9" h, 4 3/8" d base, RB 2181....................................**$45**

Moore's Patent, Dec 3D 1861, quart, aqua, correct but slightly ill-fitting lid, rounded iron yoke clamp with thumbscrew, edge flakes on lid, flakes on interior jar flange, 8 1/8" h, 3 5/8" d base, RB 2204. ....**$55**

Photo courtesy American Bottle Auctions, Sacramento, Calif.; www.AmericanBottle.com

Beaver Jar, quart, made in several colors with amber and olive amber variations being most desirable. With the original amber lid with a small button in the center, and with the typical ground lip. There is a number "10" on the base, RB 424. **$1,100**

Mason's Patent Nov 30th 1858, A62 on base, quart with embossed Tudor Rose. Lid is milk glass and also has an embossed Tudor Rose. Not the original zinc screw band with original porcelain liner. It reads "FOR MASON FRUIT JARS PORCELAIN LINED CAP." Has a series of bubbles throughout the neck area, RB 1875. **$5,500**

Owl, pint, milk glass, glass insert emb with daisy rosette, serrated screw band, 6 1/8" h, 2 1/2" d base, RB 3085 ....**$100**

Pansy, (superimposed over erased Best), quart, amber, 20 vertical panels, ground lip, glass insert, screw band, rim flaking, 5 1/4" h, 4 1/2" d base, RB 2287. ....**$220**

Patented Oct. 19, 1858, (on lid), quart, aqua, ground lip, glass lid with internal lugs, lugs on neck of jar, 7" h, 3 7/8" d base, RB 1212..**$45**

PET, half gallon, aqua, correct glass lid, spring wire clamp, lid marked "Patented Aug 21st 1869. T.G. Otterson," 9 7/8" h, 4 3/8" d base, RB 2359..**$200**

Potter & Bodine Airtight Fruit Jar, Philada, half gallon, reverse marked "Patented April 13th 1858," groove ring wax sealer, patched hole on edge of base, 2 1/4" h crack, 8 1/4" h, 4 1/4" d base, RB 2383. ....**$70**

Safety Valve, Patd May 21, 1895 HC, over triangle on base, half gallon, dark aqua, Greek Key design around shoulder and base, glass lid marked "1," ground lip, metal band clamp with bail handle, 8" h, 5 1/8" d base, RB 2539. ......**$55**

Safety Valve, Patd May 21, 1895 HC, over triangle on base, pint, emerald green, partially ground lip, emerald green

Millville Atmospheric Fruit Jar, Whitehall's Patent June 18, 1861, with original closure, pint. Small nick off the lid and a radiating potstone on the base. RB 2181. **$80**

glass lid, metal band clamp, stamped "Safety Valve Patd May 21, 1895," 5 3/4" h, 3" d base, RB 2538. ....**$210**

Sept 1st 1868," ground lip, glass insert marked "Mason's Improved May 10 1870," screw band, loss of lip flange, 12 3/8" h, 5 7/8" d base, RB 1071. ....**$880**

Smalley Full Measure, AGS (monogram), quart, amber, base marked "Patented Dec 13 1892 April 7 1896, Dec 1, 1896," 7 1/4" h, 3 5/8" sq base, RB 2648..........................**$90**

Standard, (arched), quart, light cobalt blue, reverse heel marked "W. McC & Co," applied groove ring wax sealer, four-point star under base, tin lid marked "W. McCully & Co. Glass Pittsburg," 1/2" wide chip on outer rim, 7-1/2" h, 3 3/4" d base, RB 2701-variant.................................**$880**

Star, emblem encircled by fruit, quart, aqua, ground lip, neck slopes inward to opening, zinc insert and screw band, 7 3/4" h, 3 3/4" d base, RB 2724. ....**$150**

Sun, (in circle with radiating lines) Trade Mark, quart, aqua, base marked "J. P. Barstow," and "4," ground lip, unmarked glass lid, metal yoke clamp, marked "Monier's Pat April 1 90 Mar 12 95," 7 3/4" h, 3 7/8" d base, RB 2761............**$100**

The Empire, quart, aqua, base marked "Pat Feb 13 1866," ground rim, glass lid, chipping, bruise to ground rim, 8 1/2" h, 3 3/4" d base, RB 927. ....**$80**

The Gem, gallon, aqua, base marked "H. Brooke Mould Maker NY Pat'd Nov 26th 1868. Patd Dec 17th 1861 Reis'

Sept 1st 1868," ground lip, glass insert marked "Mason's Improved May 10 1870," screw band, loss of lip flange, 12 3/8" h, 5 7/8" d base, RB 1071. ....**$880**

The Hero, half gallon, deep aqua, base marked "Patd Nov 26 1867" and "5" in center, ground lip, glass insert with "WHA" monogram on interior center, series of patent dates on exterior, screw band, two rim chips, 9" h, 4 1/2" d base, RB 1242. ....**$15**

The Hero, quart, aqua, base marked "Patd Nov 26 1867. Pat'd Dec 17 '61 Nov 4 '62 Dec 14 '69 Reis's Sept 1 '68 June 9' 69," and "87" in center, ground lip, glass insert with "WHA," monogram on interior center, series of patent dates on exterior, screw band, rim roughness, 7 1/8" h overall, 3 3/4" d base, RB 1244. ....**$25**

The Hero, quart, honey amber, base marked "Pat Nov 26 1867," and "6 (reversed) 7" in center, ground lip, metal lid with partially legible patent dates from 1862 through 1869 including Dec. 22, 1868 and Dec. 14, 1869," 7 1/2" h, 3 3/4" d base, RB 1242. ....**$6,600**

The Heroine, pint, aqua base marked "22," ground lip, glass inset marked "Pat. Feb 12.59 Dec. 17.61. Nov 4. 62.Dec 6.64. June 9.68. Jan 1.68. Sep 1.68. Sep 8.68 Dec 22.68," screw band, rim chip with flakes, 6 5/8" h, 3 1/4" d base, RB 1248. ....**$125**

The King, Pat Nov 2, 1869, quart, aqua, base marked "3," ground lip, glass lid and iron yoke clamp, one half of rim broken out, 7 1/2" h, 3 3/4" d base, RB 1418. ....**$125**

The Valve Jar Co., Philadelphia, quart, aqua, base marked "Patd Mar 1-th 1868," ground lip, glass lid, wire coil clamp, open bubble on edge of base, 7 1/2" h, 4" d base, RB 2873. ....**$385**

The Van Vliet Jar of 1881, half gallon, aqua, base marked "6," ground lip, glass lid marked "Pt May 3d 1881," metal yoke clamp with unmarked thumbscrew, attached wire extending vertically around entire jar, bruises, 9 1/4" h, 4 1/2" d base, RB 2878. ....**$525**

W. Chrysler, Pat. Nov. 21, 1865, quart, aqua, applied lip, three annealing lines, 7 3/4" h, 3 3/4" d base, RB 597-1. ....**$1,210**

Photo courtesy American Bottle Auctions, Sacramento, Calif.; www.AmericanBottle.com

Potter & Bodine's Airtight Fruit Jar/Patented April 13, 1858, quart, barrel shaped, wax sealer with sticky ball pontil. The Potter & Bodine's jars come in a few different variants. The main differences are the number of lines they used to spell out the same embossing, RB 2387-1. **$800**

Historical and Novelty Glass

Admiral Dewey, Five-Piece Water Set, colorless, consisting of a water pitcher and four tumblers. Fourth quarter 19th century. Pitcher 9" h overall, 4 7/8" d, tumblers 3 7/8" h, 2 3/4" d. Pitcher with three annealing fissures at rim, tumblers with nicks/roughness to line above pattern. **$138**

Bricks and Horse Heads, Covered Mustard, apple green, original cover with spoon slot. Fourth quarter 19th century. 3 5/8" h overall, 2 3/4" d base. One horse head with chip to one ear, two shallow chips under base. **$57**

Dog House, Two-Part Box, blue, the top being the entire house which sits on the base featuring an interior well. Fourth quarter 19th century. 3" h, 2 1/2" x 4 1/4". Top with a chip to lower front edge which does not affect the rim and a tiny potstone with light bruise to interior, base with light flake to one corner and an 1/8" annealing crack to inner rim. **$103**

English Castle-Form, Cigar Holder, opalescent, embossed "Rd 29780" in base, ribbed under base, polished table ring. Fourth quarter 19th century. 3 1/4" h, 3 1/8" sq. minor mold roughness and short annealing separations to base. **$57**

Fish Covered Dish, pale green with all-over satin finish, fully patterned on cover and base, protruding tail and one fin on base and two fins on cover. Late 19th/early 20th century. 2 1/4" h overall, 4 3/4" x 8 1/2" overall. Hint of interior mold roughness. **$36**

Jenny Lind/Columbia Statue, colorless and frosted, on a circular domed base molded with a floral wreath underneath. This is the standard illustrated in Lindsey's American Historical Glass, p. 434, fig. 424, which is wafer attached to a Beaded Panels bowl. The statue features fully molded hair on top of her head and was never attached to

Canary, Covered Dish, vaseline, round basket-weave base, signed under cover. McKee & Brothers. Late 19th/early 20th century. 3 3/4" h overall, 4 1/2" d. Two minute flakes to base rim. **$310**

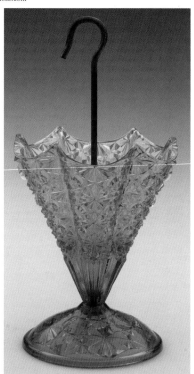

Daisy and Button Umbrella, amber, on foot, with metal handle. George Duncan & Sons. Fourth quarter 19th century. 6 5/8" h overall, 3 3/8" d rim, 2 7/8" d foot. Chip to the point of the umbrella probably done when it was ground to sit flat on the foot. **$546**

another unit. Probably Crystal Glass Co. Fourth quarter 19th century. 4 1/4" h, 4 3/4" d base. **$108**

Liberty Bell, Miniature Mug, opaque white/milk glass, embossed "1776 1876" between the bells. Fourth quarter 19th century. 2" h, 1 3/4" d rim. Minute rim flake, normal short annealing lines. **$103**

Recumbent Dog, Covered Pomade Jar, colorless, un-patterned panel on jar, presumably for a product label, remainder of jar and under cover patterned with diamonds, beaded-edge foot with rosette underneath. Fourth quarter 19th century. 4" h overall, 2" x 2 5/8" overall. Cover with a shallow chip to rear outer edge and flaking/mold roughness under rim. **$103**

Vaseline, Pressed Glass Smoking Stand, cigarette cup and horizontal-ribbed cup for matches, each on two rows of brick, on base with interior ribbing. Fourth quarter 19th century. 3" and 4" h, 3" x 5 3/4". Several flakes to the rim of each cup, a short annealing line to the rim of the match cup and another to the base. **$69**

Victorian, Gilt Brass and Glass Door Bell, exterior knotted rope-form frame with two facet-cut amber glass mounts, brass bell on interior. Fourth quarter 19th century. 6 1/4" h, 3 1/2" wide. Minor wear to gilt. **$138**

1893 World's Fair, Boat-Form Dish, colorless, embossed "Santa Maria" on sides, and "World's Fair 1893" and "Libbey Glass Co., Toledo, Ohio" under base. Libbey Glass Co. Fourth quarter 19th century. 2 1/4" h, 2 5/8" x 6 1/2". Chip to lower edge of rudder. **$300**

Milk Glass

Milk glass is a relatively recent name for opaque, milky white or colored glass that is blown or pressed into a wide variety of shapes, including animal-form covered dishes. First made in Venice in the 16th century, the white color is achieved through the addition of tin dioxide. Nineteenth-century glassmakers called milky white opaque glass "opal glass."

Alligator, Toothpick/Match Holder, opaque white/milk glass, curled tail forms handle. Fourth quarter 19th century, 2 7/8" h. **$287**

Big Owl, Salt Shaker, opaque white/milk glass, period lid. Possibly Atterbury & Co., fourth quarter 19th century, 5 3/4" h overall. Minor mold roughness, legs with manufacturing roughness/flakes. **$138**

Black Clown, Match Holder, opaque white/milk glass, ribbed circular base, remnants of original paint decoration. Fourth quarter 19th century, 3 1/4" h. **$120**

Boar's Head, Covered Dish, opaque white/milk glass, on a ribbed base, non-original applied eyes, patent date on lid interior and under base. Atterbury & Co., fourth quarter 19th century, 5 1/2" h overall, 6 1/8" x 9 3/8" rim overall. Shallow vertical chip to the rear mold line on cover and two minute flakes to base rim. **$1,150**

Canary, Covered Dish, opaque white/milk glass, round basket-weave base, signed under cover. McKee & Brothers, late 19th/early 20th century, 3 3/4" h overall, 4 1/2" d. Two minute flakes to base rim. **$780**

Duck, Covered Dish, opaque blue with light mottling, applied eyes, patent date under base. Atterbury & Co., fourth quarter 19th century, 5" h overall, 11" long overall. Hint of mold roughness and short annealing lines. **$156**

Eaglet with Eggs and Snake, Covered Dish, opaque white/milk glass with original paint decoration, interior of cover embossed "SV/2", underside of base embossed "SV/9". Late 19th/early 20th century, 5 1/4" h overall, 5 5/8" d overall. Cover with a chip under edge, base with a significant crack and glued section of rim. **$204**

Fish Pitcher, opaque white/milk glass, three-pint, molded handle, ground table ring. Atterbury & Co., fourth quarter 19th century, 7 1/4" h, 4 1/2" d rim. Trace of mold roughness to handle and table ring. **$120**

Frog Covered Dish, opaque white/milk glass, split-rib base, not signed. McKee & Brothers, late 19th/early 20th century, 3 5/8" h, 4 1/8" x 5 3/8" base. Base with rim chip and interior annealing line. **$345**

General Electric, Refrigerator-Form Covered Jar, opaque white/milk glass, name lightly embossed above doors. First quarter 20th century, 5" h overall, 2 1/8" x 3 1/2". Two minor flakes under feet. **$103**

Horse, Covered Dish, opaque white/milk glass, split-rib base, not signed. McKee & Brothers, late 19th/early 20th century, 4 1/2" h, 4 1/4" x 5 1/2" base. **$258**

Horseshoe-Form, Covered Box, opaque white/milk glass, embossed horse's head on cover, horseshoes, horn and riding crop on sides of box, somewhat worn original decoration. Probably Alton Mfg. Co., Sandwich, Mass., first

Photo courtesy Green Valley Auctions, Mt. Crawford, Va.; www.GreenValleyAuctions.com

1988 NMGCS, Commemorative Rabbit Covered Dish, green slag, a reproduction of the Greentown rabbit on a split-rib base, National Milk Glass Collector's Society logo and "NMGCS / 88 MN" embossed in base, 4 1/4" h overall. **$339**

quarter 20th century, 1 7/8" h overall, 3 1/4" x 3 5/8 overall. Minute flakes under cover. **$80**

Lion, Covered Dish, opaque white/milk glass, split-rib base possibly later, signed under cover. McKee & Brothers, late 19th/early 20th century, 4 1/4" h, 4 1/4" x 5 1/2" base. **$126**

Lion, Covered Dish, opaque white/milk glass with traces of paint decoration, split-rib base probably later, signed under cover. McKee & Brothers, late 19th/early 20th century, 4 1/4" h, 4 1/4" x 5 1/2" base. **$69**

McKinley-Roosevelt, Campaign Plate, opaque white/milk glass, intricate foliate rim. Early 20th century, 8 1/4" d. Shallow chip to the front of one rim point. **$115**

Moses in the Bulrushes, Covered Dish, opaque white/milk glass, traces of paint decoration on cover. Late 19th/early 20th century, 3" h overall, 4" x 5 3/8" base. A few light flakes. **$69**

Owl Head, Covered Dish, opaque white/milk glass, split-rib base possibly later, signed under cover. McKee & Brothers, late 19th/early 20th century, 4 1/4" h, 4 1/4" x 5 1/2" base. Chip to base table ring. **$149**

Pig, Covered Dish, opaque white/milk glass, split-rib base signed in bottom. McKee & Brothers, late 19th/early 20th century, 3 1/2" h, 4 1/8" x 5 3/8" base. Small chip and minute flake to tips of ears. **$600**

Pope Leo XIII, Covered Dish, opaque white/milk glass, round base with paneled sides. Late 19th/early 20th century, 5 1/4" h overall, 4 7/8" d. **$149**

Spaniel, Covered Dish, opaque white/milk glass showing slight opalescence, lattice on two long sides of base, stippled ends and beaded rim. Boston & Sandwich Glass Co., or one of the short-lived succeeding companies, late 19th/early 20th century, 4" h overall, 4 3/4" x 3 3/8". Cover with minute flake, base rim with two minor flakes and light mold roughness. **$149**

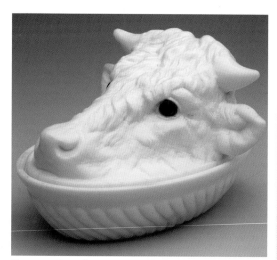

Steer's Head, Covered Dish, opaque white/milk glass, on a swirled rib base, non-original applied eyes. Challinor, Taylor & Co., fourth quarter 19th century, 5" h overall, 5 3/8" x 7 3/4" rim. Minor flake to inner rim of base, normal short annealing lines. **$3,955**

Swan, Chariot Master Salt, opaque white/milk glass, original unmarked plated-silver stand with cherub holding chain reins. Gillinder & Sons, fourth quarter 19th century, 6 3/4" h overall. **$339**

"Trilby" Foot Match Holder, opaque white/milk glass, embossed lettering on side of base, patent date under base. Fourth quarter 19th century, 2 3/4" h, 1 7/8" x 4 1/8" base. Normal short annealing lines. **$80**

Turkey, Covered Dish, opaque white/milk glass with slight pink tint, split-rib base, signed under cover. McKee & Brothers, late 19th/early 20th century, 4 1/2" h, 4 1/8" x 5 3/8" base. Several light flakes. **$258**

1989 NMGCS, Commemorative Horse Covered Dish, opaque white/milk glass, a reproduction of the McKee Horse on split-rib base, National Milk Glass Collector's Society logo and "NMGCS / ILL.89" embossed in base. With original ID card, which indicates that Summit Art Glass Co. produced slightly over 200 pieces for Society members, 4 1/4" h overall. **$126**

1999 NMGCS, Commemorative Dog Covered Dish, chocolate slag, a reproduction of the L.G. Wright spaniel dog on a split-rib base, National Milk Glass Collector's Society logo and "NMGCS / IN 99" embossed in base, also embossed under cover, 4" h overall. **$69**

Opalescent Glass

Opalescent glass, a clear or colored glass with milky white decorations, looks fiery or opalescent when held to light. This effect was achieved by applying bone ash chemicals to designated areas while a piece was still hot and then re-firing it at extremely high temperatures. There are three basic categories of opalescent glass: (1) blown (or mold blown) patterns, e.g., Daisy & Fern and Spanish Lace; (2) novelties, pressed glass patterns made in limited quantity and often in unusual shapes such as corn or a trough; and (3) traditional pattern (pressed) glass forms. Opalescent glass was produced in England in the 1870s. Northwood began the American production in 1897 at its Indiana, Pa., plant. Jefferson, National Glass, Hobbs and Fenton soon followed.

Buttons and Braids, Water Pitcher, cranberry opalescent, triangular crimped rim, colorless applied handle. Jefferson Glass Co. / Fenton Art Glass Co. Late 19th/early 20th century. 9 3/4" h overall. Two open bubbles to the interior base, small impurity at shoulder. **$920**

> **Collector's Note:** The Fenton Art Glass Co., the oldest continuously running American glass firm, was founded in 1905 by Frank L. Fenton and his brother, John W. Fenton, in an old glass factory building in Martins Ferry, Ohio. They began by painting decorations on glass blanks made by other glass manufacturers. Soon, being unable to get the glass they needed, they decided to produce their own glass. The first glass from the new Fenton factory in Williamstown, W.V., was made on Jan. 2, 1907. After a century in business, the firm announced it would close in the fall of 2007. But a surge of customer orders allowed it to remain open. See more Fenton beginning on page 461.

Carnelian/Everglades, Six-Piece Water Set, blue opalescent with bright gilt decoration, consisting of a water pitcher and five tumblers. H. Northwood Co. Early 20th century. 7 3/4" and 4" h. Light wear to rim gilt, pitcher with two small manufacturing chips to foot, which are gilded over. **$316**

Chrysanthemum Swirl, Celery Vase, blue opalescent with frosted finish, traces of gilt decoration. Late 19th/early 20th century. 6 1/2" h. Minor mold roughness and interior residue. **$80**

19th/early 20th century. 9 3/4" h overall. Light wear to exterior of body. **$115**

Daffodils, Water Pitcher, green opalescent, round crimped and ruffled rim, transparent green applied handle with pressed fan design to upper terminal. H. Northwood Co. Late 19th/early 20th century. 10 1/4" h overall. Small area of wear and scratches to shoulder. **$510**

Daisy and Fern, Water Pitcher and Six Tumblers, blue opalescent, square crimped rim, transparent blue applied handle. Northwood Glass Co. Late 19th/early 20th century. Pitcher 8 1/2" h, tumblers 3 3/4" h. Light wear and scratches to body, tumblers each with normal rim flakes/roughness and polishing. .... **$218 set**

Drapery tiebacks, four pairs, white opalescent glass floral rosettes, American, mid- to late 19th century, with white metal shanks and iron screw ends, 4 1/2" d, all have some minor chips, three have larger chips (losses) on the tri-lobed sections between the larger petals. .... **$474 all**

Double Greek Key, Three-Piece Table Set, colorless opalescent, consisting of a butter dish, covered sugar bowl and spooner. Nickel Plate Glass Co. Late 19th/early 20th century. 5 1/4" to 7" h overall, 3 1/4" to 7 1/4" d overall. Slight roughness to rims of covers and interior rim of butter base. .... **$287 set**

Photo courtesy Green Valley Auctions, Mt. Crawford, Va.; www.GreenValleyAuctions.com

Chrysanthemum Swirl, Bar Bottle, cranberry opalescent, very rare. Late 19th/ early 20th century. 12" h, 3 1/2" d overall. **$2,300**

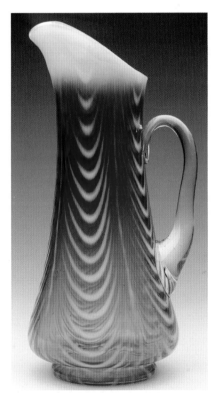

Photo courtesy Green Valley Auctions, Mt. Crawford, Va.; www.GreenValleyAuctions.com

Drapery-Blown, Tankard Water Pitcher, cranberry opalescent, colorless applied handle. Late 19th/early 20th century. 13" h overall. Manufacturing flaws to body and base, short annealing lines to spout and spots of manufacturing exfoliation around rim. **$1,035**

Chrysanthemum Swirl, Celery Vase, blue opalescent with satin finish. Late 19th/early 20th century. 6 1/2" h, 4 1/4" d overall. Minute nicks to rim. **$92**

Coin Spot-Star Crimp, Water Pitcher, blue opalescent, transparent blue applied handle, polished pontil mark. Northwood Glass Co. Late 19th/early 20th century. 8" h overall. Manufacturing flaw to lower portion of body, and a spall to pontil. **$149**
(A spall is a fragment broken off from the edge or face of a surface, and having at least one thin edge.)

Coin Spot-Star Crimp, Water Pitcher, colorless opalescent, colorless applied handle. Northwood Glass Co. and others. Late 19th/early 20th century. 8 3/4" h. Light wear and 1/4" scratch to body. **$80**

Coin Spot-Star Crimp, Water Pitcher cranberry opalescent, colorless applied handle with pressed fan design to upper terminal. Northwood Glass Co. Late 19th/ early 20th century. 8 1/2" h. Light wear to shoulder, minute irregularities to rim. **$161**

Coin Spot-Star Crimp, Water Pitcher, green opalescent, transparent green applied handle. Jefferson Glass Co. Late

Hobbs, No. 323 Dew Drop / Hobnail Jug No. 5, Ruby opalescent/cranberry opalescent, square rim, colorless applied handle, polished pontil mark. Hobbs Brockunier & Co. Late 19th/early 20th century. 7 3/4" h overall. Flake to one hob and several others with light wear. **$184**

Hobbs, No. 325 / Swirl Water Pitcher, Ruby opalescent/cranberry opalescent, square rim, colorless applied handle with pressed fan design to upper terminal, polished pontil mark. Hobbs, Brockunier & Co. Late 19th/early 20th century. 8 3/4" h. Several impurities at neck, several minute areas of polishing to rim. **$316**

Hobbs, No 326 / Windows Swirl Water Pitcher, Sapphire opalescent/blue opalescent, translucent blue applied handle with pressed fan design to upper terminal. Hobbs, Brockunier & Co. Late 19th/early 20th century. 7" h overall. Flakes and polishing to exterior and minute nicks to interior of rim, all probably done in the manufacturing process. **$1,610**

Hobbs, No. 333 / Windows Water Pitcher, Ruby opalescent/cranberry opalescent, square rim, colorless applied handle with pressed fan at upper terminal, polished pontil mark, heavy opalescence. Hobbs, Brockunier & Co. Late 19th/early 20th century. 8 1/2" h overall. **$431**

Lattice, Water Pitcher, cranberry opalescent, colorless applied handle. Late 19th/early 20th century. 9 1/4" h. Several light scratches to body and handle and a tiny spot of roughness to rim. **$1,092**

Northwood, Drapery Three-Piece Table Set, colorless opalescent, consisting of a butter dish, covered sugar bowl and creamer, butter and creamer marked with an "N" in circle on base. H. Northwood Co. First quarter 20th century. 4 1/2" to 7" h overall, 3 3/4" to 7 3/4" d overall. Sugar cover with slight interior roughness, butter cover having a single rim flake. .... **$126 set**

Opaline Brocade / Spanish Lace, Rose Bowl, vaseline, crimped rim. First quarter 20th century. 3 7/8" h, 4 1/4" d overall. **$84**

Poinsettia, Tankard Water Pitcher, opalescent, colorless applied handle with pressed fan design at upper terminal. H. Northwood Co. Late 19th/early 20th century. 13" h overall. Light scratches to lower portion of body and one side of handle, and two open bubbles to interior. **$1,955**

Poinsettia, Bride's Bowl, rubina opalescent, crimped and ruffled rim. Late 19th/early 20th century. 3 1/4" h overall, 10" d. Light interior residue. **$144**

Poinsettia, Tankard Water Pitcher, blue opalescent, blue applied handle with pressed fan design to upper terminal. H. Northwood Co. Late 19th/early 20th century. 13" h overall. Upper terminal with two cracks and 1/4" crack at body, manufacturing flaw to interior base. **$69**

Queen's Crown, Cake Stand, vaseline opalescent. English. Late 19th/early 20th century. 5 3/4" h, 10" d. Minute roughness to pattern and slight wear to plate. **$204**

Reverse Swirl, Set of Six Sauce Dishes, cranberry opalescent. Buckeye Glass Co. / Model Flint Glass Co. Late 19th/early 20th century. 1 3/4" h, 4 3/8" d. Each with rim flakes/roughness and one with a base crack. .... **$138 set**

Reverse Swirl, Water Bottle, blue opalescent. Late 19th/early 20th century. 8 1/4" h, 5" d overall. Minute nicks to rim. **$115**

Photo courtesy Green Valley Auctions, Mt. Crawford, Va.; www.GreenValleyAuctions.com

Opaline Brocade / Spanish Lace, Water Pitcher, vaseline opalescent, tri-corner crimped rim, vaseline applied handle. Late 19th/early 20th century. 9 1/2" h overall. Two small surface irregularities. **$450**

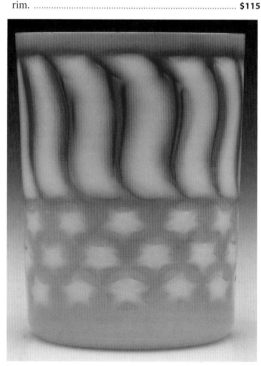

Photo courtesy Green Valley Auctions, Mt. Crawford, Va.; www.GreenValleyAuctions.com

Stars and Stripes, Tumbler, cranberry opalescent. Late 19th/early 20th century. 3 3/4" h, 2 3/4" d. **$287**

Ribbed Opal Lattice, Creamer, cranberry opalescent, colorless applied handle. Late 19th/early 20th century. 4 3/4" h. Numerous glass impurities. **$600**

Seaweed, Water Pitcher, cranberry opalescent, triangular crimped rim, colorless applied handle with lightly pressed fan design to upper terminal, polished pontil mark. Hobbs, Brockunier & Co./Beaumont Glass Co. Late 19th/early 20th century. 9" h overall. Light wear/scratches to body, interior with two open bubbles. **$805**

Stars and Stripes, Water Pitcher, blue opalescent, translucent blue applied handle with pressed fan design to upper terminal, polished pontil mark. Hobbs, Brockunier & Co. Late 19th/early 20th century. 8" h. **$2,990**

Stripe, Bottle-Form Vase, blue opalescent, tooled rim. Late 19th/ early 20th century. 9" h, 5 1/4" d overall..............**$115**

Swirl, Water Pitcher, cranberry opalescent, triangular crimped rim, colorless applied handle with pressed fan design to upper terminal, polished pontil mark. Late 19th/early 20th century. 9" h overall. Short scratch to body. **$488**

Swirl, Seven-Piece Water Set, pale cranberry opalescent, consisting of a bulbous base water pitcher with high neck, applied colorless angular handle and polished pontil mark, along with six matching tumblers with polished rims. First half 20th century. 8 3/4" and 5 3/4" h. Minor flake to one tumbler rim. .... **$488 set**

Swirl, Water Pitcher, cranberry opalescent, star-crimped rim, colorless applied handle. Late 19th/early 20th century. 8 1/2" h. Single rim flake, some impurities to interior rim, irregular shading to opalescence. **$172**

Swirl, Water Pitcher, rubina opalescent, ball form, square crimped rim, colorless applied handle. Late 19th/early 20th century. 8 1/2" h. Polishing to handle, possibly done during manufacturing. **$156**

Victor/Jeweled Heart, Water Pitcher, blue opalescent. Dugan Glass Co. Late 19th/early 20th century. 8 3/4" h overall, 5 1/4" d. Light interior haze. **$149**

Zigzag Optic/Herringbone, Water Pitcher, vaseline opalescent, colorless applied handle, polished pontil mark. Phoenix Glass Co. Late 19th/early 20th century. 7 3/4" h. **$1,610**

Salts

Beaded Scroll and Basket of Flowers, Pressed Salt (BS-2), light opalescent, on four scroll feet. Scarce. Boston & Sandwich Glass Co. 1835-1845. 1 7/8" h, 1 7/8" x 3 1/4". Minor inner-rim flake. **$113**

Blow-Over and Crack Off, Salt, deep cobalt blue, oblong octagonal form with diamond-diaper sides and ends divided by corner ribs, 30-ray base, plain ground and polished rim. Extremely rare, possibly unique. Probably New England Glass Works or South Boston Flint Glass Works. 1813-1830. 1 1/2" h, 2 1/8" x 3 1/4". Slightly disfiguring rim chip at one end, shallow chip to outer edge of opposite end, light high-point wear. **$480**

Blow-Over and Crack Off, Salt, colorless, oblong octagonal form with diamond-diaper sides and ends divided by corner ribs, 30-ray base, plain ground and polished rim. Probably New England Glass Works or South Boston Flint Glass Works. 1813-1830. 1 1/2" h, 2 1/4" x 3 1/4". Rim with one shallow chip and light mold roughness, exterior high-spot wear. **$24**

Photo courtesy Green Valley Auctions, Mt. Crawford, Va.; www.GreenValleyAuctions.com

Basket of Flowers, Pressed Salt (BF-1B), strong fiery opalescent, on four feet. Rare. Boston & Sandwich Glass Co. 1830-1840. 2" h, 1 3/4" x 3 1/8". Light chipping/mold roughness to two upper corners and feet. **$203**

Photo courtesy Green Valley Auctions, Mt. Crawford, Va.; www.GreenValleyAuctions.com

Blow-Over and Crack Off, Pedestal Salt, colorless, rectangular form with vertically ribbed sides, plain ground and polished rim, applied pressed square three-step "lemon-squeezer" pedestal with polished edges. American or Irish. 1813-1830. 2 3/4" h, 2" x 3 1/8". Minute flake to outer rim, some polishing, possibly post production. **$90**

Blow-Over and Crack Off, Pedestal Salt, colorless, rectangular form with diamond-diaper sides, notch ground and polished rim, applied pressed rectangular three-step pedestal. Possibly New England Glass Works or South Boston Flint Glass Works. 1813-1830. 3" h, 1 7/8" x 2 7/8". Rim with four small chips and flakes, foot with shallow flake to one end and two corners. **$79**

Blow-Over and Crack Off, Salts (three), colorless, each of oblong form with diamond diapering on sides, one with split ribs on ends and two with fan on ends, serrated and plain ground and polished rims, one with plain base and

Photo courtesy Green Valley Auctions, Mt. Crawford, Va.; www.GreenValleyAuctions.com

Checkered Diamond, Pattern-Molded Salt, Footed, unusual swirled purple blue, double ogee bowl with four horizontal rows of seven four-section diamonds, drawn short stem and applied sloping slightly irregular circular foot with rough pontil mark. Probably the New Bremen Glass Manufactory of John Frederick Amelung, Frederick Co., Md. Fourth quarter 18th century. 2 3/4" h, 2 1/4" d rim, 2" d foot. **$10,170**

Photo courtesy Green Valley Auctions, Mt. Crawford, Va.; www.GreenValleyAuctions.com

Covered Lyre, Pressed Salt (CD-3), colorless, on four scrolled feet, variant cover with pinecone finial and beads on rim interior arranged 10 x 20 x 10 x 20. Extremely rare. Boston & Sandwich Glass Co. 1835-1845. 2 7/8" h overall, 2" x 3 1/8" base, 1 7/8" h. Cover with a small chip under one corner and a few light flakes, base with a rim flake at one end and slight mold roughness to interior of feet. **$2,147**

two with rayed base. Possibly South Boston Flint Glass Works or New England Glass Works. 1813-1830. 1 3/4" h, 2" x 3" to 2 1/4" x 3 1/2". Minor chipping to rims. .... **$113 all**

Blown and Pressed, Pedestal Salt, colorless, unusual boat-shape bowl molded with 18 vertical ribs extending to the rolled-over rim, stuck to a pressed standard featuring a single-knop stem and an oblong quatrefoil base with triple-scallop extensions and a rosette underneath. 1820-1830. 2 3/4" h, 2 3/4" x 4 1/4" rim, 2 1/4" x 3" base. **$135**

Expanded Diamond, Pattern-Molded Footed Salt, colorless, two complete rows of 11 diamonds above elongated pointed flutes, short ribbed stem, applied circular foot tooled into five irregular petals, rough graphite pontil mark. Late 18th or early 19th century. 3" h, 2 1/4" d rim, 2 1/8" d foot. **$144**

Expanded Diamond, Pattern-Molded Footed Salts (two), colorless, first with two complete rows of 11 diamonds swirled slightly right above elongated pointed flutes, second with one complete row of 12 diamonds above elongated pointed flutes, both with short ribbed stem and applied circular foot tooled into five and six irregular petals, rough pontil marks. Late 18th or early 19th century. 2 7/8" and 3" h. First with lightly polished rim, both with light interior residue. .... **$124 both**

Free-Blown, Pedestal Salt, slightly translucent powder blue, lead content, plain slightly flared rim, short stem and circular foot with rough pontil mark. 1840-1860. 2" h, 2 3/4" d rim, 2 1/4" d foot. **$101**

"Lafayet" Steamboat, Pressed Salt (BT-5), unlisted, soft pale blue with opalescent bloom, marked "B. & S. / Glass. / Co" on stern and "Sandwich" on interior and under base. Very rare. Boston & Sandwich Glass Co. 1830-1845. 1 5/8" h, 2" x 3 5/8". Rim with a shallow chip to one paddlewheel and a chip and several flakes to interior, minor flake to table ring, light wear to some highpoints, light interior residue. **$1,320**

"Lafayet" Steamboat, Pressed Salt (BT-5), unlisted, colorless, marked "B. & S. / Glass. / Co" on stern and "Sandwich" on interior and under base. Boston & Sandwich Glass Co. 1830-1845. 1 5/8" h, 2" x 3 5/8". Rim with three V-shape chips at stern, minor mold roughness, numerous annealing lines and impurities. **$79**

Swirled Rib, Pattern-Molded Footed Salt, colorless with a gray tint, ogee bowl with 10 ribs swirled to the right, short lightly ribbed stem, applied circular foot with rough pontil mark. Late 18th or early 19th century. 2 3/4" h, 2" d rim, 2 1/8" d foot. **$158**

Glass Listed by Maker

The Sainte-Anne glassworks at Baccarat in Voges, France, was founded in 1764 and produced utilitarian soda glass. Baccarat began the production of paperweights in 1846. In the late 19th century the firm achieved an international reputation for cut-glass table services, chandeliers, display vases, centerpieces and sculptures. Products eventually included all forms of glassware.

Baccarat, cardholders (12), shell form, each signed with frosted Baccarat mark, 2 1/4" h; together with 12 individual boxes and large matching box. .... **$138 all**

Baccarat, paperweight, scattered millefiori and Gridel silhouette canes on ruffled upset muslin, with signature date cane, 1848, 2 7/8" d. **$2,040**
(*"Gridel" refers to Emile Gridel, nephew of Jean-Baptiste Toussaint, general manager of the Baccarat factory in about 1846.*)

Baccarat, paperweight, scattered millefiori and Gridel silhouette canes on ruffled upset muslin, with signature date cane, B 1848. 3 1/6" d. **$1,920**
(*"Gridel" refers to Emile Gridel, nephew of Jean-Baptiste Toussaint, general manager of the Baccarat factory in about 1846.*)

Baccarat, crystal red-wine glasses (12), signed, 7 1/2" h.
.... **$632 set**

Baccarat, crystal white-wine glasses (12), signed, 6 1/2" h.
.... **$805 set**

Baccarat, cut-glass vase and cover with ormolu fittings, its handles inset with cut beads, 20th century, 19" h. ... **$1,920**

Fenton Art Glass

The Fenton Art Glass Co. was founded in 1905 by Frank L. Fenton and his brother, John W., in an old glass factory in Martins Ferry, Ohio. They initially sold hand-painted glass made by other manufacturers, but it wasn't long before they decided to produce their own glass. The new Fenton factory in Williamstown, W.V., opened on Jan. 2, 1907. Despite economic difficulties in their 100th-anniversary year, the firm remains in business and in family hands.

Also see Carnival Glass.

1980-2005

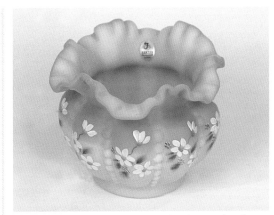

Blue Burmese beaded-melon vase, hand painted with daisies and forget-me-nots, made for QVC in 2003, 5" h. **$90**

Blue Burmese basket whimsy, with "frit" mixed into body, early 1980s, 8" h. **$150+**

Blue Burmese guest set (cup fits inside pitcher), hand painted by T. Kelly, No. 571 out of an edition of 1,950, 1999, 7 1/4" h and 3 1/2" h. **$165 set**

Blue Burmese Iridized fish whimsy, probably 1990s, 8" l and 6" h. **$100**

Blue Burmese (shiny) ribbed hexagonal vase, 1984, 5" h. **$70**

Blue, Green and Black (Ebony) shakers in a swirl pattern, hand painted, 1990s, 2 1/2" h. **$25+ each**

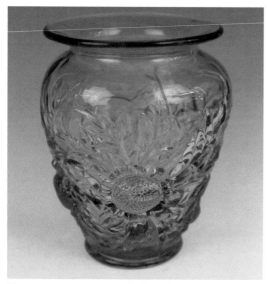

Blue-gray transparent vase (Salem Blue?) with thistle pattern, 1985, 9" h, purchased from the Fenton gift shop in Williamstown, W.Va. **$60+**

Blue, Ruby and Black (Ebony, with Autumn Leaf decoration) candlesticks, 1990s, 8 1/2" h; Blue and Ruby, **$30+** each; decorated Black. **$40+**

From left: Blue Satin covered candy jar in Wild Strawberry, 1980s, 9" h, **$30;** Blue Opalescent covered candy jar in Paneled Daisy, 1970s, 9" h. **$45**

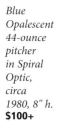

Blue Opalescent 44-ounce pitcher in Spiral Optic, circa 1980, 8" h. **$100+**

Two "tumble-ups" (carafe and cup), in glossy Burmese and Lotus Mist Burmese in Diamond Optic, with Circle of Love decoration made for Joyce Colella, 2001, 6" h and 3" h. **$200 each set**

Brown Crest basket in opalescent Hobnail, 1998 and signed by Don Fenton, made in limited numbers, 9 1/2" h, and 10" w. **$150+**

Burmese covered candy jar showing Little Brown Church in Nashua, Iowa, 1980s, 8 1/4" h. **$85+**

Blue Ridge 80th Anniversary dresser set, part of the Connoisseur Collection, limited to 1,000 sets including two perfumes, powder box and tray, 1985-86; perfumes, 5 3/4" h; powder box, 4" h; tray, 7" diameter. **$325+ set**

Burmese spherical lamp shade with hand-painted railroad motif, 1999, 13" h. **no established value**

Burmese ginger jar, three pieces with base, decorated with butterflies, 2000, designed by J.K. (Robin) Spindler, with facsimiles of Fenton family signatures, 8 1/2" h. **$275**

Burmese vase with hand-painted flowers by Martha Reynolds, 1990s, 13" h. **$350+**

Burmese vase with hand-painted floral motif by Martha Reynolds, 1997, 11" h. **$450+**

Chiffon Pink Iridized Mermaid vase, 2000, 6 1/2" h. **$90+**

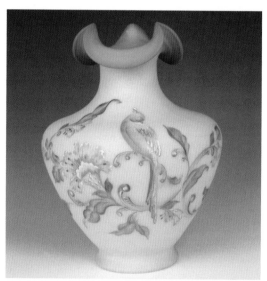

Burmese vase with hand-painted flowers and birds by Martha Reynolds, 1990s, 12" h. **$350+**

Two Christmas Compotes (using an old Dugan mold with holly pattern), 1997, in Green Radium (also called Sea Green Opalescent Iridized) and Plum Opalescent Satin, 9 1/2" diameter. **$150-$200 each**

Cobalt and Amber cornucopia candleholders, style No. 950, late 1990s, 6" h: Cobalt, **$45+;** *Amber.* **$45+**

Cobalt and Ruby candlesticks in Spiral, 1990s, 7 1/2" h. **$35+ each**

Fenton, Charleston Collection beaded melon jug, exclusive from QVC, 2002, signed by Don and Randy Fenton, marking the company's 95th anniversary, 5 1/2" h. **$130+**

Fenton, Candleglow decanter, 1980s, 11 1/2" h. **$80+**

Fenton, from left: Cobalt shoe with snowflake decoration, 2004-05, 4 1/4" l, **$30***; center: White Satin shoe with airbrush decoration and hand-painted holly leaves and berries, 2004-05, 4 1/4" l,* **$30***; right: Periwinkle Blue Bear Cub with hand-painted holly leaves and berries, 2004-05, 3 3/4" h.* **$45**

FOSTORIA GLASS

Fostoria Glass Co. began operations at Fostoria, Ohio, in 1887, and moved to Moundsville, W.V., its present location, in 1891. By 1925, Fostoria had five furnaces and a variety of special shops. In 1924, a line of colored tableware was introduced. Fostoria was purchased by Lancaster Colony in 1983.

After-dinner cup and saucer
Beverly, green	$30
June, blue	$160
Versailles, yellow	$48

Almond dish, Colony, footed $15

Ashtray
American, 2 7/8" square	$7.50
Coin, crystal	$30
Fairfax, yellow, 4" d	12
June, blue	$75

Baker, June, topaz, oval, 9" $195

Bell, Chintz, original label $130

Berry bowl, June, blue, 5" d $50

Bonbon, Bridal Wreath, #2630 Century, cut 833, three toes $75

Bouillon, Versailles, topaz $30

Bowl
American, oval, 10" l	$30
Baroque, blue, 4" square, one handle	$22
Corsage, flared, 12" d	$110
Grape Leaf, green, 12" d	$175
June, blue, 12" d	$125

Brandy inhaler, Navarre $115

Bread and butter plate, Trojan, topaz, 6" d $10

Bud vase, Coin, olive $28

Cake plate
Chintz, two handles, 10" d	$40
Coin, crystal	$135

Photo courtesy Early Auction Co. LLC.

Fostoria vase, cylindrical iridescent gold amethyst hearts and vines decoration, rolled rim, 12" h. **$500**

Cake salver
Century, crystal	$60
Coin, crystal	$98
Corsage, 10 1/2" d	$32
Navarre, crystal, handles, 10" d	$60

Fostoria, Coin, red candy dish with cover. **$70**

Candleholders, pair

Baroque, one-light, silver deposit Vintage decoration on
base, 4" h, #2496..**$75**
Baroque, two-light, removable bobeche and prisms,
8 1/2" h, 10" w, #2484...**$375**
Buttercup, 5 1/2" h, #2594, etch 340. ....**$250**
Coin, red, tall **$150**
Meadow Rose..**$185**
Trojan, topaz, 2", #2394, etch 280....................................**$145**
Trindle, #2594, three-light, Buttercup etch, 8" h, 6 1/2" w..**$250**

Candy dish, covered

Baroque, crystal...**$40**
June, yellow **$370**
Navarre, three parts **$175**
Versailles, blue, three parts..**$345**

Card tray, Brocaded Daffodil, two handles, pink, gold trim **$40**

Celery

Baroque, blue..**$85**
June, blue..**$130**

Celery tray, Trojan, topaz **$100**

Centerpiece bowl

American, 11" d...**$175**
Seascape, blue, footed **$140**

Cereal bowl, June, rose, 6" d...**$85**

Champagne

Bridal Wreath, #6051, cut 833 ....**$35**
Buttercup, #6030, etch 340 ....**$32**

Corsage, #6014, etch 325 ....**$32**
Dolley Madison..**$18**
June, saucer, petal stem..**$27**
Versailles, pink..**$40**

Cheese and cracker

Chintz **$70**
Colony **$55**
Navarre **$150**
Vernon, orchid **$90**

Cheese stand, Teardrop, 3 1/4" h **$25**

Chop plate, June, Pink, 13" d..**$230**

Cigarette box, covered

Cigarette set, Baroque, azure, #2496, five pieces **$450**
Morning Glory etching **$65**
Oriental **$170**

Cigarette urn, Coin, olive **$23**

Claret

Bridal Wreath, #6051, cut 833 ....**$38**
Camelia **$30**
June, pink..**$175**
Navarre **$80**
Trojan, yellow, 6" h...**$100**

Cocktail

Baroque, yellow **$15**
Buttercup...**$18**
Chintz **$24**
Colony **$27**

Fostoria, American pattern, bowl, 8" d. **$50**

Fairfax, #5299, yellow	$18
Hermitage, yellow, cone	$10
Meadow Rose, #6016, 3 1/2 oz, 5 1/4" h	$25
Navarre	$30
Romance	$25
Versailles, yellow, 3 1/2 oz	$25
Vesper, amber	$30

Compote
Baroque, crystal, 6"	$18
Corsage, #2496 Baroque, etch 325.	$75
Trojan, topaz, #2400, etch 280	$85

Condiment set, American, pair salt and pepper shakers, cloverleaf tray, pair cruets ... $200

Console set, Baroque, azure, #2496, pair candlesticks, 10 1/2" d bowl ... $300

Cordial
Corsage	$50
Dolley Madison	$30

Cosmetic box, covered, American, flake on bottom, 2 1/2" d ... $900

Courting lamp, Coin, amber ... $150

Creamer, individual size
Bridal Wreath, #2630 Century, cut 833	$30
Century	$9
Raleigh	$8

Creamer, table size
Baroque, azure, #2496	$55
Chintz	$20
Raleigh	$10
Trojan, topaz	$22

Creamer, sugar, tray, individual size
Camelia	$45
Century	$30
Fairfax, amber	$55
Mayfair, green	$65
Teardrop, crystal	$35

Cream soup
Colony	$95
June, blue	$100
Versailles, pink	$65
Vesper, amber	$30

Cruet, June, yellow ... $700

Crushed fruit jar, covered, America, circa 1915-25, 5 7/8" d, 6" h ... $1,600

Cup and saucer
Baroque, blue	$35
Buttercup	$34
Camelia	$20
Century	$15
Fairfax, blue	$13
Heather	$23
June, azure	$45
Lafayette, wisteria	$28
Meadow Rose	$21
Minuet, green	$55
Navarre	$24

Romance $27

Terrace, red $75

Trojan, topaz, #2375 Fairfax, etch 280. .... $40

Decanter, original stopper, Hermitage, amber, #2449 ... $125

Dinner plate

Versailles, pink, slight use $75

Vesper, amber $30

Epergne, Heirloom Opalescent, large, green $175

Figure

Deer, standing, crystal, 4 1/2" h $45

Lute and Lotus, ebony, gold highlights, price for pair,
12 1/2" h $975

Mermaid, crystal, 10 3/8" h $225

Fruit bowl

Buttercup, 13" d $75

Colony, 10" d $35

Fruit cocktail. Hermitage, topaz, #2449 .... $22

Goblet, water

American Lady, amethyst $35

Arcady $28

Baroque, azure, #2496 .... $45

Bouquet, crystal, #6033, etch 342 .... $35

Buttercup, #6030, etch 340 .... $40

Capri, cinnamon $20

Chintz, 7 5/8" h $30

Colonial Dame, green $19

Colony, 9 oz $20

Deauville, etched Indian Tree $25

Dolley Madison $20

Florentine, yellow $25

Golden Lace, gold trim $24

Jamestown, blue $80

June, blue $80

Meadow Rose $30

Navarre $40

Neo Classic, amethyst $35

Patio, Starlyte cutting $45

Shirley $25

Wilma, pink $30

Trojan, topaz $75

Grapefruit, Coronet $9

Gravy boat, liner, Kasmir, blue $180

Ice bucket, Versailles, pink $155

Iced-tea tumbler

Bouquet, crystal, #6033, etch 342 .... $35

Navarre, pink $75

Jelly, covered

Coin, amber $30

Meadow Rose, 7 1/2" d $90

Jug

Hermitage, green, #2449, three pints $145

Manor, #4020, wisteria foot $1,500

Trojan, topaz, #5000, etch 280 .... $600

Juice tumbler, June, topaz, footed $30

Lily pond, Buttercup, 12" d $55

Marmalade, covered, American $125

Mayonnaise

Baroque, azure, #2496 .... $95

Buttercup $90

Milk pitcher, Century $60

Mint, Baroque, azure, #2496, handle, 4" d $48

Nappy, handle

Baroque, azure, #2496 .... $48

Coin, blue, 5 3/8" d $30

Nut cup, Fairfax, amber $15

Oil cruet, Versailles, yellow $550

Old-fashioned tumbler, Hermitage, azure $35

Olive, Hermitage, amber, #2449 .... $32

Oyster cocktail, Hermitage, amber, #2449 .... $18

Parfait, June, pink $180

Pickle castor, American, ornate silver plated frame, 11" h $900

Pickle tray, Century, 8 3/4" $15

Pitcher, Lido, footed $225

Plate

Baroque, green, 7 1/2" d $28

Century, 9 1/2" d $30

Corsage, etch 325, 8" d $22

Rose, 9" d $15

Platter

June, topaz, oval, 12" l $145

Trojan, topaz, oval, 12" l $80

Punch bowl, footed, Baroque, crystal, original label $425

Relish dish, covered, Brocaded Summer Gardens, three
sections, white $75

Relish dish, open

Corsage, three parts, #2496, Baroque, etch 325 ... $75

June, topaz, two parts, 8 1/4" l $40

Ring holder, American, 4 1/2" l, 3" h $800

Rose bowl, American, small $18

Salad plate, Buttercup $12

Salt and pepper shakers, pair

Bridal Wreath, #2630 Century, cut 833, chrome tops ... $95

Coin, red $60

Coronet $15

Versailles, topaz, footed $200

Sauceboat, Versailles, pink, matching liner $300

Server, center handle, Trojan, topaz, etch 280 ... $135

Sherbet

Baroque, azure, #2496 .... $45

Buttercup, #6030, etch 340 .... $32

Hermitage, green, #2449 .... $22

June, azure $40

Trojan, topaz, #5099, etch 280 .... $48

Snack plate, Century, 8" d $25

Sugar, individual size, Baroque, blue. $4

Sugar, covered, table size, Trojan, topaz $22

Syrup, American, Bakelite handle. $200

Sweetmeat, Baroque, azure, #2496. .... $58

Torte plate

Baroque, azure, #2496, 14" d $125

Colony, 15" d $80

Heather, 13" d $45

Tray, Navarre, 8" l $100

Tumbler, water

Hermitage, topaz, #2449 .... $30

June, footed $55

Trojan, topaz, 5 oz, 4 1/2" h $30

Urn, covered, Coin, amber, 12 3/4" h $68

Vase

Baroque, azure, #2496, 8" h $225

Flying Fish, teal, 7" h $65

Hermitage, topaz, #2449, 6" h $45

Photo courtesy Green Valley Auctions, Mt. Crawford, Va.;www.GreenValleyAuctions.com

Greentown, No. 200 / Austrian Child's Covered Sugar and Creamer, chocolate. Indiana Tumbler and Goblet Co. Early 20th century. 3 3/4" x 3 1/4" h overall. Sugar base with mold roughness to a slight inner rim fin, creamer with normal minor annealing lines. **$536**

Greentown Glass

The Indiana Tumbler and Goblet Co. of Greentown, Ind., operated from 1894 to 1903. The company's wares in chocolate glass and "Holly Amber" are highly prized. The factory was destroyed by fire in 1903. Collectors use the term "Greentown glass" when referring to their products.

Greentown, No. 98 / Brazen Shield Covered Sugar Bowl, cobalt blue. Indiana Tumbler and Goblet Co. Fourth quarter 19th century. 6 3/4" h overall, 4" d. 5/8" chip under the edge of the base rim. **$138**

Greentown, No. 102 / Teardrop and Tassel Cordial, colorless. Indiana Tumbler and Goblet Co. Late 19th/early 20th century. 3" h. Normal annealing lines below rim.
.... **$287**

Greentown, No. 102 / Teardrop and Tassel Bowl, cobalt blue, beaded rim. Indiana Tumbler and Goblet Co. Late 19th/early 20th century. 2 5/8" h, 7 3/8" d rim. Minor mold roughness to rim. **$287**

Greentown, No. 102 / Teardrop and Tassel Sauce, Nile Green, beaded rim. Indiana Tumbler and Goblet Co. Early 20th century. 1 5/8" h, 4 5/8" d. Bruise to one bead. **$373**

Greentown, No. 140 Columbia / Herringbone Buttress Cruet, emerald green, with an appropriate stopper of a slightly different shade. Indiana Tumbler and Goblet Co. Late 19th/early 20th century. 6 1/2" h overall. Two shallow chips and roughness to tops of ribs. **$156**

Greentown, No. 200 / Austrian Child's Sugar Bowl Base, canary. Indiana Tumbler and Goblet Co. Fourth quarter 19th century. 2 3/4" h, 2 3/8" d. **$149**

Greentown, No. 350 / Cord Drapery Syrup, period lid. Indiana Tumbler and Goblet Co. Early 20th century 6 1/2" h overall. Corrosion/rust to lid. **$126**

Greentown, No. 350 / Cord Drapery Syrup, chocolate, period lid. Indiana Tumbler and Goblet Co. Early 20th century. 6 1/2" h overall. Wear to several small beads, color separation line to handle. **$138**

Greentown, No. 350 / Cord Drapery Syrup, colorless, non-period lid. Indiana Tumbler and Goblet Co. Fourth quarter 19th century. 6 1/4" h overall, 3 5/8" d overall. **$195**

Greentown, No. 375 / Cactus Mustard Pot, chocolate, plated-silver screw-on rim with hinged lid, twisted bail handle and spoon slot. Indiana Tumbler and Goblet Co. Early 20th century. 3 5/8" h overall. Shallow chip to top of foot. **$402**

Greentown, No. 375 / Cactus Water Pitcher, chocolate. Indiana Tumbler and Goblet Co. Early 20th century. 8" h overall, 5 1/2" d. Flake to the spout and minor mold roughness to the feet. **$192**

Greentown, No. 375 / Cactus Iced Tea Tumblers, Lot of Four, chocolate. Indiana Tumbler and Goblet Co. Early 20th century. 5" h. One with several pattern flakes, others with several minor to moderate annealing lines. .... **$92 set**

Greentown, No. 375 / Cactus Cruet, chocolate, appropriate well-fitting stopper of a slightly differing color. Indiana Tumbler and Goblet Co. Early 20th century. 6 5/8" h overall. Minute nicks to ribs. **$69**

Greentown, No. 375 / Cactus Sauce Dish, Golden Agate, footed. Indiana Tumbler and Goblet Co. Early 20th century. 1 7/8" h, 4 1/8" d. **$60**

Greentown, No. 400 / Leaf Bracket Cruet, chocolate, appropriate but off-color Dewey stopper. Indiana Tumbler and Goblet Co. Early 20th century. 5 1/2" h overall. Slight mold roughness. **$69**

Greentown, No. 400 / Leaf Bracket Butter Dish, chocolate. Indiana Tumbler and Goblet Co. Early 20th century. 5" h overall, 7 3/8" d overall. Shallow chip under the base rim.. .... **$46**

Greentown, No. 400 / Leaf Bracket Salt Shaker, chocolate, period lid. Indiana Tumbler and Goblet Co. Early 20th century. 3" h overall. Undamaged, normal overall annealing lines. **$92**

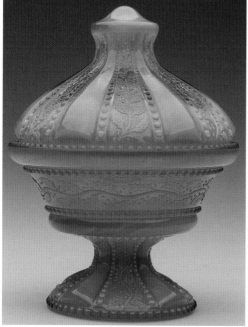

Greentown, No. 450 / Holly Low Pedestal Covered Comport, Golden Agate, beaded base rim. Indiana Tumbler and Goblet Co. Early 20th century. 6" h overall, 3 3/8" h base, 4 5/8" d base. Cover with a chip to inner flange, base with a chip to edge of foot removing one bead. **$791**

Greentown, No. 450 / Holly Bowl, Golden Agate, beaded rim. Indiana Tumbler and Goblet Co. Early 20th century. 3 1/8" h, 8 1/2" d. Minute flakes/nicks to inner rim. ... **$450**

Greentown, No. 450 / Holly Tumbler, Agate, plain rim. Indiana Tumbler and Goblet Co. Fourth quarter 19th century. 4" h, 3" d. Minute abrasion to rim. **$510**

Greentown, No. 450 / Holly Nappy, Golden Agate, single handle, beaded rim. Indiana Tumbler and Goblet Co. Early 20th century. 2" h, 4 5/8" d rim. Rim with partial loss of one bead and some minute interior flakes, light wear to handle edge. **$270**

Greentown, No. 450 / Holly Sauce Dishes, Lot of Four, Golden Agate, each with beaded rim. Indiana Tumbler and Goblet Co. Early 20th century. 1 5/8" h, 4 1/4" d. Slight inner-rim mold roughness, one with interior wear. .... **$431 all**

Greentown, No. 450 / Holly Oval Bowl, Golden Agate. Indiana Tumbler and Goblet Co. Fourth quarter 19th century. 1 7/8" h, 4 1/2" x 7 3/8". Minor roughness to interior rim. **$258**

Greentown, Bird with Berry Covered Dish, on basket-weave base. Indiana Tumbler and Goblet Co. Late 19th/ early 20th century. 4 1/2" h overall, 4 1/8" x 5 3/8". **$480**

Greentown, Buffalo Paperweight, Nile Green, without date, beaded table ring. Indiana Tumbler and Goblet Co. Early 20th century. 3 1/8" h, 4" d overall. Partial loss of one ear. **$747**

Greentown, Cat on Hamper Covered Dish, chocolate, tall version. Indiana Tumbler and Goblet Co. Early 20th century. 4 3/4" h overall, 3 1/2" sq overall. Cover with a small chip under one corner and manufacturing roughness to one ear, base with several shallow chips to rim exterior, none of which disfigure the rim profile. **$132**

Greentown, Cat on Hamper Covered Dish, chocolate, tall version. Indiana Tumbler and Goblet Co. Early 20th century. 4 3/4" h overall, 3 1/2" sq overall. Minor flake under one base corner. **$172**

Greentown, Cat on Hamper Covered Dish, emerald green, tall version. Indiana Tumbler and Goblet Co. Late 19th/ early 20th century. 4 3/4" h overall, 3 1/2" sq overall. Chip to one ear. **$192**

Greentown, Cat on Hamper Covered Dish, teal blue, tall version. Indiana Tumbler and Goblet Co. Late 19th/early 20th century. 4 3/4" h overall, 3 1/2" sq overall. Light flake to one vertical edge and a small chip under one base corner. **$218**

Greentown, Hen Covered Dish, chocolate, basket-weave pattern base. Indiana Tumbler and Goblet Co. Early 20th century. 4 1/4" h overall, 4 1/8" x 5 3/8" d base. Minor flake to one base rim bead. **$373**

Greentown, Dewey Three-Piece Table Set, amber, consisting of a covered sugar bowl, creamer and spooner. Indiana Tumbler and Goblet Co. Fourth quarter 19th century. 4 1/2" to 6 3/4" h overall. Foot flakes/roughness. .... **$92 set**

Greentown, Dewey Four-Piece Water Set, emerald green, consisting of a water pitcher and three tumblers. Indiana Tumbler and Goblet Co. Fourth quarter 19th century. Pitcher 8" h, 5 1/4" d, tumblers 3 7/8" h, 3" d. Pitcher having a chip to one foot and several open bubbles to ribbing, two tumblers with high-point wear to medallions. .... **$345 set**

Greentown, Dolphin Covered Dish, Red Agate, beaded rim. Indiana Tumbler and Goblet Co. Early 20th century. 4 1/4" h overall. Minute flake to one front fin. **$300**

Greentown, Cat on Hamper Low Covered Nappy, chocolate, base with scalloped tab handle. Indiana Tumbler and Goblet Co. Early 20th century. 3 1/2" h overall, 5 1/8" x 6 1/4" overall. Cover with what appears to be light factory grinding to the back of one ear, which does not affect the profile of the ear, base with several flakes to front edge. **$840**

Greentown, Dolphin Covered Dish, Golden Agate, beaded rim. Indiana Tumbler and Goblet Co. Early 20th century. 4 1/4" h overall. Minor flake to the tip of the front fin on cover. **$431**

Greentown, Hen Covered Dish, blue, on basket-weave base. Indiana Tumbler and Goblet Co. Late 19th/early 20th century. 4 1/2" h overall, 4 3/8" x 5 1/2". Shallow chip to base rim. **$207**

Greentown, Hen Covered Dish, chocolate, basket-weave pattern base. Indiana Tumbler and Goblet Co. Early 20th century. 4 1/4" h overall, 4 1/8" x 5 3/8" d base. Cover rim with two shallow chips to upper edge, base rim with loss of two beads. **$92**

Greentown, Indian Head Creamer, Nile Green, lacking cover. Indiana Tumbler and Goblet Co. Early 20th century. 5 3/4" h overall. With a 1/2" loss and adjacent 1" glued section at spout. **$108**

Greentown, Picture Frame Toothpick / Match Holder, pale blue, embossed "R. & M." under base. Indiana Tumbler and Goblet Co. Late 19th/early 20th century. 3 1/2" h. **$575**

Greentown, Rabbit Covered Dish, amber, on basket-weave base. Indiana Tumbler and Goblet Co. Late 19th/early 20th century. 4 1/4" h overall, 4 1/4" x 5 1/2". Minute bruise to top mold line, base rim with several flakes and normal minor roughness to interior seat. **$144**

Greentown, Rabbit Covered Dish, chocolate, on basket-weave base. Indiana Tumbler and Goblet Co. Early 20th century. 4 1/8" h overall, 4 1/8" x 5 3/8". Chip to one rim bead, normal annealing lines to cover. **$228**

Greentown, Rabbit Covered Dish, emerald green, on basket-weave base. Indiana Tumbler and Goblet Co. Late 19th/early 20th century. 4 1/8" h overall, 4 1/2" x 5 1/2". Base with a small rim chip and flake as well as a bruise to outside of rim. **$69**

Greentown, Trunk Covered Box, opaque white/milk glass, embossed "Pan American 1901" and "Put Me Off at Buffalo" on ends, slightly worn original gold decoration. Indiana Tumbler and Goblet Co. Early 20th

Greentown, Rabbit Covered Dish, teal blue, basket-weave pattern base. Indiana Tumbler and Goblet Co. Late 19th/early 20th century. 4 1/8" h overall, 4 1/4" x 5 1/2" base. Cover with light polishing under rim, base rim with an under-fill to one outer-rim scallop and several inner-rim flakes. **$226**

century. 2 1/4" h, 2 1/4" x 3 3/8". Two shallow chips to base rim. **$218**

Greentown, Trunk Covered Box, white/milk glass, no lettering on ends, worn original gold decoration. Indiana Tumbler and Goblet Co. Early 20th century. 2 1/4" h, 2 1/4" x 3 3/8". Small manufacturing chip to one upper corner of cover, which has traces of decoration, otherwise a flake to inner rim of base and short annealing lines. **$92**

Greentown, Wheelbarrow Open Salt, Green, tiny beaded diamond on front. Indiana Tumbler and Goblet Co. Late

Greentown / McKee, Daisy Covered Butter, chocolate, on three feet. Indiana Tumbler and Goblet Co. and/or McKee & Brothers. Early 20th century. 4 1/8" h overall, 4 5/8" d overall. Two minute flakes to cover rim, normal short annealing lines. **$84**

19th/early 20th century. 1 7/8" h, 1 5/8" x 2 1/4" rim.
.... **$316**

Greentown, Heron Water Pitcher, plain rim. Indiana Tumbler and Goblet Co. and possibly others. Late 19th/ early 20th century. 9" h overall. **$184**

Lalique

René Lalique (1860-1945) first gained prominence as a jewelry designer. Around 1900, he began experimenting with molded-glass brooches and pendants, often embellishing them with semiprecious stones. By 1905, he was devoting himself exclusively to the manufacture of glass articles. He produced many objects, especially vases, bowls and figurines, in the Art Nouveau and Art Deco styles.

Also see Perfume Containers.

Lalique, Champs-Élysées leaf-form bowl with a partially polished irregular rim. Engraved Lalique France, 7 1/2" x 18" x 9 3/4" d. **$960**

Lalique, Domremy vase in clear glass, circa 1926. Engraved R. Lalique France, 8 1/8" h. **$1,440**

Lalique, Esna vase of clear and frosted glass with floral design. Engraved Lalique France, 9" x 8 1/2" d. **$480**

Lalique, Font-Romeu vase of frosted glass with ferns. Engraved 'Lalique France' on base, 8 5/8" x 9 3/8" d.
.... **$570**

Lalique, Luxembourg center bowl in clear and frosted glass. Engraved Lalique France. 10 1/2" d. **$1,800**

Lalique, Marguerites center bowl of clear and frosted glass, with daisies and rays. Engraved Lalique France, 3" x 14" d.
.... **$450**

Lalique, Miroir Cygnes, swan figures on mirror, in clear and frosted glass. Engraved Lalique France. Length of mirror: 33". **$3,900**

Lalique, Saint-Francois vase of opalescent glass with sparrows and tree branches. Marked R. Lalique France on base. 7" x 6 5/8" d. **$1,200**

Lalique, Salmonides vase in opaque glass, drilled and mounted as lamp, pre-1947, vase 13 3/4" h with base.
.... **$1,080**

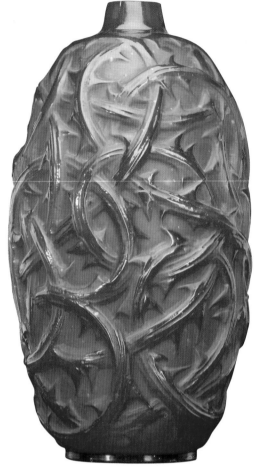

Photo courtesy Rago Arts and Auction Center, Lambertville, N.J.; www.RagoArts.com

R. Lalique, "Ronces" vase, red, molded R. LALIQUE, engraved R. Lalique, France, circa 1921, 9" h. **$5,400**

Photo courtesy Rago Arts and Auction Center, Lambertville, N.J.; www.RagoArts.com

R. Lalique, Four Seasons statuettes, "Printemps," "Ete," "Automne," and "Hiver," clear and frosted, sepia patina, chip to Automne base, engraved R. Lalique France, circa 1939. **$4,200 set**

Photo courtesy Rago Arts and Auction Center, Lambertville, N.J.; www.RagoArts.com

R. Lalique, "Languedoc" vase, emerald green, engraved R. Lalique France No. 1021, circa 1929, 8 7/8" h. **$19,200**

Photo courtesy Rago Arts and Auction Center, Lambertville, N.J.; www.RagoArts.com

R. Lalique vase, "Dahlias," clear and frosted, sepia patina, black enamel, stenciled R. LALIQUE FRANCE, circa 1923, 7" d. **$2,640**

R. Lalique vase, "Quatre Masques," clear and frosted, sepia patina, engraved R. Lalique France, circa 1911, 11 1/2". **$21,600**

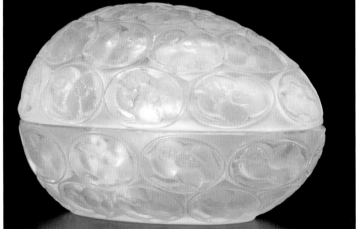

R. Lalique box, "Poussins," clear and frosted, molded R. LALIQUE FRANCE, circa 1929, 4 1/2" h. **$2,640**

R. Lalique vase, "Sauge," teal green, molded R. Lalique, circa 1923, 9 7/8" h. **$4,200**

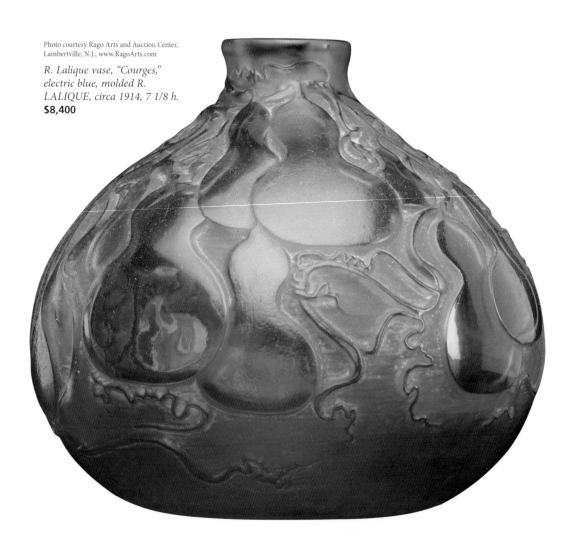

*R. Lalique vase, "Courges,"
electric blue, molded R.
LALIQUE, circa 1914, 7 1/8 h.*
$8,400

*R. Lalique berry
set, "Coquilles,"
center bowl
9 1/2" w; six
matching
individual bowls,
5" w; matching
serving plate,
12" w, signed R.
Lalique France.*
$1,400 set

Photo courtesy Rago Arts and Auction Center, Lambertville, N.J.; www.RagoArts.com

R. Lalique vase, "Milan," emerald green, engraved R. Lalique France, circa 1929, 11" h. **$15,600**

Photo courtesy Rago Arts and Auction Center, Lambertville, N.J.; www.RagoArts.com

Lalique box and cover, "Festoon," clear and frosted, blue patina, unmarked, circa 1938, 6 3/4" d. **$420**

R. Lalique vase, "Raisins," clear and frosted, sepia patina, wheel-cut R. LALIQUE FRANCE, circa 1928, 6 1/4" h. **$1,200**

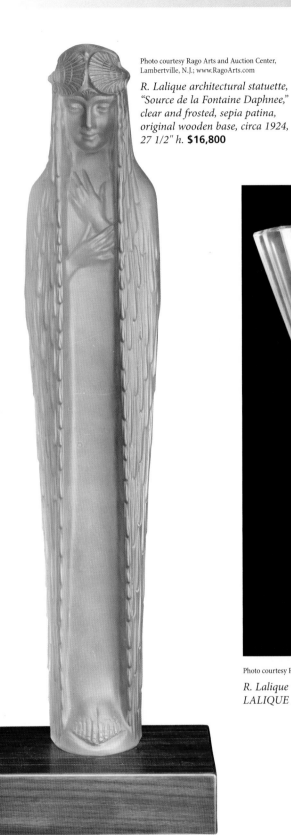

R. Lalique architectural statuette, "Source de la Fontaine Daphnee," clear and frosted, sepia patina, original wooden base, circa 1924, 27 1/2" h. **$16,800**

R. Lalique vase, "Coq," clear and frosted, stenciled R. LALIQUE FRANCE, circa 1931, 9 5/8" h. **$3,120**

R. Lalique vase, "Le Mans," cased opalescent turquoise, grayish patina, stenciled R. LALIQUE FRANCE, circa 1931, 4 1/8" h. **$2,400**

R. Lalique vase, "Albert," deep blue, wheel-cut R. LALIQUE FRANCE, circa 1925, 6 5/8" h. **$7,200**

Photo courtesy Rago Arts and Auction Center, Lambertville, N.J.;
www.RagoArts.com

*R. Lalique vase, "Poissons," emerald green,
molded R. LALIQUE, circa 1921, 9 1/8" h.*
$19,200

Photo courtesy Rago
Arts and Auction Cen-
ter, Lambertville, N.J.;
www.RagoArts.com

*R. Lalique vase, "Gui," cased
jade green, engraved R. Lalique
France No. 948, circa 1920,
6 3/4" h.* **$7,200**

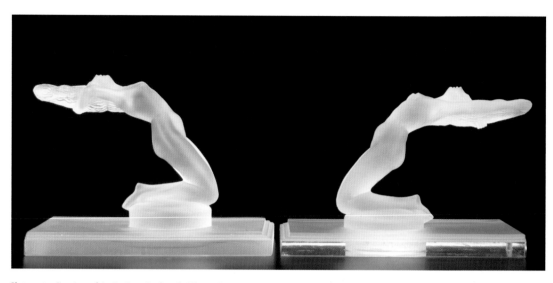

R. Lalique bookends, "Chrysis," clear and frosted, stenciled LALIQUE FRANCE, base with small edge chips, circa 1950, base 7 1/2" x 5 3/4". **$1,140**

R. Lalique vase, "Fontainebleau," deep blue, stenciled R. LALIQUE FRANCE, circa 1930, 6 7/8" d. **$8,400**

R. Lalique vase, "Ferrieres," emerald green, engraved R. Lalique France No. 1019, circa 1929, 6 1/2" h. **$5,400**

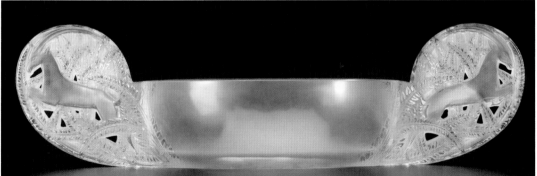

R. Lalique jardinière, "Saint-Hubert," clear and frosted, wheel-cut R. LALIQUE FRANCE, circa 1927, 18 1/2" l. **$4,500**

R. Lalique vase, "Biskra," deep blue, stenciled R. LALIQUE FRANCE, circa 1932, 11 1/2" h. **$6,600**

Photo courtesy Rago Arts and Auction Center, Lambertville, N.J.; www.RagoArts.com

R. Lalique vase, "Lierre," deep blue, whitish patina, engraved R. Lalique France No. 1041, circa 1930, 6 1/2" d. **$4,200**

Photo courtesy Rago Arts and Auction Center, Lambertville, N.J.; www.RagoArts.com

R. Lalique vase, "Pensees," clear and frosted, violet enamel, lavender patina, engraved Lalique France, circa 1920, 5 1/8" h. **$5,700**

R. Lalique vase and cover, "Fontaines," deep plum, engraved R. Lalique France, period gilt metal stand, circa 1912, 6 1/2" h overall. **$7,200**

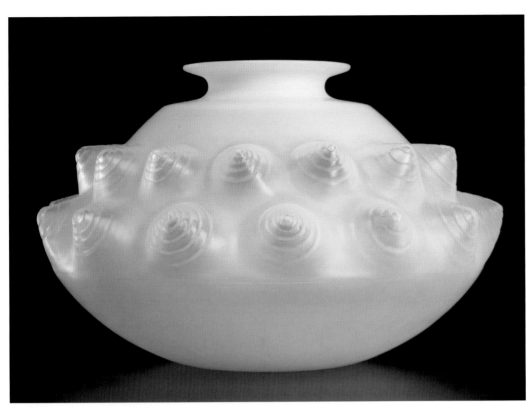

Photo courtesy Rago Arts and Auction Center, Lambertville, N.J.; www.RagoArts.com

R. Lalique vase, "Dordogne," opalescent, molded R. LALIQUE, engraved R. Lalique France, circa 1927, 10 1/2" d.
$4,800

Photo courtesy Rago Arts and Auction Center, Lambertville, N.J.; www.RagoArts.com

R. Lalique vase, "Formose," cased opalescent yellow, molded R. LALIQUE, engraved France, circa 1924, 6 3/4" h. **$7,200**

Photo courtesy Rago Arts and Auction Center, Lambertville, N.J.; www.RagoArts.com

R. Lalique vase, "Gui," plum, molded R. LALIQUE, circa 1920, 6 5/8" h. **$4,200**

Photo courtesy Rago Arts and Auction Center, Lambertville, N.J.; www.RagoArts.com

R. Lalique bowl, "Gui," opalescent, mint green, molded R. LALIQUE, circa 1921, 8 1/8" d. **$1,800**

Photo courtesy Rago Arts and Auction
Center, Lambertville, N.J.;
www.RagoArts.com

*R. Lalique, Virgin and
Child statuette, "Vierge
a L'Enfant," clear and
frosted, original wooden
base, stenciled R. Lalique
France, circa 1934,
15" h.* **$960**

Photo courtesy Rago Arts and
Auction Center, Lambertville,
N.J.; www.RagoArts.com

*R. Lalique
vase, "Orleans,"
opalescent, greenish
patina, stenciled R.
LALIQUE FRANCE,
circa 1930, 7 7/8" h.*
$3,240

Photo courtesy Rago Arts and Auction Center, Lambertville, N.J.; www.RagoArts.com

*R. Lalique port wine service,
"Dampierre," clear and frosted, sepia
patina, comprising decanter and
eight footed port glasses, stenciled
R. LALIQUE FRANCE, circa 1931.*
$2,160

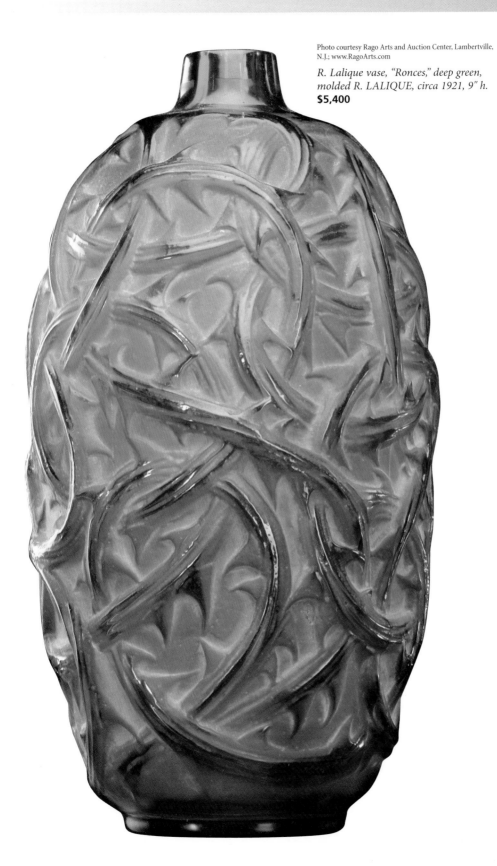

Photo courtesy Rago Arts and Auction Center, Lambertville, N.J.; www.RagoArts.com

R. Lalique vase, "Ronces," deep green, molded R. LALIQUE, circa 1921, 9" h.
$5,400

Photo courtesy Rago Arts and Auction Center, Lambertville, N.J.; www.RagoArts.com

R. Lalique vase, "Malesherbes,"
clear and frosted, heavy sepia
patina, engraved R. Lalique France
No. 1014, 1927, 9 1/8″ h. **$3,000**

Photo courtesy Rago Arts and Auction Center, Lambertville, N.J.; www.RagoArts.com

R. Lalique hood
ornament, "Longchamp
A," clear and frosted
glass, stenciled R.
LALIQUE FRANCE,
molded FRANCE, circa
1929, 4 7/8″ h. **$7,200**

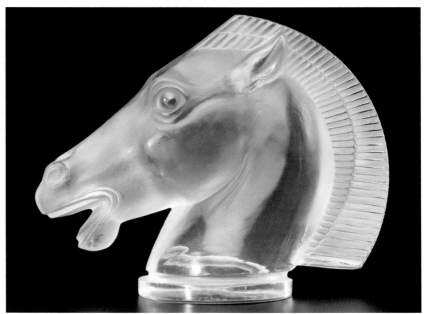

Photo courtesy Rago Arts and Auction Center, Lambertville, N.J.; www.RagoArts.com

R. Lalique hood ornament, "Coq Nain," smoky topaz glass, tail tip slightly reduced, molded R. LALIQUE, circa 1928, 8" h. **$1,440**

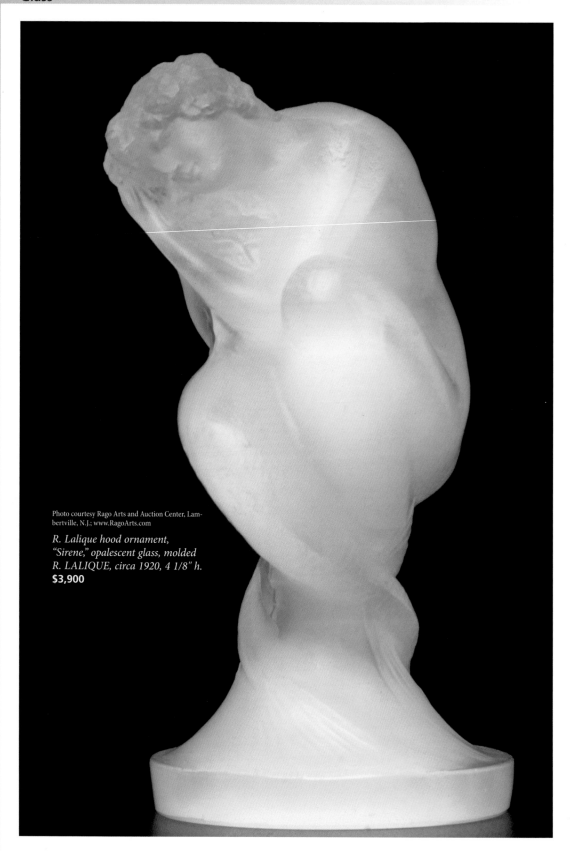

Photo courtesy Rago Arts and Auction Center, Lambertville, N.J.; www.RagoArts.com

R. Lalique hood ornament, "Sirene," opalescent glass, molded R. LALIQUE, circa 1920, 4 1/8" h.
$3,900

Photo courtesy Rago Arts and Auction Center, Lambertville, N.J.; www.RagoArts.com

R. Lalique hood ornament, "Libellule Grande," clear and frosted glass, gray patina, lucite stand, engraved R. Lalique France, circa 1928, 8 1/8" h. **$7,200**

*R. Lalique hood ornament,
"Tete De Coq," clear and
frosted glass, molded
LALIQUE, FRANCE, circa
1928, 7" h.* **$960**

*R. Lalique hood ornament,
"Cinq Chevaux," amethyst
tint glass, restorations,
molded R. LALIQUE,
engraved France, circa
1925, 6" h.* **$2,520**

QUEZAL

The Quezal Art Glass Decorating Co., named for the quetzal—a bird with brilliantly colored feathers found in tropical regions of the Americas—was organized in 1901 in Brooklyn, N.Y., by Martin Bach and Thomas Johnson, two disgruntled Tiffany workers. They soon hired Percy Britton and William Wiedebine, two more former Tiffany employees.

The first products, unmarked, were exact Tiffany imitations. Quezal pieces differ from Tiffany pieces in that they are more defined and the decorations are more visible and brighter. No new techniques were developed by Quezal.

Johnson left in 1905. T. Conrad Vahlsing, Bach's son-in-law, joined the firm in 1918, but left with Paul Frank in 1920 to form Lustre Art Glass Co,, which in turn copied Quezal pieces. Martin Bach died in 1924, and by 1925, Quezal had ceased operations.

The "Quezal" trademark was first used in 1902 and placed on the base of vases and bowls and the rims of shades. The acid-etched or engraved letters vary in size and may be found in amber, black or gold. A printed label that includes an illustration of a quetzal was used briefly in 1907.

Bowl, iridescent gold Calcite ground, stretch rim, pedestal foot, signed "Quezal," 9 1/2" d. **$800**

Candlesticks, iridescent blue, signed, 7 3/4" h. ..... **$575 pair**

Ceiling lamp shade, drop, radiating iridescent gold and green leaf decoration, domed iridescent ivory glass shade supported by brass ring suspended from three ball chains, two-socket fixture, shade inscribed "Quezal," Brooklyn, NY, early 20th century, 13 3/4" d, 21 1/2" l........................**$6,325**

Chandelier, four elaborate gilt metal scroll arms, closed teardrop gold, green, and opal shades, inscribed "Quezal" at collet rim, very minor roughness at rim edge, 14" h. **$2,000**

Cologne bottle, iridescent gold ground, Art Deco design, signed "Q" and "Melba," 7 1/2" h..................................**$250**

Finger bowl and underplate, gold iridescent bowl, pontil signed, ribbed underplate, signed "Quezal," 4 1/2" d. **$300**

Jack-in-the-pulpit vase

Green pulled-feather decoration tipped in iridescent gold, alabaster body, shiny gold interior, signed "Quezal," 6 1/2" h...**$2,250**

Green pulled-feather tipped in iridescent gold, signed "Quezal," minor wear to gold interior, 6" h. **$2,000**

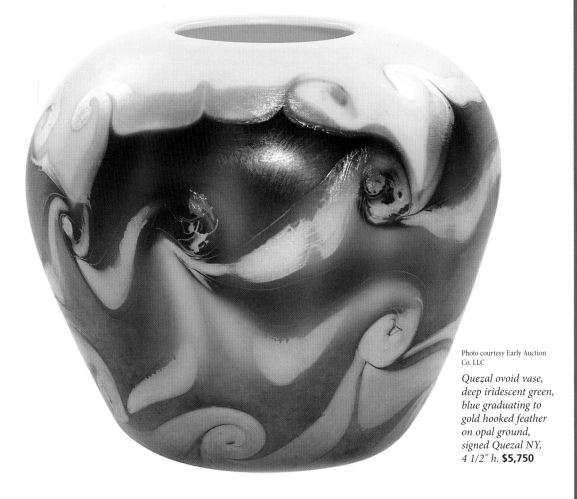

Photo courtesy Early Auction Co. LLC

Quezal ovoid vase, deep iridescent green, blue graduating to gold hooked feather on opal ground, signed Quezal NY, 4 1/2" h. **$5,750**

Lamp shade

Aperture, iridescent gold, cylindrical, ruffled rims, signed, set of three, 4 3/4" h, 1 3/4" d....................**$235 set**

Aperture, ribbed bell form, calcite exterior, gold iridescent interior, signed on rim, 4 1/2" h, 2 3/16" d..............**$180**

Low bowl, iridescent gold, ribbed shallow bowl, polished pontil, signed, 4" d..**$450**

Salt, open, shouldered, iridescent body, protruding ribs, pontil signed "Quezal," 2 1/2" d, 1 1/4" h..................**$200**

Sherbet, iridescent gold body, blue coil decoration, signed "Quezal," 4" h. **$700**

Toothpick holder, melon ribbed, pinched sides, iridescent blue, green, purple and gold, signed, 2 1/4" h..............**$200**

Urn, covered, shouldered form, marigold body, overall green "King Tut" swirl pattern, matching lid, iridescent gold foot, signed "Quezal" in silver, 13 1/2" h..............................**$5,500**

Vase

Floriform, folded iridescent gold rim, green and gold leaf decoration, signed "Quezal S 651," 5 1/4" h. **$2,350**

Footed trumpet form, opal-decorated and iridescent-tipped, green pulled feathers, signed Quezal, 8 1/2" h..........**$2,950**

Tri-fold flower form, random wintergreen loops over iridescent gold pulls, soft velvet gold iridescent interior, signed "Quezal," 5" h. **$1,750**

Tulip-form body, pinched rim, green and gold iridescent pulled feather decoration, circular foot with folded rim, base signed "Quezal," 10 1/2" h.
....**$18,800**

Whiskey taster, oval, iridescent gold, four pinched dimples, signed "Quezal" on base, 2 3/4" h. **$200**

Photo courtesy Early Auction Co. LLC

Quezal flower form vase, corset shaped, flaring ruffled rim, green pulled feathers tipped in iridescent gold decoration, signed Quezal N 397, 6 1/2" h. **$3,250**

Quezal shouldered vase, iridescent gold, green and opal pulled feathers, sgd Quezal 199, 6" h. **$2,650**

Photo courtesy Early Auction Co. LLC

Quezal vase, iridescent, opal footed urn form, everted rim with gold luster coil design, signed Quezal, 6 1/2" h. **$1,400**

Quezal cabinet vase, agate, cylindrical shouldered form, variegated gray green and amber glass, signed Quezal, 4 1/2" h.
$2,250

Corrections

Several glass listings in the 2009 edition of the Warman's guide had incorrect prices. The correct values are listed here. The Warman's staff regrets the errors. All photos are courtesy of Green Valley Auctions, Mt. Crawford, Va.

Candlestick, Petal and Loop, slightly translucent medium blue, wafer construction, two shallow chips and two flakes under base, Boston & Sandwich Glass Co., circa 1840-1860, 6 3/4" h. **$1,430**

Candlesticks, Petal and Hexagonal, deep emerald green, one with blood-red striations to base, wafer construction, Boston & Sandwich Glass Co., 1840-1860, 7 1/4" h. **$6,050 pair**

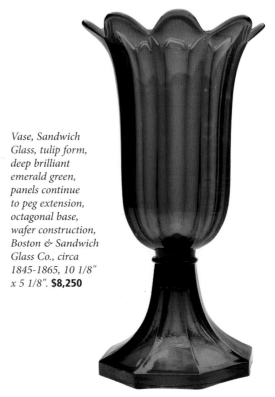

Vase, Sandwich Glass, tulip form, deep brilliant emerald green, panels continue to peg extension, octagonal base, wafer construction, Boston & Sandwich Glass Co., circa 1845-1865, 10 1/8" x 5 1/8". **$8,250**

Candlesticks, hexagonal, deep cobalt blue, wafer construction, rough snap ring under base, Boston & Sandwich Glass Co., pristine proof, 1840-1860, 7 1/2" x 4 1/4". **$3,190 pair**

Salt cover, CD-2 variant, pressed, unlisted, medium fiery opalescent, pine cone finial, interior rim beads, fitted on light opalescent BS-2 Beaded Scroll and Basket of Flowers salt, rim crack, Boston & Sandwich Glass Co., 1835-1845. **$20,900**

Salt, divided pressed, DI-1, medium amber, four paw feet, flat serrated divider top edge, New England or Continental, 1835-1850, 1 7/8" x 2" x 3 1/2". **$3,575**

Candlesticks, Petal and Columnar, alabaster/clam broth, electric blue, wafer construction, considerable alabaster impurities, three minute flakes, Boston & Sandwich Glass Co., 1850-1865, 9 1/4" x 3 5/8". **$9,900 pair**

Dish, covered, pressed hen in medium blue, cover with complex molded straw rim, dish with drape panel sides, waffle pattern base, Boston & Sandwich Glass Co., circa 1850-1870, 5 3/4" h overall. **$2,750**

Salt, Chariot pressed, mottled silvery opaque powder blue, scallop and point rim, Boston & Sandwich Glass Co., 1835-1850, 1 3/4" x 2 1/8" x 2 7/8". **$1,210**

Salt, Lyre pressed, medium blue, four scrolled feet, Boston & Sandwich Glass Co., 1835-1845, 1 7/8" x 2" x 3 1/8". **$3,850**

Salt, pedestal, free-blown, ruby, straight sides, shallow bowl, colorless knop stem, six-petal foot, rough pontil mark, encapsulated 1859 Indian Head penny, normal wear, New England, third quarter 19th century, 2 3/4" x 3 1/2" x 3". **$3,575**

Tray, "U.S.F. Constitution," lacy rectangular, colorless, alternating hearts and six-point stars border, wide scallop-and-point rim, double-rope table ring, Boston & Sandwich Glass Co., 1833-1845. **$1,870**

Vase, Sandwich Glass, trumpet form, bright citron, inward folded rim, applied wafer, hollow compressed knop stem, slightly sloping foot, polished pontil mark, rare color. **$1,540**

Vases, pair, Sandwich Glass, Four-Printie Block, brilliant canary, "gauffered" (ridged or pleated) six-flute rim, medial knop, hexagonal base, wafer construction, second factory polished under base, Boston & Sandwich Glass Co., first with shallow base edge chip, second with base edge shallow chip and two flakes, circa 1840-1860. **$1,320 pair**

GRANITEWARE

Graniteware is the name commonly given to enamel-coated iron or steel kitchenware.

The first graniteware was made in Germany in the 1830s, but was not produced in the United States until the 1860s. At the start of World War I, when European companies turned to manufacturing war weapons, American producers took over the market.

Gray and white were the most common graniteware colors, although each company made its own special colors in shades of blue, green, brown, violet, cream or red.

Older graniteware is heavier than the new. Pieces with cast-iron handles may date between 1870 to 1890; wood handles between 1900 to 1910. Other dating clues are seams, wooden knobs and tin lids.

Reproduction Alert. Graniteware still is manufactured in many of the traditional forms and colors.

Berry pail, cov, cobalt blue and white mottled, 7" d, 4 3/4" h. **$65**

Bowl, green and white, 11 3/4" d, 3 3/4" h. **$50**

Cake pan, robin's egg blue and white marbleized, 7 1/2" d. **$45**

Colander, light blue, pedestal base, 12" d. **$45**

Cookie sheet, mottled blue and white. **$225**

Cup, blue and white medium swirl, black trim and handle, 2 3/4" h. **$50**

Frying pan, blue and white mottled, white intior, 10 1/4" d. **$135**

Funnel, cobalt blue and white marbleized, large. **$50**

Grater, medium blue. **$115**

Kettle, covered, gray mottled, 9" h, 11 1/2" d. **$50**

Measure, one cup, gray. **$45**

Mixing bowls, red and white, nested set of four, 1930s. **$155**

Muffin pan, blue and white mottled, eight cups. **$250**

Pie pan, cobalt blue and white marbleized, 6" d. **$25**

Roaster, emerald green swirl, large. **$250**

Skimmer, gray mottled, 10" l. **$25**

Shovel, solid white, some usage wear, wooden handle missing. **$35**

Tube pan, octagonal, gray mottled. **$45**

Utensil rack, shaded orange, gray bowls, matching ladle, skimmer, and tasting spoon, 14 1/2" w, 22" h. ....**$400 all**

Wash basin, blue and white swirl, Blue Diamond Ware, 11 3/4" d. **$150**

Wash basin, aqua and white speckle, stamp mark "Elite Austria Reg. No. (illegible) 26," chip. **$45**

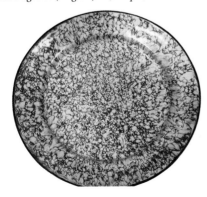

Dinner plate, dark blue and white spatter. **$30**

Teapot, sloping sides, gooseneck spout, original hinged lid and interior pouring strainer, gray and white. **$125**

Dish pan, round, deep sides, two handles, green and white spatter. **$40**

Wash basin, brown and white speckle, pierced for hanging, chips. **$55**

Roaster, three pieces, oval, green and white spatter. **$45**

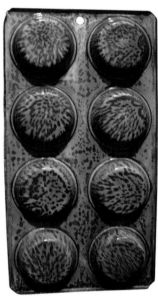

Muffin pan, eight muffins, gray and white, pierced to hang. **$85**

Photo courtesy of Dotta Auction Co. Inc.

Roaster, covered, long, oval, gray speckled. **$90**

Cup, gray, some rust. **$8**

HALLOWEEN

Due to lingering Puritan tradition, which restricted the observance of many holidays, Halloween did not become a widely celebrated holiday in the United States until the late 19th century. American almanacs of the late 18th and early 19th centuries do not include Halloween in their lists of holidays. The transatlantic migration of nearly two million Irish following the Potato Famine of 1845-1849 finally brought the holiday to the United States. Scottish emigration, primarily to Canada before 1870 and to the United States thereafter, brought the Scottish version of the holiday to each country.

Scottish-American and Irish-American societies held dinners and balls that celebrated their heritages, with perhaps a recitation of Robert Burns' poem "Halloween" or a telling of Irish legends, much as Columbus Day celebrations were more about Italian-American heritage than Columbus per se. Home parties centerd on children's activities, such as bobbing for apples, and various divination games often concerning future romance. Pranks and mischief were common as well.

The commercialization of Halloween in the United States did not start until the 20th century, beginning perhaps with Halloween postcards (featuring hundreds of designs) which were most popular between 1905 and 1915. Dennison Manufacturing Co., which published its first Hallowe'en catalog in 1909, and the Beistle Co. were pioneers in commercially made Halloween decorations, particularly die-cut paper items. German manufacturers specialized in Halloween figurines that were exported to the United States in the period between the two world wars.

Mass-produced Halloween costumes did not appear in stores until the 1930s, and trick-or-treating did not become a fixture of the holiday until the 1940s.

Advisers: Claire M. Lavin and Mark Ledenbach.

For more information, see *Vintage Halloween Collectibles,* by Mark Ledenbach, 2007.

Bogie book, Dennison
1909, perhaps a handful are extant..............................$2,000
1914 ....$1,200
1915 ....$250
1922 ....$150
Candy Containers/Nodders
  Candy container, black cat emerging from pumpkin, German, 6" h $550
  Witch pulling hay wagon, Fibro Toy, slot and tab cardboard, 1934-53, 6 3/4" h, 9 1/2" l $165
Jack-'o-lantern, tin, horn nose with original wire bail, 5 1/4" h $70
Devil nodder, composition, German, 1920s, 8 1/4" h $1,800
Diecut, paper
  Cat in candle, Dennison, near mint, circa 1920, 6" h... $125
  Floating specter, Dennison, few creases, minor surface wear, mid-1920s $125
  Lightning Wampus, aka The Halloween Devil, Beistle, circa 1931, 30" h $475
Smiling Skairo–The Hallowe'en Bug, Beistle, 1931 $475
  Pennant-shaped devil face on top diecut, German, circa 1920s, 15 1/2" $650
  Puss in Boots, German, early 1930s, 8 3/4" h $1,200
  Tiara, jack-'o-lantern man flanked by cats, 1920s, Germany, 5" h, 9 1/2" w.. $525
  Witch, bat-winged, Beistle, 1920s, 18" x 18 1/2" open . $245
Games
  "I'm a Dumbskull" game w/envelope, Beistle, 1920s.... $200
  "Ring the Belle," ring toss game, Gibson Art Company, 16" h $575
  "Fortune Wheel for Hallowe'en Parties," w/fortune cards and honeycomb base, Beistle, 1928-31, 11 1/4" h $250
  "Pick A Pumpkin" fortune game, litho paper, witch, brownie & black cat in center, 12 Pumpkin ring perimeter, Germany made for Beistle, circa 1920s. $2,300
  Owl Tell Your Fortune game, Beistle, mid-1950s, 9 1/4" h.. $125

Owl Tell Your Fortune game, USA, Beistle, (no mark), mid-1950s, 9 1/4" h x 6" w. **$110**

*Tongue Twister novelty game with
glassine envelope, USA, Gibson Art Co of
Cincinnati, 1928-1932, 5 1/2" h x 6 3/4" w,
non-embossed.* **$50**
*Sample tongue twister: Forty flagrant
fighters flayed fifty ferocious fanatics who
finally fled.*

*Large witch-head transparency, a candle would be placed
on the attached holder behind, USA, Beistle, (HE Luhrs
mark), early 1940s, 14" h x 8 1/2" w.* **$285**
*This is one of a set of three similarly sized. The others are
a cat and a JOL-head.*

*Four-sided skull & crossbones lantern, USA, Beistle, (no
mark), early 1940s-1950s, 10" h x 5" w.* **$55**
*This was made for many seasons and is plentiful. About
150 "new old stock" examples of these lanterns were
discovered in the late 1990s, which still depresses their
value considerably.*

Metal parade lantern, USA, 1905-1910, 7" diameter.
$1,100
It opens at the center and is designed for an interior candle The paper insert has almost always been burned away. This example has the original internal hardware and wooden finial.

Hard Plastic

Plastic candy container, witch rocket, pumpkin-shaped
    wheels, 1950s, 5 1/2" l, 4" h **$375**
Plastic pirate drummer, wheels, 1950s, 7 1/2" h **$500**
Plastic pirate auto with witch, Rosen/Tico **$300**

Lanterns

Jack-'o-lantern with dual-face, no stem, pulp, 1940s.... **$195**
Lantern, printed on cardboard, transparent eye, nose and
    mouth with honeycomb tissue folding sides, Beistle, fitted
    for electric or candle light, some wear, 1930s, 12" d ... **$800**
Parade jack-'o-lantern, tin, Toledo, Ohio, circa 1908, 7" d.
    .... **$1,500**
Tommy Whiskers cat face Art Deco lantern, Beistle, circa
    1938, 11" x 11 1/4"....................................... **$200**
Paper Spos'N four-sided lantern, Gibson Art Company,
    1920s **$225**

*Watermelon candy container (opens at bottom),
Germany, 1920s, 4" h.* **$425**

Miscellaneous

Ceramic, Dept. 56 Snow Village, Halloween Haunted
    Mansion, 1998, green roof, MIB **$325**
Figurines, German, boxed set of eight, original box,
    3 1/4" h.. **$1,530**
Halloween apron, crepe paper, decorated with witches,
    bats, jack-'o-lanterns, and black cats, circa 1925, 22" h
    .... **$120**
Halloween party book, orange pages, Beistle, circa 1923.
    .... **$375**
Roly-poly, witch and broom, celluloid, circa 1930, 3 1/2" h.
    .... **$775**
Sugar bowl with lid, porcelain, Germany, circa 1915,
    2 1/2" h.. **$300**
Teapot with lid, porcelain, Germany, circa 1915, 4" h **$650**

Noisemakers

Cymbals, tin litho, price for two-piece set, 1920s, 5 1/2" d.
    .... **$525**
Ratchet, tin litho, witch and bikini-clad woman, Bugle,
    1940s, 3 3/4" h **$200**

Jewelry

JEWELRY

Jewelry has been a part of every culture throughout time. It is often reflective of the times, as well as social and aesthetic movements, with each piece telling its own story through hidden clues that, when interpreted, will help solve the mysteries surrounding them.

Jewelry is generally divided into periods and styles. Each period may have several styles, with some of the same styles and types of jewelry being made in both precious and non-precious materials. Additionally, there are recurring style revivals, which are interpretations of an earlier period. For example, the Egyptian Revival that took place in the early and late 1800s, and then again in the 1920s.

Georgian, 1760-1837. Fine jewelry from this period is quite desirable, but few good-quality pieces have found their way to auction in recent years. Sadly, much jewelry from this period has been lost.

Victorian, 1837-1901. Queen Victoria of England ascended the throne in 1837 and remained queen until her death in 1901. The Victorian period is a long and prolific one; abundant with many styles of jewelry. It warrants being divided into three sub-periods: Early or Romantic period dating from 1837-1860; Mid or Grand period dating from 1860-1880; and Late or Aesthetic period dating from 1880-1901.

Sentiment and romance were significant factors in Victorian jewelry. Often, jewelry and clothing represented love and affection, with symbolic motifs such as hearts, crosses, hands, flowers, anchors, doves, crowns, knots, stars, thistles, wheat, garlands, horseshoes and moons. The materials of the time were also abundant and varied. They included silver, gold, diamonds, onyx, glass, cameo, paste, carnelian, agate, coral, amber, garnet, emeralds, opals, pearls, peridot (a green gemstone), rubies, sapphires, marcasites, cut steel, enameling, tortoise shell, topaz, turquoise, bog oak, ivory, jet, hair, gutta percha and vulcanite.

Sentiments of love were often expressed in miniatures. Sometimes they were representative of deceased loved ones, but often the miniatures were of the living. Occasionally, the miniatures depicted landscapes, cherubs or religious themes.

Hair jewelry was a popular expression of love and sentiment. The hair of a loved one was placed in a special compartment in a brooch or a locket, or used to form a picture under a glass compartment. Later in the mid-19th century, pieces of jewelry were made completely of woven hair. Individual strands of hair would be woven together to create necklaces, watch chains, brooches, earrings and rings.

In 1861, Queen Victoria's husband, Prince Albert, died. The queen went into mourning for the rest of her life, and Victoria required that the royal court wear black. This atmosphere spread to the populace and created a demand for mourning jewelry.

Mourning jewelry is typically black. When it first came into fashion, it was made from jet, fossilized wood. By 1850, there were dozens of English workshops making jet brooches, lockets, bracelets and necklaces. As the supply of jet dwindled, other materials were used such as vulcanite, gutta percha, bog oak and French jet.

By the 1880s, the somber mourning jewelry was losing popularity. Fashions had changed and the clothing was simpler and had an air of delicacy. The Industrial Revolution, which had begun in the early part of the century, was now in full swing and machine-manufactured jewelry was affordable to the working class.

Edwardian, 1890-1920. The Edwardian period takes its name England's King Edward VII. Though he ascended the throne in 1901, he and his wife, Alexandria of Denmark, exerted influence over the period before and after his ascension. The 1890s was known as La Belle Epoque. This was a time known for ostentation and extravagance. As the years passed, jewelry became simpler and smaller. Instead of wearing one large brooch, women were often found wearing several small lapel pins.

In the early 1900s, platinum, diamonds and pearls were prevalent in the jewelry of the wealthy, while paste was being used by the masses to imitate the real thing. The styles were reminiscent of the neo-classical and rococo motifs. The jewelry was lacy and ornate, feminine and delicate.

Arts & Crafts, 1890-1920. The Arts & Crafts movement was focused on artisans and craftsmanship. There was a simplification of form where the material was secondary to the design. Guilds of artisans banded together. Some jewelry was mass-produced, but the most highly prized examples of this period are handmade and signed by their makers. The pieces were simple and at times abstract. They could be hammered, patinated and acid etched. Common materials were brass, bronze, copper, silver, blister pearls, freshwater

pearls, turquoise, agate, opals, moonstones, coral, horn, ivory, base metals, amber, cabachon-cut garnets and amethysts.

Art Nouveau, 1895-1910. In 1895, Samuel Bing opened a shop called "Maison de lArt Nouveau" at 22 Rue de Provence in Paris. Art Nouveau designs in the jewelry were characterized by a sensuality that took on the forms of the female figure, butterflies, dragonflies, peacocks, snakes, wasps, swans, bats, orchids, irises and other exotic flowers. The lines used whiplash curves to create a feeling of lushness and opulence.

1920s-1930s. Costume jewelry began its steady ascent to popularity in the 1920s. Since it was relatively inexpensive to produce, there was mass production. The sizes and designs of the jewelry varied. Often, it was worn a few times, disposed of and then replaced with a new piece. It was thought of as expendable, a cheap throwaway to dress up an outfit. Costume jewelry became so popular that it was sold in both the upscale stores and the "five and dime."

During the 1920s, fashions were often accompanied by jewelry that drew on the Art Deco movement, which got its beginning in Paris at the "Exposition Internationale des Arts Décoratifs et Industriels Modernes" held in 1925. The idea behind this movement was that form follows function. The style was characterized by simple, straight, clean lines, stylized motifs and geometric shapes. Favored materials included chrome, rhodium, pot metal, glass, rhinestones, Bakelite and celluloid.

One designer who played an important role was Coco Chanel. Though previously reserved for evening wear, Chanel wore it during the day, making it fashionable for millions of other women to do so, too.

With the 1930s came the Depression and the advent of World War II. Perhaps in response to the gloom, designers began using enameling and brightly colored rhinestones to create whimsical birds, flowers, circus animals, bows, dogs and just about every other figural form imaginable.

Retro Modern, 1939-1950. Other jewelry designs of the 1940s were big and bold. Retro Modern had a more substantial feel to it and designers began using larger stones to enhance the dramatic pieces. The jewelry was stylized and exaggerated. Common motifs included flowing scrolls, bows, ribbons, birds, animals, snakes, flowers and knots.

Sterling silver now became the metal of choice, often dipped in a gold wash known as vermeil.

Designers often incorporated patriotic themes of American flags, the V-sign, Uncle Sam's hat, airplanes, anchors and eagles.

Post-War Modern, 1945-1965. This was a movement that emphasized the artistic approach to jewelry making. It is also referred to as Mid-Century Modern. This approach was occurring at a time when the Beat Generation was prevalent. These avant-garde designers created jewelry that was handcrafted to illustrate the artist's own concepts and ideas. The materials often used were sterling, gold, copper, brass, enamel, cabochons, wood, quartz and amber.

1950s-1960s. The 1950s saw the rise of jewelry that was made purely of rhinestones: necklaces, bracelets, earrings and pins.

The focus of the early 1960s was on clean lines: pillbox hats and A-line dresses with short jackets were a mainstay for the conservative woman. The large, bold rhinestone pieces were no longer the must-have accessory. They were now replaced with smaller, more delicate gold-tone metal and faux pearls with only a hint of rhinestones.

At the other end of the spectrum was psychedelic-colored clothing, Nehru jackets, thigh-high miniskirts and go-go boots. These clothes were accessorized with beads, large metal pendants and occasionally big, bold rhinestones. By the late 1960s, there was a movement back to mother nature and the "hippie" look was born. Ethnic clothing, tie dye, long skirts, fringe and jeans were the prevalent style and the rhinestone had, for the most part, been left behind.

There are other areas of jewelry collecting that aren't defined by a period per se, but more by their styles and materials.

Novelty Jewelry is popular. From the 1920s through the 1960s, new materials in jewelry featured celluloid, Bakelite, Lucite, wood, leather and ceramics to create whimsical figurals, flowers, vegetables, animals, people, western themes and geometric designs.

Mexican Silver, 1930-1970. Mexican silversmiths first made jewelry for tourists. The jewelry had pre-Hispanic and traditional Mexican motifs as well as some abstract modern designs. Artisans used silver, a combination of silver with brass or copper, alpaca, amethysts, malachite, obsidian, sodalite, tiger eye, turquoise, abalone, ebony, rosewood and enameling to create their original designs. While hundreds of artists set up their shops in the town of Taxco, Mexico, in the 30s and 40s creating a silversmith guild, there are only a relatively small number of well-known artisans who gained their reputation for their designs and craftsmanship.

Scandinavian Silver: 1900—1960. Scandinavian jewelry is another collectible manufactured in Denmark, Norway, Finland and Sweden. The jewelry has a distinct look and is often identified by its use of flowers, foliates, animals, abstract and filigree designs. The materials also included bronze, gold, amber, amethyst, chrysoprase, citrine, crystal, lapis and enamel. The jewelry was generally produced in artists' studios and workshops where the focus was on design and craftsmanship.

Value: The value of a piece of jewelry is determined by condition, craftsmanship, scarcity and rarity, age and design. Condition is first and foremost, followed by quality. Look at the design of the piece. Is it intricate and ornate? Is it handmade or machine made? Greater detail and handwork will generally make a piece more valuable.

FINE JEWELRY

Bar pin

Art Deco

Platinum and diamond, bezel and bead-set with old European and single-cut diamonds, approx. total wt. 2.74 cts.....**$1,675**

Platinum and diamond, center old European-cut diamond weighing approx. 0.75 cts, further bead and bezel-set with fourteen old European-cut diamonds, millegrain accents, gold pin.. **$1,050**

Sapphires and pearls, A.J. Hedges & Co., alternately set with nine square sapphires and two rows of seed pearls, 14k yg mount, hallmark, 2 1/2" l **$300**

Edwardian, center line of bezel-set oval rubies, surrounded by 42 old European and full-cut diamonds, approx. total wt. 2.28 cts, platinum topped 14k gold mount, hallmark "AE K," Austrian guarantee mark **$3,525**

Etruscan Revival, 14k gold, rose gold arched terminals, applied bead and wirework dec..**$260**

Victorian, 14k yg, center carnelian intaglio of three cherubs within wirework frame, applied floral, bead, and ropetwist motifs **$420**

Bracelet

Art Deco

Articulated geometric links bead and bezel-set throughout with 318 old European, square, and single-cut diamonds, approx. total wt. 11.79 cts, millegrain accents and open platinum gallery, French guarantee stamps, 7 3/8" l..**$18,800**

Articulated links composed of 96 old European-cut and full-cut diamonds, approx. total wt 5.76 cts, channel-set onyx border, millegrain accents, platinum mount, signed "Tiffany & Co.," one onyx missing, 7 1/8" l...........**$16,450**

Flexible links set with 191 full-and baguette-cut diamonds weighing approx. 5.53 cts, platinum mount, missing one small diamond, 7" l...**$8,820**

Line of 40 prong-set old European-cut diamonds, framed by lines of channel-set square-cut emeralds, approx. total diamond wt. 3.98 cts, platinum mount with 18k white gold clasp, engraved gallery, one emerald missing, 7 1/4" l.**$5,400**

Set throughout with old European, single, baguette, and marquise-cut diamonds, platinum mount, approx. total wt. 1.86 cts, 7" l...**$3,000**

Seven center old mine and European-cut diamonds, approx. total wt. 1.75 cts, flanked by rectangular pierced links, 14k white gold, 7" l...**$1,410**

Seven rectangular step-cut sapphires alternating with flexible honeycomb of bead-set old European and single-cut diamonds, approx. total wt. 4.64 cts, platinum mount, stamped "MD," French platinum guarantee stamps, 7 1/8" l...**$16,500**

Art Nouveau, 14k yg, 10 openwork plaques in floral and scroll motif each centering collet-set sapphire, hallmark for Riker Bros., 7" l..**$4,300**

Arts & Crafts, five bezel-set cushion-cut sapphires alternating with five old European-cut diamonds, approx. total diamond wt. 2.00 cts, joined by oval links, millegrain accents, circa 1915, 7 3/4" l...**$3,645**

Photo courtesy of Skinner, Inc.

Lion bracelet, 9 kt gold and diamonds, star-set with old European-cut diamond melee, ruby eyes, bracelet of oval links, mkd AS, 7 1/2" l. **$560**

Photo courtesy of Skinner, Inc.

Bracelet, lava cameo, six cameos depicting Hermes, Diana and classical figures in profile, 10 kt gold mount, small losses, 6 3/4" l. **$1,060**

Photo courtesy of Sloans & Kenyon Auctioneers and Appraisers.

Slide bracelet, Victorian, 45 yellow gold, geometric slides, triple strand, ornamented with garnets, seed pearls, opals, enamel and other embellishments, panel form tongue-and-groove clasp. **$2,950**

Photo courtesy of David Rago Auctions, Inc.

R. Lalique bracelet, "Raisins," yellow amber, engraved R. Lalique, c1919, 3 1/4" d. **$2,040**

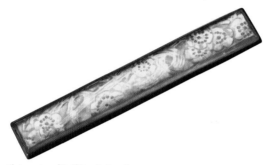

Photo courtesy of David Rago Auctions, Inc.

R. Lalique bar pin, "Barrette Aubepines," clear and frosted glass, gold reflective foil backing, orig gilt metal mount, mount stamped LALIQUE, c1912, 2 3/8" l. **$840**

Photo courtesy of Skinner, Inc.

Brooch, coral cameo, maiden with high-relief grapevine motifs, gilt-metal frame, ropetwist, engraved floral accents, 2 1/8" x 1 7/8". **$1,175**

Coin, 14k yg, heavy curb link chain suspending 1892 U.S. five-dollar coin in a wirework frame, 27.1 dwt., 6" l.....**$325**

Edwardian

Bangle, 14k yg, five bezel-set circular-cut sapphires within openwork design, 7" int. circumference.....................**$400**

Link, center old mine, European, and rose-cut diamonds in pierced and millegrain mount, flanked by knife-edge bar links, platinum-topped 18k gold, 6 1/2" l...............**$1,120**

Etruscan Revival, 18k yg, hinged bypass bangle terminating in two ram's heads, applied bead and wirework dec, 22.5 dwt, hallmark "P," evidence of solder, 6 1/2" int. circumference **$2,585**

Post-War Modern, Van Gogh, hinged bangle, 14k yg, overlapping textured gold leaves highlighted by prong-set circular-cut ruby, emerald, and sapphire accents, 13.8 dwt, signed "Van Gogh," circa 1950 ....**$530**

Retro Modern, double "tubogas"-style bracelet surmounted by bezel and bead-set old European-cut diamonds set in silver flowerheads, stems incorporating initials "H & L," 14k yg, French hallmarks...**$420**

Victorian

Bangle, 14k yg, seed pearl buckle motif, black and brown enamel accents, small dents, 6 1/4" d interior circumference...**$550**

Slide, 18k yg, mesh design with adjustable oval slide engraved with scroll and fleur-de-lis motifs, edged with palmettes dec with black tracery enamel, foxtail fringe terminals, 137.8 dwt **$1,200**

Brooch

Art Deco, diamond and platinum

Carved jade plaque depicting scrolling vines and gourds, corners accented by 22 single-cut diamonds, platinum frame, French guarantee stamps and hallmark......**$2,585**

Center old European-cut diamond weighing approx. 1.29 cts, frame of 78 French, baguette, and circular-cut diamonds, millegrain accents, platinum frame, signed "Raymond Yard"..**$5,650**

Photo courtesy of Skinner, Inc.

Brooch, 14 kt gold, hardstone cameo, maiden with upswept hair and diadem, double row of rose-cut diamond melee and seed pearls, 1 1/4" d. **$1,120**

Photo courtesy of Skinner, Inc.

Brooch, crescent, opal and diamond, fourteen cabochon opals of graduating size, old single and old mine-cut diamond melee highlights, gold mount, replaced pin stem, 1 7/8" l. estimated value **$400-$600**

Photo courtesy of Skinner, Inc.

Brooch, opal, seed pearl, and diamond crescent and starburst, 10 kt gold and opal crescent, old mine-cut diamond melee accents, 14kt gold, seed pearl, and opal starburst, latter with American maker's mk, reverse with minor evidence of solder. **$700**

Photo courtesy of Skinner, Inc.

Brooch amethyst and gold, prong-set, oval-cut amethyst 20.22 x 15.19 x 12.02 mm; frame with applied bead and ropetwist accents, minor dents, 1 1/2" x 1 1/4". **$420**

Art Nouveau

Floral spray, white-cream translucent enamel lilies centered by cultured pearls, green enamel leaves, joined by gold coiled cord, 14k polished gold stems **$750**

Orchid, light greenish-yellow and purple openwork leaves, baroque pearl and old European-cut diamond highlights, retractable bail, 14k gold **$1,275**

Arts & Crafts, Josephine Hartwell Shaw, 14k yg, center bezel-set oval amethyst surrounded by grapevine motif, signed. **$3,410**

Edwardian

Navette-form openwork brooch set with fancy-cut aquamarine and rose-cut diamonds **$600**

Photo courtesy of Skinner, Inc.

Brooch, Pietra Dura, 18kt gold, bellflower design, mount with ropetwist and wirework accents, later pin stem, 1 1/2" d. **$300**

Sword and scabbard, 14k yg, connected by trace link chain, seed pearls, four prong-set old European-cut diamond accents **$235**

Post-War Modern

Robert Altman, 14k yg, seated poodle, prong-set with ruby, emerald, and sapphire highlights, 11.7 dwt, signed **$470**

Richard Fishman, 24k yg, hand-formed openwork abstract circular brooch, signed "Richard Fishman 1979" **$940**

Renaissance Revival, T.B. Starr, 18k yg, scrolling form, black and white enamel, seven cultured pearl accents, hair compartment on verso, signed **$1,645**

Photo courtesy of Sloans & Kenyon Auctioneers and Appraisers.

Brooch, platinum and diamond, pierced geometric clips, pr, joined together as brooch, approx. 208 brilliant-cut old European cut and baguette diamonds, overall 10 ct; c1940, 3 1/4" l. **$7,080**

Photo courtesy of Sloans & Kenyon Auctioneers and Appraisers.

Earrings, pr, dangle, Victorian, yellow gold, oval citrine centered in floral stetting, granulation dec, free-swinging citrine pendant with matching floral surround, wire backs, 1 3/4" l. **$740**

Photo courtesy of Sloans & Kenyon Auctioneers and Appraisers.

Picture locket, Victorian, yellow-gold, front applied lion mask, Renaissance Revival style, jeweled eyes and gemstone clenched in paws, 1 3/8" d. **$475**

Retro Modern, Swirl, star and prong-set with full-cut diamond and ruby melee, flexible snake-chain terminals, 14k, 30.8 dwt..**$825**

Victorian, 14k yg, boss framed by rope motifs terminating in double tassels star-set with rose-cut diamond melee...... **$300**

Buckle

Edwardian, rectangular openwork buckle edged with demantoid garnets spaced by old European-cut diamonds, silver-topped gold mount..**$1,380**

Cuff links, pair

Platinum and diamond, geometric design, ten 0.10 carat round brilliant cut diamonds, 14.40 dwts **$490**

Platinum, ruby, and blue sapphire, two fine 0.40 carat rubies, two fine oval 0.40 carat blue sapphires, 12.40 dwts.........**$490**

Dress clips, pair
Art Deco

Platinum, two marquise shaped 1.20 carats diamonds, eighteen baguette cut 1.60 carats total diamonds, two 0.20 carat marquise shape diamonds, numerous small transitional round brilliant cut diamonds (2.50 carats total), 13.60 dwts..**$5,260**

18k yg, WM Wise & Son, 18k yg, shield form, bead and bezel-set with old European-cut and single-cut diamonds, approx. total wt. 0.88 cts, millegrain accents, signed..**$1,880**

Earrings

Art Deco, pendant-type, each with jadeite cabochon and bead-set single-cut diamonds suspending jadeite drop, platinum mount, later silver screw-back findings, missing one diamond..**$1,765**

Etruscan Revival, 14k yg, pendant-type, coach cover, applied bead and wirework accents, later findings.....**$1,540**

Postwar Modern

Kanaris, 18k yg, dogwood blossoms, signed "Kanaris," 14.3 dwt..**$475**

Tiffany & Co., 18k yg, aventurine quartz, carved knot, signed..**$1,000**

Retro Modern, clips, 14k yg, abstracted floral form with circular-cut sapphires and cultured pearls, signed "Tiffany & Co." **$450**

Victorian, pendant-type, gold, engraved foliate tops suspending two gold balls... **$920**

Lavaliere
Edwardian

Amethyst, 14k gold, centered by oval amethyst within openwork scrolled frame surmounted by seed pearl trefoil, suspending similar drop, joined by trace link chain, 15" l **$450**

Platinum, heart-shape aquamarine suspends two collet-set old European-cut diamonds with pear-shape aquamarine terminal, three pearl accents, fine 14k white gold ropetwist chain **$1,410**

Egyptian Revival, 14k gold, centered by amethyst intaglio scarab within shaped lotus flower mount, baroque pearl drop terminal, stylized floral links, amethyst intaglio scarabs set at intervals, 16 1/2" l **$1,380**

Locket

Art Deco, 15k gold, sq black enamel locket unfolding to reveal six pages suspended from black enamel baton and fancy link chain, 28" l.. **$650**

Art Nouveau, 14k yg, helmeted Roman warrior in center, old European-cut diamond highlight, 4.4 dwt.............. **$150**

Edwardian, Carrington & Co., circular white enamel and green guilloche enamel locket accented by an old European-cut diamond, platinum trace link chain alt. with green and white enamel baton links, hallmark, some enamel loss to locket, 20" l **$1,590**

Victorian, 14k yg

Oval, turquoise enamel and five stars with old mine-cut diamond accents, reverse with hair compartment, pendant hook, later trace link chain, evidence of solder **$325**

Pale yellow gold engraved disc surrounded by deeper gold, heavily engraved frame, rose and white gold curb-link chain, 24.7 dwt **$365**

Necklace
Art Nouveau

Butterfly with bezel-set amethysts, seed pearl border, old European-cut diamond highlight, later amethyst drop, suspended later 14k gold and amethyst bead necklace, 16 1/2" l **$1,120**

Three center shaped cartouches designed with florettes and scrolls, joined by baton-shaped fancy links, 18k yg, French guarantee stamp, 6.5 dwt, 16" l **$1,000**

Arts and Crafts, elliptical-shaped jade within conforming enamel scrolled links joined by trace link chains, similarly set pendant suspending three jade drops, 18k gold, signed "Tiffany & Co.," some enamel loss, 18" l................... **$31,050**

Edwardian

Center articulated seed pearl and old European-cut diamond scrolling floral vine, joined by ropetwist chain, 15k gold, 15" l.. **$940**

Turquoise cabochons joined by delicate trace link chain, 10k gold mount, fringe loss to central tassel, 15" l.... **$450**

Etruscan Revival, Ivy leaf and berry motif, barrel clasp, 18kt yg, 15 3/8" l.. **$2,850**

Retro Modern, 14k yg, each link designed as leaf surmounting a ring, convertible to two bracelets, 72.8 dwt, 17" l.. **$1,120**

Victorian

14k gold and garnet, three floral engraved medallions surmounted by emerald-cut garnets set in ropetwist frames, reverse with plaited hair locket, suspended from snake chain, 16 1/2" l... **$420**

18k yg, 18 concave disks centering coral bead within gold wirework frames, joined by oval-shaped links, some replaced beads and links **$1,650**

Negligee
Edwardian

Floral and foliate elements, old European and old mine-cut diamond, seed pearl accents, platinum mounts, one melee missing, later 19 1/2" l 14k white gold fancy link chain... **$3,055**

Two rose-cut diamond flower terminals framed by calibre-cut rubies suspended from knife-edge bar links highlighted by bezel-set full and rose-cut diamonds, millegrain accents, platinum and 18k gold mount, orig fitted Parisian jeweler's box, 20" l fancy link chain................................... **$4,935**

Pearls
Bracelet

Caged freshwater pearls interspersed with 18k gold beads with applied wirework, convertible to necklace with 14k gold rope chain, 8" l **$425**

Photo courtesy of David Rago Auctions, Inc.

Pendant, Edward Colonna for L'Art Nouveau Bing, Paris, light green enamel, triangular pearl and dentile pearl, mine-cut diamond, 28k yellow gold with platinum, each length of chain 9", c1900, 1 3/4" x 1 1/2". **$3,820**

Seventy-two white cultured pearls with rose overtones, measuring approx. 5.90 to 6.0 mm, 14k white gold bar spacers and clasp with 11 full-cut diamond highlights, 7 1/4" l...**$725**

Brooch, Mikimoto, 14k yg, designed as abstract leaf with clusters of cultured pearl flowers, signed........................**$420**

Earclips, pr

Button pearl suspending chain link button pearl and diamond set cap terminating in teardrop shape pearl, set in 18k white gold, probably natural pearls............**$3,300**

Elizabeth Locke, center gray pearl within 18k gold frame, hallmark..**$1,880**

Necklace

Baroque, 31 South Sea Baroque pearls graduating in size from 10.70mm to 16.20mm, 14k white gold boule with diamond melee, 19 1/2" l...................................**$4,700**

Cultured, David Webb, 31 graduated pearls measuring approx. 9.08 to 12.78 mm, invisible pearl and 14k white gold clasp, 16" l...**$1,530**

Cultured, one hundred twenty-nine pearls ranging in size from 6.7 to 7.5 mm, 14k gold gem-set clasp, 14 1/2" l....**$410**

Pendant

Art Deco

Platinum, numerous small old European cut diamonds (3.70 carats total), 18k white gold chain, 10.90 dwts..........**$4,185**

Sterling silver, coral and black enamel, Theodore Fahrner, offset by two rectangular faceted black stone panels (probably onyx), gilt chain mkd "935," pendant stamped "TF (linked) 935" **$1,880**

Art Nouveau

Collet-set sapphires and diamonds set within trefoil open wirework form, accented by rose-cut diamond points, joined by later festoons of fine trace link chain terminating in rose and circular-cut diamonds within triangular frames, later clasp, 18 1/2" l...................**$1,410**

Photo courtesy of Skinner, Inc.

Pendant brooch, emerald and diamond, Portugal, collet and bead-set, oval and step-cut foil back emeralds, rose-cut diamond highlights, silver and gold mount, hallmarks, 2 1/2" l. **$1,295**

Photo courtesy of David Rago Auctions, Inc.

Engagement ring, diamond, platinum box mount, flanked by channel-set rows of three single-cut diamonds, center European cut, 1.5 cts, size 7. **$2,940**

Photo courtesy of Sloans & Kenyon Auctioneers and Appraisers.

Lady's pendant watch, hunting case, chased floral dec front and back, 14k yellow gold, cartouche on engine-turned ground, 18k heavy rope chain with swivel, Waltham. **$740**

Plique-a-jour enamel, lavender and green irid enamel flowers, green, pink, and white plique-a-jour enamel leaves, rose-cut diamonds and pearl accents, 18k gold mount with later faux pearl chain **$1,265**

Cartier, designed as cross composed of eleven rectangular-cut aquamarines, 18k yg, signed, provenance: from estate of Reverend Thomas Mary O'Leary (1875-1949), Bishop of Springfield.. **$1,410**

Edwardian

Platinum top, 18k yg, four 3.00 mm pearls, one old European cut diamond, 24 rose-cut diamonds (0.34 carat total) 4.70 dwts.. **$1,100**

Platinum top, 18k yg, one old European 0.60 carat diamond, 59 rose-cut diamonds (0.70 carat total) suspended from 14k white gold chain, 3.40 dwts **$1,920**

Renaissance Revival, shield form with Renaissance motifs, rose-cut diamonds, rubies, pearls and emerald, cobalt blue enamel highlights, silver-topped 18k gold mount **$885**

Victorian

Circular pendant edged by gold beads and decorated with black tracery enamel, suspending gold bead pendants, fancy double trace link chain, 14k yg, 14.1 dwt., 23 1/2" l....... **$385**

Pietra dura, rose branch, one open flower, two buds, inlaid in shades of pink, varying shades of green as leaves, 14k rose gold bezel and bale **$400**

Pendant/brooch

Art Deco, platinum, navette set with five old mine and European-cut diamonds weighing approx. 5.33 cts, further surrounded by 142 bead-set old mine and European-cut diamonds weighing approx. 13.32 cts, approx. total wt. for all diamonds, 18.65 cts, provenance: accompanied by orig sketch by designer, Edmond Frisch, 336 Park Ave., New York **$9,900**

Art Nouveau, 14k yg, circular-shaped, profile of classical woman accented by chased gold hair, enameled earring and face... **$1,000**

Edwardian, 14k yg, scrolling form set throughout with rose-cut diamonds and pearls, three freshwater pearl and diamond drops **$715**

Victorian, 14k yg

Enameled inverted horseshoe framing three rounded forms, engraved accents, seed pearl highlights, 15.6 dwt, fitted box from Savage & Lyman Jewellers, Montreal **$600**

Openwork scrolling form bezel-set with three oval amethysts, suspending drop with pear-shape amethyst, chain festoons, 18.5 dwt, boxed **$1,000**

Pin

Art Nouveau

Dogwood blossom, center old European-cut diamond weighing approx. 0.50 cts, black enamel, 14k yg, American hallmark... **$775**

Lady in profile, 18k yg, rose-cut diamond accent, French guarantee stamps, signed "TW" **$325**

Edwardian, starburst, center 10.32 x 6.18 mm greenish-brown oval tourmaline, surrounded by sixteen old European-cut diamonds mounted on 14k gold rays, evidence of solder, possibly color change tourmaline, color changes to golden-olive color **$1,175**

Postwar Modern, duckling, 14k gold, freshwater pearl wings, red stone eye, signed "Ruser" **$390**

Victorian, 18k, tapering silver-topped baton with graduated bead-set rose-cut diamonds, entwined with engraved yellow gold form completed by pearl, French guarantee stamp **$350**

Ring, Lady's

Art Deco, platinum and diamond

Center rectangular step-cut emerald framed by eight full-cut diamond melee, millegrain accents, open gallery and foliate engraved shoulders **$940**

Rounded form centering bezel-set old European-cut diamond flanked by lines of channel-set sapphires, set throughout with bead-set old European-cut diamonds, approx. total wt. 0.98 cts, millegrain accents **$1,175**

Art Deco, 14k white gold, center bead-set transitional-cut diamond within raised octagonal-shaped mount, openwork gallery with millegrain accents, approx. diamond wt. 0.87 cts... **$2,350**

Art Nouveau, 18k yg, shaped rectangular plaque etched with initials "HP" flanked by stylized flowers within open and ribbed shank, inscribed "Vitaline a Hubert, 2 Jan. 1910," size 7 1/2 .... **$355**

Arts & Crafts, 14k yg, three circular-cut pink sapphires, white pearl set among swirling leaves and vines continuing to shoulders, sized **$1,175**

Edwardian

Bezel-set fancy-cut aquamarine flanked by single rose-cut diamonds, silver-topped 18k gold mounts............... **$575**

Intaglio, orange and white carnelian, winged dragon with flower in mouth, 18k yg, 7.20 dwts **$160**

Retro Modern, Birks, platinum, pave-set single-cut diamond buckle motif, channel-set with graduating line of sq step-cut sapphires.. **$2,000**

Victorian, snake, tri-color gold engraved body, (approx total 0.45 cts) old European-cut diamond, stones missing from eyes **$410**

Ring, carved oval carnelian cabochon, profile of classical warrior, Victorian, yellow gold, shank has delicate reeding and chasing. **$240**

Photo courtesy of Sloans & Kenyon Auctioneers and Appraisers.

Pin, floral bouquet form, four graduated flower heads, seven leaves and stem, three old mine cut, one brilliant cut, and numerous rose-cut diamonds, 38 round rubies, 53 round sapphires. **$1,420**

Stickpin

Art Deco, platinum

Cartier, Y-shaped form, two cultured pearls, bead-set diamond melee, no. 2608, French maker's mark, signed **$765**

Channel set rubies with diamond melee **$475**

Sugarloaf sapphire cabochon with diamond melee and ruby accents **$425**

Art Nouveau

Enameled woman, hallmark for Alling & Co., gold **$400**

Edwardian, nine bead-set old European-cut diamonds, set in platinum, centered by cultured pearl in floret design, 14k gold shank **$775**

Egyptian Revival, enameled asps framing turquoise cabochon, 14k yg **$115**

Victorian, flowerhead design centering a round opal framed by 11 old mine-cut diamonds, 14k yg setting **$360**

Suite, Lady's

Brooch and ear pendants

Coral, agate chalcedony, brooch with center coral bead within engraved reserve framed by milky agate chalcedony, ear pendants ensuite **$625**

Coral, each with carved coral rose blossoms and foliage on 14k gold stems, boxed **$235**

Pendant/brooch and earclips, all with circular-cut amethysts and foxtail fringe, 14k yg, brooch signed "W. & S.B.," boxed, earrings with later screw-back findings, evidence of solder **$1,175**

Revival-style, bracelet and ring, 14k, hinged flexible braided bangle centering three contiguous balls with wirework and applied bead decoration, ring ensuite, 14.4 dwt, bangle slightly misshaped **$470**

Victorian, demi-parure

Bracelet and earrings, bracelet composed of 15k gold florets with turquoise cabochons; pr earrings each with two 14k gold circles with turquoise cabochons suspending three small drops, 7 3/4" l bracelet **$1,765**

Watches, Pocket

History: Pocket watches can be found in many places—from flea markets to the specialized jewelry auctions. Condition of movement is the first priority; design and detailing of the case is second.

Descriptions of pocket watches may include the size (16/0 to 20), number of jewels in the movement, whether the face is open or closed (hunter), and the composition (gold, gold filled, or some other metal). The movement is the critical element, since cases often were switched. However, an elaborate case, especially if gold, adds significantly to value.

Pocket watches designed to railroad specifications are desirable. They are between 16 and 18 in size, have a minimum of 17 jewels, adjust to at least five positions, and conform to many other specifications. All are open faced.

Study the field thoroughly before buying. There is a vast amount of literature, including books and newsletters from clubs and collectors.

Pocket, Gentleman's

Aurora, Size 18, Roman numeral dial, lever set 15 jewel gilt movement #38691, Grade 3 1/2 Guild, second model, yellow gold-filled hunting case #5161726 .... **$200**

Ball, Size 16, Arabic numeral dial, lever set 17 jewel nickel movement #134015, Official Standard, Waltham model, white gold-filled Illinois hunting case #51032 .... **$500**

Borel, Size 19, Roman numeral dial, lever set 20 jewel gilt movement #15110, Minute Repeater, chronograph, 14 karat yellow gold hunting case #6947 .... **$2,650**

Burlington, Size 16, open face Arabic numeral dial, lever set 17 jewel nickel movement #3447536, Illinois, yellow gold-filled case #5001237 .... **$110**

Elgin

Size 6, Roman numeral dial, pendant set 7 jewel nickel movement #10652232, first model, yellow gold-filled Wadsworth hunting case #316391 .... **$140**

Size 12, Arabic numeral dial, pendant set 17 jewel nickel movement #16472602, yellow gold-filled Dueber hunting case #9305829.. **$120**

Size 12, open face Arabic numeral dial, pendant set 19 jewel nickel movement #25254082, C.H. Hulburd 431, platinum case #103820 .... **$1,100**

Size 16, open face Arabic numeral dial, lever set 19 jewel nickel movement #21235315, B.W. Raymond, yellow gold-filled case #8048 .... **$215**

English, brass, key-wind, swing-out case, orig paper retailer's label "Thomas Harrison Silver-Smith Danville KY Clock and Watch Maker," iron forged chain and key, early 19th century.. **$1,700**

Hamilton

Size 16, Arabic numeral dial, lever set 21 jewel nickel movement #776560, Grade 993, yellow gold-filled Illinois engraved hunting case #2922269 .... **$330**

Size 18, Roman numeral dial, lever set 17 jewel nickel movement #157179, Grade 925 The Union, yellow gold-filled hunting case **$175**

Hampden

Size 16, Arabic numeral dial, lever set 17 jewel nickel movement #1890116, William McKinley, BRDG, in a yellow gold-filled hunting case #6028660 .... **$165**

Size 16, open face Arabic numeral dial, lever set 23 jewel nickel movement #2801029, Grade 104, Bridge model, glass back nickel case.. **$350**

Size 18, Roman numeral dial, lever set 17 jewel nickel movement #1332191, Adjusted, silverine Dueber hunting case #2942431.. **$90**

Howard

Size 12, open face Arabic numeral dial, pendant set 17 jewel nickel movement #1092624, Series 8, 14 karat yellow gold monogrammed case #121454 .... **$360**

Size 16, open face Arabic numeral dial, lever set 21 jewel nickel movement #1361149, RR Chronometer Ser, white gold-filled Keystone case #1554922............................ **$300**

Illinois

Size 16, open face Arabic numeral dial, pendant set 17 jewel nickel movement #3136048, Texas Special, yellow gold-filled case #6287230..**$120**

Photo courtesy of Sloans & Kenyon Auctioneers and Appraisers.

Pocket watch, open face, railroad grade, yellow gold-plated, smooth polished case, rev engraved, old English script "G," white enamel face, Montgomery dial, serial #1182338, Howard Watch Co., Boston, c1913. **$385**

Photo courtesy of Green Valley Auctions.

Tiara, Victorian shell cameo, filigree, 18k gold, cameo set as removable brooch, 1.33 troy oz total weight, second half 19th century, cameo diameter 5/8" x 3/4". **$990**

Size 18, Roman numeral dial, lever set 11 jewel nickel movement #231676, yellow gold-filled hunting case #143231 .... **$150**

Montgomery Ward

Size 18, open face Roman numeral dial, lever set 21 jewel nickel movement #1448074, Grade 61, sixth model, 10 karat yellow rolled gold plate Illinois case #7769495.

.... **$175**

Size 18, open face Roman numeral dial, pendant set 11 jewel nickel movement #757650, 20th C, silverine Dueber case #4280 .... **$75**

Waltham

Size 14, Roman numeral dial, pendant set 13 jewel nickel movement #3127180, Chronograph, first model, coin silver American hunting case #21280 .... **$150**

Size 16, open face Arabic numeral dial, lever set 21 jewel nickel movement #20142536, Crescent St.U-D, model 1908, with wind indicator, yellow gold-filled case #9308103 .... **$900**

Pocket, Lady's

Betsy Ross, Size 0, open face Arabic numeral dial, pendant set 7 jewel nickel movement #861180, yellow gold-filled Keystone case #8186017 .... **$100**

Elgin, Size 0, Roman numeral dial, pendant set 15 jewel nickel movement #8773791, first model, yellow gold-filled Wadsworth hunting case #667982 .... **$120**

Meylan, C. H., 18k gold and enamel, open-face, white enamel dial with black Arabic numerals, fancy scrolled hands, gray guilloche enamel bezel, cover enameled with gold flowers set with diamonds, suspended from platinum and purple guilloche enamel baton link chain, crystal replaced, minor enamel loss **$850**

Vacheron & Constantin, 18k gold, hunting case, white enamel dial, Roman numerals, gilt bar movement, cylinder escapement, signed on cuvette, engraved case, size 10.

.... **$350**

Waltham, 14k yg, hunting case, white enamel dial, Arabic numeral indicators, subsidiary seconds dial, Lady Waltham jeweled nickel movement by A.W.W. Co., floral engraved case no. 224709, 0 size, gold ropetwist chain **$300**

Photo courtesy of Sloans & Kenyon Auctioneers and Appraisers

Watches, pocket, ladies, hunting cases; first designed with decorated circular dial with Roman numerals and "Louis XIV hands," within engraved scenic case set in 18k yellow gold, key wind and set; second designed with white circular dial with Roman numerals, "spade" hands, set in 14k yellow gold. **$450 pair**

Watches, Wrist

The first true wristwatch appeared about 1850. However, the key date is 1880, when the stylish, decorative wristwatch appeared to almost universal acceptance. The technology used to create the wristwatch existed in the early 19th century with Brequet's shock-absorbing "Parachute System" for automatic watches, and Adrien Philippe's winding stem.

Gentleman's

Boucheron, dress tank, A250565, white gold, reeded bezel and dial, invisible clasp, black leather Boucheron strap, French hallmarks, orig leather pouch **$2,150**

Cartier, 18k hg, rectangular convex white dial, black Roman numerals, round gold bezel, black leather strap **$1,380**

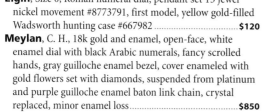

Photo courtesy of Wiederseim Associates Inc.

Pocket watch, Patek, Philippe & Co., #74501, 18k gold, with watch chain and fob, also signed "Crowell & Hubbard, Cleveland, Ohio," 1885-1890. **$2,600**

Photo courtesy of Sloans & Kenyon Auctioneers and Appraisers.

Lady's wristwatch, oval dial, Arabic numerals, platinum trim case with calibré-cut diamonds and sapphires, new leather strap, dial signed "Hamilton," c1930, 18k white gold and platinum. **$445**

Concord, Delirium, 18k gold, round goldtone dial without indicators, flat rectangular bezel, quartz movement, Swiss hallmarks, orig crocodile band, 9" l **$1,265**

Garsons, 14k gold, sq goldtone dial with simulated jewel indicators, 17-jewel nickel movement, subsidiary seconds dial, integrated mesh band, 8 1/4" l **$345**

Hamilton, 18k yg, silverized rectangular dial, applied Arabic numerals, subsidiary seconds dial, 19 jewel movement, black leather strap **$180**

Jurgensen, Jules, dress, 14k white gold, Swiss movement, silvertone brushed dial, abstract indicators, diamond-set bevel, black faux alligator strap **$290**

Longines, pale green rectangular dial, applied diamond set platinum Arabic numerals with small round and baguette cut diamonds, 15 jewel adjusted movement #3731402, case back engraved and dated 1935 .... **$2,035**

Nardin, Ulysse, 14k yg, chronometer, goldtone dial, luminescent quarter sections, applied abstract and Arabic numeral indicators, subsidiary seconds dial, lugs with scroll accents, leather strap, discoloration and scratches to dial **$270**

Omega, 18k yg, round cream dial, goldtone Arabic numeral and abstract indicators, heavy mesh bracelet, mild soil to dial, 44.80 dwt **$460**

Patek Philippe, 18k yg

Round ivory tone dial with stick indicators, later 18k gold band, circa 1960 .... **$2,700**

Silvertone metal dial, raised indicators, subsidiary seconds dial, movement #977714, reference #2470, triple signed, leather strap, circa 1949 .... **$6,230**

Frattone, 14kt yg, 18 jewel Swiss movement, black leather band **$175**

Rolex, Oyster Perpetual

14k yg, goldtone dial, abstract indicators, sweep second hand, ostrich strap, slight spotting to dial **$850**

Datejust, two tone **$2,600**

Vacheron & Constantin, 18k gold, white round dial, abstract numeral indicators, 17-jewel nickel movements, associated 18k gold brickwork band, 7 1/4" l **$1,495**

Lady's

Bulova, small round dial with Arabic and baton numerals, 17 jewel movement, 14k white gold case and bracelet set with single cut and baguette cut diamonds weighing approx 1.50 carats total **$760**

Cartier, Tank Francaise, 18k yg, rectangular ivory tone dial with Roman numeral indicators, gold band with integral clasp **$5,875**

Chanel, 18k yg, black and white dial with Roman numeral indicators, onyx cabochon winding stem, enclosing Swiss quartz movement, adjustable black alligator band and 18k gold clasp, signed **$1,300**

Elgin, platinum, rectangular ivory tone dial with Arabic numerals, 17 jewel movement, bezel, lugs, and bracelet set with single-cut and baguette diamonds, 6 1/2" l **$1,410**

Grenchen, Nivada, Swiss, 14kt white gold, 17 jewels, six 2.2 mm round diamonds, 38 1.6 mm round diamonds on watch, band with 52 diamond accents, approx 1.50 ctw, 14.4 grams **$500**

Gruen, Art Deco, platinum, rectangular silvertone dial, black Arabic numerals, bezel enhanced with 32 circular-cut diamonds, mesh strap edged by box-set single-cut diamonds, highlighted by diamond-set floret shoulders, 6 1/4" l **$4,225**

Hamilton, platinum, rectangular ivory tone dial with Arabic numeral indicators, 17 jewel movement, bezel and lugs with single-cut and baguette diamonds, joining cord band, missing winding stem **$300**

Helbros Watch Co., 17 jewels, Art Deco, combination of old European and single cut diamonds, approx 1 ct, case hinged to allow better contour when worn, calibre French cut sapphires, curved crystal, platinum setting **$995**

Movado

18k yg, rectangular gold tone dial with Arabic numeral and dot indicators, 15 jewel movement, 14k gold link band **$765**

Stainless steel, yg, mother-of-pearl dial, diamond set bezel containing thirty-six round brilliant cut diamonds weighing approx 0.72 carat total, quartz movement, deployment buckle **$525**

Pailet, Andrew, 14kt yg, diamonds around face, quartz movement, approx 1 ct TDW **$500**

Patek Philippe & Co., rectangular gold metallic enamel dial, Arabic and dot numerals, movement #940981, case # 509109; dial, movement, 18k yg, case and bracelet signed "Patek-Philippe & Co Geneve," circa 1940, 46.60 dwt, 8 1/2" l **$3,350**

Rolex, 14kt yg, Spendel band, 17 jewels, face discolored **$60**

Rolex, platinum 3 extra diamond links, diamond bezel and diamond studded band, 2.38 ctw **$2,875**

Swiss, 18k yg, Swiss movement, manual wind, domed bezel, goldtone dial, black Roman numerals, hallmark, leather strap **$920**

Watch fob

Art Nouveau

Carter Howe & Co., 14k yg, triple link chain composed of lotus buds and flowers joined by trace links suspending double griffin-head seal, hallmark **$940**

Whiteside & Blank, 14k yg, heart-shaped leaves and sinuous vine motifs joined by grosgrain strap, hallmark **$400**

COSTUME JEWELRY

Bangle/Bracelet

Bakelite, Applejuice, carved, hinged bangle with rhinestones..**$425**

Bakelite bangle, marbled green with rhinestones......**$950**

Cameo bracelet, black Bakelite and celluloid..**$350**

Jade, SS, four oval jade plaques pierced and carved with floral motifs, joined by woven foxtail chain bracelet, 7 1/4" l......**$175**

Postwar Modern, Hermes, sterling silver, heavy flattened anchor links, signed, 7 3/4" l.........................**$1,100**

Thermoplastic, yellow, five holes surrounded by aurora borealis rhinestones, hinged bangle **$225**

Victorian, French Jet snake wrap............................**$145**

Victorian, gold-filled wraparound bracelet.................**$185**

Brooch

Art Nouveau, Trout, basse-taille greenish-blue fading to pinkish-white iridescent translucent enamel................**$850**

Cameo brooch, hardstone, gold-filled frame **$195**

Edwardian, heart-shape form set throughout with seed pearls, highlighted by two bezel-set peridots, English 9k stamp, 10k gold paper clip chain, 16 3/4" l **$500**

Leaf brooch, cluster of stemmed leaves, moonglow with rhinestones on foliage **$110**

Nautical, intaglio of ship and water, Bakelite.................**$235**

Nautical, butterscotch Bakelite and wood......................**$350**

Turtle brooch, green Bakelite cabochon shell on wooden body...**$225**

Buckle

Art Nouveau, sterling silver, two repoussé plaques of female faces with flowing hair and flower blossoms, hallmark for William B. Kerr & Co. **$300**

Cameo

Pendant/brooch, Victorian, 14k gold, shell cameo habille bead-set with an old European-cut diamond set within frame, retractable bail, solder to neckchain on reverse **$180**

Pendant necklace, Victorian, 14k gold, hardstone, carnelian agate cameo within oval frame with applied foliate motifs and flexible fringe, pendant bail missing suspended element, suspended from 18" l chain...........**$450**

Earrings

Bow-shaped, brushed goldtone metal, 1960s.................**$15**

Ear cover earrings, paisley shaped, covered with clear rhinestones...**$125**

Round-shaped, red enamel flower at center, surrounded by two rings of faux pearls, followed by a ring of red enamel fleurs-de-lis and a final row of faux pearls, Robert.......**$125**

Necklace

Art Deco, negligee, faux pearl drops, purple enameled links with faux pearl spacers, 1920s.............................**$85**

Bakelite, butterscotch, beaded **$225**

Celluloid, with 21 assorted celluloid charms.................**$325**

Handmade pendant, on goldtone chain, green glass, Denmark **$195**

Victorian, locket on chain, seed pearl cross motif, circa 1880 ....**$225**

Ring, gentleman's

Cameo

Black, white, and brown agate, carved Jesus profile, yellow gold setting, 4.80 dwts, late 19th century..................**$215**

Coral, red, Socrates portrait, 14k yg, 6.30 dwts, mid-19th century **$400**

Medium blue-green beryl, bearded soldier in high relief profile, vg, Victorian, 5.80 dwts................................**$575**

Enamel, multicolored, black onyx, portrait of North African gentleman with red and green stripes, yg, Victorian, 5.00 dwts **$250**

Intaglio

Carnelian, Hermes with staff, 14k yg, 8.80 dwts **$275**

Rhodolite garnet, Romulous and Remus in profile, yg, 5.10 dwts...**$300**

Seal, black and white agate intaglio, coat of arms, 14k yg, 6.30 dwts **$120**

Figural Costume Jewelry

A popular category in figural costume jewelry is the face pin. For more information, consult *Warman's Costume Jewelry Figurals* by Kathy Flood, 2007.

Exotic 'Cambodian Prince' brooch, bronze-copper finish over pot metal, large rhinestones set into gunmetal headpiece setting, huge ruby-colored rose-montee centerpiece stone, unsigned, 1940s, 3 1/4". **$250-$500**
Possibly a Reinad piece intended for Carnegie or Eisenberg.

"Apache and Putain" fur clips, dimensional, enameled pot metal, hollow eyes, RS-accented neckerchiefs, 3-D cigarette in gigolo's mouth, signed Coro, 1942, 2 1/4" and 2 1/2". **$75-$250 each**

"La Dame aux Camellias" (Camille) brooch, enameled, gilded rhodium, mask-like face surrounded by flowers, unsigned but still tagged Coro, 1940s, 3". **$200-$250**

White Lady fur clip, pave-set RS curls, enameled face and accent flowers, hollow eyes, signed Coro, 1938-42, 2 1/8". **$150**

Jeweled Face brooch, hollow eyes, pave-set RS face, enameled eyebrows, lips, multicolor mix of square cuts, teardrops and baguettes, unsigned Reinad or Mazer design, 1938-42, 2 1/4". **$150**

Glitz Face pin, large pave-set RS, two-tone metal turban wrap, powder-blue bindi jewel, glittering earrings, 1980s-90s, 2 1/4". **$25-$50**

Turbaned head fur clip, large prong-set ruby jewel bindi, exotic hollow eyes, gilded base metal, signed Mazer, 1938-42, 3". **$250-$300**

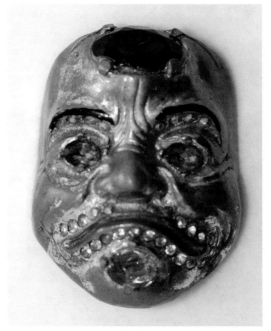

Buddha Face pin, pot metal, embedded prong-set jewels, same visage also seen gold-plated, with 'Chanel beard' (strands of Chanel-style necklace) and signed Eisenberg Original, unsigned, 1930s, 1 3/4". **$75-$150**

Brunette Beauty fur clip, gold-plated enameled lady with headdress (strongly resembles the huge Eisenberg Original so-called 'Mayan Mask'), unsigned, 1938-42, 2 1/4". **$150+**

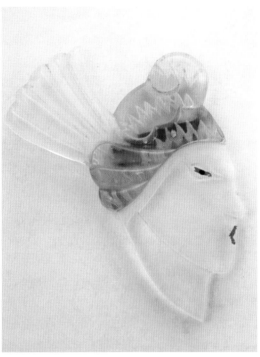

Alien Geisha face brooch, faceted navettes give an eerie or other-worldly look, highly unusual, coppery finish on deeply cast metal, 1935-42, unsigned but likely Reinad, rare, 3"+. **$500**

Feathered Flapper pin, carved and reverse-carved painted and dyed Lucite, unsigned, 1940s, 3 5/8". **$150+**

Joan of Arc brooch, helmeted, painted porcelain face/head on gilded fleur-de-lys, signed Freirich, 1960s, 2 1/4". **$100** The Maid of Orleans and the fleur-de-lys are pertinent symbol of the company's heritage and its origins as Maison David in France.

Flapper in profile, RS chain, ivory resin, illegible signature, date unknown, 2 1/4". **$50**

Jeweled headdress mask brooch, hollow, heavy, double-sided gilded face mask with two rows of inset twisted wires topped with 12 polychrome baguettes, each accented with crystal chatons; unsigned Fashioncraft Robert, 1940, 3". **$250**

Masterpiece Mask brooch, gilded metal, heavily jeweled with multi-cut, multicolor stones, elaborate array of chain strands as hair (remain partially erect and springy when brought forward), signed Fashioncraft Robert, 6". **$300-$500**

Exotic mask brooch, antiqued silver-plated metal, face with flourish or beard of 50 silver bell charms, five ruby cabochons inset into graduated raised bezels, 1970s, unsigned, 4". **$150-$200**

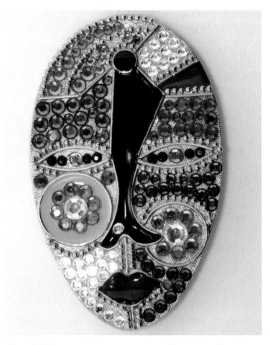

Riot of Colors mask pin, enamels and brightly colored multicolor flat-back rhinestones, 1980s, French, signed Louis Feraud, 4". **$75-$150**

Tyrolean gentleman in hat, fur clip, painted resin face prong-set into gilded rhodium frame including necktie and hat, unsigned, 1938-42, 1 1/2". **$100**
(Possibly Hobe or Napier; each company used this cast resin face, painted in different ways for greatly varying effects.)

Decoriental Dames pins, gilded sterling silver, larger size (3 1/2") with confetti fruit-salad cabochons (gold-flecked navy blue) hair ornaments, smaller size (1 7/8") plain; 1942, unsigned but identified as products of Evans Case Co. (see Brunialti, Tribute to America), marked sterling. One other piece in this series is a large, stylized, botanical-effect seahorse of gilded sterling with same navy-blue fruit-salad cabs. **$50-$250**

Cartoonish Black Faces pins, one plastic, one tin (lever makes eyes roll), unsigned, age unknown, 2" to 2 1/2". **$25 each**

Goatee Gent brooch, gilded,
exotically enameled face,
beaded drop earrings, ruby RS
mouth, RS eyebrows, colorful
headpiece, unsigned, 1940s-
50s, 2 3/4". **$150**

Moorish Pirate fur clip,
enameled, bronzed pot metal,
look of determination or shock
on face, real earring through
lobe, unsigned, 1935-42, 2".
$50-$100

JUDAICA

Judaica is any object or text used to practice and observe Jewish commandments or traditions, or celebrate and portray its customs, philosophy and way of life.

Advertising, Y. Weisberg, mid-20th century, poster for the Orient Dryer, which promises to be the "best and least expensive" solution for women concerned with the health of their family. **$207**

Antiquities Judaicae Pragenses, Prague, printed by M. Schultz, S.A., (no date) early 20th century, soft-cover booklet of twenty-five duotone photographic reproductions on card depicting scenes from Jewish Prague, (worn). ..**$59**

Beith Tephilah (prayers), Livorno, 1866 According to Sephardic rite, original calf, spine gilt-tooled in Hebrew, with printed presentation label in front: "A Present to Mordecai Fonseca in Memory of Judith, Lady Montefiore, From Sir Moses Montefiore, Bart. At Purim, 5625 [sic]." **$355**

Etrog Container, Polish silver-mounted coconut, 19th century, marked "12," coconut resting on a realistically cast leaf, hinged lid, 6 1/2" l. **$3,851**

Haggadah Shel Pessach, Passover Haggadah with Commentary of Don Yitzhak Abarbanel and others, Amsterdam, Shlomo Proops, 1712, with copper plate engravings, fold-out map, wear, rebound. ....**$7,702** *(The Haggadah is the Jewish religious text that sets out the order of the Passover Seder.)*

Hanukkah Lamp, carved stone with candle arms and facade to verso, 8" h, restoration. **$533**

Ivory Figure of a Fiddler, German, late 19th century, poised with a violin, 4" h, mounted on a carved wood base. **$1,777**

Kiddush Cup, Bohemian engraved glass, late 19th/early 20th century, beaker-form with ruby flashing and engraved Hebrew text, 5 1/4" h. **$711**

Photo courtesy Skinner Inc., Boston; www.SkinnerInc.com
Jewish Genre Group, German painted terra-cotta, Zizenhausen (Sitzenhausen), late 19th century, repairs, 6 3/4" h. **$948**

Photo courtesy Skinner Inc., Boston; www.SkinnerInc.com
Kiddush Cup, Bohemian gilt-decorated yellow glass, late 19th century, decorated with grapes and leaves and with Hebrew text, 3 1/2" h. **$1,125**

Photo courtesy Skinner Inc., Boston; www.SkinnerInc.com

Hanukkah Lamp, Italian bronze, 17th/18th century, arched form with Cohan, flanked by columns enclosing a palm tree and lions about a tray of oil wells, lacking shamus, damages, repairs, 11" h. **$3,555**

Photography, Berenice Abbott (American, 1898-1991), East Side Portrait, signed "Berenice Abbott" on mat lower right, numbered "25/40" on mat lower left, gelatin silver print, sheet size 23 1/8" x 18 3/4", not examined out of frame. **$1,422**

Scroll, Ruth (Megillah), Persian silver-cased, 19th century, with finely hand-lettered black ink on parchment text with later illumination, in a standing scroll case with bird finial and colored stone embellishments, adapted, overall 6" h. **$2,607**

Lithograph, The Jewish Welfare Board / United War Work Campaign - Week of Nove. 11, 1918, inscribed and stamped, "The Hegeman Print. N.Y. ... ," color lithograph, sheet size 14" x 22", unframed, creases, surface abrasions, tape hinged to backing mat. **$1,659**

Marriage Buckle, German silver-gilt, late 17th century, elongated clasps with heavily cast and chased foliage and fruit amidst trellis-work, gilt-metal thread and velvet belt, fully hallmarked. **$3,436**

Mezuzah, Polish-style silver, marked AR and 925., 41/4" h. **$100**

Passover Dish, tin-glazed earthenware, early 20th century, white ground with aubergine and green Hebrew text, grape clusters and a central figure of a shepherd with city in the distance, imperfections, wear, 12" d. **$1,540**

Pendant, continental enamel, 19th century, depicting Moses with the Tablets, the reverse with the Sh'ma (the central tenet of Judaism), 3/4" d. **$296**

Photography, Maison Bonfils. Jews Mourning at the Wailing Wall, Jerusalem, albumen print, signed, titled and numbered "245 Mur des Juifs un vendredi--The Jews wailing place, a Friday," in the negative, circa 1880, 8 1/2" x 11", framed, with an accompanying exhibition catalogue. **$1,185**

Scroll, Esther (Megillah), possibly Italian, 19th century, hand-lettered in black ink on parchment, in four membranes, with additional text, on ivory rollers, overall 9" l. **$1,066**

Seder saltwater egg-shaped container, transfer-decorated porcelain, late 19th/early 20th century, with polychrome decoration pertaining to the dipping of herbs in saltwater, on scrolled feet, the base marked "3H-4667/ HB-NS," 6" h. **$385**

Spice Container, Italian silver, late 18th century, cylindrical form with piercing throughout, set on a stepped circular foot, surmounted by a spire and urn-form knop, 7" h. **$3,081**

Spice Tower, Polish silver, 19th century, possibly struck with maker IW in an oval, three cylindrical tiers with pierced and engraved foliage, the lower section with a door, on a domed base ending in a square foot, surmounted by a knop and pennant flag, 8 1/2" h. **$2,488**

Timepiece, Judaic bronze, probably Germany or Austria, early 20th century, the housing formed as rampant lions holding the dial with Star of David and Hebrew numerals aloft, on an oval base, the works signed Georg Jacob Luz, Forzbein, of an earlier date, overall 6 1/2" h. **$474**

Torah Breast Plate, silver, 20th century, cartouche form with lions flanking a crown about columns and the tablet, 7 3/4" h, with suspension chain. **$562**

Torah Curtain, Hungarian, embroidered velvet and silk, 19th century, with crown and Hebrew text, some staining, loss, 64" x 44" h. **$177**

Torah Pointer, continental silver and silver gilt, mid-19th century, hallmarked, tapered form with heavily cast and chased leaves, terminating in a pointed hand, finial formed as a lion's head, 10 1/4" l, with suspension loop and chain. **$2,725**

LIGHTING

Also see Modernism, Oriental, Tiffany.

Bandstand light, Art Deco, miniature, four-piece band on green-finished, cast-metal bandstand, leaded glass backdrop, pair of orange, black and yellow striated glass "candles," 9 1/8" h (overall), 12 1/2" w, 6" deep..............**$660**

Candelabra (pair), brass and cut glass, electrified, four branches, center support ornamented with button and pad-and-spear prisms, cut-glass drip pans with button prisms cascades below, 26 1/2" h, with small cloth shades. .... **$3,450 pair**

Candelabra (pair), silver-plated, three-light, twin branches, gadrooned borders, tapered round shaft, 16" h; convertible to pair of candlesticks. .... **$287 pair**

Candelabra (pair), J. Pradier, seven lights, bronze, each with a different figure supporting seven ornate bobeches, on a black marble base. Signed J. Pradier, height to topmost bobeche, 25 1/4". .... **$1,800 pair**
(Jean-Jacques Pradier, French/Swiss, 1790-1852.)

Candleholder, Indian silver, inlaid of double bell form with a waisted center and decorated to the exterior with a dense pattern of leafy blossoms within floral bands, further foliate-patterned details on the interior rim (silver oxidized, wear), 6 1/4" h. **$100**

Candleholder, Stahl redware, brown glazed half-vase form, handle at back, 8 1/4" h; inscribed on bottom, "Made By/ J.S. Stahl/May 12th-1941/The weather/clear and very/cool." **$120**
(Three generations of the Stahl family operated a small pottery in Powder Valley, Pa., intermittently from about 1850 to 1956.)

Candleholder, Weller, Woodcraft with owls perched atop an apple tree. Impressed mark. 14 3/4". **$960**

Candle lantern, colorless free-blown cut glass and brass, hanging hall-style, France, early 19th century, with folded base rim, overall 21 1/4" h...**$503**

Candlestick, Midwestern, Free-Blown, colorless, galleried bulbous socket with pewter insert, hollow pyriform stem, and circular foot with polished pontil mark. Probably Pittsburgh. 1810-1830. 9 1/4" h, 2 1/2" d rim, 4 3/4" d foot. Undamaged with heavy usage wear under foot............ **$791**

Photo courtesy Rago Arts and Auction Center, Lambertville, N.J.; www.RagoArts.com

Candelabra, bronze, designed for candles or flame-shaped electric bulbs, by Jessie Preston, in a thistle pattern. (Exhibited at "Women Designers in the USA 1900-2000," and accompanied by a copy of the catalog.) Original patina. Stamped J PRESTON CHICAGO, 13 1/2" x 10".
$9,600
(Jessie Preston, early 20th century, Chicago.)

Photo courtesy Rago Arts and Auction Center, Lambertville, N.J.; www.RagoArts.com

Candelabra (pair), continental, each six-flame, 19th century, 26 1/2" h. **$960 pair**

Candlestick, bronze, Jarvie, complete with bobeche. Exceptional, in a original patina. Unmarked, 10 1/4" x 5 1/4". **$10,200**
(Robert Riddle Jarvie, active 1904-1920, Chicago.)

Candlestick, double, brass, Jarvie, missing bobeches. Unmarked, 11" x 8". **$2,160**
(Robert Riddle Jarvie, active 1904-1920, Chicago.)

Candlestick, Steuben Diamond Optic, blue with yellow reeding, probably shape #6593, block letter acid-stamped signature. Second quarter 20th century. 4 1/2" h, 4 3/4" d foot.................................**$103**

Candlestick, Steuben Gold Calcite shape #3581, polished table ring, original Kaufmann's paper label inscribed "#3581 / 2J / 7 ea" under base. Second quarter 20th century. 6" h, 5 1/2" d overall. **$517**

Candlesticks, (pair), Grape and Cable carnival glass, marigold, single light. Northwood Glass Co. First quarter 20th century. 5 1/2" h. One with ground top socket. ....**$23 pair**

Candlesticks (pair), brass petal-base push-up, England, first half 18th century, (imperfections), 6 1/2" h, one with a small crack on the candle cup edge, both stem bases filled with solder reinforcement. ....**$237 pair**

Candlesticks (pair), small dolphin scallop base, unrecorded deep purple blue and opaque white, each featuring a 12-petal socket and 16-scallop circular base with two pairs of concentric rings underneath, wafer construction. Probably Boston & Sandwich Glass Co., possibly Cape Cod Glass Co. or Mt. Washington Glass Co. 1860-1880. 6 3/8" and 6 5/8" h, 4" d base. Single shallow chip to one socket petal and one under-base, snap-ring flake, both standards with the usual annealing fissures and lines associated with opaque white glass. **$4,802 pair**

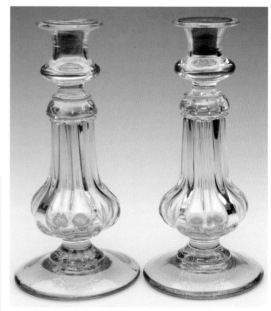

Candlesticks (pair), pillar-molded, colorless, each featuring a plain socket with wide flanged rim and pewter insert, applied to a mushroom-cap knop topping a hollow baluster stem with eight pronounced ribs, applied to a short standard and a wide slightly sloping foot with rough pontil mark. Probably Pittsburgh. Second quarter 19th century. 10 1/2" h, 2 5/8" d socket rim, 5" d foot. **$5,560 pair**

Candlesticks (pair), Roycroft, hammered copper with four riveted bands. Original dark patina, some pitting, mostly to base of one, whose bobeche is also bent and slightly torn. Orb & Cross mark, 11 1/2" and 12" h. **$2,640 pair**

Candle sconce, hammered copper, wall hanging, in the style of Carence Crafters (Chicago, circa 1910), embossed with organic design, dark patina, unmarked, 20 1/2" x 10 1/2". **$780**

Candlesticks with bells (pair), brass, tavern, England, mid- to late 19th century, with dish base, 11 1/4" h, some spots of corrosion. .... **$207 pair**

Candlesticks (two pairs), dolphin form, Boston & Sandwich Glass Co., Sandwich, Mass., circa 1845-70, in yellow and colorless glass with petal sockets over dolphin standards with large heads on square bases, 10 1/2" h; yellow candlesticks: one socket with unobtrusive crack, minor petal chip, the other stick with petal chip fairly shallow about 1/2" l, both with minor lower base edge chips; colorless candlesticks: one with a small petal chip, mold under-fill on tail tip, the other stick with a 1/2" clamshell chip to underside of one petal, both with minor base edge roughness...............................**$503 pairs**

Candle sconces (pair), glazed pottery, Henry Mercer (1856-1930), Doylestown, Pa., decorated with four birds, scrolls in beige, green ground, 11" h, 4 5/8" w, minor chips. .... **$862 pair**

Candle stand, paint-decorated, adjustable, wooden, American, late 18th/early 19th century, double-arm stand adjusts on a threaded shaft, tripod feet, with gilt linear decoration, 35 1/2" h. **$3,673**

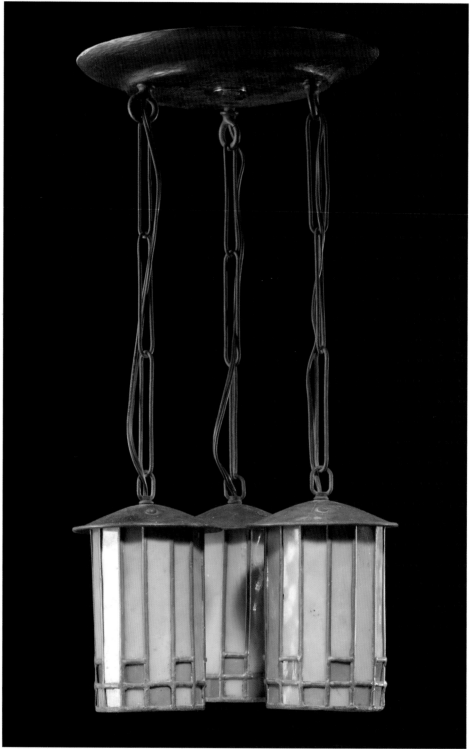

Photo courtesy Rago Arts and Auction Center, Lambertville, N.J.; www.RagoArts.com

Ceiling fixture, Roycroft, designed by Dard Hunter (1883-1966) with three cylindrical leaded-glass drops in bright green and purple glass, complete with chains and ceiling cap. Break to one piece of glass, missing finial and wear to patina on ceiling cap, 22" x 10 1/4" d. **$30,000**

Ceiling sconce, Roycroft, designed by Dard Hunter (1883-1966) with cylindrical shade of leaded glass in bright green and purple, complete with cap. Unmarked, 18" x 5". **$7,800**

Ceiling sconce, Roycroft, designed by Dard Hunter (1883-1966) with cylindrical shade of leaded glass in bright green and purple, complete with ceiling hook. Missing chain, break to two pieces. Unmarked, 10" x 5"...................**$9,000**

Chandelier, Arts & Crafts style, caramel slag glass in hammered bronze frame. Complete with ceiling cap and chain. Unmarked, 60" x 20"..**$960**

Chandelier, Arts & Crafts style, iron, with six candle fixtures, complete with chain and ceiling cap, 55" x 30". **$660**

Chandelier, brass and glass, four light with acid-etched glass panels, 20th century, 39" h, 18" d. **$900**

Chandelier, four-tiered, brass, octagonal "drip pans" on scrolled branches, electrified, 40 lights, center pedestal with paneled urn and vase forms, 20th century, 66" h, approximately 70" (greatest diameter).........................**$4,887**

Chandelier, brass and chrome, three-tiered, six octagonal "drip pans" over six, over 12 "drip pans"; all on S-scrolled branches, electrified, three-tiered center column, 30" to top of ring, approximately 46" outside diameter overall......**$575**

Chandelier, gilt metal, six-light, leaf scroll and swag bracket supports, fluted center shaft, pad prism swags at base of main body, six smaller lights, approximately 30" w around fitting at base..**$632**

Chandelier, Gothic Revival, brass, octagonal section, each side with pointed arch backed by frosted glass panel, six twin scrolled "spears" pointing upward, 53 1/8" h (overall), 24 3/8" w (overall)..**$230**

Chandelier, Handel, hollyhock motif, four-sided with pink and yellow leaded slag glass blossoms against a green geometric ground. Complete with four sockets, original chain, and floriform ceiling cap. Breaks to a few small glass pieces. Unmarked, 23 3/4" sq. x 34"...........................**$32,400**

Chandelier, Handel, with five leaded-glass shades hanging from individual arms, fastened to a square brass ceiling plate. Total: 33" x 14" sq.; shades: 4 1/2" x 5 1/2".......**$9,000**

Chandelier, Lalique, Champs-Élysées, in clear and frosted glass with chrome mounting. Engraved Lalique France. **$2,400**

Chandelier, Prairie School, with three hanging copper lantern drops lined in caramel slag glass. Unmarked, 36" x 30" x 13 3/4"...**$1,920**

Photo courtesy Green Valley Auctions, Mt. Crawford, Va.; www.GreenValleyAuctions.com

Photo courtesy Rago Arts and Auction Center, Lambertville, N.J.; www.RagoArts.com

Lamp, banquet, cut double-overlay Moorish Windows, kerosene period, cobalt blue cut to white cut to colorless font and matching stem, cast and stamped brass mounts retaining a good percentage of original gilding, double-step marble base, #2 fine line collar. Boston & Sandwich Glass Co. 1860-1880. 17" h, 5 3/8" sq base. Exceptional undamaged condition except for a few scattered flakes to edges of marble. **$6,780**

Lamp, boudoir, Handel, hammered copper conical shade suspended from hooks by chain links, pierced with stylized tulips and lined in caramel slag glass. Its single-socket base has two shafts and is lined in glass. Original dark patina. Shade stamped HANDEL. 14" x 8 1/4". **$9,000**

Chandelier, Roycroft, hammered copper, from the Roycroft Inn, with three reflective sockets, complete with original chains and ceiling cap. Fine original dark patina. Orb & Cross mark, 31" x 17"..**$7,200**

Chandelier, wrought iron, circular, each of 16 lights with stylized horse's head, electrified, ring with lower border of pendants, small ring suspended by bars; late 19th century. **$1,150**

Font, unlisted footed hanging or bracket, kerosene period, deep cobalt blue, wafer attached undersized standard with short eight-panel stem and plain circular foot, #2 fine-line collar, period burner and chimney, 5 1/4" h, 5 3/4" d overall, 3 1/2" d foot, minor mold roughness to a shoulder fin..**$4,675**

Lamp, astral, patinated brass with cut-glass shade, American, early 19th century, electrified, overall 18 1/8" h, wheel-cut shade in very good condition, the old font is a little rusty with several small cracks, there is an electric bulb socket in the center of the top with a cord attached but it was severed at one point; the ring holding the shade is affixed to the top of the font and there is a similar one attached below..........**$1,777**

Lamp, boudoir, Handel, its "chipped ice" glass shade obverse- and reverse-painted with a Nordic landscape of evergreens, over a rare single-socket tree-trunk base in bronze patina. Light spots to interior. Signed Handel with illegible number, 15" x 7"...**$6,000**

Lamp, desk, Roycroft, hammered copper with helmet shade. Cleaned patina. Orb & Cross mark, 17" x 7". **$960**

Lamp, figural, gilt bronze, with four children beneath tall trees, the tops of trees having mounted sockets, with speckled gold domed glass shade, circa 1900, Marked Brose, 23" x 10 1/2" d. **$1,200**

Lamp, figural, monumental bronze and ormolu, with gilt "socle" (a plain plinth that supports a wall) and five-arm candelabra on black painted wooden base, fitted for electricity, 19th century, 66" h. **$5,400**

Lamp, floor, Handel, its two faceted frosted-glass shades obverse-painted with a geometrical band on a plain T-base in bronze patina. Minute fleabite to lower edge of one shade. Both shades stamped HANDEL No. 2702, base has cloth label. Base: 55 1/2" x 33", shades: 4 3/4" x 6"......**$3,600**

Lamp, fluid, cut overlay glass, brass and marble with glass prisms, American, circa 1870, brass font over white cut to red glass shaft in a star and grid design, on a square double-step marble base with brass mounts, 17 3/8" h, solder repair on font, dent on font, missing one long prism, old minor edge chips on marble, overlay good............**$207**

Lamp, piano, Arts & Crafts style, hammered copper with a riveted hanging lantern, lined in raspberry and amber slag

glass. Normal cleaning to original patina. Unmarked, 8 1/2" x 10" x 17".................................**$1,020**

Lamp, stand, New York Lamp Co. "Dewdrop," kerosene period, cased red to off-white font, opaque black base, font with applied glass peg which is plastered into top of the hollow stem, #3 collar, 11" h, 5 5/8" d base, minute flake under base, two minute open bubbles to top of foot....**$2,860**

Lamp, student's, brass, acorn-shaped font, green overlay milk glass shade, two knobs marked "Duplex PA.", 21 1/4" h..............................**$690**

Lamp, table, art glass vase, pulled blue feather motif, applied threading on off-white iridescent ground, possibly Durand, gold finished hexagonal base, 9" h vase........................**$862**

Photo courtesy Green Valley Auctions, Mt. Crawford, Va.; www.GreenValleyAuctions.com

Lamp, stand, cut double-overlay Punty, kerosene period, deep rose cut to white cut to colorless font, opaque black square base with gilt decoration, brass connector, #1 brass collar. Boston & Sandwich Glass Co. Second half 19th century. 9 3/4" h, 4" sq base. Minute flake to edge of one punty and a few minute flakes to lower base, several cut-through open bubbles on lower punties, some wear to gilt. **$2,599**

Photo courtesy Rago Arts and Auction Center, Lambertville, N.J.; www.RagoArts.com

Lamp, table, Albert Berry, its four-panel shade of pierced and hammered copper with sylvan scenes lined in green and white slag glass, and garland chain suspending bone drops, over a single-socket mahogany base. Dark original patina, 3" break to one glass pane, two small corner chips to another. Unmarked, 20" x 8 3/4". **$6,600**

Lamp, table, Arts & Crafts style, eight bent-glass panels with metal overlay, supported by a column base, 19" d x 21" h, very good condition. **$425**

Lamp, table, Arts & Crafts style, domed leaded-glass shade with a multi-colored border supported by a metal base, some cracked segments, 16" d x 21" h, very good condition. **$425**

Lamp, table, Arts & Crafts style, its leaded glass shade over a two-socket oak base. Original finish. Unmarked, 25" x 19" sq...**$480**

Lamp, table, Arts & Crafts style, its helmet-shaped shade with hammered metal bands lined in curved caramel slag glass, over a two-socket faceted base, in bronze patina. Unmarked, 22 1/4" x 15 1/2". **$1,440**

Lamp, table, Arts & Crafts style, its faceted shade lined in green slag glass over a cut-out and riveted single-socket oak base. Unmarked, 24" x 18"....................................**$1,680**

Lamp, table, Dirk Van Erp, hammered copper and mica, its four-panel shade over a two-socket bulbous base. Fine original patina. Windmill stamp with remnant of D'Arcy Gaw. 16 1/2" x 15 1/2". **$8,400**
(Designer D'Arcy Gaw worked with Dirk Van Erp in his San Francisco studio in 1910-11.)

Photo courtesy Rago Arts and Auction Center, Lambertville, N.J.; www.RagoArts.com

Lamp, table, Dirk Van Erp, hammered copper and mica, its four-panel conical shade atop a two-socket trumpet-shaped base. Original patina and mica. Open box windmill mark, 18" x 17". **$14,400**

Photo courtesy Rago Arts and Auction Center, Lambertville, N.J.; www.RagoArts.com

Lamp, table, Bradley & Hubbard, its geometrical faceted shade with Greek key band, lined in green and yellow slag glass, over a three-socket base, covered in verdigris patina. One replaced socket, upper panels probably replaced. Unmarked, 22" x 15". **$900**

Photo courtesy Rago Arts and Auction Center, Lambertville, N.J.; www.RagoArts.com

Lamp, table, Fulper, rare, its ceramic shade inset with small panels of blue-green leaded slag glass on a classically-shaped, two-socket base, covered in a mirrored blue flambe glaze. Two short hairlines from rim to glass, original sockets and switch, overall excellent condition. Shade stamped 20 2 2, base has vertical stamped Fulper mark, PATENT PENDING US AND CANADA 20, 21 1/2" x 15 1/4". **$10,800**

Lamp, table, Gorham, its leaded-glass shade in a foliate pattern over a three-socket fluted base in bronze patina. (Gorham's work in leaded glass is rare). A few breaks to glass. Unmarked, 25 1/4" x 18 1/2". **$7,200**

Lamp, table, Handel, its lobed, acid-etched shade reverse-painted with a lakeside landscape at dusk, over a rare three-socket Teroma base, obverse-painted with a river landscape. Flecks to edge of shade. Shade stamped HANDEL Lamps with patent, base signed F. Gubisch, 23 1/2" x 18"...... **$10,200**

Lamp, table, Handel, its acid-etched shade reverse- and obverse-painted with an autumnal landscape, over a three-socket, orb-shaped base. Strong base and excellent original patina. Shade signed HANDEL 5209, artist signed R. Lockrow, stamped Handel Pat, stamped HANDEL on base, 24 1/2" x 18"...**$21,600**

Lamp, table, Handel, its hemispherical acid-etched shade reverse-painted by F. Gubisch with daffodils on a three-socket, bulbous bronzed base; 3/8" chip inside rim. Shade signed with HANDEL LAMPS, patent number, and HANDEL 7122 Gubisch, base stamped HANDEL, 24" x 18".
....**$8,400**

Lamp, table, Handel, its large faceted shade with brown and green cattails against caramel slag glass, over a five-socket bronze base. Fine original patina, original sockets, cap and chains. Shade unmarked, base marked HANDEL 768?, 30 1/2" x 22 1/4". **$45,000**

Lamp, table, Handel, its ribbed "chipped ice" glass shade reverse-painted with a landscape at dusk, over a matching three-socket base in bronze patina. Soft white spots inside shade do not show through the outside, restored patina, two small, flat flakes to side of shade. Base and shade stamped HANDEL, 22 1/2" x 15 1/2"..........................**$4,200**

Lamp, table, Handel, its "chipped ice" glass shade obverse-painted with a landscape, reverse-painted with shading, over a two-socket fluted base in bronze patina. Shade stamped HANDEL with patent number, 22" x 16". **$4,560**

Lamp, table, Handel, its faceted shade overlaid with Queen Anne's lace on green and caramel slag glass, over a bronzed two-socket tree trunk base. Two splits to bottom of shade, replaced cap soldered onto shade, some replaced glass panels. Base stamped HANDEL 5339, 24 1/2" x 18"...**$3,120**

Lamp, table, Jefferson/Handel, Jefferson shade of acid-etched glass reverse-painted with a bucolic landscape, over a smaller Handel two-socket base with bronzed patina.

Small nicks to edge of shade, remnants of glue from tape, replaced sockets. Shade marked 1897 and stamped Jefferson, base unmarked, 20 1/2" x 18"......................**$2,040**

Lamp, table, Jefferson, its "chipped ice" glass shade reverse-painted with a sepia tone landscape, over a two-socket bulbous chipped-ice glass base with copper finish. Shade signed 1885 Jefferson and rare artist signature M.G., 22 1/2" x 18"..**$2,400**
(Jefferson Lamp Co., Steubenville, Ohio, and Follansbee, W.V., 1900-1933.)

Lamp, table, leaded glass, mushroom-shaped shade in a tulip design on a three-light quatrefoil base with bronze patina, 19th century, couple of short breaks on glass. Unmarked, 25" x 19". **$2,760**

Lamp, table, with slag-glass shade, hexagonal paneled brown and white slag-glass shade, three sockets, bronze base with slender baluster standard, leaf-and-berry motif, circular base, 22 3/4" h (including finial), 17" w shade..............**$747**

Photo courtesy Rago Arts and Auction Center, Lambertville, N.J.; www.RagoArts.com

Lamp, table, Moe-Bridges, its hemispherical shade of acid-etched glass reverse-painted with a river landscape, on a two-socket bronze urn base. Shade signed MOE-BRIDGES CO. 186 HH, base unmarked, 23" x 18 1/4". **$4,200**
(Moe-Bridges Lamp Co. Milwaukee, early 20th century.)

Photo courtesy Rago Arts and Auction Center, Lambertville, N.J.; www.RagoArts.com

Lamp, table, Pairpoint, its "chipped ice" glass flaring shade obverse-painted with an autumnal landscape and reverse-painted in yellow, over a three-socket urn base in bronze patina. Base marked PAIRPOINT PD3034 MADE IN THE USA, 21" x 15 1/2". **$3,000**

Photo courtesy Rago Arts and Auction Center, Lambertville, N.J.; www.RagoArts.com

Lamp, table, Lillian Palmer, hammered copper, its shade of four mesh panels painted with nasturtium blossoms in polychrome, its two-socket base incised with hollyhocks. Professionally enhanced patina on base. Unmarked, 18" x 19 1/4". **$13,200**
(The Lillian Palmer Shop, San Francisco, early 20th century.)

Lamp, table, Pittsburgh, its acid-etched glass shade reverse and obverse painted with autumnal maple leaves, over an organic two-socket base with bronze patina. A few minor flecks around rim. Unmarked, 23" x 18". **$4,200** *(Pittsburgh Lamp, Brass and Glass Co., 1901-1926.)*

Lamp, table, Roycroft, hammered copper, designed by Dard Hunter (1883-1966), flaring shade of bright green and purple leaded slag glass, over a three-socket base with ring pulls. Original patina, cap and finial. A couple of short breaks to glass pieces. Base has Orb & Cross mark, 22 1/4" x 18 3/4". **$20,400**

Photo courtesy Rago Arts and Auction Center, Lambertville, N.J.; www.RagoArts.com

Lamp, table, Roycroft, by Dard Hunter (1883-1966), its flaring shade of hammered copper lined in green textured glass, over a single-socket oak base with copper fittings. (Provenance: Charles Youngers, master bookbinder at the Roycrofters and close friend of the artist.) Glass replaced some 30 years ago with Roycroft-type material; replaced or missing screws to shade, some cleaning to copper. Unmarked, 23" x 16" sq. **$12,000**

Lamp, table, Unique Lamp Co., leaded-glass shade with pink blossoms and green leaves on amber slag glass ground, over a two-socket fluted base with green leaves, 20" x 15". **$1,560**

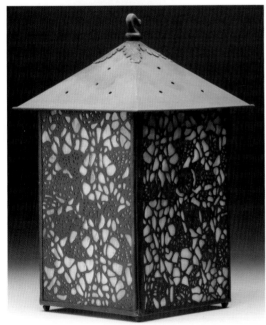

Lantern, Riviere, hanging copper in the style of Tiffany, its pierced sides in a floral pattern, lined in caramel slag glass. Unmarked, 14" x 8" sq. **$780**
(Riviere Studios, New York, early 20th century.)

Lamps (pair), floor, brass, electrified, two circular tiers with six lights and brass flame finial, larger tier below with 12 lights, ringed round shaft on domical base with three cast brass lion supports, 72" h (top of flame finial).
.... **$488 pair**

Lamps (pair), mantel, bronze, Argand style, mid-19th century, bell-form top with anthemion cresting supporting pod-and-spear prisms, cast curved arm supporting light fixture, short fluted columnar support on square base, 17 3/4" h. .... **$3,450 pair**
(Named for Ami Argand [1755-1803], a Swiss inventor.)

Lamps (pair), Murano Glass, fluted glass with controlled bubbles, "spruzzata" (spattered) gold and metal fittings, 20th century, height without socket: 23". .... **$1,080 pair**

Lamps (hand), pair, pewter, Roswell Gleason (1799-1887), Dorchester, Mass., active 1822-71, the lamps with camphene burners on acorn-shaped fonts, dish base with ring handles, impressed maker's marks, (wear), 6 1/2" h, uneven surface, fine pitting on the dish bases. ...... **$444 pair**

Lamps (stand), pair, blown-molded overshot fonts, kerosene period, cranberry fonts with medial gilt rings, each on an opaque white square base with worn gilt and American flag decoration, differing #1 fine-line collars, matching Miller burners and flattened petal-top chimneys. Probably Boston & Sandwich Glass Co., 9 3/4" h, 4" sq base. One with wear to font gilt, both with minor annealing lines to lower edge of base, one with open bubbles to base and shallow chips/roughness under base. .... **$1,870 pair**

Lamps (pair), table, porcelain, figural, girl in 18th-century costume holding basket of flowers, rocky, gilt metal base; lady wearing bonnet and flowered dress, small purse on arm, 8 1/2" h (figures), index finger of left hand of one figure broken off. .... **$230 pair**

Lamps (two), table, Bradley & Hubbard, their "chipped ice" glass shades obverse-painted with a band of stylized ivy, and reverse-painted with a mossy ground, over three-socket Arts & Crafts bases. Different bronze patinas, both caps and finials replaced. Bases marked B304, 25 1/2" x 18".
.... **$6,000 both**

Lantern, Arts & Crafts style, geometric design in metal, and mottled green and white leaded glass, unmarked, 7" w x 20" h.. **$1,500**

Lantern, Arts & Crafts style, cylindrical shape in hammered copper with oval cutouts and a mica liner, original patina, unmarked, 9 1/2" w x 13" h. **$550**

Lantern, pierced tin and glass, kerosene, marked "S. Sargent's Patent Sept. 17, 1861," with ring handle, tin font with kerosene burner, embossed brass patent label, 18 1/2" h. **$296**

Lantern, Gustav Stickley, unusual oversized wrought copper with pyramidal shade, heart cut-outs, original ceiling plate and chain, and fine original amber glass, under a rich original dark brown patina. Unmarked. Lantern to tip of hook: 15" x 9 1/2", chain to ceiling mount: 10"........ **$19,200**

Lanterns (pair), Gustav Stickley, wrought iron rectangular with pyramidal tops, with original pyramidal wall mounts. Complete with original hammered amber glass and pyramidal mounting screws. Sanded finish, replaced inner tabs. Lanterns: 5 1/2" x 6" sq. Back plate: 6" sq. .... **$3,360 pair**

Lanterns (two), Roycroft, copper, one with clear glass panes and smooth ceiling cap, the other with amber bubble glass and hammered cap. (From Elbert Hubbard's son's residence in East Aurora, N.Y.) Unmarked. With plate: 18" x 8" and 20" x 7"....................................**$2,400 both**

Sconce, hanging, Gustav Stickley, hammered copper with four hammered amber glass hanging panels, complete with chain and ceiling cap. Stamped Als-ik-kan, 42" x 7" sq.
....**$22,800**

Sconce, wall, Roycroft, designed by Dard Hunter (1883-1966) with cylindrical shade of leaded glass in bright green and purple, complete with wall cap. Unmarked, 8 1/2" x 5" x 6 1/4". **$9,600**

Sconces (four), wall, Roycroft, hammered brass, three with candle fixture. Original patina and switch. (From Elbert Hubbard's son's residence in East Aurora, N.Y.) Unmarked, 10" x 3 1/2"..**$1,680 all**

Shade, cased glass ring-top cone, kerosene period, pale blue with opal interior, 5 1/2" h, 10 3/8" d...........................**$357**

Shade, flaring, Roycroft, designed by Dard Hunter (1883-1966) of bright green and purple leaded slag glass. Unmarked, 6" x 18". **$11,400**

Shade, Handel, domed leaded glass with overall dogwood design. Marked Handel on the inside, 6 3/4" x 15 5/8".
....**$2,760**

Shade, Oregon, kerosene period, cut overlay foliate, ruby rough cut to colorless, crimped and tooled rim, 6 1/2" h, 3" fitter, two shallow chips and flake to fitter. **$825**

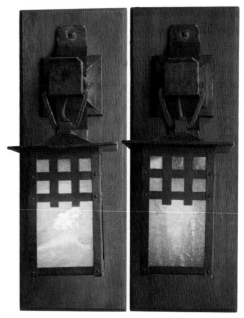

Photo courtesy Rago Arts and Auction Center, Lambertville, N.J.; www.RagoArts.com

Sconces (pair), wall, Gustav Stickley, hammered copper lined in textured agate glass. Fine original dark patina, professionally re-glued glass of the period, which may not be original, one replaced pane. Unmarked, 17" x 6". **$9,600 pair**

Photo courtesy Rago Arts and Auction Center, Lambertville, N.J.; www.RagoArts.com

Shade, Handel, leaded glass with dogwood design and a graded checkered design on top. Marked Handel on inside of shade, 9" x 18 1/2" d. **$2,520**

FAIRY LAMPS

Fairy lamps, which originated in England in the 1840s, are candle-burning night lamps. They were used in nurseries, hallways and dim corners of the home.

Two leading candle manufacturers, the Price Candle Co. and the Samuel Clarke Co., promoted fairy lamps as a means to sell candles. Both contracted with glass, porcelain and metal manufacturers to produce the needed shades and cups. For example, Clarke used Worcester Royal Porcelain Co., Stuart & Sons and Red House Glass Works in England, plus firms in France and Germany.

Fittings were produced in a wide variety of styles. Shades ranged from pressed to cut glass, from Burmese to Nailsea. Cups are found in glass, porcelain, brass, nickel and silver plate.

American firms selling fairy lamps included Diamond Candle Co. of Brooklyn, N.Y.; Blue Cross Safety Candle Co. and Hobbs-Brockunier of Wheeling, W.V.

Two-piece (cup and shade) and three-piece (cup with matching shade and saucer) fairy lamps can be found. Married pieces are common.

Clarke's trademark was a small fairy with a wand surrounded by the words "Clarke Fairy Pyramid, Trade Mark."
Reproduction Alert. Reproductions abound.

Bisque, tri-face baby girl, 3 1/2". $70
Blue and white frosted ribbon glass dome top shade, ruffled base, clear marked "S. Clarke" insert, flakes on shade, 6". $490
Blue satin mother-of-pearl shade, clear Clarke Fairy pyramid insert, 3 3/4". $225
Blue satin swirl shade, matching base, ruffled top and edge, 5". $325
Burmese
Decorated shade, clear Clark's Cricklite base, 4". $900
Egg-shaped shade, crystal insert, colorful porcelain bowl, stamped S. Clark's patent trademark, English trademark backstamp, 8". $1,380
Burmese Cricklite, dome shaped shade, pleated bowl shaped base, clear glass candle cup signed "Clarke's Cricklite Trade Mark," 7 1/2" d, 5 1/2" h. $1,350
Clarke Pyramid, light, holder, and white porcelain mug, frosted shade set on finger loop base, signed "Clarke Food Warmer," advertising slogans on mug, 8 1/2". $125
Clear molded flame shade, controlled bubbles, clear S. Clarke's Fairy Pyramid base, 4 1/2". $60
Figural green glass shade in shape of monk, set on frosted shoulders base, 4 1/2". $110
Green Nailsea shade, porcelain Doulton decorated base, signed "S. Clarke's Fairy" in center, 5 1/2". $1,300

Green opaque shade, gold and blue enamel decoration, clear pressed glass pedestal base, 8 3/4". $275
Lavender and frosted white shade, matching ruffled base, zigzag design, 5 1/2". $150
Metal, colored inset jewels, reticulated shade with bird designs, 4 1/2". $185
Ruby red, profuse white loopings, bowl-shaped base with eight turned-up scallops, clear glass candle cup holder marked "S. Clarke Patent Trade Mark Fairy," 5 3/4". ... $1,250
Ruby red, white loopings, matching piecrust crimped base, inclusion on shade, 4" d, 4 1/2" h. $585
Ruby red Cricklite, white loopings, dome-shaped shade, bowl shaped base with 26 pleats, clear glass candle cup signed "S. Clarke Patent Trade Mark Fairy," 7" d, 6" h. $975
Ruby red Cricklite, white loopings, satin dome-shaped shade, clear cup marked "S. Clarke Patent Trade Mark," 4" h. $335
Yellow satin shade, matching fitted base, clear signed "S. Clarke Fairy" insert, 6 1/4". $650
Yellow satin swirl shade, clear S. Clarke's Fairy pyramid base, 4". $150
Webb, blue shade decorated with bird and branch, clear Clarke's Cricklite insert, square blue satin base, 6 1/2". .. $1,500
White and yellow striped shade, clear S. Clarke Fairy insert, nestled on matching white and yellow ruffled base, 6" h. $500

Photo courtesy of Strawser Auction Group by Michael G. Strawser

Fairy lamp, Mount Washington, ruffled rim to base, cased peachblow glass, 6" h. **$750**

Photo courtesy of The Early Auction Company LLC.

Fairy lamp, butterscotch satin, bold stripes, matching shade and undercup with candle insert, 4 1/2" h. **$200**

Fairy lamp, Webb, Burmese, dome shade, ruffled rim base, separated with signed Clarke clear holder, double base marked with S. Clarke patent trademark, 6" h. **$650**

Fairy lamp, Webb, Burmese, four parts, shade and ruffled base, crystal candleholder, underplate marked with Clark's "Cricklite," base has Webb trademark, 6 1/2" d base, 5 1/2" h overall. **$750**

Fairy lamp, Webb, Burmese, four-part, acid finished dome shade, ruffled base, double crystal insert, marked S. Clarke Patent trademark, base stamped with circular Thomas Webb and Sons trademark, bruise to base, 6" h. **$475**

Fairy lamp, three part, Webb, Burmese, dome shade, ruffled rim, footed base decorated with oak leaves, rare Burmese insert marked S. Clarke Patent Trade Mark Fairy, Thomas Webb and Sons circular trademark, 6 1/2" h. **$2,450**

MATCH SAFES, HOLDERS

Pocket match safes are small containers used to safely carry matches in one's pocket. They were first used around the 1840s. Match safes can be found in various sizes and shapes, and were made from numerous materials such as sterling, brass, gold, ivory and vulcanite. Some of the most interesting and sought-after ones are figurals in the shapes of people, animals and almost anything else imaginable. Match safes were also a popular advertising tool around the turn of the 19th century, and were used by both large and small businesses. Match safes are known as vesta cases in England.

Collector Clubs: International Match Safe Association, PO Box 791, Malaga, NJ 08328-0791, www.matchsafe.org or IMSAoc@aol.com.

Note: While not all match safes have a striking surface, this is one test, besides size, to distinguish a match safe from a calling card case or other small period boxes. Values are based on match safes in excellent condition.

Adviser: George Sparacio

Reproduction Alert. Copycat, reproduction and fantasy match safes abound. Reproductions include Art Nouveau styles, figural/novelty shapes, nudes and many others. Fantasy and fakes include Jack Daniels and Coca-Cola.

Adophe Thiers, French statesman, figural bust, nickel plated, 2" x 1 3/8". **$388**

Alligator motif, sterling with gold interior wash, by Watson Mfg. Co., 2 1/2" x 1 1/2". **$700**

Anheuser Busch, Pullman car motif, nickel plated, 2 7/8" x 1 1/2". **$150**

Arabic designs on lid, with multi-colored enamel, scalloped lid edge, brass, 1 3/4" x 1 3/8". **$125**

Art Nouveau lady, with long hair and flowers, sterling, by Gorham Mfg. Co., no. B2-148, 2 5/8" x 1 5/8". **$145**

Automata erotica, two-figures copulating, nickel plated, 2 1/2" x 1 1/2". **$3,250**

Bamboo shaped, decorated with butterfly and flowers, probably Japanese, sterling and enamel, 2 7/8" x 1 1/4". .. **$850**

Banded black agate, rectangular shaped with agate striker, brass edging, by H. H. Tammer Curio Co., 2 3/4" x 1". **$70**

Bat, figural, Japanese, brass, 2 1/2" x 1 3/4". **$950**

Black cats driving car, trick type, plated brass and celluloid, by Joseph Walker, 2" x 2 1/2". **$325**

Book shaped, double-ender, ivory with sterling initials, 1 3/4" x 1". **$45**

Bowling motif, man smoking and holding ball, German silver, 2 1/2" x 1 5/8". **$175**

Brass with open design over glass, rectangular, 2" x 1 3/8". **$135**

Brunswick Blake Collendar Co./Monarch Cushions, white highlights, slip top, thermoplastic, 2 3/4" x 1 1/8". **$225**

Match safe, cigar and match motif, enameled on sterling, by Reeves & Sillcocks, 2 3/4" x 1 1/2". **$1,000-$1,200**

Match safe, horse motif, sterling with gold interior wash, by Gorham Mfg. Co., 2 1/2" x 1 5/8". **$300-$375**

William Jennings Bryan's image, below "For President", nickel plated brass, 2 7/8" x 1 1/2"..................................... **$150**

Buffalo Steam Rollers advertising, celluloid wrapped with b&w graphics, by Whitehead & Hoag Co., 3" x 1 1/2".
.... **$225**

Bulldog motif, sterling, by Gorham Mfg. Co., no. B2-2-02, 2 1/2" x 1 1/2".. **$375**

Butterfly and floral motif, German Silver, 2 3/4" x 1 3/4".
.... **$85**

Cawston Ostrich Farm, man riding ostrich, celluloid wrapped with multi-colored graphics, plated brass ends, by Whitehead and Hoag Co., 2 3/4" x 1 1/2"....................... **$250**

Charles Darwin, with full beard, flat back, brass, marked Rd. #89917, 2 1/8" x 1 3/8"... **$225**

Cherub and wishbone motif, sterling, by Wm. Kerr, #6, 2 5/8" x 1 1/2".. **$140**

Chicago World's Fair, 1893, image "USA Man of War" on top, litho tin with multicolored graphics, marked Bryant & May Wax Vestas, 1 1/4" x 1 7/8".................................... **$95**

Cigar, figural, sterling, by Tiffany & Co., 4" x 3/4"............ **$375**

Cigarette holder and match safe combo, sterling, by J. Gloster, Birmingham hallmarks, 2" x 2 1/4"..................... **$175**

Clam shell and coral motif, applied to sterling, clamshell and coral portion gold gilt, by Gorham Mfg. Co., no. 410, 2" x 1 1/4"... **$900**

Cobra, sterling with gold interior wash, by Gorham Mfg. Co., Providence, RI, no. 1533M, 2 1/2" x 1 1/2"....................... **$950**

Columbian World's Fair, stack of coins, figural, brass, 1893, 1 1/2" x 7/8".. **$120**

Corkscrew and knife combo, rectangular shape with mother-of-pearl side panels, nickel plated brass, 2 3/8" x 1 3/8"... **$700**

Cupid in garden, sterling with interior gold wash, by Gorham Mfg. Co., no. B1305, 2 5/8" x 1 3/4". **$400**

Diamond Match, bee and flower decoration, multicolored litho tin, by Ginna & Co., 1 1/2" x 2 1/2"........................... **$55**

Domino, figural with cigar cutter, vulcanite, 2 1/8" x 1 1/8".
.... **$175**

Door with hinge design, sterling with gold interior wash, by Webster Co., 2 3/4" x 1 5/8".. **$200**

Dragon on rampage, nickel plated brass, 2 5/8" x 1 3/8". **$85**

El Telegrafo, Key West cigar box, figural, brass, 2 1/4" x 1 1/4"... **$125**

Farmer's Friend advertising, celluloid wrapped with multicolored graphics, by J.E. Mergott, 2 3/4" x 1 1/2".... **$225**

Filigree with floral design, silver, 2 1/2" x 1 1/2". **$110**

Fireman's Fund Insurance-1915, brass with applied sterling, by Shreve & Co., 2 1/2" x 1 7/8". **$400**

Fleur-de-lis design, set with 12 diamonds, gunmetal with sapphire thumb stud, 2" x 1 1/4". **$85**

Floral motif, one side with hinged rectangular "stand", sterling, by F.S. Gilbert, 2 3/4" x 1 1/4"........................... **$115**

Footballer's leg with attached ball, figural, sterling with English hallmarks for Birmingham 1884, 2 1/4" x 1 3/8". **$1,500**

Friar holding wine basket, sterling with gold interior wash, 2 3/4" x 1 3/4". **$400**

Frog holding tobacco pouch, figural, Japanese writing that translates to "Take care with fire," brass, 2" x 1 1/8".**$325**

Gargoyle/floral motif, sterling with interior gold wash, by Wm. Kerr & Co., no. 3633, 2 1/2" x 1 3/4". **$200**

Gambling motif, whist counters plus playing-card designs, silver plated, by R. Wallace & Sons, no. 075, 2 3/4" x 1 1/2".
.... **$275**

Photo courtesy of George Sparacio, www.matchsafe.us

Match safe, Buddha, figural, silver, probably Japanese, 2 1/4" x 1 1/2". **$1,200-1,400**

Photo courtesy of George Sparacio, www.matchsafe.us

Match safe, milkmaid, sterling, by Aikin, Lambert Co., 2 1/2" x 1 1/2". **$225-$300**

Harvard University/sculling motif, sterling with gold wash inside, 2 1/4" x 1 3/4"............................ **$375**

Hidden photo, barrel shape, front hinged at bottom to reveal photo, sterling, by Battin & Co., no. 155, 2 1/2" x 1 5/8". **$260**

Holly motif, brass, possibly by Whiting Mfg. Co., 2 1/2" x 1 5/8".. **$140**

Horseshoe, with raised design and rider on horseback, figural, vulcanite, 1 7/8" x 1 1/2"............................ **$70**

Hudson-Fulton Memorial Celebration 1909, cello inserts, by J.E. Mergott, 2 7/8" x 1 1/2"...................... **$120**

Improved Order of Red Man motif, insert type, nickel plated, by August Goertz & Co., 2 3/4" x 1 1/2"........ **$45**

Indian chief, sterling, by Webster Co., 2 1/4" x 1 3/4"..... **$700**

Ironsides Company, with sailing ship logo, celluloid wrapped with multicolored graphics, plated brass ends, by J. E. Mergott Co., 2 3/4" x 1 1/2"................................... **$200**

Kappa, figural, silver plated, by Gorham Mfg. Co., no. 070, 2 1/4" x 1 1/2".. **$310**

Lady sitting on toilet, hidden by front cover, book shaped with leather cover marked "Guide", 1 5/8" x 1 1/4"......... **$300**

Lion motif, sterling, by Unger Bros., no. 32-35, 2 1/2" x 1 1/2".. **$425**

Lion and lioness, with palm trees in background, sterling with interior gold wash, by Battin & Co., no. 2-12, 2 1/2" x 1 5/8"... **$250**

Lotos Export logo, celluloid wrapped with multicolored graphics, plated brass ends, by Whitehead & Hoag Co., 2 3/4" x 1 1/2".. **$135**

Louisiana Purchase 1803-1903/Uncle Sam exchanging money for deed, brass alloy, 2 3/8" x 1 1/4". **$75**

Mail bag, figural, conforms to design patent no. 2-0586 of March 17, 1891, silver plated, by E.A. Bliss & Co., 2 3/4" x 1 1/2".. **$100**

Mauchline ware, trick-psycho box, 1893 Columbian Exposition transfer, wood, 3" x 1 1/4"........................ **$150**

Mythical figure, half man/half bird, sterling, by Carter Howe & Co., 2 1/4" x 1 1/4".................................... **$200**

Neptune & mermaid motif, with cigar cutter on lid, sterling, by F. Whiting & Co., 2 1/2" x 1 5/8"............ **$375**

Nocturnal type with candle, unpainted tin, by Charles Parker, patented June 4, 1867, 2 3/4" x 1 1/4"............ **$175**

Oriental lady holding lantern, working compass in lantern, brass, Japanese, 2 1/2" x 1 1/4"..................... **$225**

Our Heroes, (McKinley, Dewey, Sigsbee, Miles, Fitzhugh Lee), sterling, by Whiting Mfg. Co., 2 1/2" x 1 1/2"........ **$380**

Padlock, figural, "key" cutout and striker on front, plated brass, 2 1/4" x 1 3/8"... **$175**

Pearling & seaweed motif, in Persian style, kidney-shaped, sterling, by Whiting Mfg. Co., no. 2-337, 2 3/4" x 1 3/8".. **$245**

Pig running, hinged at hind quarter, figural, plated brass, 3/4" x 2 1/4".. **$170**

Psyche and Love, (winged figure and nude in flight), sterling, by Wm. Kerr, no. 10, 2 3/8" x 1 3/8"............. **$225**

Red Star Binder & Twine, bulldog and British flag, celluloid wrapped with multicolored graphics, plated brass ends, by Whitehead & Hoag Co., 2 3/8" x 1 3/8". **$85**

Richard the Lion Hearted head, figural, plated brass, by Smith Bros., no. 95195, 2" x 1 5/8".................. **$350**

Photo courtesy of George Sparacio, www.matchsafe.us

Match safe, President Benjamin Harrison, figural, plated brass, by Simon Zinn, marked "Pat. Oct. 8, 1888", push-button lid release. **$225-$275**

Robert Burns image, silver-plated brass, 1 3/4" x 1 3/8". **$90**

Roulette wheel, enamel on sterling, 2 1/4" x 1 1/2". **$450**

Rugby ball, figural, sterling, by Wm. Henry Sparrow, complete English hallmarks for Birmingham, 2 1/8" diameter. **$460**

Sailboat, plus cattails and lily pads, sterling, 2 1/2" x 1 5/8". **$225**

Scarab/stag horn beetle, figural, brass, 2 1/2" x 1 1/8". **$250**

Scottish thistle, figural, brass, 2" x 1 1/2". **$90**

Sea creatures and shells, sterling, Wm. Shiebler, no. 2-2, 2 5/8" x 1 3/8"... **$850**

Snake coiled around oval-shaped safe, brass, 2" x 1 1/4". **$65**

Soldier holding gun, gun has vesta socket, cast iron, G & V maker's mark, 3 1/8" x 1 1/2". **$200**

Steeplechase motif, silveroin, by Bristol Mfg. Co., 2 1/2" x 1 1/2". **$115**

Trick, enameled Masonic emblem on front, push to release lid, sterling, by F.S. Gilbert, 2 1/2" x 1 1/2".................. **$325**

White Mountain Refrigerators, figural, nickel-plated brass, 2 3/4" x 1 5/8".. **$135**

Xmas 1904/Collins & Co, trick type, squeeze edges to open lid, nickel plated, 1 1/2" x 2 1/2".................................**$85**

MATCH HOLDERS

The friction match achieved popularity after 1850. The early matches were packaged and sold in sliding cardboard boxes. To facilitate storage and to eliminate the clumsiness of using the box, match holders were developed.

The first match holders were cast iron or tin, the latter often displaying advertisements. A patent for a wall-hanging match holder was issued in 1849. By 1880, match holders also were being made from glass and china. Match holders began to lose their popularity in the late 1930s, with the advent of gas and electric heat and ranges.

Advertising

Ballard Flour, tin litho, figural obelisk shape, Egyptian hieroglyphics, 6 5/8" x 1 7/8"............................**$925**

Buster Brown Bread, tin litho, baker serving bread to Buster Brown and friends, wear to match basket, 6 7/8" x 2 1/8"...**$475**

Ceresota Prize Bread Flour, figural, diecut, tin litho, boy slicing bread, 5 3/8" x 2 1/2"..............................**$300**

Vulcan Plow Co., diecut, 7 7/8" x 2 3/4". **$825**

Wrigley's Juicy Fruit Gum, tin litho, red, white and black, 4 7/8" x 3 3/8". **$400**

Bisque, natural-colored rooster with beige basket, two compartments, round base with pink band, 4" h, 3 5/8" d. **$135**

Brass, bear chained to post, cast, original gilt trim, 3" h. **$225**

Bronze

Pheasants, signed "Cain," Auguste Nicolas Cain (French, 1821-1894), 4 1/4" h, 6 1/2" w. **$350**

Shoe, mouse in toe, 3" h. **$125**

Cast iron

Figural, high-button shoe, black paint, circa 1890, 5 1/2" h. **$50**

Hanging type, scrolled decoration. **$35**

Glass, satin, shaded rose to pink overlay, ball-shape, glossy off-white lining, ground pontil, 3" h, 3 1/4" d. **$155**

Majolica

Bull dog, striker, large.......................................**$440**

Happy Hooligan with suitcase, striker, rim nick to hat.**$110**

Monk, striker, hairline in base. **$140**

Papier-mâché, black lacquer, Oriental decoration, 2 3/4" h..**$25**

Porcelain, seated girl, feeding dog on table, signed "Elbogen"...**$125**

Sterling silver, hinged lid, diecut striking area, cigar cutter on one corner, lid inscription "H.R." and diamond, inside lid inscribed "Made for Tiffany & Co./Pat 12, 09/Sterling," 1 3/4" x 2 1/2". **$95**

Tin, top hat, hinged lid, original green paint, black band, 2 3/8" h..**$65**

Torquay pottery, ship scene, reads, "A match for any Man, Shankin," 2" h, 3 1/8" d. **$85**

Photo courtesy Green Valley Auctions

Match holder, figural, brass, Punch, second half 19th century, 2" h. **$125**

Photo courtesy Green Valley Auctions

Match holder, Wedgwood, Jasper, blue, bottom marked only "Wedgwood," late 19th/early 20th century, 1 1/4" h x 2" x 3 3/4". **$55**

Modernism

FUTURE OF THE MARKET: MODERNISM

The deep roots and far reach of Modern

By Noah Fleisher

There is more than a little irony in the fact that, in the world of collecting, "Modern" has a retro connotation.

It is the stuff of the 1933 Chicago World's Fair "Century of Progress," the boundless optimism of post-World War II America, the sleek comic lines and manic music of Tex Avery's MGM 1949 "House of Tomorrow" cartoons, and the ever-present acres of the suburban ranch house that subsequently spread endlessly across the nation.

The fact is that "Modernism" has never gone out of style. Its reach into the present day is as deep as its roots in the past. Just as it can be seen and felt ubiquitously in the mass media of today – on film, television, in magazines and department stores – it can be traced to the mid-1800s post-Empire non-conformity of the Biedermeier Movement, the turn of the 20th century anti-Victorianism of the Vienna Secessionists, the radical reductionism of Frank Lloyd Wright and the revolutionary post-Depression thinking of Walter Gropius and the Bauhaus school in Germany. There is no end to the ways in which the movement of Modernism, its evolution and continuing influence, can be parsed.

Photo courtesy Rago Arts and Auction Center, Lambertville, N.J.; www.RagoArts.com

Wesley Anderegg, Raku-fired figural cup and saucer, 1995. Cup signed and dated. Cup and saucer together: 5 3/4" x 6 1/4" x 4". **$1,200**

To that end, in today's economic climate, Modern is as close to a sure bet as collectors – experienced and neophyte alike – are going to get. From there, however, it's a game of names and taste; do you gravitate to Scandinavian design? American? Chairs or tables? Loveseats or sofas? Art? Sculpture? Lighting?

Ask the experts where to put your money and energy when it comes to buying Modern and you'll invariably get two answers: Put your energy into what you love, and your money into the best that you can afford. What that means on an individual basis is as varied, however, as the Modern movement itself.

"The Modernists really changed the way the world looked," said John Sollo, a partner in Sollo Rago Auction of Lambertville, N.J. "What I personally love about Modernism is that the business, as with a lot of other areas of antiques, hasn't cut it off in some arbitrary way. We've said, 'Yeah, that's cool' to anything made from 1903 to 2003. That opens it up."

There is no magic formula for determining where to put your dollars in terms of buying. Like all sectors, there are waves that favor one form over another. Ten years ago it was lounge chairs and dining room sets. As this is being written, the market is favoring Modern sculpture, ceramics, jewelry and accessories. Trying to put a finger on the pulse of the Modern market is like trying to catch lightning in a bottle.

Put another way, you'll do well at most any level and in most any sector of the market – almost all the top names in the business agree on this – but you have to have an idea going in what you personally want and like.

That openness is key, not only to the current success of Modernism as a philosophy of design, but also as an area of collecting. Sollo's partner in business, and one of the most recognizable names in the business, David Rago, takes Sollo's idea a little further by saying that Modernism is actually more about the names behind the design than the design itself, at least as far as buying goes.

"A decade ago people were buying up everything they could with the name Eames on it," Rago said (Charles and Ray Eames, husband-wife design team). "Today you can still get great deals on designs by modern masters. You just have to be informed about what you're doing. Go to major auctions and specialty Modernist shows. Talk to experts and learn as much as you can before you put money into it."

Richard Wright, the namesake of Wright20 in Chicago – a house whose Modern specialty auctions draw some of the very best examples of Modern design still available – echoes another idea that Rago put forth: that sometimes to be ahead of the curve you have to be behind it.

"There are bargains throughout the market starting at the turn of the century," said Wright. "Further, many early historical items are undervalued – or at least not hyped. Look for items out of fashion: 1930s Art Deco for example."

The word "bargain," as it refers to Modernism, must also be taken in context. A bargain can be $500, $5,000 or $50,000, depending on what, where and who you're buying. Again, it comes back to knowing your stuff. This can be accomplished by in-depth study, by association with reputable dealers and by taking your time and buying within your comfort zone.

Lisanne Dickson, Director of 1950s/Modern Design at Treadway-Toomey, goes into a little more depth on this, underscoring that a "bargain" price is relative, but certainly available.

"Classics of Modern design are undervalued and still fairly plentiful," she said. "After the 1999/2000 peak in prices, for example, designs by Charles and Ray Eames fell in value over the next seven years and have only started to firm within the last year. Prime examples can be had at fair prices, depending on how determined buyers are."

Dickson cites the current bargains in the U.S. market for big-name Scandinavian designers, and cautions entry-level buyers against going straight for the prime examples; they'll be priced out quickly.

"The closeness of an example to the original intentions of the designer is critically important," she said. "The earliest version of a design is most likely to represent the designer's true intention. Later modifications were likely made to enhance the bottom line, or ease production."

Those later designs are where an education can be had, collections formed and bargains found.

No discussion of Modern can be complete, however, without examining its genesis and enduring influence. As discussed earlier, Modernism is everywhere in today's pop culture. Austere Scandinavian furniture dominates the television commercials that hawk hotels and mutual funds. Post-war American design ranges across sit-com set dressings to movie sets patterned after Frank Lloyd Wright houses and Hollywood Modernist classics set high in the hills. What is de rigueur for any villain plotting to take over the world? A Bauhaus-inspired lair. No corporate headquarters is complete without "Modern" art on its walls, and chairs and tables straight out of the van der Rohe, Wormley and Perriand catalogs. In the same breath, however, you have to look at the dorm rooms of college students and the apartments of young people whose living spaces are packed with the undeniably Modern mass-produced products of IKEA, Target, Design Within Reach and the like.

Yet there seems to be no widespread discussion of this design influence, except among its adherents who live and breathe it. Turn to the experts and, again, you'll get as many different answers as there are Modernist forms.

Here's how Peter Loughrey, owner of Los Angeles Modern Auctions, puts it:

"Cheap rentals," he said simply. "You see a ton of print ads with Modern-designed items because rental of these things was relatively easy to come across. These are mass-produced pieces, and agencies could easily order up sets of five, 10 or 50 chairs for an ad or other marketing venture. Once these started popping up, there was no stopping it!"

This is an interesting theory, and there can be no denying that the post-World War II manufacturing techniques, and subsequent boom led to the widespread acceptance of plastic and bent plywood chairs along with low-sitting coffee tables, couches and recliners.

Wright takes this idea one step further, speaking of Modernism's appeal on an individual basis, despite its mass-production origins.

Screen, maker unknown, silver-leafed steel and wood frame with crackled finish, three panels each with suspended round and square plates that can be rotated as desired, original silver and gold finish, each panel: 20" w x 79 1/4" h, good condition. **$1,400**

"The Modern aesthetic is the culture of our times," he said. "We live in a post-Modern world that freely borrows from all past styles. In addition, art and design have become signifiers to a large group of the upper middle class. We are increasingly individually designing our world. Technology fuels this and the wide range of choices available."

"The modern aesthetic grew out of a perfect storm of post-war optimism, innovative materials and an incredible crop of designers," said Dickson. "The wide availability of the designs has made them accessible to the general public at reasonable prices."

On a more philosophic note, we can turn once more to Sollo, who posits that – even though Modern design has that "retro" feel – its time may have barely just arrived, if it's even come yet.

"I think that the people who designed the furniture were maybe ahead of society's ability to accept and understand what they were doing," he said. "It's taken people another 30 to 40 years to catch up to it, and that's what we're seeing now."

For the experienced collector of Modernism, this is well-known, and they know where and how to get their hands on good examples of Modern design at the best possible prices: Know your designers, know your tastes and spend the necessary time it takes to complete your collection.

All of the experts consulted for this article put the bottom line at almost the same place: find a dealer that you trust, go to specialty Modern auctions, sales and shows and ask as many questions as you possibly can. There is no such thing as a bad question when it comes to a "Modern" education.

Once you are well equipped with the proper knowledge of what you like and where to get it, there are tremendous deals to be had at whatever level you're buying. From $100 to $1,000 to $100,000, if you know unequivocally what you're after, then "Modern" is yours for the taking.

Noah Fleisher has written extensively for *Antique Trader Magazine, New England Antiques Journal,* and the *Northeast Journal of Antiques and Art.* He has also written for a Massachusetts style magazine called *Living Spaces,* where he wrote about a Modern-design pool house near Amherst, Mass.

Art

Macena Alberta Barton (American, 1901-1986)
"Modern Biblical Scene," circa 1940, oil on canvas, 40" x 36 1/4", signed lower left, unframed. **$325**

Harry Bertoia, (American, 1915-1978), untitled sculpture, circa 1954, gilded bronze, 10 1/2" (including base). **$8,400**

Harry Bertoia, (American, 1915-1978), untitled (Screen) sculpture, brass and steel, 23 1/2" x 21 1/2" x 4 1/2". **$33,600**

Harry Bertoia, (American, 1915-1978), untitled (Sonambient) sculpture, bronze and steel, 54 5/8" x 14" x 7". **$78,000**

Harry Bertoia, (American, 1915-1978), untitled (Zeppelin) sculpture, brass, steel and wood, 37 1/2" x 9" x 10". **$19,200**

Robert Brady, ceramic figural sculpture, "Seated Woman with Children," 1994. Signed in black ink R.B. 94, 23" x 6". **$1,920**

Karen Bresci, painted earthenware sculpture on wooden base, "Broccoli-Headed Woman," 1984. Signed and dated, 19" x 8 1/4" x 12"..**$1,320**

Photo courtesy Rago Arts and Auction Center, Lambertville, N.J.;
www.RagoArts.com

Harry Bertoia, (American, 1915-1978), untitled sculpture, circa 1954, gilded bronze, 11 3/8" (including base). **$7,200**

Photo courtesy Rago Arts and Auction Center, Lambertville, N.J.; www.RagoArts.com

Dale Chihuly / Portland Press Group, studio edition, Imperial Iris two-piece Persian set with Chartreuse Lip Wraps, 1999. Accompanied by Plexiglas display box. Signed Dale Chihuly 1234.PP2P.99., 7 1/2" x 13 1/4". **$3,360**

Mildred Lucile Crooks, (American, 1899-1972), "Modern Figures", circa 1950, oil on masonite, 18" x 30", signed lower right, framed. **$1,800**

Jill Crowley, glazed ceramic sculpture, 1980. Signed, 9" x 20"...**$1,080**

Ruth Duckworth, ceramic sculpture with tears, folds and incisions, covered in frosted white glaze with gunmetal, green and brown accents. Signed R70 in black ink, 6 1/2" x 7"...**$4,800**

Ruth Duckworth, footed porcelain sculpture covered in frosted white glaze. Signed R in black ink, 10" x 9". **$2,520**

Wharton Esherick, ink brush drawing of Hedgerow Theater (Rose Valley, Pa.) performer. Signed in pencil. Sight: Approx. 8 1/2" x 11"; framed: 18" x 22"............**$5,400**

Wharton Esherick, framed woodblock print on rice paper, "A Bright Night," circa 1925. Signed, titled and numbered. Image: 7 1/2" x 8"..**$4,800**

Richard Estes, (American, born 1932), two works of art: untitled, 1964, gouache on paper, two sheets (framed together), signed and dated, 10 1/8" x 7" (each, sight); Figures Sketched in Amsterdam, 1964, gouache on paper (framed), signed, dated, titled and inscribed, 6 1/2" x 4" (sight). ....**$960 both**

Paul Evans, welded and wrought steel fountain sculpture with abstract floral and geometric elements, circa 1956-57, 43 1/4" x 43" x 11 1/2"..................................**$42,000**

Claire Falkenstein, copper and glass fusion sculpture, executed circa 1968, (gift from the artist to a member of the Falkenstein Estate Board), 11" x 5" d.................**$30,000**

David Gilhooly, ceramic sculpture, "Breadfrog Making a Vegetable Stew of Himself," 17" x 15". **$5,700**

Photo courtesy Rago Arts and Auction Center, Lambertville, N.J.; www.RagoArts.com

Keith Haring (American, 1958-1990) Statue of Liberty, 1986, screen print in colors (framed); signed, dated and numbered P.P. 8/10, 37" x 27 3/4" (sight). **$20,400**

Photo courtesy Rago Arts and Auction Center, Lambertville, N.J.; www.RagoArts.com

LA II (Angel Ortiz, American, born 1967), untitled, acrylic on plaster bust of Tutankhamen. Signed and tagged throughout, 21 1/2" h. **$840**

Klaus Ihlenfeld, (German/American, 20th century), untitled sculpture, phosphorous bronze, signed, 14" h.
....**$3,600**

Klaus Ihlenfeld, (German/American, 20th century), Espalier, circa 2000, phosphorous bronze, signed, 13 1/2" h.
....**$2,520**

Klaus Ihlenfeld, (German/American, 20th century), Tonal, phosphorous bronze, signed, 14 1/2" h.........**$4,500**

Ilonka Karasz, (American, 1886-1981), cover Illustration for The New Yorker, July 19, 1941, gouache on paper (framed), signed, 16 7/8" x 12 1/4" (sight)...............**$9,600**

Philip and Kelvin Laverne, wall-hanging plaque in patinated metal with two women gazing from a window in sculptural relief, 1993. Engraved PHILIP KELVIN LAVERNE 93, 21 1/2" x 13 1/4"...................**$1,560**

Philip and Kelvin Laverne, acid-etched and patinated bronze plaque, "Making Love," within integrated frame. Signed Philip Kelvin Laverne, with original artist label and title on verso, 39 1/2" x 25".....................**$1,800**

Robert Loughlin, (American, born 1949), Rome IIIIX, 2007, acrylic on canvas. Signed, dated and titled, 48" x 48"; accompanied by a Brillo Box painted by the artist.
....**$1,320 both**

Photo courtesy Rago Arts and Auction Center, Lambertville, N.J.; www.RagoArts.com

Roy Lichtenstein (American, 1923-1997), Modern Sculpture with Apertures, 1967; Plexiglas with enamel screen print and silver Mylar; signed and numbered 112/200, 16 5/8" high. **$5,400**

Graham Marx, massive glazed terra-cotta ribbed sculpture with "torn" rim, approx. 23 1/2" x 34" x 23 1/2"..**$4,200**

Graham Marx, massive glazed terra cotta gourd-shaped sculpture, approx. 30" x 29" x 23".............**$16,800**

Isamu Noguchi / Gemini G.E.L., Neolithic, hot-dipped galvanized steel sculpture, 1983. Welded initials and date (i.n. 82.) Edition of 18, 72" x 26 1/2" x 16 1/2".
....**$90,000**

Albert Paley, sculpture of forged and fabricated steel, 1990. Signed PALEY with copyright, also inscribed 4/15 1990, 40" x 8" d. **$9,600**

Emile-Jacques Ruhlmann, Art Deco gilded plaster ceiling sculpture with stylized flowers from the Bon Marche department store. Approx. 47" x 29". **$3,900**

Silas Seandel, ribbon wall sculpture of forged steel. Script signature, 13 1/4" x 61 1/4". **$1,680**

Paul Soldner, slab-built, Raku-fired abstract sculpture, 1981, 14 1/2" x 35". **$22,800**

Paul Soldner, Raku fired sculpture from the Winged Series, 27" x 40" x 17". **$2,400**

Akio Takamori, ceramic sculpture, "Man with Faces," 1982, signed Akio, 11" x 16". **$7,800**

Jack Thompson, ceramic sculpture, "Dog Moses' Transition," 1981, 25" x 13" x 12". **$3,240**

Abraham Joel Tobias, (American, 1913-1996), untitled, pastel on paper, signed, 24 3/4" x 19". **$1,440**

Paul Wunderlich (German, born 1927), Torse De Femme and Torse De L'Homme, 1983, bronze, each signed and numbered 139/250, 17 1/2" h (male figure, including base), 14" high (female figure, including base); Foundry: Albrecht, Altrandsberg, Germany, 1984. ....**$3,120 pair**

Edward Zucca, wall sculpture, "A Victorian Time Machine," with tintype photographs mounted in a tiger maple frame, 1993. Signed, dated, titled, with personal inscription, verso, 7" x 53 1/2". **$1,440**

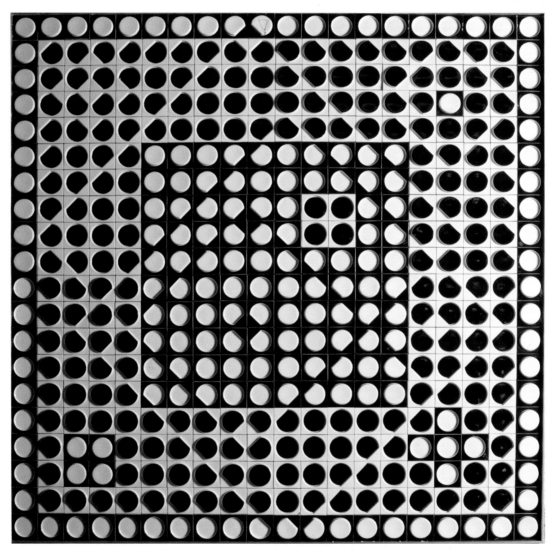

Photo courtesy Rago Arts and Auction Center, Lambertville, N.J.; www.RagoArts.com

Victor Vasarely / Rosenthal NB 22, Caope, wall-hanging sculptural relief panel composed of raised and inset black and white porcelain tiles, in metal frame. (Illustrated: Sixties Design by Philippe Garne, page 179), 78" sq. **$51,000**

Ceramics, Functional

Wesley Anderegg, Raku-fired figural earthenware cup and saucer, 1995. Signed and dated. Cup and saucer together: 5 3/4" x 6" x 3 1/4"........................ **$900**

Wesley Anderegg, Raku-fired figural cup and saucer on human sandwich base, 1996. Signed and dated. Cup and saucer together: 6 1/2" x 5 1/2" x 7 1/2"............. **$2,040**

Claude Conover, stoneware vessel, "Acalac." Signed and titled, 20 1/2" x 16 1/2"................................ **$5,400**

Richard Devore, flaring stoneware vessel, "Untitled no. 1024," with a dead-matte gray interior with small shelf, 12" x 12 3/4". **$7,200**

Richard Hirsch, large tripod ceramic vessel, 1992. Signed and dated, approx: 37 1/2" x 29" x 29". **$2,160**

Karen Karnes, stoneware winged tureen covered in deep-green matte mottled glaze. Chop mark KK., 8" x 21".
.... **$5,100**

Michael Lucero, faience sculptural double-vessel glazed in bright polychrome. Signed Michael Lucero with oversized barcode, 25-40 ML, 8 1/4" x 11 1/2" x 3 1/2"............. **$2,400**

Warren MacKenzie, stoneware platter with random white pattern on mirrored brown ground, along with porcelain covered jar in celadon glaze. Jar signed with chop mark, 2 1/2" x 12 3/4" and 3 1/2" x 4 1/2". .... **$900 both**

Marc Newsom / Cor Unum, sci-fi ceramic vase in white glaze. Decal with Cor Unum Ceramics and Art the Netherlands, stamped cipher, 13 1/2" x 12". **$720**

Picasso / Madoura, faience pitcher with abstract animal design. Signed EDITION PICASSO MADOURA, and numbered 165/200, 8" x 11 1/2" x 4 1/2"..................... **$5,400**

Picasso / Madoura, faience pitcher with abstract bird design. Signed EDITION PICASSO MADOURA, 11 1/2" x 8 1/2" x 6".. **$5,700**

Picasso / Madoura, figural faience vessel depicting a woman in black and white glaze. Signed EDITION PICASSO MADOURA, 11 1/2" x 8 1/2" x 5 1/2". **$7,200**

Picasso / Madoura, faience pitcher with abstract faces design. Signed EDITION PICASSO MADOURA, and numbered 84/300, 9 1/4" x 7 1/2" x 4 1/2"................... **$7,200**

Pillin, oval charger with circus performers on horses, signed, 10 1/2" x 16 3/4"................................... **$1,800**

Pillin, jardinere painted with horses and ladies, signed, 8 1/2" x 9 1/2".. **$2,520**

Photo courtesy Rago Arts and Auction Center, Lambertville, N.J.; www.RagoArts.com

Pillin, vase painted with ladies holding fish-laden nets, signed, 14 1/2" x 6 1/4". **$2,400**

Photo courtesy Rago Arts and Auction Center, Lambertville, N.J.; www.RagoArts.com

Picasso / Madoura, faience pitcher with abstract animal design. Signed EDITION PICASSO MADOURA, 10" x 6" x 4". **$4,200**

Mary Roehm, flaring wood-fired porcelain bowl covered in celadon semi-matte glaze. Script signature, 9" x 21 1/2" d.. **$1,200**

Paul Schreckengost, glazed earthenware Art Deco teapot and cup, 7" x 11 1/2" x 4" and 2 1/2" x 5" x 3 3/4"... **$6,000 both**

Paul Soldner, Raku-fired spherical footed vessel, circa 1965-72, 9 3/4" x 11"..................................... **$1,800**

Paul Soldner, slab-built, Raku-fired vessel, "Voco," 1981, 14 3/4" x 11 1/4"... **$1,560**

Paul Soldner, Raku-fired vessel with applied and painted floral motifs, 1981, 19" x 14" x 9".................... **$2,400**

Rudolph Staffel, flaring porcelain cup, circa 1980, 3" x 3 1/2".. **$720**

Henry Takemoto, stoneware charger with abstract brush strokes in indigo and gunmetal brown, 1959. Signed and dated, 2 1/2" x 16 1/2"..................................... **$4,200**

Peter Voulkos, wood-fired stoneware charger with three small "prunts" (ornaments) covered in ivory glaze, 1981. Signed V.O.U.L.K.O.S., 5 1/2" x 21". **$14,400**

Peter Voulkos, Shigaraki stoneware charger inscribed to the kiln in which it was fired, "FOR BIG 'AUTASH' KEEP PUFFIN AND BE GOOD Voulkos 91," 1997. Signed V.O.U.L.K.O.S. 97, U.C.F., 5 1/2" x 23".................... **$4,800**

Peter Voulkos, Raku-fired plate with torn chunks, 1995. Signed and dated, 5" x 21". **$10,800**

Peter Voulkos, stoneware plate, gas-fired, 1978. Signed V.O.U.L.K.O.S. 78, 4" x 22". **$14,400**

Betty Woodman, stoneware footed jardinere with ribbon decoration. Stamped WOODMAN, 7 1/2" x 12". **$3,120**

Photo courtesy of Treadway Toomey Galleries, Cincinnati and Oak Park, Ill.; www.TreadwayGallery.com

Ben Seibel Modern Stoneware dinnerware, by Roseville for Raymor, USA, ceramic, 12 cups, 12 saucers, 12 dinner plates, seven bread plates, three salad plates, three serving dishes, three large covered casseroles, one small covered casserole, one creamer, one covered ramekin, one pitcher, one bowl, one small handled covered dish with lid, and one bean pot, one extra lid (not shown), all in terra-cotta, signed "Raymor by Roseville", dinner plate 12" d, creamer 4 1/4" h, excellent condition. **$700 all**

Furniture

Baker, (style of), sofas (pair) with floating backrests, upholstered in white silk, 40" x 61" x 26". .... **$11,400 pair**

Garry Knox Bennett, table lamp, "A Nite on Lindquist Ridge," 1990. (Exhibited: "Made in Oakland: The Furniture of Garry Knox Bennett", American Craft Museum, New York, January 2001.) Titled/In Oakland GKB Anno 90, 20" x 22" x 20". **$1,200**

Garry Knox Bennett / Ambrose Pillphister, workstation with walnut top, chrome and metal pedestals, includes two gouache on shellacked panel paintings by Ambrose Pillphister dated 1994. Workstation signed "GKB", paintings signed "AMBROSE PILLPHISTER 1994". Workstation: 29 1/2" x 116" x 102 1/2", paintings: 17 3/4" x 26"...**$2,400**

Wendell Castle, white fiberglass Molar sofa, 26" x 48" x 29 1/2"...**$2,880**

Wendell Castle, wall hanging/table, 1992. Signed Castle '92. Table: 23 1/2" x 24" x 21 3/4", wall sculpture: 28 1/2" x 57 1/2". ....**$2,400 both**

Michael Coffey, Heron Table II, carved Wenge foyer table on single leg with hidden sliding drawer. Signed M. Coffey, 38" x 40" x 18"...**$10,800**

Danish Modern sewing table, imported by George Tanier, rosewood form with one drawer and original slide-out basket, birch-lined drawer with compartments and original pin cushion, includes original George Tanier catalog page, unsigned, original finish, 23" w x 17" d x 21" h, excellent condition.................................**$300**

Danish secretary, rosewood veneer, drop-front over four drawers with carved pulls, interior contains two drawers and various compartments, front and top drawer lock, original finish, key included, signed in drawer with Danish Furniture Makers mark, "Made in Denmark" stamp on back, original finish, 37 1/2" w x 17" d x 45" h, work surface: 28 1/2" h, very good original condition...........**$350**

Danish teak wing chairs, (pair) upholstered in white leather. Red metal tag, Made and Finished in Denmark, Imported by Selig, 40" x 34" x 29"........................**$3,600 pair**

Dining table, 1960s, possibly by Milo Baughman for Directional, parsons-style table with rosewood, walnut and veneer to top over oak legs, two 20" leaves (not shown), original finish, shown: 71 1/2" w x 39" d x 28 1/2" h, excellent condition. **$550**

Peter Dudley, entertainment cabinet in mahogany with chip-carved gallery top, enameled green interior with shelves, and two lower drawers, 81" x 40" x 21 1/2". **$3,480**

Charles Eames / Herman Miller, surfboard coffee table with black laminate top on wire base. Oval Eames/Herman Miller metal tag, 10" x 89 1/2" x 29 1/2".....................**$1,920**

Charles Eames / Herman Miller, group lounge sofa with channeled black leather upholstery, 33 1/2" x 73" x 30". **$6,000**

Wharton Esherick, walnut captain's chair with woven leather seat, accompanied by letter of authenticity from the Wharton Esherick Museum, 30 1/4" x 24 1/2" x 22". **$10,800**

Wharton Esherick, paneled wood chest with hinged lid, on casters, 1968. Signed W.E. 1968, 28" x 84" x 32".......**$18,000**

Photo courtesy Rago Arts and Auction Center, Lambertville, N.J.; www.RagoArts.com

Wendell Castle, laminated wood pedestal, 1973. Signed WC 73, 20" x 15 1/2". **$16,800**

Photo courtesy Rago Arts and Auction Center, Lambertville, N.J.; www.RagoArts.com

Charles Eames / Herman Miller, 670/671 lounge chair and ottoman in rosewood veneer with black leather upholstery. Herman Miller paper labels, 33" x 33" x 26". **$3,600 pair**

Photo courtesy Rago Arts and Auction Center, Lambertville, N.J.; www.RagoArts.com

Paul Evans, cube chair with copper, bronze and pewter patchwork covering, and gold velvet upholstery, on swivel base with casters, 28" x 32" x 31". **$9,000**

Wharton Esherick, music stand in carved cherry on three legs, 1962. Signed WE 1962, 44" x 15 1/2" x 20"......**$84,000**

Paul Evans, sculpted bronze buffet with two pieces of slate on top, and two bi-fold doors concealing two shelves, 33 1/2" x 74" x 20". **$13,200**

Paul Evans, Argente two-door cabinet with biomorphic forms in sculpted aluminum, its interior with three shelves and antiqued finish, 1968. Signed Paul Evans 68 S, 81" x 36" x 19 3/4". **$66,000**

Paul Evans, sculpted bronze dining chairs (six), two arm- and four side-, upholstered in purple crushed velvet. Armchairs: 32 1/2" x 27" x 24", side chairs: 32 1/2" x 20 1/2" x 22"...**$18,000 set**

Paul Evans, Cityscape U-shaped table with chrome covering. Marked "An Original Paul Evans," 20 1/2" x 20". **$5,100**

Paul Evans, sculpted bronze console table with inset leather-covered top, 1970. Signed P.E. '70, 24 1/4" x 60" x 18 1/4". **$6,000**

Paul Evans, sculpted bronze dining table with plate glass top on serpentine stalactite base, 1972, 29 1/4" x 82" x 40". **$11,400**

Paul Evans, sculpted bronze occasional tables (pair) with rosewood tops, 1968. One signed PE 68, 20" x 12" x 10 1/2". ....**$10,200 pair**

Dan Johnson, Gazelle chair with patinated bronze frame, caned seat and back, 32" x 19" x 17 1/2"....................**$10,800**

Dan Johnson, four-drawer, single pedestal desk with lacquered top, 30 3/4" x 54" x 24 1/4".........................**$5,700**

Finn Juhl, No. 45 teak armchair upholstered in teal wool, 32 1/4" x 28" x 26"......................**$4,500**

Finn Juhl / Niels Vodder, No.53 easy chair on sculpted teak frame upholstered in woven orange and yellow wool. Signed Niels Vodder Cabinetmaker Copenhagen, Denmark Design Finn Juhl, 28 3/4" x 28 1/4" x 26". **$3,360**

Finn Juhl / Niels Vodder, No. 45 armchairs (pair) with fabric upholstery. Branded mark, 33" x 27" x 30". ....**$9,000 pair**

Finn Juhl / France & Daverkosen, teak sofa and pair of lounge chairs with black fabric upholstery. FD metal tag, chairs branded Made in Denmark. Sofa: 28 1/4" x 72" x 28", chairs: 27 1/2" x 26 1/2" x 28"................**$7,200 all**

Finn Juhl / France & Daverkosen, teak sofas (pair) with black fabric upholstery. FD metal tag. Each: 28 1/4" x 72" x 28".....................**$14,400 pair**

Finn Juhl / Niels Vodder, Judas rosewood extension dining table with silver inlay to top, accompanied by two 22" matching leaves. Closed: 28 1/2" x 78 1/2" x 54 3/4".....................**$19,200**

Vladimir Kagan, sofa with black and white chenille upholstery on rosewood veneer base, 28 1/2" x 94 1/2" x 39 1/2". **$21,600**

Vladimir Kagan, sofa upholstered in orange wool, on walnut legs, 28" x 92" x 32"......................**$15,600**

Vladimir Kagan, serpentine sofa upholstered in cherry red fabric, 28" x 92" x 37"......................**$10,200**

Vladimir Kagan, glass-top extension dining table in rosewood and brushed aluminum, with inset plate glass top. Includes two 23 1/2" leaves. Without leaves: 29" x 84" x 34"......................**$7,800**

Vladimir Kagan / Dreyfuss, coffee table in mahogany with inset travertine top. Marked Kagan Dreyfuss New York Vladimir Kagan Design, 15" x 60" x 21 1/2".......**$1,920**

Vladimir Kagan / Kagan-Dreyfuss, small side table with carved slate top on walnut and brass frame. Kagan Dreyfuss foil label, 19" x 12" x 8". **$5,700**

Rei Kawakubo / Commes des Garcons, triangular tables (two), each with two-piece granite top on metal base with casters, designed by Kawakubo for her Comme des Garcons clothing stores, 25 1/2" x 59" x 29" and 29" x 78" x 38"......................**$1,440 both**

Florence Knoll / Knoll, oak wall-hanging credenza with painted doors, 21" x 70" x 17"......................**$1,080**

Florence Knoll / Knoll, six-drawer teak credenza with black soapstone top, on steel base. 28" x 54 3/4" x 22 1/2". **$1,500**

Florence Knoll / Knoll, four-door rosewood credenza with white marble top and eight interior shelves, on polished steel base. Knoll International label, 25 3/4" x 74 1/2" x 18". **$3,000**

Florence Knoll / Knoll, sofa with multicolored fabric upholstery and integrated two-drawer walnut end-table, on polished steel frame, 31" x 119 1/2" x 31". **$1,800**

Knoll, three-drawer rosewood desk with two slide-out shelves, on polished steel frame. Knoll Associates label, 29" x 72" x 32". **$1,680**

Philip Laverne, Madame Pompadour occasional table with polychrome floral motif. Philip Laverne Gallery paper tag, 17" x 30" x 17". **$2,400**

Philip and Kelvin Laverne, Chan Li four-door cabinet in patinated mixed metals, the doors depicting an Asian courtyard scene, concealing interior shelves and single drawer. Signed twice, Philip and Kelvin Laverne, with Philip Laverne studio paper label, 31 1/4" x 49" x 15 3/4". **$22,800**

Photo courtesy Rago Arts and Auction Center, Lambertville, N.J.; www.RagoArts.com

Vladimir Kagan, sling dining armchairs (pair) with charcoal fabric upholstery on sculpted walnut frames, 36 1/2" x 25 1/4" x 24 1/2". **$3,120 pair**

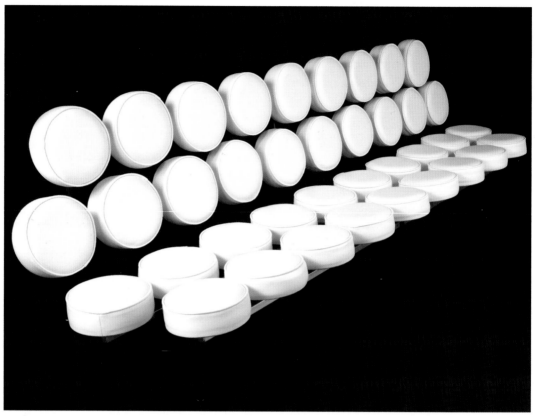

Photo courtesy Rago Arts and Auction Center, Lambertville, N.J.; www.RagoArts.com

Irving Harper / George Nelson & Associates, "Marshmallow" sofa upholstered in white vinyl on brushed and enameled steel frame. (One of only a few produced in this size.) Signed Irving Harper, 30 1/2" x 103" x 30". **$45,000**

Photo courtesy Rago Arts and Auction Center, Lambertville, N.J.; www.RagoArts.com

Wendy Maruyama, carved wood tables (pair) with shaded green and fuchsia finish, 1996. Signed Wendy Maruyama '96, 28 1/4" x 28 1/4" x 21 1/2". **$9,000 pair**

Photo courtesy Rago Arts and Auction Center, Lambertville, N.J.; www.RagoArts.com

Isamu Noguchi / Knoll, teak rocking stool with steel wire frame, circa 1954, 10 1/2" x 14". **$6,600**

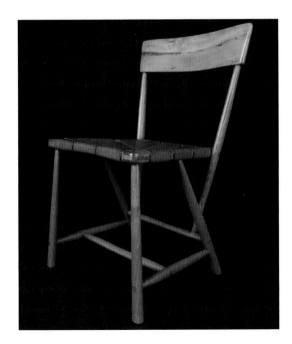

Photo courtesy Rago Arts and Auction Center, Lambertville, N.J.; www.RagoArts.com

Wharton Esherick, hickory side chair with webbed seat of brown hard leather straps, 1958. Signed W.E. 1958, 31 1/2" x 18 1/2" x 17". **$20,400**

Photo courtesy Rago Arts and Auction Center, Lambertville, N.J.; www.RagoArts.com

George Nakashima, eight-drawer walnut wall-hanging cabinet with burl-wood pulls. (An exceptional and unusual early Nakashima cabinet, the piece was originally designed as part of the interior of a residence on King's Point, Long Island, for his early patrons, the Hammer family. Nakashima served as both the architect and interior designer, and the home was heralded as a new style of modern design influenced by handmade materials.) 11 3/4" x 96 1/4" x 19 1/4". **$78,000**

Philip and Kelvin Laverne, coffee table, its scalloped top etched with Asian vignettes, 17" x 47" x 23 1/4"..........**$5,700**

Thorald Madsens / Tove and Edvard Kindt-Larsen, rosewood dining chairs (eight) with black leather upholstery. Thorald Madsens metal tags, 32" x 19 1/2" x 17"..................**$21,600 set**

Bruna Mathsson / Karl Mathsson, teak and beech expandable dining table, 28 1/2" x 60" x 43 1/2"...........**$540**

George Nakashima, walnut wall-hanging bar with glass shelves and illuminated base, 18" x 60" x 6"................**$4,200**

George Nakashima, Kornblut cabinet with burl-wood handle, 22" x 19" x 19 3/4"....................**$44,400**

George Nakashima, conoid cushion chair, in walnut with hickory spindles and black fabric cushions, 33 1/2" x 34" x 30"..................**$14,400**

George Nakashima, conoid cushion chair, in Burmese laurel with hickory spindles, 33 1/2" x 34" x 30" **$22,800**

George Nakashima, walnut conoid chairs (pair) with hickory spindles, marked with client's name, 35 1/2" x 21" x 19 1/2". ....**$19,200 pair**

George Nakashima, walnut Conoid chairs (six) with hickory spindles, marked with client's name, 35 1/2" x 21" x 20".................**$51,000 set**

George Nakashima, lounge chair with free-edge writing arm in English walnut, 1987. Signed George Nakashima April 15, 1987, and marked with client's name, 33 1/4" x 31" x 25". **$13,200**

Photo courtesy Rago Arts and Auction Center, Lambertville, N.J.; www.RagoArts.com

George Nakashima, English walnut single-pedestal desk with freeform, free-edge top incorporating four rosewood butterfly keys, over a bank of three drawers with finished back, and a rosewood cross-plank support, 29" x 78" x 40 1/2". **$132,000**

George Nakashima, "New Chair with Arms," walnut, 1970, marked SHOWROOM and signed George Nakashima 1970, 39" x 25" x 21"......................**$7,800**

George Nakashima, "New Chairs with Arms" (pair), walnut, marked with client's name. 38 1/2" x 25" x 21". ....**$10,800 pair**

George Nakashima, walnut lounge rocker with free-shaped arm. Signed STUDIO-ROCKER, 34" x 33" x 35". **$10,200**

George Nakashima, walnut credenza with four interior drawers and two shelves, and finished back, 32" x 60" x 24". **$19,200**

George Nakashima, double-pedestal desk in walnut, its free-edge top with single rosewood butterfly key, marked with client's name, 27 3/4" x 80 1/2" x 30 1/2". **$43,200**

George Nakashima, single-drawer desk in walnut on trestle base with free-edge top, 30" x 70" x 29 1/2". **$96,000**

George Nakashima, walnut four-drawer dresser with free-edge top, marked with client's name, 32" x 36" x 22". **$14,400**

George Nakashima, free-edge headboard in English walnut with five rosewood butterfly keys, 42" x 104 1/2". **$48,000**

George Nakashima, walnut two-drawer nightstands (pair), one marked with client's name, 25 1/2" x 15 1/2" x 19 1/4". ....**$24,000 pair**

George Nakashima, coffee table with free-edge walnut top, marked with client's name, 13" x 82 1/2" x 21 1/4". **$30,000**

George Nakashima, Minguren I walnut coffee table with free-form, free-edge top incorporating two rosewood butterfly keys, 1977. (Accompanied by original drawing and sales receipt.) Marked with client's name, 15 1/2" x 98 1/2" x 34 1/2". **$144,000**

George Nakashima, slab coffee table in walnut with freeform top and single butterfly key, 13 1/4" x 44" x 20". **$43,200**

George Nakashima, sled-base coffee table with free-edge Persian walnut top, 1980. Marked with client's name; also reads, "Sled-type/Persian walnut/George Nakashima 1980," 14 1/2" x 81 1/2" x 28 1/2"......................**$54,000**

George Nakashima, walnut Frenchman's Cove table, marked with client's name, 28" x 49 1/2" x 50"........**$16,800**

George Nakashima, round pedestal table in walnut, 28" x 42" d. …......................**$9,000**

George Nakashima, walnut trestle table, its top with three rosewood butterfly keys, 28" x 60" x 24". **$26,400**

George Nakashima, Wohl table with free-edge top, 1988, signed George Nakashima, June 24, 1988, 12 1/2" x 23 1/4" x 15 1/2". **$5,700**

George Nakashima / Widdicomb, high-back lounge chair upholstered with ecru fabric, 41 1/2" x 31 1/2" x 33 3/4". **$10,200**
(John Widdicomb Co., Grand Rapids, Mich.)

George Nakashima / Widdicomb, lounge chair and ottoman upholstered with ecru fabric, 33" x 32 1/4" x 33" and 16" x 25" sq. ....**$11,400 both**
(John Widdicomb Co., Grand Rapids, Mich.)

George Nakashima / Widdicomb, walnut six-drawer dresser. Branded George Nakashima inside drawer, 32" x 76" x 22". **$5,700**
(John Widdicomb Co., Grand Rapids, Mich.)

George Nakashima / Widdicomb, 12-drawer dresser with recessed brass pulls in Sundra finish. Widdicomb fabric label, 32" x 105 1/2" x 22"......................**$6,600**
(John Widdicomb Co., Grand Rapids, Mich.)

George Nakashima / Widdicomb, king-size headboard with Sundra finish, and pair of single-drawer nightstands. Headboard: 38" x 109", nightstands: 21" x 22" x 21"... **$7,200 all**
(John Widdicomb Co., Grand Rapids, Mich.)

Photo courtesy Rago Arts and Auction Center, Lambertville, N.J.; www.RagoArts.com

George Nakashima, round Minguren coffee table, in walnut with three rosewood butterfly keys, 1979, inscribed "To Alene, Abe, Merry Christmas 1979 George Nakashima," 15" x 48". **$33,600**

George Nakashima / Widdicomb, single-arm sofa and settee with slatted side panels, upholstered in ecru fabric, 25 1/2" x 103" x 34" and 25 1/2" x 62" x 34".............**$32,400** (*John Widdicomb Co., Grand Rapids, Mich.*)

George Nakashima / Widdicomb, long coffee table in Sundra finish with burl-wood veneer panel to free-form top. Widdicomb factory number, 13 1/2" x 84" x 30 1/2". **$5,700**

(*John Widdicomb Co., Grand Rapids, Mich.*)

George Nakashima / Widdicomb, side tables (two) in Sundra finish, one with spindled lower shelf. Marked George Nakashima 9/59 Sundra, with Widdicomb decal, 21 1/4" x 30" x 20" and 16 1/2" x 30" sq.............**$1,920 both** (*John Widdicomb Co., Grand Rapids, Mich.*)

George Nelson, home office desk with tan leather covering to sliding doors and to writing surface, a lift-top storage compartment, and mesh Pendaflex file, 40 1/2" x 54 1/4" x 28"...**$7,800**

George Nelson / Charles Deaton, CSS unit designed by George Nelson, consisting of 4 vertical supports with multiple drawers, cabinet and shelves, along with clock, barometer and radio unit, accompanied by L-shaped desk designed by Charles Deaton. CSS unit: 87" x 97" x 20", desk: 26" x 70" x 78".....................................**$6,000 both**

George Nelson / Herman Miller, Thin Edge two-door rosewood cabinet with porcelain pulls and single interior shelf. Herman Miller foil label, 30" x 33" x 19 1/2".....**$3,900**

George Nelson / Herman Miller, Thin Edge four-drawer rosewood chest with porcelain pulls. Herman Miller foil label, 30" x 33" x 19 1/2". **$4,200**

George Nelson / Herman Miller, Thin Edge five-drawer walnut chest with porcelain hourglass pulls, 41" x 40" x 19 1/2"..**$2,400**

George Nelson / Herman Miller, swag-leg desk with two shallow drawers, 34 1/2" x 39" x 28 3/4"..................**$4,500**

George Nelson / Herman Miller, "Marshmallow" sofa upholstered in burnt orange velvet on brushed and enameled steel frame, 31 1/2" x 51 1/2" x 31 1/2". **$10,800**

George Nelson / Herman Miller, Catenary coffee table with plate glass top on polished steel base, 15 1/4" 36" sq. **$1,500**

Norwegian, curvilinear sofa with dark-green wool upholstery and paisley fabric seat cushions, 29" x 130" x 31"...**$2,640**

Ottoman, 1950s, maker unknown, ebonized wood frame with sculptural curved legs placed on the center of each side, cushion reupholstered in beige mohair with a rectangular tufted button, refinished, 40" w x 40" d x 15" h, very good condition. **$1,300**

Albert Paley, plant stand of formed and fabricated steel with marble top, 1992. Signed Albert Paley 1992, 56" x 16" x 20"..**$21,600**

Tommi Parzinger, "American Modern" sectional sofa, by Salterini, circa 1950, two middle and two end pieces, black metal frames with circle motif to backrests, removable cushions in original leopard print fabric, (back cushions and two round bolsters included but not shown), unsigned but documented, as shown: 109" w x 30 1/2" d x 28" h, frames repainted, very good condition......................**$5,000**

Photo courtesy Rago Arts and Auction Center, Lambertville, N.J.; www.RagoArts.com

George Nelson / Herman Miller, CSS unit in rosewood veneer and brushed metal, with eight vertical supports, four black enameled metal light fixtures and numerous drawers, cupboards and shelves, 95" x 226" x 18 1/2". **$24,000**

Photo courtesy of Treadway Toomey Galleries, Cincinnati and Oak Park, Ill.; www.TreadwayGallery.com

Post-Modern barstools (three), 1993, multi-colored vinyl seats with black and white check trim, diamond plate foot rests, painted ball feet and metal coil detail to legs, titled "Jumpin' Jack" and numbered 73, 74 and 75, signature appears to read "M. Levin", dated 1993, 14" d x 26" h, very good condition. **$950 all**

Tommi Parzinger, occasional tables (pair), for Charak Modern, 1950s, two triangular forms can be used together to form a square, mahogany bases with lower shelf, leather tops with tooled edge and green/gold finish treatment, each signed with Charak label, original finish to tops, bases refinished, each is 54 1/2" w x 28" d x 18" h, used together: 40 1/4" square, very good condition. .... **$5,500 pair**

Phillip Lloyd Powell, walnut bench with woven ecru fabric cushions, and integrated marble-top table, 34 1/4" x 100 1/2" x 27"..................................**$20,400**

Phillip Lloyd Powell, two-seat walnut bench with integrated table, and woven ecru fabric cushions, 30" x 65" x 29"...**$20,400**

Phillip Lloyd Powell, two-door walnut cabinet with sculpted bi-fold doors concealing an enameled and silver-leafed interior with drawers, cabinets, shelves, and slate shelf, 92 1/2" x 48 1/2" x 21 1/4".................**$60,000**

Phillip Lloyd Powell, interchangeable three-seat settee in mahogany with integrated travertine-top tables, 30" x 120" x 29"..**$9,600**

Phillip Lloyd Powell, elliptical coffee table with slate top on mahogany base, 15 1/2" x 29 3/4" x 22 1/4"...........**$4,800**

Phillip Lloyd Powell, walnut coffee table with free-edge top, single butterfly key, and legs mortised through the top, 13 1/2" x 79" x 18 1/2".................................**$16,800**

Phillip Lloyd Powell / Paul Evans, walnut wall-hung vertical cabinet with sculpted bi-fold doors and bronze loop panel backed with beige linen, circa 1962, 54" x 30" x 19 1/4". **$60,000**

Plymouth, chest, 1940s, cherry-stained mahogany case has four recessed drawers with carved wood handles and square cutout detail, branded mark on back and metal tag in drawer, refinished, 30" w x 19 3/4" d x 33 1/2" h, very good condition..............................**$250**

John Risley, figural black wire lounge chair and ottoman. Chair: 40 1/2" x 26 1/2" x 29 3/4", ottoman: 17" x 20" x 40". ....**$6,000 pair**

John Risley, figural black wire chairs (two), one with arms, 49 1/2" x 28 3/4" x 19" and 47" x 18 3/4" x 17 1/2". ....**$4,800 both**

T.H. Robsjohn-Gibbings cabinet, for Widdicomb, bleached mahogany, five drawers with beveled edges and original brass ring pulls atop a curved platform base on hidden casters, refinished, Widdicomb Modern Originals tag in drawer, 54" w x 20 1/2" d x 32 3/4" h, very good condition. **$1,400**

Photo courtesy Rago Arts and Auction Center, Lambertville, N.J.; www.RagoArts.com

Albert Paley, coffee table with bevel-edged plate-glass top resting on a base of formed and fabricated steel, 20" x 48" sq. **$24,000**

Photo courtesy of Treadway Toomey Galleries, Cincinnati and Oak Park, Ill.; www.TreadwayGallery.com

T.H. Robsjohn-Gibbings dining set, for Widdicomb, table and six chairs, mahogany, table with round top and sunburst veneer pattern, 3 1/2" apron over curved reverse-tapered legs, lower curved stretchers, three 12" leaves, original finish, signed with cloth "Widdicomb Modern Originals" label, 48 1/4" d x 29" h, chairs with exaggerated curved backrests over oval front legs and splayed square back legs, original upholstery, original finish, 21" w x 21" d x 37 3/4" h, all in very good original condition. **$6,000 set**

T.H. Robsjohn-Gibbings dining table, for Widdicomb, rectangular bleached mahogany top with thick apron over four legs with curved stretcher to base, two 14" leaves (not shown), original finish, signed with Widdicomb Modern Original tag, 40" w x 76" d x 29" h, very good condition. **$1,800**

Gilbert Rohde / Herman Miller, seven-piece bedroom suite, consisting of a vanity and stool, two four-drawer chests with Bakelite handles (one replaced), and a king-sized headboard. Marked with metal tag and stenciled numbers. Chests: 36 1/4" x 43" x 18", headboard: 35" x 77 1/4". ....**$1,500 all**

Gilbert Rohde / Herman Miller, East Indian laurel cabinet with two doors and two drawers. Herman Miller foil label, 41" x 48" x 15". **$3,600**

Gilbert Rohde, two-piece sectional sofa with single arm and tufted white fabric upholstery on tapering wood legs, 30" x 90 1/2" x 34 1/2" and 30" x 66 1/2" x 33". **$6,000**

Gilbert Rohde, custom-designed mahogany coffee table with scallop-edged marble top, 18" x 56" x 22". **$1,800**

Gilbert Rohde / Herman Miller, "Cloud" coffee table with exotic wood veneer top, and leatherette-covered supports, 15 1/2" x 41" x 31". **$1,920**

Rustic, cast-aluminum faux antler sofa with green and white fabric upholstery, 40 1/2" x 67" x 29 1/4". **$9,600**

Sabena (Mexico), pine log bar with three matching stools, on iron frames. Branded mark. Bar: 34" x 98" x 21 1/2". ....**$3,120 all**

Sabena (Mexico), pine log magazine rack in iron frame. Branded mark, 21" x 28" x 18". **$720**

Screen, maker unknown, three mahogany panels with geometric fretwork design, unsigned, original finish, 71 1/4" w x 71 3/4" h, each panel: 23 3/4" w, very good condition. **$225**

Photo courtesy Rago Arts and Auction Center, Lambertville, N.J.; www.RagoArts.com

Eero Saarinen / Knoll, Grasshopper chair with corduroy upholstery, 34 1/2" x 27" x 32 1/2". **$2,160**

Photo courtesy Rago Arts and Auction Center, Lambertville, N.J.; www.RagoArts.com

Ludwig Mies van der Rohe / Knoll, Barcelona chairs (pair) with black leather cushions on polished steel frames. (Provenance: Seagram Building.) One with Seagram label, 30" x 31" x 28". **$5,700 pair**

Silas Seandel, primitive coffee table of cast bronze with polychrome patina, and plate glass top. Script signature, 15" x 38" x 17 1/4". **$1,560**

Silas Seandel Ironworks, dining table of fabricated and welded steel with plate glass top, 1975. Signed Silas Seandel '75 with copyright, 29" x 64" x 38 1/4".........................**$2,160**

Selig, Danish Modern high-back lounge chairs (pair), walnut frames with sculptural sides and flared arms, reupholstered in light tan leather, signed with round metal Selig tag, 34" w x 32" d x 39 1/2" h, very good condition. ....**$1,600 pair**

Jay Stanger, king-size polychrome bed in mixed wood veneers with metal accents, and two integrated nightstands. Approx. 77" x 122 3/4" x 103"................**$4,500**

Photo courtesy Rago Arts and Auction Center, Lambertville, N.J.; www.RagoArts.com

Hans Wegner / A.P. Stolen, ox chair with "horns" covered in striped fabric over original slate-gray fabric. Circular Danish Furniture control tag, 35" x 38" x 32". **$13,200**

Storage unit, 1970s, Italy, possibly by Giotto Stoppino for Heller, white molded plastic unit designed to be configured as desired, 49 pieces and 4 metal brackets for attaching to wall, overall measurement as shown: 100" w x 102" d x 73" h, large opening at left is 46 1/2" x 30 1/2" x 12" d, height of right side section is 49 1/2", also includes a letter sorter at center, which is marked "Giotto Stoppino Heller Made in Italy", six other pieces are also included: two "T" sections, one 32" straight section, one 16" straight section, and two 9" straight sections, some discoloration and yellowing, good condition...............................**$1,900 all**

Wall unit, 1960s, four black wood vertical supports with open framework support five cabinets and five shelves in rosewood, three cabinets with two doors, one cabinet with three drawers, one cabinet with a locking drop-front lined in mahogany, five shelves with spring-loaded wood pegs, includes original assembly instructions, necessary hardware and key, back is finished, unsigned, original finish, 87" w x 16 1/2" d x 73" h, very good original condition. **$1,400**

Ole Wanscher, colonial chair and ottoman in rosewood with caned seat supports and dark brown leather cushions. Danish Furniture Control Tag. Chair: 33 1/4" x 25 1/2" x 23 1/2", ottoman: 16" x 23 1/2" x 16". ....**$3,900 both**

Hans Wegner, Papa Bear armchair and ottoman upholstered in dark charcoal wool. Chair Stamped Hans J. Wegner Made in Denmark, with Danish Furniture Control tag. Chair: 39" x 31 1/2" x 29"...........................**$14,400 pair**

Hans Wegner / Fritz Hansen, oak dining chairs (four) with black vinyl seats. Stamped FH Denmark, 29" x 22 1/2" x 17 1/2". ....**$1,800 set**

Hans Wegner / Fritz Hansen, Etc., teak dining chairs (four), along with one oak armchair with black leather upholstery. Set marked with metal tag, Crafted in Denmark for Raymor, with two also marked FH Made in Denmark, 29" x 20" x 17" and 29 3/4" x 25 1/2" x 13". ....**$2,040 all**

Hans Wegner / Johannes Hansen, teak valet chair with hinged seat. Branded mark, 37 1/2" x 20" x 18"........**$15,600**

Hans Wegner / Johannes Hansen, armless settee upholstered in Jack Lenor Larsen fabric. (Accompanied by original sales receipt), 32" x 58" x 34"...........**$4,800**

Hans Wegner / Ry Mobler, two-piece rosewood sideboard with interior drawers and shelves, mid-late 1950s. Stamped Made in Denmark, 67 3/4" x 79" x 19 1/4". **$6,600**

Hans Wegner / A.P. Stolen, ox chair with striped fabric over original slate-gray fabric. Circular Danish Furniture control tag, 35" x 36" x 30".....................**$4,800**

Hans Wegner / A.P. Stolen, Papa Bear teak armchair upholstered in beige wool. Stamped mark, 39" x 35" x 28". **$8,400**

Hans Wegner / Andreas Tuck, cross-legged dining table with teak top. Branded mark, 28 1/4" x 62 1/2" x 33 1/2". **$6,600**

Hans Wegner / Andreas Tuck, teak extension dining table with two 21 3/4" leaves. Branded mark. Closed: 27 1/2" x 55" x 43". **$1,440**

Werner West / Kerava Woodworks, (Finland), lounge chairs (pair) with birch frames upholstered in mauve cotton. Stamped Made in Finland, 32 1/2" x 23" x 20". .... **$720 pair**

Edward Wormley, dining chairs, by Dunbar, set of eight, mahogany frames with original caned backrests, original upholstery, seven signed with "Dunbar for Modern" labels, original finish, 21 1/4" w x 21 1/2" d x 32 3/4" h, very good original condition......................**$3,500 set**

Edward Wormley, mirror, by Dunbar, model 5544, square form with solid brass frame, signed with green metal "Dunbar for Modern" tag and paper label, 32" w x 32" h, excellent condition......................**$600**

Frank Lloyd Wright / Henredon, Taliesin ten-drawer sideboard with recessed handles, 33" x 65 1/2" x 20 1/2". **$2,040**

Russel Wright, American Modern bookshelves (pair), by Conant Ball, solid maple, each signed with a burned mark, refinished, 39" w x 10" d x 31" h, very good condition. **$850**

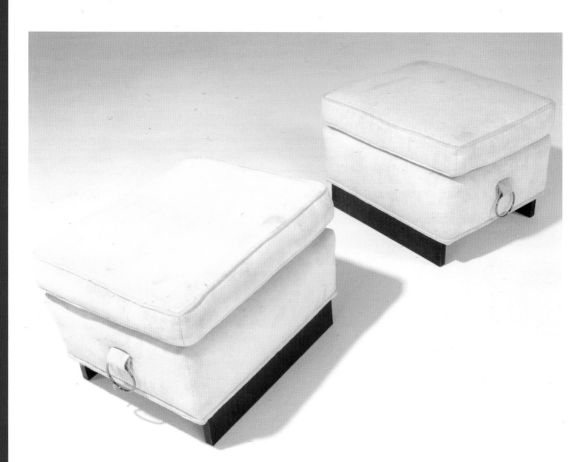

Photo courtesy Rago Arts and Auction Center, Lambertville, N.J.; www.RagoArts.com

Frank Lloyd Wright, ottomans (pair) from the Price Tower, Bartlesville, Okla., upholstered in ivory velvet on copper-clad bases, 16" x 23" x 19". **$1,800 pair**

Jewelry

Harry Bertoia, (American, 1915-1978), untitled, circa 1945, bronze bracelet, 3 1/4" d. **$3,600**

Claire Falkenstein, five abstract sculptural buttons in sterling silver. Stamped with artist's cipher. Each: 1 1/4" x 1". ....**$2,520 all**

Claire Falkenstein, abstract serpentine earrings in hammered copper. Each: 4". ....**$900 pair**

Ed Weiner, abstract spiral box brooch and earrings in sterling silver. Brooch stamped ED. Wiener, all stamped sterling. Brooch: 2 1/2", earrings: 1 1/8". ....**$1,080 all**

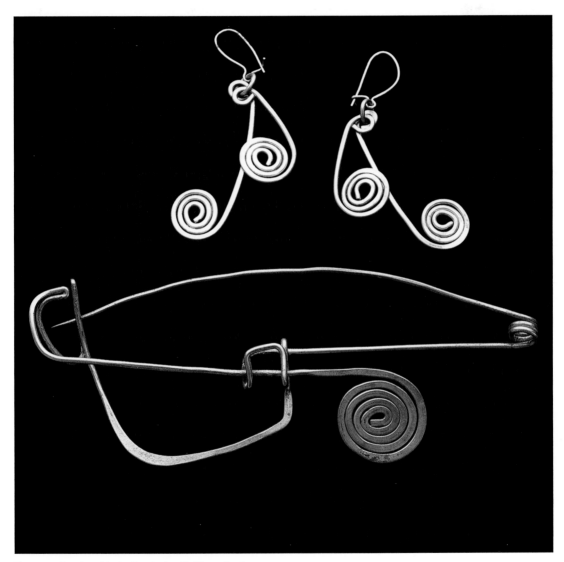

Photo courtesy Rago Arts and Auction Center, Lambertville, N.J.; www.RagoArts.com

Claire Falkenstein, abstract spiral brooch and earrings in hammered copper. Stamped signature to brooch. Brooch: 1 3/4" x 4 3/4", earrings each: 2 1/4". **$3,600 all**

Lighting

Ron Arad / One Off, tree-form floor lamp with concrete base and two flexible arms. Marked MADE IN ENGLAND MALLEABLE CH 8 BS4668, 71" h. **$14,400**

Clayton Bailey, glazed earthenware figural lamp on stand, in luster pink. (Provenance: Brooklyn Museum "Masters of American Craft," 1970.) Lamp only: 13" x 8 1/4". **$900**

Jonathan Bonner, patinated copper billfish candlestick. Signed Bonner with copyright, 11 3/4" x 5 1/2" x 3". **$660**

Mark Burns, ceramic sculptural lamp, "Mad Hatters Tea Party." Signed Burns, 22 1/2" x 17"...............**$3,900**

Photo courtesy Rago Arts and Auction Center, Lambertville, N.J.; www.RagoArts.com

Tommaso Barbi, floor lamp with leaf-shaped hammered brass reflector on coiled base, 1970s, 47 1/2" x 20". **$2,160**

Pierre Cardin, brushed steel table lamps (pair) with stamped logo to lower corner. Base: 19 1/2" x 7" x 4". ....**$2,880 pair**

Wendell Castle, candlestick in carved and gilded walnut with patinated metal. Signed W.C. 90, 16 3/4" x 3 1/4". **$1,800**

Wilhelm Hunt Diederich, (style of), iron floor lamp patterned with hunting dogs, 63" x 16" x 13"..............**$1,800**

Wharton Esherick, flame table lamp in carved walnut, 1933. Carved WE 1933, 19 1/4" x 4". **$21,600**

Richard Etts, plaster lamps (pair) with enameled ivory finish, modeled with lifelike hands, 1972. Signed, dated RICHARD ETTS with copyright, 17 1/2" x 10". ....**$3,000 pair**

A.W. and Marion Geller / Heifetz, brass and enameled metal lamp with single socket on tripod base, 36 1/2" x 20 1/2". **$5,400**

Curtis Jere, flashlight floor lamp/sculpture, 1981. Signed C. Jere 1981 with paper tag from Artisan House Inc., 67 1/2" x 26 1/4". **$4,800**

Modern Primitive, totemic candleholders (pair) in forged and fabricated iron. Both marked GRS 88, smaller also marked A.P., 24" and 18 1/2". ....**$2,520 pair**

George Kovacs Inc., black metal floor lamps (pair) with red neon tubes, 72 3/4" x 14" sq...........................**$1,200 pair**

Wendy Maruyama, mixed media wall sconce, 1981. Signed Maruyama '81, 19 1/2" x 10" x 4 3/4". **$780**

Herman Miller, E-6310 modern table lamps (pair), molded tiered shades in gray plastic with maroon bottom over black enameled bases, each: 15 1/4" d x 26 1/2" h, very good condition..**$300 pair**

Photo courtesy of Treadway Toomey Galleries, Cincinnati and Oak Park, Ill.; www.TreadwayGallery.com

Floor lamps, pair, metal tubular base supporting a broad painted paper shade with a white glass inner shade, #E1713, 25 1/2" d x 56" h. **$475 pair**

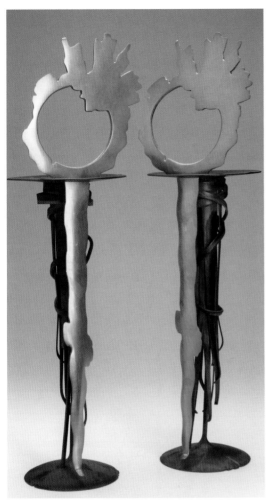

Albert Paley, Eclipse candlesticks (pair) of forged, milled steel with brass inserts, 1994. Stamped Albert Paley 1994, also numbered 36 and 27 of 50, 23 1/2" x 7" x 6 1/4". **$2,640**

Albert Paley, floor-standing candlestick of forged steel, 1970. Stamped Paley 1970, 60 1/4" x 28 1/2". **$25,200**

Albert Paley, forged steel table lamp, 1993. Stamped Albert Paley 1993 with copyright, also marked C114 and numbered 11/25, 30" x 9" d. **$14,400**

Gino Sarfatti / Arredoluce, Triennale floor lamp with enameled metal shades and handles, 69 1/2" x 42 1/2". . **$7,200**

Richard Sextone, hand-forged iron candleholder sconces (pair), 1978. Stamped R. SEXSTONE 1978, 37"......**$1,560 pair**

Table lamp, 1950s, rectangular black metal frame with four legs, supports a coated linen shade, unsigned, 6" w x 6" d x 14" h, very good condition................................**$275**

Edward Zucca, Mystery Science Lamp #8 in white oak, ebony, copper and brass with Plexiglas shades, 2003. Signed and dated, 8" x 16 1/2" x 5". **$1,800**

Edward Zucca, Mystery Science Lamp #10 in white oak, ebony, copper and brass with Plexiglas shades, 2003. Signed and dated, 13" x 15" x 9"..................**$2,280**

Roland Smith "Victor" floor lamp, circa 1948, collapsible metal base supports an adjustable boom arm with metal ball counterweight, includes catalog of the Detroit Institute of Arts An Exhibition in Modern Living from 1949 illustrating this lamp, arm as shown: 48 1/2" h x 44" w, very good original condition. **$750**

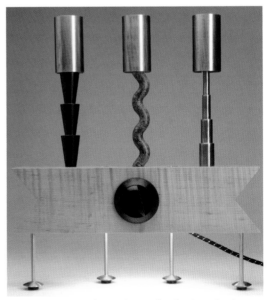

Edward Zucca, Mystery Science Lamp #4 in curly maple, ebony, copper and brass, 2003. Signed and dated, 20" x 18" x 5". **$3,120**

Edward Zucca, television lamp in painted wood and glass, 2005. Signed and dated, also marked Third Edition and numbered one of six, 14 1/2" x 11" x 10"....................**$1,320**

Metal, Functional

Jonathan Bonner, zoomorphic wood holder in stainless steel with brushed finish, 1987. Signed and dated with copyright, 16 1/2" x 18" x 9". **$2,520**

Morgan Colt, wrought-iron fireplace trivet with revolving hanging hook, 28 1/2" x 16" x 16". **$1,020**

Wilhelm Hunt Diederich, (American, 1884-1953), adjustable wrought-iron fireplace crane supporting a figural hunt scene in cast bronze, circa 1930, 38" x 44". **$15,600**

Irving Harper / George Nelson / Charles D. Briddell, Carvel Hall stainless steel flatware service for eight, complete with original case signed by Irving Harper. Stamped CARVEL HALL STAINLESS U.S.A.............**$1,020**

Albert Paley, steel door handles (pair) covered in rust patina, 11" x 6 1/2". **$2,400**

Albert Paley, four-piece fireplace tool set of forged and fabricated steel, 2005. Stamped Albert Paley 2005, 43 1/2" x 14"..**$12,000**

Albert Paley, steel paperweights (pair), 1994. Stamped Paley 1994, 8 1/2" x 4 3/4". **$660**

Russel Wright, set of silver-plated flatware for eight, with dinner and salad forks, dinner knives, dinner and soup spoons, designed 1933, produced 1987. Missing one salad fork. Stamped MMA 1987 Korea. **$4,500**

Photo courtesy Rago Arts and Auction Center, Lambertville, N.J.; www.RagoArts.com

Wilhelm Hunt Diederich, (American, 1884-1953), figural sheet-iron weathervane depicting leaping polo players, mounted on an enameled metal stand. Overall height: 87", weathervane only: 39" x 46". **$48,000**

Photo courtesy Rago Arts and Auction Center, Lambertville, N.J.; www.RagoArts.com

Albert Paley, bookends, 1993. Stamped Albert Paley 1993, numbered 4/10. Each: 9" x 13" x 3". **$2,760**

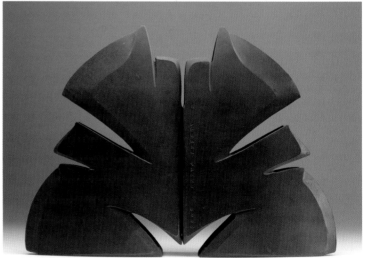

Textiles

Amacani, modern circular hooked wool rug with abstract design in oatmeal and black on mottled orange ground. Tagged Amacani, S.A, 84" d.............................**$1,140**

Alexander Calder, tapestry, "Balloons," in maguey fiber with abstract design in navy, yellow, red, peach and black, 1974. Bon Art tag, signed with embroidered copyright, CA 74 57/100, 6' x 8'. **$7,200**

Alexander Calder, tapestry, "Turquoise," in maguey fiber with abstract design in yellow, red, black and turquoise, 1975. Bon Art tag, signed with embroidered copyright, CA 75 1/100, 6' x 8'. **$5,700**

Sonia Delaunay / Articurial, assortment of five limited-edition fabrics. Each signed Sonia Delaunay and marked with an edition number. All approximately 108" long. Four cotton with 55" selvages. One cotton velvet with 45" selvage. ....**$6,600 all**

Edward Fields, rectangular wool rug with minimalist design in blue, gray and black, 1988. Signed and dated on selvage, 107" x 81 1/2".................................**$720**

Rug/tapestry, 1960s, hand-knotted wool, abstract design in yellow, brown and orange, light wear, 51" x 79", very good condition. **$250**

Elsa Rush, rectangular hooked wool rug with abstract flowers and insects in shades of brown and beige. Signed Elsa Rush, 117 1/2" x 81 1/2".....................................**$1,140**

Photo courtesy Rago Arts and Auction Center, Lambertville, N.J.; www.RagoArts.com

Alexander Calder, tapestry, "Turquoise," in maguey fiber with abstract design in yellow, red, black and turquoise, 1975. Signed with embroidered copyright, CA 75 92/100, 5' x 7'. **$4,500**

Other Objects

Harry Bertoia, (American, 1915-1978), double-sided gong, silicone bronze, 47" diameter..**$54,000**

Michael Coffey, Perceptions II laminated and carved serpentine wall-hanging mirror in African Mozambique. Signed M. Coffey, 27" x 54 1/2"..................................**$5,400**

Danish Modern bucket, round form in teak veneer with copper fasteners and swiveling handle of solid teak, unsigned, original finish, 17 1/2" d x 16" h, very good condition...**$125**

Wharton Esherick, sculptural carved walnut bowl, 1962. Marked WE 1962, 2 1/2" x 11 1/2" x 6 1/4"................**$9,000**

Wharton Esherick, mahogany tray, signed WE 1967, 1" x 23 3/4" x 13 1/2"..**$4,800**

Paul Evans, patchwork steel ice bucket, 11" x 10" x 10".. **$1,920**

Paul T. Frankl / Warren Telechron, Modernique electric clock in burnished and lacquered brass-tone metal, Bakelite and glass with detachable cord, 7 3/4" x 5 3/4" x 4"......... **$1,200**

Hans Hansen, hinged rosewood box with sterling silver insets. Stamped Hans Hansen Sterling Denmark 925 8, 1 3/4" x 8 3/4" x 5 3/4"..**$1,920**

George Nelson / Herman Miller, Thin Edge jewelry chest with nine drawers and hourglass pulls. Circular Herman Miller tag, 23 1/2" x 10 1/2" x 13"................**$8,400**

Isamu Noguchi / Knoll, collection of nine large pencil and ink blueprint drawings for Knoll. Each signed Isamu Noguchi in pencil, 27" x 36" and 32" x 40"..........**$16,800 all**

Reference literature, 1950s, including Herman Miller Illustrated Price list, 1958; *The Dunbar Book of Modern Furniture*, 1953; Chairs by Bertoia, an illustrated fold-out pamphlet; two Nessen lamp catalogs, 1959-60 and 1966; and a vintage Herman Miller postcard; plus various Herman Miller brochures, all in very good condition.
....**$300 all**

Andy Warhol books (two), and puzzle; Andy Warhol's Index (Book), First printing, 1967, Random House, with hologram cover; Andy Warhol, publication for exhibition at Moderna Museet, Stockholm, Sweden, third ed., 1970, printed in Sweden; with Andy Warhol "Red Marilyn" puzzle, 550 pieces, unopened, 12" x 12"...................**$400 all**

Russel Wright / Klise Woodworking USA, Oceana salad bowl, "Wave". Branded signature, 3 3/4" x 15" x 9 3/4".
....**$1,440**

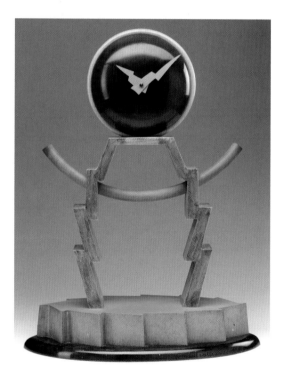

Photo courtesy Rago Arts and Auction Center, Lambertville, N.J.; www.RagoArts.com

Wendell Castle, sculptural anthropomorphic clock in maple and walnut with enameled and patinated metals, 1989. Signed and dated, 21" x 15 1/2" x 9 1/4". **$9,000**

Photo courtesy Rago Arts and Auction Center, Lambertville, N.J.; www.RagoArts.com

Isamu Noguchi / Zenith, Bakelite Radio Nurse, embossed marks, 8" x 6 1/4" x 6". **$7,200**

MUSIC BOXES

Also see Coin-Operated Devices.

Twenty-tune cylinder, which measures 3" diameter by 7 1/2" long, 40 teeth, all of which are in very good condition. Walnut and mahogany case with string inlay and decal of musical motif on lid,: 7 1/2" h x 24" w x 12" deep. Case in original condition with some wear. Mechanism probably restored years ago. All tips and dampers are present. Tone could be improved by repairing sounding board. **$575**

Continental cylinder, in rosewood case, with 10 airs, number 16677; the top of the box inlaid with an angel and drafting tools, 19th century, 6 1/4" x 18 1/4" x 8 1/2".
....**$600**

C. J. Heppe & Son, Philadelphia, tabletop model; eleven 15 1/2" discs, marring to top of case, 9 5/8" h, 21 3/4" w, 20" deep. **$1,725**

Excelsior, with six bells, 11" cylinder, inlaid case with ebony trim. Music box features zither attachment and six bells with butterfly strikers. Bells are held on with little flowers. Plays eight tunes, 10 1/2" h x 22" w x 12 1/2" deep. Inlay on top needing some repairs. Approximately a third of floral inlay in center is missing. String inlay in borders is mostly complete. Inlay in front appears complete. Card listing eight tunes has slight damage to top and corners. Lid lock is missing and top quarter of key escutcheon is broken and missing. Mechanism restored..................**$2,012**

Mira, mahogany, circa 1900, enameled urn and flowers over twin doors with conforming musical trophies, cast metal handle sides; twenty-four 18 1/2" disks; brass plate near "stop" impressed "7608", lifting veneer on back, 41" h., 28 1/2" w, 23" deep. **$7,475**

Olympia #5 disc, double comb playing 15 3/4" discs, mahogany case with elaborate molding. Lithograph winter scene inserted in the lid. Three celluloid tags complete and original, 13" h x 22" w x 20" deep. Four ball feet missing. Finish needs restoration. Mechanism is un-restored.
....**$2,990**

Polyphon upright with bells, tabletop model with walnut veneer, burl and inlay. Cornice is inlaid with "Polyphon" and flowers. Front door has burl walnut and glass, and cutout filigree to view interior. Raised on four legs, two front legs are turned and carved. The interior music box is a single comb mechanism with twelve nickel-plated bells and plays 17 1/2" discs, of which 14 are included, 32" h x 23" w x 11" deep. Slight veneer chip to back, small piece of carving loose on top; retains original crank and key for lock. Works have been restored.....**$3,910**

Reginaphone, made by the Regina Music Box Co. to compete with the phonograph popularity, phonograph included in this music box. Upright carved mahogany case with carved lions' heads, shell-and-paw feet. Lift the lid with serpentine carved front, raised panel on top, to get to the double-comb music box. Phonograph is complete with tone arm and turntable. Two curved doors slide open for the horn. Two serpentine doors open for record and disc storage. Included are 14 metal discs and a box of 78-rpm records and original crank, 50" h x 22" w x 20" deep. Slightly alligatored original finish. Mechanism is un-restored but plays well. **$12,075**

Swiss dancing doll, 6 1/4" cylinder plays three bells, snare drum and two dolls dance along to the music. Rosewood and walnut case has musical and floral inlay on lid and musical and floral decal on front. String inlay around lid and front, 11" h x 25" w x 15" deep. Minor flaking on decal. Mechanism is older restoration..................................**$2,012**

Musical Instruments

Photo courtesy James D. Julia Auctioneers, Fairfield, Maine; www.JuliaAuctions.com

Accordion, Tanzbar, roll-operated, playing 28 notes. Squeeze it back and forth like a regular accordion and it plays itself. Inlaid walnut case. With carrying case and 23 rolls, 11" h x 16" w x 9" deep. Carrying case: 12" h x 21" w x 10" deep. Case is lightly worn but clean. Rolls appear to be in good condition. **$805**

Amplifier, Fender Bassman tube, serial # A 64367, four 10" speakers, casters. Tested and working. Vintage used condition, 32" h x 25" w x 10 1/2" deep. **$225**

Amplifier, Fender Showman tube model, mid-1960s, serial # A.6911, black face. Tested and working, as-found condition, 8" h x 24" w x 9 1/2" deep. **$500**

Amplifier, Rocktron Rampage R80, serial # 00001582, one 10" speaker. Tested and working. Used condition, 18 1/2" h x 20" w x 12" deep...**$150**

Photo courtesy Leland Little Auction & Estate Sales Ltd., Hillsborough, N.C.; www.llauctions.com

Amplifier, Matchless Lightning Reverb 15 tube model, serial #F5629, two 10" Matchless Signature Series speakers, black cabinet with red face, volume, tone, treble, master and reverb knobs. Light wear from normal use, small crack in handle, in working order, 18 3/4" h x 25" w x 9 1/4" deep. **$1,450**

Banjo, Bacon Symphonie Silverbell, maple neck, pearloid floral inlays on both sides of headstock, heel and fingerboard; pot, flange and resonator are replacements. With soft-shell case. Some verdigris on tailpiece, light pitting to tone ring, chips to resonator, finish checking. **$1,000**

Banjo, Melody King Tenor, circa 1930s or later, an elaborate production with carved mahogany neck, foliate mother-of-pearl inlay on fingerboard, pearloid peg-head plate with engraved logo, early Grover tuners, ivoroid medallion showing Mercury on back of peg head, similar decoration on back and sides of mahogany resonator, with soft-shell case. Small split on pot, scratches to resonator, inlay loss to one fingerboard scroll. **$400**

Bass, Hofner Model 500/1 Beatles, circa 1960s, violin-shaped body in sunburst finish, two pickups. With hard-shell case. Cracked heel, split on headstock and lacking one tuner, normal playing wear with a few small dings.......**$575**

Bass, Univox Hi-Flyer Electric, circa early 1970s, serial # 0090659, sunburst body, two pickups. With soft-shell case. Chips to finish along edges from use, all original parts. **$300**

Dobro, Radio-Tone by Regal, circa 1930s, plywood, single cone resonator, lightning bolt sound holes, square neck, inverted tuners, Hawaiian nut, printed note sheet pasted to fretless fingerboard. With soft-shell case. Heel starting to drift a bit from the body, considerable scratching to back, good condition overall. **$350**

Guitar, 1919 Gibson Style O arch-top, serial # 63531(?) on remnants of label, factory order # 11356, blonde top, mahogany sides and back, binding throughout, dot inlay on scroll, mother-of-pearl fleur-de-lis and "The Gibson" logo on headstock. With soft-shell case. Replaced tailpiece, tuners, refinished sides and back, missing pick guard, two substantial cracks to top, split along back, 2" area of loss to binding on neck, portions of headstock inlay filled. ...**$1,250**

Guitar, Gibson ETG-150, arch-top tenor, circa 1940s-1960s, mahogany back, sides and neck, maple top with sunburst finish, rosewood fingerboard and bridge, all original hardware includes nickel-plated Kluson Deluxe tuners, four-pole P-90 pickup, white binding, tone and volume knobs. No case. Finish checking throughout, scattered dings and small scratches, slight chipping to edges of headstock and heel, light rusting to tuners. Serial number not located..........**$800**

Guitar, 1973 Gibson Dove Custom acoustic, serial # A002407, square-shouldered natural finish spruce flat top with red maple back and sides, mahogany neck, rosewood bridge and fingerboard, mother-of-pearl inlays on headstock, fingerboard, pick guard and bridge, Grover-style chrome Gibson tuners, binding on fingerboard, top and back, with Gibson hard-shell case. Wear from use, pick guard easing up from top, splits in back binding near heel. **$1,350**

Guitar, 1965 Guild Mark III classical, serial # 45422, spruce top, mahogany back, sides, binding top and back. With soft-shell case. Heavily played with worn finish on neck, numerous dings and scuffs, large crack on top does not appear to go through the wood. **$190**

Photo courtesy James D. Julia Auctioneers, Fairfield, Maine; www.JuliaAuctions.com

Drum and drumsticks with box, brass and wood, 19th century, drum having a brass center with wood top and bottom rims. Top having orange paint as well as the bottom. Bottom appears to have orange over blue and red; a clamp-tightening device on one side. Drumstick box with velvet liner and leather outside covering has original mustard edge highlighting and "Sticks" written on top and bottom. Hasp of the lock marked "Presto Lock Co. USA". Box holding a pair of 16" dark hardwood drumsticks, having 2 1/2" brass handles. Also two lighter colored drumsticks with similar brass ends. Contained in a shoulder harness with clip for drum. SIZE: Drum is 13" h x 15" d. Box is 4 1/4" h x 2" l x 6 1/2" deep. Drum intact with drumheads present, some loss to paint. Drumsticks are intact with some damage to brass, leather is dry with minor losses. **$632 all**

Photo courtesy Leland Little Auction & Estate Sales Ltd., Hillsborough, N.C.; www.llauctions.com

Drum set, Gretsch, seven piece, circa 1980s, black finish, complete outfit includes the following: 16" x 22" bass drum; four rack toms (8" x 8", 10" x 8", 12" x 10", 13" x 11"), a 16" x 16" floor tom, 4 1/2" x 14" snare drum, Camber high hat, Zildjian 20" sizzle ride, Zildjian 20" medium ride, 18" crash, three heavy-duty boom cymbal stands, bass pedal, full set of hard-shell cases and hardware, woodblock, cowbell, throne, sticks and mallets. Used, overall good condition. **$950**

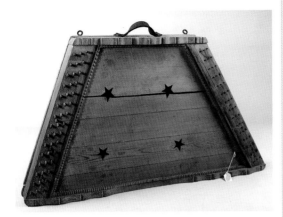

Hammered dulcimer, homemade with two-piece pine top, oak sides and back, hand carved scalloping at head and foot, top is pierced with four five-pointed stars, intricately carved beaded oak border, 48 hand-forged iron tuning pegs. Considerable wear, some splits in wood, tuners frozen. Fair condition and a "wall hanger" as is, 38 1/2" base; 19 1/2" head; 24 1/2" sides. **$80**

Guitar, Harmony Master arch-top, circa 1960s, serial # 9488H945, sunburst finish, binding to top and back, original hardware. With soft-shell case; 3" hairline crack on back, minor chips along binding, a few insignificant dings. **$325**

Guitar, Kalamazoo flat-top acoustic, serial # DK 349, circa 1940, sunburst bound spruce top, mahogany sides, v-neck, original tuners. With newer Canadian IKL hard-shell case. Three repaired top cracks, replaced bridge with evidence of original below, hairline on headstock, crackled finish. ... **$675**

Guitar, 1964 Martin 0-16NY, serial # 203664, with chipboard case, excellent condition with mahogany sides and back and tortoise binding **$1,495**

Guitar, 1969 Martin D-18, serial # 269622, with original hard-shell case, small hairline crack on top at edge of pick guard under the high E string, from sound hole to bridge, typical of guitars with pick guard shrinkage, rosewood fingerboard and bridge saddle. No strap button ever installed at the heel of the neck **$1,610**

Guitar, 1922 Martin O-18, serial # 18681, with new Martin dreadnaught hard-shell case, 12-fret neck/body, 19 frets total. Slotted headstock. Shows restoration and crack repair. ... **$1,380**

Guitar, Rickenbacher "Frying Pan" lap-steel, circa 1934, electro A-22, cast aluminum, light gold tone paint, gold "Rickenbacher Electro" name plate on open headstock, horseshoe magnet pick-up, volume control. No case. All original, as-found condition; knobs needed for volume and three tuners, inlay missing on six position dots, paint chipping throughout, 28 3/4" l, 22 1/2" deep scale. .... **$850** (Developed by George Beauchamp and Adolph Rickenbacher, the "Frying Pan" was the first commercial electric guitar.)

Guitar, Silvertone, amp-in-case electric, circa 1960s, all elements appear to be present. Fair condition with moderate wear. **$275**

Guitar, Yamaha Red Nippon Gakki FG-180, circa 1960s, serial # 143U831, spruce top, mahogany sides and back, rosewood fingerboard, bridge, bound top and back. With soft-shell case. Moderate playing wear and scuffs, including buckle marks on back. **$300**

Harp (laptop), maker unknown. Made of hardwood, decal locating notes and fancy decal around sound hole, 2" h x 13" w x 19 1/2" deep. Complete and original. Needs tuning **$23**

Hurdy Gurdy, in cart by Vincent Llinares, barrel-operated piano on a spoke-wheeled push cart. Cart has pin-striping and leather-covered handles. With one extra pinned cylinder. Piano has rosewood grain-painted case with embroidered cloth insert on top. Brass maker's plate in center and turned legs on the bottom section; 24" h x 22" w x 13" deep. (plus crank). Cart is 19" h x 50" w x 22" deep. Finish on piano is good with two or three minor scratches. Push cart very good. Insides are clean, triangle needs to be re-hung. Also has wood block. Piano needs tuning **$460**

Mandolin, 1953 Martin Style A, serial # A21075, spruce top, mahogany back, sides and neck, binding on top and back, nickel tuners and tailpiece. With hard-shell case. Heavy pick wear on both sides of sound hole, some crackling to finish, old repaired crack on upper bout **$800**

Harp guitar, 1890s, spruce top, mahogany back, sides and neck; rosewood fretted fingerboard, walnut fretless bass fingerboard, mother-of-pearl inlay on headstock, man-in-the-moon inlay on the fingerboard. Original 12-string tailpiece replaced with crude 6-string tailpiece, requiring the bass fingerboard to be unstrung, Repaired cracks on back, dings, scuffs consistent with age and use. Overall good condition and playable, comes with a concert program dated June 23, 1897, the cover of which has a photograph of this instrument in the hands of its original owner, 34 3/4" l x 12 3/4" w. **$700**

Photo courtesy Leland Little Auction & Estate Sales Ltd., Hillsborough, N.C.; www.llauctions.com

Oboe, wooden, in case. Unclear maker's stamp shows Parisian origin. Needs mouthpiece and restoration. Water-damaged case lacking cover. **$600**

Photo courtesy James D. Julia Auctioneers, Fairfield, Maine; www.JuliaAuctions.com

Organ (roll), Improved Mandolina, walnut case with elaborate gold stenciling on all sides and top. Black base. Lid opens for access to roll and swell door in front. Original directions under lid and 10 multi-tune paper rolls playing 20 notes, 14" h x 16" w x 13" deep. Original finish restored with one small corner showing how it looked originally (1" x 2"). Mechanism is rebuilt and plays well with rich tone. **$460**

Organ, concert roller, 20 note, wooden pin cylinder-operated tabletop crank organ, oak case with black base. Includes five cylinders. Crank on the front, 12 1/2" h x 18" w x 15" deep. Oak case has been refinished. Name has been re-stenciled on top and bellows have been rebuilt. Original directions inside lid. **$460**

Organ (laptop), L. H. Jones & Co., made in Brattleboro, Vt., burl mahogany veneer encases this laptop or tabletop reed organ. Having 49 notes, original ivory and ebony. Upper part of organ is to be pumped up and down as you play the keyboard. With original carrying case, felt pads and original dealer's card in lid. Organ: 8" h x 28" w x 11 1/2" deep. Original finish, two 1/8" or less chips in veneer. Bellows are original leather but work well. One dropped key. **$600**

Organ (roll), Mechanical Orguinette Co., New York, walnut case with gold stencil on all sides. Plays 14-note roll of which one fragile roll is included, 7 1/2" h x 12" w x 13" deep. Original finish, strong stencils. Bellows have been rebuilt. **$316**

Organ (roll), Chautauqua, oak case with black base. Glass door over cylinder with swell door at back, 15-pinned cylinders included, 12 1/2" h x 18" w x 15" deep. Oak case has been refinished. Stencil has been repainted by hand on top. Bellows have been rebuilt. **$517**

Organ (roll), McTammany Organette, walnut case with lots of stenciling on all sides and top. Paper-roll operated, of which five are included. Plays 14 notes on brass reeds, 9" h x 11 1/2" w x 16" deep. Case has original finish. Stenciling has been touched up. Overall good original appearance. Bellows have been rebuilt. **$460**

Piano, classical mahogany, carved, inlaid and ormolu-mounted, manufactured by Robert Nunns, Clark & Co., New York, circa 1825, sold together with an adjustable mahogany-carved stool, old refinish, both sides with severe shrinkage cracks; upper section has minor scratches to surface, 79 1/2" h. **$6,813**

Photo courtesy James D. Julia Auctioneers, Fairfield, Maine; www.JuliaAuctions.com

Photo courtesy James D. Julia Auctioneers, Fairfield, Maine; www.JuliaAuctions.com

Organ (roll), Musical Casket/Mechanical Orguinette Co., 14-note paper-roll-operated tabletop organ, walnut case with extensive gold stencils on all sides and top. Lid has swell shutter and opens to expose paper roll, 10" h x 12" w x 9 1/2" deep. Circular scratch in side from crank (very old). Mechanism appears restored. One multi-tune roll included. Small rewind crank is missing. **$540**

Piano (barrel), Pianette, tabletop, early mahogany-cased hand-cranked instrument, probably for home use. Playing six tunes on 22 notes, 37 1/2" h x 16" w x 14" deep. Mahogany case probably has original finish, few stains on the side and shelf. Piano is in need of tuning. Tuning wrench is included. **$920**

Piano, Meloutte Monographic, patented Jan. 1, 1878, playing 17 notes on bar bells by a heavy paper roll, this little instrument is made of cast iron with scrolls and musical motif. Cast iron with turquoise background and black highlights. Three rolls included, 5" h x 10" w x 13" deep. In original condition with little wear to paint. Rolls in fragile condition. **$575**

Violin, 1974 Ernst Heinrich Roth 4/4, serial # 0736 E, branded with Roth name and Bubenreuth Erlanger above label, Stradavarius copy, two-piece back. With hardshell case. - From a highly respected German shop. - Top cracks along one edge have old repairs. Set up and ready to play. Notes well and has cutting sound. **$325**

Violin, Remenyi 4/4 with Vuillaume bow; the violin, circa early 20th century with maker's name stamped on back, GERMANY stamped on right side of heel. Two old repaired cracks on the top and another on a side bout. Bow stamped VUILLAUME above frog, straight but needs new hair. ....**$225 pair**

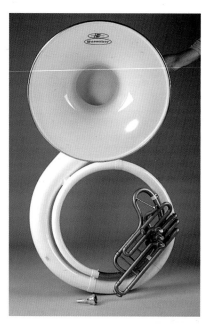

Photo courtesy Leland Little Auction & Estate Sales Ltd., Hillsborough, N.C.; www.llauctions.com

Sousaphone, Buescher-Selmer, dated Aug. 13, 1976, white fiberglass with gold painted valves. Comes with mouthpiece and dismantles for storage in custom case. New condition with very light strap abrasions on body. **$625**

Photo courtesy Leland Little Auction & Estate Sales Ltd., Hillsborough, N.C.; www.llauctions.com

Violin, 4/4 with Sacconi label, dated 1926, two-piece back, with newer hard-shell case. Repaired cracks in top, glue residue on some seams, especially noticeable between fingerboard and neck. **$2,400**
(Simone Fernando Sacconi [1895-1973] worked in Rome and later in New York.)

Photo courtesy Leland Little Auction & Estate Sales Ltd., Hillsborough, N.C.; www.llauctions.com

Xylophone, Deagan Professional 870, metal stand, rosewood bars, 3 1/2 octaves (F-C), all chimes present, stamped with four patent dates, the most recent being Feb. 2, 1915, with brass Deagan plate on one side of frame and an early Wurlitzer plate on the other side; comes with six mallets, normal playing wear, scuffs to stand, needs some tuning, 35" h x 56" w x 32.5" deep. **$1,350**

NATIVE AMERICAN OBJECTS

Native American collecting areas include intricate wood and stone carvings and masks; painted, beaded and quill-decorated hides, clothing and headpieces; pottery and basketry; weaponry, weavings and even works on paper, like Plains Indian ledger drawings.

Also see Photography.

Baskets

Photo courtesy Sanford Alderfer Auction & Appraisal, Hatfield, Pa.; www.AlderferAuction.com

California basket bowl, minor stitch loss, circa early 20th century, 15 1/2" d. **$1,150**

Photo courtesy Sanford Alderfer Auction & Appraisal, Hatfield, Pa.; www.AlderferAuction.com

Basket, large, dark brown zigzag ornaments, 7 1/8" h, 17" d. **$3,162**

Photo courtesy Sanford Alderfer Auction & Appraisal, Hatfield, Pa.; www.AlderferAuction.com

Basket, shallow, double brown scalloped bands, 12" d. **$402**

Photo courtesy Sanford Alderfer Auction & Appraisal, Hatfield, Pa.; www.AlderferAuction.com

Basket, vertical brown key ornaments, 6" h, 12" d. **$1,150**

Basket, small, dark brown vertical ornaments, 2 3/4" h, 5" d. **$51**

Pima Ola basket, fair condition, circa 1900, 12" h.......**$316**

Polychrome coiled basketry bowl, California Mission, circa 1900, the flared-side oval form with open diamond devices, 14 3/4" l, 11 3/4" w. **$2,232**

Polychrome coiled basketry bowl, Southwest Hopi, 20th century, with flared sides, decorated with geometric bands and four katchina heads, (minor loss), 15 1/2" h., 16" d..**$998**

Photo courtesy Sanford Alderfer Auction & Appraisal, Hatfield, Pa.; www.AlderferAuction.com

Native American basket, dark brown key motif, 4 1/4" h, 8 3/4" d. **$172**

Carvings, Ceramics, Textiles

Beaded belt, multicolored geometric decoration on brown field, leather backing, 35" l, (excluding tassels). **$300**

Beaded pieces (pair), Algonquin, probably off a shirt, circa 1850, 7" at longest, 5 1/4" at widest. ....**$258 pair**

Blanket, Rio Grande, center sewn, circa 1900, black and red design. **$287**

Bowl, Anasazi, prehistoric, 6 1/2" h, 3 1/4" d...............**$575**
(The cultural group often referred to as the Anasazi were a prehistoric Native American culture centered on the present-day Four Corners area of the Southwest United States. They are noted for their distinctive pottery and dwelling construction styles.)

Bowl, ceremonial, Northwest Coast, rectangular carved with two figures joining hands, 19th century, 2 1/8" x 10 1/2" x 5"...**$10,200**

Bowl, Mississippian Culture, effigy, bird form, prehistoric, 4" h, bowl opening measures 6" x 5 1/2". **$240**

(The Mississippian peoples were a mound-building, Native American culture that flourished in what is now the Midwestern, Eastern and Southeastern United States from approximately 800 to 1500 A.D.)

Bowl, Zuni, 5" h, 7 3/4" d, circa 1865. ....**$2,875**

Canteen, Acoma, circa 1920-30, 4" h, some paint loss. ... **$180**

Cup, Anasazi, prehistoric, 3 1/2" h...................................**$546**
(The cultural group often referred to as the Anasazi was a prehistoric Native American culture centered on the present-day Four Corners area of the Southwest United States. They are noted for their distinctive pottery and dwellings.)

Dance club, Shoshone, with hide cover, circa 1900, 16 1/4" long (not including fringe at both ends). **$316**

Dance dress with moccasins, suede, contemporary. Green and white beadwork repeated on dress and shoes..........**$575**

Dance roach, porcupine hair, circa early 20th century, approximately 16" long. **$172**
(A roach was attached to a bone ornament or leather base so that it stood straight up from the head like a tuft or crest.)

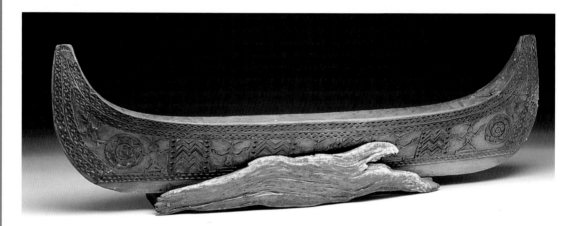

Photo courtesy James D. Julia Auctioneers, Fairfield, Maine; www.JuliaAuctions.com

Canoe (miniature), birch, chip-carved, probably Great Northwoods Region, late 19th century, carved overall with stylized figures, starburst shields within cross-hatched borders, now mounted on a carved and painted base simulating a flowing river, 8 1/2" h x 29" l x 6 3/4" w. The base is old if not original. **$1,610**

Photo courtesy High Noon, Los Angeles; www.HighNoon.com

Blanket, 1880s, Navajo, Germantown. **$74,750**

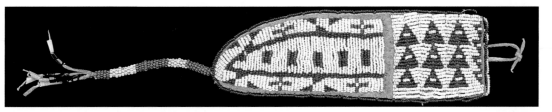

Photo courtesy James D. Julia Auctioneers, Fairfield, Maine; www.JuliaAuctions.com

Knife sheath, Plains, last quarter of the 19th century, the front side of the native tanned hide case is fully decorated in a geometric design using sinew-sewn seed beads, colors include white, dark blue and white-heart red. A 5" tassel extends from the bottom decorated in white and apple-green seed beads along with blue cut-glass trade beads and Dentalia shell, 12" l. Slight bead loss. **$345**

Headdress (medicine), Sioux buffalo-horned, circa 1920. ....**$632**

Moccasins, Algonquin, 9" long, circa 1850, one moccasin has loose upper beaded portion. **$270**

Moccasins, Plains, bead and quill decorated, last quarter of the 19th century, adult size Native-tanned uppers with hard soles. A-cut fringe decorated hide cuff with blue trade cloth has been added. Parallel lines of quillwork cover the center of the vamp, a bold geometric design in sinew-sewn beadwork surrounds the edge. Colors include white-heart red, greasy yellow, blue and dark blue, 10 1/2" l. Beadwork and hide in very good condition, much of the quill work is missing due to insect damage. **$690**

Moccasins and sheath, beaded leather pair and knife sheath; moccasins approximately 9 1/2" l. ....**$7,475 pair**

Pipe, stone figural, believed to be from the Ohio Mound culture (250-150 B.C?). **$230**

Pipe bag, Sioux, with bead and quillwork, applied cone and tassels, circa 1880-1890, 40" l. **$3,900**

Purses, (five), Iroquois, beaded, circa 1890, ranging from 4 1/2" to 5 1/2" l, beading on front and back of bags. ....**$316 all**

Rug, Navajo, regional, circa 1930, with red, brown, and tan design. **$316**

Totem, Argillite, killer whale and raven, maker signed, 6 1/4" h. **$480**

Totem, carved and polychrome wood with stacked animals and figures, 19th century, penciled on the back, "Chief Shakes", 24 3/4" h. **$6,000**

Totem, Northwest Coast, possibly Haida, carved wood with polychrome decoration, 19th/20th century, 24 1/4" h. **$6,600**

Vase, Santa Clara blackware, signed "Tomita", circa 1950, 3" h, 2 3/4" d. **$488**

Vase, Southern, wedding, Catawba or Cherokee, circa 1900, 8 1/2" h. **$316**

Water vessel, Paiute, pitch-covered, circa 1870-1880, 17" h. **$287**

Weaving, Germantown, some damage and fringe loss, circa 1910, black and red design. **$345**

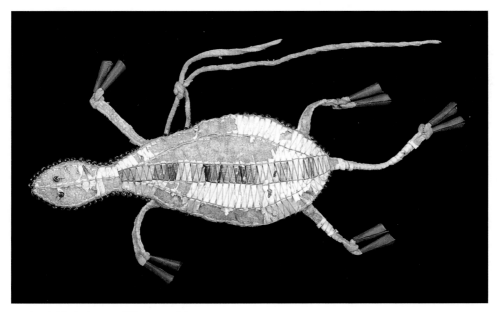

Photo courtesy James D. Julia Auctioneers, Fairfield, Maine; www.JuliaAuctions.com

Fetish (lizard form), Plains, 1860-1880s, small native-tanned hide amulet decorated with dark blue seed beads and porcupine quill embroidery. Tin cones dangle from the legs and tail, 5 1/2" l overall. Thread sewn beadwork, hide and tin cones are complete. Approximately 50% of the quillwork is missing. **$345**

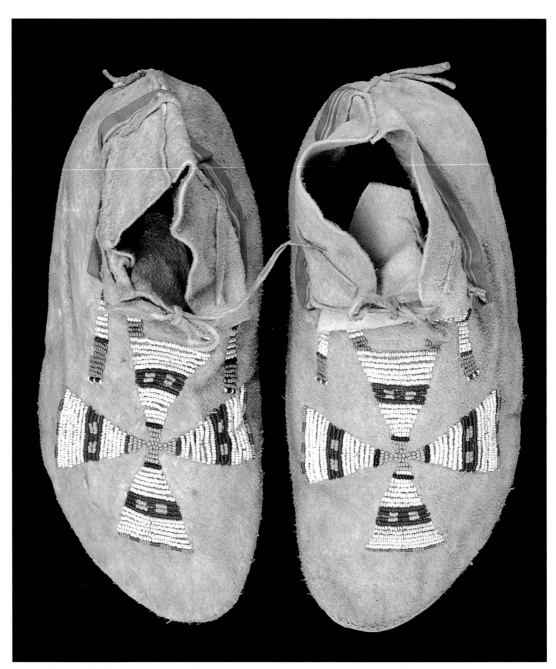

Moccasins, Southern Plains, last quarter of the 19th century, adult size, hard soles, Native-tanned and painted yellow uppers. A sinew-sewn bead work cross design covers the front. Colors include amber red, white, pink, blue and white-heart red, red and yellow commercial cloth attached to the cuff, 10 1/2" l, slight stiffness to hide cuffs. **$690**

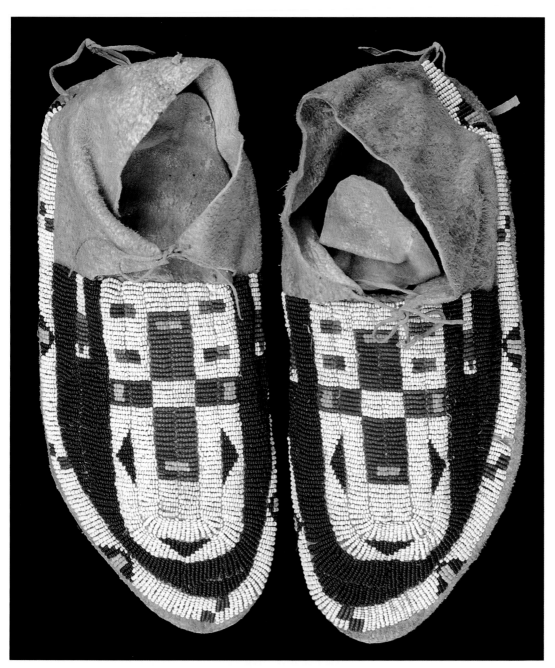

Photo courtesy James D. Julia Auctioneers, Fairfield, Maine; www.JuliaAuctions.com

Moccasins, Plains, fully beaded, the vamp is completely decorated in a geometric and cross design. Sinew-sewn lazy stitch beadwork, colors include dark blue, white, apple green, white-heart red and greasy yellow. The cuffs show evidence of old yellow paint, 10 1/2" l. The hide cuffs are slightly stiff, slight bead loss. **$1,035**

NAUTICAL

This section includes not only sailor-made objects, but also ship models, pond boats and accessories used on board a ship.

Photo courtesy James D. Julia Auctioneers, Fairfield, Maine; www.JuliaAuctions.com

Box, inlaid nautical motif, hinged cover having beveled edges and a 6" x 8 1/2" inlaid scene of two ships passing a lighthouse on green ocean. The scene has decorative string inlaid border and the sky is grained mahogany. All sides of the box have bird's-eye maple rectangular panels with similar string inlaid borders. Bottom had inset material panel, which is missing. Open interior, 4 1/2" h x 11 3/4" w x 9 1/4" deep. **$1,035**

Photo courtesy James D. Julia Auctioneers, Fairfield, Maine; www.JuliaAuctions.com

Box, paint-decorated, hinged lid, beveled top having a painted central panel of a house on a cliff with a road on another cliff. Corners are red drapes with hanging tassel. S-scroll painting on bevel. Front having a scene of boats on water nearing large castle with figures. A tall lighthouse is seen at point of land. Mid-19th century, old patina, 5 1/2" h x 13" w x 9" deep. Some open cracks at board joining. **$1,092**

Clock and barometer desk set in form of ship's wheel, circa 1927, mounted side by side, the Waterbury clock with silvered dial, time and strike movement and beveled bezel. The aneroid barometer made by Taylor Instrument Co. of Rochester, N.Y. for Waterbury Clock Co. having circular face and bezel. The two set within brass cases in the form of ship's wheels mounted on fluted mahogany columnar capstans on a stepped plinth. Suitable for desk or wall mounting, 11" h x 15 1/2" l x 4 1/2" deep. **$920**

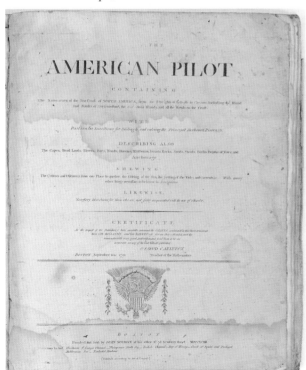

Pilot chart book, 1794, original hardboard binding with leather spine having the name "Andw (Andrew) Dunnings Book". Frontice page with title "The American Pilot" by "Osgood Carleton/ Boston, September 10th 1791. Printed and sold by John Norman at his office No. 75 Newbury Street MDCCXCIIII (1794)." Also having a 3 1/2" h x 4" w engraving of a presenting eagle with banner "E Pluribus Unum". Second page titled "Directions for Sailing Along the Coast of North America" which continues on the back. Book is 21 1/4" x 17 1/4". With some tears, losses, stains and foxing. **$408,250**

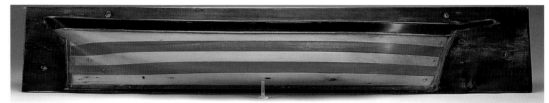

Photo courtesy James D. Julia Auctioneers, Fairfield, Maine; www.JuliaAuctions.com

Half-hull ship model, early 20th century, six laminations alternating in light and dark woods with a black top with molded edge. Affixed to a stained pine backboard, 8 3/4" h x 51 1/4" l (total). Refinished. **$920**

Captain's carry-on box, grain-painted with sliding lid, pine, American, 19th century, painted with an anchor on each side, with leather handles, surface wear, 12 3/4" h, 6 1/2" w, 16 1/4" l..**$651**

Half-hull ship model, American, late 19th/early 20th century, laminated plank construction mounted on a black-painted chamfered board, 7 1/2" x 38"......................**$1,125**

Half-hull ship model, American, late 19th/early 20th century, painted laminated wood, the hull painted green and white, overall 5" h, 25" l..**$948**

Half-hull ship model, "British Lady," Anglo-American, 19th century, laminated wood, 10 1/2" x 106"............**$2,014**

Pond boat, "Neptune," America, early 20th century, painted wood, the hull painted white, green and black, wooden stand, including sail segments, lacking mast, tears in sail segments, 15 3/4" h, 46" l..**$296**

Pond boat, "Little Rhody III," on stand, 1922, single mast, 2 sails; 61" l, 16" keel to gunwale, hatch cover marked "Little Rhody III" and "R.I.M.Y.C." (Rhode Island Miniature Yacht Club) with two pennants, sold with photo..**$3,450**

Pond boat on stand, blue, single mast, keel to top of mast 43", with ribbons, 1959 Detroit Public School Model Yacht Regatta..**$287**

Sailor's knot work, macramé swagger stick, having a metal tip, dark wrap bottom area with top having tan macramé ending in a Turk's head dark knot, 20 1/2" l.
....**$86**

Whale's teeth, nine assorted undecorated, all antique, sizes range from 7" to 3". Most have damage to end and largest has slice off tip, second largest has line gouge..........**$518 all**

Photo courtesy James D. Julia Auctioneers, Fairfield, Maine; www.JuliaAuctions.com

Dippers, coconut shell and baleen, and carved ivory: 1) 18 3/4" coconut dipper carved with clovers attached to a rope-twist baleen handle joined to a carved ivory ring-turned handle with mother of pearl insets. Shrinkage crack in handle. 2) 18" gourd dipper carved with a fish and starfish joined to a vertebrae handle with a spherical bone grip. **$805 pair**

Photo courtesy James D. Julia Auctioneers, Fairfield, Maine; www.JuliaAuctions.com

Sailor's macramé frame, with seven separate macramé strips, which when combined cover a wood base frame. Corners and center top and bottom have a braided four-string wide decoration. Macramé matte with oval window has a graduated round hole stitch which leads to the oval inner picture frame which is decorated with Turk's head knots in darker color. Overall 26" x 23", oval is 11 1/2" x 10". **$3,450**

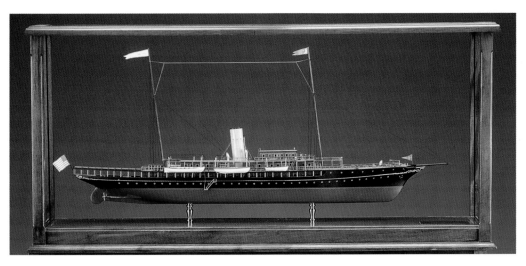

Photo courtesy James D. Julia Auctioneers, Fairfield, Maine; www.JuliaAuctions.com

Ship model of the American steam yacht "Corsair," mid-20th century, scale model with planked deck, mahogany deck houses, fully rigged with masts, full complement of assorted life craft, and full complement of sunshade framing, the hull in black paint with indigo water line, the underside in red paint, mounted within a custom-made inlaid and molded mahogany and glass display case raised on square chamfered legs and mounted with a plaque inscribed: "American Steam Yacht. 'Corsair'/Designer: Henry J. Gielow/Builder: Bath Iron Works/Owner: J. Pierpont Morgan/Captain: William B. Porter L.O.A.: 3,435 L.W.L.: 280 Beam: 42.7 Draft: 18 Lannan Ship Model Gallery, Boston", Overall: 57" h x 56 1/2" l x 16" w. Approximate size of model: 21" h x 50" l x 7 1/2" w. Fine original condition. **$3,565**

Photo courtesy James D. Julia Auctioneers, Fairfield, Maine; www.JuliaAuctions.com

Ship's wheel, American, on a wishbone capstan, circa 1890, eight-spoke wheel joined to the carved and shaped mahogany capstan, the central post with serpentine wishbone supports on a rectangular anchoring bracket, 46 1/2" h overall x 34" w overall x 30" d wheel. Weathered and faded surfaces, structurally intact, in need of cleaning. **$288**

WALLACE NUTTING

Wallace Nutting (1861-1941) was a minister, photographer, artist and antiquarian, who is most famous for his hand-colored photographs. He also was an accomplished author, lecturer, furniture maker, antiques expert and collector. His atmospheric photographs helped spur the Colonial Revival style.

Nutting studied at Phillips Exeter Academy, Harvard University, Hartford Theological Seminary and Union Theological Seminary. He graduated from Harvard with the class of 1887.

He started taking pictures in 1899 while on long bicycle rides in the countryside. In 1904 he opened the Wallace Nutting Art Prints Studio on East 23rd Street in New York. After a year he moved his business to a farm in Southbury, Conn.. He called this place "Nuttinghame." In 1912 he moved the photography studio to Framingham, Mass., in a residence he called "Nuttingholme". Nutting authored several books about the scenic beauties of New England, the United Kingdom and Ireland. In the peak of his business he employed about 200 colorists. By his own account, Wallace Nutting sold 10 million pictures.

Nutting's reproduction furniture also has developed a strong following, and are often mistaken for period pieces.

An Airing at the Haven. **$600**

All photos courtesy Michael Ivankovich Antiques & Auction Co. Inc.; www.wnutting.com

Arlington Hills – Cows. **$275**

Blowing Bubbles (untitled). **$700**

For A Bachelor

A Little house with its roof-tree

A Little fire alight for thee

A Little wife upon your knee

I wish you!

Bachelor Greeting Card. **$160**

A Cape Mill, rare Cape Cod print. **$450**

American Oaks.	$90	**Blossoms at the Bend.**	$40
A Basket Full – Floral.	$225	**Bride's Nest – Ireland.**	$400
Birch Drapery.	$50	**Broken Water.**	$70
A Bird in the Hand.	$120	**By the Wayside – Sheep.**	$80

Castle of St. Angelo, Rome. **$100**

Child Scene (untitled). **$120**

Dining Room – Went-Gardiner. **$200**

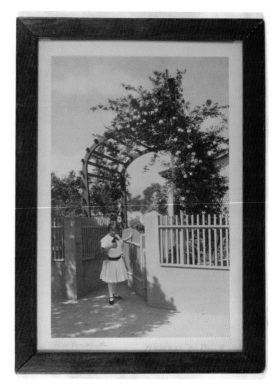

The Errand. **$80**

A Classical Maid. $45
A Cluster of Zinnias. $275
A Corner in China. $40
Drying Apples – Man. $110
Entrance, Carew Castle. $70
Evening at Killarney. $225

Fairy Tales, rare children's print. **$850**

A Figured Pitcher. **$950**

In Grandpa's Days. **$70**

The Guardian Mother. **$160**

A Jamestown Door. **$475**

A Greek Vase.. $110
Grandmother's China.. $90
The Heart of the Hills... $60
Her First "At Home".. $80
Highland Vale – Ireland.. $35
Honeymoon Stroll.. $70
In the Foothills – Spain.. $170
Into the Birchwood.. $60

Ivy and Rose Cloister. $110
Larkspur. $35
Maine Beautiful - 2nd Edition................................ $10

On the Heights (untitled). **$140**

Man and Dog, rare. **$350**

A Meadow Arch. $60
Midsummer Vale. $70
Miniature Holland Scene. $90
Mirror - Cottage on Floss. $100
Mother's Day Card. $35
A New Hampshire October. $50
New York Beautiful - 1st Ed. $3

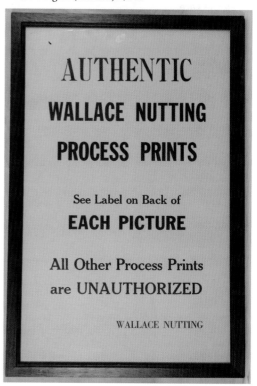

AUTHENTIC
WALLACE NUTTING
PROCESS PRINTS

See Label on Back of
EACH PICTURE

All Other Process Prints
are UNAUTHORIZED

WALLACE NUTTING

Process Print ad sign. **$120**

Stepping Stones at Bolton.
$225

On Shores of Zuyder Zee.	$1,600
Palmetto Grace – Florida.	$190
The Pasture Stream.	$50
Pennsylvania House (untitled).	$70
Pine Landing.	$70
Pinning the Lace.	$80
Red Eagle Lake.	$120
A Riffle in the Stream.	$50

The River Pasture – Cows.	$140
A Rug Pattern – England.	$90
Shadowy Orchard Curves.	$40
Sheep Scene in Pin Tray.	$130
Silhouette - Girl at Desk.	$25
Silhouette - Girl by Mirror.	$10
Silhouette - Girl by Spiral Urn.	$25
Silhouette - Girl on Fence.	$45
A Small Lily Pool.	$90
Snow Christmas Card.	$70
Spring in the Berkshires.	$30
Squirrel Bridge.	$160
Swirling Seas.	$140
Three Chums – Cat.	$170
A Touching Tale.	$90
Under Southern Oaks.	$130
Vilas Gorge.	$140

Snow Scene (untitled). **$140**

Southbury Child (untitled). **$80**

The Village Mill – France. **$225**

A Wisteria Terrace. **$90**

Who's Here? - Child Scene.	$250
A Warm Spring Day.	$120
A Warm Spring – Sheep.	$150
A Waterford Curve.	$50
Watersmeet.	$70
Wallace Nutting biography, 1st Ed., signed.	$90

With Fingers and Toes. **$60**

Nutting Furniture

#166 Maple Stool. **$350**

Mirror. **$110**

One-drawer stand. **$1,400**

#301 Side Chair.	$200
#309 Side Chair.	$225

Oak Table. **$500**

#492 Armchair. **$350**

Other Makers

Ralph Blood, Portland Head Light.............................$70
David Davidson, 1917 Calendar with Exterior. $120
David Davidson, Mayflowers of Plymouth. $90
David Davidson, My Father's Cot. $80
David Davidson, A Promise of Harvest.......................$180
David Davidson, A River of Lebanon. $40
Harris, Ausable River & Mt Whiteface. $60
Harris, Cascade Lake, Adirondacks NY. $90
Charles Sawyer, Camel's Hump & Winooski...............$110
Charles Sawyer, The Long Trail of Vermont. $40
Fred Thompson, Fireside Fancywork. $25
Fred Thompson, Where's Mother, very rare.............$2,900
Fred Thompson, Winter Surf.....................................$150

Charles Sawyer, The Last Road – Men & Oxen. **$180**

Charles R. Higgins, 2 Young Boys Fishing. **$190**

Charles Sawyer, A Maine Coast Garden. **$200**

Charles Sawyer, Advertising Sign. **$40**

Charles Sawyer - Portland Head. **$180**

Fred Thompson - Sailing Schooner Triptych. **$110**

Fred Thompson - Longfellow Triptych. **$175**

Fred Thompson, "The Pilot" (untitled). **$500**

Fred Thompson, Sunset Shadows. **$250**

Oriental

O

ORIENTAL OBJECTS

Now and Zen: Japanese woodblock prints

By Mary P. Manion

Acting director, Landmarks Gallery and Restoration Studio, Milwaukee

Reprinted from *Antique Trader* magazine

The art of Japan was unknown until Commodore Perry and his U.S. Navy flotilla sailed into Tokyo Bay in 1853. Art was probably the least of Perry's considerations behind his show of force and diplomacy, which convinced Japan's rulers to open their country to the outside world after centuries of self-imposed isolation. Perry's mission exposed Japan to the West, triggering the country's industrialization and modernization, and its rapid rise as a world power. Perry's voyage also had an unanticipated impact on Western artists, who found inspiration in the simplified lines and white space of Japanese woodblock prints. James Abbott McNeill Whistler introduced the prints to London's Pre-Raphaelites as early as 1859. Before long, Japan's influence could be seen in the work of artists across Europe and America.

The art of Japan, which found distinct expression in the medium of woodblock prints called ukiyo-e, was profoundly indebted to the contemplative spirit of Zen Buddhism. It was a meditative art that sought to strip away human complexity in exchange for glimpsing the essence of scenes. It was also a democratic art, reproduced in large numbers and reaching into every corner of the country. When Japan became a trading partner with the West, its prints were prolifically produced for export. Soon enough, Japanese artists went abroad, rendering sites familiar to Western audiences in the style of the home islands.

Perhaps the bulk of pre-World War II prints, and the legion of largely anonymous artisans who made them, accounts for their startling availability. Many antique Japanese woodblock prints can be found on eBay for under $100. However, as in any genre of visual art, the recognized masters command higher prices.

Creating a woodblock print is a three-step process involving an artist, an engraver and a printer. The artist creates the sketch on thin paper. The engraver traces the sketch onto a block of wood and carves the impression. The completed carved block is given to the printer who applies ink on the block and prints the image on a paper support. Multiple colors are achieved by repeating the ink application one color at a time within the same printed image. All steps require skilled artisans with knowledge of the process and deft handling of paper, ink and wood.

Japanese woodblock art has a long history,

originating with the propagation of Buddhist teachings and evolving into commercial production in the early 17th century. The production continued into the early 20th century. The tradition is divided between two distinct eras in Japanese history, during which the finest works of the art form were produced. The Edo period began in the 1620s, characterized by feudal military dictators known as shoguns. Their regime ended in 1867 with the restoration of imperial rule under Emperor Meiji. The Meiji period closed with the death of the emperor in 1912.

Throughout the Edo period, artists focused on Japan's insular life with depictions of the four seasons of the islands, sometimes featuring animal and plant life; iconic representations of sacred temples and landmarks; studies of women; portraits of children, shogun warriors and Sumo wrestlers; and the depiction of Japan's other popular art form, the Kabuki Theater. The Kabuki prints (called Yakusha-e) were woodblock images of elaborately costumed actors on stage and in performance. They were received in much the same way as movie and theater posters are collected today.

The Meiji period saw a great change in art as the focus turned to the western market. Japanese artists began to travel abroad for the first time in centuries and depicted Western scenes in Japanese style.

Many masters emerged from the Edo period, and among the most prolific were Katsushika Hokusai (1760-1849), Gototei Kunisada (1786-1865), Ando Hiroshige (1797-1858) and the last great master of the period, Ichiyusai Kuniyoshi (1797-1861).

Hokusai's reputation was established as a landscape painter. His masterwork, Thirty-Six Views of Mount Fuji, included a 10-print supplement featuring additional views of Mount Fuji from the interior, or 46 prints in all. Sotheby's in London sold The Great Wave Off Kanagawa, a signed print from the set, for $60,000 including buyer's premium.

Kunisada (who later signed his work as Toyokuni III)

The Great Wave Off Kanagawa, an image from Thirty-six Views of Mount Fuji, created by Katsushika Hokusai between 1826 and 1833.

shared no equal in commercial success, There was a time when the word ukiyo-e meant only one thing: Kunisada, or so it was noted during his lifetime. His series, Selection of Actors, with Scenes of the Fifty-three Stations on the Tokaido Highway, was praised in a popular song of the time. Auction prices for his prints generally range from $1,000 to $4,500.

Hiroshige (also known as Hiroshige I) produced more than 5,400 prints, many with up to several hundred impressions per image. One Hundred Views of Famous Places in Edo was one of his last, great journeys in art. His son-in-law, who became known as Hiroshige II (1826-69), was fascinated by the landscape of Japan and traveled the length of the nation for inspiration. At auction Hiroshige prices range from $500 up to the thousands, with a rare, 70-print set Views of the Province selling at Sotheby's Amsterdam for $76,692 including buyer's premium.

Many ukiyo-e prints were produced in sets, and a landscape series could bear the same title by different artists.

Both Hiroshige and Hokusai produced 53 stations on the Tokaido as well as 36 views of Mt. Fuji. Additionally, Hiroshige produced two versions of the 36 views. Titles were often descriptive if not lengthy. Kuniyoshi's Pictures of All Sorts of Places in the Eastern Capital gets to the point in a rather meandering pace. Three Great Bridges of the Eastern Capital, signed by Kuniyoshi, sold at Christie's New York for $3,000, including buyer's premium.

The Meiji period nurtured at least three great masters, Yoshitoshi Tsukioka (1839-92), Yoshiiku Ochiai (1833-1904) and Kunichika Toyohara (1835-1900). The early years expressed dark emotion and gloom with depictions of bloodthirsty battles and military heroes. Japan's war with Russia (1905) was depicted in traditional style. Afterward artists returned to more pastoral images.

Prints by some of the masters of ukiyo-e continue to be struck nowadays and are often available at modest prices. Many fine works by older woodblock artists can be found for under $1,000. Ukiyo-e remains a field of art accessible to collectors with modest budgets.

Woodblock Prints

Ikeda Eisen, (1790-1848), indigo blue (aizuri-e), a large format (oban tate-e) from the series "Modern Music Like Clusters of Pine Needles" of a maiden rendered in shades of blue, with a hint of red on her lips, signed Keisai Eisen ga, circa 1830s, (late impression, somewhat toned, rough edges), 14 1/2" h x 10" w. **$200**

Takahashi Hiroaki, (Shotei) (1871-1944), two views, each featuring Mount Fuji, one with the peak wreathed in bands of mist, the other with fishing boats pulled up on a beach, each signed "Hiroaki" and sealed "Shotei," (slightly toned, good color, slight soiling, some staining to second), 10 1/4" h x 15 1/4" w...**$1,200 pair**

Utagawa Hiroshige, (1797-1858), a mid-size horizontal sheet (aiban-yokoe) from the so-called Gyosho Tokaido Road series, depicting "Akasaka," published by Ezaki-ya/Yamada-ya, with a single censor seal (circa 1841-42), signed TL (late impression, faded, trimmed, foxed), 7 3/4" h x 12 1/2" w..**$200**

Kawano Kaoru, (1916-1965), portraying a girl holding a fan to the front, with mica-printed accents, sealed (minor tape residue to reverse, otherwise very good condition) 16 3/4" h x 11 1/4" w. **$120**

Kawano Kaoru, (1916-1965), Japanese, modern, two views, the first of a landscape with a pagoda tower silhouetted in the distance, pencil signed LL, with one seal "Kaoru," the second of a young girl seated with a small blue bird in her hands, pencil signed LR, with one seal (second with tape residue to top reverse corners), 16 3/4" h x 11 1/4" w...**$50 pair**

Kawano Kaoru, (1916-1965), Japanese, modern, two views, the first depicting a young girl in a pose of veneration, sealed "Kaoru," the second an abstract rendering of a seated maiden in red, grey and black, pencil signed LR, with one seal, 16 3/4" h x 11 1/4" w. ......**$50 pair**

Kiyochika Kobayashi, (1847-1915), titled "Honcho dori yasetsu" (Night snow, in Honcho Street), signed Kobayashi Kiyochika hitsu, right margin with date Meiji 13? (1880,

Photo courtesy Clars Auction Gallery, Oakland, Calif.; www.Clars.com

Paul Jacoulet (1896-1960), titled "Le Mandarin Aux Lunettes, Mandchoukuo," pencil signed LR, with duck seal, right margin with printer and carver cartouches of Honda and Maeda, the reverse numbered 75/150 (glue residue to top margin, some toning, especially to the margins), 19" h x 14" w. **$750**

unclear) and publisher cartouche of Fukuda Kumajiro (slightly toned and minor staining, crease to right margin), 10" h x 14 1/2" w...**$250**

Photo courtesy Clars Auction Gallery, Oakland, Calif.; www.Clars.com

Kiyochika Kobayashi (1847-1915), known as "A Steam Locomotive In Hazy Moonlight," the night scene with a steam engine proceeding down tracks parallel to the shoreline, signed Kobayashi Kiyochika hitsu, circa 1880s, no publisher cartouche (somewhat toned, creases, losses), 9" h x 13 1/2" w. **$100**

Tsukioka Kogyo, (1869-1927), two views, the first depicting a female demon in a Noh drama, the second of two figures in the kyogen play "Obake-zaki," each signed and sealed, shaped seal of the publisher (first toned and torn, second with minor matt mark), 15" h x 10" w and 10" h x 15" w.. **$60 pair**

Odake Kunikazu, (1868-1931), set of 12, from the series "Tokyo junigatsu no uchi" (The Twelve Months of Tokyo), eight with publisher notation "Shimizu-do" and date Meiji 34 (1901) on the left margin, most signed "Kunikazu-hitsu," each featuring a contemporary beauty (one in Western dress) and landscape inset of a famous place in Tokyo (center crease, some with tears along the crease, two sides with remnants of the original paper backing, otherwise relatively good condition), each sheet: 9" x 12 1/4".. **$750 set**

Utagawa Kuniyoshi, (1797-1861), a large format sheet (oban tate-e) of Shoki, the Demon Queller, pursuing a pair of oni floating above, signed "Ichiyusai Igusa Kuniyoshi," with aratame censer, date (1854) and publisher notation of Tsujioka-ya (losses, some staining, rough edges), 14" h x 9 3/4" w.. **$110**

Koichi Okumura, (Japanese, 1904-1974), six prints, signed; together with Toshi Yoshida, "From the Star, Night," 1957, with printed title, date, and signature, 2/20. Largest: 36" x 24".. **$720 all**

Kiyoshi Saito, (1907-1997), titled "Haniwa," with the clay figure in red, grey, black and mica accents, signed LR in white ink, with one seal reading "Kiyoshi," (pencil notation to reverse, otherwise excellent condition), 17" h x 11 1/4" w. **$175**

Ohara Shoson (Koson), 1877-1945, featuring a pair of bar-tailed godwits feeding in shallow waters next to reeds, signed and sealed "Shoson," 1926, circular publisher seal of Watanabe, (toned, paper tape to reverse top), 15 1/4" h x 10 1/4" w **$80**

Hiroaki Takahashi, (Japanese, 1871-1944), two color views of Mt. Fuji with lake and Torii in the foreground, signed lower right and sealed Shotei; man and child in silhouette, signed and sealed lower right Hiroaki. Both 14 5/8" x 6 1/4".. **$480 pair**

Photo courtesy Clars Auction Gallery, Oakland, Calif.; www.Clars.com

Iwata Sentaro (1901-1974), a half portrait of a Japanese beauty, signed "Sentaro-ga" (some toning, staining), 15 1/4" h x 10 1/2" w. **$110**

Ito Takashi, (1894-1982), a night scene of boats on a lake, signed and sealed "Takashi," circular publisher seal of Watanabe in the lower right corner (very slightly toned, otherwise very good condition), 10 1/4" h x 15 1/2" w. **$550**

Hiroyuki Tajima, (1911-1984), titled "Tradition" in English and Japanese, signed in pencil LR and dated '69, edition 50-8, 36 1/2" h x 27 1/2" w.. **$200**

Photo courtesy Clars Auction Gallery, Oakland, Calif.; www.Clars.com

Hiroshi Yoshida (1876-1950), titled "Naiyagara bakufu" (Niagara Falls), dated Taisho 14 (1925), from the United States Series, impressed signature LR (traces of tape residue to top reverse corners, otherwise very good condition), 10 3/4" h x 15 3/4" w. **$250**

Hiroshi Yoshida, (1876-1950), titled "Calm Wind" [in English] and "Fujo" [in Japanese], dated Showa 12 (1937), LR with printed signature and gauffrage impression of a "baren," a Japanese tool used in printmaking processes, (slightly wrinkled to top margin, very slightly toned, otherwise very good condition), 15 3/4" h x 10 1/2" w. **$175**

Toshi Yoshida, (1911-1995), titled "Cherry Blossoms" [in English] and "Sanbu Saki" [in Japanese], dated 1970, pencil signature to LR (toned, tape residue to top reverse edges, not laid down), 14 1/2" h x 21 3/4" w. **$225**

Other Art

Folding screen, Japanese, six-panel, Edo Period (1600-1868), 18th/19th century, Kano School, featuring a peacock and peahen framed by a pine and blossoming cherry trees bordering a stream overshadowed by flowering peony bushes and small song birds, unsigned, ink and color on gold-leaf applied paper ground, some blooms rendered in the dimensional moriage technique (corner tears, surface wear), 69 1/4" h x 146 3/4" w........................**$2,000**

Painting, Chinese, of bamboo, ink on paper, the upper right with a long poetic colophon with a cyclical date "yiwei" (1955), signed [unread], with three seals, framed, overall: 23" h x 30 1/4" w...**$325**

Paintings, (fan, pair), the first depicting a pair of horses in a landscape, the right with a short colophon dated "wushen" (1968), the second a poetic inscription in semi-formal script on a mica ground, signed [unread] and with two seals, overall: 17" h x 25" w.....................**$325 pair**

Paintings, ancestral portraits (pair), anonymous, Chinese, 19th Century, on brown rice cloth, half portraits show a man and woman in decorated robes with jewelry and hats. Housed in identical carved Oriental hardwood frames. Overall is 13 1/2" x 10 1/2". ....**$460 pair**

Ceramics

The history of Asian pottery spans thousands of years. By the 16th century, Chinese ceramic wares were being exported to India, Persia and Egypt. During the Ming Dynasty (1368-1643), earthenware became more highly developed. The Ch'ien Lung period (1736-1795) of the Ch'ing Dynasty marked the golden age of trade with the West.

In 1557, the Portuguese established a permanent settlement in Macau. The Dutch entered the trade early in the 17th century. With the establishment of the English East India Company, all of Europe sought Oriental-influenced pottery and porcelain. Styles, shapes, and colors were developed to suit Western tastes, a tradition that continued until the late 19th century.

Canton is a term given to porcelain made in the Canton region of China from the late 18th century to the present. It was produced largely for export. Canton china has a hand-decorated, light- to dark-blue under glaze on white ground. Design motifs include houses, mountains, trees, boats, and bridges. A design similar to willow pattern is the most common.

Borders on early Canton feature a rain-and-cloud motif (a thick band of diagonal lines with a scalloped bottom). Later pieces usually have a straight-line border.

Early plates – dating from about 1790-1840 – are often heavy and may have an unfinished bottom, while serving pieces have an overall "orange peel" bottom. Early covered pieces, such as tureens, vegetable dishes and sugars, have berry finials (also called knops) and twisted handles. Later ones have round finials and a straight, single handle. The markings "Made in China" and "China" indicate wares made after 1891.

Celadon refers to a pale, grayish-green glaze color. It is derived from the theatrical character Celadon, who wore costumes of varying shades of grayish green in Honore d'Urfe's 17th-century pastoral romance, L'Astree. French Jesuits living in China used the name to refer to a specific type of Chinese porcelain.

Celadon is divided into two types. Northern celadon, made during the Sung Dynasty up to the 1120s, has a gray-to-brownish body, with relief decoration and monochromatic olive-green glaze. Southern (Lung-ch'uan) celadon, made during the Sung Dynasty and much later, is paint-decorated with floral and other scenic designs and is found in forms that appeal to the European- and American-export market. Many of the southern pieces date from 1825 to 1885. A blue square with Chinese or pseudo-Chinese characters sometimes appear on pieces after 1850. Later pieces also have a larger and sparser decorative patterning.

Famille Rose is Chinese Export enameled porcelain on which the pink color predominates. It was made primarily in the 18th and 19th centuries. Other porcelains in the same group are Famille Jaune (yellow), Famille Noire (black), and Famille Verte (green).

Photo courtesy Clars Auction Gallery, Oakland, Calif.; www.Clars.com

Bowl, Japanese blue-glazed porcelain, square, Meiji period, thickly molded from fine white paste of Hirado type with rounded corners, its canted interior walls each displaying a raised cloud scroll and its flat floor centered with a raised kirin in white silhouette against a deep cobalt wash, all beneath a celadon-tinged glaze (minor glaze flaws), 8" sq. **$225**

Decorations include courtyard and home scenes, birds and insects. Secondary colors are yellow, green, blue, aubergine (dark purple) and black.

Imari porcelain is the collector name for Japanese wares made in the town of Arita, in the former Hizen Province, northwestern Kyūshū, and exported from the port city of Imari for the European trade. Although Imari ware was manufactured in the 17th century, the pieces most commonly encountered are those made between 1770 and 1900.

Early Imari was decorated simply, quite unlike the later heavily decorated brocade pattern commonly associated with Imari. Most of the decorative patterns are an under-glaze blue and over-glaze "seal wax" red complimented by turquoise and yellow.

The Chinese copied Imari ware. The Japanese examples can be identified by grayer clay, thicker glaze, runny and darker blue and red opaque hues.

The patterns and colors of Imari inspired many English and European potteries, such as Derby and Meissen, to adopt a similar style of decoration for their wares.

Rose Mandarin, Rose Medallion and Rose Canton are mid- to late-19th-century Chinese-export wares similar to Famille Rose.

Rose Mandarin, produced from the late 18th century to approximately 1840, derives its name from the Mandarin figures found in garden scenes with women and children. The women often have gold decorations in their hair. Polychrome enamels and birds separate the scenes.

Rose Medallion, which originated in the early 19th century and was made through the early 20th century, has alternating panels of figures, birds and flowers. The elements are four in number, separated evenly around the center medallion. Peonies and foliage fill voids.

Rose Canton, introduced somewhat later than Rose Mandarin and produced through the first half of the 19th century, is similar to Rose Medallion except the figural panels are replaced by flowers. People are present only if the medallion partitions are absent. Some patterns have been named "Butterfly and Cabbage" and "Rooster." Rose Canton actually is a catchall term for any pink enamelware not fitting into the first two groups.

Nippon, Japanese hand-painted porcelain, was made for export between 1891 and 1921. In 1891, when the McKinley Tariff Act dictated that all items of foreign manufacture be stamped with their country of origin, Japan chose to use "Nippon." In 1921, the United States decided the word "Nippon" was no longer acceptable and required all Japanese wares to be marked "Japan," ending the Nippon era.

There are more than 220 recorded Nippon back stamps or marks; the three most popular are the wreath, maple leaf and rising sun. Wares with variations of all three marks have been widely reproduced.

The majority of the marks are found in three different colors: green, blue or magenta. Colors indicate the quality of the porcelain used: green for first-grade porcelain, blue for second-grade, and magenta for third-grade. Marks were applied by two methods: decal stickers under glaze and imprinting directly on the porcelain.

Satsuma, named for a warlord who brought skilled Korean potters to Japan in the early 1600s, is a handcrafted Japanese faience (tin-glazed) pottery. It is finely crackled, has a cream, yellow-cream or gray-cream color, and is decorated with raised enamels in floral, geometric and figural motifs.

Figural Satsuma was made specifically for export in the 19th century. Later Satsuma, referred to as Satsuma-style ware, is a Japanese porcelain also hand decorated in raised enamels. From 1912 to the present, Satsuma-style ware has been mass-produced. Much of the ware on today's market is of this later period.

For details on Noritake China, see end of the ceramics section. Also see Oriental rugs in the Textiles section.

Photo courtesy Clars Auction Gallery, Oakland, Calif.; www.Clars.com

Amphora, Chinese Tang-style white glazed, the ovoid body with a tall waisted neck surmounted by a dished mouth bracketed by a pair of arching dragon-head handles extending down to the shoulder, the slightly green-tinged glaze stopping short to reveal the buff body (crazing, minor losses), 9" h. **$30**

Basket (chestnut), Chinese Export, reticulated, first half 19th century, oval form with flared rim mounted with leaf-tip handles, the reticulation of simulated bamboo, gilt-decorated overall with floral sprays, birds, butterflies and insects. Sacred bird and butterfly pattern in orange sepia, 5" h x 10" l x 8 1/2" w..**$1,725**

Bottle, Korean Punch'ong (Chosôn Dynasty, 1392-1910), sgraffito pear form with inlaid slip on a celadon ground, Yi Dynasty, 12" h...**$1,200**

Bowl, Korean Punch'ong (Chosôn Dynasty, 1392-1910), incised and stamped decoration filled with slip, the well with five spur marks, on a celadon glaze. Together with a small celadon plate stamped with flower head and leaf designs, Yi Dynasty. Larger: 7 5/8" d. ....**$1,080 pair**

Photo courtesy Clars Auction Gallery, Oakland, Calif.; www.Clars.com

Bowl, Japanese Imari, the interior well painted in polychrome enamels, gilt and under-glaze blue with a landscape medallion encircled on the side with further landscape panels alternating with floral reserves repeated on the exterior, 12 1/4" d. **$90**

Bowl (center, oval), Satsuma style, Makuzu Kozan, with four phoenix, their open wings forming the rim of the bowl, the interior with radiating petals in gosu blue centered by a dragon, on original carved base, Meiji Period. Marked in seal form Makuzu Kozan. 10 3/4" x 15 1/4" x 12". **$6,600**

Bowl, Chinese Export, blue Canton, mid-19th century, square bowl with notched corners and wavy edges, decorated overall in blue and white oriental landscapes, 4 3/4" h x 9 3/4" d..**$690**

Bowl on stand, Rose Medallion, decorated with Chinese domestic scenes; enclosures decorated with flowers, birds and fruit. Bowl is 6 1/2" h x 15 1/2" d. Stand is 6 1/2" h x 11 1/4" d. **$1,035**

Bowl (sugar), blue and white Canton, footed bowl having strap handles, medium blue decoration with a slightly domed lid and crab finial, 5" h x 4" d (without handles), small chip to edge of cover.............................**$150**

Brush box, Chinese Export Famille Rose, mid-19th century, rectangular lidded box fitted with an interior divider, decorated overall in Famille Rose design with fanciful birds and butterflies, 2 3/4" h x 7 1/4" l x 3 3/4" w.................**$518**

Candlesticks (pair), Chinese Export, inverted trumpet form, cobalt blue decorated landscape with boats, figures, trees and pagodas, flaring drip pan, 10 1/4" h.......**$540 pair**

Photo courtesy Clars Auction Gallery, Oakland, Calif.; www.Clars.com

Bowls (pair), Chinese polychrome enamel glazed, covered, Tongzhi mark and period (1861-1875), each decorated with shaped bird-and-flower reserves on a turquoise ground with a dense pattern of flowers amid leafy tendrils, the covers decorated en suite (minor rim chip), 4 1/4" d. **$120 pair**

Candlesticks (pair), Chinese Export elephant figural porcelain, China, late 18th/early 19th century, 4 1/2" h, 5 1/4" w, one with unobtrusive hairline across base at mid-belly, the other stick with glue repair where candle cup meets figure, and a chip on ear edge and saddle.............**$3,555 pair**

Candlesticks (pair), Chinese Export Rose Medallion, mid-19th century, decorated overall in Famille Rose figural, floral and bird decoration, 7 3/4" h.................**$1,380 pair**

Charger, Imari decorated porcelain, Japanese, late 19th century, scallop-rim charger decorated in under-glaze blue with polychrome enamel and gilt decoration, 16" d, unobtrusive 1/2" rim chip.............................**$325**

Charger, Japanese, blue and white, three asymmetrical reserves with bamboo, flowering branches and tree with Mount Fuji in background, 18" d. **$149**

Container, (circular, covered), Chinese Imari-inspired, Qing Dynasty, the circular exterior with a pair of short handles and painted in gilt, under-glaze blue and shades of red enamel with a sparse design of butterflies amid flowering sprays repeated on the low convex lid with a knob finial (minor rim chips), 4 1/2" d.............................**$90**

Dinnerware, Imari porcelain, iron red and cobalt blue decoration, gilt trim; some variations in patterns; six- and four-character signatures; consisting of 12 large 12" dinner plates, 19 punch cups, three cordial cups, four 3 1/2" cordial cups, four 3 1/2" sauce plates, three 9 1/2" plates, four 8" plates, twelve 5" bowls (3 chipped), four 6 1/2" bowls, six teacups and saucers, six 7 1/2" plates, nine 5" miscellaneous sauce plates, eight 4" sauce plates, 13" punch bowl, 9" bowl and 7 1/2" bowl. ....**$1,560 set**

Dish, (vegetable) with cover, Canton, rectangular dish with typical scenic decoration and notched corners, the lid with a berry knop, 5 1/2" h x 11" l x 9 1/2" w. **$518**

Dish, (vegetable), Chinese Export Canton, covered, rectangular bowl with notched corner fitted with a domed lid and knopped berry finial. Decorated overall with blue and white Oriental scenic decoration of typical form, 6 3/4" h x 11 1/2" l x 10" w.............................**$518**

Dish, (warming), Rose Medallion, four alternating floral and figural reserves, hot water well beneath, 10 1/4" d, slight chip near one spout, slight rim chip. **$460**

Dishes, (two), Chinese blue-and-white porcelain, Qing Dynasty, 19th century, the first a small plate painted with a figure on a garden terrace, the edges with fruiting scrolling vines, brown rim (rough foot), the second with the interior well painted with rocks and flowering plants, a wide floral band on the everted rim (minor chips to foot rim), 6" x 8 1/2" d. ....**$80 pair**

Photo courtesy Clars Auction Gallery, Oakland, Calif.; www.Clars.com

Charger, Japanese-style Imari, scallop edged, the interior well painted in gilt, under-glaze blue and shades of red enamel with a flower vase medallion bordered by a floral band and surrounded on the curving sides with alternating shaped floral and dragon reserves separated by vertical bands of cash-emblems, all set against a dense brocade-patterned ground, 17" d. **$425**

Photo courtesy Clars Auction Gallery, Oakland, Calif.; www.Clars.com

Cup (stem), Chinese wucai, the exterior of the circular bowl painted in under-glaze blue and bright enamels with three mythical animals flying amid cloud scrolls above stylized waves, the squared stem flaring towards the base and decorated en suite with a Lishui River border, the interior with a spurious Wanli inscription, 3 1/4" h, 2 3/4" d. **$200**

Photo courtesy Clars Auction Gallery, Oakland, Calif.; www.Clars.com

Jar (covered), Chinese Export porcelain for the Thai market, the exterior painted overall in gilt and polychrome enamels with a dense Thai-inspired floral pattern repeated on the tiered lid (hairline crack to lid), 6" h. **$500**

Figure, (nodder), Asian porcelain, seated lady in blue and white dress, nodding head, movable hands extended, 6" h, small counterbalance missing from right hand. **$632**

Jar, Japanese porcelain, blue and white painted jar with domed cover, possibly Seto, mounted as a lamp and fitted with a gilded bronze base depicting a tree trunk and flowers, Meiji Period. With base: 20" h. **$540**

Mug, Chinese Export porcelain, late 18th century, decorated with a three-masted sailing vessel carrying a British flag, 4 1/4" h, minor 1/2" hairline on rim edge, no chips or repairs. **$1,540**

Mug, Chinese Export porcelain, with American eagle and shield, late 18th/early 19th century, 3 3/8" h, spreading hairline on base, one line going up side near handle about 2 1/2". **$1,007**

Planter, Chinese Export Rose Medallion, first half 19th century, hexagonal form with flat flared edges, each side decorated in panels depicting views of daily life alternating with floral decorated panels with birds and butterflies on shaped bracket feet, 5" h x 7" d. **$690**

Platter, Chinese Export Canton, blue, mid-19th century, rectangular with canted corners decorated overall in a blue and white Oriental landscape, 16" x 12 1/2". **$575**

Platter, Canton porcelain, China, late 19th century, 14 1/4" x 17". **$503**

Platter, Chinese Export Famille Rose, oval form with canted corners, bold floral sprays, conforming border, 12 7/8" l, 9 3/4" w. **$402**

Platter, (meat), Chinese Export porcelain, blue and white, 19th century, round platter decorated with floral designs, (lacking drainer), 2 1/2" h, 17 3/8" d, 1/2" shallow rim chip. **$385**

Platter, (oval), Chinese Export porcelain, Rose Mandarin decoration with three flower, bird and butterfly reserves alternating with three figural reserves, 17 5/8" l. **$373**

Platter, (oval), Chinese Export porcelain, blue and white landscape with water, pagodas and bridge, reticulated border, 11" l, 9 5/8" w. **$258**

Platter, (oval), Famille Rose palette Chinese Export porcelain, circa 1800, decorated with flower sprigs with gilt spearhead borders, 17 5/8" d, 1/2" rim chip, scattered enamel losses. **$266**

Platters, (pair), Chinese Export Canton, cut-corner, mid-19th century, each of typical form decorated with oriental landscapes in blue and white. Both 12" l x 9 1/2" w. ....**$575 pair**

Pillow, Chinese Export porcelain, oblong with multicolored vases and assorted trophies, pierced ends, 2 1/2" h., 5 3/4" l, 4 3/4" w, chips to corners and edges. **$126**

Pot, (brush), Korean, with openwork decoration of two large roundels with Buddhistic swastika, bamboo and pomegranates in under-glaze blue enamels, 19th/20th century, 5 1/2" x 4" d. **$480**

Pot, (bough), Chinese Export porcelain, twin-handled flaring form, five-hole cover, landscape reserve with figures, interior reserve with figures, green N or Z mark on bottom, 8 1/4" h, 6 3/8" w (overall), 4 3/4" d, cover repaired. **$805**

Punchbowl, Tobacco Leaf decorated, Chinese Export, 19th century, inside and out decorated with tall green tobacco leaves, Famille Rose border, butterflies among the leaves, 6 1/4" h x 14 3/4" d, some roughness to rim. **$1,725**

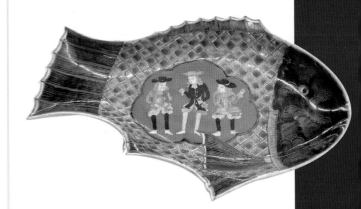

Photo courtesy Clars Auction Gallery, Oakland, Calif.; www.Clars.com

Plate, Japanese-style Imari fish form, the interior painted with a ruyi-head-shaped figural reserve of three Dutchmen on a red ground silhouetted against a geometric pattern of purple and green squares, the cobalt painted head and fins with additional gilt and red accents, 13" l. **$375**

Punchbowl, Chinese Export, Rose Mandarin, mid-19th century, rim borders profusely decorated in floral vinery with fanciful butterflies and birds. Center showing panels of domestic Oriental life outlined in Greek key borders alternating with panels of floral and butterfly decoration. Center panel decorated with a scene of scholarly learning, 5 3/4" h x 12 1/2" d, nominal wear to interior painting in bowl. **$2,242**

Punchbowl, ormolu-mounted, Rose Medallion, exterior with four multicolored painted reserves with flowers, birds and butterflies; floral band just under twin handles, four cabriole legs with scroll feet; interior with four conformingly decorated reserves and centering round reserve, 12 1/2" h., 12 1/2" d. **$1,800**

Sauceboat, Chinese Export Famille Rose, and a Rose Mandarin teapot, mid-19th century, sauceboat with applied strap handle and floral butterfly and bird decorated panel opposing a landscape-decorated panel. The drum-form teapot with polychrome-decorated lid, with panels depicting Oriental life alternating with panels of floral sprays and exotic animals. Sauceboat 3" h x 7 1/4" l. Teapot 6 1/2" h. Sauceboat with minor flakes to edge of spout. ....**$201 pair**

Tableware items, (three), Fitzhugh Pattern (blue) porcelain, China, 19th century, including a covered oval dish and two oval platters; dish 4 1/4" h, 11 d, platters 11 1/4" and 14 1/2" d. ....**$711 all**

Stoneware items, (four), Korean, Yi Dynasty: gray stoneware pedestal bowl and cover; gray water dropper with stamped designs; small vase with stamped design, and a black glaze stoneware vase. Tallest: 9 1/2". ....**$480 all**

Tableware items, (three), Chinese Export Canton, blue, cut-corner platter, 15 3/4" x 13", and two similar-shaped sauce or gravy boats, having handles and scalloped edges, each 8" l. ....**$402 all**

Teapot and trivet, Chinese Export Canton, mid-19th century, teapot with berry knopped finial and applied strap handle. Trivet of hexagonal form. Both decorated in blue and white bucolic scenes. Teapot 7" h. Trivet 5 1/4" d, teapot with very minor roughness on spout. Trivet with tiny flakes on edge. ....**$575 pair**

Tureen with cover, Chinese Export Canton, mid-19th century, cover with pointed finial fitted to the deep oval tureen with boar's head handles raised on conforming footed base, decorated overall in typical blue and white pastoral scenes, 6" h overall x 9 1/2" l x 8" w, probable small repair with missing glaze on finial, some discoloration in glaze on lid interior. **$345**

Tureen with cover, Chinese Export Canton, rectangular form, with canted corners and boar's head handles, 9 1/4" h x 12 1/2" l x 8 3/4" w, two pitting spots in lid...........**$1,035**

Vase, Chinese mirror black glazed ovoid, possibly Qing, the high shoulder body surmounted by a wide everted rim and tapering sharply to a flared foot, the base with a spurious Kangxi mark, 9" h...**$90**

Vase (garniture), Chinese Export polychrome decorated, mid-19th century, covered vase with Foo Dog finial decorated overall with stylistic raised grapevines and mice, centering polychrome painted court scenes, 12 1/2" h, finial with tiny chip on ear of dog. **$978**

Photo courtesy Clars Auction Gallery, Oakland, Calif.; www.Clars.com

Vase, Chinese, ox-blood glazed, 19th century, the ovoid exterior covered in a rich red glaze ground down on the foot (chipped foot rim, neck ground down), 15" h. **$60**

Photo courtesy Clars Auction Gallery, Oakland, Calif.; www.Clars.com

Vase, Chinese, tea dust glazed, ovoid with a long neck and low slung body (bingdu) raised on a high flaring ring foot, covered overall in the characteristic mottled olive-green glaze, the base with a spurious Qianlong cartouche, 12 1/2" h. **$1,300**

Vase, Celadon, late 19th century, with dark blue dragon, bird and flowers, stylized opposing Foo Dog handles and large upturned flaring rim: 23 1/4" h x 8 1/2" d top, some old hairlines to rim. **$172**

Vase, Japanese Hirado porcelain, painted with asters in under-glaze blue and yellow, some in moriage, Meiji period. Signed with Mikawachi Kiln marks, 13" x 5 1/4" d. **$5,100**

Vase, Kinkozan Satsuma, painted with a gilt dragon and sea spray on a mottled green glaze, Meiji period. Signed and sealed, 8 1/2" x 5". **$1,920**

Vase, Korean porcelain, squat baluster form with raised and slightly tapering neck painted with birds perched on a tree, the obverse with a bamboo stalk, Yi Dynasty, 6 3/4" h. **$8,400**

Vase, Nippon, decorated with a crane among lotus in moriage relief. Marked on the base Hand-painted Nippon, 10 1/8" h. **$2,400**

Vase, Nippon, ornate porcelain with coralene flowers and gilding on cobalt blue ground, 20th century, small losses to coralene and wear to gilding. Marked 'Patent Applied For, 38257' with three-column stamp, 8" x 5". **$1,440**

Photo courtesy Clars Auction Gallery, Oakland, Calif.; www.Clars.com

Vases (bottle, pair), Japanese-style Kutani, each of tapering square section and painted in bright enamels with figural panels alternating with flowering chrysanthemums along a fence, the angular shoulder with further flowering chrysanthemums below linked key frets, the circular neck accented with flaming jewels, the base with a recessed "fuku" cartouche, 9 3/4" h. **$450 pair** *(A cartouche is an ornate panel in the form of a tablet or shield, usually framed by foliage and scrollwork, and usually bearing an inscription or maker's name and date.)*

Photo courtesy Clars Auction Gallery, Oakland, Calif.; www.Clars.com

Vases (pair), Chinese Famille Verte-decorated phoenix-tail, the wide trumpet mouth and high-shouldered body each painted in bright enamels with a frieze of mythical birds in a lush flowering landscape within geometric patterned borders, the base with a spurious Kangxi mark (some surface wear), 16 3/4" h. **$425 pair**

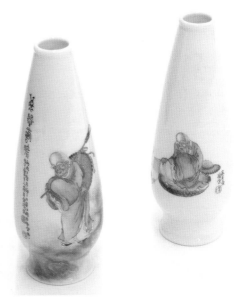

Photo courtesy Clars Auction Gallery, Oakland, Calif.; www.Clars.com

Vases (pair), Chinese polychrome enamel decorated porcelain, each pear-form body painted with Chinese immortals, one with a long colophon with a cyclical date "bingxu" and signed (unread) mark to base, 6 1/2" h. **$800 pair**

Vases (pair), Rose Mandarin porcelain, China, circa 1860, baluster-form vases decorated with gilt Kylin and Foo Dog figures around the necks, including turned wooden stands, 9 1/4" h, a 3/4" area of loose enamel is taped in place on one vase. .... **$1,066 pair**

NORITAKE CHINA

Morimura Brothers founded Noritake China in 1904 in Nagoya, Japan. The company made high-quality chinaware for export to the United States and also produced a line of china blanks for hand painting. In 1910, the company perfected a technique for the production of dinnerware and introduced streamlined production.

During the 1920s, the Larkin Co. of Buffalo, N.Y., was a prime distributor of Noritake China. Larkin offered Azalea, Briarcliffe, Linden, Modjeska, Savoy, Sheridan and Tree in the Meadow patterns as part of its premium line.

The factory was heavily damaged during World War II, and production was reduced. Between 1946 and 1948, the company sold its china under the "Rose China" mark, since the quality of production did not match the earlier Noritake China. Expansion in 1948 brought about the resumption of quality production and the use of the Noritake name once again.

There are close to 100 different marks for Noritake, and careful study is required to determine the date of production. Most pieces are marked "Noritake" with a wreath, "M," "N" or "Nippon." The use of the letter N was registered in 1953.

Bowl, fruit, Linden, 5 1/4" **$10**
Bowl, oval, Rosewin #6584 pattern, 10" l........................ **$30**
Bowl, soup, rimmed, Sheridan, 7 3/4"................................ **$14**
Bread and butter plate
   Azalea, 6 3/8" **$6**
   Briarcliffe, 6 1/2"... **$8**
   Linden, 6 3/8" **$10**
   Modjeska, 6 3/8" **$8.50**

Sheridan, 6 1/4" **$8**
Cake plate, handled, Linden, 10 1/2" **$41**
Cake set, desert scene with tent and man on camel, cobalt blue and gilt border, marked "Noritake/Made in Japan/Hand Painted," 11" d cake plate, six 6 1/4" serving plates **$770**
Candlesticks, pair, gold flowers and bird, blue luster ground, wreath with "M" mark, 8 1/4" h...................... **$125**
Celery
   Azalea, 12 3/4" **$35**
   Linden, 13"... **$40**
Coffee pot, small, lid, Rosewin, 6 3/8" **$45**
Console set, 11 3/4" d bowl, pair 8" h candlesticks, amber pearl center, 1" black rim with gold floral dec, green mark.
    .... **$465**
Creamer
   Azalea **$27**
   Linden **$30**
   Sheridan, 8 oz **$25**
Creamer and sugar, Art Deco, pink Japanese lanterns, cobalt blue ground, basket type handle on sugar, wreath with "M" mark... **$50**
Cup and saucer, Florola... **$24**
Demitasse cup and saucer, Tree in the Meadow **$45**
Dinner set, floral motif, gold rimmed, 115-piece set **$375**
Egg cup, Azalea, 3 1/8"... **$35**
Gravy boat, attached underplate, Briarcliffe.................... **$38**
Gravy boat, Tree in the Meadow................................... **$50**
Hair receiver, Art Deco, geometric designs, gold luster, wreath with "M" mark, 3 1/4" h, 3 1/2" w **$50**
Napkin ring, Art Deco man and woman, wreath with "M" mark, pair.. **$60**
Pitcher, Azalea, 28 oz **$195**
Place card holder, figural, bluebird with butterfly, gold luster, white stripes, wreath with "M" mark, pair **$35**
Plate, dinner
   Azalea, 9 7/8" **$24**
   Briarcliffe, 10" **$18**
   Linden, 10"... **$15**
   Modjeska, 9 7/8" **$25**
   Sheridan, 10 1/2" **$19**

Photo courtesy of Seeck Auctions.
Noritake, plate, Lady In Garden, 9" sq, **$325.**

Noritake Azalea pattern, lemon dish, ring handle, **$30.**

Plate, salad
  Briarcliffe, 7 1/2"..$10
  Linden, 7 5/8"..$18
  Modjeska, 7 5/8"...$11
  Rosewin, 8 1/4"..$10
  Sheridan, 8 1/4"...$10
Punch bowl set, 12" h two-part punch bowl with three-
  footed base, six 2 3/4" h cups, peacock design, cobalt blue
  and gilt borders, blue ground ext., melon and blue interior,
  "M" in wreath mark $600
Relish
  Linden, 8 5/8"...$31
  Rosewin, 9"...$17
Salt, swan, white, orange luster, pair, 3" l..........$25
Salt and pepper shakers, pair, Tree in the Meadow,
  marked "Made in Japan"...................................$35
Salt shaker, bulbous, Azalea $21
Serving platter, oval
  Briarcliffe, 11 3/4"..$50
  Linden, 11 7/8"..$58
  Linden, 13 3/4"..$80
  Rosewin, 15 1/4"..$55
  Sheridan, 13 7/8"...$38
Teapot, lid, Azalea, 3 cup size.......................$150
Tea tile, Tree in the Meadow, green mark, 5" w......$35
Toothpick holder, Azalea $80
Vegetable bowl, cov, Magnificence, #9736 ....$350
Vegetable bowl, oval, Rosewin, 10"....................$55
Vegetable bowl, round, covered, Sheridan $80
Wall pocket, butterfly, wreath with "M" mark $75

Ivory

Brush pot, probably late 18th century, depicting a
  mountainous landscape with birds in flight, the reverse
  with Chinese characters, the base segmented and
  detachable, 3 3/4" h, 3 3/4" d, base rim has an old 1/2"
  elliptic chip..$1,438
Container, of cylindrical form and finely carved to the
  exterior with diminutive figures in a landscape scattered
  with pavilions (no bottom), fixed to a wooden stand
  (wear), 4 1/2" h (overall)................................$150
Container, Meiji/Taisho period, the sections of the tusk
  carved and incised to the exterior with two felines, one of
  a lion approaching an elephant walking with trunk raised,
  pigment accents, 4" l. $100
Figure, Budai, the "Laughing Buddha," well carved and
  incised, seated on a brocade-patterned treasure sack, a
  group of five Chinese children frolicking to the top and
  back of the deity, 5 3/4" h. $225
Figure, Budai, the "Laughing Buddha," seated in a pose of
  royal ease with his left knee raised and left hand holding
  prayer beads, with finely defined facial features, 4" h...$200
Figure, bearded fisherman in an animated pose, a small dog
  to the side of the rocky outcropping (lacking pole), with a
  wooden stand, 7" h (figure only)......................$60
Figure, fisherman, mid-19th century, with inked highlights
  depicting a fisherman with bandana and floral tunic, with
  creel and bamboo spear perched on a rock plinth with a
  captured fish, height minus spear, 7 3/4", spear present,
  needs reattaching. $575

Photo courtesy Sloans & Kenyon Auctioneers and Appraisers, Chevy Chase, Md.; www.SloansandKenyon.com

Figure of deity, Chinese, carved, multi-armed, holding attributes, seated on double lotus throne, high chignon, figure of Buddha, attendants, 20th century, 11" h x 13" l x 7" w. **$945**

Photo courtesy Sloans & Kenyon Auctioneers and Appraisers, Chevy Chase, Md.; www.SloansandKenyon.com

Okimono of fisherman, holding bamboo-form stick, wearing hat, signed, late Meiji period, Japanese, 6 1/2" h. **$355**

Figure, flowering peony bush issuing from a rectangular
  container, a spray of ripe millet to one side, 6 1/2" h. ...$150
Vase, (miniature), with inlaid accents, carved and incised
  as an archaic vessel with a trumpet mouth, the ovoid body
  with archaic motifs with occasional inlay of turquoise and
  coral, with loose ring handles (possible restorations),
  2 3/4" h. $120

Jade

Bracelet, the convex sides well carved and pierced with leafy peony blossoms, the pale sea-green translucent matrix of even tone, 2 7/8" d. **$150**

Brush washer, carved and pierced as an open Buddha hand citron flanked by leafy stems to either side, the translucent olive green matrix with white striations and flecked with black, 8" l. **$700**

Clasp, archaic, well carved and incised as a dragon with a snake-form body tapering to a hooked tail, with its curving body turning back to form a narrow slot, the mottled translucent green stone with brown and white inclusions, 2" l. **$325**

Figure, elephant, carved and incised standing with its head turned to one side and trunk swaying upwards, of pale-green color mottled with white and brown fissures and inclusions, some incorporated into the design, 6 1/2" l.
.........................**$425**

Figure, Foo Lion, 20th century, in a recumbent pose with forelegs outstretched and resting on a large cash emblem, the translucent grayish-white matrix with opaque white inclusions, 3" l. **$50**

Figure (jadeite), God of Wealth, Wen Cai Shen (Bi Gan), as a bearded official holding an ingot and ruyi-head scepter in his hands, the corpulent deity surrounded by laughing children, auspicious animals, birds and symbols amid cloud scrolls, all supported on an oversize metal ingot, portions of the design picked out from the apple green and russet inclusions in the translucent mottled pale green stone, 5 3/4" h. **$650**

Figure, recumbent horse with its legs tucked close to its emaciated torso and head turned back, the greyish white translucent matrix with occasional inclusions, 2 1/4" l.
.........................**$325**

Figure, recumbent ram in a frontal pose with its legs tucked close to the body, the pale green matrix with occasional white inclusions, 2 1/4" l. **$550**

Figure, tree, with multiple blossoms fashioned from nephrite jade, agate, rose quartz and rock crystal on stems with dark green jade leaves, the rectangular container of mottled green jade (losses), 12 1/4" h. **$60**

Figure, water buffalo, carved in a recumbent posture with its head raised and turning to one side, its right foreleg held to the front, the olive-green matrix mottled with white and brown striations, incised details, 10" l. **$275**

Figures, birds, 20th century, carved and pierced as a long-tailed crested bird and its mate cavorting near a fruiting pomegranate tree, the translucent pale green stone suffused with russet in one fruit and the head of the main bird, with wooden stand, 6 1/4" h. **$120**

Figures, elephants, 20th century, realistically rendered as an African elephant attempting to comfort a calf standing to one side, the muted green stone with overall white inclusions, 7 1/2" l. **$400**

Pebble, the interior carved and undercut with a laughing figure of Shou-lao (god of longevity and luck) seated in a pose of royal ease, a youthful attendant holding a spray of peach standing to the left, the tableau picked out from the milky white interior of a red-skinned pebble, 6 3/4" l.
.........................**$225**

Photo courtesy Sloans & Kenyon Auctioneers and Appraisers, Chevy Chase, Md.; www.SloansandKenyon.com

Celedon jade vase and cover, tao tie masks, Chinese, 19th century, 5" h. **$1,770**

Pebble, 20th century, the top featuring a celestial maiden in flight with her long robes fluttering in the wind, her left hand holding a floral spray, the high-relief figure crafted from the milky white interior of a red-skinned pebble, 9" l.
.........................**$50**

Pendant, Qing Dynasty, of oval shape and carved to the front with a pair of Chinese children chasing a butterfly while playing in a fruiting melon patch, the upper portion finely carved with linked cloud scrolls, the pale green translucent matrix of even tone, 2 1/4" l. **$425**

Pendants (pair), the first of circular mutton-fat jade carved to either side with shou medallions (symbols of long life) bracketed by bats interspersed with wan-li symbols (strength), the second of rectangular shape, either side carved to the top with a pair of Mandarin ducks above a reserve of a carp in a lotus pond, reversed by an auspicious four-character seal-script inscription, the stone of even greenish-white hue, 2" d and 2 1/4" l. ....**$350 pair**

Table screens (pair), each large rectangular dark-green panel carved and incised with figures in a landscape, some traveling on horseback, working in the field or conversing in a pavilion, both reversed by two five-character poetic couplet, one with a spurious Qianlong mark, each set within a reticulated frame of foliate repeated on the separately fashioned stand, 26 1/2" h. ....**$4,250 pair**

Apple jade vase, Rouleau form, flowering lotus decoration, elephant head loose-ring handles, Chinese, 19th century. **$945.**

Vase, carved as two joined lengths of bamboo fronted by a pair of recumbent rams, the reverse with a bat amid scrolling clouds above further bamboo and a rocky outcropping, the translucent green stone with russet fissures and striations, occasional white inclusions and black flecks, 3 3/4" h..................................**$200**

Netsuke and Okimono

The traditional Japanese kimono has no pockets. Daily necessities, such as money and tobacco supplies, were carried in leather pouches, or inros, which hung from a cord with a netsuke toggle. The word netsuke comes from "ne"—to root—and "tsuke"— to fasten.

Netsuke originated in the 14th century and initially were favored by the middle class. By the mid-18th century, all levels of Japanese society used them. Some of the most famous Japanese artists, including Shuzan and Yamada Hojitsu, worked in the netsuke form.

Netsuke average from 1 to 2" in length and are made from wood, ivory, bone, ceramics, metal, horn, nutshells, etc. The subject matter is broad based, but almost always portrayed in a lighthearted, humorous manner. A net-suke must have smooth edges and balance in order to hang correctly on the sash.

Value depends on artist, region, material and the skill of the maker. Western collectors favor "katabori," pieces that represent an identifiable object.

An okimono is a Japanese carving, often small, similar to but larger than a netsuke. Unlike netsuke, which had a specific purpose, okimono were purely decorative and were displayed in the "tokonoma," a small, raised alcove. During the Meiji Period (1868-1912) many okimono were made for export to the West.

Recent reproductions are common. Some are molded resin. Newly made netsuke are carved from vegetable ivory, also known as corozo, a name used for the tagua nut in the South American rainforest.

Netsuke, (three) by Nanryu, of Oni, 20th century: one carrying Hotei's sack over his shoulder; one with Benkei's bell; and one with a large jar, all with inlaid eyes. Signed Nanryu (Keizo Kurata, born 1935). Tallest: 1 3/8" h. ....**$900 all**

(Oni are creatures from Japanese folklore, variously translated as demons, devils, ogres or trolls.)

Netsuke, three pieces, 19th/20th century: wood netsuke of a puppy, natural himotoshi, signed Toko-To, 1 1/2" h; ivory Oni emerging from lotus leaf, unsigned, 2 1/4" h; two fish with scales carved in openwork, with inlaid eyes, signed Koetsu, 1 1/2" h. ....**$720 all**

(The channel or hole carved into the netsuke for the passage of the cord is called the himotoshi. Such holes also occur naturally.)

Netsuke, three pieces, 20th century: two Shishi (stylized figure of a snarling lion) with openwork ball in negoro lacquer with traces of gilding, unsigned, 1 1/4" h; wood

Netsuke, carved wood, Shishi (stylized figure of a snarling lion) crouched over a ball, natural himotoshi, 19th century, unsigned, 1 3/4" h. **$720**
(The channel or hole carved into the netsuke for the passage of the cord is called the himotoshi. Such holes also occur naturally.)

Netsuke, by Masanao Shinzan, carved wood, of a curled-up rat with inlaid eyes, natural himotoshi and well-rendered details. Signed Shinzan (Masanao Shinzan, born 1904), 1 1/4" h. **$2,400**
(The channel or hole carved into the netsuke for the passage of the cord is called the himotoshi. Such holes also occur naturally.)

Shishi with openwork ball, signed on the base Minkoku, 1 1/4" h; ivory horse with inlaid eyes, unsigned, 1 7/8" h.
....**$540 all**

Netsuke, three carved pieces, 20th century: wood baboon holding a peach, well-rendered details, signed Yukimasa; ivory monkey and fish with inlaid eyes, signed Ippo(?); and a wood Daruma doll, signed Mitsunobu. Tallest: 1 3/4"............**$600 all**

Netsuke, ivory, six pieces, 19th-20th century: Ebisu and Daikoku riding a fish, signed; Ashinaga and Tenaga playing with children; two chicks emerging from egg, signed and sealed; group of people under a pine tree; man playing a drum with a monkey, signed; and man playing a drum. Tallest: 2"..**$780 all**

Netsuke, ivory, six pieces, Meiji period: horse emerging from a gourd, held by a bearded elder; carved horn octopus hiding in a wooden tub; scholar holding a scroll; Daruma waking from sleep; man with children at his side; and a bent figure holding a drum. All but octopus signed. Tallest: 2 1/4"..**$540 all**

Netsuke, ivory, six pieces, Meiji period: riverboat with passengers and rower sitting underneath a canopy, signed; tiger sitting on a large bamboo trunk; badger wrapped in a robe holding a fly whisk; group of five people standing under a pine tree; Okame; and swordsmith forging a blade, signed. Tallest: 1 3/8"..**$720 all**

Netsuke, ivory, six pieces, Meiji period: horse and boar; coiled snake on skull; man with gourds; monkey, signed; hunter with rabbit; and rat with purple inlaid eyes, signed. Tallest: 2"...**$600 all**

Netsuke and okimono, four pieces, carved ivory and wood; okimono: Pekinese dog holding a pierced ball; man sitting in a palanquin, being carried by two others, signed; man holding a stick; man with two children and a dog; together with four netsuke: carved wood Okame; horse, signed; water buffalo, signed, 19th/20th C. Tallest: 12". **$1,200 all**

Netsuke and tonkotsu (tobacco box), four pieces, 19th-20th century: wood netsuke of a monk piercing his chest with an ivory needle, inlaid part of himotoshi, signed on ivory tablet Ryugyoku; wood netsuke of a Sambaso dancer (part of a Kabuki theater performance) holding a fan, with metal and mother-of-pearl inlay, ivory details, signed on the box; and wood Daruma tonkotsu inlaid with mother-of-pearl eyes and ivory himotoshi, together with a wood fish pipe-holder, both unsigned. Tallest: 4 1/4". **$1,560 all**
(The channel or hole carved into the netsuke for the passage of the cord is called the himotoshi. Such holes also occur naturally.)

Photo courtesy Rago Arts and Auction Center, Lambertville, N.J.; www.RagoArts.com

Okimono, ivory and lacquered wood, Geisha with a parasol in wood with applied lacquer and carved ivory, Meiji period. Signed, 16 1/2" h. **$3,900**

Photo courtesy Rago Arts and Auction Center, Lambertville, N.J.; www.RagoArts.com

Okimono, ivory, large sectional figure of an egg tester, with an egg-filled basket strapped over his shoulder and eggs at his feet, Meiji period. Stained detail, some losses. Signed, 14 1/2" h. **$1,080**

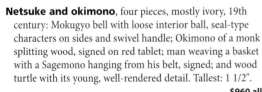

Netsuke and okimono, four pieces, mostly ivory, 19th century: Mokugyo bell with loose interior ball, seal-type characters on sides and swivel handle; Okimono of a monk splitting wood, signed on red tablet; man weaving a basket with a Sagemono hanging from his belt, signed; and wood turtle with its young, well-rendered detail. Tallest: 1 1/2". .... **$960 all**

Okimono, carved ivory and wood, man sitting on a bundle of branches, his head, hands, feet and logs carved from ivory, Meiji period. Missing accessories from hands, possibly an ax from side of bundle and signature tablet from base, 8 1/4" x 9". **$1,560**

Okimono, ivory, two pieces, 19th-20th century: three rats climbing on a mask, stained and inlaid details, 1 3/4" h; skull, 2" x 1 1/2". Both unsigned. **$960**

Okimono (three), ivory, Meiji period: rooster with hen and chicks, eyes inlaid with mother-of-pearl, one talon missing from rooster's and chick's foot, signed on base, 3" x 3 1/2" x 2 1/2"; chick emerging from broken egg, eyes inlaid with mother-of-pearl, signed on base, 2" x 4" x 2"; smaller similar to previous, one eye missing pupil, unsigned, 1 1/2" x 2 1/2" x 1 1/4". .... **$1,920 all**

Snuff Bottles

Tobacco usage spread from America to Europe to China during the 17th century. Europeans and Chinese preferred to grind the dried leaves into a powder and sniff it into their nostrils. The elegant Europeans carried their boxes and took a pinch with their fingertips. The Chinese upper class, because of their lengthy fingernails, found this inconvenient and devised a bottle with a fitted stopper and attached spoon. These utilitarian objects soon became objets d'art.

Snuff bottles were fashioned from precious and semi-precious stones, glass, porcelain and pottery, wood, metals and ivory. Glass and transparent-stone bottles often were enhanced further with delicate hand paintings, some done on the interior of the bottle.

Agate, carved

Amber, quatrefoil form, each side carved with bat and stylized ruyi design, Chinese, tiny chip and slight wear on rim, slight fissure on shoulder, 19th century, 2 1/4" h.......... **$150**

Flat rectangular shape, carved sprig of peony, reverse decorated with carved ruyi scepter, Chinese, 19th century, 2 3/8" h **$125**

Mottled brown, flattened round form, carved fisherman, reverse with cat looking up at a flying insect, red glass top, original spoon, Chinese, 19th century, 2 1/2" h **$200**

Mottled gray, flattened oval form, well carved with three men mooring boat, flower, tree decoration, Chinese, 19th century, 2 1/2" h **$575**

Amber, landscape and figures, caramel inclusions, Chinese, late 19th century, 4" l **$1,265**

Celadon, light jade, flattened ovoid short neck, 2 1/4" h . **$200**

Chrysoprase, flattened ovoid, light green, conforming stopper, 3" h..**$215**

Cinnabar lacquer, ovoid, continual scene of scholars and boys in a pavilion landscape, dark red, conforming stopper, 3 1/4" h **$230**

Cloisonné, auspicious symbols among clouds, yellow ground, lappet base border, ruyi head neck border, conforming stopper with chrysanthemum design, Qianlong four-character mark **$185**

Coral, carved, tree trunk with foliage, carved flower stopper, China, stopper glued to bottle, 19th or 20th century, 2 1/2" h **$320**

Glass

Clear, flat rectangular shape, broad oval foot, stone stopper with eye design, Chinese, 19th century, 2 1/4" h........**$125**

Interior painted with three horned goats by tree, verso with inscription, signed "Ma Shaoxian," China, no stopper, 2 1/2" h...**$480**

Opaque body, enameled peony blossoms, verso with two birds, three-characters on base, China, 3" h **$175**

Ivory, curved ivory carved with bulrushes and crocodiles, flatleaf cap with ball finial, pebbled gilt-metal lid with glass-inset neck, mounted with short neck chain, Indian, late 19th/early 20th century, 3 3/4" l...............................**$300**

Jade, carved

Flattened oval form, carved sage and pine tree on one side, reverse with man sitting under willow tree, fish on line, Chinese, 19th century, 3" h................................**$435**

Oval, carved butterfly near flowering branch, amber inclusions on one side, Chinese, design incorporates natural fissure, 18th or 19th century, 2 3/8" h **$875**

Slender oval form, carved basketweave decoration, tiger's eye stopper, Chinese, dark inclusion at base, spoon broken, 18th century, 2 3/8" h **$450**

Lapis lazuli, ovoid, relief carved, figures beneath tree, Chinese, 4" h...**$125**

Malachite, carved, gourd, Chinese, 3" h **$95**

Opal, carved sage seated before gourd, Ch'ing Dynasty, 3" h **$125**

Overlay glass, seven colors, one side with floral designs in two archaic-form vases, reverse with immortal attending a crane and deer, bats flying above, each side with animal mask and ring handles, green, blue, mauve, coral, brown, and yellow, on white ground, 19th century **$520**

Photo courtesy Sloans & Kenyon Auctioneers and Appraisers, Chevy Chase, Md.; www.SloansandKenyon.com
Snuff bottle, Chinese, rose glass, depicts qilin on brocade ground. **$445**

Photo courtesy Sloans & Kenyon Auctioneers and Appraisers, Chevy Chase, Md.; www.SloansandKenyon.com

Snuff bottle, Chinese, dark brown overlay glass, flattened ovoid form, carved, depicts flowering lotus branch above bird. **$475**

Peking glass, Snowflake

Blue overlay, each side with prancing deer, head turned with a lingchi branch in mouth, 19th century, 2 1/2" h........ **$490**

Red overlay, flattened ovoid, one side with serpent and tortoise, other with frog sitting under lily pad, 2 1/4" h **$1,265**

Porcelain

Famille Rose decoration, Chinese, Daoguang mark, iron-red seal mark... **$1,298**

Famille Rose decoration, vasiform, Chinese, marked, 19th century, 2 1/2" h **$125**

Famille Rose decoration, flattened round form, Chinese, marked, 19th century, 2 3/4" h........................... **$125**

Famille Rose decoration, raised molded dec, iron-red sacred fungus and bat mark, gilt foot rim, coral stopper, China, small chip, stopper glued to bottle, 18th or 19th century, 3 1/8" h **$95**

Famille Verte decoration, Chinese, cap loose, 19th century, 3 3/8" h **$115**

Famille Verte decoration, Chinese, 19th century, 3 3/4" h. **$150**

Famille Verte decoration, Chinese, molded boy form, Qing dynasty, 4" h.. **$355**

Gamboling lions among clouds, ruyi band on shoulder and base, carved wooden stopper and ivory spoon, gilt rims, iron-red Jiaqing four-character mark on base, China, small chips, 19th century, 3 1/4" h.......................... **$320**

Rock crystal, carved decoration of pine trees in mountainous landscape, inclusions of black crystalline in various lengths, carved coral stopper, Chinese, spoon missing, 19th century, 3 1/2" h............................. **$375**

Rose quartz, flattened ovoid, relief carved leaves and vines, Chinese, 3" h **$45**

Stag horn, flattened ovoid, one side with inset ivory panel with two laughing figures, reserve with inset panel with gold archaic script, 2 1/8" h **$175**

Turquoise, high relief carving of children and prunus trees, China. **$235**

Statuary

Figure of a bodhisattva, (one who leads an enlightened existence), Chinese, black-pigmented copper, seated on a double lotus base in long flowing robes, her hands held to the front and clutching prayer beads, the smiling face framed by an elaborate coiffure partially hidden by a cowl (some wear to finish), 13 1/2" h. **$140**

Figure of a female bodhisattva, (one who leads an enlightened existence), Nepalese, bronze, the lithe figure in a dance pose with one leg raised, the right hand holding a ghanta (ritual bell), the other with another attribute (losses), the meditative expression framed by large ear hoops and a coiffure drawn up into a tall chignon (loose), all supported on an oval double-lotus pedestal, incised details, 15 1/4" h. **$175**

Figure of Budai, (Hotei), the "Laughing Buddha," Chinese, white marble, seated with his robes partially open and holding prayer beads, his joyful face with crisply rendered features, 7" l... **$60**

Figure of a Buddha, Chinese, gilt-painted wood, seated in dhyanasana (profound meditation) with his hands to the front, the serene face with-red painted lips and crisply defined features framed by a coiffure of conical curls, 20" h... **$600**

Figure of a Buddha, Japanese, gilt lacquer, wood, 19th century, standing in monastic robe with his hands in the "fear not" and "boon granting" gestures, backed by an almond-shaped mandorla (two circles coming together) and supported on a high galleried pedestal, 10 3/4" h. **$80**

Figure of the Buddha, Southeast Asian, gilt bronze, probably Thailand, 19th century, seated in meditation on a triangular plinth with the hands joined together, the smiling face framed by a gilt diadem (restoration, wear), 6" h... **$90**

Figure of a donor, Chinese, gilt lacquered, wooden, Qing Dynasty, the chaste maiden standing in long flowing robes and holding a sacred jewel (cintamani) to the front, her face with pigment accents, all supported on a high facetted plinth (extensive wear, wormage), 15 1/2" h... **$90**

Figure of Guanyin, Chinese, celadon glazed, the deity seated with prayer beads in her right hand, the serene face framed by an elaborate diadem fronted by a small seated Buddha, the translucent bluish-green glaze pooling in the recesses, 6 1/2" h.. **$80**

Figures (two), Chinese, polychrome painted wood, Qing Dynasty, the first of Guanyin seated in a pose of royal ease with and holding prayer beads, a small figure of Amitabha Buddha to the front of his diadem; the second of a bodhisattva seated in meditation with his hands to the front and cradling a scroll (extensive wear, wormage), 9 1/2" and 8" h. .... **$50 both**

Figures (two), of deities, Indian, carved wood, the first a sandalwood image of the elephant-headed Ganesha in his four-arm manifestation, the second a larger sculpture of Vishnu in princely raiment and standing on a tiered lotus base, two of his four arms with couch and disk attributes and all backed by a foliate mandorla, 6 3/4" and 16" h. .... **$110 both**

Photo courtesy Rago Arts and Auction Center, Lambertville, N.J.; www.RagoArts.com

Figure of Kwannon, Japanese bronze, her robes finely chased with flowers and cloud designs, standing on a rockwork base, 19th century, 15 3/4" h. **$660**

PERFUME CONTAINERS

The earliest known perfume containers date back more than 4,000 years. Knowledge of perfumery came to Europe as early as the 14th century, due partially to the spread of Islam. The Hungarians introduced the first modern perfume. Made of scented oils blended in an alcohol solution, it was made in 1370 at the command of Queen Elizabeth of Hungary and was known throughout Europe as "Hungary Water."

Also see Tiffany.

Ancient glass, late Roman Empire, neck chip, body crack and cloudiness, 3" h. $28

Atomizer, green opalescent glass with gilt metal fittings and original bulb, 5 3/4" h. $57

Atomizer (travel), continental, silver and Venetian glass, circa 1900, with original bulb (loose) and carrying purse; purse 4" l. $30

Aventurine, donut shape, silver mounts with monkey stopper, black glass with copper mica flake, 3" h. $84

Baccarat, cobalt blue and clear cut-glass atomizer with original silvered metal pump fitting, stenciled mark, 3 1/2" h. $72

Photo courtesy Rago Arts and Auction Center, Lambertville, N.J.; www.RagoArts.com

Baccarat, for Delettrez "XII," pink crystal, with label, in hand-painted box, circa 1927, Marked Baccarat, 4 1/2" h. **$20,000**

Photo courtesy Rago Arts and Auction Center, Lambertville, N.J.; www.RagoArts.com

Baccarat, for Guerlain, "A Travers Champs," crystal, cord sealed, with label, in faux marble box, circa 1924, Marked Baccarat, 5" h. **$900**

Photo courtesy Rago Arts and Auction Center, Lambertville, N.J.; www.RagoArts.com

Baccarat, for J. Viard, Madhva "Ta Wao," gilded and enameled crystal, with original beaded tassel, circa 1923, marked Baccarat, 2 1/2" h. **$5,000**

Brosse Jovoy, "Hallo! Coco!", enameled glass, cord sealed, in rare cage display, with box, circa 1924, bottle 4" h. **$13,000**

Baccarat, Toujours Fidle, 3" h. $230

Bohemian glass, atomizer and perfume bottle, the amber atomizer with original bulb, the bottle with sterling silver screw cap and original stopper; taller 3 1/2" h......... **$84 pair**

Bottle and matching atomizer, Art Deco, green flash glass with original gilt metal fittings and bulbs, bottle with dauber and stopper, 4" h. .... **$144 pair**

Bourjois, Evening in Paris, presentation in blue Bakelite box modeled as an owl, 3 1/2" h...$60

Bourjois, Evening in Paris, presentation in blue Bakelite box modeled as a tall-case clock, 4 1/2" h. $115

Bouton, Piano, presentation, circa 1930s, 4 3/4" l. $57

Ciro, Bouquet Antique, circa 1932, finished in blue, black, and yellow enamel, 3 1/4" h...$517

Ciro, Bouquet Antique, with original tassel and packaging, 3" h..$330

Continental porcelain, circa 1930s, modeled as a seated cat, gilt metal replacement stopper, 3 3/4" h..................$240

Corday, Rue de la Paix, figural with ashtray base, 8" h. $103

De Vigny, Golli Wogg, circa 1930s, with original label (worn), 5 1/2" h. $120

De Vigny, Golli Wogg, 1950s, with original box, 3 1/2" h. $360

Diviblis, topaz glass atomizer with original bulb and metal fitting, 6" h. $72

Dresden porcelain, circa 1900, in 18th-century Meissen style with figures in landscape and flowers, signed Carl Theime, 3 1/2" h. $258

Czech, Art Deco, blue crystal with dauber, in unusual jeweled metalwork holder, circa 1920s, 5" h. **$1,500**

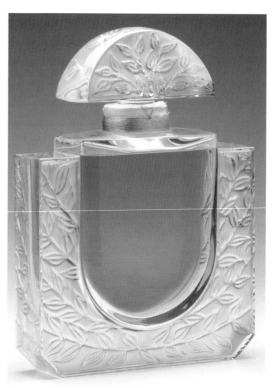

Photo courtesy Rago Arts and Auction Center, Lambertville, N.J.;
www.RagoArts.com

Lalique, "Parfum Lalique," clear and frosted crystal, circa 1992, script Lalique, 10 1/2" h.
$550

English, Victorian, opalescent glass, with brass cap and original internal stopper, horn shaped, 6" l. **$149**

English, Victorian, satin glass, with Japanese-style gilt decoration, with silver top (frozen), 3 1/4" h. **$144**

Fenton, frosted glass, 1930s with floral design, 5 1/2" h.
....**$92**

Guerlain, Liu, circa 1930, in original black and gilt Art Deco box, bottle 2 1/2" h. **$230**

Hovenvansoeg box, Danish, circa 1770, with eagle surmount, base with Latin engraving, gold wash interior, 3" h...**$240**

Kerr, American, silver pendant vial, modeled as a Renaissance baton, with cherub faces and XXX touchmark, signed Kerr, 4" h. **$195**

Collector's Note: The William B. Kerr Co. was established in Newark, N.J., in 1855. The firm was purchased by Gorham in 1906.

Kerr, American, silver pendant vial, with dolphin-shape design in Renaissance style, sprinkler form with XXX touchmark, Kerr, 3 1/4" h. **$287**

Kewpies, assembled set of five with varied hand positions, each with different pose, each with sprinkler tops, average 3" h..**$230 all**

Lalique, Coeur Joie for Ninna Ricci, 1950s, stenciled "BOTTLE MADE BY LALIQUE", 4 3/4" h. **$161**

Lalique, Enfants, 1980s, engraved Lalique France, 4 1/4" h.
....**$270**

Lalique Perfume, Limited Edition, 1996 with original packing and contents, bottle: 4" h...........................**$345**

Lalique Pour Homme, "Les Mascotes," three miniature bottles, presentation set in original box, average 2" h.
....**$161**

Lalique Society of America, Clairfontaine, 1991, in original box, stenciled marks, 4 1/2" h. **$230**

Lalique Society of America, Degas box, 1989, in original box, stenciled marks, 2 1/2" h. **$126**

Photo courtesy Rago Arts and Auction Center, Lambertville, N.J.;
www.RagoArts.com

R. Lalique, "Amphitrite," green glass, circa 1920, engraved R. Lalique France No. 514, 3 1/2" h.
$4,350

*R. Lalique, for Molinard,
"Le Baiser Du Faune,"
clear and frosted glass,
circa 1928, molded R.
LALIQUE, engraved
Molinard Paris France,
5 3/4" h.* **$4,000**

Lalique Society of America, Hestia Medallion, 1990, in
   original box, stencil marks, 5 1/2" h. **$103**
Lalique-style, Ambre Antique, presentation for Coty, 1990
   reissue, with original box, bottle 6 1/4" h. **$172**
R. Lalique, Dans La Nuit, for Worth, with original contents
   and packaging, unsigned, bottle: 3" h., box worn. **$180**
R. Lalique, figural atomizer for Marcas et Bardel, with
   green patina and original gilt metal fitting, molded 'R.
   Lalique' on bottle, 2 3/4" h. **$460**
R. Lalique, Jasmine, for Worth, molded "R. Lalique",
   2 1/2" h. **$168**
R. Lalique, Sans Adieu, for Worth, molded "R. Lalique",
   2 1/2" h. **$204**

*R. Lalique, for Roger et Gallet, "Flausa," clear
and frosted glass with sepia patina, circa 1914,
molded LALIQUE on stopper, matching engraved
control numbers, slight cloudiness to interior,
4 3/4" h.* **$3,500**

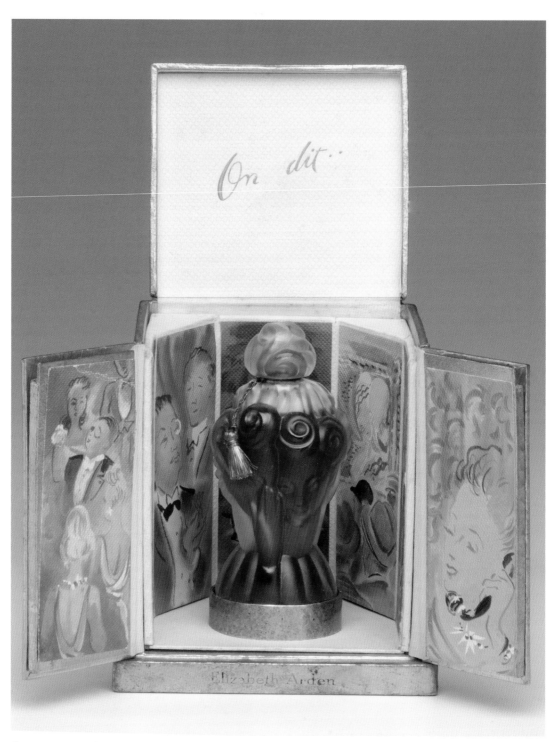

Photo courtesy Rago Arts and Auction Center, Lambertville, N.J.; www.RagoArts.com

Elizabeth Arden, "On Dit," figural frosted glass with inner stopper, in extremely rare box with graphics by Rene Bouche, circa 1948, 3 3/4" h. **$5,500**

R. Lalique, Forvil, "5 Fleurs," clear and frosted glass, cord sealed, with gray patina, circa 1929, molded R. Lalique, 4" h. **$3,000**

Lili of Bermuda, "Easter Lily," circa 1940, in original wooden box, perfume 3 1/2" h. **$168**

James McIntyre, vial, porcelain egg, circa 1885, Burslem, England, modeled as a bird's egg, with figural silver shape of baby-chicken-head screw cap, registered number 20772, 2 1/2" h. **$862**

> **Collector's Note: James MacIntyre & Co., founded circa 1860, Burslem, Staffordshire, England.**

James McIntyre, vials (three), porcelain, modeled as a walnut, acorn and hazelnut, circa 1860, two with plated screw caps (one frozen, one lacking stopper), one with silver cap (also lacking stopper), tallest 2 1/4" h. ......**$570 all**

Lanvin, display tester set, modern bottles on plastic stand, 6" h, including "My Sin" (1923), "Scandal" (1931), "Pretext" (1937), "Rumeur" (1934) and "Arpege" (1927). **$132**

Latticino, swirl pattern, with dauber stopper, missing handles, 6 1/2" h. **$92**

L'Air du Temps, in silk box, 8 oz. bottle, by Nina Ricci, doves in flight. **$510**

Lenox, porcelain for Devilbiss, with cat stopper, 3 3/4" h. **$218**

Lute form, continental, silver, lacks internal stopper, 4 1/2" l. **$373**

Mickey Mouse (pair), pottery, circa 1930, 2 1/2" h. ....**$195 pair**

Norwegian, enamel, silver gilt and guilloché, circa 1920s, signed Anderson (Norway), 5" h. **$402**
(Guilloché refers to a process of engine-turned design on metal.)

Paris Charme, a modern presentation of 13 French perfume miniatures, in original packaging. Box: 7" x 7". **$60**

Pouncet box, continental, silver, circa 1840, heart-shaped with crown surmount, gold-wash interior, 3" h. **$168**
(A pouncet box is a small perfume container with perforated top.)

Pouncet box, continental, silver, heart-shaped with floral surmount, late 19th century, silver marks on interior of cover, 2 1/2" h. **$195**
(A pouncet box is a small perfume container with perforated top.)

Pouncet box, silver, with fleur de lis touch-mark, circa 1850, heart-shaped with crown surmount, 2" h. **$149**
(A pouncet box is a small perfume container with perforated top.)

Royal Worcester, porcelain, Victoria Silver Jubilee Commemorative, dated 1887, chip and restoration to stopper and neck of bottle, 3" h. **$96**

Salvador Dali (two), black glass and plastic, taller: 2 3/4" h. ....**$184 both**

Schiaparelli, "Zut," torso of a woman in felt bag, 3 1/2". **$480**

Schuco bear, yellow mohair, jointed body, 5" h. **$373**

Schuco gnome, green hat and orange shirt, wear to face, loss to hair on top. **$402**

Steuben, Rosaline, with calcite stopper, 4 1/2" h. **$390**

Photo courtesy Rago Arts and Auction Center, Lambertville, N.J.; www.RagoArts.com

Paul Poiret, Rosine "Maharadjah," clear and black glass with label, on green glass stand, circa 1926, 4" h. **$3,750**

Schuco monkey, brown mohair, worn material, replaced foot, jointed body, 5" h. **$69**

Schuco monkey (bellboy), jointed body with red jacket and blue pants, 5" h. **$72**

Seven Dwarfs, with Cyrillic (Russian) labels, average 4 1/2" h. ....**$180 set**

Silver pendant perfume bottle case, continental, circa 1890, with micro mosaic, Italian silver plate, 3" h. **$207**

Steuben, Blue Aurene, 4 1/2" h. **$460**

Steuben, Blue Aurene, engraved Aurene J 414, 8" h. **$780**

Steuben, Blue Aurene, engraved Aurene L 835, 3" h. **$977**

Steuben, Blue Wisteria, with dauber stopper, 4 1/2" h. **$1,020**

Steuben, Crystal Yellow Cologne, with black threading and stopper, 5 1/2" h. **$570**

Steuben, glass bottle, with Alvin sterling silver overlay, 4 1/2" h. **$345**

Steuben, Gold Aurene on calcite, with engraved floral decoration, 5 1/4" h. **$1,121**

Steuben, Gold Aurene, with dauber stopper, engraved Stueben Aurene, 6 1/2" h. **$960**

Photo courtesy Rago Arts and Auction Center, Lambertville, N.J.; www.RagoArts.com

Schiaparelli, "Sans Souci," clear glass with interior blown windmill, sealed with lace cap and hang tag, with animated figural box and outer box, circa 1943, 3 1/2" h. **$6,500**

Steuben, Rosalie, with red and calcite stopper, 4 1/4" h. **$570**

Steuben, Verre de Soie, engraved with monogram C, stopper married, 8" h. **$172**

Steuben, Verre de Soie, with blue glass dauber stopper, 4 1/2" h. **$316**

Steuben, Verre de Soie, with blue jade dauber stopper, 4 1/2" h. **$373**

Steuben, Verre de Soie, with green jade stopper, 4 1/4" h. **$510**

Steuben, Verre de Soie, with green threading and green dauber stopper, 4 3/4" h. **$660**

Steuben, Yellow Jade, 4 1/2" h. **$1,725**

Stevens and Williams, vial, English, Victorian, with diamond quilted pattern, brass cap and internal stopper, 5 3/4" h. **$632**

Collector's Note: Stevens and Williams, 1880s, Stourbridge, Worcestershire, England.

Stevens and Williams, (attributed) vial, English, Victorian, Lithalyn glass with chased silver top with original internal stopper, 4 1/4" h. **$402**
(Stevens and Williams, 1880s, Stourbridge, Worcestershire, England.)

Stevens and Williams, (attributed) vial, English, Victorian, with wave pattern (Northrup Loop) in blue and white, silver screw cap lacking internal stopper, 5" h. **$480**

Stuart Manufacturing Co., Dionne Quintuplets, presentation, circa 1936, with original stand and fabric, lacking box cover, overall length: 5 1/2". **$84**

Thomas Webb, cameo glass, signed, floral design white on green, silver stopper engraved and monogrammed, internal stopper, 3" h. **$2,415**

Thomas Webb-style, cameo glass spear-shaped vinaigrette, white floral design on ruby ground, silver top is engraved and monogrammed, 4" l. **$2,300**

Thomas Webb-style, cameo glass, "Palms and Bamboo" pattern, white on pale blue, silver cap chased with Japanese floral, has original internal stopper, 3 3/4" h. **$2,587**

Collector's Note: Thomas Webb and Sons, founded 1837, Stourbridge, Worcestershire, England.

Thomas Webb, duckbill form, white over red cameo glass, flakes to bill, silver mounts, Percy Edwards and Company, Piccadilly, 5 3/4" h. **$9,200**

Thomas Webb-style, cameo glass, rare three-color, floral design in white, mauve on pale blue, silver screw cap engraved with monogram and date 1919. Lacks internal stopper. Hallmark: London 1887, 2" h. **$1,955**

Thomas Webb-style, cameo glass, floral design in white on ruby with butterfly, silver gilt stopper in Moorish taste, has original internal stopper, 3 1/4" h. **$1,920**

Thomas Webb-style, vial, cameo glass, with floral design on lemon ground, silver screw cap with monogram, lacks internal stopper, 6" l. **$960**

Thomas Webb-style vial, Victorian, gooseberry shape, with silver-chased screw top, 1 1/2" long. **$546**

Torquay, porcelain, Devon, England, with Japanese-style silver screw top, tan, turquoise, gold colors, lacks internal stopper, Registration # 74858, circa 1887-1888, 2 1/2" h. **$575**

Travel bottle, continental, silver, circa 1900, with enamel floral panel, 2 1/4" h. **$92**

Vial, Bohemian, double-ended, circa 1880, with engraved hunting scenes, brass tops, lacking internal stoppers, 5 1/2" l. **$300**

Vial, continental, opalescent glass, 19th century, with gilt metal top, 2 1/2" h. **$149**

Vial, continental porcelain, hand painted with flowers and with silver filigree overlay, modeled as a knife handle, lacks internal stopper, 4" h. **$218**

Vial, continental, silver, circa 1850, with engraved and reticulated design, in fitted wood case (not original), 4 1/4" h. **$517**

Vial, continental, silver, modeled as an owl head with glass eyes on fob chain, stopper frozen, 1 1/4" h. **$192**

Vial, English, Victorian, blue opalescent glass with silver screw top, lacks internal stopper, in original leather case, 4 1/2" l. **$373**

Vial, English, Victorian, double-ended, both silver tops and hinged center, green glass lacks internal stoppers, 5 1/4" l.
....**$373**

Vial, English, Victorian, double-ended, both silver gilt tops and hinged center, ruby glass, lacks internal stoppers, 5 1/4" l. **$345**

Vial, English, Victorian, double-ended, silver gilt tops engraved with monograms, dated 1876. ....**$345**

Vial, English, Victorian, porcelain, in the form of two blue willow pattern plates, with English silver screw cap, circa 1850, lacks internal stopper, marked with registered number 29260, 2 1/4" h. **$546**

Vial, English, Victorian, ruby flash cut glass with silver stopper and silver screw cap, lack internal stopper, 6" l.
....**$402**

Vial, French enamel, painted with a cherub and flora on deep-red ground, hinged silver gilt top, has internal stopper, gold wash interior, 3" h.......................**$1,035**

Vial, French enamel, painted with a couple in natural landscape, loss to hinge, silver gilt top, 2" h...................**$300**

Vial, French enamel, painted with figure in natural landscape, hinged silver gilt top, has internal stopper, 2" h.
....**$460**

Vial, French enamel, painted with nesting birds, deep-blue ground, hinged silver gilt top, has internal stopper, 2 1/4" h.
....**$540**

Vial, German porcelain, goat herder, circa 1900, in 18th-century Meissen style with silver-metal screw top, modeled by Vogelmann. 3" h. **$240**

Vial (scent), Victorian, cut glass and 14K gold top set with topaz and diamond jewels, has original internal stopper, 3 1/4" h. **$402**

Vial (scent), Victorian, cut glass, acorn form, in original conforming leather box, height of box: 2 1/4". **$345**

Vial (scent), Victorian, glass with silver top and internal stopper, 2" h. **$132**

Vial (scent), English, Victorian, with silver screw top, registered 72627, 2 1/4" h. **$84**

Viard, 1920s, brass top, gilt decorated with birds, molded mark, lacks internal stopper, 3" h................................**$600**

Viard, Chypre Celtic, clear with grey patina, 4 3/4" h. **$632**

Vinaigrette, Asian silver, modeled as an articulated fish, and fitted as a brooch, 3 1/2" l.......................................**$161**

Vinaigrette, continental, silver, modeled as an articulated fish, with ruby glass eyes, 19th century, 6 1/2" l.........**$1,035**

Ybry, Desir du Couer, In pink glass with original enamel cap and internal stopper (frozen), in original red Morocco leather case, bottle 4" h. **$510**

Photo courtesy Rago Arts and Auction Center, Lambertville, N.J.; www.RagoArts.com

Viard, Depinoix Boissard "Madelon," figural clear and frosted glass with enamel and multi-hued patina, circa 1919, 4" h. **$2,000**

Photo courtesy Rago Arts and Auction Center, Lambertville, N.J.; www.RagoArts.com

Viard, Depinoix, Monna Vanna "Bouquet Cavalieri," clear and frosted glass with enameled raised detail, metal pendant label, in box, circa 1900, 5" h. **$2,000**

PEWTER

Pewter is a metal alloy consisting mostly of tin with small amounts of lead, copper, antimony and bismuth added to make the shaping of products easier and to increase the hardness of the material. The metal can be cast, formed around a mold, spun, cut and soldered to form a wide variety of utilitarian articles.

Pewter was known to the ancient Chinese, Egyptians and Romans. England was the primary source of pewter for the American colonies for nearly 150 years until the American Revolution ended the embargo on raw tin, allowing the small American pewter industry to flourish until the Civil War.

Note: The listings concentrate on the American and English pewter forms most often encountered by the collector.

Basin

Attributed to John Andrew Brunstrom, Philadelphia, 1781-93, round, flared sides, single-reed brim, circular mark with facing birds and marked "LOVE" and "LONDON," minor wear, 10 1/8" d..................................$650

Circular mark with facing birds and "LOVE," "LONDON," "X" and crown mark, minor wear, 11 1/2" d..........$2,250

Partial circular mark with facing birds and marked "LOVE" and "LONDON," 8 1/8" d. $500

Basin, quart

Edward Danforth, Middletown and Hartford, Conn., 1788-94, circular form, flared sides, single reeded brim, small touch mark with lion and "ED," 7 7/8" d. $650

Richard Austin, Boston, round bowl, flared sides, single reed brim, touchmark with dove and lamb, "RICHARD AUSTIN" in shaped oval, circa 1790-1810, 8" d. $750

Beaker

Boardman & Hart, Hartford, Conn., tapered cylindrical body, incised bands, "BOARDMAN & HART" "N-YORK" touchmarks, wear, scattered small dents and pitting, second quarter 19th century, 3 1/8" h. $200

Samuel Danforth, Hartford, Conn., tapered cylindrical body, incised bands, "SD," eagle and dagger marks, 1795-1816, 5" h. $1,765

Timothy Boardman, New York City, tapered cylindrical body, incised bands, molded base, "TB&Co" and "X" quality mark, 1822-24, 5 1/4" h. $900

Bud vase, Secessionist style, original green glass insert, peacock feather embossed, stamped "WMF," 5" d, 10 1/2" h. $865

Charger, Samuel Ellis, London, monogrammed on back "MH," wear, knife, scratches, small rim repairs, 16 3/8" d. $350

Coffeepot

Rufus Dunham, Westbrook, Maine, conical cover, flared cylindrical body, incised reeding, scrolled black-painted handle, marked "R. DUNHAM," minor wear, 1837-82, 7 1/4" h. $500

Freeman Porter, Westbrook, Maine, ovoid, tooled ring at center, flared foot and rim, domed lid, wafer finial, scrolled ear handle with later black paint, circular touchmark "F. Porter Westbrook No. 1," small hole at base of handle, restored dents, 1835-60, 11" h. $320

Creamer, unmarked, American, teapot shape, 5 7/8" h. $250

Deep dish

Attributed to John Andrew Brunstrom, Philadelphia, 1781-93, circular, single reed brim, circular mark with facing birds and marked "LOVE" and "LONDON," 13" d.... $1,000

Photo courtesy Skinner Inc., Boston; www.SkinnerInc.com

Pint mug, attributed to Robert Bonnynge, Boston, 1731-1763, tapered cylindrical form with everted lip, solid molded S-scroll handle with a moon-face terminal, on a molded base, likely owners initials "AF" impressed on handle top, 4 3/8" h. **$14,100**

Photo courtesy Skinner Inc., Boston; www.SkinnerInc.com

Plate, Thomas Danforth II, Middletown, Conn., round, smooth brim, two lions in gateway touches, four small hallmarks, and "X" quality mark circa 1760-70, 9 1/2" d. **$3,172**

P

Pewter

Round, single-reed brim, circular mark with facing birds and "LOVE," crown and "X" quality mark and "LONDON" stamped twice, 13" d. **$950**

S. Kilbourn, Baltimore, eagle mark, 11" d. **$1,045**

Thomas Danforth III, Stepney (Rocky Hill), Conn., circular form, rare eagle mark, circa 1790, 6 1/8" d. **$1,650**

Flagon, one quart, Thomas D. and Sherman Boardman, Hartford, Conn., disk finial, three domes, molded cover with "chair back" thumb piece above tapered cylindrical body with fillet, scroll handle with bud terminal, molded base, "TD & SB" in rectangle and "X" quality mark, circa 1815-20, 9" h. **$4,700**

Flagon, three quarts

Boardman & Hart, Hartford, Conn., domed cover with "chair back" thumb piece, tapered cylindrical form, molded fillet and base, double scrolled handle with bud terminal, "BOARDMAN & HART," "N-YORK" and two round eagle touchmarks, circa 1825-30, 13" h. **$3,100**

Thomas D. and Sherman Boardman, Hartford, Conn., urn finial, domed and molded cover with "chair back" thumb piece, tapered cylindrical body with molded fillet and molded base, double scroll handle with bud terminal, marked with "TD & SB," eagle, and "X" quality mark, circa 1815-20, 14" h. **$4,000**

Inkwell, small circular lid, four quill holes surrounding wide flat circular base, replaced glass receptacle, 19th century, 1 3/4". **$225**

Ladle, plain pointed handle, touch mark "WH" in oval, 19th century, 13" l. **$65**

Measure

Assembled set, bellied, English, minor damage, 2 3/8" to 8" h. **$550**

John Warne, English, brass rim, battered, old repair, quart, 5 3/4" h. **$100**

Pitcher

Continental, swirl design, hinged lid, angel touch, 6 1/2" h. **$85**

Freeman Porter, Westbrook, Maine, two quart, 6" h. **$225**

Plate

Blakslee Barnes, Philadelphia, eagle touchmarks and "BB," knifemarks, dents, some edge damage, set of six, 1812-17, 7 7/8" d. .... **$980 set**

Richard Austin, Boston, circular, single reed brim, rare oval shaped touchmark with dove, lamb and "RICHARD AUSTIN," 1792-1817, 7 7/8" d. **$250**

John Skinner, Boston, round, left-facing lion touchmarks, same owner's marks on all, set of three, minor wear, 1760-90, 8 1/2" d. .... **$1,880 all**

Platter, Townsend and Compton, London, pierced insert, marked "Cotterell," 28 3/4" l. **$2,400**

Porringer

Thomas D. and Sherman Boardman, Hartford, Conn., round, boss bottom, flowered handle, "TD & SB" in rectangle touchmark, circa 1815-20, 3 1/4" d. **$715**

William Calder, Providence, R.I., round basin form, boss bottom, openwork handle with partial round eagle touchmark, dents, pitting, 1817-56, 4 1/4" d. **$360**

Samuel Hamlin Jr., Providence, R.I., circular basin form, boss bottom, flowered handle, engraved "LAH" monogram and date "1820" on bottom, round touchmark with eagle and anchor. 1801-56, 5 3/8" d. **$1,550**

Soup plate, unmarked Continental, angel touch, 8 7/8" d. . **$75**

Sugar bowl, Ashril Griswold, Meriden, Conn., eagle touch, 6" h. **$490**

Tablespoon, rattail handle, heart on back of bowl, marked "L. B.," (Luther Boardman, Massachusetts and Connecticut), set of six. .... **$330 set**

Teapot

Roswell Gleason, Dorchester, Mass., eagle touch, 6 3/4" h. **$495**

Ashbil Griswold, Meriden, Conn., eagle touch, some battering and repairs, 6 3/4" h. **$200**

Photo courtesy Skinner Inc., Boston; www.SkinnerInc.com

Coffeepot, Israel Trask, Beverly, Mass., first half 19th century, lighthouse form with reeded bands and engraved shield motifs, one shield with monogram, 10 7/8" h. **$1,175**

Photo courtesy Skinner Inc., Boston; www.SkinnerInc.com

Porringer, Gershom Jones, Providence, R.I., 1774-1809, round form with boss bottom and flowered handle, circular lion mark with "GI" initials on handle, 4 1/4" d. **$2,350**

PHONOGRAPHS

Thomas Alva Edison conceived the principle of recording and reproducing sound between May and July 1877 as a byproduct of his efforts to play back recorded telegraph messages and to automate speech sounds for transmission by telephone. He announced his invention of the first phonograph, a device for recording and replaying sound, on Nov. 21, 1877. Edison's early phonographs recorded onto a tinfoil sheet cylinder using an up-down motion of the stylus.

Baby Grand Piano-form Phonograph, by Fern-O-Grand Co., Cincinnati, Ohio, with H.J. Ellis Melodius Music Master sound box, in mahogany case with square tapering legs, 32" l x 35" h, (surface craquelure)..........................**$652**

Berliner Lever-Wind Gramophone, circa 1897, with 7" turntable, clamp, Clark-Johnson reproducer, No. J 1159 on oak traveling arm, oak case with winding lever and speed control lever on the side, transfer Berliner Gramophone, National Gramophone Co., 874 Broadway, New York City and patent dates to February 1895, underside with part of maker's operating label, and straight-flared black horn with gilt line decoration, case 9 1/2" square, (period elbow and felt, modern elbow included). Note: The lever-wound motor was designed by Eldridge Johnson and Levi Montross, and first appeared in 1896 enclosed in a circular metal case (on a rectangular baseboard like that of the hand-cranked model). **$11,850**

Columbia Model AB Graphophone, with nickel-plated, open-works mechanism, removable 5" aluminum concert mandrel, reproducer, carved oak base and matching lid with The Graphophone banner transfer and patent dates to 1897, 14 1/2" w, and aluminum witch's-hat horn. **$2,370**

Columbia Type AJ Disc Graphophone, by Columbia Phonograph Co., New York, early style, with horizontal top-wind motor, four-ball governor with threaded speed control, 7" turntable, replica sound box and arm on original bracket (repaired), oak case with corner pilasters, egg-and-dart plinth, carrying handle, banner transfer with patent dates to 1897, and brass-belled horn, case 11" square, (missing turntable clamp and brake). **$1,304**

Columbia Type AQ Graphophone, with nickel-plated, open-works mechanism, three-ball governor, floating reproducer connected to replacement horn with adapted mount, feed-screw, and shaped black enameled base with gilt line decoration, 12" l...**$415**

Columbia Type BC "Twentieth Century Premier" Graphophone, circa 1905, with Higham amplifying reproducer, 6" mandrel and massive triple-spring motor, in oak case with hinged front flap, 19" w, (case refinished), associated brass witch's-hat horn and floor stand, 57" x 23". Note: The BC took the newly introduced 6" long cylinders, and played through a mechanically amplified reproducer with a 4" diaphragm connected to the stylus via a friction wheel. **$1,778**

Columbia Type BF Graphophone, with nickel-plated bedplate, black japanned chassis (decoration worn), 6" l mandrel, reproducer, and paneled oak case with banner and exposition transfers, rounded plinth and lid, 16" w, with small nickel-plated witch's-hat horn....................**$830**

Columbia Type N Coin-Operated Graphophone, No. 43889, by American Graphophone Co., Washington, D.C., with single-spring motor, replacement aluminum reproducer, curved oak case with The Graphophone banner

Photo courtesy Skinner Inc., Boston, www.SkinnerInc.com

Berliner Improved Gramophone, with top-wind motor, speed control, sound box No. J13243 and patent date Feb. 19, 1895, turntable brake (disc and screws replaced), oak traveling arm, armrest, record clamp, oak case with replacement Berliner transfer, leather elbow and later brass horn, 9 3/4" w, (case refinished, winder replaced, arm possibly replaced). $2,015

transfer, lift-off lid, coin slot, coin drawer and marquee with modern print, 14" w...**$5,333**

Edison Concert Phonograph, No. C5623, circa 1899-1900, with Model D reproducer (cut down), 5" mandrel, Triton motor, patent dates to May 1898, plaque, Licensed by the Edison-Bell Consolidated Phonograph Co. Ltd. Not to be Used in Connection with an Automatic or Slot Device. In oak case with drawer and all-enveloping cover, 14" w, (case refinished, cover in original finish, bedplate finish restored), with brass witch's-hat horn, 31" l, two cranes and three 5" brown wax cylinders in cartons.
....**$2,844**

Edison Gem Phonograph, No. G87305, with key-wind motor, Model C reproducer, black japanned case with gilt line decoration, patent dates to 1908, oak base and domed lid, 10" w, with black octagonal horn (partly repainted) and crane...**$533**

Edison Home Phonograph, Model A, with Model C reproducer, brush, plaque with patent dates to 1893, and green oak case with banner transfer, 18" w, with crane and shaded tin flower horn with painted border..............**$1,067**

Edison Opera Phonograph, Type SM, Model A, No. 981, with Model L reproducer, brown-painted bedplate, oxidized bronze finish on mandrel and reproducer, double-spring motor, oak case with corner columns, Edison transfer, domed lid, plaque with patent dates to 1910, 18" w, and oak Music Master horn with transfer and patent date 1908, (bedplate repainted, case and horn refinished but retaining original transfers)...**$4,148**

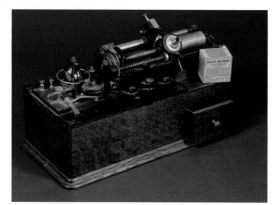

Photo courtesy Skinner Inc., Boston, www.SkinnerInc.com

Photo courtesy Skinner Inc., Boston, www.SkinnerInc.com

Edison Electric Phonograph, No. 50094, the case stamped 15, probably Victor or Balmoral model, with motor driving horizontal pulley, two-ball governor, Model C reproducer, Type D repeating attachment, black enameled bedplate with gilt line and corner decoration, plaque with patent dates to November 1903, full-length oak case with swarf tray and accessories drawer containing two oilers and an Edison recorder in maker's box, 20" w, in oak carrying case, with crane, papier-mâché Mega Phone Horn, and a case of cylinders. **$26,070**

Edison Speaking Phonograph Co. "Parlor" Tinfoil Phonograph, No. 1588, the black japanned iron base with gilt line decoration and central gilt legend, Edison's Speaking Phonograph Patented Feb 19th 1878, No. 1588, Manufactured by Brehmer Bros. Philadelphia, the mandrel with groove for foil ends (originally with rubber wedge), on threaded shaft in fixed supports with balanced crank, and the speaker in arm with adjustment for aligning the stylus with the mandrel grooves, 13" l, on mahogany base and a later glass cabinet. The Parlor model was the Edison Speaking Phonograph Co's attempt to catch a wider market for the new invention, beyond the elaborate Exhibition and Drawing Room models made by Sigmund Bergman in 1878. The first Parlor phonographs were also made by Bergmann early in 1879, but even at $15, sales were slow. The Brehmer version, slightly modified, was in production at the end of 1879, though Edison's slowness to approve the first models, followed by a fire at Brehmer's factory in April 1880, prevented rapid sales development, even though the price was now $10. ....**$22,515**

Edison Standard Phonograph, Model A, No. 40216, with H 4-minute reproducer, oak case with "suitcase" clips and rectangular lid, and brass witch's-hat horn, 12" w.
....**$563**

Edison Standard Phonograph, Model B, No. S 303078, with Model C reproducer, in refinished oak case, 13" w, (bedplate repainted)...**$296**

Edison Standard Phonograph, Model B, No. 507638, with Model K reproducer, combination gearing, oak tall case in original finish with Edison transfer, 13" w, with horn, crane and a large quantity of cylinders. **$1,126**

Edison Triumph Phonograph, Model E, No. 85500, with triple-spring motor, Model O reproducer, plaque with patent dates to 1906, oak case with domed lid, 18" w, two-

National Gramophone Co. Montross Gramophone, circa 1897-8, No. M-1617, on nickel-plated plaque, of Improved Gramophone pattern but with side-wind motor and detachable bent-rod extension arm, red turntable felt and slightly simplified oak case with red felt turntable covering and typical transfer of Berliner Gramophone, National Gramophone Co., 874 Broadway, New York City, patent dates to Feb. 19, 1895, 7" turntable, Clark-Johnson sound box, no. J 20790, stamped Pat. Applied For and Patd. Feb.19. 1895, oak arm, and straight-flared horn with gilt pin-striping, base 10" square. Note: For this model, Levi Montross was engaged not by Johnson but by Frank Seaman, whose National Gramophone Co. was Berliner's sales agent, but who sought to find improvements and lower prices for the Berliner design. It was this policy that led to the breakup of the relationship between Berliner and Seaman and the disappearance in the United States of the name Gramophone. **$11,850**

piece crane, and black No. 11 cygnet horn, (bedplate and horn repainted, case refinished). **$1,067**

Oak Phonograph Cylinder Cabinet and Contents, with six pegged drawers containing approx. 190 Edison 2-minute cylinders (untested) in a variety of genres, including opera, band, comedy and Southern titles, 37" h x 23" w. **$1,422**

Thorens Excelda Portable Gramophone, with sound box, crank and tone arm stowing in brown crackle-finish camera-form metal case with strap, 11" l, (some paint loss) and maker's instruction manual.....................................**$119**

Victor Type B Talking Machine, No. 8979, circa 1901, with 7" turntable, clamp, bolt brake, top-wind motor, Concert sound box No. 5622, oak traveling arm, oak case with applied fleur-de-lis motif and bead-and-reel carved baseboard molding, plaque on the front, Victor Made by Eldridge R. Johnson, Type B 8979, Patented U.S. and Foreign Countries. Camden, New Jersey, and black horn with gold pin-striping, base 9 1/2" square, (old split in baseboard, replacement felt and elbow)....................**$5,629**

Victor Type C Talking Machine, No. 6175, circa 1901-02, with Concert sound box No. 41420, oak traveling arm, 7" turntable with original felt and clamp, nickeled bedplate (some corrosion), side-wind motor, brass-belled black horn stamped Pat. Apl'd For, original leather elbow, oak case with fluted pilasters and metal Victor plaque. Made by Eldridge R. Johnson, Type C 6175, 11" w, horn 14 1/2" l x 9 1/2" d. Note: The first side-wind Victor, which could be wound while playing, and could also accommodate 10" records...**$2,844**

Victor Monarch Special Talking Machine, Type MS, No. 1004, with triple-spring bevel-drive motor, 10" turntable, Exhibition sound box, curved back bracket, oak traveling arm, oak case with paneled sides, rope-twist top, corner pilasters, honeysuckle plinth molding, plaque, Victor Made by Victor Talking Machine Co., Type MS 1004, Patented in U.S. and Foreign Countries, Camden, New Jersey, U.S.A., and flared brass horn, case 12 3/4" w, horn 22" l, (old splits in top, case finish rubbed down). **$2,252**

Victor Monarch Talking Machine, Type M, No. 2406, circa 1901, with single-spring bevel-drive motor, 10" turntable, Eldridge Johnson sound box on oak traveling arm, oak case with stepped plinth molding and engaged baluster corner columns, plaque, Victor Made by Eldridge R. Johnson, Type M 2406, Patented in U.S. and Foreign Countries. Camden, New Jersey, U.S.A., and brass-belled black horn, horn 21 1/2" l. Note: The first Monarch, with 10" turntable. **$2,015**

Victor Type VI Talking Machine, No. 3138, with triple-spring motor, Exhibition sound box No. 32870B, gilt fittings, transfer decorated back bracket, mahogany case with carved corner columns and gilt capitals, plaque and fluted mahogany horn, 21 1/2" d, (arm dented, missing strip of molding from front, repairs to horn). **$3,555**

Victor VV-IV Phonograph, No. 181740 F, with Exhibition sound box No. 427029A, in oak case with double-doors enclosing louvers, 13" w, (dent and pitting on tone arm). **$148**

Victor Style VV-VI Hornless Phonograph, No. 121656 F, with Exhibition sound box No. 65557 3A, in oak case with double doors enclosing louvers, 15" w. **$71**

Victrola Type VV-IX, with Exhibition sound box, in mahogany cabinet with ogee lid and double-doors enclosing louvers, 15" w, (tone arm and sound box defective)...**$95**

Victrola VV-XVI Talking Machine, No. 61169, with triple-spring motor, Exhibition sound box No. 43823G, gilt fittings, Circassian walnut cabinet with ogee lid and apron, two sets of double doors, and foliate-carved supports, 50" h. Note: Accompanied by instruction manual and record index in original envelope, and a framed letter from the Victor Talking Machine Co., to the original owner. ...**$4,148**

Victrola, Cabinet Model VV XVI, No. 121895H, with Exhibition sound box, gilt fittings, and mahogany case with two sets of double doors enclosing horn and record-storage compartment, 51" h..**$237**

Victor Electrola Type VE-XVIII, No. 555, with electric motor, Exhibition sound box, gilt fittings, retailer's transfer of Percy & Foster Piano Co., 1330 G St., Washington, D.C., and bow-fronted serpentine mahogany case with scroll-carved corners, two sets of double doors and maker's transfer, 49" h, and a box of 78 rpm records..............**$1,778**

Victrola VTLA Talking Machine, No. 788, early model, with triple-spring motor, Exhibition sound box No. 88056, gilt fittings, internal mahogany horn and upright mahogany cabinet with flat lid with transfer, ogee-form

top section and apron, and straight-sided mahogany cabinet with "L" doors enclosing drawer and ten original albums with gilt ring handles, 47" h, with maker's booklet, needle tin, needle packet and record cleaner stamped Fred. W. Peabody, Pianos, Victrolas and Kodaks. Amesbury, Newport, Mass..**$4,740**

Zon-O-Phone Type C Talking Machine, No. 6043, with 7" turntable, enclosed sound box on nickel-plated arm and bracket, papier-mâché horn, oak case with stepped plinth and celluloid plaque, Zon-O-Phone. Made Expressly for the National Gram-O-Phone Corporation, 874 Broadway, New York, by the Universal Talking Machine Co., N.Y. and pattent date Dec. 13, 1898, 9" w, horn 15" l.................**$2,844**

Zon-O-Phone Concert Talking Machine, No. 1330, circa 1903, with V-Concert sound box, steel traveling arm, 7" turntable with original felt, brass horn and rectangular oak case with Concert and Zon-O-Phone, Universal Talking Machine Mfg. Co., New York, 14 1/2" w, horn 16" l x 9" d, (attractive patina on horn, some corrosion on bedplate).
....**$2,133**

Zon-O-Phone Home Talking Machine, No. 40025, circa 1901-02, with V-Concert sound box, ornate extension arm, 27" turntable with original felt, large brass horn and oak base with celluloid plaque, Manufactured by Universal Talking Machine Mfg. Co., New York, 11" w, horn 24" l x 11" d..**$2,489**

Photo courtesy Skinner Inc., Boston, www.SkinnerInc.com

Zon-O-Phone Type A Talking Machine, by Universal Talking Machine Co., New York, with steel traveling arm, enclosed sound box, 7" turntable, brake, brass horn and oak case with glazed panels showing motor, recessed baluster corner columns and celluloid plaque, Zon-O-Phone, Made Expressly For the (Nati)onal Gram-O-Phone Corporation, 674 Broadway, New York, by the Universal Talking Machine Co., New York; base 9" x 10", horn 14 1/2" l; with three Zon-O-Phone records and a framed facsimile advertisement. **$9,480**

PHOTOGRAPHY

Modern photographic images date back to the 1820s with the development of chemical photography. The first permanent photograph was an image produced in 1826 by the French inventor Nicéphore Niépce. However, the picture took eight hours to expose, so he went about trying to find a new process. Working in conjunction with Louis Daguerre, they experimented with silver compounds based on a Johann Heinrich Schultz discovery in 1724 that a silver and chalk mixture darkens when exposed to light. Niépce died in 1833, but Daguerre continued the work, eventually culminating with the development of the daguerreotype in 1837.

Many advances in photographic glass plates and printing were made all through the 19th century. In 1884, American George Eastman developed the technology to replace photographic plates, leading to the technology used by film cameras today.

Eastman patented a photographic medium that used a photo-emulsion coated on paper rolls. The invention of roll film greatly sped up the process of recording multiple images.

Also see Autographs, Judaica.

Photo courtesy James D. Julia Auctioneers, Fairfield, Maine; www.JuliaAuctions.com

Edward S. Curtis, (American, 1868-1952), "The Vanishing Race," sepia-toned photograph showing a line of Native Americans on horseback below a mesa. The image has a blurred hue and is stamped, "Copyright 1904 by ES Curtis." Photograph is mounted on gray cut paper on top of a brown frayed-edge paper on gray backing paper in what appears to be its original frame. Photograph is 6" x 7 7/8". **$1,495**

Andersonville Prison photographs, complete set of seven, each albumen on curled mount with printed text and 1883 copyright by Theodore Wiseman from original wartime albumens taken exclusively by Southern photographer A.J. Riddle in August 1864. Wiseman, then in Lawrence, Kan., claimed to have secured the "original views in 1865, in an old chest, in old Captain Wirz's house, at Andersonville, Ga." Wisemen refers to prints, not the original negatives which, presumably, were kept by Riddle and disappeared in the 19th century. As the seven evocative Andersonville views were published with captions, Wiseman retained the exact nomenclature in marketing his later series. (Today, the Andersonville scenes remain fundamentally disturbing, but back in 1883, interest in the notorious prison was waning as evidenced by the fact that Wiseman was willing to sell the complete series at a discount, $1.00); each 6" x 4 1/4". ....**$3,450 set**

Archive, 1930s-1970s press photographs, 210 images, mostly 8" x 10" press photos, many with press stamps on reverse, includes a large number of U.S. presidents, including one each of F.D.R. and Kennedy, three of L.B.J., three of Gerald Ford, 23 of Jimmy Carter, plus more than 30 of Martin Luther King or his funeral, plus Cesar Chavez, James Earl Ray, Thurgood Marshall, Richard J. Daley, Barry Goldwater, Shirley Chisholm, Thomas Bradley. Includes many sports figures, Joe Namath, O.J. Simpson, Joe Greene, Muhammad Ali, Don King, Jackie Robinson, Hank Aaron, Tom Seaver and large group of pro-hockey images. Other topics include WWII and Vietnam; Cold War in Europe; celebrities including Diana Ross, Bill Cosby, Marilyn Horne, Sammy Davis Jr.; large group of Havana, Cuba, images; Biafra, Ethiopia, Senegal, Pakistan, India, Korea, Attica Prison and more, most with typed caption sheet. ....**$660 all**

Baker & Johnson, copy cabinet card of Geronimo, from original photograph by A. Frank Randall or George Ben Wittick, Arizona Territory, circa 1885. Geronimo is kneeling with a carbine in hand. Back mark of Baker & Johnson, Evanston, Wy. It is unusual to find Baker & Johnson circulating an image by another photographer. **$3,000**

O.S. Goff, albumen photograph of a Crow soldier and his wife, mounted on cream card stock; titled on mount in script, "Indian soldier and wife;" portrait shows a Crow man dressed as a sergeant of the 1st U.S. Calvary; his wife, wearing a gingham dress and beaded hide moccasins, stands besides him. Lacks Goff's imprint, but taken at Fort Custer, Mont., post 1885, 9" x 7 1/4". **$1,265**

Tintype, quarter plate, Making Medicine, Cheyenne ledger artist, housed in a pressed paper and wood case. Making Medicine is seated wearing a military jacket with tinted gold buttons, cut hair and he leans with his arm on a table; likely taken during his imprisonment at Fort Marion, Fla. (1875-78). **$2,300**

F.J. Haynes, President Chester A. Arthur's 1883 trip to Yellowstone, albumen image mounted on larger board. Arthur sits in the center of the scene surrounded by standing Michael V. Sheridan, Anson Stager, W.P. Clark, Dan G. Rollins and James F. Gregory; seated John S. Crosby, Phillip H. Sheridan, Arthur, Robert Lincoln, and George G. Vest, 9 1/2" x 6 1/4". **$1,035**

Photo courtesy Cowan's, Cincinnati;
www.CowanAuctions.com

Spain signing Puerto Rico over to the United States, shows interior of what is likely the Spanish Governor's palace, with five representatives of Spain/Puerto Rico on the right and five Americans on the left of a table on which is scattered treaty documents and elaborate ink stand. Seated at the table for the Americans are Gen. Nelson Miles and Rear Adm. Winfield Schley. The transfer ceremony took place Oct. 18, 1898. Imprint of F. Alonso, on 11 3/4" x 15 1/2" heavy card stock mount. **$632**

Edward S. Curtis, (American, 1868-1952), Washo Baskets, photogravure. The scene shows seven Native American baskets. Titled and numbered plate 541, "From copyright photograph, 1924 By E. S. Curtis. Photogravure Suffolk Eng. Co. Cambridge, MA." Housed in a simple wood frame with white matte. Image: 11 1/4" x 15 1/2". **$1,200**

Guide with trophy buck in canoe, hand colored, purportedly depicts Theodore Roosevelt with guide returning from a successful hunt. Titled in the image,

"Sport at Moosehead Outlet" and in lower left "2449", molded oak frame. Sight: 23 1/2" x 15". **$518**

George W. Scott, cabinet card of Sitting Bull's cabin, with his Yankton, S.D., imprint on mount, titled in manuscript below image "Waiting for Sitting Bull to come out;" in this reenactment of the attempted arrest and subsequent killing of Sitting Bull, three men are posed with rifles pointed at the open door of Sitting Bull's log cabin; a fourth man leans against the side of the house...**$920**

CAMERAS

Exakta B Camera No. 517969, Ihagee, Dresden, chrome, leather-covered body, with a Carl Zeiss, Jena Tessar f/2.8 7.5cm lens no. 2149849, in maker's everready case. Light-normal wear; not working; lens is clean and clear, minor handling marks. **$148**

Golden Ricoh "16" Subminiature Camera No. 10717, Riken Optical Industries Ltd., Japan, 16mm, gilt body, with a Riken Ricoh f/3.5 2.5cm lens, a matching Ricoh 16-Tele f/5.6 40mm lens in maker's case and embossed wood box, ever-ready case, strap, boxed and unboxed cassettes, and manual. Light signs of wear; apparently working; lens is clean and clear, minor handling marks. Note: Inspired by the spy cameras of the 1950s and '60s...**$296**

Heidoscope Stereo Camera No. 8403, Franke & Heidecke, Germany, leather-covered body, nickel magazine back, with a pair of Carl Zeiss, Jena Tessar f/4.5 5.5cm taking lenses no. 638884 and 838888, color filters and cable-release, in maker's leather case. Light-normal wear and use. **$415**

Hektor f/1.9 7.3cm Lens No. 437237, screw-fit, with caps and hood, in leather case. Light signs of wear; lens is clean and clear, minor handling marks. **$948**

Kodak Aero-Ektar f/2.5 7 in. (178mm) 5 x 5 Lens No. EE16351, engraved Delta on barrel, in wood case.
....**$148**

Photo courtesy Skinner Inc., Boston, www.SkinnerInc.com

Canon S-II Camera 15326, engraved Seiki-Kogaku, Tokyo, chrome, shutter speeds 20-500, slow speeds dial, with a Nippon Kogaku Nikkor-Q.C f/3.5 5cm lens no. 570999. Normal use and wear; apparently working; optics cloudy or require professional cleaning and servicing; body covering replaced. **$533**

Kodak Bantam Special Camera, black and chrome Art Deco-styled body, with a Kodak Anastigmat Ektar f/2 45mm lens no. 18243 in Compur-Rapid shutter, in maker's ever-ready case, in maker's box with original packaging, manual and tags. Light signs of wear; apparently working; lens is clean and clear, minor handling marks.

Note: The Bantam Special was part of Kodak's ongoing attempt to challenge the prominent German makers by producing 35mm cameras that were functional as well as sophisticated and stylish. Produced from 1936-40 with this shutter combination. **$356**

Leica I(c) Calf-skin No. 67655, black, nickel fittings, dark-red leather body covering, with a Leitz Elmar f/3.5 50mm lens (unnumbered) in standard mount, in maker's ever-ready case. Normal use and wear; apparently working; optics cloudy or require professional cleaning and servicing. **$4,740**

Leica IIIc Luftwaffen Camera No. 375858, chrome, engraved Luftwaffen-Eigentum on back and Fl. No. 38079 on top plate, red shutter blind, with a Leitz Summitar f/2 5cm lens no. 585806, in maker's ever-ready case. Normal use and wear; apparently working; lens is clean and clear, minor handling marks. Note: 1941-42. Accompanied by an USFET (United States Forces European Theater) certificate dated Aug. 12, 1945, stating that Alfred S. Resendes has been authorized to retain Leica Camera No. 375858, Summitar lens No. 585806, and three other lenses (not present). **$1,896**

Leica LHSA 25th Anniversary Summicron-M f2 90mm Lens No. 25-063, M-fit, Canada, silver chrome, with caps, warranty and plastic wrapper, in maker's soft case and box. New factory condition, apparently unused. **$1,185**

Leica IIIf Camera No. 713996, chrome, red-scale, delayed timer, with a Leitz Summarit f/1.5 5cm lens No. 1120854. ....**$652**

Leica IIIf No. 606534, chrome, black-scale. Light wear, apparently working. **$178**

Leica M4 50th Anniversary No. 1412936, black, with white paint filled engravings, the front with 50 Jahre laurel leaf motif, the back numbered 136-E, in maker's box with manual and registration certificate from Leitz, New York. New factory condition, apparently unused. Note: According to Leitz records, 1,730 units were made, 350 each with the letters L, E, I, and C, and 330 with the letter A. **$3,555**

Cameras for LHSA 25th Anniversary, grained leather body covering, with maker's case, manual and strap, in maker's box and wood presentation box. New factory condition, apparently unused. **$2,844**

Leicaflex SL Camera Outfit No. 1280021, black paint body, with a Leitz Elmarit-R f/2.8 35mm lens no. 2430683, a Summicron-R f/2 50mm lens no. 2432606, a (Canada) Elmarit-R f/2.8 135mm lens no. 2405035, and an Elmarit-R f/2.8 180mm lens no. 2456636, in maker's ever-ready case with manual. Good condition, minimal marks to camera body; apparently working; lens is clean and clear, minor handling marks. **$830**

Leitz Elmar f/4 9cm Lens No. 960783, screw-fit, chrome, with caps, in maker's keeper. Normal use and wear; lens is clean and clear, minor handling marks. **$47**

Leitz Hektor f/25 5cm Lens, no number visible, screw-fit, nickel. Normal use and wear; fine scratches on outer element. **$356**

Leitz Hektor f/2.5 12.5cm Lens No. 1223399, Midland, Ontario, Viso-fit, with caps and hood. Light signs of wear; optics cloudy or require professional cleaning and servicing. **$444**

Photo courtesy Skinner Inc., Boston, www.SkinnerInc.com

Leica M6 Platinum 150th Anniversary Camera No. 2490145, commemorative no. 1994, the top-plate engraved 150 Jahre Optik 1849-1999, Summilux-M f/1.4 35 ASPH, diced green/gray leather body covering, with a Leitz Summilux-M f/1.4 35mm, a spherical lens engraved around the rim 15 Jahre Optik 1994, in matching silk-lined polished walnut case, with warranty, manual, commemorative booklet, receipt, hood, caps, and strap, in maker's box. New factory condition, apparently unused. Note: Produced in limited edition of 30 to commemorate 150 years of the Wetzlar Optisches Institute. **$7,110**

Leitz Summarex f/1.5 8.5cm Lens No. 940241, screw-fit, with caps and hood, in maker's leather case. Good condition, minimal marks to camera body; lens with defects, may include scratches, fungal growth, separation or problems with focusing and aperture. **$1,126**

Leitz Telyt f/5 40cm Lens No. 1486413, Viso-fit, with caps, cable-release, Visoflex and two magnifiers, in maker's fitted leather case. Good condition, minimal marks to camera body; apparently working; optics cloudy or require professional cleaning and servicing. **$948**

Makinette Camera, Plaubel A.G., Germany, 127-roll film, black, folding-strut construction, with a Plaubel Anticomar f/2.7 5cm lens no. 87707; and a Plaubel & Co. Tele Makinar lens and five supplementary lenses, in fitted leather case. Normal use and wear; apparently working; lens with defects, may include scratches, fungal growth, separation or problems with focusing and aperture. **$652**

Minox B Subminiature Camera No. 744737, 16mm, chrome, with a Complan f/3.5 15mm lens, in maker's leather case with chain. Light signs of wear; apparently working; lens is clean and clear, minor handling marks. **$59**

Photo courtesy Skinner Inc., Boston, www.SkinnerInc.com

Nikon SP Camera No. 6201995, chrome, with a Nippon Kogaku Nikkor-S.C f/1.4 5cm lens no. 352600, in maker's ever-ready case with strap and manual. Good condition, minimal marks to camera body; apparently working; lens is clean and clear, minor handling marks. **$2,252**

Nikkormat FT Camera No. 4510537, chrome, with a Nikon Nikkor-H.C Auto f/2 50mm lens no. 2254909, in maker's ever-ready case. Good condition, minimal marks to camera body; apparently working; lens is clean and clear, minor handling marks. **$119**

Nikon MIOJ Variframe Finder No. 363919, chrome, engraved on the shoe Made in Occupied Japan. Normal use and wear. **$474**

Nikon Motor Drive F-36, black, with power pack, pistol grip, cables, cable-release, manuals, and guarantee dated 1968. Light signs of wear, untested. **$444**

Nikon Reflex Housing Type II No. 471292, black crackle finish, white paint-filled engravings Nippon Kogaku, Tokyo, with caps, 45 prism no. 67103, three cable-release attachments, printed instruction sheets (one annotated), and N-F adapter. Good condition, minimal marks to camera body (ding on release-housing). **$5,629**

Nippon Kogaku W-Nikkor f/4 2.5cm Lens No. 402579, Nikon rangefinder-fit, chrome, with body cap and hood, in maker's case; with promotional booklet. Good condition, minimal marks to camera body; lens is clean and clear, minor handling marks. **$1,304**

Nippon Kogaku W-Nikkor C f/4 2.5cm Lens No. 402579, Nikon rangefinder-fit, with body cap and hood, and promotional booklet. Good condition, minimal marks to camera body; lens is clean and clear, minor handling marks. **$1,422**

Nippon Kogaku Nikkor-Q.C f/4 25cm Lens No. 272114, Nikon rangefinder-fit, black, with caps, hood, leather pouch, and guarantee from Nikon Inc., New York, dated 1958. Good condition, minimal marks to camera body; lens is clean and clear, minor handling marks; small scratch and a couple of tiny edge chips on inner element. **$830**

Rollei 35 Camera No. 3020206, Germany, chrome, with a Carl Zeiss Tessar f/3.5 40mm lens no. 4529970, in maker's slipcase, manual and filters. **$207**

Rolleiflex "Baby" TLR Camera, 4 x 4 cm on 127-roll film, gray body covering, with a Heidosmat f/2.8 60mm

viewing lens and a Schneider Xenar f/3.5 60mm taking lens no. 5311877, in matching ever-ready case, with shade and manual. Good condition, minimal marks to camera body; apparently working; lens is clean and clear, minor handling marks. **$148**

Rolleiflex 3.5 TLR Camera No. 1767412, 120-roll film, with meter, a Heidosmat f/2.8 75mm viewing lens no. 2436008, and a Carl Zeiss Planar f/3.5 75mm taking lens no. 1780943, ever-ready case, strap, manual and leather reflex hood. Good condition, minimal marks to camera body; apparently working; lens is clean and clear, minor handling marks. **$504**

Schneider Symmar f/5.6 300-f/12 500mm Lens No. 4933716, in rim-set Compur shutter, with custom adaptor rings, shade and caps, in maker's box. Good condition, minimal marks to camera body; lens is clean and clear, minor handling marks. **$296**

Stecky Model III Camera No. 2210, 16mm, with a Stekinar Anastigmat f/3.5 25mm lens, in maker's ever-ready case, a Stecky f/5.6 40mm Sun-Tele # 40 lens in leather case, part of the manual, and other items. **$83**

Tessina Automatic 35mm Camera No. 463001, Concava S.A., Switzerland, chrome, with a f/2.8 25mm lens, finder and meter, in maker's ever-ready case; chain, manuals, film loader, and three film canisters. Light signs of wear; apparently working; optics cloudy or require professional cleaning and servicing. **$326**

Veriwide 100 Camera No. 60/684, Brooks-Plaubel, 120-roll film, with popup finder, frame finder, and a Schneider Super-Angulon f/8 47mm lens no. 6661243, ever-ready case (front only), and manual. Light-normal wear and use; not working, lens is clean and clear, minor handling marks. **$1,007**

Carl Zeiss (Jena) Biotar f/2 8cm Lens No. 2245038, Leica screw-fit, chrome, with meter scale. Normal use and wear; optics cloudy or require professional cleaning and servicing. **$563**

Carl Zeiss (Jena) Brass-bound Protar 690mm Lens No. 89610, with adaptor. Normal use and wear; optics cloudy or require professional cleaning and servicing (diaphragm jammed). Note: Custom conversion for use in medical photography. Handwritten notes gives directions for using the lens with Novoflex and Visoflex Leica attachments. Untested. **$830**

Carl Zeiss (Jena) Sonnar f/2.8 18cm Lens No. 2119896, Flektoscop-fit, chrome, with Zeiss Ikon shade; and a custom Leica M-fit mount. Normal use and wear; lens is clean and clear, minor handling marks. **$474**

Carl Zeiss (Jena) Tele-Tessar K f/8 30cm Lens No. 1622674, screw-fit, black, with yellow filter, shade and custom filter. Light signs of wear; optics cloudy or require professional cleaning and servicing. **$593**

Zeiss Bobette II Camera 548, roll film, leather-covered body, with an Ernostar Anastigmat f/2 4.2cm lens no. 224674. Light, normal wear. **$415**

Zeiss Contax II No. G.7313, chrome, numbered internally and on rewind knob. Light signs of wear, apparently working. **$148**

POLITICAL ITEMS

Initially, American political-campaign souvenirs were created to celebrate victories. Items issued during a campaign to show support for a candidate were actively being distributed in the William Henry Harrison election of 1840.

There is a wide variety of campaign items, as you will see here.

For more information, consult *Warman's Political Collectibles* by Dr. Enoch L. Nappen, 2008.

Ceramic Mugs

Ceramic mug with caricature of a cigar-smoking Al Smith, 4" h, 3 3/8" d, base, "Stangl," circa 1920s. **$75-$100**

Franklin Roosevelt white figural mug, 4 5/8" h, 3 x 3 1/2" d, Patriotic Products Assoc., circa 1930s. **$50-$75**

Gen. Douglas MacArthur ceramic mug with image in uniform and with sword as handle, 5 1/4" h, 3 5/8" x 3 1/8" base, "Royal Winton," circa 1944-'52. **$50-$75**

"Bobby [Kennedy] For President," mug, 3 7/8" h, 2 3/4" d, "Mann Made Mugs/ exclusive." **$25-$40**

John Kennedy mug, 3 1/8" h, 2 1/2" d, base, circa 1960-'63. **$20-$25**

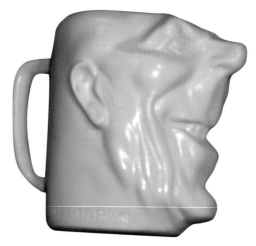

Satirical anti-Richard Nixon mug with worthless "Federal Reserve Note," 3 1/2" h, 3" d, "HH," circa 1972. **$10-$20**

Ronald Reagan caricature face mug, 3 7/8" h, 2 1/8" x 2 1/2" base, J.M. Brooks, circa 1985. **$20-$30**

Jimmy Carter caricature face mug, 4" h, 3 5/8" d, circa 1976-'80. **$15-$25**

Jimmy Carter smiling, toothy peanut mug, 4 3/8" h, 2 1/4" d, "Trimple Corp.," circa 1976-'80. **$15-$25**

Anti-Bill Clinton mug, 3 3/4" h, 3 1/8" d, First Amendment Products, circa 1993. **$5-$10 each**

PAPER CUPS

Paper campaign cup picturing Richard Nixon and George McGovern, "Maryland Cup Corp.," 1972, 3 1/8" h, 2" d. **$5-$10**

"I'm Voting for Gore" and "I'm Voting For Bush" paper cups issued in 2000 by 7-Eleven Stores, 2 3/8" d, 5 7/8" h. **$2-$5 each**

Pro-George W. Bush and pro-John Kerry "7-Election 2004" paper cups issued by 7-Eleven Stores, 2 1/2" d, 6" h. **$2-$5 each**

BEER AND SODA CANS

"I Like IKE" soda can with image of an elephant holding a pro-Dwight D. Eisenhower flag, circa 1952-'56, 2 5/8" d, 4 3/4" h. **$25-$35**

"The Right Drink For The Conservative Taste" soda can for Barry Goldwater, "Gold-water Distributing Co.," circa 1964, 2 5/8" d, 4 3/4" h. **$20-$30**

"Billy Beer" refers to Jimmy Carter's brother, Billy Carter, who received some attention during Jimmy's campaign, "The West End Brewing Co.," circa 1977-'80, 2 1/2" d, 4 3/4" h. **$5-$10**

BOTTLES

Two campaign bottles: green Hubert Humphrey-Edmund Muskie bottle, and an amber Richard Nixon-Spiro Agnew piece, "Wheaton Glass Co.," circa 1968, 7" h, 2 1/2" x 6" at base. **$15-$25 each**

"Big stick" (an apparent reference to Theodore Roosevelt's expression "walk softly but carry a big stick") glass bottle in the shape and style of a club, and with "Patented March 19, 1907" on the bottom, 6 7/8" h, 1 1/2" d. **$35-$50**

Liquor bottle celebrates the 1953 Inauguration of Dwight D. Eisenhower and Richard Nixon, 11 1/2" h, 3" d. **$35-$50**

BUBBLE GUM CIGARS

From circa-1960 to present, bubble gum political cigars have become increasingly more popular election promoters than real cigars. Unless otherwise noted, the following were produced by "Swell/Philadelphia Chewing Gum Corp."

*Five individual gum cigars: "Reagan Is Right," circa 1984, 5 3/4" l, **$5**; "The Duke In '88," circa 1988, 5 3/4" l, **$5**; "Win With Bush," circa 1988, 5 3/4" l, **$5**; "Nixon's The One," "The Donruss Co.," circa 1968, 4 3/8" l, **$10-$20**; and "Goldwater in '64," circa 1964, 4 1/4" l. **$10-$20***

Two full cases of George W. Bush and Al Gore bubble gum cigars circa 2000, 5 3/8" x 6 1/4", 1 1/2" h. **$20-$30 each**

Full case of Walter (Fritz) Mondale gum cigars, circa 1984, 5 3/8" x 6 3/8", 1 1/2" h. **$35-$50**

Display case picturing George H.W. Bush, circa 1988, 5 3/8" x 6 1/4", 1 1/2" h. **$10-$15**

METAL MATCHBOXES AND HOLDERS

Before safety matches became widely available in the early 20th century, matches were kept in metal containers, with non-safety matches too dangerous to leave uncontained.

"Teddy B" metal matchbox with embossed image of a bear holding a club and a Rough Rider hat. The reverse touts the "Congress Hotel," circa 1904-'08, 3/8" x 1 1/2", 2 3/4" h. **$100-$125**

"Hero of Manila/ May 88," Adm. George Dewey brass match holder, circa 1898-1900, 1/2" x 1 1/8", 2 3/4" h. **$25-$35**

Leather-covered metal matchbox with silver-plated copper bust of Adm. George Dewey attached to front and "Fred Muth Harmonie Hall" advertisement on reverse, circa 1899-1900, 3/8" x 1 1/2", 2 3/4" h. **$35-$50**

Adm. Dewey metal bust matchbox holder, circa 1899-1900, 1 1/2" x 2 3/8", 3 1/2" h. **$35-$50**

MATCHBOOKS

Cardboard was enough to enclose safety matches and still provide security. Printed promotional advertisements encouraged giving the matches away free, and matchbooks made great political campaign media. Every time a smoker used a match, he saw the candidate's picture and/or appeal.

Franklin Roosevelt matchbook welcoming the Chicago Democratic National Convention, circa 1940. **$15-$20**

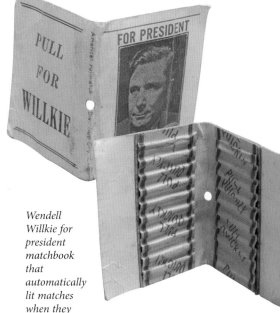

"Repeal," an anti-prohibition matchbook, circa pre-1933. **$5-$10**

"Kennedy for President," red, white and blue matchbook picturing John F. Kennedy, circa 1960. **$15-$20**

Wendell Willkie for president matchbook that automatically lit matches when they were pulled from their individual sleeves, "American Pullmatch Div.," circa 1940, 2" x 2 1/4". **$15-$20**

AIR FRESHENER

Air freshener can with elephant image and reading "Republican BS Repellent" and "Spray immediately when Republicans discuss inflation, taxes, crime, pollution, civil rights and why you should vote Republican," "American Jetway Corp.," circa 1971, 2 1/8" d, 6 3/4" h. **$15-$25**

FIRST AID KIT

Jon F. Kennedy-Lyndon B. Johnson first aid kit, including three bandages and two antiseptics, circa 1960, 2 3/4" x 1 3/4". **$10-$20**

SWITCH PLATE COVER

Switch plate cover (in original package) portraying Richard Nixon as a comic hero with "N" on his shirt, "KaKaMaMie Co.," circa 1968, 4 7/8" x 8 3/4". **$25-$35**

UTENSILS

"For A Good Measure Of Good Government, Vote For Humphrey-Muskie" plastic teaspoon and tablespoon measurer, circa 1968, 5 1/8". **$5-$10**

George Wallace double-blade penknife reading "Trust In The People 1976," "Barlow," 3 3/8". **$20-$30**

A spoon with William McKinley's image in the bowl, "Good Luck" on the front of the handle, and the reverse reading "Protection and Prosperity," circa 1896-1900; spoon with raised image of Charles Evan Hughes on handle, an eagle and "Hughes" down the handle, "Rodgers," circa 1916; similarly designed spoon, but with raised image of Woodrow Wilson and "Wilson" down the handle, "W R," circa 1916; and "Billy Possum" butter knife with raised image of a possum on the handle, circa 1908-'12. Billy Possum represented Taft. **$20-$25 each**

"Election 92 Collector's Edition" George H. W. Bush penknife in original packaging, "Case," circa 1992, 3". **$25-$35**

Razor with picture of Woodrow Wilson, an advertisement & U.S. flag on one side (under celluloid), and beautiful actresses on the other side, "Novelty Cutlery Co.," circa 1910s, 9" l, open, **$50-$75.**

Jimmy Carter-Walter Mondale double-blade penknife, 1980, 3 1/2". **$15-$20**

Penknife given as a gift by Ronald Reagan with signature across the front, "Victorinox," circa 1987-88, 3 7/8" long open. **$35-$50**

George McGovern-Robert "Sargent" Shriver double-blade penknife, 1972, 3 3/8". **$15-$20**

Knife sharpener with one edge reading "McKinley * Roosevelt," and the other side touting the virtues of being "Brave, Kind, Able, Honest," circa 1900, 1 5/8" x 3 3/8", 3/8" h. **$40-$60**

POSTCARDS

John P. Charlton of Philadelphia patented the postcard in 1861, selling the rights to H.L. Lipman, whose postcards, complete with a decorated border, were labeled "Lipman's postal card." Within a decade, European countries were also producing postcards.

The United States Postal Service began issuing pre-stamped postal cards in 1873. The postal cards came about because the public was looking for an easier way to send quick notes. The USPS was the only establishment allowed to print postcards, and it held its monopoly until May 19, 1898, when Congress passed the Private Mailing Card Act.

Initially, the United States government prohibited private companies from calling their products "postcards," so they were known as "souvenir cards." Although this prohibition was rescinded in 1901, it was not until 1908 that people were permitted to write on the address side of a postcard.

Photo courtesy Joel Edler, Iola, Wis.

Advertising, M.C. Peters Mill Co., Omaha, Neb., Alfalfa Queen, Indian maiden, circa 1910. **$35+**

Photo courtesy Joel Edler, Iola, Wis.

Advertising, Pine Tree Timothy, foldout, circa 1910. **$10+**

Photo courtesy Joel Edler, Iola, Wis.

Advertising, stork delivering Pioneer Hybrid Seed Corn, 1940s. **$8+**

Art Deco, Sorgiani, advertising for paints and inks. Excellent to near mint condition, unused. **$94**

Art Deco, (two), advertising, European "Poster Art". One has light album toning. Excellent to near mint condition. .... **$118 pair**

Art Deco, (six), glamour, "Ladies with Monkey" Series 3724 couplet set. Near mint to mint condition. .... **$129 all**

Art Deco, (six), by Levavesseur, for Moet & Chandon Champagne. Excellent to near mint condition. .... **$885 set**

Artist signed, (three), two are Mela Koehler, one is Lessieux including Wiener Werkstatte. Near mint to mint condition. .... **$271 all**

Artist signed, (six), published by Philipp & Kramer. Near mint to mint condition. .... **$354 all**

Art Nouveau, (three), two are series 1296, the other is Mucha style. Very good to near mint condition. .... **$165 all**

Art Nouveau, (three), signed Moser, Meunier. Near mint to mint condition. .... **$283 all**

Art Nouveau, (three), Napoli Expo by Gambardella, Collection des Cent by Henrida and a 1911 Rome Expo poster. Excellent to near mint condition. .... **$153 all**

Art Nouveau, (four), all are signed by T. Carson. Near mint to mint condition. .... **$188 all**

Art Nouveau women, (five), one has corner crease, four very good to excellent condition. .... **$188 set**

Art Nouveau set, (10) by Jozsa, four Kirchner cards including Byrrh advertising. Excellent to near mint condition. .... **$1,221 set**

Art Nouveau set, (10) most Kirchners. Very good to near mint condition. .... **$826 set**

Christmas, novelty mechanical, Falstaff Beer, with rotating calendar, 1931. **$300+**

Christmas, novelty, foldout tissue card. Excellent condition. **$153**

Christmas, (three), two die-cut hold-to-lights and one mechanical. All mailed. Excellent condition.............**$129 all**

Christmas, (three), Wiltd and Kray Series 2781. Very good to excellent condition.................................**$118 all**

Christmas, installment set, four cards, includes original envelope. Cards have slight album toning on reverse. Excellent condition.....................................**$118 set**

Du Pont, (13), dogs, advertising, 1916, Du Pont (Shooting) Powders, Wilmington, Del. Unused, very good to excellent condition, some minor corner wear and discoloration or scuffs on backs only, one water stain on back. ....**$826 all**

Halloween, Paul Finkenrath of Berlin, boy with ghostly radiol jack-o'-lantern, circa 1905. **$75+**

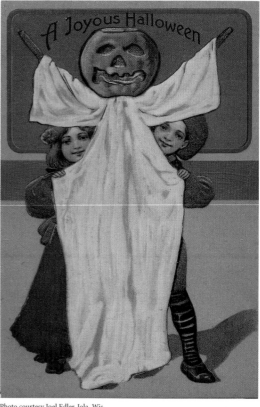

Halloween, Paul Finkenrath of Berlin, two children with ghostly radiol jack-o'-lantern, circa 1905. **$75+**

Photo courtesy Joel Edler, Iola, Wis.

Halloween, Paul Finkenrath of Berlin, two children bobbing for apples, with radiol jack-o'-lantern, circa 1905. **$75+**

Photo courtesy Joel Edler, Iola, Wis.

Halloween, John Winsch, girl in red devil costume, 1912 copyright. **$75+**

Photo courtesy Joel Edler, Iola, Wis.

Halloween, Paul Finkenrath of Berlin, two children with black cat on radiol jack-o'-lantern, circa 1905. **$75+**

Photo courtesy Joel Edler, Iola, Wis.

Halloween, John Winsch, girl with jack-o'-lantern man, 1912 copyright. **$75+**

Photo courtesy Joel Edler, Iola, Wis.

Halloween, John Winsch, girl in mummer's suit with owls, 1912 copyright. **$75+**

Photo courtesy Joel Edler, Iola, Wis.

Halloween, John Winsch, girl with floating jack-o'-lanterns, 1912 copyright. **$75+**

Halloween, (two), Clapsaddle Series #31 from Wolf Co. (scarce). Near mint condition. ....**$129 both**

Halloween, (three), Clapsaddle, very good to excellent condition. ....**$153 all**

Halloween, (three), Clapsaddle, one is Wolf Co. (scarce). Very good to excellent condition. ....**$162 all**

Halloween, (four), Clapsaddle from the Wolf Co. (scarce), including black background. ....**$200 all**

Halloween, (four), Tuck series 160. Excellent condition. ....**$212 all**

Halloween, (five), Clapsaddle Series #31, published by Wolf Co. (scarce). Excellent to near mint condition..........**$212 all**

Halloween, (six), Tuck series 150. Very good to excellent condition. ....**$224 all**

Halloween, (six), complete set Clapsaddle Series #978. Very good to excellent condition. ....**$188 set**

Halloween, (16), several different series represented, most Gibson Publ. Good to excellent condition................**$236 all**

Halloween, Schmucker Winsch, excellent to near mint condition. **$118**

Halloween, Winsch, mailed. Very good to excellent condition. **$236**

Halloween, (two), Winsch, very good to excellent condition. ....**$224 pair**

Halloween, (two), Winsch, excellent condition. ....**$767 pair**

Halloween, advertising, Collins Malto Bread. Mailed, very good condition..**$141**

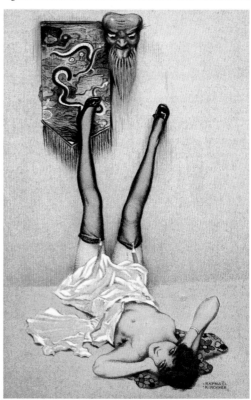

Collector's Note: "Le Masque Impassible," an example of the work of Raphael Kirchner (1876-1917), an Austrian illustrator whose pin-up art may be found on WWI-era postcards.

Raphael Kirchner, (six), "Cigarettes from the World" 1900. Corner and edge wear. Scarce set. **$354 set**

Raphael Kirchner, (six), "Perfumes," set published 1900. Very good to excellent condition. **$354 set**

Raphael Kirchner, (six), "Couples between red borders," desirable 1901 set. Excellent to near mint condition. **$295 set**

Raphael Kirchner, (six), "Girls between brown-green borders," published 1901. Couple of cards have light foxing. Excellent condition. **$129 set**

Raphael Kirchner, (nine) six small Greek heads, three misc. Excellent to near mint condition. **$767 set**

Raphael Kirchner, (10) "Heart Lady" early period, Theo. Stroefer. Excellent to near mint condition. **$590 set**

Kirchner and Kirchner designs, (nine), excellent to near mint condition. **$826 set**

Mela Koehler, for Wiener Werkstatte, #71 "Nicolo", stains on reverse. Excellent condition. **$767**

Mela Koehler, for Wiener Werkstatte, #524. Corner crease, good condition. **$708**

Mela Koehler, for Wiener Werkstatte #648. Near mint condition. **$165**

Mela Koehler, (two), for Wiener Werkstatte #580, #582, one has corner and edge wear. Excellent to near mint condition. **$460 pair**

Mela Koehler (two), for Wiener Werkstatte #592, #593, one mailed. Excellent to near mint condition. **$472 pair**

Mela Koehler, (three), "Christmas Ladies" and "Fashionable Hats". Excellent to near mint condition. **$271 all**

Henri Meunier, (12) "Les Grandes Femmes" complete set, four cards have edge foxing. Most near mint condition. **$590 set**

Alphonse Mucha, "Gismonda" Editions Cinos 1898, image of Sarah Bernhardt. Excellent to near mint condition. **$271**

Alphonse Mucha, "La Dame aux Camelius" Editions Cinos 1898, image of Sarah Bernhardt from the Champenois poster. Very good to excellent condition. Minor album marks. **$377**

Alphonse Mucha, "Lorenczaccio" Editions Cinos 1898, image of Sarah Bernhardt. Very good to excellent condition. Some foxing. **$472**

Real photo, (four), Kentucky Airport view, sellers of the "Waco" airplane, Fokker plane at Fort Bliss Field, this plane flew over North Pole. Excellent condition. **$377 all**

Real photo, (six), aviation, Kelly Field, Texas; aviator sits at wheel in bi-plane. Good to excellent condition. **$106 all**

Real photo, (eight), three Zeppelins, five vintage views of Zeppelins in flight and anchored. Excellent condition. **$70 all**

Real photo, (12), two blacks, midgets, motorcycles, two-headed cow. Fair to excellent condition. **$106 all**

Real photo, (13), three vintage CDVs, vintage printed card "The Doll Princess," nine views, plus kid with fawn and dog on blanket, midgets, political, young hunters. Excellent condition. **$129 all**

Real photo, (17), boy with gun, three young girl posed views, all young related views. Good to excellent condition. **$47 all**

Real photo, (46), 11 tinted children views, all children views with wagons, bikes, toys, twins. Fair to excellent condition. **$200 all**

Real photo, (48), all children related. Toys, Christmas trees with toys, dolls, bears. Fair to excellent condition. **$354 all**

Photo courtesy Joel Edler, Iola, Wis.

Real photo, Pabst, girl in auto-riding attire and gauntlets, circa 1915. **$25+**

Photo courtesy Joel Edler, Iola, Wis.

Santa Claus, black robe with brown trim, Art & Crafts style, marked Rotograph Co., N.Y., M3025, printed in Germany, circa 1910. **$300+**

Photo courtesy Joel Edler, Iola, Wis.

Santa Claus, blue suit, gold embossed, German, circa 1910. **$30+**

Photo courtesy Joel Edler, Iola, Wis.

Santa Claus, burgundy robe with sheepskin trim, blue umbrella, mailed, German, circa 1910. **$40+**

Photo courtesy Joel Edler, Iola, Wis.

Santa Claus, burgundy-red robe at door with boy, German, circa 1910. **$40+**

Santa Claus, burgundy-red robe with deer near house in snow, German, circa 1910. **$40+**

Santa Claus, pale green robe, carrying tree, on black background, mailed, German, circa 1910. **$40+**

Santa Claus, hold-to-light, die-cut, mailed. Very good to excellent condition. $118

Santa Claus, hold-to-light, die-cut, Mailick. Excellent condition. $153

Santa Claus, purple suit with silk insert. Excellent condition. $59

Santa Claus-Uncle Sam, die-cut hold-to-light. Seldom seen. Small corner crease, otherwise excellent condition. $2,360

Santa Claus-Uncle Sam, hold-to-light. Writing on back and just slight discoloration along the right edge, excellent to near mint condition. $1,298

Santa Claus-Uncle Sam, small stain at bottom and top left corner and writing on the back, very good condition. $413

S.L. Schmucker, (two), "The Drinkers" series, both cards with Schmucker signature (scarce). One has small corner crease. Very good to near mint condition. .... **$94 pair**

Santa Claus, green robe, looking in window, German, circa 1910. **$40+**

Santa Claus, sable robe with ermine trim, brown umbrella, mailed, circa 1910, German. **$40+**

Santa Claus-Uncle Sam, carrying tree with fenced base, toy basket with U.S. flags, circa 1910. **$400+**

Santa Claus-Uncle Sam, carrying tree with fenced base, toy bag, U.S. flags, knocking at door with children, mailed, circa 1910. **$300+**

St. Patrick's Day, Clapsaddle, maid with shamrocks, mailed, circa 1905. **$5+**

St. Patrick's Day, Clapsaddle, little girl dancing on chair, mailed, circa 1905. **$5+**

St. Patrick's Day, Clapsaddle, singing boy in top hap with shillelagh, mailed, circa 1905. **$8+**

St. Patrick's Day, Clapsaddle, little girl in bonnet with umbrella, mailed, circa 1905. **$8+**

Photo courtesy Joel Edler, Iola, Wis.

St. Patrick's Day, Schmucker Winsch, girl with crossed clay pipes, circa 1915. **$30+**

Photo courtesy Joel Edler, Iola, Wis.

St. Patrick's Day, Schmucker Winsch, girl hugging clay pipe bowl, circa 1915. **$30+**

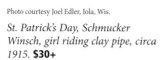

Photo courtesy Joel Edler, Iola, Wis.

St. Patrick's Day, Schmucker Winsch, girl riding clay pipe, circa 1915. **$30+**

Thanksgiving, (two), Freixas, both mailed. Very good to excellent condition. .... **$47 pair**

Trans-Miss Expo, (10), complete set sold to fund the 1898 expo in Omaha, Neb. Postcard backs. Excellent to near mint condition. .... **$224 set**

Valentines Day, (three) Winsch, all are Freixas designs, light album toning. Excellent to near mint condition.
.... **$94 all**

Valentines Day, (five), all are from series and signed H.B. Griggs. Very good to excellent condition. .... **$35 all**

Louis Wain, "Cats," "Three Blind Mice", anonymous artist. Mint condition. **$153**

Louis Wain, "Cats," Valentine Publishing "Our Club". Very good to excellent condition, with minor corner wear.
.... **$129**

Louis Wain, "Cats," advertising, David Thom & Co. Ltd (Pendleton, Manchester) "Thom's Castile Soap," anonymous artist. British back. Mint condition. **$106**

Louis Wain, "Cats," paper doll cutout, Tuck "Fairy Tale Dressing Dolls" Series 3385 - Dick Whittington. Very good condition, with corner crease. **$590**

Louis Wain, "Cats," paper doll cutout, Tuck "Fairy Tale Dressing Dolls" Series 3385 - Beauty and the Beast. Mint condition. **$590**

Louis Wain, "Cats," paper doll cutout, "Fairy Tale Dressing Dolls" Series 3385 - Little Red Riding Hood. Mint condition. **$708**

Louis Wain, "Cats," paper doll cutout, Tuck "Fairy Tale Dressing Dolls" Series 3385 – Robin Hood. Mint condition. **$708**

Louis Wain, (two), "Cats," Tuck Series 132, "A Merry Christmas" and "The Wedding Day". Excellent condition.
.... **$82 pair**

Louis Wain, (two), "Cats," Tuck, including "A Merry Christmas" Series 132, unused excellent condition. And an unsigned "The Cats at Play" W.E. Mack, London Publishing from "The Cats Academy Series" #646. Unused, very good condition with a very faint crease. .... **$70 pair**

Louis Wain, (three), "Cats," including Tuck "Diabolo" Series #9563 - Even Baby Plays It; Alphalsa Publ. #895 "Little Miss Muffet" Alpha Postcard, probably post WWI; and an

unsigned L. Salmon Pub. later issue, "The Animals' Circus". Very good to near mint condition. .... **$106 all**

Louis Wain, (four), including dog "I've met with a fine reception here", E.J. Hey & Co. Very good with some corner wear. And cats "A Bolt From the Blue" Valentine Co., excellent condition; plus two unsigned cats, one American back and one foreign back, unused very good condition.
.... **$177 all**

Wiener Werkstatte, #561. Near mint to mint condition.
.... **$295**

Wiener Werkstatte, #858. Excellent to near mint condition. **$177**

Wiener Werkstatte, #902, mailed, corner and edge wear. Very good to excellent condition. **$318**

Wiener Werkstatte, #906. Excellent to near mint condition. **$531**

St. Patrick's Day, Schmucker Winsch, girl sitting in shamrock bouquet, signed SMS, circa 1915. **$30+**

POSTERS

The advancement of printing techniques in the 18th century —including lithography, which was invented in 1796 by the German Alois Senefelder—allowed for cheap mass production and printing of posters. The invention of lithography was soon followed by chromolithography, which allowed for mass editions of posters illustrated in vibrant colors.

By the 1890s, chromolithography had spread throughout Europe. A number of noted artists created poster art in this period, foremost amongst them Henri de Toulouse-Lautrec and Jules Chéret. Chéret is considered to be the "father" of advertisement placards. He was a pencil artist and a scene decorator, who founded a small lithography office in Paris in 1866. He used striking characters, contrast and bright colors, and created more than 1,000 advertisements, primarily for exhibitions, theatres and products. The industry soon attracted the service of many aspiring painters who needed a source of revenue to support themselves.

Photo courtesy Swann Auction Galleries, New York; www.SwannGalleries.com

Be a Tight Wad!, 1925, Mather & Co., Chicago, restored punch holes in top and bottom of image; repaired tears and restoration in margins, 48" x 36". **$3,400**

Canadian Pacific, with art by Kenneth Shoesmith, showing the liner Empress of Britain. Text reads, "Canadian Pacific – To Canada or USA." Published by Sander Phillips & Co., The Bayard Press. Poster measures 40" x 25" and is framed, has been laid down and exhibits light repairs and restoration...**$1,035**

Cunard Line, with art by Odin Rosenvinge showing the liner Berengaria. Text reads, "Cunard-Europe-America." Published by Turner & Dunnett. Poster measures 40" x 24" and is framed, has been laid down and exhibits repairs, restoration and in-painting. **$1,035**

Dartmouth / Winter Carnival, 1947, by D.B. Leigh, Winthrop Printing & Offset Co., Boston, repaired tears and creases in margins and image; restored loss in top left corner; restored pinholes in top corners, 34" x 22 1/4". **$2,000**

Don't Lose Your Head, 1924, Mather & Co., Chicago, minor losses and repaired tears along lower left edge and upper left corner; restored punch holes in bottom and top of image, 48" x 36"..**$900**

French Line/French Railways, with art by Albert Sebille showing passenger train at dock with ocean liner to right. Text reads, "Paris-Havre-New York – Chemins de fer de L'etat Cie Gle TransAtlantique." Published by Novia, Paris, and printed in Paris. Poster measures 40 1/2" x 26" and is framed, exhibits repair, restoration and some in-painting. **$1,150**

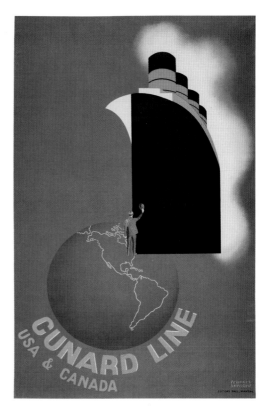

Cunard Line, circa 1935, by Francis Bernard (1900-1979), Paul Martial, repaired tears and creases in margins and image; pinholes in corners. Bernard's contribution to the world of French graphic design was considerable. In addition to the posters he designed, he was Art Director of the Paul Martial studio and in charge of advertising for the Arts Menagers exhibitions as well as for the Office Technique pour l'Utilisation de l'Acier. After World War II he became the director of communication for the French State Radio and Television. During the 1930s he was a member of the Union des Artistes Moderne. During the 1930s, Bernard was the only artist within the impressive group to use photomontage. The Cunard Line was one of the largest and most prestigious companies running ships between Europe and the United States. This exceedingly rare poster combines an impeccable stylization of an ocean liner, with a sophisticated airbrush background of white smoke, a globe, with the Americas outlined in white, and a photomontage of a man waving the vessel off. A daring and modernist image, it qualifies as one of the best travel posters of the 1930s, 39 1/4" x 24 3/4" **$24,000**

(The) Century For Xmas, 1895, by Louis John Rhead, tears and losses in margins and corners; staining in text at bottom. 21 1/2" x 14 1/2". **$500**

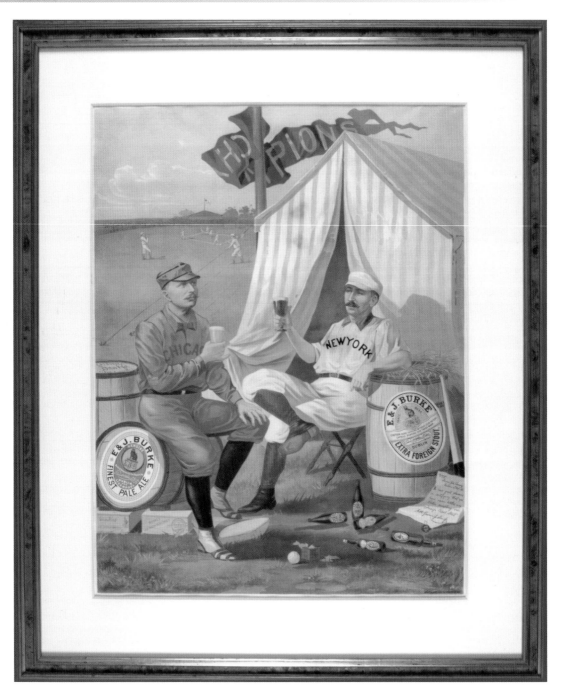

Photo courtesy Robert Edward Auctions, Watchung, N.J.; www.RobertEdwardAuctions.com

Burke Ale, lithograph, featuring Cap Anson and Buck Ewing, 1889, represents the first documented paid endorsement of a product of any kind by baseball players. It is also certainly the first advertising piece featuring players in promotion of an alcoholic beverage, which is ironic, in that the use of alcohol at games in the 1880s and 1890s was such a serious problem that there was concern for the future success of the game as a pastime suitable for attendance by the entire family. The Anson-Ewing Beer poster is exceedingly rare. Only three examples are known. All of the colors are bold, flawless and vibrant; and the poster exhibits none of the tears, creases or stains so common to similar displays of this vintage. The poster (18" x 24") has been professionally cleaned for preservation purposes (no restoration) and has been mounted and framed to total dimensions of 26" x 32". **$188,000**

Photo courtesy Swann Auction
Galleries, New York;
www.SwannGalleries.com

*Smoke Mastiff,
A. Hoen & Co.,
Richmond, Va.,
repaired tears and
creases in margins
and image. Three
sheets, 81 3/4" x
41 3/4".* **$3,600**

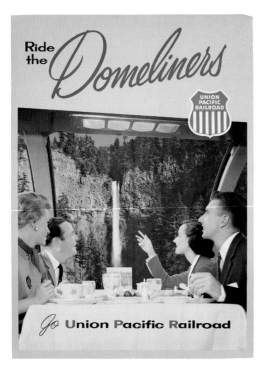

Domeliners / Union Pacific Railroad, creases in margin and image; minor loss in upper right corner; minor tears in right margin, 35 1/2" x 25". **$400**

Goal, by Joseph Leyendecker, Close Graham & Scully Inc. N.Y., light discoloration and foxing in image and margins; minor tears and creases in corners and at edges. Printed on thick stock, 26 1/2" x 20"................................**$1,800**

Inkograph, 1915, Collioud & Cie, Berne, trimmed left and right margins; creases and abrasions in image; pin holes in top and bottom margin; minor foxing in margins, 48" x 31 1/2"..**$250**

Kar-Mi Magic, one sheet of stone lithograph, titled "Kar-Mi Swallows a Loaded Gun Barrel and Shoots a Cracker from a Man's Head." Copyright 1914 by Joseph B. Hallworth, 40" w x 28" h. Vertical fold at middle; some paper loss around perimeter border. **$1,200**

Grafton Gallery, 1893, by Eugene Grasset, Verdoux, Durcourtioux & Huillard, SC., minor restoration and repaired tears in margins; abrasions in image. Matted and framed, 27" x 18 1/2". **$2,000**

German Spas, by Jupp Wiertz, Reichsbahnzentrale fur den Deutschen Reiseverkehr, Berlin, tears in margins; losses in top corners, 39 3/8" x 24 3/4". **$850**

Inman Brothers Flying Circus, circa 1929, expertly replaced bottom and right margins; minor repaired tears in margins and image. The Inman Brothers' flying circus operated a 20-passenger Boeing 80-A and a smaller Ford tri-motor. These models were used by airline companies on their airmail and passenger routes. The Inman Brothers offered novelty flights to the American public for just 50 cents. Their show also delighted visitors with a parachute jump. They called their 80-A a "Boeing Clipper." The Clipper trademark was registered by Pan American Airways in 1931 for their aircraft. The huge B-314 flying boats were the planes most remembered as Boeing Clippers. Inman had to sue to retain the rights to the Clipper name, 37 3/8" x 27 7/8". **$2,400**

Job, 1894, by Georges Meunier, Chaix, Paris, minor repaired tears at edges. Two sheets. Meunier's design in this poster is one of the best utilizing the elongated format that was current in Paris in the mid-1890s, 95" x 34 1/4". **$8,000**

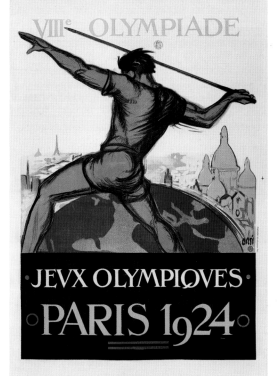

Jeux Olympiques / Paris, 1924, by Orsi, Phogor 92, Paris, vertical and horizontal folds; minor creases and abrasions in image; repaired tears and restoration in image. A taut, poised and powerful image set against the Parisian skyline. One of two posters chosen by the French Olympic Committee to advertise the 8th Olympiad. French version, 46 7/8" x 31 1/4". **$4,400**

Original Kingfisher poster. **$6,727**

Les Coulisses de L'Opera, 1891, by Jules Chéret, Chaix, Paris, text trimmed at bottom; tears and losses at edges and in image, 82 1/4" x 34". **$650**

Lorenzaccio, 1896, by Alphonse Mucha, F. Champenois, Paris, losses, wrinkles, creases and repaired tears along

Omega, circa 1910, by Leonetto Cappiello (1875-1942), Vercasson, Paris, restored tears, creases and abrasions in margins and image; restored pin holes in margins; restoration and minor losses along vertical and horizontal folds, 42 1/2" x 29". **$1,800**

Mobil Oil, 1952, by Blaise Bron (1918-?), horizontal folds, creases and abrasions in image. It is impossible to look at this image without seeing a resemblance to Roy Lichtenstein's early graphic work. However, this poster precedes Lichtenstein's first Pop Art creations by nearly 10 years. The influence of "hyper-real" Swiss posters from the late 1930s until 1960 on many Pop artists is a given, but no poster relates so closely to specific Pop Art as this one for the design-conscious Mobil Corp. Little biographical information exists on this artist. Another poster of his for Mobiloil appears in the 1952 International Poster Annual. Also in the late 1960s and early 1970s, he designed a few posters for fairs around Switzerland. This poster is a proto-Pop masterpiece that stands as an exceptional vanguard to the Pop movement of the 1960s, 50 1/8" x 35 1/2". **$28,800**

Le Petit Dauphinois. 1933, by Leonetto Cappiello (1875-1942), Devambez, Paris, vertical and horizontal folds; repaired tears at edges. Cappiello was the most influential poster artist of the first quarter of the 20th Century, and also the most prolific. Although executed towards the end of his career, this is one of Cappiello's most spectacular and rare posters, 35 1/2" x 62". **$38,400**

vertical and horizontal folds and in image. Wooden dowels affixed to top and bottom margins. Two sheets, 80" x 29".
....**$2,800**

Newcomb College, exhibition posters (two), one for Jean Bragg Gallery, New Orleans, 1998, the other "An Enterprise for Southern Women, 1895-1940, Tulane University." Both framed. Sight: 24" x 16", and 33" x 17 1/2"............**$360 both**

Pneu Michelin, M. de Brunoff et Cie., Paris, repaired tears and creases in margins and image; restored losses in right margin; repaired tears and restoration along vertical and horizontal folds; discoloration in margins and image, 42 1/2" x 58 3/4"...............................**$1,700**

Red Star Line, featuring liner Westerland at sea. Poster measures 24 1/2" x 19 1/2" and is framed, exhibits repairs, restoration...**$540**

Remington Union Metallic Cartridge, Edmund Osthaus illustration of a returning hunter being greeted at the gate. Poster retains both top and bottom metal bands, 17" w x 25" h. One horizontal roll crease near bottom edge. **$900**

Rice's Seeds, humorous stone-lithographed image of jovial gardener harvesting a colossal cabbage. Sign is captioned, "True Early Winningstadt - The Best Cabbage In The World". Lithographed by Cosack & Co., Buffalo, for the Cambridge Valley Seed Gardens, Cambridge, N.Y., circa 1890, 21 3/4 w x 27 1/2" h. Minor moisture stain on bottom left margin...**$1,093**

Savage-Stevens, with metal bands at top and bottom, this unusual poster has a central panel titled, "Nature's Rogues Gallery" with information regarding a variety of predators. The bottom center has the image of a desert wolf with a Stevens single-barrel shotgun and a Savage Sporter rifle. The outer edges have eight panels of various predators and varmints, 18" w x 26" h. Colors are vivid and bright with a few minor creases and a small gouge in the top right center, not affecting the images. Also a small tear on the right edge, again, not affecting the image. The white background is slightly yellowed with a couple water stains on left edge.
....**$120**

Sportsmen's Exposition, 1896, Liebler & Maass Litho., N.Y., repaired tears and restored minor losses in margins and along vertical and horizontal folds, 45 7/8" x 29".
....**$2,600**

Straight As An Arrow, 1929, by Willard Frederic Elmes, Mather & Co., Chicago, restored loss in lower left margin and in image; restored punch holes in top margin; abrasions in image, 43" x 35 1/2".................................**$2,000**

White Star Line/Red Star Line, featuring liner Majestic at dock with woman sitting on trunks. Text reads, "White Star Line/Red Star Line – Winter Cruises DeLuxe Around the World." Poster measures 33" x 23" and is framed, has been laid down and exhibits repairs, restoration and in-painting.
....**$1,150**

Trinkt Zürcher Löwenbrau!, 1927, by Otto Baumberger, J. C. Muller, Zurich, repaired tear though top margin, affecting image; creases in margins. Japan, 50" x 35 1/4". **$1,300**

Sun Valley / Chicago and North Western Line, 1940, by Dwight Shepler, Midwest Offset, Chicago, restored loss in upper right corner; repaired tear through margins; abrasions in image. While the Union Pacific ran trains into Sun Valley, the Chicago and North Western Line took passengers from Chicago to Omaha, where they then boarded Union Pacific trains. An extremely rare variant of this famous poster. No other copies bearing the imprint of the Chicago and North Western Line have ever surfaced, 39 3/4" x 25". **$4,800**

Bristol Steel Rod advertisement. **$3,080**

Movie Posters, Lobby Cards and Stills

American Graffiti, (Universal, 1973) One Sheet (27" x 41"). Vintage, theater-used poster for this comedy-drama that was directed by George Lucas and stars Richard Dreyfuss, Ron Howard, Cindy Williams and Mackenzie Phillips..**$138**

Angels With Dirty Faces, (Warner Brothers, 1938). French Grande (47" x 63"). One of the cornerstone films of the gangster genre, starring James Cagney, Humphrey Bogart, Pat O'Brien and the Dead End Kids. Professional restoration on linen...**$1,434**

Apocalypse Now, (United Artists, 1979). One Sheet (27" x 41"). War. Starring Marlon Brando, Martin Sheen and Robert Duvall. Un-restored poster with fresh, saturated colors. Rolled. **$167**

Dracula (Universal, 1931). Lobby Card (11" x 14"). This card features Bela Lugosi seducing the innocent Helen Chandler by feeding upon her blood. Extremely rare. **$44,812**

The African Queen (United Artists, 1952). Stills (2) (8" x 10"). Adventure. Starring Humphrey Bogart and Katharine Hepburn. Directed by John Huston. Two un-restored stills with bright color. **$155**

20,000 Years in Sing Sing (Warner Brothers, R-1950s). One Sheet (27" x 41"). Crime. Starring Spencer Tracy and Bette Davis. Un-restored poster with good color, folded. F. **$25**

Blade Runner (Warner Brothers, 1982). One Sheet (27" x 41"). Science Fiction. Starring Harrison Ford, Rutger Hauer, Sean Young and Edward James Olmos. Un-restored poster with bright color. Folded. **$262**

Photo courtesy Heritage Auction Galleries, Dallas; www.HA.com

Bullitt (Warner Brothers, 1969). One Sheet (27" x 41"). Action. Starring Steve McQueen, Robert Vaughn, Jacqueline Bisset. Restored poster with bright color on linen. **$537**

Photo courtesy Heritage Auction Galleries, Dallas; www.HA.com

Dr. No (United Artists, 1962). Six Sheet (81" x 81"). James Bond. Starring Sean Connery and Ursula Andress. Un-restored poster that displays signs of average wear and use. Folded. **$1,434**

Photo courtesy Heritage Auction Galleries, Dallas; www.HA.com

The Empire Strikes Back (20th Century Fox, 1980). One Sheet (27" x 41") Advance. Science Fiction. Starring Mark Hamill, Harrison Ford and Carrie Fisher. Directed by Irvin Kershner. A restored poster with bright color. Rolled, on linen. **$505**

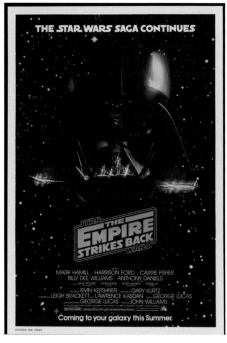

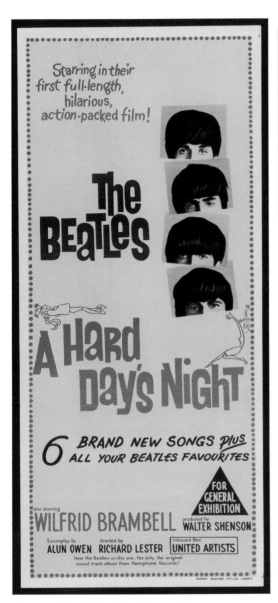

Photo courtesy Heritage Auction Galleries, Dallas; www.HA.com

A Hard Day's Night (United Artists, 1964). Australian Day Bill (13" x 30"). Rock and Roll. Starring John Lennon, Paul McCartney, George Harrison and Ringo Starr. Directed by Richard Lester. Lightly used, un-restored poster with fresh, saturated colors. Folded, Near Mint. **$836**

Fargo, (Polygram, 1996). One Sheet (27" x 40") DS. Crime. Starring Frances McDormand, William H. Macy and Steve Buscemi. Directed by Joel Coen, Ethan Coen. An unused, un-restored poster. Rolled. **$65**

The Godfather, (Paramount, 1972). One Sheet (27" x 41"). Crime. Starring Marlon Brando, Al Pacino, James Caan and Robert Duvall. Directed by Francis Ford Coppola. An un-restored poster that appears virtually unused. Folded. **$131**

The Great Dictator, (United Artists, 1940). One Sheet (27" x 41"). Directed by and starring Charlie Chaplin. One of Chaplin's last films, this was also his biggest box office success. The film garnered five Academy Award nominations. On linen. **$1,792**

Photo courtesy Heritage Auction Galleries, Dallas; www.HA.com

Giant (Warner Brothers, 1956). Lobby Card, Set of 8 (11" x 14"). Card #2 (James Dean with the house) has two pinholes in the glove. **$1,314**

Photo courtesy Heritage Auction Galleries, Dallas; www.HA.com
Citizen Kane (RKO, 1941). One Sheet (27" x 41") Style B. Starring Orson Welles. Un-restored poster, with brilliant colors and white paper. **$57,500**

Photo courtesy Heritage Auction Galleries, Dallas; www.HA.com

Gone with the Wind (MGM, R-1954). Lobby Card Set of 8 (11" x 14"). Academy Award Winner. Starring Clark Gable and Vivien Leigh. Directed by Victor Fleming. An un-restored lobby set with bright color. **$388**

Photo courtesy Heritage Auction Galleries, Dallas; www.HA.com

Houseboat (Paramount, 1958). One Sheet (27" x 41"). Comedy. Starring Cary Grant and Sophia Loren. Directed by Melville Shavelson. An un-restored poster with good color. Folded. **$95**

Photo courtesy Heritage Auction Galleries, Dallas; www.HA.com

Journey to the Center of the Earth (20th Century Fox, 1959). One Sheet (27" x 41"). Science Fiction. Starring Pat Boone and James Mason. Directed by Henry Levin. An un-restored poster with bright color. Folded. **$191**

Photo courtesy Heritage
Auction Galleries, Dallas;
www.HA.com

Lolita (MGM, 1962). Australian Day Bill (13.5" x 30"). Drama. Starring James Mason, Sue Lyon, Shelley Winters and Peter Sellers. Directed by Stanley Kubrick. A restored poster with bright color on linen. **$179**

Photo courtesy Heritage Auction Galleries, Dallas; www.HA.com

The Man Who Shot Liberty Valance (Paramount, 1962). One Sheet (27" x 41"). Western. Starring James Stewart, John Wayne, Vera Miles, Lee Marvin and Woody Strode. Directed by John Ford. An un-restored poster with bright color. Folded. **$358**

The Misfits (United Artists, 1961). Lobby Card (11" x 14"). Drama. Starring Clark Gable, Marilyn Monroe and Montgomery Clift. Directed by John Huston. An un-restored lobby card with bright color. **$68**

King Kong, (Paramount, 1976). One Sheet (27" x 41"). Horror. Starring Jeff Bridges, Charles Grodin and Jessica Lange. Directed by John Guillermin. An un-restored poster with bright color. Folded...**$57**

The Manchurian Candidate, (United Artists, 1962). One Sheet (27" x 41"). Thriller. Starring Frank Sinatra, Laurence Harvey and Janet Leigh. Directed by John Frankenheimer. An un-restored poster with bright color. Folded. **$71**

Raiders of the Lost Ark, (Paramount, 1981). One Sheet (27" x 41"). Adventure. Starring Harrison Ford and Karen Allen. Lightly used, un-restored poster with fresh, saturated colors. Folded. **$358**

The Searchers, (Warner Brothers, 1956). One Sheet (27" x 41"). Director John Ford's film of a war weary ex-Confederate soldier, John Wayne, who becomes obsessed with hunting down the Comanche tribe that has massacred his family and kidnapped his young niece, played by Natalie Wood. Restored on linen. **$4,780**

Singin' in the Rain, (MGM, 1952). One Sheet (27" x 41"). Musical. Starring Gene Kelly, Donald O'Connor, Debbie Reynolds and Jean Hagen. It received two Academy Award

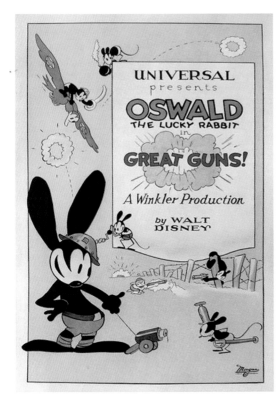

Oswald the Rabbit cartoon, 1927, for Disney's fourth cartoon featuring this character, 27" x 41". **$23,000**

The Nutty Professor (Paramount, 1963). One Sheet (27" x 41"). Comedy. Starring Jerry Lewis. Directed by Jerry Lewis. A restored poster with bright color on linen. **$95**

nominations, including Best Supporting Actress for Hagen, and Best Music..**$3,585**

The Sound of Music, (20th Century Fox, 1965). TODD-AO Six Sheet (81" x 81"). Professional restoration on linen. **$896**

Spartacus, (Universal International, 1960). One Sheet (27" x 41") Academy Awards Style. Adventure. Starring Kirk Douglas and Laurence Olivier. Directed by Stanley Kubrick. An un-restored poster with good color. Folded. **$51**

Superman the Movie, (Warner Brothers, 1978). One Sheet (27" x 41"). Action. Starring Christopher Reeve, Marlon Brando and Gene Hackman. Directed by Richard Donner. An un-restored poster with bright color. Folded. **$45**

The Treasure of the Sierra Madre, (Warner Brothers, 1948). One Sheet (27" x 41"). John Huston's epic saga of treasure and man's greed, starring Humphrey Bogart, Walter Huston and Tim Holt. John Huston won an Oscar for Best Direction and Screenplay....................................**$5,078**

Photo courtesy Heritage Auction Galleries, Dallas; www.HA.com

Mothra (Columbia, 1962). One Sheet (27" x 41"). Science Fiction. Directed by Ishirô Honda. An un-restored poster that appears virtually unused. Folded, Near Mint. **$388**

RECORDS

With the advent of the more sophisticated recording materials, earlier phonograph records became collectors' items. Condition is critical.

As with many types of collectibles, a grading scale has been developed.

Mint (M): Perfect condition, no flaws, scratches or scuffs in the grooves. The cardboard jacket will be crisp.

Near Mint (NM) or Mint-Minus (M-): The record will be close to perfect, with no marks in the grooves. The label will be clean, not marked, or scuffed. There will be no ring wear on the record or album cover.

Very Good Plus (VG+): Used for a record that has been played, but well taken care of. Slight scuffle or warps to the grooves is acceptable as long as it does not affect the sound. A faint ring wear discoloration is acceptable. The jacket may appear slightly worn, especially on the edges.

Very Good (VG): Used to describe a record that has some pronounced defects, as does the cover. The record will still play well. This usually is the lowest grade acceptable to a serious collector. Most records listed in price guides are of this grade.

Good (G): This category of record will be playable, but probably will have loss to the sound quality. The cover might be marked or torn.

Poor or Fair (P, F): Record is damaged, may be difficult to play. The cover will be damaged, usually marked, dirty or torn.

Note: Most records, especially popular recordings, have a value of less than $3. Picture sleeves will generally increase values, and often have an independent value.

45s

Pat Boone, Mono 45s, Dot
15377, "Ain't That a Shame"/"Tennessee Saturday Night," 1955 ....**$10-$20**
15443, "Tutti Frutti"/"I'll Be Home," 1956 ....**$10-$20**
15472, "I Almost Lost My Mind"/"I'm in Love with You," 1956 ....**$10-$20**
15660, "April Love"/"When the Swallows Come Back to Capistrano," 1957 ....**$7.50-$15**
15955, "Twixt Twelve and Twenty"/"Rock Boll Weevil," 1959 ....**$7.50-$15**
15982, "Fools Hall of Fame"/"The Brightest Wishing Star," 1959 ....**$7.50-$15**
16209, "Moody River"/"A Thousand Years," 1961 ....**$7.50-$15**

David Bowie, RCA Victor
APBO-0001, "Time"/"The Prettiest Star," 1973 .... **$3-$6**
PB-10152, "Young Americans"/"Knock on Wood," 1975 .... **$3-$6**
PB-10441, "Golden Years"/"Can You Hear Me," 1975 ..**$2-$4**

The Birds, Columbia
43271, "Mr. Tambourine Man"/"I Knew I'd Want You," 1965 ....**$7.50-$15**
43578, "Eight Miles High"/"Why," 1966 ....**$6-$12**

The Captain and Tennille, Butterscotch Castle 001, "The Way I Want To Touch You"/"Disney Girls" (independent first pressing), 1974 .... **$40-$80**

Creedence Clearwater Revival, Fantasy
617, "I Put A Spell On You"/"Walk on the Water," 1968 ....**$4-$8**
619, "Proud Mary"/"Born on the Bayou," 1969 .... **$3-$6**
637, "Travelin' Band"/"Who'll Stop The Rain," 1970 ... **$3-$6**

The 5th Dimension, Soul City
752, "I'll Be Loving You Forever"/"Train, Keep On Moving," 1966 ....**$30-$60**
756, "Up-Up and Away"/"Which Way To Nowhere," 1967 ....**$4-$8**

Fleetwood Mac, Reprise 1345, "Rhiannon (Will You Ever Win)"/"Sugar Daddy," 1976 ....**$2-$4**

Michael Jackson, Epic
9-50742, "Don't Stop 'Til You Get Enough"/"I Can't Help It," 1979 ....**$2-$4**
34-03509, "Billie Jean"/"Can't Get Outta the Rain," 1983 ....**$2-$4**
34-78000, "Scream"/"Childhood," 1995 ....**$1.50-$3**
34-79656, "You Rock My World" (same on both sides), 2001 ....**$1-$2**

Billy Joel, Family Productions 0900, "She's Got A Way"/ "Everybody Loves You Now," 1971 ....**$12.50-$25**

Kenny Rogers, Carlton 454, Kenneth Rogers, "That Crazy Feeling"/"We'll Always Have Each Other," 1958 ....**$50-$100**

Blues

Jackie Brenston And His Delta Cats, 78s, Chess
1458, "Rocket 88"/"Come Back Where You Belong," 1949 ....**$150-$300**
1472, "Juiced"/"Independent Woman," 1951 ....**$100-$200**

Ida Cox, 78s, Paramount
12053, "Any Woman's Blues"/"Blue Monday Blues," 1923 ....**$60-$120**
12085," Mama Doo Shea Blues"/"Worried Mama Blues," 1924 ....**$70-$140**

Lightnin' Hopkins, 45s, Jax
315, "No Good Woman"/"Been a Bad Man" (red vinyl), 1953 ....**$150-$300**
318, "Automobile"/"Organ Blues" (red vinyl), 1953 ....**$150-$300**
321, "Contrary Mary"/"I'm Begging You" (red vinyl), 1953 ....**$150-$300**

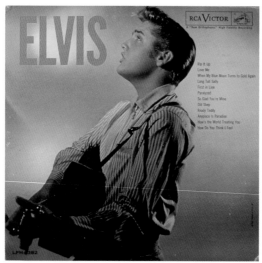

One of Elvis Presley's early albums. Some copies of this album feature an alternate take of his song "Old Shep," with the words "he grew old AND his eyes were growing dim…" Those copies can be worth $800 in near-mint condition.

Papa Charlie Jackson, 78s, Paramount
  12305, "Mama, Don't You Think I Know?"/"Hot Papa
  Blues," 1925 ....**$75-$150**
  12320, "All I Want is a Spoonful"/"Maxwell Street Blues,"
  1925 ....**$50-$100**

Blind Lemon Jefferson, 78s, Paramount
  12347, "Booster Blues"/"Dry Southern Blues," 1926
  ....**$500-$1,000**
  12493, "Weary Dog Blues"/"Hot Dogs," 1926 ....**$500-$1,000**
  12650, "Piney Woods Mama Blues"/"Low Down Mojo
  Blues" (label has a portrait of Jefferson, record is designated as "Blind Lemon Jefferson Birthday Record"), 1928
  ....**$750-$1,500**

B.B. King, 78s, Bullet
  309, "Miss Martha King"/"When Your Baby Packs Up and
  Goes," 1949 ....**$500-$1,000**
  315, "Got the Blues"/"Take a Swing with Me," 1949
  ....**$350-$700**

Bessie Smith, 78s, Columbia
  13007-D, "Far Away Blues"/"I'm Going Back to My Used To
  Be," 1924 ....**$60-$120**
  14056-D, "Reckless Blues"/"Sobbin' Hearted Blues," 1925
  ....**$80-$160**

Stevie Ray Vaughan And Double Trouble, LPs, Epic
  BFE 38734, Texas Flood, 1983 ....**$5-$10**
  FE 39304, Couldn't Stand the Weather, 1984 ....**$5-$10**

Children's
101 Dalmatians, (original motion picture soundtrack),
  LPs, Disneyland
  ST-1908, mono, 1960 ....**$12.50-$25**
  ST-4903, mono, gatefold cover with pop-up scene in center,
  1963 ....**$75-$150**
  ST-3931, mono, 1965 ....**$20-$40**
Ray Bolger, 78, Decca CU 102, "The Churkendoose," 1947
  ....**$25-$50**

The Rolling Stones, Some Girls, the images of Lucille Ball, Joan Crawford, and Marilyn Monroe were later removed in subsequent pressings, with covers featuring the words "Under Construction" or simply showing a solid color shape where a face should be, NM. **$15**

Betty Boop, 7-inch 78, Durotone R-81, Betty Boop in
  "Peter and Wendy"/Betty Boop in "She Loves Him Not,"
  193? ....**$20-$40**
Bozo The Clown, 78s, Capitol
  DAS-3046, Bozo Laughs, 1946 ....**$7.50-$15**
  BBX65, Bozo and His Rocket Ship, 2 78s with book, 1947
  ....**$10-$20**
  DBS-84, Bozo Sings, 2 78s in gatefold sleeve, 1948
  ....**$10-$20**
  DBX-3076, Bozo on the Farm, 2 78s with book, 1950
  ....**$10-$20**
The Electric Company, LP, Sesame Street 22052, The
  Electric Company, 1974 ....**$7.50-$15**
Goldilocks And The Three Bears, 78, Capitol DB-
  121, Goldilocks and the Three Bears, Margaret O'Brien,
  narrator, 1948 ....**$5-$10**
Little Nipper Series, 78-RPM records in folio, RCA Victor
  Y-383, The Adventures Of Little Black Sambo, 1949
  ....**$25-$50**
  Y-385, Pinocchio, 1949 ....**$20-$40**
  Y-397, Howdy Doody and the Air-O-Doodle, 1949
  ....**$25-$50**
  Y-414, Howdy Doody's Laughing Circus, 1949 ....**$20-$40**
  Y-438, Winnie-the-Pooh No. 1, James Stewart, narrator,
  1949 ....**$30-$60**
  Y-446, It's Howdy Doody Time, 1951 ....**$30-$60**

Country, LP
Eddy Arnold, LPs, RCA Victor
  LPM-3753, Lonely Again, mono, 1967 ....**$10-$20**
  LSP-3753, same title, stereo, 1967 ....**$7.50-$15**
Gene Autry, 78, Banner 32349, "That Silver Haired Daddy
  of Mine"/"Mississippi Valley Blues," 1931 ....**$35-$70**

The Carter Family, 78s
"Can the Circle Be Unbroken (By and By)"/"Glory to the Lamb"
(if on Perfect 13155, Oriola 8484, Banner 33465, Romeo 5484, Melotone 13432, or Conqueror 8529, value is equal), 1935 ....**$25-$50**
(if on Vocalion 03027, reissue), 1937 ....**$20-$40**
(if on OKeh 03027, reissue), 1940 ....**$15-$30**
(if on Columbia 37669, reissue), 1947 ....**$10-$20**
(if on Columbia 20268, reissue), 1948 ....**$10-$20**

Wilf Carter, 78s, Bluebird
4966, "My Swiss Moonlight Lullaby"/"The Capture Of Albert Johnson," 1933 ....**$20-$40**
4600, "My Little Swiss and Me"/"I Long for Old Wyoming," 193?? ....**$15-$30**
4624, "Old Alberta Plains"/"Won't You Be the Same Old Pal," 193?? ....**$15-$30**

Johnny Cash, 45s, Sun
241, "I Walk The Line"/"Get Rhythm," 1956 ....**$20-$40**
283, "Ballad of a Teenage Queen"/"Big River," 1958 **$12.50-$25**

Patsy Cline, 45s, Decca
30221, "Walkin' After Midnight"/"A Poor Man's Roses (Or a Rich Man's Gold)," 1957 ....**$10-$20**
31317, "Crazy"/"Who Can I Count On," 1961 ....**$6-$12**

Billy "Crash" Craddock, 45, ABC Dot 17659, "Broken Down in Tiny Pieces"/"Shake It Easy," 1976 ....**$2-$4**

Vernon Dalhart, 78, Victor 19427, "The Prisoner's Song"/"Wreck of the Old '97" (A-side recorded for several different record companies), 1924 ....**$10-$20**

Dale Evans, 78, Majestic 11025, "Under a Texas Moon"/"His Hat Cost More Than Mine," 194?? ....**$10-$20**

The Everly Brothers, 45s, Cadence
1315, "Bye Bye Love"/"I Wonder If I Care As Much," 1957 ....**$12.50-$25**
1337, "Wake Up Little Susie"/"Maybe Tomorrow," 1957 ....**$15-$30**

Merle Haggard, LPs, Capitol
ST 638, A Tribute to the Best Damn Fiddle Player in the World (Or, My Salute to Bob Wills), 1970 ....**$12.50-$25**

Emmylou Harris, 45, Jubilee 5679, "I'll Be Your Baby Tonight"/"I'll Never Fall In Love Again," 1969 ....**$10-$20**

Homer And Jethro, LP, RCA Victor LPM-1560, The Worst of Homer and Jethro (RCA Victor LPM-1560), 1958 ....**$25-$50**

Waylon Jennings, 45s
Ramco 1997, "My World"/"Another Blue Day," 1968 ....**$6-$12**
RCA PB-10924, "Luckenbach, Texas (Back to the Basics of Love)"/"Belle of the Ball," 1977 ....**$2.50-$5**

Brenda Lee, 45, Decca 31309, "Fool #1"/"Anybody But Me," 1961 ....**$7.50-$15**

Jerry Lee Lewis, LP, Mercury SR-61366, Who's Gonna Play This Old Piano ... (Think About It Darlin'), 1972 ....**$7.50-$15**

Loretta Lynn, 45s, Zero
107, "I'm A Honky Tonk Girl"/"Whispering Sea," 1960 ....**$250-$500**
112, "The Darkest Day"/"Gonna Pack My Troubles," 1961 ....**$200-$400**

Willie Nelson, 45s
Belaire 107, "Night Life"/"Rainy Day Blues," 1963 ..**$15-$30**
(if pressed on colored vinyl), 1963 ....**$30-$60**

Sarg 260, "A Storm Has Just Begun"/"When I Sing My Last Hillbilly Song," 196? ....**$25-$50**
Columbia 10176, "Blue Eyes Cryin' in the Rain"/"Bandera," 1975 ....**$2.50-$5**

Dolly Parton, 45s
Gold Band 1086, "Puppy Love"/"Girl Left Alone," 1959 ....**$300-$600**
Monument 982, "Dumb Blonde"/"The Giving and the Taking," 1967 ....**$5-$10**
RCA Victor APBO-0145, "Jolene"/"You're So Beautiful Tonight," 1973 ....**$2.50-$5**

The Sons Of The Pioneers, 78s, Decca
5047, "Tumbling Tumbleweeds"/"Moonlight on the Prairie," 1934 ....**$15-$30**
5939, "Cool Water"/"So Long to the Red River Valley," 1941 ....**$12.50-$25**

Hank Williams, LPs
MGM E-168, Moanin' the Blues (10-inch LP), 1952 ..**$200-$400**
MGM PRO-912, Reflections of Those Who Loved Him (3 LPs) (promo-only box set), 1975 ....**$125-$250**

Jazz

Cannonball Adderly, Stereo LPs, Blue Note
BST-1595, Somethin' Else
(if deep groove pressed into label), 1959 ....**$50-$100**
(if West 63rd Street address on label), 1959 ......**$37.50-$75**
(if New York USA address on label), 1963 ....**$10-$20**

Louis Armstrong, 45s
Decca 29102, "Basin Street Blues" (Pt. 1)/(Pt. 2), 1954 ....**$7.50-$15**
Kapp 573, "Hello Dolly!"/"A Lot Of Lovin' To Do," 1964 ....**$3-$6**
(with picture sleeve, add), 1964* ....**$5-$10**

Count Basie, 10-inch LPs
Clef MCG-120, Count Basie and His Orchestra Collates, 1953 ....**$100-$200**
EmArcy MG-26023, Jazz Royalty, 1954 ....**$35-$70**

Art Blakey And The Jazz Messengers, Mono LPs
Blue Note BLP-1507, At the Café Bohemia, Volume 1
(if "deep groove" indentation on label), 1956 ....**$75-$150**
(if regular version, Lexington Ave. address on label), 1956 ....**$50-$100**
Jubilee JLP-1049, Cu-Bop, 1958 ....**$40-$80**

Clifford Brown, Mono LPs
EmArcy MG-36005, Clifford Brown with Strings, 1955 ....**$60-$120**
Blue Note BLP-1526, Clifford Brown Memorial Album
(if deep groove indentation in label), 1956 ....**$100-$200**
(if regular edition, Lexington Ave. address on label), 1956 ....**$75-$150**
(if "New York, U.S.A." address on label), 196? ....**$12.50-$25**
(if W. 63rd St. address on label), 196? ....**$25-$50**

Dave Brubeck, 45s
Fantasy 524, "Stardust"/"Lulu's Back in Town," 1953 ....**$7.50-$15**
Columbia 41479, "Take Five"/"Blue Rondo A La Turk," 1960 ....**$6-$12**

Cab Calloway, 78s, Brunswick
6209, "Kickin' the Gong Around"/"Between the Devil and the Deep Blue Sea," 1931 ....**$7.50-$15**

The most popular Mouseketeer of all time, Annette Funicello's albums, 45s and picture sleeves have remained collectible for over 40 years. This picture sleeve, promotes her appearance in the movie Muscle Beach Party, NM sleeve. **$30**

6511, "Minnie the Moocher"/"Kickin' the Gong Around," 1931 .... **$10-$20**

John Coltrane, 45s

Impulse! 203, "Easy to Remember"/"Greensleeves," 1961
.... **$5-$10**

Prestige 267, "Stardust"/"Love Thy Neighbor," 1961
.... **$6-$12**

Miles Davis, 45s

Capitol F1221, "Venus de Milo"/"Darn That Dream," 1950
.... **$12.50-$25**

Columbia 42057, "It Ain't Necessarily So"/"All Blues," 1961
.... **$6-$12**

42069, "I Loves You, Porgy"/"It Ain't Necessarily So," 1961
.... **$6-$12**

Kenny Drew, 10-inch LPs

Blue Note BLP-5023, Introducing the Kenny Drew Trio, 1953 .... **$200-$400**

Norgran MGM-29, The Ideation of Kenny Drew, 1954
.... **$125-$250**

Duke Ellington, 45s

RCA Victor 47-2955, "The Sidewalks Of New York"/"Don't Get Around Much Anymore," 1949 .... **$10-$20**

Capitol F2458, "Satin Doll"/"Without A Song," 1953
.... **$6-$12**

Ella Fitzgerald, Stereo LPs

Verve V6-4053, Clap Hands, Here Comes Charley, 1962
.... **$75-$150**

Atlantic SD 1631, Ella Loves Cole, 1972 .... **$6-$12**

Stan Getz, 10-inch LPs

Savoy MG-9004, New Sounds in Modern Music, 1951
.... **$150-$300**

Prestige PRLP-102, Stan Getz and the Tenor Sax Stars, 1951
.... **$100-$200**

Roost R-407, Jazz at Storyville, 1952 .... **$75-$150**

Billie Holiday, 10-inch LPs

Columbia CL 6129, Billie Holiday Sings, 1950 ..... **$100-$200**

Decca DL 5345, Lover Man, 1951 .... **$100-$200**

Ma Rainey, 10-inch LPs, Riverside

RLP-1003, Ma Rainey, Vol. 1, 1953 .... **$125-$250**

RLP-1016, Ma Rainey, Vol. 2, 1953 .... **$125-$250**

RLP-1045, Ma Rainey, Vol. 3, 1954 .... **$125-$250**

Rock

Paul Anka, 45s, ABC-Paramount

9831, "Diana"/"Don't Gamble with Love," 1957 .... **$10-$20**

10082, "Puppy Love"/"Adam and Eve," 1960 .... **$7.50-$15**

Annette, 45s, Buena Vista

349, "First Name Initial"/"My Heart Became of Age," 1959
.... **$7.50-$15**

414, "Teenage Wedding"/"Walkin' and Talkin'," 1962
.... **$10-$20**

433, "Muscle Beach Party"/"I Dream About Frankie," 1964
.... **$7.50-$15**

Frankie Avalon, Stereo LPs, Chancellor

CHLXS 5004, Swingin' on a Rainbow, 1959 .... **$25-$50**

CHLS 5027, You're Mine, 1962 .... **$20-$40**

Chuck Berry, 45s, Chess

1604, "Maybellene"/"Wee Wee Hours," 1955 .... **$25-$50**

1626, "Roll Over Beethoven"/"Drifting Heart," 1956
.... **$25-$50**

1671, "Rock & Roll Music"/"Blue Feeling," 1957
.... **$15-$30**

1691, "Johnny B. Goode"/"Around and Around," 1958
.... **$15-$30**

1729, "Back in the U.S.A."/"Memphis Tennessee," 1959
.... **$15-$30**

Chubby Checker, 45s, Parkway

804, "The Class"/"Schooldays, Oh Schooldays," 1959
.... **$15-$30**

811, "The Twist"/"Toot" (first pressings, white label, blue print), 1960 .... **$15-$30**

811, "The Twist"/"Twistin' U.S.A.," 1961 .... **$7.50-$15**

824, "Let's Twist Again"/"Everything's Gonna Be Alright," 1961 .... **$7.50-$15**

Dee Clark, Mono LPs, Abner

LP-2000, Dee Clark, 1959 .... **$60-$120**

LP-2002, How About That, 1960 .... **$40-$80**

Bo Diddley, LPs

Checker LP 1431, Bo Diddley, 1958 .... **$75-$150**

LP 2974, Have Guitar, Will Travel, 1960 .... **$75-$150**

LP 2977, Bo Diddley Is a Gunslinger, 1961 .... **$75-$150**

Fats Domino, 45s, Imperial

45-5058, "The Fat Man"/"Detroit City Blues" (blue-label "script" logo, pressed around 1952, counterfeits exist), 1950 .... **$1,000-$2,000**

45-5209, "How Long"/"Dreaming," 1952 .... **$40-$80** (if on red vinyl), 1952 .... **$150-$300**

X5369, "Poor Me"/"I Can't Go On," 1955 .... **$12.50-$25**

X5407, "Blueberry Hill"/"Honey Chile" (black vinyl, red label), 1956 .... **$12.50-$25**

X5417, "Blue Monday"/"What's the Reason I'm Not Pleasing You," 1957 .... **$12.50-$25**

The Everly Brothers, 45s, Cadence

1337, "Wake Up Little Susie"/"Maybe Tomorrow," 1957
.... **$15-$30**

1348, "All I Have to Do Is Dream"/"Claudette," 1958
.... **$12.50-$25**

Fabian, 45s, Chancellor

1033, "Turn Me Loose"/"Stop Thief!," 1959 .... **$10-$20**

1037, "Tiger"/"Mighty Cold (To a Warm, Warm Heart)," 1959 .... **$10-$20**

Bill Haley And His Comets,

7-inch EP, Decca ED 2168, Shake, Rattle and Roll (contains "Shake, Rattle and Roll"/"A.B.C. Boogie"/"(We're Gonna) Rock Around the Clock"/"Thirteen Women (And Only One Man in Town)," value is for record and jacket), 1954
.... **$60-$120**

Buddy Holly, 45s, Decca

29854, "Blue Days, Black Nights"/"Love Me" (with star under "Decca"), 1956 .... **$150-$300**

34034, "That'll Be the Day"/"Rock Around with Ollie Vee" (with star under "Decca"), 1957 .... **$125-$250**

62074, "It Doesn't Matter Anymore"/"Raining in My Heart," 1959 .... **$20-$40**

62134, "Peggy Sue Got Married"/"Crying, Waiting, Hoping," 1959 .... **$30-$60**

62210, "True Love Ways"/"That Makes It Tough," 1960
.... **$25-$50**

Roy Orbison, Stereo LPs, Monument

SM-14002, Lonely and Blue, 1961 .... **$300-$600**

SM-14007, Crying, 1962 .... **$300-$600**

SLP-18003, In Dreams (white-rainbow label), 1963
.... **$50-$100**

The Ronettes, 45s

Colpix 601, "I Want a Boy"/"Sweet Sixteen" (as "Ronnie and the Relatives"), 1961 .... **$50-$100**

45 rpm record and picture sleeve, John Lennon, "Mind Games," Apple 1868, 1973. **$15**

45 rpm record and picture sleeve, The Grateful Dead, "Good Lovin'," Arista 0383. **$600**

ROCK 'N' ROLL

Most of the memorabilia issued during the 1950s and '60s focused on individual singers and groups. The largest quantity of collectible material is connected to Elvis Presley and The Beatles.

In the 1980s, two areas—clothing and guitars—associated with key rock 'n' roll personalities received special collector attention. Major auction houses regularly feature rock 'n' roll memorabilia as part of their collectibles sales.

It is important to identify memorabilia issued during the lifetime of an artist or performing group, as opposed to material issued after they died or disbanded.

Reproduction Alert. Records, picture sleeves, and album jackets, especially for The Beatles, have been counterfeited. When compared to the original, sound may be inferior, as may be the printing on labels and picture jackets. Many pieces of memorabilia also have been reproduced, often with some change in size, color, and design.

Backstage pass, cloth

Aerosmith, Pump Tour '89, afternoon **$10**

Bon Jovi, NJ Guest **$7**

KISS, 10th anniversary, after show, unused **$7**

Cyndi Lauper, Crew '86-87 .... **$6**

Rolling Stones, American Tour '81

.... **$15**

Book, *The Beatles Authorized Biography*, McGraw-Hill, 32 glossy black and white photos, copyright 1968 .... **$25**

Christmas card, The Partridge Family, color photo of family opening presents, Christmas tree, facsimile signatures, matching red envelope, trimmed in dark gold, c1971, 5 3/4" x 8 1/2"...**$15**

Counter display, Rolling Stones, "Made In The Shade," 1976, 3-D cardboard, bowed diecut, with four previous LP covers at left and "Rolling Stones & Tongue" logo on silver at top right, 21" x 19" **$250**

Drawing, pencil, 2 1/4" x 2 1/2" image of Jeremy the Bobb balancing on one foot, from Beatles Yellow Submarine, production notations, 1968, 12 1/2" x 16" sheet of animation paper **$150**

Drinking glass, Beatles, clear, images and text in black, 1960s, 6 1/2" h **$20**

Drumsticks
Alice in Chains...**$25**
Black Crows, concert used, logo....................................**$20**
Iron Maiden, 1985..**$50**

Fan photo, 8" x 10"
Jackson Five, full color, 1970s......................................**$10**
James Dean, black and white glossy, c1954...............**$15**

Magazine
Lennon Photo Special, Sunshine Publications, copyright 1981, 8" x 11"...**$15**
Life, Rock Stars at Home with Their Parents, Vol. 17, #13, Sept. 14, 1971 ....**$5**
Post, Mamas and Papas article, March 25, 1967 ....**$5**
The Rolling Stones Magazine, Straight Arrow Publishers, copyright 1975...**$10**

Newsletter, Rolling Stones Fan Club, four pgs, black and white, orig mailing envelope, 5" x 8".......................**$15**

Pinback button
Led Zeppelin, group logo in center, blue and white lettering: Summerfest At The Stadium Presents An Evening With Led Zeppelin, Sat, Aug. 6, 1977, Buffalo, NY, 3" d..........**$35**
Hey, Let's Twist, red lettering on white ground, striped peppermint candy design, c1961, 3 1/2" d **$20**

Portrait, Elvis Presley, by Ivan Jesse Curtain, wooden frame, 1960s...**$125**

Poster
Beatles, four sheets, each with Richard Avedon stylized portrait, 1968, 79" x 29"..**$1,840**
Family Dog, art by Victor Moscoso, second printing, Oct. 6-8, 1967 ....**$35**
Janis Joplin, Neon Rose, Matrix, San Francisco, Jan. 17-22, 1967, 13 3/4" x 20"...**$75**

Press kit, KISS, Casablanca, custom folder, three-page bio, one-page press clipping, five 8" x 10" black and white photos, orig mailing envelope with no writing or postage, 1976 ....**$500**

Scarf, Beatles, glossy fabric, half corner design, marked "The Beatles/Copyright by Ramat & Co., Ltd./London, ECI," c1964, 25" sq...**$160**

Sheet music
Jackson Five, *Mama's Pearl,* copyright 1971 Jobette Music Co..**$5**
Michael Jackson, *We're Almost There,* browntone photo cover, copyright 1974 Stone Diamond Corp **$5**

Ticket
Beatlefest '82-LA **$10**
Elvis, 9/88..**$75**
The Beatles Again Movie, 1976, 2 1/4" x 5 1/2" **$20**
Yardbirds/Doors, 1967 ....**$50**

Tour book
Depeche Mode, Devotional Tour 1993/94.......................**$10**
KISS, 10th anniversary, Vinnie V in makeup **$125**

Toy, Beatles car, battery operated tin, 1964 Ford Galaxie, vinyl Beatles-like group, "Los Yes-Yes" lithographed on hood, record inside car is bit garbled, but working, orig Rico (Spain) hangtag, orig box with insert, C.9............**$850**

T-shirt, never worn
Bon Jovi, L, Slippery When Wet.....................................**$25**
Deep Purple, L, Perfect Str…'85.....................................**$25**
Rolling Stones, XL, Steel Wheels....................................**$20**

Watch, Elvis Presley, dial with full-color illus of Elvis in elaborate white jumpsuit, blue background, copyright 1977 Boxcar Enterprises, Unique Time Co., orig blue vinyl straps, 1 1/4" d goldtone metal case.................................**$45**

45 rpm record and picture sleeve, The Byrds, "You Movin'," Sundazed Kustom Shop KS7-01, 2002. **$2.50**

45 rpm record and picture sleeve, "Keep It Together," Sire 19986, 1990. **$80**

SALT AND PEPPERSHAKERS

Rare, unique and decorative salt and peppershakers have become such popular collector's items over the years that many shaker sets are produced for the sole purpose of being a collectible and are rarely used to hold seasonings

Salt and peppershakers can be found in nearly every conceivable shape and size and are made in a variety of materials including wood, metal, ceramics, glass, and plastics. They are abundant, colorful, fun, span almost every theme, and best of all, they're often inexpensive.

Shakers in this section depict people, beings with human form or inanimate objects with human characteristics, and are the products of many makers.

This category includes "Naughties," usually anatomically incorrect women in various poses. Also see shakers made by specific makers in the glass section.

For more information, see *Antique Trader Salt and Pepper Shaker Price Guide* by Mark F. Moran, 2008.

Accordion-playing toy soldiers, 1986, can also hang as ornaments, 4 1/4" h. **$25+**

Angel with gold trim, 1940s, marked Rossware, 3 3/4" h. **$65-$75**

Little angels with gold trim, 1960s, made in Japan by Lefton, 4 1/4" and 4" h. **$25-$35**

Formal boy in top hat, 1940s, made in Japan, 4 3/4" h overall. **$45-$55**

Frowning boys with pipes in plaid caps, 1940s, made in Germany, 3 1/2" and 3 1/8" h. **$55-$65**

Boy and girl riding swans, 1950s, made in Japan, 3" h. **$25+**

Nude women, 1950s, unmarked, 3 3/4" h. **$65-$75**

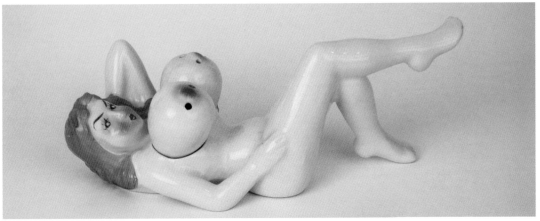

Busty woman, 1950s, made in Japan, 7" long. **$75-$85**

Glass and metal chefs, 1970s (?), maker unknown, 3 1/4" h. **$25-$35**

Children with petal collars, late 1950s, unmarked, 2 1/2" h. **$25+**

Couple in 18th-century dress with gold trim, 1950s, made in Japan, 3 3/4" and 3 7/8" h. **$25+**

Cowboy, souvenir of Eden Valley, Minn., 1960s, made in Japan, 3 3/4" h overall. **$45-$55**

Sexy black and red girl devils, 1950s, made in Japan, 4 3/4" h. **$35-$45**

Egghead couple with rhinestone eyes, 1950s, made in Japan, 3 1/4" h. **$30-$40**

Four-eyed rustic couple, 1950s, made by Enesco in Japan, 3 1/2" h. **$20-$25**

Portly gentlemen with pipes and canes, 1930s, made in Germany, 3 3/8" h. **$45-$55**

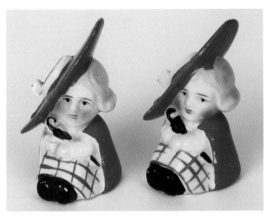

Girls in big hats with umbrellas, 1940s, made in Japan, 3 1/2" h. **$25-$35**

Girls in hats riding tropical fish, 1930s, made in Japan, 2 3/4" h. **$25-$35**

Lady riding alligator, 1950s, made in Japan, 4 1/4" h overall, 5" long. **$60**

Mr. and Mrs. Crazy Big-Head, late 1960s, unmarked, 4 3/4" h. **$25+**

Pilgrim women, 1950s, made in Japan, 3 1/4" h. **$20+**

Boy and girl pixies (?), with gold trim, 1960s, made in Japan, 3 3/4" h. **$20+**

*Pixie heads, 1960s (?),
unmarked, 3 1/4" h.* **$25-$35**

*Pixie heads, 1960s, unmarked,
3 3/4" h.* **$40-$50**

*Running spoon and fork, 1960s, made in Japan,
5 1/4" h.* **$20**

Risque arguing couple, 1950s, made in Japan, 4 3/4" h.
$55-$65

Southern belles in hoop skirts, early 1950s, souvenir of Des Moines, Iowa, made in Japan, 3" h. **$20-$25**

Showering couple, made as two pieces but sold attached, 1960s, made in Japan, 5" h. **$40+**

Tired housewives, 1960s, unmarked, 5" h. **$35-$45**

Spice of Life, 1950s, made in Taiwan, 6" long. **$55-$65**

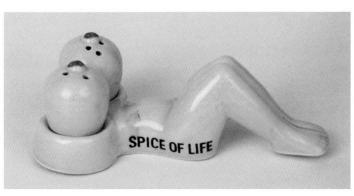

Toby couple, 1960s, made in Japan, 2 3/4" h. **$20+**

Toby bearded men (hobos?), 1960s, made in Japan, 2 1/2" h. **$20+**

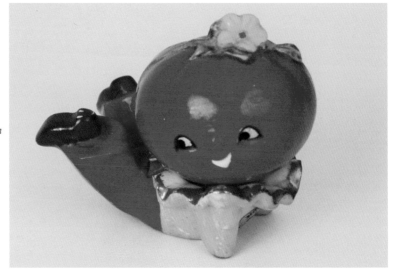

Tomato-head boy, 1940s, made in Japan, 2 1/2" h overall. **$45+**

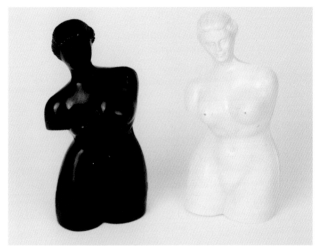

Black and white Venus de Milo, plastic, 1960s, 4" h. **$15-$25**

Victorian children, with threaded ceramic stoppers, 1930s, made in Japan, 3 1/8" and 3 1/4" h. **$35-$45**

Winter children in long coats, 1940s, Occupied Japan, 3 1/4" h. **$25-$35**

SHAVING MUGS

Shaving mugs, which hold the soap, brush and hot water used to prepare a beard for shaving, come in a variety of materials including tin, silver, glass and pottery. One style, which has separate compartments for water and soap, is the scuttle, so called because of its coal-scuttle shape.

Personalized shaving mugs were made exclusively for use in barbershops in the United Sates. They came into use shortly after the Civil War and continued to be made into the 1930s.

Unlike shaving mugs that were used at home, these mugs were personalized with the owner's name, usually in gilt lettering. The mug was kept in a rack at the barbershop, and it was used only when the owner came in for a shave. This was done for hygienic purposes, to keep from spreading a type of eczema known as "barber's itch."

The mugs were usually made on European porcelain blanks that often contained the mark of "Germany," "France" or "Austria" on the bottom. In later years, a few were made on American-made semi-vitreous blanks. Decorators who worked for major barber-supply houses did the artwork on mugs. Occasionally the mark of the barber-supply house is also stamped on the bottom of the mug.

The mugs gradually became more decorative, and included hand-painted floral decorations, as well as birds, butterflies and a wide variety of nature scenes, etc. These are classified today as "decorative" mugs.

Another category, "fraternal mugs," soon emerged. These included the emblem of an organization the owner belonged to, along with his name emblazoned in gold above or below an illustration.

"Occupational mugs" were also popular. These are mugs that contained an image illustrating the owner's occupation, such as a butcher, a bartender or a plumber. The illustration might be a man working at his job, or perhaps the tools of his trade, or a product he made or sold.

Of all these mugs, occupationals are the most prized. Their worth is determined by several factors: rarity (some occupations are rarer than others), size of mug and size of illustration (the bigger the better), quality of artwork and condition, although rare mugs with cracks or chips can still be valuable if the damage does not affect the artwork on the mug. Generally speaking, a mug showing a man at work at his job is usually valued higher than that same occupation illustrated with only the tools or finished product.

In 1901, the American inventor King Camp Gillette, with the assistance of William Nickerson, invented a safety razor with disposable blades. As a result, the need for personalized shaving mugs declined.

Prices shown are for typical mugs that have no damage and show only moderate wear on the gilt name and decoration.

Photo courtesy of Pook & Pook, Inc.

Occupational shaving mug, bicyclist on highwheeler, inscribed "P.J.," 3 4/8" h. **$700**

Fraternal

B.P.O.E., Elks, double emblem, Dr. title. **$300**
F.O.E., Fraternal Order of Eagles, eagle holding F.O.E. plaque.
....**$260**
IB of PM, International Brotherhood of Paper Makers,
    papermaking machine, clasped hands. **$275**
I.O.M., International Order of Mechanics, ark ladder. **$270**
Loyal Knights of America, eagle, flags, six-pointed star.
....**$275**
Loyal Order of the Moose, gold circle with gray moose
    head, purple and green floral dec, gilt rim and base,
    marked "Germany"..**$220**
United Mine Workers, clasped hands emblem flanked by
    crossed picks and shovels, floral dec, rose garland around
    top, marked "Germany". **$125**

Occupational

Electrician, hand-painted image of electrician wiring inside
    of electrical box, T & V Limoges, France, wear to gold
    lettering and trim, 3 5/8" d, 3 5/8" h.........................**$2,500**
Express wagon, hand painted, man driving horse drawn
    wagon, word "Express" on side, floral springs, gold rim and
    name, 4" x 3 3/4". **$400**
Fabric store, colorful hand-painted shop interior, owner
    waiting on well-dressed woman, gold trim and name,
    3 5/8" x 4 1/2"...**$700**
General store, pork, flour, and whiskey barrels, Limoges, 4"
    x 4 3/4". **$650**

Hotel clerk, clerk at desk, guest signing register. $375

House painter, detailed hand-painted image of man painting side of building, marked "Fred Dole" on bottom, light crack mark around top of handle, wear to gold lettering and trim, 3 1/2" d, 3 1/2" h. $350

Hunting

Duck hunting, hand painted, duck hunter and dog in boat, 3 1/2" x 3 1/2". $275

Ducks, hand painted, two colorful ducks at water's edge, mkd "J. & C. Bavaria," 3 5/8" x 3 5/8". $100

Hunting dogs, hand painted, two hunting dogs, brown background, mkd "St Louis Electronic Grinding Co., Barber Supplies," some wear to gold trim, crack in ring handle, 4 1/8" x 3 3/4". $120

Rabbit hunting, hand painted, large rabbits in foreground, hunter walking thru snow, factory in background, 3 1/2" x 3 1/2". $120

Sportsman, hand painted, caught fish, fishing rod, shot gun, leafy sprigs, scene of men fishing in background, name in scroll, V D Austria, 3 5/8" x 3 5/8". $130

Ice man, hand painted, horse drawn Palmer's Ice Co. delivery wagon, rim and name in gold, T & V France, 3 1/2" x 3 1/2". $825

jockey racing horse and cart, inscribed "Geo. B. Wells," 3 5/8" h. $305

Mail wagon, hand painted, postal worker driving horse drawn mail wagon, German, repair to top rim on back, gold trim lines redone, 4" x 3 3/4". $475

Mover, detailed hand-painted image of two men in moving van, gold name and trim, Royal China Int'l, 3 7/8" d, 3 5/8". $1,400

Oil derrick, hand painted, detailed oil well scene, T & V France, 3 5/8" x 3 5/8". $220

Photographer, detailed hand-colored image of portrait photographer, marked "Webb Bros" in gold, wear to gold lettering and trim, 3 5/8" d, 3 1/2" h. $700

Policeman, inscribed "H.D. Lewis," 3 5/8" h. $265

Railroad, detailed hand-painted image of two railway workers on hand car, wear to gold lettering and trim, 3 1/2" d, 3 5/8" h. $650

Serviceman fixing boiler, inscribed "M.R. Goodall," 3 5/8" h. $235

Shoemaker, hand painted, scene of shoemaker in shop, gilt foot and swags around name..................................$225

Soda fountain, hand painted, serving clerk behind counter of soda fountain, well dressed woman sitting at counter on stool, name in gold, Germany, 3 3/4" x 3 5/8". $2,500

Surveyor, hand painted, detailed land surveying instrument in center, wear to gold name and trim, D & C, 3 1/2" x 3 5/8". $550

Tugboat, boat in water, crew and captain. $750

Veteran, hand painted, US Civil War soldier holding American flag, name in gold, 3 3/4" x 3 1/2". $1,500

Writer, black desk inkwell with sander, pen, and brass handle. $350

Other

Drape and flowers, purple drape, pot of flowers, gold name..$85

Fish shape, scuttle, green and brown. $75

Skull, white, gray, black, and cream, scuttle, marked "Bavaria"...$135

Photo courtesy of Pook & Pook, Inc.

Occupational shaving mug, teamster driving horse-drawn ice wagon, "Glen Willow Ice Company," inscribed "J.R. Hinkel," 3 5/8" h. **$645**

Photo courtesy of Pook & Pook, Inc.

Occupational shaving mug, barbershop scene, inscribed "Hunter Francis," 3 1/2" h. **$645**

SILVER AND SILVER PLATE

Silver has been known since ancient times and has long been valued as a precious metal, used to make ornaments, jewelry, tableware and utensils, and coins.

Also see Lighting.

Bowl (presentation), Jarvie, hand-wrought sterling, from the Onwentsia Club (Lake Forest, Ill.) Powwow, 1918, with a repousse American Indian design and a circular medallion of a chief's head. Marked Jarvie in script, STERLING CHICAGO 2065, 2 1/2" x 5". **$4,200**
(Robert Riddle Jarvie, active 1904-1920, Chicago.)

Box, betel nut, Indian silver, of lobed contour with the hinged lid fashioned with a high-relief reserve of Krishna and Radha in a landscape, further vignettes of the life of this incarnation of Vishnu ornamenting the side, the interior with a separate segmented tray etched with floral motifs (wear), 7 1/4" l. **$130**

Cream can, 19th century, English, with decorative scroll handle, flaring shaped beaded edge base and with banner "I die for those I love". English hallmark, Sheffield, 1881-2 with hallmark "HW & Co", 5 troy oz., 4" h.................**$150**

Cream jug, sterling, London, 1831, having a tall loop handle with bright-cut decoration and square pedestal base, 5 3/4" h, some light dents and small crease.........**$259**

Creamer, silver repousse, Andrew Ellicott Warner, 1786-1870, Baltimore, the sides chased and embossed with chinoiserie motifs including pagodas, boat scenes and dense scrolled foliage, a shield-shaped cartouche below spout, angled ribbed handle with grape cluster terminals, marked "A.E.WARNER" in serrated rectangle, and 11 and an underlined 8, 5 3/4" h, approx. 13 troy oz. **$2,251**

Cup (presentation), Jarvie, hammered sterling, by George Elmslie, Harbor Point Country Club, 1915, minor and shallow dent, stamped Jarvie STERLING 2016, 7 3/4" x 5 1/4". **$8,400**
(Robert Riddle Jarvie, active 1904-1920, Chicago.)

Demitasse set, Gorham, sterling, molded oval urn form, consisting of demitasse pot, ebonized urn finial and handle side (1 1/4 pint, A2311), creamer (1/4 pint, A2314), sugar bowl (A2313), 14" oval tray (A4609); 41 total gross troy oz. ....**$600 set**

Fish set, mother-of-pearl handles, HW & Co., Sheffield; consisting of 12 knives and 12 forks, including mahogany case with brass insert, shrinkage split to top of case. ....**$805 set**

Flatware, Francis I, Reed & Barton, eight sterling dinner forks, 7 3/4" l, eight sterling hollow-handled dinner knives, 9 1/2" l, 21 troy oz. weighable silver.........................**$632 all**

Flatware, Francis I, Reed & Barton, four sterling luncheon forks, 7" l, four sterling hollow-handled luncheon knives, 9 1/8" l., 8 1/2 troy oz. weighable silver. ....**$156 all**

Flatware, Francis I, Reed & Barton, serving spoon, 8 1/4" l, fluted sugar shell, nut spoon, four flat-handled butter spreaders, three teaspoons, four 5 7/8" soup spoons, 19 troy oz..**$450 all**

Flatware, Kirk Stieff, sterling, "Williamsburg Queen Anne," 82 pieces, consisting of 25 teaspoons (5 3/4"), 10 each ice tea spoons (7") and salad forks (6 1/2"), eight each dinner forks (7 3/4") and dinner knives with old French pistol handles (9 1/4"), six butter knives with old French hollow pistol handles (6 3/4"), four dessert/soup spoons (6 3/4"), three each salad forks (6 1/4") and cocktail forks (5 1/4"), two small serving spoons (7 3/4"), cold-meat serving fork (8 1/4"), cream ladle (6 1/2"), and a gravy ladle (7 1/4"), in a felt lined box. second half 20th century, minor usage wear. **$3,575**

Inkstand, Gorham, sterling, stamp box at center flanked by two glass inkwells with sterling lids, spiral motif, pierced sides, #85 on bottom, 3 1/2" h, 7 3/4" w, 4 1/4" deep.....**$805**

Ladle, coin silver, by Ludwig Heck, Lancaster, Pa., circa 1760; "L. Heck" struck twice, monogrammed, pointed handle, 14 3/8" l, 3/4" break in edge of bowl.................**$431**

Ladle (punch), ivory handled, marked "Sterling" also having a Chinese four-character mark and maker's mark "C S" possibly for Cabot Shields, Baltimore, 1773. Ladle having a round bowl, bamboo leaf engraving to handle with water leaf ends connected to a finely carved shaped ribbed handle, 14 3/4" l..**$1,150**

Ladle (soup), silver-plated, acanthus terminal, shell bowl, Albert Coles & Co., New York, 19th century, 13 1/4" l. **$287**

Loving cup, English, two handles on pedestal, marked Peter and Ann Bateman, London, 1791. The S-scrolled lappet handles joined to the tapered cylindrical body with raised reeded mid-molding on circular pedestal

Photo courtesy Skinner Inc., Boston, www.SkinnerInc.com

Pitcher, classical, coin silver, presentation, John B. Jones, Boston, 1782-1854, the circa-1830 pitcher with double scroll cast handle, rectangular in section with applied leaf on top, bands of gadrooning on rim, middle and base, marked "J.B. Jones" on base, the side engraved with the names of five generations of males by the name of Dexter residing in or around Boston, 9 3/4" h, approx. 31 troy oz., subtle dents and several pinhead size pits on bulbous area. **$1,185**

base. Touch marks on side beneath rim, 10 troy oz., 6" h x 7 1/4" l x 3 3/4" w, form has alterations. $360

Master salts (pair), Virginia, Capt. William Richardson (1757-1809), Richmond, each of oval form with original cobalt glass insert and raised on four flaring feet, each hallmarked with a raised spread-wing Eagle and "W.R." in a rectangle, simple period script M monogram, late 18th or early 19th century, 1 7/8" h, 2" x 3 1/8" d rim, rim flake to one insert. ....**$12,100 pair**

Pitcher, hand-hammered, sterling, octagonal paneled urn form, circular molded base, Woodside Sterling Co., New York, 10 1/2" h, approximately 22 1/2 troy oz..........**$450**

Pitcher, International, sterling, urn form with helmet-form lip, repousse band of husk festoons and urns, circular base with conforming repousse decoration and flower-head border, 11" h, approximately 32 1/2 troy oz. **$805**

Pitcher, sterling, repousse, floral decoration, A.G. Schultz & Co., Baltimore, early 1900s, 8 1/2" h, approximately 21 troy oz. **$1,320**

Pitcher (presentation), Jarvie, Prairie School, faceted sterling, attributed to George Elmslie, marked, "Presented by Chicago Livestock World Iowa Poland China Futurity 1914", stamped STERLING Jarvie 2034, 9 1/2" x 7 3/4". **$25,200**

(Robert Riddle Jarvie, active 1904-1920, Chicago.)

Photo courtesy Skinner Inc., Boston, www.SkinnerInc.com

Porringer, American, probably Massachusetts, second quarter 18th century, round bowl with domed center, pierced keyhole-pattern handle with "A+B to D+A & M+W" engraved on the back of handle (an inscription on a tag attached to the handle reads: "Andrew Bowditch of Salem Mass. to Daniel Appleton and Mary Williams Boston"), 1 1/2" h, 4 1/4" d, 6 3/4" l, approx. 4 troy oz., several soft dents to bulbous area of bowl, rim a little out of round. **$651**

Platter, Stieff, sterling, oval repousse, floral border, hand chased, 16" l, approximately 36 troy oz. **$1,495**

Roast carving set, Francis I, Reed & Barton, sterling hollow-handled knife, 13 1/2" l; fork, 11 1/4". **$228**

Spoon, perforated, with receptacle, stem with gold-plated spiral band, 800 MN-marked silver spoon, 8 3/8" l; including brass-bound ceramic container with basket-weave-molded surface, 3 1/2" h........**$28 both**

Spoon (stuffing), coin silver, upward-turned handle with twin-lobe terminal, marked "R.S." in rectangle (mark not identified)........**$230**

Supper set, Sheffield silver-plate, Lazy Susan design with rotating top fitted with octagonal paneled covered center bowl with acorn finial and twin lion mask head ring handles, four covered serving dishes, two pepper urns, two open salts, bottom section with four handles, gadrooned borders, early 20th century, 30" d. ....**$1,680 set**

Photo courtesy Skinner Inc., Boston, www.SkinnerInc.com

Tea service, three pieces, coin silver, Peter Chitry, New York, early 19th century, comprising a teapot, covered sugar bowl and creamer, oval lobed bodies with fruit-form finials, shaped serpent spout, an anthemion leaf and grapevine borders on stepped oval bases, marked "P. Chitry" on bases, 7 1/4" to 9 1/2" h, approx. 55 troy oz.; together with a later plated, similarly formed, unmarked teapot and a plated rectangular tray with engraved scrolled floral and foliate design marked "Wm. Rogers 4090," teapot 9 3/4", tray 14" x 22 1/2", handles are hollow, the bases all have several small dents around them, wear to the plated pieces, the tray has surface wear. **$1,896 all**

Teapot, coin silver, Stockman & Pepper, Philadelphia, circa 1840; urn form with beaded borders, monogrammed, berry finial, applied acanthus to handle top, stepped circular base, 10 3/8" h; approximately 38 1/2 troy oz.
....**$840**

Tea and coffee service, Gorham, sterling, urn form with rococo shell and scroll borders, scrolled finial, shell feet; consisting of teapot #1142, 2 3/8 pint, 7 7/8" h; coffeepot #1141, 2 1/4 pint; covered sugar bowl #1145; creamer #1144, 5/8 pint; and waste bowl #1143; including "Extra Silver Plated" twin-handled tea tray with grapevine border, 24" across handles. Approximately 71 troy oz. total sterling silver...**$1,265 all**

Tea and coffee service, nine pieces, sterling, possibly by Galt & Bro., Washington, D.C., marked "W50", monogrammed, urn form with husk pendants and floral festoons; consisting of teapot, 3 pints, bud and leaf finial, 8" h; coffeepot, 10 1/4" h; hot water kettle on warming stand, 4 1/2 pints, 8 3/8" h; creamer, 1 pint, 6 1/4" h; covered sugar bowl, 6 1/2" h; waste bowl, gold-plated pierced brass cover, 6" h; compote, arched emblems with classical motifs, leaf-molded borders, 3 3/4" h, 11" d; and 26" oval tray and 20" oval tray. Approximately 326 total troy oz. ....**$5,100 all**

Tea and coffee service, sterling, in case with sterling tray; service: bun form, urn finials, tab feet; #950, consisting of teapot, coffee pot, creamer, sugar bowl; approximately 72 troy oz. Tray: twin-handled oval form #950, 26 5/8" across handles, approximately 79 1/2 troy oz...................**$3,000 all**

Teaspoons (six), coin silver, Sickle & Sheaf, H. McKeen, Philadelphia, circa 1823, monogrammed reverse; together with George III silver caddy spoon (of shovel form), Birmingham, 1817 (maker's mark worn).................**$345 all**

Teaspoons (12), coin silver, R. & W. Wilson, Philadelphia, 1825-1846, fiddle pattern, monogrammed, 6" l.........**$180 all**

Tray, S. Kirk & Son, Baltimore, sterling, oval repousse, floral border, 2518A, "Hand Decorated"; 18" l, approximately 51 troy oz..**$1,495**

Tray, silver-plated, twin handles, oblong with "M" monogram at center above "April 20th/1887"; floral chased field, cast floral border with square ornament at each corner; marked on reverse with "W" in circle over "86" and "26"; 28 1/4" across handles. **$207**

Trophy (sporting), sterling, campagna form, footed vase having a side hallmark at top edge marked "Edinburgh 1828" with maker's mark "GP", possibly George Purse. Trophy inscription on side reading "Lanarkshire Yeomanry Cup Given by Sir Charles McDonald Lockhart and Won by Mr. Joseph Hutchisons, Horse Sporting Bob 1831", 13.5 troy oz., 7 1/4" h x 4 3/4" d, with roughness to seams.
....**$288**

Tureen (covered), Meriden, silver-plated, boat form on oval foot, centering knop on spiraling dome, broad vertically fluted bands, twin bar-form handles, #1892/3; 6 7/8" h, 12 3/4" across handles..............................**$108**

Water urn, George III, Sheffield plate, twin loop handles, oval in section, beaded base on fluted oblong plinth, spigot side, 17" h; with card from Robert Ensko Inc. **$390**

SPORTS MEMORABILIA

Baseball

The grading of sports memorabilia, especially baseball cards, has reached such a level of detail that space does not allow for an in-depth discussion of it here. For more information, visit the Web sites of any of the professional grading services.

Also see Autographs, Posters, Toys.

Chicago Americans Giants, circa 1914 panoramic photo including Rube Foster, by Stuart Thompson, a successful commercial photographer in Vancouver, B.C., during the early 1900s. The photograph displays a few insignificant border tears, and a small corner chip in the lower right. Negro League photos dating from the early 1900s are exceedingly rare, especially those picturing prominent clubs and/or players, 16 1/2" x 6 1/2". **$35,250**

Ty Cobb, 1909-1911 T206 card, with "Ty Cobb" back, one of only about 12 known examples. With evenly rounded corners, bright colors and perfect registry. Graded fair, a couple small surface chips of paper loss do not affect Cobb's portrait. On the back is printed: "'Ty Cobb' King of the Smoking Tobacco World/Factory No. 33-4, Dist. of N.C."
....**$64,625**

Ty Cobb, 1911 M110 Sporting Life cabinet card, pastel artwork of Cobb in a classic batting stance on the front and an advertisement for Sporting Life on the reverse. Bright and clean, both front and back, with bold blue text on the reverse, 5 5/8" x 7 1/2"..**$41,125**

Cracker Jack, #144 Series, 1914 E145, complete card set, recognized as one of the most significant of all prewar baseball card issues. Total 145 cards.........................**$88,125**

George Davis, 1894 N142 Duke cabinet card, advertising Duke's Honest Tobacco brand in the lower left. There are only four ballplayers in this set. Hall of Famer Davis was one of the premier shortstops of his day, and at the time this card was issued he was a member of the New York Giants. The card has some light staining along the right border (common with Dukes), and virtually no wear to the edges and corners. Some light shading on the blank reverse. **$7,050**

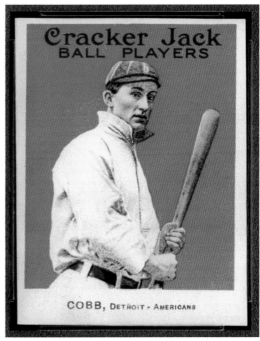

Photo courtesy Robert Edward Auctions, Watchung, N.J.; www.RobertEdwardAuctions.com

Ty Cobb, 1915 E145 Cracker Jack card, #30, pristine, crisp, with flawless registration, sharp corners, no stains. The red color of the background is particularly deep and bold. The reverse is flawless with bold black text. **$15,275**

Photo courtesy Robert Edward Auctions, Watchung, N.J.; www.RobertEdwardAuctions.com

American Tobacco Trust, 1909-1911 T206 White Border cards, near complete, a set assembled with an eye for centering and the overall visual appeal of each card. Extremely high grades, 520 cards. **$176,250**

Photo courtesy Robert Edward Auctions, Watchung, N.J.;
www.RobertEdwardAuctions.com

Mickey Mantle, 1952 Topps card, #311, ultra high-grade example, pack-fresh example with brilliant colors. The deep blue background, which is so prone to wear, is exceptionally strong. The white interlocking "NY" on the front of Mickey's cap contrasts sharply against the dark navy blue of his cap. The corners are strong and sharp. Centered 70/30 left to right and 50/50 top and bottom. Mantle's most celebrated card. **$35,250**

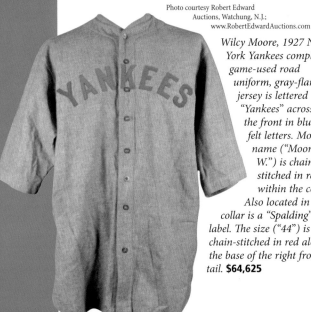

Photo courtesy Robert Edward
Auctions, Watchung, N.J.;
www.RobertEdwardAuctions.com

Wilcy Moore, 1927 New York Yankees complete game-used road uniform, gray-flannel jersey is lettered "Yankees" across the front in blue felt letters. Moore's name ("Moore W. W.") is chain-stitched in red within the collar. Also located in the collar is a "Spalding" label. The size ("44") is chain-stitched in red along the base of the right front tail. **$64,625**

Bob Feller, 1938 Goudey "Heads-Up" card, #288. Crisp and clean, with virtually perfect registration, a slightly imperfect cut along the top border (detectable only when examined closely from the reverse), four sharp corners with just the slightest hint of wear, bright colors, and a flawless reverse. **$8,225**

Goudey Gum, 1934 near complete set (89 of 96 cards), high grade, including no. 37 and no. 61 Lou Gehrig, and no. 1 Jimmy Foxx. **$64,625**

Walter Johnson, 1909 T204 Ramly Tobacco card, one of the most popular of all 1910-era tobacco issues. The card displays light rounding to the corners, and a hint of minor wear to a few spots on the edges. With 30/70 left to right centering and minor crease in the lower left corner, and a couple of very small areas of toning on the back. **$9,987**

Addie Joss, 1910 D380 Clement Bros. Bakery card, extremely rare. Joss died from meningitis on April 14, 1911, cutting short one of baseball's greatest careers. Clement Bros. cards were issued only in Rochester, N.Y. With rounded corners, no major creases, some light staining, and pencil notations on the reverse. The back of the card features advertising for Clement Bros. bread and pies. **$11,750**

Mike "King" Kelly, 1888 N162 Goodwin Champions, one the key cards from the colorful set of 50, issued by Old Judge and Gypsy Queen Cigarettes. Bright and clean, with flawless colors and perfect registration. **$9,400**

Mickey Mantle/Roger Maris, "61 in '61 or Bust" pinback. Several different pin styles were sold by vendors in 1961 commemorating, and cheering on, Mantle's and Maris' race for Ruth's record of 60 home runs in a single season. This style pin is the rarest of all. Excellent to mint condition, 3 1/2" diameter. **$3,525**

Christy Mathewson, 1904 Allegheny Card Co., extremely rare sample card from the Allegheny Card Co. set, featuring New York Giants' young star pitcher, one of Mathewson's earliest cards. Near mint appearance. **$10,575**

Christy Mathewson, 1915 E145 Cracker Jack #88, ultra high-grade example, perfectly centered, with flawless color, a perfect red background, perfect registration, an ideal "rough" Cracker Jack card surface under magnification, bright and clean, both front and back, with sharp corners. **$16,450**

Milligan and Larkin, 1887 N690 Kalamazoo Bats, Athletics, high-grade double-player pose Kalamazoo Bats tobacco card featuring catcher Jocko Milligan tagging out left fielder Henry Larkin. With misplaced canopy that covers only 70 percent of the background, accidentally exposing the wood slats that support the canopy and the cinder blocks of the building in the immediate background. The result is one of the most amusing and ridiculous photographs to appear on a 19th-century baseball card. **$17,625**

Stan Musial, 1953 St. Louis Cardinals game-used road jersey, gray zipper-front features the team name "Cardinals" embroidered on the front, above which is displayed the club's distinctive logo of two cardinals perched upon a bat. The number "6" is appliquéed on the reverse in red on navy felt. Both the name, "Musial," and the year, "53," are chain-stitched in red along the left front tail. Situated in the collar are a "Rawlings" label and an adjacent "44" size tag. Musial has inscribed the jersey, "Stan 'The Man' Musial" on the front, below which he has added his batting statistics for 1953, "Avg 337 30 HRs 113 RB's." The jersey is completely original, with no alterations, and displays moderate wear throughout. **$44,062**

Jackie Robinson, 1951 Brooklyn Dodgers game-used home jersey. **$341,779**

Alex Rodriguez, autographed 1994 Seattle Mariners rookie alternate jersey. **$29,881**

Babe Ruth, 1915 M101-5 Sporting News #151 Rookie card. Ruth had only pitched in four games with Boston in 1915 but impressed the card manufacturer enough to warrant inclusion in this issue. Near mint example. **$44,062**

Babe Ruth, 1939-1943 signed sepia Hall of Fame postcard, the first such plaque postcard set issued. Inscribed "Sincerely Babe Ruth" in black fountain pen. Sepia Hall of Fame postcards were issued in two types. The first, designated "Type-1," was issued just prior to the opening of the Hall of Fame in 1939, while "Type-2" cards (this example) were issued shortly after the dedication. The card displays a small amount of paper residue in the corners of the reverse from having once been mounted in a scrapbook album. **$44,062**

Photo courtesy Robert Edward Auctions, Watchung, N.J.; www.RobertEdwardAuctions.com

Babe Ruth, 1933 R306 Butter Cream Confectionery card, only one other example known to exist, but its whereabouts is a mystery. **$111,625**

Photo courtesy Robert Edward Auctions, Watchung, N.J.; www.RobertEdwardAuctions.com

Babe Ruth, 1914 Baltimore News rookie card. Ruth just happened to be with the Baltimore Orioles in 1914, as a complete unknown, when the Baltimore News issued the card set that included him. **$517,250**

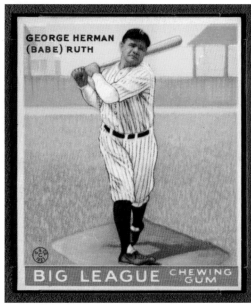

Photo courtesy Robert Edward Auctions, Watchung, N.J.; www.RobertEdwardAuctions.com

Babe Ruth, 1933 R319 Goudey #144, featuring the Babe in his classic follow-through batting pose. Four square corners with white borders and flawless colors; Ruth's image is centered slightly towards the bottom right. Crisp and clean, both front and back, with a boldly printed reverse. **$23,500**

Photo courtesy Robert Edward Auctions, Watchung, N.J.; www.RobertEdwardAuctions.com

Babe Ruth, 1934 R304 Al Demaree die-cut card, #4, exceedingly rare example of Babe Ruth from this unusual set. Issued by Chicago's Dietz Gum Co. in 1934, their unusual design combines black-and-white photographic player portraits with cartoon body art drawn by former Major League pitcher Al Demaree (hence, the name "Demaree die-cuts"). With standup tab intact. Tiny tear (less than 1/4") on the right edge (appears to be a cut, possibly relating to the die-cut process and as made). Light surface crease across Ruth's face, and a heavy horizontal crease through Ruth's foot. **$6,462**

Photo courtesy Robert Edward Auctions, Watchung, N.J.; www.RobertEdwardAuctions.com

Babe Ruth, 1938 Brooklyn Dodgers game-used cap, accompanied by two non-vintage black-and-white photos (each 10" x 8") of Ruth as a coach with the Dodgers in which he is shown wearing an identical-style cap (possibly this very one). The first of these photos pictures Ruth sitting in the dugout with Larry MacPhail, while the second captures him standing next to the grandstand as he poses with his wife and daughter. **$70,500**

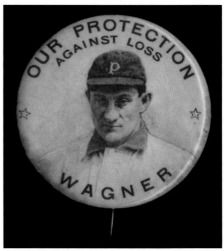

Photo courtesy Robert Edward Auctions, Watchung, N.J.; www.RobertEdwardAuctions.com

Honus Wagner, 1904 "Our Protection Against Loss" pinback, issued by a Pittsburgh insurance firm, the Commercial Oldest Accident Co. Only three known. The back paper is missing, there is rust on the reverse, and some foxing along the perimeter, 1 1/4" diameter. **$4,406**

Casey Stengel, 1910 T210 Red Border Old Mill Tobacco, shows Stengel as an outfielder with Maysville of the Blue Grass League at the beginning of his career. Bright and clean, with consistent, even wear on the corners (predominately the upper and lower left), fairly well centered (approximately 60/40 left to right), and with virtually no chipping to the fragile red borders. The front of the card has a hairline surface crease to Stengel's right (running from his shoulder to the upper left corner), and a similar surface crease in the lower right edge. The reverse has a few scattered spots...**$41,125**

Jim Thorpe, 1916 M101-5 Sporting News #176. M101-5 cards have a glossy coated surface, susceptible to creasing. This card has no creases. The front is bright and clean. The image is crisp and has perfect contrast. The corners are sharp. The card is centered approximately 70/30 left to right. The blank back is clean with a hint of toning and two tiny pinpoint chips of paper loss on the extreme edge of the top and left borders...**$41,125**

John Ward, 1887 N172 Old Judge card, hands on hips pose - "Capt. John Ward, S.S. N.Y's." Mint condition, clean front and back, with flawless square corners and strong contrast. **$29,375**

John Ward, 1888 N173 Goodwin Old Judge cabinet card, featuring Ward standing with his hands behind his back. Crisp and clean, both front and back, with particularly strong photo contrast and detail. Minor corner and edge wear. **$8,812**

1909-11 T206
HONUS WAGNER
SWEET CAPORAL

1
POOR
0005445097

Honus Wagner, 1909-1911 T206 card, American Tobacco Trust, also known as "The Beckett Wagner," compares favorably with most other low-grade examples. The colors on this card are noticeably brighter, fresher and bolder than many examples that are graded much higher. It had been stored away in ideal conditions, untouched and protected from all elements, including light, for decades. **$317,250**

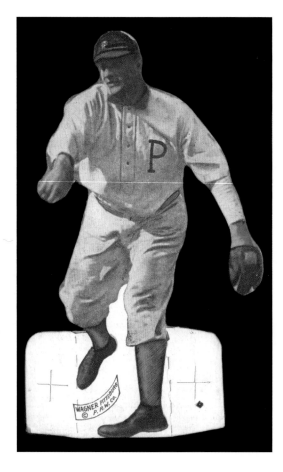

Honus Wagner, 1910 E125 American Caramel die-cut, Wagner in throwing pose, a second pose of Wagner batting is also known to exist in the set. Complete, with all flaps intact, never folded back. A very slight surface crease on Wagner's left elbow and right arm are visible only from the reverse, and there are couple of light surface creases on the folding flaps. The reverse of the card, which features a complete checklist of the Pirates in the set and advertising for American Caramels, is bright and clean, with evidence of light moisture stains on the bottom flap. **$8,225**

John Ward, 1887 N690 Kalamazoo Bats, S.S. N.Y.'s, a fresh and crisp example, one of the best of all Kalamazoo Bats or John Ward cards in existence, and one of the most desirable of all 19th-century baseball cards from any set. This set a world record for any pre-1900 card sold at auction. **$141,000**

TEXTILES

Including coverlets, embroidery, needlework, quilts, samplers, tapestries, rugs and carpets. *Also see Outsider Art.*

Coverlets

Beiderwand, William Ney, Meyerstown, Lebanon County, Pa., mid-19th century, woven red, white, green and blue wool, and cotton, one-piece coverlet with central sunburst medallion with eight-point star surrounded by eagles and stars, and borders with bird, scroll, leaf, lyre and cornucopia motifs, fringed on three edges, the bottom border with inscriptions "MADE BY WM. NEY MEYERSTOWN LEBANON CO. PA.," 86 x 90", about a 2" x 1/2" irregular shaped area of fairly unobtrusive light brown stain in center field area, fringe is good. **$1,007**

Blue and white checked, some loose seams where panels are sewn together, 79" x 82"...**$57**

Brown square and geometric decoration, on off-white ground; 96" x 72", slight tear on one edge. **$172**

Jacquard, blue and white woven wool and cotton, American, 1839, two-piece double cloth weave coverlet, the center field with rows of vase and flower designs and medallions with hearts bordered on three sides with spread-wing eagles with shields and arrows, the corner blocks inscribed "SUSAN THOMPKINS WOVE IN 1839," 92" x 78", approx. 1" x 1" loss on top right corner (not corner block), one side is longer (stretched, sagged, or woven looser) than the other...**$385**

Jacquard, Bucks County, Pa., at one corner: "M. K./ Springfi/eld: To/ Bucks: co./1843", field with eagles, flowers and geometric decoration in salmon, dark blue, and mustard, 82" x 92". **$360**

Jacquard, Fayette County, Ind., circa 1841, double lily and medallion form coverlet with cutters, oak tree and quail border, two corner panels signed "Woven in Fayette Co Indiana 1841", 7' 1" x 5' 9", minimal discoloration to fringe and outer edges...**$1,150**

Jacquard, marked "Woven by/Henry O./Overholt/1841/ For____", stylized flowers, acorns and leafage in dark blue and red on white ground, 87" x 70". **$690**

Jacquard, Pennsylvania, at one corner, "This/Coverlet/ Belongs/To/ Catherine?Diehl/1844"; field with stylized rosettes, tulips and roosters, at another corner: "S. B. Mus/ selman/ Coverlet/Weaver/Milford./ Bucks. Co/ No 473". All in red, green, and black; repetition of "Pennsylvania" in border, 80" x 88". **$600**

Embroidery, Needlework

Crewelwork panel, by Mary Balentine, western Massachusetts, 18th century, the panel with shaped hem probably a valance from a set of bed hangings, worked in polychrome wool yarns in a curvilinear floral and fruit design on a natural-colored linen ground, accompanied by an old typed exhibition card reading, "Sheffield 1733-1933/ Loaned by Mary A. Durlack/Piece of valence embroidered

Coverlet, jacquard, red, blue, green and white, border three rows of leaves and flowers, center floral and sunburst decoration, edge inscribed "John Smith J. Gackly 1838," Schaefferstown, Pa., 92" x 84". **$995**

Coverlet, jacquard, green and white, corners inscribed "M.W.M. Tenn.," borders dec with eagles, birds, potted flowers, foliage and dogs carrying flags, interior with foliage decoration, Tennessee, by Maryville Woolen Mills, late 19th century, 78" x 75". **$525**

Photo courtesy Pook & Pook Inc., Downingtown, Pa.; www.PookandPook.com

Needlework, silk on linen, verse, scene of couple, garden, sheep, and hound, flowers, Marblehead Mass., dated 1797, 14 1/2" x 9 1/2". **$3,045**

by Mary Balentine who married General John Ashley," toning, minor spots, 11 1/2" x 81"..............**$5,036**

Floral, blue vase of flowers, signed beneath "Hannah R. Knight 1837"; encircling leafy vine with tulips and other flowers, off-white ground, 23 1/4" x 23 1/4" (sight), some discoloration, maple frame...........................**$1,725**

Newcomb College, square table scarf (very rare) embroidered with stylized trees in amber and green, excellent original condition, unmarked, 15" x 15 1/4".
....**$7,200**

Picture, needlework with watercolor, two women holding lower branches of tree, third woman sitting at base of tree with lamb, house in left middle distance, 17 1/4" x 20 1/2", some damage to face of middle woman and damage to leafage near her; some rippling to paper, gilt frame......**$360**

Show towel, framed, Bucks County, Pa., needlework with spread-wing American eagle with stylized emblems in red, white and blue above "Mary Fretz/1847"; other birds, trees and flowers below; tassels at bottom, 49" x 16" (sight); bird's eye maple frame. **$1,955**

Show towel, framed Ott Family tree, Bucks County, Pa., headed by "MO"; "Elias Ott" with "1840" below; "Fredercik/Ott born/Nov. 10-1782/Eve Ott born March 26-1781" with other Otts following; asymmetrical group of stylized flowering trees in multi-colors; at bottom: "Mary Ott of Bedminster Made/This Needlework Anno Domini/1844"; 47" x 13 3/4" (sight), bird's eye maple frame. **$5,750**

Silk embroidery, of three figures under tree, two women and man nearby, 8" h, 6 1/8" w (sight). **$149**

Samplers

Hannah Bainbridge, alphabet at top, Tree of Knowledge with Adam and Eve at base; inscribed "Be/thou fait/h full unto death/and I will give thee a/crown of life"; stylized flowers and urns of flowers flanking, 10 3/4" x 8 1/4" (sight); signed lower left and right; bird's-eye maple and rosewood frame..................................**$1,265**

Keziah Jeffs, Mrs. Wetherells School, Byfield (Mass.), dated 1821, executed in a variety of green, blue, pink, and brown stitching on a cream linen ground with a central panel of floral-filled urns, stylized pine trees, perched birds and dogs beneath lines of alphabet and pious verse, all above the third panel wrought with pious verses centering a tree flanked by floral-filled baskets within a border of scrolling floral vinery. Signed at bottom, "Keziah Jeffs aged 12 years November 16 1820 Wrought this sampler at Mrs Wetherells School Byfield May 21 1821." Sight: 13 1/2" x 12", some staining and minor weakness in edges, some small holes in ground. Mounted in a later frame................................**$2,300**

Susan Magill, silk needlework with an invocation to Jesus, framed by a running border of flowers, mounted on gold foil and in wooden frame, 19th century, signed at the bottom "Susan Magill Newtown 1819," 11 1/2" x 9 1/2".
....**$1,140**

Ann Catherine Streeper, seven-line passage begins: "Jesus permit thy sacred name to stand …", green and yellow flowering trees, birds flanking tree; "Ann Catherine Streeper the daughter/Of Leonord Streeper & Sarah his Whife/Was born September the Ninth in the/Year One thousand eight hundred & 25"; birds in reeds below, followed by: "Ann Catherine Streper her work/In the 13 year of her age in the year 1838"; flowering vine border on three sides, 16 5/8" x 15 1/2" (sight). **$1,150**

Sophia Swartz, alphabet sampler, the bottom centered by a vase with flowers and a bird on a tree branch, the number 4 and ducks on either side, unframed, 19th century, signed and dated "Sophia 83 Swartz," 16 1/2" x 16 1/2". **$510**

Elizabeth Ulrick, alphabet and numerals, prose passage and "Elizabeth Ulrick 1806"; pair of birds at basket; "A rural walk in Statehouse yard"; stylized green and white flowering vine border, 20 5/8" x 15 5/8" (sight), brown letters in passage faded. **$1,610**

Tapestries

Louis Phillipe scenic tapestry, circa 1850-1860, depicting a formal garden landscape within a cartouche bordered by columns and urns beneath a foliate arch on a salmon ground. Various animals and a shepherd incorporated in scene. Whole within a border of flower heads and S-scrolls, 5' 5" x 4' 5", showing minimal and acceptable wear and fading. **$1,725**

Five tapestry seat coverings, 19th Century, one having a fox in landscape, another a deer in landscape, two with a shepherdess, another with a boy walking to school, varying from 17" x 15" to 25" x 27", some discoloration, tears and uneven edges. ....**$460 all**

Quilts

Album, pieced and appliquéd cotton, American, circa 1865, composed of 42 blocks appliquéd with flower, basket, leaf, heart, sun and moon, bird and geometric designs in solid and printed cotton fabrics on a white cotton ground, many blocks signed or stitched with the initials of the maker, one square indistinctly dated 1861 or 1867, edged and backed in white cotton, 79" x 67", several areas of light brownish stains, one square has some wool fabric with a few moth holes..**$1,125**

Album (top), pieced and appliquéd cotton, America, circa 1871, composed of 25 diamond and 21 triangle segments decorated with appliquéd and embroidered solid and printed cotton motifs including flowers, leaves fruit, Masonic emblem, shield and paisley, many squares signed by the makers, one dated 1871, edged in red cotton, 80 1/2" x 81", some of the ink signatures have run, the center diamond has a needlepoint floral design done in wool yarns and some of the stitches are missing..**$592**

American eagle, mid-19th century, appliquéd and patchwork, eagle within an oval bellflower and egg floral cartouche within a rectangular border, the whole within scrolled flowering vines. Quilted in tomato red, green and yellow calico on a cream ground, 7' 10" x 6' 7", minimal small stains in outer border...**$460**

Amish, broad open blue field with green border, 80" x 80".
....**$115**

Amish, repeating pink tree emblems, purple border, green ground, 81" x 81"..**$258**

Cotton chintz, American, early to mid-19th century, five-piece whole cloth quilt, the bottom corners removed to fit a four-poster bed, one side of the quilt is a polychrome roller-printed woven cotton fabric in a pheasant and palm tree design, the other side is roller-printed in a red and white flower and leaf design, woven braid binding, 107" x 124"...**$888**

Friendship, 30 patchwork squares with small red and yellow patterned squares, centering off-white square in each center with signature and date: "Abraham

Baltimore album, Captain Hosea C. Wyman, Civil War motif, decorated with fourteen border square panels, a large central panel with two squares below. Central large panel having a five-pointed blue star with inner white and red star. Between the upper two points is a red, white and blue American shield with owner's name "Capt. HC Wyman" and "Baltimore M.D 1863". Right side with an American flag having star-shaped field, four stars in corners. Left of American flag having crossed cannons with cannon balls. Below star on left is a displayed red eagle with blue banner in beak. Right side with a large red anchor with blue chain. Below this panel are two square panels, one with orange pot of flowers and cornucopias, the other red and yellow tulips with green leaves. Outside panels include four wreaths of red and yellow tulips; panel with rust-colored house, birds on fence and flowers signed "A.B.H."; another panel with spread wing eagle holding flowering branch with decorative banner above; another panel with colorful cornucopia of fruit and flowers; panel with red flowers and birds; panel with golden urn with flower vine; another with a green leaf heart with red dots; panel with stylized sheaf of wheat in green, yellow and red; panel with opposing green and red leaves; panel with a fruit tree with red fruit and yellow birds; and a panel with a spray of red green stemmed flowers. Appliqué work on white linen with no quilting, bound at edges with a center stitched linen backing. Colors are bright and vivid, 81" h x 64" w. Light stains to front, some minor imperfections and some additional water stains on reverse. **$13,800**

Rohn/1861," "Susan Charles/1861," "Cordelia Charles/1861," etc., 83" x 94". **$632**

Hawaiian, "The Comb of Kaiulana," circa 1850, wrought with a combination of eight-rayed combs and crowns within a stylized lei of leaves, with waffle quilting, 6' 1 1/2" x 6', with staining. **$2,300**

Oak Leaf and Flower, pieced and appliquéd cotton, American, late 19th century, with nine squares composed of four oak leaves alternating with fan-shaped flower blossoms, both surrounding a flower blossom, enclosed in an undulating flower bud and leaf vine, the motifs in red and green printed cotton on a white ground, edged and backed in white cotton, with outline and diagonal line quilting, 86" x 71", light stains, toning...........................**$385**

Pieced wool, American, early 20th century, with 35 squares set on point with four two-color stylized tulip blossoms on an off-white ground alternating with light blue squares, edged in red silk binding, off-white woven wool backing, with outline, grid, grape cluster and stylized flower blossom quilting stitches, 92" x 70", losses to edging and wool fabric around edges. **$592**

Thistle and Oak Leaf, Augusta County, Va., third quarter 19th century, the pattern repeated nine times with a diamond quilted border separating the blocks, dramatic swag and tulip border, green printed edging, each block with vine and leaf quilting, 77 1/2" x 84 1/2", small spots of fabric deterioration and some light spotting...............**$2,090**

Urn of Flowers, pieced and appliquéd cotton, American, late 19th century, composed of four large squares with an urn issuing several flower stalks bordered by carnation blossoms and leaves in solid red and green cotton fabric, some motifs embroidered with blanket stitching, the quilt edged and backed with white cotton and quilted in outline and chevron stitches, 82" x 79", some light moisture stains showing mainly on the reverse...................**$2,370**

Carpets and Rugs

Hooked

Though many have a folk-art flavor, hooked rugs were also created from popular patterns in the late 19th and early 20th centuries.

Hooked rug, wool and cotton, American, early 20th century, depicting a man and woman in the pursuit of romance, with the hooked inscription: "Take Oh! Take Those Lips Away!", mounted on a wooden frame, 33" x 50", fading, toning, scattered edge losses..........................**$1,303**

Hooked rug, wool and cotton, with a squirrel, American, early 20th century, mounted on a wooden frame, 20 3/4" x 41", minor wear, fading..**$503**

Hooked rug, wool and cotton, geometric, American, early 20th century, centered with a diamond pattern with square/triangle borders, bound with cotton twill tape, toning, 69" x 43". **$1,125**

Hooked rug, wool, geometric, American, early 20th century, with square/diamond optical illusion field with striped border, 30" x 61". **$770**

Hooked rug, wool yarn, with houses in a landscape, American, early 20th century, mounted on a wood frame, 23 1/2" x 40 1/4", couple small dark stains, small yarn loss

within orange yarn-repaired area on foreground house. **$770**

Hooked rug, Pied Piper, colorful and graphic, mounted on wood stretcher, 43 1/2" w x 25 1/2" h. **$575**

Hooked rug, with vignettes of birds and plants, all in earth tone colors with black border, 51" x approx. 60", overall scattered damage and deterioration. **$172**

Penny rug, wool, American, late 19th/early 20th century, composed of concentric discs of multicolored wool fabric edged with blanket stitching, arranged and sewn in a diamond pattern, on a woven wool backing, mounted on a wood frame, 24 1/2" x 42 1/2". **$711**

Photo courtesy James D. Julia Auctioneers, Fairfield, Maine; www.JuliaAuctions.com

Hooked rug, 19th century, yarn on burlap in a period frame, heart within a heart with anchor and cross with either side being decorated with a flowering vine. Initialed at the top "HH" and signed "Mary" and dated below "1880". The small heart in a deep blood-red coloration with the larger heart on the exterior a lighter red, the overall rug in various earth tones. Rug only, 24 1/2" w x 20" h. **$3,335**

Photo courtesy James D. Julia Auctioneers, Fairfield, Maine; www.JuliaAuctions.com

Hooked rug, starfish, first quarter of the 20th Century, woven with rows of polychrome striped squares alternating with squares depicting starfish/five petal flowers, mounted on a museum frame, 74" x 71". **$1,380**

Oriental Rugs

An authentic oriental rug or carpet is handmade, either knotted with pile or woven without pile. These rugs normally come from a broad geographical region extending from China and Vietnam in the east, to Turkey and Iran in the west, and from the Caucasus in the north to India in the south.

Bokhara, Afghanistan, with four rows of six indigo and madder red gulls on a madder red field within a lattice work and dog tooth border, 9'3" x 8'3", overall wear. **$632**

Caucasian carpet, with geometric design and alternating panels of people and animals; blue ground with yellow, green and gray, 19th/20th century, Low pile with small losses on end borders, 61" x 41 1/2". **$1,560**

Heriz, Northwest Persia, dense geometric lattice work vinery on a rose pink ground with saw tooth edge within a deep indigo guard border of stylized polychrome flower heads, 10' 1" x 7' 6", fading and discoloration throughout one quarter of end. **$1,150**

Heriz, North Persia, circa 1900, polychrome stylistic geometric latticework on a madder red field within a deep indigo main border of geometric flower heads, 10' 3" x 7', nearly full pile, ends and edges intact, some moth damage evident in corners and edges................................**$1,840**

Heriz, Northwest Persia, first quarter 20th century, indigo angular central medallion within the madder red field filled with polychrome devices centered by ivory spandrels, within the midnight-blue main border of geometric latticework, 11' 7" x 8' 6", overall general wear, losses to ends (selvage). **$345**

Isfahan prayer rug, Persia, two trees with birds centered by a vase with emerging flowers underneath a blue niche and two reserves with calligraphy, 19th/20th century, 6' 2" x 4' 5". **$1,800**

Kilim, runner, Iran, first half 20th century, typical form, comprised of a series of joined rectangular panels, each of differing geometric design. Woven in shades of red, brown, blue and cream, 9' 3" x 2' 2", minor separation of panels, minor rolling at one end. **$230**

Kuba Caucasian rug, in Lesghi star design in reds, blues, and ivory. Some wear, 3' 4" x 5' 3"...................................**$600**

Runner, Northwest Persia, central ivory scarab medallion on a midnight-blue field with dense polychrome flower heads and vinery within an ivory border of geometric designs, 10' x 3' 1"..**$460**

Sarouk, Central Persia, first quarter 20th century, indigo floral polled medallion within a wine field with scrolling polychrome floral vinery centered by turquoise spandrels, the whole within a deep indigo main border of profusely scrolling vinery and flower heads, 17' 8" x 12'...........**$8,338**

Sarouk carpet, with a floral field on a rose ground and various borders, 20th century, 12' x 8' 10"...................**$1,140**

Photo courtesy James D. Julia Auctioneers, Fairfield, Maine; www.JuliaAuctions.com

Angelis, Central Persia, circa 1910-1920, central oversized stepped medallion on a blue-black field with a grouping of nine polychrome herati design set on a madder red field with similar herati, all within a triple-stripe border, 6' 6" x 4' 5", normal wear. **$1,150**

Savonnerie carpet, with diagonal quatrefoil in ivory and caramel tones, framed by a red band and shell and leaf motif on each corner, 20th century, 18' 5" x 7' 5". **$1,140**

Collector's Note: Savonnerie is a French pile floor covering, usually large, whether made at the Savonnerie workshop or made in that manner and style. The Savonnerie factory (on the site of a former soap factory, hence the name) was established in Paris in 1627 at the Hospice de la Savonnerie at Chaillot by royal order, to provide pile carpets for use in the king's palaces and as royal gifts. The patterns are floral and architectural Renaissance conceptions, many based upon paintings and cartoons.

Tabriz, area rug with ruby red medallion and ivory spandrels, circa 1970, 6' 7" x 9' 10". **$360**

Tabriz, Persian Azerbaijan, early 20th Century, central palmette rose and pale indigo medallion within a deep indigo field of profuse floral vinery centered by pale indigo and rose spandrels, pale indigo dark border with palmettes and latticework vinery, 13' x 8' 3", minimal even wear.
....**$1,495**

Photo courtesy James D. Julia Auctioneers, Fairfield, Maine; www.JuliaAuctions.com

Dagestan, Northeast Caucasus, five differently colored octagons on a dark blue ground surrounded by a modified Kufic border, dated repeatedly "1313" in the Moslem calendar (1894). Images include saddled horses, birds, running beasts, peacocks, women in tribal dress, strange human figures, a clock telling time, combs signifying cleanliness for prayer, and other wild and diverse symbols, 12' 7" x 5'. **$6,900**

Photo courtesy James D. Julia Auctioneers, Fairfield, Maine; www.JuliaAuctions.com

Photo courtesy James D. Julia Auctioneers, Fairfield, Maine; www.JuliaAuctions.com

Lavar Kirman, Southeast Persia, circa 1900, dense polychrome floral vinery interspersed with stylized cypress trees and alternating flowering vases, the central panel forming opposing half medallions within a conforming main border of pink, beige and pale indigo flower heads, all four sides with a burnt orange cartouche in Arabic of poetic couplets, 11' 4" x 8' 1". **$14,375**

Tabriz, Northwest Persia, second quarter of the 20th Century, circular center poled medallion defined by turquoise lotus blossoms centering a floral medallion flanked by lesser urn medallions on a beige ground densely filled with vinery within a scrolling polychrome arabesque border, 18' 11" x 10' 7 1/2", staining on edge, approximately 5 1/2' from end. **$920**

Serapi, Northwest Persia, first half of the 20th century, large center red medallion with ivory and red field. Wide and thin border. Colors of brown, red, ivory with some blues and greens, 11' 10" x 9' 3", shows wear, some repairs and some small evidence of insect damage, which has been stabilized. **$920**

Tabriz, room-size carpet with a geometric floral pattern on deep red field and indigo medallion, circa 1970, 9' 7" x 12' 10". **$660**

Turkoman prayer rug, Turkmenistan, circa 1900, mihrab center containing four panels of candlestick design, the field with saw-tooth and tarantula latticework within a key and fret border, 4' 8" x 3' 10", minimal wear. **$1,610**

William Morris

William Morris (1834-1896) is the most famous of the Arts & Crafts pioneers and probably the most influential figure involved in 19th-century textile production. Key elements in Morris' designs were inspired by historic textiles that incorporated flowers found in Elizabethan gardens, and in 16th-century embroideries.

William Morris-style carpet, with floral pattern on olive green ground, 10' x 13' 9". **$1,560**

William Morris-style area rug ,with floral pattern on jade green ground, 6' x 9' 3".. **$960**

William Morris-style carpet, with a floral pattern and cream border on midnight blue ground, 8' x 10'. **$510**

William Morris-style carpet, with floral and vine pattern in deep jewel tones, 8' 2" x 10". **$840**

William Morris-style carpet, with a floral pattern in rich jewel tones, 8' 10" x 11' 9"... **$1,560**

William Morris-style runners, with floral pattern, one on indigo field, the other in greens and sand, 2' 6" x 8' and 2' 6" x 11' 5".. **$1,200 both**

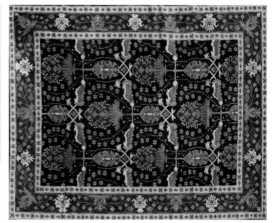

Photo courtesy Rago Arts and Auction Center, Lambertville, N.J.; www.RagoArts.com

William Morris-style carpet with a floral pattern in amber and dark plum on a black field, 9' 1" x 12' 1". **$660**

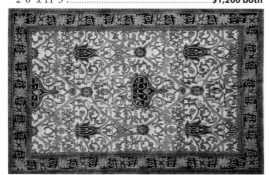

Photo courtesy Rago Arts and Auction Center, Lambertville, N.J.; www.RagoArts.com

William Morris-style area rug with floral pattern in jewel tones on a pale celadon field, 5' x 6' 10". **$480**

Tiffany

FUTURE OF THE MARKET: TIFFANY

Collecting Tiffany: Less is more

By Reyne Haines

Reyne Gallery, Cincinnati

Unfortunately, there is no crystal ball to see into the future of collecting. Collectors can be fickle and the economy can play a role in what price point people buy, and when. With that said, we can look for trends in any collecting category to help determine what markets have been stable, or volatile.

Stable markets are those that have small, but consistent, increases in value over numerous years. Volatile markets are those that have extreme highs and extreme lows. Something may enter the market at a strong price, only to cool as collecting interests wane.

Since the late 1960s, we can find a "trend" in collecting all things Tiffany. Over the last 40+ years, there has been a continued increase in value, be it 5-10 percent a year. Some types of Tiffany have increased in value in a shorter period of time. Most of these areas had little initial interest from Tiffany enthusiasts. However, as the price to obtain a piece of work by Tiffany increased, the lower-end Tiffany markets became more desirable.

My two biggest recommendations for collecting anything are 1) only buy what you like, you can never go wrong. If you buy something on speculation, and the market for such an item fades, not only does everyone else not want it, but neither do you. 2) When you find an area of collecting you do like, buy the best you can buy within your budget. In simpler terms, less is more. Buy one higher-end piece, instead of three lower-ends that equal the same price as the more expensive one. In a bad economy, the higher-end things will always sell. That market is rarely affected by economic woes. The lower to middle-of-the-road collectors tend to hold on to their money during tough times.

For many years, fine art and antiques have been a place for investors to "park" their money. A solid collection – or even a single quality piece – has often shown to increase in value at a stronger rate than that of the stock market. With that said, here are my recommendations for what to buy in the wonderful world of Louis Comfort Tiffany:

Leaded Windows: One of the more sizable and pricier categories of Tiffany collecting. While many Tiffany leaded windows sell for six figures or higher, some can still be bought on the more limited budget. Windows with religious figures or dedications were often used in churches and seem to have been all but forgotten in the Tiffany community. Perhaps an untapped market?

Lighting: Lamps, stalactites and sconces have long been a staple with Tiffany enthusiasts. The values range from the low end of a few thousand dollars to top-of-the-line at a few million. Beginning collectors should start with a desk lamp, but pursue a more rare, colored shade, or more unique base. Gold damascenes, while attractive, are the more common in the color shades. Watch for a blue or green damascene shades instead.

Photo courtesy Morphy Auctions, Denver, Pa.; www.MorphyAuctions.com

Table lamp, Russian #1910, 20" d shade has 4" aperture, "The Four Virtues" are depicted: Charitas, Veritas, Fides and Puritas. It is signed "Tiffany Studios New York #1916." Center panels are mottled in swirling multiple colors against a blue-purple background. The leading is finished in gold doré, The base is 23 1/2" h, signed "Tiffany Studios #567," finished in gold doré. Two or three hairlines in glass. **$155,000**

With leaded lamps, there are numerous factors that determine value and desirability. The first is the size and design of the shade. Is the shade common or not? Floral designs tend to be more desirable than geometric shades. The color and type of glass is another factor. You can have two identical patterned lamps, one being monochromatic, while the other is vibrant with color. This would create a dramatic difference in value. Usually (but not always), the more colorful the shade, the pricier it is.

When buyers went to Tiffany Studios to purchase a lamp for their homes, not only could they choose the style of shade they wanted and the colors, but also the type of base they wanted it to go on. Some bases were simple in design; some were more ornate. They also came in a few different patinas.

One of the more important aspects to consider when buying a Tiffany lamp is condition. If you are eyeing a great floral lamp with strong colors and a great base, but it has replacement glass, numerous loose cracks or the patina has been polished, take a moment to reconsider. With these factors in mind, make sure you pay accordingly, and know that they will make the lamp a little tough to sell down the road.

Pottery: A medium many people don't recognize as one made at Tiffany Studios. Tiffany had an interest in pottery, and this should come as no surprise considering the success of other American artists like George Ohr, or that of Newcomb College and Rookwood. While Tiffany had a passion for pottery, it was not one of his more successful ventures. Tiffany pottery was made from 1904 until 1914. It is estimated that around 2,000 pieces were made during that time.

Tiffany's pottery was quite organic in nature. The shapes, designs and glazes often imitate leaves and floral motifs. Numerous pieces can still be found today unglazed. It has been said the pieces were thrown and then left unglazed until purchased so the customer could determine the look they wanted.

This market, while still a little untapped, is gaining interest among Tiffany collectors and art-pottery enthusiasts. When acquiring a piece of Tiffany pottery, the best examples are often glazed in more than one color, or are heavily carved.

Bronze: Collecting Tiffany bronze offers something for everyone, from simple bronze figural paperweights to complete desk sets, cigar stands to planters. The sheer volume of things made in bronze by Tiffany Studios is staggering.

While the paperweights are interesting, they are not an investment-level collectible. There are also a multitude of bronze bowls, plates and compotes readily available for a few hundred dollars each. These will also stay fairly inexpensive in price due to the volume available on the market.

If you like investment-level items that have function, I would recommend collecting one of the desk sets. There are a number of different designs available, but collecting one of the more rare patterns will make finding pieces challenging, and also offer desirability with collectors when the time comes to sell. A few patterns that fall into the "rare" category would be Nautilus, Spanish or Enameled.

Tiffany also made a short run of bronze mirrors. They were very Art Nouveau in design, functional and are not often seen on the market.

Finally, there were a variety of inkwells made over the years that were not part of any desk-set series. They sometimes took form as sea life, or were a combination of two media, like glass and bronze. Finding an example can take time, and will often cost considerably more than a desk-set inkwell.

Glass: One of the most diverse categories you can collect. You can build a collection based on shape, color, decoration or period. Collecting glass can be affordable for any budget, starting with tiles selling for as low as $50 each, or a museum-quality aquamarine vase for as much as $500,000.

As with many creations, there are uncommon shapes, colors that are more desirable than others, rare techniques, and exhibition pieces that can greatly increase the value of one piece over another.

Simple gold and blue pieces, while attractive, are readily available on the market and will never increase that substantially in your lifetime. I have heard the argument many times: How one cannot afford a $10,000 piece of glass, but they have 10 pieces valued at $1,000 each in their collection. When collecting for investment, less is more. It is better to have the one highly desirable piece in your collection than a dozen common pieces. When the time comes to sell the collection, the higher-end piece will most often have increased in value faster, and will be easier to sell.

Some of the shapes and techniques recommended when collecting Tiffany glass are:

Photo courtesy Rago Arts and Auction Center, Lambertville, N.J.; www.RagoArts.com

Vase, bottle-shaped, in tomato red Favrile glass. Signed "1043 K L. C. Tiffany – Favrile," 5 3/4" h. **$5,100**

Floriforms – decorated, not plain, tall with strong color. Weak color can lower the value on what might normally be considered a desirable piece.

Tel el Amarna vases – especially in unusual colors

Engraved and Cameo vases – Cameo glass is often thought of as being a product designed by French artisans, however it was also a technique used in Tiffany glass for several years. Most cameo vases are heavily carved with padded flowers, leaves and grapes.

Agate – These vases came in colors such as blue, olive, tan/brown and were sometimes faceted.

Paperweights - Paperweight vases are quite desirable among collectors. The term "paperweight" essentially means a vase that is cased in an outer layer of clear glass. They are often internally decorated with a variety of colorful flowers and leaves. Some vases offer an iridescent interior, while others do not. Also, you may find some made with reactive glass, which seemingly changes color depending on the light.

Cypriote – Cypriote glass offers an unusual surface made to emulate that of early Roman glass.

Lava – The term best describes the outward appearance of Tiffany lava vases: Dark-colored vessels with a gold "molten lava" overflowing from the mouth of the piece.

One of the most important caveats to remember when collecting Tiffany: There are many reproductions on the market and new ones surface every year. Some are better than others. Until you have spent a good deal of time learning the difference between what is new and what is old, my strongest recommendation is to buy from a dealer you know and trust.

Reyne Haines, owner of Reyne Gallery in Cincinnati, is a regular appraiser on PBS' Antiques Roadshow. She is the author of The Art of Glass: The Collection from the Dayton Art Institute and has contributed to numerous books and articles on collecting. Haines is also the co-owner and founder of www.JustGlass.com. She may be reached at 513-504-8159.

Louis Comfort Tiffany (1849-1934) established a glass house in 1878 primarily to make stained-glass windows. In 1890, in order to utilize surplus materials at the plant, Tiffany began to design and produce "small glass," such as iridescent glass lampshades, vases, stemware and tableware in the Art Nouveau manner. Commercial production began in 1896. Tiffany developed a unique type of colored iridescent glass called Favrile, which differs from other art glass in that it was a composition of colored glass worked together while hot. The essential characteristic is that the ornamentation is found within the glass; Favrile was never further decorated. Different effects were achieved by varying the amount and position of colors. Tiffany and the artists in his studio also are well known for their fine work in other areas: bronzes, pottery, jewelry, silver and enamels. *Also see Jewelry.*

Photo courtesy Rago Arts and Auction Center, Lambertville, N.J.; www.RagoArts.com

Vase, ceramic, bottle-shaped in verdigris micro-crystalline glaze, with bronze lip around rim, 1" firing line under glaze on base. Incised "LCT," 12 1/4" x 5 1/2". **$2,040**

Art

Painting, Louis Comfort Tiffany, (American, 1848-1933), European Flower Market, oil on canvas, market set up in town square. The vendors having a variety of colorful flowers, each section with their own shade umbrella. A large building is seen in the background and a woman has selected some flowers and placed them in her basket. Signed lower right. Housed in a carved-wood stained frame, 16" x 20". **$39,100**

Ceramics

Vase, ceramic, bottle-shaped covered in a dynamic cobalt and gray crystalline glaze. Touch-ups to two small and shallow exterior chips. Signed "LCT 7," 11" x 8". **$1,920**

Vase, ceramic, deeply embossed with dogwood blossoms on a white bisque surface and a high-glaze green interior. minor staining. Marked "BP206" (for "Bronze Pottery"), 9" x 14". **$5,700**

Vase, porcelain, embossed with chestnut branches, covered in blue and green glaze dripping on an ivory ground. Opposing hairlines, one with restoration. Signed "LCT 7," remnant of foil label, 9 1/2" x 6 1/2". **$5,400**

Clocks

Clock (shelf), bronze, Tiffany & Co., with Roman figures and winged griffins in all over gilding, circa 1900, 24" h.
....**$4,200**

Glass

Bowl, Favrile Pastel Rib Optic, shaded green with opalescent feather panels, signed "5 - 1925 L.C.T. Favrile" around a polished pontil mark. First quarter 20th century. 1 7/8" h, 5 3/4" d...**$488**

Bowl, Favrile Rib Optic, gold iridescent, ruffled rim, signed "L.C.T." within the polished pontil mark. First quarter 20th century. 2" h, 4 1/2" d...**$287**

Center bowl, gold Favrile glass with green leaves and tendrils, complete with double flower frog. Bowl and frog etched "8064K L.C. Tiffany Favrile," 4" x 10 3/4".
....**$3,120 both**

Open Salt, Favrile, gold iridescent, scalloped rim, signed "L.C.T.", polished pontil mark. First quarter 20th century. 1" h, 2 5/8" d...**$161**

Perfume bottle, Favrile glass, with trailing-vine decoration, engraved "L.C. Tiffany Favrile 1926G" and with paper label, 4 1/4" h. **$5,462**

Vase (baluster), blue Favrile glass, some burst bubbles near rim. Etched "1154 6163 J L.C. Tiffany Favrile," 10 1/4" x 8"...**$2,400**

Vase, Favrile glass, gold-ribbed vase with flaring lip, circular base; incised under base: "1523-4962M L.C. Tiffany Inc. Favrile," 7" h. **$862**

Vase, Favrile glass with gold pulled-feather decoration on heat-reactive glass with a lustrous pale-yellow ground. Calcium deposits and scratching to interior. Etched "L.C. Tiffany Favrile F140" and circular paper label, 9 1/2" x 4".
....**$1,560**

Clock (desk), bronze, in the Art Deco pattern with red enamel squares, in brass wash. Minor pitting to finish. Stamped "Tiffany & Co. New York Louis C. Tiffany Furnaces Inc. 360" and circular stamp, 5 1/2" x 5 3/4" x 4". **$8,400**

Coupe, Favrile glass, floriform with green pulled-feather decoration and gold luster interior. Etched "8206E L.C. Tiffany – Favrile," 4 1/2" x 5 1/2". **$2,280**

Trivet (circular), Favrile glass mosaic, depicting a dragonfly in gold tones against a blue and green mottled glass swirl. In original copper frame. Script signature "Tiffany Studios," 7" d. **$10,800**

Vase (miniature), Favrile glass, two-handled form with green pulled-feather decoration on orange and lime green ground. Etched "L.C.T. N2011," 2 3/4" x 3 1/4". **$2,520**

Vase (miniature), Favrile glass, agate, etched "L.C.T. R543," 2 1/2" h. **$7,800**

Vase (miniature), Favrile glass, agate. Paper label, 3 1/2". **$3,480**

Vase (miniature), Favrile glass, agate. Etched "L.C.T. Favrile 328X," 3 1/4" h. **$9,000**

Vase (miniature), Favrile glass, with blue and gold luster finish. Etched "L.C.T. N1907," 3" h. **$5,400**

Vase (miniature), Favrile glass, floriform, with green hearts and vines on gold iridescent ground. Signed "4167L L.C. Tiffany – Favrile," 6" h. **$2,640**

Vase (miniature), Favrile glass, floriform with green pulled-feather decoration on opalescent ground. Signed "L.C. Tiffany - Y 7226 – Favrile," 6" h. **$2,520**

Vase (miniature), Favrile glass, in a luster agate pattern. Etched "L.C.T. M6407," paper label, 4 1/4" h. **$3,600**

Vase (miniature), Favrile glass, in a luster agate pattern. Etched "L.C.T. N6422," paper label, 3 1/4" h. **$2,280**

Vase (miniature), Tel El Amarna blue Favrile glass, Etched "L.C.T. N2673," remnants of two paper labels, 2 1/2". **$2,640**

Vase (miniature), Favrile glass, "zipper" form. Etched "L.C.T.," paper label, 3 3/4" h. **$3,900**

Vase (miniature), red Favrile glass, "zipper" form with blue iridescent pattern. Marked, "T 2037 L. C. T.," 3 3/4" h. **$3,600**

Window, leaded glass in a geometric pattern. One short break to glass. Unmarked. Frame: 25" x 32 3/4". **$3,600**

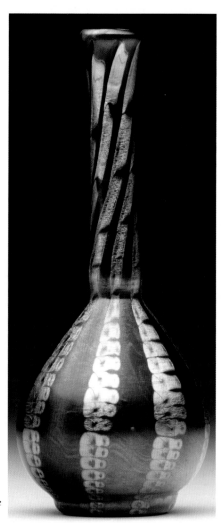

Vase (miniature), red Favrile glass, "zipper" form with blue iridescent pattern. Etched "L.C.T. 0300," 4 3/4". **$3,600**

Tiffany vase, gold Favrile, footed shouldered form, tapered flaring rim, signed "4335F L.C. Tiffany-Favrile," circa 1911, 13" h. **$3,200**

Tiffany vase, Favrile, attenuated onion-form cup, ribbed sides, short knopped standard, domed ribbed circular foot, golden iridescence, inscribed "L.C. Tiffany-Favrile 1646G," circa 1912, 15" h. **$2,750**

Tiffany vase, decorated Favrile, bottle form, opaque yellow with gold and purple pulled feathers, signed "T5227 L.C.T.," 7" h. **$2,950**

Tiffany gold Favrile vase, cylindrical form, bulging crimps in chain pattern, half moon iridescent gold rim, signed "O6369 L.C.T.," circa 1901, 6 1/2" h. **$1,750**

Tiffany cabinet vase, blue Favrile, corset-shaped body, double applied chain design, bright rich gold overtones, button pontil, signed "220G L.C. Tiffany-Favrile," 3 1/2" h. **$1,650**

Tiffany metal and glass paperweight, green stained Favrile glass, Grapevine pattern, signed "Tiffany Studios New York 936," 3 3/4" d. **$300**

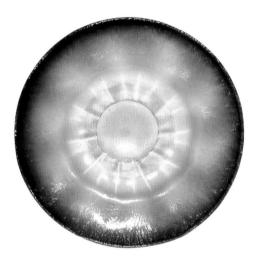

Tiffany compote, green pastel, amber optic ribbed, bright green iridescent green stretch border, signed "1278 L.C. Tiffany Inc. Favrile," 8" w. **$650**

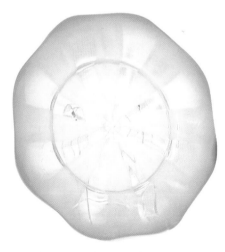

Tiffany dinner plate, green pastel, scalloped rim, alternating green and opalescent bands, 11" w. **$600**

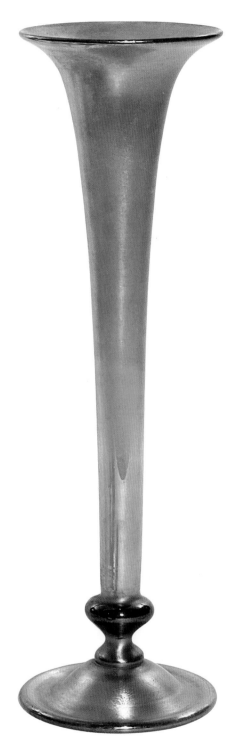

Tiffany trumpet vase, gold Favrile, footed, knopped standard, flaring trumpet rim, blue overtones, signed "1511-8203L L.C. Tiffany-Favrile," circa 1917, 18" h. **$2,200**

Tiffany finger bowl and underplate, gold Favrile, signed "L.C.T. Favrile," 6" d. **$300**

Tiffany low bowl, blue Favrile, scalloped rim, diagonally ribbed, signed "1277 L.C. Tiffany Favrile," 6" w. **$400**

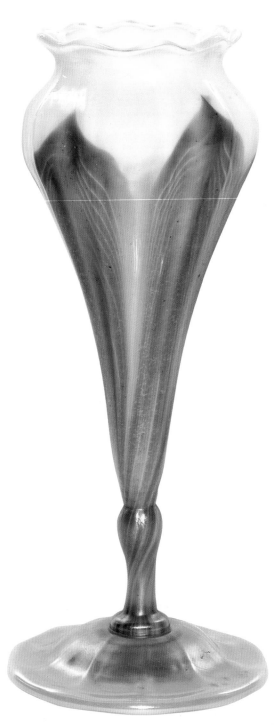

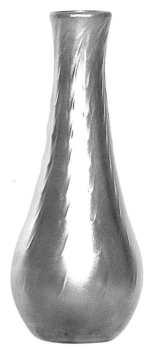

Tiffany vase, Favrile floriform, creamy-white opalescent elongated onion form, emerald green striated feathering decoration, short knopped stem, raised on slightly domed circular foot, inscribed "L.C.T. 4744A," 9 1/2" h. **$5,000**

Tiffany vase, gold Favrile, bulbous tick form, internal zipper pattern, signed "1540-1490N L.C. Tiffany-Inc. Favrile," circa 1919, 12" h. **$1,100**

Photo courtesy Early Auction Co. LLC

Tiffany vase, diminutive Favrile, ovoid form in opal, green and iridescent gold pulled feather decoration, signed "9833E L.C.T. Favrile," circa 1911, 1 1/4" h. **$1,100**

Photo courtesy Early Auction Co. LLC

Tiffany vase, squatty iridescent green body, gold Favrile chain pattern dec, lemon interior, signed "L325 L.C. Tiffany-Favrile," 6 1/4" w. **$3,250**

Photo courtesy Early Auction Co. LLC

Tiffany paperweight vase, cylindrical bulbous translucent form, internal decoration with white-stemmed daffodils with red and yellow stamens, green striated leaves, button pontil, signed "2973G L.C. Tiffany-Favrile," 7 1/2" h. **$18,000**

Tiffany cabinet vase, shouldered form, green iridescent pulled feather on gold ground, blue overtones, circa 1898, signed "L.C. Tiffany J4833," 2 3/4" h. **$850**

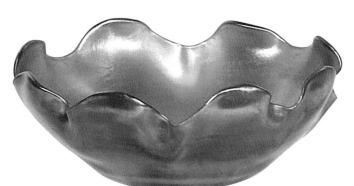

Tiffany bowl, iridescent gold Favrile, scalloped rim, signed "L.C.T.," 7" w. **$700**

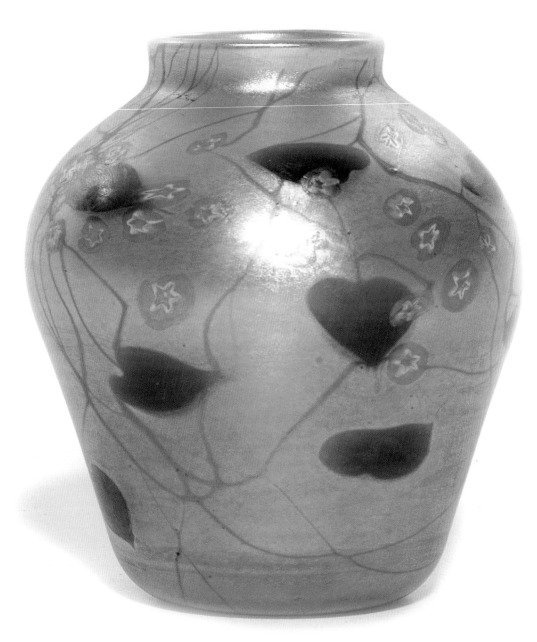

Photo courtesy Early Auction Co. LLC

Tiffany gold Favrile shouldered vase, ovoid body, green hearts and vines, white millifiori, signed "8529C L.C. Tiffany-Favrile," circa 1908, 4 1/4" h. **$2,000**

Photo courtesy Early Auction Co. LLC

Tiffany vase, iridescent green, double gourd form, gold pulled feather decoration, button pontil, partial label, 6" w. **$2,500**

Tiffany diminutive vase, Favrile, opal, ovoid, shouldered form, green and iridescent gold pulled feather dec, signed "6051 L.C.T. Favrile," circa 1912, 1 1/4" h. **$950**

Tiffany vase, Favrile decorated, green ovoid form, gold pulled feather, opal rim, button pontil, signed "L.C.T. O5127," circa 1901, 6" h. **$2,100**

Tiffany ovoid cabinet vase, creamy opal with gold and green pulled feather dec, 3" h. **$750**

Tiffany cabinet vase, bulbous form, iridescent green, gold heart and vines decoration, spatter of white millifiori, signed clockwise "V9280 L.C.T." **$3,500**

Lighting

Table lamp, bronze, with electrified oil font, topped by a pebbled shade by unknown maker. Base stamped "Tiffany Studios New York," 14 1/2" x 12"..................**$9,600**

Table lamp, Black Eyed Susan, on a three-socket fluted base. A couple of minor breaks to glass, fine original bronze patina. Stamped "Tiffany Studios New York 370S182," 22 1/2" x 16"..................**$48,000**

Table lamp, Geometric its conical shade of leaded amber slag glass over a four-socket base in bright gold finish. Patina compromised on base. Stamped "Tiffany Studios New York 1493," 25" x 20 1/2". **$12,000**

Photo courtesy Morphy Auctions, Denver, Pa.; www.MorphyAuctions.com

Bronze latticework base for a no. 29727 Tiffany Studios lamp, "studded" with glass cabochons replicating jade stones, in original condition with finial switch, six original sockets and cap. **$92,000**

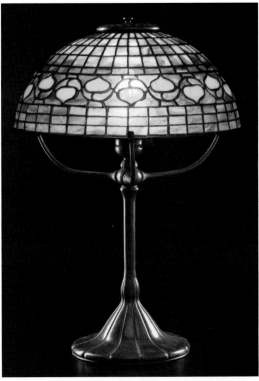

Photo courtesy Rago Arts and Auction Center, Lambertville, N.J.; www.RagoArts.com

Table lamp, Acorn, shade with blue, green and yellow slag glass over a three-arm, single-socket fluted bronze base. Fine original patina, several short breaks to glass. Shade and base stamped "Tiffany Studios New York," base with "TGDCo 259," 21" x 14". **$13,200**

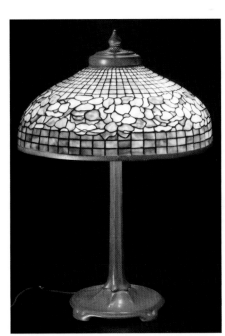

Photo courtesy Rago Arts and Auction Center, Lambertville, N.J.; www.RagoArts.com

Table lamp, Dogwood, on a four-socket elongated organic base (Taller version of this form). A couple short lines to glass, original bronze patina. Stamped "Tiffany Studios New York 531," 31" x 21". **$45,000**

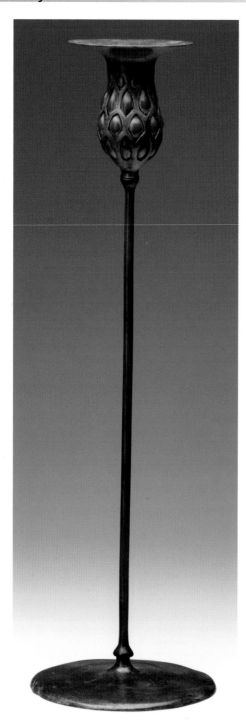

Candlestick, bronze floriform with blown-in green glass, complete with bobeche. Stamped "Tiffany Studios New York 91100," 20". **$2,280**

Metalware, Watches

Cane, semi-crook sterling handle is 2 1/3" high and 3 1/4" to the side. It has a hammered texture and two raised rings near the bottom, as well as a scalloped edge at the base. It is initialed "D.H.H." for the owner and it is marked "Tiffany Co., Sterling". The shaft is snakewood that has a slight curve from age. It ends with a 1 1/3" white metal and iron ferrule. The overall length is 36". It is circa 1890.
....**$1,725**

Cane handle, gold and enamel with moonstone and diamonds. The cylindrical handle is 2" high and 3/4" in diameter. A cabochon moonstone is set in a gold bezel on the top that is seated on white enamel with guilloche. The body of the handle is royal-blue enamel with guilloche. Applied on the blue enamel is a gold swallow in flight. It is inlaid with tiny rose-cut diamonds. A 1/4" gold band at the base is marked "Tiffany & Co., 14k". Mounted on anebony shaft of the same period and there is a 1 1/2" brass and iron ferrule. The overall length is 36 1/2". It is circa 1890.
....**$10,350**

Desk set, 11 pieces, gold doré, in the Bookmark pattern: cigar box, letter opener, inkwell, blotter ends, notebook holder, stamp box, rocker blotter, two letter holders, and a calendar. Stamped "Tiffany Studios New York," and numbered. Cigar box: 2 1/2" x 6" x 5 1/2". ....**$3,600 all**

Wristwatch, Art Deco, platinum and diamond, rect ivory-tone dial with Arabic numeral indicators, 17 jewel International Watch Co. movement, bezel and lugs with bead-set diamond melee, engraved accents, black cord band, case with Krementz hallmark, 7" l.. **$940**

Watch, pocket, Tiffany, hunting case, sterling silver. **$250.**

TOOLS

Before the advent of the assembly line and mass production, practically everything required for living was handmade at home or by a local tradesman or craftsman. The cooper, the blacksmith, the cabinetmaker and the carpenter all had their special tools.

Early examples of these hand tools are collected for their workmanship, ingenuity, place of manufacture or design. Modern-day craftsmen often search out and use old hand tools in order to authentically recreate an object.

Arithmometer, Burkhardt, black-enameled plate, eight slides, crank and 16-digit display, oak case, German operating instructions, retail transfer of Carl H. Reuter, Philadelphia, 23". **$1,528**

Auger, E. C. Stearns, No. 4, adjustable, hollow, 70% japanning. **$60**

Axe head, ship builder's, Campbell's, XXX, New Brunswick, 6" w. **$55**

Balance, brass beam, solid arm, two trays, brass pillar with finial and lever adjustment, mahogany base, F. Attwood, Brimingham, 16" h. **$235**

Bicycle wrench, Billings & Spencer Co., made for Pope Mfg. Co., patent Jan. 15, 1895, adjusting screw on side, 5 1/2". **$95**

Brace

    P. S. & W., No. 1202, Samson patent ball bearing chuck, rose-wood handle, 1895 patent date, 12" sweep. **$40**

    Stanley, No. 923-8, 8" sweep. **$55**

    Yankee, No. 2101-10, 10" sweep. **$65**

Chamfer knife, cooper's, L. & I. J. White, laminated blade. **$65**

Chisel

    Buck Bros., 3/8" bevel edge, cast steel..............................**$45**

    Stanley, No. 750, 5/8" bevel edge, markd "Stanley, D., Made in USA," 9 1/4" l..**$35**

Clamp, wood, adjustable. **$45**

Clapboard marker, Stanley, No. 88, 80% nickel remains. **$25**

Photo courtesy of Green Valley Auctions.

Plane, iron and wood combination, embossed "STANLEY/No45," incomplete set of 14 irons, orig wooden box with paper label, with modern dovetailed box, fine. **$99**

Photo courtesy of Green Valley Auctions

Plane, wooden cornice/crown molding, stamped "P.CHAPIN/ MAKER/BALTo" and "5 1/2 INCH," loss of one handle. **$285**

Compass, surveyor's type, 5 1/2" d compass card divided 0-90 in four quadrants, brass needle clamp, mahogany body, straight maple arm, two bubble levels, bone vernier w/screw thread adjustment, two horizontal sights, two vertical sights, George Leighton Whitehouse, Dover, NH, fitted green box, 14" l. **$2,350**

Doweling machine, Stanley, No. 77, 3/8" cutter. **$375**

Draw knife

C. E. Jennings, pattern maker's type, black egg-shaped handles, 4". **$40**

Whitherby, Winstead, Connecticut, folding handles, 8". .**$70**

Fret saw, Miller Falls Co., No. 2, deep throat, extra blades, orig box, 12" l. **$175**

Hammer

Claw, Stanley, 7 oz, bell face. **$25**

Magnetic tack, Stanley, No. 601, original decal. **$40**

Hand drill

Miller Falls, No. 353, ratchet, three-jaw chuck, solid steel frame, 11" l. **$50**

North Bros., Yankee No. 1530A, right and left hand ratchet movement, remnants of orig decal, original box. **$175**

Jeweler's vice, Stevens Patent, c1900, 2" jaws. **$175**

Jointer and raker gauge, Simonds, No. 342, adjustable. **$30**

Nippers, W. Schollhorn, Bernard's patent, Pat. Oct 24, 90% nickel plating, 1899. ....**$25**

Nut wrench

Boos Tool Corp, Kansas City, Missouri, screw adjust, orig box, 6" l. **$85**

Boston Wrench Co., Boston, Massachusetts, quick adjust nut, patent Oct. 2, 1906, 6" l. **$195**

Octant, ebony, brass index arm, ivory vernier, double pinhole, three shades, finial and scale engraved SBR (Spencer, Browning & Co.), stained oak case, two printed labels, "John Kehew, Nautical Instrument Maker, 69 North Water St., New Bedford," 11" radius. **$940**

Pipe wrench

Balin Tool Co., Los Angeles, California, patent no. 2210274, spring-loaded jaw, 10". **$165**

Eaton, Cole & Burnham, Franklin patent, July 20, 1886 ....**$135**

Plane

Preston & Sons, miniature, beech, 4" l. **$95**

Record, No. 050, "Improved Combo," metallic, Sheffield, England, orig cutters, orig wood box, 9" l. **$185**

Stanley, No. 3, made in USA logo, rosewood handle, circa 1950. ....**$100**

Photo courtesy of Skinner Inc.

Radius octant, ebony, R.W.S. Stevens, bone scale divided 0-100, brass index arm, mirror double pinhole sight, three shades, adjustable magnifier, bone plaque and two of three brass feet, 12" radius. **$295**

Photo courtesy of Green Valley Auctions

Plane, wooden plow, stamped "A. HOWLAND & Co/ N.Y." and "NO.96," 12". **$240**

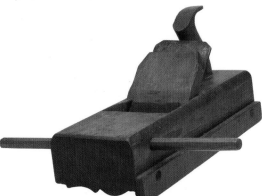

Photo courtesy of Green Valley Auctions

Plane, wooden cornice/crown molding, 13 1/4" l. **$290.**

Stanley, No. 4, type 11, three patent dates cast in bed, dark rosewood handle. **$115**

Stanley, No. 5, Jack, 1910 patent date cast in bed, dark rosewood handle, tall knob. **$135**

Stanley, No. 9-1/2, block, adjustable throat and cutter. **$40**

Stanley, No. 20, Circular, locking screw, '92 patent date on cutter. **$225**

Stanley, No. 72, chamfer, cast cap screw, brass star-wheel date, rosewood handle and knob, 1886 patent date on cutter. **$395**

Stanley, No. 271, router, 3" l. **$65**

Pliers, W. Schollhorn, Bernard's patent, parallel jaws, top nippers, blued, 6 1/2" l. **$25**

Protractor, brass sector rule, two quadrant arcs, Price, No. 726625, 24". **$294**

Putty knives, Stanley, Handyman, cocobolo handles, six-pc set, original box. **$95**

Ratchet brace, Stanley No. 2101, Yankee, 14" l. **$75**

Rip saw, Henry Disston & Sons, No. 12, London Spring steel, four-screw apple wood handle with early wheat carving, 1896-1917 medallion, 28" l. **$145**

Saw jointer, Atkins. **$30**

Saw set, Stanley, No. 43, pistol-grip, original box. **$60**

Saw vise, Sears, Roebuck & Co., No. 4920, Dunlap, original box, 11" l. **$55**

Screwdriver, spiral ratchet, North Bros. Mfg. Co., Philadelphia Yankee No. 30A, three orig straight bits, original box. ...**$50**

Yankee No. 35, one orig bit, 12" l. **$35**

Ship caulking mallet, oak head, 15-1/2" l **$85**

Shipwright's slick, L. H. Watts, New York, 2 1/2" size, 22 1/2" l. **$245**

Slide rule, boxwood, circa 1800, 24" l. **$395**

Socket gouge, Zenith, 1/4", 12 1/2" l. **$30**

Spoke pointer, Hargrave, Cincinnati Tool Co., No. 343, 90% enamel remains. **$65**

Sweep gouge, J. B. Addis & Sons, No. 9, rosewood handle, 5/8" medium sweep. **$30**

Swivel vice, North Bros., Yankee No. 1993, quick adjusting swivel base, cam-action lock, 2 3/4" jaws. **$115**

Tap and die set, Greenfield No. AA-4, two-piece adjustable die screw plate. **$45**

Toolbox, machinist's, Gerstner, walnut, 11 drawers, 26" w, 9" d, 15 1/2" h. **$390**

Yard rule, Stanley, No. 41, maple. **$45**

Wire gauge, Starrett Co., L. S., Athol, Massachusetts, No. 283, U.S. standard, 3 1/2" l. **$15**

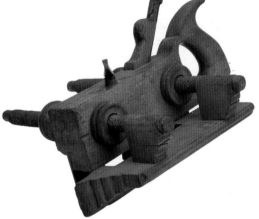

Photo courtesy of Green Valley Auctions

Workbench, wooden, full-length storage trough at back, shelf below, bench vise at right end, second vise, iron hold fast, 116" l x 35" h x 25 1/4" deep. **$880**

Photo courtesy of Green Valley Auctions

Plane, wooden plow, stamped "SANDUSKY TOOL CO," and "611", 11 1/2". **$155**

Photo courtesy of Joy Luke Auctions

Plane, Stanley, cast iron, type 2, circular, No. 113, 10" l. **$70**

Photo courtesy of Green Valley Auctions

Plane, wooden cornice/crown molding, 14 3/4". **$85**

Stair saw, 11 1/2". **$60**

Wooden croze, tiger maple and ivory, 15" l. **$220**

Hatchet, adze, 21 3/4". **$85**

Toys

TOYS

Barbie

Barbie the fashion doll was launched in 1959. The doll is produced by Mattel Inc., founded in 1945 by Harold "Matt" Matson and Elliot Handler. Handler's wife, Ruth, is regarded as the creator of Barbie.

In the early 1950s, Ruth Handler watched her daughter, Barbara, at play with paper dolls, and noticed that she often gave them adult roles. At the time, most children's toy dolls were representations of infants.

During a trip to Europe in 1956 with her children, Barbara and Kenneth, Ruth Handler came across a German doll called Bild Lilli. She purchased three of the adult-figured dolls, gave one to her daughter and took the others back to Mattel.

Ruth Handler redesigned the doll (with help from engineer Jack Ryan) and named her Barbie, after Handler's daughter. The doll made its debut at the American International Toy Fair in New York on March 9, 1959. This date is also used as Barbie's official birthday. Mattel acquired the rights to the Bild Lilli doll in 1964 and production of Lilli was halted.

Barbie's full name is Barbara Millicent Roberts. In a series of novels published by Random House in the 1960s, her parents' names are given as George and Margaret Roberts from the fictional town of Willows, Wis. Her beau, Ken Carson, first appeared in 1961.

Photo courtesy McMasters Harris Auction Co., Cambridge, Ohio; www.McMastersHarris.com

#1 Ponytail Barbie, with stand, blonde hair, black/white eyes, red lips, straight legs. Gold hoop earrings. Hair has replaced rubber band in ponytail. Torso slightly stained. One metal reinforcement missing from hole in foot. Pedestal stand prongs slightly bent. **$3,450**

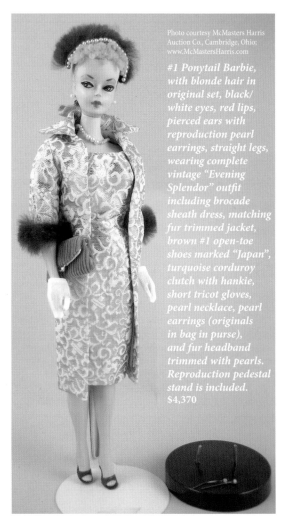

Photo courtesy McMasters Harris Auction Co., Cambridge, Ohio; www.McMastersHarris.com

#1 Ponytail Barbie, with blonde hair in original set, black/white eyes, red lips, pierced ears with reproduction pearl earrings, straight legs, wearing complete vintage "Evening Splendor" outfit including brocade sheath dress, matching fur trimmed jacket, brown #1 open-toe shoes marked "Japan", turquoise corduroy clutch with hankie, short tricot gloves, pearl necklace, pearl earrings (originals in bag in purse), and fur headband trimmed with pearls. Reproduction pedestal stand is included. $4,370

#1 Ponytail Barbie, brunette hair, black/white eyes, red lips, cheek blush, pierced ears with hoop earrings, straight legs, wearing black/white striped swimsuit and black "Japan" marked open-toe shoes, in box with black pedestal stand and booklet. Ponytail is loose and rubber band is replaced, left leg does not move and appears to be "welded" to body. Stand is slightly scuffed and has a couple of tiny scratches, prongs are rusted. Box insert is replaced; box is creased and worn and corners are split, two have been repaired with tape. 11 1/4" doll. **$8,050**

#2 Ponytail Barbie, in original box with pedestal stand. Blonde hair, black/white eyes, red lips, faint cheek blush, pierced ears, wearing original black/white striped swimsuit and black "Japan" marked #1 open-toe shoes, in box with black wire and pedestal stand. Feet stained from shoes, hair appears to be in original set, bottom rubber band replaced in ponytail. Black wire stand is discolored, pedestal is slightly scuffed. Box insert is replaced, box not mint, writing on box bottom. **$6,900**

#3 Brunette Ponytail Barbie. Brunette hair, blue eyes, red lips, pierced ears, straight legs. Wearing Commuter Set, navy jacket with matching skirt, white satin body blouse, blue/white checked body blouse, floral silk hat, "Japan" marked open-toe shoes, crystal necklace with matching bracelet, short white nylon gloves; red cardboard hatbox. One shoe is navy, the other is black. **$1,035**

#4 Blond Ponytail Barbie. Blonde hair, blue eyes, red lips, pierced ears, straight legs. Wearing original black/white striped swimsuit and black open-toe shoes (both marked "Japan"). Feet are stained from shoes. **$201**

#4 Ponytail Barbie, wearing "Theatre Date". Straight legs, blonde hair in original top knot (bottom rubber band replaced), pierced ears, blue eyes, light cheek blush. Wearing complete outfit of green satin skirt and jacket with matching hat, white satin blouse and green "Japan" marked open toe shoes. Skirt has small amount of dark discoloration on front. **$172**

#5 Ponytail Barbie, in original swimsuit. Titian hair, blue eyes, red lips, pierced ears, faded eyebrows. Wearing original one-piece black/white striped swimsuit and black "Japan" marked open-toe shoes. Discoloration on back of right leg. **$201**

#5 Ponytail Barbie, with black wire stand, blonde hair, blue eyes, red lips with some color loss, pierced ears, straight legs. Wearing homemade dress with blue corduroy purse, unmarked black o/t shoes (one strap split). Black wire stand included. **$115**

American Girl Barbie, wearing "Swingin' Easy", blonde hair, blue eyes, yellow lips, bendable legs. Wearing green floral print dress. **$258**

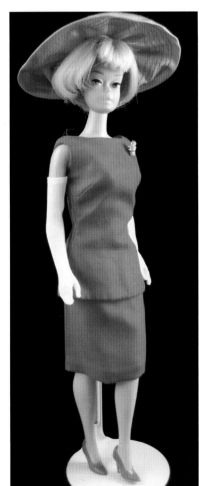

Blonde American Girl Barbie. Blonde hair, blue eyes, cream lips, pierced ears, bendable legs. Wearing "Music Center Matinee", two-piece outfit of red chiffon over taffeta with diamond look pin, rose colored picture hat, and red closed toe spikes marked "Japan". Sides of head are dark. **$460**

American Girl Barbie, brunette side-part hair, blue eyes, beige lips, wearing original multicolored stripe swimsuit. Head is dark, legs are very loose, several small pin-sized holes in feet and left toe chip. Scratch on back. Swimsuit has small section of stitching missing at seam. **$805**

American Girl Barbie, wearing "Fashion Luncheon". Bendable legs, brunette hair, blue eyes, pale yellow lips. Wearing pink knit and satin dress with matching jacket, pink satin hat with floral decoration, white long sleeved gloves. Pink "Japan" marked closed toe shoes. Left leg extremely loose and joint broken, face slightly dark; outfit age discolored with stain on collar of jacket. **$258**

Bubblecut Barbie wearing "After Five" with vinyl case. Barbie has golden blonde hair, pierced ears, blue eyes, pink lips, straight legs. Wearing black dress with white organdy collar, matching organdy hat with black velvet hat band, and replaced black open toe shoes. Case has Bubblecut Barbie graphic, circa 1963. Case is scuffed, but with no tears in vinyl. **$92**

Bubblecut Barbie, wearing "Friday Night Date", Barbie has straight legs, titian hair, blue eyes, light red lips and pierced ears. Face is slightly dark. Wearing white cotton underdress with blue corduroy jumper decorated with felt appliques and black "Japan" marked open-toe shoes. Included are her serving tray and one glass (has crack) and two straws. **$143**

Photo courtesy McMasters Harris Auction Co., Cambridge, Ohio; www.McMastersHarris.com

Fashion Queen Barbie, wearing "Let's Dance". Doll has molded brown hair with blue vinyl headband, blue eyes, red lips, pierced ears, straight legs. Wearing blue floral print dress. In black vinyl Fashion Queen Barbie case. Circa 1963. Case is scuffed and worn with no noted tears in vinyl. Plastic inside has several cracks and holes. **$69**

Bubblecut Barbie, boxed, in original swimsuit. Black bubble cut hair, red lips. Includes original box, stand and brochure. **$103**

Color Magic Barbie, yellow hair with blue clip, blue eyes, dark pink lips, bendable legs. **$287**

Color Magic Barbie, yellow hair with blue clip and multi-colored scarf, blue eyes, red lips, cheek blush, bendable legs, wearing print skirt and blouse. Left leg is slightly loose, small split in left toes. **$345**

Hair Fair Brunette Barbie, Brunette bob cut, blue eyes, real lashes, a few nicks and marks. Wearing original green dress tagged "Barbie". **$46**

Swirl Ponytail Barbie, wearing orange nylon swimsuit, brunette hair, blue eyes, dark pink lips, pierced ears, and straight legs. Wearing orange one-piece nylon swimsuit. Small scratches on backs of legs. Swimsuit is missing some stitching and has small "runs." **$115**

Talking Barbie, in original outfit. Brunette hair in original set with pink bow, blue eyes, real lashes, pink lips. String does not work, a few nicks and marks. Wearing original swimsuit tagged "Barbie", 1968. ....**$103**

Talking Barbie, NRFB. Brunette hair, blue eyes, coral lips, rooted eyelashes, bendable legs, wearing original swimsuit with net cover-up, wrist tag, in box with clear plastic stand. Vinyl attachments for arms in box are split, box has a few small creases. **$258**

Talking Barbie head on Twist 'N' Turn Body, blonde hair, blue eyes, coral lips, cheek blush, rooted eyelashes, bendable legs, wearing black nylon swimsuit. Head has slight yellow tone. **$46**

Twist 'N' Turn Barbie, wearing original outfit. Brunette hair with bright orange hair tie, pierced ears, blue eyes, sparse rooted eyelashes, pink lips, faded cheek blush, bendable legs. Wearing original bright orange two-piece swimsuit with net cover. Head has slight yellow tone and left ear is discolored. **$92**

Twist 'N' Turn Barbie, in original outfit. Brunette hair with orange ribbon tie, blue eyes, red/orange lips, cheek blush, rooted eyelashes, bendable legs, wearing orange vinyl two-piece swimsuit with net cover-up. Face and hands are slightly yellowed. Swimsuit waist is stretched and back discolored. **$143**

Twist 'N' Turn Barbie, Wearing original swimsuit with mesh cover (no bikini top), matching hair ribbon. Swimsuit bottom is stained. 1966. ....**$69**

Twist 'N' Turn Barbie and Hair Happenin's Francie, Twist 'n turn Barbie has Living Barbie head with shoulder length hair, real lashes (several lashes missing), wearing off the shoulder body suit. Hair Happenins Francie wearing original dress tagged "Francie", brown eyes framed by real lashes, pink lips. 1969. ....**$69 pair**

Walking Miss America & Drum Major Ken, Barbie includes original gown, bouquet of flowers, wand, cloak, crown, and sash. Hair is in original set and she walks gracefully. Ken includes uniform, hat, shoes marked "Japan" and baton. ....**$46 pair**

Barbie: Family, Friends

Allan, in original box, red painted hair, brown eyes, straight legs, wearing multicolored striped jacket and blue swim trunks. **$46**

Twist 'N' Turn Casey, Blonde hair, wearing tagged one-piece outfit with belt. Open mouth, real lashes. Some wear to outfit. Uneven skin tone. **$57**

Talking Christie, in original box, oxidized red hair, brown eyes, pink lips, wearing orange vinyl two-piece swimsuit and multi-colored cover-up, wrist tag, in box with clear plastic stand. Doll is loose in box, box not mint. **$287**

Twist 'N' Turn Christie, in original box, brunette hair, brown eyes, rooted eyelashes, bright pink lips, wrist tag. Wearing yellow, pink and orange one-piece swimsuit, in box with clear plastic stand. Original cellophane on box. **$345**

Francie, with "Growin' Pretty Hair", in orig. outfit. Bendable legs, blonde hair, brown eyes, rooted eyelashes, hot pink lips, cheek blush. Wearing pink lame and satin dress with pink netting overskirt and attached panty. Original rubber band in hair is in fragments, head is slightly dark and has yellow tone. Color is faded on back of lame. **$46**

Francie, in original box, blonde hair with plastic cover, brown eyes, cheek blush, bright pink lips, straight legs. Wearing original red/white two-piece swimsuit in box with gold wire stand, booklet, comb and red closed toe shoes. Face is slightly yellow and arms are light. **$402**

Black Francie, with real lashes wearing tagged dress. 1965. ....**$460**

Black Francie, in original swimsuit. Brunette hair, brown eyes, rooted eyelashes, bright pink lips, twist 'n turn waist, bendable legs, attached wrist tag. Wearing original swimsuit and has booklet. Nose is slightly light.........**$1,610**

Growin' Pretty Hair Francie, wearing original dress tagged "Francie". Brown eyes framed by real lashes, pink lips. Hair does not retract. 1970. ....**$34**

Twist 'N' Turn Francie, in original outfit, blonde hair with hot pink hair ribbon, brown eyes, rooted eyelashes, cheek blush, dark pink lips, and bendable legs. Wearing floral print with lace trim top and hot pink panties. Nose is light, small blue discoloration on right ankle. **$345**

Walking Jamie, in original outfit, light brown hair and brown eyes framed by real lashes. Wearing original outfit. Walking mechanism in working order. A few nicks on back of legs...**$69**

T'NT Julia, in original outfit, oxidized red hair, brown eyes, rooted eyelashes, pink lips, bendable legs, wearing two-piece white nurse's uniform and cap, white pilgrim shoes, wrist tag. Tag is creased and has tear at wrist, cap is discolored..**$143**

T'NT Julia, wearing "Apple Print Sheath", oxidized red hair, brown eyes, rooted eyelashes, cheek blush, pink lips, bendable legs, wearing apple print Barbie dress and black "Japan" marked open-toe shoes (split straps)..................**$57**

Ken, in original box. Brunette painted hair Ken wearing original red/white striped jacket and red trunks in box with booklet. Box not mint; replaced insert. **$46**

Ken, in original box. Brunette painted hair, straight legs, wearing white knit shirt and red shorts with white polka dots, cork sandals with red straps. Box not mint. **$69**

Ken, in original box. Painted hair, blue eyes, wearing "Tuxedo Ken" outfit including white shirt, black slacks with matching jacket, maroon cummerbund and bow tie, black

Photo courtesy McMasters Harris Auction Co., Cambridge, Ohio; www.McMastersHarris.com

Francie, with bendable legs, wearing "Gad-Abouts", Brunette hair, brown eyes, rooted eyelashes, cheek blush, plum lips. Wearing blue and green printed knit shirt with matching hose, green knit skirt with matching hat, soft green ankle boots, and rare white plastic glasses with green stripe. Francie's nose and ears are slightly light. Right arm is light and light spots on left arm. Hair is stiff. **$172**

Photo courtesy McMasters Harris Auction Co., Cambridge, Ohio; www.McMastersHarris.com

Julia, wearing one-piece white nurse uniform. Julia has brown eyes, dark red hair, rooted eyelashes, twist 'n' turn waist, bendable legs, cheek blush, pink lips. Wearing white cotton dress with matching nurse cap and white pilgrim shoes. A few small blue marks on back of right leg. **$92**
  (Not part of the Barbie line. Based on the 1968 TV character, Julia, played by Diahann Carroll.)

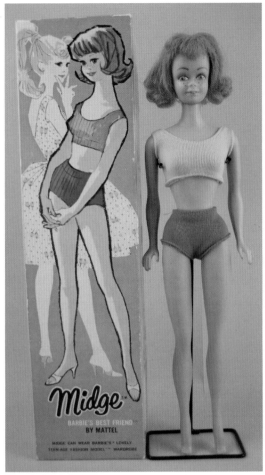

Photo courtesy McMasters Harris Auction Co., Cambridge, Ohio; www.McMastersHarris.com

Midge, in original box, blonde hair, blue eyes, plum lips with painted teeth, pierced ears, straight legs, wearing two piece turquoise and blue swimsuit, in box with black wire stand. Box insert replaced. **$115**

socks and shoes, and corsage. Booklet included. Box not mint, insert missing. $80

Flocked Hair Ken, in original box. Flocked blonde hair, blue eyes, straight legs, wearing red swim trunks and cork sandals with red vinyl straps. Yellow terry cloth towel also included. Box insert replaced, box not mint. $80

MOD Hair Ken, NRFB, brunette hair Ken wearing brown/white checked jacket over white turtleneck, brown slacks and shoes. In box with white plastic stand. Box edges are worn... $57

Midge, in original box, straight legs. Midge has straight legs, titian hair, blue eyes, dark plum lips. Wearing two-piece swimsuit with pale aqua top and orange bottom. She comes with box marked "Blonde" in good condition. Also included are a gold wire stand and booklet. $57

Midge, in original swimsuit and box with stand, titian hair, blue eyes, dark pink lips, straight legs. Wearing original

two-piece yellow and orange swimsuit and red "Japan" marked open toe shoes. Black wire stand included. Box not mint. $69

Bendable Leg Midge, in original swimsuit. Brunette hair in original set with headband. Deep coral lips with light brown freckles. Both bendable legs work smoothly. 1964. .... $230

Brunette Midge, in original box. Brunette hair, blue eyes, pierced ears, straight legs, wearing two-piece pink and red swimsuit, red open-toe shoes, in box with booklet and black wire stand. Box not mint, three split corners repaired with tape, replaced box insert. $57

Titian Midge, in original box, titian hair, blue eyes, pink lips, straight legs, wearing yellow and orange two-piece swimsuit. Replaced box insert, box not mint. $46

Titian Bendable Leg Midge, in original swimsuit. Titian hair with faded blue ribbon headband, blue eyes, plum lips, pierced ears. Wearing original multi-colored stripe one-piece knit swimsuit. Legs are loose and right leg has pin-sized hole. Both feet and ankles have several pin-sized holes.. $143

Midge and Ken, Midge has titian hair, blue eyes, straight legs, and is wearing original orange and yellow two-piece swimsuit. Ken has blonde painted hair, blue eyes, and is wearing original red/white striped swimsuit and red swim trunks. .... $46 pair

Straight Leg Midge & Blonde Bubblecut Barbie, Brunette straight-leg Midge wearing pink and red two-piece swimsuit. Minor wear to swim top and small stain on bottom. Coral lips, coral fingernails and toenails, light brown freckles. Blonde bubble cut Barbie wearing original red swimsuit. Red lips and fingernails. Pierced ears with no green ear.. $115 pair

P.J., in original outfit. Blonde hair with bead ties, brown eyes, rooted eyelashes, bright pink lips, cheek blush, twist 'n' turn waist and bendable legs. Wearing hot pink one-piece nylon swimsuit with crocheted skirt and orange vinyl waistband. $46

Live Action P.J., with microphone, wearing orange dress, sheer blouse and tights, silver knee-high boots, "suede" vest with long tassels. Also includes microphone. $80

Skipper, in original box. Boxed Skipper with original swimsuit, shoes marked Japan, sandals, headband, comb, brush, wrist tag, pamphlet and stand. 1964. .... $172

Skipper, in original swimsuit with 3 extra outfits. Blonde hair, rooted eyelashes, blue eyes, pink lips, cheek blush, a twist 'n' turn waist and bendable legs. "Pink Princess" outfit includes pink crepe dress with three gold buttons and lace trim, green crepe coat with gold buttons trimmed with pink velvet, and pink nylon panty hose. Hat and shoes not included; items are slightly age discolored; "Budding Beauty" includes hot pink/white taffeta with floral print dress only; "Daisy Crazy" is complete with hot pink knit dress and yellow floral print tricot, matching socks and yellow "Japan" marked flats.. $103

Blonde Skipper, in original box. Blonde hair, blue eyes, pink lips, straight legs, wearing original red/white one-piece swimsuit and red "Japan" marked flats, in box with booklet. Box bottom has small tear.............................. $103

Quick Curl Skipper, NRFB, circa 1962. Age discolored but in excellent condition.. $70

Photo courtesy McMasters Harris Auction Co., Cambridge, Ohio; www.McMastersHarris.com

Photo courtesy McMasters Harris Auction Co., Cambridge, Ohio; www.McMastersHarris.com

Brunette Skipper, MIB. Brunette hair with metal headband and plastic wrap, blue eyes, pink lips, straight legs, wearing original red/white one-piece swimsuit, wrist tag. Gold wire stand and cellophane packet containing booklet, white comb and brush, and red "Japan" marked flats included in box. Box insert has small tears. Box label has creased edge. **$201**

Skooter, in "Hearts 'n' Flowers", two versions. Straight legs, blonde hair, brown eyes, wearing green cotton print skirt with yellow knit bodice and matching jacket and cap, yellow knit knee socks, and yellow "Japan" marked boots. Skooter has her "Arithmetic" and "English" books in black vinyl book strap and a yellow vinyl purse with shoulder strap. Also included is the "blue" version of this outfit, dress with jacket only. Small discoloration on lower front of skirt. This outfit is hard to find. One rubberband in hair is broken. **$172 all**

Skooter and Skipper, in original boxes. Blonde hair, with red ties, brown eyes, cream lips, straight legs, wearing original red/white two-piece swimsuit and red "Japan" marked flats, in box with detached wrist tag (torn) and booklet. Box not mint. Skipper has titian hair, blue eyes, pink lips and straight legs, wearing original red/white one-piece swimsuit and red "Japan" marked flats, in box with booklet. Booklet is creased, no box insert, box is worn and has areas of discoloration and repairs on cover.... **$103 pair**

Twist 'N' Turn Stacey, blonde hair with ribbon tie, blue eyes, rooted eyelashes, dark pink lips with teeth, cheek blush, bendable legs. Wearing two-piece multi-colored swimsuit. Head is slightly yellow....................................**$201**

Twist 'N' Turn Stacey, in original box. Box labeled "Copper Penny," blue eyes, dark pink lips with teeth, cheek blush, rooted eyelashes, bendable legs. Wearing multi-colored one-piece swimsuit, in box with clear plastic stand. Circa 1967. Original cellophane on box..........................**$575**

Talking Stacey & TNT Casey, Talking Stacey wearing original swimsuit, blonde hair, blue eyes and real lashes; string does not work. Twist N' Turn Casey wearing swimsuit tagged "Francie", brunette bob cut, blue eyes and real lashes...**$80 pair**

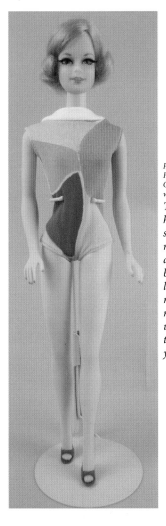

Twist 'n' Turn Stacey, hair with attached string, blue eyes, rooted eyelashes, dark pink lips, cheek blush, and bendable legs. Wearing multicolored one-piece nylon swimsuit and unmarked blue open-toe shoes. Head is yellowed. **$172**

Brunette "Walk Lively" Steffie, in original outfit. Dark brunette hair, brown eyes, bright orange lips, cheek blush, bendable legs, and attached wrist tag. Wearing original multicolored print nylon outfit, red chiffon scarf, and red pilgrim shoes. She also has her stand and instructions sheet. **$201**

Barbie: Accessories

Barbie shoes (24 pairs), includes 13 pairs of closed-toe and 11 pairs of open-toe shoes marked "Japan". Variety of colors. .... **$230 all**

"Bouncy Flouncy", "Tenterrific" Outfits. "Bouncy Flouncy" Barbie outfit: Multicolored floral print dress with matching purse and orange closed-toe shoes on card with label. Complete. "Tenterrific" Francie outfit: Multicolored floral print dress with matching hat, white vinyl purse with green ribbon straps, and green low heel shoes to complete the outfit on card with label. .... **$230 pair**

"Commuter Set" Barbie Outfit, white silk body blouse, blue/white checked body blouse, navy knit suit, black #1 open-toe shoes (both marked "Japan"), crystal necklace and bracelet, red floral hat, short white nylon gloves, and red hat box. White blouse has discolored spots. **$230**

Formal Occasion Barbie Fashion, #1697. Complete with dress, regal hooded cape, closed-toe pumps marked "Japan". 1967. .... **$115**

Furry Go Round, Sears Exclusive Barbie Fashion, orange suede cloth coat with rows of brown fur, hood, matching lace stockings, orange boots marked "Japan", 1967. ..... **$125**

"Gay Parisienne" Barbie Outfit, blue "bubble" dress, white fur stole, blue net hat, gold velvet clutch, pearl earrings, pearl necklace, long white nylon gloves, blue #1 "Japan" marked open-toe shoes. **$977**

Picnic Set #967 and After Five #934, Complete Fashions, Picnic Set is complete and includes shirt, jeans, hat, wedge shoes, woven picnic basket, bamboo fishing pole with fish, 1959. After Five fashion is also complete with dress, hat and shoes marked "Japan", 1962. .... **$115 both**

Roman Holiday Barbie Fashion, #968. Includes dress, coat and high-heeled shoes marked "Japan", 1959. .... **$172**

"Student Teacher" Outfit, for Barbie and Midge, NRFB. Box is in very good condition. **$373**

Vintage Barbie Stands, four black pedestal bases (three marked TM, one marked R), three black wire attachments, one black wire base. One base is chipped, all are scuffed. .... **$316 all**

Dolls, General

Bru Jne bébé with wardrobe, circa 1885, bisque socket head, blue paperweight eyes and a dimpled chin, 19" h. **$40,250**

F.G. French Fashion, late 1880's, Gauthier doll with bisque swivel head on kid-lined separate bisque shoulder plate. Head is incised "2", shoulder has "F" on one side and "G" on the other. Pale blue paperweight eyes and pale bisque with rosy cheeks. The all-leather fashion body is gusseted at the elbows, hips and knees and she wears her original dark blonde mohair wig in upswept braids and black antique leather slippers, as well as a two-piece patterned cotton dress with silk ribbon and lace trim, 16 1/2" h. Bisque head and shoulder are very good to excellent. Body has some wear and minor patching with both hands whitewashed and two fingers loose on right hand. **$1,035**

Gebruder Heubach Character Boy, closed mouth boy with all molded and painted features, intaglio eyes, incised "5 7602 Germany" and Heubach fan mark. He is on his original fully jointed wood and composition body with elongated upper legs and dressed in a two-piece green and white cotton suit with waist belt and newer suede shoes, 17" h. (44cm). **$480**

Martha Chase, "Chester" doll, circa 1910, with steamer trunk filled with clothes, and provenance from the Atlanta Toy Museum, 37" h. **$5,750**

Halopeau, French bébé, circa 1880, 24" h. **$109,250**

Jumeau, First Series Portrait, with head incised "1" and an unmarked body. She has spiral blue paperweight eyes, mauve shading on the upper eyelids, outlined lips and is on her original body with eight separate ball joints and straight wrists. Redressed in a pink silk and lace dress, wearing slightly later marked "Jumeau" shoes, which are stamped "6 Paris" as well as an antique blond mohair wig over cork pate: 17" h. Minor kiln dust on bisque, minor chip near left earring hole, and body has had an old repaint. **$12,650**

Kammer & Reinhardt, Googly, largest size made with head incised "K * R Simon & Halbig 131" with blue glass set eyes looking to the right, closed smiling mouth on fully jointed toddler body made of wood and composition. Dressed in red cotton print outfit with matching bandanna and blonde human hair wig and white oil cloth shoes, 15 1/2" h. Eyes have been reset, uneven coloring with large white spot on right side of face and above left ear and discolored area on neck socket, possibly from metal rust. Body has been repainted with replaced hands, possibly French.............................. **$5,750**

Kestner, Hilda Toddler, cabinet-size character is incised "B. Made in Germany 6 245 J.D.K. Jr 1914 Copyright Hilda". She is on a fully jointed toddler body with diagonal hip joints and has dark brown glass sleep eyes, open mouth with two upper teeth and wears a blond mohair wig, antique white cotton dress with pink ribbon inserts and newer white oilcloth shoes, 13" h. Minor color loss on left cheek and slight speckling on chin; arms and hands have old light repaint. **$2,012**

Male French Fashion, glass-eyed, shoulder head, elaborately dressed to represent a late-18th-century gentleman or military figure. Clothing is all sewn to the body, which by touch appears to be a solid hard carton with knee-high black leather boots, wooden hands; the right holding a baton. He has white flax hair pulled into a long braid in the back and is covered by a cardboard pillbox hat with red and blue ribbon. The left knee is purposely bent so that the left leg stretches slightly back and outward, 13 1/2" h..**$3,600**

Armand Marseilles, Googly, bisque head incised "Germany 323 A 10/0 M" with blue side-glancing sleeping eyes, closed smiling mouth on five-piece papier-mache body with painted shoes and socks. She wears her original cotton Art Deco dress and an elaborate red satin wide brimmed hat with cloth flowers and feathers, 7" h. Typical wear to body..**$632**

Kathe Kruse doll, circa 1927, with painted cloth head, brown painted eyes and all-cloth jointed body, 14" h. **$10,925**

Simon & Halbig, peddler doll, circa 1880, with twill body and bisque head, offers her tiny wares from a woven basket. **$8,625**

Dollhouses

Altoona, Pa., dollhouse, circa 1900, white clapboard house is a copy of a full-sized Altoona home, built by the foreman for the Pennsylvania railroad shops. Both sides of the house are hinged and when opened, there are four rooms on the left side and three rooms on the right with a hall on the right side. Rooms have old wallpaper inside but may not be original, 38" h x 36" w x 34" deep. Needs tightening of joints, floors and walls are somewhat slack. **$575**

Amish-built dollhouse, circa 1895, simulated brick, made in the Lancaster, Pa., area. There is a front and back porch, the roofs have hand-split shingles and the dark-green shutters have raised panels with workable hinges. The house opens from the left side to reveal two large rooms with rafters. The interior of the house has dark-stained woodwork with pastel painted walls. Floors are crudely made planks of wood. Top floor has vaulted ceilings, overall 32" h x 25 1/2" w x 39" deep. **$575**

Christian Hacker dollhouse, six rooms, opens from the front and has had decals of flowers and angels glued on the exterior and interior of the house. The porches, doors and roof brackets remain in their original condition. Instead of a lithograph paper roof, there are shingles applied. An electric elevator is found in the center rooms of the house, which moves from the first to the second floors (needs repair). The house has its original wiring for electricity. Floor papers are missing in most rooms with remnants in the halls. Overall approx. 43" w x 33" deep x 42" h. Has been over-painted. The widow's walk, railing at the front dormer and on the main roof of the porch are missing. **$4,140**

Christian Hacker dollhouse, circa 1910, front facade has half-timbering on the second story, a long balcony with railing and a bay window and front entrance below. All painted surfaces are original as well as the brick-papered sides to the house. The roof papers are in near excellent condition throughout the house. The house opens from the front to reveal three rooms with original wallpapers. Some decals on second floor papers were added, as were the floor coverings and curtains. Overall 23 1/2" l x 26" h x 15" deep. One front hinge needs replacement..............................**$270**

German dollhouse, circa 1910, two-story clapboard house has its original paint in cream with green trim and a red roof. It opens from the back and front to reveal eight rooms, including upstairs and downstairs hallways with a staircase. There are long porches across the entire front with cutout decorative railings (one piece missing on lower right porch) with two large openings (one on first floor and on second floor) that appear to have missing doors or windows). Columns and railings on porches have some repaint in places. A widow's walk and chimneys are found at the peak of the roof. The interior rooms have their original surfaces with interconnecting doors. Decals, fabrics and curtains have been added. The house has its original wiring for electricity. Overall 39" l x 37" h x 29" deep (not including detachable porch)......................................**$575**

Wooden doll bungalow, reminiscent of Schoenhut, this three-room house with porch features one large room and two smaller rooms. Exterior has faux brick and stone pattern and removable roof. Access is gained by two hinged walls on sides, 19" w x 18 1/2" h x 25" deep...................**$300**

Photo courtesy Morphy Auctions, Denver, Pa.; www.MorphyAuctions.com

Mystery Dolls' House, circa 1880, American Victorian detailing, fine condition with often-missing original wallpaper intact, 29" h x 25" w x 15 1/2" deep. **$11,500**

Photo courtesy of Skinner Inc.

Dollhouse, Bliss, Queen Anne Cottage, red roof, paper-covered gabled house, porch, balcony, original wall and floor coverings, façade opens to reveal ground floor room, one on the first, side opens to a single room extension on the left, some losses, circa 1911, 24 1/2" h x 18" w x 18" d. **$2,115**

Photo courtesy of Skinner Inc.

Dollhouse with contents, Christian Hacker, Germany, three bays and stories, original brick papers, cream trim, paper-covered mansard roof, blue/gray tiles, two rooms and central hall on ground floor, first-floor drawing room, two rooms under second floor eaves, most rooms with period wall coverings, curtains, original floor treatments, kitchen with painted dresser, hutch and stove, metal dishes, serving pieces, pots and pans, wooden tubs with produce, soft metal toaster, bisque head cook, many other items, opening façade, exterior surface wear, lifting roof paper, damage and losses to furniture, 29" h, 24 3/8" w x 13 1/2" d. **$8,225**

Photo courtesy of Skinner Inc.

Dollhouse and contents, Schoenhut, Model 5/1000 E, two story colonial style, light tan, cream trim, green shutters, red fiber-board shingled roof, off-center front door, one window on ground floor, two windows on first floor, colonnaded porch on right with balcony above, back opens to reveal two rooms on each floor, cream interior, printed parquet floor covering, electrified fittings, roof and balcony railings damaged, furniture losses, four-figure German bisque head family, Schoenhut furniture, 20" h x 24" w x 15" d, 1932. **$355**

Toys, General

Althoff Bergman, camel on platform, American, tin, circa 1880, in original yellow paint with red mouth, mounted on a green base with small cast-iron wheels, 9" l x 7 1/4" h. Scattered paint flaking all over the surface of the camel and base. A piece of the tin on one side of the leg missing. **$1,035**

Arcade, Andy Gump Car, elaborate version features a crank, license plates, painted comic figure and additional highlighting to wheels and trim, 7 1/2" l, some damage to rear license plate...**$840**

Arcade, Buick sedan, enameled in blue and black with white rubber tires, circa 1930s, 8 3/4" l. Overall paint is very fine with some restoration to hood. **$1,552**

Arcade, Chevy sedan, black with silver grille and gold headlights. Nickel-plated wheels with black hubs, 8 1/4" l. Replaced spare tire. **$2,520**

Arcade, gas pumps (pair), one is yellow with red trim, with moveable gas indicator on front and stenciled "Arcade Gas" at top; second is red with gold highlights and has its original hose, 6 1/4" and 6 1/2" h, respectively. Yellow pump has minor chipping. Red pump with some rusting to front...**$805 pair**

Arcade, Mack coal dump truck, painted red with "coal" stenciled on back dump. Has cast-iron wheels painted white with red hubs. Also has an original Arcade decal on bed of dump, 10 1/4" l, most of its wear to wheels and sides of bed and hood of truck. Figure is a replacement.....**$1,150**

Arcade, Mack tank truck, with Mack decal on grille. This version has a cast-iron tank, it also came with a tin tank and has dual wheels on the back of truck. Painted red with spoke steel wheels and a nickel-plated driver, 13" l. Overall paint chipping and wear to truck especially on the grille. **$920**

Arcade, Plymouth (?) coupe, one of the largest toy coupes made by Arcade, it features a removable spare tire mounted to the trunk, 8 1/2" l. Old paint restoration and probable replaced spare. **$747**

Arcade, "Red Baby" dump truck, with original stencil on front doors, "International Harvester Trucks". Contains original nickel-plated driver, four cast-iron, nickel-plated wheels with red hubs, and a working nickel-plated wrench used to lift the dump body, 10 3/4" l............................**$1,200**

Arcade, red-top cab, usually found in black and orange. Enameled in black with a white center section and red windows and roof, it sports white hubs and gray tires, 5" l. Overall very good, heavier paint loss due to flaking on roof. **$805**

Arcade, T-Bar Mack dump truck, painted gray with nickel-plated spoke wheels and nickel-plated driver. Also

Photo courtesy Old Town Auctions LLC, Boonsboro, Md.; www.OldTownAuctions.com

A&A American Metal Toy Co., Desi Arnaz, conga drum, retains original tag copyrighted 1952 by Lucille Ball – Desi Arnaz; bottom metal band has dent; small dent to body at top band; drum head intact with some wrinkling; rare original box: complete, split on one seam. **$6,600**

Photo courtesy Morphy Auctions, Denver, Pa.; www.MorphyAuctions.com

Arcade, Checker Cab, cast iron, orange with nickel grille and driver, white rubber tires are firm and bright. No cracks or breaks. Moderate scratching and wear, some orange shows through the black on the roof, 9" l. **$25,300**

Photo courtesy James D. Julia Auctioneers, Fairfield, Maine; www.JuliaAuctions.com

Arcade, Brinks Express Co. armored truck, only a handful of these toys are known to exist. Believed to have been originally made for the Brinks Co. for promotional purposes. It weighs 5 pounds and is an accurate portrayal of a real-life vehicle, including gun turrets on the sides and rear. The rear of the truck opens up to a cast-iron bed, unlike many of the other panel trucks that have a tin bed. Painted in a deep red with gold highlighting, red hubs and white rubber tires, 12" l, overall normal wear and chipping to paint. Lacking the rubber tire on one iron wheel. **$34,500**

Arcade, Yellow Cab, painted orange and black with steel wheels, also ink-stamped "Yellow Cab" on passenger doors, 8" l. Roof of cab has been broken and re-glued. **$345**

has "Mack" embossed on driver door, 12" l. Heavy wear throughout. **$360**

Bandai, Ford Custom Ranch Wagon with original box, wagon is lithographed yellow with dark blue roof, chromed bumpers and headlights, rubber tires and celluloid windshield and hubcaps that read "Ford". Box is brightly lithographed, 11 1/2" l. Car has a few rub marks. Friction motor inoperative. Box lid with minor soiling and creases. **$517**

Battleship, scale model, tin, ram front with many gun turrets, ventilators, railings, lifeboats, riggings, etc. Meant to be operational with an electric motor, it was powered in

Atom, Batman, Superhero Walking Toy with original box, Japanese, tin and vinyl, wind-up, 1960s. Working, original cape, made by Atom, Tokyo, Japan. Vinyl head and arms. tin body. Only sold in Japan. "Spindle legs" version. Moderate scratching on legs. Box has minor restoration. Some creasing and light staining. Box has original cardboard inserts, 13" h. **$13,800**

the water with three propellers. Of unknown vintage, but most likely made in the 1920s, primarily out of tin with some wood, and painted in proper colors. At the stern of the ship, the name "Liberte" is applied, suggesting that this was a French vessel, 53" l. In need of re-rigging, partial front mast, no motor present. Bottom shows some damage with replacement keel. **$6,000**

Bing, touring car, tin, lithographed red with white and peach wheels. Marked "GBN" on back of car. Also has a lithographed driver/chauffeur with goggles, 9 1/4" l. Considerable amount of rust to fenders and floor of car. **$747**

British, limousine, lithographed olive green with tan running boards, black and green lithographed wheels and cream bumpers. Stamped on side, "MADE IN GT. BRITAIN", 13 1/2" l. Some scratching to roof, hood and fenders and some minor denting to roof. **$345**

British, town car, late 1920s, with chauffeur, having wind-up motor and is stamped on back, "MADE IN GB, MADE IN ENGLAND", 9 1/4" l. Some rusting to roof, back of one fender detached. **$300**

Buddy L, aerial ladder truck, electric headlights, separate steel grille and pressed-disk simulated spoke tires. With a pull-along wire handle. Overall painted red with original "Buddy L" decals, 29" l. Some discoloration and some areas lacking paint. Minor rust. **$1,380**

Buddy L, cement mixer, and heavy steam shovel painted red and black. Shovel has two pistons that help move it up and down. Cement mixer is painted gray and is on steel wheels. Larger is 18" l. Shovel appears to be intact, heavy wear throughout. Cement mixer is lacking door on boiler. Having partial original decals with heavy overall wear. .... **$977 both**

Buddy L, coal truck, with opening doors and headlamps, simulated pressed tires. Painted black and has original Buddy L decals and original coal chute, 11" h x 25" l. Some rusting and wear to fenders. **$6,325**

Buddy L, express line truck, 1920s, some paint loss to roof area, where either a child sat or pushed on the truck with hands. Still retains original tailgate and opening/closing doors on rear, 24 1/2" l. Also with wear to internal bed and dashboard decal...................................**$2,185**

Buddy L, railway express truck, green removable roof and sides, two back opening doors. Cab painted black and has red disk steel wheels, 24" l. Decals are of more recent vintage. Bed and cab of truck over-painted. **$805**

Buddy L, road roller, as toy is pulled, the pistons go back and forth and the roller smooths the ground in front of it. Painted green and retains all original decals, 18" l. Some rusting to the roller and wheels, uniform wear to roof, and wear to decals. **$1,840**

Buddy L, sand and gravel truck with opening doors. Deluxe version has headlights, two opening doors and pressed-disk simulated spoke tires, 26" l. Black body of truck has been repainted. **$3,450**

Buddy L, tank truck, cab is painted black with green tank. Also has original spout and cap on tanker. With original decals, "Buddy L Tank Line" on both sides, 23 1/2" l. Some minor flaking to tank. Front fenders are slightly. **$2,587**

Buddy L, fire trucks (two), aerial ladder truck painted red with nickel-plated extension ladders. With original decals and brass bell. Hook and ladder truck also painted red with original decals, ladder racks, reel and ladders. Longer is 30". Aerial ladder appears all original with original decals and bell, with most of its wear on fenders and high points. The hook and ladder is all original with original ladders, even wear throughout. ....**$1,150 both**

Buddy L, flivvers (two), a flivver truck painted black with steel spoke tires. Also has the earlier Buddy L decal on bottom. Along with a Buddy L dump flivver. Longer is 12". Truck is all original in poor to fair condition with significant paint wear and rusting. Dump (rarer) over-painted..**$840 both**

Cap gun, monkey with coconut, animated, when coconut in monkey's hand is raised, cap is placed on top of gun and trigger is pulled. Coconut slams down and explodes cap, 4" h x 4" l. Retains more than half of its original japanned finish and is in working condition.................................**$230**

Carette, limousine, rubber-tired wheels, four original headlights, and beveled glass windows. Lithographed in dark green with opening doors to passenger compartment, with chauffeur, 16" l. Minor flaking to lithograph sides and driver and typical chipping around the doors. **$6,325**

Carette, limousine, lithographed red with a blue roof, white spoke tires. Has a brake and a reverse, also has two original head lamps and a hand-painted chauffeur, 13" l. With some minor discoloration to hood and some wear around the doors. **$2,587**

Carette, ocean liner, with four funnels, three crow's nests, search light, 12 ventilators. Painted cream, tan, black and white, 15" h x 27" l. The boat has been over-painted and has replaced string. **$4,200**

Carousel, European, tin clockwork, circa 1900, Turn of the Century, horses with riders and gondolas with passengers. With dual flags (replacements) atop a cloth canopy protecting the passengers from the elements. When wound, the carousel propels in a counterclockwise fashion, 14" h. Some significant flaking to various horses and riders. Clockwork mechanism appears to have been repaired. **$2,300**

Photo courtesy Old Town Auctions LLC, Boonsboro, Md.; www.OldTownAuctions.com

Chein, Popeye "Heavy Hitter," lithographed tin, wind-up, scattered minor play wear, small spot of litho wear on left side panel, light tarnishing to bell, working, 11 5/8" h. **$5,500**

Carousel, German, hand-painted tin, circa 1910, likely by Mueller & Kaderer, containing four pressed-cardboard horses and riders. The toy is activated by either a hand crank or is attached to a live steam engine. When activated, the carousel goes around in a counterclockwise motion while emitting "plink plank" music (inoperative). Three glass and tin lights suspended from an internal canopy would illuminate the platform for nighttime rides. Still retains original flag at top, 17" h. Significant flaking to tin. One lamp missing, but tin shade is present. **$690**

Charlie Chaplin, wind-up walker, lithographed German tin features a blue coat, black pants and black trademark derby with cane in his right hand. Charlie stands on cast-iron feet, and when he is wound, he does his famous penguin shuffle, 9" h. Left arm appears to be a replacement. Wear on high spots with some minor scratches, and Charlie's face has some discoloration. **$540**

Photo courtesy James D. Julia Auctioneers, Fairfield, Maine; www.JuliaAuctions.com

Boycraft, pedal car, by Steelcraft, modeled after the 1935 Chrysler Airflow. Having separate windshield, steel rims with rubber tires, separate working headlights with glass inserts and original Boycraft label on seat of car. Approx. 45" l. All original including bumper, headlights, windshield, tires and hubs. Retains most of its original paint. Windshield present but missing celluloid insert. Missing rear view mirror. Some light rusting and scratching. **$3,737**

Photo courtesy Noel Barrett, Carversville, Pa.; www.NoelBarrett.com

Marklin, circa-1905 enameled tinplate clockwork side-wheeler Providence. **$99,000**; *Carette, 2350 O-gauge clockwork passenger train set.* **$35,750**

Photo courtesy James D. Julia Auctioneers, Fairfield, Maine; www.JuliaAuctions.com

Buddy L, ice delivery truck, 1920s, open black cab and yellow bed with its original canvas cover, 25" l. One original ice block. Retains all original decals. Wear to the fenders. **$2,587**

Photo courtesy James D. Julia Auctioneers, Fairfield, Maine; www.JuliaAuctions.com

Kingsbury, #8 fire station, 1920s with clockwork motor that, when wound, would automatically open its doors so the engine could exit, 13" l. Motor inoperative, lacking call box on side. **$720**

Erhard & Sohne, squirrel cage with wax squirrel, ormolu, 2" h. **$3,737**

Fisher-Price, "Push-Cart Pete," #740, wood, hand-painted face and legs. Head moves as he is pushed. Only known example, 9" l. **$14,400**

Chess set, cased, Bakelite, set in red and ochre in green felt-lined case. King is 4" h. **$840**

Dent, police patrol truck, painted blue with black roof and embossed "police patrol" on side panel of truck. Has four steel wheels and fifth wheel side-mounted to driver's side of truck, 8 3/4" l. Assembled in the 1970s. Wear to roof and some light oxidation to tires. **$1,320**

Doepke, Rossmoyne aerial ladder fire truck, authentic recreation of the American La France truck, in the original box. The paint is vibrant, the aluminum painted ladders are shiny and bright. With original brochure featuring many other Doepke toys, 33" l. Like new in box, some

Fire hose reel model carriage, 1860s (?), wheels and hose reel frame each have been cut and trimmed from a single piece of steel and/or brass. Hose reel has been adorned with elliptical cutouts and mirrored center sections. The original toolbox is still present on the back as well as a crescent-shaped emblem attached to a pole that would support the fire marker. Carefully engraved upon the emblem is the name "Suffolk". Of unknown manufacture, but believed to be Continental, untouched condition, 21" l. Lacking one bell. Eisenglass lacking from fire lantern. Original hose shows signs of deterioration. **$3,565**

minor soiling. Box condition overall is very fine with some staining and minor tearing to flaps on one end. **$1,265**

Doepke, Rossmoyne ladder truck, with extension ladder and extra ladders and spare tire, wind up working siren, steerable front wheels, 33 1/2" l. Significant overall chipping, possibly clear coated. **$120**

Fallows, horse-drawn trolley, with original painted and stenciled decoration, red trolley with green roof stenciled "Central Transportation". Has four delicate cast-iron wheels and pulled by two brown horses with white manes and red saddles, 16" l. Roof still retains its gold-decorated stencil design. Paint flaked and pitted in places and scattered flaking and pitting over the trolley and horses. **$2,587**

Fallows, horse-drawn trolley, car painted green, red and yellow with four cast-iron wheels being pulled by two black horses, 19" l. With rusting and paint loss to the horses and some fading to the back of trolley. **$1,265**

Fallows, tin bell toy with Cupid astride a butterfly's body, as the toy is propelled along the floor, the butterfly's wings flap, Cupid rises and falls, and the bell rings. Luminescent, large multicolored embossed wings, Cupid is in flesh-tone paint with gilt wings and sash about his midsection and highlighted with brown hair, on an embossed orange-red painted tin base with iron wheels. Period catalog cut from Conway Brothers of Philadelphia refers to this toy as #1032 "Mechanical Cupid Butterfly with Gong Attachment", 8" l x 8 1/2" h. Untouched condition. **$6,325**

Fisher-Price, Donald Duck Cart, #544, with car and base painted blue. Lithographed Donald on wood and when toy is pulled, Donald's arms swing up and down and toy clicks, 10" l. Minor discoloration to paper. **$143**

Football players, hollow lead, unknown origin and manufacture, probably from 1920s, 11 opposing figures on two teams, one in red, the other in blue. Finely cast and lightweight. Each team consists of six crouched players, four standing, and one crouched player with ball. Range

General Grant Smoker clockwork toy (left), Ives, 14" h, cloth uniformed with cast-metal head and hands and cast-iron feet. **$18,700**; *Banjo Player, Jerome Secor, clockwork, cloth-dressed wood and metal figure with painted-tin banjo on cast-iron stool.* **$22,000**

from 1 3/4" to 3 1/4" h. Heavy damage to one red player and one blue player. ....**$575 set**

George Brown, double ox cart, tin toy features original painted and stenciled design on the cream cart being drawn by two cream-colored oxen. The cart rides on original cast-iron wheels. Approximately 9 1/2" l. Scattered paint flaking over the entire surface of the cart and oxen. **$2,645**

George Brown, toy carts (two), red cart with mustard interior being drawn by a small white-painted horse; with its original delicate cast-iron wheels. The second, a covered green cart being pulled by a brown horse with red saddle having its original delicate cast-iron wheels. Red cart approximately 7 3/4" l, the green colored cart approximately 8" l. Much scattered paint loss and scratches on the red cart. The green cart with some flaking to the roof. ....**$287 both**

Giraffe, wooden, circa 1950s-60s, multi-ball joints in crackled black and yellow paint. Partial decal on bottom of foot reads "Oakland", 14" h. Various paint chips, predominantly to head...**$150**

Gunthermann, clockwork trolley, lithographed, embossed doors and windows, 8 1/2" l. Some staining and/or corrosion to roof. Mechanism intact, but does not appear to catch. **$575**

Gunthermann, Foxy Grampa, tin, depicting a young man astride Foxy Grampa, who is on all fours and is propelled forward by the boy raising and lowering his legs, pushing

Harris, goat cart, two white goats with black and red trappings pulling a blue buckboard with bright yellow wheels, being driven by a woman in a white and blue dress, 5" h x 13" l. Minor chipping and general wear, replaced driver. **$2,070**

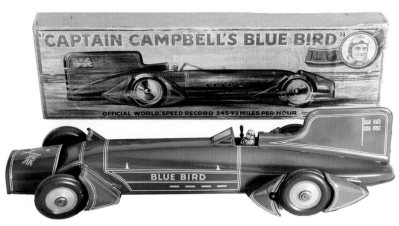

Gunthermann, Captain Campbell's Blue Bird racer, German, sold by Minitoy U.K., tin, with original pictorial box, working, general light play wear, 16" l. **$7,700**

his feet against the floor, 8" l. Mechanism functioning, paint is poor, lacking one leg and one arm. **$1,552**

Haji, Japanese, car with boat, trailer and original box, friction, 1950s, red lithographed car with orange trailer and bright multicolored boat has an outboard motor, 16" l (total). **$460**

Harris, buckboard, two black prancing horses on wheels pulling a red buckboard with yellow enamel wheels and a polychrome driver in gray and flesh tones, 5" h x 13 1/2" l. Some overall wear. **$1,495**

Horseless carriage, cast iron and wood, simulating a turn-of-the-century vehicle with a large friction weight that would propel it forward. Finely detailed cast-iron canopy and kickboard with a female driver and her Buster Brown-type passenger atop a wooden chassis enameled in red with pinstripes. Of unknown manufacture, perhaps by Scheibel or Dayton Friction, 6 1/4" l. **$1,035**

Hubley, general digger, with green and red body, with nickel shovel on swivel rear. White rubber tires with wooden hubs, 10" l. CONDITION: Some minor flattening to tires. **$1,035**

Hubley, Lindy airplane, in gray paint with "Lindy" emblazoned in red across the wings. Celebrating Lindbergh's flight from the U.S. to France, 13 1/4" wingspan. Overall paint chips with pitting to nickel-plated nose and propeller. Underside shows some rust and replaced pulley string. **$977**

Hubley, phaeton, white carriage being pulled by a prancing black horse, with yellow wheels and a blue-painted woman driver. 5" h x 16 3/4" l. Color of back wheels does not match the front wheels. The figure is old but is not original to this toy. The white cart has heavy wear. The black horse is in excellent condition. **$632**

Hubley, #5 racer, large steel wheels that simulate the look of balloon tires, hunched-over driver, and hoods emblazoned with the number 5 that lift to reveal the engine, 9 1/2" l. Left and right hoods have been replaced. **$840**

Hubley, racer with moveable flames, rubber tires. When racer is rolled, twelve flames shoot from engine, 11" l. Colors on racer are bright with four original wheels and hubs. Paint is above average. **$3,600**

Hubley, crash car and Harley Davidson cycle, crash car painted red with gold highlights and nickel plated iron wheels; together with a green civilian Harley Davidson cycle with nickel-plated wheels. Crash car 5" h x 9" l, Harley is 4" h x 6" l. Crash car is very good to excellent, still has a partial Hubley decal on back step; replaced hose reel. Harley is in near excellent condition. .... **$2,415 pair**

Ideal, three-horse pumper, with two silver horses and one brown, all three in full gallop pulling a nickel-plated boiler and an electroplated airbag with four red enameled wheels, one original driver, 9" h x 22" l. **$2,760**

Ives, clockwork runabout, rare to find cast-iron toys with clockwork motors, with steerable front wheels, 7" h x 7 1/2" l. Repainted, with a reproduction driver. **$747**

Japanese, wooden boat with dragon, battery power, boat with two head lamps, two horns and life preserver. Painted white and brown with a large dragon painted on either side, 17 1/2" l. Some minor cracking on the deck boards and wear at the high points. **$360**

JEP, Citroen roadster, painted green with black running boards, electric head lamps, spare tire with license plate, 15 1/2" l. Minor flaking and distress on bottom of car. **$977**

JEP, Hispana Suiza open-air car, big clockwork motor and original JEP tag on side. Painted yellow with red running boards, electric headlights and two original composition figures, 7" h x 20" l. Some paint loss to seats and minor rusting to windshield and some chipping to fenders and car body. One rubber tire split in half. **$4,600**

Photo courtesy James D. Julia Auctioneers, Fairfield, Maine; www.JuliaAuctions.com

Hubley, Packard, intricate detailing including opening doors and hoods, nickel-plated chauffeur is poised upon a simulated tufted leather seat, 12-cylinder nickel-plated engine, nickel-plated radiator with attached lights projecting over the front bumper with the license plate marked "Iowa 1927". Spare is fastened to the rear of car, the tires being of iron simulating balloon tires with blue hubs, 11" l. Overall paint is very fine plus, passenger door has had paint touch-up and is a possible replacement. Appears to have had a small repair to chassis under spare tire. **$12,650**

Photo courtesy James D. Julia Auctioneers, Fairfield, Maine; www.JuliaAuctions.com

JEP, Rolls Royce Open Phaeton, circa 1930, detailed radiator grille with rare custom Flying Lady sterling hood ornament, spring bumpers, forward and reverse gears, brake mechanism, electric headlamps, powerful motor, propeller shaft and rear axle and differential. Also included is a composition driver/chauffeur with articulated arms, 20" l. Older professional restoration. **$3,600**

Karl Bubb, limousine, has slip-on headlamps, side brake, side lever for forward and reverse, glass windshield and side windows, and a lithographed chauffeur. Lithographed brown with black roof and brown fenders, 13 3/4" l. Has been exposed to elements, light oxidation and rust throughout. One of the side windows has a crack. **$1,610**

Karl Bubb, limousine, lithographed red with black roof and fenders with white and brown lithographed tires, 11" l. With bright litho, a superior example. **$2,012**

Kelmet, White crane truck, painted black and red with a nickel-plated crane that moves up and down. Also comes with rubber tires over cast-iron spoke wheels. Marked "WHITE" on radiator and side fenders, 27" l. Some wear and light oxidation and some separation to the red paint. **$5,175**

Kenton, horse-drawn farm wagon with black driver wearing simulated straw hat, detachable cart, being pulled by a black and white horse, 6 3/4" h x 14" l. Bright enameling. **$1,150**

Kenton, Overland circus bandwagon, with six musicians, driver and a red-painted rider on each horse. Wagon is red with gold highlights, yellow and silver wheels. It has white horses with gold trappings, 7" h x 14" l. **$632**

Kenton, Overland circus wagon and circus truck, truck painted yellow with a white bear and silver driver. The circus wagon with a white bear and a blue driver with gold cap. Truck is 5 3/4" h x 9" l and wagon 6 3/4" h x 13" l. Truck appears all original with overall wear especially to the tires. Wagon is in very good condition. ....**$862 both**

Keystone, fire vehicles (two), water tower with original ladders, side horn and bell. Also has original decals. With a Mack City Fire Department fire truck, 31" l. Both appear to be all original. Water tower has its ladders, tank, cap, bell and horn. Fire Department truck has its original ladders and reels. ....**$1,800 both**

Keystone, water tower, water could be put in the tank and it could be pumped out through the water tower nozzle. Has original tank, painted red with original decals, 31" l. Some parts of more recent vintage. Paint is faded. **$660**

Kingsbury, coupe, painted blue with a tan roof and black and silver running boards. With moveable front wheels, taillights and headlights and luggage box on rear bumper. Also has a lift-out rumble seat, 12 7/8" l. Noticeable flaking to the passenger side of car, but with bright enameled paint. **$1,667**

Kingsbury, hook and ladder with original wooden box, with a molded tin seat, nickel-plated ladders, white rubber tires, red enameling with black and silver fenders. Turn crank for a full range of movement, 31" l. Toy with moderate wear throughout. Box has some staining. ...**$1,380**

Kingsbury, motor-driven stake truck, with rubber tires, orange and green polychrome paint with gilt and silver trimming, it is driven by a clockwork motor cranked from the front bumper, 24" l. Exposed to the elements, retains some orange on the bed, but most other original paint is lacking. **$1,610**

Kingsbury, motor-driven stake truck, with rubber tires, orange and green polychrome paint with gilt and silver trimming, it is driven by a clockwork motor cranked from the front bumper, 24" l. Professionally restored. **$3,450**

Kingsbury, motor-driven stake truck, with rubber tires, orange and green polychrome paint with gilt and silver trimmings, driven by clockwork motor cranked from the front bumper. In original paint, also features a decal of the American Flag on top of the cab roof, which is probably original or added at the point of sale, 24" l. **$5,175**

Lehmann, Mixtum Toy with Box, German, tin wind-up, working, rare black version. Minor overall wear, minor scratching, 5" l. **$6,900**

Kingsbury, panel truck, painted blue with black running boards. Has electric headlights and swivel front wheels, white rubber tires with orange hubs,13" l. With minor rusting and paint flaking throughout. **$1,150**

Kingsbury, Sunbeam Racers (pair), one in original box, 1930s, both in red. Both with original figure and Dunlop Cord racing tires. One comes with highly lithographed original box, 19" l. Both with some paint loss and soiling. One missing steering wheel. Box with professional restoration. ....**$3,000 pair**

Kyser & Rex, Philadelphia, Miss Liberty bell toy, painted cast-iron, 8" l...**$29,700**

Lehmann, autobus, colorful lithograph in reds and yellows with a white roof. Has Lehmann logo on front grill, 8 1/4" l. Minor discoloration to sides and some wear at the high points. **$1,552**

Lehmann, "Naughty Boy," car in which mischievous boy tries to take tiller from the driver, 4 1/2" l. The litho on the toy is bright with some minor scratches and slight oxidation on wheels. **$230**

Lehmann, Oho Car, lithographed green with brown lithographed driver and has white and red spoke wheels, 4" l. Some minor flaking on back of car...............................**$690**

Lehmann, Titania limousine, red and blue lithographed tin limo has electric head lamps, coil-spring clockwork drive, adjustable and lockable wheels, chauffeur, detailed graphics and lithography, 11" l. Slight oxidation and some minor wear to wheels. **$3,680**

Little Nemo bisque comic character figurines (five), early 20th century, German made, with movable arms. **$22,412 all**

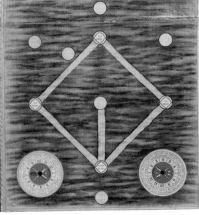

Photo courtesy Old Town Auctions LLC, Boonsboro, Md.;
www.OldTownAuctions.com

*Marx, "New York" wind-up, lithographed tin,
with multiple action and original box; some rubs
and scratches, working; box is missing two inner
flaps, has tears and creases, one box flap re-
attached, 9 1/2" d.* **$3,520**

Photo courtesy Morphy Auctions, Denver, Pa.;
www.MorphyAuctions.com

*McLoughlin Bros.,
Parlor Base Ball
Game, 1897, two
spinners, nine yellow,
nine blue game pieces.
Only known example.
Scratching and water
stains on front cover,
edge wear. Box:
17 1/2" x 18 1/2".*
$13,800

Marklin, large brougham with original horse, enameled in dark blue and black with a multitude of trim colors and carried by the trademark Marklin red undercarriage, large lanterns (possible replacements) adorn the exterior, 44" l. Glass possibly replaced, and the horse lacking some trappings (some detached but included)................**$24,150**

Milton Bradley, Motor Cycle Game, lithographed box lid depicting a cyclist on a 1905 cycle, 9" square. Lithograph is bright and shiny................**$425**

Modern Toys, Japanese Super Buick in original box, lithographed red with blue stripes. With chrome-plated bumpers, headlights and hood ornament and rubber tires. When friction motor is engaged, a siren sound is emitted, 11" l. Slight oxidation on chrome. Box is in near excellent condition................**$517**

Moxie, "Horsemobile," rare blue version, double-sided color lithographed toy from the Moxie Co., patented Feb. 27, 1917. Depicting a man on horseback alongside an early roadster, 8 1/2" l x 6 1/2" h. A few soft bends to the driver and front of car, with a few scattered paint chips and scuffs.................**$1,495**

Mustang Fastback, 1967, in original box, blue plastic car with rubber tires and a metal undercarriage. Toy is complete with assembly instructions, manual, decals and extra parts, 16" l. Box is soiled and missing one end flap.................**$210**

Photo courtesy Morphy Auctions, Denver, Pa.; www.MorphyAuctions.com

Mechanical band, French, circa 1860, in elaborately inlaid brass and wood box, papier-mâché musicians in Middle Eastern dress. **$7,475**

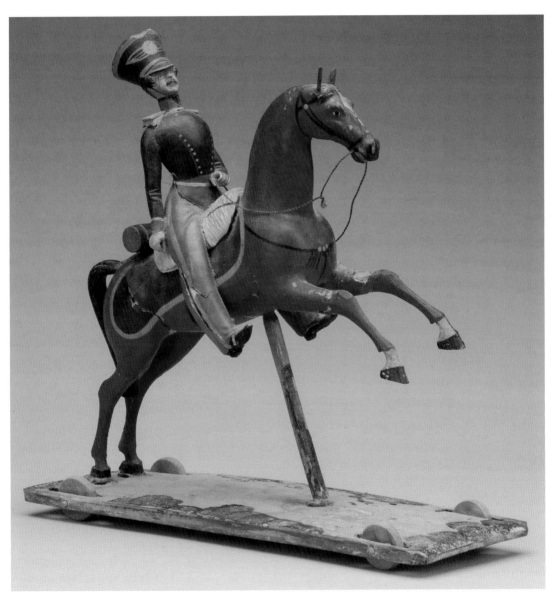

Photo courtesy Morphy Auctions, Denver, Pa.; www.MorphyAuctions.com

Soldier riding horse, German, probably Nuremberg, early 19th century, painted composition Prussian officer in full dress atop a rearing horse, wooden platform, 11" h. **$12,650**

Photo courtesy Hake's Americana & Collectibles, York, Pa; www.Hakes.com
Nifty, Mickey Mouse on Scooter and box, prewar Japanese wind-up, celluloid and tin, it's believed that only two boxed examples exist. **$37,041**

P & L/Wilkins, Deluxe Pumper, brown and white horse sitting on erratic wheels so when the toy is pulled, the horses seem to gallop pulling a pumper with red wheels. When the toy is pulled, a bell rings under carriage, 6 3/4" h x 18" l. Overall chipping and wear to toy, wheels may be replacements. **$1,265**

Schoenhut, carnival tent, with side banner depicting period attractions (1900s-1930s) featuring the Wild Man, the Bearded Lady, Siamese Twins. Inside, the bleachers are packed with spectators who gawk at the show below. Tent, 42" w x 26" h x 18" d. Banner, 49" w x 18" h. Wood on sideshow banner has been expertly redone. Tent lacking some flags and banners on top. **$2,875**

Schoenhut, farmer and wife, original clothing on the wife. Farmer has replaced pants, belt and hat, 7 1/2" and 8" h, respectively. Heads appear to have paint restoration. ...**$270**

Schoenhut, glass-eye polar bear and brown bear; polar bear with open mouth is in fine original condition, the brown bear features an open/closed mouth, 8" and 7 1/2" h. respectively. Brown bear lacking one ear. .... **$862 both**

Photo courtesy Noel Barrett, Carversville, Pa.; www.NoelBarrett.com
Renou, automaton, lady magician who conjures an illusion in which puppet-show heads (in rear theater) disappear from stage and appear in the die-shape box. **$30,800**

Photo courtesy Morphy Auctions, Denver, Pa.; www.MorphyAuctions.com
Paper theater setting, French, 19th century, recreates Les Adventures du Chat Botté du Marquis de Carabas, or Puss in Boots. **$4,600**

Photo courtesy James D. Julia Auctioneers, Fairfield, Maine; www.JuliaAuctions.com

Schoenhut, kangaroo and bison, original-condition, painted-eye kangaroo with open mouth, and a carved-hair bison, 7 1/2" and 5 1/2" h, respectively. Overall kangaroo is excellent. Bison with some wear to high spots. ..... **$690 both**

Schuco, wind-up dancers, Bavarian boy with green felt hat lifts his partner (made of celluloid) over his head, 5" h. Some wear to the paint on the top of the girl's head. Lacking key. **$172**

Sled, painted wooden "CHIEF" Child's, America, early 20th century, with iron runners, the underside inscribed, "EAC DEC 25 1910," paint wear, 4 1/4" h, 10 1/2" w, 36 1/2". **$118**

Smith-Miller, Mack Army truck, green cab with wooden body, 19" l. Minor flaking to decals on cab. **$402**

Smith-Miller, Mack Bell Telephone truck, two-tone green Mack cab with a wooden body and canvas top, 19" l. Minor corrosion to aluminum parts. **$1,955**

Smith-Miller, Mack West Coast Fast Freight truck, all original box freight truck. Tin back end labeled, "West Coast Fast Freight", 20" l. **$1,265**

Smith-Miller, Mobiloil tractor-trailer, all-original oil tanker in red with Mobiloil decals, 22" l. **$517**

Smith-Miller, Pie Mack tractor-trailer, all original truck with red cab and aluminum back end, 28" l. Overall box wear, some flaking to decals on side of trailer. **$1,265**

Smith-Miller, MIC dump truck, yellow with lever inside to activate dumping mechanism, 17 1/2" l. Minor corrosion to aluminum parts. **$1,380**

Smith-Miller, MIC flatbed with lumber, yellow cab with green frame with a chained load of lumber and lever to activate lift bed, 19 1/2" l. Minor corrosion to aluminum parts, some soiling to cab of truck. **$1,440**

Smith-Miller, MIC L.A.F.D. aerial ladder fire truck, with working ladders that extend through a series of gears, 26" l. Minor corrosion to aluminum parts. **$747**

Smith-Miller, MIC stake body truck, all original with power tailgate lift, 18" l. Minor corrosion to aluminum parts. **$1,020**

Schoenhut, Supplee Milk wagon, with dapple horse on its platform, has all of its original trappings and tail. The wagon painted white and green with a black roof has a marquee on top "Ask for Supplee Ice Cream". Comes with an original figure and case of milk. Back folds down and has three original awnings, 13" h x 25" l. Some minor wear to the wheels. **$10,350**

Photo courtesy James D. Julia Auctioneers, Fairfield, Maine; www.JuliaAuctions.com

Steiff, Felix the Cat on Irish Mail, Felix sitting upon his bellows seat will propel the Irish Mail forward, pumping and leaning back as the bellows (non-functional) make a squeaking sound. Believed to be of 1920s vintage, retaining its original script Steiff button with remnants of paper tag, 9 1/2" h. Near mint, tail is intact but appears wire within is broken. **$10,350**

Smith-Miller, MIC tractor-trailer, red tractor with Fruehauf trailer in polished aluminum, 28" l. Minor corrosion to aluminum parts...**$920**

Smith-Miller, MIC wrecker, white with boom, marked, "Official tow car–24 hour service," 16" l. Minor corrosion to aluminum parts, some corrosion to tow boom. **$1,200**

> **Collector's Note: Margarete Steiff (1847-1909) was born in Giengen, Germany. She was a seamstress and confined to a wheelchair due to polio she contracted as a baby. She started making stuffed animals as a hobby in 1880.**
>
> **These toys began as elephants, based on a design Steiff found in a magazine, and were originally sold as pincushions to her friends. However, children began playing with them, and in the years following she went on to design many other successful animal-themed toys for children, such as dogs, cats and pigs. She designed and made most of the prototypes herself.**
>
> **By 1903, the firm she established with her brother, Fritz, was producing a jointed mohair teddy bear, whose production dramatically increased to more than 970,000 units in 1907. The famed "button in ear" was devised by Margarete's nephew, Franz, in 1904, to keep counterfeits from being passed off as authentic Steiff toys.**

Steiff, Bear, blond mohair, ear button, shoe-button eyes, vertically stitched nose, embroidered mouth and claws,

long arms and body, large feet, non-functioning growler, 16" h, one paw pad recovered, stuffing compressed, minor fur loss, soiled. **$4,200**

Steiff, Bear, blond mohair, rattle, no button, black shoe-button eyes, fully jointed, embroidered nose and mouth, overall wear, stains, rip on arm, working rattle, excelsior stuffing, no pad style, circa 1910, 5" h............**$410**

Steiff, Bear, blond mohair, script ear button, glass eyes, embroidered nose, mouth, claws excelsior stuffed, fully jointed, felt feet pads have scattered moth holes, break at sides, mid-19th century, 30" h......................**$1,955**

Steiff, Bear, blond mohair, shoe-button eyes, fully jointed, embroidered nose and claws, excelsior stuffing, loss to fur, stuffing and fiber, circa 1905, 9 1/2" h...........**$710**

Steiff, Bear, white mohair, fully jointed, long curly fur, embroidered brown nose, mouth, and claws, glass eyes, felt pads, excelsior stuffing, circa 1910, 20" h, slight fur loss on snout...**$7,100**

Steiff, Bear, cinnamon mohair, swivel head, black shoe-button eyes, cotton floss stitched nose with vertical stitching, stitched mouth, center seam body and head, no button in ear, original felt pads on paws, 20" h. **$9,500**

Steiff, Bear, golden mohair, 100th anniversary, ear button, fully jointed, plastic eyes, black embroidered nose, mouth, and claws, peach felt pads, excelsior stuffing, certificate no. 3934, original box, 17" h. **$210**

Steiff, Bear, golden mohair, ear button, black embroidered nose and claws, mouth missing, black shoe button eyes, squeaker, fully jointed body, excelsior stuffing, original felt pads, 1" fabric tear right front arm joint, minor fur loss, overall soiling, circa 1905, 14" h...........................**$1,955**

Steiff, Bear, golden mohair, shoe-button eyes, embroidered nose, mouth and claws, fully jointed, excelsior stuffing, no pad arms, moth damage to foot pads, circa 1915, 8 1/2" h.
....**$1,380**

Photo courtesy Skinner Inc., Boston, www.SkinnerInc.com

Steiff Bear, gold shaggy mohair, ear button and cloth tags, fully jointed, glass eyes, black embroidered nose, mouth and claws, yellow felt pads, moth damage, fur wear and matting, late 1920s, 14" h. **$265**

Photo courtesy Wiederseim Associates Inc.

Steiff, Bear, w/underscored button, gold mohair, 12" h. **$950**

Steiff, Bear, light apricot mohair, ear button, fully jointed, shoe-button eyes, embroidered nose, mouth, and claws, excelsior stuffing, felt pads, fur loss to lower back and back of legs, slight moth damage on pads, circa 1905, 12 1/2" h. **$1,610**

Steiff, Bear, light golden mohair, underscored ear button, black shoe-button eyes, center seam, black embroidered nose, mouth and claws, fully jointed, tan felt pads, holes in pads, circa 1905, 14" h **$4,890**

Steiff, Bison, mohair, ear button, chest tag, post WWII, 9 1/2" l. **$200**

Steiff, Boxer, beige mohair coat, black trim, glass eyes, leather collar marked "Steiff," head turns, minor wear, straw stuffing, 16 1/2" l, 15 1/2" h................**$165**

Steiff, Boxer puppy, paper label "Daly," 4 1/4" h. **$130**

Steiff, Cat, pull toy, white mohair coat, gray stripes, glass eyes, worn pink ribbon with bell, pink felt ear linings, button, cast iron wheels, 14" l **$1,980**

Steiff, Cocker spaniel, sitting, glass eyes, ear button, chest tag, post WWII, 5 3/4" h. **$125**

Steiff, Cocker spaniel puppy, button, 4 3/4" h. **$90**

Steiff, Dalmatian puppy, paper label "Sarras," 4 1/4" h. ..**$145**

Steiff, Dog, pull toy, orange and white mohair coat, glass eyes, steel frame, cast iron wheels, one ear missing, button in remaining ear, voice box does not work, 15 1/2" l, 14" h. **$280**

Steiff, Frog, velveteen, glass eyes, green, sitting, button and chest tag, 3 3/4" l. **$125**

Steiff, Goat, ear button, 6 1/2" h. **$150**

Steiff, Horse on wheels, ear button, glass eyes, white and brown, wear and breaks to fabric, on solid metal wheels, non-functioning pull-ring, circa 1930, 21" l, 17" h. **$215**

Steiff, Kanga and Roo, shaded mohair, glass eyes, swivel neck and arms, 21" h kangaroo, 4" h velveteen joey in pouch..**$450**

Steiff, Kitten, Gussy, white and black, glass eyes, ear button, chest tag, post WWII 6 1/2" l.............................**$125**

Steiff, Koala, glass eyes, ear button, chest tag, post WWII, 7 1/2" h. **$135**

Steiff, Lion, pull toy, worn gold mohair coat, glass eyes, worn streaked mane incomplete, no tail, ring-pull voice box, steel frame, sheet metal wheels with white rubber treads marked "Steiff," 21" l, 18" h. **$500**

Steiff, Owl, Wittie, glass eyes, ear button, chest tag, post WWII, 4 1/2" h. **$95**

Steiff, Parakeet, Hansi, bright lime green and yellow, airbrushed black details, plastic eyes, button tag, chest tag, plastic beak and feet, 4 3/4" h..............................**$115**

Steiff, Rabbit, unmarked, wear, 9 1/2" h..........................**$220**

Steiff, Soldier, slight moth damage, hat and equipment missing, circa 1913, 14" h. **$460**

Steiff, Turtle, Slo, plastic shell, glass eyes, ear button, chest tag, post WWII, 7" l...**$85**

Steiff, Walrus, Paddy, plastic tusk, glass eyes, ear button, chest tag, post WWII, 6 1/2" l..............................**$145**

Strauss, Ham & Sam "The Minstrel Team", when wound, Sam plays the piano while Ham dances and plays the banjo, 6 1/2" l. Overall fading with rust spots on the piano and figures...**$480**

Thimble Drome, Prop Rod Racer, futuristic, circa 1960s, with a red plastic body on a die-cast metal chassis, black

Tippco, motorcycle, with sidecar and passengers, German, tin wind-up, 9" l. **$6,900**

Vielmetter, Clown Artist, German, tin with original box, hand-crank mechanism, clown actually creates several different drawings through use of special interchangeable cams to be inserted into toy, retains all discs; some wear to high points; 4 7/8" square base. **$5,225**

rubber tires, and a propeller in the back, 12 3/4" l. Stress cracks to plastic where propeller is attached...................**$57**

Tricycle, Victorian, cast iron with two large spoke wheels and one smaller wheel in front to which tiller is attached. Oilcloth-covered seat with backrest, 45" l x 26" w x 27" h. Rubber that wraps iron wheels shows some hardening and flattening. Front wheel is missing rubber. Black-painted finish shows age-appropriate wear. Seat has some slight tears. **$540**

Vindex, Bates 40 bulldozer, painted gray throughout and embossed on side, "The Bates 40". Also has a nickel-plated driver, 6 1/4" l. Overall wear and has a replaced driver. **$3,162**

Vindex, case plow, red with swivel guiding front wheel in embossed case with green wheels, 4" h x 9 1/2" l. Most of its wear to wheels. **$1,092**

Vis-a-Vis, German, clockwork, early horseless carriage, automobile had a driver and woman passenger (now missing). Lead headlights are still intact as well as the rubber tires on the cast-lead wheels, 7" l. Overall paint condition is poor..**$4,800**

Wilkins, dump cart, horse enameled in black pulling a red dump cart with yellow wheels. The driver is polychrome in blue and flesh tones. Also comes with a cartful of cast-iron shovels, rakes, picks etc. Also has its original back

Photo courtesy Old Town Auctions LLC, Boonsboro, Md.; www.OldTownAuctions.com

Yamada, Clown Pony Trainer, prewar Japanese, tinplate toy, wind-up, retains original flag, 6" across; 6 1/4" h. **$6,050**

gate, 5" h x 13" l. Some paint loss to horse, wheels and figure... **$2,760**

Wilkins, hay rake, tin and bent-wire back with a handle. Also has a black cast-iron horse, red frame and yellow wheels. The driver is painted brown/black and has flesh-tone face and hands, 5" h x 9" l. Wear to wheels and horse. The figure is old but not original to this toy. **$2,012**

Wilkins, hay tedder (only about five or six known), black horse, yellow cast-iron frame with red wheels. When toy is pulled, the tedder arms turn. 5 1/2" h x 9 1/4" l. Even wear throughout. **$6,325**

Wilkins, horse-drawn fire chief wagon, single horse pulling robust fireman, 5" h x 12" l. Considerable paint loss, but no breaks or repairs.. **$1,092**

Wilkins, horse-drawn plow, black horse with gold and red highlights and a red frame with yellow wheels and an

original figure. When lever is pressed, plow blade drops, 4 3/4" h x 10" l, plow blade appears to be an old recast. **$5,175**

Willkins, horse-drawn wagon, two horses painted black, wagon and wheels are yellow. 6" h x 13" l. Professionally restored.. **$287**

Wilkins, mower, cast iron with moveable tin and iron mowing blades. Two black horses pulling mower with yellow and black wheels driven by a farmer with a derby cap, 5 1/2" h x 9 3/4" l. Even wear throughout. Driver is repainted. **$2,070**

Wilkins, two-horse pumper, two big black horses (detachable) in full prance pulling the pumper with a robust fireman leading the horses on, 6 3/4" h x 19" l. Heavy overall wear.. **$1,725**

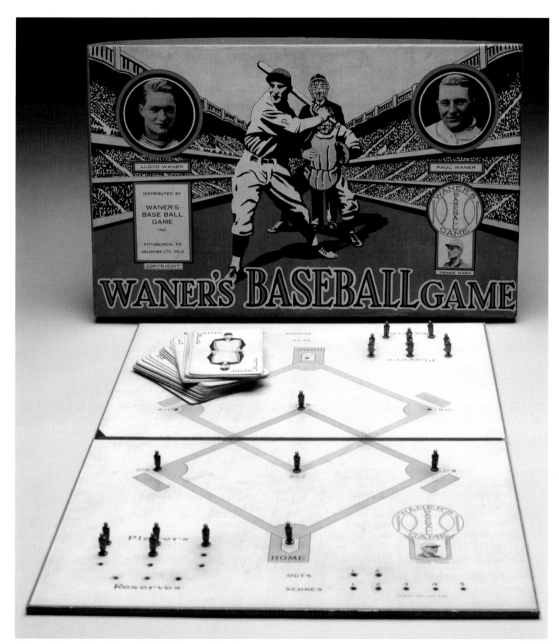

Photo courtesy James D. Julia Auctioneers, Fairfield, Maine; www.JuliaAuctions.com

Waner's Baseball Game, in original box, with lid depicting a batter ready to swing at the pitch. Shows the grandstands behind him. Also on the lid are pictures of the two Waner brothers, Lloyd and Paul. The game board is two diamonds with playing cards and metal pegs in the form of players, 14 1/2" l. Retains playing board, cards and pegs. Lid with minor soiling and scuffing. **$632**

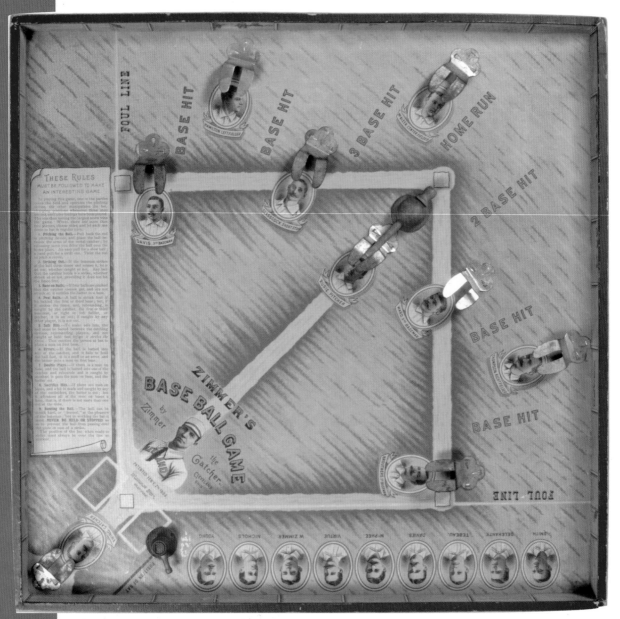

Photo courtesy Robert Edward Auctions, Watchung, N.J.; www.RobertEdwardAuctions.com

Zimmer's Base Ball Game, 1894, designed to "pitch" a wooden ball launched by a wooden spring-loaded "pitcher." When the ball is hit, metal pieces above each player's portrait in the field are designed to "catch" the ball. This example has absolutely no surface wear on the playing surface. The small wooden bat necessary for play is missing. Dimensions: 21 1/4" *square, surrounded on all four sides by wood "stadium walls," which are 1 1/2" high (detail below).* **$19,975**

Gas-Powered Racers

"Tether cars" were developed in the 1930s and still are built, raced and collected today. The vehicles are tethered to a central post. Unlike radio-control cars, there is no remote control over the model's speed or steering. First made by hobby craftsmen, these little gas-powered racers were later produced in small numbers by commercial manufacturers such as Dooling Brothers (California), Dick McCoy (Duro-Matic Products), B.B. Korn and many others. Original examples of the early cars, made from 1930s-60s, are avidly collected today and can command prices in the thousands of dollars.

Banana Wagon Speedway Pacemaker, gas-powered racer, made for Peter DePaolo, presented to him by the factory in 1951. DePaolo's cars were always yellow in color, always numbered "12", and always known as "Banana Wagon". Powered by a .60 Hornet engine. With letter of provenance from DePaolo's son confirming that this racer was given to his father and was in his collection for many years, 17" l. Some minor crazing and paint chips around graphics, wear to hubs, small corner cracks to paint at seat corners. **$3,162**

Richard Beggs, contemporary Indy gas-powered racer, faithful copy of B.B. Korn's supercharged racer with Twin Super Cyclone .60 engine and four-wheel drive, graphics done by Beggs. Enameled in yellow with stylized black flames down the hood with graphics of Felix the Cat and "Double Trouble" on the side with "4" at the tail, 20 1/2" l. **$3,565**

Jim Carmellini, gas-powered racer, with rare Black Panther 10cc gas ignition engine. Boat-tail racer with exposed engine is in silver aluminum with red-painted highlights and wood trim and is numbered "2" at the tail, 20" l. **$4,887**

Don Edmunds, "Felix" Chevrolet gas-powered racer, with late-model Saito 4-cycle overhead valve glow engine, this is one of Edmunds' all-hammered aluminum "Hisso II" racecars. Decorated in bright red and white with image of Felix the iconic comic character on the hood and "5" on tail. Features Firestone tires and composition driver created by Don Edmund's wife, Garnet, 18 1/2" l. Heat marks and light corrosion to pipe. **$4,312**

Don Edmunds, "Polly Gas" Special, gas-powered racer, made from hand-hammered aluminum with graphics of a parrot with "Polly Gas" along hood. Powered by a 4-stroke .60 OS engine, this "one-off" car has considerable variations from his previous "Hisso" series. Compete with handmade driver behind the wheel, 18 1/2" l. Small heat mark to pipe, light surface scratches. **$4,312**

Don Edmunds, Trackmaster gas-powered racer, circa 1975, powered by an Atwood Champion .60 ignition engine. Body is formed by hand-hammered aluminum and is marked "Bowes Seal Fast Special" and "23" on the tail. Complete with full cockpit, instrumentation, and steering wheel. There is a small plaque on the bottom that reads "Don Edmunds Autoresearch", 19" l **$3,220**

B.B. Korn, "Beggs Special" gas-powered racer, contemporary, Richard Beggs' faithful representation of B.B. Korn's Twin Supercharged Indy-type racer. Twin blowers supply boost to output of gas engine Full instrumentation, steering wheel and engineering throughout. Black racer with tufted red leather seat. Marked "Twin Supercharged" and "7" on the sides, 20 1/2" l. Windshield has slight cracking. **$3,335**

B.B. Korn, "Meteor" gas powered racer, 1938, powered by an early .60 Brown Jr. ignition engine. This was Barney

Don Edmunds, "Elcar Special" gas-powered racer, modeled after the Indianapolis racing car driven by John Duff, winner of the Indy 500 in 1926. It is equipped with a scale non-operating Model 8-cylinder Miller engine. Suspension detail, hand-laced wire wheels. Details include complete instrumentation, scale steering wheel, hinged hood and red and yellow paint, lettered "Elcar Special". Complete with driver made by Edmund's wife, Garnet, 20 1/2" l. Some distress to leather straps. **$5,462**

Butch Marx, 1933 Gus Schrader Special gas-powered racer, with Dooling .29 ignition engine, museum-quality throughout and one of three ever built. Decorated in deep red with white center stripe and numbered "5" at the tail, 17 1/2" l. **$5,750**

Korn's first racecar. The body was formed from sheet metal emblazoned with "Korn Spl" and "3" on the tail. Very few of these were ever produced, 18" l. Slight surface wear to body and graphics. **$4,542**

J.L. Special, contemporary gas-powered racer, black front-wheel drive racer powered by an ignition .60 Super Cyclone engine is marked "J.L. Special" on side and "7" on tail. Complete with crescent windshield and aluminum hubs, 18 1/2" l. **$1,955**

Butch Marx, 1952 Sprint Car gas-powered racer, marked with Bowes Seal Fast logo on side with Mobil horse at nose and "26" on tail. Graphics by Buz McKim. Decorated in black and white with blue trim, 18" l. **$5,750**

Butch Marx, Caruso Midget gas-powered racer, late 1930s, powered by a McCoy .19 gas ignition engine. Enameled in black with "Caruso" across the hood and "2" at the tail, 15 3/4" l. **$4,025**

Butch Marx, DePalma gas-powered racer, using an original car from which patterns for the cast parts were made to assure accuracy of sizes. The body is carved wood and painted yellow as the original was. It is mounted on the correct strapped steel chassis. The snap rings that hold the dust felts in place and six bearings have been fitted just as on the original car. Power is supplied by a .60 Super Cyclone engine of the correct vintage. Coil, condenser and fuel shut-off mechanism complete the running components. This car is featured in the Eric Zausner "Spindizzies" book on page 23 where it is listed as "extremely rare," 16" l. Couple minor scratches. **$1,380**

Butch Marx, "Finish Line Engineering Offy" special gas-powered racer. One of the greats of the 1940s-1950s, Butch Marx created this car faithfully down to the frame, wire wheels and suspension, it could be considered a scale model of an Offenhauser-powered racing car. With a .29 Dooling gas ignition engine. Enameled in black with "88" at the tail, 17" l. **$4,600**

Popp Special, gas-powered racer, circa 1940, powered by an ignition .60 Super Cyclone engine. The Popp cars were made in Milwaukee and bore a resemblance to the Bremer Whirlwind, also made in Milwaukee; few were made. In 1998, Mr. Popp's widow sold the last parts stock and four cars were assembled from them, including this one, 20" l. Heat marks to pipe. **$2,880**

Rexner, 1939 "Bowes Seal Fast Special" gas-powered racer, with a .60 Atwood Champion gas ignition engine, includes graphics of Bowes Seal Fast logo and "33" on tail, 18 1/2" l. **$4,715**

Rexner, First Series gas-powered racer, circa 1979-1980, powered by a .60 Super Cyclone ignition gas engine, this is the first gas powered racer built by Marvin Reichert and was raced by him for many years, 17 1/2" l. Windshield has small crack, minor paint chips to graphics. Left front tire has much of the tread worn off. **$2,047**

Synchro Rocket, 1939 gas-powered racer, with rare Synchro Rocket Super Ace gas ignition engine. The wire wheels are hand-strung and the fit and finish details are extraordinary. The transmission lever is the ignition switch and lights the small lamp on the dash as well as brings up power for the engine. Enameled in white with "Gilmore Oil Co. Ltd" and "41" on the sides. 20" l. **$2,300**

Photo courtesy James D. Julia Auctioneers, Fairfield, Maine; www.JuliaAuctions.com

Synchro Rocket, gas-powered racer, built on an original Synchro Rocket chassis and powered by the seldom-seen correct Synchro Ace gas ignition engine with the original working centrifugal clutch. The wooden body was carved by Marvin Reichert for Willie Chambers in the earliest period of the hobby. Decorated in white with red highlights and leather trim, 20" l. Minor crazing to paint. **$1,725**

Marbles

Glass marbles were invented around 1848 in Germany and went into mass production in the early 20th century, but World War I cut off their importation from Europe. American makers introduced mechanized glass-marble production, which became the most common manufacturing method in the world.

Aqua Blue Mica Marble, 2 1/8". Extremely rare large size and color. Loaded with mica. **$6,325**

Aqua Tornado Latticino Swirl Marble, 1 1/16". Unusual aqua tornado latticino swirl with outer white latticino cage. **$1,150**

Blue Glass Swirl Marble, 7/8". Blue glass with latticino swirl in center and four bands of red edged by white. **$460**

Caramel Swirl with Mica, 1 1/16". Caramel colored with mica. **$258**

Cobalt Ribbon Core Marble, 11/16". Dark cobalt-blue ribbon core with outer white latticino bands. **$316**

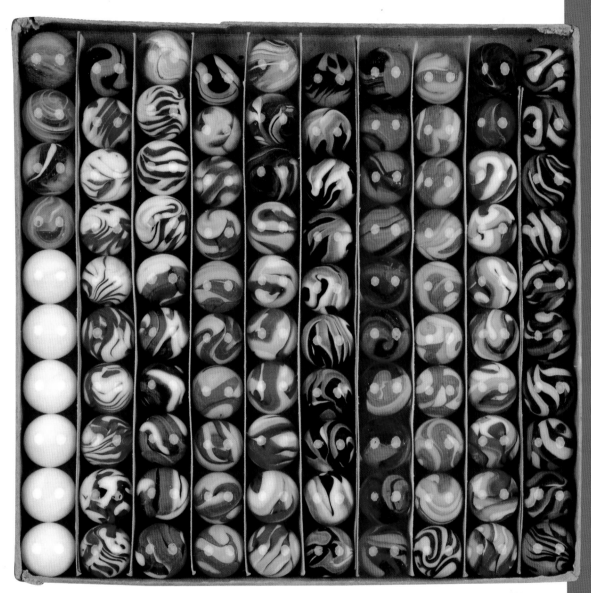

Christensen Agate Box, an extremely rare, 100-count marble box. Included are a number of colorful flames. Marbles range in size from 5/8" to 11/16". This box is one of a few known. All of the marbles are in "wet mint" and unused condition. Box is 7" x 7". **$18,400**

All marble images courtesy Morphy Auctions, Denver, Pa.; www.MorphyAuctions.com

Double Ribbon Marble, 7/8". Nude double ribbon. White ribbon with transparent red ribbon. **$1,035**

Double Ribbon Marble, 1 5/8". Unusual double ribbon with white tightly corkscrewed ribbons. Transparent red that flows in twists give it a pink appearance. Two sets of yellow latticino lines. **$8,050**

Double Ribbon Swirl Marble, 13/16". Double ribbon with one white latticino and one yellow latticino ribbon. Two wide transparent red bands alternating with two wide bands of white latticino. **$517**

Emerald Green Glass Swirl Marble, 7/8". Unusual emerald green glass. White latticino center with outer white lines. **$460**

End of Cane Swirl Marble, 22/32". With multicolored bands and a layer of latticino. **$402**

Four-Lobed Solid Core Marble, 1 15/16". Four lobes with a red/orange solid core. Four white lines on outer edge of peaks. Two outer lines of blue and green. Four outer lines of orange. **$1,035**

Four-Stage Yellow Lobe Core Marble, 2 7/16". Yellow lobe core with white valleys. Four sets of three latticino lines in the next stage. Five red, white, blue and white bands in the next stage. Four bands of yellow, white, yellow latticino strands on the surface. **$3,162**

Indian Mag Lite Marble, 1 9/16". Deep cobalt blue with strong outer bands of yellow, white, blue, purple, green and orange lines. Rare. **$9,200**

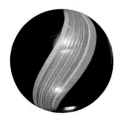

Indian Marble, 1 25/32". Wide bands of blue, orange, yellow and green. Rare. **$7,475**

Latticino Cased Core Marble, 29/32". Unusual white latticino core cased in aqua blue with red and white outer lines. **$575**

Multi-lobed Solid Core Marble, 2 3/16". Multi-lobed solid-core valleys alternating blue and turquoise. Red highlights on each. Outer yellow lines. **$6,900**

Naked Corkscrew Ribbon Swirl Marble, pontil to pontil center with white bands and red running through the middle. Flanked on both sides by pink line, followed by blue, turquoise, yellow, and burnt orange. Opposing side of ribbon has a pink line running down the center band, 1 5/8" d. **$14,950**

Naked Divided Core Marble, 1 3/4". With two ribbons of latticino and two ribbons of opaque. Unusual pattern. **$517**

Naked Swirl Marble, 15/16". Unusual naked clear glass swirl with latticino core. **$517**

Onionskin with Mica Marble, 2 1/4". Unusual in that the one end of the marble has tighter twisting than the other. **$402**

Red Latticino Core Marble, 1 1/16". Bright red latticino core with four mid-layer bands of orange/white, olive/white, blue/white, and grey/white. **$632**

Ribbon Core Marble, 11/16". Unusual ribbon core with four distinct panels. **$258**

MOR-Ribbon Core Marble, 11/16". Alternating bands of blue/white and red/white. Outer layer of yellow latticino. **$115**

Ribbon Core Marble, 11/16". Two sets of red/white and blue/white ribbons with outer yellow latticino bands. **$115**

Ribbon Core Marble, 11/16". Red and green single ribbon with outer pink/white bands. **$172**

Ribbon Core Swirl Marble, 21/32". Tight ribbon core with multicolored bands. **$230**

Ribbon Core Swirl Marble, 2". Unusual thick white ribbon core capped with yellow outer decoration. Outer red/white, green/white and blue/white bands. **$805**

Ribbon Marble, 23/32". Unusual red-ribbed yellow ribbon with green jelly core. **$805**

Single Ribbon Marble, 25/32". Three-stage single ribbon. White ribbon with four latticino lines above the face. Four outer red lines. **$316**

Single Ribbon Marble, 7/8". Single ribbon of yellow latticino capped by white bands. Two outer sets of three yellow latticino and four transparent red lines. **$287**

Single Ribbon Swirl Marble, 15/16". Single ribbon with alternating blue, red, green and white. Outer layer latticino panel of white and yellow. Both edges of the ribbon have alternating blue and red lines. **$201**

Single Ribbon Swirl Marble, 13/16". Turquoise and white ribbon with deep red center. Outer bands of red/yellow/green and red/white/blue. Unusual colors. **$517**

Solid Core Swirl Marble, 2". White solid core enclosed by tight red lines. Outer layer of white lines. **$1,035**

Submarine-Type Marble, 1 1/4". Turquoise glass submarine-type marble. Opaque surface bands of yellow and white. Inner bands of same yellow and white. **$575**

Suspended Mica Marble, 1 15/32". Suspended mica in blue glass. **$9,200**

Three-Stage Divided Core Marble, 7/8". Three ribbons of green outlined in yellow. Second stage is yellow latticino cage. Third stage is four bright red outer bands. **$632**

Three-Stage Red Jelly Core Marble, 11/16". Three-stage red jelly core. Yellow latticino lines. Outer red, red/white and green/yellow bands. **$517**

Three-Stage Solid Core Marble, 1 7/8". Three-stage emerald green solid core. Yellow latticino cage with four outer red and white bands. Rare core color. **$5,462**

Three-Stage Swirl Marble, 13/16". Three-stage red jelly core. Yellow latticino lines. Outer red/green/red and blue/pink/blue bands. **$747**

Three-Stage Swirl Marble, 13/16". Three-stage green jelly core. Second stage of yellow latticino cage. Third stage with two outer pink/red bands and two pink, blue and white bands. **$862**

Three-Stage Swirl Marble, 2 1/2". Three stage with white, blue, yellow and turquoise center. Cage of closely spaced red transparent lines. Outer alternating yellow and white lines that fall in between the red transparent lines. **$2,875**

Tornado Twisting Marble, 13/16". Four tornado-twisting ribbons. Loaded with multiple colored strands. **$575**

Triple Twist Swirl Marble, 7/8". Naked triple-twist ribbon. Red transparent center with blue, yellow, green, red and turquoise. **$920**

White Corkscrew Ribbon Marble, 13/16". White corkscrew ribbon with multicolored outer bands circling the ribbon from pontil to pontil. **$4,312**

Star Trek

Captain Kirk, plastic figure w/cloth costume, Mego, 1975, 8" h..**$55**

Colorforms Set, 1975. ....**$20**

Communicators, blue plastic walkie talkies, Mego, 1976. ....**$150**

Controlled Space Flight, plastic Enterprise, battery-operated, Remco, 1976. ....**$125**

Enterprise Model Kit, from Star Trek: The Motion Picture, Mego/Grand Toys, 1980. ....**$100**

Figurine Paint Set, Milton Bradley, 1979. ....**$25**

Helmet, plastic w/sound and lights, Remco, 1976. ....**$80**

Kirk Costume, Ben Cooper, 1975. ....**$30**

Paint-By-Numbers Set, Hasbro, 1972. ....**$35**

Phaser, black plastic, battery operated, Remco, 1975.....**$100**

Spock Wristwatch, from Star Trek: The Motion Picture, Bradley, 1979. ....**$30**

Tricorder, blue plastic tape recorder, Mego, 1976. ....**$135**

Vulcan Shuttle Model Kit, from Star Trek III, Ertl, 1984. ....**$20**

Water Pistol, white plastic shaped like the Enterprise, Azarak-Hamway, 1976. ....**$30**

Kirk Bank, Kirk standing in front of a computer console holding a closed Communicator in his right hand while gripping a handle from the console in his left. **$55-$75**

Spock Bank, Spock standing in front of a copper-colored computer console. **$65-$85**

Star Wars

3 3/4" Figures, 1977-78

Boba Fett **$19**
C-3PO **$20**
Chewbacca **$13**
Darth Vader **$15**
Death Squad Commander **$12**
Death Star Droid **$30**
Greedo **$18**
Hammerhead **$15**
Han Solo **$22**
Jawa, cloth cape **$20**
Jawa, vinyl cape **$250**
Luke as X-Wing Pilot **$15**
Luke Skywalker **$45**
Luke w/Telescoping Lightsaber **$185**
Obi-Wan Kenobi **$21**
Power Droid **$11**
Princess Leia Organa **$28**
R2-D2 ....**$26**
R5-D4 ....**$17**
Sand People **$17**
Snaggletooth, red body **$10**
Stormtrooper **$30**
Walrus Man **$15**

12" Figures, 1978-79

Boba Fett **$175**
C-3PO **$35**
Chewbacca **$50**
Darth Vader **$75**
Han Solo **$110**
Jawa **$55**
Luke Skywalker **$125**
Obi-Wan Kenobi **$125**
Princess Leia Organa **$85**
R2-D2 ....**$45**
Stormtrooper **$95**

Creatures/Play Sets, 1977-78

Creature Cantina **$25**
Death Star Station **$75**
Droid Factory **$50**
Land of the Jawas **$45**
Patrol Dewback **$20**

Vehicles

Darth Vader's TIE Fighter **$45**
Imperial TIE Fighter **$25**
Imperial Troop Transport **$35**
Jawa Sandcrawler **$220**
Land Speeder **$13**
Millennium Falcon **$80**
X-Wing Fighter **$35**

Photo courtesy James D. Julia Auctioneers, Fairfield, Maine; www.JuliaAuctions.com

Bing for Bassett-Lowke, Flying Scotsman, live steam engine, 4-6-2 locomotive with an eight-wheel tender. British-outline train comes with its original test track. Overall length is 43", engine and tender measure 38". Approximate outside width of track is 2 3/4". Minimal paint loss to the engine and minor paint lifting to small section of tender top. **$5,750**

Toy Trains

American Flyer, STD gauge train set with accessories, includes Loco 4692, tender 4663, gondola 4017, flatcar 4023, tank car 4010 and caboose 4021. Each piece retains the original box and is accompanied by various pieces of track, X-crossings, transformer and several village accessories and related magazines and catalogs. Locomotive's drive rod has been repaired, showing some distress to the paint. Caboose shows some flaking to one side. Remainder generally good.............................**$2,185 set**

Biaggi, 1-gauge Crocodile engine, 32" l. Two detached lamps (but present) at one end of the locomotive. **$6,095**

Biaggi, passenger cars (five), two German sleeping wagons, a Swiss passenger car, Swiss mail car and an Italian parlor car, 37" l each. One German sleeping wagon has extensive silver paint lost to roof.............................**$3,220 all**

Bing, Grand Central Station, almost a direct copy of the earlier Ives station, this example manufactured by Bing in the 1920s was made for the American market, probably to accompany the American-outline trains that they also sold in the U.S. Bing logo is high under the roof on both ends of the station. Interior is equipped for a single candle for nighttime use. Finely lithographed with a simulated stone siding and tiled roofing 19 1/2" l x 8 1/2" deep x 8 1/2" h. Some wear and thinness of lithograph, most prevalent on roof. **$402**

Bing for Bassett-Lowke, clockwork Duchess of Montrose with original box, 4-6-2 British-outline engine in virtually un-played-with condition. Typical of Bassett-Lowke, their toy train models were more like scale models. Accompanied by four pieces of Bassett-Lowke literature, including original catalog picturing the Duchess of Montrose, 21" l. Lacking right side windshield to front of locomotive. Box shows fading and staining to top and some warping. **$4,025**

Buddy L, outdoor train set (seven pieces), including a #963 engine, tender, two cattle cars, flat bed (early), tank car and a caboose. Overall 140" l. Some rusting and paint loss on some pieces. Tanker missing cap and retains about 50% original paint. ....**$2,357 set**

Buddy L, outdoor train set (seven pieces), consisting of #963 engine, cattle car, boxcar, a hopper, a tanker, a tender and caboose. Overall 140" l. Caboose is repainted and boxcar has heavy rusting and pitting..................................**$1,725 set**

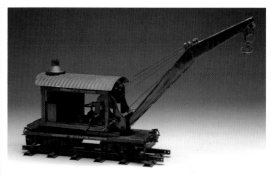

Photo courtesy James D. Julia Auctioneers, Fairfield, Maine; www.JuliaAuctions.com

Buddy L, crane car, made as an accessory for the Buddy L railroad. Car sits on a flatbed car with wheels to be used on the Buddy L track. Painted black with a red roof and partial original decals, 17" l. Minor wear and oxidation. **$2,070**

Buddy L, outdoor train set (eight pieces), set consists of an engine, tender, cattle car, boxcar, flatbed, tanker, hopper and caboose. Total length approx. 160" l. Most of the set is over-painted. Heavy wear and rusting throughout. ....**$2,415 set**

English-outline, live steam engine and tender, large gauge, scratch-built brass locomotive with a 4-6-2 wheel configuration, engineer's cab with an opening roof vent, intricate drive rods and simulated springs and journal boxes on the tender. The engine is marked "4472" in applied brass numbers and the tender was marked "L.N.E.R" in similar brass letters (no longer present). Boiler shows minor heat buildup and discoloration.............**$1,322**

Fallows, four-piece train set, stenciled "SKIP" on boiler. Having a gold-washed tender and two cars, overall 20" l. Retains more than 50 percent original finish. **$115**

Live steam engines (two), the first is of German manufacture and is a traction-style engine with a nickel-plated boiler. Retains an original tag that instructs the operator that it is a reversible engine as well. Chain-driven flywheel activates the rear drive, propelling the vehicle forward. Second is a J. & E. Stevens upright steam engine decorated in green with a multitude of highlighting colors. Included is the original wooden dovetail box for this toy with original label, each is 8 1/2" h. Both engines show little evidence of wear.................................**$3,737 both**

Marklin, Eagle set, O gauge, solid-wheel, American-outline engine drawing two Eagle cars. Total length 21". Overall is poor to fair, the engine is in need of straightening and adjustments. Orange Eagle car paint is good. Blue Eagle car has minimal paint, but strong decals. Some end rails missing from both passenger cars. Missing two wheels and an axle. ....**$7,200 set**

Marklin, HO gauge turntable and engine house, circa 1950s/60s, with three bays and accompanied by an electrified turntable of slightly earlier vintage. Roundhouse is 13" and turntable is 12"......................................**$517 both**

Marklin, Stuttgart train station, HO scale, two-part embossed tin with simulated brick and pillars. Complete with typical 1930s oval logo stamped on base, 33" l x 14" h. Soiling and uniform wear throughout. Lacking flag at top of tower. A fair amount of crazing to paint.................**$1,680**

OBB Reihe, 214 live steam scale model train, Bobner's first model that took 5,000 hours over the course of 19 years to complete. Fitted with electric water heater, it is believed to be fully functional including forward/reverse. Handcrafted in cast iron and metal and accompanied by a custom display track with tilted mirror that allows the viewer to see the underside and all its intricate workings, 41" l. **$7,475**

Southern Pacific, Super Power Daylight scale model, colored in red and orange over a black background, the long cylinder with 4-8-4 wheel arrangement is followed by a matching tender lettered "Southern Pacific Lines". Locomotive 49" l, tender 35" l. **$3,450**

Union Pacific, 1940, "Big Boy" with tender scale model. In 1940, Union Pacific required a train that could handle the rugged mountain terrain, yet sustain speeds of 50 mph on flat land. This cutaway version shows the intricate inner workings. With 4-4-8 wheel arrangement, it pulls a 16-wheel tender. Locomotive 69" l, tender 37" l.............**$4,255**

Photo courtesy of Skinner Inc.

Chad Valley boxed Clockwork train, "O" gauge, bright green and black lithographed tin engine, No. 3402 and tender, two log carriers, two red freight bodies which become freight cars when attached to carrier bases, three curved track sections, two straight pieces, slight wear on one building roof, cover edge damage on box, 1950s. **$385**

VIETNAM WAR COLLECTIBLES

The Vietnam War is a unique part of the American experience. Because of the controversy surrounding U.S. involvement in the conflict, it is not surprising that many returning veterans discarded their uniforms and gear, or stowed them away in footlockers in dusty attics or damp basements. New generations are now asking about the Vietnam War and the objects associated with it.

The values given are for new or excellent-condition, unissued items in most instances. Items known to have been used in Vietnam, with documented provenance, command premium prices, but that provenance is essential.

For more information, consult *Warman's Vietnam War Collectibles* by David Doyle, 2008.

QUARTERMASTER CORPS

The U.S. military is organized so that it is almost self-contained. The objective is to be able to keep an army of thousands of men in the field operating independently of local supplies of any type of material. Much of this material—food, clothing, petroleum products among them—are the responsibility of the Quartermaster Corps.

The Second Continental Congress established the position of Quartermaster General on June 16, 1775. The Quartermaster Corps proper was created by Congress in 1912 by merging the Subsistence, Pay and Quartermaster departments. The responsibility of the Quartermaster Corps in Vietnam was to provide supplies needed by the individual combat soldier in the field.

In this section of the book are grouped the items typically supplied by the Quartermaster Corps for use by Army personnel in the field. Specialized items used by MP, Medics, etc., are found in their respective sections. Within the Quartermaster section of this book, the collectibles are further broken down

Boots

During the Vietnam War a variety of footwear was distributed and worn by U.S. forces. The "classic" footwear was the jungle boot. Development of what was to become the jungle boot began in 1955, with the intent to eliminate a longstanding problem with U.S. combat boots. At least as far back as WWII, the army had experienced problems with the stitching in conventional boots deteriorating rapidly when worn in tropical environments.

www.vietnamgear.com

Jungle Boots DMS
The Tropical Combat Boot was a considerable improvement over its predecessors, but was far from ideal. The extremely moist and hot conditions of the tropics brought about stitching failure at the sole. Sometimes these failures could occur after only one month of service. Hence, the Direct Molded Sole (DMS) began to be used. In this manufacturing technique, the sole was vulcanized to the upper rather than stitched to it. The uppers of these boots were made from nylon duck and leather, and laced all the way up, rather than using a combination of laces and buckles. Both the top stay as well as the backstay were leather-reinforced. On the inside arch of each boot were a pair of screened brass drainage eyelets countersunk into the boot. **$125-175**

www.vietnamgear.com

Tropical Combat Boots
The earliest of the U.S. jungle boots featured canvas uppers, and two buckle fasteners held the boot to the leg. These fasteners were among the shortcomings of this boot style, as they became entangled in the dense undergrowth found in Southeast Asia. **$150-200**

HEADGEAR

The primary purpose of military headgear is to protect the soldier's head from sun, rain, and of course, from wounds. A secondary function is to provide distinctive identification to friend and foe. Despite regulations, troops in the field have long tended to personalize their headgear by shaping their caps, and making other subtle changes. In Vietnam, such trends reached record highs. Straps on helmets and hats were often festooned with cigarettes, repellents and other lightweight items that needed to be kept dry and easily accessible. Helmet covers and "boonie" hats became canvases for trench art—with decorations drawn or sewn on—often to the dismay of officers.

Such customized items warrant a premium—sometimes substantial—over pristine as-issued items. However, fraudulent items are frequently encountered. Was a helmet cover decorated with a ballpoint pen in the Central Highlands four decades ago, or was it decorated in a basement in Cleveland four days ago? Provenance is critical in establishing that a premium is warranted.

M1 Helmet

The classic M1 Helmet, which dated to WWII, remained the primary headgear for U.S. troops in combat areas during the Vietnam War. However, the Vietnam-era "steel pots" differed from the ones their fathers wore. An aggregate had long been added to the paint applied to the steel cover to decrease luster. During WWII, this aggregate was ground cork; during the Vietnam era it was sand. Through 1967, helmets were painted OD 319; after 1967 the helmets were painted Munsell 10Y 3/3.

COVER, HELMET CAMOUFLAGE
CONTRACT No. DSA 100-68-C-2188
E.S.N. 8415-261-6833

Camouflage covers, which the Marine Corps had begun to use during WWII, became standard with the army as well in Vietnam. The M1 shown here is covered with the Camouflage Helmet Cover, Leaf Pattern, which was introduced in 1959 and was used until 1977. Local foliage was to be inserted in the buttonholes visible in the cover to aid in camouflage.

Helmet, with liner, chinstrap, and band. **$30-70**

Also visible in the photo is the 23-inch circumference camouflage helmet band. Though intended to secure additional concealment items, it most frequently was used to secure personal items such as insect repellent, matches, etc.

Chinstraps were issued with helmets, but were not always used.

Resin-impregnated cotton duck was used to form the M1 Helmet Liner until 1969. However, in 1962, experiments began with laminated nylon liners that offered improved protection with only a moderate increase in weight. The nylon units, known as Combat Helmet Liners, were tested in the field in Vietnam, and by 1964 the new liners were being mass produced. Production of liners with removable suspensions did not begin until late 1972, and production of liners with permanent suspensions did not end until 1974.

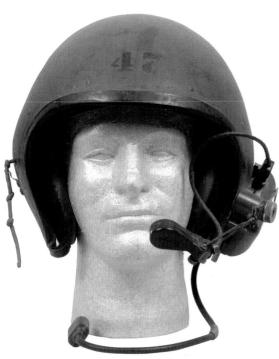

SPH-4 Flyer's Helmet

The SPH-4 began replacing the earlier APH-5 flying helmet in July 1969. Both acrylic and polycarbonate visors have been used on these helmets; however, the latter were not available until late in 1972. These helmets included an M87 microphone as well as headset, and were used by both helicopter and scout aircraft pilots. **$75-200**

Combat Vehicle Crewman Helmet

This bullet-resistant helmet is made of ballistic nylon. The wide-open frontal area allowed the wearer to use vision and sighting systems installed in armored vehicles without having to remove the helmet. The helmet included microphone and headset. The integral cable plugged directly into the vehicle's communication system. **$30-60**

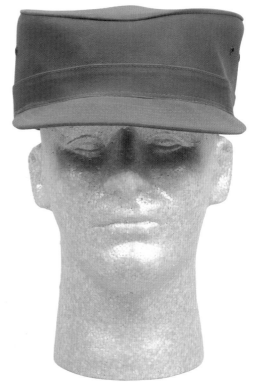

Ridgeway Cap

In 1953, Army Chief of Staff Matthew Bunker Ridgeway directed that troops have a neat appearance, which often involved inserting cardboard stiffeners in their M1951 cotton field caps. A commercially available substitute with spring reinforcements became popular with the troops, who were willing to spend the few dollars to buy this rather than deal with stiffening their issue M1951. This commercial replacement is commonly known as the "Ridgeway Cap." This hat was used in Vietnam until July 1, 1964. **$20-30**

Tropical Hat, aka "Boonie Hat"

Perhaps the quintessential piece of Vietnam war head gear is the Tropical Hat, sometimes referred to as a hot-weather hat or jungle hat—but known universally to GIs and collectors as the boonie hat. Field-testing of this hat began in Vietnam during 1966, with mass production beginning the next year. However, in July 1968, General Creighton Abrams took command of MACV, and he strongly disliked the boonie hat, largely because it lent itself to individualization and because of its non-rigid shape. By late 1971, Abrams and his staff had, for all intents and purposes, eliminated the boonie hat. The boonie hat was most commonly found in olive drab **$20-30**

Camouflaged Tropical Hat

A limited number of the boonie hats were produced with the ERDL camouflage pattern. These hats were not widely used in Vietnam, in part because they were not produced in this pattern until immediately before Abram's virtual ban on this style of cover. **$40-60**

Bush Hat

Vietnamese-made "bush" hats were popular with advisors from 1962-66. The advent of the tropical "boonie" hat contributed to the demise of the bush hat, which typically had only local authorization. The example shown here has the tiger-stripe camouflage pattern. **$75-125**

Black Beret

Black berets were worn by a host of units in Vietnam. Among these were advisors to ARVN tank and mechanized units, National Police Force, Mobile Advisory Teams, as well as U.S. scout dog and combat tracker teams and certain Ranger units. **$40-60**

Green Beret

Made famous by the Army Special Forces, the Rifle Green Army shade 297 wool beret is arguably the most famous piece of headgear to come out of the war. It is also the only beret officially approved for wear by men in the Army during the Vietnam War. **$250-350**

SHIRTS/JACKETS

Maybe 1952-pattern utility jacket

This is what is commonly referred to as a second-pattern Jungle Fatigue Coat. It differed from the first-pattern jacket by having hidden rather than exposed buttons, and did not have a gas flap. The official nomenclature is Jungle Fatigue Coat, Man's, Combat, Tropical DSA100-1387. **$30-60**

The third pattern of the Jungle Fatigue Coat was made of wind-resistant cotton poplin dyed OG-107. Unlike its predecessors, it did not have shoulder tabs. These were introduced in 1967 and were from the 8405-935-4702 series. **$30-60**

Coat, Bush, Hot-Wet, T-54-4, Experimental

Lightweight green coat with four flapped pockets on front. Dark brown plastic buttons. Cotton belt with gold gilt sliding buckle. Experimental hot-weather bush jacket that was not adopted. **Too rarely traded to establish accurate value**.

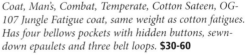

Coat, Man's, Combat, Temperate, Cotton Sateen, OG-107 Jungle Fatigue coat, same weight as cotton fatigues. Has four bellows pockets with hidden buttons, sewn-down epaulets and three belt loops. **$30-60**

Shirt, man's cotton, OG-107, special warfare. Epaulets added in the field. **$15-25**

This long-sleeve, OG-107 single-breasted jungle jacket, with four cargo pockets with flaps and buttons on each side at chest and one on each side at waist, was known as Coat, Man's, Cotton, Water-Resistant, Poplin. The jacket, part of series FSN 8405-082-5569, fastens in front with five concealed buttons. **$30-60**

This Coat, Man's, Combat, Tropical, dyed OG-107 was made of lightweight wind-resistant, rip-stop cotton poplin. The single-breasted garment with concealed buttons was designed to be worn with the tail outside of trousers. The cargo pockets featured flaps and double buttons. **$30-60**

Coat, Man's, Combat, Tropical, Camouflage, Lightweight wind-resistant cotton poplin. Single-breasted. The ERDL (Engineer Research and Development Laboratory) camo-pattern jacket was designed to be worn with the tail outside of trousers. It had concealed buttons, cargo pockets with flaps and double buttons. Several variations of this pattern, with different colors dominant in each variation. **$300-450**

CHEST, OUTFIT, OFFICER'S MESS, M-1937
STOCK NO. 63-C-553
1952
MILLER MANUFACTURING CO.
GLEN COVE, N.Y.

When eating together, officers in the field did not use a Field Mess Kit. Rather they used the Chest, Outfit, Officer's Mess, — essentially an eight-officer Mess Set in box. Included was a teapot, coffee pot, two serving bowls, salt and pepper shakers, and eight of each of the following items: teaspoon, fork, knife, spoon, plate, bowl, cup. **$150-250**

WESTERN, COWBOY

The myths and realities of the American Old West continue to captivate collectors.

Areas of interest often focus on the latter half of the 19th century, between the Civil War and the start of the 20th century. But the entire 19th century, when the nation grew from an agrarian society to an industrialized power, holds many treasures for collectors.

Book of Western Expansion, "Laws of the Territory of the United States North-West of the Ohio." Perhaps the most storied book of the first American "West," the Maxwell Code was printed in the Ohio River settlement of Cincinnati in 1796, at a time when the village was little more than a collection of crude log buildings serving as shelter for 200 inhabitants surrounding the government outpost of Fort Washington. With the Treaty of Greenville in 1795 marking the end of the Indian Wars, the government permitted, and actually encouraged, settlement of the territory. As settlers began to make their way into the territory, the need for a printing of civil and criminal laws required for regulating behavior soon became apparent. While the ordinance establishing the Northwest Territory (what is now Ohio, Indiana, Michigan, Illinois and parts of Wisconsin and Minnesota) had been established in 1787, there was no body of written law that could be called upon in the event of legal disputes. Printer William Maxwell produced the volume containing the new laws. The exact number of copies printed is unknown. **$103,500**

Brand book, 1915, Montana, "The American Brand Book For Big Horn, Rosebud, Custer, Fallon, Prairie, Dawson, Richland and Wibaux Counties, published by The American Printing Company, Miles City, Montana, October 1, 1913," with stiff printed wraps, staple binding, 167 pages, illustrating all the brands in use in these counties with owners' names. **$1,725**

Business archive, for the Martin Valley Livestock Co., Buffalo Gap, S.D., including a ledger book for the business and a book of stock certificates for the company. Entries seem to cover all aspects of the company, including May 1887 lists of breeding stock, along with the names of the cattle themselves. Included is an entry for an August 1902 meeting of the stockholder's held in Deadwood, at which time a decision was made to issue paper stock for the company. The folio ledger contains shares of stock for the company. **$1,725**

California Gold Rush diary, A B. Vincent, spanning 1848-1851, diary and 13 documents. Vincent left his wife behind as he worked his way to California aboard ship in late June 1850, heading out to the gold fields to make his fortune. His experience in the Gold Rush was similar to that of many others: hardship following upon hardship in a rough and almost lawless land. Working with a company of fellow gold-seekers, he stopped first at Green Spring Diggings where he "slept under the sky and on the lap of Mother Earth," and from then into August, he dug holes and found little gold, but a good deal of despair. With only 64 dollars remaining, he "concluded on leaving the diggings ... very discouraging I tell you and no prospect of doing better. O Father of mine, protect and assist my family and enable me to provide for them ... " Vincent's notes,

Photo courtesy High Noon LA Inc., Los Angeles; www.HighNoon.com

Edward H. Bohlin, Machris pictorial saddle ensemble with matching spurs and gun belt, circa 1940, sterling silver and gold. **$129,500 all**

however, suggest that as time went on, he was able to send shipments of cash to his wife back east, suggesting that his tribulations might have eased. ....**$10,350 all**

The Comstock Lode, "Its Character, and the Probable Mode of its Continuance in Depth. Richthofen, Ferdinand Baron, PhD. San Francisco: Sutro Tunnel Co., 1866." Printed paper wraps, 83 pages, in custom "clamshell" box with leather spine with gilt lettering, cloth boards, marbled paper edges. The German-born von Richthofen (1833-1905) traveled most of the world, but seemed to focus on Asia and North America for his research. He is credited with coining the term "Silk Road" for the route from China west to Europe. **$180**

Fort Laramie treaty document, 1866, signed by Big Head, Oglala Sioux Chief, partially printed document, 11 1/2" x 9", with printed heading "United States of America" above a spread-winged American eagle clutching a ribbon with "E Pluribus Unum issued by the office of the Commissioner of Indian Affairs, Department of the Interior. Issued June 28, 1866, at Fort Laramie, Wyoming Territory to Big Head, Chief of the Band of Ogallallah [sic], with printed obligation of both Big Head and the U.S. Government, signed for the Government by R.N.M. Larew, President Pro Tem Peace Commission." This document is an exceptionally rare record of the first failed post-Civil War attempt by the U.S. Government to bring peace to the Northern Plains. Throughout the early 1860s Northern Plains tribes were constantly marauding mail and stage lines along the Bozeman Trail. Fear of a large scale uprising prompted Washington to mount a peace initiative in the winter of 1866, with Fort Laramie, Wyoming Territory, to be the site of a meeting between tribal and Government officials with the aim of negotiating a lasting peace. **$6,900**

Frontier Fighter, "The Autobiography of George W. Coe, Who Fought and Rode with Billy the Kid. Coe, George W. 1934," first edition, Boston: Houghton Mifflin Company. Inscribed under frontis portrait "Geo. W. Coe/ Sept 30 - 1936/ Glenem(?), New Mex." Coe is most noted as the last survivor of the Lincoln County War (1878-1879) and best friend of Henry McCarty, a.k.a. William H. Bonney, a.k.a. Billy the Kid. **$747**

James's Traveler's Companion, "Being a Complete Guide Through the Western States to the Gulf of Mexico and the Pacific, Via the Great Lakes, Rivers, Canals, Etc. ...With Numerous Maps and Illustrations. Massey, S. L. Cincinnati: J.A. & U.P. James, 1851." Green cloth with gilt steamboats and title front, gilt spine, 224 pages, frontis foldout map of Mississippi River, smaller maps and illustrations within text, including views of New Orleans and Louisville, plan of Cincinnati, illustration of steamboat, map of lower Louisiana, etc. **$1,495**

Letter book, and presidential appointment, of Enoch Hoag, Superintendent of Indians, 11" x 9", watered silk boards, with red leather backing, gilt lettering on spine letter book, with pastedown label on front cover "No. 1. Miscellaneous Letters & Documents" (copies), containing letter tabbed index A-Z index, followed by numbered pages 29-499, covering the years 1872-74, belonging to Enoch Hoag (1812-1884). Includes his folio appointment, signed by Ulysses S. Grant, as President of the United States. Hoag, a Quaker, was appointed Superintendent of Indian Affairs for the Central Superintendency located in Kansas and the Indian Territory by Ulysses S. Grant in April 1869. From his office in Lawrence, Kan., Hoag's charges included the Kickapoo, Shawnee, Potawatomi, Kansas, Osage, Quapaw, Sac and Fox, Cheyenne, Arapaho, Wichita, Kiowa, Comanche and Plains Apache. In his role as superintendent, Hoag was responsible for establishing schools, distributing supplies and payment of annuities. Hoag's tenure ended with the election of Rutherford B. Hayes as president. **$2,990**

Mountain Meadow Massacre, letters (two) by C. R. Savage discussing the events and images of Mormon leaders. Both with their 1889 transmittal envelopes from Savage's Art Bazaar in Salt Lake City. The massacre occurred in September 1857. Mormon militia and Paiute Indians attacked and besieged a wagon train of immigrants bound for California. More than 127 men, women and

Photo courtesy High Noon LA Inc., Los Angeles; www.HighNoon.com

Paul Newman, gray wool jacket and vest, worn in "Butch Cassidy and the Sundance Kid" (1969) **$17,250**

children were executed after they had surrendered to their attackers. **$3,220**

Patent medicine salesman's broadside, 10" x 15 3/4", with lithograph of "The Diamond King, Dr. J.I. Lighthall, the Indian Medicine Man," and announcing that he "Is at Richmond, Ind., Curing hundreds of people daily, at his Camp on Main St. Come Immediately and be Cured. Don't Delay. Printed by Cullaton & Co., Richmond, IN." Lighthall was a consummate showman, dressing in Liberace style, one night a full-length sealskin coat, the next, a red velvet Colonial-style suit, many glittering with "diamonds" to increase the spectacle. In his "last stand" in San Antonio, the Daily Express touted/advertised, in addition to free tooth extraction: "On Monday night he will appear on one of the plazas wearing $300,000 worth of diamonds, the largest collection in the possession of any one individual in the world." While in San Antonio, Lighthall contracted smallpox. He died less than a week after his 30th birthday. **$2,415**

Robert Redford, coat worn in "Butch Cassidy and the Sundance Kid" (1969). **$13,800**

Roy Rogers, fringed shirt created by Nudie Cohn. **$7,475**

Territory directory, 1883, "Tucson and Tombstone General and Business Directory for 1883 and 1884. Containing A Complete List of All the Inhabitants. ... Cobler and Co., Daily Citizen Steam Printing Establishment." Original cloth spine and printed boards with advertisements on both front and rear, 224 pages, errata, and index. Only four other copies known. **$11,500**

Gustav Stickley, 268, 315, 329, 376, 378-382, 386-388, 390, 392, 396, 549-550
L. and J.G. Stickley, 382, 387
Stickley Brothers, 312, 374, 379, 381
Sugar Shaker, 438
Superman, 106, 109-110, 113, 125, 684

T

Taylor Tilery, 196
Teco, 196
Teddy Bear, 258, 768
Fred Thompson, 609-610
Jim Thorpe, 708
Tintype, 564, 645
Tippco, 769
Tonkotsu, 626
Torah, 534
Train, 4, 31, 55, 65, 123, 169, 171, 361, 669, 685, 756, 780-781, 793
Tramp Art, 356, 358

U

Uncle Sam, 98, 103, 309, 514, 555
Unique Lamp Co., 549
Union Pacific, 672, 676, 781
Union Porcelain Works, 196
United Features Syndicate, 320
University City, 196

V

Valentino, 282
Van Briggle, 197-198
Vance/Avon, 198
Mies van der Rohe, 577
Dirk Van Erp, 14, 312-315, 543
Victor Vasarely, 564
Versace, 288
Viard, 630, 638
Victor, 73, 80, 105, 123, 439, 459, 564, 581, 642-643, 681, 685-688, 690
Victrola, 643
Vielmetter, 769
Vietnam, 3-4, 6, 120, 124-125, 300, 644, 715, 782-787
Vinaigrette, 637-638

W

Vivienne Westwood, 288
Eugene Von Bruenchenhein, 76-77
Kurt Vonnegut, 93
Louis Wain, 667
George Wallace, 655
W.J. Walley, 198

Walrath, 198
Walther, 325
Honus Wagner, 708-710
Waner's, 771
John Ward, 709-710
Ward Brothers, 333
Andy Warhol, 40, 584
Wave Crest, 411
Waverly Studios, 317
Watt, 261
Weathervane, 355, 357, 364-365, 582
Thomas Webb & Sons, 396, 411-412
Wedgwood, 219, 221, 228-229, 231, 234-235, 237-238, 556
Weller, 4, 176, 199-204, 535
Wheatley, 204
Wheeling, 229-231, 233, 412, 433, 444, 551
Wendell Willkie, 654
Western, Cowboy, 3, 6, 272, 792-793
Whimsy bottle, 361
Whirligig, 356, 361
James Abbott McNeill Whistler, 68, 72, 612
Wiener Werkstatte, 657, 661, 667
Guy Carleton Wiggins, 61
Willkins, 770
Woodrow Wilson, 655-656
Winchester, 69, 326-327, 342
John Winsch, 12, 659-660
Wonder Woman, 109, 111, 283
Tiger Woods, 93
Frank Lloyd Wright, 38, 374, 558-559, 578
Russel Wright, 578, 582, 584
Wurlitzer, 310-311, 590
Andrew Nathaniel Wyeth, 62

X

X-Men, 111

Y

Yamada, 625, 770
Yamaha, 587
Yves Saint Laurent, 279

Z

Zane, 177, 353
Zanesville, 31, 140, 176-177, 184, 199, 425, 430
Zark, 204
Zeiss, 646, 648
Zimmer's, 772
Zon-O-Phone, 643
Zsolnay, 221, 225, 228
Edward Zucca, 564, 581-582

Manage Your Collection with Expertise

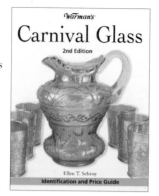
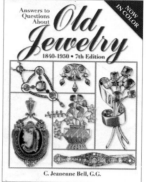
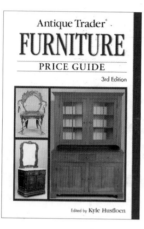

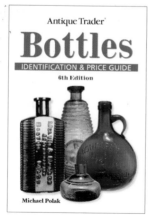
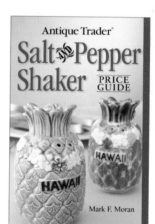